The Annotated Bibliography of Canada's Major Authors

The Annotated Bibliography of Canada's Major Authors

Volume Eight

Edited by Robert Lecker
and Jack David

ECW PRESS

Canadian Cataloguing in Publication Data

Lecker, Robert, 1951–
    The annotated bibliography of Canada's major
authors

Includes index.

ISBN 1-55022-044-6 (v. 8: bound)
ISBN 1-55022-043-8 (v. 8: pbk.)

1. Canadian literature – Bibliography.
I. David, Jack, 1946– .   II. Title.

Z1375.L35 1979 016.81 C79-094602-5 rev

Published with the assistance of the Ontario Arts Council
and The Canada Council.

Printed and bound in Canada by Imprimerie Gagné Ltée.;
typeset by ECW Type & Art.

Cover (paper edition): "Canada Tree II," by John K. Esler.

Published by
    ECW PRESS
    2120 Queen Street East, Suite 200
    Toronto, Ontario M4E 1E2.

Distributed in Canada by
    General Distribution Services
    30 Lesmill Road,
    Toronto, Ontario M3B 2T6.

Distributed outside Canada by
    G.K. Hall & Co.
    An Imprint of Macmillan Publishing Company
    866 Third Avenue
    New York, New York 10022.

For Tom Spall

And to the dedicated, patient work of Laura Groening, Francis Mansbridge, and Mary MacPherson

Contents

Introduction

This is Volume Eight, the final book of a multi-volume series entitled *The Annotated Bibliography of Canada's Major Authors* (*ABCMA*). The series is the first collection of annotated bibliographies of works by and on French- and English-Canadian authors from the nineteenth and twentieth centuries. *ABCMA* contains four volumes devoted to prose, and four to poetry. Each volume, in turn, includes discrete, annotated bibliographies of works by and on specific writers. This volume, for example, meets the demand for primary and secondary information on three of Canada's most respected writers: Irving Layton, Dennis Lee, and D.C. Scott.

Although no bibliography can compensate for individual research, *ABCMA* does provide both the scholar and the general reader with two unique tools. First, the series presents listings of works by the important Canadian authors covered in each volume. These listings cover books, broadsides, manuscripts, contributions to periodicals and books (including poems, short stories, articles, reviews, and a selection of reprinted anthology contributions), audio-visual material, and miscellaneous works. This presentation of primary sources includes all book editions and indicates where and when material has been reprinted, revised, translated, excerpted, or retitled. Second, the series contains an annotated list of works on the author — including books, articles and sections of books, theses and dissertations, interviews, audio-visual material, awards and honours, plus book reviews (on the author's individual works) selected

according to such criteria as critical importance, regional response, idiosyncratic perspective, and international evaluation. The annotations in the sections devoted to critical writings are designed to furnish an informed, but objective, summary of the arguments advanced in each secondary source. Throughout the series, the sections devoted to primary and secondary works are organized chronologically within genres so as to provide the reader with a sense of the relation between creative output and shifting critical response. An index to critics listed in each bibliography provides alphabetical cross-references to secondary sources.

ABCMA compilers have obtained information regarding primary and secondary material up to 31 December 1990 (for Layton), 1991 (Lee), and 1988 (Scott). The editors recognize that the thoroughness of *ABCMA* may be determined only after a considerable period of time; they also acknowledge the fact that bibliographies on living authors must be subject to constant scrutiny and revision.

The bibliographical principles which have been applied to the series are those established by the Modern Language Association as set forth in the *MLA Handbook* (New York: Modern Language Association, 1977). The parts and sections of each bibliography are organized chronologically within genre; in the case of chronological duplication, alphabetical ordering is employed.

Each bibliography contains the following basic components:

Table of Contents

Part I

Works by the Author

A   Books, Broadsides, Audio-Visual Material, and Manuscripts

B   Contributions to Periodicals and Books (Poems, Short Stories, Articles, Reviews, and Reprinted Anthology Contributions: A Selection), Audio-Visual Material, and Miscellaneous Works

Part II

Works on the Author

C   Books, Articles and Sections of Books, Theses and Dissertations, Interviews, Audio-Visual Material, and Awards and Honours

D   Selected Book Reviews (plus selected reviews of audio-visual works and dramatic works where applicable)

Index to Critics Listed in the Bibliography

The organization of each component is more fully described as follows:

Table of Contents: The Table of Contents lists the components of each bibliography and indicates the pages on which these components are to be found. The components are also designated by the citation numbers used to identify entries in the bibliography.

Part I: Part I of each bibliography is devoted to works by the author. These works are listed chronologically within genres under the subsections and headings described below.

A. Books, Broadsides, Audio-Visual Material, and Manuscripts: This section contains a list of all books published by the author (organized chronologically within genres according to date of publication), a list of all broadsides by the author (organized chronologically according to the date of publication), a list of audio-visual materials published by the author (organized chronologically according to the date of publication or production), and a list of the author's manuscripts held privately or by institutions (ordered according to the extensiveness of each manuscript collection). When an author has published in one genre only, the section devoted to books and manuscripts contains only those two headings; however, when an author has published books in several genres (e.g., poetry, prose, criticism, drama, travel books) or has edited books, separate sub-headings indicating each kind of work are presented within the section. These too are organized chronologically.

Primary titles are cited as follows: the *original title* of the first edition is followed, consecutively, by the *place of the publication*, the *name of the publisher*, the *date of the publication*, and *the number of pages* in the edition. (In the case of simultaneous publication in several places, alphabetical ordering is employed.) After this initial entry, the same information is provided for all subsequent editions and translations of the original work. When an edition contains a critical introduction or foreword, this fact is noted in the entry, and the page references are given for this before the total number of pages in the book. Within this section, annotations are also provided to indicate features particular to a given edition. Audio-visual material that is self-contained (i.e., a play or a recording, but not a contribution to a larger collection of audio-visual material), is also listed in Section A. Audio-visual material in a collection of works by more than one author is included in Section B. The entries include such items as producer, director, duration, and cast. Revisions in any later productions are also noted.

The section devoted to manuscripts offers a description of the contents and location of manuscript collections. The location is followed by a short list of the contents comprising the collection. This list varies according to the extent that manuscript materials have been catalogued. The data are accompanied by an annotation which comments on the comprehensiveness of the collection. The compiler has listed the material in the collection according to the manner in which the manuscripts are stored; thus, the identification of the contents ranges from a list of all manuscripts (organized in relation to the system employed by the cataloguing institution) to a summary of previously unidentified material contained in boxes, folders, files, and the like. In all cases the compilers have sought to convey the scope of any given manuscript collection.

B. *Contributions to Periodicals and Books, Audio-Visual material, and Miscellaneous Works:* This section provides listings of poems, short stories, articles, reviews, audio-visual material, and miscellaneous material by the author which have been published in books and periodicals, broadcast on radio or television, or recorded on tapes or records that include works by other authors as well. Since the nature of the author's contributions to these sources differs, the headings in the section also differ from bibliography to bibliography. Generally speaking, however, the organization of headings in this section corresponds to the works' degree of importance (as reflected by critical opinion indicated in Part II). Thus, when an author's contributions to periodicals, books, and anthologies are primarily poems, followed by the next most important area of contribution, and so on. The section also includes (when applicable) a listing of audio-visual materials published or aired by the author. Once again, the citations which appear under each heading are organized chronologically.

Contributions to selected anthologies are arranged in chronological order by anthology, while the author's contributions to each anthology are alphabetized to expedite identification. This compilation is included for the information of readers who wish to gain some sense of the works which have been most widely anthologized, and some idea of how the selections made by various editors have altered over time.

Section B also provides details on material which has been reprinted, revised, retitled, translated, excerpted, or reprinted in one of the author's own books. When an item has been reprinted, full information as to publication data pertaining to the reprint is given. The fact that an original publication has been reprinted in *revised* form is indicated parenthetically thus: Rpt. (revised). When a work has been *reprinted and retitled*, the new title is indicated parenthetically in quotation marks: Rpt. ("New Title"). *Translated reprints* are indicated as: Rpt. trans. ("New Title"). *Excerpted reprints* are indicated as: Rpt. (excerpt). *Abridged reprints* are indicated as: Rpt. (abridged). When a work has been *reprinted, revised, retitled,* and *excerpted,* the entry reads: Rpt. (revised, excerpt — "New Title"). Finally, the fact that a work reappears in one of the author's books is indicated at the end of the entry by an abbreviation which refers to the title of the author's book. A full list of abbreviations precedes the citations in Section B. Audiovisual work is ordered according to date of release. Such technical information as duration, film size, tape speed, and contents is also provided where the information is available.

Part II: Part II of each bibliography is devoted to works *on* the author. These works are listed chronologically under the subsections and headings described below.

C. *Books, Articles and Sections of Books, Theses and Dissertations, Interviews, Audio-Visual Material, and Awards and Honours:* As in Section B, the actual headings in Section C vary according to the nature of the critical works which exist on each author. Entries in this section are annotated with a description of the critical viewpoints expressed in each secondary work. Publication data are given for all secondary sources, including reprinted forms. The format governing the citation of these reprints is identical to that described in Section B of Part I above. Theses and dissertations are identified according to the year that they were completed and the institutions at which they were presented. Awards and honours are listed chronologically, as are interviews with the author and audio-visual material on the author's work.

D. *Selected Books Reviews:* This section contains a list of selected book reviews on the author's books listed in Part I, Section A. The sub-headings in this section correspond to the title of the work. Beneath each sub-heading is presented, in chronological order and with annotations, a representative cross-section of reviews. The book reviews have been chosen according to the following criteria: a) critical excellence (reviews which offer significant insight), b) regional response (reviews which assess the impact of the book from the viewpoint of particular regions), c) idiosyncratic appeal (reviews which offer unconventional interpretations or which display engaging critical biases), and d) international evaluation (foreign reviews which attempt to place the work in a literary context extending beyond Canada).

Index to Critics Listed in the Bibliography: This index provides an alphabetical cross-reference to the names of critics listed in Part II.

The editors welcome the submission of corrections, additions, and queries. Correspondence should be addressed to the publisher.

Irving Layton
An Annotated Bibliography

Francis Mansbridge

Part 1

Works by Irving Layton

Part II

Works on Irving Layton

Acknowledgements

For more than seven years, while I have worked on this bibliography, I have benefitted from the resources of university libraries from Victoria to Fredericton, as well as dozens of other libraries and individuals who are far too numerous to name here. I would like to express my thanks to all who responded so generously to my many requests. Thanks especially to Joy Bennett and the Layton collection at Concordia University, which made an impossible job only difficult. I have also appreciated the extensive help of my hometown library at East Kootenay Community College, which has shown that smaller can be better. Thanks also to the assistance of Irving and his wife Anna for answering much that would otherwise be unanswerable. And, finally, thanks to the editorial finesse of Ellen Quigley, who brought it all together.

Introduction

In a career that has spanned over half a century, Irving Layton's prodigious energies have helped transform Canadian poetry from the preserve of a WASP elite to a forum where multiple and diverse voices from every facet of our society collide vigorously. In the words of Joan Finnigan, he has "done the most to upset the public stereotype of the Canadian poet" (C71). Or, as Al Purdy put it in his more pungent manner, before Layton "everyone sounded like your aunt Martha" (C382).

Irving Layton was born Israel Pincus Lazarovitch in 1912 in Tirgul Neamt, Romania, the youngest of seven children. A year after Israel's birth the Lazarovitch family moved to a new life in Montreal, where they settled in the Jewish ghetto. His early life was a struggle against poverty and anti-semitism, although he soon acquired the personality and skills to combat these obstacles, skills on which he would draw in his many subsequent battles.

Layton attended Baron Byng High School, immortalized by Mordecai Richler in *The Apprenticeship of Duddy Kravitz* as Fletcher's Field High School, but was expelled two months before graduation in a dispute over unpaid tuition fees. A schoolmate, David Lewis, later leader of Canada's New Democratic Party, introduced him to a young poet named A.M. Klein. Klein's tutoring Layton in Latin, along with David Lewis lending him ten dollars for the exam fee, enabled Irving to graduate.

Although Irving had become interested in poetry in high school, and published his first poem when he was nineteen (B1), a more serious commitment to writing began after his enrolling in 1933 as a student at Macdonald College. An agricultural college on the western fringes of Montreal, this was an unlikely venue for an aspiring writer, but a combination of government subsidy and the scarcity of opportunities in depression Montreal was enough to secure Layton's enrolment. Numerous poems, articles, reviews, and short stories appeared over the next decade, during which Layton acquired a B.Sc. from Macdonald College and an M.A. in Political Science from McGill University. He also became intensely involved with a group of young poets, especially Louis Dudek, who congregated in the 1940s around John Sutherland and his little magazine *First Statement*.

From the very beginning the critical reception of Layton's writing has been varied, quite often depending on the background of the reviewer. Those in the Anglo-Saxon literary mainstream often expressed reservations concerning the conscious roughness of his expression, and by what was often seen as an unbecoming egotism. His supporters tended to come from those who shared his belief that poetry should be passionately engaged with ideas and emotions. Most often his advocates were themselves poets.

His first book of poetry, *Here and Now* (A1), was published in 1945. Klein remained an ardent supporter, noting in Layton's first book "a power of expression which is unique and personal, and a social awareness which endows poetic utterance with base and substance" (D2). Other critics were less impressed with his penchant for social realism and a perceived deficiency in technique. E.K. Brown considered the poems "saturated . . . with the political and social problems of the immediate present" (D5). Alfred Ames felt that Layton should acquire more "disciplined expression" and "elevation of feeling" (D4), and Margaret Avison similarly felt that Layton needed more "technical competence or developing conviction" (D1).

For another decade Layton continued to bash away at Canadian WASP gentility with his aggressively passionate poetry, although few outside the literary community paid much attention. Contacts with American writers beginning in the early 1950s, however, opened up new possibilities for the exchange of ideas and wider publication. In 1954 American poet Robert Creeley published Layton's *In the Midst of My Fever* (A5), and in 1956 Jonathan Williams published the first retrospective collection of Layton's poetry, *The Improved Binoculars* (A10), with a foreword by William Carlos Williams. With the latter book, especially, Layton was in a position to demand and receive serious attention from major critics. In 1958 American critic Hugh Kenner described the Layton-Dudek-Souster group as central to poetic activity of the 1950s (C41).

Response to *The Improved Binoculars*, especially outside Canada, greatly exceeded the cautious reactions to his earlier brief books. Many praised his sensuality and lyric gift. Even Northrop Frye, who had been gradually warming to Irving Layton in reviews of earlier books, "strongly recommended" (D43) this volume. American critic Richard Eberhart praised his youthful exuberance (D42), and *The Times Literary Supplement* of London was similarly impressed by "his leaping vitality" (D44). Hardest to impress were fellow Canadians like Kildare Dobbs, who in the *Canadian Forum* objected to poems that saw "the poet slobbering over girls," or indulging in "lofty pity for his suffering fellow-men" (D46). Throughout his life Layton has drawn strength from his war against the gentility and puritanism that he sees endemic in Canadian literature and its criticism, positing against it an iconoclastic Hebrew sensuality.

Layton's roots in the Jewish ghetto had given him a different frame of reference from that of the predominantly WASP Canadian literary establishment, and the mandarins were slow to welcome him into the poetic fold. But in 1955 A.J.M. Smith, one of Layton's most cherished WASP enemies, published the first major article on Layton (C24), which praised the "mastery of rhythm" and "ability to combine seemingly incompatible images" in his more recent poems. Excluded from the two earlier versions of Smith's influential *The Book of Canadian Poetry*, Layton was finally inducted into the 1957 edition (B1070).

Layton's major breakthrough to a Canadian audience came with *A Red Carpet for the Sun* (A13), published in 1959 by McClelland and Stewart, as were many of his later books. Most critics responded to an exuberant energy and variety in these poems. Alden Nowlan saw "awesome wonder, honesty, joy, beauty, and brutality" (D66), while Eli Mandel found the book "continuously exciting and disturbing" (D68). American critics were also generous in their praise, with John Ciardi urging the bright young men to "put the book into their pockets and Layton into their minds" (D70). More negative notes were sounded by Northrop Frye, who always had difficulty accepting aspects of Layton's work; he felt Layton was "tired of his present achievements" (D69). Dudek's attack, which indicted Layton for "illiteracy," "barbarism," and lack of craft (D63) widened the rift between the two poets and friends who had worked closely together since the early 1940s to renew Canadian poetry. Personal and poetic differences drove them apart, and the rift became permanent in the early 1960s.

During the late 1950s Layton's public profile was further raised by his exposure in the media. Frequent appearances on television and radio, especially on *Fighting Words*, his frequent public readings, and numerous articles and letters in the popular press made his views on sex, poetry, and politics known to many who had never read a poem. His energetic avowal of the salutary nature of sex shocked the puritanical, while his support of American involvement in Viet Nam offended the liberal. Layton derived intense satisfaction from his frequent engagements with the representatives of Canadian gentility.

George Woodcock's 1966 article "A Grab at Proteus: Notes on Irving Layton" (C141) provided a benchmark for many of Layton's later critics. Woodcock noted Layton's stance as a modern-day prophet who at times wrote brilliantly, but at other times adopted a clown-like mask that led him to publish work which would have been best kept private. Many of his best poems stem from an identification with the animal world and those people who are "outside the herd of hostile humanity."

The first book *on* Layton was published in 1969 by friend and fellow poet Eli Mandel (C3), and revised and expanded (C8) in 1981. Layton worked more, in Mandel's view, from the literary traditions of the United States and Europe than Britain. His poetry did not so much fuse discordant elements as hold them in ironic balance, particularly between the poet and the world, and imagination and fact. His revised monograph described him as "the richest, most well-stored, most energetic poet of this century."

Layton financed his writing during these years through teaching, mostly at Herzliah, a Jewish parochial high school in Montreal. His tenure there ended in June of 1960 when he was fired for union activities which brought him into conflict with the school administration. During the 1960s he taught part-time at various places, mostly Sir George Williams University (now Concordia), but also for Ross Tutorial School and the Chambly County Protestant School Board. In 1967, a major Canada Council award enabled him to abandon these constraints to set off on travels which over the next two years took him to France, Greece, Israel, and India.

Layton's 1965 *Collected Poems* (A16) appeared to mixed reviews, with Louis Dudek dismissing his "crudity and vulgarity" (D91), and Hayden Carruth saying these poems gave the impression "of having been written off the cuff by an intelligent, well-educated, observant, cheerful gas-meter-inspector" (D94). But most recognized it as a major achievement in the development of Canadian poetry. For Bruce Nesbitt this was one of the half-dozen most important volumes of Canadian poetry since 1950 (D96), while Al Purdy considered it "the most substantial body of good work published in this country" (D93). The revolutionary Layton had become, in John Robert Colombo's view, "a sweet-voiced Theodore Roethke" (D92).

Response to *The Collected Poems of Irving Layton* (A20), which remains the closest to a collection of Layton's com-

plete poems, was almost universally positive; in X.J. Kennedy's opinion it had a good chance of making himself and his subjects immortal (D135). Frank Watt considered it one of the most important poetic achievements in English-Canadian poetry this century (D133); Al Purdy praised Layton as "a poet as close to genius as any alive" (D125). For Frank Davey, Layton had helped break "the Puritan embargo on image, magic, and sexuality," although his poetry was more concerned with "opinions, thoughts, and feelings" than that of the next generation (D129).

Layton's perennial interest in expressing ideas naturally led him to writing prose. Articles, letters, reviews, short stories, and introductions have been interspersed with his poems throughout his writing career. A selection of these appeared in *Engagements: The Prose of Irving Layton* (A53), edited by Seymour Mayne, in 1972. Reactions to this book were mixed, with Arnold Ages welcoming Layton's "hard-hitting cogent prose" (D303), but Jim Christy finding it ranging from the "ridiculous" to the "workaday mediocre" (D310). For many, Layton was, in Fulford's words, difficult to take in a "pure state, unadulterated by the poetic process" (D304).

A second collection of Layton's prose, *Taking Sides: The Collected Social and Political Writings* (A54), was published in 1978, edited by Howard Aster. While some appreciated the added information this book gave on Layton's career, others, like Doug Fetherling, found the editing "slapdash" (D313). Patricia Keeney Smith considered the collection "maddeningly uneven" (D315), although Sandra Djwa appreciated the way this book "chronicles Layton's concept of the function of the artist within the context of his changing political and social thought" (D316).

Layton's affinity for warmer climates and the greater sensuality and passion that is often associated with the cultures of southern Europe was reflected in his later years by frequent trips to these areas and numerous publications, especially in Italian. The first translation of his poems into Italian was *Il freddo verde elemento* (A23), published by

Giulio Einaudi in 1974, with an introduction by Northrop Frye. Later translations into Italian include *Il puma ammansito/The Tamed Puma* (A32) in 1978, *In un'eta ghiaccio* (A39) in 1981, *Le poesie d'amore di Irving Layton* in 1983 (A33), and *Tutto sommato: poesie 1945–1989* (A49) in 1989. Critical attention has included a collection of essays on Layton, *Italian Critics on Irving Layton* (1988) (C12), edited by Alfredo Rizzardi and translated into English, and a book by Valerio Bruni, *Danza Sulla Fune* (1990) (C13) (in Italian). In addition, book-length selections of his poems have been published in Greek, Spanish, and Korean translations. Nominations for the Nobel prize in the 1980s were proposed jointly by the Italians and South Koreans.

Layton continued to write prolifically during his tenure teaching at York University from 1969 to 1978. With the publication of *For My Brother Jesus* (A26) in 1976 he found a new club with which to beat Canadian gentility — the complicity of Christianity in laying the psychological base which led to the murder of six million Jews. While George Jonas found this book fulfilled even Layton's "own grandiose claims to significance" (D185), more typical was Patricia Morley's dismissal of the poems as "fatuous" (D194). Stephen Hatfield viewed them as "watery, pleonastic and unengaging" (D189), while Patrick O'Flaherty lamented Layton's decline "into the spleen of senescence" (D187).

All the time Layton was engaged in literary activities, he was also living intensely. An early marriage to Faye Lynch was short-lived, but a later marriage to Betty (later Boscka) Sutherland, and then a long-term relationship with Aviva Ravel provided underpinnings for much of his writing. A brief marriage to Harriet Bernstein in 1978 quickly ended with a nasty separation; since 1982 he has been living with and is now married to Anna Pottier.

Layton's real and imagined experiences with women have occasioned numerous imaginative flights. Many of the resulting poems were collected in *The Love Poems of Irving Layton* (A31), which was reviewed with remarkable consensus as a major addition to the Layton canon, characterized by a variety of feeling and a delicate balance between the lyric and the ironic. Fraser Sutherland described "I Would for Your Sake Be Gentle" as having the quality of "a gifted translation from the classical Greek of a great poet" (D208), while Patricia Keeney Smith noted "the fearless touch of one who has loved both wisely and too well" (D209). One of the few dissenting voices, Douglas Barbour, found the book "decidedly anerotic" (D207).

Apart from the monographs by Eli Mandel, Wynne Francis (C420), and Valerio Bruni, critics have either concentrated on particular aspects of Layton's work or contented themselves with relatively superficial discussions. So it was with much anticipation that members of the academic community and others awaited the publication of Elspeth Cameron's *Irving Layton: A Portrait* (C9), the first major book on Layton and one of the first full-length biographies on any Canadian literary figure. Initial response to the book was generally positive, with William French describing it as "dispassionate and remarkably comprehensive" (C451) and Robert Fulford as an "excellent book" which helped to revive Layton's sagging reputation (C455). But Layton, objecting to factual inaccuracies and a perceived negative tone, viewed the book as slanderous. His strenuous counterattack attempted to discredit Cameron through numerous letters (B944–B951) and appearances in the media. Here again was an incarnation of the WASP mentality to destroy.

During the past decade Layton's publishing career has slowed little, although many of his books have been largely collections of previously published work. One of his most important books of new poems in the past decade was *The Gucci Bag* (A41), in which several critics perceived a new subdued note of loneliness and poignancy. Joseph Kertes praised his "roundness of vision" and "unprecedented wisdom" (D259) and Sheila Martindale noted he "has lost none of his brilliance and fire" (D260).

Layton now lives with Anna Pottier, who has been sharing his life for the past decade, in a quiet area of Montreal's

NDG. The remarkable variety of his life and the imaginative achievement of his best poetry have no parallel in Canada. More than any writer of his generation, Layton stretched the bonds that inhibited the movement of Canadian poetry, revealing through example the poetic possibilities engendered by new facets of thought and feeling.

Part 1

Works by Irving Layton

A   Books (Poetry, Poetry and Prose, Prose, Memoir, Translation, and Books Edited), Pamphlets and Portfolios, Broadsides, Editorial Work, Audio-Visual Material, and Manuscripts

Poetry

A1   *Here and Now.* New Writers Series, No. 1. Montreal: First Statement, 1945. [36] pp.
  Includes "Boarding House" (B33), "Change [Empty of all meaning]," "Church Parade" (B51), "De Bullion Street" (B55), "Drill Shed" (B54), "Epitaph for a Christian" (B22), "Epitaph for a Communist" (B23), "Epitaph for a Philosopher" (B28), "Epitaph for a Wit" (B29), "Gents' Furnishings" (B53), "Jeremiad," "Jewish Main Street" (B59), "Lady Remington" (B45), "The Modern Poet [Since Auden set the fashion]" (B36), "Mortuary" (B46), "Mother, This Is Spring," "My Father" (B12), "Newsboy" (B42), "Night," "Petawawa" (B43), "Proof Reader" (B63), "Providence" (B26), "Restaurant De Luxe" (B31), "Returning with an Annual Passion" (B58), "Spinoza" (B57), "Stolen Watch" (B64), "The Swimmer" (B60), "Upper Water Street" (B50), "Waterfront" (B62), "We Have Taken the Night" (B56), "Winter Scene" (B47), and "Words without Music" (B61).

A2   *The Black Huntsmen.* Montreal: Privately printed, 1951. 55 pp.
  Includes "Aerolites [Up there, up there on high]" (B30), "The Ape and the Pharisee," "Auspex" (B78), "The Black Huntsmen" (B79), "Blood on the Moon," "Butchevo, the Critic," "Church Parade" (B51), "Compliments of the Season" (B58), "Crisis" (B52), "De Bullion Street" (B55), "Elan," "Existentialist" (B537), "Fog" (B50), "Gents Furnishings" (B53), "Gonorrhea Racetrack" (B49), "Gothic Landscape" (B76), "Intransitive Verb," "Lenin" (B68), "The Modern Poet [Since Eliot set the fashion]" (B36), "Mont Rolland" (B81), "Mrs. Fornheim, Refugee," "Mrs. Potiphar," "Newsboy" (B42), "Nightfall" (B56), "The Poet and the Statue," "Poet Killed in Action" (B77), "Poplars," "Proof Reader" (B63), "Schoolteacher in Late November" (B72), "Songs of a Half-Crazed Nihilist" (B82), "Stolen Watch" (B64), "Suum Cuique," "The Swimmer" (B60), "To Be Played on a Broken Virginal" (B74), "Ville Marie" (A50 — "Montreal"), "Weekend Special" (B61), "Woman in the Square" (B75), "The World's a Tavern" (B83), and "The Yard" (B67).
  ———. Montreal: Privately printed, 1951. i–xii, 56 pp.
  A second edition of this book contains all the poems listed in the previous edition plus the following: "Afternoon of a Coupon Clipper," "Change [Empty of all meaning]" (A1), "Community" (B33), "Drill Shed" (B54), "English for Immigrants" (B65), "Lady Enfield" (B45), "Epitaphs: Communist" [B23], "Mild Gentleman, Philosopher [B28], Wit [B29]," "Ice Follies" (A50), "Jewish Main Street" (B59), "North Country" (B70), "Sudden Thaw" (B66), and "Training Camp" (B43).

A3   ———, Louis Dudek, and Raymond Souster. Preface Irving Layton. *Cerberus.* Toronto: Contact,

1952, pp. 45–46, 47–72.

Layton's contributions include "Anacreon" (B88), "Bishop Berkeley Goes to Bed," "Call Me Ferdinand," "Crone," "The Excessively Quiet Groves" (B85), "The Execution," "Ex-Nazi," "Genius Love and Poetry" (B89), "Good-Bye Bahai," "Hymn to the Rising Sun," "January Love" (B84), "Letter to Raymond Souster," "Lines on the Massey Commission," "Little David: For E.B.," "News of the Phoenix: For A.S.," "Poetess [Her talk is pert]," "Rembrandt," "Terrene" (B87), "To a Very Old Woman" (B90), "Trumpet Daffodil" (B96), and "Vignette."

A4   *Love the Conqueror Worm*. Toronto: Contact, 1953. 49 pp.

Includes "Ah Rats! (A Political Extravaganza of the 30's)" (B11), "Battle of the (S)ages," "Beauty [Omah who keeps house]," "Cemetery in August," "Corypheus," "Death of Moishe Lazarovitch: For Anica Fellegi" (B180), "Eros [With the best side of my tongue]," "Esto Perpetua," "Fable for Adults," "For Adlai Stevenson," "For Dulla, Who Unexpectedly Came into Some Money," "For Governor Stevenson," "Had I the Talent," "In Memory of Fred Smith" (B91), "Letter to Louis Dudek" (B97), "The Literary Life," "Love the Conqueror Worm" (B94), "Miniatures with a Meaning," "Moses Talked to Jupiter" (B92), "Odysseus in Limbo" (B83), "Overheard in a Barbershop," "Paideia" (B101), "The Perverse Gulls," "Philosophy 34" (B355), "A Pocketful of Rye," "Reconciliation" (B225), "Smoke Rings," "Soleil de Noces" (B98), "Street Funeral" (B95), "To the Girls of My Graduation Class" (B93), "Vexata Quaestio" (B140), and "A Vision."

A5   *In the Midst of My Fever*. Palma de Mallorca: Divers, 1954. [35] pp.

Includes "Against This Death" (B590), "The Ants" (B129), "Bacchanal" (B105), "The Birth of Tragedy" (B171), "Composition in Late Spring" (B104), "Early Morning in Cote St. Luc," "First Snow: Lake Achigan" (B131), "For Priscilla," "How Poems Get Written" (B356), "In the Midst of My Fever" (B102), "It's All in the Manner" (B106), "Lachine, Que.," "Lacquered Westmount Doll" (B132), "The Longest Journey," "The Madonna of the Magnificat" (B107), "Maxie," "Metzinger: Girl with a Bird" (B108), "Mildred," "Motet" (B136), "Mr. Ther-Apis" (B103), "Paraclete" (B109), "Portrait of Aileen" (B134), "Sancta Simplicitas" (B135), and "Seven O'Clock Lecture: For Neil Compton" (B99).

A6   *The Long Pea-Shooter*. Montreal: Laocoon, 1954. 68 pp.

Includes "Address to the Undernourished," "Admonition to a Young Poet," "All-Too-Human," "Author, with a Pipe in His Mouth," "Brief Encounter," "Canadian Spring," "Cyril Tishpish" (B100), "Eros Where the Rents Aren't High," "Flaubertism, Trillingism, Or," "For an Older Poet in Despair with the Times," "Henry Crockett, M.P." (B118), "How to Look at an Abstract" (B315), "Impotence" (B119), "June Weather," "Latria," "The Law," "Lines on Myself," "Look, the Lambs Are All Around Us!", "Marie," "Marius," "The Masked Marvel," "Mediocrity and Genius," "Metropolis," "Misunderstanding" (B335), "New Tables," "No Moby Dick," "Now That I'm Older," "O.B.E." (B122), "On First Looking into Stalin's Coffin," "On Mr. and Mrs. Y's Reactions to Z's Misfortune," "On Reading the Holmes-Laski Letters," "Part of a Letter," "Pine Avenue Analyst," "Poet Turned Novelist (For E.B.)," "Poetess [This thumping cow]," "Processed," "Prologue to the Long Pea-Shooter" (B139), "Quiz Show," "Rain at La Minerve," "The Ravens [Where's the poem]," "S.A. Collection," "Sensibility," "Silver Lining," "Simon O'Bowd," "Spousal Grief," "T.S. Eliot" (B127), "This Fact of Feeling," "Two Poets in Toronto," "University Buildings," "Veteran," "What Ulysses Said to Circe on the Beach of Aeaea," and "Young Man in Earnest."

A7 *The Blue Propeller.* Toronto: Contact, 1955. [38] pp.
Includes "Admonition and Reply," "Afternoon Tea" (B145), "Alexandra School Revisited," "Apeswatch," "Canadian Skiers" (B153), "Canadiana," "Christmas Day," "Death of a Poet," "Defence Enough," "English Prof: For H.W. Wells," "Epitaph for an Ugly Servitor to Three Queens" (B115), "For My Detractors," "Golfers" (B117), "The Greeks Had a Word for It," "Human Being," "Love's Diffidence" (B154), "The Lusts of the Spirit," "May Day Orators," "Metamorphosis" (B517), "Mount Royal," "Mute in the Wind," "My Favourite Colour's Green," "Noblesse Oblige," "Not Blown Away," "On the Death of A. Vishinsky" (B143), and "Portrait [Pay small attention to the chin]" (B137).

———— . Illus. Toronto: Contact, 1955. [36] pp.
A second version of this book contains all the poems listed in the previous edition, plus three tipped-in orange leaves on which there are two engravings, plus the following additional poems: "Enigma" (B161), "Fell Horatio: For George Woodcock," "For an Anniversary of Shaw's Death," "For the More Devotional," "Georgie, Am I Concrete Enough," "Horsley-Trevor," "Love Dream of Alfred Smythe, Magnate," "More Canadiana," and "When I See a Giant."

A8 *The Cold Green Element.* Toronto: Contact, 1955. [50] pp.
Includes "Birds at Daybreak" (B110), "Boys in October" (B287), "The Buffaloes" (B142), "The Cold Green Element: For Lorne Pierce" (B111), "The Comic Element" (B112), "The Dancers" (B113), "The Dark Plebeian Mind" (B146), "Death of a Construction Worker" (B114), "Enemies" (B141), "The Executioner," "Factorytown Mist," "For Louise, Age 17" (B116), "God, When You Speak," "Harlequin and Virgin," "The Improved Binoculars" (B500), "Keewaydin Poetry Festival" (B120), "Me, the P.M., and the Stars" (B133), "Metaphysical" (B147), "La Minerve" (B121), "Orpheus" (B123), "Poem [I would for your sake be gentle]" (B138), "Poet and Dancer," "The Poet Entertains Several Ladies" (B124), "The Poetic Process" (B125), "The Quill in Tranquillity," "The Red and the Black," "Saratoga Beach" (B144), "The Satyr," "Song for Naomi" (B792), "Summer Idyll: For William Goodwin" (B126), "Theology" (B148), "When It Came to Santayana's Turn" (B128), and "Winter Fantasy."

A9 *The Bull Calf and Other Poems.* Toronto: Contact, 1956. 49 pp.
Includes "Abel Cain" (B155), "After the Chinese," "Arachnid," "Astarte," "Boardwalk at Verdun" (B166), "Boys Bathing," "The Bull Calf" (B149), "Chokecherries," "The Dark Nest," "Disunity," "Earth Goddess," "The Fertile Muck" (B173), "Fiat Lux," "Firecrackers," "First Walk in Spring," "Halos at Lac Marie Louise" (B156), "Intersections," "Lesbia" (B167), "Letter from a Straw Man" (B162), "Maurer: Twin Heads" (B150), "The Mosquito," "On Seeing the Statuettes of Ezekiel and Jeremiah in the Church of Notre Dame" (B151), "One View of Dead Fish," "Red Chokecherries" (B165), "Rose Lemay," "Sacrament by the Water" (B160), "Song for a Late Hour," "Spikes," "Sutherland: Portrait of A.C." (B152), "Thoughts in the Water" (B157), "Undine," and "The Way of the World" (B158).

A10 *The Improved Binoculars.* Introd. William Carlos Williams. Jargon, No. 18. Highlands, N.C.: Jonathan Williams, 1956. 9–10, 106 pp.

Includes "After the Chinese" (A9), "Afternoon Tea" (B145), "The Ants" (B129), "Bacchanal" (B105), "The Birth of Tragedy" (B171), "Boys Bathing" (A9), "Boys in October" (B287), "The Bull Calf" (B149), "By Ecstasies Perplexed" (A11), "Cafe Politics in Spring" (B159), "Cemetery in August" (A4), "Chokecherries" (A9), "The Cold Green Element" (B111), "The Comic Element" (B112), "Compliments of the Season" (B58), "Composition in Late Spring" (B104), "Concourse at Cataraqui" (A11), "The Dancers" (B113), "De Bullion Street" (B55), "Death of Moishe Lazarovitch" (B180), "Earth Goddess" (A9), "Enemies" (B141), "Excursion" (B61), "The Fertile Muck" (B173), "First Snow: Lake Achigan" (B131), "First Walk in Spring" (A9), "For Louise, Age 17" (B116), "From Colony to Nation" (B748), "God, When You Speak" (A8), "Golfers" (B117), "Haruspex" (B78), "How Poems Get Written" (B356), "The Improved Binoculars" (B500), "In Memory of Fred Smith" (B91), "In the Midst of My Fever" (B102), "It's All in the Manner" (B106), "Latria" (A6), "The Longest Journey" (A5), "Love's Diffidence" (B154), "The Madonna of the Magnificat" (B107), "Maurer: Twin Heads" (B150), "Maxie" (A5), "Metaphysical" (B147), "Metzinger: Girl with a Bird" (B108), "Mildred" (A5), "La Minerve" (B121), "Mont Rolland" (B81), "Mrs. Fornheim, Refugee" (A2), "Nausicäa" (A11), "Newsboy" (B42), "Odysseus in Limbo" (B83), "On Seeing the Statuettes of Ezekiel and Jeremiah in the Church of Notre Dame" (B151), "Original Sin" (A11), "Orpheus" (B123), "Overheard in a Barbershop" (A4), "Paraclete" (B109), "Poem [I would for your sake be gentle]" (B138), "The Poet Entertains Several Ladies" (B124), "The Poetic Process" (B125),

"Portrait of Aileen" (B134), "Rain at La Minerve" (A6), "The Ravens [Where's the poem]" (A6), "Reconciliation" (B225), "The Red and the Black" (A8), "Rose Lemay" (A9), "Sacrament by the Water" (B160), "Saratoga Beach" (B144), "The Satyr" (A8), "Seven O'Clock Lecture" (B99), "Song for a Late Hour" (A9), "Song for Naomi" (B792), "Street Funeral" (B95), "Summer Idyll" (B126), "Sutherland: Portrait of A.C." (B152), "The Swimmer" (B60), "Thanatos and Eros" (A11), "Thoughts in the Water" (B157), "To the Girls of My Graduating Class" (B93), "To a Very Old Woman" (B90), "Undine" (A9), "Vexata Quaestio" (B140), "The Way of the World" (B158), "The Way the World Ends" (A11), "Westmount Doll" (B132), "When It Came to Santayana's Turn" (B128), "Winter Fantasy" (A8), and "Woman" (B168).

———. Introd. William Carlos Williams. Jargon, No. 18. Highlands, N.C.: Jonathan Williams, 1956. 9–10, 139 pp.

A second version of this book contains all the poems listed in the previous edition plus the following: "Admonition and Reply" (A7), "Anti-Romantic" (B174), "Astarte" (A9), "Black, Black," "The Dark Nest" (A9), "The Dark Plebeian Mind" (B146), "Early Morning in Cote St. Luc" (A5), "For Phyllis Who Snatched Her Poem in Anger" (A11), "For Priscilla" (A5), "Harlequin and Virgin" (A8), "Holiday" (B164), "Lady Enfield" (B45), "Lesbia" (B167), "Letter from a Straw Man" (B162), "Look, the Lambs Are All Around Us!" (A6), "Macdonald College 1905–1955" (A11), "Marie" (A6), "Me, the P.M., and the Stars" (B133), "Metamorphosis" (B517), "The Mosquito" (A9), "Motet" (B136), "My Favourite Colour's Green" (A7), "Now That I'm Older" (A6), "Obit," "On First Looking into Stalin's Coffin" (A6), "Philosophy 34" (B355), "Poet and Dancer" (A8), "Two Ladies at Traymore's"

(A11), "What Ulysses Said to Circe on the Beach of Aeaea" (A6), and "The Widows."

A11 *Music on a Kazoo.* Toronto: Contact, 1956. 59 pp.

Includes "Anglo-Canadian," "Archetypes," "Bargain," "Bibilus, Poetaster," "Bookseller," "By Ecstasies Perplexed," "Cafe Politics in Spring" (B159), "The Cold War: Saxon vs. Slav," "Concourse at Cataraqui," "Dionysius," "The Dwarf," "Enigma" (B161), "Esthetique" (B747), "Flags," "For Phyllis Who Snatched Her Poem in Anger," "From Colony to Nation" (B748), "From a Lawn-Chair," "Gathering of Poets," "Holiday" (B164), "The Human Condition [And not ten years ago]," "Imaginary Conversation," "Joseph K — ," "A Life," "Macdonald College 1905-1955," "A Marriage [What does your husband do for you?]," "Meeting," "Modern Love," Nausicaa," "The Newer Critics," "On Being Bitten by a Dog," "On Reading Spender's Collected Poems," "Original Sin," "Prescription," "Project," "The Puma's Tooth," "Snivellization," "Strategy," "Suzanne," "Teachers" (A4 — "Corypheus"), "Thanatos and Eros," "To the Cypriots," "Two Ladies at Traymore's," "The Way the World Ends," "When I See a Giant," and "Woman" (B168).

A12 *A Laughter in the Mind.* Jargon, No. 28. Highlands, N.C.: Jonathan Williams, 1958. 54 pp.

Includes "Autumn Lines for My Son," "Berry Picking" (B195), "Black, Black" (A10), "Cain" (B193), "Captives" (B192), "Cat Dying in Autumn" (B179), "Chatterers" (B194), "Climbing" (B182), "Côte des Neiges Cemetery" (B186), "E.P. on His Critics," "Family Portrait" (B172), "Garter Snake," "How Domestic Happiness Is Achieved," "If You Can't Scream" (B181), "Individualists" (B196), "Laurentian Rhapsody" (B188), "Letter to a Librarian," "Love Dream of W.P. Turner, English Poet," "The

Myth of Smith," "Olives for Jay MacPherson" (B183), "On the Jones Biography of Sigmund Freud," "Paging Mr. Superman" (B197), "Parting" (B184), "Poem for the Next Century" (B189), "Poetic Fame" (B185), "Rain," "A Roman Jew to Ovid," "Sheep" (B190), "The Toy Gun," "Two Songs for Sweet Voices" (B169), "Venetian Blinds," "Victory," "Whatever Else Poetry Is Freedom" (B191), and "The Widows" (A10).

———. Preface Irving Layton. Montreal: Orphée, 1959. [11-13], 97 pp.

A second version of this book contains all the poems listed in the previous edition plus the following: "Aesthete," "Anti-Romantic" (B174), "A Bonnet for Bessie," "Dance, My Little One" (B192), "Difference" (B163), "Divinity" (B198), "Enigma" (B161), "For Mao Tse-Tung" (B199), "For the More Devotional," "Heaven and Earth," "Love Is an Irrefutable Fire" (B200), "My Flesh Comfortless" (B201), "Obit" (A10), "Olives for Jay Macpherson" (B183), "Poem for the Year 2058" (B189), "Post Crematoria," "Providence" (B26), "The Transmogrification (For F.M.)," "The Transparency," "The Warm Afterdark" (B202), "When I See a Giant" (A7), "A Word from Diogenes" (B175), and "Young Girls Dancing" (B203).

A13 *A Red Carpet for the Sun.* Foreword Irving Layton. Toronto: McClelland and Stewart, 1959. [4], [240] pp.

———. Foreword Irving Layton. Jargon Books, No. 35. Highlands, N.C.: Jonathan Williams, 1959. [4], [240] pp.

Includes "Abel Cain" (B155), "Admonition and Reply" (A7), "After the Chinese" (A9), "Afternoon Tea" (B145), "Against This Death" (B590), "Anglo-Canadian" (A11), "Anti-Romantic" (B174), "The Ants" (B129), "Astarte" (A9), "Autumn Lines for

My Son" (A12), "Bacchanal" (B105), "Bargain" (A11), "Beauty [Omah who keeps house]" (A4), "Berry Picking" (B195), "The Birth of Tragedy" (B171), "Black, Black" (A10), "The Black Huntsmen" (B79), "Boardwalk at Verdun" (B166), "A Bonnet for Bessie" (A12), "Boys Bathing" (A9), "Boys in October" (B287), "The Buffaloes" (B142), "The Bull Calf" (B149), "By Ecstasies Perplexed" (A11), "Café Politics in Spring" (B159), "Cain" (B193), "Canadian Skiers" (B153), "Cat Dying in Autumn" (B179), "Cemetery in August" (A4), "Chatterers" (B194), "Chokecherries" (A9), "Christmas Day" (A7), "Climbing" (B182), "The Cold Green Element" (B111), "The Comic Element" (B112), "Compliments of the Season" (B58), "Composition in Late Spring" (B104), "Concourse at Cataraqui" (A11), "Côte des Neiges Cemetery" (B186), "Crone" (A3), "Dance, My Little One" (B192), "The Dancers" (B113), "The Dark Nest" (A9), "The Dark Plebeian Mind" (B146), "De Bullion Street" (B55), "Death of a Construction Worker" (B114), "Death of Moishe Lazarovitch" (B180), "Dionysius" (A11), "Divinity" (B198), "Drill Shed" (B54), "The Dwarf" (A11), "Early Morning in Côte St. Luc" (A5), "Earth Goddess" (A9), "Enemies" (B141), "Epitaphs: Philosopher [B28], Poet Killed in Action [B77], An Ugly Servitor to Three Queens [B115], Wit [B29]," "Eros [With the best side of my tongue]" (A4), "Esthetique" (B747), "Excursion" (B61), "The Execution" (A3), "The Executioner" (A8), "Ex-Nazi" (A3), "Family Portrait" (B172), "The Fertile Muck" (B173), "Fiat Lux" (A9), "First Snow: Lake Achigan" (B131), "First Walk in Spring" (A9), "For Louise, Age 17" (B116), "For Mao Tse-Tung: A Meditation on Flies and Kings" (B199), "For My Detractors" (A7), "For Phyllis, Who Snatched Her Poem in Anger" (A11), "For Priscilla" (A5), "From Colony to Nation" (B748), "Garter Snake" (A12), "God, When You Speak" (A8), "Golfers" (B117), "Good-bye Bahai" (A3), "Gothic Landscape" (B76), "Halos at Lac Marie Louise" (B156), "Harlequin and Virgin" (A8), "Haruspex" (B78), "Holiday" (B164), "How Domestic Happiness Is Achieved" (A12), "How Poems Get Written" (B356), "How to Look at an Abstract" (B315), "I Would for Your Sake Be Gentle" (B138), "If You Can't Scream" (B181), "Imperial" (B122), "The Improved Binoculars" (B500), "In Memory of Fred Smith" (B91), "In the Midst of My Fever" (B102), "Individualists" (B196), "Intersections" (A9), "It's All in the Manner" (B106), "Jewish Main Street" (B59), "Joseph K —" (A11), "Keewaydin Poetry Festival" (B120), "Lachine, Que." (A5), "Lady Enfield" (B45), "Latria" (A6), "Laurentian Rhapsody" (B188), "Lesbia" (B167), "Letter from a Straw Man" (B162), "Letter to a Librarian" (A12), "The Longest Journey" (A5), "Look, the Lambs Are All Around Us" (A6), "Love Is an Irrefutable Fire" (B200), "Love the Conqueror Worm" (B94), "Love's Diffidence" (B154), "Macdonald College 1905–1955" (A11), "The Madonna of the Magnificat" (B107), "Marie" (A6), "Maurer: Twin Heads" (B150), "Maxie" (A5), "May Day Orators" (A7), "Me, the P.M., and the Stars" (B133), "Metamorphosis" (B517), "Metaphysical" (B147), "Metzinger: Girl with a Bird" (B108), "Mildred" (A5), "La Minerve" (B121), "Misunderstanding" (B335), "Modern Love" (A11), "Mortuary" (B46), "Motet" (B136), "Mont Rolland" (B81), "Mr. Ther-Apis" (B103), "Mrs. Fornheim, Refugee" (A2), "My Flesh Comfortless" (B201), "Nausicäa" (A11), "New Tables" (A6), "Newsboy" (B42), "Not Blown Away" (A7), "Now That I'm Older" (A6), "Obit" (A10), "Odysseus in Limbo" (B83), "On Being Bitten by a Dog" (A11), "On First Looking into Stalin's Coffin" (A6), "On My Way to School," "On Seeing the Statuettes of Ezekiel and Jeremiah in the Church of Notre Dame" (B151), "On the Death of A. Vishinsky" (B143), "One View of Dead Fish" (A9), "Original Sin" (A11), "Orpheus" (B123), "Overheard in a Barbershop" (A4), "Paging Mr. Superman" (B197), "Paraclete" (B109), "Parting" (B184), "Philosophy 34" (B355), "Poem for the Next Century" (B189), "Poet and Dancer" (A8), "The Poet Entertains Several Ladies" (B124), "Poetic Fame" (B185), "The Poetic Process" (B125), "Portrait [Pay small attention to the chin]" (B137), "Portrait of Aileen" (B134), "Project" (A11), "Providence" (B26), "The Puma's Tooth" (A11), "Rain" (A12), "Rain at La Minerve" (A6), "The Ravens [Where's the poem]" (A6), "Reconciliation" (B225), "Red Chokecherries" (B165), "Rembrandt" (A3), "A Roman Jew to Ovid" (A12), "Rose LeMay" (A9), "Sacrament by the Water" (B160), "Saratoga Beach" (B144), "The Satyr" (A8), "Seven O'Clock Lecture" (B99), "Sheep" (B190), "Song for a Late Hour" (A9), "Song for Naomi" (B792), "A Spider Danced a Cosy Jig" (B30), "Spikes" (A9), "Street Funeral" (B95), "Summer Idyll" (B126), "Sutherland: Portrait of A.C." (B152), "Suzanne" (A11), "The Swimmer" (B60), "T.S. Eliot" (B127), "Terrene" (B87), "Thanatos and Eros" (A11), "Theology" (B148), "Thoughts in the Water" (B157), "To a Very Old Woman" (B90), "To the Girls of My Graduating Class" (B93), "The Toy Gun" (A12), "Trumpet Daffodil" (B96), "Two Ladies at Traymore's" (A11), "Two Poets in Toronto" (A6), "Undine" (A9), "Venetian Blinds" (A12), "Veteran" (A6), "Vexata Quaestio" (B140), "Victory" (A12), "A Vision" (A4), "The Warm Afterdark" (B202), "The Way of the World" (B158), "The Way the World Ends" (A11), "Westmount Doll" (B132), "Whatever Else Poetry Is Freedom" (B191), "What Ulysses Said to Circe on the Beach at Aeaea" (A6), "When It Came

to Santayana's Turn" (B128), "The Widows" (A12), "Winter Fantasy" (A8), "Woman" (B168), and "Young Girls Dancing at Camp Lajoie" (B203).

A14   *Balls for a One-Armed Juggler*. Foreword Irving Layton. Toronto: McClelland and Stewart, 1963. xviii–xxii, 121 pp.

Includes "Advice for Two Young Poets" (B269), "Agnus Dei," "Ambiguities of Conduct," "Androgyne" (B270), "The Architect" (B325), "At Desjardins," "Baudelaire in a Summer Cottage," "The Bishopric" (B261), "Breakdown" (B275), "Butterfly on Rock" (B271), "The Cage" (B254), "Change [We were looking at the October landscape]," "Crazy Jack" (B278), "The Dazed Steer: For Norman Mailer" (B272), "Dining Out" (B210), "The Disguise," "The Divine Madman," "Drunk on McGill Campus: For Sabine" (B276), "Elegy for Marilyn Monroe" (B277), "Epigram for Roy Daniells" (B264), "Five Women," "The Fool's Song," "For Alexander Trocchi, Novelist" (B249), "For Aviva, Because I Love Her" (B255), "For My Friend Who Teaches Literature," "Free Djilas," "Friends S—— loves you, I said," "Gifts," "The Gods Speak Out" (B252), "A Grotesque Pair," "The Hag," "A Harsh Karsh," "History as a Slice of Ham" (B265), "Homo Oeconomicus: For Nikita," "If I Lie Still" (B591), "The Imbecile" (B273), "Involvement," "Lazarus," "Lilith" (B256), "Love Among the Cannibals [Having enjoyed]," "Make Mine Vodka," "Man Going Up and Down," "Mashed Potatoes," "Merlin Perverse" (B262), "Mixed Metaphors," "Moral with a Story" (B274), "Neighbour Love [A grove]," "No Cause for Jealousy," "No Shish Kebab" (B257), "No Wild Dog," "Not in Vain," "On a Clothing Manufacturer," "On Rereading the Beats" (B280), "The Pillar" (B247), "Poem for the Peerless Queen," "Political Economy"

(B266), "Portrait of an English Prof" (B267), "The Predator" (B285), "Questions" (B253), "The Real Values" (B260), "The Ritual Cut," "Silence: For Ernest Hemingway [The word betrays the act]" (B258), "Sören Kierkegaard," "The Sparks Fly" (B268), "Still Life," "Stranger in Town," "Supernatural Event at Cedar Pond," "Sutra," "A Tall Man Executes a Jig: For Malcolm Ross" (B248), "Thanatos," "Therapy" (B439), "There Were No Signs" (B250), "This Machine Age" (B170), "To a Lily: For A.J.M. Smith" (B259), "Le Tombeau de la mort," "The Well-Wrought Urn" (B263), "What Does It Matter?", "Whom I Write For" (B251), "Who's Crazy?", and "Why I Can't Sleep Nights."

A15   *The Laughing Rooster.* Preface Irving Layton. Toronto: McClelland and Stewart, 1964. 17–25, 112 pp.

Includes "Aftermath," "Ambivalency," "And These Live," "At the Alhambra," "At the Iglesia de Sacromonte" (B302), "At the Pier in Denia" (B288), "Ballad of the Old Spaniard" (B289), "Betrayal," "Bicycle Pump" (B300), "Blue and Lovely, My Love," "The Cactus," "El Caudillo" (B293), "Coal" (B281), "Courtesies of Love," "Creation [I fashioned you]" (B306), "The Daimon," "Das Wahre Ich" (B282), "A Dedication" (B744), "Discourse on Christian Love," "Diversion," "Done on Both Sides," "Encounter," "Equation," "Everywhere, the Stink" (B438), "F.R. Scott" (B286), "Food for Thought" (B299), "For My Former Students" (B290), "For My Green Old Age" (B301), "For Princess Sally," "Fornalutx," "Friends: For Nancy [The person I most admire]," "Gift," "The Giraffe," "El Gusano [From the place where I was sitting]" (B294), "Homage to Ben Jonson," "Homage to Lucullus" (B283), "I Saw a Faun," "Icarus," "In Memory of Stephen Ward" (B303), "Injustice," "The

Laughing Rooster," "Life in the 20th Century," "The Lizard" (B291), "Lust," "Lyric [The rains will come]," "The Maddened Lover" (B284), "Man and Wife," "Mexico as Seen by the Reverent Dudek" (B212), "Montgo," "My Queen, My Quean," "On Reading Moby Dick," "On Spanish Soil" (B295), "On the Assassination of President Kennedy" (B292), "Pins & Splinters," "Plaza de Toros" (B296), "Pleasure," "Portrait of a Genius" (B305), "Portrait of Nolady," "Prussian Blue," "Redemption" (B437), "Release [I shall rejoice]" (B10), "Requiem for an Age" (B13), "Second Thought on the Armada" (B304), "The Seduction [First he knocks her down]," "Silly Rhymes for Aviva," "The Song of Thrift," "Spring Exultances: For Aviva" (B297), "Stone-Splitters in Alicante" (B298), "Success," "The Tragic Poet," "Vigil" (B1), "Why I Believe in God," "Why the Hares Stare and Run," "Winter Light," "The Worm [The filthy rain]," and "Wrong End of Telescope."

A16   *Collected Poems.* Foreword Irving Layton. Toronto: McClelland and Stewart, 1965. xix–xxii, 354 pp.

Includes "Abel Cain" (B155), "Admonition and Reply" (A7), "Advice for Two Young Poets" (B269), "After the Chinese" (A9), "After Theognis" (B228), "Aftermath" (A15), "Afternoon Tea" (B145), "Against This Death" (B590), "Amaduce, the Critic" (A2 — "Butchevo, the Critic"), "Ambiguities of Conduct" (A14), "Ambivalency" (A15), "Androgyne" (B270), "Anglo-Canadian" (A11), "Anti-Romantic" (B174), "The Ants" (B129), "Arachnid" (A9), "Arboreal Nature" (B229), "Archetypes" (A11), "The Architect" (B325), "Astarte" (A9), "At Desjardins" (A14), "At the Alhambra" (A15), "At the Iglesia de Sacromonte" (B302), "At the Pier in Denia" (B288), "Autumn Lines for My Son" (A12), "Bacchanal" (B105), "Ballad of the Old Spaniard"

(B289), "Bargain" (A11), "Baudelaire in a Summer Cottage" (A14), "Beauty [Omah who keeps house]" (A4), "Because My Calling Is Such" (B204), "Berry Picking" (B195), "Betrayal" (A15), "Beutel's Name Is Inscribed for Eternal Life" (B230), "Bicycle Pump" (B300), "Birds at Daybreak" (B110), "The Birth of Tragedy" (B171), "Bishop Berkeley Goes to Bed" (A3), "The Bishopric" (B261), "Black, Black" (A10), "The Black Huntsmen" (B79), "Blue and Lovely, My Love" (A15), "Boardwalk at Verdun" (B166), "Boys Bathing" (A9), "Boys in October" (B287), "Breakdown" (B275), "Brief Encounter" (A6), "The Buffaloes" (B142), "The Bull Calf" (B149), "Butterfly on Rock" (B271), "By Ecstasies Perplexed" (A11), "The Cactus" (A15), "Café Politics in Spring" (B159), "The Cage" (B254), "The Caged Bird" (B206), "Cain" (B193), "Canadian Skiers" (B153), "Casca, or Suum Cuique" (A2 — "Suum Cuique"), "Cat Dying in Autumn" (B179), "El Caudillo" (B293), "Cemetery in August" (A4), "Chatterers" (B194), "Chloris" (A4 — "Had I the Talent"), "Clibus, the Poetaster," "Climbing" (B182), "Coal" (B281), "The Cold Green Element" (B111), "The Comic Element" (B112), "Community" (B33), "Compliments of the Season" (B58), "Composition in Late Spring" (B104), "Concourse at Cataraqui" (A11), "Conference Man," "The Convertible" (B231), "Corypheus" (A4), "Côte des Neiges Cemetery" (B186), "Courtesies of Love" (A15), "Creation [I fashioned you]" (B306), "Crone" (A3), "Dance, My Little One" (B192), "The Dancers" (B113), "Dans le Jardin" (B207), "The Dark Nest" (A9), "The Dark Plebeian Mind" (B146), "Das Wahre Ich" (B282), "The Day Aviva Came to Paris" (B208), "De Bullion Street" (B55), "Death of a Construction Worker" (B114), "Death of Moishe Lazarovitch" (B180), "A Dedication" (B744), "Defence Enough" (A7), "Dialogue with a Young and Pretty Wife" (A51), "Dion-

ysus" (A11), "Discourse on Christian Love" (A15), "Disunity" (A9), "Diversion" (A15), "Divine Image" (B238), "Divinity" (B198), "Drill Shed" (B54), "Dudelus, Poetaster" (A11 — "Bibilus, Poetaster"), "The Dwarf" (A11), "Early Morning in Côte St. Luc" (A5), "Earth Goddess" (A9), "Élan" (A2), "Elegy for Marilyn Monroe" (B277), "Elpinor" (A7 — "Horsley-Trevor"), "Encounter" (A15), "Enemies" (B141), "Epitaphs: Philosopher [B28], Poet Killed in Action [B77], An Ugly Servitor to Three Queens [B115], Wit [B29]," "Eros [With the best side of my tongue]" (A4), "Eros Where the Rents Aren't High" (A6), "Esthetique" (B747), "Everywhere, the Stink" (B438), "Excursion" (B61), "The Execution" (A3), "The Executioner" (A8), "Ex-Nazi" (A3), "F.R. Scott" (B286), "Family Portrait" (B172), "The Fertile Muck" (B173), "Fiat Lux" (A9), "The Fictive Eye" (A51), "First Snow: Lake Achigan" (B131), "First Walk in Spring" (A9), "Food for Thought" (B299), "The Fool's Song" (A14), "For Adlai Stevenson" (A4), "For Alexander Trocchi, Novelist" (B249), "For Aviva, Because I Love Her" (B255), "For Dulla Who Unexpectedly Came into Some Money" (A4), "For Louise, Age 17" (B116), "For Mao Tse-Tung: A Meditation on Flies and Kings" (B199), "For My Detractors" (A7), "For My Former Students" (B290), "For My Friend Who Teaches Literature" (A14), "For My Green Old Age" (B301), "For Phyllis Who Snatched Her Poem in Anger" (A11), "For Priscilla" (A5), "For Prof. F.M. Heichelheim" (B239), "For the More Devotional" (A7), "Fornalutx" (A15), "Free Djilas" (A14), "From Colony to Nation" (B748), "Garter Snake" (A12), "Gathering of Poets" (A11), "Genius Love and Poetry" (B89), "Gift" (A15), "The Giraffe" (A15), "God, When You Speak" (A8), "Golfers" (B117), "Good-bye Bahai" (A3), "Gothic Landscape" (B76), "The Greeks Had a Word for It" (A7),

"El Gusano [From the place where I was sitting]" (B294), "Halos at Lac Marie Louise" (B156), "Harlequin and Virgin" (A8), "Haruspex" (B78), "History as a Slice of Ham" (B265), "Holiday" (B164), "Homage to Lucullus" (B283), "Hostia" (B232), "How Domestic Happiness Is Achieved" (A12), "How Poems Get Written" (B356), "How to Look at an Abstract" (B315), "Human Being" (A7), "I Know the Dark and Hovering Moth" (B205), "I Saw a Faun" (A15), "I Would for Your Sake Be Gentle" (B138), "Icarus" (A15), "If I Lie Still" (B591), "If You Can't Scream" (B181), "The Imbecile" (B273), "The Improved Binoculars" (B500), "In Memory of Fred Smith" (B91), "In Memory of Stephen Ward" (B303), "In Rattlesnake Country," "In the Midst of My Fever" (B102), "Individualists" (B196), "Injustice" (A15), "Innocence," "Intersections" (A9), "It's All in the Manner" (B106), "Jewish Main Street" (B59), "Joseph K — " (A11), "Karl Marx" (B69), "Keewaydin Poetry Festival" (B120), "Keine Lazarovitch 1870–1959" (B220), "Lady Enfield" (B45), "Latria" (A6), "The Laughing Rooster" (A15), "Laurentian Rhapsody" (B188), "Lazarus" (A14), "Lesbia" (B167), "Letter from a Straw Man" (B162), "Letter to a Librarian" (A12), "A Life" (A11), "Life in the 20th Century" (A15), "Lilith" (B256), "The Lizard" (B291) "Logos" (B307), "The Longest Journey" (A5), "Look, the Lambs Are All Around Us!" (A6), "Love Is an Irrefutable Fire" (B200), "Love the Conqueror Worm" (B94), "Love's Diffidence" (B154), "Lust" (A15), "Macdonald College 1905–1955" (A11), "The Maddened Lover" (B284), "The Madonna of the Magnificat" (B107), "Man and Wife" (A15), "Man Going Up and Down" (A14), "Marie" (A6), "Marius" (A6), "Mashed Potatoes" (A14), "Maurer: Twin Heads" (B150), "Maxie" (A5), "May Day Orators" (A7), "Me, the P.M., and the Stars" (B133), "Metamorphosis" (B517), "Metaphysical" (B147), "Metzinger: Girl with a Bird" (B108), "Mexico as Seen by the Reverent Dudek" (B212), "Mildred" (A5), "La Minerve" (B121), "Misunderstanding" (B335), "Mixed Metaphors" (A14), "Modern Love" (A11), "The Modern Poet [Since Eliot set the fashion]" (B36), "Mont Rolland" (B81), "Montgo" (A15), "Moral with a Story" (B274), "Mortuary" (B46), "The Mosquito" (A9), "Motet" (B136), "Mount Royal" (A7), "Mr. Beutel Lays a Cornerstone" (B214), "Mr. Ther-Apis" (B103), "Mrs. Fornheim, Refugee" (A2), "Mute in the Wind" (A7), "My Flesh Comfortless" (B201), "My Queen, My Quean" (A15), "Nausicäa" (A11), "New Tables" (A6), "Newsboy" (B42), "No Shish Kebab" (B257), "No Wild Dog" (A14), "Not Blown Away" (A7), "Now That I'm Older" (A6), "O.B.E." (B122), "O Say Can You See" (B308), "Obit" (A10), "Odysseus in Limbo" (B83), "On Being Bitten by a Dog" (A11), "On First Looking into Stalin's Coffin" (A6), "On My Way to School" (A13), "On Seeing the Statuettes of Ezekiel and Jeremiah in the Church of Notre Dame" (B151), "On Spanish Soil" (B295), "On the Assassination of President Kennedy" (B292), "On the Death of A. Vishinsky" (B143), "One View of Dead Fish" (A9), "Original Sin" (A11), "Orpheus" (B123), "Overheard in a Barbershop" (A4), "Paging Mr. Superman" (B197), "Paraclete" (B109), "Parting" (B184), "Paysage" (A8 — "The Red and the Black"), "Personae," "Philosophy 34" (B355), "Piazza San Marco" (B221), "The Pillar" (B247), "Pine Avenue Analyst" (A6), "Plaza de Toros" (B296), "Pleasure" (A15), "A Pocketful of Rye" (A4), "Poem for the Next Century" (B189), "Poet and Dancer" (A8), "The Poet Entertains Several Ladies" (B124), "Poetic Fame" (B185), "The Poetic Process" (B125), "Political Economy" (B266), "Poplars" (A2), "Portrait [Pay small attention to the chin]" (B137), "Portrait of a Genius"

(B305), "Portrait of Aileen" (B134), "Portrait of Nolady" (A15), "Post-Crematoria" (A12), "The Predator" (B285), "Processed" (A6), "Project" (A11), "Prologue to the Long Pea-Shooter" (B139), "Providence" (B26), "The Puma's Tooth" (A11), "Questions" (B253), "Rain" (A12), "Rain at La Minerve" (A6), "The Ravens [Where's the poem]" (A6), "The Real Values" (B260), "Reconciliation" (B225), "Red Chokecherries" (B165), "Redemption" (B437), "Rembrandt" (A3), "The Ritual Cut" (A14), "A Roman Jew to Ovid" (A12), "Rose Lemay" (A9), "Sacrament by the Water" (B160), "Sagebrush Classic" (B227), "Sancta Simplicitas" (B135), "Saratoga Beach" (B144), "The Satyr" (A8), "Schoolteacher in Late November" (B72), "Second Thoughts on the Armada" (B304), "The Seduction [First he knocks her down]" (A15), "Sensibility" (A6), "Seven O'Clock Lecture" (B99), "Sheep" (B190), "Silence: For Ernest Hemingway [The word betrays the act]" (B258), "Silly Rhymes for Aviva" (A15), "Silver Lining" (A6), "Snivellization" (A11), "Soleil de Noces" (B98), "Song" (B235), "Song for a Late Hour" (A9), "Song for Naomi" (B792), "The Sparks Fly" (B268), "A Spider Danced a Cosy Jig" (B30), "Spikes" (A9), "Still Life" (A14), "Stocktaking on the Day of Atonement" (B244), "Stolen Watch" (B64), "Stone-Splitters in Alicante" (B298), "A Strange Turn" (B311), "Street Funeral" (B95), "Success" (A15), "Summer Idyll" (B126), "Sutherland: Portrait of A.C." (B152), "Suzanne" (A11), "The Swimmer" (B60), "T.S. Eliot" (B127), "A Tall Man Executes a Jig" (B248), "Terrene" (B87), "Thanatos and Eros" (A11), "Theology" (B148), "Therapy" (B439), "There Were No Signs" (B250), "Thersites," "This Machine Age" (B170), "Thoughts in the Water" (B157), "To a Very Old Woman" (B90), "To the Girls of My Graduating Class" (B93), "The Toy Gun" (A12), "The Tragic Poet" (A15), "Trilliums after a Party" (B219), "Trumpet Daffodil" (B96), "Two Ladies at Traymore's" (A11), "Two Poets in Toronto" (A6), "Two Songs for Sweet Voices" (B169), "Undine" (A9), "University Buildings" (A6), "Venetian Blinds" (A12), "Veteran" (A6), "Vexata Quaestio" (B140), "Victoria Square" (A51), "Vigil" (B1), "A Vision" (A4), "The Warm Afterdark" (B202), "The Way of the World" (B158), "The Way the World Ends" (A11), "The Well-Wrought Urn" (B263), "Westmount Doll" (B132), "What Ulysses Said to Circe on the Beach of Aeaea" (A6), "Whatever Else Poetry Is Freedom" (B191), "When It Came to Santayana's Turn" (B128), "Whom I Write For" (B251), "Why I Believe in God" (A15), "Why I Don't Make Love to the First Lady" (B245), "Why the Hares Stare and Run" (A15), "The Widows" (A12), "Winter Fantasy" (A8), "Winter Light" (A15), "With the Money I Spend" (A51), "Woman" (B168), "Woman in the Square" (B75), "Women of Rome" (B223), "The Wooden Spoon" (B224), "A Word from Diogenes" (B175), "The Worm [The filthy rain]" (A15), "The Yard" (B67), "Young Girls Dancing at Camp Lajoie" (B203), and "Zoroastrian" (B309).

A17 *Periods of the Moon.* Foreword Irving Layton. Toronto: McClelland and Stewart, 1967. 11–14, 127 pp.

Includes "Above All, Avoid Halitosis" (B347), "The Air Is Sultry" (B312), "Animal Behaviour," "Apparition" (B351), "At the Belsen Memorial" (B326), "Ballad of the Stones," "Beach Acquaintance: For Henri Lamonde," "Beach Romance," "Chairman, Board of Education: For Ben Beutel," "Clochards: For Wynne Francis" (B352), "Collaboration" (B345), "The Coming of the Messiah," "Confederation Ode" (B327), "Crisis Theology," "Erich Kästner," "Euphoria," "Faces of the Young,"

"Fair Musia," "Fidelity," "For David's Second Birthday on July 24th," "For Miss Cézanne" (B316), "For Musia's Grandchildren" (B317), "For the Editor of the Jewish Canadian Eagle," "For the Record: For Mark Schwartz" (B318), "For the Stinker Who Called Me an Apologist for Nazi Crimes: For Peter Lust" (B328), "Freedom" (B319), "Games" (B353), "Gratitude" (B333), "Gypsies," "Holiday in the South" (B334), "The Human Condition: For A.W. [Hope for the human race?]" (B321), "Improved Vision," "Insect Blood," "Insomnia," "Invention" (B329), "Light," "Look Homeward, Angel," "Love Rhymes with Dove," "Mahogany Red" (B322), "Mammoths" (B342), "Memo to Herbert Spencer," "Mutability," "Mystery," "Myth," "National Virtues" (B336), "New Year's Eve: For Marion" (B343), "Nice," "North and South" (B330), "Nothing Less: For Aviva," "An Old Nicoise Whore: For Germaine D — " (B354), "Olympia Kaput" (B314), "On the Naming of Streets," "On the Quay with My Mother's Ghost," "Pigeons" (B518), "Pilgrim" (B344), "Plage Neptune," "Poetry," "Poros," "Portrait Done with a Steel Pen" (B331), "Presbyterian Church Signboard," "Professional Jew," "Quay Scene," "Repetition" (B337), "Reply to a Rhyming Notary," "Rhine Boat Trip" (B332), "Ruins" (B349), "Rules," "The Sad Madonna" (B346), "Sight Seeing," "A Song about Woman" (B338), "Song of a Frightened Jewish Boy," "Sophisticates Abroad," "Speculators," "Street Violinist," "Sun-Bathers" (B339), "Three on a Park Bench," "Time's Velvet Tongue" (B357), "To a Beautiful Unknown Girl" (B358), "Vacation in Nice," "The Wave: For Sam Tata" (B340), "Westminster Abbey," "Winter Lyric" (B324), "Women of the Back Streets of Europe" (B341), and "The World [First and foremost]."

A18 *The Shattered Plinths.* Foreword Irving Layton.

Toronto: McClelland and Stewart, 1968. 12–16, 95 pp.

Includes "Arabs," "Autopsy on Aberfan," "Bad Dream," "The Best Proof" (B373), "Brief Dialogue Between Negro Father and Son," "Counsel for My Stung Love," "Dorothy Parker (1893–1967)" (B359), "Elegy for Strul" (B374), "End of the Summer" (B365), "Epiphany," "Fantasia in Black," "For My Two Sons, Max and David" (B361), "For the Cause," "For the Girl with Wide-Apart Eyes," "The Graveyard" (B380), "Haiku: For Eleanor Stober," "He Saw Them, at First," "Heraclitos," "Homage to Roumania," "If Whales Could Think on Certain Happy Days" (B516), "Iroquois in Nice" (B570), "Kamerad" (B366), "The Larger Issue," "Lesson for Today" (B367), "Like a Mother Demented: For Frank Scott" (B368), "Love Poem with an Odd Twist" (B362), "Marché Municipale: For Desmond Pacey" (B348), "Mediterranean Cemetery" (B369), "Merited," "Modern Greek Poet: For A. Vavrikos," "Modern Lyric" (B375), "The New Sensibility," "The Next Time Does It" (B370), "Oil Slick on the Riviera: For Milton Wilson" (B371), "On a Negro Rioter in Buffalo," "On Seeing the Guillotine at Madame Tussaud's," "On This Far Shore" (B363), "One Last Try at a Final Solution," "Peacemonger," "Poet at Sinai," "Poetess [She has a voice]," "Prelude," "Proper Reading Light," "Queer Hate Poem" (B376), "The Red Moujhik" (B360), "Rumberto," "Soapflakes," "Songs Out of Season," "A Sort of After-Dinner Speech," "The Sweet Light Strikes My Eyes: For Wynne Francis," "Talk at Twilight" (B377), "Tamed Birds," "To a Generation of Poets," "To the Russians at the U.N.," "To Write an Old-Fashioned Poem" (B364), "Vignettes," "Village Funeral" (B372), "The Way Keats Never Would Have Told It," "Who Will Give Me Back," and "Yet What if the Survivors" (B378).

A19 *Selected Poems*. Ed. and preface Wynne Francis. Toronto: McClelland and Stewart, 1969. [xiii–xiv], 140 pp.

———. Ed. and preface Wynne Francis. London: Charisma, 1974. [xiii–xiv], 140 pp.

Includes "At the Iglesia de Sacromonte" (B302), "Ballad of the Old Spaniard" (B289), "Bargain" (A11), "Because My Calling Is Such" (B204), "Berry Picking" (B195), "The Birth of Tragedy" (B171), "The Black Huntsmen" (B79), "The Bull Calf" (B149), "Butterfly on Rock" (B271), "By Ecstasies Perplexed" (A11), "The Cage" (B254), "Cain" (B193), "Cat Dying in Autumn" (B179), "El Caudillo" (B293), "Cemetery in August" (A4), "Chokecherries" (A9), "Climbing" (B182), "Clochards" (B352), "The Cold Green Element" (B111), "Compliments of the Season" (B58), "Composition in Late Spring" (B104), "The Convertible" (B231), "Côte des Neiges Cemetery" (B186), "Dans le Jardin" (B207), "The Day Aviva Came to Paris" (B208), "De Bullion Street" (B55), "Death of Moishe Lazarovitch" (B180), "A Dedication" (B744), "Elegy for Strul" (B374), "Enemies" (B141), "Excursion to Ottawa" (B61), "The Execution" (A3), "Family Portrait" (B172), "The Fertile Muck" (B173), "The Fool's Song" (A14), "For Mao Tse-Tung: A Meditation on Flies and Kings" (B199), "For Musia's Grandchildren" (B317), "For My Detractors" (A7), "For My Two Sons, Max and David" (B361), "From Colony to Nation" (B748), "Gothic Landscape" (B76), "The Graveyard" (B380), "El Gusano [From the place where I was sitting]" (B294), "I Know the Dark and Hovering Moth" (B205), "I Would for Your Sake Be Gentle" (B138), "If Whales Could Think on Certain Happy Days" (B516), "The Improved Binoculars" (B500), "In the Midst of My Fever" (B102), "Invention" (B329), "Karl Marx" (B69), "Keine Lazarovitch: 1870–1959" (B220), "Laurentian Rhapsody" (B188), "Letter from a Straw Man" (B162), "Like a Mother Demented" (B368), "Look, the Lambs Are All Around Us!" (A6), "Love Poem with an Odd Twist" (B362), "Love the Conqueror Worm" (B94), "Mahogany Red" (B322), "Marché Municipale" (B348), "Maxie" (A5), "Metamorphosis" (B517), "Metzinger: Girl with a Bird" (B108), "Misunderstanding" (B335), "Mont Rolland" (B81), "Mortuary" (B46), "Mrs. Fornheim, Refugee" (A2), "My Flesh Comfortless" (B201), "Nausicäa" (A11), "New Tables" (A6), "Newsboy" (B42), "No Wild Dog" (A14), "Oil Slick on the Riviera" (B371), "An Old Nicoise Whore" (B354), "On Being Bitten by a Dog" (A11), "On First Looking into Stalin's Coffin" (A6), "On Seeing the Statuettes of Ezekiel and Jeremiah in the Church of Notre-Dame" (B151), "On the Quay with My Mother's Ghost" (A17), "Paging Mr. Superman" (B197), "Parting" (B184), "Pigeons" (B518), "Plaza de Toros" (B296), "Portrait of a Genius" (B305), "Prologue to the Long Pea-Shooter" (B139), "Proof Reader" (B63), "Rain" (A12), "Rain at La Minerve" (A6), "Red Chokecherries" (B165), "Rhine Boat Trip" (B332), "Sacrament by the Water" (B160), "Sagebrush Classic" (B227), "Seven O'Clock Lecture" (B99), "Song for a Late Hour" (A9), "Song for Naomi" (B792), "Speculators" (A17), "The Sweet Light Strikes My Eyes" (A18), "The Swimmer" (B60), "A Tall Man Executes a Jig" (B248), "There Were No Signs" (B250), "This Machine Age" (B170), "To a Very Old Woman" (B90), "To the Girls of My Graduating Class" (B93), "Trumpet Daffodil" (B96), "Vexata Quaestio" (B140), "The Way of the World" (B158), "Westminster Abbey" (A17), "Whatever Else Poetry Is Freedom" (B191), "Whom I Write For" (B251), "Why I Don't Make Love to the First Lady" (B245), "With the Money I Spend" (A51), "Woman" (B168), "Women of Rome"

(B223), "The World's a Tavern" (B83), "The Worm [The filthy rain]" (A15), "The Yard" (B67), and "Yet What if the Survivors" (B378).

A20   *The Collected Poems of Irving Layton*. Foreword Irving Layton. Toronto: McClelland and Stewart, 1971. [i–vi], 589 pp.
———. [Limited ed.] Foreword Irving Layton. Illus. Harold Town. Toronto: McClelland and Stewart, 1971. [viii–xiii], 589 pp.

Includes "Abel Cain" (B155), "Absence" (A21), "Admonition and Reply" (A7), "Advice for Two Young Poets" (B269), "Aerolites [Up there, up there on high]" (B30), "After Auschwitz" (B386), "After the Chinese" (A19), "After Theognis" (B228), "Aftermath" (A15), "Afternoon Tea" (B145), "Against This Death" (B590), "The Air Is Sultry" (B312), "Ambiguities of Conduct" (A14), "Ambivalency" (A15), "Androgyne" (B270), "Anglo-Canadian" (A11), "Anti-Romantic" (B174), "The Ants" (B129), "The Ape and the Pharisee" (A2), "Apparition" (B351), "Arabs" (A18), "Arachnid" (A9), "Aran Islands" (B429), "Arboreal Nature" (B229), "Archetypes" (A11), "The Architect" (B325), "As Seen through a Glass Darkly" (B440), "At Desjardins" (A14), "At the Alhambra" (A15), "At the Belsen Memorial" (B326), "At the Iglesia de Sacromonte" (B302), "At the Pier in Denia" (B288), "Attachments" (B403), "Autopsy on Aberfan" (A18), "Autumn Lines for My Son" (A12), "Bacchanal" (B105), "Ballad of the Old Spaniard" (B289), "Ballad of the Stones" (A17), "Bargain" (A11), "Baudelaire in a Summer Cottage" (A14), "Beach Acquaintance" (A17), "Beach Romance" (A17), "Beauty [How does one tell]" (B310), "Because My Calling Is Such" (B204), "Berry Picking" (B195), "The Best Proof" (B373), "Betrayal" (A15), "Beutel's Name Is Inscribed for Eternal Life" (B230),

"Bicycle Pump" (B300), "Birds at Daybreak" (B110), "The Birth of Tragedy" (B171), "Bishop Berkeley Goes to Bed" (A3), "The Bishopric" (B261), "Black, Black" (A10), "The Black Huntsmen" (B79), "Blood on the Moon" (A2), "Blue and Lovely, My Love" (A15), "Boardwalk at Verdun" (B166), "Boudha Nath" (A52), "Boys Bathing" (A9), "Boys in October" (B287), "Breakdown" (B275), "The Bridge" (B381), "Brief Dialogue Between Negro Father and Son" (A18), "Brief Encounter" (A6), "The Brothers Lazarovitch" (B458), "The Buffaloes" (B142), "Bugs" (A52), "The Bull Calf" (B149), "Butterfly on Rock" (B271), "By Ecstasies Perplexed" (A11), "The Cactus" (A15), "Café Politics in Spring" (B159), "The Cage" (B254), "The Caged Bird" (B206), "Cain" (B193), "Canadian Skiers" (B153), "Cat Dying in Autumn" (B179), "El Caudillo" (B293), "Cemetery in August" (A4), "Changeling" (B418), "Chatterers" (B194), "Chokecherries" (A9), "Cleavages" (B382), "Climbing" (B182), "Climbing Hills" (A52), "Clochards" (B352), "Coal" (B281), "The Cold Green Element" (B111), "Collaboration" (B345), "The Comic Element" (B112), "The Coming of the Messiah" (A17), "Community" (B33), "Compliments of the Season" (B58), "Composition in Late Spring" (B104), "Concourse at Cataraqui" (A11), "Confederation Ode" (B327), "Consider the Lilies" (B447), "The Convertible" (B231), "Côte des Neiges Cemetery" (B186), "Counsel for My Stung Love" (A18), "Courtesies of Love" (A15), "Creation [I fashioned you]" (B306), "Creation [The pregnant cat]" (B398), "Crisis Theology" (A17), "Crone" (A3), "Dance, My Little One" (B192), "Dance with a Watermelon" (B242), "The Dancers" (B113), "Dans le Jardin" (B207), "The Dark Nest" (A9), "The Dark Plebian Mind" (B146), "Das Wahre Ich" (B282), "The Day Aviva Came to Paris" (B208), "De Bullion Street" (B55), "Death of a Construction

Worker" (B114), "Death of Moishe Lazarovitch" (B180), "A Dedication" (B744), "Dialogue with a Young and Pretty Wife" (A51), "Dionysian Reveller" (A21), "Dionysus" (A11), "Dionysus in Hampstead" (B442), "Discourse on Christian Love" (A15), "Disunity" (A9), "Diversion" (A15), "Divine Ground" (A52), "Divine Image" (B238), "Divinity" (B198), "Done on Both Sides" (A15), "Dorothy Parker (1893–1967)" (B359), "Drill Shed" (B54), "Drunk on McGill Campus" (B276), "Dudelus, Poetaster" (A11 — "Bibilus, Poetaster"), "The Dwarf" (A11), "Early Morning in Côte St. Luc" (A5), "Earth Goddess" (A9), "Élan" (A2), "Elegy for Marilyn Monroe" (B277), "Elegy for Strul" (B374), "Elephant" (B395), "Encounter" (A15), "End of the Summer" (B365), "End of the White Mouse" (B446), "Ends" (A52), "Enemies" (B141), "English for Immigrants" (B65), "Entry" (B545), "Epiphany" (A18), "Epitaph for a Poet [I sang of thighs]" (A21), "Epitaphs: Philosopher [B28], Poet Killed in Action [B77], An Ugly Servitor to Three Queens" [B115], Wit [B29]," "Erich Kästner (1899–)" (A17), "Eros [With the best side of my tongue]" (A4), "Eros [So expertly did he teach]" (B451), "Esthetique" (B747), "Eternal Recurrence [Even that leaf as it falls]" (B443), "Euphoria" (A17), "Everywhere, the Stink" (B438), "Excursion" (B61), "The Execution" (A3), "The Executioner" (A8), "Ex-Nazi" (A3), "F.R. Scott" (B286), "Fair Musia" (A17), "Family Portrait" (B172), "Fanatic in San Feliu" (B430), "Fantasia in Black" (A18), "Farewell [I said to her: 'I no longer want]" (B408), "The Fertile Muck" (B173), "Fiat Lux" (A9), "The Fictive Eye" (A51), "The Final Peace" (B609), "Firecrackers" (A9), "First Snow: Lake Achigan" (B131), "First Walk in Spring" (A9), "Fish" (B399), "Fishermen" (B421), "The Fool's Song" (A14), "For Adlai Stevenson" (A4), "For Alexander Trocchi, Novelist" (B249), "For Anna" (A76), "For Aviva" (B409), "For Aviva, Because I Love Her" (B255), "For Dulla Who Unexpectedly Came into Some Money" (A4), "For Governor Stevenson" (A4), "For John Slavin's Birthday" (B404), "For Julie" (B415), "For Louise, Age 17" (B116), "For Mao Tse-Tung: A Meditation on Flies and Kings" (B199), "For Miss Cézanne" (B316), "For Musia's Grandchildren" (B317), "For My Detractors" (A7), "For My Former Students" (B290), "For My Friend Who Teaches Literature" (A14), "For My Green Old Age" (B301), "For My Two Sons, Max and David" (B361), "For Natalya Correia" (B431), "For Phyllis Who Snatched Her Poem in Anger" (A11), "For Priscilla" (A5), "For Some of My Student Militants" (B449), "For the Cause" (A18), "For the Girl with Wide-Apart Eyes" (A18), "For the More Devotional" (A7), "For the Record" (B318), "For the Stinker Who Called Me an Apologist for Nazi Crimes" (B328), "Fornalutx" (A15), "Free Djilas" (A14), "Free Expression" (B452), "Freedom" (B319), "Friends [The person I most admire]" (A15), "From Colony to Nation" (B748), "Frost and Fences" (B432), "Games" (B353), "The Gardener" (B450), "Garter Snake" (A12), "Gathering of Poets" (A11), "Genius Love and Poetry" (B89), "Gents Furnishings" (B53), "Gift" (A15), "Gifts" (A14), "The Giraffe" (A15), "God Is Love" (B453), "God, When You Speak" (A8), "Golfers" (B117), "Good-Bye Bahai" (A3), "Gothic Landscape" (B76), "Gratitude" (B333), "The Graveyard" (B380), "The Greeks Had a Word for It" (A7), "Grey Morning in Lisbon" (B426), "El Gusano [From the place where I was sitting]" (B294), "Gypsies" (A17), "Haiku" (A18), "Halos at Lac Marie Louise" (B156), "Harlequin and Virgin" (A8), "Haruspex" (B78), "The Haunting" (B444), "He Saw Them, at First" (A18), "Heraclitos" (A18), "Hero of Babi Yar" (A52), "Hierophants" (B187), "Hills and Hills: For Aviva"

(B400), "His Holiness Is Right" (B410), "History as a Slice of Ham" (B265), "Holiday" (B164), "Holocaust" (B411), "Homage to Ben Johnson [sic]" (A15), "Homage to Lucullus" (B283), "Homage to Onassis" (B448), "Homo Oeconomicus" (A14), "Hostia" (B232), "How Domestic Happiness Is Achieved" (A12), "How Poems Get Written" (B356), "How to Look at an Abstract" (B315), "Human Being" (A7), "The Human Condition [Hope for the human race?]" (B321), "The Human Condition [And not ten years ago]" (A11), "I Can Sleep Beside My Lady" (B435), "I Know the Dark and Hovering Moth" (B205), "I Owe This to St. Paul" (A52), "I Saw a Faun" (A15), "I Would for Your Sake Be Gentle" (B138), "Icarus" (A15), "Ice Follies" (A50), "If Euclid Were Your Analyst" (B610), "If I Lie Still" (B591), "If Whales Could Think on Certain Happy Days" (B516), "If You Can't Scream" (B181), "The Imbecile" (B273), "The Improved Binoculars" (B500), "In Memory of Fred Smith" (B91), "In Memory of Stephen Ward" (B303), "In Praise of Benefactors" (B226), "In Rattle snake Country" (A16), "In the Midst of My Fever" (B102), "Individualists" (B196), "Inishmore" (B424), "Injustice" (A15), "Innocence" (A16), "Insect Blood" (A17), "Insomnia" (A17), "Intersections" (A9), "Invention" (B329), "Irish Luck" (A52), "Israelis" (B394), "It's All in the Manner" (B106), "Jasmine, Anyone?" (B389), "Jewish Main Street" (B59), "Joseph K —" (A11), "July 21, 1969" (A21), "June Weather" (A6), "Kamerad" (B366), "Karl Marx" (B69), "Keewaydin Poetry Festival" (B120), "Keine Lazarovitch 1870–1959" (B220), "Kilmurvey Strand" (B425), "Lachine, Que." (A5), "Lady Enfield" (B45), "Lake Selby" (B454), "The Larger Issue" (A18), "Latria" (A6), "The Laughing Rooster" (A15), "Laura Cunneyflow" (A21), "Laurentian Rhapsody" (B188), "Lazarus" (A14), "Leave-

taking" (A52), "Lesbia" (B167), "Lesson for Today" (B367), "Lester" (B40), "Letter from a Straw Man" (B162), "Letter to a Librarian" (A12), "Letter to Louis Dudek" (B97), "Librarian at Asheville" (A51), "A Life" (A11), "Life in the 20th Century" (A15), "Light" (A17), "Like a Mother Demented" (B368), "Lilith" (B256), "Lines on Myself" (A6), "The Lizard" (B291), "Logos" (B307), "The Longest Journey" (A5), "Look Homeward, Angel" (A17), "Look, the Lambs Are All Around Us!" (A6), "Love Is an Irrefutable Fire" (B200), "Love Poem with an Odd Twist" (B362), "Love the Conqueror Worm" (B94), "Love's Diffidence" (B154), "Lust" (A15), "Lyric [The rains will come]" (A15), "Macdonald College 1905–1955" (A11), "The Maddened Lover" (B284), "The Madonna of the Magnificat" (B107), "Magda" (B240), "Mahogany Red" (B322), "Make Mine Vodka" (A14), "Mammoths" (B342), "Man and Wife" (A15), "Man Going Up and Down" (A14), "Marché Municipale" (B348), "Marie" (A6), "Marius" (A6), "Mashed Potatoes" (A14), "Maurer: Twin Heads" (B150), "Maxie" (A5), "May Day Orators" (A7), "Me, the P.M., and the Stars" (B133), "Mediterranean Cemetery" (B369), "Memo to My Sons" (A21), "Merited" (A18), "Metamorphosis" (B517), "Metaphysical" (B147), "Metzinger: Girl with a Bird" (B108), "Mexico as Seen by the Reverent Dudek" (B212), "Mildred" (A5), "La Minerve" (B121), "Misunderstanding" (B335), "Mixed Metaphors" (A14), "Modern Greek Poet" (A18), "Modern Love" (A11), "Modern Lyric" (B375), "Modern Miracle" (A52), "The Modern Poet [Since Eliot set the fashion]" (B36), "Mont Rolland" (B81), "Montgo" (A15), "Montreal" (A50), "Moral with a Story" (B274), "Mortuary" (B46), "Moses Talked to Jupiter" (B92), "The Mosquito" (A9), "Motet" (B136), "Mount Royal" (A7), "Mr. Beutel Lays a Cornerstone" (B214), "Mr. Ther-Apis" (B103),

"Mrs. Fornheim, Refugee" (A2), "Mrs. Potiphar" (A2), "Mutability" (A17), "Mute in the Wind" (A7), "My Eyes Are Wide Open" (A51), "My Flesh Comfortless" (B201), "My Queen, My Quean" (A15), "Myth" (A17), "Nail Polish" (B455), "National Virtues" (B336), "Nausicäa" (A11), "Neanderthal" (A52), "Neighbour Love [A grove]" (A14), "Nepalese Woman and Child" (B396), "The New Sensibility" (A18), "New Tables" (A6), "New Year's Eve" (B343), "Newsboy" (B42), "The Next Time Does It" (B370), "Nightfall" (B56), "Nightmare" (A52), "No Curtain Calls" (B459), "No Shish Kebab" (B257), "No Wild Dog" (A14), "Nocturne" (A52), "North and South" (B330), "Not Blown Away" (A7), "Now That I'm Older" (A6), "O.B.E." (B122), "O Say Can You See" (B308), "Obit" (A10), "Odysseus in Limbo" (B83), "Oedipus" (B401), "Ohms" (B436), "Oil Slick on the Riviera" (B371), "An Old Nicoise Whore" (B354), "Olives for Jay Macpherson" (B183), "Olympia Kaput" (B314), "On Being Bitten by a Dog" (A11), "On First Looking into Stalin's Coffin" (A6), "On My Way to School" (A13), "On Rereading the Beats" (B280), "On Seeing the Statue of Sappho on the Quay of Mitylene" (A52), "On Seeing the Statuettes of Ezekiel and Jeremiah in the Church of Notre Dame" (B151), "On Spanish Soil" (B295), "On the Assassination of President Kennedy" (B292), "On the Death of A. Vishinsky" (B143), "On the Naming of Streets" (A17), "On the Quay with My Mother's Ghost" (A17), "On This Far Shore" (B363), "One Last Try at a Final Solution" (A18), "One View of Dead Fish" (A9), "Original Sin" (A11), "Orpheus" (B123), "Osip Mandelshtam (1891–1940)" (B427), "Our Common Future" (B233), "Overheard in a Barbershop" (A4), "Paging Mr. Superman" (B197), "Paraclete" (B109), "Parting" (B184), "Paul Verlaine" (A21), "Paysage" (A8 — "The Red and the Black"), "Peacemonger" (A18),

"Personae" (A16), "The Perverse Gulls" (A4), "Philosophy 34" (B355), "Piazza San Marco" (B221), "Pigeons" (B518), "Pilgrim" (B344), "The Pillar" (B247), "Pine Avenue Analyst" (A6), "The Pit" (B416), "Plaza de Toros" (B296), "Plea for My Lady" (A21), "Pleasure" (A15), "A Pocketful of Rye" (A4), "Poem for the Next Century" (B189), "Poet and Dancer" (A8), "The Poet and the Statue" (A2), "Poet at Sinai" (A18), "The Poet Entertains Several Ladies" (B124), "Poetic Fame" (B185), "The Poetic Process" (B125), "Political Economy" (B266), "Pomegranates" (A52), "Poplars" (A2), "Portrait [Pay small attention to the chin]" (B137), "Portrait Done with a Steel Pen" (B331), "Portrait of Aileen" (B134), "Portrait of a Genius" (B305), "Portrait of Nolady" (A15), "Post-Crematoria" (A12), "Postscript to Empire" (B390), "A Prayer" (A51), "The Predator" (B285), "Prelude" (A18), "Presbyterian Church Signboard" (A17), "Prizes" (B237), "Processed" (A6), "Project" (A11), "Prologue to the Long Pea-Shooter" (B139), "Proof Reader" (B63), "Protest" (B402), "Providence" (B26), "Prussian Blue" (A15), "The Puma's Tooth" (A11), "Quay Scene" (A17), "Queer Hate Poem" (B376), "Questions" (B253), "Rain" (A12), "Rain at La Minerve" (A6), "The Ravens [Where's the poem]" (A6), "The Real Values" (B260), "Recipe for a Long and Happy Life" (A21), "Reconciliation" (B225), "Red Chokecherries" (B165), "Redemption" (B437), "Release [I shall rejoice]" (B10), "Rembrandt" (A3), "Repetition" (B337), "Requiem for an Age" (B13), "Rhine Boat Trip" (B332), "Right Conduct" (B407), "The Ritual Cut" (A14), "A Roman Jew to Ovid" (A12), "Rose Lemay" (A9), "Ruins" (B349), "Sacrament by the Water" (B160), "The Sad Madonna" (B346), "Sagebrush Classic" (B227), "Sancta Simplicitas" (B135), "Saratoga Beach" (B144), "Satan in Utopia" (B441), "The Satyr" (A8), "Schoolteacher in Late November" (B72), "Second Thought on the Armada" (B304), "The Seduction [First he knocks her down]" (A15), "Seduction [I said: 'I am too']" (B423), "Seven O'Clock Lecture" (B99), "Shakespeare" (B445), "Sheep" (B190), "Sight Seeing" (A17), "Silence [The word betrays the act]" (B258), "Silent Joy" (B405), "Silly Rhymes for Aviva" (A15), "Silver Lining" (A6), "The Skull" (B417), "The Smell" (B412), "Soapflakes" (A18), "Soleil de Noces" (B98), "Song" (B235), "A Song about Woman" (B338), "Song for a Late Hour" (A9), "Song for Naomi" (B792), "Songs Out of Season" (A18), "A Sort of After-Dinner Speech" (A18), "Sourwine Sparkle" (B413), "The Sparks Fly" (B268), "Speculators" (A17), "A Spider Danced a Cosy Jig" (B30), "Spikes" (A9), "Spring Exultances" (B297), "Still Life" (A14), "Stocktaking on the Day of Atonement" (B244), "Stolen Watch" (B64), "Stone-Splitters in Alicante" (B298), "Storm at Ydra" (B391), "The Straight Man" (A21), "A Strange Turn" (B311), "Street Funeral" (B95), "Street Violinist" (A17), "Success" (A15), "Sudden Thaw" (B66), "Summer Idyll" (B126), "Sun Bathers" (B339), "Supernatural Event at Cedar Pond" (A14), "Sutherland: Portrait of A.C." (B152), "Sutra" (A14), "Suzanne" (A11), "The Sweet Light Strikes My Eyes" (A18), "The Swimmer" (B60), "The Swinging Flesh," "T.S. Eliot" (B127), "Taj Mahal" (A52), "Talk at Twilight" (B377), "A Tall Man Executes a Jig" (B248), "Tamed Birds" (A18), "Terrene" (B87), "Thanatos and Eros" (A11), "Theology" (B148), "Therapy" (B439), "There Were No Signs" (B250), "This Machine Age" (B170), "Thoughts in the Water" (B157), "Thoughts of a Senile Revolutionist" (B456), "Three on a Park Bench" (A17), "Time's Velvet Tongue" (B357), "To a Beautiful Unknown Girl" (B358), "To a Very Old Woman" (B90), "To the Girls of My Graduating Class" (B93), "To the Lawyer Handling My Divorce Case" (B537), "To the Priest Who Kept My Wife Awake All Night, Farting" (A21), "To the Russians at the U.N." (A18), "To Write an Old-Fashioned Poem" (B364), "The Toy Gun" (A12), "The Tragic Poet" (A15), "The Tragic Sense" (B222), "Tribal Tic" (A52), "Trilliums After a Party" (B219), "Trumpet Daffodil" (B96), "Two Ladies at Traymore's" (A11), "Two Poets in Toronto" (A6), "Two Songs for Sweet Voices" (B169), "Undine" (A9), "University Buildings" (A6), "Variations on a Theme by Shakespeare" (A51), "Venetian Blinds" (A12), "Veteran" (A6), "Vexata Quaestio" (B140), "Victoria Square" (A51), "Victory" (A12), "Vigil" (B1), "Vignettes" (A18), "Village Funeral" (B372), "A Vision" (A4), "The Warm Afterdark" (B202), "The Wave" (B340), "The Way of the World" (B158), "The Way the World Ends" (A11), "The Way to Go" (A52), "The Well-Wrought Urn" (B263), "Westminster Abbey" (A17), "Westmount Doll" (B132), "What Does It Matter" (A14), "What Ulysses Said to Circe on the Beach of Aeaea" (A6), "Whatever Else Poetry Is Freedom" (B191), "When I See a Giant" (A7), "When It Came to Santayana's Turn" (B128), "Whom I Write For" (B251), "Why I Can't Sleep Nights" (A14), "Why I Don't Make Love to the First Lady" (B245), "Why the Hares Stare and Run" (A15), "The Widows" (A12), "Winter Fantasy" (A8), "Winter Light" (A15), "Winter Lyric" (B324), "With the Money I Spend" (A51), "Woman" (B168), "Woman in the Square" (B75), "Women of Rome" (B223), "Women of the Back Streets of Europe" (B341), "The Wooden Spoon" (B224), "A Word from Diogenes" (B175), "The World [First and foremost]" (A17), "The Worm [The filthy rain]" (A15), "The Yard" (B67), "Yesterday" (A21), "Yet What if the Survivors" (B378), "You and the 20th Century" (B457), "Young Girls Dancing at Camp Lajoie" (B203), and "Zoroastrian" (B309).

A21 *Nail Polish.* Toronto: McClelland and Stewart, 1971. 87 pp.

Includes "Absence," "Advice for David," "Aran Islands" (B429), "As Seen through a Glass Darkly" (B440), "The Brothers Lazarovitch: After Margaret Atwood" (B458), "Cemeteries," "Consider the Lilies" (B447), "Dark Lady," "Dionysian Reveller," "Dionysus in Hampstead" (B442), "Easy Rider," "End of the White Mouse" (B446), "Entry" (B545), "Epitaph for a Poet [I sang of thighs]," "Eros [So expertly did he teach]" (B451), "Eternal Recurrence [Even that leaf as it falls]" (B443), "Fanatic in San Feliu" (B430), "Fertility Rite," "For Anna" (A76), "For Natalya Correia" (B431), "For Some of My Student Militants" (B449), "Free Expression" (B452), "Frost and Fences" (B432), "The Gardener" (B450), "God Is Love" (B453), "Grey Morning in Lisbon" (B426), "The Haunting: For George Woodcock" (B444), "Homage to Onassis" (B448), "Hungry Christians," "I Can Sleep Beside My Lady: After Leonard Cohen" (B435), "Ibn Gabirol," "Inishmore" (B424), "Irish Song," "July 21, 1969," "Kilmurvey Strand" (B425), "Lake Selby" (B454), "Laura Cunneyflow," "Legend," "Marxist" (B433), "Meleager Wonders," "Memo to My Sons," "Nail Polish" (B455), "No Curtain Calls" (B459), "Notes for a Suite: For the Ladies in B — complex," "Ohms" (B436), "Osip Mandelshtam (1891–1940)" (B427), "Paul Verlaine," "Pith & Vinegar," "Plea for My Lady," "Portraits Drawn from Life," "Qualitas Occulta," "Recipe for a Long and Happy Life," "Rochel" (B37), "Satan in Utopia" (B441), "Shakespeare" (B445), "Short Sermon on God and Nature by the Rabbi Who Survived Auschwitz," "The Straight Man," "Thoughts of a Senile Revolutionist" (B456), "To the Priest Who Kept My Wife Awake All Night, Farting," "Tragic Irony," "Yesterday," and "You and the 20th Century" (B457).

A22 *Lovers and Lesser Men.* Toronto: McClelland and Stewart, 1973. 109 pp.

Includes "Ad Majorem Dei Gloriam," "Advice to a Young Poet," "The Antipodeans" (B479), "An Aubade" (B480), "The Baroness" (B481), "The Benediction" (B472), "Bennie," "Bigamist," "The Burning Bush" (B473), "The Cockroach," "The Dovecote," "Early Morning in Mithymna," "Economy Please, Toronto," "Edmund Wilson (1895–1972)," "Elegy for Nathan Ralph" (B485), "End of the Affair [Wisdom is the decay of youth]" (B486), "The Establishment," "Farewell [She's gone. The one I swore up and down]" (B687), "The Fine Excess," "For Auld Lang Syne: For Saul Berman," "For Max Who Showed Me His First Good Poem," "Fortuna et Cupidas," "A Greek's View of Canadians" (B487), "Hiccups," "Holy Stinkfinger," "I Don't Like It," "I Think of Ovid," "Idealists," "The Incarnation" (B474), "Inspiration," "Let Me Not" (B467), "A Letter to No One in Particular" (B488), "Liars," "Limpets" (B612), "Look Here, Doktor Freud," "Love's Philosophy," "The Luck of an Old Fart," "Mad Cripple," "Magic" (B464), "Marriage [It is not love]," "Memo to a Suicide" (B471), "Modern Poet [His mouth]," "My Eyes Have Seen the Glory" (B489), "Narcissus," "Necrophiles," "New Year's Eve, Zihuatanejo" (B465), "No Exit" (B463), "Old Dubrovnik: For Pero Santic" (B616), "On Reading Cohen's 'The Energy of Slaves,' " "On Seeing an Old Poet and His Wife" (B490), "Party at Hydra: For Marianne," "Poetry and Truth" (B491), "Poetry as the Fine Art of Pugilism: For Jack McClelland," "A Political Dream," "Post-Auschwitz Jew" (B475), "Refutation," "Rupert Brooke *1887–1915*" (B614), "The Sages," "Saviour," "Signs and Portents: For Eli Mandel," "Silence [The language of silence]," "The Silence [It grew from nothing]" (B714), "Snowman" (B492), "Some Canadian Birds in October" (B460),

"Stella" (B482), "Stella Ioannou *(1894–1972)*" (B483), "Sunflower: For Lynne Stean," "Tale of Two Cities," "A Tale with Teeth in It" (B615), "The Terrorist" (B493), "Teufelsdrockh Concerning Women" (B496), "That Is the Question" (B476), "Tide" (B469), "To Maoists," "To the Gov-Gen's Poetry Awards Committee for 1971–1972," "The Tower," "The Transfiguration," "Two for One" (B466), "Vampire," "A Walk to Chora," "Walt's Reply" (B484), "Why I'm Not an Atheist" (B494), "The World: For Alexander Solzhenitsyn [In heaven it's different, here below]," "Xmas Eve 1971, Zihuatanejo: For William Goodwin" (B470), and "York University" (B478).

A23   *Il freddo verde elemento*. Trans. Amleto Lorenzini. Introd. [in Italian] Northrop Frye. Turin: Giulio Einaudi, 1974. v–viii, 88 pp.

Includes English and facing-page Italian translations of the following: "Archetypes / Archetipi" (A11), "As Seen through a Glass Darkly / Visto oscuramente in uno specchio" (B440), "The Birth of Tragedy / La nascita della tragedia" (B171), "Cain / Caino" (B193), "Clochards: For Wynne Francis / Clochards: Per Wynne Francis" (B352), "The Cold Green Element / Il freddo verde elemento" (B111), "Heraclitos / Eraclito" (A18), "How to Look at an Abstract / Come guardare un quadro astratto" (B315), "The Improved Binoculars / Il binocolo perfezionato" (B500), "Insomnia / Insonnia" (A17), "Keine Lazarovitch 1870–1959" (B220), "Laura Cunneyflow" (A21), "Like a Mother Demented / Come madre demente" (B368), "Love Poem with an Odd Twist / Poesia d'amore d'uno strano piglio" (B362), "Misunderstanding / Malinteso" (B335), "Nausicäa / Nausicaa" (A11), "Now That I'm Older / Ora che invecchio" (A6), "Paging Mr. Superman / Rintracciando Mr Superman" (B197), "Piazza San Marco" (B221), "Poetry / Poesia" (A17), "Ruins / Rovine" (B349), "Shakespeare" (B445), "Sun Bathers / Il bagno di sole" (B339), "T.S. Eliot" (B127), and "The Well-Wrought Urn / L'urna ben lavorata" (B263).

A24   *The Pole-Vaulter*. Foreword Irving Layton. Toronto: McClelland and Stewart, 1974. 9–11, 94 pp.

Includes "Adam and Eve," "Afternoon of a Dying Satyr," "American Young Woman in Patmos" (B525), "Analogue" (B461), "The Animal Across the Street," "Apokalypsis," "Archilochus Curses the Woman Who Jilted Him," "Asian Suite," "Australian Bush," "The Basin," "Bedbugs" (B512), "The Black Queen" (B526), "Bodhidharma," "Budapest," "Ch'an Artist" (B527), "The Coastal Mind," "Conversion" (B520), "Corncrakes," "Departed" (B498), "Encounter with a Reptile," "Epigram for A.M. Klein" (B502), "The Final Solution" (B532), "For a Young Poet Who Hanged Himself," "For Andrei Amalrik" (B521), "For Anne Frank" (B499), "For Nadezhda Mandelshtam" (B528), "For the Fraulein from Hamburg" (B522), "Funeraria 'Olea' " (B497), "Ganymede" (B519), "Greek Epigram: For Peggy Sylvia," "Greek Fly," "Harry Truman 1884–1972" (B495), "Hit Parade," "Honeymoon," "The Ideal among Vacationists" (B503), "Jijimuge," "Leviathan," "Lillian Roxon" (B504), "Lines for My Grandchildren," "Lullaby," "Lures," "Madman," "Madonna and Dionysos" (B505), "Marriage [The lover of the treacherous wife]" (B523), "Mary" (B533), "Mexican Guerilas" (B462), "Midsummer's Dream in the Vienna Stadpark" (B511), "Mithymna Cemetery," "Molibos Cat" (B569), "Museum at Iraklion" (B506), "My Fair Lady from Bremen," "Peacock," "Poet on Cos: For 'Mike' Varvarikos," "Poetry and the Class War," "Poet's Bust" (B524), "Pole-Vaulter" (B513), "Portrait of Someone I Know

Too Well," "Portrait of the Artist as a Young Bull" (B477), "Postcard: For Aviva," "Proteus and Nymph: For Molly," "Ravens [A luxury meal]," "Religious Poet 1973 A.D.," "Requiem for A.M. Klein" (B507), "Revolution," "September Woman" (B514), "The Shadow" (B515), "The Solitary," "Some Other Day," "A Tailor's View of History," "Terrorists" (B508), "Thoughts of a Male Chauvinist Pig" (B529), "The Three Sisters," "To the Woman with the Speaking Eyes: For Rae Sampson" (B501), "The Transfiguration" (A22), "The Ventriloquist" (B546), "What I Told the Ghost of Harold Laski" (B530), and "Young Couple at the Lum Fong Hotel."

A25 *Seventy-Five Greek Poems 1951–1974.* Athens: Hermias, 1974. [60] pp.

Includes "Alas, Too Noiseless: For Andy and Sheila," "American Young Woman in Patmos" (B525), "Apokalypsis" (A24), " 'Archilochos' Complaint,' " "Archilocos vs Homer," "The Basin" (A24), "The Beard," "Blackout," "Byron Exhibition at the Benaki Museum," "The Castle," "Climbing Hills" (A52), "Dionysos" (A11), "Dionysos in Hampstead" (B442), "A Dream in Pangrati," "Early Morning in Mithymna" (A22), "End of the Affair [Wisdom is the decay of youth]" (B486), "Eros [With the best side of my tongue]" (A4), "The Final Peace" (B609), "Fishermen" (B421), "Flytrap" (B534), "Ganymede" (B519), "Greek Epigram: For Peggy Sylvia" (A24), "Greek Fly" (A24), "Helios," "Hellenes: For Nassos and Lydia," "Her Mediterranean Mind," "Heraclitos" (A18), "Hills and Hills: For Aviva" (B400), "Homage to Onassis" (B448), "I Owe This to St. Paul" (A52), "Icarus" (A15), "The Ideal Among Vacationists" (B503), "If Euclid Were Your Analyst" (B610), "Inspiration" (A22), "Ithaca: For Marsha Kinder" (B611), " 'Kazantzakis: God's Athlete,' " "Leavetaking" (A52), "Limpets" (B612),

"Madonna and Dionysos" (B505), "Mithymna Cemetery" (A24), "Modern Greek Poet: For A. Vavrikos" (A18), "Molibos Cat" (B569), "Museum at Iraklion" (B506), "Myth" (A17), "Nausicäa" (A11), "Odysseus in Limbo" (B83), "Oedipus" (B401), "Olympia Kaput" (B314), "On Seeing the Statue of Sappho on the Quay of Mitylene" (A52), "Orpheus" (B123), "Party at Hydra: For Marianne" (A22), "Peacemonger" (A18), "Poet on Cos: For 'Mike' Varvarikos" (A24), "Pomegranates" (A52), "Poros" (A17), "Protest" (B402), "Proteus and Nymph" (A24), "Reunion at the Hilton," "Ruins" (B349), "Rupert Brooke 1887–1915" (B614), "The Satyr" (A8), "The Shark" (B571), "Silent Joy" (B405), "The Skull" (B417), "Sophisticates Abroad" (A17), "Stella" (B482), "Stella Ioannou (1894–1972)" (B483), "Storm at Ydra" (B391), "Take It All In," "A Tale with Teeth in It" (B615), "Thanatos and Eros" (A11), "That Is the Question" (B476), "The Unwavering Eye" (B536), "A Vision" (A4), and "What Ulysses Said to Circe on the Beach of Aeaea" (A6).

A26 *The Darkening Fire: Selected Poems 1945–1968.* Preface Wynne Francis. Toronto: McClelland and Stewart, 1975. xi–xv, 176 pp.

Includes "Against This Death" (B590), "The Ants" (B129), "At the Iglesia de Sacromonte" (B302), "Ballad of the Old Spaniard" (B289), "Bargain" (A11), "Beach Acquaintance" (A17), "Because My Calling Is Such" (B204), "Berry Picking" (B195), "The Birth of Tragedy" (B171), "The Black Huntsmen" (B79), "Blue and Lovely, My Love" (A15), "Boys Bathing" (A9), "The Bull Calf" (B149), "Butterfly on Rock" (B271), "By Ecstasies Perplexed" (A11), "The Cage" (B254), "The Caged Bird" (B206), "Cain" (B193), "Cat Dying in Autumn" (B179), "El Caudillo" (B293), "Cemetery in August" (A4), "Chokecherries" (A9), "Climbing" (B182), "Clochards" (B352), "The Cold Green Element" (B111), "Compliments of the Season" (B58), "Composition in Late Spring" (B104), "Confederation Ode" (B327), "The Convertible" (B231), "Côte des Neiges Cemetery" (B186), "Dans le Jardin" (B207), "Das Wahre Ich" (B282), "The Day Aviva Came to Paris" (B208), "De Bullion Street" (B55), "Death of a Construction Worker" (B114), "Death of Moishe Lazarovitch" (B180), "A Dedication" (B744), "Divine Image" (B238), "Elegy for Marilyn Monroe" (B277), "Elegy for Strul" (B374), "Enemies" (B141), "Excursion" (B61), "The Execution" (A3), "The Executioner" (A8), "Family Portrait" (B172), "The Fertile Muck" (B173), "First Snow: Lake Achigan" (B131), "First Walk in Spring" (A9), "For Alexander Trocchi, Novelist" (B249), "For Louise, Age 17" (B116), "For Mao Tse-tung: A Meditation on Flies and Kings" (B199), "For Miss Cézanne" (B316), "For Musia's Grandchildren" (B317), "For My Two Sons, Max and David" (B361), "For the Girl with Wide-Apart Eyes" (A18), "Fornalutx" (A15), "From Colony to Nation" (B748), "God, When You Speak" (A8), "Golfers" (B117), "Gothic Landscape" (B76), "The Graveyard" (B380), "El Gusano [From the place where I was sitting]" (B294), "Halos at Lac Marie Louise" (B156), "Heraclitos" (A18), "How to Look at an Abstract" (B315), "I Know the Dark and Hovering Moth" (B205), "I Would for Your Sake Be Gentle" (B138), "Icarus" (A15), "If I Lie Still" (B591), "If Whales Could Think on Certain Happy Days" (B516), "The Imbecile" (B273), "The Improved Binoculars" (B500), "In the Midst of My Fever" (B102), "Insomnia" (A17), "Invention" (B329), "Karl Marx" (B69), "Keewaydin Poetry Festival" (B120), "Keine Lazarovitch 1870–1959" (B220), "Letter to a Librarian" (A12), "Like a Mother Demented" (B368), "Look, the Lambs Are All Around Us!" (A6), "Love's Diffidence" (B154), "Love the Conqueror Worm" (B94), "Mahogany Red" (B322), "Marché Municipale" (B348), "Maurer: Twin Heads" (B150), "Maxie" (A5), "Metamorphosis" (B517), "Metzinger: Girl with a Bird" (B108), "La Minerve" (B121), "Misunderstanding" (B335), "Mont Rolland" (B81), "Mortuary" (B46), "The Mosquito" (A9), "Mrs. Fornheim, Refugee" (A2), "Mutability" (A17), "My Flesh Comfortless" (B201), "Nausicäa" (A11), "New Tables" (A6), "Newsboy" (B42), "North and South" (B330), "Now That I'm Older" (A6), "Odysseus in Limbo" (B83), "An Old Nicoise Whore" (B354), "On Being Bitten by a Dog" (A11), "On First Looking into Stalin's Coffin" (A6), "On Seeing the Statuettes of Ezekiel and Jeremiah in the Church of Notre Dame" (B151), "Orpheus" (B123), "Paging Mr. Superman" (B197), "Paraclete" (B109), "Peacemonger" (A18), "Piazza San Marco" (B221), "Pigeons" (B518), "Plaza de Toros" (B296), "The Poet Entertains Several Ladies" (B124), "The Poetic Process" (B125), "Poetry" (A17), "Political Economy" (B266), "Portrait of a Genius" (B305), "Portrait of Aileen" (B134), "The Predator" (B285), "Prelude" (A18), "Prologue to the Long Pea-Shooter" (B139), "Proof Reader" (B63), "Rain" (A12), "Rain at La Minerve" (A6), "Red Chokecherries" (B165), "Rembrandt" (A3), "Repetition" (B337), "Rhine Boat Trip" (B332), "Ruins" (B349), "Sacrament by the Water" (B160), "Seven O'Clock Lecture" (B99), "Sheep" (B190), "Song for a Late Hour" (A9), "Song for Naomi" (B792), "Still Life" (A14), "A Strange Turn" (B311), "Street Funeral" (B95), "Sun-Bathers" (B339), "The Sweet Light Strikes My Eyes" (A18), "The Swimmer" (B60), "A Tall Man Executes a Jig" (B248), "Thanatos and Eros" (A11), "There Were No Signs" (B250), "To a Very Old Woman" (B90), "To the Girls of My Graduating Class" (B93),

"Trumpet Daffodil" (B96), "Vexata Quaestio" (B140), "The Well-Wrought Urn" (B263), "Westminster Abbey" (A17), "Whatever Else Poetry Is Freedom" (B191), "When It Came to Santayana's Turn" (B128), "Whom I Write For" (B251), "With the Money I Spend" (A51), "Woman" (B168), "Women of Rome" (B223), "The Worm [The filthy rain]" (A15), "The Yard" (B67), and "Yet What if the Survivors" (B378).

A27 *The Unwavering Eye: Selected Poems 1969–1975.* Foreword Eli Mandel. Toronto: McClelland and Stewart, 1975. x–xi, 161 pp.

Includes "Absence" (A21), "Ad Majorem Dei Gloriam" (A22), "After Auschwitz" (B386), "The Antipodeans" (B479), "Aran Islands" (B429), "As Seen through a Glass Darkly" (B440), "An Aubade" (B480), "Australian Bush" (A24), "The Baroness" (B481), "The Beard" (A25), "The Benediction" (B472), "The Black Queen" (B526), "Blackout" (A25), "Bodhidharma" (A24), "Bugs" (A52), "Byron Exhibition at the Benaki Museum" (A25), "The Castle" (A25), "Cemeteries" (A21), "Ch'an Artist" (B527), "Changeling" (B418), "Climbing Hills" (A52), "The Coastal Mind" (A24), "The Cockroach" (A22), "Creation [The pregnant cat]" (B398), "Departed" (B498), "Dionysos in Hampstead" (B442), "A Dream at Pangrati" (A25), "Early Morning at Mithymna" (A22), "Elephant" (B395), "End of the White Mouse" (B446), "Ends" (A52), "Entry" (B545), "Epigram for A.M. Klein" (B502), "Eternal Recurrence [Even that leaf as it falls]" (B443), "Farewell [She's gone. The one I swore up and down]" (B687), "The Final Peace" (B609), "The Final Solution" (B532), "Fishermen: For Peggy Sylvia" (B421), "Flytrap" (B534), "For Andrei Amalrik" (B521), "For Anna" (A76), "For Auld Lang Syne: For Saul Berman" (A22), "For Max Who Showed Me His First Good Poem" (A22), "For Natalya Correia" (B431), "For the Fraulein from Hamburg" (B522), "Fortuna et Cupidas" (A22), "Funeraria 'Olea'" (B497), "Ganymede" (B519), "The Gardener" (B450), "Greek Fly" (A24), "The Haunting" (B444), "Helios" (A25), "The Hellenes" (A25), "Her Mediterranean Mind" (A25), "Hills and Hills" (B400), "His Holiness Is Right" (B410), "Holocaust" (B411), "I Can Sleep Beside My Lady" (B435), "I Think of Ovid" (A22), "The Ideal among Vacationists" (B503), "If Euclid Were Your Analyst" (B610), "Inspiration" (A22), "Israelis" (B394), "Ithaca" (B611), "Kilmurvey Strand" (B425), "Lake Selby" (B454), "Laura Cunneyflow" (A21), "Leavetaking" (A52), "Lillian Roxon" (B504), "Marriage [The lover of the treacherous wife]" (B523), "Memo to a Suicide" (B471), "Midsummer's Dream in the Vienna Stadpark" (B511), "Mithymna Cemetery" (A24), "Molibos Cat" (B569), "Nepalese Woman and Child" (B396), "No Exit" (B463), "O Jerusalem" (B531), "Ohms" (B436), "On Seeing an Old Poet and His Wife" (B490), "On Seeing the Statue of Sappho on the Quay of Mitylene" (A52), "Osip Mandelshtam (1891–1940)" (B427), "Party at Hydra: For Marianne" (A22), "Peacock" (A24), "Plea for My Lady" (A21), "Poetry and Truth" (B491), "Poet's Bust" (B524), "Pole-Vaulter" (B513), "Pomegranates" (A52), "Postcard: For Aviva" (A24), "Postscript to Empire" (B390), "Protest" (B402), "Proteus and Nymph: For Molly" (A24), "Recipe for a Long and Happy Life" (A21), "Requiem for A.M. Klein" (B507), "Reunion at the Hilton" (A25), "Rupert Brooke 1887–1915" (B614), "Saviour" (A22), "The Shadow" (B515), "Shakespeare" (B445), "The Shark" (B571), "Signs and Portents: For Eli Mandel" (A22), "The Silence [It grew from nothing]" (B714), "Silent Joy" (B405), "The Skull" (B417), "The Smell" (B412), "Snowman"

(B492), "Some Other Day" (A24), "Sourwine Spar-kle" (B413), "Stella" (B482), "Storm at Ydra" (B391), "Take It All In" (A25), "A Tale with Teeth in It" (B615), "The Terrorist" (B493), "Terrorists" (B508), "That Is the Question" (B476), "Tide" (B469), "To Maoists" (A22), "To the Woman with the Speaking Eyes: For Rae Sampson" (B501), "The Transfiguration" (A22), "The Unwavering Eye" (B536), "The Ventriloquist" (B546), "A Walk to Chora" (A22), "What I Told the Ghost of Harold Laski" (B530), "Xmas Eve 1971, Zihuatanejo: For William Goodwin" (B470), and "Young Couple at the Lum Fong Hotel" (A24).

A28 *For My Brother Jesus.* Foreword Irving Layton. Toronto: McClelland and Stewart, 1976. xv–xviii, 128 pp.

Includes "Act of Creation: For Leonard Cohen," "Adam: For Amleto Lorenzini" (B538), "Adonis" (B539), "The Arch," "Asylums," "At the Barcelona Zoo" (B548), "Beauty and Genius," "La Belle France," "Break Up Your Words," "Brief Letter to Cervantes," "C'est Fini," "Crazy Jenny Talks to the Bishop," "Daphnis and Chloë," "Desmond Pacey: In Memoriam" (B541), "Discothèque: For Zephyra," "Displaced Person," "The Door," "L'Envoi," "Excelsior," "Fiasco," "Florence" (B557), "For Edda" (B542), "For Francesca" (B510), "For Jesus Christ," "For My Brother Jesus" (B816), "For My Distant Woman" (B564), "For My Incomparable Gypsy: For Sparkles" (B558), "For Some of My Best Friends" (B563), "For Yannis Ritsos," "Galim," "Go to the Ant," "The Graduate," "The Haemorrhage," "The Hallowing" (B552), "Ha-Nagid's Admonition to Jewish Scholars," "How Many Days" (B559), "The Human Cry" (B837), "In Praise of Older Men," "Incident at the Cathedral" (B606), "Island Circe," "Jeshua" (B560), "Jesus and Saint Paul," "Judea

Eterna," "June Bug," "Kazantzakis: God's Athlete" (A25), "The Last Dryad," "Lord Shiva," "The Neolithic Brain," "No Visitor from Outer Space," "North American Poet," "O Jerusalem" (B531), "Of the Man Who Sits in the Garden," "Old Cemetery," "On Revisiting Poros After an Absence of Ten Years: For Aviva," "On the Survival of the Fittest" (B549), "Parque de Montjuich: For Jack Bernstein" (B547), "The Plaka: For John and Ruth Colombo" (B561), "Poet at Ramblas," "The Red Geranium," "Release" (B555), "The Revolving Door" (B556), "Runts," "Saint Antipop" (B565), "Saint John the Baptist," "Saint Pinchas" (B543), "Salim," "Saved" (B562), "Saviours" "Seduction of and by a Civilized Frenchwoman" (B535), "A Spanish Episode," "The Stain," "Sublimation: 1975," "Survivor," "Tabletalk," "To Margaret," "True Love" (B544), "Ulysses in Spetsai," "La Vie Religieuse," "The Violent Life: For Pier Paolo Pasolini," and "Warrior Poet" (B550).

A29 *The Uncollected Poems of Irving Layton 1936–59.* Ed. and Afterword W. David John. Preface Seymour Mayne. Oakville / Ottawa: Mosaic / Valley, 1976. 11–13, 145–46, 153 pp.

Includes "Accept This Day" (B19), "Address to the Undernourished" (A6), "Admonition to a Young Poet" (A6), "Aesthete" (A12), "Ah Rats! (A Political Extravaganza of the 30s)" (B11), "Alexandra School Revisited" (A7), "All-Too-Human" (A6), "Anacreon" (B88), "Apeswatch" (A7), "Author, with a Pipe in His Mouth" (A6), "Battle of the (S)ages" (A4), "Beneath the Bridge" (B24), "Bookseller" (A11), "Call Me Ferdinand" (A3), "Canadian Spring" (A6), "Canadiana" (A7), "Change [Empty of all meaning]" (A1), "Church Parade" (B51), "The Cold War: Saxon vs. Slav" (A11), "Corypheus" (A4), "Cyril Tishpish" (B100), "Day" (B41), "Days of Wrath" (B9), "Death of a Poet" (A7), "Debacle"

(B21), "Difference" (B163), "Doubting Thomas" (B176), "E.P. on His Critics" (A12), "English Prof.: For H.W. Wells" (A7), "Enigma" (B161), "Epitaph for a Brigadier," "Epitaph for a Christian" (B22), "Epitaph for a Common Grave" (B38), "Epitaph for a Communist" (B23), "Esto Perpetua" (A4), "The Excessively Quiet Groves" (B85), "Fable for Adults" (A4), "Factorytown Mist" (A8), "Fell Horatio: For George Woodcock" (A7), "Flags" (A11), "Flaubertism, Trillingism, Or" (A6), "Fog" (B50), "For an Anniversary of Shaw's Death" (A7), "For an Older Poet in Despair with the Times" (A6), "Forecast" (B39), "From a Lawn-chair" (A11), "Georgie? Am I Concrete Enough?" (A7), "Gonorrhea Racetrack" (B49), "Heaven and Earth" (A12), "Henry Crockett, M.P." (B118), "House to Let" (B25), "Hymn to the Rising Sun" (A3), "Imaginary Conversation" (A11), "Impotence" (B119), "Inebriate" (B35), "Intransitive Verb" (A2), "January Love" (B84), "Jeremiad" (A1), "Jones on Sigmund Freud" (A12 — "On the Jones Biography of Sigmund Freud"), "The Law" (A6), "Lenin" (B68), "Letter to Raymond Souster" (A3), "Lines on the Massey Commission" (A3), "The Literary Life" (A4), "Literary Smoothie," "Love Dream of W.P. Turner" (A12 — "Love Dream of W.P. Turner, English Poet"), "The Lusts of the Spirit" (A7), "Lyrics" (B14), "A Marriage [What does your husband do for you?]" (A11), "The Masked Marvel" (A6), "Masquerade" (B2), "Mediocrity and Genius" (A6), "Medley for Our Times" (B15), "Meeting" (A11), "Metropolis" (A6), "Miniatures with a Meaning" (A4), "More Canadiana" (A7), "Mother, This Is Spring" (A1), "My Favourite Colour's Green" (A7), "The Myth of Smith" (A12), "The Newer Critics" (A11), "News of the Phoenix" (A3), "Night" (A1), " — 1943 — " (B52), "No Moby Dick" (A6), "Noblesse Oblige" (A7), "Obstacle Course" (B40), "Old Halifax Cemetery" (B16), "On Mr. and Mrs. Y's Reaction to Z's Misfortune" (A6), "On Reading Spender's Collected Poems" (A11), "On Reading the Holmes-Laski Letters" (A6), "On the Proposed Air Pact Outlawing the Bombing of Cities" (B3), "Paideia" (B101), "Part of a Letter" (A6), "Plain Words" (B177), "Poem [A little child]" (B44), "Poet Turned Novelist: For E.B." (A6), "Poetess [Her talk is pert and entertains]" (A3), "Poetess [This thumping cow]" (A6), "Portrait of a Pseudo-Socialist" (B4), "Prescription" (A11), "Queer Poem" (B71), "The Quill in Tranquillity" (A8), "Quiz Show" (A6), "Restaurant De Luxe" (B31), "S.A. Collection" (A6), "Say It Again, Brother" (B48), "Simon O'Bowd" (A6), "Smells" (B178), "Smoke Rings" (A4), "Songs of a Half-Crazed Nihilist" (B82), "Spinoza" (B57), "Spousal Grief" (A6), "Strategy" (A11), "Thaumaturge" (B5), "This Fact of Feeling" (A6), "To ———" (B6), "To Be Played on a Broken Virginal" (B74), "To L.B." (B8), "To My Wife," "To R.E." (B37), "To the Cypriots" (A11), "Training Camp" (B43), "The Transmogrification: For R.E." (A12), "The Transparency" (A12), "Vignette" (A3), "Voltaire Jezebel" (B7), "Waterfront" (B62), "Winter Scene" (B47), and "Young Man in Earnest" (A6).

A30   *The Covenant*. Foreword Irving Layton. Toronto: McClelland and Stewart, 1977. xii–xv, 112 pp.

Includes "Aetna" (B574), "The Arcade" (B575), "At the Beach," "Aviva," "The Awakening," "Bacillus Prodigiosus," "The Bald Tartar," "Bambino," "Because You Squeezed Back," "Calligraphy," "Catacombe dei Capuccini: For William Goodwin" (B551), "Caveat," "Christos-Dionysos" (B775), "The Circumcision," "Come Closer, Brothers," "Come Out Come Out Wherever You Are," "Contemporary Poet," "Covenant," "The Crucifixion," "The Curse: For David," "The Day God Was Looking After the Little Sparrow," "El Diablo: For Nicholas Haines" (B576), "Dialogue" (B719), "Dialogue with an Italian Christian Democrat," "Digby Dolben," "Disguises," "Distinctions," "Elysium: For Carmine Crudo," "An Epigram for Martial," "Europe 1976" (B582), "The Exorcist," "Fathers and Sons," "Faustein" (B566), "The Fire-Gutted Church on Avenue Road" (B584), "For Susan E. Rothney, Cosmetician," "For the Golden Boy," "For the Roman Who Stole Three Hundred Dollars," "Freaks: For Beth Marcilio," "The Galilean," "The Glass Dancer: For 'Bull' (D.D. Redwood)" (B567), "The Golden Age of Spanish Painting," "Gone" (B573), "Heinrich Heine," "Hidden Worlds" (B577), "Homecoming [Nor have I seen a toad]," "Idiots," "Innocents," "Invocation," "Judean Epigrams," "King Kong" (B578), "King of the Jews," "Lady on the Piazza," "Laurentia," "Letter to an Irish Poet," "Letter to the Soviet Cultural Attaché," "Letting Go," "Like Once I Lost," "Love-Lament of a Mesomorph: For Adrienne Clarkson," "The Luminous Bagel" (B583), "Magdalena," "Mary, Mary, Quite Contrary," "Meditation of an Aging Lebanese Poet," "Minden, Ont.," "Moments of Election: For Jacques Montpetit" (B579), "Morning Sounds," "Necrophilia," "Night Thoughts" (B553), "Nouvelle Vague," "O Cureless Rapture," "On Seeing an Old Man Praying in the Duomo," "Oracabessa, Xmas Eve 1975" (B568), "Paul Sextus," "The Perfect Cleft: For Susan Kulpaka," "The Phylactery Box," "Poet on the Square," "The Presence" (B670), "The Progress of Poesy," "A Psalm of David," "The Quill" (B572), "Requiem for an Unknown," "Review of 'Bravo, Layton,'" "Runcible: For Linda Sobel Halbert," "The Sabbath," "The Sacrifice," "Scylla," "Sicilian Vespers," "The Sinner," "Smoke [I've come to the tavern]," "Snowdrift: For Jo," "Son of Man," "A Song for Ancients: For Jerry and May Cohen" (see B1288), "Soviet Broilerism 2000 AD" (B581), "Sunset," "Sylvia," "The Tamed Puma," "There Was a Sound of Revelry, Once: For Naim Kattan," "Thoughts on Titling My Next Book 'Bravo, Layton,'" "Toronto, Xmas 1976," "A Walk to Nowhere" (B585), and "Xianity" (B580).

A31   *The Poems of Irving Layton*. Ed. and introd. Eli Mandel. New Canadian Library Original, No. O12. Toronto: McClelland and Stewart, 1977. 4–8, 63 pp. *The Selected Poems of Irving Layton*. Introd. Hugh Kenner. Ed. Eli Mandel. New York: New Directions, 1977. 5–8, 64 pp.

Includes "Adam" (B538), "Aran Islands" (B429), "The Baroness" (B481), "Berry Picking" (B195), "The Birth of Tragedy" (B171), "Blackout" (A25), "Butterfly on Rock" (B271), "The Cage" (B254), "Cain" (B193), "Chokecherries" (A9), "The Cockroach" (A22), "The Cold Green Element" (B111), "Divinity" (B198), "Elegy for Marilyn Monroe" (B277), "Elegy for Strul" (B374), "Family Portrait" (B172), "For Mao Tse-Tung: A Meditation on Flies and Kings" (B199), "For My Brother Jesus" (B816), "For My Distant Woman" (B564), "Golfers" (B117), "El Gusano [From the place where I was sitting]" (B294), "The Haunting" (B444), "The Improved Binoculars" (B500), "In the Midst of My Fever" (B102), "Inspiration" (A22), "Israelis" (B394), "Keine Lazarovitch 1870–1959" (B220), "Lillian Roxon" (B504), "Mahogany Red" (B322), "Misunderstanding" (B335), "O Jerusalem" (B531), "An Old Nicoise Whore" (B354), "On Seeing the Statuettes of Ezekiel and Jeremiah in the Church of Notre Dame" (B151), "Osip Mandelshtam (1891–1940)" (B427), "Paraclete" (B109), "Parque de Montjuich" (B547), "Pole-Vaulter" (B513), "Recipe for a Long and Happy Life" (A21), "Rhine Boat Trip" (B332), "Seduction of and by a Civilized Frenchwoman"

(B535), "Shakespeare" (B445), "The Shark" (B571), "Song for Naomi" (B792), "Survivor" (A28), "The Swimmer" (B60), "A Tall Man Executes a Jig" (B248), "The Ventriloquist" (B546), "The Well-Wrought Urn" (B263), "Whatever Else Poetry Is Freedom" (B191), and "With the Money I Spend" (A51).

A32 *Il Puma Ammansito.* Trans. Francesca Valente. Illus. Carlo Mattioli. Milan: Trentadue, 1978. 56 pp.
The Tamed Puma. Trans. Francesca Valente. Illus. Carlo Mattioli. Milan / Toronto: Trentadue / Virgo, in co-operation with the Italian Cultural Institute of Toronto, 1979. 56 pp.

Includes both original English and Italian translations of the following: "The Arcade / La Galleria" (B575), "Catacombe Dei Cappuccini: For William Goodwin / Catacombe dei Cappuccini: A William Goodwin" (B551), "For Edda / A Edda" (B542), "For Francesca / A Francesca" (B510), "For Sassu and His Horse / Per Sassu e il suo cavallo," "For 751-0329 / Per 751-0329" (B586), "Lady on the Piazza / Donna in Piazza di Spagna" (A30), "Laurentia," "Night Music / Musica notturna" (B594), "Poet on the Square / Il poeta sulla piazza," "Puppet Show with Dialogue / Spettacolo di burrattini con dialogo," "Smoke [I've come to the tavern] / Fumo" (A30), "The Tamed Puma / Il puma ammansito" (A30), and "Women of Rome / Donne romane" (B223).

A33 *The Love Poems of Irving Layton.* [Limited ed.] Foreword Irving Layton. Lithographs Graham Coughtry. Toronto: Canadian Fine Editions, 1978. [v–vi], 101 pp.
———. [Limited ed.] Foreword Irving Layton. Handwritten prefatory poem "[I sang of thighs]" (A20 — "Epitaph for a Poet [I sang of thighs]") Irving Layton. Lithographs Graham Coughtry. Toronto: Canadian Fine Editions, 1978. [ii], [vii–viii], 101 pp.

"The Air Is Sultry" (B312), "Androgyne" (B270), "An Aubade" (B480), "Bargain" (A11), "Because My Calling Is Such" (B204), "Berry Picking" (B195), "Blue and Lovely, My Love" (A15), "The Bridge" (B381), "By Ecstasies Perplexed" (A11), "Coal" (B281), "Creation [I fashioned you]" (B306), "Dans Le Jardin" (B207), "The Dark Nest" (A9), "David and Bathsheba," "The Day Aviva Came to Paris" (B208), "Discotheque" (A28), "Disguises" (A30), "Divinity" (B198), "Divorce," "End of the Affair [Wisdom is the decay of youth]" (B486), "Fanatic in San Feliu" (B430), "Farewell [She's gone. The one I swore up and down]" (B687), "Fata Morgana," "For Anna" (A76), "For Artemis," "For Aviva, Because I Love Her" (B255), "For Francesca" (B510), "For Miss Cézanne" (B316), "For Musia's Grandchildren" (B317), "For My Distant Woman" (B564), "For My Green Old Age" (B301), "For My Incomparable Gypsy" (B558), "For Priscilla" (A5), "For Sandra," "Gone" (B573), "Goodnight, Sweet Lady," "Hidden Worlds" (B577), "Holiday" (B164), "I Know the Dark and Hovering Moth" (B205), "I Would for Your Sake Be Gentle" (B138), "If I Lie Still" (B591), "In Praise of Older Men" (A28), "Inspiration" (A22), "Lady on the Piazza" (A30), "The Last Dryad" (A28), "Laurentia," "Letter from a Straw Man" (B162), "Letter to a Lost Love," "Love in a Cold Climate," "Love Poem with an Odd Twist" (B362), "Madman on Mithymna Beach" (B613), "Mahogany Red" (B322), "La Minerve" (B121), "Misunderstanding" (B335), "Musia," "Nightfall" (B56), "Of the Man Who Sits in the Garden" (A28), "One Day in the Life of Pincu Lazarovich," "The Perfect Mouth," "Proteus and Nymph" (A24), "The Quill" (B572), "Rain" (A12), "Return to Eden," "Sacrament by the Water" (B160), "Seduction of and by a Civilized Frenchwoman" (B535), "Smoke [I've come to the tavern]" (A30), "Snowdrift" (A30), "Song for a Late Hour" (A9), "A Strange Turn" (B311), "Talk at Twilight" (B377), "The Tamed Puma" (A30), "To Blow a Man Down," "To Margaret" (A28), "Two Songs for Sweet Voices" (B169), "Undine" (A9), "The Way to Go" (A52), "With the Money I Spend" (A51), "Woman" (B168), "The Worm [The filthy rain]" (A15), and "You and the 20th Century" (B457).

Poemas de amor. Trans. Salustiano Masó. Prólogo Irving Layton. Madrid: Hiperión, 1983. 9–11, 206 pp.

Includes English versions in a paragraph at the bottom of the Spanish text.

Includes "A Enriqueta" ["For Harriet"], "A Francesca" ["For Francesca"] (B510), "A Luisa, de 17 años" [For Louise, Age 17"] (B116), "A Margaret" ["To Margaret"] (A28), "A mi gitana incomparable" ["For My Incomparable Gypsy"] (B558), "A mi mujer lejana" ["For My Distant Woman"] (B564), "A mi verde ancianidad" ["For My Green Old Age"] (B301), "A Miss Cézanne" ["For Miss Cézanne"] (B316), "A Priscila" ["For Priscilla"] (A5), "A Sandra" ["For Sandra"], "El aire es asfixiante" ["The Air Is Sultry"] (B312), "Alborada" ["An Aubade"] (B480), "Ambivalencia" ["Ambivalency"] (A15), "Amor en clima gélido" ["Love in a Cold Climate"], "Amor moderno" ["Modern Love"] (A11), "Andrógino" ["Androgyne"] (B270), "Anochecer" ["Nightfall"] (B56), "Arándanos y frambuesas" ["Berry Picking"] (B195), "Asunto concluido" ["End of the Affair (Wisdom is the decay of youth)"] (B486), "Ausente" ["Gone"] (B573), "Aviva" (A30), "Azules y bellas, amor mío" ["Blue and Lovely, My Love"] (A15), "Bígamo" ["Bigamist"] (A22), "La boca perfecta" ["The Perfect Mouth"], "Buenas noches, señora mía" ["Goodnight, Sweet Lady"], "Canción para una hora postrera" ["Song for a Late Hour"] (A9), "Carbón" ["Coal"] (B281), "Carta a un amor perdido" ["Letter to a Lost Love"], "Carta de un hombre de paja" ["Letter from a Straw Man"] (B162), "Cerros y cerros" ["Hills and Hills"] (B400), "El cipo" ["The Pillar"] (B247), "Clic, clic" ["Click, Click"], "Cómo se escriben los poemas" ["How Poems Get Written"] (B356), "Como una vez que perdí" ["Like Once I Lost"] (A30), "Con el dinero que me gasto" ["With the Money I Spend"] (A51), "Conozco la oscura mariposa que revuela en la noche" ["I Know the Dark and Hovering Moth"] (B205), "El converso" ["The Convert"], "Creación" ["Creation (I fashioned you)"] (B306), "Dans le jardin" (B207), "David y Besabé" ["David and Bathsheba"], "Del hombre que se sienta en el jardin" ["Of the Man Who Sits in the Garden"] (A28), "Despedida" ["Farewell (She's gone. The one I swore up and down)"] (B687), "El día en que Aviva llegó à Paris" ["The Day Aviva Came to Paris"] (B208), "Día de fiesta" ["Holiday"] (B164), "Discoteca" ["Discothèque"] (A28), "Disfraces" ["Disguises"] (A30), "Divinidad" ["Divinity"] (B198), "Divorcio" ["Divorce"], "Dos canciones para voces melifluas" ["Two Songs for Sweet Voices"] (B169), "En loor de los viejos" ["In Praise of Older Men"] (A28), "Eros" ["Eros (With the best side of my tongue)"] (A4), "Eterno retorno" ["Eternal Recurrence (Even that leaf as it falls)"] (B443), "Fanático en San Feliu" ["Fanatic in San Feliu"] (B430), "Fata Morgana," "El gusano" ["The Worm (The filthy rain)"] (A15), "Humo" ["Smoke (I've come to the tavern)"] (A30), "Insomnio" ["Insomnia"] (A17), "Inspiración" ["Inspiration"] (A22), "Lady en la piazza" ["Lady on the Piazza"] (A30), "La lanzadera" ["The Quill"] (B572), "Latría" ["Latria"] (A6), "Lírica invernal" ["Winter Lyric"] (B324), "Lluvia" ["Rain"] (A12), "Loco en la playa de Mithymna" ["Madman on

Mithymna Beach"] (B613), "Los años de mortifica-
ción" ["The Chastening Years"], "La madriguera
oscura" ["The Dark Nest"] (A9), "Malentendido"
["Misunderstanding"] (B335), "Manera de morir"
["The Way to Go"] (A52), "Memorándum a un
suicida" ["Memo to a Suicide"] (B471), "Metamorfosis" ["Changeling"] (B418), "Mi reina, mi coima"
["My Queen, My Quean"] (A15), "La Minerve"
(B121), "¡Mira, todos los borregos a nuestro alred-
edor!" ["Look, the Lambs Are All Around Us!"]
(A6), "Mujer" ["Woman"] (B168), "Mundos escon-
didos" ["Hidden Worlds"] (B577), "Musia," "Nau-
sicaa" ["Nausicäa"] (A11), "Ondina" ["Undine"]
(A9), "Ortodoxia" ["Orthodoxy"], "Pacifista a
cualquier precio" ["Peacemonger"] (A18), "Para
Ana" ["For Anna"] (A76), "Para Artemisa" ["For
Artemis"], "Para Aviva, porque la quiero" ["For
Aviva, Because I Love Her"] (B255), "Para la joven
de ojos espaciados" ["For the Girl with Wide-Apart
Eyes"] (A18), "Para los nietos de Musia" ["For
Musia's Grandchildren"] (B317), "Parloteo entre dos
luces" ["Talk at Twilight"] (B377), "Poema de amor
con un giro insospechado" ["Love Poem with an
Odd Twist"] (B362), "Poeta y mujer" ["Poet and
Woman"], "Por éxtasis turbado" ["By Ecstasies Per-
plexed"] (A11), "Por ti quisiera ser un hombre
afable" ["I Would for Your Sake Be Gentle"] (B138),
"Porque tal es mi vocación" ["Because My Calling Is
Such"] (B204), "Preludio" ["Prelude"] (A18), "Pro-
teo y ninfa" ["Proteus and Nymph"] (A24), "El
Puente" ["The Bridge"] (B381), "El puma domado"
["The Tamed Puma"] (A30), "Retorno al Edén"
["Return to Eden"], "Retraimiento del amor"
["Love's Diffidence"] (B154), "Rojo caoba"
["Mahogany Red"] (B322), "Sacramento en la
ribera" ["Sacrament by the Water"] (B160), "La
seducción" ["The Seduction (First he knocks her
down)"] (A15), "Seducción de y por una francesa

civilizada" ["Seduction of and by a Civilized Frenchwoman"] (B535), "Si yazgo sosegado" ["If I Lie
Still"] (B591), "La transfiguración" ["The Transfiguration"] (A22), "Trato" ["Bargain"] (A11), "Tú y
el siglo xx" ["You and the 20th Century"] (B457),
"Tumbar a un hombre" ["To Blow a Man Down"],
"La última driada" ["The Last Dryad"] (A28), "Un
día en la vida de Pincu Lazarovich" ["One Day in the
Life of Pincu Lazarovich"], "Un lance insolito" ["A
Strange Turn"] (B311), and "Ventisquero" ["Snowdrift"] (A30).

The Love Poems of Irving Layton. Foreword Irving
Layton. Toronto: McClelland and Stewart, 1980.
[7–8], 139 pp.

Includes "The Air Is Sultry" (B312), "Ambival-
ency" (A15), "Androgyne" (B270), "An Aubade"
(B480), "Aviva" (A30), "Bargain" (A11), "Because
My Calling Is Such" (B204), "Berry Picking" (B195),
"Bigamist" (A22), "Blue and Lovely, My Love"
(A15), "The Bridge" (B381), "By Ecstasies Per-
plexed" (A11), "Changeling" (B418), "The Chasten-
ing Years," "Click, Click," "Coal" (B281), "The
Convert," "Creation [I fashioned you]" (B306),
"Dans Le Jardin" (B207), "The Dark Nest" (A9),
"David and Bathsheba," "The Day Aviva Came to
Paris" (B208), "Discothèque" (A28), "Disguises"
(A30), "Divinity" (B198), "Divorce," "End of the
Affair [Wisdom is the decay of youth]" (B486), "Eros
[With the best side of my tongue]" (A4), "Eternal
Recurrence [Even that leaf as it falls]" (B443),
"Fanatic in San Feliu" (B430), "Farewell [She's gone.
The one I swore up and down]" (B687), "Fata Morg-
ana," "For Anna" (A76), "For Artemis," "For Aviva,
Because I Love Her" (B255), "For Francesca" (B510),
"For Harriet," "For Louise, Age 17" (B116), "For
Miss Cézanne" (B316), "For Musia's Grandchildren"
(B317), "For My Distant Woman" (B564), "For My
Green Old Age" (B301), "For My Incomparable

Gypsy" (B558), "For Priscilla" (A5), "For Sandra," "For the Girl with Wide-Apart Eyes" (A18), "Gone" (B573), "Goodnight, Sweet Lady," "Hidden Worlds" (B577), "Hills and Hills" (B400), "Holiday" (B164), "How Poems Get Written" (B356), "I Know the Dark and Hovering Moth" (B205), "I Would for Your Sake Be Gentle" (B138), "If I Lie Still" (B591), "In Praise of Older Men" (A28), "Insomnia" (A17), "Inspiration" (A22), "Lady on the Piazza" (A30), "The Last Dryad" (A28), "Latria" (A6), "Letter from a Straw Man" (B162), "Letter to a Lost Love," "Like Once I Lost" (A30), "Look, the Lambs Are All Around Us!" (A6), "Love in a Cold Climate," "Love Poem with an Odd Twist" (B362), "Love's Diffidence" (B154), "Madman on Mithymna Beach" (B613), "Mahogany Red" (B322), "Memo to a Suicide" (B471), "La Minerve" (B121), "Misunderstanding" (B335), "Modern Love" (A11), "Musia," "My Queen, My Quean" (A15), "Nausicäa" (A11), "Nightfall" (B56), "Of the Man Who Sits in the Garden" (A28), "One Day in the Life of Pincu Lazarovich," "Orthodoxy," "Peacemonger" (A18), "The Perfect Mouth," "The Pillar" (B247), "Poet and Woman," "Prelude" (A18), "Proteus and Nymph" (A24), "The Quill" (B572), "Rain" (A12), "Return to Eden," "Sacrament by the Water" (B160), "The Seduction [First he knocks her down]" (A15), "Seduction of and by a Civilized Frenchwoman" (B535), "Smoke [I've come to the tavern]" (A30), "Snowdrift" (A30), "Song for a Late Hour" (A9), "A Strange Turn" (B311), "Talk at Twilight" (B377), "The Tamed Puma" (A30), "To Blow a Man Down," "To Margaret" (A28), "The Transfiguration" (A22), "Two Songs for Sweet Voices" (B169), "Undine" (A9), "The Way to Go" (A52), "Winter Lyric" (B324), "With the Money I Spend" (A51), "Woman" (B168), "The Worm [The filthy rain]" (A15), and "You and the 20th Century" (B457).

Le poesie d'amore di Irving Layton. Introd. and trans. Alfredo Rizzardi. Designed Ernesto Treccani e Ettore De Conciliis. Abano Terme, Italy: Piovan, 1983. 5–11, 156 pp.

Includes English and facing-page translations of the following: "The Air Is Sultry / L'aria è afosa" (B312), "Ambivalency / Ambivalenza" (A15), "Bargain / Baratto" (A11), "Blue and Lovely, My Love / Azzurre e leggiadre, amore" (A15), "The Bridge / Il ponte" (B381), "Changeling / Sostituzione" (B418), "The Convert / Convertito," "Creation [I fashioned you] / Creazione" (B306), "Disguises / Travestimenti" (A30), "Divinity / Attributi divini" (B198), "End of the Affair [Wisdom is the decay of youth] / Fine della storia" (B486), "Fanatic in San Feliu / Fanatico a San Feliu" (B430), "For Artemis / Per Artemide," "For Aviva, Because I Love Her / Per Aviva, perché l'amo" (B255), "For Harriet / Per Harriet," "For Priscilla / Per Priscilla" (A5), "Gone / Partita" (B573), "Goodnight, Sweet Lady / Buonanotte, dolce signora," "Hills and Hills / Colline e colline" (B400), "How Poems Get Written / Come si scrivono le poesie" (B356), "I Sang of Thighs / Cantai le cosce" (A21 — "Epitaph for a Poet [I sang of thighs]"), "If I Lie Still / Se giaccio immobile" (B591), "Insomnia / Insonnia" (A17), "Latria" (A6), "Look, the Lambs Are All Around Us! / Guarda, gli agnelli sono tutti intorno a noi!" (A6), "Love's Diffidence / Incertezza d'amore" (B154), "Misunderstanding / Incomprensione" (B335), "Nightfall / Imbrunire" (B56), "Orthodoxy / Ortodossia," "Poet and Woman / Poeta e Donna," "Proteus and Nymph / Proteo e Ninfa" (A24), "Rain / Pioggia" (A12), "Return to Eden / Ritorno all'Eden," "Sacrament by the Water / Sacramento presso l'acqua" (B160), "Seduction of and by a Civilized Frenchwoman / Seduzione di (e da parte di) una colta francese" (B535), "Smoke [I've come to the tavern] / Fumo" (A30), "Snowdrift /

Mucchio di neve" (A30), "Song for a Late Hour / Canto per un'ora tarda" (A9), "A Strange Turn / Strano cambiamento" (B311), "Talk at Twilight / Conversazione al crepuscolo" (B377), "The Tamed Puma / Il puma domato" (A30), "To Margaret / A Margherita" (A28), "Winter Lyric / Lirica invernale" (B324), "With the Money I Spend / Con i soldi che spendo" (A51), "Woman / Donna" (B168), "The Worm [The filthy rain] / Il verme" (A15), and "You and the 20th Century / Tu e il xx secolo" (B457).

A34 *The Tightrope Dancer.* Foreword Irving Layton. Toronto: McClelland and Stewart, 1978. 9–11, 112 pp.

Includes "The Accident," "After a Sleepless Night," "Arab Hara-Kiri," "At the Chill Centre," "Beatitude," "Before the Millenium Comes," "Blackbird," "Bravo, Death. I Love You," "Bridegroom," "Checkmate: For Vladimir Nabokov," "Comrade" (B588), "Danke Schön: For Nicky Fisher," "Death Washes the Face of the World," "The Descent of Man," "Dialectical Leap" (B618), "Dr. Spock Please Answer," "Don't Blame the Apple," "Eden," "England 1977," "The Expanding Universe," "Fascination," "Figs," "The Final Memo," "The Final Poem" (B605), "Flies" (B598), "Flowers He'll Never Smell: John Angus McDougald," "For Another Who Squeezed Back: For Rita," "For Artemis," "For Masha Cohen," "For My Brother Oscar," "For Old Rabbi Schachter," "For Sassu and His Horse" (A32), "For 751–0329" (B586), "The Goat," "God Is Not Dead," "Goodnight, Sweet Lady" (A33), "Grand Finale" (B599), "Greek Dancer," "The Greek Light," "Hangover" (B593), "The Happening" (B600), "Harrietia," "Hummingbird," "Intimations," "The Journey," "Late Invitation to the Dance" (B601), "The Latest Wrinkle," "Madman on Mithymna Beach" (B613), "The Male-

diction" (B602), "Medusas" (B607), "Memo to Sir Mortimer," "Mishnah and the Eternal Shmuck," "Mockingbird," "The Monster," "Night Music" (B594), "Odd Couple," "Opium" (B619), "The Oracle," "The Papal Election" (B620), "The Perfect Mouth," "Poetry," "The Prize," "The Professional," "Provender," "Puppet Show with Dialogue" (A32), "Rabbi Simeon Comforts His Flock," "Return to Eden," "Sandcrab," "Schadenfreude," "Sir," "Sir Mortimer," "Smoke [Père Lachaise is so peaceful]" (B604), "Star Trek," "Sunflight," "Sunstroke," "Tell It to Peggy," "Theatre" (B595), "The Tightrope Dancer," "To Blow a Man Down" (A33), "To the Victims of the Holocaust" (B596), "Trapped Faun," "Tropical Flowers" (B608), "Two Women: For Bobby Maslen," "The Voyage," "Watch Out for His Left: For Leonid Brezhnev," "When Death Comes for You" (B597), "Yeats in St. Lucia," "You Allowed the Generalissimo: For F. Franco," "You Come to Me," and "Zorba the Jew."

A35 *Droppings from Heaven.* Foreword Irving Layton. Toronto: McClelland and Stewart, 1979. 11–14, 111 pp.

Includes "The Absurd Animal," "Antimonies" (B617), "Autumn Seen as My Lady," "The Banff Centre: For Neill M. Armstrong," "The Black Tom," "Cabalist," "Calibrations," "The Canadian Epic," "Carib Sun," "The Chastening Years: For Sandra Beaudin" (A33), "Click, Click" (A33), "The Convert: For Harriet," "Cosmic Religion," "Cuisine Canadienne" (B622), "The Dark Underside: For David Jeffrey," "David and Bathsheba" (A33), "The Deer Hunter," "Deodorants," "Divine Madman," "Divorce" (A33), "Droppings from Heaven" (B623), "Expurgated Edition," "Fantasia in C Sharp," "Fata Morgana" (A33), "Father and Daughter: For Naomi," "For Harriet" (A33), "For Sandra" (A33),

"Freud with All His Knowledge," "Froth," "The Garburetor," "Gazpacho," "The Halo: For David Staines," "Hanging in There" (B625), "The Happy Hooker: For Peter Gzowski," "Homecoming [The apartment is empty except]," "How a Poem Moves," "Hurrah for the Elephant," "The Idols," "In Great Gatsby Country," "In Plato's Cave," "Inverness," "Jane Eyre," "The Lesson," "Letter from a Young Roman Existentialist," "Letter to a Lost Love" (A33), "Libido: For Joyce Carol Oates" (B637), "The Literary Mind" (B626), "The Magician," "Man and Woman," "Misogynist," "Molibos," "Musia," "NBC: Late Night News," "Narcissus" (B638), "The New Piety," "The New Pope Gives Us Hope," "News from Nowhere: For William Morris" (B603), "No More Chicken Soup" (B634), "No Vacancy," "Not All Canucks Are Schmucks," "One Day in the Life of Pincu Lazarovich" (A33), "Operation Barbarossa," "Orthodoxy," "Paradise: For Kevin McVeigh," "Poet and Woman," "Praise the Lord," "Prayer for My Old Age," "Senile, My Sister Sings" (B713), "The Sex Drive," "Shit," "Shlemihl: For Reinhard Pummer" (B628), "The Sign of the Cross: For Anatoli Shcharansky," "The Slaughterhouse," "Snake Goddess: For Heidi Compagnat," "Stillness," "Synagogue in West Palm Beach: For Mary and Jack Bernstein" (B639), "Takeoff," "To the Jewish Dissenters," "Transcendence," "2028," "What Crazy Jenny Sings in Her Golden Ghetto," "Where Was Your Shit-Detector, Pablo?", and "A Wild Peculiar Joy" (B630).

A36   *There Were No Signs*. [Deluxe ed.] Etchings Aligi Sassu. Milan / Toronto: Trentadue / Madison Gallery, 1979. 17 folded leaves.

Each poem is signed: Irving Layton. Each etching is signed: Aligi Sassu.

———— . Etchings Aligi Sassu. Milan / Toronto:

Trentadue / Madison Gallery, 1979. [39] pp.

Includes "Catacombe dei Cappuccini: For William Goodwin" (B551), "De Bullion Street" (B55), "Divinity and John Dewey" (B776), "Flies" (B598), "For Francesca" (B510), "For Sassu and His Horse" (A32), "For 751-0329" (B586), "The Galilean" (A30), "Hidden Worlds" (B577), "If Whales Could Think on Certain Happy Days" (B516), "Lady on the Piazza" (A30), "Plaza de Toros" (B296), "Saviour" (A22), "There Were No Signs" (B250), and "Women of Rome" (B223).

A37   *For My Neighbours in Hell*. Oakville, Ont.: Mosaic / Valley, [1980]. 94 pp.

Includes "The Abyss," "Anti-Abortionist," "Antisemites" (B641), "Apocalypse" (B654), "Ashes and Diamonds" (B640), "Bright's Wines," "The Burning Remnant," "Civilizations," "The Comedian" (B656), "La Condition Humaine" (B635), "The Cracked Mirror," "Criticaster," "Dirty Old Man," "Dracula" (B642), "The Dysphasiac," "Egalitarian" (B653), "The Election," "The Fifth International," "The Final Coming" (B651), "Finally, the Final Solution" (B671), "Florida Nights" (B621), "For Don Carlos" (B663), "For My Neighbours in Hell [Hate, your adrenalin]" (B643), "Ghouls," "[God made the viper, the shark, the tsetse fly]" (B776), "God's Mysterious Ways," "Greek Fishermen," "Greek Tragedy," "Greetings," "Guru" (B624), "Hamilton Journalist: For David McFadden," "The Hex," "The High Cost of Living," "Homage to Sir Mortimer," "Kitchen Serenade," "Lady with a Recorder" (B644), "The Last Survivor," "The Long Shade" (B657), "The Lyric [As moles construct]" (B631), "Male Chauvinist" (B645), "The Mildewed Maple," "Mount Royal Cemetery" (B646), "Mountain Playhouse" (B647), "Mr. Teng Goes to Washington," "Music Hath Such Charms: For Marc Bernstein,"

"Natural Selection" (B627), "Nature's Sculpture," "Never in Rosedale" (B658), "Next Year, in Jerusalem," "Niagara-on-the-Lake," "No Tiger Lily," "Not with a Whimper," "Old Codgers in a Gym" (B632), "Old Men" (B659), "On Becoming a Brigadier," "On the Death of Pope Paul VI," "On the Sudden Death of a Relative" (B636), "Orangemen's Parade," "Overheard in a Lavabo," "The Painted Bird: For Jerzy Kosinski," "Paradox," "Pardon Me, Lady," "Passing Through the Rockies: For Ruth Fraser" (B660), "The Passionate WASP" (B633), "The Petits Hommes," "Plato Was an Asshole," "The Poet on His Detractors," "Progress of an Affair," "Queen Street," "The Red Chamberpot," "Reflections in an Old Ontario Cemetery" (B664), "Rumination of an Aging Millionaire," "The Second Coming," "Self-Interview" (B648), "Soda Water," "Stalin" (B649), "Sunbather," "To a Young Girl Sunbathing," "The True Picture" (B650), "Tuthankhamen," "20th Century Sadist," "Two Communist Poets" (B629), "United Church Signboard," "When Death Says 'Come,'" "With All Due Respect," and "Words from an Old Greek Poet."

A38 *Europe and Other Bad News*. Foreword Irving Layton. Toronto: McClelland and Stewart, 1981. 9–11, 96 pp.

Includes "Anarch" (B676), "The Annunciation" (B678), "Ashtoreth" (B675), "Balloon," "Beach Scene," "Beginnings and Other Starts," "Being," "Being There" (B679), "Bitch," "Blitzkrieg," "Comrade Trotsky" (B688), "The Consummation" (B680), "Conversos," "Credo: For William Goodwin," "Cruising" (B662), "Death of God," "Death, Where's your Sting-a-Ling?", "Definitions" (B682), "Deliverance" (B666), "Disgrace Abounding," "Divine Egotist" (B689), "Early Morning Sounds" (B690), "Eine Kleine Nachtmusik" (B673), "Endan-

gered Species," "The Enlightenment," "Eternal Recurrence [The sleepwalkers are advancing on Armageddon]" (B683), "Flora," "For Antonio Machado" (B684), "For Else Lasker-Schuler" (B691), "For Erich Muhsam" (B667), "For Hans, Maybe Klaus or Tadeusz" (B672), "For Marina Ivanovna Tsvetayeva" (B692), "For Reverend B.A. Wurm," "Friends, My Delight," "Gay Sunshine Anthology," "The Glimpse," "Goodbye to All That," "The Great Hatred," "Gulag," "Hells," "Herzl," "In an Ice Age," "Isla Mujeres," "The Itch," "The Joker," "Junk" (B668), "Koré" (B669), "Malachi," "Masterpiece," "Mayan Blue," "Memo to Max and David," "Michal," "The Nativity," "No Absolute Joy," "Nominalist," "North of Eden," "One Day, My Love," "Other Beginnings and Starts," "Palmtree," "Platyhelminths," "Poet," "The Presence" (B670), "A Psalm in Niagara," "The Pulse," "The Queen of Hearts" (B685), "Reingemacht" (B674), "The Release [Before the cancer bugs]" (B652), "The Ring," "Ruina Maya," "The Search" (B709), "Sempre" (B693), "Smells," "Sunflowers" (B676), "To a Shmuck with Talent" (B681), "Transfiguration," "Universalist," "Vikki," "The Wheel," "The Wretched of the Earth," and "Xian."

A39 *In un'età di ghiaccio*. Ed. and trans. Alfredo Rizzardi. Illus. Ettore De Conciliis. Foreword (in English and Italian) Irving Layton. Introd. (in Italian) Alfredo Rizzardi. Roma: Lerici, [1981]. 5–7, 9–11, 192 pp.

Includes English and facing-page Italian translations of the following: "Adam / Adamo" (B538), "Aetna / Etna" (B574), "The Arcade / La galleria" (B575), "At the Iglesia de Sacromonte / Alla Iglesia de Sacromonte" (B302), "The Cage / La gabbia" (B254), "Catacombe dei Cappuccini: For William Goodwin / Catacombe dei cappuccini: Per William Goodwin" (B551), "Clochards: For Wynne Francis /

Clochards: Per Wynne Francis" (B352), "The Cockroach / La blatta" (A22), "De Bullion Street / Via de Bullion" (B55), "Early Morning in Mithymna / Di primo mattino a Mitimna" (A22), "Eine Kleine Nachtmusik" (B673), "Elegy for Marilyn Monroe / Elegia per Marilyn Monroe" (B277), "The Final Solution / La soluzione finale" (B532), "Florence / Firenze" (B557), "For Andrei Amalrik / Per Andrei Amalrik" (B521), "For Edda / Per Edda" (B542), "For Erich Muhsam / Per Erich Muhsam" (B667), "For My Brother Jesus / Per mio fratello gesù" (B816), "For My Neighbours in Hell [Hate, your adrenalin] / Per il mio prossimo all'inferno" (B643), "For 751–0329 / Per 751–0329" (B586), "God Is Not Dead / Dio non è morto" (A34), "Hells / Inferni" (A38), "Heraclitos / Eraclito" (A18), "The Improved Binoculars / Il binocolo potenziato" (B500), "In an Ice Age / In un'età di ghiaccio" (A38), "Keine Lazarovitch 1870–1959" (B220), "Lady on the Piazza / Donna in Piazza di Spagna" (A30), "Late Invitation to the Dance / Tardo invito alla danza" (B601), "Laura Cunneyflow" (A21), "Like a Mother Demented / Madre uscita di senno" (B368), "Paraclete" (B109), "Piazza San Marco" (B221), "The Plaka / La plaka" (B561), "Poet on the Square / Il poeta sulla piazza" (A32), "Pole-Vaulter / Saltatore con l'asta" (B513), "Reflections in an Old Ontario Cemetery / Riflessioni in un vecchio cimitero dell'Ontario" (B664), "Rhine Boat Trip / In barca sul Reno" (B332), "Seduction of and by a Civilized Frenchwoman / Seduzione di (e da parte di) una colta francese" (B535), "Senile, My Sister Sings / Senile, canta mia sorella" (B713), "September Woman / Donna in settembre" (B514), "The Sinner / Il peccatore" (A30), "Sun Bathers / Bagnanti" (A37), "Survivor / Sopravvissuto" (A28), "A Tall Man Executes a Jig / Un uomo alto esegue una giga" (B248), "To the Victims of the Holocaust / Alle vittime dell'Olo-

causto" (B596), "2028" (A35), "The Violent Life: For Pier Paolo Pasolini / La vita violenta: Per Pier Paolo Pasolini" (A28), "Women of Rome / Donne romane" (B223), and "Whatever Else Poetry Is Freedom / Quant'alto la poesia è liberta" (B191).

A40   *A Wild Peculiar Joy: Selected Poems 1945–82.* Toronto: McClelland and Stewart, 1982. 224 pp.
———. Toronto: McClelland and Stewart, 1982. 224 pp.
    Includes "Absence" (A21), "After Auschwitz" (B386), "Against This Death" (B590), "Anarch" (B677), "The Annunciation" (B678), "The Arch" (A28), "Ballad of the Old Spaniard" (B289), "Bargain" (A11), "Berry Picking" (B195), "The Birth of Tragedy" (B171), "The Black Huntsmen" (B79), "Blossom" (B698), "Bodhidharma" (A24), "Boys Bathing" (A9), "The Breaststroke" (B705), "The Bull Calf" (B149), "Butterfly on Rock" (B271), "Cabalist" (A35), "The Cage" (B254), "Cain" (B193), "Cat Dying in Autumn" (B179), "Catacombe dei Capuccini" (B551), "Centennial Ode" (B327), "The Cold Green Element" (B111), "La Commedia" (B696), "Composition in Late Spring" (B104), "The Convertible" (B231), "Côte des Neiges Cemetery" (B186), "The Dark Underside" (A35), "The Day Aviva Came to Paris" (B208), "Dialogue" (B719), "Divine Image" (B238), "Dracula" (B642), "Early Morning Sounds" (B690), "Eine Kleine Nachtmusik" (B673), "End of the White Mouse" (B446), "L'Envoi" (A28), "Europe 1976" (B582), "Everything in the Universe Has Its Place," "Family Portrait" (B172), "The Fertile Muck" (B173), "Figs" (A34), "Flies" (B598), "Flytrap" (B534), "For Auld Lang Syne" (A22), "For Louise, Age 17" (B116), "For Mao Tse-Tung: A Meditation on Flies and Kings" (B199), "For Musia's Grandchildren" (B317), "For My Brother Jesus" (B816), "For My

Neighbours in Hell [God made the viper, the shark, the tsetse fly]" (B776), "For My Sons, Max and David" (B361), "For Natalya Correia" (B431), "For 7515–03296" (B586), "From Colony to Nation" (B748), "The Galilean" (A30), "The Garburetor" (A35), "The Garden" (B725), "Golfers" (B117), "Grand Finale" (B599), "The Graveyard" (B380), "Greetings" (A37), "El Gusano [From the place where I was sitting]" (B294), "The Haemorrhage" (A28), "The Haunting" (B444), "Hells" (A38), "Heraclitus" (A18), "How a Poem Moves" (A35), "The Human Cry" (B837), "The Improved Binoculars" (B500), "In the Midst of My Fever" (B102), "Iroquois in Nice" (B570), "Israelis" (B394), "Ithaca" (B611), "Journey into the Long Night on Castors," "Keewaydin Poetry Festival" (B120), "Keine Lazarovitch: 1870–1959" (B220), "Letter to a Librarian" (A12), "Like a Mother Demented" (B368), "Look, the Lambs Are All Around Us!" (A6), "Love the Conqueror Worm" (B94), "The Luminous Bagel" (B583), "Maxie" (A5), "Meditation of an Aging Lebanese Poet" (A30), "Midsummer's Dream in the Vienna Stadtpark" (B511), "La Minerve" (B121), "Misunderstanding" (B335), "Mont Rolland" (B81), "The Mosquito" (A9), "My Flesh Comfortless" (B201), "Narcissus" (B638), "Nausicäa" (A11), "New Tables" (A6), "Night Music" (B594), "Nominalist" (A38), "North of Eden" (A38), "Now That I'm Older" (A6), "O Jerusalem" (B531), "An Old Niçoise Whore" (B354), "On Being Bitten by a Dog" (A11), "On Seeing the Statuettes of Ezekiel and Jeremiah in the Church of Notre Dame" (B151), "Osip Mandelshtam (1891–1940)" (B427), "Paging Mr. Superman" (B197), "Paraclete" (B109), "Parque de Montjuich" (B547), "Plaza de Toros" (B296), "The Poetic Process" (B125), "Political Economy" (B266), "The Predator" (B285), "Proteus and Nymph" (A24), "The Puma" (A30 — "The Tamed Puma"), "Rain at La Minerve" (A6), "Recipe for a Long and Happy Life" (A21), "Rhine Boat Trip" (B332), "Samantha Clara Layton" (B686), "The Search" (B709), "Sempre" (B693), "Senile, My Sister Sings" (B713), "Seven O'Clock Lecture" (B99), "Shakespeare" (B445), "The Shark" (B571), "Sheep" (B190), "Signs and Portents" (A22), "The Silence [It grew from nothing]" (B714), "The Sinner" (A30), "The Skull" (B417), "The Slaughterhouse" (A35), "Song for a Late Hour" (A9), "Song for Naomi" (B792), "Stella" (B482), "Still Life" (A14), "A Strange Turn" (B311), "Street Funeral" (B95), "Sunflowers" (B676), "The Swimmer" (B60), "Synagogue in West Palm Beach" (B639), "A Tall Man Executes a Jig" (B248), "There Were No Signs" (B250), "To Maoists" (A22), "To the Girls of My Graduating Class" (B93), "To the Victims of the Holocaust" (B596), "Vexata Quaestio" (B140), "Vita Aeterna," "Whatever Else Poetry Is Freedom" (B191), "The Wheel" (A38), "When Hourly I Praised," "Where Was Your Shit-Detector, Pablo?" (A35), "A Wild Peculiar Joy" (B630), "Woman" (B168), "Xianity" (B580), and "Yeats in St. Lucia" (A34).

———. Toronto: McClelland and Stewart, 1989. 315 pp.

A second edition of this book contains all the poems listed in the previous edition plus the following: "Arabs" (A18), "Aristocrats" (B760), "Attending Suzanne's Funeral" (B836), "August Strindberg" (B752), "Beutel's Name Is Inscribed for Eternal Life" (B230), "Black Tourist in Tinos" (B807), "Blind Man's Bluff" (A41), "Boris Pasternak" (A41), "Boschka Layton: 1921–1984" (B791), "Bottles: For Giorgio Morandi" (B812), "Bridegroom" (A34), "Budapest" (A24), "The Carillon" (B706), "The Cockroach" (A22), "La Condition Humaine" (B635), "The Dazed Fly" (A41), "Dead Souls"

(B718), "Descent from Eden" (A41), "Dionysians in a Bad Time" (B804), "Elegy for Marilyn Monroe" (B277), "Elephant" (B395), "Epistle to Catullus" (B778), "Eternal Recurrence [The sleepwalkers are advancing on Armageddon]" (B683), "Etruscan Tombs: For Dante Gardini" (B796), "Fascination" (A34), "Fellini" (B805), "Final Reckoning: After Theognis" (B824), "For Ettore, with Love and Admiration" (B777), "For the Wife of Mr. Milton" (B701), "Fortuna et Cupidas" (A22), "From the Nether World" (B706), "Funeraria 'Olea'" (B497), "Greek Fly" (A24), "I Take My Anna Everywhere" (B753), "I Think of Ovid" (A22), "In Plato's Cave" (A35), "Inspiration" (A22), "Kali in the Suburbs" (A41), "Late Invitation to the Dance" (B601), "The Lesson" (A35), "Letter to a Lost Love" (A35), "Medusas" (B607), "Molibos" (A35), "Music Hath Such Charms: For Marc Bernstein" (A37), "New Shining Worlds: For S. Ross" (A41), "Nostalgia When the Leaves Begin to Fall" (B757), "Odd Obsession: For Lisa" (B766), "Old Men" (B659), "On the Death of Pope Paul VI" (A37), "Operation Barbarossa" (A35), "Out of Pure Lust: For Vivian" (A41), "Party at Hydra: For Marianne" (A22), "Paul Verlaine" (A21), "Peacock" (A24), "Perfection" (B749), "Portrait of a Modern Woman" (B726), "The Prize" (A34), "Reinfemacht" (B674), "Rupert Brooke: 1887–1915" (B614), "Sandcrab" (A34), "The Seesaw" (B720), "Sex Appeal" (B759), "The Tightrope Dancer" (A34), "To Make an End: For Malka Cohen 1897–1981" (B699), "Tristezza" (B704), "Twentieth Century Gothic" (B827), "Two Women: For Bobby Maslen" (A34), "When Death Comes for You" (B597), "With the Money I Spend" (A51), "Yeats at Sixty-Five" (B763), and "Zucchini" (B695).

A41   *The Gucci Bag.* [Limited ed.] Foreword Irving Layton. Oakville, Ont.: Mosaic / Valley, 1983. 1–5, [105] pp.

Includes "Ah, Nuts," "Los Americanos" (B715), "The Amnesty," "And There Was Light," "Apodoxis," "Apostate" (B716), "The Black Thread" (B702), "Blind Man's Bluff," "Blossom" (B698), "Bonded," "Boris Pasternak," "Bottles: For Giorgio Morandi" (B812), "The Breast Stroke: For Diane Parent" (B705), "A Brief History of the Jews [Once they talked to God]" (B728), "The Camera Eye," "The Captive," "The Carillon" (B706), "The Carved Nakedness" (B717), "Central Heating" (B764), "La Commedia" (B696), "The Courage to Be," "Dancing Man" (B746), "Day in Court" (B743), "The Dazed Fly," "Dead Souls" (B718), "Descent from Eden," "The Divine Touch," "Dung Beetle" (B734), "An End in View," "The End of the Matter," "Everything in the Universe Has Its Place" (A40), "Fabrizio: for William Goodwin" (B741), "Fire Warden: For Boris Pasternak" (B711), "First Violet: For Kim Yang Shik," "The Flaming Maple" (B769), "Flights" (A80), "For the Great Wrong," "For the Wife of Mr. Milton" (B701), "From the Nether World" (B707), "The Furrow," "The Garden" (B725), "The Hairy Monster: For Earl and Erika" (B737), "Journey into the Long Night on Castors," "Kali in the Suburbs," "Letting Go," "The Lone Ranger," "Make Room William Blake" (B745), "Manikins: For Veneranda McGrath," "Medusa," "Memo to a Tall Two-Footed Swine" (B731), "More Champagne, Darling: For Patrick Crean" (B765), "Mountains: For Sid Marty," "Moutarde," "Murders at the Rue Bathurst" (B720), "Nearer to Thee" (B738), "Needles," "Neighbour Love [A malicious, pot-bellied arthritic Jew]" (B730), "New Shining Worlds: For S. Ross," "Odd Obsession: For Lisa" (B766), "Of Leaves & Loves," "Of One Fairy & Three Goddesses," "An Old Man's Wet Dream," "Orpheus in Old Forest Hill," "Out of Pure Lust: For Vivian," "Perfection" (B749), "A Poet from Tibilsi Complains," "Poetry Conference"

(B703), "Portrait of a Modern Woman" (B726), "A Prayer to Colette," "Recovery" (B733), "The Remnant" (B708), "Samantha Clara Layton" (B686), "Saxophonist: For Simon Stone," "The Seal: For Alice Duarte," "The Seesaw" (B721), "Self Fulfillment," "Self-Overcoming," "Seventeen Lines and Three Kisses: For Veneranda," "The Swamp" (B727), "The Talisman," "Thank You Veneranda," "There's Always Job" (B722), "They Also Serve" (B712), "To Make an End: For Malka Cohen 1897–1981" (B699), "Tragedy: For Annette Pottier" (B739), "Trees in Late Autumn" (B767), "The Vacuum" (B729), "Vita Eterna" (A40), "What Do You Think of Mitterand? For Lisa Ross" (B740), "When Hourly I Praised" (A40), "Where Has the Glory Fled" (B771), "The Winged Horse: For Doug Beardsley" (B710), "With Undiminished Fire" (B694), "Youth and Age 1981" (B768), and "Zucchini" (B695).

——— . Foreword Irving Layton. Toronto: McClelland and Stewart, 1983. 9–13, 143 pp.

Includes "Ah, Nuts," "Los Americanos" (B715), "Apostate" (B716), "Aristocrats" (B760), "August Strindberg" (B752), "The Black Thread" (B702), "Blind Man's Bluff," "Blossom" (B698), "Bonded," "The Book Burning," "Boris Pasternak," "Bottles: For Giorgio Morandi" (B812), "The Breast Stroke: For Diane Parent" (B705), "A Brief History of the Jews [Once they talked to God]" (B728), "The Camera Eye," "The Captive," "The Carillon" (B706), "The Carved Nakedness" (B717), "Central Heating" (B764), "La Commedia" (B696), "Comrade Undershaftsky" (B742), "Culture Shock," "Dancing Man" (B746), "The Dazed Fly," "Dead Souls" (B718), "Descent from Eden," "The Divine Touch," "Dung Beetle" (B734), "The End of the Matter," "The Essence of Judaism," "Everything in the Universe Has Its Place" (A40), "Fabrizio: For William Goodwin" (B741), "Fill in the Blank" (B773), "Fire Warden: For Boris Pasternak" (B711), "First Violet," "The Flaming Maple" (B769), "Flights," "For the Great Wrong," "For the Wife of Mr. Milton" (B701), "From the Nether World" (B707), "The Furrow," "The Garden" (B725), "The Hairy Monster" (B737), "Holiday Inn: Tokyo," "I Take My Anna Everywhere" (B753), "The Immortals" (B774), "Jude the Obscure" (B787), "Kali in the Suburbs," "Kidney Pie," "Klaus Englehart," "Letting Go," "The Lone Ranger," "Make Room, William Blake" (B745), "Manikins," "Medusa," "More Champagne, Darling: For Patrick Crean" (B765), "The Mountains: For Sid Marty," "Moutarde," "Murders at the Rue Bathurst" (B720), "The Music of Energy" (B756), "Nearer to Thee" (B738), "Needles," "Neighbour Love [A malicious, pot-bellied arthritic Jew]" (B730), "New Shining Worlds: For S. Ross," "New Year's Poem for Veneranda" (B788), "Nostalgia When the Leaves Begin to Fall" (B757), "Odd Obsession: For Lisa" (B766), "Of Leaves and Loves," "Of One Fairy and Two Goddesses," "Orpheus in Old Forest Hill," "Out of Pure Lust: For Vivian," "Perfection" (B749), "Poetry Conference" (B703), "Portrait of a Modern Woman" (B726), "A Prayer to Colette," "Psychologists" (B762), "Recovery" (B733), "The Remnant" (B708), "Rendezvous at the Coffee Mill: For Sarah" (B758), "Samantha Clara Layton" (B686), "Saxophonist: For Simon Stone," "The Seal: For Alice Duarte," "The Seesaw" (B721), "Self-Overcoming," "Seventeen Lines and Three Kisses: For Veneranda," "Sex Appeal" (B759), "The Swamp" (B727), "The Talisman," "There's Always Job" (B722), "They also Serve" (B712), "Tick Tock" (B772), "To Make an End: For Malka Cohen, 1897–1981" (B699), "Tragedy: For Annette Pottier" (B739), "Trees in Late Autumn" (B767), "The Vacuum" (B729), "Veneranda Dancing," "Vita

Aeterna" (A40), "What Do You Think of Mitterand? For Lisa Ross" (B740), "When Hourly I Praised" (A40), "Where Has the Glory Fled?" (B771), "Whitehern: For Joe Kertes" (B779), "The Winged Horse: For Doug Beardsley" (B710), "With Undiminished Fire" (B694), "Yeats at Sixty-Five" (B763), "Youth and Age 1981" (B768), and "Zucchini" (B695).

———. [2nd ed.] Foreword Irving Layton. Oakville, Ont.: Mosaic, 1984. 13–17, 143 pp.

Includes "Advice to a Young Poet" (A22), "Ah Nuts," "Los Americanos" (B715), "The Amnesty," "Apodoxis," "Apostate" (B716), "Aristocrats" (B760), "August Strindberg" (B752), "The Black Thread" (B702), "Blind Man's Bluff," "Blossom" (B698), "Bonded," "The Book Burning," "Boris Pasternak," "Boschka Layton 1921–1984" (B791), "Bottles: For Giorgio Morandi" (B812), "The Breast Stroke: For Diane Parent" (B705), "A Brief History of the Jews [Once they talked to God]" (B728), "The Camera Eye," "The Captive," "The Carillon" (B706), "Carmen," "The Carved Nakedness" (B717), "Central Heating" (B764), "La Commedia" (B696), "Comrade Undershaftsky" (B742), "Culture Shock," "The Cyst: For Ettore de Conciliis" (B789), "Dancing Man" (B746), "The Dazed Fly," "Dead Souls" (B718), "Descent from Eden," "Dionysians in a Bad Time," "The Discrete Charm of the Bourgeois," "The Divine Touch," "Dung Beetle" (B734), "Empty Words," "The End of the Matter," "Epistle to Catullus" (B778), "The Essence of Judaism," "Everything in the Universe Has Its Place" (A40), "Fabrizio: For William Goodwin" (B741), "Fire Warden: For Boris Pasternak" (B711), "First Violet: For Kim Yang Shik," "The Flaming Maple" (B769), "Flights," "For Ettore, with Love and Admiration," "For the Great Wrong," "For the Wife of Mr. Milton" (B701), "From the Nether World" (B707), "The

Furrow," "The Garden" (B725), "The Hairy Monster: For Earl and Erika" (B737), "Holiday Inn: Tokyo," "I Am Who I Am," "I Take My Anna Everywhere" (B753), "The Immortals" (B774), "Journey into the Long Night on Castors," "Jude the Obscure" (B787), "Juvenal Redivivus" (B790), "Kidney Pie," "Klaus Englehart," "Lady Aurora" (B803), "Lady Macbeth" (B761), "Letting Go," "The Lone Ranger," "Major Canadian Poet: For George Woodcock" (B750), "Make Room, William Blake" (B745), "Manikins," "Medusa," "Monsters" (B732), "More Champagne, Darling: For Patrick Crean" (B765), "The Mountains: For Sid Marty," "Moutarde," "Murders at the Rue Bathurst" (B720), "The Music of Energy" (B756), "Nearer to Thee" (B738), "Needles," "Neighbour Love [A malicious, pot-bellied arthritic Jew]" (B730), "New Shining Worlds: For S. Ross," "New Year's Poem for Veneranda" (B788), "Nostalgia When the Leaves Begin to Fall" (B757), "Odd Obsession: For Lisa (B766), "Of Leaves and Loves," "Of One Fairy and Two Goddesses," "Orpheus in Old Forest Hill," "Out of Pure Lust: For Vivian," "Perfection" (B749), "Poetry Conference" (B703), "Portrait of a Modern Woman" (B726), "A Prayer to Colette," "Psychologists" (B762), "Recovery" (B733), "The Remnant" (B708), "Rendezvous at the Coffee Mill: For Sarah" (B758), "Samantha Clara Layton" (B686), "The Seal," "The Seesaw" (B721), "Self-Overcoming," "Seventeen Lines and Three Kisses: For Veneranda," "Sex Appeal" (B759), "The Swamp" (B727), "The Talisman," "There's Always Job" (B722), "They also Serve" (B712), "To Make an End: For Malka Cohen 1897–1981" (B699), "Tragedy: For Annette Pottier" (B739), "Trees in Late Autumn" (B767), "Trench Mouth," "The Vacuum" (B729), "Veneranda Dancing," "Vita Aeterna" (A40), "What Do You Think of Mitterand? For Lisa Ross" (B740), "When Hourly I

Praised" (A40), "Where Has the Glory Fled?" (B771), "Whitehern: For Joe Kertes" (B779), "The Winged Horse: For Doug Beardsley" (B710), "With Undiminished Fire" (B694), "Yeats at Sixty-Five" (B763), "Youth and Age 1981" (B768), and "Zucchini" (B695).

A42 *A Spider Danced a Cosy Jig.* Ed. Elspeth Cameron. Illus. Miro Malish. Toronto: Stoddart, 1984. [27] pp.

Includes "Ah Nuts!" (A41), "Bugs" (A52), "The Bull Calf" (B149), "Encounter with a Reptile" (A24), "Fish" (B399), "Greetings" (A37), "If Whales Could Think on Certain Happy Days" (B516), "King Kong" (B578), "The Laughing Rooster" (A15), "Peacock" (A24), "The Perverse Gulls" (A4), "Runcible: For Linda Sobel Halbert" (A30), "A Spider Danced a Cosy Jig" (B30), and "Whose Zoo?" (B776).

A43 *The Love Poems of Irving Layton: With Reverence & Delight.* Foreword Irving Layton. Oakville, Ont.: Mosaic, 1984. 7–8, 140 pp.

Includes "The Air Is Sultry" (B312), "Androgyne" (B270), "An Aubade" (B480), "Aviva" (A30), "Bargain" (A11), "Because My Calling Is Such" (B204), "Berry Picking" (B195), "Blind Man's Bluff" (A41), "Blue and Lovely, My Love" (A15), "Bonded" (A41), "The Breaststroke: For Diane Parent" (B705), "By Ecstasies Perplexed" (A11), "Changeling" (B418), "The Chastening Years" (A33), "Click, Click" (A33), "Coal" (B281), "The Convert" (A35), "Creation [I fashioned you]" (B306), "Dans Le Jardin" (B207), "The Dark Nest" (A9), "David and Bathsheba" (A33), "The Day Aviva Came to Paris" (B208), "Discotheque" (A28), "Divinity" (B198), "Divorce" (A33), "End of the Affair [Wisdom is the decay of youth]" (B486), "Eternal Recurrence [Even that leaf as it falls]" (B443), "Fanatic in San Feliu" (B430), "Farewell [She's gone. The one I swore up and down]" (B687), "Fata Morgana" (A33), "For Anna" (A76), "For Artemis" (A34), "For Aviva, Because I Love Her" (B255), "For Francesca" (B510), "For Harriet" (A33), "For Louise, Age 17" (B116), "For Miss Cézanne" (B316), "For Musia's Grandchildren" (B317), "For My Distant Woman" (B564), "For My Green Old Age" (B301), "For My Incomparable Gypsy" (B558), "For Priscilla" (A5), "For Sandra" (A33), "For the Girl with Wide-Apart Eyes" (A18), "Gone" (B573), "Goodnight, Sweet Lady" (A33), "Hidden Worlds" (B577), "Hills and Hills" (B400), "Holiday" (B164), "How Poems Get Written" (B356), "I Know the Dark and Hovering Moth" (B205), "I Take My Anna Everywhere" (B753), "I Would for Your Sake Be Gentle" (B138), "If I Lie Still" (B591), "In Praise of Older Men" (A28), "Insomnia" (A17), "Inspiration" (A22), "Lady Aurora" (B803), "Lady on the Piazza" (A30), "The Last Dryads" (A28), "Latria" (A6), "Letter from a Straw Man" (B162), "Letter to a Lost Love" (A33), "Look, the Lambs Are All Around Us!" (A6), "Love Poem with an Odd Twist" (B362), "Love's Diffidence" (B154), "Madman on Mithymna Beach" (B613), "A Madrigal for Anna," "Mahogany Red" (B322), "Memo to a Suicide" (B471), "La Minerve" (B121), "Misunderstanding" (B335), "Modern Love" (A11), "Nausicäa" (A11), "New Year's Poem for Veneranda" (B788), "Nightfall" (B56), "Odd Obsession: For Lisa" (B766), "Of Leaves and Loves" (A41), "Of the Man Who Sits in the Garden" (A28), "One Day in the Life of Pincu Lazarovich" (A33), "Orpheus in Old Forest Hill" (A41), "Orthodoxy" (A35), "Out of Pure Lust: For Vivian" (A41), "Peacemonger" (A18), "The Perfect Mouth" (A33), "Poet and Woman" (A33), "Prelude" (A18), "Proteus and Nymph" (A24), "The Puma" (A30 — "The

59

Tamed Puma"), "The Quill" (B572), "Rain" (A12), "Rendezvous at the Coffee Mill: For Sarah" (B758), "Return to Eden" (A33), "Sacrament by the Water" (B160), "The Seduction [First he knocks her down]" (A15), "Seduction of and by a Civilized Frenchwoman" (B535), "Seventeen Lines and Three Kisses: For Veneranda," "Smoke [I've come to the tavern]" (A30), "Snowdrift" (A30), "Song for a Late Hour" (A9), "A Strange Turn" (B311), "Talk at Twilight" (B377), "To Blow a Man Down" (A33), "To Margaret" (A28), "Tragedy: For Annette Pottier" (B739), "The Transfiguration" (A22), "Two Songs for Sweet Voices" (B169), "Undine" (A9), "Veneranda Dancing" (A41), "The Way to Go" (A52), "When Hourly I Praised" (A40), "Winter Lyric" (B324), "With the Money I Spend" (A51), "Woman" (B168), "The Worm [The filthy rain]" (A15), "Yeats at Sixty-Five" (B763), and "You and the 20th Century" (B457).

A44 [*The Selected Poems of Irving Layton.*] Trans. Jaihuin Kim. Introd. Seoul, Korea: Hyongsol Publishing, 1985. 185 pp.

Includes both English and Korean versions of "Absence" (A21), "After Auschwitz" (B386), "Los Americanos" (B715), "Apocalypse" (B654), "An Aubade" (B480), "The Benediction" (B472), "Butterfly on Rock" (B271), "Cat Dying in Autumn" (B179), "Caveat: For Sharon" (A30), "Ch'an Artist" (B527), "The Chastening Years" (A33), "Crazy Jenny Talks to the Bishop" (A28), "Creation [The pregnant cat]" (B398), "The Day God Was Looking After the Little Sparrow" (A30), "The Deer Hunter" (A35), "End of the Affair [Wisdom is the decay of youth]" (B486), "Eternal Recurrence [Even that leaf as it falls]" (B443), "Family Portrait" (B172), "Farewell [She's gone. The one I swore up and down]" (B687), "The Fertile Muck" (B173), "The Final Peace" (B609), "The Fool's Song" (A14), "For Auld Lang Syne: For Saul Berman" (A22), "For Harriet" (A35), "For Reverend B.A. Wurm" (A38), "Friends, My Delight" (A38), "Greetings" (A37), "The Haemorrhage" (A28), "Hidden Worlds" (B577), "Hills and Hills" (B400), "Homecoming [The apartment is empty except]" (A35), "I Would for Your Sake Be Gentle" (B138), "If I Lie Still" (B591), "The Improved Binoculars" (B500), "Insomnia" (A17), "The Last Dryad" (A28), "Laurentia" (A30), "Leavetaking" (A52), "Love Lament of a Mesomorph: For Adrienne Clarkson" (A30), "Madman on Mithymna Beach" (B613), "Metamorphosis" (B517), "Morning Sounds" (A30), "Mortuary" (B46), "No Absolute Joy" (A38), "Nominalist" (A38), "Old Men" (B659), "An Old Nicoise Whore" (B354), "On the Death of Pope Paul VI" (A37), "Palmtree" (A38), "Perfection" (B749), "Plaza de Toros" (B296), "Poet and Woman" (A35), "Poetry and Truth" (B491), "Postcard: For Aviva" (A24), "The Presence" (B670), "The Progress of Poesy" (A30), "Proteus and Nymph: For Molly" (A24), "Rain" (A12), "Red Chokecherries" (B165), "Reflections in an Old Ontario Cemetery" (B664), "Requiem for an Unknown" (A30), "Rhine Boat Trip" (B332), "Rumination of an Aging Millionaire" (A37), "The Shark" (B571), "The Silence [It grew from nothing]" (B714), "The Skull" (B417), "Smoke [I've come to the tavern]" (A30), "Some Other Day" (A24), "Song for a Late Hour" (A9), "Song for Naomi" (B792), "Take It All In" (A25), "There Were No Signs" (B250), "Transcendence" (A35), "True Love" (B544), "Two Songs for Sweet Voices" (B169), "The Unwavering Eye" (B536), "The Way of the World" (B158), "When Death Says 'Come'" (A37), "Woman" (B168), and "Young Couple at Lum Fong Hotel" (A24).

A45 ΕΔΩ ΑΓΑΠΗΣΕ ΦΛΕΓΟΜΕΝΗ Η ΣΑΠΦΩ / *Where Burning Sappho Loved.* Trans. ΚΑΤΕΡΙΝΑ ΑΓΓΕΛ–

AKH–POYK / Katerina Angelaki-Rooke. Athens: Libro, 1985. 147 pp.

Includes English and facing-page Greek translations of the following: "After a Sleepless Night / Μετα απο μια αυπνη νυχτα" (A34), "Archilochos vs. Homer / Ἀρχιλοχος εναντιον Ὁμηρου" (A25), "Blackout / Συσκοτιση" (A25), "The Castle / Το Καστρο" (A25), "Dionysos / Διονυσος" (A11), "A Dream at Pangrati / "Ονειρο στο Παγκρατι" (A25), "Early Morning in Mithymna / Νωρις καποιο πρωι στην Μηθυμνα" (A22), "End of the Affair [Wisdom is the decay of youth] / Το τελος μιας ερωτικης ιστοριας" (B486), "Figs / Τα Συκα" (A34), "Fishermen / Ψαραδες" (B421), "Flytrap / Μυγοπαγιδα" (B534), "Ganymede / Γανυμηδης" (B519), "Greek Dancer / Ελληνας χορευτης" (A34), "Greek Fly / Ἑλληνικη μυγα" (A24), "The Greek Light / Το Ἑλληνικο φως" (A34), "Helios / Ὁ Θεος "Ηλιος" (A25), "Hellenes: For Nassos and Lydia / "Ελληνες" (A25), "Heraclitos / Ἡρακλειτος" (A18), "Hills and Hills: For Aviva / Λοφοι και Λοφοι" (B400), "Hummingbird / Το κολιμπρι" (A34), "Icarus / "Ικαρος" (A15), "Inspiration / Ἐμπνευση" (A22), "Ithaca: For Marsha Kinder / Ἰθακη" (B611), "Late Invitation to the Dance / Καθυστερημενη προσκληση στο χορο" (B601), "Leavetaking / Ἀποχαιρετισμος" (A52), "Mithymna Cemetery / Νεκροταφειο στη Μηθυμνα" (A24), "Molibos Cat / Στο Μολυβο μια γατα" (B569), "The Monster / Το τερας" (A34), "Nausicaa / Ναυσικα" (A11), "Night Music / Νυχτερινη Μουσικη" (B594), "On Seeing the Statue of Sappho on the Quay of Mitylene / Ἀντικρυζοντας το ἀγαλμα της Σαπφους" (A52), "Orpheus / Ὀρφεας" (B123), "Party at Hydra: For Marianne / Παρτυ στην "Υδρα" (A22), "Poetry / Ποιηση" (A17), "Protest / Διαμαρτυρια" (B402), "Proteus and Nymph / Πρωτευς και νυφη" (A24), "Rupert Brooke / Rupert Brooke (1887–1915)"

(B614), "The Satyr / Σατυρος" (A8), "The Shark / Ὁ Καρχαριας" (B571), "The Skull / Το Κρανιο" (B417), "Stella / Ἡ Στελλα" (B482), "Storm at Hydra / Καταιγιδα στην "Υδρα" (B391), "Take It All In / Ρουφειχτε τα ολα" (A25), "Thanatos and Eros / Θανατος και ερως" (A11), "That Is the Question / Ἰδου το ερωτημα" (B476), "Theatre / Θεατρο" (B595), "Two Women: For Bobby Maslen / Δυο γυναικες" (A34), "The Unwavering Eye / Το Ἀκλονητο Ματι" (B536), "What Ulysses Said to Circe on the Beach of Aeaea / Τι ειπε ο Ὀδυσσεας στην Κιρκη . . ." (A6), "When Death Comes for You / "Ο]ταν ο θανατος ερθει για σενα" (B597).

A46 *Dance with Desire: Love Poems.* Toronto: McClelland and Stewart, 1986. 165 pp.

Includes "Absence" (A21), "Androgyne" (B270), "The Annunciation" (B678), "Apparition" (B351), "Archilocos Versus Homer" (A25), "Aristocrats" (B760), "Ashtoreth" (B675), "Bargain" (A11), "Because My Calling Is Such" (B204), "Because You Squeezed Back" (A30), "Berry Picking" (B195), "Bicycle Pump" (B300), "The Bishopric" (B261), "Black Tourist in Tinos" (B807), "Blind Man's Bluff" (A41), "Bonded" (A41), "Boschka Layton 1921–1984" (B791), "The Breast Stroke" (B705), "By Ecstasies Perplexed" (A11), "Carmen," "The Castle" (A25), "Central Heating" (B764), "The Chastening Years" (A33), "The Convertible" (B231), "Creation [I fashioned you]" (B306), "Dans le Jardin" (B207), "David and Bathsheba" (A33), "The Day Aviva Came to Paris" (B208), "Discothèque" (A28), "Diverse Pleasures," "The Divine Touch" (A41), "Divorce" (A33), "Elegy for Marilyn Monroe" (B277), "Epitaph for a Poet [I sang of thighs]" (A21), "Farewell [She's gone. The one I swore up and down]" (B687), "Fata Morgana" (A33), "The Final Coming" (B651), "The Fine Excess" (A22), "For

Aviva, Because I Love Her" (B255), "For Edda" (B542), "For Francesca" (B510), "For Harriet" (A33), "For Louise, Age 17" (B116), "For Musia's Grandchildren" (B317), "For My Distant Woman" (B564), "For My Green Old Age" (B301), "For My Incomparable Gypsy" (B558), "For Sandra" (A33), "The Hairy Monster" (B737), "Hidden Worlds" (B577), "Hills and Hills" (B400), "Holiday" (B164), "How Poems Get Written" (B356), "Hummingbird" (A34), "I Take My Anna Everywhere" (B753), "I Think of Ovid" (A22), "I Would for Your Sake Be Gentle" (B138), "Insomnia" (A17), "Inspiration" (A22), "The Investiture," "Jude the Obscure" (B787), "Lady Macbeth" (B761), "Lady on the Piazza" (A30), "Laurentia" (A30), "Letter from a Straw Man" (B162), "Letter to a Lost Love" (A33), "Love Lament of a Mesomorph" (A30), "Love's Diffidence" (B154), "Marie" (A6), "Medusa" (A41), "Memo to a Suicide" (B471), "La Minerve" (B121), "Misunderstanding" (B335), "More Champagne, Darling: For Patrick Crean" (B765), "Nausicäa" (A11), "New Year's Poem for Veneranda" (B788), "Obit" (A10), "Odd Obsession" (B766), "Of Leaves and Loves" (A41), "Of the Man Who Sits in the Garden" (A28), "An Old Niçoise Whore" (B354), "Orpheus" (B123), "Out of Pure Lust" (A41), "Poet and Woman" (A33), "Portrait of a Modern Woman" (B726), "Portrait of Aileen" (B134), "Proteus and Nymph" (A24), "The Puma" (A30 — "The Tamed Puma"), "Puppet Show with Dialogue" (A32), "Rain" (A12), "Rendezvous at the Coffee Mill" (B758), "Reunion at the Hilton" (A25), "Sacrament by the Water" (B160), "The Seduction [First he knocks her down]" (A15), "Seduction of and by a Civilized Frenchwoman" (B535), "September Woman" (B514), "Smoke [I've come to the tavern]" (A30), "Snake Goddess: For Heidi" (A35), "A Song about Woman" (B338), "Song for a Late Hour"

(A9), "Stella" (B482), "A Strange Turn" (B311), "Sylvia" (A30), "Talk at Twilight" (B377), "Thanatos and Eros" (A11), "The Tightrope Dancer" (A34), "To a Beautiful Unknown Girl" (B358), "To Margaret" (A28), "To the Girls of My Graduating Class" (B93), "To the Woman with the Speaking Eyes" (B501), "Undine" (A9), "Vampire" (A22), "Veneranda Dancing" (A41), "Vikki" (A38), "The Way to Go" (A52), "The Well-Wrought Urn" (B263), "When Death Comes for You" (B597), "With the Money I Spend" (A51), "Woman" (B168), "You and the Twentieth Century" (B457), and "Young Couple at Lum Fong Hotel" (A24).

A47 *Final Reckoning: Poems 1982–1986.* "Acknowledgments" Irving Layton. Oakville, Ont.: Mosaic, 1987. 7–8, 81 pp.

Includes "Aesthetic Cruelty," "Alison Parrott 1975–1986," "And There Was Light" (A41), "And They All Fall Down," "Apodoxis" (A41), "Approaching Doomsday," "Black Tourist in Tinos" (B807), "Boschka Layton 1921–1984" (B791), "Burnt Offering" (B818), "Carmen," "Casa Cacciatore" (B823), "Cracks in the Acropolis" (B795), "The Cyst" (B789), "Devotion: For Vito Riviello" (B828), "Dionysians in a Bad Time" (B804), "Diverse Pleasures" (B822), "Epistle to Catullus" (B778), "Etruscan Tombs: For Dante Gardini" (B796), "Fellini" (B805), "Final Reckoning: After Theognis" (B824), "For Ettore, with Love and Admiration" (B777), "Functional Illiterates," "The Gelded Lion" (B829), "Herbert Vunce" (B813), "High Fidelity," "I Am Who I Am" (B780), "Immortelles for a Literary Strumpet," "Imperfection" (B784), "Inter-View" (B830), "The Investiture" (B808), "Judgement at Murray's" (B797), "Juvenal Redivivus" (B790), "Kitch" (B819), "Lady Aurora" (B803), "Lady Macbeth" (B761), "Leopardi in Montreal" (B806), "A Madrigal for Anna" (B825), "Maimonidean Perplexity," "Major Canadian Poet" (B750), "The Massacre" (B798), "Memo to a Literary Pimp: For Robert Fulford" (B831), "Monsters" (B732), "Mustering All His Wit," "Nightmare in the Annex" (B826), "No Bird But Lighter Than One," "Olympic Stewardess" (B821), "Omnipresence," "Opiums" (B820), "Overman," "The Paddler" (B809), "The Piles of Greece, the Piles of Greece" (B810), "Poem That Says It All" (B817), "Popcorn" (B793), "Principessa Anna" (B799), "Saturday Night Farticle" (B833), "Sciatica" (B794), "Simpson," "Socrates at the Centaur" (B834), "Soft Porn," "Terry Fox," "The Theatre of Dionysos: For Don and Sheila" (B811), "Trench Mouth," "Tristezza: For F. Ruberti" (B704), "Twentieth Century Gothic" (B827), "Two for the Road, Frank" (B802), "Una Scopata" (B800), and "Wagschal Exhibition" (B801).

A48 *Fortunate Exile*. Toronto: McClelland and Stewart, 1987. 168 pp.

Includes "Adam" (B538), "After Auschwitz" (B386), "Anarch" (B677), "The Annunciation" (B678), "Antimonies" (B617), "At the Belsen Memorial" (B326), "The Benediction" (B472), "The Best Proof" (B373), "The Black Huntsmen" (B79), "Boris Pasternak" (A41), "Boschka Layton: 1921–1984" (B791), "A Brief History of the Jews [So what if you gave the world]" (B655), "Burnt Offering" (B818), "Cabalist" (A35), "Cain" (B193), "C'est Fini" (A28), "Comrade Trotsky" (B688), "Conversos" (A38), "The Crucifixion" (A30), "The Dark Underside" (A35), "Das Wahre Ich" (B282), "David and Bathsheba" (A33), "Death of Moishe Lazarovitch" (B180), "Departed" (B498), "Divine Image" (B238), "Dorothy Parker (1893–1967)" (B359), "Eine Kleine Nachtmusik" (B673), "Elan" (A2), "The Elec-

tion" (A37), "Entry" (B545), "Eternal Recurrence [The sleepwalkers are advancing on Armageddon]" (B683), "Etruscan Tombs: For Dante Gardini" (B796), "Father and Daughter," "Final Reckoning" (B824), "The Final Solution" (B532), "For Anne Frank" (B499), "For Else Lasker-Schuler" (B691), "For Erich Muhsam" (B667), "For Hans, Maybe Klaus or Tadeusz" (B672), "For Jesus Christ" (A28), "For My Brother Jesus" (B816), "For My Neighbours in Hell [Hate, your adrenalin]" (B643), "For My Sons, Max and David" (B361), "For Nadezhda Mandelstam" (B528), "For 7515–03296" (B586), "The Galilean" (A30), "The Golden Age of Spanish Painting" (A30), "Gothic Landscape" (B76), "Grand Finale" (B599), "The Graveyard" (B380), "The Haemorrhage" (A28), "Ha-Nagid's Admonition to Jewish Scholars" (A28), "Hear, O Israel," "Heinrich Heine" (A30), "Hells" (A38), "Herzl" (A38), "Ibn Gabriol" (A21), "The Improved Binoculars" (B500), "Incident at the Cathedral" (B606), "The Interloper," "Israelis" (B394), "Jeshua" (B560), "Jesus and Saint Paul" (A28), "Jew" (B428), "Jewish Main Street" (B59), "Judea Eterna" (A28), "Keine Lazarovitch: 1870–1959" (B220), "King Kong" (B578), "The Latest Wrinkle," "The Lesson" (A35), "The Luminous Bagel" (B583), "The Lyric [As moles construct]" (B631), "Magdalena" (A30), "The Magician" (A35), "Maimonidean Perplexity" (A47), "Memo to My Sons" (A21), "Midsummer's Dream in the Vienna Stadpark" (B511), "Mrs. Fornheim, Refugee" (A2), "My Father" (B12), "Next Year, in Jerusalem" (A37), "The New Sensibility," "Nightmare in the Annex" (B826), "No Wild Dog" (A14), "O Jerusalem" (B531), "On Seeing the Statuettes of Ezekiel and Jeremiah in the Church of Notre Dame" (B151), "On the Death of Pope Paul VI" (A37), "On the Sudden Death of a Relative" (B636), "Osip Mandelstam (1891–1940)" (B427), "Parque de Montjuich" (B547), "Paul Sextus" (A30), "The Phylactery Box" (A30), "Poet at Sinai" (A18), "Post-Crematoria" (A12), "The Predator" (B285), "Proper Reading Light" (A18), "Rabbi Simeon Comforts His Flock" (A34), "Recipe for a Long and Happy Life" (A21), "Reingemacht" (B674), "Requiem for A.M. Klein" (B507), "Rhine Boat Trip" (B332), "The Sabbath" (A30), "Saint Pinchas" (B543), "Sancta Simplicitas" (B135), "The Search," "Senile, My Sister Sings" (B713), "The Shadow" (B515), "Shalom Shalom," "Shlemihl" (B628), "The Sign of the Cross" (A35), "Sightseeing," "The Sinner" (A30), "The Subversive" (B665), "Sunflowers" (B676), "Survivor" (A28), "Terrorists" (B508), "To Maoists" (A22), "To the Jewish Dissenters" (A35), "To the Victims of the Holocaust" (B596), "This Machine Age" (B170), "The True Picture" (B650), "Twentieth-Century Gothic" (B827), "Wagschal Exhibition" (B801), "Warrior Poet" (B550), "The Wheel" (A38), "Whom I Write For" (B251), "A Wild Peculiar Joy" (B630), "Xianity" (B580), and "You Never Can Tell."

A49   *Tutto sommato: poesie 1945–1989.* Ed. and introd. Alfredo Rizzardi. Preface Leonard Cohen. Abano Terme, Italy: Piovan, 1989. 5–9, 10–11, 282 pp.

Includes English with facing-page Italian translations of the following: "Adam / Adamo" (B538), "Aetna / Etna" (B574), "The Arcade / La galleria" (B575), "At the Iglesia De Sacromonte / Alla Iglesia De Sacromonte" (B302), "Attending Suzanne's Funeral / Seguendo il funerale di Suzanne" (B836), "August Strindberg / Augusto Strindberg" (B752), "Beatitude / Beatitudine" (A34), "Birthday Poem for John Newlove / Per il compleanno di John Newlove," "The Black Tom / Tom il nero" (A35), "Black Tourist in Tinos / Una turista negra a Tinos" (B807), "Boris Pasternak" (A41), "The Cage / La gabbia" (B254), "Catacombe dei Cappuccini: For William Goodwin / Catacombe dei Cappuccini: Per William Goodwin" (B551), "Clochards: For Wynne Francis / Clochards: Per Wynne Francis" (B352), "The Cockroach / La blatta" (A22), "The Comedian / Il comico" (B656), "La Condition Humaine" (B635), "The Dark Underside / L'oscuro rovescio" (A35), "De Bullion Street / Via de Bullion" (B55), "Early Morning in Mithymna / Di primo mattino a Mitimna" (A22), "Eine Kleine Nachtmusik" (B673), "Elegy for Marilyn Monroe / Elegia per Marilyn Monroe" (B277), "Elephant / L'elefante" (B395), "Eternal Recurrence [Even that leaf as it falls] / Eterni ricorsi" (B443), "Etruscan Tombs: For Dante Gardini / Tombe Etrusche: Per Dante Gardini" (B796), "Fellini" (B805), "Figs / Fichi" (A34), "The Final Solution / La soluzione finale" (B532), "Final Reckoning: After Theognis / Rendiconto finale: da Teognide" (B825), "Florence / Firenze" (B557), "For Andrei Amalrik / Per Andrei Amalrik" (B521), "For Erich Muhsam / Per Eric Muhsam" (B667), "For Edda / Per Edda" (B542), "For Ettore, with Love and Admiration / Per Ettore con amore e ammirazione" (B777), "For My Brother Jesus / Per mio fratello Gesù" (B816), "For My Brother Oscar / Per mio fratello Oscar" (A34), "For My Neighbours in Hell [Hate, your adrenalin] / Per il mio prossimo all'inferno" (B643), "For 751–0329 / Per 751–0329" (B586), "Funeraria 'Olea' / Funeraria olea" (B497), "The Garburetor / Il carburatore" (A35), "God Is Not Dead / Dio non è morto" (A34), "Greek Fly / Mosca greca" (A24), "Hells / Inferni" (A38), "Heraclitos / Eraclito" (A18), "The High Cost of Living / Il prezzo alto del vivere" (A37), "The Improved Binoculars / Il binocolo potenziato" (B500), "In an Ice Age / In un'età di ghiaccio" (A38), "Keine Lazarovitch" (B220), "Lady on the Piazza / Donna in Piazza di Spagna" (A30), "Lake Selby / Lago Selby" (B454), "Late Invitation to the Dance / Tardo invito alla danza" (B601), "Laura Cunneyflow

/ Laura Conneyflow" (A21), "Like a Mother Demented / Madre uscita di senno" (B368), "The Lone Ranger / Cavaliere Solitario" (A41), "Midsummer's Dream in the Vienna Stadpark / Sogno di mezza estate nello Stadpark di Vienna" (B511), "Molibos Cat / La gatta di Molibos" (B569), "Music Hath Such Charms: For Marc Bernstein / Tale incanto ha la musica: Per Marc Bernstein" (A37), "Night Music / Musica notturna" (B594), "Paraclete / Paracleto" (B109), "Peacock / Pavone" (A24), "Piazza San Marco" (B221), "The Plaka / La Plaka" (B561), "Poet on the Square / Il poeta sulla piazza" (A30), "Poetry / Poesia" (A17), "Pole-Vaulter / Saltatore con l'asta" (B513), "Portrait of a Modern Woman / Ritratto di una donna moderna" (B725), "Recovery / Guarigione" (B733), "Reflections in an Old Ontario Cemetery / Riflessioni in un vecchio cimitero dell'Ontario" (B663), "Reingemacht" (B674), "Rhine Boat Trip / In barca sul Reno" (B332), "Seduction of and by a Civilized Frenchwoman / Seduzione di, (e da parte di) una colta francese" (B535), "Senile My Sister Sings / Senile canta mia sorella" (B713), "September Woman / Donna di settembre" (B514), "The Sinner / Il peccatore" (A30), "Sir / Madame" (A34), "Stillness / Quiete" (A35), "Sun Bathers / Bagnanti" (B339), "Sunflowers / Girasoli" (B676), "Survivor / Sopravvissuto" (A28), "A Tall Man Executes a Jig / Un uomo alto esegue una giga" (B248), "The Tightrope Dancer / Danza sulla fune" (A34), "To the Victims of the Holocaust / Alle vittime dell'Olocausto" (B596), "Tristezza" (B704), "2028" (A35), "The Violent Life: For Pier Paolo Pasolini / La vita violenta: Per Pier Paolo Pasolini" (A28), "Whatever Else Poetry Is Freedom / Ma Soprattutto la poesia è libertà" (B191), "With the Money I Spend / Con i soldi che spendo" (A51), "Women of Rome / Donne romane" (B223), "Young Couple at Lum Fong Hotel / Giovane coppia all'Hotel Lum Fong" (A24), "Zucchini / Zucchine" (B695).

Poetry and Prose

A50 *Now Is the Place.* Foreword Irving Layton. New Writers Series, No. 6. Montreal: First Statement, 1948. 2, 57 pp.

Includes the following poems: "Afternoon of a Coupon Clipper" (A2), "Church Parade" (B51), "Compliments of the Season" (B58), "De Bullion Street" (B55), "Drill Shed" (B54), "The Eagle" (B68), "English for Immigrants" (B65), "Epitaph for a Christian" (B22), "Excursion to Ottawa" (B61), "Gents' Furnishings" (B53), "Ice Follies," "Jewish Main Street" (B59), "Karl Marx" (B69), "Lady Remington" (B45), "The Modern Poet [Since Eliot set the fashion]" (B36), "Montreal," "Newsboy" (B42), "North Country" (B70), "Petawawa" (B43), "A Poor Poet Is Grateful for a Sudden Thaw" (B66), "Proof Reader" (B63), "Schoolteacher in Late November" (B72), "Stolen Watch" (B64), "The Swimmer" (B60), "To the Lawyer Handling My Divorce Case" (B537), "Winter Scene" (B47), and "The Yard" (B67).

Includes the following short stories: "A Death in the Family" (B1058) and "Vacation in La Voiselle" (B1057).

The foreword has been excised from many copies of this book by Layton. The text has been printed by Wynne Francis in her monograph on Layton (C420).

A51 *The Swinging Flesh.* Foreword Irving Layton. Toronto: McClelland and Stewart, 1961. ix–xv, 190 pp.

Includes the following poems: "After Theognis" (B228), "Arboreal Nature" (B229), "The Atonement" (B234), "Because My Calling Is Such" (B204),

"Beutel's Name Is Inscribed for Eternal Life" (B230), "Bitter Almonds" (B209), "The Caged Bird" (B206), "The Convertible" (B231), "Dance with a Watermelon" (B242), "Dans le Jardin" (B207), "The Day Aviva Came to Paris" (B208), "Dialogue with a Young and Pretty Wife," "Divine Image" (B238), "The Fall" (B243), "The Fictive Eye," "For Prof. F.M. Heichelheim" (B239), "Hierophants" (B187), "Hostia" (B232), "I Know the Dark and Hovering Moth" (B205), "In Praise of Benefactors" (B226), "Keine Lazarovitch 1870–1959" (B220), "Librarian at Asheville," "Magda" (B240), "Maria Poidinger" (B236), "Mr. Beutel Lays a Cornerstone" (B214), "My Eyes Are Wide Open," "Our Common Future or The Progress of Satire" (B233), "Overture, Opus, and Coda," "Piazza San Marco" (B221), "A Prayer," "Prizes" (B237), "Sagebrush Classic" (B227), "Song" (B235), "Stocktaking on the Day of Atonement" (B244), "Today I Am a Man" (B241), "The Tragic Sense" (B222), "Trilliums after a Party" (B219), "Variations on a Theme by Shakespeare," "Victoria Square," "Why I Don't Make Love to the First Lady" (B245), "With the Money I Spend," "Women of Rome" (B223), and "The Wooden Spoon" (B224).

Includes the following short stories: "A Death in the Family" (B1058), "The English Lesson" (B1056), "A Game of Chess" (B1055), "Osmeck" (B1061), "Piety" (B1056a), "Mrs. Polinov" (B1060), "The Philistine" (B1054), "A Plausible Story" (B1059), "Unemployed" (B1053), and "Vacation in La Voiselle" (B1057).

A52   *The Whole Bloody Bird (Obs, Aphs & Pomes)*. Foreword Irving Layton. Toronto: McClelland and Stewart, 1969. 9–12, 155 pp.

Includes the following "Pomes": "After Auschwitz" (B386), "At Wenger's, New Delhi," "Attach-ments" (B403), "Boudha Nath," "The Bridge" (B381), "Bugs," "Changeling" (B418), "Cleavages" (B382), "Climbing Hills," "Creation [The pregnant cat]" (B398), "Depth Charge" (B419), "Dialogue with a Dick: For Richard Sommers," "Divine Ground," "Elephant: For Northrop Frye" (B395), "Ends," "The Equalizer" (B420), "Farewell [I said to her: 'I]" (B408), "The Final Peace" (B609), "Fish" (B399), "Fishermen: For Peggy Sylvia" (B421), "For Aviva" (B409), "For John Slavin's Birthday" (B404), "For Julie" (B415), "For One Far Away," "Hero of Babi Yar: For Degtyarev," "Hills and Hills: For Aviva" (B400), "His Holiness Is Right" (B410), "Holocaust" (B411), "Hymn to the Republic" (B379), "I Owe This to St. Paul," "If Euclid Were Your Analyst" (B610), "In Excelsis: For John Slavin," "Incarnation," "Incident at New Delhi" (B397), "Incomplete Syllogism" "Incongruity," "Incubus," "Irish Luck," "Israelis" (B394), "It's a Riot, Boys" (B383), "Jasmine, Anyone?" (B389), "Leavetaking," "Memo from a Modern Biographee," "Modern Miracle," "National Vices," "Neanderthal," "Nepalese Woman and Child" (B396), "The New Breed," "Nightmare," "No One Asked," "Nocturne," "Oedipus" (B401), "On Seeing the Statue of Sappho on the Quay of Mitylene," "The Pit" (B416), "A Poet Curses Pigeons," "Poets," "Pomegranates," "Postscript to Empire" (B390), "Protest" (B402), "Reb Yitzhok Elucidates," "Right Conduct" (B407), "Seduction [I said: 'I am too]" (B423), "The Shrinking General" (B384), "Silent Joy" (B405), "The Skull" (B417), "The Smell" (B412), "Sourwine Sparkle" (B413), "Storm at Ydra: For Leonard Cohen" (B391), "Taj Mahal," "Tribal Tic," "The Way to Go," "What's New, Kathmandu?" (B392), "When I Consider" (B422), "The Whole Bloody Bird," "Whose Zoo [Who ever heard of a pimp]" (B385), "Wonder," and "Yoga" (B393).

Also includes "Aphs" [aphorisms] (B1000, B1005, B1006), "Obs I" [observations] (B1000), and "Obs II" (B1000).

Prose

A53   *Engagements: The Prose of Irving Layton.* Ed. Seymour Mayne. Preface Irving Layton. Toronto: McClelland and Stewart, 1972. x–xvi, 336 pp.

Includes the following articles and reviews: "Cemeteries Are Where I Am Most Dionysian" (B1004), "Crepe Hanger's Carnival" (B1145), "Elephant" (B1008), "Forever Honeyless: Canadian Criticism" (B992), "Harold Laski" (B970), "Let's Win the Peace" (B972), "Poets: The Conscience of Mankind" (B983), "Poets with Cameras in Their Fists" (B986), "Politics and Poetry" (B971), "Rev. of *At the Long Sault and Other New Poems*, by Archibald Lampman" (B1140), "Rev. of *The Colour as Naked*, by Patrick Anderson" (B1144), "Rev. of *A History of Western Philosophy*, by Bertrand Russell" (B1143), "Rev. of *The Hitleriad*, by A.M. Klein" (B1141), "Rev. of *The Picnic and Other Stories*, by Desmond Pacey" (B1146), "Rev. of *Poems*, by A.M. Klein" (B1142), "Shaw, Pound and Poetry" (B975), and "A Tall Man Executes a Jig" (B980).

Includes the following Forewords, Prefaces, and Introductions: "By Way of an Introduction, *Poems for 27 Cents*" (A62), "Foreword, *Balls for a One-Armed Juggler*" (A14), "Foreword, *Collected Poems (1965)*" (A16), "Foreword, *The Collected Poems of Irving Layton (1971)*" (A20), "Foreword, *i Side Up*" (B1011), "Foreword, *Magadan*" (B1010), "Foreword, *Periods of the Moon*" (A17), "Foreword, *A Red Carpet for the Sun*" (A13), "Foreword, *The Shattered Plinths*" (A18), "Foreword, *The Swinging Flesh*" (A51), "Introduction, *Poems to Color*" (B1009), "Introductory Note, *Canadian Poems*

1850–1952" (A60), "Note, *A Laughter in the Mind*, 2nd ed." (A12), "Preface, in *The Laughing Rooster*" (A15), "Untitled Preface, *Cerberus*" (A3), and "What Canadians Don't Know About Love" (B982).

Includes the following letters: "Letter, *First Statement*" [April 1943] (B839), "Correspondence, *The Canadian Forum*" [June 1945] (B840), "Letter to Cid Corman, *Origin*" (B841), "Correspondence, *The Canadian Forum*" [Oct. 1956] (B842), "Letter, *McGill Daily*" [11 Feb. 1957] (B843), "Correspondence, *The Canadian Forum*" [March 1957] (B844), "Correspondence, *The Canadian Forum*" [Sept. 1957] (B845), "Correspondence, *The Canadian Forum*" [Feb. 1958] (B846), "Letter, *The Montreal Star*" [25 Oct. 1961] (B848), "Correspondence, *The Canadian Forum*" [March 1962] (B850), "Correspondence, *The Canadian Forum*" [May 1962] (B851), "An Open Letter to Louis Dudek" [*Cataract*, Winter 1962] (B849), "Reply, *Cataract*" (B853), "Letter, *The Montreal Star*" [12 Dec. 1962] (B854), "Correspondence, *The Canadian Forum*" [May 1963] (B858), "Letter, *The Tamarack Review*" (B859), "Letter, *The Montreal Star*" [4 Nov. 1964] (B862), "Letter, *The Montreal Star*" [15 Dec. 1964] (B864), "Letter, *The Montreal Star*" [4 Oct. 1969] (B886), and "Letter, *Saturday Night*" (B900).

Includes the following short stories: "A Death in the Family" (B1058), "The English Lesson" (B1056), "A Game of Chess" (B1055), "Osmeck" (B1061), "Piety" (B1056a), "Mrs. Polinov" (B1060), "The Philistine" (B1054), "A Plausible Story" (B1059), "Unemployed" (B1053), and "Vacation in La Voiselle" (B1057).

Also includes Clara Thomas' "A Conversation with Margaret Laurence and Irving Layton" (excerpt) (C587). The poem "[In this cold realm]" (B187) is included in the February 1958 letter to *The Canadian Forum*.

A54 *Taking Sides: The Collected Social and Political Writings.* Ed. and introd. Howard Aster. Oakville, Ont.: Mosaic / Valley, 1977. 5–8, 222 pp.

Because this book includes pieces by Layton as well as about Layton, each piece has been listed separately in Sections B and C of this bibliography. But, because the critical works about Layton are all interviews and discussions, this book is also listed in Section A and reviews are listed under this title in Section D.

Includes the following prose by Layton: "Epigrams," "Essays, Reviews, Lectures, 1943–1977 ['Canada's Poetic Riches' (B1007), 'Canadian Poetry: Modern' (B974), Foreword to *Modern Romanian Poetry* (B1019), Introduction to *Anvil Blood* (B1015), Introduction to *Ontario College of Art Yearbook* (1967) (B994), Lecture, 6 Sept. 1967 (B996), Lecture, 7 Sept. 1967 (B997), 'My Troublesome Compatriates' (B1018), 'Nietzsche and Poetry: A Discussion' (B1014), 'A Philosopher's Analysis' (B985), 'Politics and Poetry' (B971), 'Prince Hamlet and the Beatniks' (B981), 'The Role of the Teacher' (B976)]," "A First View, 1935–1937 ['Current History,' 25 Oct. 1935 (B958), 'Current History,' 22 Nov. 1935 (B960), 'Current History,' 6 Dec. 1935 (B962), 'Current History,' 27 March 1936 (B963), 'The Farmer Thinks: Will Fascism Conquer?' (B967)]," "Harold Laski: The Paradoxes of a Liberal Marxist, 1946" (B1020), "Ruminations [*Canada Month*, 1967, *Le Chien D'Or / The Golden Dog*, 1972, *Cyclic*, 1966, *The Gateway*, 1965, *A Georgian Supplement*, 1965, *Northword Magazine*, 1971, 'On and Off St. Catharine Street, Two Artists of the World' (B988)]," and "Views on the World: Letters, Articles, Travels, 1960–1977. Accuses Dr. Rowse of Falsifying the Record [B855], Advises Dealing with Germany with 'Compassion, Intelligence' [B857], Another Danger Fills Mr. Layton's Mind to Exclusion of Proclaimed Nazi Rebirth [B876], Arabs and

Jews [B897], Books and Bookmen [B979], CBC Back-Down 'Act of Poltroonery' [B875], A Champion for Fellini [B919], Course of Events in Santo Domingo Demonstrates U.S. Moderation [B867], East Berlin Impressions [B991], Excerpts from Two Letters on a First Trip to Israel [B880], Germany's New Chancellor Exhibiting Sincere Desire to Reassure Doubters [B874], Germany's Searching Students [B989], The Great Mortgage Hanging Over Israel [B998], A High Price to Pay for Survival [B1001], House Windbags Not Fit to Lace Trudeau's Ski-Boots, Poet Says [B895], In the Morning, the Snow Was Like the Beginning of Creation [B1003], Israel [B898], The Kaleidoscope That Is India [B1002], Lacombe, Lucien [B908], Last Tango in Paris [B906], Lays Summit Failure to Calculated U.S. Act [B847], Layton on Eayrs [B890], Layton Says He Supports, Not Opposes, French-Canadian Manifestation [B885], Layton Says Three Films Are Masterpieces But Reviewer Is Bland, Smug [B909], Minority Rights Key Mid-East Issue [B999], Mr. Layton Defends His Insights into Germany's Mind against Criticism [B871], Nixon's Courageous Decision to Act in Cambodia as Unqualified Success [B891], No Room for Myth [B904], Poet Irving Layton on Cambodia [B889], Poet Layton Says Hockey Hysteria Is 'A Ridiculous Emotional Binge' [B901], The Quebec Situation [B893], Reclaiming Irving Layton, Rev. of *This England*, by James Edward Ward [B1137], Review of Latest Book Astonishing, Dismaying Irving Layton Charges [B913], Shaw Review Missed the Point [B899], Situation in Germany Today Unlike That Leading to Fall of Weimar Republic [B873], Teach-In [B872], Throwaways, Laryngeals, Simple-Simons [B1017], The Time for Illusions Is Over, the Confrontation Is Here [B878], Trudeau's Good Sense Put an End to Reign of Terror [B894], U.S. Effort in Viet Nam and Its Scope Justified by

Mounting External Threat [B869], Viet Nam Reverse Giving Communists a Lesson They Will Not Soon Forget [B879], A View of Germany [B993], Visitor to Germany Thoroughly Convinced Nation's Abhorrence of Hitlerism Sincere [B870], Widely Condemned U.S. Policy Defended as Wise and Right [B866], Yahooville Spawned Critic: Layton [B903], Zest for Life in German Cities [B990]."

For works about Layton, see Howard *Aster*'s Introduction (C283), Jack *Doupe*'s "Irving Layton: U.S.A. & Viet Nam" (C572), "Interview with Irving Layton" (C565), Tom *Laing*'s "Irving Layton" (C592), Rose *Lax*'s and Elliot *Newman*'s "Irving Layton Is:" (C569), Lawrence J. *Resnitzsky*'s "Interview with Irving Layton" (C594), and John *Thompson*'s, with Jon *Whyte*, Dianne *Woodman*, and Linda *Strand*, "An Asexual Interview with Irving Layton" (C564).

A55 ———, and Dorothy Rath. *An Unlikely Affair.* Introd. Adrienne Clarkson. Oakville, Ont.: Mosaic / Valley, 1980. 230 pp.

Includes the following poems among the letters of correspondence: "Boudha Nath: For Robert F. Kennedy," "Byron Exhibition at the Benaki Museum," and "Jasmine Anyone?" (B389).

A56 *Wild Gooseberries: The Selected Letters of Irving Layton.* Ed., introd., and notes Francis Mansbridge. Toronto: Macmillan, 1989. v–xii, 424 pp.

Includes Layton's letters for the period 1939–1989.

A57 *Irving Layton & Robert Creeley: The Complete Correspondence, 1953–1978.* Ed., introd., and notes Ekbert Faas and Sabrina Reed. Montreal / Kingston: McGill-Queen's Univ. Press, 1990. i–xxxii, 312 pp.

Memoir

A58 ———, with David O'Rourke. *Waiting for the Messiah: A Memoir.* Toronto: McClelland and Stewart, 1985. 264 pp.
——— . Toronto: Totem, 1986. 264 pp.

Translation

A59 ———, Francesca Valente, Greg Gatenby, Giorgio Bassani, and Portia Prebys. *Rolls Royce and Other Poems.* By Giorgio Bassani. Introd. Northrop Frye. Toronto: Aya, 1982. [7–9, 47 pp.]

Books Edited

A60 ———, and Louis Dudek. Introd. Irving Layton and Louis Dudek. *Canadian Poems 1850–1952.* Toronto: Contact, 1952. 13–17, 127 pp.
——— . Rev. ed. Introd. Irving Layton and Louis Dudek. Toronto: Contact, 1953. 15–20, 160 pp.

A61 *Pan-ic: A Selection of Contemporary Canadian Poems.* [*Pan* (4 Issues of Poetry) (New York), No. 2 (1958)]. [42] pp.

A62 ———, and introd. Irving Layton. *Poems for 27 Cents.* Montreal: Privately printed, 1961. 2–4, 32 pp.

A63 *Love Where the Nights Are Long: Canadian Love Poems.* Illus. Harold Town. Toronto: McClelland and Stewart, 1962. 78 pp.
——— , and introd. ["What Canadians Don't Know About Love"]. *Love Where the Nights Are Long: An Anthology of Canadian Love Poems.* [Limited ed.] Illus. Harold Town. Toronto: McClelland and Stewart, 1962. viii–xi, 72 pp.

A64   *Anvil*. Montreal: Privately printed, 1966. 67 pp.

A65   ———, and introd. *Poems to Color*. Toronto: York Univ., 1970. [70 pp.]

A66   ———, and foreword. *i side up*. Toronto: York Poetry Workshop, 1971. 1-3, 48 pp.

A67   ———, and introd. *Anvil Blood*. Toronto: [York Univ. Poetry Workshop], 1973. 3-5, 57 pp.

A68   ———, and foreword. *New Holes in the Wall*. Toronto: York Univ., 1975. 55 pp.

A69   *Shark Tank*. Toronto: [York Univ. Poetry Workshop], 1977. 98 pp.

A70   *Handouts from the Mountain*. Toronto: York Poetry Workshop, 1978. 414 pp.

A71   ———, and foreword. *Rawprint*. Montreal: Concordia Univ., 1989. 63 pp.

Pamphlets and Portfolios

A72   Untitled. Victoria: Univ. of Victoria, Dept. of Creative Writing, 2 Oct. 1974. 4 pp.
       Includes "For the Fraulein from Hamburg" (B522) and "The Ventriloquist" (B546).

A73   *Shadows on the Ground: A Portfolio*. [Limited ed.] Oakville, Ont.: Mosaic / Valley, 1982. 6 leaves.
       Includes "The Annunciation" (B678), "Everything in the Universe Has Its Place," "Make Room, William Blake" (B745), "Portrait of a Modern Woman" (B726), and "Samantha Clara Layton" (B686).

A74   *Love Poems*. Lithographs Salvatore Fiume. Milan: Teodorani, 1985. 8 leaves.
       Includes "The Cage / La gabbia" (B254), "The Improved Binoculars / Il binocolo potenziato"

(B500), and "A Tall Man Executes a Jig / Un uomo alto esegue una giga" (B248).

Broadsides

A75   *On the Assassination of President Kennedy*. Offprint from *Queen's Quarterly*, 70 (Winter 1963). 1 leaf. (B292)

A76   *For Anna*. Orange Bear Reader, No. 4. Windsor, Ont.: n.p., 1970. 1 leaf.

A77   *Epiphany*. Designed David Brown. Quarryposters, 2. Kingston, Ont.: Quarry, [1968]. 1 leaf. (A18)

A78   *Catacombe dei Cappucini*. Palermo: n.p., 1976. 2 leaves. (B551)

A79   *Reflections in an Old Ontario Cemetery*. Designed Gustave Tellering. N.p.: n.p., [c.1980]. 1 leaf. (B664)

A80   *The Cost and Consequences of a Two-Year Marriage to an Enchanting Jewish American Princess*. N.p.: n.p., Sept. 1982. 1 leaf.
       Includes "Flights" (A41) and list of alleged financial costs of Layton's marriage to Harriet Bernstein.

A81   *The Well-Wrought Urn*. Canadian Poets on Posters. N.p.: n.p., n.d. 1 leaf. (B263)

Editorial Work

A82   Editorial board member. *First Statement*, 1, No. 13 [1943]-3, No. 1 (June–July 1945).

A83   Editorial board member. *Northern Review*, 1, No. 1 (Dec.–Jan. 1945–46)-2, No. 2 (July–Aug. 1948).

A84 Contributing editor. *Black Mountain Review* [Black Mountain, N.C.], No. 1 (Spring 1954)–No. 7 (Autumn 1957).

A85 Guest editor. *Origin* [Featuring New Canadian Poetry], Ser. 1, No. 18 (Winter–Spring 1956). 64 pp.

A86 Supervisor. *The Pioneer*, 2, No. 1 (n.d.).
Done by Grade 9 students under Layton's supervision.

Audio-Visual Material

A87 *Irving Layton at Le Hibou*. Narr. Irving Layton. Posterity, PTR 13001, [c.1962]. (L.p.; approx. 36 min.)
Includes "Admonition and Reply" [35 sec.] (B1211), "Bargain" [20 sec.] (B1274), "The Birth of Tragedy" [1 min., 25 sec.] (B1169), "Cemetery in August" [51 sec.] (see A4), "The Cold Green Element" [1 min., 50 sec.] (B1161), "Composition in Late Spring" [1 min., 39 sec.] (see B104), "Death of Moishe Lazarovitch" [1 min., 5 sec.] (B1154), "Family Portrait" [55 sec.] (B1238), "Fertile Muck" [1 min., 41 sec.] (B1171), "First Walk in Spring" [58 sec.] (see A9), "For My Detractors" [55 sec.] (see A7), "From Colony to Nation" [1 min.] (B1193), "God, When You Speak" [1 min., 16 sec.] (B1163), "How Poems Get Written" [20 sec.] (see B356), "Imperial" [16 sec.] (see B122 — O.B.E."), "The Improved Binoculars" [58 sec.] (B1172), "It's All in the Manner" [53 sec.] (see B106), "Letter from a Straw Man" [1 min., 29 sec.] (see B162), "Love's Diffidence" [41 sec.] (see B154), "Marie" [1 min., 8 sec.] (see A6), "Me, the P.M., and the Stars" [2 min., 30 sec.] (see B133), "Misunderstanding" [12 sec.] (B1215), "On Being Bitten by a Dog" [28 sec.] (B1217), "On My Way to School" [17 sec.] (B1218),

"On Seeing the Statuettes of Ezekiel and Jeremiah in the Church of Notre Dame" [1 min., 28 sec.] (B1209), "Philosophy 34" [56 sec.] (see B355), "Song for Naomi" [1 min., 5 sec.] (B1191), "The Swimmer" [1 min., 5 sec.] (B1221), "To the Girls of My Graduating Class" [1 min.] (B1224), "The Way of the World" [1 min., 4 sec.] (see B158), "The Way the World Ends" [1 min., 27 sec.] (see A11), "What Ulysses Said to Circe on the Beach of Aeaea" [35 sec.] (see A6), "When It Came to Santayana's Turn" [55 sec.] (see B128), and "Women of Rome" [2 min., 45 sec.] (see B223).

A88 *Poems of Irving Layton*. Narr. Irving Layton. Montreal: Jewish Public Library, [c.1965]. (Audiocassette; approx. 36 min.)
Includes "After Auschwitz" [58 sec.] (see B386), "The Birth of Tragedy" [1 min., 30 sec.] (B1169), "The Bull Calf" [1 min., 30 sec.] (B1170), "Cat Dying in Autumn" [55 sec.] (B1174), "Clochards" [1 min., 46 sec.] (see B352), "The Day Aviva Came to Paris" [4 min., 12 sec.] (see B208), "The Executioner" [42 sec.] (see A8), "Family Portrait" [53 sec.] (B1238), "For Musia's Grandchildren" [1 min., 19 sec.] (see B317), "Free Djilas" [31 sec.] (B1212), "Gothic Landscape" [58 sec.] (see B76), "The Graveyard" [1 min., 26 sec.] (see B380), "If Whales Could Think on Certain Happy Days" [36 sec.] (B1296), "The Improved Binoculars" [1 min.] (B1172), "Israelis" [1 min., 30 sec.] (B1235), "Keine Lazarovitch 1870–1959" [1 min., 38 sec.] (B1208), "Lady Enfield" [18 sec.] (B1234), "Leavetaking" [35 sec.] (B1240), "Me, the P.M., and the Stars" [2 min., 20 sec.] (see B133), "Misunderstanding" [12 sec.] (B1215), "On First Looking into Stalin's Coffin" [50 sec.] (see A6), "On My Way to School" [18 sec.] (B1218), "Poplars" [18 sec.] (see A2), "Rhine Boat Trip" [36 sec.] (B1241), "Song for Naomi" [1 min.,

10 sec.] (B1191), "A Spider Danced a Cosy Jig" [33 sec.] (B1220), "There Were No Signs" [40 sec.] (B1228), "This Machine Age" [46 sec.] (B1223), "To the Girls of My Graduating Class" [58 sec.] (B1224), "Whatever Else, Poetry Is Freedom" [2 min., 40 sec.] (B1190), and "Whom I Write For" [2 min., 25 sec.] (see B251).

A89 *Irving Layton*. Narr. Irving Layton. Montreal: Sir George Williams Univ., 18 March 1967. (Audio-cassette; approx. 32 min.)

Includes "Archetypes" [45 sec.] (see A11), "At the Alhambra" [49 sec.] (see A15), "Bacchanal" [47 sec.] (B1173), "Bargain" [22 sec.] (B1274), "The Birth of Tragedy" [1 min., 26 sec.] (B1169), "The Black Huntsmen" [1 min., 7 sec.] (see B79), "The Bull Calf" [1 min., 50 sec.] (B1170), "Cemetery in August" [54 sec.] (see A4), "The Cold Green Element" [1 min., 52 sec.] (B1161), "De Bullion Street" [1 min., 5 sec.] (B1233), "Death of a Construction Worker" [34 sec.] (see B114), "For Louise, Age 17" [1 min., 2 sec.] (B1175), "For My Green Old Age" [55 sec.] (B1226), "Free Djilas" [30 sec.] (B1212), "Gathering of Poets" [18 sec.] (see A11), "Gothic Landscape" [56 sec.] (see B76), "The Improved Binoculars" [1 min., 3 sec.] (B1172), "Keine Lazarovitch 1870–1959" [1 min., 40 sec.] (B1208), "Look Homeward Angel" [24 sec.] (see A17), "Love the Conqueror Worm" [39 sec.] (see B94), "Misunderstanding" [11 sec.] (B1215), "Mrs. Fornheim, Refugee" [48 sec.] (B1165), "Mutability" [50 sec.] (see A17), "On My Way to School" [19 sec.] (B1218), "Orpheus" [1 min., 8 sec.] (see B123), "Plaza de Toros" [33 sec.] (B1205), "The Predator" [1 min., 20 sec.] (see B285), "Seven O'Clock Lecture" [2 min., 20 sec.] (see B99), "Soleil de Noces" [20 sec.] (see B98), "Song for Naomi" [1 min., 7 sec.] (B1191) "Summer Idyll" [56 sec.] (B1177), "There Were No

Signs" [40 sec.] (B1228), "This Machine Age" [44 sec.] (B1223), "Time's Velvet Tongue" [23 sec.] (see B357), "To a Beautiful Unknown Girl" [49 sec.] (see B358), and "To the Girls of My Graduating Class" [1 min.] (B1224).

A90 *Irving Layton Reads His Poetry*. Narr. Irving Layton. Montreal: Jewish Public Library, [c.1967]. (Audio-cassette; approx. 39 min.)

Includes "Archetypes" [44 sec.] (see A11), "Bacchanal" [49 sec.] (B1173), "Bargain" [20 sec.] (B1274), "The Birth of Tragedy" [1 min., 30 sec.] (B1169), "The Black Huntsmen" [1 min., 10 sec.] (see B79), "The Bull Calf" [1 min., 42 sec.] (B1170), "Cemetery in August" [55 sec.] (see A4), "The Cold Green Element" [1 min., 48 sec.] (B1161), "Confederation Ode" [1 min., 12 sec.] (see B327), "De Bullion Street" [1 min., 7 sec.] (B1233), "Family Portrait" [55 sec.] (B1238), "For Musia's Grandchildren" [1 min., 38 sec.] (see B317), "For My Green Old Age" [54 sec.] (B1226), "Free Djilas" [33 sec.] (B1212), "Gathering of Poets" [20 sec.] (see A11), "Gothic Landscape" [56 sec.] (see B76), "Gratitude" [55 sec.] (see B333), "The Improved Binoculars" [58 sec.] (B1172), "Keine Lazarovitch 1870–1959" [1 min., 35 sec.] (B1208), "Look Homeward Angel" [58 sec.] (see A17), "Love the Conqueror Worm" [42 sec.] (see B94), "Maxie" [1 min., 25 sec.] (B1156), "Misunderstanding" [14 sec.] (B1215), "Mutability" [52 sec.] (see A17), "On My Way to School" [20 sec.] (B1218), "On Spanish Soil" [50 sec.] (B1204), "Plaza de Toros" [30 sec.] (B1205), "Poets of a Distant Time" [1 min., 42 sec.], "Predator" [1 min., 25 sec.] (see B285), "Rhine Boat Trip" [38 sec.] (B1241), "Seven O'Clock Lecture" [2 min., 30 sec.] (see B99), "Soleil de Noces" [22 sec.] (see B98), "The Swimmer" [1 min., 8 sec.] (B1221), "There Were No Signs" [42 sec.] (B1228), "This Machine Age" [48 sec.] (B1223), "Time's Velvet Tongue" [30 sec.] (see B357), "To a Beautiful Unknown Girl" [55 sec.] (see B358), "To the Girls of My Graduating Class" [1 min., 2 sec.] (B1224), "Vexata Quaestio" [37 sec.] (see B140), and "The Well-Wrought Urn" [22 sec.] (B1225).

A91 *An Evening with Irving Layton.* Narr. Irving Layton. Guelph, Ont.: Massey Hall, Univ. of Guelph, 29 Jan. 1969. (Audiocassette; approx. 46 min.)

Includes "The Birth of Tragedy" [1 min., 35 sec.] (B1169), "The Bull Calf" [1 min., 58 sec.] (B1170), "Chokecherries" [43 sec.] (see A9), "Death of Moishe Lazarovitch" [1 min., 6 sec.] (B1154), "A Dedication" [1 min., 39 sec.] (see B744), "The Fertile Muck" [1 min., 43 sec.] (B1171), "For Musia's Grandchildren" [1 min., 21 sec.] (see B317), "I Would for Your Sake Be Gentle" [1 min., 14 sec.] (B1213), "The Improved Binoculars" [1 min., 8 sec.] (B1172), "In the Midst of My Fever" [2 min., 33 sec.] (B1164), "Invention" [2 min., 32 sec.] (see B329), "Letter from a Straw Man" [1 min., 51 sec.] (see B162), "Red Chokecherries" [37 sec.] (B1219), "Rhine Boat Trip" [41 sec.] (B1241), "Sacrament by the Water" [44 sec.] (B1176), "Seven O'Clock Lecture" [2 min., 39 sec.] (see B99), "Song for Naomi" [1 min., 6 sec.] (B1191), "The Swimmer" [1 min., 3 sec.] (B1221), "There Were No Signs" [40 sec.] (B1228), "To a Very Old Woman" [1 min., 44 sec.] (see B90), "Whatever Else, Poetry Is Freedom" [2 min., 39 sec.] (B1190), "With the Money I Spend" [3 min., 23 sec.] (see A51), "The World's a Tavern" [2 min., 37 sec.] (see B83), "The Yard" [1 min., 32 sec.] (see B67), and "Yet What if the Survivors" [1 min., 42 sec.] (see B378).

A92 *Irving Layton.* Narr. Irving Layton. Toronto: High Barnet, [c.1972]. (Audiocassette; approx. 37 min.)

"After Auschwitz" [1 min.] (see B386), "The Birth of Tragedy" [1 min., 22 sec.] (B1169), "The Bull Calf" [1 min., 42 sec.] (B1170), "Cat Dying in Autumn" [57 sec.] (B1174), "Clochards" [1 min., 44 sec.] (see B352), "The Day Aviva Came to Paris" [4 min., 16 sec.] (see B208), "The Executioner" [1 min., 40 sec.] (see A8), "Family Portrait" [46 sec.] (B1238), "For Louise, Age 17" [1 min., 3 sec.] (B1175), "For Musia's Grandchildren" [1 min., 9 sec.] (see B317), "Free Djilas" [29 sec.] (B1212), "Gothic Landscape" [59 sec.] (see B76), "The Graveyard" [1 min.] (see B380), "If Whales Could Think on Certain Happy Days" [36 sec.] (B1296), "The Improved Binoculars" [56 sec.] (B1172), "Israelis" [1 min., 36 sec.] (B1235), "Keine Lazarovitch 1870–1959" [1 min., 29 sec.] (B1208), "Lady Enfield" [20 sec.] (B1234), "Leavetaking" [31 sec.] (B1240), "Me, the P.M., and the Stars" [2 min., 13 sec.] (see B133), "Misunderstanding" [10 sec.] (B1215), "Mrs. Fornheim, Refugee" [43 sec.] (B1165), "On First Looking into Stalin's Coffin" [50 sec.] (see A6), "On My Way to School" [20 sec.] (B1218), "Poplars" [16 sec.] (see A2), "Rhine Boat Trip" [36 sec.] (B1241), "Silent Joy" [21 sec.] (B1242), "Song for Naomi" [1 min., 4 sec.] (B1191), "A Spider Danced a Cosy Jig" [34 sec.] (B1220), "There Were No Signs" [36 sec.] (B1228), "This Machine Age" [43 sec.] (B1223), "To the Girls of My Graduating Class" [57 sec.] (B1224), "Whatever Else Poetry Is Freedom" [2 min., 46 sec.] (B1190), and "Whom I Write For" [2 min., 27 sec.] (see B251).

A93 *Layton.* Narr. Irving Layton. "Foreword to *The Collected Poems*," Irving Layton [back container]. Introd. Irving Layton (49 sec.) Caedmon, ML7002, [c.1973]. (L.p., 47 min., 37 sec.)

Includes "Arabs" [1 min., 26 sec.] (see A18), "Ballad of the Old Spaniard" [1 min., 51 sec.] (B1197),

"Berry Picking" [1 min., 35 sec.] (B1185), "The Birth of Tragedy" [1 min., 14 sec.] (B1169), "The Bull Calf" [1 min., 42 sec.] (B1170), "Cain" [2 min., 50 sec.] (B1186), "Clochards" [1 min., 50 sec.] (see B352), "The Cold Green Element" [1 min., 47 sec.] (B1161), "Composition in Late Spring" [1 min., 42 sec.] (see B104), "Epitaph for a Poet [I sang of thighs]" [29 sec.] (see A21), "The Fertile Muck" [1 min., 31 sec.] (B1171), "For Louise, Age 17" [1 min., 9 sec.] (B1175), "How Poems Get Written" [21 sec.] (see B356), "I Would for Your Sake Be Gentle" [1 min., 8 sec.] (B1213), "If I Lie Still" [1 min., 4 sec.] (see B591), "The Improved Binoculars" [62 sec.] (B1172), "Innocence" [31 sec.] (see A16), "Israelis" [1 min., 35 sec.] (B1235), "Keine Lazarovitch 1870–1959" [1 min., 38 sec.] (B1208), "On Seeing the Statuettes of Ezekiel and Jeremiah in the Church of Notre Dame" [1 min., 24 sec.] (B1209), "Plaza de Toros" [31 sec.] (B1205), "The Predator" [1 min., 37 sec.] (see B285), "Rain" [1 min., 10 sec.] (see A12), "Rhine Boat Trip" [38 sec.] (B1241), "Song for Naomi" [1 min., 11 sec.] (B1191), "Spikes" [1 min., 22 sec.] (see A9), "Therapy" [48 sec.] (B1222), "There Were No Signs" [41 sec.] (B1228), "This Machine Age" [1 min., 28 sec.] (B1223), "To the Girls of My Graduating Class" [1 min., 41 sec.] (B1224), "Vigil" [45 sec.] (see B1), "What Does It Matter" [2 min., 13 sec.] (see A14), "Whom I Write For" [2 min., 28 sec.] (see B251), and "Xmas Eve 1971, Zihuatanejo" (1 min., 28 sec.) (see B470).

A94   *A Red Carpet for the Sun.* Foreword Irving Layton. Audiocassette. Peterborough: Trent Audio Library, Trent Univ., Feb. 1975. (260 min.)
       Includes "Abel Cain" (see B155), "Admonition and Reply" (B1211), "After the Chinese" (see A9), "Afternoon Tea" (see B145), "Against This Death" (B1250), "Anglo-Canadian" (B1184), "Anti-

Romantic" (see B174), "The Ants" (see B129), "Astarte" (see A9), "Autumn Lines for My Son" (see A12), "Bacchanal" (B1173), "Bargain" (B1274), "Beauty [Omah who keeps house]" (see A4), "Berry Picking" (B1185), "The Birth of Tragedy" (B1169), "Black, Black" (see A10), "The Black Huntsmen" (see B79), "Boardwalk at Verdun" (see B166), "A Bonnet for Bessie" (see A12), "Boys Bathing" (see A9), "Boys in October" (see B287), "The Buffaloes" (see B142), "The Bull Calf" (B1170), "By Ecstasies Perplexed" (see A11), "Café Politics in Spring" (see B159), "Cain" (B1186), "Canadian Skiers" (see B153), "Cat Dying in Autumn" (B1174), "Cemetery in August" (see A4), "Chatterers" (see B194), "Chokecherries" (see A9), "Christmas Day" (see A7), "Climbing" (see B182), "The Cold Green Element" (B1161), "The Comic Element" (see B112), "Compliments of the Season" (see B58), "Composition in Late Spring" (see B104), "Concourse at Cataraqui" (see A11), "Côte des Neiges Cemetery" (see B186), "Crone" (see A3), "Dance, My Little One" (B1187), "The Dancers" (see B113), "The Dark Nest" (see A9), "The Dark Plebeian Mind" (see B146), "De Bullion Street" (B1233), "Death of a Construction Worker" (see B114), "Death of Moishe Lazarovitch" (B1154), "Dionysius" (see A11), "Divinity" (see B198), "Drill Shed" (see B54), "The Dwarf" (see A11), "Early Morning in Côte St. Luc" (see A5), "Earth Goddess" (see A9), "Enemies" (see B141), "Epitaphs: Philosopher [see B28], Poet Killed in Action [see B77], An Ugly Servitor to Three Queens [see B115], Wit [see B29]," "Eros [With the best side of my tongue]" (see A4), "Esthetique" (see B747), "Excursion" (see B61), "The Execution" (see A3), "The Executioner" (see A8), "Ex-Nazi" (see A3), "Family Portrait" (B1238), "The Fertile Muck" (B1171), "Fiat Lux" (see A9), "First Snow: Lake Achigan" (B1162), "First Walk in Spring" (see A9),

"For Louise, Age 17" (B1175), "For Mao Tse-Tung: A Meditation on Flies and Kings" (B1254), "For My Detractors" (see A7), "For Phyllis, Who Snatched Her Poem in Anger" (see A11), "For Priscilla" (see A5), "From Colony to Nation" (B1193), "Garter Snake" (see A12), "God, When You Speak" (B1163), "Golfers" (B1207), "Good-bye Bahai" (see A3), "Gothic Landscape" (see B76), "Halos at Lac Marie Louise" (see B156), "Harlequin and Virgin" (see A8), "Haruspex" (see B78), "Holiday" (see B164), "How Domestic Happiness Is Achieved" (see A12), "How Poems Get Written" (see B356), "How to Look at an Abstract" (see B315), "I Would for Your Sake Be Gentle" (B1213), "If You Can't Scream" (see B181), "Imperial" (see B122), "The Improved Binoculars" (B1172), "In Memory of Fred Smith" (see B91), "In the Midst of My Fever" (B1164), "Individualists" (see B196), "Intersections" (see A9), "It's All in the Manner" (see B106), "Jewish Main Street" (B1214), "Joseph K —" (see A11), "Keewaydin Poetry Festival" (see B120), "Lachine, Que." (see A5), "Lady Enfield" (B1234), "Latria" (see A6), "Laurentian Rhapsody" (see B188), "Lesbia" (see B167), "Letter from a Straw Man" (see B162), "Letter to a Librarian" (see A12), "The Longest Journey" (see A5), "Look, the Lambs Are All Around Us" (see A6), "Love Is an Irrefutable Fire" (see B200), "Love the Conqueror Worm" (see B94), "Love's Diffidence" (see B154), "Macdonald College 1905–1955" (see A11), "The Madonna of the Magnificat" (see B107), "Marie" (see A6), "Maurer: Twin Heads" (see B150), "Maxie" (B1156), "May Day Orators" (see A7), "Me, the P.M., and the Stars" (see B133), "Metamorphosis" (see B517), "Metaphysical" (see B147), "Metzinger: Girl with a Bird" (see B108), "Mildred" (see A5), "La Minerve" (see B121), "Misunderstanding" (B1215), "Modern Love" (see A11), "Mont Rolland" (see B81), "Mortuary" (see B46),

"Motet" (see B136), "Mr. Ther-Apis" (see B103), "Mrs. Fornheim, Refugee" (B1165), "My Flesh Comfortless" (see B201), "Nausicäa" (see A11), "New Tables" (see A6), "Newsboy" (see B42), "Not Blown Away" (see A7), "Now That I'm Older" (B1271), "Obit" (see A10), "Odysseus in Limbo" (see B83), "On Being Bitten by a Dog" (B1217), "On First Looking into Stalin's Coffin" (see A6), "On My Way to School" (B1218), "On Seeing the Statuettes of Ezekiel and Jeremiah in the Church of Notre Dame" (B1209), "On the Death of A. Vishinsky" (see B143), "One View of Dead Fish" (see A9), "Original Sin" (B1256), "Orpheus" (see B123), "Overheard in a Barbershop" (see A4), "Paging Mr. Superman" (see B197), "Paraclete" (see B109), "Parting" (see B184), "Philosophy 34" (see B355), "Poem for the Next Century" (see B189), "Poet and Dancer" (see A8), "The Poet Entertains Several Ladies" (see B124), "Poetic Fame" (see B185), "The Poetic Process" (see B125), "Portrait [Pay small attention to the chin]" (see B137), "Portrait of Aileen" (see B134), "Project" (see A11), "Providence" (see B26), "The Puma's Tooth" (see A11), "Rain" (see A12), "Rain at La Minerve" (see A6), "The Ravens [Where's the poem]" (see A6), "Reconciliation" (see B225), "Red Chokecherries" (B1219), "Rembrandt" (see A3), "A Roman Jew to Ovid" (see A12), "Rose LeMay" (see A9), "Sacrament by the Water" (B1176), "Saratoga Beach" (see B144), "The Satyr" (see A8), "Seven O'Clock Lecture" (see B99), "Sheep" (B1189), "Song for a Late Hour" (see A9), "Song for Naomi" (B1191), "A Spider Danced a Cosy Jig" (B1220), "Spikes" (see A9), "Street Funeral" (B1159), "Summer Idyll" (B1177), "Sutherland: Portrait of A.C." (see B152), "Suzanne" (see A11), "The Swimmer" (B1221), "T.S. Eliot" (see B127), "Terrene" (see B87), "Thanatos and Eros" (see A11), "Theology" (see B148), "Thoughts in the Water" (see B157), "To a Very Old Woman" (see B90), "To the Girls of My Graduating Class" (B1224), "The Toy Gun" (see A12), "Trumpet Daffodil" (see B96), "Two Ladies at Traymore's" (see A11), "Two Poets in Toronto" (B1229), "Undine" (see A9), "Venetian Blinds" (see A12), "Veteran" (see A6), "Vexata Quaestio" (see B140), "Victory" (see A12), "A Vision" (see A4), "The Warm Afterdark" (see B202), "The Way of the World" (see B158), "The Way the World Ends" (see A11), "Westmount Doll" (see B132), "Whatever Else Poetry Is Freedom" (B1190), "What Ulysses Said to Circe on the Beach at Aeaea" (see A6), "When It Came to Santayana's Turn" (see B128), "The Widows" (B1178), "Winter Fantasy" (see A8), "Woman" (see B168), and "Young Girls Dancing at Camp Lajoie" (see B203).

A95   *An Evening with Irving Layton.* Narr. Irving Layton. Chair Shulamis Yelin. Montreal: Jewish Public Library, 15 Feb. 1976. (Audiocassette; approx. 47 min.)

Includes "Admonition and Reply" [35 sec.] (B1211), "After Auschwitz" [1 min.] (see B386), "Auld Lang Syne" [40 sec.] (B1273), "Bargain" [22 sec.] (B1274), "The Birth of Tragedy" [1 min., 30 sec.] (B1169), "The Bull Calf" [1 min., 45 sec.] (B1170), "Departed" [37 sec.] (see B498), "Early Morning in Mithymna" [1 min., 2 sec.] (see A22), "Elegy for Strul" [1 min., 56 sec.] (B1285), "Family Portrait" [51 sec.] (B1238), "The Fertile Muck" [1 min., 43 sec.] (B1171), "For Jesus Christ" [55 sec.] (B1277), "For My Brother Jesus" [2 min., 19 sec.] (B1282), "The Improved Binoculars" [55 sec.] (B1172), "Incident at the Cathedral" [52 sec.] (see B606), "Israelis" [1 min., 47 sec.] (B1235), "Jesus and St. Paul" [1 min., 9 sec.] (see A28), "Keine Lazarovitch 1870–1959" [1 min., 43 sec.] (B1208), "Mrs. Fornheim, Refugee" [48 sec.] (B1165), "O Jerusalem" [1 min., 25 sec.] (see B531), "On Being

Bitten by a Dog" [29 sec.] (B1217), "On Seeing the Statuettes of Ezekiel and Jeremiah in the Church of Notre Dame" [1 min., 25 sec.] (B1209), "The Pole-Vaulter" [48 sec.] (see B513), "Requiem for A.M. Klein" [1 min., 57 sec.] (see B507), "Rhine Boat Trip" [35 sec.] (B1241), "The Shadow" [3 min., 58 sec.] (see B515), "The Shark" [1 min., 3 sec.] (see B571), "Song for Naomi" [1 min., 15 sec.] (B1191), "There Were No Signs" [37 sec.] (B1228), "To a Beautiful Unknown Girl" [55 sec.] (see B358), and "Warrior Poet" [49 sec.] (B1278).

A96   *My Brother Jesus.* Narr. Irving Layton. Montreal: Saidye Bronfman Center, 16 May 1976. (Audiocassette; 90 min.)

Includes "Displaced Person" [55 sec.] (B1280), "For Jesus Christ" [57 sec.] (B1277), and "For My Brother Jesus" [2 min., 10 sec.] (B1282).

Layton also talks of Christian persecution of Jews and his aim of reclaiming Jesus for the Jews (86 min.).

A97   *An Evening with Irving Layton.* Host Ann Morgenstar. Montreal: Jewish Public Library, 8 Feb. 1981. (Audiocassette; approx. 16 min.)

Includes "Bright's Wines" [6 sec.] (see A37), "Click, Click" [1 min., 7 sec.] (see A33), "The Dark Underside" [1 min., 10 sec.] (see A35), "Father and Daughter" [1 min., 41 sec.] (see A35), "For My Neighbours in Hell [Hate, your adrenalin]" [1 min., 9 sec.] (see B643), "[God made the viper]" [14 sec.] (see B776), "The Graveyard" [1 min., 30 sec.] (see B380), "Keine Lazarovitch 1870–1959" [1 min., 45 sec.] (B1208), "Male Chauvinist" [15 sec.] (see B645), "On Seeing the Statuettes of Ezekiel and Jeremiah in the Church of Notre Dame" [1 min., 28 sec.] (B1209), "Rhine Boat Trip" [36 sec.] (B1241), "Senile, My Sister Sings" [2 min., 14 sec.] (see B713), "Song for Naomi" [1 min., 5 sec.] (B1191), "Sunday

Service, 11 a.m." [13 sec.], "Synagogue in West Palm Beach" [1 min., 31 sec.] (see B639), and "There Were No Signs" [36 sec.] (B1228).

A98   *Irving Layton*. Narr. Irving Layton. TV Ontario Council of Ministers of Education, 1984. (1/2" and 3/4" VHS; colour; 14 min.)
Includes "The Carved Nakedness" [31 sec.] (see B717), "Eine Kleine Nachtmusik" [1 min., 1 sec.] (see B673), "The Lone Ranger" [1 min., 1 sec.] (see A41), and "Veneranda Dancing" [27 sec.] (see A41).
Layton also comments on his work.

A99   *A Poetry Reading by Irving Layton*. Narr. Irving Layton. Prod. Rick Curtis. Modern Canadian Poets: A Recorded Archive. League of Canadian Poets. Toronto, [1982]. (Audiocassette; approx. 32 min.)
Includes "Berry Picking" [1 min., 40 sec.] (B1185), "The Birth of Tragedy" [1 min., 22 sec.] (B1169), "Blackout" [1 min., 13 sec.] (see A25), "The Bull Calf" [1 min., 45 sec.] (B1170), "Cain" [2 min., 58 sec.] (B1186), "Divinity and John Dewey" [17 sec.] (see B776), "For Andrei Amalrik" [1 min., 47 sec.] (see B521), "For Another Who Squeezed Back" [1 min., 11 sec.] (see A34), "For Masha Cohen" [56 sec.] (see A34), "For My Brother Oscar" [42 sec.] (see A34), "For 751-0329" [1 min., 19 sec.] (B1300), "From Colony to Nation" [59 sec.] (B1193), "The Improved Binoculars" [1 min.] (B1172), "Keine Lazarovitch 1870–1959" [1 min., 33 sec.] (B1208), "Lillian Roxon" [1 min., 22 sec.] (see B504), "Molibos Cat" [59 sec.] (see B569), "O Jerusalem" [1 min., 18 sec.] (see B531), "On Seeing the Statuettes of Ezekiel and Jeremiah in the Church of Notre Dame" [1 min., 23 sec.] (B1209), "Orpheus" [1 min., 11 sec.] (see B123), "Paraclete" [1 min., 17 sec.] (see B109), "Red Chokecherries" [36 sec.] (B1219), "Rhine Boat Trip" [37 sec.] (B1241), "Sacrament by

the Water" [39 sec.] (B1176), "Song for Naomi" [1 min., 6 sec.] (B1191), "The Swimmer" [1 min., 4 sec.] (B1221), "Theatre" [42 sec.] (see B595), and "There Were No Signs" [40 sec.] (B1228).
Also includes an interview by Timothy Wilson (12 min.) (C641).

A100 *A Tall Man Executes a Jig*. Narr. Irving Layton. Dir. Donald Winkler. Prod. Bill Brind. NFB, 1987. (Colour; 16 mm; 1/2"; VHS; Beta; 25 min., 58 sec.)
Includes "A Tall Man Executes a Jig" (see B248) and Layton's commentary on this poem.

A101 *A Wild Peculiar Joy: Selected Poems 1945–82*. Narr. Irving Layton. Toronto: McClelland and Stewart, 1990. (Audiocassette.)
Includes "Bargain" (B1274), "Berry Picking" (B1185), "The Birth of Tragedy" (B1169), "The Bull Calf" (B1170), "Cat Dying in Autumn" (B1174), "The Cold Green Element" (B1161), "Composition in Late Spring" (see B104), "Côte des Neiges Cemetery" (see B186), "The Dark Underside" (see A35), "Dracula" (see B642), "Eine Kleine Nachtmusik" (see B673), "Elegy for Marilyn Monroe" (see B277), "Family Portrait" (B1238), "The Fertile Muck" (B1171), "Final Reckoning: After Theognis" (see B824), "For Louise, Age 17" (B1175), "For Musia's Grandchildren" (see B317), "For 7515–03296" (B1300), "Golfers" (B1207), "Grand Finale" (see B599), "Hells" (see A38), "I Take My Anna Everywhere" (see B753), "In Plato's Cave" (see A35), "Keine Lazarovitch: 1870–1959" (B1208), "La Minerve" (see B121), "Misunderstanding" (B1215), "The Mosquito" (see A9), "Night Music" (see B594), "Now That I'm Older" (B1271), "O Jerusalem" (see B531), "On Seeing the Statuettes of Ezekiel and Jeremiah in the Church of Notre Dame" (B1209), "Out of Pure Lust" (see A41), "Political

Economy" (see B266), "The Predator" (see B285), "Rhine Boat Trip" (B1241), "Samantha Clara Layton" (see B686), "Senile, My Sister Sings" (see B713), "Shakespeare" (B1287), "The Shark" (see B571), "Song for Naomi" (B1191), "The Swimmer" (B1221), "There Were No Signs" (B1228), "Whatever Else Poetry Is Freedom" (B1190), and "Whom I Write For" (see B251).

Manuscripts

Note: Because archival holdings for Layton are so numerous, I have listed the four major holdings in order of importance (Concordia University Library, Jewish Public Library, University of Saskatchewan Library, and Thomas Fisher Rare Book Library), but the rest appear in alphabetical order according to the title of the collection. In the case of an individual's collection of papers, the last name, rather than the first word, has been alphabetized.

A102 Irving Layton Collection
Concordia University Library
Concordia University
Montreal, Quebec

As the major repository of Layton's work, this collection aims to include all material by and about Layton. It has a complete collection of books by Layton, an extensive collection of periodicals in which his work has appeared, as well as alphabetically filed copies of most of his poems from periodicals. An extensive collection of material on Layton is kept up-to-date through a clipping service. Some theses, scrapbooks, and photographs are also included. The audio-visual part of the collection includes tapes and transcripts made by David O'Rourke for Layton's *Waiting for the Messiah: A*

Memoir. Audiotapes include CBC appearances, interviews, and poetry readings. There are also a number of videotapes. The collection contains 1 box of letters by Layton, which includes correspondence by Layton to Cid Corman, George Woodcock, Louis Dudek, Wynne Francis, and others. There is also a collection of letters by Layton to Kathleen C. Moore (then editor of *Athanor*) and 2 envelopes of letters from Cid Corman to Raymond Souster. The collection includes the major portion of Layton's manuscripts, including those of *The Improved Binoculars*, *The Laughing Rooster*, and *Balls for a One-Armed Juggler*, and poems that appeared in *The Unwavering Eye: Selected Poems 1969–1975*, *The Darkening Fire: Selected Poems 1945–1968*, *For My Brother Jesus*, and *The Covenant*. There are 11 notebooks and 4 scrap-books, as well as 3 filing cabinet drawers containing letters to Layton. A fourth drawer contains restricted correspondence. The letters to Layton include copies of Desmond Pacey's contribution to the Pacey-Layton correspondence. Much of this material has been catalogued. See C7 and C11.

A103 Jewish Canadiana Collection
Jewish Public Library
Montreal, Quebec

Although the Jewish Public Library holds little previously unpublished material, it has a large collection of Layton material as part of its collection on Canadian Jewish authors. It also subscribes to a clipping service. The Layton material is contained in ten boxes.

Boxes 1–4:
Books by Layton.

Box 5:
Periodicals with poems by Layton — *The Canadian*

Forum, CIV/n, *The Fiddlehead*, *First Statement*, *Intercourse*, *Northern Review*, *Origin*, *Quarry*, and *The Tamarack Review*.

Box 6:
Miscellaneous periodicals with poems by Layton.

Box 7:
Prose by Layton, mainly articles and letters in newspapers; also some material about him.

Box 8:
Articles on Layton, mostly from newspapers.

Box 9:
Periodical articles on Layton and reviews of his books.

Box 10:
Miscellaneous material on Layton.

A104 Layton Papers
University of Saskatchewan Library
University of Saskatchewan
Saskatoon, Saskatchewan

The Layton material is contained in 4 manuscript boxes and 1 oversized item (the deluxe edition of *Love Where the Nights Are Long: An Anthology of Canadian Love Poems*). The collection is catalogued.

Box 1:
Books by Layton (15), from *Here and Now* to *Balls for a One-Armed Juggler*, a complete collection of books to 1963 except for *Now Is the Place* and *The Black Huntsmen*.

Box 2:
Cerberus, *Cerberus* (mounted galley proofs), *Canadian Poems 1850–1952*, 1st ed. (1952), 2nd ed. (1953), *Love Where the Nights Are Long: An Anthology of Canadian Love Poems*; recordings of

Layton's lecture "Prince Hamlet and the Beatniks" delivered at the David B. Steinman Festival, St. Lawrence University, 18 Feb. 1962 (2 reels) and of Layton reading his poetry (2 reels).

Box 3:
Photocopies of poetry and prose by Layton from the *Macdonald College Failt-Ye Times* and the *McGill Daily*; copies of *First Statement*, *The Canadian Forum*, *Northern Review*, *Commentary*, CIV/n, *Black Mountain Review*, *Bulletin of Montreal Teachers Federation of Jewish Schools*, *Origin*, *Pan-ic*, *Exchange*, and *The Tamarack Review* in which Layton's work appeared; some critical material on Layton, mostly book reviews and newspaper clippings.

Box 4:
Manuscripts by Layton including essays on Machiavelli (1938) (10 pp.) and "Poetry Outlets in Canada" (Montreal 1957); 3 notebooks; typescript drafts of *Music on a Kazoo*, *The Bull Calf and Other Poems*, and *A Laughter in the Mind*; and numerous drafts of poems and short stories. Correspondence includes letters to J.S. Caplan (30 April 1960), Mrs. J. Kennedy (19 April 1961), 8 letters and 3 postcards by William Carlos Williams (14 Jan. 1955–19 Feb. 1960), and 1 letter by Hugh MacLennan (18 March 1960). Material on Layton includes Patricia Porth's "The Poetry of Irving Layton" and copies of Herzliah Junior High School graduation exercises 19 June 1952 and 24 June 1955 inscribed by students.

A105 Irving Layton Papers
Thomas Fisher Rare Book Library
University of Toronto
Toronto, Ontario

This collection includes material on *Lovers and Lesser Men* and *A Wild Peculiar Joy: Selected Poems*

1945–1982. *Lovers and Lesser Men*: drafts of poems dated 10 June–26 July 1972 (233 leaves); holograph drafts, usually accompanied by typed copies; some leaves have holographs on both sides; most are included in *Lovers and Lesser Men*. Poetry workbooks for *Lovers and Lesser Men*, 1972 (2 vols.); holograph, with numerous additions and corrections by the author. Typescript of *Lovers and Lesser Men* with holograph notes and corrections (167 leaves); some poems are signed; many duplicate poems are included, some of which are xerox copies. *A Wild Peculiar Joy: Selected Poems 1945–1982* (191 leaves): page proofs with corrections.

A106   Earle Birney Papers
Thomas Fisher Rare Book Library
University of Toronto
Toronto, Ontario

The Earle Birney Papers include 24 letters from Layton to Birney (22 July 1951–7 Nov. 1966); 12 postcards (1 Nov. 1957–27 Dec. 1968); 1 telegram (24 July 1951); 2 testimonial letters from students (21 and 22 April 1962); and 1 postcard to Esther Birney (6 Feb. 1967).

A107   Paul Blackburn Papers
Department of Special Collections
The University Library
University of California at San Diego
La Jolla, California

The Paul Blackburn Papers contain 2 letters from Layton to Blackburn (12 July 1954 and 30 Oct. 1961); as well as the typescript of "The Red and the Black" by Irving Layton.

A108   George Bowering Papers
Literary Manuscript Collection

National Library of Canada
395 Wellington Street
Ottawa, Ontario

The George Bowering Papers contain 3 postcards from Layton to Bowering (18 July 1962, 21 Aug. 1962, and n.d.); 3 letters (29 Sept. 1962, 8 Nov. 1962, and 20 Nov. 1965); and 1 letter from Layton to the Canada Council (28 Feb. 1963).

A109   Leonard Cohen Papers
Thomas Fisher Rare Book Library
University of Toronto
Toronto, Ontario

This collection includes a holograph copy of the television comedy *Enough of Fallen Leaves*, by Leonard Cohen and Irving Layton [Montreal, c.1961] (125 leaves); a holograph copy of the television play *Lights on the Black Water*, by Leonard Cohen and Irving Layton [Montreal, c.1961] (43 leaves) (leaf 23 is missing, and leaf 33 is numbered twice); and a holograph copy of the television play *A Man Was Killed*, by Leonard Cohen and Irving Layton [Montreal, c.1961] (29 leaves). Six personal notes by Layton discuss Layton's and Cohen's writing. Also included are 1 letter from Nina Froud to Irving Layton; and 1 letter from David Peddie to Irving Layton and Leonard Cohen.

A110   Cid Corman Collection
Harry Ransom Humanities Research Centre
The University of Texas
Austin, Texas

The following correspondence from Irving Layton to Cid Corman is included: 8 holograph letters, signed; 23 typed letters, signed; 2 holograph postcards, signed (8 are undated; the remaining are dated

1953–54); included with the letters are both attachments and enclosures. Also included are 1 holograph letter, signed (27 July 1955); 2 typed letters, signed (9 Jan. 1956 and 22 Feb. 1956).

A111 Alan Crawley Papers
Kathleen Ryan Hall
Queen's University Archives
Queen's University
Kingston, Ontario

The Alan Crawley Papers contain 1 letter from Layton to Floris McClaren (c.1951).

A112 Harold Files Papers
McLennan Library
McGill University
Montreal, Quebec

The following poems by Layton form part of a collection in the papers of Professor of English Harold Files (M.G. 1037, c. 7) offered to Ryerson Press in 1947 under the title "McGill's Younger Poets: An Anthology of Student Verse": "Church Parade," "Drill Shed," "Petawawa," "St. Lawrence Blvd.," "Spinoza," "Waterfront," and "Winter Scene." The anthology was never published.

A113 R.A.D. Ford Literary Papers
Literary Manuscript Collection
National Library of Canada
395 Wellington Street
Ottawa, Ontario

The R.A.D. Ford Literary Papers contain 1 letter from Layton to Ford (17 Sept. 1971).

A114 Gary Geddes Papers
Literary Manuscript Collection
National Library of Canada
395 Wellington Street
Ottawa, Ontario

The Gary Geddes Papers contain 6 letters from Layton to Geddes (4 Jan. 1974, 22 Jan. 1974, 16 Oct. 1974, 10 Nov. 1977, 7 Dec. 1977, and 10 April 1985). The material is restricted.

A115 John Glassco Papers
National Archives of Canada
395 Wellington Street
Ottawa, Ontario

The John Glassco Papers contain 5 letters from Layton to Glassco (23 Nov. 1963, 7 Jan. 1964, 31 Jan. 1964, 2 Feb. 1964, and 17 March 1964).

A116 Michael Gnarowski Papers
Literary Manuscript Collection
National Library of Canada
395 Wellington Street
Ottawa, Ontario

The Michael Gnarowski Papers contain 4 letters from Layton to Gnarowski (15 March 1962, 6 Nov. 1970, 9 Dec. 1970, and 11 Jan. 1972); 1 letter from Layton to Glen Siebrasse (n.d.); 3 copies of Louis Resnitsky's interview with Layton (C361); a published but unlocated review of Layton's *The Shattered Plinths* and Louis Dudek's *Atlantis*; and signed typescripts of Layton's poems "For the More Devotional," "Family Portrait," and "Woman."

A117 Phyllis Gotlieb Papers
National Archives of Canada
395 Wellington Street
Ottawa, Ontario

The Phyllis Gotlieb Papers contain 1 letter from Layton to Gotlieb (20 April 1962).

A118 Ralph Gustafson Collection
University of Saskatchewan Library
University of Saskatchewan
Saskatoon, Saskatchewan

The Ralph Gustafson Collection includes 12 letters and 3 postcards from Layton to Gustafson (Feb. 1943–11 July 1962); 10 letters from Gustafson to Layton (10 Feb. 1943–25 July 1962); 2 letters to R.G. Everson (19 Feb. 1960 and 20 Feb. 1960); 2 letters to Louis Dudek (21 Feb. 1960 and an undated open letter). Typescripts of several poems by Layton, an item on Layton's Governor-General's award in *The Gazette* [Montreal] (29 March 1960) (C57), and an article from Bishop University's *Campus* (14 March 1962) (C72) in which Layton compares Northrop Frye to a eunuch in a harem.

A119 Ralph Gustafson Papers
Kathleen Ryan Hall
Queen's University Archives
Queen's University
Kingston, Ontario

The Ralph Gustafson Papers contain 14 letters and 2 postcards from Layton to Gustafson (4 Jan. 1964–30 May 1981).

A120 Kenneth Hertz Papers
National Archives of Canada
395 Wellington Street
Ottawa, Ontario

The Kenneth Hertz Papers contain 1 letter from Layton to Hertz (9 Nov. 1964).

A121 George Johnston Papers
National Archives of Canada
395 Wellington Street
Ottawa, Ontario

The George Johnston Papers contain 8 letters from Layton to Johnston (4 Feb. 1956, 10 Feb. 1956, 16 March 1956, 17 Feb. 1958, 6 April 1958, 3 May 1958, 27 March 1960, and 16 Nov. 1965).

A122 A.M. Klein Papers
National Archives of Canada
395 Wellington Street
Ottawa, Ontario

The A.M. Klein Papers contain 1 letter from Layton to Klein (10 Aug. 1948).

A123 Pat Lane Papers
Special Collections Division
University of British Columbia
Vancouver, British Columbia

The Pat Lane Papers contain 9 letters and 1 postcard from Layton to Lane; and 2 letters from Lane to Layton.

A124 Layton, Irving — ZB Collection
National Archives
Canadian Jewish Congress
1590 Avenue Docteur Penfield
Montreal, Quebec

The National Archives contains 2 letters to Ms. Ruth Lazarus (7 Sept. and 25 Sept. 1976); 2 letters to Rabbi Kirshenbaum (23 June 1970 and 31 March 1976); 1 letter to H.M. Caiserman (18 May 1939); a postcard to Mrs. Goldberg (23 May 1964); a letter of recommendation from W.H. Brittain, Dean of MacDonald College (3 May 1939); a letter of recommendation from J.E. Lattimer, Professor of Agricultural Economics (16 Dec. 1938); and a copy of a letter from Sr. Marie Noelle of the Montreal committee for Jewish Catholic Relations concerning *For My Brother Jesus*.

A125 Norman Levine Papers
York University Archives
Scott Library
York University
North York, Ontario

The Norman Levine Papers contain 1 letter from Layton to Levine (30 June 1958).

A126 Hugh MacLennan Papers
Department of Rare Books and Collections
University of Calgary Library
University of Calgary
Calgary, Alberta

The Hugh MacLennan Papers contain 1 letter from Layton to MacLennan (13 Feb. 1969).

A127 Manuscript Archives / Special Collections,
Contemporary Literature Collection,
Inventory No. MsC16
W.A.C. Bennett Library
Simon Fraser University
Burnaby, British Columbia

This collection contains 3 letters from Layton to R.E. Jennings, student (16 Nov. 1960, 28 March 1961, and 20 April 1961) (8 leaves); and a letter from Layton to Bob Anderman, student (1983) (1 leaf).

A128 Tom Marshall Papers
Literary Manuscript Collection
National Library of Canada
395 Wellington Street
Ottawa, Ontario

The Tom Marshall Papers contain 16 letters from Layton to Marshall (28 Oct. 1963, 12 Oct. 1965, 18 July 1966, 20 Sept. 1966, 5 Feb. 1969, 28 July 1969, 3 Aug. 1969, 4 July 1970, n.d. (c.Nov. 1970), 7 Jan.

1974, 22 Feb. 1974, 16 Sept. 1975, 20 July 1977, 18 Aug. 1977, 11 Oct. 1977, and 10 May 1978); 1 postcard (31 July 1977); 1 letter to John Trachuk (13 Oct. 1973); a signed typescript of "Inishmore"; typescripts of "Marxist," "Rewards," "Conversion in the Hotel Regente," "Free Expression," "Epigram on Ireland," "Sunflight," and "Intimations"; a copy of Leonard Michael's review of *The Selected Poems of Irving Layton* (D196); and an invitation to the Kingston launching of *There Were No Signs*.

A129 Robin Mathews Papers
National Archives of Canada
395 Wellington Street
Ottawa, Ontario

The Robin Mathews Papers contain correspondence with Irving Layton (1962–77). The material is restricted.

A130 McClelland and Stewart Papers
The William Ready Division of
Archives and Research Collections
Mills Memorial Library
McMaster University
Hamilton, Ontario

The McClelland and Stewart Papers contain 100 letters and 19 postcards from Layton to Jack McClelland; letters from McClelland to Layton; and assorted other communications and material by McClelland and Stewart relevant to the publication of Layton's books (1959–74).

A131 *Northern Journey* Collection
York University Archives
Scott Library
York University
North York, Ontario

The records of *Northern Journey* contain 4 letters from Layton to Fraser Sutherland (1976); 1 letter from Layton to A.J.M. Smith (23 May 1976); and 2 versions of "A Poem to Calm the Nervous Fears of the Very Reverend A.J.M. Smith."

A132 Alden Nowlan Papers
Department of Rare Books and Special Collections
University of Calgary Library
University of Calgary
Calgary, Alberta

The Alden Nowlan Papers contain 9 letters from Layton to Nowlan (22 Oct. 1966–10 Oct. 1981); and a copy of a letter from John Nowlan (Alden's son) to Layton (7 Oct. 1970), with original containing a brief reply by Layton.

A133 Charles Olson Papers
Special Collections Department
Homer Babbidge Library
University of Connecticut
Storrs, Connecticut

The Charles Olson Papers contain 1 letter from Layton to Robert Creeley (n.d.); 6 letters from Layton to Charles Olson (3 Jan. 1953–15 April 1955); 1 postcard (n.d.); and typescripts of the poems "Lacquered Westmount Doll" and "First Snow at Lake Achigan."

A134 Michael Ondaatje Papers
Literary Manuscript Collection
National Library of Canada
395 Wellington Street
Ottawa, Ontario

The Michael Ondaatje Papers contain 1 note from Layton to Ondaatje (12 Jan. 1978).

A135 Desmond Pacey Papers
Harriet Irving Library
University of New Brunswick
Fredericton, New Brunswick

The Desmond Pacey Papers contain 402 letters from Layton to Pacey (1955–74) comprising 1,050 leaves. The collection also includes 8 letters from Pacey to Layton, 9 letters by Layton to the editor of various newspapers, and letters by Layton to R.G. Everson, The Council for Jewish Education, and Louis Dudek. There are letters to Layton from C.A. Chabot, K. Olive, and several admirers, and correspondence between Pacey and Laurie Lerew, George Edelstein, Aviva Layton, and Ann Saddlemyer. In addition to letters, the collection includes 91 poems by Layton, mostly in typescript, 35 articles and interviews on Layton, 9 reviews of Layton's work, an article by Layton titled "On Evil as the Necessary Extension of Being," and various other miscellaneous items. The material is catalogued.

A136 *Poetry Canada Review* Papers
Literary Manuscript Collection
National Library of Canada
395 Wellington Street
Ottawa, Ontario

The *Poetry Canada Review* Papers contain 1 letter from Layton to Clifton Whiten and Ted Plantos (3 June 1979); 7 letters from Layton to Clifton Whiten (14 Oct. 1979, 5 Nov. 1979, 7 Dec. 1980, 3 Nov. 1982, 2 April 1983, 10 Sept. 1983, and n.d.); 1 postcard from Layton to Whiten (23 Dec. 1983); and typescripts of "Kakania" and "The Conquest of Death."

A137 *Prism International* Papers
Special Collections Division

University of British Columbia Library
Vancouver, British Columbia

Adams, Michele, and Christel Josephy. "An Inventory of the Records 1958–1975 of *Prism International*." Contains manuscripts of the following Layton poems: "At the Iglesia de Sacromonte," "Like a Mother Demented," and "The Next Time Does It."

A138   A.W. Purdy Collection
University of Saskatchewan Library
University of Saskatchewan
Saskatoon, Saskatchewan

The A.W. Purdy Collection includes 16 letters and 5 postcards from Layton to Purdy (8 June 1955–9 Dec. 1964).

A139   Al Purdy Papers
Kathleen Ryan Hall
Queen's University Archives
Queen's University
Kingston, Ontario

The Al Purdy Papers contain 2 letters and 1 postcard from Layton to Purdy (4 Jan. 1967–30 Sept. 1967).

A140   Mordecai Richler Papers
Department of Rare Books and Collections
University of Calgary Library
University of Calgary
Calgary, Alberta

The Mordecai Richler Papers contain a copy of a letter from Layton to the editor of *Holiday* [Philadelphia] (28 March 1964) (B861).

A141   Joe Rosenblatt Papers
National Archives of Canada

395 Wellington Street
Ottawa, Ontario

The Joe Rosenblatt Papers contain typescript copies of "At the Barcelona Zoo" and "Warrior Poet," submitted to *Jewish Di-al-ŏg*, and 1 letter from Layton to Rosenblatt (26 Feb. 1974).

A142   Malcolm Ross Papers
Department of Rare Books and Special Collections
University of Calgary Library
University of Calgary
Calgary, Alberta

The Malcolm Ross Papers contain letters from Layton to Ross (27 March 1960–10 Dec. 1962); a postcard (9 June 1965); and copies of the poems "Androgyne," "Collaboration," and "For Mao Tse-Tung: A Meditation on Flies and Kings."

A143   F.R. Scott Papers
National Archives of Canada
395 Wellington Street
Ottawa, Ontario

The F.R. Scott Papers contain 5 letters from Layton to Scott (13 Nov. 1956–28 June 1974); 1 letter from Layton to Floris McLaren (c.1951); 9 postcards and 2 other cards to Scott (1955–5 June 1973); numerous clippings and other material related to Layton, including book reviews of his own work and typescripts and holographs of several poems.

A144   Reuben Slonim Papers
National Archives of Canada
395 Wellington Street
Ottawa, Ontario

The Reuben Slonim Papers contain 2 printed copies of "The Cost and Consequences of a Two-Year Marriage to an Enchanting Jewish Princess" and 1 signed typescript of "Idds." They include copies of letters to Layton's former wife Harriett (15 March 1983), to her father Jack Bernstein (n.d.), and an open letter to Prime Minister Trudeau (n.d.), as well as 1 letter to Slonim (21 Jan. 1982). The material is restricted.

A145 A.J.M. Smith Papers
Thomas Fisher Rare Book Library
University of Toronto
Toronto, Ontario

The A.J.M. Smith Papers contain 15 letters from Layton to Smith (2 Jan. 1943–2 Feb. 1964) and 1 to Adrian Jaffe (19 April 1963).

A146 A.J.M. Smith Papers
University Archives
Thomas J. Bata Library
Trent University
Peterborough, Ontario

The A.J.M. Smith Papers contain 1 note (n.d.) and 1 letter from Layton to A.J.M. Smith (16 March 1956).

A147 Raymond Souster Papers
Thomas Fisher Rare Book Library
University of Toronto
Toronto, Ontario

The Raymond Souster Papers include 1 letter (7 June 1961) and 1 Christmas card (Dec. 1964) from Layton to Souster, discussing Souster's collected poems and the possibility of Layton giving a reading as part of the Contact poetry reading series.

A148 Elizabeth Spencer Papers
Literary Manuscript Collection
National Library of Canada

395 Wellington Street
Ottawa, Ontario

The Elizabeth Spencer Papers contain 2 letters from Layton to Spencer (2 March 1981 and 16 March 1981). The material is restricted.

A149 Anne Wilkinson Papers
Thomas Fisher Rare Book Library
University of Toronto
Toronto, Ontario

The Anne Wilkinson Papers contain 3 letters from Layton to Wilkinson (1956–58).

A150 Jonathan Williams Papers
Poetry / Rare Books Collection
University Libraries
State University of New York at Buffalo
Buffalo, New York

The Jonathan Williams Papers contain 102 letters from Layton to Williams (17 Dec. 1953–16 March 1969); 77 postcards from Layton to Williams, most of them undated (1954–69); 2 telegrams from Layton to Williams (3 Feb. 1957 and 4 March 1957); and 1 letter from Layton to R.G. Everson (25 Feb. 1960). Also included are typescripts of several poems and other enclosures.

A151 George Woodcock Papers
Kathleen Ryan Hall
Queen's University Archives
Queen's University
Kingston, Ontario

The George Woodcock Papers contain 11 letters and 12 postcards from Layton to Woodcock (24 Oct. 1959–10 Aug. 1978).

B Contributions to Periodicals and Books (Poetry, Published Correspondence, Articles, Short Stories, Excerpts, Reprinted Anthology Contributions: A Selection, Reviews, Translations, and Play) and Audio-Visual Material

Note: When an item is reprinted in one of Layton's books or recorded on one of his recordings, this fact is noted in the entry through one of the following abbreviations:

Balls for a One-Armed Juggler . . . .   BOAJ
The Black Huntsmen . . . .   BH
The Black Huntsmen (second edition) . . .   BH2
The Blue Propeller . . . .   BP
The Blue Propeller (second edition) BP2
The Bull Calf and Other Poems . . . .   BCOP
Catacombe dei Cappucini   CC
Cerberus . . . .   Cerb.
The Cold Green Element . . . .   CGE
Collected Poems (1965) . . . .   CP
The Collected Poems of Irving Layton
    (1971) . . . .   CPIL
The Covenant . . . .   Cov.
Dance with Desire: Love Poems . . . .   DD

The Darkening Fire: Selected Poems
    1945–1968 . . . .   DF
Droppings from Heaven . . . .   DH
Engagements: The Prose of Irving
    Layton . . . .   E:PIL
Europe and Other Bad News . . . .   EOBN
An Evening with Irving Layton
    (1969) EIL69
An Evening with Irving Layton
    (1976) EIL76
An Evening with Irving Layton
    (1981) EIL81
Final Reckoning: Poems 1982–1986 . . . . . .   FR
For My Brother Jesus . . . .   MBJ
For My Neighbours in Hell . . . .   MNH
Fortunate Exile . . . .   FE
Il freddo verde elemento . . . .   fve
The Gucci Bag (limited edition) . . . . .   GB (l.ed)
The Gucci Bag . . . .   GB
The Gucci Bag (second edition) GB2
Handouts from the Mountain . . . .   HM
Here and Now . . . .   HN
The Improved Binoculars . . . .   IB
The Improved Binoculars (second edition) . .   IB2
In the Midst of My Fever . . . .   MMF
In un'età di ghiaccio . . . .   eg
Irving Layton (Montreal) . . . . . .   IL (Montreal)
Irving Layton (Toronto) . . . .   IL (Toronto)
Irving Layton (TV Ontario) . . . .   IL (TV)
Irving Layton at Le Hibou . . . .   ILH
Irving Layton Reads His Poetry . . . .   ILRH
The Laughing Rooster . . . .   LR
A Laughter in the Mind . . . .   LM
A Laughter in the Mind (second edition) . .   LM2
Layton . . . .   Layton
The Long Pea-Shooter . . . .   LPS
Love Poems (Italian Portfolio) . . . .   LP
The Love Poems of Irving Layton . . . . . .   LPIL

The Love Poems of Irving Layton
  (limited edition) . . . . *LPIL* (l.ed)
The Love Poems of Irving Layton:
  With Reverence & Delight . . . . . . *LPIL:RD*
Love the Conqueror Worm . . . . *LCW*
Love Where the Nights Are Long: An
  Anthology of Canadian Love Poems
  (limited edition) . . . . *LWNA* (l.ed)
Lovers and Lesser Men . . . . *LLM*
Music on a Kazoo . . . . *MK*
My Brother Jesus (cassette) . . . . *MBJ* (cas.)
Nail Polish . . . . *NP*
Now Is the Place . . . . *NIP*
On the Assassination of President
  Kennedy . . . . *OAPK*
Periods of the Moon . . . . *PM*
Poemas de amor . . . . *Pa*
The Poems of Irving Layton . . . . *PIL*
Poems of Irving Layton (1965) *PIL65*
Le poesie d'amore di Irving Layton . . . . . *paIL*
A Poetry Reading by Irving Layton . . . . . *PRIL*
The Pole-Vaulter . . . . *PV*
A Red Carpet for the Sun . . . . *RCS*
A Red Carpet for the Sun (cassette) . . *RCS* (cas.)
Reflections in an Old Ontario Cemetery *ROOC*
Selected Poems (1969) *SP69*
The Selected Poems of Irving Layton
  (Introd. Hugh Kenner) . . . . *SPIL*
[*The Selected Poems of Irving Layton*]
  (Korean ed.) . . . . *SPIL(K)*
Seventy-Five Greek Poems 1951–1974 . . . *SFGP*
Shadows on the Ground . . . . *SG*
The Shattered Plinths . . . . *SP*
A Spider Danced a Cosy Jig . . . . *SDCJ*
The Swinging Flesh . . . . *SF*
Taking Sides: The Collected Social and
  Political Writings . . . . *TS:CS*
A Tall Man Executes a Jig . . . . *TMEJ*

The Tamed Puma . . . . *TP*
There Were No Signs . . . . *TWNS*
The Tightrope Dancer . . . . *TD*
Tutto sommato: poesie 1945–1989 . . . . *Ts:p*
The Uncollected Poems of Irving Layton
  1936–59 . . . . *UPIL*
[*University of Victoria Pamphlet*] . . . . *UVP*
An Unlikely Affair . . . . *UA*
The Unwavering Eye: Selected Poems
  1969–1975 . . . . *UE*
Waiting for the Messiah: A Memoir . . . . . . *WM*
The Well-Wrought Urn . . . . *WWU*
Where Burning Sappho Loved /
  ΕΔΩ ΑΓΑΠΗΣΕ ΦΛΕΓΟΜΕΝΗ Η
  ΣΑΠΦΩ . . . . *WBSL*
The Whole Bloody Bird (Obs, Aphs, &
  Pomes) . . . . *WBB*
Wild Gooseberries: The Selected Letters
  of Irving Layton . . . . *WG*
A Wild Peculiar Joy: Selected Poems
  1945–82 . . . . *WPJ*
A Wild Peculiar Joy: Selected Poems
  1945–82 (second edition) *WPJ2*
A Wild Peculiar Joy: Selected Poems
  1945–82 (cassette) . . . . *WPJ* (cas.)

Poetry

B1   "Vigil." *The McGilliad*, April 1931, p. 108. Rpt. (revised) in *McGill Daily*, 26 Jan. 1938, p. 4. Rpt. (revised) in *First Statement*, 1, No. 12 [1943], 10. *LR* (revised); *CP*; *CPIL*.
     Originally signed: Irvine Layton. See *Layton*.

B2   "Masquerade." *Macdonald College Failt-Ye Times* [Montreal], 21 Feb. 1936, p. 2. *UPIL* (revised).
     Originally signed: Irving Lazarovitch.

B3 "On the Proposed Air Pact Outlawing the Bombing of Cities." *McGill Daily*, 3 Nov. 1937, p. 4. *UPIL*. Originally signed: Irvine Layton.

B4 "Portrait of a Pseudo-Socialist." *McGill Daily*, 3 Nov. 1937, p. 4. *UPIL* (revised). Originally signed: Irvine Layton.

B5 "Thaumaturge." *McGill Daily*, 18 Nov. 1937, p. 2. *UPIL*. Originally signed: Irvine Layton.

B6 "To –." *McGill Daily*, 19 Nov. 1937, p. 4. *UPIL*. Originally signed: Irvine Layton.

B7 "Voltaire Jezebel." *McGill Daily*, 26 Nov. 1937, p. 4. *UPIL*. Originally signed: Irvine Layton.

B8 "To L.B." *McGill Daily*, 2 Dec. 1937, p. 2. *UPIL*. Originally signed: Irvine Layton.

B9 "Days of Wrath." *McGill Daily*, 8 Dec. 1937, p. 4. *UPIL*. Originally signed: Irvine Layton.

B10 "De Mortuis." *McGill Daily*, 2 Feb. 1938, p. 4. *LR* (revised — "Release [I shall rejoice]"); *CPIL*. Originally signed: Irvine Layton.

B11 "Ah Rats!!! A Political Extravaganza." *McGill Daily*, 5 Oct. 1938, p. 2. *LCW* [revised — "Ah Rats! (A Political Extravaganza of the 30's)"]; *UPIL* [revised — "Ah Rats! (A Political Extravaganza of the 30s)"].

B12 "A Jewish Rabbi." *McGill Daily*, 8 Nov. 1938, p. 2. Rpt. in *First Statement*, 1, No. 9 [1943], 2. *HN* (revised — "My Father"); *FE*. Originally signed: Irvine Layton.

B13 "Meditations of a Liberal." *McGill Daily*, 8 Nov. 1938, p. 2. *LR* ("Requiem for an Age"); *CPIL*. Originally signed: Irvine Layton.

B14 "Lyrics [Come, my love, since life is short]." *McGill Daily*, 15 Nov. 1938, p. 2. *UPIL* (revised). Originally signed: Irvine Layton.

B15 "Medley for Our Times." *McGill Daily*, 28 Nov. 1938, p. 2. *UPIL* (revised). Originally signed: Irvine Layton.

B16 "Old Halifax Cemetery." *McGill Daily*, 25 Oct. 1939, p. 2. *UPIL*. Originally signed: Irving Peter Layton.

B17 "New Horizons." *McGill Daily*, 1 Nov. 1940, p. 2.

B18 "Metastasis." *McGill Daily*, 28 Nov. 1940, p. 2.

B19 "Accept This Day." *McGill Daily*, 13 Dec. 1940, p. 2. Rpt. in *First Statement*, 1, No. 9 [1943], 1. *UPIL*. Originally signed: I.L.

B20 "To a Fallen Airman." *McGill Daily*, 13 Dec. 1940, p. 2. Originally signed: I.L.

B21 "Debacle." *The Canadian Forum*, April 1941, p. 19. *UPIL*.

B22 "Epitaph for a Christian." *The Canadian Forum*, Sept. 1941, p. 176. *HN* (revised); *UPIL* (revised); *NIP* (revised).

B23 "Epitaph for a Communist." *The Canadian Forum*, Sept. 1941, p. 176. *HN*; *BH2* (revised — "Epitaphs: Communist"); *UPIL* ("Epitaph for a Communist").

B24 "Beneath the Bridge." *Saturday Night*, 18 Oct. 1941, p. 21. *UPIL*.

B25 "House to Let." *McGill Daily*, 27 Oct. 1941, p. 2. Rpt. in *First Statement*, 1, No. 9 [1943], 1. *UPIL*.

B26 "Providence." *Saturday Night*, 1 Nov. 1941, p. 29. Rpt. in *First Statement*, 1, No. 12 [1943], 9–10. Rpt. in *Voices* [New York], No. 113 (Spring 1943), p. 40. *HN*; *LM2* (revised); *RCS*; *CP*; *CPIL*.
　　See *RCS* (cas.).

B27 "Denouement." *McGill Daily*, 11 Nov. 1941, p. 2.

B28 "Epitaph for a Philosopher." *McGill Daily*, 11 Nov. 1941, p. 2. Rpt. ("Three Epitaphs: For a Philosopher") in *The Canadian Forum*, May 1942, p. 55. *HN* ("Epitaph for a Philosopher"); *BH2* ("Epitaphs: Philosopher"); *RCS*; *CP*; *CPIL*.
　　See *RCS* (cas.).

B29 "Epitaph for a Wit." *McGill Daily*, 11 Nov. 1941, p. 2. Rpt. ("Three Epitaphs: For a Wit") in *The Canadian Forum*, May 1942, p. 55. *HN* ("Epitaph for a Wit"); *BH2* ("Epitaphs: Wit"); *RCS*; *CP*; *CPIL*.
　　See *RCS* (cas.).

B30 "My Love, a Miracle." *McGill Daily*, 12 Nov. 1941, p. 2. Rpt. in *Saturday Night*, 19 Sept. 1942, p. 9. *BH* (revised, expanded — "Aerolites [Up there, up there on high]"); *BH2*; *RCS* (excerpt — "A Spider Danced a Cosy Jig"); *CP*; *CPIL*; *SDCJ*.
　　See *PIL65*, *IL* (Toronto), *RCS* (cas.), and B1220.

B31 "Restaurant de Luxe." *McGill Daily*, 21 Jan. 1942, p. 2. Rpt. in *The Canadian Forum*, July 1942, pp. 120–21. *HN* (revised — "Restaurant De Luxe"); *UPIL* (revised).

B32 "Were I an Artificer." *McGill Daily*, 22 Jan. 1942, p. 2.

B33 "Boarding House." *McGill Daily*, 28 Jan. 1942, p. 2. Rpt. in *The Canadian Forum*, May 1942, p. 49. *HN*; *BH2* (revised — "Community"); *CP*; *CPIL*.
　　Originally signed: I.L.

B34 "Mars." *McGill Daily*, 28 Jan. 1942, p. 2.

B35 "Inebriate." *McGill Daily*, 13 Feb. 1942, p. 2. *UPIL*.

B36 "The Modern Poet [Since Auden set the fashion]." *McGill Daily*, 20 Feb. 1942, p. 2. Rpt. in *First Statement*, 2 April 1943, p. 4. *HN*; *BH* (revised — [Since Eliot set the fashion]); *BH2*; *CP*; *CPIL*; *NIP*.

B37 "To R.E." *McGill Daily*, 27 Feb. 1942, p. 2. *NP* (revised — "Rochel"); *UPIL* (revised — "To R.E.").

B38 "Three Epitaphs: For a Common Grave." *The Canadian Forum*, May 1942, p. 55. *UPIL* (expanded — "Epitaph for a Common Grave").

B39 "Forecast." *McGill Daily*, 11 Nov. 1942, p. 2. Rpt. in *First Statement*, Aug. 1943, p. 16. *UPIL*.
　　Originally signed: Lieut. Irving Layton, R.C.A.

B40 "Obstacle Course." *McGill Daily*, 11 Nov. 1942, p. 2. Rpt. in *First Statement*, 1, No. 12 [1943], 10. *CPIL* ("Lester"); *UPIL* ("Obstacle Course").

B41 "Day." *First Statement*, 1, No. 12 [1943], 9. *UPIL*.

B42 "Newsboy." *Direction* [Scoudouc, N.B.], No. 2 [1943], p. 9. Rpt. in *Poetry* [Chicago], 63 (1944), 256–57. *HN*; *BH*; *BH2*; *IB*; *IB2*; *RCS*; *CP*; *SP69*; *CPIL*; *DF*; *NIP*.
　　See *RCS* (cas.).

B43 "Petawawa." *Direction* [Scoudouc, N.B.], No. 3 [1943], p. 5. Rpt. in *The Canadian Forum*, Jan. 1944, p. 234. Rpt. (revised) in *First Statement*, Feb. 1944, p. 8. *HN*; *BH2* ("Training Camp"); *UPIL*; *NIP* ("Petawawa").
    The Canadian Forum publication is signed: Lt. Irving Layton.

B44 "Poem [A little child]." *Direction* [Scoudouc, N.B.], No. 3 [1943], p. 5. *UPIL*.

B45 "Lady Remington." *The Canadian Forum*, Jan. 1943, p. 303. Rpt. in *Voices* [New York], No. 113 (Spring 1943), p. 40. *HN* (revised); *BH2* ("Lady Enfield"); *IB2*; *RCS*; *CP*; *CPIL*; *NIP* ("Lady Remington").
    Originally signed: Lieutenant Irving Layton. See *PIL65* ("Lady Enfield"), *IL* (Toronto), *RCS* (cas.), and *B1234*.

B46 "Mortuary." *The Canadian Forum*, Feb. 1943, p. 333. *HN*; *RCS*; *CP*; *SP69*; *CPIL*; *DF*; *SPIL*(K).
    Originally signed: Lieut. Irving Layton. See *RCS* (cas.).

B47 "Winter Scene." *The Canadian Forum*, Feb. 1943, p. 333. *HN* (revised); *UPIL*; *NIP*.
    Originally signed: Lieut. Irving Layton.

B48 "Say It Again, Brother." *First Statement*, 14 May 1943, pp. 7–8. *UPIL*.

B49 "Gonorrhea Racetrack." *First Statement*, June 1943, p. 2. *BH* (revised); *BH2*; *UPIL* (revised).

B50 "Upper Water Street." *First Statement*, June 1943, pp. 2–3. *HN*; *BH* (revised — "Fog"); *BH2*; *UPIL*.

B51 "Church Parade." *The Canadian Forum*, Aug. 1943, p. 115. *HN* (revised); *BH* (revised); *BH2*; *UPIL*; *NIP* (revised).
    Originally signed: Lt. Irving Layton.

B52 "1943." *First Statement*, Sept. 1943, p. 21. *BH* (revised — "Crisis"); *BH2*; *UPIL* (" — 1943 — ").

B53 "Gents' Furnishings." *First Statement*, Oct. 1943, pp. 16–17. *HN* (revised); *BH* (revised — "Gents Furnishings"); *BH2*; *CPIL* (revised); *NIP* (revised — "Gents' Furnishings").

B54 "Drill Shed." *Poetry* [Chicago], 63 (Feb. 1944), 256. *HN* (revised); *BH2* (revised); *RCS*; *CP*; *CPIL*; *NIP*.
    See *RCS* (cas.).

B55 "De Bullion Street." *First Statement*, March 1944, p. 3. *HN*; *BH*; *BH2*; *IB*; *IB2*; *RCS*; *CP*; *SP69*; *CPIL*; *DF*; *TWNS*; *eg* ("De Bullion Street / Via de Bullion"); *Ts:p*; *NIP* ("De Bullion Street").
    See *IL* (Montreal), *ILRH*, *RCS* (cas.), and *B1233*.

B56 "We Have Taken the Night." *First Statement*, April 1944, p. 2. *HN* (revised); *BH* (revised — "Nightfall"); *BH2*; *CPIL*; *LPIL* (l.ed); *Pa* ("Anochecer"); *LPIL* ("Nightfall"); *paIL* ("Nightfall / Imbrunire"); *LPIL:RD* ("Nightfall").

B57 "Spinoza." *The Canadian Forum*, July 1944, p. 90. *HN*; *UPIL*.

B58 "April." *First Statement*, 2, No. 8 (Aug. 1944), 16–17. *HN* (revised — "Returning with an Annual Passion"); *BH* (revised — "Compliments of the Season"); *BH2*; *IB*; *IB2*; *RCS* (revised); *CP*; *SP69*; *CPIL*; *DF*; *NIP* (revised).
    See *RCS* (cas.).

B59 "Jewish Main Street." *First Statement*, 2, No. 8 (Aug. 1944), 8–9. *HN* (revised); *BH2*; *RCS*; *CP*; *CPIL*; *FE*; *NIP*.
See *RCS* (cas.) and B1214.

B60 "The Swimmer." *First Statement*, 2, No. 10 (Dec.–Jan. 1944–45), 8. Rpt. in *Poetry* [Chicago], 66 (June 1945), 123. *HN*; *BH*; *BH2*; *IB*; *IB2*; *RCS*; *CP*; *SP69*; *CPIL*; *DF*; *PIL*; *SPIL*; *WPJ*; *WPJ2*; *NIP*.
See *ILH*; *ILRH*, *EIL69*, *RCS* (cas.), *PRIL*, *WPJ* (cas.), and B1221.

B61 "Words without Music." *First Statement*, 2, No. 10 (Dec.–Jan. 1944–45), 22–23. *HN*; *BH* (revised — "Weekend Special"); *BH2*; *IB* (revised — "Excursion"); *IB2*; *RCS*; *CP*; *SP69* ("Excursion to Ottawa"); *CPIL* (revised — "Excursion"); *DF*; *NIP* (revised — "Excursion to Ottawa").
See *RCS* (cas.) ("Excursion").

B62 "Waterfront." *The Canadian Forum*, Feb. 1945, p. 258. Rpt. in *The Pottersfield Portfolio* [Porters Lake, N.S.], 3 (1981–82), 26. *HN*; *UPIL*.

B63 "Proof Reader." *The Canadian Forum*, March 1945, p. 286. *HN* (revised); *BH* (revised); *BH2*; *SP69* (revised); *CPIL*; *DF*; *NIP*.

B64 "Young Thief." *The Canadian Forum*, April 1945, p. 24. *HN* ("Stolen Watch"); *BH* (revised); *BH2*; *CP*; *CPIL*; *NIP* (revised).

B65 "English for Immigrants." *Northern Review*, 1, No. 1 (Dec.–Jan. 1945–46), 22. *BH2* (revised); *CPIL*; *NIP*.

B66 "A Poor Poet Is Grateful for a Sudden Thaw." *Northern Review*, 1, No. 5 (Feb.–March 1947), 25. *BH2* ("Sudden Thaw"); *CPIL*; *NIP* ("A Poor Poet Is Grateful for a Sudden Thaw").

B67 "The Yard." *Northern Review*, 1, No. 5 (Feb.–March 1947), 24. *BH* (revised); *BH2*; *CP* (revised); *SP69*; *CPIL*; *DF*; *NIP* (revised).
See *EIL69*.

B68 "Eagle." *Northern Review*, 1, No. 6 (Aug.–Sept. 1947), 15. *BH* ("Lenin"); *BH2*; *UPIL*; *NIP* ("The Eagle").

B69 "Karl Marx." *Northern Review*, 1, No. 6 (Aug.–Sept. 1947), 14. *CP* (revised); *SP69*; *CPIL*; *DF*; *NIP*.

B70 "North Country." *Contemporary Verse*, No. 24 (Spring 1948), p. 6. *BH2*; *NIP*.

B71 "Queer Poem." *Contemporary Verse*, No. 24 (Spring 1948), p. 7. *UPIL*.

B72 "Schoolteacher in Late November." *Contemporary Verse*, No. 24 (Spring 1948), p. 7. *BH* (revised); *BH2*; *CP*; *CPIL*; *NIP* (revised).

B73 "One, and Two." *Northern Review*, 2, No. 2 (July–Aug. 1948), 25–26.

B74 "Music for Two Pianos." *Northern Review*, 2, No. 3 (Sept.–Oct. 1948), 23. *BH* ("To Be Played on a Broken Virginal"); *BH2*; *UPIL*.

B75 "Woman in the Square." *Northern Review*, 2, No. 3 (Sept.–Oct. 1948), 24. *BH* (revised); *BH2*; *CP* (revised); *CPIL*.

B76 "Gothic Landscape." *Commentary* [New York], July 1950, p. 41. *BH*; *BH2*; *RCS*; *CP*; *SP69*; *CPIL*; *DF*; *FE*.
See *PIL65*, *IL* (Montreal), *ILRH*, *IL* (Toronto), and *RCS* (cas.).

B77 "Poet Killed in Action." *The Canadian Forum*, May 1951, p. 43. *BH*; *BH2*; *RCS* ("Epitaphs: Poet Killed in Action"); *CP*; *CPIL*.
See *RCS* (cas.).

B78 "Haruspex." *Commentary* [New York], July 1951, p. 75. *BH* ("Auspex"); *BH2*; *IB* (revised — "Haruspex"); *IB2*; *RCS*; *CP*; *CPIL*.
See *RCS* (cas.).

B79 "The Black Huntsmen." *Contact*, 1, No. 1 (Jan. 1952), 8. *BH*; *BH2*; *RCS*; *CP*; *SP69*; *CPIL*; *DF*; *WPJ*; *WPJ2*; *FE*.
See *IL* (Montreal), *ILRH*, and *RCS* (cas.).

B80 "The Drunken Poet." *Contact*, 1, No. 1 (Jan. 1952), 8.

B81 "Mont Rolland." *Contact*, 1, No. 1 (Jan. 1952), 8. Rpt. in *ellipse*, No. 11 (1972), p. 68. Rpt. trans. Jean-Jacques Granger in *ellipse*, No. 11 (1972), p. 69. *BH*; *BH2*; *IB*; *IB2*; *RCS*; *CP*; *SP69*; *CPIL*; *DF*; *WPJ*; *WPJ2*.
See *RCS* (cas.).

B82 "Songs of a Half-Crazed Nihilist." *Contact*, 1, No. 1 (Jan. 1952), 7. *BH* (revised); *BH2*; *UPIL* (revised).

B83 "The World's a Tavern." *Contact*, 1, No. 1 (Jan. 1952), 6. *BH*; *BH2*; *LCW* ("Odysseus in Limbo"); *IB*; *IB2*; *RCS*; *CP*; *SP69* ("The World's a Tavern"); *CPIL* ("Odysseus in Limbo"); *SFGP*; *DF*.
See *EIL69* ("The World's a Tavern") and *RCS* (cas.) ("Odysseus in Limbo").

B84 "January Love." *Contact*, 1, No. 1 (March 1952), 6. *Cerb.*; *UPIL*.

B85 "Mr. Butchevo Phrie." *Contact*, 1, No. 2 (March 1952), 5. *Cerb.* ("The Excessively Quiet Groves"); *UPIL*.

B86 "Portrait [Playing blind man's bluff]." *Contact*, 1, No. 2 (March 1952), 7.

B87 "Terrene." *Contact*, 1, No. 2 (March 1952), 6. Rpt. in *New Directions in Prose and Poetry* [New York], No. 14 (1953), p. 133. *Cerb.*; *RCS*; *CP*; *CPIL*.
See *RCS* (cas.).

B88 "Anacreon." *Contact*, 1, No. 3 (May–July 1952), 3. *Cerb.*; *UPIL*.

B89 "Genius, Love, and Poetry." *Contact*, 1, No. 3 (May–July 1952), 8. *Cerb.* (revised — "Genius Love and Poetry"); *CP*; *CPIL*.

B90 "To a Very Old Woman." *Contact*, 1, No. 4 (Aug.–Oct. 1952), 16. Rpt. ("To a Very Old Lady") in *New Directions in Prose and Poetry* [New York], No. 14 (1953), pp. 133–34. *Cerb.* ("To a Very Old Woman"); *IB*; *IB2*; *RCS*; *CP*; *SP69*; *CPIL*; *DF*.
See *EIL69*, *RCS* (cas.), and C665.

B91 "In Memory of Fred Smith." *Contact*, 2, No. 1 (Nov.–Jan. 1952–53), 1. *LCW*; *IB*; *IB2*; *RCS*; *CP*; *CPIL*.
See *RCS* (cas.).

B92 "Moses Talked to Jupiter." *Contact*, 2, No. 1 (Nov.–Jan. 1952–53), 2. *LCW* (revised); *CPIL*.

B93 "To the Girls of My Graduating Class." *Contact*, 2, No. 1 (Nov.–Jan. 1952–53), 1. Rpt. in *Congress Bulletin* [Canadian Jewish Congress], May 1959, p. 3. Rpt. in *Cyclic*, 1, No. 3 (1966), 6. Rpt. in *The*

Human Voice Quarterly [Miami], 2, No. 3 (Aug. 1966), [18]. Rpt. in *Story* [New York], 1, No. 1 (May 1967), 32. *LCW* ("To the Girls of My Graduation Class"); *IB* ("To the Girls of My Graduating Class"); *IB2*; *RCS*; *CP*; *SP69*; *CPIL*; *DF*; *WPJ*; *WPJ2*; *DD*.
See *ILH*, *PIL65*, *IL* (Montreal), *ILRH*, *IL* (Toronto), *Layton*, *RCS* (cas.), and B1224.

B94 "Love the Conqueror Worm." *CIV/n*, No. 1 (Jan. 1953), p. 11. *LCW*; *RCS*; *CP*; *SP69*; *CPIL*; *DF*; *WPJ*; *WPJ2*.
See *IL* (Montreal), *ILRH*, and *RCS* (cas.).

B95 "Street Funeral." *CIV/n*, No. 1 (Jan. 1953), p. 12. *LCW*; *IB*; *IB2*; *RCS*; *CP*; *CPIL*; *DF*; *WPJ*; *WPJ2*.
See *RCS* (cas.) and B1159.

B96 "The Trumpet Daffodil." *New Directions in Prose and Poetry* [New York], No. 14 (1953), p. 132. *Cerb.* ("Trumpet Daffodil"); *RCS*; *CP*; *SP69*; *CPIL*; *DF*.
See *RCS* (cas.).

B97 "Letter to Louis Dudek." *Contact*, 2, No. 2 (Feb.–April 1953), 9. *LCW*; *CPIL*.

B98 "Soleil des Noces." *Contact*, 2, No. 2 (Feb.–April 1953), 13. *LCW*; *CP*; *CPIL*.
See *IL* (Montreal) and *ILRH*.

B99 "Seven O'Clock Lecture: For Neil Compton." *CIV/n*, No. 2 (April 1953), pp. 1–2. Rpt. ("Seven O'Clock Lecture") in *ellipse*, No. 11 (1972), pp. 80–81. Rpt. trans. Joseph Bonenfant ("Le cours de sept heures") in *ellipse*, No. 11 (1972), pp. 82–83. Rpt. ("Seven O'Clock Lecture") in *The Illustrated Companion History of Sir George Williams University*. Montreal: Concordia Univ., 1977, p. 27. *MMF* ("Seven O'Clock Lecture: For Neil Compton"); *IB* ("Seven O'Clock Lecture"); *IB2*; *RCS*; *CP*; *SP69*; *CPIL*; *DF*; *WPJ*; *WPJ2*.
See *IL* (Montreal), *ILRH*, *EIL69*, and *RCS* (cas.).

B100 "Canadian Aesthete." *Contact*, 2, No. 3 (May–Aug. 1953), 4–5. *LPS* (revised — "Cyril Tishpish"); *UPIL*.

B101 "Paideia." *Contact*, 2, No. 3 (May–Aug. 1953), 3–4. *LCW* (revised); *UPIL*.

B102 "In the Midst of My Fever." *CIV/n*, No. 3 (July–Aug. 1953), pp. 9–10. Rpt. in *Artisan* [Liverpool, Eng.], No. 6 (Autumn 1954), pp. 1–2. *MMF*; *IB*; *IB2*; *RCS*; *CP*; *SP69*; *CPIL*; *DF*; *PIL*; *SPIL*; *WPJ* (revised); *WPJ2*.
See *EIL69*, *RCS* (cas.), and B1164.

B103 "Mr. Ther-Apis." *CIV/n*, No. 4 (Oct. 1953), p. 5. *MMF*; *RCS* (revised); *CP*; *CPIL*.
See *RCS* (cas.).

B104 "Composition in Late Spring." *Contact*, No. 8 (Sept.–Dec. 1953), p. 20. Rpt. in *Artisan* [Liverpool, Eng.], No. 6 (Autumn 1954), pp. 4–5. Rpt. in *ellipse*, No. 11 (1972), pp. 70–71. Rpt. trans. Marc Lebel ("Composition en fin de Printemps") in *ellipse*, No. 11 (1972), pp. 72–73. *MMF* ("Composition in Late Spring"); *IB*; *IB2*; *RCS*; *CP*; *SP69*; *CPIL*; *DF*; *WPJ*; *WPJ2*.
See *ILH*, *Layton*, *RCS* (cas.), and *WPJ* (cas.).

B105 "Bacchanal." *Origin*, Ser. 1, No. 12 (Spring 1954), pp. 200–01. *MMF*; *IB*; *IB2*; *RCS*; *CP*; *CPIL*.
See *IL* (Montreal), *ILRH*, *RCS* (cas.), and B1173.

B106 "It's All in the Manner." *Origin*, Ser. 1, No. 12 (Spring 1954), p. 200. *MMF*; *IB*; *IB2*; *RCS*; *CP*; *CPIL*.
See *ILH* and *RCS* (cas.).

B107 "The Madonna of the Magnificat: For Marian Scott." *Origin*, Ser. 1, No. 12 (Spring 1954), p. 202. Rpt. in *Artisan* [Liverpool, Eng.], No. 6 (Autumn 1954), p. 3. *MMF* ("The Madonna of the Magnificat"); *IB*; *IB2*; *RCS*; *CP*; *CPIL*.
See *RCS* (cas.).

B108 "Metzinger: Girl with a Bird." *Origin*, Ser. 1, No. 12 (Spring 1954), pp. 202–03. *MMF*; *IB* (revised); *IB2*; *RCS*; *CP*; *SP69*; *CPIL*; *DF*.
See *RCS* (cas.).

B109 "The Paraclete." *Origin*, Ser. 1, No. 12 (Spring 1954), pp. 201–02. *MMF* ("Paraclete"); *IB*; *IB2*; *RCS*; *CP*; *CPIL*; *DF*; *PIL*; *SPIL*; *eg*; *WPJ*; *WPJ2*; *Ts:p* ("Paraclete / Paracleto").
See *RCS* (cas.) ("Paraclete") and *PRIL*.

B110 "Birds at Daybreak." *Origin*, Ser. 1, No. 14 (Autumn 1954), pp. 72–73. *CGE*; *CP*; *CPIL*.

B111 "The Cold Green Element." *Origin*, Ser. 1, No. 14 (Autumn 1954), pp. 68–69. Rpt. in *The Humanities Association Review* [Kingston, Ont.], 1960, pp. 8–9. Rpt. in *ellipse*, No. 11 (1972), pp. 72, 74. Rpt. trans. Joseph Bonenfant ("La froide verdure") in *ellipse*, No. 11 (1972), pp. 73, 75. Rpt. trans. Oláh Janos and Tótfalusi István ("Hideg zőld elem") in *Gótika a vadonban: Kanadai angol nyelvű Költők, modern Könyvtár*. Ed. James Steele. Introd. Béla Köpeczi. Debrecenben: Europa Konyvkiado, 1983, pp. 116–17. Rpt. ("Il freddo verde elemento") in *Poesia canadese del Novocento*. Ed. and trans. Caterina Ricciardi. Napoli: Liguori, 1986, pp. 111, 113. *CGE* ("The Cold Green Element: For Lorne Pierce"); *IB* ("The Cold Green Element"); *IB2*; *RCS*; *CP*; *SP69*; *CPIL*; *fve* ("The Cold Green Element / Il freddo verde elemento"); *DF* ("The Cold Green Element"); *PIL*; *SPIL*; *WPJ*; *WPJ2*.

For the English contributions to the 1986 anthology, see B1126. See also *ILH*, *IL* (Montreal), *ILRH*, *Layton*, *RCS* (cas.), *WPJ* (cas.), and B1161.

B112 "The Comic Element." *Origin*, Ser. 1, No. 14 (Autumn 1954), p. 79. *CGE*; *IB*; *IB2*; *RCS*; *CP*; *CPIL*.
See *RCS* (cas.).

B113 "The Dancers." *Origin*, Ser. 1, No. 14 (Autumn 1954), p. 77. *CGE*; *IB*; *IB2*; *RCS*; *CP*; *CPIL*.
See *RCS* (cas.).

B114 "Death of a Construction Worker." *Origin*, Ser. 1, No. 14 (Autumn 1954), p. 78. Rpt. trans. Oláh Janos and Tótfalusi István ("Egy épí tő munkás halála") in *Gótika a vadonban: Kanadai angol nyelvű Költők, modern Könyvtár*. Ed. James Steele. Introd. Béla Köpeczi. Debrecenben: Europa Konyvkiado, 1983, p. 112. *CGE* (revised — "Death of a Construction Worker"); *RCS*; *CP*; *CPIL*; *DF*.
See *IL* (Montreal) and *RCS* (cas.).

B115 "Epitaph for an Ugly Servitor to Three Queens." *Origin*, Ser. 1, No. 14 (Autumn 1954), p. 84. *BP*; *BP2*; *RCS* ("Epitaphs: An Ugly Servitor to Three Queens"); *CP*; *CPIL*.
See *RCS* (cas.).

B116 "For Louise, Age 17." *Origin*, Ser. 1, No. 14 (Autumn 1954), pp. 73–74. *CGE*; *IB*; *IB2*; *RCS*; *CP*; *CPIL*; *DF*; *Pa* ("A Luisa, de 17 años"); *LPIL* ("For Louise, Age 17"); *WPJ*; *WPJ2*; *LPIL:RD*; *DD*.
See *IL* (Montreal), *IL* (Toronto), *Layton*, *RCS* (cas.), *WPJ* (cas.), and B1175.

B117 "Golfers." *Origin*, Ser. 1, No. 14 (Autumn 1954), p. 76. Rpt. ("Golfistaa") in *Antología de la poesia anglocanadiense contemporánea.* Ed. and trans. Bernd Dietz. Barcelona: Los libros de la frontera, 1985, p. 69. *BP* ("Golfers"); *BP2*; *IB*; *IB2*; *RCS*; *CP*; *CPIL*; *DF*; *PIL*; *SPIL*; *WPJ*; *WPJ2*.

For the English contributions to the 1985 anthology, see B1123. See also *RCS* (cas.), *WPJ* (cas.), and B1207.

B118 "Henry Crockett, M.P." *Origin*, Ser. 1, No. 14 (Autumn 1954), p. 79. *LPS*; *UPIL*.

B119 "Impotence." *Origin*, Ser. 1, No. 14 (Autumn 1954), p. 83. *LPS*; *UPIL*.

B120 "Keewaydin Poetry Festival." *Origin*, Ser. 1, No. 14 (Autumn 1954), pp. 69–70. *CGE*; *RCS* (revised); *CP*; *CPIL*; *DF*; *WPJ*; *WPJ2*.
See *RCS* (cas.).

B121 "La Minerve." *Origin*, Ser. 1, No. 14 (Autumn 1954), pp. 74–75. *CGE*; *IB*; *IB2*; *RCS*; *CP*; *CPIL*; *DF*; *LPIL* (l.ed); *Pa*; *LPIL*; *WPJ*; *WPJ2*; *LPIL:RD*; *DD*.
See *RCS* (cas.) and *WPJ* (cas.).

B122 "O.B.E." *Origin*, Ser. 1, No. 14 (Autumn 1954), p. 84. *LPS*; *RCS* ("Imperial"); *CP* ("O.B.E."); *CPIL*.
See *ILH* ("Imperial") and *RCS* (cas.).

B123 "Orpheus." *Origin*, Ser. 1, No. 14 (Autumn 1954), p. 82. *CGE*; *IB*; *IB2*; *RCS*; *CP*; *CPIL*; *SFGP*; *DF*; *WBSL* ("Orpheus / Ὀρφεας"); *DD* ("Orpheus").
See *IL* (Montreal), *RCS* (cas.), and *PRIL*.

B124 "The Poet Entertains Several Ladies." *Origin*, Ser. 1, No. 14 (Autumn 1954), pp. 80–81. *CGE*; *IB*; *IB2*; *RCS*; *CP*; *CPIL*; *DF*.
See *RCS* (cas.).

B125 "The Poetic Process (For G.W.)." *Origin*, Ser. 1, No. 14 (Autumn 1954), pp. 71–72. *CGE* ("The Poetic Process"); *IB*; *IB2*; *RCS*; *CP*; *CPIL*; *DF*; *WPJ*; *WPJ2*.
See *RCS* (cas.).

B126 "Summer Idyll." *Origin*, Ser. 1, No. 14 (Autumn 1954), p. 67. *CGE* (revised — "Summer Idyll: For William Goodwin"); *IB* ("Summer Idyll"); *IB2*; *RCS*; *CP*; *CPIL*.
See *IL* (Montreal), *RCS* (cas.), and B1177.

B127 "T.S. Eliot." *Origin*, Ser. 1, No. 14 (Autumn 1954), p. 83. Rpt. trans. Ion Caraion in *Romania Literara* [Bucharest], 23 April 1970, p. 22. *LPS* (revised); *RCS*; *CP*; *CPIL*; *fve*.
See *RCS* (cas.).

B128 "When It Came to Santayana's Turn." *Origin*, Ser. 1, No. 14 (Autumn 1954), p. 81. *CGE*; *IB*; *IB2*; *RCS*; *CP*; *CPIL*; *DF*.
See *ILH* and *RCS* (cas.).

B129 "The Ants." *Contact*, No. 9 (Jan.–April 1954), p. 21. *MMF*; *IB*; *IB2*; *RCS*; *CP*; *CPIL*; *DF*.
See *RCS* (cas.).

B130 "End of the Affair [Composedly she rests]." *Contact*, No. 10 (March 1954), p. 5.

B131 "First Snow: Lake Achigan." *Black Mountain Review* [Black Mountain, N.C.], No. 1 (Spring 1954), p. 33. Rpt. in *Poetry Pilot* [New York], Aug. 1961, p. 8. *MMF*; *IB*; *IB2*; *RCS*; *CP*; *CPIL*; *DF*.
See *RCS* (cas.) and B1162.

B132 "Lacquered Westmount Doll." *Black Mountain Review* [Black Mountain, N.C.], No. 1 (Spring 1954), p. 19. *MMF*; *IB* ("Westmount Doll"); *IB2*; *RCS*; *CP*; *CPIL*.
See *RCS* (cas.).

B133 "Me, the P.M., and the Stars." *civ/n*, No. 5 (March 1954), pp. 1–2. *CGE* (revised); *IB2*; *RCS*; *CP*; *CPIL*. See *ILH*, *PIL65*, *IL* (Toronto), and *RCS* (cas.).

B134 "Portrait of Aileen." *Contact*, No. 9 (Jan.–April 1954), p. 20. *MMF*; *IB*; *IB2*; *RCS*; *CP*; *CPIL*; *DF*; *DD*.
See *RCS* (cas.).

B135 "Sancta Simplicitas." *Contact*, No. 10 (March 1954), p. 5. *MMF* (revised); *CP*; *CPIL*; *FE*.

B136 "Motet." *Black Mountain Review* [Black Mountain, N.C.], No. 2 (Summer 1954), p. 7. *MMF*; *IB2*; *RCS*; *CP*; *CPIL*.
See *RCS* (cas.).

B137 "Portrait [Pay small attention to the chin]." *Black Mountain Review* [Black Mountain, N.C.], 1, No. 2 (Summer 1954), 38. *BP*; *BP2*; *RCS*; *CP*; *CPIL*.
See *RCS* (cas.).

B138 "Poem [I would for your sake be gentle]." *Black Mountain Review* [Black Mountain, N.C.], No. 3 (Fall 1954), p. 39. Rpt. in *The New York Times Book Review*, 18 Jan. 1959, p. 2. Rpt. ("I Would for Your Sake Be Gentle") on inside cover of menu for "Valentine's Day at the Mill, 1981." The Old Mill [restaurant], Toronto. *CGE* ("Poem [I would for your sake be gentle]"); *IB*; *IB2*; *RCS* ("I Would for Your Sake Be Gentle"); *CP*; *SP69*; *CPIL*; *DF*; *LPIL* (l.ed); *Pa* ("Por ti quisiera ser un hombre afable"); *LPIL* ("I Would for Your Sake Be Gentle"); *LPIL:RD*; *SPIL*(K); *DD*.
See *EIL69*, *Layton*, *RCS* (cas.), and B1213.

B139 "Prologue to the Long Pea-Shooter." *civ/n*, No. 6 (Sept. 1954), pp. 19–23. *LPS* (revised); *CP* (revised); *SP69*; *CPIL*; *DF*.

B140 "Vexata Quaestio." *Artisan* [Liverpool, Eng.], No. 6 (Autumn 1954), pp. 2–3. Rpt. in *ellipse*, No. 11 (1972), p. 66. Rpt. trans. Marc Lebel in *ellipse*, No. 11 (1972), p. 67. *LCW*; *IB*; *IB2*; *RCS*; *CP*; *SP69*; *CPIL*; *DF*; *WPJ*; *WPJ2*.
See *ILRH* and *RCS* (cas.).

B141 "Enemies." *Black Mountain Review* [Black Mountain, N.C.], 1, No. 4 (Winter 1954), pp. 3–4. Rpt. trans. Oláh Janos and Tótfalusi István ("Ellenségek") in *Gótika a vadonban: Kanadai angol nyelvű Költők, modern Könyvtár.* Ed. James Steele. Introd. Béla Köpeczi. Debrecenben: Europa Konyvkiado, 1983, pp. 109–11. *CGE* (revised — "Enemies"); *IB*; *IB2*; *RCS*; *CP*; *SP69*; *CPIL*; *DF*.
See *RCS* (cas.).

B142 "The Buffaloes." *civ/n*, No. 7 (Winter 1955), p. 19. *CGE*; *RCS*; *CP* (revised); *CPIL*.
See *RCS* (cas.).

B143 "On the Death of A. Vishinsky." *civ/n*, No. 7 (Winter 1955), p. 21. *BP*; *BP2*; *RCS*; *CP*; *CPIL*.
See *RCS* (cas.).

B144 "Saratoga Beach." *civ/n*, No. 7 (Winter 1955), p. 20. *CGE* (revised); *IB*; *IB2*; *RCS*; *CP*; *CPIL*.
See *RCS* (cas.).

B145 "Afternoon Tea." *Black Mountain Review* [Black Mountain, N.C.], 2, No. 5 (Summer 1955), 88. *BP*; *BP2*; *IB*; *IB2*; *RCS*; *CP*; *CPIL*.
See *RCS* (cas.).

B146 "The Dark Plebian Mind." *Black Mountain Review* [Black Mountain, N.C.], 2, No. 5 (Summer 1955), 89. Rpt. in *Cyclic*, 1, No. 3 (1966), 9. *CGE*; *IB2*; *RCS*; *CP*; *CPIL*.
See *RCS* (cas.).

B147 "Metaphysical." *Black Mountain Review* [Black Mountain, N.C.], 2, No. 5 (Summer 1955), 57. *CGE; IB; IB2; RCS; CP; CPIL.*
See *RCS* (cas.).

B148 "Theology." *Black Mountain Review* [Black Mountain, N.C.], 2, No. 5 (Summer 1955), 50. *CGE; RCS; CP; CPIL.*
See *RCS* (cas.).

B149 "The Bull Calf." *Origin*, Ser. 1, No. 17 (Fall 1955), pp. 23–24. *BCOP* (revised); *IB; IB2; RCS; CP; SP69; CPIL; DF; WPJ; WPJ2; SDCJ.*
See *PIL65, IL* (Montreal), *ILRH, EIL69, IL* (Toronto), *Layton, RCS* (cas.), *EIL76, PRIL, WPJ* (cas.), and B1170.

B150 "Maurer: Twin Heads." *Origin*, Ser. 1, No. 17 (Fall 1955), p. 24. *BCOP; IB; IB2; RCS; CP; CPIL; DF.*
See *RCS* (cas.).

B151 "On Seeing the Statuettes of Ezekiel and Jeremiah in the Church of Notre Dame, Montreal." *Origin*, Ser. 1, No. 17 (Fall 1955), p. 22. Rpt. in *Congress Bulletin* [Canadian Jewish Congress], May 1959, p. 3. Rpt. in *The New Montrealer*, Autumn 1983, p. 13. *BCOP* ("On Seeing the Statuettes of Ezekiel and Jeremiah in the Church of Notre Dame"); *IB* (revised); *IB2; RCS; CP; SP69* ("On Seeing the Statuettes of Ezekiel and Jeremiah in the Church of Notre-Dame"); *CPIL* ("On Seeing the Statuettes of Ezekiel and Jeremiah in the Church of Notre Dame"); *DF; PIL; SPIL; WPJ* (revised); *WPJ2; FE.*
See *ILH, Layton, RCS* (cas.), *EIL76, EIL81, PRIL, WPJ* (cas.), and B1209.

B152 "Sutherland: Portrait of A.C." *Origin*, Ser. 1, No. 17 (Fall 1955), p. 21. *BCOP; IB; IB2; RCS; CP; CPIL.*
See *RCS* (cas.).

B153 "Canadian Skiers." *The Fiddlehead*, No. 26 (Nov. 1955), pp. 10–11. *BP; BP2; RCS; CP; CPIL.*
See *RCS* (cas.).

B154 "Love's Diffidence." *The Fiddlehead*, No. 26 (Nov. 1955), p. 10. Rpt. trans. Ion Caraion ("Smerenïa dragoste̦i") in *Romania Literara* [Bucharest], 23 April 1970, p. 22. *BP* ("Love's Diffidence"); *BP2; IB; IB2; RCS; CP; CPIL; DF; Pa* ("Retraimiento del amor"); *LPIL* ("Love's Diffidence"); *paIL* ("Love's Diffidence / Incertezza d'amore"); *LPIL:RD* ("Love's Diffidence"); *DD.*
See *ILH* and *RCS* (cas.).

B155 "Abel Cain." *Origin*, Ser. 1, No. 18 (Winter–Spring 1956), p. 86. *BCOP; RCS; CP; CPIL.*
See *RCS* (cas.).

B156 "Halos at Lac Marie Louise: For Adrien Ste. Marie." *Origin*, Ser. 1, No. 18 (Winter–Spring 1956), p. 84. *BCOP* ("Halos at Lac Marie Louise"); *RCS; CP; CPIL; DF.*
See *RCS* (cas.).

B157 "Thoughts in the Water." *Origin*, Ser. 1, No. 18 (Winter–Spring 1956), p. 85. *BCOP; IB; IB2; RCS; CP; CPIL.*
See *RCS* (cas.).

B158 "The Way of the World." *Origin*, Ser. 1, No. 18 (Winter–Spring 1956), pp. 83–84. Rpt. trans. Oláh Janos and Tótfalusi István ("Így êl a világ") in *Gótika a vadonban: Kanadai angol nyelvű Költők, modern Könyvtár.* Ed. James Steele. Introd. Béla Köpeczi. Debrecenben: Europa Konyvkiado, 1983, pp. 106–07. *BCOP* ("The Way of the World"); *IB; IB2; RCS; CP; SP69; CPIL; SPIL(K).*
See *ILH* and *RCS* (cas.).

B159 "Café Politics in Spring." *The Fiddlehead*, No. 27 (Feb. 1956), p. 6. *IB* ("Cafe Politics in Spring"); *IB2*; *MK*; *RCS* ("Café Politics in Spring"); *CP*; *CPIL*.
See *RCS* (cas.).

B160 "Sacrament by the Water." *The Fiddlehead*, No. 27 (Feb. 1956), pp. 6–7. Rpt. in *Maclean's*, 20 Oct. 1962, p. 33. Rpt. in *The Brandon Sun*, 7 June 1975, p. 4. *BCOP*; *IB*; *IB2*; *RCS*; *CP*; *SP69*; *CPIL*; *DF*; *LPIL* (l.ed) *Pa* ("Sacramento en la ribera"); *LPIL* ("Sacrament by the Water"); *paIL* ("Sacrament by the Water / Sacramento presso l'acqua"); *LPIL:RD* ("Sacrament by the Water"); *DD*.
See *EIL69*, *RCS* (cas.), *PRIL*, and B1176.

B161 "Enigma." *Black Mountain Review* [Black Mountain, N.C.], No. 6 (Spring 1956), p. 112. *BP2*; *MK*; *LM2*; *UPIL*.

B162 "Letter from a Straw Man." *Black Mountain Review* [Black Mountain, N.C.], No. 6 (Spring 1956), pp. 110–11. *BCOP*; *IB2*; *RCS*; *CP*; *SP69*; *CPIL*; *LPIL* (l.ed); *Pa* ("Carta de un hombre de paja"); *LPIL* ("Letter from a Straw Man"); *LPIL:RD*; *DD*.
See *ILH*, *EIL69*, and *RCS* (cas.).

B163 "Difference." *Adventurer* [Herzliah High School, Montreal], No. 2 (May 1956), p. 12. Rpt. in *Yes*, 2, No. 2 (Summer 1957), 4. *LM2*; *UPIL*.

B164 "Holiday." *The Fiddlehead*, No. 28 (May 1956), p. 6. *IB2*; *MK*; *RCS*; *CP*; *CPIL*; *LPIL* (l.ed); *Pa* ("Día de fiesta"); *LPIL* ("Holiday"); *LPIL:RD*; *DD*.
See *RCS* (cas.).

B165 "Red Chokecherries." *The Fiddlehead*, No. 28 (May 1956), p. 6. *BCOP*; *RCS*; *CP*; *SP69*; *CPIL*; *DF*; *SPIL*(K).
See *EIL69*, *RCS* (cas.), *PRIL*, and B1219.

B166 "Boardwalk at Verdun." *The Canadian Forum*, Aug. 1956, p. 109. *BCOP*; *RCS*; *CP*; *CPIL*.
See *RCS* (cas.).

B167 "Lesbia." *The Fiddlehead*, No. 29 (Aug. 1956), pp. 2–3. *BCOP* (revised); *IB2*; *RCS*; *CP*; *CPIL*.
See *RCS* (cas.).

B168 "Woman." *Yes*, 1, No. 2 (Aug. 1956), 5. Rpt. in *The Brandon Sun*, 7 June 1975, p. 4. *IB*; *IB2*; *MK*; *RCS*; *CP*; *SP69*; *CPIL*; *DF*; *LPIL* (l.ed); *Pa* ("Mujer"); *LPIL* ("Woman"); *paIL* ("Woman / Donna"); *WPJ* ("Woman"); *WPJ2*; *LPIL:RD*; *SPIL*(K); *DD*.
See *RCS* (cas.).

B169 "Two Songs for Sweet Voices." *The Fiddlehead*, No. 30 (Nov. 1956), p. 7. *LM*; *LM2*; *CP*; *CPIL*; *LPIL* (l.ed); *Pa* ("Dos canciones para voces melifluas"); *LPIL* ("Two Songs for Sweet Voices"); *LPIL:RD*; *SPIL*(K).

B170 "This Machine Age." *University of Alberta Gateway*, 24 Nov. 1956, p. 6. *BOAJ*; *CP*; *SP69*; *CPIL*; *FE*.
See *PIL65*, *IL* (Montreal), *ILRH*, *IL* (Toronto), *Layton*, and B1223.

B171 "The Birth of Tragedy." *Encounter* [London, Eng.], Dec. 1956, p. 38. Rpt. in *The Humanities Association Review* [Kingston, Ont.], 1960, p. 8. Rpt. in *Cyclic*, 1, No. 3 (1966), 6. Rpt. in *ellipse*, No. 3 (1966), p. 76. Rpt. trans. Monique Grandmangin ("La naissance de la tragédie") in *ellipse*, No. 11 (1972), p. 77. Rpt. ("The Birth of Tragedy") in *The Malahat Review* [Univ. of Victoria], No. 24 (Oct. 1972), p. 22. Rpt. in *Waves*, 3, No. 3 (Spring 1975), 4. Rpt. in *The Brandon Sun*, 7 June 1975, p. 4. Rpt. in *The Gazette* [Univ. of Western Ontario], 26 March

1982, p. 6. Rpt. trans. Oláh Janos and Tótfalusi István ("A tragédia születése") in *Gótika a vadonban: Kanadai angol nyelvű Költők, modern Könyvtár*. Ed. James Steele. Introd. Béla Köpeczi. Debrecenben: Europa Konyvkiado, 1983, pp. 117–18. Rpt. trans. Branko Gorjup ("Rodenje Tragedije") in *Republika* [Zagreb, Yugoslavia], Nos. 10–12 (1984), p. 170. *MMF* ("The Birth of Tragedy"); *IB*; *IB2*; *RCS*; *CP*; *SP69*; *CPIL*; *fve* ("The Birth of Tragedy / La nascita della tragedia"); *DF* ("The Birth of Tragedy"); *PIL*; *SPIL*; *WPJ*; *WPJ2*.

See *ILH*, *PIL65*, *IL* (Montreal), *ILRH*, *EIL69*, *IL* (Toronto), *Layton*, *RCS* (cas.), *EIL76*, *PRIL*, *WPJ* (cas.), and B1169.

B172 "Family Portrait." *Yes*, 1, No. 3 (Dec. 1956), [9]. Rpt. in *Congress Bulletin* [Canadian Jewish Congress], May 1959, p. 3. *LM*; *LM2*; *RCS*; *CP*; *SP69*; *CPIL*; *DF*; *PIL*; *SPIL*; *WPJ*; *WPJ2*; *SPIL*(K).

See *ILH*, *PIL65*, *ILRH*, *IL* (Toronto), *RCS* (cas.), *EIL76*, *WPJ* (cas.), and B1238.

B173 "The Fertile Muck." *Queen's Quarterly*, 62 (Winter 1956), 528. Rpt. in *ellipse*, No. 11 (1972), p. 78. Rpt. trans. Marc Lebel ("La Fiente féconde") in *ellipse*, No. 11 (1972), p. 79. Rpt. trans. Oláh Janos and Tótfalusi István ("Termő mocsok") in *Gótika a vadonban: Kanadai angol nyelvű Költők, modern Könyvtár*. Ed. James Steele. Introd. Béla Köpeczi. Debrecenben: Europa Konyvkiado, 1983, pp. 105–06. Rpt. ("Fertile concime") in *Poesia canadese del Novocento*. Ed. and trans. Caterina Ricciardi. Napoli: Liguori, 1986, p. 115. *BCOP* ("The Fertile Muck"); *IB*; *IB2*; *RCS*; *CP*; *SP69*; *CPIL*; *DF*; *WPJ*; *WPJ2*; *SPIL*(K).

For the English contributions to the 1986 anthology, see B1126. See also *ILH*, *EIL69*, *Layton*, *RCS* (cas.), *EIL76*, *WPJ* (cas.), and B1171.

B174 "Anti-Romantic." *Combustion*, No. 1 (Jan. 1957), p. 8. *IB2*; *LM2*; *RCS*; *CP*; *CPIL*.
See *RCS* (cas.).

B175 "Diogenes on the Human Clod." *Combustion*, No. 1 (Jan. 1957), p. 8. *LM2* ("A Word from Diogenes"); *CP*; *CPIL*.

B176 "Doubting Thomas." *Combustion*, No. 1 (Jan. 1957), p. 8. *UPIL*.

B177 "Plain Words." *Combustion*, No. 1 (Jan. 1957), p. 8. *UPIL*.

B178 "Smells." *Combustion*, No. 1 (Jan. 1957), p. 8. *UPIL*.

B179 "Cat Dying in Autumn." *Yes*, 2, No. 1 (April 1957), 11. Rpt. in *ellipse*, No. 11 (1972), p. 86. Rpt. trans. Sylvie Theriault ("La mort de la chatte à l'automne") in *ellipse*, No. 11 (1972), p. 87. *LM* ("Cat Dying in Autumn"); *LM2*; *RCS*; *CP*; *SP69*; *CPIL*; *DF*; *WPJ*; *WPJ2*; *SPIL*(K).
See *PIL65*, *IL* (Toronto), *RCS* (cas.), *WPJ* (cas.), and B1174.

B180 "Death of Moishe Lazarovitch." *The New York Times Book Review*, 4 Aug. 1957, p. 2. *LCW* ("Death of Moishe Lazarovitch: For Anica Fellegi"); *IB* ("Death of Moishe Lazarovitch"); *IB2*; *RCS*; *CP*; *SP69*; *CPIL*; *DF*; *FE*.
See *ILH*, *EIL69*, *RCS* (cas.), and B1154.

B181 "If You Can't Scream." *Delta*, No. 1 (Oct. 1957), p. 11. *LM*; *LM2*; *RCS*; *CP*; *CPIL*.
See *RCS* (cas.).

B182 "Climbing." *The Canadian Forum*, Nov. 1957, p. 182. Rpt. in *The New York Times Book Review*,

19 July 1959, p. 2. *LM; LM2; RCS; CP; SP69; CPIL; DF.*
See *RCS* (cas.).

B183 "Olives for Jay MacPherson." In *Pan-ic: A Selection of Contemporary Canadian Poems.* Ed. Irving Layton. [*Pan, 4 Issues of Poetry* (New York), No. 2 (1958)], n. pag. Rpt. in *Yes*, No. 14 (1965), pp. 34–35. *LM; LM2* ("Olives for Jay Macpherson"); *CPIL.*

B184 "Parting." *The Fiddlehead*, No. 35 (Winter 1958), pp. 10–11. *LM; LM2; RCS; CP* (revised); *SP69; CPIL.*
See *RCS* (cas.).

B185 "Poetic Fame." In *Pan-ic: A Selection of Contemporary Canadian Poems.* Ed. Irving Layton. [*Pan, 4 Issues of Poetry* (New York), No. 2 (1958)], n. pag. *LM; LM2; RCS; CP; CPIL.*
See *RCS* (cas.).

B186 "Côte des Neiges Cemetery." *The Canadian Forum*, Feb. 1958, p. 253. Rpt. in *The Human Voice Quarterly* [Miami], 2, No. 3 (Aug. 1966), [15–16]. *LM; LM2; RCS; CP; SP69; CPIL; DF; WPJ; WPJ2.*
See *RCS* (cas.) and *WPJ* (cas.).

B187 "[In this cold realm]." Letter. *The Canadian Forum*, Feb. 1958, p. 255. *CPIL* (revised — "Hierophants"); *SF* (revised); *E:PIL* ("Correspondence: *The Canadian Forum*" [Feb. 1958]: "[In this cold realm]").
See B846 (Letter).

B188 "Laurentian Rhapsody." *The Canadian Forum*, Feb. 1958, pp. 252–53. *LM; LM2; RCS; CP; SP69; CPIL.*
See *RCS* (cas.).

B189 "Poem for the Next Century." *The Canadian Forum*, Feb. 1958, p. 253. *LM; LM2* ("Poem for the Year 2058"); *RCS* ("Poem for the Next Century"); *CP; CPIL.*
See *RCS* (cas.).

B190 "Sheep." *The Canadian Forum*, Feb. 1958, p. 252. *LM; LM2; RCS; CP; CPIL; DF; WPJ; WPJ2.*
See *RCS* (cas.) and B1189.

B191 "Whatever Else Poetry Is Freedom." *The Canadian Forum*, Feb. 1958, p. 252. Rpt. (revised—"Whatever Else, Poetry Is Freedom") in *The Journal of Canadian Fiction*, 1, No. 1 (Winter 1972), 68–69. *LM* (revised—"Whatever Else Poetry Is Freedom"); *RCS; CP; SP69; CPIL; DF; PIL; SPIL; eg* ("Whatever Else Poetry Is Freedom / Quant'altro la poesia è liberta"); *WPJ* ("Whatever Else Poetry Is Freedom"); *WPJ2; Ts:p* ("Whatever Else Poetry Is Freedom / Ma Soprattutto la poesia è libertá").
See *PIL65* ("Whatever Else Poetry Is Freedom"), *EIL69, IL* (Toronto), *RCS* (cas.), *WPJ* (cas.), and B1190.

B192 "Captives." *The Fiddlehead*, No. 36 (Spring 1958), pp. 24–25. *LM; LM2* ("Dance, My Little One"); *RCS; CP* (revised); *CPIL.*
See *RCS* (cas.) and B1187 ("Captives").

B193 "Cain." *Queen's Quarterly*, 65 (Summer 1958), 294–95. Rpt. ("Caino") in *Poesia canadese del Novocento.* Ed. and trans. Caterina Ricciardi. Napoli: Liguori, 1986, pp. 117, 119, 121. *LM* ("Cain"); *LM2; RCS; CP; SP69; CPIL; fve* ("Cain / Caino"); *DF* ("Cain"); *PIL; SPIL; WPJ; WPJ2; FE.*
For the English contributions to this anthology, see B1126. See also *Layton, RCS* (cas.), *PRIL*, and B1186.

B194 "Chatterers." *Delta*, No. 4 (July 1958), p. 23. *LM; LM2; RCS; CP; CPIL.*
See *RCS* (cas.).

B195 "Berry Picking." *The Tamarack Review*, No. 9 (Autumn 1958), p. 25. Rpt. in *ellipse*, No. 11 (1972), p. 84. Rpt. trans. Claudine Richetin ("Cueillette") in *ellipse*, No. 11 (1972), p. 85. Rpt. trans. Oláh Janos and Tótfalusi István ("Bogyószedeś") in *Gótika a vadonban: Kanadai angol nyelvű Költők, modern Könyvtár.* Ed. James Steele. Introd. Béla Köpeczi. Debrecenben: Europa Konyvkiado, 1983, pp. 107–08. *LM* (revised — "Berry Picking"); *LM2*; *RCS*; *CP*; *SP69*; *CPIL*; *DF*; *PIL*; *SPIL*; *LPIL* (l.ed); *Pa* ("Arándanos y frambuesas"); *LPIL* ("Berry Picking"); *WPJ* (revised); *WPJ2*; *LPIL:RD*; *DD*.
See *Layton*, *RCS* (cas.), *PRIL*, *WPJ* (cas.), and B1185.

B196 "Individualists." *The Tamarack Review*, No. 9 (Autumn 1958), p. 24. *LM*; *LM2*; *RCS*; *CP*; *CPIL*.
See *RCS* (cas.).

B197 "Paging Mr. Superman." *The Tamarack Review*, No. 9 (Autumn 1958), pp. 26–28. *LM*; *LM2*; *RCS*; *CP*; *SP69*; *CPIL*; *fve* ("Paging Mr. Superman / Rintracciando Mr Superman"); *DF* ("Paging Mr. Superman"); *WPJ* (revised); *WPJ2*.
See *RCS* (cas.).

B198 "Divinity." *The Canadian Forum*, Nov. 1958, p. 178. *LM2*; *RCS*; *CP*; *CPIL*; *PIL*; *SPIL*; *LPIL* (l.ed); *Pa* ("Divinidad"); *LPIL* ("Divinity"); *paIL* ("Divinity / Attributi divini"); *LPIL:RD* ("Divinity").
See *RCS* (cas.).

B199 "For Mao Tse Tung: A Meditation on Flies and Kings." *The Canadian Forum*, Nov. 1958, p. 179. *LM2* ("For Mao Tse-Tung"); *RCS* ("For Mao Tse-Tung: A Meditation on Flies and Kings"); *CP*; *SP69*; *CPIL*; *DF* ("For Mao Tse-tung: A Meditation on Flies and Kings"); *PIL* ("For Mao Tse-Tung: A Meditation on Flies and Kings"); *SPIL*; *WPJ*; *WPJ2*.
See *RCS* (cas.) and B1254 ("Power and Poetry: For Mao Tse-Tung: A Meditation on Flies and Kings").

B200 "Love Is an Irrefutable Fire." *The Canadian Forum*, Nov. 1958, p. 178. *LM2*; *RCS*; *CP*; *CPIL*.
See *RCS* (cas.).

B201 "My Flesh Comfortless." *The Canadian Forum*, Nov. 1958, p. 179. *LM2*; *RCS*; *CP*; *SP69*; *CPIL*; *DF*; *WPJ*; *WPJ2*.
See *RCS* (cas.).

B202 "The Warm Afterdark." *The Canadian Forum*, Nov. 1958, p. 178. *LM2*; *RCS*; *CP*; *CPIL*.
See *RCS* (cas.).

B203 "Young Girls Dancing at Camp Lajoie." *The Canadian Forum*, Nov. 1958, p. 178. *LM2* ("Young Girls Dancing"); *RCS* ("Young Girls Dancing at Camp Lajoie"); *CP*; *CPIL*.
See *RCS* (cas.).

B204 "Because My Calling Is Such." *Queen's Quarterly*, 66 (Spring 1959), 26. Rpt. in *Congress Bulletin* [Canadian Jewish Congress], May 1959, p. 3. *CP*; *SP69*; *CPIL*; *DF*; *LPIL* (l.ed); *Pa* ("Porque tal es mi vocación"); *LPIL* ("Because My Calling Is Such"); *LPIL:RD*; *DD*; *SF*.

B205 "I Know the Dark and Hovering Moth (For William Blake)." *Queen's Quarterly*, 66 (Summer 1959), 284–85. *CP* ("I Know the Dark and Hovering Moth"); *SP69*; *CPIL*; *DF*; *LPIL* (l.ed); *Pa* ("Conozco la oscura mariposa que revuela en la noche"); *LPIL* ("I Know the Dark and Hovering Moth"); *LPIL:RD*; *SF*.

B206 "The Caged Bird." *The Canadian Forum*, Aug. 1959, p. 109. *CP*; *CPIL*; *DF*; *SF*.

B207 "Dans le Jardin." *The Canadian Forum*, Dec. 1959, p. 201. *CPJ*; *SP69*; *CPIL*; *DF*; *LPIL* (l.ed) ("Dans Le Jardin"); *Pa* ("Dans le jardin"); *LPIL* ("Dans Le Jardin"); *LPIL:RD*; *DD* ("Dans le Jardin"); *SF*.

B208 "The Day Aviva Came to Paris." *Galley Sail Review* [San Francisco], Winter 1959–60, pp. 35–37. Rpt. (revised) in *The Canadian Forum*, Feb. 1960, pp. 256–27. Rpt. in *The Human Voice Quarterly* [Miami], 2, No. 3 (Aug. 1966), [14–15]. Rpt. in *ellipse*, No. 11 (1972), pp. 90, 92, 94. Rpt. trans. Monique Grandmangin ("Le jour où Aviva vint à Paris") in *ellipse*, No. 11 (1972), pp. 91, 93, 95. *CP* ("The Day Aviva Came to Paris"); *SP69*; *CPIL*; *DF*; *LPIL* (l.ed); *Pa* ("El día en que Aviva llegó a Paris"); *LPIL* ("The Day Aviva Came to Paris"); *WPJ*; *WPJ2*; *LPIL:RD*; *DD*; *SF*.
See *PIL65* and *IL* (Toronto).

B209 "Consistency." *Moment* [New Glasgow, P.E.I.], No. 3 (1960), p. 9. *SF* (expanded — "Bitter Almonds").

B210 "Dining Out." *Moment* [New Glasgow, P.E.I.], No. 3 (1960), p. 9. *BOAJ* (revised).

B211 "In Defence of Mr. Beutel." *Moment* [New Glasgow, P.E.I.], No. 3 (1960), p. 9.

B212 "Mexico as Seen by Looie the Lip." *Moment* [New Glasgow, P.E.I.], No. 1 (1960), p. 8. *LR* (revised — "Mexico as Seen by the Reverent Dudek"); *CP*; *CPIL*.

B213 "Mr. Beutel Is Weary of Life." *Moment* [New Glasgow, P.E.I.], No. 3 (1960), p. 9.

B214 "Mr. Beutel Lays a Cornerstone." *Moment* [New Glasgow, P.E.I.], No. 3 (1960), p. 9. Rpt. in *The Canadian Forum*, Sept. 1960, p. 137. *CP*; *CPIL*; *SF*.

B215 "Mr. Kaplan's Prayer on the High Holidays." *Moment* [New Glasgow, P.E.I.], No. 3 (1960), p. 9.

B216 "Misfortunes." *Moment* [New Glasgow, P.E.I.], No. 3 (1960), p. 9.

B217 "Why Gurus Have Grey Eyebrows." *Moment* [New Glasgow, P.E.I.], No. 3 (1960), p. 8.

B218 "How I Cured Myself of Homesickness." *The Canadian Forum*, Jan. 1960, p. 227.

B219 "Trilliums after a Party (For Maxwell Cohen)." *The Canadian Forum*, Jan. 1960, p. 226. *CP* ("Trilliums after a Party"); *CPIL* ("Trilliums After a Party"); *SF* ("Trilliums after a Party").

B220 "Keine Lazarovitch 1870–1959." *The Tamarack Review*, No. 15 (Spring 1960), p. 22. *CP*; *SP69* ("Keine Lazarovitch: 1870–1959"); *CPIL* ("Keine Lazarovitch 1870–1959"); *fve*; *DF*; *PIL*; *SPIL*; *eg*; *WPJ* ("Keine Lazarovitch: 1870–1959"); *WPJ2*; *FE*; *Ts:p* ("Keine Lazarovitch"); *SF* ("Keine Lazarovitch 1870–1959").
See *PIL65*, *IL* (Montreal), *ILRH*, *IL* (Toronto), *Layton*, *EIL76*, *EIL81*, *PRIL*, *WPJ* (cas.) ("Keine Lazarovitch: 1870–1959"), and B1208 ("Keine Lazarovitch 1870–1959").

B221 "Piazza San Marco." *The Tamarack Review*, No. 15 (Spring 1960), p. 26. Rpt. trans. Ion Caraion in *Romania Literara* [Bucharest], 23 April 1970, p. 22. Rpt. ("Piazzo San Marco / Piazza S. Marco") in *Nuovo Mundo* [Toronto], Marzo 1978, p. 11. *CP* ("Piazza San Marco"); *CPIL*; *fve*; *DF*; *eg*; *Ts:p*; *SF*.

B222 "The Tragic Sense." *The Tamarack Review*, No. 15 (Spring 1960), p. 23. *CPIL*; *SF*.

B223 "Women of Rome." *The Tamarack Review*, No. 15 (Spring 1960), pp. 24-25. *CP* (revised); *SP69*; *CPIL* (revised); *DF*; *TP* (revised — "Women of Rome / Donne romane"); *TWNS* ("Women of Rome"); *eg* ("Women of Rome / Donne romane"); *Ts:p*; *SF* ("Women of Rome").
  See *ILH*.

B224 "The Wooden Spoon." *The Tamarack Review*, No. 15 (Spring 1960), pp. 27-28. Rpt. (revised) in *The Human Voice Quarterly* [Miami], 2, No. 3 (Aug. 1966), [16-17]. *CP*; *CPIL*; *SF*.

B225 "Reconciliation." *Liberté*, 60, No. 2 (mars–avril 1960), 92. Rpt. trans. Georges Cartier in *Liberté*, 60, No. 2 (mars–avril 1960), 93. *LCW*; *IB*; *IB2*; *RCS*; *CP*; *CPIL*.
  See *RCS* (cas.).

B226 "In Praise of Benefactors." *The Canadian Forum*, June 1960, p. 60. *CPIL*; *SF*.

B227 "Craps: Sagebrush Classic." *The Canadian Forum*, Aug. 1960, p. 118. *CP* ("Sagebrush Classic"); *SP69*; *CPIL*; *SF*.

B228 "After Theognis." *The Canadian Forum*, Sept. 1960, p. 137. Rpt. trans. Ion Caraion ("Dupǎ Theognis") in *Romania Literara* [Bucharest], 23 April 1970, p. 22. *CP* ("After Theognis"); *CPIL*; *SF*.

B229 "Arboreal Nature." *The Canadian Forum*, Sept. 1960, p. 137. *CP*; *CPIL*; *SF*.

B230 "Beutel's Name Is Inscribed for Eternal Life." *The Canadian Forum*, Sept. 1960, p. 137. *CP*; *CPIL*; *WPJ2*; *SF*.

B231 "The Convertible." *The Canadian Forum*, Sept. 1960, p. 137. Rpt. in *The Human Voice Quarterly* [Miami], 2, No. 3 (Aug. 1966), [15]. Rpt. trans. Jarosław Sokół and Florian Smieja ("Kabriolet") in *Literatura na Świecie* [Warsaw] [No. 4 (225)], Kwiecień [April] 1990, p. 77. *CP* ("The Convertible"); *SP69*; *CPIL*; *DF*; *WPJ*; *WPJ2*; *DD*; *SF*.

B232 "Hostia." *The Canadian Forum*, Sept. 1960, p. 137. *CP*; *CPIL*; *SF*.

B233 "Our Common Future: Or the Progress of Satire." *The Canadian Forum*, Sept. 1960, p. 137. *CPIL* ("Our Common Future"); *SF* ("Our Common Future or The Progress of Satire").

B234 "The Atonement." *The Fiddlehead*, No. 46 (Autumn 1960), p. 7. *SF*.

B235 "For You." *The Fiddlehead*, No. 46 (Autumn 1960), p. 5. *CP* ("Song"); *CPIL*; *SF*.

B236 "Maria Poidinger." *The Fiddlehead*, No. 46 (Autumn 1960), p. 6. *SF*.

B237 "Prizes." *The Fiddlehead*, No. 46 (Autumn 1960), p. 8. *CPIL*; *SF*.

B238 "Divine Image." *The Montrealer*, Jan. 1961, p. 37. Rpt. in *The Canadian Forum*, Feb. 1961, p. 248. *CP*; *CPIL*; *DF*; *WPJ* (revised); *WPJ2*; *FE* (revised); *SF*.

B239 "For Prof. F.M. Heichelheim." *The Tamarack Review*, No. 18 (Winter 1961), p. 80. *CP*; *SF*.

B240 "Magda." *The Tamarack Review*, No. 18 (Winter 1961), p. 79. *CPIL*; *SF*.

B241 "Today I Am a Man." *The Tamarack Review*, No. 18 (Winter 1961), pp. 79–80. *SF*.

B242 "Dance with a Watermelon." *The Canadian Forum*, Feb. 1961, p. 248. *CPIL* (revised); *SF*.

B243 "The Fall." *The Canadian Forum*, Feb. 1961, p. 248. *SF*.

B244 "Stock-Taking on the Day of Atonement." *The Canadian Forum*, Feb. 1961, p. 248. *CP* ("Stock-taking on the Day of Atonement"); *CPIL*; *SF*.

B245 "Why I Don't Make Love to the First Lady." *The Canadian Forum*, March 1961, p. 267. *CP* (revised); *SP69*; *CPIL*; *SF*.

B246 "The Wave of the Future." *The Canadian Forum*, Sept. 1961, p. 122.

B247 "The Pillar." *Evidence*, No. 3 (Fall 1961), p. 35. *BOAJ*; *CP*; *CPIL*; *Pa* ("El cipo"); *LPIL* ("The Pillar").

B248 "A Tall Man Executes a Jig: For Malcolm Ross." *Queen's Quarterly*, 86 (Autumn 1961), 456–58. Rpt. in *The Human Voice Quarterly* [Miami], 2, No. 3 (Aug. 1966), [17–18]. Rpt. ("Un uomo alto esegue una giga") in *Poesia canadese del Novocento*. Ed. and trans. Caterina Ricciardi. Napoli: Liguori, 1986, pp. 121, 123, 125. *BOAJ* ("A Tall Man Executes a Jig: For Malcolm Ross"); *CP* ("A Tall Man Executes a Jig"); *SP69*; *CPIL*; *DF*; *PIL*; *SPIL*; *eg* ("A Tall Man Executes a Jig / Un uomo alto esegue una giga"); *WPJ* (revised — "A Tall Man Executes a Jig"); *WPJ2*; *Ts:p* ("A Tall Man Executes a Jig / Un uomo alto esegue una giga"); *LP*.

For the English contributions to this anthology, see B1126. See also *TMEJ* ("A Tall Man Executes a Jig").

B249 "For Alexander Trocchi." *The Canadian Forum*, Oct. 1961, p. 158. *BOAJ* ("For Alexander Trocchi, Novelist"); *CP*; *CPIL*; *DF*.

B250 "There Were No Signs." Rpt. ("There Were No Signs") in *Concordia University Magazine*, May, June, July 1982, p. 25. *The Canadian Forum*, Oct. 1961, p. 158. Rpt. in *Amethyst* [Acadia Univ.], 2, No. 4 (Summer 1963), 14. Rpt. in *ellipse*, No. 1 (Fall 1969), p. 62. Rpt. trans. Gerald Backland and Gilles Carrier ("Sans indices") in *ellipse*, No. 1 (Fall 1969), p. 63. Rpt. trans. Bogusław Rostworowski ("Nie Było Znaków") in *Życie Literackie* [Krakow], 14 April 1974, p. 11. Rpt. trans. Branko Gorjup ("Bez Putokaza" / "There Were No Signs") in *Naše novine*, 18 Oct. 1978, p.12. Rpt. trans. Branko Gorjup ("Bez Putokaza") in *Republika* [Zagreb, Yugoslavia], Nos. 10–12 (1984), p. 169. *BOAJ* ("There Were No Signs"); *CP*; *SP69*; *CPIL*; *DF*; *TWNS*; *WPJ*; *WPJ2*; *SPIL*(K).

See *PIL65*, *IL* (Montreal), *ILRH*, *EIL69*, *IL* (Toronto), *Layton*, *EIL76*, *EIL81*, *PRIL*, *WPJ* (cas.), and B1228.

B251 "Whom I Write For." *The Canadian Forum*, Oct. 1961, p. 158. Rpt. in *The Human Voice Quarterly* [Miami], 2, No. 3 (Aug. 1966), [17]. Rpt. in *ellipse*, No. 1 (Fall 1969), pp. 64, 66. Rpt. trans. Gerald Backland and Gilles Carrier ("Pour qui j'écris") in *ellipse*, No. 1 (Fall 1969), pp. 65, 67. Rpt. ("Para quiene escribo") in *Antología de la poesía anglo canadiense contemporánea*. Ed. and trans. Bernd Dietz. Barcelona: Los libros de la frontera, 1985, pp. 71, 73. *BOAJ* ("Whom I Write For"); *CP*; *SP69*; *CPIL*; *DF*; *FE*.

For the English contributions to the 1985 anthology, see B1123. See also *PIL65*, *IL* (Toronto), *Layton*, and *WPJ* (cas.).

B252 "The Gods Speak Out." *Exchange*, 1, No. 1 (Nov. 1961), 24. *BOAJ* (revised).

B253 "Questions." *Exchange*, 1, No. 2 (Dec. 1961), 7. *BOAJ*; *CP*; *CPIL*.

B254 "The Cage." *The Tamarack Review*, No. 22 (Winter 1962), p. 37. *BOAJ*; *CP*; *SP69*; *CPIL*; *DF*; *PIL*; *SPIL*; *eg* ("The Cage / La gabbia"); *WPJ* ("The Cage"); *WPJ2*; *Ts:p* ("The Cage / La gabbia"); *LP* ("The Cage").

B255 "For Aviva, Because I Love Her." *The Fiddlehead*, No. 51 (Winter 1962), p. 4. *BOAJ* (revised); *CP*; *CPIL*; *LPIL* (l.ed); *Pa* ("Para Aviva, porque la quiero"); *LPIL* ("For Aviva, Because I Love Her"); *paIL* ("For Aviva, Because I Love Her / Per Aviva, perché l'amo"); *LPIL:RD* ("For Aviva, Because I Love Her"); *DD*.
See B1286 ("Portrait of a One-Armed Juggler: For Aviva, Because I Love Her").

B256 "Lilith." *The Fiddlehead*, No. 51 (Winter 1962), pp. 4–5. *BOAJ* (revised); *CP*; *CPIL*.

B257 "No Shish Kebab." *The Tamarack Review*, No. 22 (Winter 1962), pp. 38–39. *BOAJ*; *CP*; *CPIL*.

B258 "Silence: For Ernest Hemingway [The word betrays the act]." *The Tamarack Review*, No. 22 (Winter 1962), p. 36. Rpt. trans. Panteies Trogades ("ΣΙΩΠΗ") in *Nea Hestia* [Athens], 1 May 1967, p. 597. *BOAJ* ("Silence: For Ernest Hemingway [The word betrays the act]"); *CP*; *CPIL* ("Silence [The word betrays the act]").
See B1210.

B259 "To a Lily: For A.J.M. Smith." *Cataract*, 1, No. 2 (Winter 1962), 22. *BOAJ*.

B260 "The Real Values." *Exchange*, 2, No. 3 (Feb.–March 1962), 11. *BOAJ*; *CP*; *CPIL*.

B261 "The Bishopric." *The Canadian Forum*, June 1962, p. 61. Rpt. in *The Mirror* [Univ. of Saskatchewan], 14 Feb. 1973, Topics, p. 2. *BOAJ*; *CP*; *CPIL*; *DD*.

B262 "Merlin Perverse." *The Canadian Forum*, June 1962, p. 67. *BOAJ*.

B263 "The Well-Wrought Urn." *The Canadian Forum*, June 1962, p. 67. Rpt. trans. Ion Caraion ("Urna cea cu har lucrata") in *Romania Literara* [Bucharest], 23 April 1970, p. 22. *BOAJ* ("The Well-Wrought Urn"); *CP*; *CPIL*; *fve* ("The Well-Wrought Urn / L'urna ben lavorata"); *DF* ("The Well-Wrought Urn"); *PIL*; *SPIL*; *DD*; *WWU*.
See *ILRH* and B1225.

B264 "Epigram for Roy Daniells." *Cataract*, 1, No. 3 (July 1962), 38. Rpt. ("Brief Review: Epigram for Roy Daniells") in *TISH*, Sept. 1962, p. 273. *BOAJ* ("Epigram for Roy Daniells").

B265 "History as a Slice of Ham." *Cataract*, 1, No. 3 (July 1962), p. 36. *BOAJ*; *CP*; *CPIL*.

B266 "Political Economy." *Cataract*, 1, No. 3 (July 1962), p. 39. *BOAJ*; *CP*; *CPIL*; *DF*; *WPJ*; *WPJ2*.
See *WPJ* (cas.).

B267 "Portrait of an English Prof." *Cataract*, 1, No. 3 (July 1962), p. 37. *BOAJ*.

B268 "The Sparks Fly." *The Canadian Forum*, Aug. 1962, p. 120. *BOAJ*; *CP*; *CPIL*.

B269 "Advice for Two Young Poets." *The Tamarack Review*, No. 25 (Autumn 1962), p. 85. Rpt. in *Ame-*

thyst [Acadia Univ.], 2, No. 4 (Summer 1963), 39. *BOAJ* (revised); *CP*; *CPIL*.

B270 "Androgyne." *Queen's Quarterly*, 69 (Autumn 1962), 427. *BOAJ*; *CP*; *CPIL*; *LPIL* (l.ed); *Pa* ("Andrógino"); *LPIL* ("Androgyne"); *LPIL:RD*; *DD*.

B271 "Butterfly on Rock." *The Tamarack Review*, No. 25 (Autumn 1962), p. 83. Rpt. in *ellipse*, No. 11 (1972), p. 88. Rpt. trans. Claudine Richetin ("Le Papillon sur le rocher") in *ellipse*, No. 11 (1972), p. 89. Rpt. trans. Jurosław Sokół and Florian Smieja ("Motyl na Skale") in *Literatura na Świecie* [Warsaw] [No. 4 (225)], Kwiecień [April] 1990, p. 76. *BOAJ* ("Butterfly on Rock"); *CP*; *SP69*; *CPIL*; *DF*; *PIL*; *SPIL*; *WPJ*; *WPJ2*; *SPIL*(K).
See B1252 ("Power and Poetry: Butterfly on Rock").

B272 "The Dazed Steer: For Norman Mailer." *The Tamarack Review*, No. 25 (Autumn 1962), p. 86. *BOAJ*.

B273 "The Imbecile." *The Tamarack Review*, No. 25 (Autumn 1962), pp. 84–85. *BOAJ* (revised); *CP*; *CPIL*; *DF*.

B274 "Moral with a Story." *The Tamarack Review*, No. 25 (Autumn 1962), p. 86. *BOAJ*; *CP*; *CPIL*.

B275 "A Poet's Advice: Breakdown." *McGill Daily*, 26 Sept. 1962, p. 5. *BOAJ* ("Breakdown"); *CP*; *CPIL*.

B276 "A Poet's Advice: Drunk on McGill Campus." *McGill Daily*, 26 Sept. 1962, p. 5. *BOAJ* ("Drunk on McGill Campus: For Sabine"); *CPIL* (revised — "Drunk on McGill Campus").

B277 "Elegy for Marilyn Monroe." *Evidence*, No. 6 (1963), pp. 84–87. *BOAJ*; *CP*; *CPIL*; *DF*; *PIL*; *SPIL*; *eg* ("Elegy for Marilyn Monroe / Elegia per Marilyn Monroe"); *WPJ2* ("Elegy for Marilyn Monroe"); *DD*; *Ts:p* ("Elegy for Marilyn Monroe / Elegia per Marilyn Monroe").
See *WPJ* (cas.) ("Elegy for Marilyn Monroe").

B278 "Crazy Jack." *Something Else* [Ottawa], No. 1 (March 1963), p. 15. *BOAJ*.

B279 "Mystery." *Amethyst* [Acadia Univ.], 2, No. 4 (Spring 1963), 37.

B280 "on re-reading the beats." *The Outsider* [New Orleans], 1, No. 3 (Spring 1963), 42–43. *BOAJ* (revised — "On Rereading the Beats"); *CPIL*.

B281 "Coal." *The Canadian Forum*, May 1963, p. 39. *LR*; *CP*; *CPIL*; *LPIL* (l.ed); *Pa* ("Carbón"); *LPIL* ("Coal"); *LPIL:RD*.

B282 "Das Wahre Ich." *The Canadian Forum*, May 1963, p. 50. Rpt. trans. Oláh Janos and Tótfalusi István in *Gótika a vadonban: Kanadai angol nyelvű Költők, modern Könyvtár*. Ed. James Steele. Introd. Béla Köpeczi. Debrecenben: Europa Konyvkiado, 1983, p. 115. *LR*; *CP*; *CPIL*; *DF*; *FE*.

B283 "Homage to Lucullus." *The Fiddlehead*, No. 57 (Summer 1963), pp. 62–63. Rpt. in *The Canadian Forum*, Aug. 1963, p. 110. *LR*; *CP*; *CPIL*.

B284 "The Maddened Lover." *The Fiddlehead*, No. 57 (Summer 1963), p. 63. *LR*; *CP*; *CPIL*.

B285 "The Predator." *Amethyst* [Acadia Univ.], 2, No. 4 (Summer 1963), 6–7. Rpt. ("Orillia Reader Says Layton Poem Sums Up Need to Protect") in *Orillia*

Sun, 7 April 1987, p. 5. *BOAJ* ("The Predator"); *CP*; *CPIL*; *DF*; *WPJ*; *WPJ*2; *FE*.
  See *IL* (Montreal) ("Predator"), *ILRH*, *Layton* ("The Predator"), and *WPJ* (cas.).

B286 "F.R. Scott." *The Canadian Forum*, Aug. 1963, p. 110. *LR*; *CP*; *CPIL*.

B287 "Boys in October." *The New York Times Book Review*, 17 Nov. 1963, p. 2. *CGE*; *IB*; *IB*2; *RCS* (revised); *CP*; *CPIL*.
  See *RCS* (cas.).

B288 "At the Pier in Denia." *The Canadian Forum*, Dec. 1963, p. 197. *LR*; *CP*; *CPIL*.

B289 "Ballad of the Old Spaniard." *The Canadian Forum*, Dec. 1963, p. 197. *LR*; *CP*; *SP*69; *CPIL*; *DF*; *WPJ* (revised); *WPJ*2.
  See *Layton* and B1197.

B290 "For My Former Students." *The Canadian Forum*, Dec. 1963, p. 197. *LR*; *CP*; *CPIL*.
  See B1201.

B291 "The Lizard." *The Canadian Forum*, Dec. 1963, p. 198. *LR*; *CP*; *CPIL*.
  See B1203.

B292 "On the Assassination of President Kennedy." *Queen's Quarterly*, 70 (Winter 1963), 514. Rpt. in *The Holy Blossom Temple Bulletin* [Toronto], 23 March 1965, p. 7. Rpt. in *The Atlantic Mirror*, 1, No. 1 (Jan.–March 1967), 14. *LR*; *CP*; *CPIL*; *OAPK*.

B293 "El Caudillo." *The Tamarack Review*, No. 30 (Winter 1964), p. 45. *LR*; *CP*; *SP*69; *CPIL*; *DF*.
  See B1199.

B294 "El Gusano [From the place where I was sitting]." *The Tamarack Review*, No. 30 (Winter 1964), pp. 46–47. *LR*; *CP* (revised); *SP*69; *CPIL*; *DF*; *PIL*; *SPIL*; *WPJ*; *WPJ*2.
  See B1202.

B295 "On Spanish Soil." *The Tamarack Review*, No. 30 (Winter 1964), p. 44. *LR*; *CP*; *CPIL*.
  See *ILRH* and B1204.

B296 "Plaza de Toros." *The Tamarack Review*, No. 30 (Winter 1964), p. 47. Rpt. trans. Branko Gorjup in *Republika* [Zagreb, Yugoslavia], Nos. 10–12 (1984), p. 174. *LR*; *CP*; *SP*69; *CPIL*; *DF*; *TWNS*; *WPJ*; *WPJ*2; *SPIL*(K).
  See *IL* (Montreal), *ILRH*, *Layton*, and B1205.

B297 "Spring Exultances." *Evidence*, No. 8 (1964), p. 113. *LR* (revised — "Spring Exultances: For Aviva"); *CPIL* ("Spring Exultances").

B298 "Stone-Splitters in Alicante." *The Fiddlehead*, No. 59 (Winter 1964), p. 17. *LR*; *CP*; *CPIL*.

B299 "Food for Thought." *Catapult*, 1, No. 1 (Winter-Spring 1964), 7. *LR*; *CP*.

B300 "Bicycle Pump." *The Fiddlehead*, No. 60 (Spring 1964), p. 20. *LR*; *CP*; *CPIL*; *DD*.

B301 "For My Green Old Age." *The Fiddlehead*, No. 60 (Spring 1964), p. 20. *LR*; *CP*; *CPIL*; *LPIL* (l.ed); *Pa* ("A mi verde ancianidad"); *LPIL* ("For My Green Old Age"); *LPIL:RD*; *DD*.
  See *IL* (Montreal), *ILRH*, and B1226.

B302 "At the Iglesia de Sacromonte." PRISM *international*, 4, No. 1 (Summer 1964), 32. *LR*; *CP*; *SP*69; *CPIL*; *DF*; *eg* ("At the Iglesia de Sacromonte / Alla Iglesia de Sacromonte"); *Ts:p* ("At the Iglesia De Sacromonte / Alla Iglesia De Sacromonte").

See B1251 ("Power and Poetry: At the Iglesia de Sacromonte").

B303 "In Memory of Stephen Ward." *Catapult*, 1, No. 2 (Summer 1964), 2. *LR*; *CP*; *CPIL*.

B304 "Second Thought on the Armada." *Catapult*, 1, No. 2 (Summer 1964), 6. *LR*; *CP* ("Second Thoughts on the Armada"); *CPIL* ("Second Thought on the Armada").

B305 "Portrait of a Genius." *The Canadian Forum*, June 1964, p. 60. *LR*; *CP*; *SP69*; *CPIL*; *DF*.

B306 "Creation [I fashioned you]." *Envoi* [Cheltenham, Eng.], No. 23 (Sept. 1964), p. 2. *LR*; *CP*; *CPIL*; *LPIL* (l.ed); *Pa* ("Creación"); *LPIL* ("Creation [I fashioned you]"); *paIL* ("Creation [I fashioned you] / Creazione"); *LPIL:RD* ("Creation [I fashioned you]"); *DD*.
See B1200.

B307 "Logos." *Yes*, No. 13 (Dec. 1964), p. 19. *CP*; *CPIL*.

B308 "O Say Can You See." *Yes*, No. 13 (Dec. 1964), p. 21. *CP*; *CPIL*.

B309 "Zoroastrian." *Yes*, No. 13 (Dec. 1964), p. 20. *CP* (revised); *CPIL*.

B310 "Beauty [How does one tell]." *The Literary Review* [Fairleigh Dickinson Univ., Teaneck, N.J.], 8 (Summer 1965), 547. *CPIL*.

B311 "A Strange Turn." *The Literary Review* [Fairleigh Dickinson Univ., Teaneck, N.J.], 8 (Summer 1965), 547. *CP* (revised); *CPIL*; *DF*; *LPIL* (l.ed); *Pa* ("Un lance insolito"); *LPIL* ("A Strange Turn"); *paIL* ("A Strange Turn / Strano cambiamento"); *WPJ* ("A Strange Turn"); *WPJ2*; *LPIL:RD*; *DD*.

B312 "The Air Is Sultry." *Quarry*, 15, No. 2 (Nov. 1965), 6. *PM*; *CPIL*; *LPIL* (l.ed); *Pa* ("El aire es asfixiante"); *LPIL* ("The Air Is Sultry"); *paIL* ("The Air Is Sultry / L'aria è afosa"); *LPIL:RD* ("The Air Is Sultry").

B313 "Innocents Abroad." *Quarry*, 15, No. 2 (Nov. 1965), 6.

B314 "Olympia Kaputt." *The Canadian Forum*, Dec. 1965, p. 195. *PM* ("Olympia Kaput"); *CPIL*; *SFGP*.

B315 "How to Look at an Abstract." *Cyclic*, 1, No. 3 (March 1966), 9. Rpt. in *The Human Voice Quarterly* [Miami], 2, No. 3 (Aug. 1966), 18. *LPS*; *RCS* (revised); *CP*; *CPIL*; *fve* ("How to Look at an Abstract / Come guardare un quadro astratto"); *DF* ("How to Look at an Abstract").
See *RCS* (cas.).

B316 "For Miss Cézanne." *The Canadian Forum*, March 1966, p. 280. *PM*; *CPIL*; *DF*; *LPIL* (l.ed); *Pa* ("A Miss Cézanne"); *LPIL* ("For Miss Cézanne"); *LPIL:RD*.

B317 "For Musia's Grandchildren." *The Tamarack Review*, No. 39 (Spring 1966), p. 16. *PM* (revised); *SP69*; *CPIL*; *DF*; *LPIL* (l.ed); *Pa* ("Para los nietos de Musia"); *LPIL* ("For Musia's Grandchildren"); *WPJ*; *WPJ2*; *LPIL:RD*; *DD*.
See *PIL65*, *ILRH*, *EIL69*, *IL* (Toronto), and *WPJ* (cas.).

B318 "For the Record: For Mark Schwartz." *The Tamarack Review*, No. 39 (Spring 1966), p. 18. *PM*; *CPIL* ("For the Record").

B319 "Freedom." *The Tamarack Review*, No. 39 (Spring 1966), p. 18. Rpt. trans. Kim Yang Shik in *Wor Kan Men Ha* [Seoul], Jan. 1974, p. 128. *PM*; *CPIL*.

B320 "Fried Fish, My Love." *Intercourse*, No. 2 (Spring 1966), pp. 16–17.

B321 "The Human Condition: For A.W. [Hope for the human race?]." *The Tamarack Review*, No. 39 (Spring 1966), p. 17. *PM* (revised); *CPIL* ("The Human Condition [Hope for the human race?]").

B322 "Mahogany Red." *The Tamarack Review*, No. 39 (Spring 1966), pp. 19–21. *PM*; *SP69*; *CPIL*; *DF* (revised); *PIL*; *SPIL*; *LPIL* (l.ed) (revised); *Pa* ("Rojo caoba"); *LPIL* ("Mahogany Red"); *LPIL:RD*.

B323 "Poetry Workshop." *Intercourse*, No. 2 (Spring 1966), p. 16.

B324 "Winter Lyric." *The Tamarack Review*, No. 39 (Spring 1966), p. 15. *PM*; *CPIL*; *Pa* ("Lírica invernal"); *LPIL* ("Winter Lyric"); *paIL* ("Winter Lyric / Lirica invernale"); *LPIL:RD* ("Winter Lyric").

B325 "The Architect." *The Human Voice Quarterly* [Miami], 2, No. 3 (Aug. 1966), [16]. *BOAJ*; *CP*; *CPIL*.

B326 "At the Belsen Memorial." *The Tamarack Review*, No. 41 (Autumn 1966), pp. 72–73. Rpt. in *Karussell*, Nov. 1966, p. 6. Rpt. in *Congress Bulletin* [Canadian Jewish Congress], Feb. 1967, p. 6. *PM*; *CPIL*; *FE*.
    The *Karussell* reprint is part of an interview with Layton (C568).

B327 "Confederation Ode." *The Tamarack Review*, No. 41 (Autumn 1966), pp. 71–72. *PM* (revised); *CPIL*; *DF*; *WPJ* ("Centennial Ode"); *WPJ2*.
    See *ILRH* ("Confederation Ode").

B328 "For the Stinker Who Called Me an Apologist for Nazi Crimes: For Peter Lust." *Intercourse*, No. 4 (Fall 1966), p. 24. *PM*; *CPIL* ("For the Stinker Who Called Me an Apologist for Nazi Crimes").

B329 "Invention." *The Tamarack Review*, No. 41 (Autumn 1966), pp. 70–71. *PM* (revised); *SP69*; *CPIL*; *DF*.
    See *EIL69*.

B330 "North and South." *The Tamarack Review*, No. 41 (Autumn 1966), pp. 65–66. *PM*; *CPIL*; *DF*.

B331 "Portrait Done with a Steel Pen." *The Tamarack Review*, No. 41 (Autumn 1966), pp. 66–68. *PM* (revised); *CPIL*.

B332 "Rhine Boat Trip." *Queen's Quarterly*, 73 (Autumn 1966), 381. Rpt. in *Karussell*, Nov. 1966, p. 6. Rpt. in *Congress Bulletin* [Canadian Jewish Congress], Feb. 1967, p. 6. Rpt. in *Black Moss* [Windsor, Ont.], 1, No. 2 (Spring 1969), 7. Rpt. trans. Branko Gorjup ("Brodom Po Rajni") in *Republika* [Zagreb, Yugoslavia], Nos. 10–12 (1984), p. 171. *PM* ("Rhine Boat Trip"); *SP69*; *CPIL*; *DF*; *PIL*; *SPIL*; *eg* ("Rhine Boat Trip / In barca sul Reno"); *WPJ* ("Rhine Boat Trip"); *WPJ2*; *SPIL*(K); *FE*; *Ts:p* ("Rhine Boat Trip / In barco sul Reno").
    The *Karussell* reprint is part of an interview with Layton (C568). See *PIL65* ("Rhine Boat Trip"), *ILRH*, *EIL69*, *IL* (Toronto), *Layton*, *EIL76*, *EIL81*, *PRIL*, *WPJ* (cas.), and B1241.

B333 "Gratitude." *The Canadian Forum*, Sept. 1966, pp. 129–30. *PM*; *CPIL*.
    See *ILRH*.

B334 "Holiday in the South." *The Canadian Forum*, Sept. 1966, p. 130. *PM*.

B335 "Misunderstanding." *University of Calgary Tally Stick*, Sept. 1966, p. 112. Rpt. in *Marianopolis College Marianews* [Montreal], 28 Feb. 1967, p. 7. Rpt. in *The Montreal Sunday Express*, 10 Dec. 1978, p. 21. Rpt. in *The Gazette* [Univ. of Western Ontario], 26 March 1982, p. 6. *LPS*; *RCS*; *CP*; *SP69*; *CPIL*; *fve* ("Misunderstanding / Malinteso"); *DF* ("Misunderstanding"); *PIL*; *SPIL*; *LPIL* (l.ed); *Pa* ("Malentendido"); *LPIL* ("Misunderstanding"); *paIL* ("Misunderstanding / Incomprensione"); *WPJ* ("Misunderstanding"); *WPJ2*; *LPIL:RD*; *DD*.
See *ILH*, *PIL65*, *IL* (Montreal), *ILRH*, *IL* (Toronto), *RCS* (cas.), *WPJ* (cas.), and B1215.

B336 "National Virtues." *The Canadian Forum*, Sept. 1966, p. 129. *PM*; *CPIL*.

B337 "Repetition." *The Canadian Forum*, Sept. 1966, p. 129. *PM*; *CPIL*; *DF*.

B338 "A Song about Woman." *The Canadian Forum*, Sept. 1966, p. 129. *PM* (revised); *CPIL*; *DD*.

B339 "Sun-Bathers." *The Canadian Forum*, Sept. 1966, p. 130. *PM*; *CPIL* ("Sun Bathers"); *fve* ("Sun Bathers / Il bagno di sole"); *DF* ("Sun-Bathers"); *Ts:p* ("Sun Bathers / Bagnanti").

B340 "The Wave." *The Tamarack Review*, No. 41 (Autumn 1966), pp. 68–69. *PM* ("The Wave: For Sam Tata"); *CPIL* ("The Wave").

B341 "Women of the Back Streets of Europe." *Intercourse*, No. 4 (Fall 1966), p. 8. *PM* (revised); *CPIL*.

B342 "Mammoths." *Quarry*, 16, No. 1 (Oct. 1966), 9. *PM*; *CPIL*.

B343 "New Year's Eve." *Quarry*, 16, No. 1 (Oct. 1966), 8–9. *PM* ("New Year's Eve: For Marion"); *CPIL* ("New Year's Eve").

B344 "Pilgrim." *Quarry*, 16, No. 1 (Oct. 1966), 7. *PM* (revised); *CPIL*.

B345 "Collaboration." *Queen's Quarterly*, 72 (Winter 1966), 625. Rpt. in *The Atlantic Mirror*, 1, No. 1 (Jan.–March 1967), 14. *PM*; *CPIL*.

B346 "The Sad Madonna." *The Telegram* [Toronto], 24 Dec. 1966, p. 25. *PM*; *CPIL*.

B347 "Above All, Avoid Halitosis." *Intercourse*, No. 5 (Winter 1967), p. 24. *PM* (revised).

B348 "Marché Municipal." *Adam International Review* [London, Eng.], Nos. 313-314-315 (1967), p. 23. *SP* ("Marché Municipale: For Desmond Pacey"); *SP69* ("Marché Municipale"); *CPIL*; *DF*.

B349 "Ruins." *Intercourse*, No. 5 (Winter 1967), p. 4. *PM* (revised); *CPIL*; *fve* ("Ruins / Rovine"); *SFGP* ("Ruins"); *DF*.

B350 "Deadalive: For Charles Lazarus." *Canadian Jewish Chronicle Review* [Montreal], 10 Feb. 1967, p. 8.

B351 "Apparition." *Edge*, No. 6 (Spring 1967), pp. 37–38. *PM*; *CPIL*; *DD*.

B352 "Clochards." *Edge*, No. 6 (Spring 1967), pp. 36–37. Rpt. (revised) in *Poetry Australia* [Sydney], 16 (June 1967), 21. *PM* ("Clochards: For Wynne Francis"); *SP69* ("Clochards"); *CPIL*; *fve* ("Clochards: For Wynne Francis / Clochards: Per Wynne Francis"); *DF* ("Clochards"); *eg* ("Clochards: For Wynne Francis / Clochards: Per Wynne Francis"); *Ts:p*.
See *PIL65* ("Clochards"), *IL* (Toronto), and *Layton*.

B353 "Games." *Edge*, No. 6 (Spring 1967), p. 35. *PM*; *CPIL*.

B354 "An Old Niçoise Whore." *Edge*, No. 6 (Spring 1967), pp. 35-36. *PM* ("An Old Nicoise Whore: For Germaine D— "); *SP69* ("An Old Nicoise Whore"); *CPIL*; *DF*; *PIL*; *SPIL*; *WPJ* ("An Old Niçoise Whore"); *WPJ2*; *SPIL*(K) ("An Old Nicoise Whore"); *DD* ("An Old Niçoise Whore").

B355 "Philosophy 34." *The Malahat Review* [Univ. of Victoria], No. 2 (April 1967), pp. 121-23. *LCW*; *IB2*; *RCS*; *CP*; *CPIL*.
See *ILH* and *RCS* (cas.).

B356 "How Poems Get Written." *Story* [New York], 1, No. 1 (May 1967), 31. Rpt. in *Queen's University Journal*, n.d., p. 3. Rpt. trans. Ion Caraion ("Cuma de se scriu poezii") in *Romania Literara* [Bucharest], 23 April 1970, p. 22. *MMF* ("How Poems Get Written"); *IB*; *IB2*; *RCS*; *CP*; *CPIL*; *Pa* ("Cómo se escriben los poemas"); *LPIL* (revised — "How Poems Get Written"); *paIL* ("How Poems Get Written / Come si scrivono le poesie"); *LPIL:RD* ("How Poems Get Written"); *DD*.
See *ILH*, *Layton*, and *RCS* (cas.).

B357 "Time's Velvet Tongue." *Story* [New York], 1, No. 1 (May 1967), 29. *PM*; *CPIL*.
See *IL* (Montreal) and *ILRH*.

B358 "To a Beautiful Unknown Girl." *Story* [New York], 1, No. 1 (May 1967), 29. *PM*; *CPIL*; *DD*.
See *IL* (Montreal), *ILRH*, and *EIL76*.

B359 "Dorothy Parker (1893-1967)." Letter. *The Montreal Star*, 23 June 1967, [Sec. Entertainment], p. 15. *SP* (revised); *CPIL*; *FE*.

B360 "The Red Moujhik." *Canadian Jewish Chronicle Review* [Montreal], 7 July 1967, p. 5. Rpt. in *The Tamarack Review*, No. 45 (Autumn 1967), p. 8. *SP*.

B361 "To My Two Sons, Max and David." *The Canadian Forum*, Sept. 1967, p. 133. Rpt. in *Fraternally Yours: Official Publication of the New Fraternal Jewish Association* [Toronto], 14, No. 2 (June 1973), 5. *SP* (revised — "For My Two Sons, Max and David"); *SP69*; *CPIL*; *DF*; *WPJ* ("For My Sons, Max and David"); *WPJ2*; *FE*.

B362 "Love Poem with an Odd Twist." *The Canadian Forum*, Sept. 1967, p. 133. *SP*; *SP69*; *CPIL*; *fve* ("Love Poem with an Odd Twist / Poesia d'amore d'uno strano piglio"); *LPIL* (l.ed) ("Love Poem with an Odd Twist"); *Pa* ("Poema de amor con un giro insospechado"); *LPIL* ("Love Poem with an Odd Twist"); *LPIL:RD*.

B363 "On This Far Shore." *The Canadian Forum*, Sept. 1967, p. 132. *SP*; *CPIL*.

B364 "To Write an Old-Fashioned Poem." *The Canadian Forum*, Sept. 1967, p. 132. *SP* (revised); *CPIL*.

B365 "End of Summer." *Quarry*, 17, No. 1 (Fall 1967), 33. *SP* ("End of the Summer"); *CPIL*.

B366 "Kamerad." *The Tamarack Review*, No. 45 (Autumn 1967), p. 9. *SP* (revised); *CPIL*.

B367 "Lesson for Today." *The Tamarack Review*, No. 45 (Autumn 1967), p. 9. *SP*; *CPIL*.

B368 "Like a Mother Demented." PRISM *international*, 7, No. 2 (Autumn 1967), 48. *SP* ("Like a Mother Demented: For Frank Scott"); *SP69* ("Like a Mother Demented"); *CPIL*; *fve* ("Like a Mother Demented

/ Come madre demente"); *DF* ("Like a Mother Demented"); *eg* ("Like a Mother Demented / Madre uscita di senno"); *WPJ* ("Like a Mother Demented"); *WPJ2*; *Ts:p* ("Like a Mother Demented / Madre uscita di senno").

B369 "Mediterranean Cemetery." *Quarry*, 17, No. 1 (Fall 1967), 32. *SP*; *CPIL*.

B370 "The Next Time Does It." PRISM *international*, 7, No. 2 (Autumn 1967), 49. *SP*; *CPIL*.

B371 "Oil Slick on the Riviera." *The Tamarack Review*, No. 45 (Autumn 1967), p. 7. *SP* ("Oil Slick on the Riviera: For Milton Wilson"); *SP69* (revised — "Oil Slick on the Riviera"); *CPIL*.

B372 "Village Funeral." *The Tamarack Review*, No. 45 (Autumn 1967), p. 9. *SP*; *CPIL*.

B373 "The Best Proof." *The Telegram* [Toronto], 23 Sept. 1967, Showcase, p. 19. *SP*; *CPIL*; *FE*.
      See B1275.

B374 "Elegy for Strul" (excerpts). *The Telegram* [Toronto], 23 Sept. 1967, Showcase, p. 19. *SP* (revised, expanded); *SP69*; *CPIL* (revised); *DF*; *PIL*; *SPIL*.
      See *EIL76* and B1285 ("Portrait of a One-Armed Juggler: Elegy for Strul").

B375 "Modern Lyric." *The Telegram* [Toronto], 23 Sept. 1967, Showcase, p. 19. *SP*; *CPIL*.

B376 "Queer Hate Poem." *The Telegram* [Toronto], 23 Sept. 1967, Showcase, p. 19. *SP*; *CPIL*.

B377 "Talk at Twilight." *The Telegram* [Toronto], 23 Sept. 1967, Showcase, p. 19. *SP*; *CPIL*; *LPIL* (l.ed); *Pa* ("Parloteo entre dos luces"); *LPIL* ("Talk at Twi-

light"); *paIL* ("Talk at Twilight / Conversazione al crepuscolo"); *LPIL:RD* ("Talk at Twilight"); *DD*.

B378 "Yet What if the Survivors." *The Telegram* [Toronto], 23 Sept. 1967, Showcase, p. 19. *SP*; *SP69*; *CPIL*; *DF* (revised).
      See *EIL69*.

B379 "Hymn to the Republic." In *The New Romans: Candid Canadian Opinions of the U.S.* Ed. A.W. Purdy. Edmonton: Hurtig, 1968, pp. 62–64. *WBB*.

B380 "The Graveyard." *Queen's Quarterly*, 74 (Winter 1967), 700. *SP*; *SP69*; *CPIL* (revised); *DF*; *WPJ*; *WPJ2*; *FE*.
      See *PIL65*, *IL* (Toronto), and *EIL81*.

B381 "The Bridge." *Pluck* [Univ. of Alberta], 1, No. 1 (Jan. 1968), 16. *CPIL*; *LPIL* (l.ed); *Pa* ("El Puente"); *LPIL* ("The Bridge"); *paIL* ("The Bridge / Il ponte"); *WBB* ("The Bridge").

B382 "Cleavages." *Quarry*, 17, No. 2 (Winter 1968), 40. *CPIL*; *WBB*.

B383 "It's a Riot, Boys." *Quarry*, 17, No. 2 (Winter 1968), 41. *WBB*.

B384 "The Shrinking General." *Pluck* [Univ. of Alberta], 1, No. 1 (Jan. 1968), 17. *WBB*.

B385 "Whose Zoo [Who ever heard of a pimp]." *Quarry*, 17, No. 2 (Winter 1968), 41. *WBB*.

B386 "After Auschwitz." *The Canadian Forum*, March 1968, p. 276. *CPIL*; *UE*; *WPJ* (revised); *WPJ2*; *SPIL*(K) (revised); *FE* (revised); *WBB* (revised).
      See *PIL65*, *IL* (Toronto), and *EIL76*.

B387 "Words for an Anxious Age." *The Tamarack Review*, No. 47 (Spring 1968), pp. 7–8.

B388 "At Wenger's." *The Telegram* [Toronto], 20 July 1968, p. 51.

B389 "Jasmine, Anyone?". *The Telegram* [Toronto], 20 July 1968, Books Section, p. 51. Rpt. in *The Canadian Forum*, Sept. 1968, p. 135. *CPIL*; *WBB*; *UA*.

B390 "Postscript to Empire." *The Telegram* [Toronto], 20 July 1968, Books Section, p. 51. *CPIL*; *UE*; *WBB*.

B391 "Storm at Ydra: For Leonard Cohen." *The Telegram* [Toronto], 20 July 1968, Books Section, p. 51. Rpt. trans. Branko Gorjup ("Oluja Nad Idrom") in *Republika* [Zagreb, Yugoslavia], Nos. 10–12 (1984), p. 173. *CPIL* ("Storm at Ydra"); *SFGP*; *UE*; *WBSL* ("Storm at Hydra / Καταιγιδα στην Ύδρα"); *WBB* ("Storm at Ydra: For Leonard Cohen").

B392 "What's New, Kathmandu?". *The Telegram* [Toronto], 20 July 1968, Books Section, p. 51. *WBB* (revised).

B393 "Yoga." *The Telegram* [Toronto], 20 July 1968, Books Section, p. 51. *WBB*.

B394 "Israelis." *Jerusalem Post Magazine*, 2 Aug. 1968, p. 9. Rpt. in *Quarry*, 18, No. 4 (Fall 1968), 26–27. *CPIL*; *UE*; *PIL*; *SPIL*; *WPJ*; *WPJ2*; *FE*; *WBB*.
    See *PIL65*, *IL* (Toronto), *Layton*, *EIL76*, and B1235.

B395 "Elephant." *The Canadian Forum*, Sept. 1968, p. 135. *CPIL* (revised); *UE*; *WPJ2*; *Ts:p* ("Elephant / L'elefante"); *WBB* ("Elephant: For Northrop Frye").

B396 "Nepalese Woman and Child." *The Canadian Forum*, Sept. 1968, p. 135. *CPIL*; *UE*; *WBB*.

B397 "Incident at New Delhi." *Quarry*, 18, No. 4 (Fall 1968), 27–28. *WBB*.

B398 "Creation [The pregnant cat]." *The Telegram* [Toronto], 23 Nov. 1968, Weekend / Showcase, p. 5. Rpt. in *The McGill News*, 56, No. 3 (Fall 1975), 32. *CPIL*; *UE*; *SPIL*(K); *WBB*.

B399 "Fish." *The Telegram* [Toronto], 23 Nov. 1968, Weekend / Showcase, p. 5. *CPIL*; *SDCJ*; *WBB*.

B400 "Hills and Hills: For Aviva." *The Telegram* [Toronto], 23 Nov. 1968, Weekend / Showcase, p. 5. *CPIL*; *SFGP*; *UE* (revised — "Hills and Hills"); *Pa* ("Cerros y cerros"); *LPIL* (revised — "Hills and Hills"); *paIL* ("Hills and Hills / Colline e colline"); *LPIL:RD* ("Hills and Hills"); *SPIL*(K); *WBSL* ("Hills and Hills: For Aviva / Λοφοι και Λοφοι"); *DD* ("Hills and Hills"); *WBB* ("Hills and Hills: For Aviva").

B401 "Oedipus." *The Telegram* [Toronto], 23 Nov. 1968, Weekend / Showcase, p. 5. *CPIL*; *SFGP*; *WBB*.

B402 "Protest." *The Telegram* [Toronto], 23 Nov. 1968, Weekend / Showcase, p. 5. *CPIL*; *SFGP*; *UE*; *WBSL* ("Protest / Διαμαρτυρια"); *WBB* ("Protest").

B403 "Attachments." *Folio* [Toronto], 4, No. 1 [Dec. 1968], [9]. *CPIL*; *WBB*.

B404 "For John Slavin's Birthday." *Folio* [Toronto], 4, No. 1 [Dec. 1968], [9]. Rpt. in *Intercourse*, No. 10 (Feb. 1969), p. 22. *CPIL*; *WBB*.

B405 "Silent Joy." *Folio* [Toronto], 4, No. 1 [Dec. 1968], [9]. *CPIL*; *SFGP*; *UE*; *WBB*.
See *IL* (Toronto) and B1242.

B406 "In Praise of Silhouette." *N.D.G. Monitor* [Montreal], 4 Dec. 1968.

B407 "Right Conduct." *Canadian Dimension*, 5, No. 7 (Dec.–Jan. 1968–69), p. 2. *CPIL*; *WBB*.

B408 "Farewell [I said to her: I]." *Bishop's University Nuevue*, 1, No. 1 (1969), 13. *CPIL* ("Farewell [I said to her: 'I no longer want]"); *WBB* ("Farewell [I said to her: 'I]").

B409 "For Aviva." *Bishop's University Nuevue*, 1, No. 1 (1969), 14. *CPIL*; *WBB*.

B410 "His Holiness Is Right." *Bishop's University Nuevue*, 1, No. 1 (1969), 14. *CPIL*; *UE*; *WBB*.

B411 "Holocaust." *Quarry*, 18, No. 2 (Winter 1969), 4–5. *CPIL*; *UE*; *WBB*.

B412 "The Smell." *Quarry*, 18, No. 2 (Winter 1969), 5–6. *CPIL*; *UE*; *WBB*.

B413 "Sourwine Sparkle." *Quarry*, 18, No. 2 (Winter 1969), 4. *CPIL*; *UE*; *WBB*.

B414 "To Irving Layton Sans Love." *The Ontarion* [Univ. of Guelph], 23 Jan. 1969.
Layton rewrites "To irving sans love" (C715).

B415 "For Julie." *Intercourse*, No. 10 (Feb. 1969), p. 22. *CPIL*; *WBB*.

B416 "The Pit." *Intercourse*, No. 10 (Feb. 1969), p. 22. *CPIL*; *WBB*.

B417 "The Skull." *Intercourse*, No. 10 (Feb. 1969), p. 21. *CPIL*; *SFGP*; *UE*; *WPJ*; *WPJ2*; *SPIL*(K); *WBSL* ("The Skull / To Κρανιο"); *WBB* ("The Skull").

B418 "Changeling." *Inner Space* [Carleton Univ.], Spring 1969, n. pag. *CPIL*; *UE*; *Pa* ("Metamorfosis"); *LPIL* ("Changeling"); *paIL* ("Changeling / Sostituzione"); *LPIL:RD* ("Changeling"); *WBB*.

B419 "Depth Charge." *Inner Space* [Carleton Univ.], Spring 1969, n. pag. *WBB*.

B420 "The Equalizer." *Inner Space* [Carleton Univ.], Spring 1969, n. pag. *WBB*.

B421 "Fishermen." *Queen's Quarterly*, 76 (Spring 1969), 10. *CPIL*; *SFGP*; *UE* ("Fishermen: For Peggy Sylvia"); *WBSL* ("Fishermen / Ψαραδες"); *WBB* ("Fishermen: For Peggy Sylvia").

B422 "When I Consider." *Inner Space* [Carleton Univ.], Spring 1969, n. pag. *WBB*.

B423 "Seduction [I said: 'I am too]." *Intercourse*, No. 11 (April 1969), p. 6. *CPIL*; *WBB*.

B424 "Inishmore." *Quarry*, 19, No. 1 (Fall 1969), 34. *CPIL* (revised); *NP* (revised).

B425 "Kilmurvey Strand." *Quarry*, 19, No. 1 (Fall 1969), 32–33. *CPIL*; *NP*; *UE*.

B426 "Grey Morning in Lisbon." *Diario Popular* [Lisbon], 27 Nov. 1969, p. 13. Rpt. in *The Canadian Forum*, Jan. 1970, p. 234. *CPIL*; *NP* (revised).

B427 "Osip Mandelshtam (1891–1940)." *Hanukah Magazine* [*The Canadian Jewish News*] [Toronto], 12

Dec. 1969, p. 4. Rpt. in *The Tamarack Review*, No. 54 (Second Quarter 1970), pp. 47–48. *CPIL*; *NP*; *UE*; *PIL*; *SPIL*; *WPJ* (revised); *WPJ2*; *FE* ["Osip Mandelstam (1891–1940)"].

B428 "Jew." *Hanukah Magazine* [*The Canadian Jewish News*] [Toronto], 12 Dec. 1969, p. 4. *FE*.

B429 "Aran Islands." *Queen's Quarterly*, 76 (Winter 1969), 648–49. *CPIL* (revised); *NP*; *UE*; *PIL*; *SPIL*.

B430 "Fanatic in San Feliu." *The Canadian Forum*, Jan. 1970, p. 235. *CPIL* (revised); *NP*; *LPIL* (l.ed); *Pa* ("Fanático en San Feliu"); *LPIL* ("Fanatic in San Feliu"); *paIL* ("Fanatic in San Feliu / Fanatico a San Feliu"); *LPIL:RD* ("Fanatic in San Feliu").

B431 "For Natalia Correia." *The Canadian Forum*, Jan. 1970, p. 234. Rpt. ("For Natalya Correia") in *The Tamarack Review*, No. 54 (Second Quarter 1970), p. 49. *CPIL* (revised); *NP*; *UE* (revised); *WPJ*; *WPJ2*.

B432 "Frost and Fences." *Anonym* [Buffalo], Nos. 5–6 (1970), p. 131. *CPIL*; *NP*.

B433 "Marxist." *The Canadian Forum*, Jan. 1970, p. 234. *NP*.

B434 "Reversion." *Anonym* [Buffalo], Nos. 5–6 (1970), p. 133.

B435 "I Can Sleep Beside My Lady: After Leonard Cohen." *The Tamarack Review*, No. 54 (Second Quarter 1970), pp. 50–51. *CPIL* ("I Can Sleep Beside My Lady"); *NP* ("I Can Sleep Beside My Lady: After Leonard Cohen"); *UE* (revised — "I Can Sleep Beside My Lady").

B436 "Ohms." *The Tamarack Review*, No. 54 (Second Quarter 1970), pp. 51–52. Rpt. in *Anonym* [Buffalo], Nos. 5–6 (1970), p. 132. *CPIL*; *NP*; *UE*.

B437 "Mîntuire." Trans. Ion Caraion. *Romania Literara* [Bucharest], 23 April 1970, p. 22. *LR* ("Redemption"); *CP*; *CPIL*.

B438 "Pretutindeni, put." Trans. Ion Caraion. *Romania Literara* [Bucharest], 23 April 1970, p. 22. *LR* ("Everywhere, the Stink"); *CP*; *CPIL*.

B439 "Terapie." Trans. Ion Caraion. *Romania Literara* [Bucharest], 23 April 1970, p. 22. *BOAJ* ("Therapy"); *CP*; *CPIL*.
See *Layton* and B1222.

B440 "As Seen through a Glass Parkly [sic]." *The Canadian Forum*, April–May 1970, p. 8. *CPIL* ("As Seen through a Glass Darkly"); *NP*; *fve* ("As Seen through a Glass Darkly / Visto oscuramente in uno specchio"); *UE* ("As Seen through a Glass Darkly").

B441 "Satan in Utopia." *The Canadian Forum*, April–May 1970, p. 93. *CPIL* (revised); *NP* (revised).

B442 "Dionysus in Hampstead." *The Tamarack Review*, No. 55 (Third Quarter 1970), pp. 10–11. *CPIL*; *NP*; *SFGP* ("Dionysos in Hampstead"); *UE*.

B443 "Eternal Recurrence [Even that leaf as it falls]." *The Tamarack Review*, No. 55 (Third Quarter 1970), p. 13. *CPIL*; *NP*; *UE*; *Pa* ("Eterno retorno"); *LPIL* (revised — "Eternal Recurrence [Even that leaf as it falls]"); *LPIL:RD*; *SPIL*(K); *Ts:p* ("Eternal Recurrence / Eterni ricorsi").

B444 "The Haunting." *The Tamarack Review*, No. 55 (Third Quarter 1970), p. 12. *CPIL*; *NP* ("The

Haunting: For George Woodcock"); *UE* ("The Haunting"); *PIL*; *SPIL*; *WPJ*; *WPJ*2.

B445 "Shakespeare." *The Tamarack Review*, No. 55 (Third Quarter 1970), pp. 7–10. *CPIL*; *NP*; *fve*; *UE*; *PIL*; *SPIL*; *WPJ*; *WPJ*2.
  See *WPJ* (cas.) and B1287 ("Portrait of a One-Armed Juggler: Shakespeare").

B446 "End of the White Mouse." *Queen's Quarterly*, 77 (Winter 1970), 576–77. Rpt. in *The Canadian Forum*, Feb. 1971, p. 380. *CPIL*; *NP*; *UE*; *WPJ*; *WPJ*2.

B447 "Consider the Lilies." *Jewish Di-al-ŏg*, Hanukkah 1970, p. 11. *CPIL*; *NP*.

B448 "Homage to Onassis." *Jewish Di-al-ŏg*, Hanukkah 1970, p. 11. *CPIL*; *NP*; *SFGP*.

B449 "For My Student Militants." *Quarry*, 20, No. 1 (Winter 1971), 16–17. *CPIL* ("For Some of My Student Militants"); *NP*.

B450 "The Gardener." *Quarry*, 20, No. 1 (Winter 1971), 15. Rpt. in *The Canadian Forum*, Feb. 1971, p. 378. *CPIL*; *NP*; *UE*.

B451 "Eros [So expertly did he teach]." *Ingluvin*, No. 2 (Jan.–March 1971), p. 54. *CPIL* (revised); *NP*.

B452 "Free Expression." *Ingluvin*, No. 2 (Jan.–March 1971), p. 53. *CPIL* (revised); *NP*.

B453 "God Is Love." *The Canadian Forum*, Feb. 1971, p. 380. *CPIL* (revised); *NP* (revised).

B454 "Lake Selby." *The Canadian Forum*, Feb. 1971, p. 379. *CPIL*; *NP*; *UE*; *Ts:p* ("Lake Selby / Lago Selby").

B455 "Nail Polish." *The Canadian Forum*, Feb. 1971, p. 379. Rpt. in *Gossip!* [Toronto], March 1971, p. 4. *CPIL*; *NP*.
  See B1255 ("Power and Poetry: Nail Polish").

B456 "Thoughts of a Senile Revolutionist." *The Canadian Forum*, Feb. 1971, p. 379. *CPIL*; *NP*.

B457 "You and the 20th Century." *The Canadian Forum*, Feb. 1971, p. 378. *CPIL*; *NP*; *LPIL* (l.ed); *Pa* ("Tú y el siglo xx"); *LPIL* ("You and the 20th Century"); *paIL* ("You and the 20th Century / Tu e il xx secolo"); *LPIL:RD* ("You and the 20th Century"); *DD* ("You and the Twentieth Century").

B458 "The Brothers Lazarovitch: After Margaret Atwood." *The University of Windsor Review*, 6, No. 2 (Spring 1971), 2. *CPIL* ("The Brothers Lazarovitch"); *NP* ("The Brothers Lazarovitch: After Margaret Atwood").

B459 "No Curtain Calls." *The University of Windsor Review*, 6, No. 2 (Spring 1971), 1. *CPIL*; *NP*.

B460 "Some Canadian Birds in October." *Saturday Night*, Oct. 1971, p. 45. *LLM*.

B461 "Analogue." *Manna* [Toronto], No. 4 (1972), p. 24. *PV*.

B462 "Mexican Guerillas." *Manna* [Toronto], No. 4 (1972), p. 24. *PV*.

B463 "Mexico Poems: No Exit." *Impulse*, 1, No. 2 (Winter 1972), 5–6. Rpt. ("No Exit") in *Waves*, 1, No. 1 (Spring 1972), 42. Rpt. (" 'No Exit' ") in *Queen's Quarterly*, 79 (Summer 1972), 146. Rpt. in *The Unmuzzled Ox* [New York], 1, No. 3 (Summer 1972), 53–54. *LLM* ("No Exit"); *UE*.

B464 "Magic." *The Unmuzzled Ox* [New York], 1, No. 2 (Feb. 1972), 56–57. Rpt. (revised) in *Impulse*, 1, No. 3 (Spring 1972), 32. *LLM.*

B465 "New Year's Eve, Zihuatanejo." *Waves*, 1, No. 1 (Spring 1972), 40. Rpt. ("New Year's Eve Zihuatanejo") in *Impulse*, 1, No. 3 (Spring 1972), 30–31. *LLM* ("New Year's Eve, Zihuatanejo").

B466 "Two for Aviva." *Waves*, 1, No. 1 (Spring 1972), 41. Rpt. ("Two for One") in *Quest*, May 1972, p. 46. Rpt. in *Counter / Measures* [Bedford, Mass.], No. 2 (1973), p. 5. Rpt. in *Excalibur* [York Univ.], 15 March 1973, p. 7. Rpt. in *The Dalhousie Gazette*, 12 Feb. 1981, p. 16. *LLM.*

B467 "Let Me Not." *Quest*, May 1972, p. 46. *LLM.*

B468 "My Lovely Angel." *Quest*, May 1972, p. 46.

B469 "Tide." *Quest*, May 1972, p. 46. Rpt. ("Mexico Poems: Tide") in *Impulse*, 1, No. 2 (Winter 1972), 7. Rpt. ("Tide") in *Counter / Measures* [Bedford, Mass.], No. 2 (1973), p. 4. *LLM; UE.*

B470 "Xmas Eve 1971, Zihuatanejo." *Queen's Quarterly*, 79 (Summer 1972), 145. Rpt. in *Counter / Measures* [Bedford, Mass.], No. 2 (1973), p. 7. *LLM* ("Xmas Eve 1971, Zihuatanejo: For William Goodwin"); *UE.*

See *Layton* ("Xmas Eve 1971, Zihuatanejo").

B471 "Memo to a Suicide." *The Unmuzzled Ox* [New York], 1, No. 4 (Autumn 1972), 70. Rpt. in *Rufus* [Los Angeles], No. 3 (Spring 1973), p. 5. Rpt. in *The McGill News*, 56, No. 3 (Fall 1975), 32. *LLM* (revised); *UE* (revised); *Pa* ("Memorándum a un suicida"); *LPIL* ("Memo to a Suicide"); *LPIL:RD*; *DD.*

B472 "The Benediction." *The Chronicle Review* [Montreal], Oct. 1972, p. 15. *LLM* (revised); *UE*; *SPIL*(K); *FE.*

B473 "The Burning Bush." *The Chronicle Review* [Montreal], Oct. 1972, p. 16. *LLM.*

B474 "The Incarnation." *The Chronicle Review* [Montreal], Oct. 1972, p. 16. *LLM.*

B475 "Post-Auschwitz Jew." *The Chronicle Review* [Montreal], Oct. 1972, p. 15. *LLM.*

B476 "That Is the Question." *Saturday Night*, Oct. 1972, p. 48. Rpt. in *Origin*, Ser. 4, No. 5 (Oct. 1978), p. 44. Rpt. in *The Dalhousie Gazette*, 12 Feb. 1981, p. 16. *LLM; SFGP; UE; WBSL* ("That Is the Question / Ἰδού τὸ ἐρώτημα").

B477 "Portrait of the Artist as a Young Bull." *Toronto Daily Star*, 6 Oct. 1972, p. 7. Rpt. in *Time*. Can. Ed., 16 Oct. 1972, p. 13. Rpt. in *Excalibur* [York Univ.], 19 Oct. 1972, p. 9. Rpt. (revised) in *The Stuffed Crocodile* [London, Ont.], 1, No. 5 (Jan. 1973), 110. *PV* (revised).

See B1258.

B478 "York University." *Saturday Night*, Dec. 1972, p. 10. *LLM.*

B479 "The Antipodeans." *Queen's Quarterly*, 79 (Winter 1972), 503. *LLM; UE.*

B480 "An Aubade." *Chicago Review*, 24, No. 3 (Winter 1972), 127. Rpt. in *The Canadian Forum*, Jan. 1973, p. 18. *LLM; UE; LPIL* (l.ed); *Pa* ("Alborada"); *LPIL* ("An Aubade"); *LPIL:RD; SPIL*(K).

B481 "The Baroness." *Chicago Review*, 24, No. 3 (Winter 1972), 125–26. *LLM; UE; PIL; SPIL.*

B482 "Stella." *Queen's Quarterly*, 79 (Winter 1972), 503–04. Rpt. trans. Effihia Psimenatov, Dino Siotis, and George Thaniel in *The Amaranth: Bulletin of Modern Greek Studies Program* [Univ. of Toronto], No. 7 (1984), pp. 10–12. *LLM; SFGP; UE; WPJ; WPJ2; WBSL* ("Stella / Ἡ Στελλα"); *DD* ("Stella").

B483 "Stella Ioannou (1894–1972)." *Queen's Quarterly*, 79 (Winter 1972), 504. *LLM; SFGP.*

B484 "Walt's Reply." *Chicago Review*, 24, No. 3 (Winter 1972), 126. *LLM.*

B485 "Elegy for Nathan Ralph." *The Canadian Forum*, Jan. 1973, p. 21. *LLM* (revised).

B486 "End of the Affair [Wisdom is the decay of youth]." *The Stuffed Crocodile* [London, Ont.], 1, No. 5 (Jan. 1973), 109. *LLM; SFGP; LPIL* (l.ed); *Pa* ("Asunto concluido"); *LPIL* ("End of the Affair [Wisdom is the decay of youth]"); *paIL* ("End of the Affair [Wisdom is the decay of youth] / Fine della storia"); *LPIL:RD* ("End of the Affair [Wisdom is the decay of youth]"); *SPIL*(K); *WBSL* ("End of the Affair [Wisdom is the decay of youth] / Το τελος μιας ερωτικης ιστοριας").

B487 "A Greek's View of Canadians." *The Stuffed Crocodile* [London, Ont.], 1, No. 5 (Jan. 1973), 112. *LLM.*

B488 "A Letter to No One in Particular." *The Canadian Forum*, Jan. 1973, p. 20. *LLM.*

B489 "My Eyes Have Seen the Glory." *The Canadian Forum*, Jan. 1973, p. 19. *LLM.*

B490 "On Seeing an Old Poet and His Wife." *Counter / Measures* [Bedford, Mass.], No. 2 (1973), p. 6. *LLM; UE.*

B491 "Poetry and Truth." *The Canadian Forum*, Jan. 1973, p. 19. *LLM; UE; SPIL*(K).

B492 "Snowman." *Counter / Measures* [Bedford, Mass.], No. 2 (1973), p. 6. *LLM; UE.*

B493 "The Terrorist." *The Canadian Forum*, Jan. 1973, pp. 18–19. *LLM; UE.*

B494 "Why I'm Not an Atheist." *Counter / Measures* [Bedford, Mass.], No. 2 (1973), p. 6. Rpt. in *The Stuffed Crocodile* [London, Ont.], 1, No. 5 (Jan. 1973), p. 111. *LLM.*

B495 "Harry Truman 1884–1972." *Saturday Night*, Feb. 1973, p. 12. *PV.*

B496 "Teufelsdrockh Concerning Women." *Excalibur* [York Univ.], 8 March 1973, p. 7. Rpt. in *The London Free Press*, 28 April 1973, p. 15. *LLM.*

B497 "Funeraria 'Olea.'" *Ariel* [Univ. of Calgary], No. 4 (July 1973), p. 47. *PV; UE; WPJ2; Ts:p* ("Funeraria 'Olea' / Funeraria olea").

B498 "Departed." *The Chronicle Review* [Montreal], Sept. 1973, p. 9. *PV; UE; FE.*
See *EIL*76.

B499 "For Anne Frank." *The Chronicle Review* [Montreal], Sept. 1973, p. 9. *PV; FE.*
See *B*1267.

B500 "The Improved Binoculars." *Hong Kong Sunday Post Herald*, 4 Nov. 1973, p. 3. Rpt. trans. Oláh Janos and Tótfalusi István ("A tökéletesített távcső") in *Gótika a vadonban: Kanadai angol nyelvű Költők, modern Könyvtár.* Ed. James Steele. Introd. Béla Köpeczi. Debrecenben: Europa Konyvkiado, 1983, p. 114. Rpt. trans. Jurosław Sokół and Florian Smieja ("Naprawiona Lornetka") in *Literatura na Świecie* [Warsaw] [No. 4 (225)], Kwiecień [April] 1990, p. 73. *CGE* ("The Improved Binoculars"); *IB*; *IB2*; *RCS*; *CP*; *SP69*; *CPIL*; *fve* ("The Improved Binoculars / Il binocolo perfezionato"); *DF* ("The Improved Binoculars"); *PIL*; *SPIL*; *eg* ("The Improved Binoculars / Il binocolo potenziato"); *WPJ* ("The Improved Binoculars"); *WPJ2*; *SPIL*(K); *FE*; *Ts:p* ("The Improved Binoculars / Il binocolo potenziato"); *LP*.

See *ILH* ("The Improved Binoculars"), *PIL65*, *IL* (Montreal), *ILRH*, *EIL69*, *IL* (Toronto), *Layton*, *RCS* (cas.), *EIL76*, *PRIL*, and B1172.

B501 "For the Woman with the Speaking Eyes." *New* [Trumansburg, N.Y.], Nos. 22–23 (Fall–Winter 1973–74), p. 64. *PV* ("To the Woman with the Speaking Eyes: For Rae Sampson"); *UE*; *DD* ("To the Woman with the Speaking Eyes").

B502 "Epigram for A.M. Klein." *Canadian Literature*, No. 59 (Winter 1974), p. 39. *PV*; *UE*.

B503 "The Ideal among Vacationists." *Counter / Measures* [Bedford, Mass.], No. 3 (1974), p. 54. *PV*; *SFGP*; *UE*.

B504 "Lillian Roxon." *Counter / Measures* [Bedford, Mass.], No. 3 (1974), p. 55. Rpt. in *The Sydney Morning Herald* [Australia], 7 March 1974. Rpt. in *Canberra Poetry* [Australian National University], 1, No. 4 (Autumn 1974), 50. *PV*; *UE*; *PIL*; *SPIL*. See *PRIL*.

B505 "Madonna and Dionysos." *The Unmuzzled Ox* [New York], 2, No. 3 (1974), 34. *PV*; *SFGP*.

B506 "Museum at Iraklion." Trans. Kim Yang Shik. *Wor Kan Men Ha* [Seoul], Jan. 1974, p. 129. *PV*; *SFGP*.

B507 "Requiem for A.M. Klein." *Canadian Literature*, No. 59 (Winter 1974), pp. 38–39. *PV*; *UE*; *FE*. See *EIL76*.

B508 "Terrorists." *Saturday Night*, Jan. 1974, p. 6. *PV*; *UE*; *FE*.

B509 "To First Violet." Trans. Kim Yang Shik. *Wor Kan Men Ha* [Seoul], Jan. 1974, p. 129.

B510 "For Francesca." *Chatelaine*, March 1974, p. 91. *MBJ*; *TP* ("For Francesca / A Francesca"); *LPIL* (l.ed) ("For Francesca"); *Pa* ("A Francesca"); *LPIL* ("For Francesca"); *TWNS*; *LPIL:RD*; *DD*.

B511 "Midsummer's Dream in the Vienna Stadpark." *The Chronicle Review* [Montreal], March 1974, p. 11. *PV*; *UE*; *WPJ* ("Midsummer's Dream in the Vienna Stadtpark"); *WPJ2*; *FE* ("Midsummer's Dream in the Vienna Stadpark"); *Ts:p* ("Midsummer's Dream in the Vienna Stadpark / Sogno di mezza estate nello Stadpark di Vienna").

B512 "Bedbugs." *Waves*, 2, No. 3 (Spring 1974), 8. *PV* (revised).

B513 "Pole-Vaulter." *Waves*, 2, No. 3 (Spring 1974), 9. Rpt. trans. Amleto Lorenzini, Carla Plevano, and Francesca Valente ("Il Saltatore con L'Asta") in *Almanaco Dello Specchhio 6*. Ed. Marco Forti. N.p.: Mondadori, 1977, pp. 191, 193. *PV* ("Pole-Vaulter"); *UE*; *PIL*; *SPIL*; *eg* ("Pole-Vaulter / Saltatore con l'asta"); *Ts:p*.

For the English contributions to the 1977 anthology, see B1101. See also *EIL76* ("The Pole-Vaulter").

B514 "September Woman." *Waves*, 2, No. 3 (Spring 1974), 10. *PV* (revised); *eg* ("September Woman / Donna in settembre"); *DD* ("September Woman"); *Ts:p* ("September Woman / Donna di settembre").

B515 "The Shadow." *Inscape* [Univ. of Ottawa], 11, No. 2 (Spring 1974), 48–50. Rpt. trans. Amleto Lorenzini, Carla Plevano, and Francesca Valente ("L'Ombra") in *Almanaco Dello Specchhio 6*. Ed. Marco Forti. N.p.: Mondadori, 1977, pp. 185, 187, 189. *PV* ("The Shadow"); *UE*; *FE*.
   For the English contributions to the 1977 anthology, see B1101. See also *EIL76*.

B516 "Gdyby Wieloryby Umiały Myśleć W Pewne Radosne Dni." Trans. Bogusław Rostworowski. *Życie Literackie* [Krakow], 14 April 1974, p. 11. Rpt. ("If Whales Could Think on Certain Happy Days") in *New Books*. Vancouver: J.J. Douglas, Spring 1977, [front cover]. Rpt. in *The Ontario Beaver* [Oakville, Ont.], 7 Sept. 1977. Rpt. in *Weekend Magazine*, 17 Sept. 1977, p. 9. *SP*; *SP69*; *CPIL*; *DF*; *TWNS*; *SDCJ*.
   See *PIL65*, *IL* (Toronto), and B1296.

B517 "Metamorfoza." Trans. Bogusław Rostworowski. *Życie Literackie* [Krakow], 14 April 1974, p. 11. *BP* ("Metamorphosis"); *IB2* (revised); *RCS*; *CP*; *SP69*; *CPIL*; *DF*; *SPIL*(K).
   See *RCS* (cas.).

B518 "Gołębi." Trans. Bogusław Rostworowski. *Życie Literackie* [Krakow], 14 April 1974, p. 11. *PM* ("Pigeons"); *SP69*; *CPIL*; *DF*.

B519 "Canymede." *Inscape* [Univ. of Ottawa], 11, No. 3 (Fall 1974), 27. *PV* ("Ganymede"); *SFGP*; *UE*; *WBSL* ("Ganymede / Γανυμηδης").

B520 "Conversion." *Inscape* [Univ. of Ottawa], 11, No. 3 (Fall 1974), 29. *PV*.

B521 "For Andrei Amalrik." *Inscape* [Univ. of Ottawa], 11, No. 3 (Fall 1974), 31. *PV*; *UE*; *eg* ("For Andrei Amalrik / Per Andrei Amalrik"); *Ts:p*.
   See *PRIL* ("For Andrei Amalrik").

B522 "For the Fraulein from Hamburg." *Canberra Poetry* [Australian National Univ.], 1, No. 4 (Autumn 1974), 49. Rpt. in *The Canadian Forum*, Oct. 1974, p. 31. *PV*; *UE*; *UVP*.

B523 "Marriage [The lover of the treacherous wife]." *Inscape* [Univ. of Ottawa], 11, No. 3 (Fall 1974), 28. *PV*; *UE*.

B524 "Poet's Bust." *Inscape* [Univ. of Ottawa], 11, No. 3 (Fall 1974), 30. *PV* (revised); *UE*.

B525 "American Young Woman in Patmos." *The Canadian Forum*, Oct. 1974, p. 31. *PV*; *SFGP*.

B526 "The Black Queen." *The Canadian Forum*, Oct. 1974, p. 30. *PV*; *UE*.

B527 "Ch'an Artist." *The Canadian Forum*, Oct. 1974, p. 31. Rpt. in *The McGill News*, 56, No. 3 (Fall 1975), 32. Rpt. trans. Amleto Lorenzini, Carla Plevano, and Francesca Valente ("L'Artista Ch'an") in *Almanaco Dello Specchhio 6*. Ed. Marco Forti. N.p.: Mondadori, 1977, p. 191. *PV* ("Ch'an Artist"); *UE*; *SPIL*(K).
   For the English contributions to the 1977 anthology, see B1101.

B528 "For Nadezhda Mandelshtam." *The Canadian Forum*, Oct. 1974, p. 30. *PV* (revised); *FE* ("For Nadezhda Mandelstam").

B529 "Thoughts of a Male Chauvinist Pig." *The Canadian Forum*, Oct. 1974, p. 31. Rpt. in *The Brandon Sun*, 7 June 1975, p. 4. *PV*.

B530 "What I Told the Ghost of Harold Laski." *The Canadian Forum*, Oct. 1974, p. 31. *PV; UE*.
See B1289 ("Portrait of a One-Armed Juggler: What I Told the Ghost of Harold Laski").

B531 "O Jerusalem." *The Chronicle Review* [Montreal], Nov. 1974, p. 7. Rpt. in *The Ontario Review*, No. 2 (Spring–Summer 1975), p. 16. Rpt. trans. Amleto Lorenzini, Carla Plevano, and Francesca Valente ("O Gerusaleme") in *Almanaco Dello Specchhio 6*. Ed. Marco Forti. N.p.: Mondadori, 1977, pp. 173, 175. Rpt. trans. Branko Gorjup ("O Jeruzaleme") in *Republika* [Zagreb, Yugoslavia], Nos. 10–12 (1984), p. 174. Rpt. trans. Jurosław Sokół and Florian Smieja ("O Jerozolimo") in *Literatura na Świecie* [Warsaw] [No. 4 (225)], Kwiecień [April] 1990, p. 74. Rpt. ("O Jerusalem") in *The Canadian Jewish News, Viewpoints*, 30 Aug. 1990, p. 8. *UE; MBJ* (revised); *PIL; SPIL; WPJ; WPJ2; FE*.
For the English contributions to the 1977 anthology, see B1101. See also *EIL76, PRIL*, and *WPJ* (cas.).

B532 "The Final Solution." *Jewish Di-al-ŏg*, Hanukkah 1974, p. 32. *PV* (revised); *UE; eg* ("The Final Solution / La soluzione finale"); *FE* ("The Final Solution"); *Ts:p* ("The Final Solution / La soluzione finale").

B533 "Mary." *Jewish Di-al-ŏg*, Hanukkah 1974, p. 47. *PV*.

B534 "Flytrap." *Waves*, 3, No. 2 (Winter 1975), 40. Rpt. trans. Amleto Lorenzini, Carla Plevano, and France-sca Valente ("Acchiappamosche") in *Almanaco Dello Specchhio 6*. Ed. Marco Forti. N.p.: Mondadori, 1977, pp. 175, 177. *SFGP* ("Flytrap"); *UE; WPJ; WPJ2; WBSL* ("Flytrap / Μυγοπαγιδα").
For the English contributions to the 1977 anthology, see B1101.

B535 "Seduction of and by a Civilized Frenchwoman." *Exile* [York Univ.], 3, No. 1 (1975), 113. Rpt. ["Seduzione di (e da parte di) una colta francese"] in *Poesia canadese del Novocento*. Ed. and trans. Caterina Ricciardi. Napoli: Liguori, 1986, pp. 129, 131. *MBJ* ("Seduction of and by a Civilized Frenchwoman"); *PIL; SPIL; LPIL* (l.ed); *Pa* ("Seducción de y por una francesa civilizada")' *LPIL* ("Seduction of and by a Civilized French Woman"); *paIL* ["Seduction of and by a Civilized French Woman / Seduzione di (e da parte di) una colta francese"]; *eg; LPIL:RD* ("Seduction of and by a Civilized French Woman"); *DD; Ts:p* ["Seduction of and by a Civilized French Woman / Seduzione di, (e da parte di) una colta francese"].
For the English contributions to this anthology, see B1126.

B536 "The Unwavering Eye." *Waves*, 3, No. 2 (Winter 1975), 41. Rpt. trans. Amleto Lorenzini, Carla Plevano, and Francesca Valente ("L'Occhio Fermo") in *Almanaco Dello Specchhio 6*. Ed. Marco Forti. N.p.: Mondadori, 1977, p. 173. Rpt. trans. Branko Gorjup ("Nepokolebljivo Oko") in *Republika* [Zagreb, Yugoslavia], Nos. 10–12 (1984), p. 171. *SFGP* ("The Unwavering Eye"); *UE; SPIL*(K); *WBSL* ("The Unwavering Eye / Το ’Ακλονητο Ματι").
For the English contributions to the 1977 anthology, see B1101.

B537 "To the Lawyer Handling My Divorce Case." *The Toronto Sun*, 11 Feb. 1975, p. 3. *BH* ("Existentialist"); *BH2*; *CPIL* ("To the Lawyer Handling My Divorce Case"); *NIP*.

B538 "Adam: For Amleto Lorenzini." *Waves*, 3, No. 3 (Spring 1975), 8–9. Rpt. in *Iconomatrix: A Polemical & Iconoclastic Quarterly*, 1, No. 1 (Sept. 1975), 24–25. Rpt. trans. Amleto Lorenzini, Carla Plevano, and Francesca Valente ("Adamo") in *Almanaco Dello Specchhio* 6. Ed. Marco Forti. N.p.: Mondadori, 1977, pp. 181, 183. *MBJ* ("Adam: For Amleto Lorenzini"); *PIL* ("Adam"); *SPIL*; *eg* ("Adam / Adamo"); *FE* ("Adam"); *Ts:p* ("Adam / Adamo").
For the English contributions to the 1977 anthology, see B1101. See also B1279 ("Adam").

B539 "Adonis." *Iconomatrix: A Polemical & Iconoclastic Quarterly*, 1, No. 1 (Sept. 1975), 22. *MBJ*.

B540 "Amo Amas Tit Loves an Ass." *Iconomatrix: A Polemical & Iconoclastic Quarterly*, 1, No. 1 (Sept. 1975), 21–22.

B541 "Desmond Pacey: In Memoriam." *Iconomatrix: A Polemical & Iconoclastic Quarterly*, 1, No. 1 (Sept. 1975), 3. *MBJ*.

B542 "For Edda." *Iconomatrix: A Polemical & Iconoclastic Quarterly*, 1, No. 1 (Sept. 1975), 22–23. *MBJ* (revised); *TP* ("For Edda / A Edda"); *eg* ("For Edda / Per Edda"); *DD* ("For Edda"); *Ts:p* ("For Edda / Per Edda").

B543 "Saint Pinchas." *Iconomatrix: A Polemical & Iconoclastic Quarterly*, 1, No. 1 (Sept. 1975), 23–24. *MBJ* (revised); *FE*.

B544 "True Love." *Iconomatrix: A Polemical & Iconoclastic Quarterly*, 1, No. 1 (Sept. 1975), 23. *MBJ*; *SPIL*(K).

B545 "Perspective: Entry." *The McGill News*, 56, No. 3 (Fall 1975), 32. *CPIL* ("Entry"); *NP*; *UE*; *FE*.

B546 "Perspective: The Ventriloquist." *The McGill News*, 56, No. 3 (Fall 1975), 32. *PV* ("The Ventriloquist"); *UE*; *PIL*; *SPIL*; *UVP*.

B547 "Parque de Montjuiche (For Jack Bernstein)." *The Chronicle Review* [Montreal], Oct. 1975, p. 65. *MBJ* (revised — "Parque de Montjuich: For Jack Bernstein"); *PIL* ("Parque de Montjuich"); *SPIL*; *WPJ* (revised); *WPJ2*; *FE*.

B548 "At the Barcelona Zoo." *Jewish Di-al-ŏg*, Hanukkah 1975, p. 29. *MBJ*.

B549 "On the Survival of the Fittest." *Jewish Di-al-ŏg*, Hanukkah 1975, p. 28. *MBJ* (revised).

B550 "Warrior Poet." *Jewish Di-al-ŏg*, Hanukkah 1975, p. 29. *MBJ*; *FE*.
See *EIL76* and B1278.

B551 "Catacombe Dei Cappucini: For William Goodwin." *Exile* [York Univ.], 4, No. 1 (1976), 71–72. *Cov.* ("Catacombe dei Capuccini: For William Goodwin"); *TP* ("Catacombe Dei Cappuccini: For William Goodwin / Catacombe dei Cappuccini: A William Goodwin"); *TWNS* ("Catacombe dei Cappuccini: For William Goodwin"); *eg* ("Catacombe dei Cappuccini: For William Goodwin / Catacombe dei cappuccini: Per William Goodwin"); *WPJ* ("Catacombe dei Capuccini"); *WPJ2*; *Ts:p* ("Catacombe dei Cappuccini: For William Goodwin

/ Catacombe dei Cappuccini: Per William Goodwin"); *CC* ("Catacombe dei Cappucini").

B552 "The Hallowing." *Waves*, 4, No. 2 (Winter 1976), 40. *MBJ*.

B553 "Night Thoughts." *Exile* [York Univ.], 4, No. 1 (1976), 73–74. *Cov*.

B554 "A Poem to Calm the Nervous Fears of the Very Reverend Arthur Smith." *Northern Journey*, Nos. 7–8 (1976), p. 105.

B555 "Release." *Waves*, 4, No. 2 (Winter 1976), 41. *MBJ*.

B556 "The Revolving Door." *Waves*, 4, No. 2 (Winter 1976), 38–39. *MBJ*.

B557 "Florence." *The Tamarack Review*, No. 68 (Spring 1976), p. 37. *MBJ*; *eg* ("Florence / Firenze"); *Ts:p*.

B558 "For My Incomparable Gypsy." *The Tamarack Review*, No. 68 (Spring 1976), pp. 40–41. *MBJ* ("For My Incomparable Gypsy: For Sparkles"); *LPIL* (l.ed) ("For My Incomparable Gypsy"); *Pa* ("A mi gitana incomparable"); *LPIL* ("For My Incomparable Gypsy"); *LPIL:RD*; *DD*.

B559 "How Many Days." *The Tamarack Review*, No. 68 (Spring 1976), p. 42. *MBJ*.

B560 "Jeshua." *The Tamarack Review*, No. 68 (Spring 1976), pp. 34–36. *MBJ*; *FE*.

B561 "The Plaka." *The Tamarack Review*, No. 68 (Spring 1976), pp. 38–39. *MBJ* ("The Plaka: For John and Ruth Colombo"); *eg* ("The Plaka / La plaka"); *Ts:p* ("The Plaka / La Plaka").

B562 "Saved." *The Tamarack Review*, No. 68 (Spring 1976), p. 33. *MBJ*.

B563 "For Some of My Best Friends." *Fraternally Yours* [Official Publication of the New Fraternal Jewish Association, Toronto], April 1976, p. 9. Rpt. in *The Canadian Forum*, June–July 1976, p. 59. *MBJ*.

B564 "For My Distant Woman." *The Ontario Review*, No. 4 (Spring–Summer 1976), p. 19. *MBJ*; *PIL*; *SPIL*; *LPIL* (l.ed); *Pa* ("A mi mujer lejana"); *LPIL* ("For My Distant Woman"); *LPIL:RD*; *DD*.

B565 "St. Antipop." *The Canadian Forum*, June–July 1976, p. 59. *MBJ* ("Saint Antipop").

B566 "Faustein." *Inscape* [Univ. of Ottawa], 13, No. 1 (Fall 1976), 19. *Cov*.

B567 "The Glass Dancer: For 'Bull' (D.D. Redwood)." *Inscape* [Univ. of Ottawa], 13, No. 1 (Fall 1976), 20–21. *Cov*.

B568 "Oracabessa, Xmas Eve 1975." *Inscape* [Univ. of Ottawa], 13, No. 1 (Fall 1976), 22. *Cov*.

B569 "La gatta di Molibos." Trans. Amleto Lorenzini, Carla Plevano, and Francesca Valente. In *Almanaco Dello Specchhio 6*. Ed. Marco Forti. N.p.: Mondadori, 1977, p. 189. *PV* ("Molibos Cat"); *SFGP*; *UE*; *WBSL* ("Molibos Cat / Στο Μολυβο μια γατα"); *Ts:p* ("Molibos Cat / La gatta di Molibos").
  For the English contributions to the 1977 anthology, see B1101. See also *PRIL* ("Molibos Cat").

B570 "Irochese a Nizza." Trans. Amleto Lorenzini, Carla Plevano, and Francesca Valente. In *Almanaco Dello Specchhio 6*. Ed. Marco Forti. N.p.: Mondadori,

1977, pp. 177, 179, 181. *SP* ("Iroquois in Nice");
WPJ; *WPJ*2.

For the English contributions to the 1977 anthology, see B1101.

B571 "Il pescecane." Trans. Amleto Lorenzini, Carla Plevano, and Francesca Valente. In *Almanaco Dello Specchhio 6*. Ed. Marco Forti. N.p.: Mondadori, 1977, p. 171. Rpt. trans. Branko Gorjup ("Morski Pas") in *Republika* [Zagreb, Yugoslavia], Nos. 10–12 (1984), p. 172. *SFGP* ("The Shark"); *UE*; *PIL*; *SPIL*; *WPJ*; *WPJ*2; *SPIL*(K); *WBSL* ("The Shark / 'Ο Καρχαριας").

For the English contributions to the 1977 anthology, see B1101. See also *EIL*76 ("The Shark") and *WPJ* (cas.).

B572 "The Quill." *Chatelaine*, Jan. 1977, p. 78. *Cov.*; *LPIL* (l.ed); *Pa* ("La lanzadera"); *LPIL* ("The Quill"); *LPIL:RD*.

B573 "Gone." *Chatelaine*, March 1977, p. 116. *Cov.*; *LPIL* (l.ed); *Pa* ("Ausente"); *LPIL* ("Gone"); *paIL* ("Gone / Partita"); *LPIL:RD* ("Gone").

B574 "Aetna." *Chicago Review*, 28, No. 4 (Spring 1977), p. 142. Rpt. in *CV/II*, 3, No. 3 (Jan. 1978), 35. *Cov.*; *eg* ("Aetna / Etna"); *Ts:p*.

B575 "The Arcade." *Chicago Review*, 28, No. 4 (Spring 1977), 143–44. Rpt. in *Waves*, 5, Nos.2–3 (Spring 1977), 60. *Cov.* (revised); *TP* ("The Arcade / La Galleria"); *eg* ("The Arcade / La galleria"); *Ts:p*.

B576 "El Diablo: For Nicholas Haines." *Chicago Review*, 28, No. 4 (Spring 1977), 141. Rpt. in *CV/II*, 3, No. 3 (Jan. 1978), 35. *Cov.*

B577 "Hidden Worlds." *Waves*, 5, Nos. 2–3 (Spring 1977), 61. *Cov.* (revised); *LPIL* (l.ed); *Pa* ("Mundos escondidos"); *LPIL* ("Hidden Worlds"); *TWNS*; *LPIL:RD*; *SPIL*(K); *DD*.

B578 "King Kong." *Chicago Review*, 28, No. 4 (Spring 1977), 143. *Cov.*; *SDCJ*; *FE*.

B579 "Moments of Election: For Jacques Montpetit." *Waves*, 5, Nos. 2–3 (Spring 1977), 58–59. Rpt. in *CV/II*, 3, No. 3 (Jan. 1978), 34. *Cov.*

B580 "Xianity." *Waves*, 5, Nos. 2–3 (Spring 1977), 57. Rpt. trans. Branko Gorjup ("Xianty") in *Republika* [Zagreb, Yugoslavia], Nos. 10–12 (1984), p. 175. *Cov.* (revised — "Xianity"); *WPJ*; *WPJ*2; *FE*.
See B1295.

B581 "Broilerism, 2000 AD." *The English Quarterly* [Oromocto, N.B.], 10, No. 2 (Summer 1977), 113. *Cov.* (revised — "Soviet Broilerism 2000 AD").

B582 "Europe 1976." *Toronto Life*, Oct. 1977, p. 69. *Cov.*; *WPJ*; *WPJ*2.

B583 "The Luminous Bagel." *Toronto Life*, Oct. 1977, p. 69. *Cov.*; *WPJ* (revised); *WPJ*2; *FE* (revised).

B584 "The Fire-Gutted Church on Avenue Road." *The Ontario Review*, No. 7 (Fall–Winter 1977–78), p. 66. *Cov.*

B585 "A Walk to Nowhere." *The Ontario Review*, No. 7 (Fall–Winter 1977–78), p. 67. *Cov.*

B586 "For 751–0329." *Toronto Life*, Dec. 1977, p. 68. *TP* ("For 751–0329 / Per 751–0329"); *TD* ("For 751–0329"); *TWNS*; *eg* ("For 751–0329 / Per 751–

0329"); *WPJ* ("For 7515–03296"); *WPJ2*; *FE*; *Ts:p*
("For 751–0329 / Per 751–0329").
See *PRIL* ("For 751–0329"), *WPJ* (cas.) ("For
7515–03296"), and B1300 ("For 751–0329").

B587 "Canucky Shmuck: For Douglas Barbour." *Intrinsic*,
No. 3 (Winter 1978), p. 17. Rpt. in *Books in Canada*,
March 1978, p. 5.

B588 "Comrade." In *Handouts from the Mountain*. Ed.
Irving Layton. Toronto: York Univ. Poetry Work-
shop, 1978, p. 39. *TD*.
See B1105 for reprinted material in this book.

B589 "For Oscar Latch." *Intrinsic*, No. 3 (Winter 1978),
p. 16.

B590 "Contra esta muerte." Trans. Manuel Santos. In
Antología de la Poésia Actual Canadiense Inglesa.
Ed. Manuel Santos. Mexico: Universidad Autonoma
de San Luis Potosi, 1978, p. 78. Rpt. in *Antología de
la poesía anglo canadiense contemporánea*. Ed. and
trans. Bernd Dietz. Barcelona: Los libros de la
frontera, 1985, p. 59. Rpt. ("Contro Questa Morte")
in *Poesia canadese del Novocento*. Ed. and trans.
Caterina Ricciardi. Napoli: Liguori, 1986, p. 111.
MMF ("Against This Death"); *RCS*; *CP*; *CPIL*; *DF*;
WPJ; *WPJ2*.
For the English contributions to the 1985 anthology, see B1123. For the English contributions to the
1986 anthology, see B1126. See also *RCS* (cas.) and
B1250 ("Poetry and Power: Against This Death").

B591 "Si Yo Me Acuesto Inmovil." Trans. Manuel Santos.
In *Antología de la Poésia Actual Canadiense Inglesa*.
Ed. Manuel Santos. Mexico: Universidad Autonoma
de San Luis Potosi, 1978, pp. 79–80. Rpt. ("Si me
trendo y no me muevo") in *Antología de la poesía*

anglo canadiense contemporánea. Ed. and trans.
Bernd Dietz. Barcelona: Los libros de la frontera,
1985, pp. 61, 63. *BOAJ* ("If I Lie Still"); *CP*; *CPIL*;
DF; *LPIL* (l.ed); *Pa* ("Si yazgo sosegado"); *LPIL* ("If
I Lie Still"); *paIL* ("If I Lie Still / Se giaccio immo-
bile"); *LPIL:RD* ("If I Lie Still"); *SPIL*(K).
For the English contributions to the 1985 anthol-
ogy, see B1123. See also *Layton*.

B592 "George Woodcock Is Not a Shmuck." *Intrinsic*, No.
3 (Winter 1978), p. 14.

B593 "Hangover." *Intrinsic*, No. 3 (Winter 1978), p. 15.
TD (revised).

B594 "Night Music." *Waves*, 6, Nos. 2–3 (Spring 1978),
71. *TP* ("Night Music / Musica notturna"); *TD*
("Night Music"); *WPJ*; *WPJ2*; *WBSL* ("Night Music
/ Νυχτερινη Μουσικη"); *Ts:p* ("Night Music /
Musica notturna").
See *WPJ* (cas.) ("Night Music").

B595 "Theatre." *Waves*, 6, Nos. 2–3 (Spring 1978), 31.
TD (revised); *WBSL* ("Theatre / Θεατρο").
See *PRIL* ("Theatre").

B596 "To the Victims of the Holocaust." *Waves*, 6, Nos.
2–3 (Spring 1978), 70. Rpt. in *The Canadian Jewish
News* [Toronto], 14 March 1985, p. 11. *TD*; *eg* ("To
the Victims of the Holocaust / Alle vittime
dell'Olocausto"); *WPJ* ("To the Victims of the Holocaust"); *WPJ2*; *FE*; *Ts:p* ("To the Victims of the
Holocaust / Alle vittime dell'Olocausto").

B597 "When Death Comes for You." *Waves*, 6, Nos. 2–3
(Spring 1978), 31. *TD*; *WPJ2*; *WBSL* ("When Death
Comes for You / "Οταν ο θανατος ερθει για σενα");
DD ("When Death Comes for You").

B598 "Flies." *The Canadian Forum*, April 1978, p. 22. *TD*; *TWNS*; *WPJ*; *WPJ2*.

B599 "Grand Finale." *The Canadian Forum*, April 1978, p. 23. *TD*; *WPJ* (revised); *WPJ2*; *FE* (revised).
See *WPJ* (cas.).

B600 "The Happening." *The Canadian Forum*, April 1978, p. 23. *TD*.

B601 "Late Invitation to the Dance." *The Canadian Forum*, April 1978, p. 23. *TD*; *eg* ("Late Invitation to the Dance / Tardo invito alla danza"); *WPJ2* ("Late Invitation to the Dance"); *WBSL* ("Late Invitation to the Dance / Καθυστερημενη προσκληση στο χορο"); *Ts:p* ("Late Invitation to the Dance / Tardo invito alla danza").

B602 "The Malediction." *The Canadian Forum*, April 1978, p. 22. *TD*.

B603 "News from Nowhere: For William Morris." *The Canadian Forum*, April 1978, p. 22. *DH*.

B604 "Smoke [Père Lachaise is so peaceful]." *The Canadian Forum*, April 1978, p. 23. *TD*.

B605 "The Final Poem." *Canadian Literature*, No. 77 (Summer 1978), p. 41. *TD*.

B606 "Incident at the Cathedral." *McGill News*, Summer 1978, p. 3. *MBJ*; *FE*.
See *EIL76*.

B607 "Medusas." *Canadian Literature*, No. 77 (Summer 1978), p. 93. *TD*; *WPJ2*.

B608 "Tropical Flowers." *Canadian Literature*, No. 77 (Summer 1978), p. 49. *TD*.

B609 "The Final Peace." *Origin*, Ser. 4, No. 5 (Oct. 1978), p. 39. *CPIL*; *SFGP*; *UE*; *SPIL*(K); *WBB*.

B610 "If Euclid Were Your Analyst." *Origin*, Ser. 4, No. 5 (Oct. 1978), p. 40. *CPIL*; *SFGP*; *UE*; *WBB*.

B611 "Ithaca: For Marsha Kinder." *Origin*, Ser. 4, No. 5 (Oct. 1978), p. 48. *SFGP*; *UE* ("Ithaca"); *WPJ*; *WPJ2*; *WBSL* ("Ithaca: For Marsha Kinder / Ἰθακη").

B612 "Limpets." *Origin*, Ser. 4, No. 5 (Oct. 1978), p. 41. *LLM*; *SFGP*.

B613 "Madman on Mithymna Beach." *Origin*, Ser. 4, No. 5 (Oct. 1978), p. 47. *LPIL* (l.ed); *Pa* ("Loco en la playa de Mithymna"); *LPIL* ("Madman on Mithymna Beach"); *TD*; *LPIL:RD*; *SPIL*(K).
See B1297.

B614 "Rupert Brooke 1887–1915." *Origin*, Ser. 4, No. 5 (Oct. 1978), pp. 45–46. *LLM*; *SFGP*; *UE*; *WPJ2* ("Rupert Brooke: 1887–1915"); *WBSL* ["Rupert Brooke / Rupert Brooke (1887–1915)"].

B615 "A Tale with Teeth in It." *Origin*, Ser. 4, No. 5 (Oct. 1978), pp. 42–43. *LLM*; *SFGP*; *UE*.

B616 "Stari Dubrovnik." Trans. Branko Gorjup. *Naše novine*, 18 Oct. 1978, p. 17. Rpt. ("Olal Dubrovnik") in *Kultura* [Warsaw], 18 Oct. 1978, p. 17. Rpt. trans. Branko Gorjup ("Stari Dubrovnik") in *Republika* [Zagreb, Yugoslavia], Nos. 10–12 (1984), p. 172. *LLM* ("Old Dubrovnik: For Pero Santic").

B617 "Antimonies." *Zero: Contemporary Buddhist Life and Thought* [Los Angeles], 2 (1979), 123. Rpt. in *Matrix*, No. 9 (Spring–Summer 1979), p. 8. *DH*; *FE*.

B618 "Dialectical Leap." CV/II, 4, No. 1 (Winter 1979), 15. *TD*.

B619 "Opium." CV/II, 4, No. 1 (Winter 1979), 15. *TD*.

B620 "The Papal Election." CV/II, 4, No. 1 (Winter 1979), 15. *TD*.

B621 "Caesar Is Dead! Long Live Caesar." *Matrix*, No. 9 (Spring–Summer 1979), p. 12. *MNH* (revised — "Florida Nights").

B622 "Cuisine Canadienne." *Matrix*, No. 9 (Spring–Summer 1979), p. 9. *DH*.

B623 "Droppings from Heaven." *Matrix*, No. 9 (Spring–Summer 1979), p. 6. *DH*.

B624 "Guru." *Matrix*, No. 9 (Spring–Summer 1979), p. 13. Rpt. in *Poetry Canada Poésie*, 1, No. 1 (Fall 1979), 5. *MNH* (revised).

B625 "Hanging in There." *Matrix*, No. 9 (Spring–Summer 1979), p. 10. *DH*.

B626 "The Literary Mind." *Matrix*, No. 9 (Spring–Summer 1979), p. 6. *DH* (revised).

B627 "Natural Selection." *Matrix*, No. 9 (Spring–Summer 1979), p. 9. *MNH* (revised).

B628 "Shlemihl: For Reinhard Pummer." *Matrix*, No. 9 (Spring–Summer 1979), p. 10. *DH*; *FE* ("Shlemihl").

B629 "Two Communist Poets." *Matrix*, No. 9 (Spring–Summer 1979), p. 11. *MNH* (revised).

B630 "A Wild Peculiar Joy." *Matrix*, No. 9 (Spring–Summer 1979), p. 7. Rpt. in *The Canadian Jewish News, Viewpoints*, 30 Aug. 1990, p. 8. *DH*; *WPJ*; *WPJ2*; *FE*.

B631 "The Lyric [As moles construct]." *Poetry Canada Poésie*, 1, No. 1 (Fall 1979), 5. Rpt. in *Athanor* [Concordia Univ.], 1, No. 1 (Nov. 1979), 16. *MNH*; *FE*.

B632 "Old Codgers in a Gym." *Poetry Canada Poésie*, 1, No. 1 (Fall 1979), 5. *MNH*.

B633 "The Passionate Wasp." *Poetry Canada Poésie*, 1, No. 1 (Fall 1979), 5. Rpt. in *Athanor* [Concordia Univ.], 1, No. 1 (Nov. 1979), 17. *MNH* ("The Passionate WASP").

B634 "No More Chicken Soup." *Toronto Life*, Oct. 1979, p. 85. *DH*.

B635 "La Condition Humaine." *Athanor* [Concordia Univ.], 1, No. 1 (Nov. 1979), 16. Rpt. in *Poetry Canada Review*, 1, No. 2 (Winter 1979–80), 4. Rpt. in *Anthos*, 2, Nos. 1–2 (1980), 107. *MNH*; *WPJ2*; *Ts:p*.

B636 "On the Sudden Death of a Relative." *Athanor* [Concordia Univ.], 1, No. 1 (Nov. 1979), 17. *MNH* (revised); *FE*.

B637 "Libido." *The Ontario Review*, No. 11 (Fall–Winter 1979–80), p. 17. *DH* ("Libido: For Joyce Carol Oates").

B638 "Narcissus." *The Ontario Review*, No. 11 (Fall–Winter 1979–80), p. 16. *DH*; *WPJ*; *WPJ2*.

B639 "Synagogue in West Palm Beach." *The Ontario Review*, No. 11 (Fall–Winter 1979–80), p. 15. *DH* ("Synagogue in West Palm Beach: For Mary and Jack Bernstein"); *WPJ* ("Synagogue in West Palm Beach"); *WPJ2*.
   See *EIL81*.

B640 "Ashes and Diamonds." *Poetry Canada Review*, 1, No. 2 (Winter 1979–80), 4. *MNH*.

B641 "Antisemites." *Anthos*, 2, Nos. 1–2 (1980), 107. *MNH* (revised).

B642 "Dracula." *Anthos*, 2, Nos. 1–2 (1980), 111–12. Rpt. in *Trends: The Paisley College of Technology Literary Magazine* [Paisley, Scotland], 5, No. 10 (1984), 7. *MNH*; *WPJ*; *WPJ*2.
   See *WPJ* (cas.).

B643 "For My Neighbours in Hell [Hate, your adrenalin]." *Anthos*, 2, Nos. 1–2 (1980), 108. Rpt. in *Trends: The Paisley College of Technology Literary Magazine* [Paisley, Scotland], 5, No. 10 (1984), 9. *MNH*; *eg* ("For My Neighbours in Hell [Hate, your adrenalin] / Per il mio prossimo all'inferno"); *FE* ("For My Neighbours in Hell [Hate, your adrenalin]"); *Ts:p* ("For My Neighbours in Hell [Hate, your adrenalin] / Per il mio prossimo all'inferno").
   See *EIL81* ("For My Neighbours in Hell [Hate, your adrenalin]").

B644 "Lady with a Recorder." *Anthos*, 2, Nos. 1–2 (1980), 108. *MNH*.

B645 "Male Chauvinist." *Anthos*, 2, Nos. 1–2 (1980), 110. Rpt. in *Athanor* [Concordia Univ.], 1, No. 2 (Feb. 1980), 25. *MNH*.
   See *EIL81*.

B646 "Mount Royal Cemetery." *Anthos*, 2, Nos. 1–2 (1980), 110. *MNH*.

B647 "Mountain Playhouse." *Anthos*, 2, Nos. 1–2 (1980), 106. *MNH* (revised).

B648 "Self-Interview." *Anthos*, 2, Nos. 1–2 (1980), 109. *MNH* (revised).

B649 "Stalin." *Anthos*, 1, Nos. 1–2 (1980), 106. *MNH*.

B650 "The True Picture." *Anthos*, 2, Nos. 1–2 (1980), 110–11. *MNH*; *FE*.

B651 "The Final Coming." *Athanor* [Concordia Univ.], 1, No. 2 (Feb. 1980), 25. *MNH*; *DD*.

B652 "The Release [Before the cancer bugs]." *Athanor* [Concordia Univ.], 1, No. 2 (Feb. 1980), 25. Rpt. in *The Canadian Forum*, April 1980, p. 17. *EOBN*.

B653 "Egalitarian." *Poetry Canada Review*, 1, No. 3 (Spring 1980), 8. *MNH*.

B654 "Apocalypse." *The Canadian Forum*, April 1980, p. 16. *MNH*; *SPIL*(K).

B655 "A Brief History of the Jews [So what if you gave the world]." *The Canadian Forum*, April 1980, p. 17. *FE*.

B656 "The Comedian." *The Canadian Forum*, April 1980, p. 16. Rpt. in *Trends: The Paisley College of Technology Literary Magazine* [Paisley, Scotland], 5, No. 10 (1984), 8. *MNH*; *Ts:p* ("The Comedian / Il comico").

B657 "The Long Shade." *The Canadian Forum*, April 1980, p. 17. *MNH*.

B658 "Never in Rosedale." *The Canadian Forum*, April 1980, p. 17. *MNH*.

B659 "Old Men." *The Canadian Forum*, April 1980, p. 17. *MNH*; *WPJ*2; *SPIL*(K).

B660 "Passing Through the Rockies: For Ruth Fraser." *The Canadian Forum*, April 1980, p. 16. *MNH*.

B661 "Woody Allen." In "Canada Is in Danger of Being Gobbled Up." *The Globe and Mail* [Toronto], 19 April 1980, p. 7.

This poem is included in the article "Canada Is in Danger of Being Gobbled Up" (B931).

B662 "Cruising." *The Globe and Mail* [Toronto], 22 April 1980, p. 7. *EOBN*.

B663 "For Don Carlos." *Poetry Canada Review*, 1, No. 4 (Summer 1980), 5. *MNH* (revised).

B664 "Reflections in an Old Ontario Cemetery." *Poetry Canada Review*, 1, No. 4 (Summer 1980), 3. *MNH*; *eg* ("Reflections in an Old Ontario Cemetery / Riflessioni in un vecchio cimitero dell'Ontario"); *SPIL*(K) ("Reflections in an Old Ontario Cemetery"); *Ts:p* ("Reflections in an Old Ontario Cemetery / Riflessioni in un vecchio cimitero dell'Ontario"); *ROOC* ("Reflections in an Old Ontario Cemetery").

B665 "The Subversive." *Poetry Canada Review*, 1, No. 4 (Summer 1980), 3. *FE*.

B666 "Deliverance." *Athanor* [Concordia Univ.], 1, No. 3 (Aug. 1980), 28. *EOBN*.

B667 "For Erich Muhsam." *Athanor* [Concordia Univ.], 1, No. 3 (Aug. 1980), 29. *EOBN*; *eg* ("For Erich Muhsam / Per Erich Muhsam"); *FE* ("For Erich Muhsam"); *Ts:p* ("For Erich Muhsam / Per Erich Muhsam").

B668 "Junk." *Athanor* [Concordia Univ.], 1, No. 3 (Aug. 1980), 27. *EOBN* (revised).

B669 "Kore." *Athanor* [Concordia Univ.], 1, No. 3 (Aug. 1980), 27. *EOBN* (Koré).

B670 "The Presence." *Athanor* [Concordia Univ.], 1, No. 3 (Aug. 1980), 30. *Cov.*; *EOBN*; *SPIL*(K).

B671 "Finally, the Final Solution." *Poetry Canada Review*, 2, No. 1 (Fall 1980), 10. *MNH*.

B672 "For Hans, Maybe Klaus or Taddeuz." *Waves*, 9, No. 1 (Autumn 1980), 50–51. *EOBN* ("For Hans, Maybe Klaus or Tadeusz"); *FE*.

B673 "Eine Kleine Nachtmusik." *Waves*, 9, No. 1 (Autumn 1980), 53. Rpt. trans. Alessandro Gebbia in *A cultura* [Italy], 12 Aprile 1981, p. iv. *EOBN*; *eg*; *WPJ*; *WPJ2*; *FE*; *Ts:p*.
See *IL* (TV) and *WPJ* (cas.).

B674 "Reingemacht." *Waves*, 9, No. 1 (Autumn 1980), 52. *EOBN*; *WPJ2*; *FE*; *Ts:p*.

B675 "Ashtoreth." *Athanor* [Concordia Univ.], 1, No. 4 (Dec. 1980), 79. *EOBN*; *DD*.

B676 "Sunflowers." *Athanor* [Concordia Univ.], 1, No. 4 (Dec. 1980), 80. Rpt. in *The Eye* [Montreal], Dec. 1982, p. 2. *EOBN*; *WPJ*; *WPJ2*; *FE*; *Ts:p* ("Sunflowers / Girasoli").

B677 "Anarch." *Canadian Literature*, No. 87 (Winter 1980), p. 66. *EOBN* (revised); *WPJ*; *WPJ2*; *FE*.

B678 "The Annunciation." *Canadian Literature*, No. 87 (Winter 1980), p. 102. *EOBN*; *WPJ* (revised); *WPJ2*; *DD* (revised); *FE*; *SG*.

B679 "Being There." *Canadian Literature*, No. 87 (Winter 1980), p. 51. *EOBN*.

B680 "The Consummation." *Canadian Literature*, No. 87 (Winter 1980), p. 67. *EOBN*.

B681 "To a Shmuck with Talent." *Poetry Canada Review*, 2, No. 2 (Winter 1980–81), 10. *EOBN*.

B682 "Definitions." *Cross-Canada Writers' Quarterly*, 3, No. 1 (Winter 1981), 13. Rpt. in *Poetry Canada Review*, 2, No. 3 (Spring 1981), 13. Rpt. in *The Canadian Jewish News* [Toronto], 15 April 1982, p. 5. *EOBN*.

B683 "Eternal Recurrence [The sleepwalkers are advancing on Armageddon]." *Cross-Canada Writers' Quarterly*, 3, No. 1 (Winter 1981), 12. *EOBN*; *WPJ2*; *FE*.

B684 "For Antonio Machado." *Cross-Canada Writers' Quarterly*, 3, No. 1 (Winter 1981), 13. *EOBN*.

B685 "The Queen of Hearts." *Cross-Canada Writers' Quarterly*, 3, No. 1 (Winter 1981), 12. *EOBN*.

B686 "[Into the ordinary day you came]." *The Globe and Mail* [Toronto]. "McLuhan Tribute Planned," 28 Jan. 1981, p. 14. Rpt. ("Samantha Clara Layton") in *Canadian Literature*, No. 90 (Autumn 1981), p. 5. Rpt. in *The Toronto Sun*, 2 May 1982, p. G26. *WPJ*; *WPJ2*; *GB* (l.ed); *GB*; *GB2*; *SG*.
   Originally published in Zena Cherry's column, but signed Irving Layton in the text. See *WPJ* (cas.).

B687 "Farewell [She's gone. The one I swore up and down]." *The Dalhousie Gazette*, 12 Feb. 1981, p. 16. *LLM*; *UE*; *LPIL* (l.ed); *Pa* ("Despedida"); *LPIL* ("Farewell [She's gone. The one I swore up and down]"); *LPIL:RD*; *SPIL*(K); *DD*.

B688 "Comrade Trotsky." *Poetry Canada Review*, 2, No. 3 (Spring 1981), 13. *EOBN*; *FE*.

B689 "Divine Egotist." *Poetry Canada Review*, 2, No. 3 (Spring 1981), 13. *EOBN*.

B690 "Early Morning Sounds." *Poetry Canada Review*, 2, No. 3 (Spring 1981), 13. *EOBN*; *WPJ*; *WPJ2*.

B691 "For Else Lasker-Schuler." *Poetry Canada Review*, 2, No. 3 (Spring 1981), 13. *EOBN*; *FE*.

B692 "For Marina Ivanovna Tsvetayeva." *Poetry Canada Review*, 2, No. 3 (Spring 1981), 13. *EOBN*.

B693 "Sempre." *Poetry Canada Review*, 2, No. 3 (Spring 1981), 13. *EOBN*; *WPJ*; *WPJ2*.

B694 "With Undiminished Fire." *Waves*, 10, Nos. 1–2 (Summer–Fall 1981), 92–93. *GB* (l.ed); *GB*; *GB2*.

B695 "Zucchini." *Waves*, 10, Nos. 1–2 (Summer–Fall 1981), 94. *WPJ2*; *GB* (l.ed); *GB*; *GB2*; *Ts:p* ("Zucchini / Zucchine").

B696 "La Commedia." *The Canadian Forum*, Aug. 1981, p. 30. *WPJ*; *WPJ2*; *GB* (l.ed); *GB*; *GB2*.

B697 "They Sleep Without Dreams or Nightmares." *New Edition* [Toronto], 15 Sept. 1981, p. 7.

B698 "Blossom." *The Canadian Author & Bookman*, 57, No. 1 (Fall 1981), 29. *WPJ* (revised); *WPJ2*; *GB* (l.ed); *GB*; *GB2*.

B699 "To Make an End (For Malka Cohen 1897–1981)." *Canadian Literature*, No. 90 (Autumn 1981), p. 13. *WPJ2* ("To Make an End: For Malka Cohen 1897–1981"); *GB* (l.ed); *GB*; *GB2*.

B700 "The Quality of Mercy . . . ." *The Whig-Standard* [Kingston, Ont.], 29 Oct. 1981, p. 6.

B701 "For the Wife of John Milton." *Canadian Literature*, No. 91 (Winter 1981), p. 96. Rpt. ("For Malka Cohen 1897–1981") in *Shirim: A Jewish Poetry*

Journal [Los Angeles], 2, No. 2 (Fall 1983), 19. *WPJ2* ("For the Wife of Mr. Milton"); *GB* (l.ed); *GB*; *GB2*.

B702 "The Black Thread." *The Pottersfield Portfolio* [Porters Lake, N.S.], 3 (1981–82), 37. *GB* (l.ed); *GB*; *GB2*.

B703 "Poetry Conference." *The Pottersfield Portfolio* [Porters Lake, N.S.], 3 (1981–82), 5. *GB* (l.ed); *GB*; *GB2*.

B704 "Tristessa." *The Pottersfield Portfolio* [Porters Lake, N.S.], 3 (1981–82), 9. *WPJ2* ("Tristezza"); *FR* ("Tristezza: For F. Ruberti"); *Ts:p* ("Tristezza").

B705 "The Breast Stroke." *Exile* [York Univ.], 9, No. 1 (1982), 45. *WPJ* ("The Breaststroke"); *WPJ2*; *GB* (l.ed) ("The Breast Stroke: For Diane Parent"); *GB*; *GB2*; *LPIL:RD* ("The Breaststroke: For Diane Parent"); *DD* ("The Breast Stroke").

B706 "The Carillon." *Exile* [York Univ.], 9, No. 1 (1982), 46. Rpt. in *ellipse*, No. 40 (1988), p. 94. Rpt. trans. Jean Antonin Billard ("Le Carillon") in *ellipse*, No. 40 (1988), p. 95. *WPJ2* ("The Carillon"); *GB* (l.ed) (revised); *GB*; *GB2*.

B707 "From the Nether World." *Matrix*, No. 14 (Winter 1982), p. 22. *WPJ2*; *GB* (l.ed); *GB*; *GB2*.

B708 "The Remnant." *Exile* [York Univ.], 9, No. 1 (1982), 44. *GB* (l.ed); *GB*; *GB2*.

B709 "The Search." *Canadian Ethnic Studies / etudes ethnique au Canada*, 14, No. 1 (1982), 74. *EOBN* (revised); *WPJ*; *WPJ2*.

B710 "The Winged Horse." *Matrix*, No. 14 (Winter 1982), p. 23. *GB* (l.ed) ("The Winged Horse: For Doug Beardsley"); *GB*; *GB2*.

B711 "Fire Warden." *Graduate* [Univ. of Toronto Alumni], 9, No. 3 (Jan.–Feb. 1982), 14. *GB* (l.ed) ("Fire Warden: For Boris Pasternak"); *GB*; *GB2*.

B712 "They Also Serve." *Poetry Canada Review*, 3, No. 3 (Spring 1982), 4. *GB* (l.ed); *GB*; *GB2*.

B713 "Senile, My Sister Sings." *The Gazette* [Univ. of Western Ontario], 26 March 1982, p. 6. *DH*; *eg* ("Senile, My Sister Sings / Senile, canta mia sorella"); *WPJ* ("Senile, My Sister Sings"); *WPJ2*; *FE*; *Ts:p* ("Senile My Sister Sings / Senile canta mia sorella"). See *EIL81* ("Senile, My Sister Sings") and *WPJ* (cas.).

B714 "The Silence [It grew from nothing]." *The Gazette* [Univ. of Western Ontario], 26 March 1982, p. 6. *LLM*; *UE*; *WPJ*; *WPJ2*; *SPIL*(K).

B715 "Los Americanos." *The Canadian Forum*, April 1982, p. 22. *GB* (l.ed); *GB*; *GB2*; *SPIL*(K).

B716 "Apostate." *Origins* [Hamilton, Ont.], 12, No. 1 (April 1982), 25. *GB* (l.ed); *GB*; *GB2*.

B717 "The Carved Nakedness." *Origins* [Hamilton, Ont.], 12, No. 1 (April 1982), 27. *GB* (l.ed); *GB*; *GB2*. See *IL* (TV).

B718 "Dead Souls." *The Canadian Forum*, April 1982, p. 22. *WPJ2*; *GB* (l.ed); *GB*; *GB2*.

B719 "Dialogue." *The Canadian Jewish News* [Toronto], 15 April 1982, p. 5. *Cov.*; *WPJ*; *WPJ2*. See B1291.

B720 "Murders at the Rue Bathurst." *The Canadian Forum*, April 1982, p. 22. *GB* (l.ed); *GB*; *GB2*.

B721 "The Seesaw." *The Canadian Forum*, April 1982, p. 23. *WPJ2*; *GB* (l.ed) (revised); *GB*; *GB2*.

B722 "There's Always Job." *The Canadian Forum*, April 1982, p. 23. *GB* (l.ed) (revised); *GB*; *GB2*.

B723 "The Wanting Proof." *Origins* [Hamilton, Ont.], 12, No. 1 (April 1982), 24.

B724 "An Ideal Husband." *The Canadian Jewish News* [Toronto], 15 April 1982, p. 5.

B725 "The Garden." PRISM *international*, 20, No. 4 (Summer 1982), 44–45. *WPJ*; *WPJ2*; *GB* (l.ed); *GB*; *GB2*.

B726 "Portrait of a Modern Woman." *Poetry Canada Review*, 3, No. 4 (Summer 1982), 5. *WPJ2*; *GB* (l.ed); *GB*; *GB2*; *DD*; *Ts:p* ("Portrait of a Modern Woman / Ritratto di una donna moderna"); *SG* ("Portrait of a Modern Woman").

B727 "The Swamp." PRISM *international*, 20, No. 4 (Summer 1982), 43. Rpt. in *The Pottersfield Portfolio* [Porters Lake, N.S.], 4 (1982–83), 25. Rpt. in *Mamashee* [Wyoming, Ont.], 6, No. 2 (Winter 1983), [11]. *GB* (l.ed); *GB*; *GB2*.

B728 "A Brief History of the Jews [Once they talked to God]." *The Canadian Forum*, Aug. 1982, p. 14. *GB* (l.ed); *GB*; *GB2*.

B729 "The Vacuum." *Poetry Canada Review*, 4, No. 1 (Fall 1982), 11. Rpt. in *The Canadian Literary Review*, No. 1 (Fall–Winter 1982), p. 7. *GB* (l.ed); *GB*; *GB2*.

B730 "Love Your Neighbour [A malicious, pot-bellied arthritic Yid]." *The Canadian Literary Review*, No. 1 (Fall–Winter 1982), p. 6. Rpt. ("Neighbour Love [A malicious, pot-bellied arthritic Yid]") in *The Lunatic Gazette* [Erin, Ont.], 1, No. 2 (Nov.–Dec. 1982), 2. *GB* (l.ed) (revised — "Neighbour Love [A malicious, pot-bellied arthritic Jew]"); *GB*; *GB2*.

B731 "Memo to a Tall Two-Footed Swine." *The Canadian Literary Review*, No. 1 (Fall–Winter 1982), p. 51. *GB* (l.ed).

B732 "Monsters." *The Canadian Literary Review*, No. 1 (Fall–Winter 1982), p. 51. *GB2*; *FR*.

B733 "The Recovery." *The Canadian Literary Review*, No. 1 (Fall–Winter 1982), pp. 5–6. *GB* (l.ed) ("Recovery"); *GB*; *GB2*; *Ts:p* ("Recovery / Guarigione").

B734 "Dung Beetle." *The Lunatic Gazette* [Erin, Ont.], 1, No. 2 (Nov.–Dec. 1982), 2. *GB* (l.ed); *GB*; *GB2*.

B735 "Electra." *The Lunatic Gazette* [Erin, Ont.], 1, No. 2 (Nov.–Dec. 1982), 2.

B736 "Empty Words." *The Lunatic Gazette* [Erin, Ont.], 1, No. 2 (Nov.–Dec. 1982), 2.

B737 "The Hairy Monster." *The Lunatic Gazette* [Erin, Ont.], 1, No. 2 (Nov.–Dec. 1982), 2. *GB* (l.ed) ("The Hairy Monster: For Earl and Erika"); *GB* ("The Hairy Monster"); *GB2* ("The Hairy Monster: For Earl and Erika"); *DD* ("The Hairy Monster").

B738 "Nearer to Thee." *The Lunatic Gazette* [Erin, Ont.], 1, No. 2 (Nov.–Dec. 1982), 2. *GB* (l.ed); *GB*; *GB2*.

B739 "Tragedy." *The Lunatic Gazette* [Erin, Ont.], 1, No. 2 (Nov.–Dec. 1982), 2. *GB* (l.ed) ("Tragedy: For Annette Pottier"); *GB*; *GB2*; *LPIL:RD*.

B740 "What Do You Think of Mitterand?". *The Lunatic Gazette* [Erin, Ont.], 1, No. 2 (Nov.–Dec. 1982), 2. Rpt. in *The Literary Half-Yearly* [Univ. of Mysore, India], [Canadian Issue], 24, No. 2 (July 1983), 66. *GB* (l.ed) ("What Do You Think of Mitterand? For Lisa Ross"); *GB*; *GB2*.

B741 "Fabrizio: For William Goodwin." *Canadian Literature*, No. 95 (Winter 1982), p. 6. *GB* (l.ed); *GB*; *GB2*.

B742 "Comrade Undershaftsky." *Poetry Canada Review*, 4, No. 2 (Winter 1982–83), 10. *GB*; *GB2*.

B743 "Day in Court." *The Pottersfield Portfolio* [Porters Lake, N.S.], 4 (1982–83), 34. *GB* (l.ed).

B744 "Ajánlás." Trans. Oláh Janos and Tótfalusi Istvan. In *Gótika a vadonban: Kanadai angol nyelvű Költők, modern Könyvtár*. Ed. James Steele. Introd. Béla Köpeczi. Debrecenben: Europa Konyvkiado, 1983, p. 113. *LR* ("A Dedication"); *CP*; *SP69*; *CPIL*; *DF*. See *EIL69*.

B745 "Make Room William Blake." *Argo* [Oxford, Eng.], 4, No. 3 [*Delta*, No. 66] (1983), 29. *GB* (l.ed); *GB* ("Make Room, William Blake"); *GB2*; *SG*.

B746 "Dancing Man." *Mamashee* [Wyoming, Ont.], 6, No. 2 (Winter 1983), [10]. *GB* (l.ed); *GB*; *GB2*.

B747 "Esztétika." Trans. Oláh Janos and Tótfalusi Istvan. In *Gótika a vadonban: Kanadai angol nyelvű Költők, modern Könyvtár*. Ed. James Steele. Introd. Béla Köpeczi. Debrecenben: Europa Konyvkiado, 1983, pp. 115–16. *MK* ("Esthetique"); *RCS*; *CP*; *CPIL*. See *RCS* (cas.).

B748 "Gyarmatból nemzetté." Trans. Oláh Janos and Tótfalusi Istvan. In *Gótika a vadonban: Kanadai angol nyelvű Költők, modern Könyvtár*. Ed. James Steele. Introd. Béla Köpeczi. Debrecenben: Europa Konyvkiado, 1983, pp. 108–09. Rpt. ("Da colonia a nazione") in *Poesia canadese del Novocento*. Ed. and trans. Caterina Ricciardi. Napoli: Liguori, 1986, p. 117. *IB* ("From Colony to Nation"); *IB2*; *MK*; *RCS*; *CP*; *SP69*; *CPIL*; *DF*; *WPJ*; *WPJ2*.

For the English contributions to the 1986 anthology, see B1126. See also *ILH*, *RCS* (cas.), *PRIL*, and B1193.

B749 "Perfection." *Mamashee* [Wyoming, Ont.], 6, No. 2 (Winter 1983), [9]. *WPJ2*; *GB* (l.ed); *GB*; *GB2*; *SPIL*(K).

B750 "Major Canadian Poet: For George Woodcock." *The Lunatic Gazette* [Erin, Ont.], 1, No. 3 (Jan.–Feb. 1983), 8. *GB2*; *FR* ("Major Canadian Poet").

B751 "New Year's Resolution." *The Lunatic Gazette* [Erin, Ont.], 1, No. 3 (Jan.–Feb. 1983), 8.

B752 "August Strindberg." *Poetry Canada Review*, 4, No. 4 (Summer 1983), 8. *WPJ2*; *GB*; *GB2*; *Ts:p* ("August Strindberg / Augusto Strindberg").

B753 "I Take My Anna Everywhere." *Poetry Canada Review*, 4, No. 4 (Summer 1983), 8. *WPJ2*; *GB*; *GB2*; *LPIL:RD*; *DD*.
See *WPJ* (cas.).

B754 "Kakania." *Poetry Canada Review*, 4, No. 4 (Summer 1983), 9.

B755 "Lawyers: For Linda Dranoff." *Poetry Canada Review*, 4, No. 4 (Summer 1983), 9.

B756 "The Music of Energy." *Poetry Canada Review*, 4, No. 4 (Summer 1983), 8. *GB* (revised); *GB2*.

B757 "Nostalgia When the Leaves Begin to Fall." *Poetry Canada Review*, 4, No. 4 (Summer 1983), 9. *WPJ2*; *GB*; *GB2*.

B758 "Rendezvous at the Coffee Mill: For Sarah." *Poetry Canada Review*, 4, No. 4 (Summer 1983), 9. *GB*; *GB2*; *LPIL:RD*; *DD* ("Rendezvous at the Coffee Mill").

B759 "Sex Appeal." *Poetry Canada Review*, 4, No. 4 (Summer 1983), 9. *WPJ2*; *GB*; *GB2*.

B760 "Three Poems: Aristocrats." *The Antigonish Review*, No. 54 (Summer 1983), p. 54. *WPJ2* ("Aristocrats"); *GB*; *GB2*; *DD*.

B761 "Three Poems: Lady Macbeth." *The Antigonish Review*, No. 54 (Summer 1983), p. 55. *GB2* ("Lady Macbeth"); *DD*; *FR*.

B762 "Three Poems: Psychologists." *The Antigonish Review*, No. 54 (Summer 1983), p. 54. *GB* ("Psychologists"); *GB2*.

B763 "Yeats at Sixty-Five." *Poetry Canada Review*, 4, No. 4 (Summer 1983), 8. *WPJ2*; *GB*; *GB2*; *LPIL:RD*.

B764 "Central Heating." *The Literary Half-Yearly* [Univ. of Mysore, India], [Canadian Issue], 24, No. 2 (July 1983), 63–64. *GB* (l.ed); *GB*; *GB2*; *DD*.

B765 "More Champagne, Darling: For Patrick Crean." *The Literary Half-Yearly* [Univ. of Mysore, India], [Canadian Issue], 24, No. 2 (July 1983), 65. *GB* (l.ed); *GB*; *GB2*; *DD*.

B766 "Odd Obsession: For Lisa." *The Literary Half-Yearly* [Univ. of Mysore, India], [Canadian Issue], 24, No. 2 (July 1983), 59–60. *WPJ2*; *GB* (l.ed); *GB*; *GB2*; *LPIL:RD*; *DD* ("Odd Obsession").

B767 "Trees in Late Autumn." *The Literary Half-Yearly* [Univ. of Mysore, India], [Canadian Issue], 24, No. 2 (July 1983), 57–58. *GB* (l.ed); *GB*; *GB2*.

B768 "Youth and Age 1981." *The Literary Half-Yearly* [Univ. of Mysore, India], [Canadian Issue], 24, No. 2 (July 1983), 61–62. *GB* (l.ed); *GB*; *GB2*.

B769 "The Flaming Maple." *Poetry Canada Review*, 5, No. 1 (Fall 1983), 16. *GB* (l.ed); *GB*; *GB2*.

B770 "Hedges." *Poetry Canada Review*, 5, No. 1 (Fall 1983), 16.

B771 "O Israel, Where Are Your Poets?". *Shirim: A Jewish Poetry Journal* [Los Angeles], 2, No. 2 (Fall 1983), 18. *GB* (l.ed) (revised — "Where Has the Glory Fled"); *GB* ("Where Has the Glory Fled?"); *GB2*.

B772 "Tick Tock." *Poetry Canada Review*, 5, No. 1 (Fall 1983), 16. *GB*.

B773 "Fill in the Blank." *The Canadian Forum*, Oct. 1983, p. 21. *GB*.

B774 "The Immortals." *The Canadian Forum*, Oct. 1983, p. 42. *GB*; *GB2*.

B775 "Chrisos-Dionysos." Trans. Branko Gorjup. *Republika* [Zagreb, Yugoslavia], Nos. 10–12 (1984), p. 175. *Cov.* ("Christos-Dionysos").

B776 "Divinity and John Dewey [God made the viper, the shark, the tsetse fly]." *Trends: The Paisley College of Technology Literary Magazine* [Paisley, Scotland], 5, No. 10 (1984), 10. Rpt. ("For My Neighbours in Hell

[God made the viper, the shark, the tsetse fly]") in *The Canadian Jewish News, Viewpoints*, 30 Aug. 1990, p. 8. *TWNS* ("Divinity and John Dewey [God made the viper, the shark, the tsetse fly]"); *MNH* ("[God made the viper, the shark, the tsetse fly]"); *WPJ* ("For My Neighbours in Hell [God made the viper, the shark, the tsetse fly]"); *WPJ2*; *SDCJ* ("Whose Zoo?").

See *EIL81* ("[God made the viper]") and *PRIL* ("Divinity and John Dewey [God made the viper, the shark, the tsetse fly]").

B777   "To Ettore, with Love and Admiration." *Conjunctions* [New York], No. 6 (1984), p. 165. Rpt. in *Matrix*, No. 18 (Spring 1984), p. 25. *WPJ2* ("For Ettore, with Love and Admiration"); *FR*; *Ts:p* ("For Ettore, with Love and Admiration / Per Ettore con amore e ammirazione").

B778   "Epistle to Catullus." *The Canadian Forum*, March 1984, p. 42. *WPJ2*; *GB2*; *FR*.

B779   "Whitehern: For Joe Kertes." *The Canadian Forum*, March 1984, p. 40. *GB*; *GB2*.

B780   "I Am Who I Am." *Matrix*, No. 18 (Spring 1984), p. 27. *FR*.

B781   "[In the faculty room]." *Matrix*, No. 18 (Spring 1984), p. 27.

B782   "January Spleen: Advice to a Young Poet." *Matrix*, No. 18 (Spring 1984), p. 26.

B783   "January Spleen: The Discrete Charm of the Bourgeois." *Matrix*, No. 18 (Spring 1984), p. 26.

B784   "January Spleen: Imperfection." *Matrix*, No. 18 (Spring 1984), p. 26. *FR* ("Imperfection").

B785   "January Spleen: Love Among Cannibals [He lost his heart to a woman]." *Matrix*, No. 18 (Spring 1984), p. 26. Rpt. ("Love Among the Cannibals [He lost his heart to a woman]") in *Noovo Masheen* [Ottawa], No. 2 (1985), p. 18.

B786   "January Spleen: Sewage." *Matrix*, No. 18 (Spring 1984), p. 26.

B787   "Jude the Obscure." *Canadian Literature*, No. 100 (Spring 1984), p. 198. *GB*; *GB2*; *DD*.

B788   "New Year's Poem for Veneranda." *Canadian Literature*, No. 100 (Spring 1984), p. 198. *GB*; *GB2*; *LPIL:RD*; *DD*.

B789   "Two Poems: The Cyst." *The Antigonish Review*, No. 58 (Summer 1984), p. 116. *GB2* ("The Cyst: For Ettore de Conciliis"); *FR* ("The Cyst").

B790   "Two Poems: Juvenal Redidivus." *The Antigonish Review*, No. 58 (Summer 1984), p. 115. *GB2* ("Juvenal Redivivus"); *FR*.

B791   "Boschka Layton 1921–1984." *The Canadian Forum*, Aug.–Sept. 1984, p. 49. Rpt. trans. Young Girl Lee (English and Korean versions) in *Anthology: Poets of the Pacific Countries 1* [Shimunhaksa] [Seoul, Korea], 15 April 1985, p. 29. *WPJ2* ("Boschka Layton: 1921–1984"); *GB2* ("Boschka Layton 1921–1984"); *DD*; *FR*; *FE* ("Boschka Layton: 1921–1984").

B792   "Canción para Naomi." In *Antología de la poesía anglo canadiense contemporánea*. Ed. and trans. Bernd Dietz. Barcelona: Los libros de la frontera, 1985, pp. 65, 67. *CGE* ("Song for Naomi"); *IB*; *IB2*; *RCS*; *CP*; *SP69*; *CPIL*; *DF*; *PIL*; *SPIL*; *WPJ*; *WPJ2*; *SPIL(K)*.

For the English contributions to the 1985 anthology, see B1123. See also *ILH, PIL65, IL* (Montreal), *EIL69, IL* (Toronto), *Layton, RCS* (cas.), *EIL76, EIL81, PRIL, WPJ* (cas.), and B1191.

B793 "Popcorn." *Noovo Masheen* [Ottawa], No. 2 (1985), p. 17. Rpt. trans. Young Girl Lee (English and Korean versions) in *Anthology: Poets of the Pacific Countries 1* [*Shimunhaksa*] [Seoul, Korea], 15 April 1985, p. 28. Rpt. ("Five Poems: v. Popcorn") in The *Idler* [Toronto], May 1986, p. 40. *FR* ("Popcorn").

B794 "Sciatica." *Noovo Masheen* [Ottawa], No. 2 (1985), p. 17. *FR.*

B795 "Cracks in the Acropolis." *Matrix*, No. 20 (Spring 1985), p. 33. *FR.*

B796 "Etruscan Tombs: For Dante Gardini." *Descant*, No. 48 [16, No. 1] (Spring 1985), p. 25. *WPJ2; FR; FE; Ts:p* ("Etruscan Tombs: For Dante Gardini / Tombe Etrusche: Per Dante Gardini").

B797 "Judgement at Murray's." *Descant*, No. 48 [16, No. 1] (Spring 1985), p. 28. *FR.*

B798 "The Massacre." *Descant*, No. 48 [16, No. 1] (Spring 1985), p. 27. *FR.*

B799 "Principessa Anna." *Montréal Now*, 2, No. 2 (Spring 1985), n. pag. *FR.*

B800 "Una Scopata." *Descant*, No. 48 [16, No. 1] (Spring 1985), p. 26. *FR.*

B801 "Wagschal Exhibition." *Matrix*, No. 20 (Spring 1985), p. 32. *FR; FE.*

B802 "Two for the Road, Frank." *The Canadian Forum*, April 1985, p. 21. *FR.*

B803 "Lady Aurora" (English and Korean versions). Trans. Young Girl Lee. *Anthology: Poets of the Pacific Countries 1* [*Shimunhaksa*] [Seoul, Korea], 15 April 1985, p. 27. *GB2; LPIL:RD; FR.*

B804 "Dionysians in a Bad Time." *Canadian Literature*, No. 105 (Summer 1985), p. 43. *WPJ2; FR.*

B805 "Fellini." *Canadian Literature*, No. 106 (Fall 1985), p. 15. Rpt. in *The Canadian Jewish News, Viewpoints*, 30 Aug. 1990, p. 8. *WPJ2; FR; Ts:p.*

B806 "Leopardi in Montreal." *Canadian Literature*, No. 106 (Fall 1985), p. 55. *FR.*

B807 "Black Tourist in Tinos." *The Canadian Forum*, Nov. 1985, p. 23. Rpt. in *Aegean Review* [photocopy Layton Collection, Concordia Univ.; source unavailable]. *WPJ2; DD; FR; Ts:p* ("Black Tourist in Tinos / Una turista negra a Tinos").

B808 "The Investiture." *The Canadian Forum*, Nov. 1985, p. 23. *FR.*

B809 "The Paddler." *The Canadian Forum*, Nov. 1985, p. 23. *FR.*

B810 "The Piles of Greece, the Piles of Greece." *The Canadian Forum*, Nov. 1985, p. 23. *FR.*

B811 "The Theatre of Dionysos: For Don and Sheila." *The Canadian Forum*, Nov. 1985, p. 22. *FR.*

B812 "Bottiglie." In *Poesia canadese del Novocento*. Ed. and trans. Caterina Ricciardi. Napoli: Liguori, 1986, pp. 131, 133. Rpt. ("Bottles: For Giorgio Morandi") in *The Canadian Jewish News, Viewpoints*, 30 Aug. 1990, p. 8. *WPJ2*; *GB* (l.ed); *GB*; *GB2*.

For the English contributions to the 1986 anthology, see B1126.

B813 "Herbert Vunce." In *The Bumper Book*. Ed. John Metcalf. Toronto: ECW, 1986, pp. 128–29. Rpt. in *Poetry Canada Review*, 7, No. 4 (Summer 1986), 29. *FR*.

B814 "I am a Hotel." In *The Bumper Book*. Ed. John Metcalf. Toronto: ECW, 1986, p. 39.

B815 "O Cureless Rapture: for Robert Fulford." In *The Bumper Book*. Ed. John Metcalf. Toronto: ECW, 1986, pp. 26–27.

B816 "Per mio fratello Gesù." In *Poesia canadese del Novocento*. Ed. and trans. Caterina Ricciardi. Napoli: Liguori, 1986, pp. 127, 129. *MBJ* ("For My Brother Jesus"); *PIL*; *SPIL*; *eg* ("For My Brother Jesus / Per mio fratello gesù"); *WPJ* ("For My Brother Jesus"); *WPJ2*; *FE*; *Ts:p* ("For My Brother Jesus / Per mio fratello Gesù").

For the English contributions to the 1986 anthology, see B1126. See also *EIL76* ("For My Brother Jesus"), *MBJ* (cas.), *WPJ* (cas.), and B1282.

B817 "Poem That Says It All." Trans. Dino Siotis. Νέα Πορεία [New Way] [Thessalonika], April–June 1986, pp. 78–79. *FR*.

B818 "Five Poems: I. Burnt Offering." *The Idler* [Toronto], May 1986, p. 38. *FR* ("Burnt Offering"); *FE*.

B819 "Five Poems: II. Kitch." *The Idler* [Toronto], May 1986, p. 38. *FR* ("Kitch").

B820 "Five Poems: III. Opiums." *The Idler* [Toronto], May 1986, p. 39. *FR* ("Opiums").

B821 "Five Poems: IV. Olympic Stewardess." *The Idler* [Toronto], May 1986, p. 40. *FR* ("Olympic Stewardess").

B822 "Diverse Pleasures." *Poetry Canada Review*, 7, No. 4 (Summer 1986), 29. *FR*.

B823 "Casa Cacciatore." *The Antigonish Review*, Nos. 66–67 (Summer–Autumn 1986), p. 199. *FR*.

B824 "Final Reckoning: After Theognis." *The Antigonish Review*, Nos. 66–67 (Summer–Autumn 1986), p. 198. *WPJ2*; *FR*; *FE* ("Final Reckoning"); *Ts:p* ("Final Reckoning: After Theognis / Rendiconto finale: da Teognide").

See *WPJ* (cas.) ("Final Reckoning: After Theognis").

B825 "A Madrigal for Anna." *The Antigonish Review*, Nos. 66–67 (Summer–Autumn 1986), p. 200. *FR*.

B826 "Nightmare in the Annex." *The Canadian Jewish News, Viewpoints*, 4 Sept. 1986, p. 2. *FR*; *FE*.

B827 "Twentieth Century Gothic." *The Canadian Jewish News, Viewpoints*, 4 Sept. 1986, p. 2. *WPJ2*; *FR*; *FE* ("Twentieth-Century Gothic").

B828 "Devotion: For Vito Riviello." *Acta Victoriana*, 111, No. 1 (Fall 1986), 23. *FR*.

B829 "The Gelded Lion." *Acta Victoriana*, 111, No. 1 (Fall 1986), 24. *FR*.

B830 "Inter-View." *Acta Victoriana*, 111, No. 1 (Fall 1986), 25. Rpt. in *Cross-Canada Writer's Quarterly*, 9, No. 2 (1987), 13. *FR*.

B831 "Memo to a Literary Pimp." *Acta Victoriana*, III, No. 1 (Fall 1986), 22. *FR* ("Memo to a Literary Pimp: For Robert Fulford").

B832 "Niagara-on-the-Lake Sewage." *Acta Victoriana*, III, No. 1 (Fall 1986), 24.

B833 "Saturday Night Farticle: For Robert Fulford." *Acta Victoriana*, III, No. 1 (Fall 1986), 23. *FR* ("Saturday Night Farticle").

B834 "Socrates at the Centaur." *Canadian Literature*, No. 112 (Spring 1987), pp. 16–17. *FR*.

B835 "Birthday Poem for John Newlove." *Canadian Literature*, No. 119 (Winter 1988), p. 56.

B836 "Attending Suzanne's Funeral." *Canadian Literature*, No. 120 (Spring 1989), p. 63. *WPJ2*; *Ts:p* ("Attending Suzanne's Funeral / Seguendo il funerale di Suzanne").

B837 "Krzyk Człowieka." Trans. Jurosław Sokół and Florian Smieja. In *Literatura na Świecie* [Warsaw] [No. 4 (225)], Kwiecień [April] 1990, p. 75. *MBJ* ("The Human Cry"); *WPJ*; *WPJ2*.

Published Correspondence

B838 "An Explanation." *McGill Daily*, 30 Nov. 1938, p. 2.
Signed: Irvine Layton. Layton interprets his poem "Medley for Our Times" (B15).

B839 Letter. *First Statement*, 2 April 1943, pp. 7–8. *E:PIL* ("Letter, *First Statement*" [April 1943]).
Signed: Lt. Irving Layton. Layton replies to Patrick Waddington's criticism of his poetry (C15).

B840 "So I'm Honest but Not Beautiful." *The Canadian Forum*, June 1945, p. 65. *E:PIL* ("Correspondence, *The Canadian Forum*" [June 1945]).
Layton replies to Margaret Avison's criticism of *Here and Now* (D1). Avison's response (C17) follows.

B841 Letter. *Origin*, Ser. 1, No. 14 (Autumn 1954), p. 75. *E:PIL* ("Letter to Cid Corman, *Origin*").
The writing of poetry is discussed.

B842 Letter. *The Canadian Forum*, Oct. 1956, pp. 160–62. Rpt. in *Forum: Canadian Life and Letters 1920–70. Selections from* The Canadian Forum. Ed. J.L. Granatstein and Peter Stevens. Toronto: Univ. of Toronto Press, 1972, pp. 306–07. *E:PIL* ("Correspondence, *The Canadian Forum*" [Oct. 1956]).
Layton replies to A.G. Christopher's response (July 1956) (C30) to Millar MacLure's review of *The Bull Calf and Other Poems* (D35). See also B844 and C34.

B843 "Bull Calves and Kazoos." *McGill Daily*, 11 Feb. 1957, p. 2. *E:PIL* ("Letter, *McGill Daily*" [11 Feb. 1957]).
The McGill University Library refused to catalogue *The Bull Calf and Other Poems* and *Music on a Kazoo*.

B844 Letter. *The Canadian Forum*, March 1957, p. 282. *E:PIL* ("Correspondence, *The Canadian Forum*" [March 1957]).
Layton's response is occasioned by A.J.M. Smith's reply (C34) to Layton's earlier letter (B842).

B845 Letter. *The Canadian Forum*, Sept. 1957, pp. 137–38. *E:PIL* ("Correspondence, *The Canadian Forum*" [Sept. 1957]).

Layton replies to Kildare Dobbs's review of *The Improved Binoculars* (D46).

B846 Letter. *The Canadian Forum*, Feb. 1958, p. 255. E:PIL ("Correspondence, *The Canadian Forum*" [Feb. 1958]).

Taking inspiration from the poems about him by Kildare Dobbs (C685) and A.J.M. Smith (C34), Layton responds with a comment on critics in general. This letter includes a poem "[In this cold realm]" (B187).

B847 "Lays Summit Failure to Calculated U.S. Act." *The Montreal Star*, 27 May 1960, p. 12. TS:CS ("Views of the World: Letters, Articles, Travels, 1960–1977. Lays Summit Failure to Calculated U.S. Act").

B848 "More in Anger Than in Sorrow: Genius Answers Mediocrity." *The Montreal Star*, 25 Oct. 1961, p. 10. E:PIL ("Letter, *The Montreal Star*" [25 Oct. 1961]).

Layton responds to Walter O'Hearn's critical poem "To a Slopshire Lad" (21 Oct. 1961) (C696).

B849 "An Open Letter to Louis Dudek." *Cataract*, 1, No. 2 (Winter 1962), 23–26. E:PIL.

Layton criticizes Louis Dudek's poetry.

B850 Letter. *The Canadian Forum*, March 1962, pp. 281–82. E:PIL ("Correspondence, *The Canadian Forum*" [March 1962]).

Layton responds to Peter Dale Scott's review of *Poems for 27 Cents* (D349).

B851 Letter. *The Canadian Forum*, May 1962, pp. 41–42. E:PIL ("Correspondence, *The Canadian Forum*" [May 1962]).

Layton replies to John Robert Colombo's article "A Conference on Creative Writing" (C73).

B852 Letter. *Teangadóir*, 5, No. 4, Ser. 2, 1, No. 4 [No. 40] (May 1962), p. 148.

Layton congratulates the editors on "an interesting mag."

B853 "Irving Layton Replies." *Cataract*, 1, No. 3 (July 1962), 42. E:PIL ("Reply, *Cataract*").

Layton responds to George Ellenbogen's "An Open Letter to Irving Layton" (C74).

B854 "Two Poets of Love Don't Love a Critic." *The Montreal Star*, 12 Dec. 1962, p. 8. E:PIL ("Letter, *The Montreal Star*" [12 Dec. 1962]).

Layton responds to Stanley Handman's 8 December critical review of *Love Where the Nights Are Long*.

B855 "Accuses Dr. Rowse of Falsifying Record." *The Montreal Star*, 5 Feb. 1963, p. 8. TS:CS ("Views of the World: Letters, Articles, Travels, 1960–1977. Accuses Dr. Rowse of Falsifying Record").

Layton disagrees with historian A.L. Rowse's statement, in a talk at McGill University, that Germany was solely responsible for WW II.

B856 "On Mr. O'Hearn's View of Mr. Layton's Book." *The Montreal Star*, 13 Feb. 1963, p. 10.

Layton replies to Walter O'Hearn's review of *Balls for a One-Armed Juggler* (D73).

B857 "Advises Dealing with Germany with 'Compassion, Intelligence.'" *The Montreal Star*, 14 Feb. 1963, p. 8. TS:CS ("Views of the World: Letters, Articles, Travels, 1960–1977. Advises Dealing with Germany with 'Compassion, Intelligence'").

Layton advises a more compassionate attitude towards Germany in this reply to Sam Katz's defense of A.L. Rowse's views (see B855).

B858 Letter. *The Canadian Forum*, May 1963, pp. 30–31. *E:PIL* ("Correspondence, *The Canadian Forum*" [May 1963]).
Layton replies to Peter Dale Scott's comments on "Keine Lazarovitch 1870–1959" (C88), Hugh MacLean's reading of *Lawrence of Arabia* in the April issue, and Pádraig O' Broin's review of *Balls for a One-Armed Juggler* (D63).

B859 Letter. *The Tamarack Review*, No. 28 (Summer 1963), pp. 94–95. *E:PIL* ("Letter, *The Tamarack Review*").
Layton responds to Gerald Taaffe's article "Diary of a Montreal Newspaper Reader" (C86).

B860 "A Cliché Strikes Back." *Maclean's*, 16 May 1964, p. 10.
Layton responds to Mordecai Richler's criticisms (C99).

B861 "Contention in Canada." *Holiday* [Philadelphia], July 1964, p. 4.
Layton responds to Mordecai Richler's article "Canadiana: One Man's View" (C98).

B862 "Unflattering Review Elicits Equally Uncomplimentary Reply." *The Montreal Star*, 4, Nov. 1964, p. 14. *E:PIL* ("Letter, *The Montreal Star*" [4 Nov. 1964]).
Layton replies to Louis Dudek's review of *The Laughing Rooster* (D83).

B863 "Layton Replies." *The Georgian* [Sir George Williams Univ.], 17 Nov. 1964, p. 6. Rpt. in *McGill Daily*, 17 Nov. 1964.
Layton replies to Brian Robinson's challenge to a debate on Layton's poetry (C108).

B864 "What About 'Genius and Devotion'?". *The Montreal Star*, 15 Dec. 1964, p. 6. *E:PIL* ("Letter, *The Montreal Star*" [15 Dec. 1964]).

Layton responds to Professor Miller's article, which suggests that it is possible to teach poetry.

B865 "Layton Springs Back." *McGill Daily*, 3 March 1965, pp. 4–5.
Layton replies to Brian Robinson's letter of 24 February (see B863).

B866 "Widely Condemned U.S. Policy Defended as Wise and Right." *The Montreal Star*, 17 May 1965, p. 5. *TS:CS* ("Views of the World: Letters, Articles, Travels, 1960–1977. Widely Condemned U.S. Policy Defended as Wise and Right").
Layton defends American policy in Latin America.

B867 "Course of Events in Santo Domingo Demonstrates U.S. Moderation." *The Montreal Star*, 26 May 1965, p. 8. *TS:CS* ("Views of the World: Letters, Articles, Travels, 1960–1977. Course of Events in Santo Domingo Demonstrates U.S. Moderation").
Layton defends American policy in Santo Domingo.

B868 "Upright Citizen's Belief in Law Sorely Tried by Police Conduct." *The Montreal Star*, 8 Dec. 1965, p. 6.

B869 "U.S. Effort in Viet Nam and Its Scope Justified by Mounting External Threat." *The Montreal Star*, 22 Dec. 1965, p. 6. *TS:CS* ("Views of the World: Letters, Articles, Travels, 1960–1977. U.S. Effort in Viet Nam and Its Scope Justified by Mounting External Threat").
Layton defends American response to Hanoi's escalation of the war in Viet Nam.

B870 "Visitor to Germany Thoroughly Convinced Nation's Abhorrence of Hitlerism Sincere." *The*

Montreal Star, 19 May 1966, p. 8. *TS:CS* ("Views of the World: Letters, Articles, Travels, 1960–1977. Visitor to Germany Thoroughly Convinced Nation's Abhorrence of Hitlerism Sincere").

Layton writes from Germany praising its commitment to freedom and democracy.

B871 "Mr. Layton Defends His Insights into Germany's Mind against Criticism." *The Montreal Star*, 21 June 1966, p. 8. *TS:CS* ("Views of the World: Letters, Articles, Travels, 1960–1977. Mr. Layton Defends His Insights into Germany's Mind against Criticism").

Layton again defends Germany's repudiation of Naziism.

B872 "Teach-In." *The Globe and Mail* [Toronto], 27 Oct. 1966, p. 6. *TS:CS* ("Views of the World: Letters, Articles, Travels, 1960–1977. Teach-In").

Layton expresses his "disgust and anger" at a teach-in on American foreign policy held at the University of Toronto.

B873 "Situation in Germany Today Unlike That Leading to Fall of Weimar Republic." *The Montreal Star*, 28 Nov. 1966, p. 8. *TS:CS* ("Views of the World: Letters, Articles, Travels, 1960–1977. Situation in Germany Today Unlike That Leading to Fall of Weimar Republic").

Layton defends his view that Germany is no longer a threat to the rest of the world.

B874 "Germany's New Chancellor Exhibiting Sincere Desire to Reassure Doubters." *The Montreal Star*, 16 Dec. 1966, p. 8. *TS:CS* ("Views of the World: Letters, Articles, Travels, 1960–1977. Germany's New Chancellor Exhibiting Sincere Desire to Reassure Doubters").

Layton defends Germany.

B875 "CBC Back-Down 'Act of Poltroonery.' " *The Montreal Star*, 20 Jan. 1967, p. 6. *TS:CS* ("Views of the World: Letters, Articles, Travels, 1960–1977. CBC Back-Down 'Act of Poltroonery' ").

The CBC had planned to carry a taped interview with Adolf Von Thadden, but backed down in the face of opposition. Layton disagrees with this decision.

B876 "Another Danger Fills Mr. Layton's Mind to Exclusion of Proclaimed Nazi Rebirth." *The Montreal Star*, 31 Jan. 1967, p. 6. *TS:CS* ("Views of the World: Letters, Articles, Travels, 1960–1977. Another Danger Fills Mr. Layton's Mind to Exclusion of Proclaimed Nazi Rebirth").

Layton reaffirms his belief that Germany is no longer a Nazi threat.

B877 "Layton on Lust." *Canadian Jewish Chronicle Review* [Montreal], 10 Feb. 1967, p. 4.

Layton replies to Peter Lust's letter in the 27 January issue of this newspaper, accusing him of misquotation and misinterpretation (C140).

B878 "The Time for Illusions Is Over, the Confrontation Is Here." *The Montreal Star*, 17 June 1967, p. 6. *TS:CS* ("Views of the World: Letters, Articles, Travels, 1960–1977. The Time for Illusions Is Over, the Confrontation Is Here").

The Western world should have confidence in the power of the United States to help resolve the Middle East conflict.

B879 "Viet Nam Reverse Giving Communists a Lesson They Will Not Soon Forget." *The Montreal Star*, 28 Nov. 1967, p. 8. *TS:CS* ("Views of the World: Letters, Articles, Travels, 1960–1977. Viet Nam Reverse Giving Communists a Lesson They Will Not Soon Forget").

Layton comments on the American successes against aggression in Viet Nam and the Middle East.

B880 "Excerpts from Two Letters on a First Visit to Israel." *The Telegram* [Toronto], 16 March 1968, p. 78. *TS:CS* ("Views of the World: Letters, Articles, Travels, 1960–1977. Excerpts from Two Letters on a First Trip to Israel").
The present situation of the Jews in Israel is discussed.

B881 "From Tel Aviv, Irving Layton Has a Word for a Critic." *The Montreal Star*, 15 July 1968, p. 8.
Layton defends the views expressed in his article "The Kaleidoscope That Is India" (B1002).

B882 Letter. In "Word from Lesbos and the Senate." By Kildare Dobbs. *Toronto Daily Star*, 26 Sept. 1968, p. 85.
Layton objects to Kildare Dobbs terming him a "dollar-dazzled Whitman" (C160) in his review of *The New Romans: Candid Canadian Opinions of the U.S.*, edited by Al Purdy.

B883 "The Return of the Civilized Killer." *Canadian Dimension*, 5, No. 7 (Dec.–Jan. 1968–69), 2.
Layton responds to Richard Sommer's review of *The Shattered Plinths* (D110).

B884 Letter. *Collage* [McMaster Univ.], 7 Feb. 1969, p. 4.
Layton demands an apology for the attack on him in *Collage* (C167).

B885 "Layton Says He Supports, Not Opposes, French Canadian Manifestation." *The Montreal Star*, 21 April 1969, p. 8. *TS:CS* ("Views of the World: Letters, Articles, Travels, 1960–1977. Layton Says He Supports, Not Opposes, French-Canadian Manifestation").

Layton replies to criticism of his leaving Montreal for a teaching position at York University.

B886 Letter. *The Montreal Star*, 4 Oct. 1969, p. 50. *E:PIL* ("Letter, *The Montreal Star*" [4 Oct. 1969]).
Layton criticizes Warren Tallman's "Robert Duncan, Poet of Passion," in *The Montreal Star*, 13 September.

B887 "Governor-General's Awards." *The Globe and Mail* [Toronto], 10 April 1970, p. 6.
With sixteen other people, Layton co-signs a letter objecting to criticism of Warren Tallman's appointment to the Governor-General's awards selection committee.

B888 Letter. *The Globe and Mail* [Toronto], 10 April 1970, p. 6. Rpt. ("The Canada Council Needs a Vigorous Housecleaning") in *The Toronto Star*, 10 April 1970, First Sec., p. 6.
Layton criticizes Warren Tallman for his lack of interest in Canadian poetry as anything more than an extension of American work. Layton also calls for a "vigorous housecleaning" of The Canada Council, "to root out the dead wood and the high-handed incompetents who have managed to secure for themselves positions of authority."

B889 "Poet Irving Layton on Cambodia." *The Montreal Star*, 14 May 1970, p. 10. *TS:CS* ("Views of the World: Letters, Articles, Travels, 1960–1977. Poet Irving Layton on Cambodia").
Layton supports American policy in Viet Nam.

B890 "Layton on Eayrs." *Toronto Daily Star*, 16 May 1970, Insight, p. 19. *TS:CS* ("Views of the World: Letters, Articles, Travels, 1960–1977. Layton on Eayrs").

Layton responds to James Eayrs' views (*Toronto Daily Star*, 12 May) on President Nixon's position in Cambodia.

B891 "Nixon's Courageous Decision to Act in Cambodia an Unqualified Success." *The Montreal Star*, 3 June 1970, p. 10. *TS:CS* ("Views of the World: Letters, Articles, Travels, 1960–1977. Nixon's Courageous Decision to Act in Cambodia an Unqualified Success").

The invasion of Cambodia is the one unqualified American success of the war.

B892 "The Toronto Mind Baffles Montrealer." *Toronto Daily Star*, 9 Oct. 1970, First Sec., p. 7.

Layton protests the receipt of a parking ticket.

B893 "The Quebec Situation." *The Globe and Mail* [Toronto], 24 Oct. 1970, p. 6. Rpt. in *Shocked and Appalled: A Century of Letters to* The Globe and Mail. Ed. Jack Kapica. Toronto: Lester & Orpen Dennys, 1985, pp. 223–24. *TS:CS* ("Views of the World: Letters, Articles, Travels, 1960–1977. The Quebec Situation").

Layton supports the Canadian government's policy towards the Quebec terrorists. See B1246.

B894 "Trudeau's Good Sense Put an End to Reign of Terror." *Toronto Daily Star*, 30 Oct. 1970, First Sec., p. 7. *TS:CS* ("Views of the World: Letters, Articles, Travels, 1960–1977. Trudeau's Good Sense Put an End to Reign of Terror").

Layton supports Prime Minister Trudeau's implementation of the War Measures Act.

B895 "House Windbags Not Fit to Lace Trudeau's Ski-Boots, Poet Says." *The Globe and Mail* [Toronto], 31 Oct. 1970, p. 7. *TS:CS* ("Views of the World: Letters, Articles, Travels, 1960–1977. House Windbags Not Fit to Lace Trudeau's Ski-Boots, Poet Says' ").

Layton again defends Prime Minister Trudeau's actions against the FLQ.

B896 "Layton Says Students Are Reading Canadian Writers Despite Some Teachers." *The Montreal Star*, 5 March 1971, p. 8.

Layton replies to Bob Adams' letter in the 15 February issue of *The Montreal Star*, which stated that Canadian students "do not read Canadian literature because it is not very good."

B897 "Arabs and Jews." *The Globe and Mail* [Toronto], 13 April 1971, p. 7. *TS:CS* ("Views of the World: Letters, Articles, Travels, 1960–1977. Arabs and Jews").

Layton objects to Donald V. Stirling's 7 April letter to *The Globe and Mail* [Toronto], which states that Israel is a major threat to world peace.

B898 "Israel." *The Globe and Mail* [Toronto], 23 April 1971, p. 7. *TS:CS* ("Views of the World: Letters, Articles, Travels, 1960–1977. Israel").

Layton replies to Donald Stirling's 19 April letter to *The Globe and Mail* [Toronto], which argues that Israel is "a potential catalyst to East-West calamity."

B899 "Shaw Review Missed the Point." *Toronto Daily Star*, 1 March 1972, First Sec., p. 7. *TS:CS* ("Views of the World: Letters, Articles, Travels, 1960–1977. Shaw Review Missed the Point").

Layton disagrees with Urjo Kareda's 23 February review in *Toronto Daily Star* of *Arms and the Man* by George Bernard Shaw.

B900 "Layton Elucidates." *Saturday Night*, May 1972, p. 3. *E:PIL* ("Letter, *Saturday Night*").

Layton replies to Barry Callaghan's review of *The Collected Poems of Irving Layton* (D128).

B901 "Poet Layton Says Hockey Hysteria Is 'A Ridiculous Emotional Binge.' " *Toronto Daily Star*, 6 Oct. 1972, First Sec., p. 7. *TS:CS* ("Views of the World: Letters, Articles, Travels, 1960–1977. Poet Layton Says Hockey Hysteria Is 'A Ridiculous Emotional Binge' ").
Layton comments on Team Canada.

B902 Letter. *The Windsor Star*, 10 Oct. 1972, p. 13.
Layton comments on the Canada-Russia hockey games.

B903 "Yahooville Spawned Critic." *Excalibur* [York Univ.], 1 Nov. 1972, p. 8. *TS:CS* ("Views of the World: Letters, Articles, Travels, 1960–1977. Yahooville Spawned Critic: Layton").
Layton responds to Wayne Cannon's "Layton Abuses Canadians; Prof." (C206).

B904 "No Room for Myth." *The Globe and Mail* [Toronto], 10 Jan. 1973, p. 7. *TS:CS* ("Views of the World: Letters, Articles, Travels, 1960–1977. No Room for Myth").
Layton replies to Robert Martin's 30 December 1972 article about him (C209).

B905 "Words Falsely Put in My Mouth: Irving Layton." *The Toronto Star*, 21 April 1973, Insight, p. 21.
Layton comments on his fee for reading poetry.

B906 "Last Tango in Paris." *The Globe and Mail* [Toronto], 27 June 1973, p. 7. *TS:CS* ("Views of the World: Letters, Articles, Travels, 1960–1977. Last Tango in Paris").
Layton reviews *Last Tango in Paris*, produced by Alberto Grimaldi and directed by Bernardo Bertolucci.

B907 Letter. *Waves*, 2, No. 3 (Spring 1974), 75.
Layton congratulates the editors.

B908 "Lacombe, Lucien." *The Globe and Mail* [Toronto], 18 Nov. 1974, p. 6. *TS:CS* ("Views of the World: Letters, Articles, Travels, 1960–1977. Lacombe, Lucien").
Layton reviews the film *Lacombe, Lucien*, produced and directed by Louis Malle.

B909 "Layton Says Three Films Are Masterpieces, but Reviewer Is Bland, Smug." *The Globe and Mail* [Toronto], 11 Jan. 1975, p. 7. *TS:CS* ("Views of the World: Letters, Articles, Travels, 1960–1977. Layton Says Three Films Are Masterpieces But Reviewer Is Bland, Smug").
Layton reviews *Amarcord*, produced by Franco Cristaldi and directed by Feddrico Fellini; *The Night Porter*, produced by Robert Gordon Edward and Esa de Simone and directed by Liliana Cavani; and *Phantom of Liberté*, produced by Serge Silberman and directed by Louis Bunuel. See also C254 and C255.

B910 "His Beams Bemocked . . . ." *Books in Canada*, Nov. 1975, pp. 44–45.
Layton objects to Len Gasparini's review of Seymour Mayne's *Name* in the August 1975 issue of *Books in Canada*.

B911 "On the Originality of Irving Layton." *Saturday Night*, Nov. 1975, p. 6.
Layton dissociates himself from Louis Dudek and Raymond Souster; he denies any imitation on his part of William Carlos Williams, Robert Creeley, or Cid Corman.

B912 "Open Letter to A.J.M. Smith." *Northern Journey*, Nos. 7–8 (1976), p. 104.

Layton responds to A.J.M. Smith's poem "On Reading Layton's 'Poetry as the Fine Art of Pugilism'" (C729). See also B554.

B913 "Review of Latest Book Astonishing, Dismaying Irving Layton Charges." *The Toronto Star*, 25 March 1976, p. B5. Rpt. ("Layton Blasts Critic Fulford for Panning His Poems") in *The Citizen* [Ottawa], 27 March 1976, p. 83. TS:CS ("Views of the World: Letters, Articles, Travels, 1960–1977. Review of Latest Book Astonishing, Dismaying Irving Layton Charges").
Layton objects to Robert Fulford's review of *For My Brother Jesus* (D179).

B914 "First Gasp." *Books in Canada*, April 1976, p. 34.
Layton defends his comments on Len Gasparini (B910).

B915 "Asinine Imputation." *Books in Canada*, Nov. 1976, p. 40.
Layton responds to Lela Parlow's letter in the August issue of *Books in Canada* (C280), which was critical of the views expressed in *For My Brother Jesus*.

B916 "Re Mother Oracle." *Canadian Magazine*, 6 Nov. 1976, p. 28.
Layton denies Margaret Atwood's statement that he said "women are only good for screwing." His falling asleep during her reading was not, he said, a comment on her poetry.

B917 "The Birth of Anti-Semitism: Jesus' Brother Replies to His Critics." *Canadian Magazine*, 13 Nov. 1976, p. 10.
Layton defends his opinion that Christians were responsible for the Nazi holocaust.

B918 "Critics." *The Globe and Mail* [Toronto], 8 March 1977, p. 7.
Layton responds to Donald Creighton's "Only a Few Steady Book Buyers" (5 March), reminding him of the many fine reviews currently being done by poets and writers and comments on Robert Martin's review of *Islands in the Stream*, by Ernest Hemingway.

B919 "A Champion for Fellini." *The Globe and Mail* [Toronto], 26 March 1977, p. 7. TS:CS ("Views of the World: Letters, Articles, Travels, 1960–1977. A Champion for Fellini").
Layton reviews Federico Fellini's *Casanova*, produced by Alberto Grimaldi.

B920 "Artists." *The Globe and Mail* [Toronto], 11 April 1977, p. 6.
Layton replies to a letter by Alan Coates (C290), stating there can be more important things on an artist's mind than a relationship with a woman.

B921 "For His Brother Gary." *Books in Canada*, Jan. 1978, pp. 32–33.
Layton objects to Gary Geddes' review of *The Covenant* (D192).

B922 "Film Banned by Censor Board a Masterpiece, Poet Contends." *The Toronto Star*, 15 April 1978, p. C3.
Layton reviews *Pretty Baby*, produced and directed by Louis Malle.

B923 "Wasps on the Needle." *Books in Canada*, Oct. 1978, p. 39.
Layton decries academics who churn out lifeless poems.

B924 "Poet Calls for Action against Bigotry." *The Toronto Star*, 14 April 1979, p. B3.

CBC's *Connections* portrays the involvement of the non-WASP in organized crime. It should be balanced by positive portraits of the non-WASP — for example, his own collaboration with Aligi Sassu on *There Were No Signs*.

B925 "Character & Leadership." *The Toronto Star*, 18 May 1979, p. A9.
Layton discusses televised political debates.

B926 "Don't Be Fooled." *The Montreal Star*, 7 July 1979, p. B7. Rpt. ("Little Changes") in *The Windsor Star*, 16 July 1979, p. 9. Rpt. ("Dissidents Released but Others Jailed Since") in *Belleville Intelligencer*, 16 July 1979. Rpt. ("Don't Be Fooled") in *The Herald* [Dauphin, Man.], 18 July 1979.
The Windsor Star and *The Herald* reprints are signed: Dr. Irving Layton. Layton discusses reports that the Soviet Union is relaxing its harsh treatment of Soviet Jews.

B927 "Dracula Differs Only in Choice of Food in Our Murderous Quest for Immortality." *The Globe and Mail* [Toronto], 21 July 1979, p. 7.
Layton compares Dracula to Everyman.

B928 "Apocalypse Now: Ruthless Ideals Challenge Western Values." *The Globe and Mail* [Toronto], 20 Oct. 1979, p. 7.
Layton reviews the movie *Apocalypse Now*, produced and directed by Francis Ford Coppola.

B929 "Apocalypse Now." *The Globe and Mail* [Toronto], 6 Nov. 1979, p. 6.
Layton qualifies his review of the movie *Apocalypse Now*, produced and directed by Francis Ford Coppola (B928).

B930 "Anglophone Arrogance Is My Target, Says Irving Layton." *The Globe and Mail* [Toronto], 9 April 1980, p. 7.
Layton objects to Dennis Duffy's review of *An Unlikely Affair* (D319).

B931 "Canada Is in Danger of Being Gobbled Up." *The Globe and Mail* [Toronto], 19 April 1980, p. 7.
Layton discusses the insensitivity of English Canadians. The poem "Woody Allen" (B661) is included.

B932 "CBC 'Censors' News, Says Layton." *The Globe and Mail* [Toronto], 3 May 1980, p. 7.
Layton discusses the CBC's distortion of his comments concerning Volker Schlondorff's film, *The Tin Drum*, produced by Franz Seitz.

B933 "Review Leaves Reader Wavering." *The Gazette* [Montreal], 29 Aug. 1980, p. 47.
Layton comments on Louis Dudek's review of *Lives of the Poets*, by William H. Pritchard; *Ezra Pound and the Cantos: A Record of Struggle*, by Wendy Flory; and *Wallace Stevens: A Celebration*, ed. Frank Doggett and Robert Buttal (*The Gazette*, 2 August).

B934 "Bergman Illuminates Psyche." *The Globe and Mail* [Toronto], 7 Feb. 1981, p. 7.
Layton discusses Ingmar Bergman's *From the Life of the Marionettes*.

B935 "Trudeau Towers Above Pygmies." *The Toronto Star*, 10 Feb. 1981, p. A7.
Layton discusses the Canadian constitution and energy policy.

B936 "Irving Layton: Open Letter to PCR." *Poetry Canada Review*, 2, No. 3 (Spring 1981), 13.

Layton decries the absence in Canada of knowledgeable critics, such as Alfred Kazin, Lionel Trilling, and Irving Howe. He discusses his vision of poetry.

B937 "Book Review Is Mindless Drivel." *The Gazette* [Montreal]. "You Be the Critic," 15 May 1981, p. 50.
Layton strongly objects to Susan Stromberg-Stein's review of *Europe and Other Bad News* (D242).

B938 "Droppings from Layton." *Books in Canada*, Aug.–Sept. 1981, pp. 30–31.
Layton responds to Tecca Crosby's critical review of *Europe and Other Bad News* (D243).

B939 "Two Major Errors in Layton Article." *The Toronto Star*, 13 May 1982, p. A19.
Layton corrects factual errors in Olivia Ward's article (C371).

B940 "Israel." *The Globe and Mail* [Toronto], 24 June 1982, p. 6.
Layton discusses Israel and the PLO.

B941 Letter. *The Lunatic Gazette* [Erin, Ont.], 1, No. 1 (Oct.–Nov. 1982), 2.
Layton suggests the benefits of publishing his work in *The Lunatic Gazette*.

B942 "Poet Responds to 'Not Nice' Comments." *The Gazette* [Montreal], 5 April 1984, p. B6.
Layton objects to Michael Mirolla's suggestion (*The Gazette* [Montreal], 17 March 1984) that he was not nice to Louis Dudek.

B943 "His Poem for Zundel." *The Canadian Jewish News* [Toronto], 14 March 1985, p. 11.
Layton discusses Ernst Zundel and what he stands for. The poem "To the Victims of the Holocaust" follows. See B596.

B944 "Another View of the Genesis." *Quill & Quire*, Sept. 1985, p. 2.
Layton comments on Elspeth Cameron's biography (C9) and its limitations. A brief response by Cameron follows (C442).

B945 "Poet Claims Fiction in Biography." *The Gazette* [Montreal], 8 Oct. 1985, p. B2.
Elspeth Cameron is more third-rate novelist than scholar.

B946 "Biography Filled with 'Unevaluated Gossip.' " *The Toronto Star*, 5 Nov. 1985, p. A14.
Elspeth Cameron's book concentrates on and fictionalizes Layton's personal relationships.

B947 "Vital Invective." *Maclean's*, 11 Nov. 1985, p. 4.
Layton objects to Brian D. Johnson's review of Elspeth Cameron's biography (D333) and the biography itself (C9).

B948 Letter. *The Globe and Mail* [Toronto], 9 Jan. 1986, p. A6.
Layton responds to William French's column (C460), concerning his alleged attempts to damage Elspeth Cameron's reputation.

B949 "Layton Denies 'Hate Mail.' " *The Canadian Jewish News* [Toronto], 23 Jan. 1986, p. 11
Layton denies Joel Yanosky's assertion that Layton sent hate mail to Elspeth Cameron (C459).

B950 "The Layton Challenge." *The Globe and Mail* [Toronto], 3 Feb. 1986, p. A6.
Layton challenges Elspeth Cameron to appear before three Canadian literature scholars to defend his accusations of inaccuracy in her biography.

B951 "Speaking of WASPS." *The Globe and Mail* [Toronto], 14 Feb. 1986, p. A6.
Layton responds to Heather Robertson's letter (C470), denying that he preaches hatred of the WASP.

B952 "Critic Disappoints." *The Citizen* [Ottawa], 18 Feb. 1986, p. A9.
Layton expresses disappointment at Sharon Drache's review of *Essential Words: An Anthology of Jewish Canadian Poetry*, edited by Seymour Mayne.

B953 "Layton's Reply: Kiss of the Spiderman." *Influence*, April–May 1986, p. 10.
Layton responds to Peter Worthington's "A Case of Hate Literature" (C471).

B954 "Layton's Lament." *Toronto*, July 1986, p. 6.
Ray Conlogue's article (C474) substantiates Layton's position, but Conlogue remains blind to the truth.

B955 "Beethovenesque Layton." *The Canadian Jewish News* [Toronto], 6 Nov. 1986, p. 11.
Layton states that Frank Rasky's article (C479) is one of the few ever written "that did not misquote me outrageously or misrepresent my views."

B956 "Column 'Bright Searching Light' on Crisis." *The Gazette* [Montreal], 8 July 1990, p. B3.
Responding to Norman Webster's column in *The Gazette* 30 June, Layton comments on Meech Lake.

Articles

B957 "Current History." *Macdonald College Failt-Ye Times* [Montreal], 18 Oct. 1935, p. 2.
Signed: Pero. The Canadian federal election, in which William Lyon Mackenzie King defeated Richard Bennett, is discussed.

B958 "Current History." *Macdonald College Failt-Ye Times* [Montreal], 25 Oct. 1935, pp. 2–3. *TS:CS* ("A First View, 1935–1937 ['Current History,' 25 Oct. 1935]").
Originally signed: Pero. The political situations in France and Italy are discussed.

B959 "Current History." *Macdonald College Failt-Ye Times* [Montreal], 1 Nov. 1935, p. 2.
Japan's aggression in northern China is discussed.

B960 "Current History." *Macdonald College Failt-Ye Times* [Montreal], 22 Nov. 1935, p. 2. *TS:CS* ("A First View, 1935–1937 ['Current History,' 22 Nov. 1935]").
The political situation in Britain is discussed.

B961 "Current History." *Macdonald College Failt-Ye Times* [Montreal], 29 Nov. 1935, p. 2.
The Quebec provincial election, in which Premier Taschereau was re-elected, is discussed.

B962 "Current History." *Macdonald College Failt-Ye Times* [Montreal], 6 Dec. 1935, p. 2. *TS:CS* ("A First View, 1935–1937 ['Current History,' 6 Dec. 1935]").
The social situation in Germany and the communist system in Russia is discussed.

B963 "Current History." *Macdonald College Failt-Ye Times* [Montreal], 27 March 1936, p. 2. *TS:CS* ("A First View, 1935–1937 ['Current History,' 27 March 1936]").
Signed: Irving Lazarovitch. Adolf Hitler's remilitarization of the Rhine is discussed.

B964 "The Farmer Thinks: Co-Operation in Nova Scotia." *McGill Daily*, 3 Nov. 1937, p. 4.
Signed: Irvine Layton.

B965 "The Farmer Thinks: Mr. Hepburn's Re-Election." *McGill Daily*, 10 Nov. 1937, p. 4.
Signed: Irvine Layton.

B966 "The Farmer Thinks: The New Deal for Agriculture." *McGill Daily*, 19 Nov. 1937, p. 4.
Signed: Irvine Layton.

B967 "The Farmer Thinks: Will Fascism Conquer?". *McGill Daily*, 24 Nov. 1937, p. 4. *TS:CS* ("A First View, 1935–1937 ['The Farmer Thinks: Will Fascism Conquer?']").
Originally signed: Irvine Layton.

B968 "The Farmer Thinks: The Wheat Situation." *McGill Daily*, 31 Jan. 1938, p. 4.
Signed: Irvine Layton.

B969 "The Farmer Thinks: Culture and Capitalism." *McGill Daily*, 2 Feb. 1938, p. 4.
Signed: Irvine Layton.

B970 "Harold Laski." *Forge*, Dec. 1941, pp. 36–40. *E:PIL*.

B971 "Politics and Poetry." *First Statement*, Aug. 1943, pp. 17–21. *E:PIL*; *TS:CS* ("Essays, Reviews, Lectures, 1943–1977 ['Politics and Poetry']").

B972 "Let's Win the Peace." *First Statement*, May 1944, pp. 11–15. *E:PIL*.

B973 "Ghitta Caiserman." *Modern Review* [New York], 1, No. 6 (Aug.–Sept. 1947), 17–18.

B974 "Canadian Poetry: Modern." *Prism* [Sir George Williams College Literary Society], (1955), pp. 18–20. *TS:CS* ("Essays, Reviews, Lectures, 1943–1977 ['Canadian Poetry: Modern']").

B975 "Shaw, Pound and Poetry." *CIV/n*, No. 7 (Winter 1955), pp. 11–12. *E:PIL*.

B976 "The Role of the Teacher." *Bulletin of the Montreal Teachers Federation of Jewish Schools*, 1, No. 1 (Oct. 1955), 4–5. *TS:CS* ("Essays, Reviews, Lectures, 1943–1977 ['The Role of the Teacher']").

B977 "Irving Layton Remembers Chopped Liver and Humble Pie." *Maclean's*, 31 Jan. 1959, p. 30.

B978 Introductory "Note" to *A Laughter in the Mind*. *Congress Bulletin* [Canadian Jewish Congress], May 1959, p. 3. *LM* (expanded — Preface).

B979 "Books and Bookmen." *The Vancouver Sun*, 13 Aug. 1960, p. 5. *TS:CS* ("Views of the World: Letters, Articles, Travels, 1960–1977. Books and Bookmen").

B979a Introduction. In *Poems for 27 Cents*. Montreal: Privately printed, 1961, pp. 2–4.

B980 "A Tall Man Executes a Jig." In *Poet's Choice*. Ed. Paul Engle and Joseph Langland. New York: Dial, 1962, pp. 122–23. *E:PIL*.

B981 "Prince Hamlet and the Beatniks." David B. Steinman Festival, St. Lawrence Univ., Canton, N.Y. 18 Feb. 1962. *TS:CS* ("Essays, Reviews, Lectures, 1943–1977 ['Prince Hamlet and the Beatniks']").

B982 "Love Where the Nights Are Long." *Maclean's*, Oct. 1962, pp. 32–33. Rpt. (expanded — "Love Is Layton's Answer to Canada's Long, Cold, Winter Nights") in *The Vancouver Sun*, 7 Dec. 1962, [First sec.], p. 5. *E:PIL* ("What Canadians Don't Know about Love"); *LWNA* (l.ed).

B983 "Poets: The Conscience of Mankind." *The Globe Magazine* [*The Globe and Mail*] [Toronto], 15 June 1963, pp. 5, 17. *E:PIL*.

B984 "The Creative Process." Foster Poetry Conference, McGill Univ., Montreal. 12–14 Oct. 1963. Printed in *English Poetry in Quebec: Proceedings of the Foster Poetry Conference, October 12–14 1963*. Ed. John Glassco. Montreal: McGill Univ. Press, 1965, pp. 24–42.

B985 "A Philosopher's Analysis." *Moderator* [New Haven, Conn.], 3, No. 1 (Spring 1964), 17–18. *TS:CS* ("Essays, Reviews, Lectures, 1943–1977 ['A Philosopher's Analysis']").

B986 "Poets with Cameras in Their Fists." *The Montreal Star*, 20 June 1964, p. 4. *E:PIL*.

B987 "Tragedies to Help Keep One Sane." *The Globe Magazine* [*The Globe and Mail*] [Toronto], 25 Dec. 1965, p. 13.

B988 "On and Off St. Catharine Street, Two Artists of the World." *New-Generation-Nouvelle* [Baron Byng High School, Montreal], April 1966. *TS:CS* (abridged — "Ruminations ['On and Off St. Catharine Street, Two Artists of the World']").

B989 "Germany's Searching Students." *The Montreal Star*, 26 May 1966, p. 7. *TS:CS* ("Views of the World: Letters, Articles, Travels, 1960–1977. Germany's Searching Students").

B990 "Zest for Life in German Cities." *The Montreal Star*, 7 June 1966, p. 9. *TS:CS* ("Views of the World: Letters, Articles, Travels, 1960–1977. Zest for Life in German Cities").

B991 "East Berlin Impressions." *The Montreal Star*, 8 July 1966, p. 7. *TS:CS* ("Views of the World: Letters, Articles, Travels, 1960–1977. East Berlin Impressions").

B992 "Canadian Criticism? Stark, Raving, Mad! A Baneful Influence." *The Telegram* [Toronto], 8 Oct. 1966, p. 12. *E:PIL* ("Forever Honeyless: Canadian Criticism").

B993 "Two Views of Germany." *Maclean's*, 19 Nov. 1966, pp. 18, 26, 28, 30, 31. *TS:CS* ("Views of the World: Letters, Articles, Travels, 1960–1977. A View of Germany").

B994 Introduction. *Ontario College of Art Yearbook*, 1967, p. 1. *TS:CS* ("Essays, Reviews, Lectures, 1943–1977 [Introduction to *Ontario College of Art Yearbook* (1967)]").

B995 "Dear Harris & Freedman." In *Poems from Ritual / Through the Telemeter*. By Michael Harris and Michael Freedman. Montreal: Ransack, 1967, n. pag.

B996 Lecture. Le poète dans la société contemporaine / The Poet and the World of Man, Montreal, 6 Sept. 1967. Printed in *études littéraires* [Univ. Laval], 1 (Dec. 1968), 351–53. *TS:CS* ("Essays, Reviews, Lectures, 1943–1977 [Lecture, 6 Sept. 1967]").

B997 Lecture. Le poète dans la société contemporaine / The Poet and the World of Man, Montreal, 7 Sept. 1967. Printed in *études littéraires* [Univ. Laval], 1 (Dec. 1968), 395–96. *TS:CS* ("Essays, Reviews, Lectures, 1943–1977 [Lecture, 7 Sept. 1967]").

B998 "The Great Mortgage Hanging Over Israel." *The Montreal Star*, 15 March 1968, p. 8. *TS:CS* ("Views of the World: Letters, Articles, Travels, 1960–1977. The Great Mortgage Hanging Over Israel").

B999 "Minority Rights Key Mid-East Issue." *The Montreal Star*, 27 March 1968, p. 14. *TS:CS* ("Views of the World: Letters, Articles, Travels, 1960–1977. Minority Rights Key Mid-East Issue").

B1000 "Some Observations and Aphorisms." *The Tamarack Review*, No. 47 (Spring 1968), pp. 5–7. *WBB* (expanded — "Aphs," "Obs I," and "Obs II").

B1001 "A High Price to Pay for Survival." *The Montreal Star*, 1 April 1968, p. 6. *TS:CS* ("Views of the World: Letters, Articles, Travels, 1960–1977. A High Price to Pay for Survival").

B1002 "The Kaleidoscope That Is India." *The Montreal Star*, 25 May 1968, p. 6. *TS:CS* ("Views of the World: Letters, Articles, Travels, 1960–1977. The Kaleidoscope That Is India").

B1003 "In the Morning, the Snow Was Like the Beginning of Creation." *The Telegram* [Toronto], 31 Aug. 1968, Sec. 4, p. 5. *TS:CS* ("Views of the World: Letters, Articles, Travels, 1960–1977. In the Morning, the Snow Was Like the Beginning of Creation").

B1004 "Cemeteries Are Where I Am Most Dionysian." *The Telegram* [Toronto], 21 Sept. 1968, p. 5. *E:PIL*.

B1005 "Aphorisms." *The Telegram* [Toronto], 23 Nov. 1968, Weekend / Showcase, p. 5. *WBB* (expanded — "Aphs").

B1006 "More Aphorisms." *The Telegram* [Toronto], 23 Nov. 1968, Weekend / Showcase, p. 5. *WBB* (expanded — "Aphs").

B1007 "Canada's Poetic Riches." *The Montreal Star*, 29 March 1969, Supplement, pp. 3–4. *TS:CS* ("Essays, Reviews, Lectures, 1943–1977 ['Canada's Poetic Riches']").

B1008 [Introduction to] "Elephant." In *How Do I Love Thee: Sixty Poets of Canada (and Quebec) Select and Introduce Their Favourite Poems from Their Own Work*. Ed. John Robert Colombo. Edmonton: Hurtig, 1970, p. 20. *E:PIL*.

B1009 Introduction. In *Poems to Color*. Ed. Irving Layton. Toronto: York Univ. 1970, pp. 6–9. *E:PIL* (" 'Introduction,' *Poems to Color*").

B1010 Foreword. In *Magadan*. By Michael Solomon. Montreal: Chateau, 1971, pp. ix–x. Rpt. New York: Vertex, 1971, pp. ix–x. *E:PIL* ("Foreword, *Magdan*").

B1011 Foreword. In *i Side Up*. Ed. Irving Layton. Toronto: York Univ. 1971, pp. 1–3. *E:PIL* ("Foreword, *i Side Up*").

B1012 Foreword. In *Within Two*. By Anna Shirley. Ottawa: The Anna Shirley Foundation, 1971, pp. 13–14.

B1013 "Irving Layton's Canada." *Maclean's*, Sept. 1971, pp. 14, 80.

B1014 ———, and Eli Mandel. "Nietzsche and Poetry: A Discussion." *The Malahat Review* [Univ. of Victoria], No. 24 (Oct. 1972), pp. 23–29. *TS:CS* ("Essays, Reviews, Lectures, 1943–1977 ['Nietzsche and Poetry: A Discussion']").
See B1257.

B1015 Introduction. In *Anvil Blood*. Ed. Irving Layton. Toronto: [York Univ. Poetry Workshop], 1973, pp. 3–5. *TS:CS* ("Essays, Reviews, Lectures, 1943–1977 [Introduction to *Anvil Blood*]").

B1016 "Poet Says Many Things Beyond the Obvious." *Excalibur* [York Univ.], 15 March 1973, p. 7.

B1017 Foreword. In *New Holes in the Wall*. Toronto: York Univ., 1975, pp. i–iii. *TS:CS* ("Views of the World: Letters, Articles, Travels, 1960–1977. Throwaways, Laryngeals, Simple-Simons").

B1018 "My Troublesome Compatriots." *Iconomatrix: A Polemical & Iconoclastic Quarterly*, 1, No. 1 (Sept. 1975), 19–21. *TS:CS* ("Essays, Reviews, Lectures, 1943–1977 ['My Troublesome Compatriates']").

B1019 Foreword. In *Modern Romanian Poetry*. Ed. Nicholas Catanoy. Oakville, Ont.: Mosaic / Valley, 1977, pp. 9–11. *TS:CS* ("Essays, Reviews, Lectures, 1943–1977 [Foreword to *Modern Romanian Poetry*]").

B1020 "Harold Laski: The Paradoxes of a Liberal Marxist." *Canadian Journal of Political and Social Theory* [Concordia Univ.], 1, No. 1 (Winter 1977), 71–90. *TS:CS* (expanded — "Harold Laski: The Paradoxes of a Liberal Marxist, 1946").

B1021 "Self-Images: Reflections from the Celebrated. More Magnificent Obsessions. "Irving Layton Lover at the Holocaust." *Toronto Life*, Dec. 1977, pp. 47, 64, 66.

B1022 "An Epistolary Preface." In *Moon without Light*. By Len Gasparini. Toronto: York Publishing, 1978, n. pag.

B1023 "Laytonisms." In *Handouts from the Mountain*. Ed. Irving Layton. Toronto: York Univ. Poetry Workshops, 1978, p. 44.
 See B1105 for reprinted material in this book.

B1024 "Leading with a 5,000-Year-Old Chin." *Books in Canada*, March 1978, p. 5.

B1025 Foreword. In *Irving Layton: A Bibliography 1935–1977*. By Joy Bennett and James Polson. Montreal: Concordia Univ. Press, 1979, p. [v].

B1026 Foreword. In *Piece Work*. By Mona Adilman. Ottawa: Borealis, 1979, pp. vii–viii.

B1027 "*Dropping from Heaven* Forward [sic]." *Matrix*, No. 9 (Spring–Summer 1979), pp. 3–5. *DH* (revised — Foreword).

B1028 "A Day in the Life." *Weekend Magazine*, 25 Aug. 1979, p. 7.

B1029 "A Personal Memoir." *Viewpoints: The Canadian Jewish Quarterly*, 2, No. 4 (Spring 1981), 3–4.

B1030 "Am I Cheering to Empty Bleachers?". *The Globe and Mail* [Toronto], 25 April 1981, p. 6.

B1032 "A Chess Master in Control." *Descant*, [Dennis Lee Special Issue], No. 39 [14, No. 1] (Winter 1982), p. 31. Rpt. in *Tasks of Passion: Dennis Lee at Mid-Career*. Ed. Karen Mulhallen, Donna Bennett, and Russell Brown. Toronto: Descant, 1982, p. 31.

B1033 "Foreword to *The Tightrope Dancer*." In *The Insecurity of Art*. Ed. Ken Norris and Peter Van Toorn. Montreal: Véhicule, 1982, pp. 86–88. *TD* (Foreword).

B1034 "Foreword to the Gucci Bag." *The Lunatic Gazette* [Erin, Ont.], 1, No. 1 (Oct.–Nov. 1982), 6–7. Rpt. ("Jack the Ripper as Metaphor") in *The Canadian Literary Review*, No. 1 (Fall–Winter 1982), pp. 45–50. *GB* (l.ed) (revised — Foreword); *GB* (revised); *GB2*.

B1035 "Recalling the 50's." In CIV/n: *A Literary Magazine of the 50's*. Ed. Aileen Collins and Simon Dardick. Montreal: Véhicule, 1983, pp. 249–51.

B1036 "Varied Hues." In *Celebrate Our City. Toronto: 150th Anniversary*. Ed. Barbara Amiel and Lorraine Monk. Introd. Mike Filey. Toronto: McClelland and Stewart, 1983, p. 28.

B1037 "Oh! Montreal." *The New Montrealer*, Autumn 1983, pp. 11, 13.

B1038 [Tribute to Alden Nowlan.] *Poetry Canada Review*, 5, No. 1 (Fall 1983), 3.

B1039 "Why Layton Is Coming Home to Montreal." *The Gazette* [Montreal], 26 Nov. 1983, p. I1.

B1040 "Where's Poetry? On the Screen." *The Globe and Mail* [Toronto], 25 Feb. 1984, First Sec., p. 6.

B1041 "A Poet's Perspective." *Toronto Life*. "Papal Perspectives," Sept. 1984, p. 51.

B1042 "Remembering the Dean of Canadian Poets." *The Gazette* [Montreal], 2 Feb. 1985, p. B11.

B1043 "Pourquoi Ecrivez-Vous? 400 Ecrivains Repondent: Irving Layton." *Libération*, March 1985, p. 28.

B1044 "Books for Christmas; Montrealers Make a Gift of Reading. Irving Layton: Poet." *The Gazette* [Montreal], 14 Dec. 1985, p. E2.
    Layton recommends *Freud for Historians*, by Peter Gay; *Essential Words: An Anthology of Jewish Canadian Poetry*, ed. Seymour Mayne; and *Frida Kahlo: A Portrait*, by Hayden Herrera.

B1045 "Reminiscence: Some Words About Milton Acorn." *Cross-Canada Writers' Quarterly*, 8, Nos. 3–4 (1986), 8.

B1046 "Writer's Writers." *Books in Canada*, Jan.–Feb. 1987, p. 10.

B1047 "The Forties: Irving Layton." *Brick* [Toronto], [Special Issue on F.R. Scott], No. 30 (Summer 1987), pp. 32–34.

B1048 "Friendships: Irving Layton." *Brick* [Toronto], [Special Issue on F.R. Scott], No. 30 (Summer 1987), p. 51.

B1049 "Recollected: Irving Layton." *Brick* [Toronto], [Special Issue on F.R. Scott], No. 30 (Summer 1987), p. 58.

B1050 Foreword. In *Rawprint*. Montreal: Concordia Poetry Workshop, 1989, pp. 5–6.

B1051 [Introduction to] "Piety." In *Montreal Mon Amour: Short Stories from Montreal*. Ed. and introd. Michael Benazon. Toronto: Deneau, 1989, p. 34.

Short Stories

B1052 "Silhouette of a Man." *McGill Daily*, 17 Dec. 1937, p. 1. Rpt. in *McGill Daily*, 24 Jan. 1938, pp. 2, 4. Originally signed: Irvine Layton.

B1053 "A Parasite." *First Statement*, 1, No. 14 [1943], 3–9. SF (revised — "Unemployed"); E:PIL.

B1054 "The Philistine." *First Statement*, April 1944, pp. 5–13. SF; E:PIL.

B1055 "A Game of Chess." *First Statement*, May 1944, pp. 1–8. Rpt. (revised) in *The Tamarack Review*, No. 18 (Winter 1961), pp. 60–70. *SF; E:PIL*. Originally signed: Jim Dorken.

B1056 "The English Lesson." *First Statement*, 2, No. 12 (April–May 1945), 3–13. *SF; E:PIL*.

B1056a "Piety." *First Statement*, 3 No. 1 (June–July 1945), 23–36. *SF; E:PIL*.

B1057 "Vacation in La Voiselle." *Northern Review*, 1, No. 2 (Feb.–March 1946), 2–16. *NIP; SF* (revised); *E:PIL*.

B1058 "A Death in the Family." *Northern Review*, 1, No. 4 (Dec.–Jan. 1946–47), 2–11. *NIP; SF; E:PIL*.

B1059 "A Plausible Story." *Origin*, Ser. 1, No. 14 (Autumn 1954), pp. 91–104. *SF* (revised); *E:PIL*.

B1060 "Mrs. Polinov." *Origin*, Ser. 1, No. 17 (Fall–Winter 1955–56), pp. 25–40. *SF* (revised); *E:PIL*.

B1061 "Osmeck." *The Canadian Forum*, Feb. 1961, pp. 249–52. *SF; E:PIL*.

Excerpts

B1062 "My Father and I." *The Canadian Jewish News*, *Viewpoints*, 14 June 1984, pp. 1, 2, 7. *WM* (revised, expanded — Ch. ii).

B1063 "Waiting for the Messiah." *Canadian Literature*, No. 101 (Summer 1984), pp. 7–14. *WM* (revised — Ch. i).

B1064 "Irving Layton — the Macdonald College Years" (excerpt from *Waiting for the Messiah*). *The Gazette* [Montreal], 12 Oct. 1985, pp. B5–B6. *WM* (Ch. x).

B1065 *Waiting for the Messiah* (excerpt). *Poetry Canada Review*, 7, No. 2 (Winter 1985–86), 3–4, 9. *WM* (Ch. xiii).

B1066 "Irascible, Irrepressible, Irritable: Irving Layton" (excerpt from *Wild Gooseberries: The Selected Letters of Irving Layton*). *Saturday Magazine, The Toronto Star*, 19 Aug. 1989, pp. M12–M13. *WG* (Earle Birney, 22 July 1951, 24 July 1951; Louis Dudek, Sept. 1954; Desmond Pacey, 22 June 1955; Jack McClelland, 27 May 1967; Musia Schwartz, 10 June 1980; Harriet Bernstein, 15 Jan. 1982; Elspeth Cameron, 8 March 1985, 15 Sept. 1985).

Reprinted Anthology Contributions: A Selection

B1067 "De Bullion Street," "Jewish Main Street," "Newsboy," "Petawawa," "Returning with an Annual Passion," "Stolen Watch," "The Swimmer," and "Words without Music." In *Other Canadians: An Anthology of New Canadian Poetry in Canada*. Ed. and introd. John Sutherland. Montreal: First Statement, 1947, pp. 54–60.

B1068 "Mont Rolland," "The Swimmer," "To a Very Old Woman," and "Vexata Quaestio." In *Canadian Poems 1850–1952*. Ed. and introd. Louis Dudek and Irving Layton. Toronto: Contact, 1952, pp. 89–92.

B1069 "In the Midst of My Fever" and "Vexata Quaestio." In *New Canadian Poetry*. Preface Gael Turnbull. Artisan, No. 6. London, Eng.: Heron, 1954, pp. 1–3.

B1070 "The Birth of Tragedy," "The Fertile Muck," "In the Midst of My Fever," "Metzinger: Girl with a Bird," "Newsboy," "Poem," and "Rain at La Minerve." In *The Book of Canadian Poetry: A Critical and His-*

torical Anthology. 3rd ed. Ed. and introd. A.J.M. Smith. Toronto: Gage, 1957, pp. 405–12.

B1071 "The Birth of Tragedy," "The Bull Calf," "Composition in Late Spring," "For Louise, Age 17," and "The Swimmer." In *The Penguin Book of Canadian Verse.* Ed. and introd. Ralph Gustafson. Harmondsworth, Eng.: Penguin, 1958, pp. 183–87.

B1072 "Cain" and "Golfers." In *The Art of Poetry.* Ed. and introd. Hugh Kenner. New York: Holt, Rinehart & Winston, 1959, pp. 26–27, 33–34.

B1073 "Bacchanal," "The Birth of Tragedy," "Boys in October," "The Bull Calf," "The Cold Green Element," and "The Fertile Muck." In *The Oxford Book of Canadian Verse: In English and French.* Ed. and introd. A.J.M. Smith. Toronto: Oxford Univ. Press, 1960, pp. 303–10.

B1074 "Vacation in La Voiselle" (story). In *Canadian Short Stories.* Ed. and introd. Robert Weaver. Toronto: Oxford Univ. Press, 1960, pp. 248–69.

B1075 "Café Politics in Spring," "Holiday," and "Parting." In *A Canadian Anthology (Poems from* The Fiddlehead: *1945–1959).* Ed. and preface Fred Cogswell. [*The Fiddlehead*, No. 50 (Fall 1961)], pp. 29–31.

B1076 "The Bishopric," "The Day Aviva Came to Paris," "Divinity," "Sacrament by the Water," and "Song for a Late Hour." In *Love Where the Nights Are Long: An Anthology of Canadian Love Poems.* Ed. and introd. Irving Layton. Toronto: McClelland and Stewart, 1962, pp. 18, 36–38, 59, 65, 71.

B1077 "Foreword to *A Red Carpet for the Sun.*" In *Masks of Poetry: Canadian Critics on Canadian Verse.* Ed.

and introd. A.J.M. Smith. New Canadian Library Original, No. O3. Toronto: McClelland and Stewart, 1962, pp. 139–43.

B1078 "A Plausible Story" (story). In *A Book of Canadian Stories.* Ed. Desmond Pacey. Rev. ed. Toronto: Ryerson, 1962, pp. 244–59.

B1079 "Keine Lazarovitch (1870–1959)." In *An Anthology of Commonwealth Verse.* Ed. and introd. Margaret O'Donnell. London: Blackie, 1963, p. 185.

B1080 "The Architect," "Berry Picking," "The Birth of Tragedy," "Cain," "Cat Dying in Autumn," "Cemetery in August," "The Cold Green Element," "Composition in Late Spring," "The Convertible," "Côte des Neiges Cemetery," "The Day Aviva Came to Paris," "Enemies," "Family Portrait," "Golfers," "Keewaydin Poetry Festival," "Look, the Lambs Are All Around Us!", "Maurer: Twin Heads," "Misunderstanding," "Mont Rolland," "Song for Naomi," "The Swimmer," "A Tall Man Executes a Jig," "To the Girls of My Graduating Class," "Vexata Quaestio," "The Well-Wrought Urn," "Whatever Else Poetry Is Freedom," "Whom I Write For," and "The Wooden Spoon." In *Poetry of Mid-Century 1940–1960.* Ed. and introd. Milton Wilson. New Canadian Library Original, No. O4. Toronto: McClelland and Stewart, 1964, pp. 47–83.

B1081 "Piety" (story). In *Modern Canadian Stories.* Ed. Giose Rimanelli and Roberto Ruberto. Foreword Earle Birney. Toronto: Ryerson, 1966, pp. 373–88.

B1082 "Anglo-Canadian," "Concourse at Cataraqui," "From Colony to Nation," "Golfers," "The Improved Binoculars," "Jesus Saves," "Letter to a Librarian," "Misunderstanding," and "The Way the

World Ends." In *The Blasted Pine: An Anthology of Satire, Invective, and Disrespectful Verse*. Rev. and enl. ed. Ed. and introd. F.R. Scott and A.J.M. Smith. Toronto: Macmillan, 1967, pp.3–4, 32, 43–44, 72, 75, 109–10, 122, 132, 147.

B1083 "Berry Picking," "The Birth of Tragedy," "Cain," "The Day Aviva Came to Paris," and "A Tall Man Executes a Jig." In *Modern Canadian Verse: In English and French*. Ed. and introd. A.J.M. Smith. Toronto: Oxford Univ. Press, 1967, pp. 149–59.

B1084 "Overheard in a Barbershop." In *The New Modern Poetry: British and American Poetry Since WW II*. Ed. M.L. Rosenthal. London: Macmillan, 1967, p. 132.

B1085 "Berry Picking," "Conference Man," "On My Way to School," "Veteran," and "The Well-Wrought Urn." In *Impact*. Ed. and foreword William Eckersley. Toronto: Dent, 1968, pp. 45, 67, 128, 141, 142.

B1086 "Song for Naomi" and "A Spider Danced a Cosy Jig." In *The Wind Has Wings: Poems from Canada*. Ed. Mary Alice Downie and Barbara Robertson. Illus. Elizabeth Cleaver. Toronto: Oxford Univ. Press, 1968, pp. 43, 80.

B1087 "Berry Picking," "The Birth of Tragedy," "The Bull Calf," "Butterfly on Rock," "The Cold Green Element," "The Fertile Muck," "In the Midst of My Fever," "Keine Lazarovitch 1870–1959," "On Being Bitten by a Dog," "Song for Naomi," "A Spider Danced a Cosy Jig," and "There Were No Signs." In *Five Modern Canadian Poets*. Ed. and introd. Eli Mandel. Toronto: Holt, Rinehart and Winston, 1970, pp. 23–37.

B1088 "Elephant." In *How Do I Love Thee: Sixty Poets of Canada (and Quebec) Select and Introduce Their Favourite Poems from Their Own Work*. Ed. and preface John Robert Colombo. Edmonton: Hurtig, 1970, p. 19–20.
See B1008.

B1089 "Aran Islands," "For Anna," "For Natalya Correia," "The Haunting," "Ohms," and "Osip Mandelstam (1891–1940)." In *New American and Canadian Poetry*. Ed. and introd. John Gill. Boston: Beacon, 1971, pp. 129–35.

B1090 "Unemployed" (story). In *Great Canadian Short Stories*. Ed. and introd. Alec Lucas. New York: Dell, 1971, pp. 140–47.

B1091 "Lady Remington," "Layton on Layton" (letter), "There Were No Signs," and "Three Poems: Cote Des Neiges Cemetery; Sheep; Whatever Else Poetry Is Freedom." In *Forum: Canadian Life and Letters 1920–70. Selections from* The Canadian Forum. Ed. and preface J.L. Granatstein and Peter Stevens. Toronto: Univ. of Toronto Press, 1972, pp. 214, 306–07, 312–13, 344.

B1092 "Above All, Avoid Halitosis," "The Birth of Tragedy," "The Bull Calf," "Confederation Ode," "Foreword to *A Red Carpet for the Sun*," "Keine Lazarovitch, 1870–1959," "On Seeing the Statuettes of Ezekiel and Jeremiah in the Church of Notre Dame," "Song for Naomi," "A Tall Man Executes a Jig," and "Whatever Else Poetry Is Freedom." In *The Evolution of Canadian Literature in English 1945–1970*. Ed. and introd. Paul Denham. Preface Mary Jane Edwards. Toronto: Holt, Rinehart and Winston, 1973, pp. 57–71.

B1093 "Analogue" and "Mexican Guerrillas." In *Anvil Blood*. Ed. and introd. Irving Layton. Toronto: [York Univ. Poetry Workshop], 1973, p. 57.

B1094 "Against This Death," "Berry Picking," "The Birth of Tragedy," "The Bull Calf," "Cain," "The Cold Green Element," "Keine Lazarovitch 1870–1959," "Look, the Lambs Are All Around Us!", "Sacrament by the Water," "A Tall Man Executes a Jig," and "Whatever Else Poetry Is Freedom." In *20th-Century Poetry & Poetics*. 2nd ed. Ed. and preface Gary Geddes. Toronto: Oxford Univ. Press, 1973, pp. 243–56.

B1095 "Berry Picking," "The Birth of Tragedy," "Keine Lazarovitch 1870–1959," "On Seeing the Statuettes of Ezekiel and Jeremiah in the Church of Notre Dame," and "Shakespeare." In *The Oxford Anthology of Canadian Literature*. Ed. and preface Robert Weaver and William Toye. Toronto: Oxford Univ. Press, 1973, pp. 265–73.

B1096 "Berry Picking," "The Birth of Tragedy," "The Black Huntsmen," "The Bull Calf," "Butterfly on Rock," "Cat Dying in Autumn," "Cemeteries," "The Cold Green Element," "Foreword to *A Red Carpet for the Sun*," "Keine Lazarovitch, 1870–1959," "Misunderstanding," "Newsboy," "Song for Naomi," "A Tall Man Executes a Jig," and "Whatever Else Poetry Is Freedom." In *Canadian Anthology*. 3rd rev. ed. Ed. and preface Carl F. Klinck and Reginald E. Watters. Toronto: Gage, 1974, pp. 389–400.

B1097 "Berry Picking," "The Birth of Tragedy," "The Bull Calf," "Composition in Late Spring," "First Snow, Lake Achigan," "On Seeing the Statuettes of Ezekiel and Jeremiah in the Church of Notre Dame," "Song for Naomi," and "Stella." In *Selections from Major Canadian Writers: Poetry and Creative Prose in English*. Ed. and preface Desmond Pacey. Toronto: McGraw-Hill Ryerson, 1974, pp. 87–95.

B1098 "Early Morning in Mithymna," "End of the Affair," "The Final Peace," "Hills and Hills," "I Owe This to St. Paul," "Leavetaking," "Limpets," "Modern Greek Poet," "Oedipus," "Olympia Kaput," "Poros," "Storm at Ydra," and "That Is the Question." In *Five Canadian Poets in Greece*. Ed. and introd. Theodore Sampson. Preface G.P. Kournoutos. Athens: Hellenic Ministry of Culture and Sciences, 1974, pp. 26–42.

B1099 "The Cold Green Element," "Epitaph for an Ugly Servitor to Three Queens," "Golfers," "Letter to Cid Corman," "The Madonna of the Magnificat," "Metzinger: Girl with a Bird," "La Minerve," "A Plausible Story" (story), and "The Way of the World." In *The Gist of Origin 1951–1971*. Ed. and introd. Cid Corman. New York: Grossman, 1975, pp. 68–69, 81–95, 122–23.

B1100 "Apokalysis" and "The Protest." In *Events: Greece 1967–1974*. Ed. Michael Harlow. Athens: Anglo-Hellenic, [1976], pp. 44–45.

B1101 "Adam," "Ch'an Artist," "Flytrap," "Iroquois in Nice," "Molibos Cat," "O Jerusalem," "Pole-Vaulter," "The Shadow," "The Shark," and "The Unwavering Eye." In *Almanaco Dello Specchhio 6*. Ed. Marco Forti. Introd. and trans. Amleto Lorenzini, Carla Plevano, and Francesca Valente. N.p.: Mondadori, 1977, pp. 170, 172, 174, 176, 178, 180, 182, 184, 186, 188, 190, 192.

See B513, B515, B527, B531, B534, B536, B538, B569, B570, and B571 for original Italian translations of these poems.

B1102 "The Black Huntsmen," "Bodhidharma," "Cat Dying in Autumn," "Death of Moishe Lazarovitch," "End of the White Mouse," "For Musia's Grandchildren," "Golfers," "The Haunting," "Osip Mandelshtam (1891–1940)," "Saint Pinchas," "Seven O'Clock Lecture," and "Terrorists." In *Canadian Poetry: The Modern Era*. Ed. and preface John Newlove. Toronto: McClelland and Stewart, 1977, pp. 119–31.

B1103 "Contemporary Poet," "O Cureless Rapture," "Heinrich Heine," and "To the Editors of the Tamarack Review." In *Shark Tank*. Ed. Irving Layton. Toronto: York Poetry Workshop, 1977, pp. 95–98.

B1104 "Against This Death," "Berry Picking," "Cain," "The Cold Green Element," "The Fertile Muck," "If I Lie Still," "Israelis," "Keine Lazarovitch 1870–1959," "Look, the Lambs Are All Around Us!", "Marché Municipale," "On Seeing the Statuettes of Ezekiel and Jeremiah in the Church of Notre Dame," "Rhine Boat Trip," "Sacrament by the Water," "A Tall Man Executes a Jig," and "Whatever Else Poetry Is Freedom." In *15 Canadian Poets Plus 5*. Ed. and preface Gary Geddes and Phyllis Bruce. Toronto: Oxford Univ. Press, 1978, pp. 72–90.

B1105 "After a Sleepless Night," "Comrade," "Greek Dancer," and "Intimations." In *Handouts from the Mountain*. Ed. Irving Layton. Toronto: York Univ. Poetry Workshop, 1978, pp. 39–42.
    See B588 and B1023 for original contributions to this book.

B1106 "The Black Huntsmen," "The Birth of Tragedy," "Butterfly on Rock," "Cemetery in August," "For Mao Tse-Tung: A Meditation on Flies and Kings," "The Haunting," "The Human Cry," "O Jerusalem," "Pole-Vaulter," "Red Chokecherries," "The Swimmer," "A Tall Man Executes a Jig," and "The Unwavering Eye." In *Literature in Canada*. Ed. and preface Douglas Daymond and Leslie Monkman. Vol. II. Toronto: Gage, 1978, 277–90.

B1107 "F.R. Scott," "George Woodcock Is Not a Shmuck," "Portrait of a Genius," "Requiem for A.M. Klein," and "To the Editors of the Tamarack Review." In *Tributaries. An Anthology: Writer to Writer*. Ed. and introd. Barry Dempster. Oakville, Ont.: Mosaic / Valley, 1978, pp. 28–29, 50, 82, 84, 96.

B1108 "Keine Lazarovitch 1870–1959." In *The Poets of Canada*. Ed. and preface John Robert Colombo. Edmonton: Hurtig, 1978, pp. 131–32.

B1109 "Divine Image," "Epigram for A.M. Klein," "In Rattlesnake Country," "Prussian Blue," and "Refutation." In *To Say the Least: Canadian Poets from A to Z*. Ed. and introd. P.K. Page. Toronto: Porcépic, 1979, pp. 28, 73, 74, 99, 113.

B1110 "Jewish Main Street." In *Voices Within the Ark: The Modern Jewish Poets*. Ed. and introd. Howard Schwartz and Anthony Rudolf. Yonkers, N.Y.: Pushcart, 1980, p. 760.

B1111 "The Black Huntsman," "For My Brother Jesus," "Israelis," and "The Search." In *The Spice Box: An Anthology of Jewish Canadian Writing*. Ed. and introd. Gerri Sinclair and Morris Wolfe. Toronto: Lester & Orpen Denys, 1981, pp. 187–91.

B1112 "I Would for Your Sake Be Gentle." In *The Lines of the Poet. 13 Poems*. Ed. and introd. D.G. Jones. Preface Morton Rosengarten. Lithographs Morton Rosengarten. Toronto: Monk Bretton Books, 1981. 1 leaf.

B1113 "Letter to a Librarian." In *Tygers of Wrath: Poems of Hate, Anger and Invective*. Ed. and introd. X.J. Kennedy. Athens: Univ. of Georgia Press, 1981, pp. 186–87.

B1114 "The Birth of Tragedy," "Butterfly on Rock," "The Cold Green Element," "End of the White Mouse," "The Fertile Muck," "For Mao Tse-Tung: A Meditation on Flies and Kings," "Keine Lazarovitch 1870–1959," "Newsboy," "O Jerusalem," "Song for Naomi," "A Tall Man Executes a Jig," and "Whatever Else, Poetry Is Freedom." In *An Anthology of Canadian Literature in English*. Ed. and introd. Russell Brown and Donna Bennett. Vol. 1. Toronto: Oxford Univ. Press, 1982, 56–82.

B1115 "Brief Letter to Cervantes," "Florida Nights," "Greetings," "The High Cost of Living," and "Runcible." In *Cross / Cut: Contemporary English Quebec Poetry*. Ed. and preface Peter Van Toorn and Ken Norris. Montreal: Véhicule, 1982, pp. 142–46.

B1116 "The Bull Calf," "The Cold Green Element," "The Fertile Muck," "For My Brother Jesus," "Keine Lazarovitch, 1870–1959," "The Search," "The Swimmer," "A Tall Man Executes a Jig," and "Whatever Else Poetry Is Freedom." In *Canadian Poetry*. Ed. Jack David and Robert Lecker. Introd. George Woodcock. Vol. 1. New Press Canadian Classics. Toronto / Downsview, Ont.: General / ECW, 1982, 238–50.

B1117 "Butterfly on Rock," "The Cold Green Element," "The Fertile Muck," "For Mao Tse-Tung: A Meditation on Flies and Kings," "For Musia's Grandchildren," "From Colony to Nation," "Grand Finale," "The Improved Binoculars," and "A Tall Man Executes a Jig." In *The New Oxford Book of Canadian Verse: In English*. Ed. and introd. Margaret Atwood. Toronto: Oxford Univ. Press, 1982, pp. 148–58.

B1118 "A Poet's Advice to His Friends." In *Jewish History: Moments and Methods*. Ed. Sorel Goldberg Loeb and Barbara Binder Kadden. Denver, Col.: Alternatives in Religious Education, 1982, p. 36.

B1119 "The Buffaloes," "Crêpe Hanger's Carnival" (review), "Death of Moishe Lazarovitch," "In the Midst of My Fever," "Love the Conqueror Worm," "Me, the P.M., and the Stars," "Metzinger: Girl with a Bird," "Mr. Ther-Apis," "On the Death of A. Vishinsky," "Prologue to the Long Pea-Shooter," rev. of *The Colour as Naked*, by Patrick Anderson, "Saratoga Beach," "Seven O'Clock Lecture," "Shaw, Pound and Poetry" (article), "Street Funeral," "Trans Canada" (translation), and "Yiddish Poetry in Canada" (translation)." In *CIV/n: A Literary Magazine of the 50's*. Ed. Aileen Collins and Simon Dardick. Introd. Aileen Collins. Montreal: Véhicule, 1983, pp. 21–22, 37–38, 72–73, 78–81, 101–02, 131–32, 152–53, 183–87, 207–09, 216–18, 224–25.

B1120 "Song for Naomi" and "Wit." In *Poetry in Focus*. Ed. Bob Cameron, Margaret Hogan, and Patrick Lashmar. Toronto: Globe / Modern Curriculum, 1983, pp. 92, 105.

B1121 "The Worm." In *The Third Taboo: A Collection of Poems on Jealousy*. Ed. Heather Cadsby and Maria Jacobs. Foreword Don Coles. Toronto: Wolsak and Wynn, 1983, p. 46.

B1122 "Jude the Obscure" and "New Year's Poem for Veneranda." In *Canadian Writers in 1984: The 25th Anniversary Issue of* Canadian Literature. Ed. and introd. W.H. New. Vancouver: Univ. of British Columbia Press, 1984, p. 198.

B1123 "Against This Death," "Golfers," "If I Lie Still," "Song for Naomi," and "Whom I Write For." In *Antología de la poesía anglocanadiense contemporánea.* Ed., trans., and introd. Bernd Dietz. Barcelona: Los libros de la frontera, 1985, pp. 58, 60, 62, 64, 66, 68, 70, 72.

See B117, B251, B590, B591, and B792 for original Spanish translations in this book.

B1124 "Das Wahre Ich," "For My Two Sons, Max and David," "Post Crematoria," "The Real Values," and "Synagogue in West Palm Beach." In *Mirror of a People: Canadian Jewish Experience in Poetry and Prose.* Ed. Sheldon Oberman and Elaine Newton. Foreword Elaine Newton. Introd. Murray Goldenberg. Winnipeg: Jewish Educational Publishers of Canada, Inc., 1985, pp. 140–43, 167, 198–200.

B1125 "The Final Solution," "For My Brother Jesus," "Israelis," "Osip Mandelshtam (1891–1940)," "Requiem for A.M. Klein," and "Rhine Boat Trip." In *Essential Words: An Anthology of Jewish Canadian Poetry.* Ed. and introd. Seymour Mayne. Ottawa: Oberon, 1985, pp. 74–83.

B1126 "Against This Death," "Bottles," "Cain," "The Cold Green Element," "The Fertile Muck," "For My Brother Jesus," "From Colony to Nation," "Seduction of and by a Civilized Frenchwoman," and "A Tall Man Executes a Jig." In *Poesia canadese del Novocento.* Ed. and trans. Caterina Ricciardi. Napoli: Liguori, 1986, pp. 109, 110, 112, 114, 116, 118, 120, 122, 124, 126, 128, 130, 132.

See B111, B173, B193, B248, B535, B590, B748, B812, and B816 for the original Italian translations of these poems.

B1127 "Elegy for Strul," "Keine Lazarovitch 1870–1959," and "Maxie." In *Relations: Family Portraits.* Ed. and introd. Kenneth Sherman. Oakville, Ont.: Mosaic, 1986, pp. 19, 82–83, 117.

B1128 "Berry Picking." In *The CanLit Foodbook: From Pen to Palate — A Collection of Tasty Literary Fare.* Ed., introd., and illus. Margaret Atwood. Toronto: Totem, 1987, pp. 44–45.

B1129 "Butterfly on Rock," "The Cold Green Element," "A Tall Man Executes a Jig," and "Whatever Else Poetry Is Freedom." In *Introduction to Literature: British, American, Canadian.* Ed. and preface Robert Lecker, Jack David, and Peter O'Brien. New York: Harper & Row, 1987, pp. 375–80.

B1130 "Keine Lazarovitch 1870–1959." In *To Read Literature: Fiction, Poetry, Drama.* 2nd ed. Toronto: Holt, Rinehart and Winston, 1987, pp. 645–46.

B1131 "Overman" and "Soft Porn." In *The Moosehead Anthology: A Collection of Contemporary Writing.* Ed. staff of *The Moosehead Review.* Montreal: D.C., 1988, pp. 8–9.

B1132 "Catacombe Dei Cappuccini," "A Champion for Fellini" (published correspondence), "Layton Says Three Films Are Masterpieces But Reviewer Is Bland, Smug" (published correspondence), and "Women of Rome." In *Canadian Travellers in Italy.* Ed. Barry Callaghan. Scarborough, Ont.: Exile, 1989, pp. 134, 184–89, 256.

B1133 "Eine Kleine Nachtmusik," "Keine Lazarovitch: 1870–1959," "The Swimmer," and "Woman." In *The Other Language: English Poetry of Montreal.* Ed. Endre Farkas. Dorion, P.Q.: Muses / Compagni des Muses, 1989, pp. 18–21.

B1134 "Piety." In *Montreal Mon Amour: Short Stories from Montreal*. Ed. and introd. Michael Benazon. Toronto: Deneau, 1989, pp. 33–47.

B1135 "The Terrorist." In *Themes for All Times*. Ed. and preface Ron Clarke, Roy Bonisteel, Betty King, and Judy Gibson. St. John's: Jesperson, 1989, pp. 332–34.

B1136 "Birthday Poem for John Newlove," "I Take My Anna Everywhere," "Review of Bravo, Layton," and "Thoughts of Titling My Next Book Bravo, Layton." In *The Third Macmillan Anthology*. Ed. John Metcalf and Kent Thompson. Toronto: Macmillan, 1990, pp. 55–61.

Reviews

B1137 Rev. of *This England*, by James Edward Ward. *First Statement*, Aug. 1943, pp. 21–22. *TS:CS* ("Views of the World: Letters, Articles, Travels, 1960–1977. Rev. of *This England*, by James Edward Ward").
    Originally signed: I.P.L.

B1138 Rev. of *The Night Is Ended*, by J.S. Wallace. *First Statement*, Sept. 1943, p. 22.
    Originally signed: I.P.L.

B1139 Rev. of *Who Dare to Live*, by Frederick B. Watt. *First Statement*, Oct. 1943, p. 22.
    Originally signed: I.P.L.

B1140 Rev. of *At the Long Sault and Other New Poems*, by Archibald Lampman, ed. Duncan Campbell Scott and E.K. Brown. *First Statement*, March 1944, pp. 16–17. *E:PIL*.
    Originally signed: I.P.L.

B1141 Rev. of *The Hitleriad*, by A.M. Klein. *First Statement*, 2, No. 9 (Oct.–Nov. 1944), 17–20. *E:PIL*.

B1142 Rev. of *Poems*, by A.M. Klein. *First Statement*, 2, No. 12 (April–May 1945), 35–36. Rpt. in *A.M. Klein*. Critical Views on Canadian Writers, No. 4. Ed. and introd. Tom Marshall. Toronto: Ryerson, 1970, pp. 23–25. *E:PIL*.
    Originally signed: I.P.L.

B1143 Rev. of *A History of Western Philosophy*, by Bertrand Russell. *Northern Review*, 1, No. 2 (Feb.–March 1946), 43–46. *E:PIL*.

B1144 Rev. of *The Colour as Naked*, by Patrick Anderson. *CIV/n*, No. 5 (March 1954), p. 15. *E:PIL*.

B1145 "Crêpe Hanger's Carnival." Rev. of *A Dream That Is Dying, Shake Hands with the Hangman*, and *Walking Death*, by Raymond Souster. *CIV/n*, No. 7 (Winter 1955), pp. 26–27. *E:PIL* ("Crepe Hanger's Carnival").

B1146 Rev. of *The Picnic and Other Stories*, by Desmond Pacey. *The Fiddlehead*, No. 39 (Winter 1959), p. 41. *E:PIL*.

B1147 "Bare Essentials." Rev. of *New Poems*, by Henry Moscovitch. *Matrix*, No. 16 (Spring 1983), pp. 62–64.

B1148 "Christians, Jews Are Closer Than They Think, Rabbi Says." Rev. of *The Christian Problem: A Jewish View*, by Rabbi Stuart E. Rosenberg. *The Gazette* [Montreal], 28 Feb. 1987, Books, p. H9.

B1149 "Red Wounds." Rev. of *A Soviet Odyssey*, by Suzanne Rosenberg. *Saturday Night*, April 1988, pp. 59–61.

Translations

B1150 "Yiddish Poetry in Canada." *CIV/n*, No. 3 (July–Aug. 1953), pp. 14–17.
  Translated from the original Yiddish by Melech Ravitch.

B1151 "Trans Canada." *CIV/n*, No. 3 (July–Aug. 1953), pp. 17–18.
  Translated from the original Yiddish poem by Melech Ravitch.

Play

B1152 ———, and Leonard Cohen. *A Man Was Killed*. *Canadian Theatre Review* [York Univ.], No. 14 (Spring 1977), pp. 56–68.

Audio-Visual Material

B1153 On the 35th Anniversary of the Jewish Public Library. CFCF Radio [Montreal], 26 Nov. 1949. (15 min.)

B1154 "Death of Moishe Lazarovitch." Narr. Irving Layton. *Anthology*. Prod. Robert McCormack. CBC Radio, 28 Dec. 1954. (1 min.) Rebroadcast ("Portrait of a One-Armed Juggler: Death of Moishe Lazarovitch"). Narr. Irving Layton. *A Special Occasion*. Prod. Malka. CBC-FM Radio, 21 July 1977. (1 min., 3 sec.) Rebroadcast. CBC Radio, 24 July 1977. (1 min., 3 sec.) *ILH* ("Death of Moishe Lazarovitch"); *EIL69*; *RCS* (cas.).
  See *LCW* ("Death of Moishe Lazarovitch: For Anica Fellegi"), *IB* ("Death of Moishe Lazarovitch"), *IB2*, *RCS*, *CP*, *SP69*, *CPIL*, *DF*, *FE*, and B180. Layton also comments on his poems in the 1954 broadcast. The two 1977 broadcasts include a

critical discussion among fourteen contributors (C667).

B1155 "Letter to Raymond Souster." Narr. Irving Layton. *Anthology*. Prod. Robert McCormack. CBC Radio, 28 Dec. 1954. (2 min., 34 sec.)
  See *Cerb.* and *UPIL*. Layton also comments on his poems.

B1156 "Maxie." Narr. Irving Layton. *Anthology*. Prod. Robert McCormack. CBC Radio, 28 Dec. 1954. (1 min., 24 sec.) Recorded. Narr. Irving Layton. In *Six Montreal Poets*. Folkways, FL9805, 1957. (L.p.; 1 min., 29 sec.) Rebroadcast. Narr. Irving Layton. *In a Manner of Speaking*. Comp. Hugh Webster. CBC Radio, 2 Nov. 1961. (1 min., 26 sec.) *ILRH*; *RCS* (cas.).
  See *MMF*, *IB*, *IB2*, *RCS*, *CP*, *SP69*, *CPIL*, *DF*, *WPJ*, and *WPJ2*. Layton also comments on his poems in the *Anthology* broadcast.

B1157 "Metropolis." Narr. Irving Layton. *Anthology*. Prod. Robert McCormack. CBC Radio, 28 Dec. 1954. (50 sec.)
  See *LPS* and *UPIL*. Layton also comments on his poems.

B1158 "Silver Lining." Narr. Irving Layton. *Anthology*. Prod. Robert McCormack. CBC Radio, 28 Dec. 1954. (1 min., 11 sec.)
  See *LPS*, *CP*, and *CPIL*. Layton also comments on his poems.

B1159 "Street Funeral." Narr. Irving Layton. *Anthology*. Prod. Robert McCormack. CBC Radio, 28 Dec. 1954. (55 sec.) *RCS* (cas.).
  See *LCW*, *IB*, *IB2*, *RCS*, *CP*, *CPIL*, *DF*, *WPJ*, *WPJ2*, and B94. Layton also comments on his poems.

B1160 "Young Man in Earnest." Narr. Irving Layton. *Anthology*. Prod. Robert McCormack. CBC Radio, 28 Dec. 1954. (1 min., 36 sec.)

See *LPS* and *UPIL*. Layton also comments on his poems.

B1161 "The Cold Green Element." Narr. Irving Layton. *Anthology*. Prod. Robert McCormack. CBC Radio, 15 Nov. 1955. (1 min., 50 sec.) Recorded. Narr. Irving Layton. In *Six Montreal Poets*. Folkways, FL9805, 1957. (L.p.; 1 min., 50 sec.) Rebroadcast. *In a Manner of Speaking*. Comp. Hugh Webster. CBC Radio, 2 Nov. 1961. (1 min., 45 sec.) *ILH*; *IL* (Montreal); *ILRH*; *Layton*; *RCS* (cas.); *WPJ* (cas.).

See *CGE* ("The Cold Green Element: For Lorne Pierce"), *IB* ("The Cold Green Element"), *IB2*, *RCS*, *CP*, *SP69*, *CPIL*, *fve* ("The cold green element / Il freddo verde elemento"), *DF* ("The Cold Green Element"), *PIL*, *SPIL*, *WPJ*, *WPJ2*, and B111. Layton also comments on his poems in the *Anthology* broadcast.

B1162 "First Snow: Lake Achigan." Narr. Irving Layton. *Anthology*. Prod. Robert McCormack. CBC Radio, 15 Nov. 1955. (48 sec.) Recorded. Narr. Irving Layton. *Canadian Poets 1*. Toronto: CBC, 1966. (L.p.; 47 sec.) Rebroadcast. Narr. Irving Layton. *Ideas*. CBC Radio, 7 Nov. 1966. (45 sec.) *RCS* (cas.).

See *MMF*, *IB*, *IB2*, *RCS*, *CP*, *CPIL*, *DF*, and B131. Layton also comments on his poems in the *Anthology* broadcast.

B1163 "God, When You Speak." Narr. Irving Layton. *Anthology*. Prod. Robert McCormack. CBC Radio, 15 Nov. 1955. (1 min., 14 sec.) *ILH*; *RCS* (cas.).

See *CGE*, *IB*, *IB2*, *RCS*, *CP*, *CPIL*, and *DF*. Layton also comments on his poems.

B1164 "In the Midst of My Fever." Narr. Irving Layton. *Anthology*. Prod. Robert McCormack. CBC Radio, 15 Nov. 1955. (2 min., 30 sec.) *EIL69*; *RCS* (cas.).

See *MMF*, *IB*, *IB2*, *RCS*, *CP*, *SP69*, *CPIL*, *DF*, *PIL*, *SPIL*, *WPJ*, *WPJ2*, and B102. Layton also comments on his poems.

B1165 "Mrs. Fornheim, Refugee." Narr. Irving Layton. *Anthology*. Prod. Robert McCormack. CBC Radio, 15 Nov. 1955. (47 sec.) Recorded. Narr. Irving Layton. *Canadian Poets 1*. Toronto: CBC, 1966. (L.p.; 46 sec.) Rebroadcast. Narr. Irving Layton. *Saturday Evening*. Host Robin Skelton. CBC Radio, 2 April 1966. (41 sec.) Rebroadcast. Narr. Irving Layton. *Ideas*. CBC Radio, 7 Nov. 1966. (47 sec.) Rerecorded. Narr. Irving Layton. *Birney / Layton*. Toronto: Ontario Institute for Studies in Education, 1969. (Audiocassette; 46 sec.) Rebroadcast ("Portrait of a One-Armed Juggler: Mrs. Fornheim, Refugee"). Narr. Irving Layton. *A Special Occasion*. Prod. Malka. CBC-FM Radio, 21 July 1977. (45 sec.) Rebroadcast. CBC Radio, 24 July 1977. (45 sec.) *IL* (Montreal) ("Mrs. Fornheim, Refugee"); *IL* (Toronto); *RCS* (cas.); *EIL76*.

See *BH*, *BH2*, *IB*, *IB2*, *RCS*, *CP*, *SP69*, *CPIL*, *DF*, and *FE*. Layton comments on his poems in the *Anthology* broadcast. The *Saturday Evening* broadcast includes an interview by Robin Skelton (C566). The *A Special Occasion* broadcast includes a critical discussion among fourteen contributors (C667).

B1166 "University Buildings." Narr. Irving Layton. *Anthology*. Prod. Robert McCormack. CBC Radio, 15 Nov. 1955. (29 sec.)

See *LPS*, *CP*, *CPIL*. Layton also comments on his poems.

B1167 ———, Ted Allan, Douglas Grant, and Morley Callaghan. Panellists. *Fighting Words*. Moderator

Nathan Cohen. CBC TV, 9 Dec. 1956. (30 min.)

B1168 ———, Don Henshaw, and Ray Godfrey. Panellists. *Citizens' Forum*. Chair Pierre Berton. Summary Carlton Williams. CBC Radio, 20 Dec. 1956. (90 min.)

B1169 "The Birth of Tragedy." Narr. Irving Layton. In *Six Montreal Poets*. Folkways, FL9805, 1957. (L.p.; 1 min., 26 sec.) Broadcast. Narr. Irving Layton. *Anthology*. CBC Radio, 4 March 1960. (1 min., 30 sec.) Rebroadcast. Narr. Irving Layton. *In a Manner of Speaking*. Comp. Hugh Webster. CBC Radio, 2 Nov. 1961. (1 min., 29 sec.) Rerecorded. Narr. Irving Layton. *Canadian Poets* 1. Toronto: CBC, 1966. (L.p.; 1 min., 37 sec.) Rebroadcast. Narr. Irving Layton. *Saturday Evening*. Host Robin Skelton. CBC Radio, 2 April 1966. (1 min., 27 sec.) Rebroadcast ("An Hour with Irving Layton: The Birth of Tragedy"). Narr. Irving Layton. Host Sylvia Spring. *Venture*. CBC Radio, 3 July 1966. (1 min., 25 sec.) Rebroadcast ("The Birth of Tragedy"). Narr. Irving Layton. *Ideas*. CBC Radio, 1 Nov. 1966. (1 min., 32 sec.) Rebroadcast. Narr. Irving Layton. *Ideas*. CBC Radio, 7 Nov. 1966. (1 min., 32 sec.) Rerecorded. Narr. Irving Layton. *Birney / Layton*. Toronto: Ontario Institute for Studies in Education, 1969. (Audiocassette; 1 min., 28 sec.) Rebroadcast ("Power and Poetry: The Birth of Tragedy"). Narr. Len Berman. *Ideas*. CBC Radio, 22 Nov. 1971. CBC Learning Systems, No. 765. (1 min., 29 sec.) Rebroadcast ("Nietzsche and Poetry: The Birth of Tragedy"). Narr. Irving Layton. *Ideas*. CBC Radio, 1972. CBC Radio Learning Systems, No. 339, [c.1973]. (1 min., 30 sec.) *ILH* ("The Birth of Tragedy"); *PIL65*; *IL* (Montreal); *ILRH*; *EIL69*; *IL* (Toronto); *Layton*; *RCS* (cas.); *EIL76*; *PRIL*; *WPJ* (cas.).
    See *MMF, IB, IB2, RCS, CP, SP69, CPIL, fve*

("The birth of tragedy / La nascita della tragedia"), *DF* ("The Birth of Tragedy"), *PIL, SPIL, WPJ, WPJ2*, and B171. The *Saturday Evening* broadcast includes an interview by Robin Skelton (C566); the *Venture* broadcast includes an interview by Sylvia Spring (C567); the 1971 *Ideas* broadcast also includes an interview (C593); the "Nietzsche and Poetry" broadcast on *Ideas* also includes a discussion with Eli Mandel (B1257).

B1170 "The Bull Calf." Narr. Irving Layton. In *Six Montreal Poets*. Folkways, FL9805, 1957. (L.p.; 1 min., 56 sec.) Broadcast. Narr. Irving Layton. *In a Manner of Speaking*. Comp. Hugh Webster. CBC Radio, 2 Nov. 1961. (1 min., 54 sec.) Rerecorded. *Canadian Poets* 1. Toronto: CBC, 1966. (L.p.; 1 min., 52 sec.) Rebroadcast. Narr. Irving Layton. *Saturday Evening*. Host Robin Skelton. CBC Radio, 2 April 1966. (1 min., 54 sec.) Rebroadcast. Narr. Irving Layton. *Ideas*. CBC Radio, 1 Nov. 1966. (1 min., 40 sec.) Rebroadcast. Narr. Irving Layton. *Ideas*. CBC Radio, 7 Nov. 1966. (1 min., 40 sec.) Rerecorded. Narr. Irving Layton. *Birney / Layton*. Toronto: Ontario Institute for Studies in Education, 1969. (Audiocassette; 1 min., 54 sec.) *PIL65*; *IL* (Montreal); *ILRH*; *EIL69*; *IL* (Toronto); *Layton*; *RCS* (cas.); *EIL76*; *PRIL*; *WPJ* (cas.).
    See *BCOP, IB, IB2, RCS, CP, SP69, CPIL, DF, WPJ, WPJ2, SDCJ*, and B149. The *Saturday Evening* broadcast includes an interview by Robin Skelton (C566).

B1171 "The Fertile Muck." Narr. Irving Layton. In *Six Montreal Poets*. Folkways, FL9805, 1957. (L.p.; 1 min., 41 sec.) Broadcast. Narr. Irving Layton. *In a Manner of Speaking*. Comp. Hugh Webster. CBC Radio, 2 Nov. 1961. (1 min., 38 sec.) *ILH*; *EIL69*; *Layton*; *RCS* (cas.); *EIL76*; *WPJ* (cas.).

See *BCOP, IB, IB2, RCS, CP, SP69, CPIL, DF, WPJ, WPJ2, SPIL*(K), and B173.

B1172 "The Improved Binoculars." Narr. Irving Layton. In *Six Montreal Poets*. Folkways, FL9805, 1957. (L.p.; 1 min., 4 sec.) Broadcast. Narr. Irving Layton. *Anthology*. CBC Radio, 19 Feb. 1957. (51 sec.) Rebroadcast. Narr. Irving Layton. *In a Manner of Speaking*. Comp. Hugh Webster. CBC Radio, 2 Nov. 1961. (1 min., 1 sec.) Rebroadcast. Narr. Irving Layton. *Saturday Evening*. Host Robin Skelton. CBC Radio, 2 April 1966. (1 min., 1 sec.) Rerecorded. Narr. Irving Layton. *Birney / Layton*. Toronto: Ontario Institute for Studies in Education, 1969. (Audiocassette; 1 min., 1 sec.) Rebroadcast ("City Soundscapes: The Improved Binoculars"). Narr. Irving Layton. *Ideas*. Prod. Mary Ann Hammond. CBC Radio, 7 Nov. 1972. (50 sec.) Rebroadcast ("The Improved Binoculars"). Narr. Irving Layton. *Quebec Now*. CBC Radio, 16 Sept. 1973. (50 sec.) *ILH; PIL65; IL* (Montreal); *ILRH; EIL69; IL* (Toronto); *Layton; RCS* (cas.); *EIL76; PRIL*.

See *CGE, IB, IB2, RCS, CP, SP69, CPIL, fve* ("The improved binoculars / Il binocolo perfezionato"), *DF* ("The Improved Binoculars"), *PIL, SPIL, eg* ("The Improved Binoculars / Il binocolo potenziato"), *WPJ* ("The Improved Binoculars"), *WPJ2, SPIL*(K), *FE, Ts:p* ("The Improved Binoculars / Il binocolo potenziato"), *LP*, and B500 ("The Improved Binoculars"). Layton comments on his poems in the *Anthology* broadcast. The *Saturday Evening* broadcast includes an interview by Robin Skelton (C566). The *Quebec Now* broadcast includes an interview by David McPherson (C599).

B1173 "Bacchanal." Narr. Irving Layton. *Anthology*. CBC Radio, 19 Feb. 1957. (51 sec.) *IL* (Montreal); *ILRH; RCS* (cas.).

See *MMF, IB, IB2, RCS, CP, CPIL*, and B105. Layton also comments on his poems.

B1174 "Cat Dying in Autumn." Narr. Irving Layton. *Anthology*. CBC Radio, 19 Feb. 1957. (1 min., 7 sec.) Recorded. Narr. Irving Layton. *Birney / Layton*. Toronto: Ontario Institute for Studies in Education, 1969. (Audiocassette; 51 sec.) *PIL65; IL* (Toronto); *RCS* (cas.); *WPJ* (cas.).

See *LM, LM2, RCS, CP, SP69, CPIL, DF, WPJ, WPJ2, SPIL*(K), and B179. Layton comments on his poems in the *Anthology* broadcast.

B1175 "For Louise, Age 17." Narr. Irving Layton. *Anthology*. CBC Radio, 19 Feb. 1957. (1 min., 12 sec.) *IL* (Montreal); *IL* (Toronto); *Layton; RCS* (cas.); *WPJ* (cas.).

See *CGE, IB, IB2, RCS, CP, CPIL, DF, Pa* ("A Luisa, de 17 años"), *LPIL* ("For Louise, Age 17"), *WPJ, WPJ2, LPIL:RD, DD*, and B116. Layton also comments on his poems.

B1176 "Sacrament by the Water." Narr. Irving Layton. *Anthology*. CBC Radio, 19 Feb. 1957. (42 sec.) *EIL69; RCS* (cas.); *PRIL*.

See *BCOP, IB, IB2, RCS, CP, SP69, CPIL, DF, LPIL* (l.ed), *Pa* ("Sacramento en la ribera"), *LPIL* ("Sacrament by the Water"), *paIL* ("Sacrament by the Water / Sacramento presso l'acqua"), *LPIL:RD* ("Sacrament by the Water"), *DD*, and B160. Layton also comments on his poems.

B1177 "Summer Idyll." Narr. Irving Layton. *Anthology*. CBC Radio, 19 Feb. 1957. (1 min., 22 sec.) *IL* (Montreal); *RCS* (cas.).

See *CGE* ("Summer Idyll: For William Goodwin"), *IB* ("Summer Idyll"), *IB2, RCS, CP, CPIL*, and B126. Layton also comments on his poems.

B1178 "The Widows." Narr. Irving Layton. *Anthology*. CBC Radio, 19 Feb. 1957. (1 min., 41 sec.) *RCS* (cas.).
See *IB2*, *LM*, *LM2*, *RCS*, *CP*, *CPIL*. Layton also comments on his poems.

B1179 ———, Karl Stern, Arthur Mizener, and Douglas Grant. Panellists. *Fighting Words*. Moderator Nathan Cohen. CBC Radio, 3 Dec. 1957. (28 min., 45 sec.)

B1180 ———, Carl Polanyi, John Irving, and Morley Callaghan. Panellists. *Fighting Words*. Moderator Nathan Cohen. CBC Radio, 28 Jan. 1958. (28 min., 15 sec.)

B1181 ———, William Blatz, J.K. Galbraith, and John Saywell. Panellists. *Fighting Words*. Moderator Nathan Cohen. CBC Radio, 5 March 1958. (23 min., 45 sec.)

B1182 ———, and Jonathan Williams. Discussion. *Assignment*. CBC Radio, 15 April 1958. (5 min.)

B1183 ———, William Bothwell, Anthony Prisch, and Jean Tweed. Panellists. *Fighting Words*. Moderator Nathan Cohen. CBC Radio, 22 April 1958. (28 min., 20 sec.)

B1184 "Anglo-Canadian." Narr. Bill McNeil. *Assignment*. Co-hosts Maria Barrett and Bill McNeil. CBC Radio, 11 June 1958. (18 sec.) Rebroadcast. Narr. Irving Layton. *Judy*. Host Judy LaMarsh. CBC Radio, 13 Nov. 1975. (18 sec.) *RCS* (cas.).
See *MK*, *RCS*, *CP*, and *CPIL*.

B1185 "Berry Picking." Narr. Irving Layton. *Anthology*. CBC Radio, 11 Nov. 1958. (1 min., 33 sec.) Rebroadcast. Narr. Irving Layton. *Saturday Evening*. Host

Robin Skelton. CBC Radio, 2 April 1966. (1 min., 35 sec.) *Layton*; *RCS* (cas.); *PRIL*; *WPJ* (cas.).
See *LM*, *LM2*, *RCS*, *CP*, *SP69*, *CPIL*, *DF*, *PIL*, *SPIL*, *LPIL* (l.ed) *Pa* ("Arándanos y frambuesas"), *LPIL* ("Berry Picking"), *WPJ*, *WPJ2*, *LPIL:RD*, *DD*, and B195. The *Saturday Evening* broadcast includes an interview by Robin Skelton (C566).

B1186 "Cain." Narr. Irving Layton. *Anthology*. CBC Radio, 11 Nov. 1958. (1 min., 30 sec.) *Layton*; *RCS* (cas.); *PRIL*.
See *LM*, *LM2*, *RCS*, *CP*, *SP69*, *CPIL*, *fve* ("Cain / Caino"), *DF* ("Cain"), *PIL*, *SPIL*, *WPJ*, *WPJ2*, *FE*, and B193.

B1187 "Captives." Narr. Irving Layton. *Anthology*. CBC Radio, 11 Nov. 1958. (1 min., 5 sec.) *RCS* (cas.) ("Dance, My Little One").
See *LM* ("Captives"), *LM2* ("Dance, My Little One"), *RCS*, *CP*, *CPIL*, and B192 ("Captives").

B1188 ———, Marya Mannes, George McCowan, and Ayn Rand. Panellists. *Fighting Words*. Moderator Nathan Cohen. CBC Radio, 11 Nov. 1958. (30 min.)

B1189 "Sheep." Narr. Irving Layton. *Anthology*. CBC Radio, 11 Nov. 1958. (1 min., 35 sec.) *RCS* (cas.).
See *LM*, *LM2*, *RCS*, *CP*, *CPIL*, *DF*, *WPJ*, *WPJ2*, and B190.

B1190 "Whatever Else Poetry Is Freedom." Narr. Irving Layton. *Anthology*. CBC Radio, 11 Nov. 1958. (1 min., 32 sec.) *PIL65*; *EIL69*; *IL* (Toronto); *RCS* (cas.); *WPJ* (cas.).
See *LM*, *LM2*, *RCS*, *CP*, *SP69*, *CPIL*, *DF*, *PIL*, *SPIL*, *eg* ("Whatever Else Poetry Is Freedom / Quant'altro la poesia è liberta"), *WPJ* ("Whatever Else Poetry Is Freedom"), *WPJ2*, *Ts:p* ("Whatever Else

Poetry Is Freedom / Ma Soprattutto la poesia è libertá"), and B191 ("Whatever Else Poetry Is Freedom").

B1191 "Song for Naomi." Narr. Irving Layton. *Anthology.* CBC Radio, 1 May 1959. (1 min., 10 sec.) Rebroadcast. CBC *Sunday Night: A Program of Contemporary Canadian Poetry.* Music Tibor Polgar with Jan Rubes. CBC Radio, 19 Sept. 1965. (3 min., 20 sec.) Recorded. Narr. Irving Layton. *Canadian Poets* 1. Toronto: CBC, 1966. (L.p.; 1 min., 15 sec.) Rebroadcast. Narr. Irving Layton. *Saturday Evening.* Host Robin Skelton. CBC Radio, 2 April 1966. (1 min., 8 sec.) Rebroadcast. Narr. Irving Layton. *Ideas.* CBC Radio, 1 Nov. 1966. (1 min., 12 sec.) Rebroadcast. Narr. Irving Layton. *Ideas.* CBC Radio, 7 Nov. 1966. (1 min., 12 sec.) Rerecorded. Narr. Irving Layton. *Birney / Layton.* Toronto: Ontario Institute for Studies in Education, 1969. (Audiocassette; 1 min., 13 sec.) *ILH; PIL65; IL* (Montreal); *EIL69; IL* (Toronto); *Layton; RCS* (cas.); *EIL76; EIL81; PRIL; WPJ* (cas.).
    See *CGE, IB, IB2, RCS, CP, SP69, CPIL, DF, PIL, SPIL, WPJ, WPJ2, SPIL*(K), and B792 ("Canción para Naomi"). The *Saturday Evening* broadcast includes an interview by Robin Skelton (C566).

B1192 ——, Hugh Garner, Earle Birney, and Frank Tumpane. Panellists. *Fighting Words.* Moderator Nathan Cohen. CBC TV, 19 June 1960. (30 min.)

B1193 "From Colony to Nation." Narr. Irving Layton. FM *News.* CBC-FM Radio, 27 Feb. 1961. (1 min., 2 sec.) Recorded. Narr. Irving Layton. *Birney / Layton.* Toronto: Ontario Institute for Studies in Education, 1969. (Audiocassette; 1 min.) *ILH; RCS* (cas.); *PRIL.*
    See *IB, IB2, MK, RCS, CP, SP69, CPIL, DF, WPJ, WPJ2,* and B747 ("Gyarmatból nemzetté").

B1194 ——, Ron Hambleton, Kenneth Rexroth, and Morley Callaghan. Panellists. *Fighting Words.* Moderator Nathan Cohen. CBC TV, 4 June 1961. (30 min.) Rebroadcast. *Fighting Words.* CBC TV, 6 June 1961. (30 min.)

B1195 Panellist. *I.Q.* CBC Radio, 24 March 1963. (7 min.) On censorship.

B1196 "Aftermath." Narr. Irving Layton. *Sunday Night Anthology.* Host Robert Fulford. CBC Radio, 15 Dec. 1963. (30 sec.)
    See *LR, CP,* and *CPIL.*

B1197 "Ballad of the Old Spaniard." Narr. Irving Layton. *Sunday Night Anthology.* Host Robert Fulford. CBC Radio, 15 Dec. 1963. (2 min., 3 sec.) *Layton.*
    See *LR, CP, SP69, CPIL, DF, WPJ, WPJ2,* and B289.

B1198 "The Cactus." Narr. Irving Layton. *Sunday Night Anthology.* Host Robert Fulford. CBC Radio, 15 Dec. 1963. (1 min., 23 sec.)
    See *LR, CP,* and *CPIL.*

B1199 "El Caudillo." Narr. Irving Layton. *Sunday Night Anthology.* Host Robert Fulford. CBC Radio, 15 Dec. 1963. (1 min., 12 sec.) Recorded. *Canadian Poets* 1. Toronto: CBC, 1966. (L.p.; 1 min., 17 sec.) Rebroadcast. Narr. Irving Layton. *Ideas.* CBC Radio, 1 Nov. 1966. (1 min., 15 sec.) Rebroadcast. Narr. Irving Layton. *Ideas.* CBC Radio, 7 Nov. 1966. (1 min., 15 sec.)
    See *LR, CP, SP69, CPIL, DF,* and B293.

B1200 "Creation [I fashioned you]." Narr. Irving Layton. *Sunday Night Anthology.* Host Robert Fulford. CBC Radio, 15 Dec. 1963. (34 sec.) Rebroadcast ("An

Hour with Irving Layton: Creation [I fashioned you]"). Narr. Irving Layton. *Venture*. Host Sylvia Spring. CBC Radio, 3 July 1966. (35 sec.)

See *LR* ("Creation [I fashioned you]"), *CP*, *CPIL*, *LPIL* (l.ed), *Pa* ("Creación"), *LPIL* ("Creation [I fashioned you]"), *paIL* ("Creation [I fashioned you] / Creazione"), *LPIL:RD* ("Creation [I fashioned you]"), *DD*, and B306. The *Venture* broadcast includes an interview by Sylvia Spring (C567).

B1201 "For My Former Students." Narr. Irving Layton. *Sunday Night Anthology*. Host Robert Fulford. CBC Radio, 15 Dec. 1963. (42 sec.) Rebroadcast ("An Hour with Irving Layton: For My Former Students"). Narr. Irving Layton. *Venture*. Host Sylvia Spring. CBC Radio, 3 July 1966. (42 sec.)

See *LR* ("For My Former Students"), *CP*, *CPIL*, and B290. The *Venture* broadcast includes an interview by Sylvia Spring (C567).

B1202 "El Gusano [From the place where I was sitting]." Narr. Irving Layton. *Sunday Night Anthology*. Host Robert Fulford. CBC Radio, 15 Dec. 1963. (1 min., 11 sec.)

See *LR*, *CP*, *SP69*, *CPIL*, *DF*, *PIL*, *SPIL*, *WPJ*, *WPJ2*, and B294.

B1203 "The Lizard." Narr. Irving Layton. *Sunday Night Anthology*. Host Robert Fulford. CBC Radio, 15 Dec. 1963. (1 min., 3 sec.)

See *LR*, *CP*, *CPIL*, and B291.

B1204 "On Spanish Soil." Narr. Irving Layton. *Sunday Night Anthology*. Host Robert Fulford. CBC Radio, 15 Dec. 1963. (1 min., 2 sec.) *ILRH*.

See *LR*, *CP*, *CPIL*, and B295.

B1205 "Plaza de Toros." Narr. Irving Layton. *Sunday Night Anthology*. Host Robert Fulford. CBC Radio, 15 Dec.

1963. (31 sec.) *IL* (Montreal); *ILRH*; *Layton*.

See *LR*, *CP*, *SP69*, *CPIL*, *DF*, *TWNS*, *WPJ*, *WPJ2*, *SPIL*(K), and B296.

B1206 "Silly Rhymes for Aviva." Narr. Irving Layton. *Sunday Night Anthology*. Host Robert Fulford. CBC Radio, 15 Dec. 1963. (1 min., 44 sec.)

See *LR*, *CP*, and *CPIL*.

B1207 "Golfers." Narr. Irving Layton. *Canadian Poets 1*. Toronto: CBC, 1966. (L.p.; 35 sec.) Broadcast. Narr. Irving Layton. *Ideas*. CBC Radio, 1 Nov. 1966. (35 sec.) Rebroadcast. Narr. Irving Layton. *Ideas*. CBC Radio, 7 Nov. 1966. (35 sec.) *RCS* (cas.); *WPJ* (cas.).

See *BP*, *BP2*, *IB*, *IB2*, *RCS*, *CP*, *CPIL*, *DF*, *PIL*, *SPIL*, *WPJ*, *WPJ2*, and B117.

B1208 "Keine Lazarovitch 1870–1959." Narr. Irving Layton. *Canadian Poets 1*. Toronto: CBC, 1966. (L.p.; 1 min., 42 sec.) Broadcast. Narr. Irving Layton. *Saturday Evening*. Host Robin Skelton. CBC Radio, 2 April 1966. (1 min., 35 sec.) Rebroadcast. Narr. Irving Layton. *Ideas*. CBC Radio, 7 Nov. 1966. (1 min., 40 sec.) Rerecorded. Narr. Irving Layton. *Birney / Layton*. Toronto: Ontario Institute for Studies in Education, 1969. (Audiocassette; 1 min., 32 sec.) Rebroadcast ("Portrait of a One-Armed Juggler: Keine Lazarovitch 1870–1959"). Narr. Irving Layton. *A Special Occasion*. Prod. Malka. CBC-FM Radio, 21 July 1977. (1 min., 36 sec.) Rebroadcast. CBC Radio, 24 July 1977. (1 min., 36 sec.) *PIL65* ("Keine Lazarovitch 1870–1959"); *IL* (Montreal); *ILRH*; *IL* (Toronto); *Layton*; *EIL76*; *EIL81*; *PRIL*; *WPJ* (cas.) ("Keine Lazarovitch: 1870–1959").

See *CP* ("Keine Lazarovitch 1870–1959"), *SP69* ("Keine Lazarovitch: 1870–1959"), *CPIL* ("Keine Lazarovitch 1870–1959"), *fve*, *DF*, *PIL*, *SPIL*, *eg*, *WPJ* ("Keine Lazarovitch: 1870–1959"), *WPJ2*, *FE*,

Ts:p ("Keine Lazarovitch"), *SF* ("Keine Lazarovitch 1870–1959"), and B220. The *Saturday Evening* broadcast includes an interview by Robin Skelton (C566). The *A Special Occasion* broadcast includes a critical discussion among fourteen contributors (C667).

B1209 "On Seeing the Statuettes of Ezekiel and Jeremiah in the Church of Notre Dame." Narr. Irving Layton. *Canadian Poets* 1. Toronto: CBC, 1966. (L.p.; 1 min., 30 sec.) Broadcast. Narr. Irving Layton. *Ideas*. CBC Radio, 7 Nov. 1966. Rebroadcast ("City Soundscapes: On Seeing the Statuettes of Ezekiel and Jeremiah in the Church of Notre Dame"). Narr. Irving Layton. *Ideas*. Prod. Mary Ann Hammond. CBC Radio, 7 Nov. 1972. (1 min., 15 sec.) Rebroadcast ("On Seeing the Statuettes of Ezekiel and Jeremiah in the Church of Notre Dame"). Narr. Irving Layton. *Quebec Now*. CBC Radio, 16 Sept. 1973. (1 min., 15 sec.) Rebroadcast ("Portrait of a One-Armed Juggler: On Seeing the Statuettes of Ezekiel and Jeremiah in the Church of Notre Dame"). Narr. Irving Layton. *A Special Occasion*. Prod. Malka. CBC-FM Radio, 21 July 1977. (1 min., 20 sec.) Rebroadcast. CBC Radio, 21 July 1977. (1 min., 20 sec.) *ILH* ("On Seeing the Statuettes of Ezekiel and Jeremiah in the Church of Notre Dame"); *Layton*; *RCS* (cas.); *EIL76*; *EIL81*; *PRIL*; *WPJ* (cas.).
   See *BCOP, IB, IB2, RCS, CP, SP69, CPIL, DF, PIL, SPIL, WPJ, WPJ2, FE*, and B151 ("On Seeing the Statuettes of Ezekiel and Jeremiah in the Church of Notre Dame, Montreal"). The *Quebec Now* broadcast includes an interview by David McPherson (C599). The *A Special Occasion* broadcast includes a critical discussion among fourteen contributors (C667).

B1210 "Silence [The word betrays the act]." Narr. Irving Layton. *Canadian Poets* 1. Toronto: CBC, 1966. (L.p.; 56 sec.) Broadcast. Narr. Irving Layton. *Ideas*. CBC Radio, 7 Nov. 1966. (58 sec.)
   See *BOAJ* ("Silence: For Ernest Hemingway [The word betrays the act]"), *CP, CPIL* ("Silence [The word betrays the act]"), and B258 ("Silence: For Ernest Hemingway [The word betrays the act]").

B1211 "Admonition and Reply." Narr. Irving Layton. *Saturday Evening*. Host Robin Skelton. CBC Radio, 2 April 1966. (38 sec.) *ILH; RCS* (cas.); *EIL76*.
   See *BP, BP2, IB2, RCS, CP*, and *CPIL*. This broadcast includes an interview by Robin Skelton (C566).

B1212 "Free Djilas." Narr. Irving Layton. *Saturday Evening*. Host Robin Skelton. CBC Radio, 2 April 1966. (31 sec.) Rebroadcast. Narr. Irving Layton. *Judy*. Host Judy LaMarsh. CBC Radio, 13 Nov. 1975. (31 sec.) *PIL65; IL* (Montreal); *ILRH; IL* (Toronto).
   See *BOAJ, CP*, and *CPIL*. The *Saturday Evening* broadcast includes an interview by Robin Skelton (C566).

B1213 "I Would for Your Sake Be Gentle." Narr. Irving Layton. *Saturday Evening*. Host Robin Skelton. CBC Radio, 2 April 1966. (1 min., 13 sec.) *EIL69; Layton; RCS* (cas.).
   See *CGE* ("Poem [I would for your sake be gentle]"), *IB, IB2, RCS* ("I Would for Your Sake Be Gentle"), *CP, SP69, CPIL, DF, LPIL* (l.ed), *Pa* ("Por ti quisiera ser un hombre afable"), *LPIL* ("I Would for Your Sake Be Gentle"), *LPIL:RD, SPIL*(K), *DD*, and B138 ("Poem [I would for your sake be gentle]"). This broadcast includes an interview by Robin Skelton (C566).

B1214 "Jewish Main Street." Narr. Irving Layton. *Saturday Evening*. Host Robin Skelton. CBC Radio, 2 April

1966. (1 min., 1 sec.) Rebroadcast. Narr. Irving Layton. *Quebec Now*. CBC Radio, 16 Sept. 1973. (1 min.) *RCS* (cas.).

See *HN*, *BH2*, *RCS*, *CP*, *CPIL*, *FE*, *NIP*, and B59. The *Saturday Evening* broadcast includes an interview by Robin Skelton (C566). The *Quebec Now* broadcast includes an interview by David McPherson (C599).

B1215 "Misunderstanding." Narr. Irving Layton. *Saturday Evening*. Host Robin Skelton. CBC Radio, 2 April 1966. (12 sec.) Rebroadcast ("An Evening with Irving Layton: Misunderstanding"). Narr. Irving Layton. *Venture*. Host Sylvia Spring. CBC Radio, 3 July 1966. (14 sec.) Rebroadcast. Narr. Irving Layton with Italian voice-over translation [Amleto Lorenzini]. *Identities*. CBC Radio, 10 Feb. 1975. (11 sec.) Rebroadcast ("Misunderstanding"). Narr. Irving Layton. Host Judy LaMarsh. CBC Radio, 13 Nov. 1975. (10 sec.) Rebroadcast ("Portrait of a One-Armed Juggler: Misunderstanding"). Narr. Irving Layton. *A Special Occasion*. Prod. Malka. CBC-FM Radio, 21 July 1977. (12 sec.) Rebroadcast. CBC Radio, 24 July 1977. (12 sec.) *ILH* ("Misunderstanding"); *PIL65*; *IL* (Montreal); *ILRH*; *IL* (Toronto); *RCS* (cas.); *WPJ* (cas.).

See *LPS*, *RCS*, *CP*, *SP69*, *CPIL*, *fve* ("Misunderstanding / Malinteso"), *DF* ("Misunderstanding"), *PIL*, *SPIL*, *LPIL* (l.ed), *Pa* ("Malentendido"), *LPIL* ("Misunderstanding"), *paIL* ("Misunderstanding / Incomprensione"), WPJ ("Misunderstanding"), *WPJ2*, *LPIL:RD*, *DD*, and B335. In the *Identities* broadcast, Layton also comments on Amleto Lorenzini's literary qualifications as a translator. The *Saturday Evening* broadcast includes an interview by Robin Skelton (C566); the *Venture* broadcast includes an interview by Sylvia Spring (C567). The *A Special Occasion* broadcast includes a critical discussion among fourteen contributors (C667).

B1216 "No Wild Dog." Narr. Irving Layton. *Saturday Evening*. Host Robin Skelton. CBC Radio, 2 April 1966. (35 sec.)

See *BOAJ*, *CP*, *SP69*, *CPIL*, and *FE*. This broadcast includes an interview by Robin Skelton (C566).

B1217 "On Being Bitten by a Dog." Narr. Irving Layton. *Saturday Evening*. Host Robin Skelton. CBC Radio, 2 April 1966. (27 sec.) Recorded. Narr. Irving Layton. Musical setting Amanta. In *A Continental Hug: Canadian Poetry Set to Chilean Music*. [Dunvegan, Ont.] Cormorant, 1989. *ILH*; *RCS* (cas.); *EIL76*.

See *MK*, *RCS*, *CP*, *SP69*, *CPIL*, *DF*, *WPJ*, and *WPJ2*. The *Saturday Evening* broadcast includes an interview by Robin Skelton (C566).

B1218 "On My Way to School." Narr. Irving Layton. *Saturday Evening*. Host Robin Skelton. CBC Radio, 2 April 1966. (19 sec.) Rebroadcast. Narr. Irving Layton. *Judy*. Host Judy LaMarsh. CBC Radio, 13 Nov. 1975. (17 sec.) *ILH*; *PIL65*; *IL* (Montreal); *ILRH*; *IL* (Toronto); *RCS* (cas.).

See *RCS*, *CP*, and *CPIL*. The *Saturday Evening* broadcast includes an interview by Robin Skelton (C566).

B1219 "Red Chokecherries." Narr. Irving Layton. *Saturday Evening*. Host Robin Skelton. CBC Radio, 2 April 1966. (37 sec.) *EIL69*; *RCS* (cas.); *PRIL*.

See *BCOP*, *RCS*, *CP*, *SP69*, *CPIL*, *DF*, *SPIL*(K), and B165. This broadcast includes an interview by Robin Skelton (C566).

B1220 "A Spider Danced a Cosy Jig." Narr. Irving Layton. *Saturday Evening*. Host Robin Skelton. CBC Radio, 2 April 1966. (34 sec.) Rebroadcast. Narr. Irving Layton. *National School Broadcasts*. Canadian Writers and Their Themes. CBC Radio, 14 April

1967. (33 sec.) *PIL65*; *IL* (Toronto); *RCS* (cas.).

See *BH* (expanded — "Aerolites"), *BH2*, *RCS* ("A Spider Danced a Cosy Jig"), *CP*, *CPIL*, *SDCJ*, and B30 ("My Love, a Miracle"). The *Saturday Evening* broadcast includes an interview by Robin Skelton (C566).

B1221 "The Swimmer." Narr. Irving Layton. *Saturday Evening*. Host Robin Skelton. CBC Radio, 2 April 1966. (1 min., 6 sec.) Recorded. Narr. Irving Layton. *Birney / Layton*. Toronto: Ontario Institute for Studies in Education, 1969. (Audiocassette; 1 min., 10 sec.) Rebroadcast ("Portrait of a One-Armed Juggler: The Swimmer"). Narr. Irving Layton. *A Special Occasion*. Prod. Malka. CBC-FM Radio, 21 July 1977. (1 min., 8 sec.) Rebroadcast. CBC Radio, 24 July 1977. (1 min., 8 sec.) *ILH* ("The Swimmer"); *ILRH*; *EIL69*; *RCS* (cas.); *PRIL*; *WPJ* (cas.).

See *HN*, *BH*, *BH2*, *IB*, *IB2*, *RCS*, *CP*, *SP69*, *CPIL*, *DF*, *PIL*, *SPIL*, *WPJ*, *WPJ2*, *NIP*, and B60. The *Saturday Evening* broadcast includes an interview by Robin Skelton (C566). The *A Special Occasion* broadcast includes a critical discussion among fourteen contributors (C667).

B1222 "Therapy." Narr. Irving Layton. *Saturday Evening*. Host Robin Skelton. CBC Radio, 2 April 1966. (48 sec.) *Layton*.

See *BOAJ*, *CP*, *CPIL*, and B439 ("Terapie"). This broadcast includes an interview by Robin Skelton (C566).

B1223 "This Machine Age." Narr. Irving Layton. *Saturday Evening*. Host Robin Skelton. CBC Radio, 2 April 1966. (45 sec.) Rebroadcast. Narr. Irving Layton. *Judy*. Host Judy LaMarsh. CBC Radio, 13 Nov. 1975. (44 sec.) *PIL65*; *IL* (Montreal); *ILRH*; *IL* (Toronto); *Layton*.

See *BOAJ*, *CP*, *SP69*, *CPIL*, *FE*, and B170. The *Saturday Evening* broadcast includes an interview by Robin Skelton (C566).

B1224 "To the Girls of My Graduating Class." Narr. Irving Layton. *Saturday Evening*. Host Robin Skelton. CBC Radio, 2 April 1966. (1 min.) Rebroadcast ("An Hour with Irving Layton: To the Girls of My Graduating Class"). *Venture*. Host Sylvia Spring. CBC Radio, 3 July 1966. (59 sec.) Recorded ("To the Girls of My Graduating Class"). Narr. Irving Layton. *Birney / Layton*. Toronto: Ontario Institute for Studies in Education, 1969. (Audiocassette; 1 min., 10 sec.) *ILH*; *PIL65*; *IL* (Montreal); *ILRH*; *IL* (Toronto); *Layton*; *RCS* (cas.).

See *LCW* ("To the Girls of My Graduation Class"), *IB* ("To the Girls of My Graduating Class"), *IB2*, *RCS*, *CP*, *SP69*, *CPIL*, *DF*, *WPJ*, *WPJ2*, *DD*, and B93. The *Saturday Evening* broadcast includes an interview by Robin Skelton (C566); the *Venture* broadcast includes an interview by Sylvia Spring (C567).

B1225 "The Well-Wrought Urn." Narr. Irving Layton. *Saturday Evening*. Host Robin Skelton. CBC Radio, 2 April 1966. (20 sec.) *ILRH*.

See *BOAJ*, *CP*, *CPIL*, *fve* ("The well-wrought urn / L'urna ben lavorata"), *DF* ("The Well-Wrought Urn"), *PIL*, *SPIL*, *DD*, *WWU*, and B263. This broadcast includes an interview by Robin Skelton (C566).

B1226 "An Hour with Irving Layton: For My Green Old Age." Narr. Irving Layton. *Venture*. Host Sylvia Spring. CBC Radio, 3 July 1966. (58 sec.) *IL* (Montreal) ("For My Green Old Age"); *ILRH*.

See *LR*, *CP*, *CPIL*, *LPIL* (l.ed), *Pa* ("A mi verde ancianidad"), *LPIL* ("For My Green Old Age"),

LPIL:RD, DD, and B301. This broadcast includes an interview by Sylvia Spring (C567).

B1227 "An Hour with Irving Layton: Success." Narr. Irving Layton. *Venture.* Host Sylvia Spring. CBC Radio, 3 July 1966. (7 sec.)
See *LR* ("Success"), *CP,* and *CPIL.* This broadcast includes an interview by Sylvia Spring (C567).

B1228 "An Hour with Irving Layton: There Were No Signs." Narr. Irving Layton. *Venture.* Host Sylvia Spring. CBC Radio, 3 July 1966. (36 sec.) Recorded ("There Were No Signs"). Narr. Irving Layton. *Birney / Layton.* Toronto: Ontario Institute for Studies in Education, 1969. (43 sec.) *PIL65; IL* (Montreal); *ILRH; EIL69; IL* (Toronto); *Layton; EIL76; EIL81; PRIL; WPJ* (cas.).
See *BOAJ, CP, SP69, CPIL, DF, TWNS, WPJ, WPJ2, SPIL*(K), and B250. The *Venture* broadcast includes an interview by Sylvia Spring (C567).

B1229 "An Hour with Irving Layton: Two Poets Entering Toronto." Narr. Irving Layton. *Venture.* Host Sylvia Spring. CBC Radio, 3 July 1966. (42 sec.) *RCS* (cas.) ("Two Poets in Toronto").
See *LPS, RCS, CP* and *CPIL.* This broadcast includes an interview by Sylvia Spring (C567).

B1230 Contributor. TBA. CBC TV, 12 Dec. 1966. (3 min.)
Irving Layton and German-Canadian Peter Lust talk to Peter Desbarats about the possibility of Nazi resurgence in Germany.

B1231 "Revolution Plus Fifty." Host Patrick Watson. *Take 30.* Prod. Moses Znaimer. CBC TV, 22 Jan. 1967. [Audiotape in CBC Radio Archives.] (4 min., 50 sec.)
Layton comments on Russia fifty years after the revolution. He also reads poetry by Vladimir May-

akovsky, Isaac Babel, Osip Mandelshtam, and Anna Akhmatova.

B1232 "Canadian Writers and Their Themes." *National School Broadcasts.* Script Len Peterson. Music William McCauley. Prod. Eithne Black. CBC Radio, 14 April 1967. (5 min., 40 sec.)

B1233 "De Bullion Street." Narr. Irving Layton. *Modern Canadian Poetry.* Host Phyllis Webb. Prod. John Kennedy. CBC Television Extension, 30 April 1967. [Audiotape in CBC Radio Archives.] (1 min., 3 sec.) Recorded ("A Conversation with Irving Layton: De Bullion Street"). Narr. Irving Layton. Instructional Media Centre. Toronto: Univ. of Toronto, 1971. (1 min., 8 sec.) *IL* (Montreal) ("De Bullion Street"); *ILRH; RCS* (cas.).
See *HN, BH, BH2, IB, IB2, RCS, CP, SP69, CPIL, DF, TWNS, eg* ("De Bullion Street / Via de Bullion"), *Ts:p, NIP* ("De Bullion Street"), and B55. The *Modern Canadian Poetry* broadcast includes an interview by Phyllis Webb (C571); the Instructional Media Centre recording also includes an interview by Christine Lavigne and Lawrence Stevenson (C585).

B1234 "Lady Enfield." Narr. Irving Layton. *Modern Canadian Poetry.* Host Phyllis Webb. Prod. John Kennedy. CBC Television Extension. 30 April 1967. [Audiotape in CBC Radio Archives.] (17 sec.) *PIL65; IL* (Toronto); *RCS* (cas.).
See *HN* ("Lady Remington"), *BH2* ("Lady Enfield"), *IB2, RCS, CP, CPIL, NIP* ("Lady Remington"), and B45. This broadcast includes an interview by Phyllis Webb (C571).

B1235 "Israelis." Narr. Irving Layton. CBC *Tuesday Night.* Host Pearl Sheffy. CBC-FM Radio, 26 Nov. 1968. (1 min., 28 sec.) *PIL65; IL* (Toronto); *Layton; EIL76.*

See *CPIL, UE, PIL, SPIL, WPJ, WPJ2, FE, WBB*, and B394. The 1968 broadcast includes an interview by Pearl Sheffy (C574).

B1236 "The New Breed." Narr. Irving Layton. CBC *Tuesday Night*. Host Pearl Sheffy. CBC-FM Radio, 26 Nov. 1968. (1 min., 5 sec.)
See *WBB*. This broadcast includes an interview by Pearl Sheffy (C574).

B1237 ———, and C.V. Ponomareff. Discussion on the Russian poet Sergey Esenin. Toronto: Dept. of Slavic Studies, Univ. of Toronto, 1969. (Black-and-white; 3/4" videocassette; 43 min.)

B1238 "Family Portrait." Narr. Irving Layton. *Birney / Layton*. Toronto: Ontario Institute for Studies in Education, 1969. (Audiocassette; 51 sec.) Broadcast. Narr. Irving Layton. *Judy*. Host Judy LaMarsh. CBC Radio, 13 Nov. 1975. (51 sec.) Rebroadcast ("Portrait of a One-Armed Juggler: Family Portrait"). Narr. Irving Layton. *A Special Occasion*. Prod. Malka. CBC-FM Radio, 21 July 1977. (53 sec.) Rebroadcast. CBC Radio, 24 July 1977. (53 sec.) *ILH* ("Family Portrait"); *PIL65; ILRH; IL* (Toronto); *RCS* (cas.); *EIL76; WPJ* (cas.).
See *LM, LM2, RCS, CP, SP69, CPIL, DF, PIL, SPIL, WPJ, WPJ2, SPIL*(K), and B172. The two 1977 broadcasts include a critical discussion among fourteen contributors (C667).

B1239 "For My Friend Who Teaches Literature." Narr. Irving Layton. *Birney / Layton*. Toronto: Ontario Institute for Studies in Education, 1969. (Audiocassette; 59 sec.)
See *BOAJ, CP*, and *CPIL*.

B1240 "Leavetaking." Narr. Irving Layton. *Birney / Layton*. Toronto: Ontario Institute for Studies in Education,
1969. (Audiocassette; 30 sec.) *PIL65; IL* (Toronto).
See *CPIL, SFGP, UE, SPIL*(K), and *WBB*.

B1241 "Rhine Boat Trip." Narr. Irving Layton. *Birney / Layton*. Toronto: Ontario Institute for Studies in Education, 1969. (Audiocassette; 35 sec.) *PIL65; ILRH; EIL69; IL* (Toronto); *Layton; EIL76; EIL81; PRIL; WPJ* (cas.).
See *PM, SP69, CPIL, DF, PIL, SPIL, eg* ("Rhine Boat Trip / In barca sul Reno"), *WPJ* ("Rhine Boat Trip"), *WPJ2, SPIL*(K), *FE, Ts:p* ("Rhine Boat Trip / In barco sul Reno"), and B332 ("Rhine Boat Trip").

B1242 "Silent Joy." Narr. Irving Layton. *Birney / Layton*. Toronto: Ontario Institute for Studies in Education, 1969. (Audiocassette; 48 sec.) *IL* (Toronto).
See *CPIL, SFGP, UE, WBB*, and B405.

B1243 ———, Paul Lavigne, and Peter Smith. "The Return of the Mask." *Ideas*. CBC Radio [c.1970]. (1 hr.) CBC Learning Systems, No. 405 [c.1972]. (Reel-to-reel; 1 hr.)

B1244 "The Artist as Worker." *Ideas*. CBC Radio, 27 Feb. 1970. (30 min.)
Reflections on artistic creation with Layton, painter John Tiby, and musician and composer Milton Barnes.

B1245 ———, Jack Ludwig, and Andy Wainwright. *Anthology*. CBC Radio, 29 Aug. 1970.
A discussion of Israel today.

B1246 "The Quebec Situation." Narr. Irving Layton. *Sunday Magazine*. Written, prod., and ed. Joan Donaldson, Angus McLellan, and Lloyd Bulmer. CBC Radio, 1 Nov. 1970. (2 min.)
See *TS:CS* ("Views of the World: Letters, Articles, Travels, 1960–1977. The Quebec Situation") and B893 ("The Quebec Situation").

B1247 "A Conversation with Irving Layton: For the More Devotional." Narr. Irving Layton. Instructional Media Centre. Toronto: Univ. of Toronto, 1971. (38 sec.)

See *BP2* ("For the More Devotional"), *LM2*, *CP*, and *CPIL*.

B1248 ———, Ted Milner, and Andrew Wernick. Panellists. *Fighting Words*. Moderator Nathan Cohen. CHCH TV [Hamilton], 5 March 1971. (22 min.)

B1249 ———, Harry L. Wolfson, and Allen Spraggett. Panellists. *Fighting Words*. Moderator Nathan Cohen. CHCH TV [Hamilton], 26 March 1971. (21 min., 10 sec.)

B1250 "Power and Poetry: Against This Death." Narr. Len Berman. *Ideas*. CBC Radio, 22 Nov. 1971. CBC Learning Systems, No. 765. (43 sec.) *RCS* (cas.) ("Against This Death").

See *MMF*, *RCS*, *CP*, *CPIL*, *DF*, *WPJ*, *WPJ2*, and B590 ("Contra esta muerte"). The 1971 broadcast includes an interview (C593).

B1251 "Power and Poetry: At the Iglesia de Sacromonte." Narr. Len Berman. *Ideas*. CBC Radio, 22 Nov. 1971. CBC Learning Systems, No. 765. (43 sec.)

See *LR* ("At the Iglesia de Sacromonte"), *CP*, *SP69*, *CPIL*, *DF*, *eg* ("At the Iglesia de Sacromonte / Alla Iglesia de Sacromonte"), *Ts:p* ("At the Iglesia De Sacromonte / Alla Iglesia De Sacromonte"), and B302 ("At the Iglesia de Sacromonte"). Also includes an interview (C593).

B1252 "Power and Poetry: Butterfly on Rock." Narr. Len Berman. *Ideas*. CBC Radio, 22 Nov. 1971. CBC Learning Systems, No. 765. (50 sec.).

See *BOAJ* ("Butterfly on Rock"), *CP*, *SP69*, *CPIL*, *DF*, *PIL*, *SPIL*, *WPJ*, *WPJ2*, *SPIL*(K), and B271. Also includes an interview (C593).

B1253 "Power and Poetry: Elan." Narr. Len Berman. *Ideas*. CBC Radio, 22 Nov. 1971. CBC Learning Systems, No. 765. (29 sec.)

See *BH* ("Elan"), *BH2*, *CP* ("Élan"), *CPIL*, and *FE* ("Elan"). Also includes an interview (C593).

B1254 "Power and Poetry: For Mao Tse-Tung: A Meditation on Flies and Kings." Narr. Len Berman. *Ideas*. CBC Radio, 22 Nov. 1971. CBC Learning Systems, No. 765. (2 min., 59 sec.) *RCS* (cas.) ("For Mao Tse-Tung: A Meditation on Flies and Kings").

See *LM2* ("For Mao Tse-Tung"), *RCS* ("For Mao Tse-Tung: A Meditation on Flies and Kings"), *CP*, *SP69*, *CPIL*, *DF* ("For Mao Tse-tung: A Meditation on Flies and Kings"), *PIL* ("For Mao Tse-Tung: A Meditation on Flies and Kings"), *SPIL*, *WPJ*, *WPJ2*, and B199 ("For Mao Tse Tung: A Meditation on Flies and Kings"). Also includes an interview (C593).

B1255 "Power and Poetry: Nail Polish." Narr. Len Berman. *Ideas*. CBC Radio, 22 Nov. 1971. CBC Learning Systems, No. 765. (1 min., 15 sec.)

See *CPIL* ("Nail Polish"), *NP*, and B455. Also includes an interview (C593).

B1256 "Power and Poetry: Original Sin." Narr. Len Berman. *Ideas*. CBC Radio, 22 Nov. 1971. CBC Learning Systems, No. 765. (41 sec.) *RCS* (cas.) ("Original Sin").

See *IB*, *IB2*, *MK*, *RCS*, *CP*, and *CPIL*. Also includes an interview (C593).

B1257 ———, and Eli Mandel. "Nietzsche and Poetry: A Discussion." *Ideas*. CBC Radio, 1972. CBC Learning Systems, No. 339.

See *TS:CS* ("Essays, Reviews, Lectures, 1943–1977 ['Nietzsche and Poetry: A Discussion']") and B1014 ("Nietzsche and Poetry: A Discussion"). Layton also reads "The Birth of Tragedy" (B1169).

B1258 "Portrait of the Artist as a Young Bull." Narr. James Eayrs. *Weekend.* CBC TV, 8 Oct. 1972. [Audiotape in CBC Radio Archives.] (2 min.)
See *PV* and B477.

B1259 ———, and Malcolm Muggeridge. Debate. *Arts Magazine.* Introd. Helen Hutchinson. CBC TV, 28 Oct. 1972. [Audiotape in CBC Radio Archives.] (16 min.) Rebroadcast. *Arts '73.* CBC TV, 22 March 1973. (16 min.)

B1260 *Ideas.* "City Soundscapes." Prepared by David Mac-Pherson. Prod. Mary Ann Hammond. Announcer Warren Davis. CBC Radio, 7 Nov. 1972. (6 min.)
A collage of music, poetry, and speech projects an image of Montreal. Layton talks about Mount Royal and reads "The Improved Binoculars" (B1172) and "On Seeing the Statuettes of Ezekial and Jeremiah in the Church of Notre Dame" (B1209).

B1261 "[I no longer understand]." Narr. Irving Layton. *Take 30.* Host Adrienne Clarkson. CBC TV, 14 Feb. 1973. Rebroadcast. *Take 30.* CBC TV, 14 Feb. 1974. [Audiotape in CBC Radio Archives.] (42 sec.)
Layton also comments on love and writing.

B1262 "Lady." Narr. Irving Layton. *Take 30.* Host Adrienne Clarkson. CBC TV, 14 Feb. 1973. Rebroadcast. *Take 30.* CBC TV, 14 Feb. 1974. [Audiotape in CBC Radio Archives.] (1 min., 23 sec.)
Layton also comments on love and writing.

B1263 "The Way to Go." Narr. Irving Layton. *Take 30.* Host Adrienne Clarkson. CBC TV, 14 Feb. 1973. Rebroadcast. *Take 30.* CBC TV, 14 Feb. 1974. [Audio-

tape in CBC Radio Archives.] (45 sec.)
See *CPIL*, *LPIL* (l.ed.), *Pa* ("Manera de morir"), *LPIL* ("The Way to Go"), *LPIL:RD*, *DD*, and *WBB.* Layton also comments on love and writing.

B1264 Debater. *Weekend.* Moderator James Eayrs. CBC TV, 15 April 1973. [Audiotape in CBC Radio Archives.] (4 min.)
On Canadian-American union.

B1265 "Mount Royal." Narr. Irving Layton. *Quebec Now.* Host David McPherson. CBC Radio, 16 Sept. 1973. (1 min., 22 sec.)
See *BP*, *BP2*, *CP*, and *CPIL.* The 1973 broadcast also includes an interview by David McPherson (C599).

B1266 Contributor. "A.M. Klein: A Portrait of the Poet." CBC *Tuesday Night.* Prod. Seymour Mayne. Ed. Robert Weaver. Supervising ed. Alex Smith. CBC Radio, 6 Nov. 1973.

B1267 "For Anne Frank." Narr. Kildare Dobbs. *Anthology.* Ed. Robert Weaver. Supervising ed. Alex Smith. CBC Radio, 16 Nov. 1974. (1 min.) Rebroadcast ("Portrait of a One-Armed Juggler: For Anne Frank"). Narr. Irving Layton. *A Special Occasion.* Prod. Malka. CBC-FM Radio, 21 July 1977. (1 min., 2 sec.) Rebroadcast. CBC Radio, 24 July 1977. (1 min., 2 sec.)
See *PV* ("For Anne Frank"), *FE*, and B499. The two 1977 broadcasts include a critical discussion among fourteen contributors (C667).

B1268 Contributor. "Why I Love the U.S.A." *Up Canada.* Host Rob Parker. Exec. prod. George Robertson. CBC TV, 3 Dec. 1974. [Audiotape in CBC Radio Archives.] (30 sec.)

B1269 Contributor. "A Documentary Portrait of American Poet William Carlos Williams." Ed. Patrick Hyman. Prod. Howard Engel. CBC *Tuesday Night*. CBC Radio, 7 Jan. 1975. (1 min.) Rebroadcast. CBC *Tuesday Night*. CBC-FM Radio, 9 Jan. 1977. (1 min.)

Allen Doremus and Colin Fox also read poems by Williams.

B1270 ———, and John Hofsess. Debaters. *As It Happens*. Hosts Barbara Frum and Alan Maitland. CBC Radio 22 Jan. 1975. (18 min.)

On the merits of the film *The Night Porter*.

B1271 "Now That I'm Older." Narr. Irving Layton with Italian voice-over translation [Amleto Lorenzini]. *Identities*. CBC Radio, 10 Feb. 1975. (49 sec.) *RCS* (cas.); *WPJ* (cas.).

See *LPS, IB2, RCS, CP, CPIL, fve* ("Now that I'm older / Ora che invecchio"), *DF* ("Now That I'm Older"), *WPJ*, and *WPJ2*. Layton also comments on Amleto Lorenzini's literary qualifications as a translator.

B1272 Contributor. *This Country in the Morning*. Host Peter Gzowski. CBC Radio, 21 April 1975. (38 sec.)

Layton and other alumni who attended the reunion at Baron Byng High School present their reminiscences.

B1273 "Auld Lang Syne." Narr. Irving Layton. *Judy*. Host Judy LaMarsh. CBC Radio, 13 Nov. 1975. (40 sec.) *EIL76*.

See *LLM* ("For Auld Lang Syne: For Saul Berman"), *UE, WPJ* ("For Auld Lang Syne"), *WPJ2*, and *SPIL*(K) ("For Auld Lang Syne: For Saul Berman").

B1274 "Bargain." Narr. Irving Layton. *Judy*. Host Judy LaMarsh. CBC Radio, 13 Nov. 1975. (19 sec.) Rebroadcast ("Portrait of a One-Armed Juggler: Bargain"). Narr. Irving Layton. *A Special Occasion*. Prod. Malka. CBC-FM Radio, 21 July 1977. (20 sec.) Rebroadcast. CBC Radio, 24 July 1977. (20 sec.) *ILH* ("Bargain"); *IL* (Montreal); *ILRH*; *RCS* (cas.); *EIL76*; *WPJ* (cas.).

See *MK, RCS, CP, SP69, CPIL, DF, LPIL* (l.ed.), *Pa* ("Trato"), *LPIL* ("Bargain"), *paIL* ("Bargain / Baratto"), *WPJ* ("Bargain"), *WPJ2, LPIL:RD*, and *DD*. The two 1977 broadcasts include a critical discussion among fourteen contributors (C667).

B1275 "The Best Proof." Narr. Irving Layton. *Judy*. Host Judy LaMarsh. CBC Radio, 13 Nov. 1975. (11 sec.)

See *SP, CPIL, FE*, and B373.

B1276 "In Rattlesnake Country." Narr. Irving Layton. *Judy*. Host Judy LaMarsh. CBC Radio, 13 Nov. 1975. (9 sec.)

See *CP* and *CPIL*.

B1277 "For Jesus Christ." Narr. Irving Layton. *Judy*. Host Judy LaMarsh. CBC Radio, 27 Feb. 1976. (51 sec.) *EIL76*; *MBJ* (cas.).

See *MBJ* and *FE*. Irving Layton and Eli Mandel discuss the "poet as Jew."

B1278 "Warrior Poet." Narr. Irving Layton. *Judy*. Host Judy LaMarsh. CBC Radio, 27 Feb. 1976. (45 sec.) *EIL76*.

See *MBJ, FE*, and B550. Irving Layton and Eli Mandel discuss the "poet as Jew."

B1279 "Adam." Narr. Irving Layton. *Gzowski on* FM. Guest host Bob McKeown. Prod. Nancy Buttons. CBC-FM Radio, 13 April 1976. (1 min., 47 sec.)

See *MBJ* ("Adam: For Amleto Lorenzini"), *PIL* ("Adam"), *SPIL, eg* ("Adam / Adamo"), *FE* ("Adam"), *Ts:p* ("Adam / Adamo"), and B538

("Adam: For Amleto Lorenzini"). The 1976 broadcast includes an interview by Bob McKeown (C605).

B1280 "Displaced Person." Narr. Irving Layton. *Gzowski on* FM. Guest host Bob McKeown. Prod. Nancy Buttons. CBC-FM Radio, 13 April 1976. (49 sec.) *MBJ* (cas.).
　　See *MBJ*. The 1976 broadcast includes an interview by Bob McKeown (C605).

B1281 "North American Poet." Narr. Irving Layton. *Gzowski on* FM. Guest host Bob McKeown. Prod. Nancy Buttons. CBC-FM Radio, 13 April 1976. (22 sec.)
　　See *MBJ*. The 1976 broadcast includes an interview by Bob McKeown (C605).

B1282 "For My Brother Jesus." Narr. Irving Layton. *The Eric Friesen Show*. CBC Radio, 26 Jan. 1977. (2 min., 15 sec.) *EIL76*; *MBJ* (cas.).
　　See *MBJ*, *PIL*, *SPIL*, *eg* ("For My Brother Jesus / Per mio fratello gesù"), *WPJ* ("For My Brother Jesus"), *WPJ2*, *FE*, and *Ts:p* ("For My Brother Jesus / Per mio fratello Gesù"). The 1976 broadcast includes an interview by Eric Friesen (C607).

B1283 "Idiots." Narr. Irving Layton. *90 Minutes Live*. Host Peter Gzowski. Exec. prod. Alex Frame. CBC TV, 10 March 1977. (49 sec.)
　　See *Cov*. The 1977 broadcast includes an interview by Peter Gzowski (C608).

B1284 "Letter to the Soviet Cultural Attaché." Narr. Irving Layton. *90 Minutes Live*. Host Peter Gzowski. Exec. prod. Alex Frame. CBC TV, 10 March 1977. (1 min., 15 sec.)
　　See *Cov*. The 1977 broadcast includes an interview by Peter Gzowski (C608).

B1285 "Portrait of a One-Armed Juggler: Elegy for Strul." Narr. Irving Layton. *A Special Occasion*. Prod. Malka. CBC-FM Radio, 21 July 1977. (1 min., 15 sec.) Rebroadcast. CBC Radio, 24 July 1977. (1 min., 15 sec.) *EIL76* ("Elegy for Strul").
　　See *SP*, *SP69*, *CPIL*, *DF*, *PIL*, *SPIL*, and B374. The two 1977 broadcasts include a critical discussion among fourteen contributors (C667).

B1286 "Portrait of a One-Armed Juggler: For Aviva, Because I Love Her." Narr. Irving Layton. *A Special Occasion*. Prod. Malka. CBC-FM Radio, 21 July 1977. (36 sec.) Rebroadcast. CBC Radio, 24 July 1977. (36 sec.)
　　See *BOAJ* ("For Aviva, Because I Love Her), *CP*, *CPIL*, *LPIL* (l.ed), *Pa* ("Para Aviva, porque la quiero"), *LPIL* ("For Aviva, Because I Love Her"), *paIL* ("For Aviva, because I love her / Per Aviva, perché l'amo"), *LPIL:RD* ("For Aviva, Because I Love Her"), *DD*, and B255. The two 1977 broadcasts include a critical discussion among fourteen contributors (C667).

B1287 "Portrait of a One-Armed Juggler: Shakespeare." Narr. Irving Layton. *A Special Occasion*. Prod. Malka. CBC-FM Radio, 21 July 1977. (2 min., 40 sec.) Rebroadcast. CBC Radio, 24 July 1977. (2 min., 40 sec.) *WPJ* (cas.) ("Shakespeare").
　　See *CPIL*, *NP*, *fve*, *UE*, *PIL*, *SPIL*, *WPJ*, *WPJ2*, and B445. The two 1977 broadcasts include a critical discussion among fourteen contributors (C667).

B1288 "Portrait of a One-Armed Juggler: A Song for Ancients." Narr. Irving Layton. *A Special Occasion*. Prod. Malka. CBC-FM Radio, 21 July 1977. (34 sec.) Rebroadcast. CBC Radio, 24 July 1977. (34 sec.)
　　See *Cov*. ("A Song for Ancients"). The two 1977 broadcasts include a critical discussion among fourteen contributors (C667).

B1289 "Portrait of a One-Armed Juggler: What I Told the Ghost of Harold Laski." Narr. Irving Layton. *A Special Occasion*. Prod. Malka. CBC-FM Radio, 21 July 1977. (1 min., 18 sec.) Rebroadcast. CBC Radio, 24 July 1977. (1 min., 18 sec.)
See *PV* ("What I Told the Ghost of Harold Laski"), *UE*, and B530. The two 1977 broadcasts include a critical discussion among fourteen contributors (C667).

B1290 ——, John Newlove, and William Glenesk. Discussion on Layton's *The Covenant*. *The Eric Friesen Show*. Host Eric Friesen. CBC Radio, 21 Sept. 1977. (30 min.)

B1291 "Dialogue." Narr. Irving Layton. *The Eric Friesen Show*. Host Eric Friesen. CBC Radio, 21 Sept. 1977. (47 sec.)
See *Cov.*, *WPJ*, *WPJ2*, and B719.

B1292 "Sin." Narr. Irving Layton. *The Eric Friesen Show*. Host Eric Friesen. CBC Radio, 21 Sept. 1977. (48 sec.)

B1293 "The Sinner." Narr. Irving Layton. *The Eric Friesen Show*. Host Eric Friesen. CBC Radio, 21 Sept. 1977. (1 min., 14 sec.)
See *Cov.*, *WPJ*, *WPJ2*, and *FE*.

B1294 "Smoke [I've come to the tavern]." Narr. Irving Layton. *The Eric Friesen Show*. Host Eric Friesen. CBC Radio, 21 Sept. 1977. (40 sec.)
See *Cov.*, *TP* ("Smoke [I've come to the tavern] / Fumo"), *LPIL* (l.ed.) ("Smoke [I've come to the tavern]"), *Pa* ("Humo"), *LPIL* ("Smoke [I've come to the tavern]"), *LPIL:RD*, *SPIL*(K), and *DD*.

B1295 "Xianity." Narr. Irving Layton. *The Eric Friesen Show*. Host Eric Friesen. CBC Radio, 21 Sept. 1977. (40 sec.)
See *Cov.*, *WPJ*, *WPJ2*, *FE*, and B580.

B1296 "If Whales Could Think on Certain Happy Days." Narr. Irving Layton. *Science Magazine*. Host David Suzuki. CBC TV, 22 March 1978. (39 sec.) Retelecast. *Science Magazine*. Host David Suzuki. CBC TV, 25 Aug. 1980. (39 sec.) *PIL65*; *IL* (Toronto).
See *SP*, *SP69*, *CPIL*, *DF*, *TWNS*, *SDCJ*, and B516 ("Gdyby Wieloryby Umiały Myśleć W Pewne Radosne Dni").

B1297 "Madman on Mithymna Beach." Narr. Irving Layton. *Canada after Dark*. Hosts Paul Soles and Paul Grigsby. CBC TV, 28 Sept. 1978. (48 sec.)
See *LPIL* (l.ed), *Pa* ("Loco en la playa de Mithymna"), *LPIL* ("Madman on Mithymna Beach"), *TD*, *LPIL:RD*, *SPIL*(K), and B613. The 1978 telecast also includes an interview by Paul Soles and Paul Grigsby (C618).

B1298 Contributor. *The Jesus Trial*. Prod. and dir. Tad Jaworski. TV Ontario, 5 Nov. 1978.

B1299 "Irving Layton." In *Toronto Today*. Aircheck. 1979. (3/4" videocassette.) [Layton Collection, Concordia Univ.]

B1300 "For 751–0329." Narr. Irving Layton. *Authors: Irving Layton*. Host Joyce Davidson. CBC TV, 7 Sept. 1979. (59 sec.) *PRIL*; *WPJ* (cas.) ("For 7515–03296").
See *TP* ("For 751–0329 / Per 751–0329"), *TD* ("For 751–0329"), *TWNS*, *eg* ("For 751–0329 / Per 751–0329"), *WPJ* ("For 7515–03296"), *WPJ2*, *FE*, *Ts:p* ("For 751–0329 / Per 751–0329"), and B586 ("For 751–0329"). The 1979 telecast also includes an interview by Joyce Davidson (C625).

B1301 Contributor. *Bob McLean Show*. Host Bob McLean. CBC TV, 26 Sept. 1979. (12 min.)

Layton discusses his new home in Niagara-on-the-Lake.

B1302 Contributor. *Arts National: The Sound of the Seventies*. Pt. 1. CBC Radio, 7 Jan. 1980. (2 min.)
Layton gives his view of the world.

B1303 "A.M. Klein: The Poet as Landscape." *Spectrum*. Prod. and dir. David Kaufman. CBC TV, 9 Jan. 1980. (3 min.)

B1304 "The Song of Leonard Cohen." *Spectrum*. Prod. and dir. Harry Rasky. CBC TV, 5 Nov. 1980.
Layton discusses Cohen's work and reads Cohen's poem "Death of a Lady's Man."

B1305 "Love and Marriage." *Man Alive*. Prod. Mai Zetterling. CBC TV, 29 Nov. 1981.

B1306 ——, Robert Haynes, and Elizabeth Kilbourn. Panellists. "Sanctity of Life." *Fraser's Edge*. Hosts Fraser Kelly and Susan Ormiston. CBC TV, 6 Dec. 1982. (27 min., 50 sec.)
A discussion on test-tube babies, abortion, surrogate motherhood, euthanasia, and suicide.

B1307 Actor. *Wildfire: The Story of Tom Longboat*. Prod. and dir. David Tucker. CBC TV, 29 May 1984. (1 hr.)
Irving Layton plays the part of Longboat's promoter, Harry Rosenthal.

B1308 ——, and Elspeth Cameron. Contributors. *The Journal*. Host Barbara Frum. CBC TV, 15 Oct. 1985. (12 min., 8 sec.)
Irving Layton expresses his resentment in a confrontation with Elspeth Cameron after her publication of *Irving Layton: A Portrait*.

B1309 "Diary." *The Journal*. CBC TV, 17 Dec. 1985. (6 min., 7 sec.)
Irving Layton plans to collect material to write a biography of Elspeth Cameron.

B1310 *City Lights*. Pts. 1–11. N.d. (3/4" videocassette; 60 min.) [Layton Collection, Concordia Univ.]

B1311 "Irving Layton on A.M. Klein." Montreal: Jewish Public Library. N.d. (55 min.)

Part II

Works on Irving Layton

C   Books, Articles and Sections of Books, Theses and Dissertations, Interviews and Profiles, Miscellaneous Audio-Visual Material, Poems about Layton, Miscellaneous, and Awards and Honours

Books

C1   Whalley, Peter. *Lust Where the Summer's Short: All Canadian Love Poems*. Poems by Ivy Peyton. Engravings Harrieta Nowt. [Hỹpẽrbóle] (Morin Heights, P.Q.), No. 11 (Oct. 1963)]. [20 pp.]
     Whalley writes a series of poems under the name Ivy Peyton, satirizing Layton's love poems.

C2   Robinson, Brian. *Laytonic Love*. Montreal: Three Star, 1965. [14 pp.]
     Robinson's preface to his pamphlet of six poems indicates they "are meant as satirical lashings at love à la Irving Layton." Robinson satirizes the emphasis on the instinctual, especially in its sexual aspect, which he states is predominant in Layton's poetry and in our society generally.

C3   Mandel, Eli. *Irving Layton*. Ed. William French. Toronto: Forum House, 1969. 82 pp. Rpt. (excerpt)
in *Modern Commonwealth Literature: A Library of Literary Criticism*. Ed. John H. Ferres and Martin Tucker. New York: Frederick Ungar, 1977, pp. 302–03.
     One of Layton's legitimate claims to uniqueness is that he works from the literary traditions of the United States and Europe rather than the British tradition of T.S. Eliot and W.H. Auden. But, like William Blake, his work is characterized by "excess" and "exuberance." Layton is "teacher, prophet, visionary." His major thematic "concerns are the nature of the creative process, the ambiguities and perplexities of individual desire, and the social implications of both human perversity and creativity." For Layton, poetry does not so much fuse discordant elements as hold them in ironic balance, particularly between the poet and the world, and imagination and fact. The Dionysian-Apollonian tension also pervades his work. Ambiguity is particularly characteristic of his imagery, which "finally settles . . . into a symbolic pattern of delicate precision." Often ". . . the way down is the way up," with many poems seeking "a continuing confrontation with evil." Irony is his main tool for his Blakean attack on civilization. Imagination enables the poet to confront the evil within society and within himself and, thus, attain freedom. Fantasy is another "structural principle of Layton's poetry." He is "acutely aware of poetry as craft."

C4   Osterlund, Steven. *Fumigator: An Outsider's View of Irving Layton*. Cleveland: Rumple Studios, 1975. 17 pp. Rpt. ("Fumigator: An Outsider's View of Irving Layton") in *Irving Layton: The Poet and His Critics*. Ed. Seymour Mayne. Toronto: McGraw-Hill Ryerson, 1978, pp. 260–71.
     Osterlund gives a personal account of his correspondence and subsequent friendship with Layton.

Osterlund arrived in Canada from the United States in 1967, and his account extends from that date to the early 1970s. Layton impressed him with his generosity, vitality, and perceptive intelligence. His attitude towards other writers is generously supportive and free from personal assaults. Layton's efforts have brought out the best in Osterlund's poetic talents.

C5 Bennett, Joy. *Eight Irving Layton Notebooks 1968–1972 in the Concordia University Library*. Montreal: University Archives, McGill Univ., 1976. 44 pp.

Done as an assignment for library science course 405–645A given by Professor John Andreassen at McGill University, this book includes a preface, a short biographical note, and catalogues of eight of Layton's notebooks, which "contain the original workings and drafts for most of Irving Layton's publications for the period from 1968 to 1973." For each notebook, a brief description is followed by a list of the items that appear on each page of the notebook. "These notebooks represent a record of poetry and observations written while Layton travelled through Portugal, Greece and other parts of Europe." Many were later published in *The Whole Bloody Bird (Obs, Aphs, & Pomes)*, *Nail Polish*, and *The Pole-Vaulter*.

C6 Mayne, Seymour, ed. and introd. *Irving Layton: The Poet and His Critics*. Toronto: McGraw-Hill Ryerson, 1978. 1–22, 291 pp.

Because this collection includes reprints of earlier articles and reviews, each item is listed separately in the appropriate section of this bibliography. The collection includes Richard *Adams*' rev. of *Engagements: The Prose of Irving Layton* (D306), Charles *Bukowski*'s rev. of *The Laughing Rooster* (D82), June *Callwood*'s "The Lusty Laureate from the Slums" (C55), Hayden *Carruth*'s rev. of *Collected Poems* (D94), John *Ciardi*'s rev. of *A Red Carpet for the Sun* (D70), Fred *Cogswell*'s rev. of *The Long Pea-Shooter* (D26), Robert *Creeley*'s rev. of *Cerberus*, *The Black Huntsmen*, *Love the Conqueror Worm*, and *Canadian Poems 1850–1952* (D10, D17, D20, D346), Frank *Davey*'s rev. of *The Collected Poems of Irving Layton* (D129), Robertson *Davies*' rev. of *A Red Carpet for the Sun* (D60), Kildare *Dobbs*'s rev. of *The Improved Binoculars* (D46), Stan *Dragland*'s rev. of *Lovers and Lesser Men* (D150), Louis *Dudek*'s "Layton Now and Then: Our Critical Assumptions" (C29), rev. of *Collected Poems* (D91), rev. of *A Red Carpet for the Sun* (D63), rev. of *The Swinging Flesh* (D289), and "The Transition in Canadian Poetry" (C51), Wynne *Francis*' "Layton and Nietzsche" (C281), Northrop *Frye*'s Introduction to *Il freddo verde elemento* (C232), rev. of *The Black Huntsmen* (D9), rev. of *Cerberus* (D15), rev. of *The Cold Green Element* and *The Blue Propeller* (D29, D31), rev. of *A Laughter in the Mind* (D57), rev. of *The Long Pea-Shooter* and *In the Midst of My Fever* (D23, D29), rev. of *Music on a Kazoo*, *The Bull Calf and Other Poems*, and *The Improved Binoculars* (D39, D43, D49), and rev. of *A Red Carpet for the Sun* (D69), Robert *Fulford*'s rev. of *Engagements: The Prose of Irving Layton* (D304), Roy *Fuller*'s rev. of *A Red Carpet for the Sun* (D59), A.D. *Hope*'s rev. of *A Red Carpet for the Sun* (D67), X.J. *Kennedy*'s rev. of *The Collected Poems of Irving Layton* (D135), Hugh *Kenner*'s rev. of *A Laughter in the Mind* (D58), A.M. *Klein*'s rev. of *Here and Now* (D2), Edward *Lacey*'s rev. of *Lovers and Lesser Men* (D152), Gwendolyn *MacEwen*'s rev. of *The Unwavering Eye: Selected Poems 1969–1975* (D172), Eli *Mandel*'s rev. of *A Laughter in the Mind* (D55), rev. of *A Red Carpet for the Sun* (D61), rev. of *Selected Poems* and *The Whole Bloody Bird (Obs, Aphs, & Pomes)*

(D119, D294), rev. of *The Shattered Plinths* (D109), and rev. of *The Swinging Flesh* (D293), Gilles *Marcotte*'s rev. of *A Red Carpet for the Sun* (D62), Anne *Marriott*'s rev. of *Love the Conqueror Worm* (D19), Tom *Marshall*'s rev. of *Selected Poems* and *The Whole Bloody Bird (Obs, Aphs & Pomes)* (D121, D299), Seymour *Mayne*'s Introduction (C299) and "Selected Bibliography" (C300), Susan *Musgrave*'s rev. of *The Pole-Vaulter* (D163), Alden A. *Nowlan*'s rev. of *A Red Carpet for the Sun* (D66), Pádraig O' *Broin*'s "Fire Drake" (C553), Steven *Osterlund*'s "Fumigator: An Outsider's View of Irving Layton" (C4), Desmond *Pacey*'s rev. of *The Bull Calf and Other Poems* (D37), rev. of *Periods of the Moon* (D104), and rev. of *The Swinging Flesh* (D286), A.W. *Purdy*'s rev. of *Balls for a One-Armed Juggler* (D76), rev. of *Collected Poems* (D93), and rev. of *The Collected Poems of Irving Layton* (D125), James *Reaney*'s rev. of *Music on a Kazoo* (D50), Harry *Roskolenko*'s "Two Reviews of *Now Is the Place* (1948)" (D282), Robin *Skelton*'s rev. of *The Laughing Rooster* (D86), A.J.M. *Smith*'s "The Recent Poetry of Irving Layton" (C24), Patricia Keeney *Smith*'s "Irving Layton and the Theme of Death" (C189), Richard *Sommer*'s rev. of *The Shattered Plinths* (D110), Raymond *Souster*'s rev. of *The Black Huntsmen* (D7), John *Sutherland*'s rev. of *Now Is the Place* (D281), Warren *Tallman*'s "Wonder Merchants: Modernist Poetry in Vancouver during the 1960s" (C244), Elizabeth *Waterston*'s rev. of *Nail Polish* (D142), F.W. *Watt*'s rev. of *The Collected Poems of Irving Layton* (D133), Phyllis *Webb*'s rev. of *The Swinging Flesh* (D287), William Carlos *Williams*' "A Note on Layton" (C26), Milton *Wilson*'s "Notebook on Layton" (C227), "Other Canadians and After" (C42), rev. of *Balls for a One-Armed Juggler* (D81), and rev. of *A Red Carpet for the Sun* (D65), and George *Woodcock*'s "A Grab at Proteus:

Notes on Irving Layton" (C141), rev. of *The Long Pea-Shooter* and *In the Midst of My Fever* (D22, D27).

C7   Bennett, Joy, and James Polson. *Irving Layton: A Bibliography 1935–1977*. Introd. Joy Bennett and James Polson. Foreword Irving Layton. Montreal: Concordia Univ. Libraries, 1979. i–iv, vii, 200 pp.

This book "is, in essence, a guide to one section of Concordia University Library's Irving Layton Collection." Works by Layton are listed under books, editions, plays, articles and reviews, short stories, correspondence, and poetry. The poetry section aims at listing all poems published by Layton to the end of 1977, including books in which they have been reprinted. Works about Layton are listed under critical articles, book reviews, newspaper clippings, unlocated clippings, dissertations, and bibliographies. Arrangement of the material is generally chronological, except for the section of poems by Layton, which is alphabetical. See A102 and C11.

C8   Mandel, Eli. *The Poetry of Irving Layton*. Toronto: Coles, 1981. 121 pp.

This book is a revised and substantially expanded version of Mandel's earlier *Irving Layton* (C3). In an additional chapter, Mandel discusses Layton's poetry of the past decade, emphasizing his unabated energy and the hostility and lack of understanding evinced by the English-Canadian cultural establishment. The main subject of his recent poetry, which is "in the tradition of European moral satire and vision" is "the story of the Jewish writer or poet in Canada." Layton is most characterized in his recent poetry by an "affirmation of ecstasy" while "confronting the void." He is "the richest, most well-stored, most energetic poet of this century."

C9 Cameron, Elspeth. *Irving Layton: A Portrait*. Don Mills, Ont.: Stoddart, 1985. 518 pp. Rpt. (excerpt — "The Tumultuous Loves of Irving Layton") in *Chatelaine*, Oct. 1985, pp. 66–67, 108, 110, 112–13.

This full-length biography begins with Layton's family background in Roumania and ends with a 6 September 1983 reading at Harbourfront in Toronto. Cameron portrays his life as a zig-zag, full "of sudden twists and about-faces." A key to his character lies in his attempts to balance possibilities and avoid making final choices, whether in his women, his career, or his art. "Even as a boy Layton created the world to suit himself in order to avoid suffering." Cameron describes Layton's literary career as reaching its peak in the late 1950s and early 1960s, with his writing since then steadily declining both in imaginative power and popularity. His attempt, beginning about 1970, to reclaim Jesus for the Jews, was an ill-fated effort to "astonish his public and revivify his sagging reputation."

C10 Francis, Wynne. *Irving Layton and His Works*. [Toronto: ECW, 1985.] 92 pp.

This is an offprint of Francis' essay in *Canadian Writers and Their Works* (C420).

C11 Bennett, Joy. *A Catalogue of the Manuscripts in the Irving Layton Collection, Concordia University*. Calgary: Univ. of Calgary Press, 1988. 229 pp.

This catalogue of the Irving Layton collection at Concordia includes 528 entries following standard archival cataloguing procedures. Most entries are poems, although some of Layton's prose, including several versions of *Waiting for the Messiah: A Memoir*, is catalogued. A second volume including "correspondence and ephemeral material" is planned. See A102 and C7.

C12 Rizzardi, Alfredo, ed. *Italian Critics on Irving Layton*. Abano Terme, Italy: Piovan, 1988. 194 pp.

Includes Sylvia *Albertazzi*, "Misunderstandings: A Note on Layton's and Cohen's Love Poems," pp. 75–87; Valerio *Bruni*, "An Agnostic Faust: Redemptive Transgression in the Work of Irving Layton," pp. 49–71 (rpt. ["La Transgressione Come Riscato"] in his *Danza Sulla Fune: Studio Sulla Poesia di Irving Layton*. Abano Terme, Italy: Piovan, 1990, pp. 81–103); Giorgia *Caprani*, "Man and Superman: Eli Mandel and Irving Layton," pp. 169–91; Elio *Chinol*, "A Voice from Canada," pp. 13–17; Carla *Comellini*, "D.H. Lawrence's and I. Layton's Vitalism," pp. 123–37; Lilla Maria *Crisafulli Jones*, "Irving Layton: Poetry of the Body," pp. 107–19; Mario *Domenichelli*, "Irving Layton: Laughter and Death," pp. 33–45; Caterina *Ricciardi*, "Irving Layton: On Poetry. A Conversation," pp. 91–103; Alfredo *Rizzardi*, "Foreword: Layton's Italy and the Italian Readers' Layton," p. 9, "An Italian Bibliography of Irving Layton," p. 193, and "The Love Song of Irving Layton," pp. 21–29; and Biancamaria *Rizzardi*, "The Unwavering Eye: Layton's Poetic Conception of Life," pp. 141–65.

Albertazzi: The poetry of Irving Layton and Leonard Cohen reduces women to their physical attributes. Love is often a joke, sex "a ritual for the celebration of man's virility." This awareness of the transience of physical love leads to "a conscious fear of loneliness and darkness and an unconscious awe of the potentialities hidden in the woman's body." In their work love becomes "an attempt to escape from the everlasting void."

Bruni: Layton's image of Faust is Dracula, a mask for the poet that is parodied by bourgeois greed and cruelty. While human fury is gratuitous, the natural world is governed by unavoidable ferocity. Many of the figures in his poems are united by their "inability to tolerate the finiteness of human experience." Some poems like "New Tables" suggest the possibility of rejecting the "power and arrogance" of contemporary society for "ecstasy arising from complete fusion with everything."

Caprani: While Irving Layton projects confidence and firmness in his poetry, Eli Mandel's work is suffused with desolation, despair, and suffering. Mandel is "forbidden the knowledge of the glorious burning body in whose abysses Layton shameless[ly] celebrates life." But they share the "desire to pierce the veils of appearance until truth is finally revealed."

Chinol: Layton's links are with such writers as D.H. Lawrence, "who attempt to bring into literature the emotion of an authentic human experience." Like W.B. Yeats, he reveals the world's "unlimited misery and countless atrocities, but [is] united, despite all, to a deep, reverent acceptance of life." The bourgeois and totalitarian worlds are "expressions of a death-wish"; the poet must "discover a more authentic order of values." (This article was previously published as "Une voce dal Canada" [see C364].)

Comellini: Both Layton and D.H. Lawrence believe poetry should discomfort the reader. "Lawrence's . . . search for glimpses of God in men finds fulfillment in Layton's theme of the gifted poet." His "debt to Lawrence can be seen in his imagery, in the idea of the poet as a prophet."

Crisafulli Jones: In his poetry Layton assumes the masks of warrior, lover, thief, and prophet. His poems are often conversations with a silent listener, using point of view to achieve unusual effects. His love poems are distinguished by an expression of a "tremendous will to survive," although some also suggest that "women and words may suddenly turn into the black hole itself and be the real threat to the poet."

Domenichelli: In Layton's poetry, laughter is always linked with death. Laughter may be either sado-masochistic, if coming from someone else, or bitter if the poet is laughing. Laughter is "the freezing, threatening noise of the clash between Eros and Thanatos . . . the noise of the clash between illusion and reality. Although laughter is conditioned by death, it "can, in its turn, condition death and become the laughter which mythically marks rebirth." (This article was previously published [see C417].)

Ricciardi: Layton agrees that Canada has been slow to come of age culturally, partly because of its linguistic divisions. Northrop Frye has had little influence on creative writers; all criticism is "ancillary to the creative act." The Hebrew prophets, W.B. Yeats, and Constantine Cavafy are the most important influences on Layton's work. "Jews are the Christ symbol for our vicious age." (This conversation was previously published [see C631].)

Alfredo *Rizzardi*, Foreword: For Layton, Italy serves as "an imaginary Eden to stage the endless comedy of love balancing . . . and making up for the grim tragedy of hatred." For the Italian reader he provides rare insights into "the great issues of our century." His poetry reveals "commitment to the highest human values — those values that the twentieth century has everywhere betrayed."

Alfredo *Rizzardi*, "An Italian Bibliography": Primary and secondary material is included.

Alfredo *Rizzardi*, "The Love Song": The Italian translation of *The Love Poems of Irving Layton* shows Layton's love poetry to be "a private diary into which a total and real erotic experience is outpoured." His "main chords are lust and mirth." The sexual urge is presented as a "desperate attempt at filling the void underlying human existence." But "beauty has the power to exorcise death." (This article was previously published [see C388].)

Biancamaria *Rizzardi*: "From the paradox between form and energy which is at the root of Layton's and Nietzsche's thought spring conflicts at various levels which determine . . . the themes of both." In both, the Apollonian-Dionysian conflict is manifested on three levels: biological, psychological-social, and the making of poetry. We must strive, both say, to accept the world in all its aspects, going beyond the negative to become a superman. But when confronted by the Nietzschean tragedy of eternal recurrence, Layton retreats to Spinoza and Hume and a more intellectualized vision of the world.

C13   Bruni, Valerio. *Danza Sulla Fune: Studio Sulla Poesia di Irving Layton.* Abano Terme, Italy: Piovan, 1990. 134 pp.

Bruni's book opens with a discussion of Layton's important position in contemporary poetry. While his technique has become more refined, his major themes are present from his earliest work. Successive chapters discuss Layton's violence, his lyricism, and the theme of transgression. Layton delineates two ways of facing existence: passive acceptance or constructive transgression. In his work the Jew becomes a symbol for all those who were victims of violence and imposition. Parts of this book were previously published (see C12 and C462).

Articles and Sections of Books

C14   Sutherland, John. "Three New Poets." *First Statement*, 1, No. 12 ([1943]), 1, 2, 3, 4.

Sutherland discusses Layton along with Kay Smith and Louis Dudek, all of whom have poetry appearing in the same issue of *First Statement*. "Layton . . . speaks with . . . directness and a masculine vigour." Like Klein, he has "a love of romantic beauty."

"Dudek, Layton, and Miss Smith . . . represent a fusion of modern and traditional elements."

C15   Waddington, Patrick. Letter to John Sutherland. *First Statement*, 2 April 1943, pp. 5–7.

Waddington criticizes "Day," "Providence," and "Obstacle Course," poems by Layton published in *First Statement*, No. 12. "Day" is full of clichés, while "Obstacle Course" betrays the poverty of Layton's muse. In the story "A Parasite," published in *First Statement*, No. 14, ". . . the thought, the feeling, the conclusion are all false," "partly because Mr. Layton is speaking of himself." Layton's reply follows (B839).

C16   Dudek, Louis. "Poets of Revolt . . . or Reaction." *First Statement*, 11 June 1943, pp. 3–5.

Dudek discusses Carl Sandburg as a representative of the healthy American poetic tradition of an affirmative point of view associated with a working-class background and mentality. In contrast, he poses such writers as T.S. Eliot and e.e. cummings, who are upper class and often negative. Irving Layton, along with Raymond Souster, Patrick Anderson, and a number of other poets (including Dudek himself) is criticized for a similar undesirable negative tendency in some of his poems.

C17   Avison, Margaret. Letter. *The Canadian Forum*, June 1945, p. 65.

Replying to Layton's response (B840) to her review (D1), Avison insists on high standards for poetry.

C18   Weaver, Robert. "Notes on Canadian Literature." *The Nation* [New York], 16 Feb. 1946, p. 200.

Although Layton draws on Jewish backgrounds, he has developed along more proletarian lines than A.M. Klein. Layton's poems of the slums, in *Here and*

Now, "are filled with effectively contrasted poetic expression and blunt social statement."

C19 Sutherland, John. "Introduction: The Old and the New." In *Other Canadians: An Anthology of the New Poetry of Canada 1940–46*. Ed. John Sutherland. Montreal: First Statement, 1947, pp. 15, 19. Rpt. ("Introduction to *Other Canadians*") in *The Making of Modern Poetry in Canada: Essential Articles on Contemporary Canadian Poetry in English*. Ed. Louis Dudek and Michael Gnarowski. Toronto: Ryerson, 1967, pp. 56, 60.

Layton is mentioned as one of several writers who is indifferent "to the art-religion hypothesis of our escapist writers and critics." His work "is distinguished by a hard-fisted proletarianism."

C20 Pacey, Desmond. *Creative Writing in Canada: A Short History of English-Canadian Literature*. Toronto: Ryerson, 1952, pp. 115, 141, 144, 149. Rpt. (expanded) in rev. and enl. ed. Toronto: McGraw-Hill Ryerson, 1961, pp. 124, 153, 156, 163–67, 170, 176, 185, 233, 234, 235, 236, 245, 246, 251, 268.

In the first edition, Layton receives a brief mention. His "dominant note" is anger. In the new revised and enlarged edition, Pacey notes that Layton believes poetry must be passionate, against convention, and the product of the poet's own experience. He is versatile, the most successful of Canadian poets at writing of sex, and capable of portraying both "the glory and horror of life on earth." He is the major Canadian poet of the mid-twentieth century and the "chief prophet of the Montreal social-realist group."

C21 Pacey, Desmond. "English-Canadian Poetry 1944–54." *Culture*, 15 (Sept. 1954), 257, 261–62, 264. Rpt. in *Essays in Canadian Criticism: 1938–1968*.

By Desmond Pacey. Toronto: Ryerson, 1969, pp. 103, 107, 108, 111.

Layton's "poems are sometimes rough and ready in technique, but his frequent revision of them is proof that he has an artistic conscience."

C22 Dudek, Louis. "The State of Canadian Poetry: 1954." *The Canadian Forum*, Oct. 1954, pp. 153, 154. Rpt. in *The Making of Modern Poetry in Canada: Essential Articles on Contemporary Canadian Poetry in English*. Ed. Louis Dudek and Michael Gnarowski. Toronto: Ryerson, 1967, pp. 170, 171, 172, 173, 174. Rpt. in *Selected Essays and Criticism*. By Louis Dudek. Ottawa: Tecumseh, 1978, pp. 45, 47, 48, 50.

Irving Layton, who exemplifies the "wave of creative work in poetry" of the past fifteen years, is one of the best of the modern Canadian poets.

C23 "Canadian Writers Come into Their Own." *The Times Literary Supplement* [London], 5 Aug. 1955, p. iii.

Layton has a "direct, hard style," "but until now his poems are only occasions for poems."

C24 Smith, A.J.M. "The Recent Poetry of Irving Layton: A Major Voice." *Queen's Quarterly*, 62 (Winter 1955–56), 587–91. Rpt. ("A Salute to Layton: In Praise of His Earliest Masterpieces") in *On Poetry and Poets: Selected Essays of A.J.M. Smith*. By A.J.M. Smith. New Canadian Library, No. 143. Toronto: McClelland and Stewart, 1977, pp. 70–75. Rpt. ("The Recent Poetry of Irving Layton") in *Irving Layton: The Poet and His Critics*. Ed. Seymour Mayne. Toronto: McGraw-Hill Ryerson, 1978, pp. 43–48. Rpt. (excerpt) in *Contemporary Literary Criticism: Excerpts from Criticism of the Work of Today's Novelists, Poets, Playwrights, and Other*

Creative Writers. Ed. Sharon R. Gunton and Laurie Lanzen Harris. Vol. xv. Detroit: Gale, 1980, 318–19.

Layton emerges as an accomplished poet with the 1954 volumes, *The Long Pea-Shooter* and *In the Midst of My Fever.* While much of his earlier work was "arrogant, puerile, or deliberately offensive," these more recent poems display "a mastery of rhythm," a firm respect for his "personal here and now," "a sense of freedom," an ability to combine "seemingly incompatible images," "a power to generate fantasy out of reality," and "elegance."

C25   Smith, A.J.M. "Poet." In *Writing in Canada: Proceedings of the Canadian Writers' Conference, Queen's University, 28–31 July 1955.* Ed. George Whalley. Introd. F.R. Scott. Toronto: Macmillan, 1956, p. 17.

The first stanza of Layton's "The Birth of Tragedy" is quoted as evidence of the poet's "responsibility to the nature of reality."

C26   Williams, William Carlos. "A Note on Layton." [Introduction]. In *The Improved Binoculars.* By Irving Layton. Highlands, N.C.: Jonathan Williams, 1956, pp. 9–10. Rpt. (abridged) in *Congress Bulletin* [Canadian Jewish Congress], May 1959, p. 3. Rpt. (expanded, original) in *The Making of Modern Poetry in Canada: Essential Articles on Contemporary Canadian Poetry in English.* Ed. Louis Dudek and Michael Gnarowski. Toronto: Ryerson, 1967, pp. 233–34. Rpt. (excerpt) in *Modern Commonwealth Literature: A Library of Literary Criticism.* Ed. John H. Ferres and Martin Tucker. New York: Frederick Ungar, 1977, p. 299. Rpt. (expanded, original) in *Irving Layton: The Poet and His Critics.* Ed. Seymour Mayne. Toronto: McGraw-Hill Ryerson, 1978, pp. 52–53.

Layton is a good poet, full of celebration and a protean versatility. He combines a broad range of vocabulary and technique with modesty, is "capable of anything," and may become "one of the west's most famous poets."

C27   Frye, Northrop. "Preface to an Uncollected Anthology." Royal Society of Canada, Sec. II, Toronto. 11 June 1956. Printed in *Studia Varia: Royal Society of Canada, Literary and Scientific Papers.* Ed. G.D. Murray. Toronto: Univ. of Toronto Press, 1957, pp. 22, 25, 35. Rpt. (abridged) in *Canadian Anthology.* Rev. ed. Ed. Carl F. Klinck and Reginald E. Watters. Toronto: Gage, 1966, pp. 516, 517–18, 523. 3rd ed., 1974, pp. 596, 597, 603. Rpt. (expanded, original) in *The Bush Garden: Essays on the Canadian Imagination.* By Northrop Frye. Toronto: House of Anansi, 1971, pp. 164, 168, 179. Rpt. in *Contexts of Canadian Criticism: A Collection of Critical Essays.* Ed. Eli Mandel. Patterns of Literary Criticism, No. 9. Chicago: Univ. of Chicago Press, 1971, pp. 182, 186, 197. Rev. ed. Toronto: Univ. of Toronto Press, 1971, pp. 182, 186, 197.

Some of Layton's poetry expresses "arrogant defiance of the landscape." "Golfers" is typical of Canadian satiric light verse. "The Cold Green Element" is a key poem.

C28   Dudek, Louis. Letter. *The Canadian Forum,* June 1956, p. 68.

Dudek responds to Millar MacLure's contention that Layton was influenced by Pound (D35), stating that Layton has never read the cantos or been enthusiastic about Pound's poetry.

C29   Dudek, Louis. "Layton Now and Then — Our Critical Assumptions." *Queen's Quarterly,* 63 (Summer 1956), 291–93. Rpt. in *Selected Essays and Criticism.* By Louis Dudek. Ottawa: Tecumseh, 1978, pp. 52–55. Rpt. ("Layton Now and Then: Our Critical Assumptions") in *Irving Layton: The Poet and His Critics*. Ed. Seymour Mayne. Toronto: McGraw-Hill Ryerson, 1978, pp. 49–51.

A.J.M. Smith's recent praise of Layton (C24) is as overdone as his previous neglect was unjustified. Layton's "relevance to life" and "energy," as well as his Jewish proletarian background, make it difficult for more traditional critics to give him his due estimate.

C30 Christopher, A.G. Letter. *The Canadian Forum*, July 1956, p. 86. Rpt. in *Forum: Canadian Life and Letters 1920–70. Selections from* The Canadian Forum. Ed. J.L. Granatstein and Peter Stevens. Toronto: Univ. of Toronto Press, 1972, p. 306.

Christopher responds to Millar MacLure's review of *The Bull Calf and Other Poems* (D35), berating the critics for being too overwhelmed by Layton's successful propaganda.

C31 Daniells, Roy. "Literature I: Poetry and the Novel." In *The Culture of Contemporary Canada*. Ed. Julian Park. Ithaca, N.Y.: Cornell Univ. Press, 1957, pp. 71, 73–74.

Layton's "vigour and fecundity are making him the most exciting of contemporary Canadian poets." More than any other of his Canadian contemporaries, he has a "consciously Hebrew sensibility."

C32 Pacey, Desmond. "Canadian Literature: Poetry and Drama." In *The New International 1957 Year Book: A Compendium of the World's Progress for the Year 1956*. Ed. Henry E. Vizetelly. New York: Funk & Wagnalls, 1957, p. 73.

With his "frank, vigorous and colloquial verse," Layton, along with E.J. Pratt, "is gaining recognition as Canada's leading poet."

C33 Rexroth, Kenneth. "The World Is Full of Strangers." In *New Directions in Prose and Poetry*. No. 16. New York: New Directions, 1957, pp. 198–99.

Layton is the only Canadian representative on Rexroth's list of the significant younger North American poets.

C34 Smith, A.J.M. Letter. *The Canadian Forum*, Jan. 1957, p. 237.

Smith versifies Layton's earlier letter to *The Canadian Forum* (B842). ". . . Layton and Dudek are rapidly making themselves the ideal objects of classical satire . . . ." (For Layton's response, see B844.)

C35 Dempsey, Lotta. "Poet Attacks Publisher's Attitude." *The Globe and Mail* [Toronto], 14 Jan. 1957, p. 17.

Layton is angered that Ryerson would not distribute *The Improved Binoculars*, as originally arranged, because of alleged obscenity.

C36 Dudek, Louis. "The Montreal Poets." *Forge*, Feb. 1957, pp. 3–6. Rpt. in *Culture*, 18 (June 1957), 150, 151, 152, 154. Rpt. in *The McGill Movement: A.J.M. Smith, F.R. Scott, and Leo Kennedy*. Ed. Peter Stevens. Critical Views on Canadian Writers, No. 2. Toronto: Ryerson, 1969, pp. 7, 9, 11. Rpt. in *Selected Essays and Criticism*. By Louis Dudek. Ottawa: Tecumseh, 1978, pp. 60, 61, 62, 63, 64.

Layton views Montreal "with a tortured and distorting passion." Like many other Montreal poets, he is often satirical.

C37 Eckman, Frederick. *Cobras and Cockle Shells: Modes in Recent Poetry*. Vagrom Chap Book, No. 5. Flushing, N.Y.: n.p., 1958, pp. 34, 35–36, 45.

Eckman quotes Layton's "Poetess" and "Lines on Myself" as examples of the "kinetic" mode of writing, which is distinguished "by its ability to create the illusion of rapid movement." Layton's poems cited here are examples of the "conventional," rather than the "modernist," manner.

C38 Frye, Northrop. "Poetry." In *The Arts in Canada: Stocktaking at Midcentury*. Ed. Malcolm Ross. Toronto: Macmillan, 1958, p. 89.

In Layton's work ". . . the body . . . is closer to spirit than the intellect." He is "an academic rather than a romantic poet."

C39 Rashley, R.E. *Poetry in Canada: The First Three Steps*. Toronto: Ryerson, 1958, pp. 133, 134–35, 147, 159.

Layton's early work is impelled by a destructive attitude towards "religion and romance and the formal structure of civilization." His more recent poetry retains this attitude, but conveys it in a more "clear, forceful, poetic manner."

C40 [Biographical Note.] *Canadian Author & Bookman*, 34, No. 1 (Spring 1958), 11.

Brief biographical data.

C41 Kenner, Hugh. "Columbus's Log-Book." Rev. of *The Selected Letters of William Carlos Williams*. Ed. John C. Thirlwall. *Poetry* [Chicago], 92 (June 1958), 177.

Along with poets writing in England and America, the Layton-Dudek-Souster group is central to the poetic activity of the 1950s.

C42 Wilson, Milton. "Other Canadians *and After*." Association of Canadian University Teachers of English, Edmonton. June 1958. Printed in *The Tamarack Review*, No. 9 (Autumn 1958), pp. 84, 86–89, 90, 92. Rpt. in *Masks of Poetry: Canadian Critics on Canadian Verse*. Ed. A.J.M. Smith. New Canadian Library Original, No. O3. Toronto: McClelland and Stewart, 1962, pp. 130, 132–35, 137, 138. Rpt. (abridged) in *Irving Layton: The Poet and His Critics*. Ed. Seymour Mayne. Toronto: McGraw-Hill Ryerson, 1978, pp. 70–73, 74, 76.

Two myths are examined and discredited: Layton is a neglected genius, and he learned to write through hard work and prolific output. Layton is a "learned poet" who does not distinguish between literature and life. Like Canadian poetry in general, Layton's work is not a product of historical development, so he can draw from whatever sources he sees fit.

C43 "Arts and Letters: Far Out." *Time*, Can. Ed., 7 July 1958, p. 9.

With Aviva Cantor, Irving Layton has written twenty-three songs, five of which have been put under contract by Peer International Corp., an American song-publishing company.

C44 Dahlberg, Edward. Letter to Jonathan Williams. 3 Aug. 1958. Printed in *Edward Dahlberg: A Tribute. Essays, Reminiscences, Correspondences, Tributes*. Ed. Jonathan Williams. New York: David Lewis, 1970, p. 95.

Layton's "vernacular affectation" lacks authenticity, but he "has feeling." "He is afraid of being serious . . . ."

C45 Dudek, Louis. "Patterns in Recent Canadian Poetry." *Culture*, 19 (Dec. 1958), 404, 406, 407, 409, 411, 413. Rpt. in *The Making of Modern Poetry in Canada: Essential Articles on Contemporary Canadian Poetry in English*. Ed. Louis Dudek and Michael Gnarowski. Toronto: Ryerson, 1967, pp. 276, 278, 279, 280, 282, 284. Rpt. in *Selected Essays and Criticism*. By Louis Dudek. Ottawa: Tecumseh, 1978, pp. 99, 102, 103, 104, 106, 109.

Layton, along with Raymond Souster and Louis

Dudek, was the first poet to write "truly Canadian and realistic modern poetry." His latest poetry, however, is "wellnigh demented."

C46 "The Canadian Muse." *The Times Literary Supplement* [London], 19 Dec. 1958, p. 735.
In a review of Ralph Gustafson's *The Penguin Book of Canadian Verse*, Layton is described as the " 'father-figure' " of Canadian poetry, with poetry now as natural to him "as the very things he writes about."

C47 Rome, David. *A Selected Bibliography of Jewish Canadiana*. Introd. Samuel Bronfman. Montreal: Canadian Jewish Congress and The Jewish Public Library, 1959, Literature Sec., pp. 5–6.
A list of Layton's books to 1959 and several poems published in periodicals.

C48 "Irving Layton to Address Sisterhood Meeting." *Shaare Zion Congregation* [Montreal], 2 Jan. 1959, p. 4.
Layton will speak at the Sisterhood Hospitality Tea. A short biographical portrait is sketched.

C49 Cohen, Leonard. "Irving Layton." *Congress Bulletin* [Canadian Jewish Congress], May 1959, p. 3.
Brief biographical information.

C50 Wilson, Milton. "Recent Canadian Verse." *Queen's Quarterly*, 66 (Summer 1959), 271. Rpt. in *Recent Canadian Verse*. Gen. ed. Milton Wilson. Kingston: Jackson, [1959], p. 4.
Layton's poetry abounds with "unresolved contradiction," the "mixture of cruelty and compassion at the heart of things." While death is a curse, it is also a consolation.

C51 Dudek, Louis. "The Transition in Canadian Poetry." *Culture*, 20 (Sept. 1959), 284, 293–94, 295. Rpt. (abridged) in *Irving Layton: The Poet and His Critics*. Ed. Seymour Mayne. Toronto: McGraw-Hill Ryerson, 1978, p. 77.
Layton has been a key figure in freeing Canadian poetry from "outworn values." Until 1953, he "proclaimed the shocking unpuritanical values of an overturned morality"; after 1953, he tried with limited success to communicate his own "dynamic conception of reality."

C52 Ciardi, John. "Sounds of the Poetic Voice." *Saturday Night* [New York], 24 Oct. 1959, p. 53.
The voice of Canadian poetic maturity, "not only matured but personal," may be heard in the poetry of Irving Layton.

C53 Fairbairn, Dave. "The Hotbed." *The Brunswickian* [Univ. of New Brunswick], 15 Jan. 1960, p. 3.
Layton is praised for his frankness and versatility.

C54 Maag, Trudy. "Layton: Outspoken Poet at Art Centre Tomorrow Night." *The Brunswickian* [Univ. of New Brunswick], 15 Jan. 1960, p. 3.
Layton is praised for his energy, vitality, and poetic talents.

C55 Callwood, June. "The Lusty Laureate from the Slums." *Toronto Star Weekly* [*Toronto Daily Star*], 6 Feb. 1960, pp. 10–12, 21. Rpt. in *Irving Layton: The Poet and His Critics*. Ed. Seymour Mayne. Toronto: McGraw-Hill Ryerson, 1978, pp. 107–16.
Callwood describes Layton's atypical (for a poet) nature and his skill as a teacher. She depicts his home background and traces his development as both a person and a writer to his present level of accomplishment.

C56 Bernstein, Nat. "'Canadians Not Aware of Tradition,' Layton." *The Monitor* [Montreal], 17 March 1960, pp. 1, 19.

Layton criticizes the Canadian public for its philistinism and the educational system for the way it stifles talent.

C57 "Literature Awards." *The Gazette* [Montreal], 29 March 1960.

Layton is pictured along with Hugh MacLennan, Governor-General Vanier, and Chairman of the Canada Council Brooke Claxton on the occasion of his winning of the Governor-General's Award for poetry.

C58 West, Paul. "Ethos and Epic: Aspects of Contemporary Canadian Poetry." *Canadian Literature*, No. 4 (Spring 1960), pp. 8, 9, 15.

"The Bull Calf" illustrates the distinctive Canadian manner of utterance, which has a "thumping, emphatic and non-iambic quality."

C59 Burridge, T.D. "Feels Canada 'Immune' to Layton Malaise." Letter. *The Montreal Star*, 1 June 1960, p. 10.

Burridge disagrees with Layton's contention concerning the failure of the summit (B847).

C60 Birney, Earle. "Books and Bookmen." *The Vancouver Sun*, 20 Aug. 1960, p. 5.

Birney compares Mordecai Richler's and Irving Layton's attitudes toward being a Canadian writer. Birney prefers Layton's positive attitude to Richler's disdain. But where a poet lives is not important. The poet's "roots are . . . in his language."

C61 Wilson, Milton. "Klein's Drowned Poet: Canadian Variations on an Old Theme." *Canadian Literature*, No. 6 (Autumn 1960), pp. 11, 16–17.

Wilson closes his article with some thoughts on the relation of Layton's poetry to the theme of the drowned poet, particularly as shown in "The Cold Green Element" and "Whatever Else Poetry Is Freedom."

C62 Watt, F.W. "Canada." In *The Commonwealth Pen: An Introduction to the Literature of the British Commonwealth*. Ed. A.L. McLeod. Ithaca, N.Y.: Cornell Univ. Press, 1961, p. 31.

Layton's defiance of self-conscious literary styles has not prevented him from "technical experiments" and "traditional verse."

C63 Webster, Norman. "'Significant' Beatniks Give a Boost to Poetry — Layton." *Sherbrooke Daily Record*, 12 Jan. 1961, pp. 1, 5.

On the occasion of a visit to Bishop's University, Layton praises the beat poets for depicting a "different America," but feels there is not much good poetry being written at present.

C64 "Nature and Fantasy." Rev. of *The Oxford Book of Canadian Verse: In English and French*, ed. A.J.M. Smith. *The Times Literary Supplement* [London], 13 Jan. 1961, p. 24.

In this review, the writer observes that Layton has the same energy, faith, and optimism as E.J. Pratt, but lacks his compassion.

C65 Farrell, Alexander. "Golden Age of Poetry." *Winnipeg Free Press*, 28 April 1961, p. 56.

During a seminar conducted at Bishops University by Desmond Pacey and Ralph Gustafson, Pacey cites *A Red Carpet for the Sun* as "probably the best single volume of verse published anywhere in the world during the decade."

C66 "Competition in Arts Draws Fire from Poet." *Toronto Daily Star*, 8 May 1961, p. 8.

In a talk to the First Unitarian Congregation, Layton is critical of The Canada Council's competitive nature. He comments also on the importance of the writer's function in today's society and the necessity for enthusiastic teachers in our schools.

C67 Schecter, Bayla. "Layton Enumerates Enemies." *McGill Daily*, 17 Nov. 1961, p. 2.

The writer's main enemies are the public, "which is conventional and herd-like," and journalists, who cannot understand the unrespectable and the unconventional.

C68 Pearson, Alan. "Lost in the Feud: Is It Worth 27 Cents?". *Canada Month*, Dec. 1961, pp. 39–40.

Pearson describes Walter O'Hearn's "To a Slopshire Lad" (C696), a poem in *The Montreal Star*, criticizing Layton for his introduction to *Poems for 27 Cents*, and Layton's response (B848).

C69 "Layton, Irving." *The Reader's Encyclopaedia of American Literature* (1962).

A brief bio-critical note. Layton's poetry is "full of protest."

C70 Mathews, John Pengwerne. *Tradition in Exile: A Comparative Study of Social Influences on the Development of Australian and Canadian Poetry in the Nineteenth Century*. Toronto: Univ. of Toronto Press, 1962, p. 148.

While Layton has denounced academic poetry, his work remains "intellectual in conception and not concerned with reaching a mass audience."

C71 Finnigan, Joan. "Canadian Poetry Finds Its Voice in a Golden Age." *The Globe Magazine* [*The Globe and Mail*] [Toronto], 20 Jan. 1962, pp. 11, 14. Rpt. ("Joan Finnegan") in *The Making of Modern Poetry in Canada: Essential Articles on Contemporary Canadian Poetry in English*. Ed. Louis Dudek and Michael Gnarowski. Toronto: Ryerson, 1967, pp. 235, 238, 240.

Layton "stole the day" in his reading at the Canadian Conference of the Arts at the O'Keefe Centre in May of 1961. He has "done the most to upset the public stereotype of the Canadian poet."

C72 "Layton Compares Frye to Harem Eunuch." *The Campus* [Bishop's Univ.], 14 March 1962.

At a student conference on creative writing held in Toronto, Layton lashes out at academic critics, particularly Northrop Frye, for teaching without creating.

C73 Colombo, John Robert. "A Conference on Creative Writing." *The Canadian Forum*, April 1962, pp. 13, 15.

Layton was a vocal member of the last day's panel (along with Desmond Pacey, Jay Macpherson, and Pierre Trudeau) at the first Student Conference on Creative Writing at the University of Toronto in February 1962. Layton responds in the May issue of *The Canadian Forum* (B851).

C74 Ellenbogen, George. "An Open Letter to Irving Layton." *Cataract*, No. 3 (July 1962), pp. [40–41].

Ellenbogen criticizes Layton for taking potshots at Louis Dudek, who has done much for many young poets. Layton is still a great fighter, but should direct his attacks at more appropriate targets.

C75 Francis, Wynne. "Montreal Poets of the Forties." *Canadian Literature*, No. 14 (Autumn 1962), pp. 21–34. Rpt. in *A Choice of Critics: Selections from* Canadian Literature. Ed. George Woodcock. Toronto: Oxford Univ. Press, 1966, pp. 36–52.

Layton played an important role in *First Statement*; he was one of the last of John Sutherland's friends to break with him. Canada's "most significant" poet, Layton had his poetic development strongly influenced by both the *Preview* and *First Statement* poets.

C76 Davey, Frank. "Brief Review." TISH, Sept. 1962, p. 14. Rpt. in TISH: *No. 1–19*. Ed. Frank Davey. Vancouver: Talonbooks, 1975, pp. 273–74.

Layton's "Epigram for Roy Daniells" is flawed on many counts. This type of "unreasoned, clumsy, archaic, dull and cliché'd poem" is typical of the decline of Layton's powers to "personal invective." Continued in C77.

C77 Davey, Frank. " — More of Brief Review." *tish*, Oct. 1962, p. 9. Rpt. in TISH: *No. 1–19*. Ed. Frank Davey. Vancouver: Talonbooks, 1975, p. 290.

Although Tony Friedson and George Bowering defend Layton's "Epigram for Roy Daniells," Davey finds the poem either "unrefined anger" or "unrecognizable parody." Continued from C76.

C78 Dudek, Louis. "Canada's Literature of Revolt." *The Nation* [New York], 27 Oct. 1962, p. 270.

Irving Layton's early poetry lashes out at the social landscape. A probing of "the dark reaches of modern thought . . . becomes glaringly explicit" in some of his poetry.

C79 Fenson, Melvin. "Poet & Purse." *Canada Month*, Nov. 1962, p. 30.

Especially in his poems critical of Ben Beutel, Layton is representative of the resentment often felt by Jewish intellectuals against the traditionalism and bourgeois values of the Jewish community. The Canadian Jewish Congress provided a forum for this discussion, agreeing that Jews "have a right to revolt against their community's tradition and values."

C80 "Layton, Irving (Peter) 1912– ." In *Contemporary Authors: A Bio-Bibliographical Guide to Current Authors and Their Works*. Ed. James M. Ethridge. Vol. III. Detroit: Gale, 1963, 120. Rpt. (expanded) in *Contemporary Authors: A Bio-Bibliographical Guide to Current Authors and Their Works*. Ed. James M. Ethridge and Barbara Kopala. First Revision. Vols. I–IV. Detroit: Gale, 1967, 572–73. Rpt. (expanded) in *Contemporary Authors: A Bio-Bibliographical Guide to Current Writers in Fiction, General Nonfiction, Poetry, Journalism, Drama, Motion Pictures, Television, and Other Fields*. Ed. Ann Evory. New Revision. Vol. II. Detroit: Gale, 1981, 403–04.

Bio-bibliographical data.

C81 Katz, Sam. "Defends Rowse Views on Europe's History." Letter. *The Montreal Star*, 11 Feb. 1963, p. 10.

Katz defends A.L. Rowse's view of Europe's history as opposed to Layton's (B855).

C82 Belsen, A. "Layton's Competence as Historian Disputed." Letter. *The Montreal Star*, 12 Feb. 1963, p. 8.

Belsen disputes Layton's historical competence in his letter criticizing A.L. Rowse (B855).

C83 Lust, [Peter]. "Takes Layton to Task for Attack on Rowse." Letter. *The Montreal Star*, 12 Feb. 1963, p. 8.

Lust disagrees with Layton's criticism of A.L. Rowse (B855).

C84 Goodwin, Wm. Letter. *The Montreal Star*, 13 Feb. 1963, p. 10.

Goodwin supports Layton in his struggle against Walter O'Hearn (D73, B856), whom he says is behaving like a "tired schoolmaster."

C85 Hopkinson, Pauline. Letter. *The Montreal Star*, 13 Feb. 1963, p. 10.

In response to Layton's criticism of A.L. Rowse (B855), Hopkinson advises Layton to stick to poetry and leave history to the historians.

C86 Taaffe, Gerald. "Diary of a Montreal Newspaper Reader." *The Tamarack Review*, No. 27 (Spring 1963), pp. 49–62.

From October 1962 to February 1963 the readers of *The Montreal Star*'s "Letters to the Editor" column were treated to several controversies fostered by the eccentric and provincial nature of English-speaking Montrealers. Layton, one of the most frequent and effective contributors to the various debates, objects vigorously to Stanley Handman's harsh review of *Love Where the Nights Are Long* (B854) and to British historian A.L. Rowse's attack on Germany (B855). His main battle is with Walter O'Hearn, associate editor and critic for *The Montreal Star*. Layton's response to O'Hearn's derogatory review of *Balls for a One-Armed Juggler* (B856) is more hurt than belligerent.

C87 Bell, Del. " 'Maverick Poet' Provides Lively Evening for 200." *The London Free Press*, 22 March 1963, p. 4.

Layton's reading at the London Public Library was a great success. The contemporary poet, says Layton, should bring "awakening to the fact that a tragic situation is here."

C88 Scott, Peter Dale. Rev. of *The First Five Years: A Selection from* The Tamarack Review, ed. Robert

Weaver. *The Canadian Forum*, April 1963, p. 19.

"... the angry dignity of the poem to his [Layton's] dead mother ["Keine Lazarovitch 1870–1959"] is spoiled with the inane Thomas rhetoric" of the last line. (For Layton's response, see B858.)

C89 "Irving Layton (1912–   )." In *Écrivains Canadiens / Canadian Writers: A Biographical Dictionary*. Ed. Guy Sylvestre, Brandon Conron, and Carl F. Klinck. Toronto: Ryerson, 1964, pp. 79–80. Rpt. in *Canadian Writers / Écrivains Canadiens: A Biographical Dictionary*. Rev. and enl. ed. Ed. Guy Sylvestre, Brandon Conron, and Carl F. Klinck. Toronto: Ryerson, 1966, pp. 89–90.

Layton has a command of "originality and freshness of imagery, a telling irony and prophetic indignation, frequently coupled with surprising sympathy and tenderness, and a versatility of form and technique."

C90 Rome, David. *Jews in Canadian Literature: A Bibliography*. Rev. ed. Vol. 1. Montreal: Canadian Jewish Congress and Jewish Public Library, 1964, 139–56 [plus 27 inserted leaves.]

More than just an enumeration of works by and about Layton, this entry takes the form of a running commentary on Layton's work based on a chronological overview of his writing career to 1964.

C91 Woodcock, George. "Away from Lost Worlds." In *On Contemporary Literature*. Ed. Richard Kostelanetz. New York: Avon, 1964, pp. 100, 105–06. Rpt. ("Away from Lost Worlds: Notes on the Development of a Canadian Literature") in *Odysseus Ever Returning: Essays on Canadian Writers and Writing*. By George Woodcock. Introd. W.H. New. Toronto: McClelland and Stewart, 1970, pp. 4, 9. Rpt. in *Readings in Commonwealth Literature*. Ed. William

Walsh. Oxford: Clarendon, 1973, pp. 212, 217–18.

Although a lot of other rubbish sometimes obscures Layton's best poems, he can, at his best, communicate "a joy in the glory of life or a devastating contempt of life's enemies."

C92 Stern, Karl. "Berton, Layton Called Western Nihilists." *The Globe and Mail* [Toronto], 2 March 1964, p. 5.

Stern criticizes Pierre Berton and Irving Layton for their "pathological views on sex."

C93 Tumpane, Frank. "Sincerely Yours." *The Telegram* [Toronto], 3 March 1964, Fourth Sec., p. 31.

Layton's comments on sex (C558) are an insensitive effort for publicity.

C94 Allen, A.W. "Mr. Layton on Sex." Letter. *The Globe and Mail* [Toronto], 7 March 1964, p. 6.

Allen objects to Layton's suggestion of loosening sexual restraint.

C95 Mason, Grace A. Letter. *The Globe and Mail* [Toronto], 7 March 1964, p. 6.

Layton's views present the inner moral decay of our society.

C96 Young, C. Letter. *The Globe and Mail* [Toronto], 7 March 1964, p. 6.

Concentration on sex, as evident in Layton's letter, will ensure society's destruction.

C97 Harvey, John. "Mankind: The Conscience of Poets." *The Marxist Quarterly* [Toronto], No. 9 (Spring 1964), pp. 4–15.

Harvey criticizes Layton's "Poets: The Conscience of Mankind" (B983) for his anti-Soviet, anti-proletarian bias. The average Canadian is not, as Layton argues, indifferent to poetry. Unlike A.Y. Jackson, who believed in his community with the working man, Layton does not understand "the interrelationship of social interests." Once the "cold war propaganda" by people like Layton is swept away, debate in poetry and science will reach new heights.

C98 Richler, Mordecai. "Canadiana: One Man's View." *Holiday* [Philadelphia], April 1964, pp. 46–47.

". . . Layton is primarily an entertainer" on the Canadian literary scene. He and Leonard Cohen travel across the country giving readings "as a quasi-cultural Dean Martin and Jerry Lewis act."

C99 Richler, Mordecai. "Anyone with a Thick Accent Who'd Steal Milk Money from Little Children Can't Be *All* Bad." *Maclean's*, 4 April 1964, p. 52.

Much of today's writing is "pseudoserious," littered by half truths and stale conventions. Layton, more than any other Canadian poet, "illustrates the stylish cliché, the ill-thought-out rebellion."

C100 Schmidt, Adolph. "Die Kriegschuld der Deutschen." *Der Courier* [Toronto], 30 July 1964.

Schmidt discusses Layton's disagreement with A.L. Rowse over German war guilt (B855).

C101 Francis, Wynne. "A Critic of Life: Louis Dudek as Man of Letters." *Canadian Literature*, No. 22 (Autumn 1964), pp. 8, 10, 13, 14, 15, 16, 20, 21.

The literary friendship between Louis Dudek and Irving Layton began with their editorial association, along with John Sutherland, in the publication of *First Statement*. Associations by Dudek with Lionel Trilling and others in New York led him to break with Layton and his "doctrinaire Marxism" about 1947. In 1951, with Dudek's return to Montreal, a reconciliation took place. But an attack on Dudek by Layton published in the Winter 1962 issue of *Cataract* (B849) finalized the rift that had been widening since 1956.

C102 Maltby, G.M. "Balls! A One-Armed Juggler." *The Carleton* [Carleton Univ.], 25 Sept. 1964, p. 5.

Maltby was disappointed with Layton's reading at Carleton, finding him "too comfortable." "He has sold out much of irreverence and ferocity for three meals a day."

C103 Vineberg, Dusty. "Poetic Quartet Ends Campus Tour." *The Montreal Star*, 31 Oct. 1964, p. 4.

Irving Layton, Earle Birney, Leonard Cohen, and Phyllis Gottlieb have just completed a poetry reading tour. Vineberg describes the final reading and his impressions of the poets.

C104 Goodwin, William. "Dudek Predictions Already Disproven." Letter. *The Montreal Star*, 5 Nov. 1964, p. 10.

Layton's inclusion in anthologies edited by Milton Wilson and Paul Engle disproves Louis Dudek's assertions (D83).

C105 Nathan, C. "Even Sick Poets May Turn Out Good Work." Letter. *The Montreal Star*, 5 Nov. 1964, p. 10.

A poet's sickness is completely irrelevant to an understanding of his poetry. (See B862 and D83.)

C106 "Letters: Poet's Progress." *Time*, Can. ed., 6 Nov. 1964, p. 16.

In the reading tour by Irving Layton, Earle Birney, Leonard Cohen, and Phyllis Gottlieb, Layton's flamboyant presence on and off stage was noteworthy.

C107 Stone, Sheila. "Dudek Credentials as Critic Defended." Letter. *The Montreal Star*, 6 Nov. 1964, p. 6.

Contrary to Layton's accusations, Louis Dudek's wisdom and concern still make him a centre of energy for many people. (See B862 and D83.)

C108 Robinson, Brian. "Brian Robinson Writes: November 7, 1964." *McGill Daily*, 11 Nov. 1964, p. 5. Rpt. ("Robinson vs. Layton") in *The Georgian* [Sir George Williams Univ.], 17 Nov. 1964, p. 6.

Layton had attacked Robinson for his review of Seymour Mayne's *That Monocycle the Moon*. Robinson responds by challenging Layton to a debate on the value of his poetry.

C109 Needemyer, Margot. " 'Plain Person' Finds Layton Stimulating." Letter. *The Montreal Star*, 14 Nov. 1964, p. 8.

Layton's "vision and judgement of today's life and morals is only an inspiration for the youth of tomorrow to try and make the world we live in a less narrow-minded, less backward and less prejudiced place." (See B862 and D83.)

C110 Buchan, Patricia. "Prof. Dudek Rated as Competent Critic." Letter. *The Montreal Star*, 9 Nov. 1964, p. 8.

Louis Dudek is a courageous reviewer and Layton's personal attacks on him are "highly distasteful and insensitive." (See B862 and D83.)

C111 Gale, B. "Mr. Layton's Letters Are Not Ingratiating." Letter. *The Montreal Star*, 13 Nov. 1964, p. 6.

Layton's reactions to criticism are childish and will only do him harm. (See B862 and D83.)

C112 Baglow, John. "Counsels Mr. Layton to Show Discretion." Letter. *The Montreal Star*, 18 Nov. 1964, p. 8.

Layton would be well advised to stick to poetry and forget the prose. (See B862 and D83.)

C113 Berke, C.S. "Considers Dudek Winner of 'Joust.' " Letter. *The Montreal Star*, 20 Nov. 1964, p. 6.

Layton's name-calling and exploitation of the press has had an adverse effect on public opinion. (See B862 and D83.)

C114 Robinson, Brian. "Robinson vs. Layton: Round Two." *McGill Daily*, 26 Nov. 1964, p. 5.
Layton refuses to debate because he is "plain stupid." "Elegy for Marilyn Monroe" is a confused poem full of banal language.

C115 [Biographical Note.] *Yes*, No. 13 (Dec. 1964), n. pag.
Layton possesses a "combination of worldly and academic experience." He is angry at "the abdication of poetry from the fact of life."

C116 Gnarowski, Michael. "Of Prophets and Multiple Visions." *Yes*, No. 13 (Dec. 1964), n. pag.
Gnarowski summarizes the controversy occasioned by Louis Dudek's scathing review of Layton's *The Laughing Rooster* in *The Montreal Star* (D83). Layton's response (B862) was followed by seven others, three on Layton's side (C104, C105, C109) and four against (C107, C110, C111, C112).

C117 Whittal, A.E. "A Paradox Evident in Layton Behaviour." Letter. *The Montreal Star*, 21 Dec. 1964, p. 8.
Whittal responds to Layton's letter (B864), stating that his behaviour is paradoxical.

C118 Rosebery, M.A. "Attack on Miller Discussion of Poetry Due to Misconception." Letter. *The Montreal Star*, 24 Dec. 1964, p. 8.
Layton's attack (B864) is the result of a misconception on the part of Layton.

C119 Paradis, F.X. "Layton Fulminations Draw Strong Protest." Letter. *The Montreal Star*, 26 Dec. 1964, p. 8.
Paradis protests against Layton's "Goebbels-like, but puerile and vituperative tirades" (B864).

C120 Beattie, Munro. "Poetry (1935–1950)." In *Literary History of Canada: Canadian Literature in English*. Gen. ed. Carl F. Klinck. Toronto: Univ. of Toronto Press, 1965, pp. 768, 769, 776, 778, 779, 781–83. 2nd ed., 1976. Vol. III, 279, 280, 287, 288, 290, 292–94. Rpt. (excerpt) in *Contemporary Literary Criticism: Excerpts from Criticism of the Work of Today's Novelists, Poets, Playwrights, and Other Creative Writers*. Ed. Sharon R. Gunton and Laurie Lanzen Harris. Vol. xv. Detroit: Gale, 1980, 323.
The descriptive Layton of the 1940s changes to the denunciatory Layton of the 1950s. While his poetic myth has its deficiencies, *The Improved Binoculars* "contains poems as good as any written in this country."

C121 Clark, Gerald. *Canada: The Uneasy Neighbour*. Toronto: McClelland and Stewart, 1965, pp. 382–83.
Nationalist Layton differs from internationalist Mordecai Richler in his concept of the ideal relationship between Canada and the United States. In his analysis, Layton "shows more maturity and discipline" than Richler.

C122 Frye, Northrop. "Conclusion." In *Literary History of Canada: Canadian Literature in English*. Gen. ed. Carl F. Klinck. Toronto: Univ. of Toronto Press, 1965, pp. 834, 846. Rpt. in *The Bush Garden: Essays on the Canadian Imagination*. By Northrop Frye. Toronto: House of Anansi, 1971, pp. 230–31, 246–47.
Some of Layton's work expresses a North American rebellion against repression. He demonstrates "not only the cruelty but the vulgarity of the death-wish consciousness." "The imminence of the natural world" is central to Canadian writing and much of Layton's work.

C123 "Irving Layton: A Catalogue Based on an Exhibition of Books from the Harris Collection of American Poetry and Plays in Brown University Library, Fall

1964." John Hay Library, Providence, Rhode Island, 1965. 4 pp.

Bibliographical data with a brief bio-critical note.

C124 Rhodenizer, Vernon Blair. *Canadian Literature in English*. Montreal: Quality, 1965, pp. 944–45, 963, 1047.

Brief bio-critical information.

C125 Wilson, Edmund. *O Canada: An American's Notes on Canadian Culture*. New York: Farrar, Straus, and Giroux, 1965, p. 91.

Layton has helped to rid Canadian verse of "Presbyterian inhibitions." Although his poetry is "audacious and full of high spirits," it is "not very arresting" and is "fearfully imitative."

C126 Davey, Frank. "Black Days on Black Mountain." *The Tamarack Review*, No. 35 (Spring 1965), pp. 63, 64, 67, 68.

The Black Mountain influence first entered Canada in the 1940s through Irving Layton, Louis Dudek, and Raymond Souster and has flourished here more than it has in the United States. (For Dudek's response see C132.)

C127 Gnarowski, Michael. "Anti-Intellectualism in Canadian Poetry." *Canadian Author & Bookman*, 40, No. 3 (Spring 1965), 4, 5.

Irving Layton and Raymond Souster are the best examples of the poet as Canadian proletarian. Layton's attack on Louis Dudek in *Cataract* is "abusive rather than critical"; his attack on Robert Finch lacks "freshness, originality or illumination."

C128 Goodger-Hill, Trevor. "To Urge Support of U.S. Policy Termed Compromise of Ideals." Letter. *The Montreal Star*, 27 May 1965, p. 6.

Layton's support of U.S. policy (B866) is a compromise of ideals.

C129 Hertz, K.V. "Irving Layton, Ferocious Poet." *Montreal '65*, June 1965, p. 23.

Perhaps no other contemporary poet confronts the nature of mid-twentieth-century man with the "ferocity and zeal" of Layton. He combines "delight and energy," confronting both "the horror and the light of human existence."

C130 Jones, D.G. "The Sleeping Giant, or the Uncreated Conscience of the Race." Annual Meeting of the Association of Canadian University Teachers of English, Vancouver. June 1965. Printed in *Canadian Literature*, No. 26 (Autumn 1965), pp. 11, 12–14, 20. Rpt. (revised) in *Butterfly on Rock: A Study of Themes and Images in Canadian Literature*. By D.G. Jones. Toronto: Univ. of Toronto Press, 1970, pp. 21–23, 26, 31.

Layton is one of those poets who reveals the limitations of such critical views as those held by W.P. Wilgar, T.E. Farley, and Warren Tallman, who argue that Canadian literature is essentially negative. In poems such as "The Birth of Tragedy" and "The Cold Green Element," the poet becomes like A.M. Klein's "nth Adam" or a "Christ-figure." Layton's "Mount [sic] Rolland" is an optimistic view of the mountain "opposed to a commercial and industrial society which tries to tame it."

C131 Thériault, Yves. "Irving Layton, Homme et Poète." *Montreal '65*, June 1965, pp. 22–23.

The French-Canadian novelist gives his impressions of Layton and the way Montreal is universalized in his work. "Irving Layton est celui de nos poètes qui porte présentement l'image canadienne le plus loin, et le plus vastement."

C132 Dudek, Louis. "Lunchtime Reflections on Frank Davey's Defence of the Black Mountain Fort." *The Tamarack Review*, No. 36 (Summer 1965), pp. 59, 61, 63. Rpt. in *Selected Essays and Criticism*. By Louis Dudek. Ottawa: Tecumseh, 1978, pp. 212, 214, 216.

Responding to Frank Davey's article (C126), Dudek states that Layton has been influenced by neither Ezra Pound nor William Carlos Williams. Layton writes "archaic stuff" in an "outdated metrical line" "that goes back to [A.M.] Klein and then to Marlowe rather than to any modern poet."

C133 McPherson, Hugo. "Canadian Writing: Present Declarative." *English* [London, Eng.], 15 (Autumn 1965), 213, 214.

Layton is "the dominant figure" in the recent flowering of Canadian literature. He "affirms the complementary creative forces of poetry and sex."

C134 Robertson, Heather. "Most of the Shock Has Gone Out of Sex." *The Winnipeg Tribune*, 6 Nov. 1965, Showcase, p. 1.

Irving Layton has now become respectable. In this article, which is based on an interview, Layton discusses the use of a persona in his poetry which is distinct from his personal life, and the importance for his work of being a Jew in Montreal.

C135 Gnarowski, Michael. "Notes on the Background and History of *Contact* Magazine." In Contact 1952–1954: *Notes on the History and Background of the Periodical and an Index*. Ed. Michael Gnarowski. Montreal: Delta, 1966, pp. 5, 7, 11, 27–28.

Layton's contributions to *Contact* receive brief mention.

C136 Klinck, Carl F., and Reginald E. Watters. "Irving Layton (1912–   )." In *Canadian Anthology*. Rev. ed. Ed. Carl F. Klinck and Reginald E. Watters. Toronto: Gage, 1966, p. 385. 3rd ed., 1974, pp. 388–89.

Klinck and Watters sketch a brief bio-critical introduction.

C137 Watters, R.E. "Bibliography: Irving Layton (1912–)." In *Canadian Anthology*. Rev. ed. Ed. Carl F. Klinck and Reginald E. Watters. Toronto: Gage, 1966, pp. 584–85. 3rd ed., 1974, pp. 682–83.

Brief bibliographical data including secondary sources.

C138 Watters, Reginald Eyre, and Inglis Freeman Bell. "Layton, Irving, 1912–   ." In *On Canadian Literature 1806–1960: A Check List of Articles, Books and Theses on English-Canadian Literature, Its Authors and Language*. Toronto: Univ. of Toronto Press, 1966, p. 116.

Brief bio-bibliographical data.

C139 Wetzstein, Ross. "The Sound of Silence Emerged Loud and Clear." *The Village Voice* [New York], 31 March 1966, p. 17.

During the final session of the International Writers Conference, Layton insisted that the writer must be hostile to society. He incurred a "bitterly hostile" attack from poet Norman MacCuaig.

C140 Lust, Peter. "Some Doubt Cast on Completeness of Germans' Repudiation of Naziism." Letter. *The Montreal Star*, 25 May 1966, p. 6.

Lust disagrees with Layton's views on Naziism in Germany (B876).

C141 Woodcock, George. "A Grab at Proteus: Notes on Irving Layton." *Canadian Literature*, No. 28 (Summer 1966), pp. 5–21. Rpt. in *Odysseus Ever Returning: Essays on Canadian Writers and Writing*. By

George Woodcock. Introd. W.H. New. Toronto: McClelland and Stewart, 1970, pp. 76–92. Rpt. ("Poursuite de Protée: Propos d'Irving Layton") trans. Rodolphe LaCasse. *ellipse*, No. 11 (1972), pp. 96–115. Rpt. ("A Grab at Proteus: Notes on Irving Layton") in *Poets and Critics: Essays from Canadian Literature 1966–1974*. Ed. George Woodcock. Toronto: Oxford Univ. Press, 1974, pp. 53–70. Rpt. in *Irving Layton: The Poet and His Critics*. Ed. Seymour Mayne. Toronto: McGraw-Hill Ryerson, 1978, pp. 156–73. Rpt. (excerpt) in *Contemporary Literary Criticism: Excerpts from Criticism of the Work of Today's Novelists, Poets, Playwrights, and Other Creative Writers*. Ed. Sharon R. Gunton and Laurie Lanzen Harris. Vol. XV. Detroit: Gale, 1980, 321–23.

While Layton has published much bad poetry, his best is sufficiently good and plentiful to make him an important poet. He adopts a romantic, rebellious stance, writing as a modern prophet whose divine inspiration puts him beyond criticism. His energy and inspiration leads him to write with great brilliance at times, although his emphasis on poetry as freedom leads him to adopt a clown-like mask and write many pieces which should not have been published. Layton writes as both lover and misanthrope; many of his best poems stem from an identification with the animal world and those people who are "outside the herd of hostile humanity."

C142 McCracken, Melinda. "Erotic, Sensual, Carnal, but Not Obscene." *Weekend Magazine*, 30 July 1966, pp. 16, 17.

McCracken narrates Layton's personal and poetic development to his present position as the " 'white-haired daddy of modern Canadian poetry,' " to use Layton's own words. Layton indicates pleasure at the way his Montreal roots have nourished a poetic vision of life and the way poetry is becoming more acceptable in Canada.

C143 Story, Norah. "Layton, Irving." In her *The Oxford Companion to Canadian History and Literature*. Toronto: Oxford Univ. Press, 1967, p. 444.

Layton "expresses the concept of the poet as a man in tune with nature, oriented toward the sun as a creative force, and agonized by the blindness, pettiness, and stupidities of men whose faces are turned to waste and destruction."

C144 Story, Norah. "Poetry in English." In her *The Oxford Companion to Canadian History and Literature*. Toronto: Oxford Univ. Press, 1967, pp. 647, 648, 649, 651.

Layton's contribution to the development of Canadian poetry in English receives brief mention.

C145 Handman, Susan. "Neo-Nazi 'Fact' Defies Dismissal." Letter. *The Montreal Star*, 23 Jan. 1967, p. 6.

Layton cannot deny the fact of the neo-Nazi movement (B875).

C146 Lust, Peter. "That CBC Interview." *Canadian Jewish Chronicle Review*, 27 Jan. 1967, p. 10.

Responding to Layton's letter (B875), Lust accuses Layton of being "more German than the West German government."

C147 Callaghan, Barry. "Irving Layton, the Pagan Pilgrim." *The Telegram* [Toronto], 4 Feb. 1967, Showcase, p. 22.

Layton has a keen awareness of evil, but, like the gypsies, he survives with gaiety. What sets him apart from other Jews and poets is his refusal to give way to either sentimentality or despair.

C148 Vineberg, Dusty. "Layton Engaged in Poetic Feud." *The Montreal Star*, 22 Feb. 1967, p. 62.

Layton, back from a visit to Germany as a guest of the Bonn government, has been criticized for his favourable views of modern Germany. In this article, based on a televised interview with Pierre Berton, Layton explains the reasons for his views.

C149 "Layton to Speak at Q.C.C." *Communique* [Bayside, N.Y.], 2 March 1967, pp. 1–2.

Layton will be reading at Queensborough Community College. "The poet is known for his lively style, vibrant personality and spirited attacks on orthodoxy, philistinism and hypocrisy."

C150 Lund, K.A. "Satyric Layton." *The Canadian Author & Bookman*, 42, No. 3 (Spring 1967), 8.

Layton's great energy finds its main outlet in his content rather than in any innovations in form. His central symbol is the sun, whose creative aspects are paralleled on the human scale by the phallus. Sexual love and the writing of poetry frequently merge, as both are aspects of creativity.

C151 Johnston, Grant. "Poet at the Pen — They Liked Layton." *The Gazette* [Montreal], 25 April 1967, p. 7.

Layton's reading at the LeClerc Institute (a prison) was highly successful. The reading was followed by nearly an hour of questions. Layton commented that they were "my most critical audience"; they asked him if he would return as poet-in-residence.

C152 "The Inner Voice." *Story* [New York], No. 1 (May 1967), p. 28.

This is a brief account of the changes of poetic and personal fortunes for Irving Layton and Leonard Cohen between 1958 and 1967.

C153 Bain, Freda. "Mr. Layton's Views Inspire Wonder." Letter. *The Montreal Star*, 21 June 1967, p. 8.

Layton's letter (B878) is a joke. His view of the struggle between communism and democracy is grossly oversimplified.

C154 Francis, Wynne. "Irving Layton." *The Journal of Commonwealth Literature* [London, Eng.], No. 3 (July 1967), pp. 34–48.

Layton burst on the Canadian poetic scene when poets like Bliss Carman and Archibald Lampman were the accepted norm. While many of his poems were written mainly for shock value, a significant number even from his earliest work are "perceptive and carefully wrought." While he is an innovator in subject matter, his style is "well within the conventions of nineteenth-century English poetry." Layton is capable of writing about love without being erotic. He views death as "a natural transformation of . . . [life's] energy"; ". . . his concern for crippled and dying animals" is original. His concept of the poet as both "a spokesman and guide" has drawn many readers, as have his vigorous personal and literary quarrels with critics and censors. While "The peak of Layton's influence is over," his poetic powers may not be.

C155 Purdy, Al. "Canadian Poetry in English since 1867." *Journal of Commonwealth Literature* [London, Eng.], No. 3 (July 1967), pp. 26–28.

Layton is a tradition-breaker in content, but a traditionalist in form. He "is a striking and magnificent poet."

C156 French, William. "Poets' Conference: Not Exactly Socko." *The Globe and Mail* [Toronto], 9 Sept. 1967, p. 13.

At Expo's World Conference of Poets, Layton

objected strenuously to A.J.M. Smith's suggestion that poetry should not attempt to be popular.

C157 Hauer, Benjamin. "Poet Irving Layton's Survey on Israel Found Sadly Wanting." Letter. *The Montreal Star*, 21 March 1968, p. 10.

Layton's article (B998) is wrong in attributing agnostic views to the majority of Israelis.

C158 Attwood, D.W. "Irving Layton's View of India Found Taken from Wrong Grandstand." Letter. *The Montreal Star*, 4 June 1968, p. 8.

Layton's article (B1002) is grossly misleading. His image of Indians as "the carefree slave is really meant to console the conscience of westerners."

C159 Shapiro, Sraya. "Canadian View of Israelis." *Jerusalem Post Magazine*, 2 Aug. 1968, p. 9.

Occasioned by Layton's trip to Israel, Shapiro discusses various views that Layton holds. Layton may be attracted to Israel because of its "inseparable link between politics and life."

C160 Dobbs, Kildare. "Eagle Is Readied for Chopping Block." *Toronto Daily Star*, 5 Sept. 1968, p. 23.

In a review of *The New Romans: Candid Canadian Opinions of the U.S.*, Dobbs terms Irving Layton a "dollar-dazzled Whitman," and his "Hymn to the Republic" obsequious bootlicking. (For Layton's response, see B882.)

C161 New, William H. "A Wellspring of Magma: Modern Canadian Writing." *Twentieth Century Literature*, 14 (Oct. 1968), 125–26.

Poems like Layton's "Misunderstanding" express a "Canadian ironic arrogance."

C162 Sommer, Richard. "Richard Sommer Replies." *Canadian Dimension*, 5, No. 7 (Dec.–Jan. 1968–69), 2.

Sommer's review of Layton's *The Shattered Plinths* (D110) occasioned an energetic response from Layton (B883), which this letter immediately follows. The glorification of violence in Layton's work and his confusion of ambition with devotion to his art is especially objectionable. Sommer regrets that the inbred nature of the Canadian literary world makes honest criticism difficult.

C163 Francis, Wynne. Preface. In *Selected Poems*. By Irving Layton. Ed. Wynne Francis. Toronto: McClelland and Stewart, 1969, n. pag. Rpt. (excerpt) in *Modern Commonwealth Literature: A Library of Literary Criticism*. Ed. John H. Ferres and Martin Tucker. New York: Frederick Ungar, 1977, pp. 301–02.

Although Layton's indifference to editing, his polemical forewords, and his "protean nature" have discouraged critics, he deserves greater critical consideration. Passion, "with its connotation of both suffering and joy," is the common denominator of his work. ". . . suffering rage and defiant exultation suffuse all his poetry . . . ."

C164 Geddes, Gary. "Irving Layton (b. 1912)." In *20th Century Poetry and Poetics*. Ed. Gary Geddes. Toronto: Oxford Univ. Press, 1969, p. 589. 2nd ed., 1973, pp. 630–31.

Layton's poetry combines violence with sentimentality; with the exception of a few poems, it suffers from his inability to reconcile the opposing roles of the poet as "public spokesman" and "clear-thinking analyst."

C165 Moisan, Clément. *L'âge de la littérature canadienne: essai*. Collection Constantes, Vol. XIX. Montréal: HMH, 1969, 113, 120, 121, 128.

"Le vrai Layton n'est pas un satirique, c'est un

poète élégiaque, le poète de l'amour, dont la technique consiste à unir sans cesse romantisme et ironie."

C166 [Veldhuis, B.A.] "Rant #1." Editorial. *Collage* [McMaster Univ.], 23 Jan. 1969, p. 2. Rpt. in *The Ontarion* [Univ. of Guelph], 23 Jan. 1969. Rpt. in *Collage* [McMaster Univ.], 7 Feb. 1969, pp. 4–5.

Layton's poetry is "hugely insipid and consistently inconsequential." As a writer-in-residence at the University of Guelph, he is only "a pleasant peacock mascott."

C167 [Veldhuis, B.A.] "Anapestics." *Collage* [McMaster Univ.], 7 Feb. 1969, p. 3.

In a parody of new criticism, Veldhuis ironically dissects the various levels of meanings possible in each statement in the following line from Layton's letter in the same issue (B884): "Certainly I find the interest in that area of my body significant, as I do the reference to my codpiece which since I am unable to locate it on my person, appears to have gotten stuck in his throat."

C168 Chapin, Jane. "Layton." *Campus* [Univ. of Guelph], 1, No. 4 (Feb. 1969), 9.

Layton's salary, while a poet-in-residence at the University of Guelph, is being paid by the student association. He is living in residence next to thirty students who are interested in poetry.

C169 Veldhuis, B.A. "Layton vs. Veldhuis." *Collage* [McMaster Univ.] 7 Feb. 1969, p. 5.

Veldhuis replies to Layton's letter (B884), which was written in response to Veldhuis' "Rant #1" (C166), dismissing Layton's comments as arrogant name-calling.

C170 McDonald, Marci. "Irving Layton Finally Forgives Toronto Its Stuffy Past." *Toronto Daily Star*, 16 April 1969, Entertainment, p. 20.

On the occasion of Layton's taking up a professorship at York University, he says that the centre for English-Canadian poetry has now shifted from Montreal to Toronto.

C171 Solomon, Michael. "The Jewish Light Goes On in Israel as Diaspora Candles Flicker Out." *The California Jewish Voice*, 9 May 1969, pp. 4, 5.

Layton states that "Diaspora Jewry is doomed." "The young generations must be taught that the essence of beauty, righteousness and poetry are to be found in the Bible."

C172 Dudek, Louis. "Poetry in English." *Canadian Literature*, No. 41 (Summer 1969), pp. 111–16, 118. Rpt. in *The Sixties: Canadian Writers and Writing of the Decade. A Symposium to Celebrate the Tenth Anniversary of* Canadian Literature. Ed. George Woodcock. Vancouver: Univ. of British Columbia Press, 1969, pp. 111–16, 118. Rpt. in *Readings in Commonwealth Literature*. Ed. William Walsh. Oxford: Clarendon, 1973, pp. 257–59, 261, 263, 264. Rpt. ("Poetry of the Sixties") in *Selected Essays and Criticism*. By Louis Dudek. Ottawa: Tecumseh, 1978, pp. 269–74, 276, 278.

Along with Al Purdy and Leonard Cohen, Layton is among the most popular poets of the 1960s. All three have indulged in self-promotion, although ". . . they haven't quite 'sold out.'" All belong to "the school of direct speech," "a reaction to the refinement of our predecessors." Layton has "visceral vitality," but he lacks the sophisticated complexity of poets like Margaret Avison and James Reaney.

C173 Correia, Natália. "Quem É Irving Layton." *Diario Popular* [Lisbon], 27 Nov. 1969, pp. 1, 3.

Correia writes, in Portuguese, on the occasion of Layton's visit to read in Lisbon.

C174 Geddes, Gary, and Phyllis Bruce. "Irving Layton." In *15 Canadian Poets*. Ed. Gary Geddes and Phyllis Bruce. Toronto: Oxford Univ. Press, 1970, pp. 278–79. Rpt. (revised) in *15 Canadian Poets Plus 5*. Ed. Gary Geddes and Phyllis Bruce. Toronto: Oxford Univ. Press, 1978, pp. 390–92. Rpt. [revised — "Irving Layton (b. 1912)"] in *15 Canadian Poets X2*. Ed. Gary Geddes. Toronto: Oxford Univ. Press, 1988, pp. 539–41.

Canada's most controversial poet, Irving Layton, has done much to extend the range of subject matter of Canadian poetry in work that at its best is "a perfect blend of passion and restraint." His main subjects are "sexual love, power, and imagination."

C175 Jones, D.G. *Butterfly on Rock: A Study of Themes and Images in Canadian Literature*. Toronto: Univ. of Toronto Press, 1970, pp. 11–12, 21–23, 26, 83, 88, 111, 128, 129–33, 134, 136, 138, 139, 163, 165, 183.

"The Birth of Tragedy" and "Butterfly on Rock" illustrate the present vitality of Canadian poetry. Layton's best poetry celebrates both life and death. In "A Tall Man Executes a Jig," he identifies "with a cosmic power that contains both creation and destruction, the darkness and the light." "Butterfly on Rock" combines a sense of "triumphant affirmation of life" with "insistence of the reality and individuality of death." In "The Birth of Tragedy," Layton adopts the role of Adam naming creation; in "The Cold Green Element," he becomes the swimmer, a common image in Canadian poetry.

C176 Jones, Joseph, and Johanna Jones. *Authors and Areas of Canada*. People and Places in World-English

Literature, No. 1. Austin, Tex.: Steck-Vaughan, 1970, pp. 3, 34–35.

Layton is more concerned with nature than are some of his Montreal associates.

C177 Smith, A.J.M. "Layton, Irving Peter." In *Contemporary Poets of the English Language*. Ed. Rosalie Murphy. New York: St. Martin's, 1970, pp. 632–34. Rpt. in *Contemporary Poets*. Rev. ed. Ed. James Vinson. New York: St. Martin's, 1975, pp. 879–92. 3rd ed. Ed. James Vinson. London: Macmillan, 1980, pp. 884–87. 4th ed. Ed. James Vinson and D.L. Kirkpatrick. New York: St. Martin's, 1985, pp. 481–83.

Layton is an "uneven poet," but his best poetry ranks with the best written in English today. He has a "romantic conception of the poet," but in "his handling of language, metre, and poetic techniques" he is "a thoroughly classical poet."

C178 Lieberman, Dina. "Dear Mr. Layton." *The Paper* [Loyola College], 26 Jan. 1970, p. 12.

Layton is marvelled at for his "sensitivity," "sensuality," and generally overwhelming insight into life.

C179 Rodriguez, Elizabeth. "A Report on the Poets at Festival 70 (Bishop's University)." *The Fiddlehead*, No. 84 (March–April 1970), p. 124.

Layton spent much of his time at Festival 70 "explaining his poetry to his circle of groupies."

C180 Richmond, John. "Four Montrealers Win Literary Honors." *The Montreal Star*, 14 April 1970, p. 70.

Layton objects to the presence of Warren Tallman, an American with little interest in Canadian poetry, on the jury to decide the winner of the Governor-General's Medal for poetry. He considers that Milton Acorn, not George Bowering, should have won the award.

C181 Dwyer, Peter. "The Canada Council Did Not Select the Poetry Award Jury." Letter. *Toronto Daily Star*, 18 April 1970, p. 13.

Layton's letter (B887) ignores the fact that the jury itself appointed Warren Tallman to the jury for the Governor-General's Awards as a replacement for the retiring Henry Kreisel.

C182 Gold, Jack R. "Let the Poet Stick to His Verse." Letter. *The Montreal Star*, 19 May 1970, p. 6.

Layton's support of American policy in Viet Nam (B889) is misguided. He should stick to poetry.

C183 Mandel, Eli. "Modern Canadian Poetry." *Twentieth Century Literature*, 16 (July 1970), 176, 181.

For Layton, as for many other Canadian poets, exotic landscapes become metaphors for the here and now. But Layton's "flamboyant assertiveness" is less central to Canadian poetry than the more objective work of Raymond Souster or Al Purdy.

C184 Djwa, Sandra. "Canadian Poetry and the Computer." *Canadian Literature*, No. 46 (Autumn 1970), pp. 44, 54.

Along with a number of other poets' works, Layton's poetry was entered on a computer to assess the frequency with which certain words were used. Viewing his work in the context of Canadian poetry will help explain his "image of man as a 'dis-eased animal.' "

C185 Scott, Don. Letter. *The Globe and Mail* [Toronto], 28 Oct. 1970, p. 7.

Layton's letter (B893) demonstrates a deficient knowledge of history. He should stick to writing poems.

C186 Gnarowski, Michael. *Contact Press 1952–1967: A Note on Its Origins and a Check List of Titles.* Montreal: Delta, 1971, pp. [2, 4, 10, 11, 12, 17, 19, 21, 22].

Gnarowski chronicles Layton's involvement and publications with Contact Press.

C187 Wad[dington]., M[iriam]. "Layton, Irving (1912–)." *Encyclopaedia Judaica* [Jerusalem]. Vol. IV (1971).

Layton is "Hellenistic rather than Judaic in his ethical approach." His writing is characterized by "aggressive masculinity" and concern with the role of the poet.

C188 T[homson]., P[eter]. "Layton, Irving (1912–)." In *Britain and the Commonwealth.* Vol. I of *The Penguin Companion to Literature.* Ed. David Daiches. Harmondsworth, Eng.: Penguin, 1971, p. 308.

A brief bio-critical note. Layton's "influence on the younger Canadian poets has been profound."

C189 Smith, Patricia Keeney. "Irving Layton and the Theme of Death." *Canadian Literature*, No. 48 (Spring 1971), pp. 6–15. Rpt. in *Irving Layton: The Poet and His Critics.* Ed. Seymour Mayne. Toronto: McGraw-Hill Ryerson, 1978, pp. 189–98.

Layton's vision of life and poetry as an expression of opposites leads him to explore both the positive power of the sun and life, and its opposite, death. Much of his poetry portrays a fascination with a creative figure closely allied to the Nietzschean "overman." While many elements of our society are life-denying, others, such as the protagonists of "For Mao Tse-Tung: A Meditation on Flies and Kings" and "A Tall Man Executes a Jig" express possibilities of creation, even though this implies destruction. The cycle of life and death, which occurs naturally in nature, is complicated in man by his awareness of death. Art and erotic love also imply both death and rebirth.

C190 Waterston, Elizabeth. "Irving Layton: Apocalypse in Montreal." *Canadian Literature*, No. 48 (Spring 1971), pp. 16–24.

"... Layton has moved from mystic contemplation of a moment in his experience in Montreal into a powerful universal vision." The sense of place in Layton's poetry is important, especially the symbolic use he makes of the city. In the 1950s, his vision of the city becomes more universalized. This view was further encouraged by trips to Europe during the 1960s. From the late 1950s through the 1960s, his attitude is one of ironic disillusionment, but his most recent poems reflect a calmer, more affirmative vision.

C191 Rosenthal, J. "Irving Layton Criticized, Praised for His Stand on Israeli Conflict." Letter. *The Globe and Mail* [Toronto], 16 April 1971, p. 7.

Layton's jingoistic attitudes (B897) run counter to the Judaic tradition of humanism and "deplete the moral capital Jews have so painfully accumulated."

C192 Stirling, Donald V. "Arabs and Jews." Letter. *The Globe and Mail* [Toronto], 19 April 1971, p. 6.

Layton's letter (B897), with its attacks on Stirling and the Christian church, is not the way to solve the complex Arab-Israeli situation.

C193 Gallimore, Ian. "Irving Layton." Letter. *The Globe and Mail* [Toronto], 3 May 1971, p. 6.

"There is ... no justification whatsoever for the vitriolic remarks Layton makes against Gentiles." (See B897.)

C194 Waterston, Elizabeth. "The Haloing Snake." *Alphabet*, Nos. 18–19 (June 1971), pp. 24–29.

"A Tall Man Executes a Jig" "returns poetically to the theme of anguish and suffering, and constructs a work that is both metaphysically and aesthetically satisfying and successful." "Analogical structure" aligns the elements of the poem into a suggestion of "mystic experience." The halo gives the poem "visual shape" and "conceptual unity." The snake is "the central, crucial item in the cosmos" and "the image of the mystic poet's poetic self."

C195 Ower, John. "An Over-Riding Metaphor: Images of Exile, Imprisonment and Home in Modern Canadian Poetry." MOSAIC: *A Journal for the Comparative Study of Literature and Ideas* [Univ. of Manitoba], 4, No. 4 (Summer 1971), 81, 82–84, 85.

Layton's "The Fertile Muck" and "Seven O'Clock Lecture" are "evidence that a sense of banishment and entrapment still haunts our society." The former "turns on the ironic and paradoxical notion of an exile from a suburban prison which is essential if the poet is to remain spiritually centred and freely creative." The latter suggests "that the cultural potential of the university may be frustrated, making it simply another place of imprisonment and exile."

C196 Jones, D.G. "Adam's Inventory: Aspects of Contemporary Canadian Literature." *Social Education* [Richmond, Va.], 35 (Oct. 1971), 595, 596, 599, 600, 601. Rpt. in *Readings in Commonwealth Literature*. Ed. William Walsh. Oxford: Clarendon, 1973, pp. 241, 243, 251–52.

In many of Layton's poems, he speaks as a mythic figure, representing "a vitality, an imaginative vision that does not die when Irving Layton dies."

C197 Ross, Alexander. "Irving Layton's Latest Exile: The Suburbs." *The Toronto Star*, 7 Dec. 1971, p. 39.

Layton has survived his rise to eminence and his move to Toronto. Much of his time is spent in reading manuscripts from would-be poets and helping people with their personal problems.

C198 Atwood, Margaret. *Survival: A Thematic Guide to Canadian Literature*. Toronto: House of Anansi, 1972, pp. 64, 77, 84–85, 189–90.

While many of Layton's poems are locked into positions of anger, in some of his nature poems, such as "For Mao Tse-Tung: A Meditation of Flies and Kings" and "The Birth of Tragedy," he transcends these alternatives. "A Tall Man Executes a Jig" is noteworthy for the protagonist's refusal to either curse or identify with the dying snake as victim.

C199 Geggie, Mary, and Peter Whalley. *Northern Blights: More Than Anyone Needs to Know about Canadian Poetry and Painting*. Morin Heights, P.Q.: Upbank, 1972, pp. 3, 6, 31.

Under the guise of Scurving Blayton, Layton's concerns with sex and his non-academic view of poetry are gently satirized. A poem by "Scurving Blayton" is also included (C720).

C200 New, W.H. Introduction. In his *Articulating West: Essays on Purpose and Form in Modern Canadian Literature*. [Three Solitudes: Contemporary Literary Criticism in Canada, No. 1.] Toronto: new, 1972, pp. xxii–xxiii, xxiv, xxv.

Layton's poems are committed to physical fact but are also free "from the world of everyday conventions," which has no vitality or myth.

C201 Reference Division, McPherson Library, University of Victoria, B.C., comp. "Layton, Irving Peter* 1912– ." In *Creative Canada: A Biographical Dictionary of Twentieth-Century Creative and Performing Artists*. Vol. II. Toronto: Univ. of Toronto Press, 1972, 157–58.

Bio-bibliographical data.

C202 Thomas, Clara. "Irving Layton." In her *Our Nature — Our Voices: A Guidebook to English-Canadian Literature*. Vol. 1 of *Our Nature — Our Voices*. Toronto: new, 1972, pp. 134–37.

Thomas' account of Layton's life and work emphasizes his fusion of the poet-seer and the Hebraic prophet. ". . . no one in our literature has expressed himself so forcibly, so unselfconsciously and, therefore, so effectively."

C203 Waddington, Miriam. Introduction. In *John Sutherland: Essays, Controversies and Poems*. Ed. Miriam Waddington. New Canadian Library Original, No. 81. Toronto: McClelland and Stewart, 1972, pp. 7, 8, 9, 10, 12, 14.

Waddington recounts Layton's associations with John Sutherland. He attempted to influence Sutherland towards Marxism.

C204 Watters, Reginald Eyre. "Layton, Irving, 1912– ." In his *A Checklist of Canadian Literature and Background Materials, 1628–1960*. 2nd ed. Toronto: Univ. of Toronto Press, 1972, pp. 11, 225.

Brief bibliographical data.

C205 Doyle, Mike. "The Occasions of Irving Layton." *Canadian Literature*, No. 54 (Autumn 1972), pp. 70–83. Rpt. (excerpt) in *Contemporary Literary Criticism: Excerpts from Criticism of Today's Novelists, Poets, Playwrights, and Other Creative Writers*. Ed. Carolyn Riley and Barbara Harte. Vol. II. Detroit: Gale, 1974, 236–37.

Layton, a traditionalist in technique, responds with complexity and ambivalence to the world around him. The most prominent aspects of his poetic personality are "poet, cocksman, teacher and misanthrope," which Doyle discusses in a number of Layton's poems. His criticisms of our society are not particularly original, and he does not, in his poetry, articulate a consistent alternate vision. Yet, there is a richness to his work and a combined awareness and defiance of his own mortality.

C206 Cannon, Wayne. "Layton Abuses Canadians; Prof." *Excalibur* [York Univ.], 19 Oct. 1972, p. 9.

Layton's criticism of the conduct of the Canadian hockey team in the U.S.S.R.-Canada series, and of Canadians generally (B901), reveals his deficient understanding of Canadian history. The day is past for such denigration of things Canadian.

C207 Mantle, K. "Canadians Are Spineless if Layton Cultural Leader." *Excalibur* [York Univ.], 9 Nov. 1972, p. 8.

Layton's letter (B903) proves that he is completely devoid of talent and should be ousted from his post as writer-in-residence.

C208 Craig, Jamie. "Poet Flashes His Ego to Expose His Talent." *The Vancouver Sun*, 17 Nov. 1972, p. 35.

Layton denies that age is diminishing his poetic fervour. He states ". . . he is never so fully alive as when writing a poem."

C209 Martin, Robert. "The Silver Seems to Mellow the Satyr-Poet Layton." *The Globe and Mail* [Toronto], 30 Dec. 1972, pp. 27–28.

Age has mellowed Layton, who is also now a Toronto professor. Much of his polemics and reputation was, in any case, more a mask than reality.

C210 D[avey]., F[rank]. "Layton, Irving (1912–)." In *Supplement to The Oxford Companion to Canadian History and Literature.* Ed. William Toye. Toronto: Oxford Univ. Press, 1973, pp. 184–86. Rpt. (revised) in *The Oxford Companion to Canadian Literature.* Ed. William Toye. Toronto: Oxford Univ. Press, 1983, pp. 436–38.

Layton incorporates the irrational in his poetry for the first time since Archibald Lampman and Bliss Carman. For Layton, ". . . the poem must convey truth, and truth can reside in the most ignoble and 'unpoetic' subjects and be expressed in blatantly non-poetic forms."

C211 Denham, Paul. Introduction. In *The Evolution of Canadian Literature in English 1945–1970.* Ed. Paul Denham. Toronto: Holt, Rinehart and Winston, 1973, pp. 1, 2, 3, 4–5, 6, 8, 11.

Layton is one of the few Canadian poets since A.M. Klein to examine the cultural conflict in Quebec. He has helped introduce some of the Black Mountain poets to a Canadian audience, and his refusal "to consider poetry as the preserve of an intellectual élite" has helped to widen the poetic audience in Canada. His work is difficult to classify.

C212 Gnarowski, Michael. "Layton, Irving, 1912——." In his *A Concise Bibliography of English Canadian Literature.* Toronto: McClelland and Stewart, 1973, pp. 63–66. 2nd rev. ed., 1978, pp. 74–77.

Bibliographical data.

C213 MacCulloch, Clare. "Cock of the Walk." *Alive* [Guelph, Ont.], No. 27 (1973), pp. 45–46.

Layton speaks with "effrontery, candour, and directness." For him, the poet is priest and poetry religion, deeply rooted in the rabbinic tradition. The current flourishing state of Canadian poetry, since 1945 the most substantial in the English-speaking world, is due in large part to Layton's efforts.

C214 MacCulloch, Clare. *The Neglected Genre: The Short Story in Canada.* Guelph, Ont.: Alive, 1973, pp. 12, 63–67.

MacCulloch discusses Layton's short story "Vacation in La Voiselle." There is a bond "between him and Ethel Wilson as social critic and commentator." His "concept of writer as prophet can be best witnessed" in the short story.

C215 S[tevens]., P[eter]. "Poetry in English." In *Supplement to The Oxford Companion to Canadian History and Literature*. Ed. William Toye. Toronto: Oxford Univ. Press, 1973, pp. 247, 253.

Layton's poetry has not changed much, but his more recent work does reveal a "new mellowness."

C216 Seymour-Smith, Martin. "Canadian Literature." In *Funk & Wagnalls Guide to Modern World Literature*. New York: Funk & Wagnalls, 1973, p. 335. Rpt. (revised) in *The New Guide to Modern World Literature*. 3rd rev. ed., London: Macmillan, 1985, pp. 353–54. Rpt. New York: Peter Bedrick, 1985, pp. 353–54.

Layton's "immense energy tends to obscure his incapacity . . . to organize his emotions." While "highly gifted," he is "overrated" and full of clichés and "childish rage."

C217 Strickland, David. *"Quotations" from English Canadian Literature*. Modern Canadian Library. Toronto: Pagurian, 1973, pp. 9, 10, 11, 32, 41, 46, 49, 61, 66, 70, 79, 92, 102, 106, 109, 125, 127, 128, 150, 151, 155, 159, 164, 165, 171.

Layton's works are quoted under the categories "Acceptance," "Action," "Adult," "City," "Death," "Dreams," "Egotism," "Freedom," "God," "Happiness," "Idealist," "Life," "Love," "Man," "Mediocrity," "People," "Poets," "Poetry," "Strength," "Success," "Time," "Virtue," "Woman," "Women," and "Writers."

C218 Walsh, William. "Canada." In *Commonwealth Literature*. New York: Oxford Univ. Press, 1973, p. 91.

Rpt. (revised — "The Shape of Canadian Poetry") in *The Sewanee Review* [Univ. of the South, Sewanee, Tenn.], 87 (Jan.–March 1979), 76–77.

Although Layton's poetry suffers from "an inappeasable interest in himself," he has "a rare rhythmic gift and a modern voice capable of song."

C219 Waterston, Elizabeth. *Survey: A Short History of Canadian Literature*. Methuen Canadian Literature Series. Toronto: Methuen, 1973, pp. 126, 138, 140, 146, 150–54, 163, 179.

". . . Layton faces and voices all the evil and the suffering in the world." While in some poems like "Composition in Late Spring" Layton sees himself as the "archetypal hero," others such as "De Bullion Street" convey a nightmarish vision of the city. ". . . particularly in his poems on death, [he] explores the dark destructive forces in the universe . . . ." Like the artists of his generation, Layton gives "voice to the inarticulate creation."

C220 Jones, D.G. "Myth, Frye and Canadian Writers." *Canadian Literature*, No. 55 (Winter 1973), pp. 8, 9, 11, 12–13, 15, 17–18, 20, 21. Rpt. (abridged) in *Contemporary Literary Criticism: Excerpts from Criticism of Today's Novelists, Poets, Playwrights, and Other Creative Writers*. Ed. Carolyn Riley and Barbara Harte. Vol. II. Detroit: Gale, 1974, 237.

Along with A.M. Klein and Robert Kroetsch, Layton is among the first Canadian writers to express "a confidence rooted in a clear conception of the function and capital importance of the imagination." He "is probably our first important poet . . . [to write] with an absolute conviction as to the significance of poetry and the power of the word." Layton's antagonism towards Northrop Frye stems from the contrast between the Dionysian imagination of the former with the Apollonian imagination of the latter.

C221 Mayne, Seymour. "Irving Layton: A Bibliography in Progress 1931–1971." *West Coast Review* [Simon Fraser Univ.], 7, No. 3 (Jan. 1973), 23–32.

Mayne's intentionally selective bibliography contains many items not found in later bibliographies. It consists of an introduction followed by three main sections: "Books," "Individual Items," and "Writings about Layton."

C222 Wall, Chris. "Crucified by Religion and Science, Love Is a Dying Art." *The Mirror* [Univ. of Saskatchewan], 14 Feb. 1973, Topics, pp. 2–3.

Layton says that love has become debased in our society to its physiological elements. Our modern puritanism inhibits the body and spirit working together in joyful sex.

C223 Granite, M.J. "Laytonmania." *Canadian Jewish Outlook*, March 1973, pp. 12–13.

Once a poet, Layton has been spoiled by success. His right-wing political stance, including his support of American foreign policy in Viet Nam and the imposition of the War Measures Act in Canada, is naïve and unconvincing.

C224 Anderson, Patrick. "A Poet Past and Future." *Canadian Literature*, No. 56 (Spring 1973), p. 20.

To Anderson's "surprise," he finds on returning to Canada that Layton is "writing like a *Preview* poet somewhat matured."

C225 Koenig, Wendy. "Maverick Poet Regards Himself as 'National Aphrodisiac.' " *The London Free Press*, 28 April 1973, p. 15.

Koenig interweaves an account of Layton's life with his attitudes to women. Layton inveighs against modern women who attempt to become like men. "They're clawing away at men in the damn competitive ruthlessness that they should be trying to fight."

C226 Elliott, Jas D. "Last Tango in Toronto." Letter. *The Globe and Mail* [Toronto], 2 July 1973, p. 7.

Elliott reacts with disgust to both the film *Last Tango in Paris* and Layton's letter (B906). "I resent Mr. Layton's slur on WASPS."

C227 Wilson, Milton. "Notebook on Layton." *The Tamarack Review*, No. 61 (Nov. 1973), pp. 56–73. Rpt. in *Irving Layton: The Poet and His Critics*. Ed. Seymour Mayne. Toronto: McGraw-Hill Ryerson, 1978, pp. 221–36.

Basing his discussion on *The Collected Poems of Irving Layton*, Wilson notes that many of the 1950s poems "took their occasion from a painting or a sculpture," or treat "objects and people as elements in a sharply defined visual design." Poems from *The Laughing Rooster* depict his Spanish experiences. *Periods of the Moon* is "technically the most accomplished" volume, containing many of his "best fantasies," while *The Shattered Plinths* faces "the shattering of political violence." Unfortunately, *The Collected Poems of Irving Layton* is arranged in a half-chronological manner, "which is far more meaningless than downright chaos."

C228 Gibney, Dee. "Modern Society Lashed as Beehive Utopia." *Hong Kong Sunday Post Herald*, 4 Nov. 1973, p. 3.

Layton criticizes "materialism and the death of emotion." "The poet is the person who insists on the validity and the right of each individual's dreams."

C229 Colombo, John Robert. *Colombo's Canadian Quotations*. Edmonton: Hurtig, 1974, pp. 335–36. Rpt. (revised). *Colombo's Concise Canadian Quotations*. Edmonton: Hurtig, 1976, pp. 51, 67, 88, 99, 108, 114, 115, 126, 127, 134, 141, 152, 173, 185, 191, 202, 210, 216.

Colombo selects quotations from Layton's prose and poetry.

C230   Davey, Frank. "Irving Layton." In his *From There to Here: A Guide to English-Canadian Literature since 1960*. Vol. II of *Our Nature — Our Voices*. Erin, Ont.: Porcépic, 1974, pp. 160–65.

Layton counters the concept of the poem as "cold" and "static" with "passionate, personal lyrics." His poetry is built around the interdependence of Dionysian raw energy with Apollonian form and intelligence. His poetry of "personal opinions, thoughts, feelings" differs from that of John Newlove, George Bowering, or Margaret Atwood, in whose work the tone and "the nature of the consciousness which they project is more important than their overt content." A brief bibliography is included.

C231   Fisher, Neil H. First Statement *1942–1945: An Assessment and an Index*. Ottawa: Golden Dog, 1974, pp. 5, 6, 9, 14, 16, 19, 20, 21, 22, 23, 24, 39, 40, 42, 43, 49, 50, 54, 55, 57, 60, 61, 62, 63–65, 66, 69, 71, 73, 74, 75, 77, 87, 88, 90, 91, 98.

Fisher discusses Layton's contribution to *First Statement*. An index to *First Statement* is included.

C232   Frye, Northrop. "Introduzione." Trans. Amleto Lorenzini. In *Il freddo verde elemento*. By Irving Layton. Trans. Amleto Lorenzini. Turin: Guilio Einaudi, 1974, pp. v–viii. Rpt. trans. [English] ["Introduction to *Il freddo verde elemento* (1974)"] in *Irving Layton: The Poet and His Critics*. Ed. Seymour Mayne. Toronto: McGraw-Hill Ryerson, 1978, pp. 251–54.

Layton survives translation well, often becoming "gentler and more delicate" in Italian. He is both lyricist and satirist, attacking those "who wish to castrate everybody with more love of life than they have, who make refined efforts to ignore their own bodies and so can only try to possess the body of others." With modern totalitarian states "merely a further development of the bourgeois death-wish," the poet must keep imaginatively free from the world. His image of the swimmer represents abandonment of "the separating consciousness."

C233   Mandel, Eli. "Criticism as Ghost Story." *Impulse*, 3, No. 2 ([Winter 1974]), 2–3. Rpt. in *Another Time*. By Eli Mandel. Three Solitudes: Contemporary Literary Criticism in Canada, No. 3. Erin, Ont.: Porcépic, 1977, p. 147.

Mandel locates the development of "thematic and cultural criticism in Canada" in essays by Northrop Frye, "Marshall McLuhan, James Reaney, Milton Wilson, Warren Tallman, D.G. Jones, and Irving Layton. The list is not random. . . . it suggests that a peculiarly literary version of Canadian personality has been developing for some time . . . ."

C234   Stevens, Peter. "Canada." In *Literatures of the World in English*. Ed. Bruce King. London: Routledge & Kegan Paul, 1974, p. 55.

Layton's poetry builds on the uneasy balance of Apollonian and Dionysian forces; ". . . the poet's mission . . . [is] essentially tragic because he recognizes that there can be no permanent reconciliation of the divided things."

C235   Shik, Kim Yang. "Canadian Poet Irving Layton and His Poetry." *Wor Men Ha* [Seoul], Jan. 1974, pp. 124–29.

Shik provides a general introduction in Korean to Layton's work.

C236   Crommelin, Jill. "Following a Long Tradition." *The West Australian*, 19 March 1974, p. 3.

Layton is not impressed by Australia's backwardness in sexual liberation, but admires the "lovely long legs" of the Australian girls.

C237 "Evidence of Opinion." IPLO *Quarterly* [Institute of Professional Librarians of Ontario, Toronto], 15, No. 4 (April 1974), 135–47.

Layton acted as an expert witness for the defence in the trial of Nathan Houser and Michael Haberlin for possession of obscene books for distribution. This entry is an edited transcript of the evidence.

C238 Pomeroy, Graham. "Latent Layton: A Male Chauvinist." *Canadian Review*, 1, No. 2 (April 1974), 3–5.

Much of Layton's poetry is "only pointed to subjugate Woman to the tyranny of Man." While he is not a misogynist, he characterizes woman by "banality, vanity, triviality, lasciviousness, and infidelity." When his "chauvinistic quackery" is revealed, his popularity will fade.

C239 Morley, Patricia. "Layton Stalks a 'Rare Bird.'" *The Ottawa Journal*, 11 May 1974, p. 40.

At the symposium on A.M. Klein's work held at the University of Ottawa, Layton criticized Klein for "an inability to assimilate the experience of man's capability for destruction." David Lewis leaped to Klein's defence.

C240 Dudek, Louis. "A Letter re 'First Statement.'" 13 June 1974. Printed in *Open Letter*, Ser. 4, Nos. 8–9 (Spring–Summer 1981), pp. 213, 214, 215, 216.

Both Neil Fisher's book on *First Statement* (C231) and Miriam Waddington's on John Sutherland (C203) lead to misconceptions of Layton's role in *First Statement* by dating his involvement several months later than it actually occurred.

C241 Shik, Kim Yang. *Shik Men Ha* [Seoul], July 1974, pp. 158–59.

Shik provides a general introduction in Korean to Layton's work.

C242 De Villiers, Marc. "The Apprenticeship of Irving Layton." *The Globe and Mail Weekend Magazine* [Toronto], 27 July 1974, pp. 8–9.

In an article based on an interview, Layton discusses his manner of writing, particularly his care with revision, and his successful rise from the Montreal slums. One weakness of Margaret Atwood's *Survival: A Thematic Guide to Canadian Literature*, Layton says, is that it ignores the affirmative Hebrew tradition in Canadian literature.

C243 Mayne, Seymour. "A Conversation with Patrick Anderson." *Inscape*, 11, No. 3 (Fall 1974), pp. 57–58, 63, 75.

Anderson states that he and Layton share a mutual admiration for each other's work.

C244 Tallman, Warren. "Wonder Merchants: Modernist Poetry in Vancouver During the 1960's." *boundary 2* [State Univ. of New York at Binghamton] [A Canadian Issue], 3, No. 1 (Fall 1974), 67, 68–71, 74, 77, 79. Rpt. in *Open Letter*, [Godawful Streets of Man, essays by Warren Tallman], Ser. 3, No. 6 (1976), pp. 185, 186–89, 192, 195, 197. Rpt. in *Godawful Streets of Man*. By Warren Tallman. Toronto: Coach House, 1977, pp. 185, 186–89, 192, 195, 197. Rpt. (abridged — "Wonder Merchants: Modernist Poetry in Vancouver during the 1960s") in *Irving Layton: The Poet and His Critics*. Ed Seymour Mayne. Toronto: McGraw-Hill Ryerson, 1978, pp. 246–50.

Unlike the Vancouver Modernists, Layton "concentrated upon himself as object and scarcely at all upon the language innovations necessary in order to enter Modernist writing." William Carlos Williams admired Layton's energy, but Layton remains stalled in humanism. He did, however, "break the hold over poetry in Canada of genteel ersatz English versification."

C245 "Trustees Ban Book on Canadian Poetry." *The Standard* [Elliot Lake, Ont.], 14 Nov. 1974, p. 1.
Layton's "Whom I Write For" was the main reason *Poetry of Mid-Century 1940–1960* was deemed unfit for use by Grade 13 students at Elliot Lake Secondary School, as judged by the Board of Trustees.

C246 Kropp, Marsha. "Lacombe, Lucien." Letter. *The Globe and Mail* [Toronto], 25 Nov. 1974, p. 6.
Layton's analysis of *Lacombe, Lucien* (B908) is "incredibly naive and arrogant."

C247 "Mid-Winter Meeting." *Ontario Bar News*, 3, No. 8 (Dec. 1974), 5.
Layton will be one of the speakers at the mid-winter meeting of the Ontario branch of lawyers.

C248 Richmond, John. "Italians Venerate Layton." *The Montreal Star*, 19 Dec. 1974, p. A14.
Layton discusses his highly favourable impressions of Italy after a successful week there in connection with the publication of *Il freddo verde elemento*.

C249 "Canadian Literature in Italy." *Italy Canada Trade* [Toronto], 10, No. 4 (Winter 1974), 68.
Layton is cited as one of the Canadian authors now becoming known in Italy.

C250 "Irving Layton in Italy: A Breakthrough in the Cultural Relations Between Italy and Canada." *Italy Canada Trade* [Toronto], 10, No. 4 (Winter 1974), 68–69.

Aided by the efforts of Amleto Lorenzini, Layton received an enthusiastic welcome for his readings in Milan, Vicenza, and Venice.

C251 Francis, Wynne. Preface. In *The Darkening Fire: Selected Poems 1945–1968*. By Irving Layton. Toronto: McClelland and Stewart, 1975, pp. xi–xv.
Layton's poetic vision is of "a world of becoming in which strife and tension are the mark of vitality and growth." Nature, death, and love are explored on a number of different levels. Man is not at home in the universe, but at his best aspires to a greatness that results in his separation from the masses. The poet often appears as a "social outcast." "The art of poetry is the crowning theme in Layton's work."

C252 Mandel, Eli. Foreword. in *The Unwavering Eye: Selected Poems 1969–1975*. By Irving Layton. Toronto: McClelland and Stewart, 1975, pp. x–xi.
This volume highlights the "development in his writing and vision." He demonstrates here his "imperial voice," which brings us "to a recognition of the historical and symbolic significance of the Jewish experience for our understanding of contemporary society and its values." Raging "like an old prophet," he helps us "know ourselves anew."

C253 New, William H. *Critical Writings on Commonwealth Literature: A Selective Bibliography to 1970, with a List of Theses and Dissertations*. University Park: Pennsylvania State Univ. Press, 1975, pp. 136, 153, 162–63, 298, 299.
Brief bibliographical data.

C254 Neice, David C. "Movie Criticism." Letter. *The Globe and Mail* [Toronto], 18 Jan. 1975, p. 7.
Martin Knelman is a world-class movie critic, far preferable to the "philosophical posturings" of Layton (B909).

C255 Wainwright, A. "Film Criticism." Letter. *The Globe and Mail* [Toronto], 31 Jan. 1975, p. 7.
Layton's insight into film warrants his being offered the post of film critic for *The Globe and Mail*.

C256 Wismer, Cathy. "Canadian Literature Comes of Age." *Canadian Mosaico*, Feb. 1975, pp. 24, 25, 27, 28.
The Italians received Layton's *Il freddo verde elemento* with enthusiasm; translator Amleto Lorenzini played an important role in bridging the gap between Italy and Canada.

C257 Francis, Wynne. " 'The Birth of Tragedy:' A Nietzschean Reading." *Waves*, 3, No. 3 (Spring 1975), 5–8.
This poem embodies the Nietzschean aesthetic that writing poetry "is a redemptive act, an affirmation of life." The circular structure of the poem suggests the inextricable relationship between birth and death. Unlike many of Layton's poems, this has "a sapient tranquility," and "the exquisite economy of line and the radiant translucence of a fine watercolour."

C258 Francis, Wynne. "Layton's Red Carpet: A Reading of 'For Mao Tse-Tung: A Meditation on Flies and Kings.' " *Inscape* [Univ. of Ottawa], 12, No. 1 (Spring 1975), 50–56.
"For Mao Tse-Tung: A Meditation on Flies and Kings" is one of those "imaginative keys" to a poet's work that Northrop Frye describes in his "Preface to an Uncollected Anthology." Images of insects, haloes, dancing, fire, and sun are at the core of Layton's vision, illuminating the themes of creative imagination, creative suffering, and the possibility of imposing aesthetic order on this suffering through a "triumph of the life force."

C259 Mandel, Eli. "The Months of Fire: Contemporary Canadian Poetry." *The English Quarterly* [Oromocto, N.B.], 8, Nos. 1–2 (Spring–Summer 1975), 3, 4, 7, 8.
However humble his beginnings, and whatever John Sutherland's claims, Layton is now more aristocratic than proletarian. He "defines for us one major aspect of modernism, its traditionalism, its humanistic assertion of man's centrality and his creativity."

C260 Wintrobe, Wanda L. "Layton Inspired by His Heritage." *The Canadian Jewish News* [Toronto], 28 Nov. 1975, p. 7.
In a speech given at the Associated Hebrew Schools, Layton discusses the way Christianity is responsible for anti-Semitism and the way his own work is rooted in the Jewish tradition.

C261 Gasparini, Leonard. "A 'Pretzel' Replies." *Books in Canada*, Dec. 1975, p. 40.
Gasparini defends himself and the state of Canadian book reviewing from Layton's attack (B910).

C262 Buri, S.G., and Robert Enright. "Perspective: Selection from an Interview with Al Purdy." CV/II, 2, No. 1 (Jan. 1976), 51, 55.
"Thank god for Layton," who was a salutary influence in the otherwise deadly 1950s.

C263 Farley, T.E. *Exiles & Pioneers: Two Visions of Canada's Future 1892–1975*. Ottawa: Borealis, 1976, pp. 135, 136, 137, 147–49, 150, 153, 156, 160, 195.
The poems in *A Red Carpet for the Sun* only partly bear out the bold declarations of the Preface; they are more "a rage to live, based, it would seem, on fear." As do many Canadian poets, Layton depicts the sun more as destroyer than as life-giver.

C264 John, W. David. Afterword. In *The Uncollected Poems of Irving Layton 1936–59*. Ed. W. David John. Ottawa: Mosaic / Valley, 1976, pp. 145–46.

This volume's goal is to include all of Layton's poems published to 1959 that were not included in *A Red Carpet for the Sun*. The arrangement is chronological by date of publication.

C265 Fee, Margery, and Ruth Cawker. *Canadian Fiction: An Annotated Bibliography*. Toronto: Peter Martin, 1976, pp. 147, 149, 150–51, 160.

Brief bibliographical data.

C266 Mantz, Douglas. *Landscape in Canadian Poetry: Major Authors Edition*. Toronto: n.p., 1973–79, pp. 21, 25, 30, 49–50, 69–70, 83, 88, 101, 109–10.

An annotated bibliography on the use of landscape in Canadian poetry based upon the works of major poets published in single-author book form.

C267 Mayne, Seymour. Preface. In *The Uncollected Poems of Irving Layton 1936–59*. Ed. W. David John. Ottawa: Mosaic / Valley, 1976, pp. 11–13.

"These uncollected poems serve as the seedbed from which spring the signature and major poems." They affirm Layton's range, development, and rejection of all forms of "genteel sensibility." Layton has changed "the literary sensibility of English Canada."

C268 McCullagh, Joan. *Alan Crawley and* Contemporary Verse. Foreword Dorothy Livesay. Vancouver: Univ. of British Columbia Press, 1976, pp. 1, 24, 39, 45, 51.

Layton is critical of P.K. Page's poems for being "blurred, misty, full of damp crawling things." Jay Macpherson's criticism of the unpoetic qualities of Layton's "the Girls of his Graduating Class" [sic; "To the Girls of My Graduating Class"] is also quoted.

C269 Purdy, Al. "The Ego Has It Both Ways: Poets in Montreal." *Northern Journey*, Nos. 7–8 (1976), pp. 127–34, 136–37, 138, 139–40, 146.

Purdy discusses his relationships with and impressions of Irving Layton, along with Milton Acorn, Louis Dudek, and other poets he encountered in Montreal. Layton "is childish and trivial, egocentric and overbearing, boastful and dangerously harmful to others influenced by him — but he remains in my mind as close to a great poet as any I know of who is still living."

C270 Woodcock, George. "Poetry." In *Literary History of Canada: Canadian Literature in English*. Gen. ed. Carl F. Klinck. 2nd ed. Toronto: Univ. of Toronto Press, 1976. Vol. III, 288, 291, 296, 298, 309–10, 312.

Layton's work has neither changed nor developed. The decline of his lyrical urge makes the *Collected Poems* of 1965 the most important volume published between 1960 and 1973.

C271 Slopen, Beverley. "Irving Layton's Crown of Thorns." *The Canadian* [*The Toronto Star*], 20 March 1976, pp. 4–6, 8.

Slopen describes the roots of Layton's concern with anti-Semitism, especially in his own life and the lives of his children. "The treatment of the Jew is a telltale sign of where mankind is going," which leaves little cause for optimism.

C272 Bauer, David. "Layton, Hitler Make the Same Point." Letter. *The Toronto Star*, 25 March 1976, p. B5.

Robert Fulford's review (D179) did not go far enough. Layton shares with Hitler a "leering contempt for the Christian spirit."

C273 Anderson, A.H. *The Toronto Star*, 31 March 1976, p. B5.

Contrary to Layton's "contempt for the human spirit," Christians helped many Jews at the time of the Holocaust. (See B913 and D179.)

C274 Fulford, Robert. "Why Did Layton Let Me Go On So Long, Critic Asks." Letter. *The Toronto Star*, 31 March 1976, p. B5.

Layton's criticism (B913) of Fulford's recent review (D179) and critical ability comes a little late in view of the number of Layton books Fulford has reviewed favourably in the past.

C275 Nielsen, Mary L. "Christianity Not 'Anti-Life.'" Letter. *The Toronto Star*, 31 March 1976, p. B5.

Evidence of the New Testament refutes Layton's criticism of Christianity as anti-life. (See B913 and D179.)

C276 Obodiac, Stan. "Millions of Christians Were Also Killed." Letter. *The Toronto Star*, 31 March 1976, p. B5.

Layton's attacks on Christianity avoid the fact that without the sacrifice of millions of Christians, Hitler could not have been defeated. (See B913 and D179.)

C277 Mandel, Eli. "A Hard Year to Scan." *Books in Canada*, April 1976, p. 5.

The Unwavering Eye: Selected Poems 1969–1975 and *The Darkening Fire: Selected Poems 1945–1968* "remind us of 30 years in which he [Layton] moulded the lines and images and forged the forms of contemporary writing in Canada."

C278 Layton, Aviva. "Steely Eye vs. Steely Eye." *Weekend Magazine* [*The Globe and Mail*] [Toronto], 8 May 1976, pp. 16–18.

Layton's former wife recounts the two meetings she and her husband had with Australian novelist Patrick White. The first was disastrous, but the second was more pleasant, with the writers sharing a "remarkably similar" vision of the world.

C279 Stevens, Peter. "The Fiery Eye: The Poetry of Irving Layton." *The Ontario Review*, No. 4 (Spring–Summer 1976), pp. 51–58.

In *The Darkening Fire: Selected Poems 1945–1968* and *The Unwavering Eye: Selected Poems 1969–1975*, Layton is both "detached observer" and "drawn into the whirling chaos of life and its terrifying paradoxes." His poems combine the transcendence of experience with "ordinariness." He is moving towards "a more clarified language"; some poems in *The Whole Bloody Bird (Obs, Aphs & Pomes)* possess a "meditative simplicity." His more recent poems show "a fiercely joyous approach to life" and "an acceptance of himself as man / poet in a search for communion beyond self."

C280 Parlow, Lela. "Advising Layton." Letter. *Books in Canada*, Aug. 1976, p. 26.

Parlow objects to attitudes expressed by Layton in *For My Brother Jesus*. She includes a poem "For My Brother Layton."

C281 Francis, Wynne. "Layton and Nietzsche." *Canadian Literature*, No. 67 (Winter 1976), pp. 39–52. Rpt. in *Irving Layton: The Poet and His Critics*. Ed. Seymour Mayne. Toronto: McGraw-Hill Ryerson, 1978, pp. 272–86.

Layton combines a fresh and original poetic vision with a close kinship to Nietzsche. His poetic output increased markedly in the early 1950s when Marx's influence gave way to that of Nietzsche. Nietzsche gave him a mythic structure for his poetry, including sun symbolism, the concept of art as a creation of the conflict between Apollonian reason and Dionysian chaos, and the concept of the superman. "The Birth of Tragedy" is the most lucid rendering of Nietzschean aesthetic. The Dionysian figure appears in his poetry as buffoon, crippled poet, caged artist, child, dwarf, and madman and is opposed to the spirit of rationalism, which is embodied in the bourgeois, the philistine, the bureaucrat, the academic, and the critic. Both Layton and Nietzsche become more Dionysian in their later work.

C282 Atwood, Margaret. Letter. *The Canadian Magazine*, 18 Dec. 1976, p. 22.
   Atwood replies to Layton's letter (B916), stating that Irving said ". . . women were good for nothing but f. . . ."

C283 Aster, Howard. Introduction. In *Taking Sides: The Collected Social and Political Writings*. Ed. Howard Aster. Oakville, Ont.: Mosaic / Valley, 1977, pp. 5–8.
   This book provides "the debate with public reality from which the major themes of Layton's poetic world have been molded." The dialectic between love and politics is at the heart of his work. Love, imagination, and politics are all means through which Layton confronts reality. This book "provides a composite portrait of a Canadian poet deeply engaged in the dilemmas and conflicts of our time."

C284 Jaihuin, Kim. "Irving Layton: Erotic Poetry — Commitment and Consciousness of Human Solidarity." In *College of Arts and Sciences Thesis Collection*. Vol. VI. Chonbuk, Korea: Chonbuk National Univ., 1977, pp. 13–29.
   An overall view of Layton's poetry in Korean. Jaihuin centres on the poet's theory of eroticism plus Layton's ideas on his own poetry, culminating in his ideas on the artifice of imagination.

C285 Kenner, Hugh. Introduction. In *The Selected Poems of Irving Layton*. Ed. Eli Mandel. New York: New Directions, 1977, pp. 5–8.
   "Layton's art is always to sound artless," but, whether done consciously or not, his poems here and elsewhere display a fine technical virtuosity. Living in Canada has provided him with a suitable freedom. Layton expects little from life, but the lover and poet may sometimes "break free."

C286 Mandel, Eli. *Another Time*. Three Solitudes: Contemporary Literary Criticism in Canada, No. III. Erin, Ont.: Porcépic, 1977, pp. 119, 120–21, 128, 130.
   The city Montreal appears frequently in Canadian poetry; it is transformed by Layton in the "fiery furnace of imagination."

C287 Mandel, Eli. "The Ethnic Voice in Canadian Writing." In *Identities: The Impact of Ethnicity on Canadian Writing*. Ed. Wsevolod Isajiw. Canadian Ethnic Studies Association. Vol. V. Toronto: Peter Martin, 1977, pp. 59, 62–63. Rpt. in *Another Time*. By Eli Mandel. Three Solitudes: Contemporary Literary Criticism in Canada, No. III. Erin, Ont.: Porcépic, 1977, pp. 93, 96–97. Rpt. in *Figures in a Ground: Canadian Essays in Modern Literature Collected in Honor of Sheila Watson*. Ed. Diane Bessai and David Jackel. Saskatoon: Western Producer Prairie, 1978, pp. 266, 270–72.
   Layton's version of ethnicity equates the poet with the Jew and creates "a male-female dialectic that constantly demands his assertion of masculinity."

C288 Mandel, Eli. Introduction. In *The Poems of Irving Layton*. New Canadian Library Original, No. O12. Toronto: McClelland and Stewart, 1977, pp. 4–8. Rpt. ("Introducing Irving Layton") in *The Family*

Romance. By Eli Mandel. Winnipeg: Turnstone, 1986, pp. 141–46.

Layton manages to arouse both admiration and annoyance in his readers. He is both "a troubled and troubling writer," expressing through his continuing evolution the incompleteness of life. The "grand design" of his work first became evident with *A Red Carpet for the Sun.* Between 1963 and 1969 his poetry changed to communicate a darker vision of the deficiencies of Europe and Christianity. Layton's work is "the most important body of poetry in our time; . . . it has given us knowledge of ourselves in visions struck like fire out of rock."

C289 Norris, Ken. Introduction. In *Montreal English Poets of the Seventies.* Ed. Ken Norris and Andre Farkas. Montreal: Véhicule, 1977, pp. x, xi. Rpt. (revised, expanded — "Poetic Honey: The English Poetry Scene in Montreal") in *Essays on Canadian Writing,* No. 6 (Spring 1977), pp. 67–68, 69, 72. Rpt. (revised — "Montreal English Poetry in the Seventies") in cv/II, 3, No. 3 (Jan. 1978), 8, 9, 10.

Younger Montreal poets of the 1960s followed either Louis Dudek's social realism, the Jewish tradition, or "poetry of personality" as practised by Leonard Cohen and Irving Layton. But none "could eclipse their [Dudek's, Cohen's, and Layton's] lyrical mastery or come close to cultivating more engaging poetic personalities."

C290 Coates, Alan. "Irving Layton." Letter. *The Globe and Mail* [Toronto], 18 March 1977, p. 6.

Coates responds to Layton's letter of 8 March (B918). Layton's involvement in this newspaper debate is a sad indication of his insecurity.

C291 Amiel, Barbara. "Much Ado about Irving." *Maclean's,* 4 April 1977, pp. 78–79.

Layton's sixty-fifth birthday party at the Casa Loma was highlighted by Sylvia Fraser bursting from a cardboard cake and the "force and attractiveness" of the poet himself.

C292 Frayne, Helen. "On Quebec: An Interview with Louis Dudek." CBC Radio, 10 July 1977. Printed in cv/II, 3, No. 3 (Jan. 1978), 38.

Dudek briefly mentions Layton as a "strongly political" writer and notes that he introduced Black Mountain poetry to Layton.

C293 Ross, Malcolm. "The Imaginative Sense and the Canadian Question." MOSAIC: *A Journal for the Interdisciplinary Study of Literature* [Univ. of Manitoba], 11, No. 1 (Fall 1977), 7–8. Rpt. in *The Impossible Sum of Our Traditions: Reflections on Canadian Literature.* By Malcolm Ross. Introd. David Staines. Toronto: McClelland and Stewart, 1986, pp. 154–55.

Irony is a distinctive note in Canadian literature. "Perhaps in no other Canadian writer is the mode of irony so complex, so many-faceted as in the work of Irving Layton."

C294 Hunt, Peter. "Irving Layton, Pseudo-Prophet — A Reappraisal." *Canadian Poetry: Studies, Documents, Reviews* [Univ. of Western Ontario], No. 1 (Fall–Winter 1977), pp. 1–27.

Layton's current exalted status in Canadian poetry is unwarranted. He is "a major symptom of much that is diseased in the modern sensibility." While he has a "lyrical gift" and "inborn intensity," his poetry is deficient on both stylistic and moral grounds. It does not stand comparison with the best Canadian poetry, let alone the best elsewhere. Too much of his work is cynical or barbaric, characterized by "a lack of compassion as well as intolerance." His understanding of Nietzsche is superficial, and his positions on religious, literary, and political questions are hardly revolutionary in today's society. Many similarities exist between his position and that of Northrop Frye; both "are really in the falsely prophetic traditions of gnosticism." Neither does the view of him as a "Swiftian satirist," held by Frye and Eli Mandel, stand up to analysis.

C295 Capone, Giovanna. *Canada il villaggio della terra: letteratura canadese di lingua inglese.* Bologna: Pàtron, 1978, pp. 5, 6, 17, 37–38, 39, 40, 49, 144, 172.

"I principali aspetti della sua poetica sono l'aspetto satirico e l'aspetto lirico: il primo motiva anche la sulta del suo linguaggio, fatto di vocaboli communi, di strutture non ricercate, di immagini spesso oltraggiosamente sessuali."

C296 Francis, Wynne. "The Farting Jesus: Layton and the Heroic Vitalists." cv/II, 3, No. 3 (Jan. 1978), 46–51.

Layton's emphasis on prophecy makes him atypical of contemporary Canadian writing, but links him with the tradition of "Heroic Vitalism" exemplified by Blake, Carlyle, Nietzsche, Lawrence, and Yeats. Francis focuses mainly on poems in *The Covenant*, showing that Layton's values are Heraclitean and Dionysian; he values freedom, reveres great men, abhors systems, and is committed to power, chaos, and a life of passion and virility. He attacks Christianity for its spiritual and physical aridity, claiming Jesus as a Jewish hero.

C297 Mathews, Robin. *Canadian Literature: Surrender or Revolution.* Ed. Gail Dexter. Toronto: Steel Rail, 1978, pp. 151, 152, 159.

Although Layton has rebelled against Canadian sexual inhibition, his "personalist" stance prevents him from being a true revolutionary.

C298 Mathews, Robin. "Developing a Language of Struggle: Canadian Literature and Literary Criticism." In *In Our Own House: Social Perspectives on Canadian Literature.* Ed. Paul Cappon. Toronto: McClelland and Stewart, 1978, p. 139.

Although Layton is often presented as a liberator from repression, his "love poems are usually powerful chauvinist statements of the male speaker's right to employ the female as a sexual object quite unrelated to anything but an erotic contact."

C299 Mayne, Seymour. Introduction. In *Irving Layton: The Poet and His Critics.* Ed. Seymour Mayne. Toronto: McGraw-Hill Ryerson, 1978, pp. 1–22.

Layton has received neither the amount nor the kind of critical attention that his poetry warrants. In the first phase of his career, which closes with the publication of *The Improved Binoculars*, he received little critical attention. In the second phase, culminating with the 1965 *Collected Poems*, Layton's audience widens, but the focus of criticism is more often his public personality than his poems. In the third phase of his career, his "unpopular political stance interfered with a judicious reception to his work." "Layton's body of work is the most considerable in Canadian poetry"; the many poems about him by other poets attest to the nature of his influence. Still, much critical work remains to be done in order to delineate the nature of his achievement.

C300 [Mayne, Seymour.] "Selected Bibliography." In *Irving Layton: The Poet and His Critics.* Ed. Seymour Mayne. Toronto: McGraw-Hill Ryerson, 1978, pp. 287–91.

A list of books by Layton and a brief selection of secondary material.

C301 Naaman, Antoine, et Léo A. Brodeur. *Répertoire des thèses littéraires canadiennes de 1921 à 1976.*

Sherbrooke: Naaman, 1978, pp. 185, 193–94.
Brief bibliographical data.

C302 Stevens, Peter. "Layton, Irving Peter [Lazarovitch] (1912–)." In his *Modern English-Canadian Poetry: A Guide to Informational Sources*. Vol. xv of *American Literature, English Literature and World Literatures in English*. Detroit: Gale, 1978, pp. 2, 10, 14, 21, 22, 23, 34, 37, 127–32, 135, 146, 165, 167.

Stevens includes bio-bibliographical information and notes that Layton's poetry "is often flamboyant and rhetorically charged, centering on the self-image of the poet."

C303 Ross, Malcolm. "The Ballot." The Calgary Conference on the Canadian Novel, Univ. of Calgary, Calgary. 18 Feb. 1978. Printed in *Taking Stock: The Calgary Conference on the Canadian Novel*. Ed. Charles R. Steele. Downsview, Ont.: ECW, 1982, p. 141.

Irving Layton's *Selected Poems* did not make the top ten works of various genres, but was number eleven on the ballot.

C304 Freedman, Adele. "Who Says Only God Can Make a Poet?". *The Globe and Mail* [Toronto], 18 March 1978, p. 41.

Anthologies such as *Shark Tank* are apt expressions of Layton's poetry workshops. These workshops begin with an examination of past masterpieces and proceed to an analysis of the students' own poems. Students report that he is a good teacher, intensely involved, trying to help them achieve a balance between thought and feeling.

C305 Pesnoy, R. " 'Just Another Exploitation of Young.' " Letter. *The Toronto Star*, 22 April 1978, p. C3.

We need the Ontario Censor Board to protect us from the filth, in the form of films like *Pretty Baby*, that surround us, and people like Layton who promote them (see B922).

C306 Strong, Daniel. " 'Naive Interpretation of Sick Movie.' " Letter. *The Toronto Star*, 22 April 1978, p. C3.

Pretty Baby is a sick movie, and Layton's interpretation (B922) is naïve.

C307 Tepper, Rhonda. " 'Layton Sees Things as They Really Are.' " Letter. *The Toronto Star*, 22 April 1978, p. C3.

Layton shows our hypocritical attitudes to films like *Pretty Baby* for what they are. (See B922.)

C308 Lisinski, E. " 'Nauseating View of the World.' " Letter. *The Toronto Star*, 25 April 1978, p. A9.

Layton's tirade against the Ontario Board of Censors (B922) is pathetic and arrogant.

C309 Plomish, Stan. " 'Wallowing in Literary Stench.' " Letter. *The Toronto Star*, 25 April 1978, p. A9.

Layton's praise of *Pretty Baby* (B922) shows him "wallowing in a self-created atmosphere of literary stench."

C310 Baker, Howard. "Jewish Themes in the Works of Irving Layton." *Essays on Canadian Writing*, No. 10 (Spring 1978), pp. 43–54.

Layton is devoted to the secular rather than religious aspects of Jewish culture; he identifies himself with the sensual Hebrew tradition rather than the stunted Jews of modern ghetto life. In poems like "For My Two Sons Max and David," he demonstrates a deep understanding of Jewish history. Jesus is portrayed positively as a vital, sensual figure, but Christianity "is a false, superstition-ridden parody of its original values." Christians' repression of their vital energies has resulted in the perversions of anti-Semitism. In contrast, modern day Israelis express Layton's "ideal of the strong and the sensual."

C311 Van Wilt, Kurt. "Layton, Nietzsche and Overcoming." *Essays on Canadian Writing*, No. 10 (Spring 1978), pp. 19–42.

Layton believes that "The poet's primary aim is to awaken man to his present limitation and his future possibility — of becoming a creator rather than a destroyer, a whole rather than a partial being." The ideal poet must be a Nietzschean Overman, a strong individual, experiencing continual death and rebirth in his life and work, and integrating within himself energy and passion with form and reason. Van Wilt discusses a number of poems that illustrate Layton's concept of the Overman. The reader must be sensitive to irony in Layton's work, avoiding the trap of identifying the poem's view with the poet's.

C312 Wayne, Joyce. "Defending the WASP." Letter. *Books in Canada*, April 1978, p. 32.

"Layton's crack about ethnic writers being the only good writers in Canada is nonsense." Wayne questions Layton's racial and ethnic chauvinism.

C313 Skelton, Robin. Letter. *Books in Canada*, May 1978, pp. 47–48.

Layton deserves the Leacock award for his genius as a parodist.

C314 Vardon, John F. "Forever Irving." Letter. *Books in Canada*, May 1978, p. 47.

In response to Layton's letter (B921), Vardon sardonically points out how successful Jewish writers have been in Canada.

C315 Webb, Phyllis. Letter. *Books in Canada*, May 1978, p. 48.

In reaction to Layton's supposedly chauvinistic letter in *Books in Canada* (B921), Webb parodies Shakespeare's "Hath not a Jew . . ." as "Hath not a WASP . . . ," suggesting that "WASPS" are no less human than Jews.

C316 "Poet and Prophet." In "What the Martlet Hears." *McGill News*, Summer 1978, p. 3.

Layton read and discussed his work at a Hillel society event; Layton emphasized the role Christians have played in the persecution of the Jews.

C317 Ward, Olivia. "Layton's Taking All His Love Away." *The Toronto Star*, 2 July 1978, p. D5.

On the occasion of his departure from Toronto for Montreal, Layton says people in Toronto are too concerned with success, but Montreal people show more "warmth" and "acceptance."

C318 Richler, Mordecai. "Be It Ever So (Increasingly) Humble, There's No Place Like Home." *Maclean's*, 7 Aug. 1978, p. 54.

Richler welcomes Layton back to Montreal.

C319 Buckowski, Denise. "Shakespeare and I . . . ." *Books in Canada*, Aug.–Sept. 1978, pp. 7–9.

Buckowski, Layton's editor with McClelland and Stewart, tells of her editorial experiences with Layton. She has not found him chauvinistic, contrary to his reputation. Although he is cunning at getting his own way, he is thoroughly professional in his relationship with his editor and quite receptive to reasonable criticism. He is also a terrible speller.

C320 Horgan, Denys. "Controversy Haunts Trial." *The Globe and Mail* [Toronto], 23 Sept. 1978, p. 17.

Layton says that the exposure of negative Jewish-Christian feelings in the film *The Jesus Trials* is healthy.

C321 "O Irvingu Laytonu." *Naše novine*, 18 Oct. 1978, p. 17.
This article is written in Croatian.

C322 Douglas, Marcia. "Intolerance on Trial, and the Jury's Still Out." *Maclean's*, 30 Oct. 1978, pp. 53-54.
Layton appeared in Ted Jaworski's TV series, *The Jesus Trial*, which "traces Jesus' life and death and the persecution that followed in his name." Layton appeared as one of Jaworski's scholars and is quoted in support of the series.

C323 "People." *Maclean's*, 4 Dec. 1978, p. 51.
On Layton's marriage to Harriet Bernstein.

C324 Ackerman, Marianne. "At Last Canadians Have Woken Up." *Sunday Post of Canada* [Toronto], 10 Dec. 1978, p. 16.
Layton expresses pleasure at the increase of poetry's popularity in Canada. Making fun of religion, he says, is only objected to by those whose religion is itself unsure.

C325 Marshall, Tom. *Harsh and Lovely Land: The Major Canadian Poets and the Making of a Canadian Tradition.* Vancouver: Univ. of British Columbia Press, 1979, pp. xiv, 6, 12, 46, 57, 58, 59, 65, 67-75, 76, 77, 79, 89, 90, 91, 97, 101, 108, 112, 135, 136, 139, 150, 168, 169, 178, 179.
In some ways following on from A.M. Klein, Layton has carried the symbolic activity of swimming and diving further than any other Canadian poet. He communicates both "the possibility of liberation into a larger, freer life" and also a "vision of tragedy." "The Birth of Tragedy" and "The Cold Green Element" develop a "tension between life and death in surrealistic fashion." Later poems, particularly "A Tall Man Executes a Jig," "develop a myth of the poet as conquering hero." While Layton's technique is "too traditional and eclectic and not exploratory enough," he has managed to "reveal the horror as well as the glory of existence and also the fierce joy of living in the face of the horror."

C326 Moisan, Clément. *Poésie des frontières: étude comparée des poésies canadienne et québécoise.* Quebec: Hurtubise, 1979, pp. 15, 22n., 25, 26, 27, 63, 73, 74, 96, 97, 129, 131, 132, 133, 134, 143-50, 151, 152n., 253, 273, 276, 297, 298, 301, 323, 327, 328. Rpt. trans. George Lang and Linda Weber (revised) in *A Poetry of Frontiers: Comparative Studies in Quebec / Canadian Literature.* Victoria, B.C.: Porcépic, 1983, pp. x, 36, 37, 51, 52, 76, 77, 78, 85-90, 91, 159, 175, 177, 190, 193, 194, 205, 208.
Moisan compares Layton's poetry to that of Paul Marie Lapointe. Layton is "violent and crude" far more often than Lapointe. But, while their tone is different, they speak of the same realities. They both write of "violence, sacred revolt and love." Both use "biting satire" and convey an awareness of time, setting themselves against society. Layton's language "keeps the reader earthbound," while Lapointe's "draws the reader out of the real world."

C327 Pacey, Desmond. *Essays: Canadian Literature in English.* Ed. and preface by A.L. McLeod. Foreword H.H. Anniah Gowda. Powre above Powres, No. 4. Mysore, India: Centre for Commonwealth Literature and Research, Univ. of Mysore, 1979, pp. 123-25.
"Fearless honesty and its pervasive theme that life must be lived to the full" are the great strengths of

Layton's poetry. But the rhetorical forewords and publication of too many inferior poems have harmed his reputation.

C328 Stenbaek-Lafon, Marianne, and Ken Norris. "An Interview with Joe Rosenblatt." CV/II, 4, No. 1 (Winter 1979), 34.

In the last thirty years, Layton has "written some of the best poems in the English language." Since him there has been "no major breakthrough."

C329 Amiel, Barbara. "Poetry: Capsule Comments on Canada." *Maclean's*, 15 Jan. 1979, pp. 49, 50.

Layton has helped demolish many of the barriers erected by our puritanical society.

C330 Dudek, Louis. "The Poetry of the Forties." Conference on Canada in the Forties, York Univ., Downsview, Ont. 9 Feb. 1979. Printed in *Open Letter*, Ser. 4, Nos. 8–9 (Spring–Summer 1981), pp. 288, 289, 290, 291, 294–95, 296.

Layton anticipated by at least fifteen years the "revolt and vulgarization" of the 1960s. ". . . Layton in the forties already represented a large element of that liberation as it applies to poetry."

C331 Brownstein, Bill. "Love Is Lucrative for Layton." *The Gazette* [Montreal], 14 Feb. 1979, p. 33.

Brownstein describes Layton's current literary activities, especially the deluxe editions of *The Love Poems of Irving Layton*. Layton expatiates on his marital bliss.

C332 Person, A.D. "Thoughts on a Native Land." *The Canadian Forum*, April 1979, pp. 15–16.

Layton says he is returning to Quebec because of his admiration for " 'humanist' " René Levesque.

C333 "Book Combines Poetry, Art." *The London Free Press*, 7 April 1979, p. B6.

The collaboration between Irving Layton and Aligi Sassu on Layton's *There Were No Signs* has been close and fruitful.

C334 Hunt, Peter. "Boo to the Belly-Dancers." Letter. *Books in Canada*, June–July 1979, p. 33.

In a discussion of censorship of Canadian literature in the schools, Hunt notes "Many students are made to read Alice Munro, Al Purdy, Irving Layton, Margaret Atwood *et al.* but know nothing of the fine work of Carman, Roberts, Lampman, D.C. Scott, Callaghan, and Gabrielle Roy."

C335 Ellman, Eugene. "A Poet Picks Niagara-on-the-Lake Where Nostalgia Elevated to Style." *The St. Catharines Standard*, 14 July 1979, pp. 1–2.

Layton discusses the dehumanizing effects of our society and his intention to retire from teaching to live at Niagara-on-the-Lake.

C336 Thompson, Lee Briscoe, and Deborah Black. "The Dance of a Pot-Bellied Poet: Explorations into 'A Tall Man Executes a Jig.' " *Concerning Poetry* [Western Washington Univ.], 12, No. 2 (Fall 1979), 33–43.

"A Tall Man Executes a Jig" is a key Layton poem in its exploration of the poet's concept of an antinomial universe. The "tall man" is Moses, Joshua, Adam, and the poet himself. Here the antinomies are brought to at least momentary resolution, which for Layton is what poetry should achieve.

C337 Murphy, Brian K. " 'Apocalypse' Analysis Is Too Simple." *The Globe and Mail* [Toronto], 27 Oct. 1979, p. 7.

Layton's analysis of *Apocalypse Now* (B928) oversimplifies the conflict between East and West.

C338 Brennan, Patrick. "Layton Speaks Out on Separation Bid." *The Daily Mercury* [Guelph, Ont.], 7 Nov. 1979, p. 21.

Layton argues against the separation of Quebec.

C339 Govier, Katherine. "Couples Today: Do Age Gaps Matter?". *Chatelaine*, Jan. 1980, p. 103.

Layton's current wife Harriet comments on the joys of marriage to an older man.

C340 Weisner, Kenneth. "The Liberation of Poetry." *Miami International*, March 1980, p. 20.

Brief bio-critical information prepares the way for Layton's visit and reading in Miami.

C341 Clever, Glenn. "Layton on Layton." CV/II, 4, No. 4 (Spring 1980), 18–19.

Layton places too much emphasis on the function of poetry as rhetorical persuasion and self-expression and not enough on its function "as verbal symbol of man." His poems, rather than his inconsistent polemics, are the best testimonials of what he believes poetry to be.

C342 O'Rourke, David. "A Second Look at English Poetry in Montreal." CV/II, 4, No. 4 (Spring 1980), 24, 25–27.

Responding to Ken Norris' "Montreal English Poetry in the Seventies" (C289), O'Rourke finds Norris' assessment of Layton's role deficient. Layton has much more ongoing significance and influence than Norris recognizes.

C343 Howitt, Eaton. "Sticks and Stones." *The Vancouver Sun*, 17 April 1980, p. C8.

Dennis Duffy's negative review of *An Unlikely Affair* (D319) led to a response by Layton in *The Globe and Mail* [Toronto], on 9 April (B930). Howitt describes the respective positions.

C344 Reid, James. "Layton Verse Has Common Sense." *The Globe and Mail* [Toronto], 26 April 1980, p. 7.

Reid comments, tongue-in-cheek, on Layton's poem "Cruising."

C345 Stroud, Carston. "Caught with Paper Lover: The Unlikely Correspondence of Irving Layton and Dorothy Rath." *Toronto Life*, May 1980, pp. 48, 82, 84, 141, 142, 145, 147.

Based on their correspondence published in *An Unlikely Affair: The Irving Layton-Dorothy Rath Correspondence*, Stroud summarizes the stages through which the Layton-Rath relationship passed.

C346 Blaise, Clark. "The Truth Is: We Are All Laytons." *The Globe and Mail* [Toronto], 3 May 1980, p. 6.

Blaise's *Lunar Attractions*, as well as other good Canadian books, do not get the attention they deserve. Canadian writers are all Laytons in their disappointment with the Canadian public.

C347 Alderman, Tom. "A Poem Is Not a Four-Letter Word." *Today Magazine* [*The Toronto Star*], 17 May 1980, p. 9.

In this article, based on an interview, Layton says that the way poetry is taught in our schools kills it. He recommends starting with a book like *Canadian Poetry: The Modern Era*, edited by John Newlove, and following your interests from there.

C348 Norris, Ken. "An Open Letter to David O'Rourke Concerning Montreal Poetry." CV/II, 5, No. 1 (Autumn 1980), 52–53.

Responding to David O'Rourke's "A Second Look at English Poetry in Montreal" (C342), Norris states that David Solway and Michael Harris "have followed Layton in seeing the world in terms of sex and death for so long that I don't think they're now able to distinguish between the two."

C349 Ruggles, Terry. "The Many Faces of Irving Layton." *The Oakville Journal Record*, 1 Oct. 1980, p. 18.

This article was occasioned by a series of lectures, on the theme "What Is the Modern Sensibility," given by Layton at Sheridan College.

C350 O'Rourke, David. "The Lion in Winters: Irving Layton at York." *Canadian Literature*, No. 87 (Winter 1980), pp. 52–65.

O'Rourke presents Layton's comments towards the end of his 1977–78 graduate course on Montreal poetry at Winters College, in which Layton lectured on Layton. These comments are divided into "Biographical Notes," "Fourteen Poems" (critical comments by Layton on several of his poems), and "Last Class at York." Layton attacks gentility, emphasizes his sympathy with bravery in the face of hardship, and denies influence by any others, including A.M. Klein, Nietzsche, and D.H. Lawrence. While acknowledging that the Montreal poets Michael Harris and David Solway do excellent work, he criticizes them for returning to the Archibald Lampman landscape tradition. The poet must also prophesy.

C351 Moore, Kathleen C. "Signature Marks and Burnt Pearls: An Interview with Seymour Mayne." *Athanor*, 1, No. 4 (1981), 7, 8, 9, 10, 11, 12.

The quarrel between Irving Layton and Louis Dudek disrupted the "community of discourse" in the Montreal poetic scene. Like a number of other Canadian poets, Layton is able to integrate his personal vision with a larger world.

C352 Monkman, Leslie. *A Native Heritage: Images of the Indian in English-Canadian Literature*. Toronto: Univ. of Toronto Press, 1981, pp. 94–95, 128, 179n.

Layton's "Iroquois in Nice" shows the Indian in contrast with the corrupt European world, by which he is destroyed.

C353 Nadel, Ira Bruce. "Irving Layton, 1912–   ." In his *Jewish Writers of North America: A Guide to Information Sources*. Vol. VIII of *American Studies Information Guide Series*. Detroit: Gale, 1981, 155–58.

Nadel lists Layton's books to 1980 and includes a selective list of secondary sources.

C354 Rizzardi, Alfredo. Introduzione. In *In un'età di ghiaccio*. Ed. and trans. Alfredo Rizzardi. Rome: Lerici, 1981, pp. 9–11. Rpt. (revised, expanded — "Ancora Irving Layton") in *Tutto sommato: poesie 1945–1989*. Preface Leonard Cohen. Ed. Alfredo Rizzardi. Abano Terme, Italy: Piovan, 1989, pp. 5–9.

"Ebbro di fumi erotici e esaltato in una visione perenne di libertà creativa," Layton's work is "un massiccio isolato." For him, ". . . la poesia non sia un oggetto verbale, ma la voce viva del poeta," "per incidere con lorza l'ipocrisia, l'ingiustizia, la crudeltà."

C355 Spriet, P[ierre]. "Les Poètes juifs de Montréal et le christianisme." In *Le Facteur religieux en Amérique du Nord, No. 2: Apocalypse et autres trauvaux*. Ed. Jean Béranger. Bordeaux: Maison des Sciences de l'Homme d'Aquitaine, Univ. de Bordeaux III, 1981, pp. 177–80, 183–93.

Spriet focuses on the different views of Christianity expressed in the poetry of Layton and A.M. Klein. "La vision chrétienne de Layton est en définitive une vision encore plus juive que celle de Klein." While they share a sympathy for Quebec, Klein approves French Canada's acceptance of traditional values, while Layton, writing later, approves their rejection of the same values. "La vision de Klein comme celle de Layton est 'mystique' parce qu'elle intègre tout et donne à ce tout un sens et un seul."

C356 Woodcock, George. *Taking It to the Letter*. Montreal: Quadrant, 1981, pp. 40–41, 62–63.

Woodcock includes two letters to Layton. In the first, he praises Layton's poem "Funeraria Olea" and asks for a "reminiscent piece on A.M. Klein" for *Canadian Literature*. In the second, he agrees with Layton's low opinion of the Australians and expresses his anger at Solzhenitsyn's arrest.

C357 Marchand, Blaine. "wQ Interviews Dorothy Rath." *Cross-Country Writers' Quarterly*, 3, No. 1 (Winter 1981), 13–14.

Dorothy Rath describes her ambivalent feelings about the publication of *An Unlikely Affair: The Irving Layton-Dorothy Rath Correspondence*, both prior and subsequent to its publication. Rath states she is no longer writing poetry.

C358 Gallivan, Kathleen. "Welcome Back, Mr. Layton." Letter. *The Globe and Mail* [Toronto], 14 Feb. 1981, p. A7.

A sardonic response to Layton's article on Bergman (B934), suggesting his writing would benefit from a closer attention to grammar.

C359 Kang, Shin-Bong. " 'Let's Build United Nation.' " Letter. *The Toronto Star*, 17 Feb. 1981, p. A9.

Kang agrees with Layton (B935) and the need to build a strong federal government.

C360 McCulloch, Peter B. "Layton's Opinion 'Not One Bit Better.' " Letter. *The Toronto Star*, 17 Feb. 1981, p. A9.

McCulloch objects to Layton's letter (B935). Layton gets more coverage than he deserves in the *Toronto Star*, and Pierre Trudeau is no champion of the people.

C361 Smith, Roger. "Every 'Pygmy' Has One Vote." Letter. *The Toronto Star*, 18 Feb. 1981, p. A9.

Pierre Trudeau's power is dangerous, and Layton's misplaced emotional support will only evoke an equal and opposite reaction in favour of democracy.

C362 Plomish, Stan. " 'Pygmies' Not Disturbed." Letter. *The Toronto Star*, 21 Feb. 1981, p. B3.

Layton's views (B935) are ignorant, and Pierre Trudeau's time has not yet arrived.

C363 Richard, Laurie. "Pierre Trudeau 'a Great Patriot.' " Letter. *The Toronto Star*, 21 Feb. 1981, p. B3.

Layton's praise of Pierre Trudeau (B935) is "fearless, honest, brilliant."

C364 Chinol, Elio. "Une voce dal Canada." *Il Giornale* [Milan], 3 May 1981. Rpt. (trans. into English) in *Italian Critics on Irving Layton*." Ed. Alfredo Rizzardi. Abano Terme, Italy: Piovan, 1988, pp. 13–17.

See C12.

C365 Smith, P.K. "Poets Find a Voice to Stage Their Words." *Performing Arts in Canada*, Dec. 1981, p. 43.

Layton's "style is rhetorical," but "the poetic self is magnanimous, addressing itself to universal pain, joy, and beauty."

C366 Atwood, Margaret. Introduction. In *The New Oxford Book of Canadian Verse: In English*. Toronto: Oxford Univ. Press, 1982, pp. xxxvi, xxxvii.

In Canadian poetry, Layton's "exuberance of spirit," "vigour of imagery," and "sexuality" are unprecedented.

C367 Billings, Robert. "Irving Layton 1912–   ." In *Canadian Poetry*. Ed. Jack David and Robert Lecker. Vol. 1. New Press Canadian Classics. Toronto / Downsview, Ont.: General / ECW, 1982, 312–14.

Layton is an eclectic poet whose adopted roles include those of "victim, confessor, penitent, sensitive sensualist, boor, outraged human being, Jewish prophet, bon vivant, revolutionary, and Antichrist." He has a great range of thought, vocabulary, and feeling.

C368 Brown, Russell, and Donna Bennett. "Irving Layton, b. 1912." In *An Anthology of Canadian Literature in English*. Ed. Russell Brown and Donna Bennett. Vol. 1. Toronto: Oxford Univ. Press, 1982, 566–68.

Layton's "exuberance and his desire to enlighten his readers" have always characterized his poetry. Many of his public stances are contradicted by his private actions.

C369 Caplan, Usher. *Like One That Dreamed: A Portrait of A.M. Klein*. Toronto: McGraw-Hill Ryerson, 1982, pp. 98–100, 114, 206–09, 217–18.

A.M. Klein was Layton's earliest mentor; they met frequently to share their poetry. After Klein's breakdown Layton remained one of his closest friends. He felt Klein's tragedy was his inability to face "the evil realities of twentieth century existence."

C370 Metcalf, John. *Kicking against the Pricks*. Downsview, Ont.: ECW, 1982, pp. 52, 53, 58, 147, 167, 181.

Layton is "a considerable poet," who, with Leonard Cohen, found the Montreal female population in the early 1960s particularly open to "instruction."

C371 Ward, Olivia. "Layton Fights to See His Daughter." *The Toronto Star*, 2 May 1982, p. C1.

Layton tells of his difficulties in seeing his daughter, placing most of the blame on the inadequacies of the legal system.

C372 Farrell, Crook. "Poet's Wife Loses Bid to Gag Husband Over Break-Up." *The Toronto Star*, 11 May 1982, p. A8.

Although the material circulated by Layton about his ex-wife Harriet is "uncomplimentary," the judge of the Ontario Supreme Court ruled that it did not constitute harassment.

C373 Baernstein, Tsigane. "Irving Layton Photos Like Night and Day." *The Toronto Star*, 27 May 1982, p. A19.

Baernstein objects to the Layton photograph in the paper on 13 May.

C374 Bentley, D.M.R. "Drawers of Water; Notes on the Significance and Scenery of Fresh Water in Canadian Poetry." Pt. 1. CV/II, 6, No. 4 (Aug. 1982), 17, 19.

Like some of Canada's most thoughtful poets, Layton has followed the river upstream towards the Dionysian.

C375 Chanin, Lawrence. Letter. CV/II, 6, No. 4 (Aug. 1982), 61.

Responding to Peter Herman's review of *For My Neighbours in Hell* (D239), Chanin defends Layton's misanthropy as being "in the noble tradition of the Old Testament prophets." "*For My Neighbours in Hell* harmonizes perfectly with the madness, violence and perversion that are running rampant throughout the world."

C376 Weinstein, Ann. "Irving Layton: The Raging Bull-Calf, A Personal Look at an Old Book Friend." *The Eye* [Montreal], Dec. 1982, pp. 3–5, 15.

Compared to Mordecai Richler, Layton is more accepting of his roots. Opposing forces within him are more reconciled. He is bent on eradicating the schism between Jews and Gentiles. For him "each poem is like the act of love."

C377 Clarke, Cera. "Ron Mann's Poetry Film Lacks Emotion." Letter. *Now* [Toronto], 2–8 Dec. 1982, p. 4.

Layton "was left on the cutting room floor" in Ron Mann's film, *Poetry in Motion*, "mainly because he doesn't belong in a movie with a cast of vipers . . . and other organ-centred males."

C378 Lane, M. Travis. "Contemporary Canadian Verse: The View from Here." *University of Toronto Quarterly*, 52 (Winter 1982–83), 188, 189.

Layton is one of those poets who often values "poetic feeling over poetic production."

C379 Bentley, D.M.R. "The Mower and the Boneless Acrobat: Notes on the Stances of Baseland and Hinterland in Canadian Poetry." *Studies in Canadian Literature*, 8 (1983), 18, 22, 37, 42.

Layton is a "baseland" poet whose main commitments are to order and closed form.

C380 Cena, Adele. "Il ruolo del poeta in Irving Layton." In *Canada: Testi e contesti*. Ed. and premessa Alfredo Rizzardi. Abano Terme, Italy: Piovan, 1983, pp. 261–77.

"Poeta come spia, ribelle, critico, profeta, clown, martire: tutti gli accostamenti svelano sfaccettature che sembrano costituirsi come rete all'opera di Layton, le cui maglie vanno man mano infittendosi fino ad isolare un'immagine: il poeta che celebra la vita in tutta la sua pienezza."

C381 Collins, Aileen. Introduction. In *CIV/n: A Literary Magazine of the 50's*. Ed. Aileen Collins. Montreal: Véhicule, 1983, pp. 7, 8, 10.

Irving Layton and Louis Dudek were involved with *CIV/n* as editorial advisors. Many of the editorial meetings were held at the Laytons' house.

C382 Cooney, Seamus, ed. *The Bukowski-Purdy Letters 1964–1974: A Decade of Dialogue*. Sutton West, Cal.: Paget, 1983, pp. 15, 29, 32, 88, 89, 102.

In a letter dated 9 January 1965, Al Purdy describes Layton as "pretty well washed up," although he has written some fine poetry. Charles Bukowski refers to him as "your tinselled craftsman." Purdy states that before Layton came along, ". . . everyone sounded like your aunt Martha . . . ."

C383 Hošek, Chaviva. "Poetry in English: 1950 to 1982." In *The Oxford Companion to Canadian Literature*. Ed. William Toye. Toronto: Oxford Univ. Press, 1983, pp. 662, 667.

Layton "hit his stride in the fifties." His "satire and invective" is balanced "by more lyrical and self-examining poems."

C384 Hoy, Helen. In her *Modern English-Canadian Prose: A Guide to Information Sources*. Vol. 38 of *American Literature, English Literature and World Literatures in English*. Detroit: Gale, 1983, pp. 21, 46, 212, 247, 525.

Brief bibliographical data.

C385 Keith, W.J. "The Function of Canadian Criticism at the Present Time." Univ. of Alberta, 1983. Printed (revised) in *Essays on Canadian Writing*, [10th Anniversary Issue], No. 30 (Winter 1984–85), pp. 8–9, 10.

In a discussion of Puritanism and gentility in Canadian literature, Keith recalls "Layton attacking the Toronto that was still — just! — 'Toronto the Good' . . ." and notes "Some of Irving Layton's poems . . . employ a 'fine' rhetoric to communicate 'crude' material, while some are crude in both senses . . . ."

C386 Norris, Ken. "The Significance of *Contact* and *CIV/n*." In *CIV/n: A Literary Magazine of the 50's*. Ed. Aileen Collins. Montreal: Véhicule, 1983, pp. 253,

254, 255, 256, 257, 258, 259, 260, 261, 262, 263, 264, 265, 266.

Layton's role in *Contact* and *civ/n* is described in the context of the editors' efforts to resist "the regressive tendency in poetry that stemmed out of the late forties" and to push "poetry forward to a condition of Modernism resting on the most solid of foundations."

C387 Ripley, Gordon, and Anne V. Mercer. "Layton, Irving." *Who's Who in Canadian Literature 1983–1984* (1983). Rpt. (revised) in *Who's Who in Canadian Literature* (1987).

Ripley and Mercer include brief bio-bibliographical data.

C388 Rizzardi, Alfredo. "Il canto d'amore di Irving Layton." In *Le poesie d'amore*. Ed. Alfredo Rizzardi. Abano Terme, Italy: Piovan, 1983, pp. 5–11. Rpt. (revised and trans. — "The Love Song of Irving Layton") in *Canada: The Verbal Creation / la creazione verbale*. Ed. Alfredo Rizzardi. Abano Terme, Italy: Piovan, 1985, pp. 55–62. Rpt. in *Italian Critics on Irving Layton*. Ed. Alfredo Rizzardi. Abano Terme, Italy: Piovan, 1988, pp. 19–29. See C12.

C389 Stromberg-Stein, Susan. *Louis Dudek: A Biographical Introduction to His Poetry*. Ottawa: Golden Dog, 1983, pp. 20, 21–23, 26, 39, 52, 53, 55, 57, 60, 66–67, 73, 103, 108, 116, 124, 128.

Irving Layton's and Louis Dudek's early association and contributions to *First Statement* and Contact Press are discussed. Layton criticized Ezra Pound's influence on Dudek, claiming that " 'meeting Pound was hard on Dudek because in trying to reach up to Pound's level he never developed his own poetic voice.' " Layton's and Dudek's friendship has been described as " 'the acquaintance that ended in slander.' " The final explosive rift between them in the early 1960s resulted from "the clash of their egos and their ideals." (Layton responds [B942] when Michael Mirolla quotes Stromberg-Stein in *The Gazette* [Montreal], 17 March 1984, p. I3.)

C390 Wilson, Carolin. "The Passionate Poet." *What's Up* [St. Catharines, Ont.], Jan. 1983, pp. 6–11.

Layton comments on aspects of his life and works.

C391 "Poet Layton Must Pay for Sewer Use." *The Gazette* [Montreal], 19 Jan. 1983, p. B1.

The town fathers of St. Catharines decline Layton's offer of an ode in payment for a sewer bill.

C392 Ackerman, Marianne. "*civ/n*'s Rebellious 'Mission' Recalled." *The Globe and Mail* [Toronto], 8 March 1983, Entertainment, p. 15.

At the launching party for the reprinting of *civ/n*, Layton states that poetry no longer matters; "Filmmakers are the real modern poets." His friend Venny McGrath later comments that Layton "can't decide between the ham sitting on his knee and the one on the table."

C393 Giller, Doris. "Flashforward to the 1980s: The Mood Is Much Mellower Now." *The Gazette* [Montreal], 12 March 1983, p. I1.

The cast and crew from the days of *civ/n* can still generate excitement, with Layton one of the star attractions.

C394 Stewart, Robert. "Flashback to the 1950s: Poets Brooded with Gusto." Rev. of *civ/n: Literary Magazine of the 50's*, ed. Aileen Collins. *The Gazette* [Montreal], 12 March 1983, p. I1.

While the *civ/n* poets often ignored "the often ugly

realities of the 1950s" in favour of a more immediate world, this book "makes a valuable addition to the record of Canadian literary life."

C395 Fitzgerald, Judith. "A Brief Blossom, Impressive Results." Rev. of CIV/n: A Literary Magazine of the 50's, ed. Aileen Collins. The Globe and Mail [Toronto], 19 March 1983, Sec. Entertainment, p. 14.
    While some of Layton's sentiments now appear cliché, they were important in their time.

C396 Scanlon, Kevin. "Do You Believe This Is the Brunswick?". The Toronto Star, 25 March 1983, p. C1.
    Irving Layton is one of the stars at the new literary venue of The Brunswick House.

C397 Somerville, H.W. "Clip Job on Hairdos." Letter. The Globe and Mail [Toronto], 26 March 1983, p. 7.
    Somerville responds to Layton's comments reported in the 8 March issue of The Globe and Mail [Toronto] (C392), disagreeing with his views of men and women expressed at that time.

C398 Homel, David. "Field Notes: Cane-Banging and Camaraderie 30 Years after the Dawn of CIV/n." Books in Canada, May 1983, pp. 3–4.
    On the occasion of the republication of CIV/n, Layton argues that modern poetry broke through in Montreal because the tensions produced by divergent groups made fertile ground for poetry.

C399 Milner, Phil. Rev. of CIV/n: A Literary Magazine of the 50's, ed. Aileen Collins. The Antigonish Review, No. 54 (Summer 1983), pp. 35, 36, 37.
    Layton's presence in CIV/n is pervasive, with much of his writing providing the stimulus for other writers.

C400 Mandel, Eli. "The New Phrenology: Developments in Contemporary Canadian Writing." The Literary Half-Yearly [Univ. of Mysore, India], 24 (July 1983), 103.
    Layton's "A Tall Man Executes a Jig" and "The Cold Green Element" are cited as examples of the work of modern Canadian writers who represent the eastern-centralist myth of Canadian consciousness.

C401 Corley, Carol. "Irving Layton Starring in Film Shot at Whitehern." The Spectator [Hamilton], 13 July 1983, p. A7.
    Layton is enjoying his first movie role as the manager of Tom Longboat in the film Wildfire: The Story of Tom Longboat (B1307). Both film-making and poetry, he says, "require a little imagination and a little reality."

C402 Woodcock, George. "Queen's Quarterly and Canadian Culture." Queen's Quarterly, 90 (Autumn 1983), 618–19.
    Some of Layton's contributions to Queen's Quarterly are mentioned, and the closing stanza of "A Tall Man Executes a Jig" is quoted.

C403 Colombo, John Robert. Canadian Literary Landmarks. Toronto: Hounslow, 1984, pp. 62, 64, 65–66, 67, 71, 72, 75, 76, 84, 86–87, 128, 144, 145, 181, 183, 206, 208, 243.
    Layton is mentioned under the headings "Lachine, Que.," "Montreal, Que.," "Kingston, Ont.," "Niagara-on-the-Lake, Ont.," "Oakville, Ont.," "Toronto, Ont.," and "Saskatoon, Sask."

C404 Faas, Ekbert. "Layton and Creeley: Chronicle of a Literary Friendship." In Robert Creeley: The Poet's Workshop. Ed. Caroll F. Terrell. Orono, Me.: National Poetry Foundation Univ. of Maine at Orono, 1984, pp. 249–73.

Faas discusses the personal and literary relationship between Irving Layton and Robert Creeley as revealed in their correspondence between 1953 and 1957. Crises such as that caused by Creeley's strenuous criticism of Louis Dudek's poetry were survived through Creeley's and Layton's conviction of each other's talents. Creeley was an astute critic and editor of Layton's poetry; while he liked their "tight firm structures," he objected to their occasional "lack of dynamic action."

C405 Giguère, Richard. *Exil, révolte et dissidence: étude comparée des poésies québécoise et canadienne (1925-1955).* Vie des Lettres québécoises, No. 23. Québec: Les Presses de l'Univ. Laval, 1984, pp. 8, 54, 83, 86-87, 91, 118n., 152, 155-59, 160, 169, 183, 194-97, 199, 201, 204, 212, 226, 230, 250-52.

An introduction in Yugoslavian to Layton's work, followed by translations of eleven of his poems (B171, B250, B296, B332, B391, B531, B536, B571, B580, B774, B776).
Layton has a transitional position in English-Canadian poetry parallel to that of Alain Grandbois in French-Canadian poetry. "Dans le combat de l'amour et de l'imagination opposés aux puissances destructices, de la 'Beauté,' face à la 'Mort,' le poète se sait invincible parce qu'il possède le pouvoir de créer." "Pour Layton . . . la poésie dont tenir compte de toutes les couches de la société, mais surtout des gens les plus démunis." Giguère's book is based on his dissertation (C541).

C406 Gorjup, Branko. "Irving Layton." *Republika* [Zagreb, Yugoslavia], Nos. 10-12 (1984), pp. 166-68.

An introduction in Yugoslavian to Layton's work, followed by translations of eleven of his poems (B171, B250, B296, B332, B391, B531, B536, B571, B580, B774, B776).

C407 McQuarrie, Jane, Anne Mercer, and Gordon Ripley. *Index to Canadian Poetry in English.* Toronto:

Reference, 1984, pp. 12, 18, 21, 22, 24, 25, 26, 28, 30, 31, 32, 33, 34, 35, 36, 37, 39, 40, 43, 44, 45, 47, 48, 50, 52, 53, 54, 55, 57, 58, 59, 61, 62, 64, 65, 68, 70, 71, 74, 76, 78, 81, 82, 83, 85, 87, 90, 91, 92, 93, 97, 99, 103, 104, 107, 110, 111, 113, 117, 119, 120, 122, 123, 125, 128, 130, 134, 135, 136, 138, 139, 144, 148, 150, 153, 154, 155, 156, 159, 162, 164, 166, 171, 172, 173, 179, 182, 185, 191, 192, 196, 197, 199, 200, 201, 204, 205, 208, 210, 211, 212, 213, 246-47, 321.

Information on anthologies containing poems by Layton.

C408 Powe, Bruce W. "Raging Bull: The Poetry, Politics and Polemics of Irving Layton." In his *A Climate Charged.* Oakville, Ont.: Mosaic, 1984, pp. 95-116.

". . . Layton's best lyrics are the most indispensable of any Canadian poet of his generation," but his ". . . entrapment in his role . . . had a devastating effect on his writings." Layton is full of paradoxes, combining romanticism with satire. His poetry shows little development and can most profitably be read as one long work. His prose is not generally successful, as "The Carlyle-like tone collides with the practical school teacher." "The value of Layton's work is that he has made himself and his poetry integral to our imaginations." His "failure is that he never reconciled the tension between the demands of craft and his desire to change his world"; ". . . his gift is that he never broke faith with life."

C409 Stouck, David. "Irving Layton." In his *Major Canadian Authors: A Critical Introduction.* Lincoln, Neb.: Univ. of Nebraska Press, 1984, pp. 179-95, 241, 252, 298. Rpt. Rev. ed., 1988, pp. 179-95, 241, 252, 320.

Following a brief sketch of Layton's poetic and personal background, Stouck discusses the "amazing energy and range" of Layton's poetry. Layton reveals "a compassionate identification with the innocent creatures of the world," balancing poems on "human depravity" with others which reveal "strong, positive feelings." "A Tall Man Executes a Jig" is a central poem in its probing the question of whether one should "transcend materiality" or "accept the life processes." While his public personality hinders appreciation of his work, ". . . Layton has an ear for the rhetoric and rhythms of great poetry and has produced several pieces that will surely live on."

C410 Coates, Darlene. "Poetic Injustice." Letter. *Books in Canada*, May 1984, p. 33.

If the public has lost interest in poetry, Layton's own self-indulgence is in a large part to blame.

C411 Harris, Michael. "Irving Layton: An Unforgettable Poet and Teacher." *The Record* [Sherbrooke], 2 Nov. 1984, p. 5.

Harris recalls a creative-writing class taken at Sir George Williams University with Layton in 1967. Layton conveyed "fierce curiosity" and "passion" and "made his point of view credible" without forcing it on his students.

C412 Benazon, Michael. "Layton: Taking the Underpants Off Canadian Poetry." *The Record* [Sherbrooke], 16 Nov. 1984, pp. 6–7.

Montreal, Layton says, has produced more good poets than Toronto because it is more cosmopolitan and embodies within it more tensions. He and others, like Leonard Cohen and Seymour Mayne, have burst the puritanical restraints on Canadian poetry. Poets today have craft, but lack either the power of prophecy or the grasp of contemporary issues. The craft of poetry can be taught, but only by an accomplished poet.

C413 Francis, Wynne. "A Dramatic Story Missed." Rev. of *Northern Review 1945–1956: A History and an Index*, ed. Hilda Vanneste; and *civ/n: A Literary Magazine of the 50's*, ed. Aileen Collins. *Canadian Poetry: Studies, Documents, Reviews*, No. 15 (Fall–Winter 1984), pp. 85, 90–92, 93.

The story of civ/n derives from the tensions between Louis Dudek and Irving Layton. While Dudek aspired to be the Ezra Pound of Canada, Layton saw himself in line with the Old Testament and European prophetic tradition.

C414 Whiteman, Bruce. "Two Little Magazines." Rev. of *Northern Review, 1945–1956: A History and an Index*, by Hilda M.C. Vanneste; and *civ/n: A Literary Magazine of the 50's*, ed. Aileen Collins. *Essays on Canadian Writing*, [10th Anniversary Issue], No. 30 (Winter 1984–85), pp. 126, 127, 128, 129.

In this review of Hilda M.C. Vanneste's book on *Northern Review* and the reprint of civ/n, Whiteman also mentions Layton's role and development *vis-à-vis* these two magazines. John Sutherland, through *Northern Review*, "gave much needed encouragement . . . to spark a number of poets who gradually developed lasting reputations: Layton, [Miriam] Waddington, [Raymond] Souster, et al. . . . Louis Dudek and Irving Layton, though never on the masthead [of civ/n], were clearly the grey eminences behind the magazine . . . ." Layton's and Dudek's involvement with civ/n came from "increasing dissatisfaction with their input into *Contact* . . . ." Layton's poems "stand out head and shoulders above the rest . . . ." Souster thought the demise of civ/n was a result of the falling out between Layton and Dudek. Layton wrote "a piece about some earlier Souster books which he (Layton) called 'Crêpe Hanger's Carnival.' Souster later appropriated the title for his selected poems 1955–58."

C415 Barbour, Douglas. "Poetry in English, 1960–1980s." *The Canadian Encyclopedia*. Vol. III (1985). Rpt. 2nd ed. Vol. III (1988).

While Layton is a major poet, his conservatism in form has prevented him from becoming a major influence on later writers.

C416 Cameron, Elspeth. "Layton, Irving Peter." *The Canadian Encyclopedia*. Vol. II (1985). Rpt. (expanded) 2nd ed. Vol. II (1988).

"Layton was the most outspoken and flamboyant" of the poets who emerged from Montreal in the 1940s.

C417 Domenichelli, Mario. "Irving Layton: Laughter and Death." In *Canada: The Verbal Creation / la creazione verbale*. Ed. and premessa / foreword Alfredo Rizzardi. Abano Terme, Italy: Piovan, 1985, pp. 81–93. Rpt. in *Italian Critics on Irving Layton*. Ed. Alfredo Rizzardi. Abano Terme, Italy: Piovan, 1988, pp. 31–45.

See C12.

C418 Goldie, Terry. "Louis Dudek." In *Canadian Writers and Their Works*. Poetry Series. Vol. V. Ed. Robert Lecker, Jack David, and Ellen Quigley. Introd. George Woodcock. Toronto: ECW, 1985, pp. 76, 77, 79, 81, 82, 84–85, 87, 89, 93, 94–95, 122, 124, 125. Rpt. *Louis Dudek and His Works*. [Toronto: ECW, 1985; offprint.]

In their early careers, until about 1956, Layton and Dudek shared "vaguely left-wing and anti-establishment" attitudes.

C419 Fee, Margery. *Canadian Poetry in Selected English-Language Anthologies: An Index and Guide*. Halifax: Dalhousie Univ. School of Library Service, 1985, pp. 8, 46–48, 76, 86, 88, 90, 92, 93, 94, 96, 98, 99, 100, 101, 102, 104, 105, 106, 107, 108, 109, 110, 111, 112, 113, 115, 116, 117, 118, 119, 120, 121, 124, 125, 127, 128, 129, 131, 133, 134, 135, 136, 138, 139, 140, 142, 143, 144, 145, 146, 147, 149, 151, 152, 153, 154, 155, 156, 157, 160, 162, 163, 165, 167, 168, 169, 170, 171, 173, 175, 176, 177, 179, 180, 182, 184, 186, 187, 188, 190, 191, 192, 193–94, 197, 198, 200, 201, 202, 203, 204, 205, 206, 210, 211, 212, 213, 214, 217, 218, 220, 222, 224, 226, 227, 228, 229, 231, 232, 237, 238, 240, 241, 242, 243, 244, 246, 247.

Information on Layton's poetry in anthologies.

C420 Francis, Wynne. "Irving Layton." In *Canadian Writers and Their Works*. Ed. Robert Lecker, Jack David, and Ellen Quigley. Introd. George Woodcock. Poetry Series. Vol. V. Toronto: ECW, 1985, 141–234.

Following the format for this series, Francis introduces her subject with a brief biography followed by placing him in regard to his "Tradition and Milieu." Layton does not fit into a Canadian tradition, drawing as he does from such a wide spectrum of literary sources. She chronicles his struggle for acceptance, his battles with the critics, and outlines some of the main conflicts in which he has been involved. Layton rejected the ineffectual sentimentality of A.M. Klein and his (Layton's) father, and the "moneytheistic" attitude of his brother-in-law Strul Goldberg, leaning more towards the defiance and courage symbolized in his mother. In the early 1950s, Layton moved from Marxism to Nietzscheism, both of which became accommodated in his Hebraism. As early as "Song of a Frightened Jewish Boy" in *Periods of the Moon* (1966), there were indications that Layton would eventually reclaim Jesus as his kinsman. The Six Day War served to confirm his insights and make him a more militant poet. From 1970 on, Layton directed his attacks against Christianity, with Nietzscheism and Hebraism blended into a "cosmic Judaism." A selected bibliography is included. This is also published as an offprint (C10).

C421 Geddes, Gary. "Old Poetics: Or, Feeding a New Line." *Waves*, 13, Nos. 2–3 (Winter 1985), 5–6.

Geddes comments on the line "And the inescapable lousiness of growing old" from Layton's "Keine Lazarovitch." The line acquires its brilliance through the juxtaposition of the colloquial "lousiness" with the formal "inescapable." The impressive rhythmic effect of the line comes both from the play of speech rhythms against poetic rhythms, and "a semi-conscious element of recognition and surprise at the way the stresses fall and the way the sounds themselves build up."

C422 Gnarowski, Michael. "Poetry in English, 1918–1960." *The Canadian Encyclopedia*. Vol. III (1985). Rpt. 2nd ed. Vol. III (1988).

Layton was one of the *First Statement* poets whose work was marked by a strong "social concern and a more direct sense of urban experience." His publication in 1959 of *A Red Carpet for the Sun* helped make Canadian poetry, particularly his own work, more popular.

C423 Keith, W.J. *Canadian Literature in English*. Longman Literature in English. London: Longman, 1985, pp. 6, 57, 61, 75, 76, 84, 91–94, 96, 98, 208, 210, 259–60.

Layton is the "pre-eminent poetic figure" of mid-century. His range of subject matter is extraordinary, and he has a "wonderful capacity for creating unforgettable lines." Layton is both romantic and a classicist, both a traditionalist and a poetic revolutionary. While an uneven poet, he is memorable for his "passionate realism."

C424 Kröller, Eva-Marie. "Nineteenth Century Canadians and the Rhine Valley." In *Gaining Ground: European Critics on Canadian Literature*. Ed. Robert Kroetsch and Reingard M. Nischik. Western Canadian Literary Documents Series, Vol. VI. Edmonton: NeWest, 1985, p. 243.

The response of nineteenth-century Canadians to the Rhineland provides a backdrop to such contemporary poems as Layton's "Rhine Boat Trip."

C425 Mayne, Seymour. Introduction. In *Essential Words: An Anthology of Jewish Canadian Poetry*. Ed. Seymour Mayne. Ottawa: Oberon, 1985, pp. 12–13, 14.

While A.M. Klein celebrated "tradition and community," Layton "disaffiliated himself from accepted traditions and from the community." His "tough-minded earthiness" has had a widespread influence on Canadian poetry.

C426 McGregor, Gaile. *The Wacousta Syndrome: Explorations in the Canadian Langscape*. Toronto: Univ. of Toronto Press, 1985, pp. 119, 294–95, 405.

As one of the few who represent that the Canadian poet's mission is "to 'liberate' society from stifling convention," even Layton projects " 'a self threatened by images of castration or engulfment' . . . [and] reveals a certain covert anxiety."

C427 New, W.H. "Literature in English." *The Canadian Encyclopedia*. Vol. II (1985). Rpt. 2nd ed. Vol. II (1988).

Layton is mentioned for his connection with the *First Statement* group.

C428 Platnick, Phyllis. *Canadian Poetry: Index to Criticisms (1970–1979) / Poésie Canadienne: Index de Critiques (1970–1979)*. [Toronto]: Canadian Library Association, 1985, pp. 182–89.

Includes information on theses, articles, reviews, and other material on Layton's work published between 1970 and 1979.

C429 Wiens, Erwin. "The Horses of Realism: The Layton-Pacey Correspondence." *Studies in Canadian Literature*, 10, Nos. 1–2 (1985), 183–207.

The correspondence between Irving Layton and Desmond Pacey spans the years from 1954 to 1974, with the majority of letters written between 1954 and 1965. Pacey and Layton were drawn together through their affinities with social realism, with Pacey being particularly attracted by Layton's energy. Taking a generally chronological approach, Wiens shows how this correspondence documents the development of Canadian poetry and criticism, as well as being full of exchanges on a wide variety of personal and literary topics, and rich in personal drama. While Pacey was not an astute analyst of Layton's poetry, "He regarded Layton's ideas and opinions as worthy to be challenged, and he responded with 'Dionysian' relish and a kind of fearless sincerity."

C430 Woodcock, George. Introduction. In *Canadian Writers and Their Works*. Poetry Series. Vol. v. Ed. Robert Lecker, Jack David, and Ellen Quigley. Toronto: ECW, 1985, pp. 2–3, 4, 5, 12–16, 19.

For Layton, the poet must be a prophet, but much of his work is romantic and traditional. He is at his best "in his passionate and compassionate poems of identification with the suffering world," such as "A Tall Man Executes a Jig."

C431 Precosky, Don. "Reassessing *Other Canadians*." CV/II, 8, No. 4 (Feb. 1985), 26, 27.

"... Layton's poems are closest to the spirit of ... [Sutherland's] introduction ...." "The Swimmer"

embodies "the merging of self and nature which is the central theme of his best works."

C432 Goddard, John. "Other People's Lives." *Books in Canada*, March 1985, pp. 6–8.

Layton expresses his reservations on Elspeth Cameron's forthcoming biography of him (C9), but Cameron feels she can "make the form and style expressive of the subject."

C433 Goldsworthy, Frederick. "The Rampant 'I': Irving Layton Reassessed." *World Literature Written in English* [Univ. of Guelph], 25 (Spring 1985), 137–44.

Viewing Layton in the context of the Romantic tradition gives his work cohesion. He distances himself from the rest of humanity through his portrait of himself as an alien Jew and his Nietzschean interests. The role of the "I" in his poetry, a "distanced and hostile prophet," helps him preserve his alienation and write the way he does.

C434 Wiens, Erwin. "From Apocalypse to Black Mountain: The Contexts of Layton's Early Criticism." *Canadian Poetry: Studies, Documents, Reviews*, No. 16 (Spring–Summer 1985), pp. 1–20.

Wiens examines "Layton's criticism in the context of prominent developments in poetry and criticism during the decade that followed World War II." In the 1940s, he uses Herbert Read and the Apocalyptics to attack the T.S. Eliot-W.H. Auden-Dylan Thomas eclecticism of the *Preview* group. In the 1950s, he asserts a modern American tradition "against the disaffected, Movement-influenced, formalism of the 'mythopeic' poets." He shifted his critical position as soon as Black Mountain poetics became established in Canada. "What remained consistent was his conviction that poetry must function at the centre of both public and private life."

C435 French, William. "A Double Dose of Layton." *The Globe and Mail* [Toronto], 21 May 1985, p. M9.
French briefly notes that the coincident publication in the coming fall of Elspeth Cameron's biography (C9) and Layton's memoirs is unusual and perhaps unprecedented. Cameron states that Layton may be surprised when he sees the book.

C436 Kertes, Joseph. " 'Brief Are the Days of Beauty': The Wisdom of Irving Layton's 'The Gucci Bag.' " *Canadian Literature*, No. 105 (Summer 1985), pp. 32–42.
The Gucci Bag conveys "a prevailing sense of finality" in a manner similar to that of W.B. Yeats's *Last Poems*. A "sense of calm and reconciliation" and "images of transformation" pervade the volume, although Layton is still distressed "by avarice and covetousness," which he symbolizes in the gucci bag. Vituperative poems are balanced by "expressions of almost boyish wonder and vulnerability" in poems like "Samantha Clara Layton." Layton provides "us with insight into the state of the world and some suggestions as to how to improve it."

C437 Slopen, Beverley. "An Outrageous Life . . . Respectable Protest . . . East Meets West." *Quill & Quire*, July 1985, p. 36.
Elspeth Cameron discusses the writing of biographies in general and the experience of writing on Layton (C9) in particular.

C438 Shein, Brian. "Among the Immortals." *Toronto Life*, Aug. 1985, p. 15.
Shein describes Layton's activities while in Greece being filmed for the documentary *Poet: Irving Layton Observed*.

C439 Slopen, Beverley. "Layton's Life Being Told Twice Over." *The Sunday Star* [*The Toronto Star*]. "Book World," 4 Aug. 1985, Books, p. G11.
Elspeth Cameron's biography of Layton (C9) and Layton's memoirs promise to be intriguing accounts of his life.

C440 Adachi, Ken. "The Scaling of Irving Layton." *The Toronto Star*, 18 Aug. 1985, p. A20.
Elspeth Cameron states that she admires Layton's energy and poetic achievement, although he has contempt for himself. Her forthcoming book "does make Layton terribly human."

C441 Bennett, Joy. "Getting Permission." *Quill & Quire*, Sept. 1985, p. 2.
Bennett defends Concordia University's policy requiring researchers using the Layton collection to get permission from authors of letters to Layton. (See also C446.)

C442 Cameron, Elspeth. [Letter.] *Quill & Quire*, Sept. 1985, p. 2.
Cameron responds to Layton's letter (B944), affirming her version of the genesis of the biography.

C443 Adachi, Ken. "The Tumultuous Life of Irving Layton." *The Toronto Star*. "Books," 23 Sept. 1985, p. D3.
Layton's literary feud with Elspeth Cameron is an overreaction, but "literary feuds are as old as literature itself."

C444 Slopen, Beverley. "The True Art of Insult, by Irving Layton." *The Toronto Star*, 29 Sept. 1985, p. G10.
Slopen communicates some of Layton's strenuous objections to Elspeth Cameron's biography (C9).

C445 Cameron, Elspeth. "The Tumultuous Loves of Irving Layton." *Chatelaine*, Oct. 1985, pp. 66–67, 108,

110, 112–13. Rpt. (revised) in *Irving Layton: A Portrait*. By Elspeth Cameron. Don Mills, Ont.: Stoddart, 1985, pp. 101–03, 136–38, 141–43, 166–70, 226–27, 259–64, 410, 412, 433, 447–48, 457–58, 460–61.

Layton's relationships with Faye, Betty, Aviva, Harriet, and Anna are summarized.

C446 Cameron, Elspeth. "Unusual Policy an Obstacle." *Quill & Quire*, Oct. 1985, p. 2.

The requirement that researchers obtain written permission from authors of letters to Layton before viewing them is unusually stringent. (See also C441.)

C447 Chodan, Lucinda. "Layton's Biography Blues: Poet Launches Campaign to Discredit Book." *The Gazette* [Montreal], 2 Oct. 1985, p. H11. Rpt. (abridged — "Layton Out to Discredit Biography by Cameron") in *Calgary Herald*, 5 Oct. 1985, p. A12.

Layton criticizes the accuracy and tone of Elspeth Cameron's biography (C9), but Cameron stands firm.

C448 "'. . . Most Malevolent Book': Layton Attacks New Biography." *The Globe and Mail* [Toronto], 3 Oct. 1985, p. D5.

Layton criticizes Elspeth Cameron's biography (C9) for inaccuracies and innuendos. Cameron defends her statements.

C449 Cameron, Elspeth. "Matter of Scholarship." Letter. *The Globe and Mail* [Toronto], 12 Oct. 1985, p. A7.

Cameron takes issue with Layton's examples of errors in her biography (C9), specifically her description of his attitudes towards communism and capitalism.

C450 Pietkiewicz, Karen J. *The Gazette* [Montreal], 18 Oct. 1985, p. B2.

Elspeth Cameron has distorted Pietkiewicz's comments to fit her own image of Layton as a sexual predator.

C451 French, William. "Passion and a Lot of Poetry." Rev. of *Irving Layton: A Portrait*, by Elspeth Cameron; and *Waiting for the Messiah: A Memoir*, by Irving Layton. *The Globe and Mail* [Toronto], 19 Oct. 1985, p. J3.

These two books are complementary. Elspeth Cameron's "dispassionate and remarkably comprehensive" biography (C9) is balanced by Layton's "earthy, passionate and bombastic" approach.

C452 Richardson, Jeff. "Irving Layton Waxes Poetic in the Land of Homer." *Saturday Night*, Nov. 1985, p. 84.

On the occasion of launching Layton's ΕΔΩ ΑΓΑΠΗΣΕ ΦΛΕΓΟΜΕΝΗ Η ΣΑΠΦΩ / *Where Burning Sappho Loved*, Layton gives a reading to a group of diplomats and Canadian expatriates. The reactions of various people are wryly noted; Canada's cultural attaché suggests that he is also in the "writing business." " 'I write dispatches.' "

C453 Whiteway, Doug. "Cameron vs. Layton." *Winnipeg Free Press*, 6 Nov. 1985, p. 34.

In spite of their ongoing battle, Elspeth Cameron recognizes that Layton is a seminal if now somewhat anachronistic figure in Canadian poetry. His breaking of taboos led, for example, to Marian Engel deciding to write about menstruation.

C454 McGoogan, Kenneth. "Layton, Biographer Slug It Out." *Calgary Herald*, 10 Nov. 1985, p. F7.

Elspeth Cameron states that writing Layton's biography (C9) turned her into a feminist. Between biographer and subject, McGoogan notes three sources of friction: "First, he's a Jew and she's a WASP.

Second, he's a man of passionate extremes . . . she's a university-trained scholar . . . he's a let-it-all-hang-out man's man and she's an articulate contemporary woman."

C455 Fulford, Robert. "Smoking Mr. Layton Out of His Own Woods." *The Toronto Star*, 23 Nov. 1985, "Books," p. M7.

Elspeth Cameron's biography of Layton (C9) is an "excellent book," which has helped revive Layton's sagging reputation.

C456 Lefeuvre, Linda. Letter. *Chatelaine*, Dec. 1985, p. 200.

The excerpt (C445) from Elspeth Cameron's book (C9) printed in *Chatelaine* on October 1985 (C445) shows that Layton never grew up in his relation with women.

C457 McWhirter, George. "Creativity at UBC." Letter. *The Globe and Mail* [Toronto], 3 Dec. 1985, p. A7.

McWhirter responds to Bronwyn Drainie's article "The New Patronage of Literature" in the Literary Supplement of *The Globe and Mail* [Toronto], 16 November 1985. "Irving Layton has learned from Hemingway that to be a great writer, you not only have to travel, but you have to open your shirt collar and show your chest to let those people know how great a writer you are."

C458 Goddard, John. "Lecture by Layton Biographer Ends in Shouts, Booing." *The Gazette* [Montreal], 9 Dec. 1985, p. D10.

After a public lecture on Layton by Elspeth Cameron, his bride-to-be, Anna Pottier, vehemently criticized Cameron. Cameron states that she has received hate mail from Layton every day for three months.

C459 Yanofsky, Joel. "Author Accused of Doing a Hatchet Job on Poet." *The Canadian Jewish News* [Toronto], 19 Dec. 1985, p. 31.

Elspeth Cameron's lecture at the Jewish Public Library was disrupted by Anna Pottier's denunciations of Cameron and her book (C9). Cameron responded that Layton's anger stems from her accurate depiction of his mercurial nature. (For Layton's response see B949.)

C460 French, William. "Book Break-Ins and Zesty Thrills." *The Globe and Mail* [Toronto], 28 Dec. 1985, p. D21.

French mentions Layton's alleged attempt to damage Elspeth Cameron's reputation. "Layton launched an attack by mail on Cameron that has no precedent in this country for venom and scurrilous implications." (For Layton's response see B948.)

C461 Adachi, Ken. "A Year of Double Talk and Toil." *The Sunday Star* [*The Toronto Star*]. "Books," 29 Dec. 1985, p. E11.

Layton's invective against Elspeth Cameron's biography (C9) continues. His most recent letter indicates he will write a biography of Cameron's life.

C462 Bruni, Valerio. "La redenzione nel sole: L'elemento costruttivo nell'opera di Irving Layton." In *Lo specchio magico: studi sulla poesia canadese*. Ed. Alfredo Rizzardi. Abano Terme, Italy: Piovan, 1986, pp. 106–32. Rpt. in *Danza Sulla Fune: Studio Sulla Poesia di Irving Layton*. By Valerio Bruni. Abano Terme, Italy: Piovan, 1990, pp. 55–79.

Layton's poetry takes issue with the inhumanity he sees pervading the modern world. "La poesia di Layton sembra dunque suggerire che, benchè la 'resurrezione' sia lontana in un mondo che sembra avviata sempre più verso l'autodistruzione, essa è possibile soltonto attraverso il recupero delle forze vitali insite nell'uomo, della sua capacità creativa, della libertà di godere pienamente dei piaceri dell'esistenza, dell'ebbrezza del sesso, del contatto assoluto con la natura, in quella che potremmo definire una redenzione nel sole."

C463 Dudek, Louis. "Can Lit Notes — 1." In *The Bumper Book*. Ed. John Metcalf. Toronto: ECW, 1986, p. 41.

Dudek briefly notes "It's odd that the two poets in Canada who write obsessively about Jesus are Jews .... If Layton ever had an original idea it probably came out of Nietzsche or Bernard Shaw."

C464 Knickers, Suzi [Darling, Michael]. "Suzi Knickers' Book Bits." In *The Bumper Book*. Ed. John Metcalf. Toronto: ECW, 1986, p. 117.

Darling satirically notes, "Poet Irving Layton ... will ... have himself crucified on Good Friday" in order to win the Nobel Prize.

C465 Sutherland, Fraser. "In Defence of Laura Secord." In *The Bumper Book*. Ed. John Metcalf. Toronto: ECW, 1986, p. 8.

Earle Birney, Irving Layton, and Al Purdy "have adapted foreign influences to the Canadian landscape and psyche." This tension between local and cosmopolitan influences sometimes produces poetry that is ironic and "a little too slick."

C466 Hrywnak, Luboslaw. "Poetry an Achievement." Letter. *The Gazette* [Montreal], 2 Jan. 1986, p. B2.

Elspeth Cameron's description of Layton's personality in her biography (C9) is not justified. "I believe strongly his person is beyond reproach."

C467 Carson, Ed. "Irving Layton the Loser?". Letter. *The Globe and Mail* [Toronto], 22 Jan. 1986, p. A7.

Layton's unfounded attacks on Elspeth Cameron's biography (C9) will not prevent its being "valued for its compassion, accuracy and insight."

C468 Adachi, Ken. "Brave Little *Contact* Helped Fledgling Poets." *The Toronto Star*. "Books," 27 Jan. 1986, p. D3.

Layton "lent an enthusiastic hand for a while, particularly after the magazine ... evolved into Contact Press ...."

C469 Heward, Burt. "Layton's Life Sells Poorly But Thrives." *The Citizen* [Ottawa], 8 Feb. 1986, p. E3.

Some booksellers have reported that poor sales of *Waiting for the Messiah: A Memoir* and Elspeth Cameron's *Irving Layton: A Portrait* (C9) were partly due to the controversy.

C470 Robertson, Heather. "Enough of 'Reverse Racism.'" *The Globe and Mail* [Toronto], 8 Feb. 1986, p. A7.

Layton's letter (B950) is an example of reverse racism.

C471 Worthington, Peter. "A Case of Hate Literature." *Influence*, Feb.–March 1986, p. 62.

Layton's attacks on Elspeth Cameron have "passed the bounds of decency," rivalling the actions of Jim Keegstra and Ernst Zundel. The Canadian cultural establishment is remiss for not coming to Cameron's support.

C472 Allen, P.R. "Proof of Charge Is Missing." *The Globe and Mail* [Toronto], 15 March 1986, p. A7.

Layton gives no indication of how he can prove his accusation (B950) of Elspeth Cameron's anti-semitism.

C473 Mortimer, Rick. Letter. *The Globe and Mail* [Toronto], 15 March 1986, p. A7.

Responding to Layton's letter (B950), Mortimer states that as a WASP, he is tired of being blamed for everything that is wrong in the world.

C474 Conlogue, Ray. "Layton's Complaint." *Toronto*, May 1986, pp. 51–53, 82–85.

Although Layton over-reacted, he was genuinely hurt by his portrayal in Elspeth Cameron's book (C9). Cameron did not do a particularly good job of coping with the complexities of Layton's character, particularly his self-dramatization of himself as a womanizer.

C475 Ackerman, Marianne. "Toga-Wearing Layton Enlivens Old Debate." *The Gazette* [Montreal], 5 May 1986, Entertainment, p. B13.

In The Symposium at Centaur Theatre, Layton was one of a cast of eight re-enacting "the 2,000 year old debate on the nature of eros, its relation to beauty, pleasure and the good life."

C476 Herman, Peter. Rev. of *Essential Words: An Anthology of Jewish Canadian Poetry*. Ed. Seymour Mayne. RUBICON [McGill Univ.], No. 7 (Summer 1986), pp. 219, 220.

Layton's influence in *Essential Words: An Anthology of Jewish Canadian Poetry* is pervasive, felt especially in the language and the concept of Jew as poet / prophet.

C477 Barsky, Lesley. "Holy Hormones . . . Male Pregnancy." *Chatelaine*, Aug. 1986, p. 63.

Layton is one of several men asked their opinion on male pregnancy. Layton states ". . . it would be a marvellous experience."

C478 Yanofsky, Joel. "The Great Canadian Literary Feud." *The Gazette* [Montreal], 30 Aug. 1986, p. B8.

The conflict between Elspeth Cameron and Irving Layton was unprecedented in Canadian literary history.

C479 Rasky, Frank. "Layton Claims He's Been Leading Double Life." *The Canadian Jewish News* [Toronto], 9 Oct. 1986, p. 39.

At the Jewish book fair, Layton claims that his image as a womanizer was created by him to get people to read his books. He also comments on his idyllic marriage to Anna, the Elspeth Cameron biography (C9), his place in the poetic hierarchy, and the meaning Jewishness has for him.

C480 Fraser, Matthew. "Layton Dominates Montreal Connections." *The Globe and Mail* [Toronto], 27 Oct. 1986, p. D9.

Of the three NFB documentaries on Irving Layton, Mordecai Richler, and Brian Moore, Layton's (C673) makes the greatest impression. Layton is the "self-proclaimed Dionysius of Canadian poetry." Layton is a man "who exults in himself at least as well as he writes poems."

C481 [Baernstein], Tsigane. " 'Women Make Men, Men Make Art . . .' Debunking the Bards." HERizons, Oct.–Nov. 1986, pp. 18–19, 31.

Layton's ideas and some of his poems are used as examples of the ways in which the creativity of women has been suppressed.

C482 Levy, David. "Layton: Canada's Kahane?". *Canadian Jewish News* [Toronto], 6 Nov. 1986, p. 11.

Frank Rasky's praise of Layton (C479) takes his "graceless slander" of Elspeth Cameron as objective fact. "His [Layton's] noisy vengefulness, lack of grace, forbearance and humility . . . are the very opposite of Jewish virtue."

C483 Ward, Olivia. "Life's 'Disappointing' but Layton's Smiling Again." *The Toronto Star*, 16 Nov. 1986, p. G5.

Layton considers his battle with Elspeth Cameron now behind him. Anna discusses her meeting with Layton and their life together.

C484 Djwa, Sandra. *The Politics of the Imagination: A Life of F.R. Scott*. Toronto: McClelland and Stewart, 1987, pp. 212–13, 216, 272, 275–83, 286, 290, 295–96, 412.

Layton's encounters with F.R. Scott are discussed with special attention to Layton's militant involvement with the Kingston Writers Conference in 1954, of which Scott was the chief organizer.

C485 "Irving Layton (b. 1912)." In *Introduction to Literature: British, American, Canadian*. Ed. and preface Robert Lecker, Jack David, and Peter O'Brien. New York: Harper & Row, 1987, p. 374.

Bio-critical information. "Layton is a prophet, satirist and lyricist."

C486 Moritz, Albert, and Theresa Moritz. *The Oxford Illustrated Literary Guide to Canada*. Toronto: Oxford Univ. Press, 1987, pp. 69–70, 71–72, 100, 108, 133, 164, 175, 178–79, 204.

Layton is indexed under "Montreal," "Ste.-Anne-de-Bellevue," "Bancroft," "Niagara-on-the-Lake," "Toronto," and "Saskatoon."

C487 Nash, Knowlton. *Prime Time at Ten: Behind-the-Camera Battles of Canadian TV Journalism*. Toronto: McClelland and Stewart, 1987, pp. 55–56, 84–85.

Nash discusses the uproar occasioned by Layton's reading of "The Farting Jesus" on *Ninety Minutes Live*.

C488 Woodcock, George. "Canadian Poetry: The Emergent Tradition." In his *Northern Spring: The Flowering of Canadian Literature*. Vancouver: Douglas & McIntyre, 1987, pp. 190, 191.

Layton is a "hyper-romantic, reaching a poetic extravagance of diction and a density of imagery that are far removed from anything Pound or Williams would have accepted."

C489 Gold, Jack. "Forgive Him, Lord, He's Just a Bit Confused." *The Gazette* [Montreal], 17 March 1987, p. B2.

Layton's attacks on Christianity in his review of Rabbi Stuart E. Rosenberg's *The Christian Problem: A Jewish View* (B1148) are overly simplified and ignore the evidence of the New Testament.

C490 Lang, Allen A. "Layton's Holocaust View Nonsense." *The Gazette* [Montreal], 17 March 1987, p. B2.

Layton's contention that Christianity was responsible for the holocaust is nonsense. Any persecution of Jews by Christians is against the spirit of their religion. (See B1148.)

C491 Meyer, Bruce, and Brian O'Riordan. "Two Windows: An Interview with D.G. Jones." *Poetry Canada Review*, 8, Nos. 2–3 (Spring 1987), 5.

Jones briefly notes that ". . . in the late 50s and early 60s, the so-called myth makers — Louis Dudek and Irving Layton presumably (Layton is as close to Northrop Frye as anybody) — they were trying to move Canadian poets away from the bias towards social realism."

C492 "3rd Annual Best-Dressed List." *Chatelaine*, April 1987, p. 81.

Layton has been dressing better since his battle

with Elspeth Cameron. Perhaps he is trying to show her he can look bourgeois too.

C493 Greenstein, Michael. "Canadian Poetry after Auschwitz." *Canadian Poetry: Studies, Documents, Reviews*, No. 20 (Spring–Summer 1987), pp. 1, 2–6, 9, 10, 14, 15. Rpt. in *Third Solitudes: Tradition and Discontinuity in Jewish Canadian Literature*. By Michael Greenstein. Montreal: McGill-Queen's Univ. Press, 1989, pp. 35–53.

Layton, along with Leonard Cohen and Eli Mandel, has been more successful than A.M. Klein in confronting the holocaust poetically. Layton's "more modern techniques" are better suited for the subject than Klein's "medieval parallels and historical allusions." ". . . Layton the prophet declaims against forgetfulness in order to avenge the ghosts of innocent children, while Layton the poet employs metaphoric disguise to imprint images of absence, like tattooed arms, indelibly in his reader's mind."

C494 Dreschel, Andrew. "Angry Words." *The Spectator* [Hamilton], 23 May 1987, p. D3.

Layton's comments on various topics are combined with biographical information. Canada, argues Layton, puts the United States into perspective. "The tundra, and the snow, and the darkness . . . [give] a bronx cheer to the civilization to the south."

C495 "Layton, Irving Peter." *Marquis Who's Who in the World*. 8th ed. (1987–88).

Bio-bibliographical data.

C496 O'Rourke, David. "A Memoir of Layton and Callaghan: On the Target." *Poetry Canada Review*, 9, No. 1 (Fall 1987), pp. 14–15.

O'Rourke recounts his student days and early friendship with Layton, as well as his editorial contacts with Layton. He also discusses a meeting among Layton, Barry Callaghan, and himself. Layton and Callaghan have a similar energy and courage and a frustration with the limitations of Canadian society.

C497 Miner, Michael. "Coming Curmudgeon." *The Reader* [Chicago], Oct. 1987.

Layton states that while he has thought of coming to the United States, he has always been able to make a living teaching in Canada. His forthcoming readings in Chicago have evoked little interest.

C498 Curran, Ann. "Canadian Writer Mixes Poetry with Controversy." *The Pittsburgh Press*, 3 Oct. 1987.

On the occasion of his forthcoming reading at the Carnegie Lecture Hall in Oakland, Layton comments on the necessity of passion and imagination. His way of writing poetry is instinctual, starting sometimes with rhythm and sometimes with words.

C499 Curran, Ann. "Irving Layton's Love Poems Produce a Feast of Love at Poetry Forum." *The Pittsburgh Press*, 8 Oct. 1987.

Layton's reading at the Carnegie Lecture Hall was well received. "An unusual warmth was evident in the closing session as people asked Layton about his mother."

C499a Brenner, Rachel Feldhay. "The Canadian Jew and the State of Israel: Explorations in Canadian Jewish Writing." *Viewpoints*, 15, No. 5, Supplement to *The Canadian Jewish News*, 26 Nov. 1987, pp. 1, 2.

The Jew today is caught between the conflicting options of "a powerful national system operating primarily in the interests of Jewish independence" and "a universal system striving to guarantee freedom and protection for humanity at large." Layton takes a humanist approach, preaching reconciliation with the past. But he also "wholeheartedly supports the image of Jewish strength represented by the State of Israel."

C500 Billard, Jean Antonin. "Irving Layton." *ellipse*, No. 40 (1988), p. 93.
In a preface to his translation of Layton's "The Carillon" (B705), Billard describes him as "un poète impitoyable pour un monde sans piété, sans mémoire."

C501 "Irving Layton 1912– ." In *The Cambridge Guide to Literature in English*. Ed. Ian Ousby. Foreword Margaret Atwood. Cambridge: Cambridge Univ. Press, 1988, p. 567.
Brief biographical data.

C502 Kirk, Heather. "Anecdotes of Canadian Literary Life." *Cross-Canada Writers' Magazine*, 10, No. 1 (1988), 3.
Kirk recollects her associations with several Canadian writers. Layton was both generous and demanding as a person and a teacher.

C503 Lewis, Joanne. "Irving's Women: A Feminist Critique of the Love Poems of Irving Layton." *Studies in Canadian Literature*, 13, No. 2 (1988), 142–56.
"A feminist critique makes it imperative" that the life of the poet not be separated from his poems. Layton is "a misogynist, with a particular hatred and fear of the woman artist." Their genitalia are "dirty and repulsive": violence and death are often linked with sex, with the female "destructive and castrating" character. The male poet's power over language provides him with power over women; he feels threatened by woman's power to create.

C504 Mansbridge, Francis. "Irving Layton 1912– ." In *The New Canadian Anthology*. Ed. and preface Robert Lecker and Jack David. Introd. George Woodcock. Scarborough, Ont.: Nelson, 1988, pp. 103–04.
Mansbridge briefly introduces Layton's life and work. Layton is a figure full of apparent contradictions. "A full appreciation of his achievement requires an ability to keep these various and sometimes conflicting aspects in balance."

C505 Mezei, Kathy, with Patricia Matson and Maureen Hole. *Bibliography of Criticism on English and French Literary Translations in Canada 1950–1986. Annotated / Bibliographie de la Critique des Translations Littéraires Anglaises et Francaises au Canada de 1950 à 1986. Avec Commentaires*. Pref. Viviane F. Launay. Introd. Kathy Mezei. Ottawa: Univ. of Ottawa Press / Canadian Federation for the Humanities, 1988, p. 144.
Brief comments on translations of Layton's foreword to *The Swinging Flesh* and some of his poems in Suzanne Guertin's thesis (C536).

C506 Mills, John. "A Rigmarole: Memoirs of a Mud Wrestler." In *The Macmillan Anthology 1*. Ed. John Metcalf and Leon Rooke. Toronto: Macmillan, 1988, pp. 241, 245, 246, 247, 253–58, 262–63, 266–71, 273, 275–76.
In this memoir of his early life, Mills discusses his tempestuous relationship with Irving and Aviva. "Canadian Literature can be said to have entered the modern world with Layton's *The Swinging Flesh* and Leonard Cohen's *Beautiful Losers*.

C507 "N.F.B. — Films about Canadian Literature." CM: *A Reviewing Journal of Canadian Materials for Young People*, Jan. 1988, pp. 10–11.
In *Poet: Irving Layton Observed* and, in the shorter version, *Irving Layton: An Introduction* (C673), ". . . Layton exudes the zest and passion that inform his verse." In *A Tall Man Executes a Jig* (A100), he

"reads and discusses one of his best-known sonnet sequences . . . ."

C508 Rosenberg, Suzanne. *A Soviet Odyssey*. Toronto: Oxford Univ. Press, 1988, pp. 24, 25–28. Rpt. (abridged — "Poet's Socialism Led to Arguments") in *The Globe and Mail* [Toronto], 16 April 1988, p. D5.

Rosenberg recounts her youthful friendship with Layton. He possessed "breadth of heart and mind from which trifling things were hastily dismissed." "Like Antaeus he drew his strength from the earth and was opening himself up to the realities of living."

C509 Weiss, Allan. "Layton, Irving (1912–   )." In his *A Comprehensive Bibliography of English-Canadian Short Stories 1950–1983*. Toronto: ECW, 1988, pp. 389–90.

Weiss lists Layton's short stories, including reprinted anthology contributions.

C510 Mader, Phil. "Irving Layton at Le Hibou." *The Archivist* [Ottawa], 15, No. 1 (Jan.–Feb. 1988), 10–11.

The National Archives recently acquired the recording *Irving Layton at Le Hibou*, which is "as complete a reflection of Layton's ethos as any other collection of his work."

C511 Adachi, Ken. "Anthology Producers Try, Try, Try Again." *The Toronto Star*, 23 April 1988, p. M4.

Layton's contribution to *The Macmillan Anthology 1*, edited by John Metcalf and Leon Rooke, "is all very pathetic stuff."

C512 Wilkins, Charles. "ECW: Making Bibliography Pay." *Quill & Quire*, June 1988, p. 9.

In this article, based on an interview with Jack David, co-owner of ECW PRESS, David comments that Layton's bibliography has "been an enormous headache," but after three different bibliographers have taken a stab at it, a fourth is finally "bringing it all together."

C513 Ayre, John. *Northrop Frye: A Biography*. Toronto: Random House, 1989, pp. 235, 277.

The "fiercely ideological" differences between Northrop Frye and Irving Layton were exacerbated by Frye's attacks on Layton's early poetry. "Layton believed as dogmatically in the inspirational power of real experience as Frye believed in the power of literary convention."

C514 Cohen, Leonard. "To the Reader / Al Lettore." In *Tutto sommato: poesie 1945–1989*. By Irving Layton. Ed. and trans. Alfredo Rizzardi. Abano Terme, Italy: Piovan, 1989, pp. 10–11.

Layton "is the greatest living poet in the English language." In his work you will "refresh your imagination in the continual exercise of his sublime refusal to submit."

C515 Mansbridge, Francis. Introduction. In *Wild Gooseberries: The Selected Letters of Irving Layton*. Ed. Francis Mansbridge. Toronto: Macmillan, 1989, pp. v–xii, 3–4, 79–80, 171, 247, 305.

This book includes a general introduction and shorter introductions to each of the book's five sections. These letters reveal a complex person, "in opposition to society and in conflict within himself." Often he writes of people as "suitable embodiments of the characteristics he admires or detests." While his letters become more thoughtful and introspective as he grows older, righteous indignation, never far away, often erupts.

C516 Miki, Roy. *A Record of Writing: An Annotated and Illustrated Bibliography of George Bowering*. Vancouver: Talonbooks, 1989, pp. 36, 40, 50, 64, 113, 133, 155, 162, 170, 198, 217, 220, 255–56, 257, 289, 290, 308.

Layton is mentioned in connection with writings by and about George Bowering.

C517 New, W.H. *A History of Canadian Literature*. London: Macmillan, 1989, pp. 185–87, 194–96, 198, 258.

In Layton's poetry, "system is an agent of death" and "language . . . the agent of fertility." "Layton excels at expressing the immediacy of rage and joy."

C518 Hunter, Tim. "The North American States: Charles Olson's Letters to Irving Layton." *Line* [Simon Fraser Univ.], No. 13 (Spring 1989), pp. 123–52.

This article includes reprints of the eight letters and one postcard extant from Charles Olson to Irving Layton, dating from 1952 to 1957. Olson's brief articles "The Celts, and Plato" and "The Crisis of the Third Foot" are included, as are a brief introduction and extensive annotation.

C519 Todd, Jack. "Irving Layton: Shotgun Blast in China Shop." *The Gazette* [Montreal], 10 Oct. 1989, p. A3.

While Layton is a decent performer, his work does not stand scrutiny. His social satires are "wickedly funny," but his use of language is often imprecise or "lyrically overheated."

C520 Faas, Ekbert, and Sabrina Reed. Introduction. In *Irving Layton & Robert Creeley: The Complete Correspondence 1953–1978*. Ed. Ekbert Fass and Sabrina Reed. Montreal / Kingston: McGill-Queen's Univ. Press, 1990, pp. i–xxxii.

Faas and Reed outline the Irving Layton-Robert Creeley correspondence. Creeley's influence, as friend, publisher, and poet, is discussed, including Creeley's influence on Layton's relationship with Louis Dudek and others. Creeley greatly encouraged Layton's writing and literary career.

C521 "Publishers Reject Poems by Layton." *The Citizen* [Ottawa], 1 March 1990, p. B7.

Toronto writer and hoaxer Crad Kilodney submitted a manuscript of Layton poems to twenty-six Canadian publishers. Only two recognized them as Layton's.

C522 Arnold, Janice. "Concordia Creates Layton Award." *Canadian Jewish News* [Montreal], 28 June 1990, p. 2.

In honour of Layton's long association with Concordia, two awards of $500 each have been established for undergraduates who demonstrate excellence in poetry and short fiction.

C523 Fraser, Hugh. "Sweet Harmony: Evening of Passion and Wit." *The Spectator* [Hamilton], 10 July 1990, p. C1.

Poet Irving Layton and cellist Ofra Harnoy combine at the Hamilton Art Gallery to produce "a wonderfully passionate musicality."

Theses and Dissertations

C524 Edelstein, George. "Irving Layton: A Study of the Poet in Revolt." M.A. Thesis Montreal 1962.

This biography by one of Layton's ex-army mates attempts "to isolate and examine some of the motives underlying Layton's actions." Having rejected Communism and religion, all that is left is his belief in the self and "gratification of his ego."

C525 Rogers, Amos Robert. "American Recognition of Canadian Authors Writing in English 1890–1960." 2 vols. Diss. Michigan 1964.

Layton's recognition in the United States to 1960 receives brief documentation.

C526 Lyons, Roberta. "Jewish Poets from Montreal: Concepts of History in the Poetry of A.M. Klein, Irving Layton, and Leonard Cohen." M.A. Thesis Carleton 1966.

The poetry of Irving Layton, A.M. Klein, and Leonard Cohen is examined "to determine how their possession of a common Montreal Jewish background has created in the writing of each a strong and distinctive concept of history." Layton's strong reaction against Judaism is mixed with Marxism and "Nietzschean hedonism."

C527 Reif, Eric Anthony. "Irving Layton: The Role of the Poet." M.A. Thesis Toronto 1966.

Reif examines Layton's prose statements "to see how he himself formulates the reasons and impulses behind his work." He examines the poems for the ways in which they "go beyond or contradict what Layton has said in his prose." In his poetry he examines attitudes "to nature, love, death, society, poetry and in general to the various ways men choose to live."

C528 Munro, Patricia Jane. "Seas, Evolution and Images of Continuing Creation in English-Canadian Poetry." M.A. Thesis Simon Fraser 1970.

Layton is one of nine poets whose work is examined for the way in which seas have often become the typical location of genesis. Chapter vi, "Irving Layton: The Swimmer's Neighbourhood," looks at examples of the drowned poet.

C529 Smith, P.K. "The Theme of Death in Irving Layton's Poetry." M.A. Thesis Sir George Williams 1970.

Death, for Layton, is a necessary part of the creative process. The cycle of life and death, as expressed in nature, is particularly important. By illustrating this cycle in Layton's poetry, Smith traces "the similarities between Layton's story of the poet and Nietzsche's story of the 'overman.'"

C530 Adams, Richard. "The Poetic Theories of Irving Layton: A Study in Polarities." M.A. Thesis New Brunswick 1971.

Layton regards the poet as a special person who stands for freedom against the repression of society. He uses the god Apollo "to represent the forces of society which attempt to stifle individuality." Dionysos, like the poet, combats society with "the doctrine of exuberance and freedom." Layton's poetry acts as a bridge between the two worlds.

C531 Seymour, Thomas Henry. "The Widening Gyre: Politics in the Poetry of Yeats. O How the Mighty Have Fallen!: Hemingway and the Deterioration of Style. *First Statement*'s first statements: 'romanticism, yes, but . . . .'" M.A. Thesis Simon Fraser 1971.

The last of these three essays analyzes the first seven issues of *First Statement*. Layton's essay "Politics and Poetry" receives particular attention for the way it brings together the major characteristics of *First Statement*.

C532 Mayne, Seymour. "A Study of the Poetry of Irving Layton." Diss. British Columbia 1972.

Mayne divides Layton's poetic career into eight chronological phases. Each of the phases "moves out from an initial stance and vision, and then completes itself in a manner that offers a new point of departure." The image of the poet is the centre around which Layton's poetics revolve.

C533 Rowe, Margaret Lillian. "Art and Life: A Study of the Poetry of Irving Layton." M.A. Thesis Dalhousie 1972.

Rowe discusses the relationship between artistic performance and social concern in Layton's poetry. As both artist and prophet, the poet must reconcile his artistic consciousness with his duty to humanity. Poems should be, for Layton, "a synthesis of formal beauty and relevance of idea." In the first section of the thesis, Rowe studies Layton's poetic theory; in the second, she examines his main themes; in the third, she discusses aspects of his technique.

C534 Burgess, G.C. Ian. "Irving Layton's Poetry: A Catalogue and Chronology." M.A. Thesis McGill 1973.

By establishing the first publication date of each poem, Burgess "provides a starting point for the analysis of Layton's poetic development." The publishing history of each poem includes a cross-reference to poems with changed titles. "This catalogue describes the books, lists the poems, dates the poems, and provides a beginning for those who wish to explore Layton's development from 1945 to 1973." In the first section of the thesis, Burgess lists and describes Layton's books; in the second section, he lists each poem alphabetically and provides its publishing history. Periodical publication is not included.

C535 Ferrari, Jean Dominique. "The Prophet and the Coke Bottle: A Study of Irving Layton's Poetic Vision of Common Life." M.A. Thesis PAU 1973.

The general character of Layton's work is marked by its being rooted "in a world of solid objects." One of these solid objects is the coke bottle, which "suggests common daily life" and "symbolizes the vulgar character of the world chosen by the poet." The poet is also a prophet who "tries to reach men by means of his admonitions and revelations."

C536 Guertin, Suzanne. "Irving Layton: de L'Anglais au Français." M.A. Thesis Montréal 1974.

This thesis is a translation of poems from *The Swinging Flesh* and a selection of thirty poems from *The Selected Poems of Irving Layton*. "Nous reproduirons le texte anglais qui sera suivi de la traduction française et des commentaires et annotations relatifs à cette traduction. Pour la gouverne du lecteur, sont reproduites en exegue les dates de composition des différents recueils d'où sont tirés les poèmes."

C537 Féral, Jeanine. "Aspects Sociaux de la Poésie Montréalaise de 1935 à 1955." M.A. Thesis Carleton 1975.

Féral applies formal and sociological approaches to Montreal poetry from 1935 to 1955. Irving Layton's "Mortuary" is one of five poems that highlight some complexes of themes and formal tendencies peculiar to the period.

C538 Hoadley, Jocelyn M. "Fire Imagery in the Poetry of Irving Layton." M.A. Thesis Concordia 1975.

Fire imagery in Layton's poetry "becomes the measure whereby the poet defines the universe, society and himself." In the first part of the thesis, Hoadley traces "Layton's attempts to understand, dominate, and inter-relate with reality." In the second section, she shows "Layton's struggle to measure himself as passionate poet against the masses."

C539 Morton, Mary Lee Bragg. "*First Statement* and *Contemporary Verse*: A Comparative Structure." M.A. Thesis Calgary 1977.

In this comparative study of Alan Crawley's *Contemporary Verse* with John Sutherland's *First Statement* and *Northern Review*, Morton focuses, in the third section, on the work of Dorothy Livesay, P.K. Page, Earle Birney, Irving Layton, and Louis Dudek to demonstrate the different editorial policies of these magazines.

C540 Sherwood, Lyn Elliot. "Innocence and Experience: An Analysis of the Sun Image in Some Modern Canadian Poetry." M.A. Thesis Carleton 1977.

Layton is one of nine Canadian poets in whose work ". . . the sun is a symbol of archetypal significance whose variations create a pattern which expresses a dialectic of innocence and experience." Several of his poems are discussed under the chapter headings "Innocence," "Experience," "Transformation," and "Higher Innocence."

C541 Giguère, Richard. "Une poésie de dissidence: Étude comparative de l'évolution des poésies québécoise et canadienne moderne à Montréal, 1925-1955." Diss. British Columbia 1978.

This dissertation is published in revised form in Giguère's book (C405).

C542 Kriepans-McGrath, Veneranda. "Love and Loathing: The Role of Woman in Irving Layton's Vision." M.A. Thesis Concordia 1981.

In Irving Layton's poetry, woman helps man achieve "the discovery of the inner self and unity with the cosmos." In a world where destruction rules, redemption is yet possible through the experience of sensual love. Woman "serves as a source of inspiration to man and poet."

C543 Adams, Richard Gordon. "Irving Layton: The Early Poetry, 1931-1945." Diss. New Brunswick 1983.

Layton began writing poetry when he was nine or ten, shortly after his father's death. While his political writing was polished by the time he was in university, his poetry was "weak and derivative." Layton developed rapidly as a poet after becoming involved with *First Statement* in 1943. The best of his poems of this time are more concerned with moral than political prophecy.

C544 Wiens, Erwin. "The Criticism of Irving Layton." Diss. Ottawa 1983.

By using forewords from Layton's books, public correspondence, lectures, films, reviews, and interviews, Wiens "demonstrates that Layton has maintained a consistent didactic emphasis in his criticism." He has "asserted the vital role of poetry," "discerned what was crucial," and "has been the main spokesman for the prophetic and realist traditions in Canadian poetry." Layton's debates with Desmond Pacey, Louis Dudek, and Northrop Frye receive special emphasis.

C545 Ierfino-Adornato, Maria. "The Poetry of Irving Layton: A Scatological Dimension." M.A. Thesis Concordia 1984.

Layton uses scatology "to shock the reader into an awareness of the human condition." His "writing ranges from the humorous and vituperative to the profoundly philosophic and religious." "Love and art are the aspects of redemption that allow us to transcend" material disaster.

C546 Lemm, Richard. "Polished Lens and Improved Binoculars: Moral Vision in the Poetry of A.M. Klein and Irving Layton." Diss. Dalhousie 1986.

A.M. Klein and Irving Layton "are intensely and critically concerned with issues of good and evil in human experience and history." Layton believes that only death and sometimes love can achieve a unity of the opposites within humanity and nature. Moral vision in both Klein's and Layton's poetry "is incisive, vital and relevant to many of the crises and dilemmas that have faced humanity throughout history and that challenge humanity in our own era."

Interviews and Profiles

C547 Engel, Raoul. Interview with Irving Layton. *Assignment.* CBC Radio, 25 Oct. 1957. (4 min.)

Layton talks to Engel about the new *Six Montreal Poets* Folkways record and how important a place for writing Montreal is.

C548 Abrams, Tevia. "Layton Lashes Western Spiritual Decline." *The Georgian* [Sir George Williams Univ.], 4 March 1958, p. 4.

Russia's success in scientific endeavours comes from its not being shackled by the "feudal, aristocratic and Christian ideologies" that hamper scientific research in the West. Modern writers reflect this anti-scientific spirit. "Art is the last bastion of humanism; we must not let it die."

C549 Engel, Raoul. Interview with Irving Layton and Jonathan Williams. *Assignment.* CBC Radio, 15 April 1958. (5 min.)

Irving Layton and Jonathan Williams discuss the contemporary poetry scene.

C550 Davidson, Joyce, and John O'Leary. Interview with Aviva Cantor and Irving Layton. *Tabloid.* CBC TV, 10 May 1958. (5 min.)

Aviva Cantor and Irving Layton discuss their collaboration as song writers. (See C43.)

C551 Engel, Raoul. "The Night People." CBC Radio, 26 Sept. 1958. (4 min., 16 sec.)

For Layton the night is aristocratic, while ". . . the sun is far too democratic." Women do not necessarily become vampires at night; they may become creatures of extraordinary romance.

C552 Fairbairn, Dave. "Irving Layton versus Dave Fairbairn." *The Brunswickan* [Univ. of New Brunswick], 22 Jan. 1960, p. 5.

Layton criticizes our "pathetic" universities and the way our society degrades sex. Religion should embody "an attitude of wonderment" rather than a set of rules.

C553 O' Broin, Pádraig. "Fire-Drake." *Teangadóir*, 5, No. 2, Ser. 2, 1, No. 2 [No. 38], 1 Nov. 1961, 73–80. Rpt. in *Irving Layton: The Poet and His Critics*. Ed. Seymour Mayne. Toronto: McGraw-Hill Ryerson, 1978, pp. 125–29.

Layton talks of what it was like being a Jew growing up in Montreal and comments on the nature of the Jewish culture, particularly its nonconformist attitude. While A.M. Klein has no equal in Canadian writing for his "colour, rhythm, complexity, density, . . . he hasn't found the spiritual, aesthetic, moral values to sustain himself as a writer." Modern Jewish writers are too optimistic; they reject the baseness of humanity. Leonard Cohen rejects Jewish morality, which gives his work "an element of unreality and insincerity." For Layton, the human mixture of spirit and dirt "is the central riddle of human existence."

C554 Sherwood, Martin. "The News Talks to Irving Layton, the Montreal Poet." *Loyola News* [Loyola College, Montreal], 16 March 1962, p. 3.

Layton says that Canada, and Montreal in particular, is producing the best poetry in the world today. Poets need passion, but bad teaching inhibits students. Layton's outlook is strongly anti-academic.

C555 Traynor, Tim. "Two Views of Canadian Literature." "An Angry Poet." *The Interpreter* [Univ. of Western Ontario], Feb.–March 1963.

Frye's influence on poetry, says Layton, is pernicious because it diverts attention away from the poem to criticism. Academic and poetic lives are incompatible. North American culture is too concerned with comfort; poetry must fight this tendency.

C556 "What Canada Means to Me." *Telescope*. Prod. and dir. Ross McLean. CBC TV, 1 July 1963. (3 min.)

On the occasion of Dominion Day, Layton expresses his feelings about Canada.

C557 Anechstein, Julie. "Profile of a One-Armed Juggler." *McGill Daily*, 1 Nov. 1963, Panorama, p. 1.

Layton displays his views in support of separatism, universities as middle-class finishing schools, and the little value our society places on selfhood. He sees little cause for optimism in our society, or in the relations between men and women. But the poetry in Canada "is the most vital poetry now being written."

C558 Grant, Maggie. "Sex at 16, Fanny for Newlyweds." *The Globe and Mail* [Toronto], 29 Feb. 1964, [Entertainment], p. 18.

Layton criticizes the teaching of English and the puritanical attitude of Canadians towards sex. His statement "I hope my 14-year-old daughter has had six lovers before she's 16" caused considerable furore in this Toronto paper.

C559 Vineberg, Dusty. "Sir George Williams Appoints First Poet-in-Residence." *Weekend Magazine* [*The Montreal Star*], 3 July 1965, Entertainment, p. 5.

Layton discusses his appointment as poet-in-residence and the ways in which he hopes he will be able to help the less conventional student.

C560 Jackson, Paul C. "Layton Claims Canadians Repressed, Lacking in Passion." *Star-Phoenix* [Saskatoon], 8 Nov. 1965, p. 10.

Canadians suffer from repression and over-emphasis on external things, although poetry and the arts are gradually becoming more popular. "Leisure is only unemployment with a halo around it."

C561 "An Interview with Irving Layton." *The Sheaf* [Univ. of Saskatchewan], 12 Nov. 1965, Mosaic, pp. 17, 20.

Modern poetry should give us more illumination than it generally does; it is becoming irrelevant in the type of society that is developing. The only thing he works at, Layton says, "is to be in love all the time." The interview is continued in C563.

C562 Ross, Alexander. "The Man Who Copyrighted Passion." *Maclean's*, 15 Nov. 1965, pp. 22, 45–47, 49.

In this overview of Layton's life, Ross comments on Layton's early years, his war experiences, his three marriages, his ventures into real estate, and his generally controversial nature.

C563 "An Interview with Irving Layton." *The Sheaf* [Univ. of Saskatchewan], 19 Nov. 1965, Mosaic, p. 20.

This concludes the interview commenced in C561. Layton argues that too much modern poetry depresses; good poetry should be vital. Like that of many other poets, his popular lecherous image fills a psychological void in the Canadian consciousness, although the truth of his life does not conform to this image.

C564 Thompson, John, Jon Whyte, Dianne Woodman, and Linda Strand. "An Asexual Interview with Irving Layton." *The Gateway* [Univ. of Alberta], 24 Nov. 1965, pp. 6–7. Rpt. (abridged) in *Taking Sides: The Collected Social and Political Writings*. Ed. Howard Aster. Oakville, Ont.: Mosaic / Valley, 1977, pp. 177–79.

Good education depends on the teacher rather than the system. Layton notes that his being lumped with the Black Mountain poets is inaccurate; actually, he is the one who has influenced Robert Creeley, rather than the reverse.

C565 "Interview with Irving Layton." *Cyclic*, 1, No. 3 (March 1966), 7–9. Rpt. (abridged) in *Taking Sides: The Collected Social and Political Writings*. Ed. Howard Aster. Oakville, Ont.: Mosaic / Valley, 1977, pp. 187–91.

Layton distinguishes between his roles as man and poet. In his poetry, he attempts to give a sense of the atrocities of the age. Art "is an expression of vitality." A love of poetry or the other arts is no guarantee of virtue. Tragedy is of a higher order than satire, but Layton claims great poems written in both genres.

C566 Skelton, Robin. Interview with Irving Layton. *Saturday Evening*. Prod. David Errington. CBC Radio, 2 April 1966. (40 min.)

The poet must give expression to what is in the minds and hearts of his contemporaries and also discover those forces making for new life. Sex and death together form the major substance of Layton's poetry. Too many teachers spoil the student's enjoyment of poetry; analysis should always lead to enjoyment. Poetic language is different from that of prose; rhythmic expression and voice are important. Layton also reads twenty-one poems (B1165, B1169–B1170, B1172, B1185, B1191, B1208, B1211–B1225).

C567 Spring, Sylvia. "An Hour with Irving Layton." *Venture*. Prod. Elizabeth Barry. Exec. prod. Harry Boyle. CBC Radio, 3 July 1966. (52 min.)

In today's society, the poet is a clown, although recently the Canadian public has been paying more attention. Most teaching of poetry errs in ignoring the genesis of the poem in the poet's personality. Layton's main influences have been his mother, God, and Shakespeare. Poets are chosen, but fewer women get picked because to be poets they must sacrifice their vanity for ambition. Layton also reads nine poems (B1169, B1200–B1201, B1215, B1224, B1226–B1229).

C568 "An Interview with Irving Layton." *Karussell*, Nov. 1966, pp. 5–7.

Layton discusses his recent trip to Germany and his efforts there to promote Canadian poetry. He finds little to worry about in any resurgence of Nazi feeling. He was impressed by the anti-Nazi poet Erich Kastner and looks forward to a return to Germany. Also includes "At the Belsen Memorial" (B326) and "Rhine Boat Trip" (B332).

C569 Lax, Rose, and Elliot Newman. "Irving Layton Is:". *The Georgian* [Sir George Williams Univ.], 2 Dec. 1966, Op. Ed., pp. 1, 3. Rpt. (abridged) in *Taking Sides: The Collected Social and Political Writings*. Ed. Howard Aster. Oakville, Ont.: Mosaic / Valley, 1977, pp. 179–85.

The university is an artificial environment, whose main function for poets is to enable them to avoid repeating what has already been said. The poet should be interested in the poem, not in culture or the Canadian identity. While the writing of poetry cannot be taught, it is possible to teach prospective poets short-cuts. Today's mood of anxiety makes it difficult for love and imagination to survive.

C570 Freeman, Barbara. "Sent by the Angels of God . . . ." *Marianews* [Marianopolis College], 28 Feb. 1967, pp. 7–8.

Layton discusses his early career and his differences with Louis Dudek and Brian Robinson of McGill University. The situation for Canadian poetry has improved greatly in recent years; between 1945 and 1965, the best poetry in the world was being written in Canada.

C571 Webb, Phyllis. Interview with Miriam Waddington, Irving Layton, and F.R. Scott. *Modern Canadian Poetry.* Host Phyllis Webb. Prod. John Kennedy. CBC Television Extension, 30 April 1967. (30 min.)

The poets interviewed reminisce on the nature of poetic activity in Canada in the 1940s, especially the roles of John Sutherland and Alan Crawley. The influences of Dylan Thomas, Ezra Pound, William Carlos Williams, and E.J. Pratt are discussed. Layton says that he and his Canadian contemporaries were not interested in Pratt because their concerns were different. The broadcast also includes a reading of "De Bullion Street" (B1233) and "Lady Enfield" (B1234).

C572 Doupe, Jack. "Irving Layton: U.S.A. & Viet Nam." *Canada Month,* June 1967, pp. 22–25. Rpt. (abridged) in *Taking Sides: The Collected Social and Political Writings.* Ed. Howard Aster. Oakville, Ont.: Mosaic / Valley, 1977, pp. 191–99.

Layton defends American involvement in Viet Nam, because it is neutralizing rather than controlling this area. The major conflict between China and the Soviet Union is evidence that the monolithic front of Communism is crumbling; relations between Russia and the United States are correspondingly improving. Subsequent events have justified American involvement in the Dominican Republic, as they will justify American involvement in Viet Nam.

C573 [Article.] *The Ontarion* [Univ. of Guelph], 15 Nov. 1968, p. 18. Rpt. in *Collage* [McMaster Univ.], 7 Feb. 1969, p. 4.

There should be no bounds on poetic subjects. The poet must be totally committed to "creativity, love, joy, and freedom."

C574 Sheffy, Pearl. Interview with Irving Layton. CBC *Tuesday Night.* Announcer Gordon Jones. Prod. Ter-

rence Gibbs. CBC Radio, 26 Nov. 1968. (30 min.)

Layton talks with Pearl Sheffy in Tel Aviv about Judaism in Israel and the Israeli people. He is impressed by the variety of time and space in Israel, but disappointed with the literature. This broadcast also includes a reading of "Israelis" (B1235) and "The New Breed" (B1236).

C575 Brown, Lyal, and Jacques Langlois. Interview with Irving Layton. *Sunday Supplement.* Prod. David Humphries. CBC Radio, 15 Dec. 1968. (10 min.)

Brown and Langlois discuss with Layton his recent trip to Israel. His visit there has resolved for him the differences between poetry and power, making him more of a "soldier-poet."

C576 Zolf, Larry. "Books of the Year 1968." *Anthology.* Ed. Robert Weaver. Prod. Alex Smith. Supervising prod. Terrence Gibbs. CBC Radio, 28 Dec. 1968. (3 min.)

Layton's favourite book of 1968 is Leonard Cohen's *Selected Poems.*

C577 Ascroft, Sheila. "Canadian Poetry: Does It Exist?". *Bishop's University Nuevue,* 1, No. 1 (1969), 12–13.

Layton states that the hallmark of the modern poet is complete freedom. Poetry must be emotionally moving; "slickness, sentimentality and rhetoric" are presently endangering the craft.

C578 Fulford, Robert. Interview with Irving Layton. *This Is Robert Fulford.* Host Robert Fulford. CBC Radio, 7 Jan. 1969. (15 min.)

Layton tells Fulford that teaching creative writing is worthwhile, both to encourage the real poet and discourage the non-poet. He expects his forthcoming residence at Guelph University will be fruitful. He also defends his support of American policy in Viet Nam.

C579 Morton, Caroline. "Irving Layton — A Poet with Sex in One Eye and Death in the Other." *Daily Ryersonian* [Ryerson Polytechnical Institute], 14 Jan. 1969, p. 4.

Critics are acceptable only if they act as "a middleman or merchant" between the writer and his public.

C580 Rosenblood, Norman. "Interview with Irving Layton." *The Spectator* [Hamilton], 1 Feb. 1969, p. 20.

Layton finds the new freedom flourishing in today's society encouraging. In Quebec, especially, a "creative ferment" imparts a joy to life. Imagination, power, and love may lead to the creation of a new and better society.

C581 Hutchinson, Helen. Interview with Irving Layton. *Matinée*. CBC Radio, 9 April 1969. (12 min.)

Layton notes, "I inherited my father's mystical nature and my mother's personality." Canadian poetry has been the best in the English-speaking world since 1945, but today's young poets do not "learn their craft."

C582 "In Quebec: Total Blindness Complete Failure of Thought." *Hanukah Magazine* [*The Canadian Jewish News*] [Toronto], 12 Dec. 1969, pp. 2–4.

In Quebec today, the Jewish people should no longer identify themselves with the English Canadians. Layton expresses satisfaction with the increasing popularity of poetry, although there are dangers attendant on the poet becoming a public figure. Critics are all right if they do necessary work, like preparing bibliographies, but they should not criticize living writers. The poet must suffer for his creativity; no one has manifested this truth more than the Jews.

C583 "Les Juifs les minorities parmi les Canadiens français." *Nouveau Monde*, March 1970, pp. 13–17.

Left-wing terrorists, including extreme separatists, are often anti-Zionist, with much encouragement coming from the Soviet Union. The poet today "devient le symbole de l'individu qui a échappé au monde moderne et à sa richesse." "Le Juif a une sympathie et une compréhension de la totalité et de l'expérience humaine." Suffering is a price the creative artist must pay.

C584 Hutchinson, Helen. Interview with Irving Layton, *Anthology*. CBC Radio, 30 Sept. 1970.

Layton is one of several artists whose views on critics are solicited. He states that critics often help the reader, but not the poet. The critic often reviews the poet, rather than the poem, and does not have the same ecstasy of creation as the poet.

C585 Lavigne, Christine, and Lawrence Stevenson. "A Conversation with Irving Layton." Dir. Bert Laale. Prod. Instructional Media Centre. Host Michael Keefer. Toronto: Univ. of Toronto, SC213-B, 1971. Rerecorded, 3 May 1978. (Videocassette; black-and-white; 62 min.)

In Part I, Layton notes that the poet is concerned with the destiny of humanity and is, in that sense, a prophet. All poetry tries to lead people to the promised land. The poet must personally experience the anguish of the twentieth century to write with authority. Nature is a symbol of humanity's radical innocence. Layton also comments on the United States and how it differs from Canada. In Part II, Layton comments on the different position of the poet in today's society compared with the time he started writing. British poetry at present is not worth considering; Canadian poetry combines qualities from both its British and American roots. The best poetry in the English-speaking world since 1945 has been written in Canada. Our culture is the main means through which our country can define itself. Layton emphasizes the necessity of revision in his poetry, even in short poems of a few lines. Anything after his collected poems will not be an anti-climax — he'd "rather be climaxing aunties." Layton also reads "De Bullion Street" (B1233).

C586 Thomas, Clara. "Conversations Between Clara Thomas and Irving Layton." Toronto: York Univ. [1971?]. (Audiotape; 30 min.)

Layton discusses his early life and the beginnings of his writing career. The artist's job is to prevent society from stagnating. Good teachers should inspire love for and understanding of poetry in their students. Layton's early readings in the Romantics have given him a sense of form and rhythm that has benefited him in his later work and that too many younger poets lack.

C587 Thomas, Clara. "In Conversation with Irving Layton and Margaret Laurence." Toronto: York Univ., [1971?]. (Audiotape; 30 min.) Printed ("A Conversation about Literature: An Interview with Margaret Laurence and Irving Layton") in *Journal of Canadian Fiction*, 1, No. 1 (Winter 1972), 65–69. Rpt. (abridged — "A Conversation with Margaret Laurence and Irving Layton") in *Engagements: The Prose of Irving Layton*. Ed. Seymour Mayne. Toronto: McClelland and Stewart, 1972, pp. 65–68.

Taking as a focal point the idea of universality, Irving Layton and Margaret Laurence comment on their life and work. Laurence sees affinities between her background and Layton's, particularly between Layton's crude but indomitable brother-in-law Strul Goldberg and her maternal grandfather, who served as a model for Grandfather O'Connor in her collection entitled *A Bird in the House*. Both, especially Layton, emphasize the links between universality,

freedom, and mythology in their works. The figures of his past have become archetypal.

C588 Anderson, Allan. "Poets of Canada: 1920 to the Present." Interview with Milton Acorn, Margaret Atwood, Margaret Avison, Earle Birney, George Bowering, Victor Coleman, Leonard Cohen, Joan Finnigan, John Glassco, George Jonas, Irving Layton, Dorothy Livesay, Gwendolyn MacEwen, Eli Mandel, Alden Nowlan, Michael Ondaatje, P.K. Page, Al Purdy, James Reaney, and A.J.M. Smith. *Anthology*. Supervising prod. Alex Smith. Ed. Robert Weaver. CBC Radio, 15 May 1971. (2 min., 40 sec.)

Part I of a seven-part series. Anderson interviews the above poets on the way they write their poetry and what they do when they suffer dry periods. Layton states that his poetry demands to be written, and written in a particular form. Poetry affirms the uniqueness of the individual.

C589 Anderson, Allan. "Poets of Canada: 1920 to the Present." Interview with Milton Acorn, George Bowering, Leonard Cohen, Victor Coleman, Doug Fetherling, Northrop Frye, Len Gasparini, Irving Layton, Dennis Lee, Gwendolyn MacEwen, David McFadden, bpNichol, and Michael Ondaatje. *Anthology*. Supervising prod. Alex Smith. Ed. Robert Weaver. CBC Radio, 12 June 1971. (2 min., 18 sec.)

Part V of a seven-part series. This program features the younger poets. Layton criticizes the younger poets for their lack of humour, lack of reading or a sense of tradition, and their arrogance.

C590 Anderson, Allan. "Poets of Canada: 1920 to the Present." Interview with Margaret Atwood, Margaret Avison, Nelson Ball, Victor Coleman, Northrop

Frye, John Glassco, Irving Layton, Dennis Lee, Dorothy Livesay, Gwendolyn MacEwen, Eli Mandel, Anne Marriott, John Newlove, Glen Siebrasse, Francis Sparshott, Peter Stevens, Miriam Waddington, Milton Wilson, and George Woodcock. *Anthology*. Supervising prod. Alex Smith. Ed. Robert Weaver. CBC Radio, 19 June 1971. (2 min., 43 sec.)

Part VI of a seven-part series. Anderson interviews the above writers on small presses and literary criticism. Layton feels that while Northrop Frye's generalizations about the garrison and the wilderness may be true about some writers, they are not true about him. Critics, because they do not, like the poet, possess passion, are unaware of the true nature of poetry.

C591 Anderson, Allan. "Poets of Canada: 1920 to the Present." Interview with Milton Acorn, Margaret Avison, Henry Beissel, Earle Birney, George Bowering, John Robert Colombo, Frank Davey, Ronald Everson, Joan Finnigan, John Glassco, Phyllis Gotlieb, David Helwig, George Johnston, George Jonas, Irving Layton, Anne Marriott, John Newlove, Alden Nowlan, Michael Ondaatje, James Reaney, Miriam Waddington, and Robert Weaver. Supervising prod. Alex Smith. Ed. Robert Weaver. CBC Radio, 26 June 1971. (2 min., 18 sec.)

Part VII of a seven-part series. Anderson interviews the above poets and critics on the practical aspects of being a poet. In talking about poetry and success, Layton says that he is concerned about the esteem he gets, because every poet is in the race for immortality.

C592 Laing, Tom. "Irving Layton." *Northword Magazine* [Grimsby, Ont.], July 1971, pp. 43–47, 62–64. Rpt. (abridged) in *Taking Sides: The Collected Social and Political Writings*. Ed. Howard Aster. Oakville, Ont.: Mosaic / Valley, 1977, pp. 199–210.

Canadian poets may be distinguished from their American counterparts by a distinctive interest in individuals and a perspective and sense of form. The Canadian characteristics of gentility and kindliness are fatal to the poet. Layton's lack of critical attention is a reflection of the state of Canadian criticism. "The uncritical, unthinking acceptance of a herd emotion" is an anathema to him. The job of the poet is to wake people up; he is prophetic in the sense of being intuitive. The stereotypes of Layton as sex maniac and megalomaniac are simply not true; the opposites of love and death inform his life and work.

C593 "Power and Poetry." *Ideas*. CBC Radio, 22 Nov. 1971. CBC Learning Systems, No. 765. (30 min.)

Layton defines power as "disciplined passion" or "spiritualized energy." Christianity has caused the emasculation of the individual. Everything in this world is endowed with energy, but many are crippled early in life by authority. All nature is striving to become self-conscious; God is striving to become man. Man too often "gets his kicks" through the misuse of power. True power comes through imagination and love. Len Berman also reads eight of Layton's poems (B1169, B1250–B1256).

C594 Resnitzky, Lawrence J. "Interview with Irving Layton." *The Golden Dog / Le Chien d'or*, No. 1 (Jan. 1972), n. pag. Rpt. (abridged) in *Taking Sides: The Collected Social and Political Writings*. Ed. Howard Aster. Oakville, Ont.: Mosaic / Valley, 1977, pp. 211–17.

Layton attacks those critics who would approve only one period or one type of his poetry. If other poets have influenced him, it is only in the general sense of providing him with "a modern sensibility and a modern idiom." As a poet, he is both prophet and clown; too many critics attack the man rather than the poet. His manner of writing "is the dominant style of writing in Canada today," its uniqueness lying in its "combination of metaphysics and psychology." Over the years, his craft has become more "complex" and "full-throated," although the nature of his poetic vision has not changed. He has always attacked Canadian "gentility" and "snobbishness."

C595 Marsh, Bruce. Interview with Irving Layton. *Concern*. Ed. Bruce Lawson. CBC Radio, 20 Sept. 1972. (26 min.)

Layton says that he changed from Marxism to a broader, more humanistic philosophy because of his experience in marriage. He is trying to combine the innocence of youth with the wisdom of age.

C596 Fulford, Robert. Interview with Irving Layton. *This Is Robert Fulford*. Host Robert Fulford. CBC Radio, 28 Oct. 1972. (26 min.)

Fulford's interview focuses on Layton's prose collected in *Engagements: The Prose of Irving Layton*. The poet, as a prophet, has for Layton a sense of passion and urgency. Layton discusses his battles with Northrop Frye and Louis Dudek and his present admiration for the former. Reading *Engagements: The Prose of Irving Layton* now gives him both "pleasure and melancholy."

C597 Clarkson, Adrienne. Interview with Irving Layton. *Take 30*. CBC TV, 14 Feb. 1973. Rebroadcast, 14 Feb. 1974. (17 min.)

Writing poems helps Layton live through dark and painful emotions, as any experience can be transformed into poetry. Men are inherently more creative than women; women's creativity is largely biological. Canadians think they are being moral when mostly they are just uncomfortable. Everything but making love and writing poetry bores him.

C598 Allard, Kerry. "Conversation: Jewish Layton, Catholic Hood, Protestant Bowering." *Open Letter*, Ser. 2, No. 5 (Summer 1973), pp. 30–39.

Layton feels that exile is a necessary part of his life. "... the artist *is* sinful ..." in the sense that he asserts his superiority to God. Any great writer is a priest or prophet, although Layton regards himself as less optimistic than George Bowering.

C599 McPherson, David. Interview with Irving Layton. *Quebec Now*. CBC Radio, 16 Sept. 1973. (29 min.)

Layton recalls how his early life in Montreal has made him the poet that he is. He discusses the anti-Semitism he experienced, his move to Toronto, and the egotistical nature of modern cities. Layton also reads four poems (B1172, B1209, B1214, B1265).

C600 Fulford, Robert. Interview with Irving Layton. *Speaking of Books*. TV Ontario, [c.1974]. (30 min.)

Layton talks about politics and sex in his poetry, as well as the influence of his Jewish heritage on his poetry.

C601 Brooks, David. "Interview with Irving Layton." *Canberra Poetry* [Canberra, Australia], 1, No. 4 (Autumn 1974), 53–57.

Australia needs to give more public support to its poets through publicly funded readings and university positions, as Canada does. Canadian poetry has greater breadth, eroticism, and psychological awareness than Australian. Layton also discusses the nature of Leonard Cohen's links with the Black Mountain poets.

C602 Purnis, Mieta Pagella. Interview with Irving Layton. Voice-over translation. *Identities*. CBC Radio, 10 Feb. 1975. (4 min., 20 sec.)

Layton describes Amleto Lorenzini's literary qualifications for translating his poetry. Layton trusts him because of his great breadth of culture.

C603 D'Agostino, Sara. "The War Goes On: A Conversation with Irving Layton." *Acta Victoriana* [Victoria College, Univ. of Toronto], 100, No. 1 (Fall 1975), 9–16.

While Layton feels that good poetry continues to be written, most is by those who have not been to universities. Gentility and the absence of a "religious element" hamper much modern poetry. The poet's job is to make people uncomfortable.

C604 Strasman, Gavriel. "A Warning to the Christians: Irving Layton Discusses *For My Brother Jesus*." *The Canadian Zionist*, March–April 1976, pp. 11–12.

Layton wishes to reclaim Jesus as a Jewish prophet. The persecution of the Jews throughout history has been a direct result of the anti-Semitism preached by Christianity. The great contribution of the Jew is his rejection of idols, which is one of the main reasons why, in a world that worships idols, he is persecuted.

C605 McKeown, Bob. *Gzowski on* FM. Prod. Nancy Buttons. CBC-FM Radio, 13 April 1976. (40 min.)

Layton defends *For My Brother Jesus* against McKeown's criticisms. He writes against the life-denying attitudes of this country. His stamina has kept him from the fate of many other poets, enabling him to withstand the repressive forces of society. Christianity has been used as an excuse for the persecution of the Jews for two thousand years, culminating with the holocaust. Layton is saying something that "nobody has had the guts to say." "Adam," "Displaced Person," and "North American Poet" (B1279–B1281) are read.

C606 Finlay, Mary Lou. Interview with Irving Layton. *Take 30*. Dir. John Evelyn. CBC TV, 14 April 1976. (30 min.)

Layton says his bitterness towards Christians is based on his belief that Christianity's promotion of anti-Semitism for the past two thousand years was responsible for the Jewish holocaust in Nazi Germany.

C607 Friesen, Eric. Interview with Irving Layton. *The Eric Friesen Show*. Host Eric Friesen. CBC Radio, 26 Jan. 1977. (12 min.)

Layton is glad that *For My Brother Jesus* outraged so many people, because it is the poet's job "to probe into the diseased tissue with the scalpel of the imagination and intellect." He admires true Christianity, which is a way of life, but despises Xianity, which is a repressive creed, destroying eroticism. "For My Brother Jesus" is also read (B1282).

C608 Gzowski, Peter. Interview with Irving Layton. *90 Minutes Live*. Host Peter Gzowski. Exec. prod. Alex Frame. CBC TV, 10 March 1977. (12 min.)

Layton talks of his past, his present favourite activities, and reads "Idiots" and "Letter to the Soviet Cultural Attaché" (B1283–B1284).

C609 Brown, Harry, and Maxine Crook. Interview with Irving Layton. *Morningside*. Prod. Janet Russell. CBC Radio, 31 March 1977. (25 min.)

Layton talks about the opening of a three-month seminar on Canadian studies in Bologna, Italy, presented by the city, the University of Bologna, and the Canadian Cultural Institute in Rome. He heard many Italian academics delivering papers on Canadian authors, a practice Canadians do not reciprocate. Leonard Cohen is much better known in Italy than in Canada. The fact that the seminar was held in

Bologna, a city with a Communist government for the past thirty years, means that the Communists wish to maintain ties and affiliations with Western democracies. He compares Bolognese to Canadian sensuality, and criticizes a critical review of the film *Casanova*.

C610 "An Interview with Irving Layton." *Canadian Theatre Review* [York Univ.], No. 14 (Spring 1977), pp. 54–55.
This interview precedes Irving Layton's and Leonard Cohen's play, *A Man Was Killed*, published in the same issue (B1152). This is one of five or six plays on which he and Cohen collaborated. Layton complains about the CBC's lack of encouragement for their dramatic works and praises his and Cohen's work for its anticipation of the issues of the 1960s.

C611 Hyman, Patrick. "Irving Layton at Sixty-Five." *Anthology*. Host Harry Mannis. Prod. Alex Smith. CBC Radio, 28 May 1977. (30 min.)
Layton states that he is now writing more than ever, making as many as thirty-five drafts of one poem. He discusses the recent publication of *The Uncollected Poems of Irving Layton*, the American publication of his selected poems, *Taking Sides: The Collected Social and Political Writings*, and the correspondence with Dorothy Rath, which was published in *An Unlikely Affair*. Rath was a *hausfrau* magically transformed into a poet. Poetry should be taught by communicating the experience behind the poem, not the scholastic dissection practised in the schools.

C612 Rasky, Frank. "We Jews Can Identify with French Canada." *The Toronto Star*, 15 June 1977, p. B3.
Layton is optimistic about the future of the relationship between French- and English-speaking Canada, especially if they listen to representatives of the

third solitude who, like himself, are neither English nor French.

C613 Mantz, Douglas. "An Interview with Irving Layton: An Example of Overcoming Distance and Restricted Budgets." *The English Quarterly* [Oromocto, N.B.], 10, No. 2 (Summer 1977), 1–12.
Mantz recounts his experience of setting up a telephone conference between his students and Layton. An edited transcript of the interview shows Layton responding to questions about specific poems, as well as to more general matters such as his attitude towards women and his concept of divinity.

C614 Gzowski, Peter. Interview with Irving Layton. *90 Minutes Live*. Host Peter Gzowski. Exec. prod. Alex Frame. CBC TV, 30 Nov. 1977. (25 min.)
The humanity of Jesus and his teaching of love and enjoyment of life are themes in many of Layton's poems. Layton defends himself against the charge of blasphemy.

C615 Thornton, Russell. "Interview with Irving Layton." *McGill Daily*, 8 Dec. 1977, pp. 30–31.
Jesus on the cross representing the power of the individual to defy brute force and the holocaust representing the endurance of the Jewish people are potent symbols for our day. Justice, equality, freedom, and creativity are all Hebrew ethical principles. Layton himself is a prophet; where he once attacked the surface gentility of Christianity, he now attacks the underlying mendaciousness and hypocrisy.

C616 Gzowski, Peter, and Judy LaMarsh. Interview with Irving Layton. *90 Minutes Live*. Host Peter Gzowski. Exec. prod. Alex Frame. CBC TV, 30 Jan. 1978. (23 min.)
Irving Layton, Peter Gzowski, and Judy LaMarsh discuss the Francis Fox scandal. Layton also talks

about his poetry, his image as a poet in Canadian society, and his feelings about Jesus being a man.

C617 Sherman, Kenneth. "An Interview with Irving Layton." *Essays on Canadian Writing*, No. 10 (Spring 1978), pp. 7–18.

Layton defends his view that "... Christendom, by publicizing a stereotype of the Jew for nearly two thousand years, prepared the soil on which the death camps and the crematoria could spring-up and flourish." While there is more poetry today, it lacks the range and ambition of the 1940s and 1950s. The influence of the Black Mountain poets has contributed to this narrowing of scope. Biological differences lead to essential differences in creativity between men and women; men are the better poets. Layton also comments on the nature of his public image and his attempt to combine argument with poetry.

C618 Soles, Paul, and Paul Grigsby. Interview with Irving Layton. *Canada after Dark*. CBC TV, 28 Sept. 1978. (14 min.)

Layton discusses the differences between Toronto and Montreal, Jewish and French communities in Montreal, the difference between sexuality and eroticism, and love, poetry, and death. Layton also reads "Madman on Mithymna Beach" (B1297).

C619 Smith, Beverly. "The Gospel According to Irving Layton." *Thursday Report* [Concordia Univ.], 26 Oct. 1978, pp. 1, 5.

Layton talks about his approach to teaching creative writing, the political situation in Quebec, and his attitude to Christianity.

C620 Camus, Susann. "The Passion of Irving Layton." *The Fulcrum* [Univ. of Ottawa], 9 Nov. 1978, p. 15.

Layton discusses various topics, especially poetry, Christianity, and Canada.

C621 Abrams, Judy. "Poet as Prophet." *The Georgian* [Sir George Williams Univ.], 1 Dec. 1978, p. 35.

Layton lashes out at the poor way in which poetry is taught and the philistine nature of Canadian society. Poetry combats the philistinism of our society.

C622 Brown, Harry. Interview with Irving Layton. *Take 30*. Dir. Ron Evenden. CBC TV, 25 Jan. 1979. (15 min.)

Layton discusses his recent move to Montreal from Toronto, the future of the Jewish community in Montreal, and the varied reactions of the Canadian public to his poetry over the years.

C623 Davidson, Joyce. "Irving Layton." *Authors*. Dir. Robbie Leggatt. Prod. Sandra Faire. CBC TV, 16 July 1979. (30 min.)

Sex and death, according to Layton, are the only things worth writing about. His role as a poet / prophet is to ask the uncomfortable questions about civilization and the nature of man as revealed by the holocaust. Layton also discusses his recent collaboration with the Italian artist Aligi Sassu, in *There Were No Signs*, and his current marriage.

C624 Sherman, David. "Irving Layton Warns Us That We Can Be Monsters." *The Gazette* [Montreal], 18 Aug. 1979, p. 66.

In this article, which is based on an interview, Sherman comments on Layton's current literary activities. Layton comments on the presence of evil in man, life in Niagara-on-the-Lake, and his feud with Louis Dudek.

C625 Davidson, Joyce. Interview with Irving Layton. *Authors: Irving Layton*. CBC TV, 7 Sept. 1979. (30 min.)

Layton discusses the role of the poet as prophet asking the uncomfortable questions about civilization and the nature of humanity. He also discusses his recent portfolio *There Were No Signs*, his recent marriage to Harriet Bernstein, and reads "For 751-0329" (B1300).

C626 Henighan, Tom. "Freedom and the Life of Poetry: An Interview with Irving Layton." *Journal of Canadian Poetry*, 2, No. 2 (Autumn 1979), 5–12.

Layton discusses his rejection of Louis Dudek's Poundian influence and his feeling that the Black Mountain poets lacked a "philosophical and metaphysical element." Neither E.J. Pratt nor A.J.M. Smith influenced his work. A.M. Klein was overwhelmed by the holocaust and the world's indifference to it. WASP gentility, with its repression of much experience, still pervades Canadian poetry. The most important thing in life is freedom, which goes hand in hand with creativity.

C627 Thornton, Russell. "A Message for Supermen: An Interview with Irving Layton." *Athanor* [Concordia Univ.], 1, No. 1 (Nov. 1979), 5–10.

Poetry and living in general are acts of aggression which may manifest either a destructive or a creative power. Chance, Appetite, and Death are Layton's three gods. The true artist is the one who keeps growing; ". . . his life becomes the central symbol," conveying both extravagance and unity.

C628 "Profile: Irving Layton." *The Lictor* [Queen's Univ.], 8 Nov. 1979, p. 8.

While the greatest danger facing our society is "paralysis," the future gives cause for optimism, since ". . . technology can never breed despots and suppression and survive."

C629 Shackleton, Deborah. "Click! Another Poem is Born." *The Sunday Star* [Toronto], 4 May 1980,

p. D10. Rpt. in "Canadian Energy Series: Irving Layton." *Descant*, Nos. 27–28 (1980), pp. 114–17.

Writing poetry is marked by compression and unpredictability. The artist grows from intuition to intelligence; the great artist must have energy, intelligence, and form, and the energy to fight against the pressures of society to conform.

C630 Gervais, Marty. "Canada's Angry Prophet." *The Windsor Star*. "The Book Page," 7 March 1981, p. C7.

On the occasion of the publication of *Europe and Other Bad News*, Layton discusses the "overriding gentility in Canadian poetry which has stunned the senses and cloistered us from reality." Layton defines himself as both a European and a religious poet and a prophet who imparts his beliefs joyously.

C631 Ricciardi, Caterina. "Irving Layton: On Poetry. A Conversation." *Litteratura D'America*, No. 7 (Spring 1981), pp. 155–67. Rpt. in *Italian Critics on Irving Layton*. Ed. Alfredo Rizzardi. Abano Terme, Italy: Piovan, 1988, pp. 89–103.

See C12.

C632 Gebbia, Alessandro. " 'I miei maestri sono insieme i profeti ebrei del passato e Dante.' " *A cultura* [Italy], 12 Aprile 1981, p. IV.

"Credo che i grandi poeti debbano occuparsi di problemi piu importanti del genere umano." "La mia e una poesia molto visuale e l'artista, il pittore, puo vedere l'immagine che ho in mente. Se ancora non si e capito, la mia poesia non e astratta, e concreta e l'artista puo visualizzarla."

C633 Henighan, Tom. "Creativity and the Experience of the Holocaust: An Interview with Irving Layton." *Matrix*, No. 13 (Spring–Summer 1981), pp. 20–26.

The violence that disrupts our world is a result of the discontent most people feel. Fear of death, rather than a Freudian sexual repression "breeds sadism, cruelty and the desire to humiliate others." While Jewish culture has exerted a powerful beneficial influence on the culture of the United States, the WASP mentality still predominates in Canada. People should strive for freedom and creativity, for they are the keys to happiness.

C634 "Due Mondi Poetici: Layton, desiderio e crudeltà." *Canada Contemporaneo* [Canadian Embassy, Rome], 11, No. 6 (July–Aug. 1981), 6–7.

This interview follows the publication of Layton's *In un'età di ghiaccio*. The desire and cruelty in his poetry have their roots in his Jewishness and his own heart. His style has become more direct in its need to express the human urge toward self-destruction. "In Canada il mio vero nemico è 'la tradizione gentile.'"

C635 Meyboom, Jan Peter. "An Afternoon with Irving Layton." *The New Edition* [Toronto], 15 Sept. 1981, pp. 6–7.

Layton hammers away at the puritanism of Canadians and the perniciousness of critics who often slow the recognition of good writers. The poet's "job is to be aware of those things that threaten the human spirit."

C636 Bennett, Michael. "A Canadian Poet? Now That's Italian." *The Toronto Sun*, 8 Oct. 1981, p. 20.

Layton's recent nomination for a Nobel Prize in literature, the first for a Canadian author, is due to Italian efforts. In this article, based on an interview, Layton comments that ". . . a lot of Canadians get off on my escapades." "All of us have a desire for immortality."

C637 Ward, Olivia. "Is This a Humble Irving Layton?". *The Toronto Star*, 1 Nov. 1981, pp. C1–C2.

In an article based on an interview, Layton expresses a sense of vindication at his nomination for the Nobel Prize, but longs for the day when he can stop marrying. Now that his fourth marriage has collapsed, he doubts he will get married again.

C638 Zosky, Brenda. "The Poet's Paid His Dues." *The Gazette* [Montreal], 13 Nov. 1981, p. 41.

In this article, based on interviews with Irving Layton and Aviva Layton, Layton says he is as angry as ever — but not bitter — about Canada. "Every writer writes to get out of hell." Aviva Layton, his former wife, says she still talks to him every day and that "He has more integrity to his talent than anybody I know."

C639 Sullivan, Rosemary, and panel of students, Erindale College, Univ. of Toronto. *Canadian Poetry Eh!*. Prod. Ian O'Neill and Rosemary Sullivan. Graham Cable TV / FM Radio [Toronto] [c.1982]. [Held at Univ. of Toronto.] (3/4" videocassette; colour)

Layton speaks of his work, his public persona, and the media distortion of both.

C640 Knelman, Judith. "Irving Layton: 'Drown Yourself in the Sounds of Your Time' Counsels Our Poet-in-Residence." *Graduate* [Univ. of Toronto], Jan.–Feb. 1982, pp. 11, 13.

This profile is based on an interview held in Layton's office. Layton, currently poet-in-residence, talks of techniques that can improve poems. The poet's task is "to articulate the experience and sensibility" of his age. Our society is marred by materialism and repression.

C641 Wilson, Timothy. Interview with Irving Layton. In *A Poetry Reading by Irving Layton*. Prod. Rick Curtis.

Modern Canadian Poets: A Recorded Archive. League of Canadian Poets. Toronto [1982]. (Audiocassette; 12 min.)

The main object of Layton's attack continues to be WASP gentility, which is a running away from the facts. Most Canadian poets ignore the realities of the Holocaust and the Gulag death camps, although David Solway and Seymour Mayne have some of his prophetic fervour. He has never been without the feeling that he has been inspired. Also includes poems read by Layton (A99).

C642 Peterson, Leslie. "Literary Lion in Winter." *The Vancouver Sun*, 26 March 1982, p. C6.

Layton's three lawsuits are described: one about statements made by William French in a review; one about property settlement with his estranged wife, Harriet; one against his lawyer's $11,000 legal bill. Layton would be a filmmaker if he was starting over, but he enjoys the adulation he is now receiving.

C643 Stern, Beverley. "Irving Layton Celebrates Birthday; Continues Nipping at Middle-Class." *The Canadian Jewish News* [Toronto], 15 April 1982, p. 5.

The battle against "anti-eroticism and linguistic repression" has been won. Layton finds people are now more open to new ideas.

C643a Hendry, Donald. "Biding Time." *Concordia University Magazine*, May, June, July 1982, pp. 25, 26, 27.

Layton discusses his recent nomination for the Nobel Prize, the special difficulty of being a poet in this century, and the subject of love in his poetry.

C644 Lees, David. "The Creative Chaos of Irving Layton." *Chatelaine*, Sept. 1982, pp. 52–53, 86, 88, 90–92, 98.

Layton is sensitive and vulnerable, his life an emotional chaos through a series of relationships with women, starting with his mother, and continuing through four wives and assorted others. Lees discusses Aviva Layton's semi-autobiographical novel *Nobody's Daughter* (C770) at some length, sympathizing more with Irving Layton than with his ex-wife. Irving Layton states that the artist must endure chaos as a condition for the creation of art.

C645 Mozel, Howard. "European Tour Confirms Poet's Values." *Oakville Beaver* [Oakville, Ont.], 3 June 1983, p. 13.

Layton's reading tour of Europe was a resounding success.

C646 [Whiten, Clifton.]"PCR Interview with Irving Layton." *Poetry Canada Review*, 4, No. 4 (Summer 1983), 8–9.

Layton describes himself as an angry man, but not sad or embittered. He comments on women ("a great principle of vitality"), his Jewishness, and his belief that modern poetry should embody freedom rather than adherence to some particular form or school of thought. He also discusses his dislike of academics (they "use literature as a substitute for living"), his pessimistic view of human nature, and his reasons for not joining the League of Canadian Poets.

C647 Meyer, Bruce, and Brian O'Riordan. "Irving Layton." In their *In Their Words: Interviews with Fourteen Canadian Writers*. Toronto: House of Anansi, 1984, pp. 10–24.

Canada was built on the concept of negation, which is why it cannot accept a great poet (like Layton). A.M. Klein influenced Layton in a general way, but Pound is a "minor poet." "With the young poets I always look to see if they have any poems about fucking, about death. If they don't, they're not poets." Genius is the ability to combine wisdom with passion. Layton's support of American involvement in Viet Nam and the Canadian employment of the War Measures Act has been vindicated by subsequent events. The poet is a prophet "who addresses himself to the moral, the psychological, the social and political dilemmas of his time." The poet's fight is for "the waywardness and the dignity of the human being."

C647a Butska, Nina. "Interview: The Poet in Society." *Dialogue* [Humber College], 2, No. 5 (Feb. 1984), 1–2.

To kill the human spirit for me is the greatest crime of all"; the poet must be passionately involved in its defense. Betrayal and disharmony are inevitable attributes of our world, but the creative individual is often able to find nurturing in wife and children.

C648 Martin, Donald. "Interview: Poetic Activity Is at a High Point, Says Irving Layton, but There Are Few Great Poems, Because Society Has Smothered Passion." *Books in Canada*, March 1984, pp. 26–28.

Layton called his latest book *The Gucci Bag* as a warning against materialism. He changed his name to Layton "because it rhymes with Satan," and prefers Montreal to Toronto because of its joy and European affiliations. Today's poetry is more notable for its competence than its passion. "As far as Canadian poets are concerned, Gulag never happened."

C649 Powe, B.W. "An Interview with Irving Layton." *Conjunctions* [New York], No. 6 (Spring 1984), pp. 154–64.

Layton talks of his battles with critics, of the indifferent public, and his efforts to make himself visible. The filmmakers today, rather than the poets, are making the big statements. "American poetry lacks a metaphysical dimension." The true poet "is passionately concerned with the fate, fortune, and adventure of the human spirit." Layton is a successor to the Hebrew prophets of the Old Testament.

C650 Benazon, Michael. "Irving Layton and the Montreal Poets." *Matrix*, No. 20 (Spring 1985), pp. 16–20.

Layton discusses his early years in Montreal. He admired A.M. Klein most of the Montreal poets, for he had a "world consciousness" his contemporaries lacked. David Solway, Michael Harris, and Seymour Mayne are among the most significant Montreal poets of their generation. Too much modern poetry is "formless," lacking passion and emotion.

C651 Gabereau, Vicky. Interview. *The Vicky Gabereau Show*. CBC Radio, Oct. 1985. Printed (abridged) in *This Won't Hurt a Bit*. By Vicky Gabereau. Don Mills, Ont.: Collins, 1987, pp. 185–89.

On the occasion of his publication of *Waiting for the Messiah: A Memoir*, Layton describes his life as characterized by "creative restlessness." He immediately recognized Leonard Cohen as a poet, for "... one eye has death and the other eye has sexuality."

C652 Interview with Irving Layton. *Midday*. CBC TV, 16 Oct. 1985.

Layton is interviewed on the occasion of his recently completed memoirs.

C653 Gzowski, Peter. Interview with Irving Layton. *Morningside*. Host Peter Gzowski. CBC Radio, 22 Oct. 1985. (23 min., 45 sec.)

Gzowski and Layton discuss Elspeth Cameron's biography of Layton (C9) and Layton's *Waiting for the Messiah: A Memoir*.

C654 Pivato, Joe. "I don't know anything that equalled my delight, astonishment, and terror at discovering I was a poet." *Athabasca University Magazine*, 10, No. 4 (Winter 1986–87), 6–10.

Layton voices his objections to Elspeth Cameron's deficiencies in scholarship and poetic comprehension in her biography of him (C9). He is gratified that Italians have nominated him for the Nobel Prize, but sad that the Canadian WASP establishment continues to ignore him. The poet must be a prophet. Too much contemporary poetry is mere word play.

C655 Purdy, Al. "Irving Layton Speaking." *Waves*, 15, No. 3 (Winter 1987), 5–13.

The social awareness that characterized the poetry of Layton and older poets is lacking in younger poets. *TISH* and its followers are devitalizing Canadian poetry. Layton's large fund of anger from the past, combined with discipline, enables him to continue writing. The poet must make his experience accessible to future generations through access to the unconscious, which is the creative aspect of the human personality.

C655a "A Chat with Irving Layton: A New Book of Poems on Judaism." *Lifestyles*, 1988, pp. 53–56.

In a discussion of *Fortunate Exile* Layton states that "the Jew is the human condition writ large." It is the nature of the spirit not to be at home in our world. The symbiosis of the Jews with other cultures occasioned by the Diaspora has resulted in the rich cross-fertilization of the work of many writers— including his own.

C656 Smith, Leslie. "Layton Returns to Halifax to Talk Shop with Writers." *The Chronicle-Herald* [Halifax], 2 Nov. 1988, p. 6-L.

On the occasion of his reading at the Writers' Federation of Nova Scotia Literary Symposium 4-5 November, Layton talks of his career and how impressed he is with his young poetry students.

C656a Scavetta, Tony. "Irving Layton Reading at Humber College, Oct. 19, 1988." *The Plowman* [Humber College], No. 3 (Jan. 1989), p. 10.

C657 Homel, David. "Mask and Man." *Books in Canada*, Nov. 1989, pp. 19–21.

Jewish writers of the younger generation lack the commitment Layton's generation had to humanism and internationalism. His own outrageous behaviour was a persona to get himself and poetry generally accepted by the Canadian public. Music and metaphysics are essential for good poetry.

C658 Marchand, Philip. "Layton Sees a Movie in Berlin Symbol." *The Toronto Star*, 16 Nov. 1989, p. B3.

Layton discusses how he feels films have taken the place of poetry as today's art form; too much poetry today is written by women and is obsessively concerned with language.

C659 Pringle, Valerie, and Ralph Benmergui. Interview with Irving Layton. *Midday*. CBC TV, 29 Nov. 1989. (7 min., 8 sec.)

Layton discusses *Wild Gooseberries: The Selected Letters of Irving Layton*.

C660 Norris, Gary. "Layton No Longer Poetry's Wild Man: Provocative Poet Looks Forward to New Impulses and Wonderful Times." *The Gazette* [Montreal], 7 Jan. 1990, p. F5.

On tour to promote *Wild Gooseberries: The Selected Letters of Irving Layton*, Layton expresses pessimism on the future of poetry. Imaginative understanding of the world is now mainly the province of film.

C661 Cameron, B. *Interview with Irving Layton*. Medea Productions, n.d. (Videocassette; colour)

Layton compares *Heart of Darkness* with *Apocalypse Now*, produced and directed by Francis Ford Coppola.

Miscellaneous Audio-Visual Material

C662 Shane, George. "Poet of Passion." In his *Canada in Caricature*. Winnipeg: Greywood, 1967, p. 22.
In this cartoon of Layton, Shane profiles Layton's views on love and politics."

C663 Mandel, Eli. "Maypoles and Whipping Posts." *Celebration: Ideas*, CBC Radio, 8 May 1967. (1 min.)
In Layton's "The Birth of Tragedy" the broken world of objects is made whole in the mouth of the poet. Death itself is a birth day.

C664 Aislin [Mosher, Terry]. "Aislin's Cross-Hatch." *The Montreal Star*, 26 April 1969, p. 27.
A cartoon on Layton's departure to Toronto.

C665 Quigley, Paul, adapted. *A Sense of Poetry: To a Very Old Woman*. Prod. Cinematica Canada. Distrib. Marvin Melnyk, 1974. (16 mm.; 10 min., 30 sec.)
A dramatic adaptation of Layton's poem "To a Very Old Woman."

C666 Whyte, Rich. "The Temptation of Saint Irving." *Books in Canada*, Nov. 1976, p. 40.
A cartoon of Layton.

C667 Francis, Wynne, Gertie Goldberg, Bill Goodwin, Michael Harris, Irving Layton, David Lewis, Eli Mandel, Seymour Mayne, Alden Nowlan, Dora Pleat, Melech Ravitch, Musia Schwartz, David Solway, and Eleanor Stober. "Portrait of a One-Armed Juggler." *A Special Occasion*. Prepared and prod. Malka. CBC-FM Radio, 21 July 1977. (2 hrs.) Rebroadcast. CBC Radio, 24 July 1977. (2 hrs.)

On the occasion of Layton's sixty-fifth birthday, the contributors discuss Layton's importance in Canadian poetry. Perspectives on his politics, women, poetry, Jewishness, and his family are interwoven with his readings of fourteen poems (B1154, B1165, B1208–B1209, B1215, B1221, B1238, B1267, B1274, B1285–B1289).

C668 Tata, Sam. "The Plates by Sam Tata: Irving Layton." *Canadian Fiction Magazine*, No. 29 (1979), pp. 30–31.
A photographic portrait of Layton, dated Montreal 1960, preceded by a list of his books.

C669 Aislin [Mosher, Terry]. Cartoon. *The Gazette* [Montreal], 29 Nov. 1983, p. B2.
A cartoon on Layton's return to live in Montreal.

C670 Maggs, Arnaud. "Arnaud Maggs' Literary Portraits: Irving Layton." *Canadian Fiction Magazine*, Nos. 50–51 (1984), p. [134].
This photograph of Layton, dated 20 July 1983, appeared on the cover of Elspeth Cameron's biography of Layton (C9).

C671 Gzowski, Peter. Interview with Elspeth Cameron. *Morningside*. Host Peter Gzowski. CBC Radio, 23 Oct. 1985. (24 min.)
Gzowski and Cameron discuss Layton's life and its relation to Cameron's biography of Layton (C9).

C672 Gzowski, Peter. Interview with Robert Fulford, Gwendolyn MacEwen, and Eli Mandel. *Morningside*. Host Peter Gzowski. CBC Radio, 24 Oct. 1985. (25 min.)
Gzowski, Fulford, MacEwen, and Mandel discuss Irving Layton's life and its relation to Elspeth Cameron's biography of Layton (C9).

C673 *Poet: Irving Layton Observed.* Life Transformed: Canadian Writers at Work. Dir. Donald Winkler. Prod. William Brind. Exec. prod. Barrie Howells. NFB, [1986]. (Colour; beta and VHS videocassette; 52 min., 3 sec.) Broadcast. CBC TV, 30 July 1987. (52 min., 3 sec.) Rerecorded (abridged). *Irving Layton: An Introduction.* Dir. Donald Winkler. Prod. William Brind. Exec. prod. Barrie Howells. NFB, n.d. (27 min., 27 sec.)

In this film, which is shot mainly in Greece, Layton discusses the role of the poet in our society. Poets are like the canaries that used to be kept in mines; they sense impending disaster sooner than most.

Poems about Layton

C674 Creeley, Robert. "For Irving." *CIV/n*, No. 5 (March 1954), p. 4. Rpt. in *The Collected Poems of Robert Creeley: 1945–1975.* By Robert Creeley. Los Angeles: Univ. of California Press, 1982, p. 64. Rpt. in *CIV/n: A Literary Magazine of the 50's.* Ed. Aileen Collins. Montreal: Véhicule, 1983, p. 134.

C675 Smith, A.J. M. "Astraea Redux." *CIV/n*, No. 6 (Sept. 1954), p. 11. Rpt. (revised — "Astraea Redux: Keewaydin Poetry Conference") in *Collected Poems.* By A.J.M. Smith. Toronto: Oxford Univ. Press, 1962, n. pag. Rpt. in his *Poems: New and Collected.* Toronto: Oxford Univ. Press, 1967, pp. 110–11. Rpt. (original) in *CIV/n: A Literary Magazine of the 50's.* Ed. Aileen Collins. Montreal: Véhicule, 1983, p. 175.

C676 Walton, George. "Buttocks and Buttercups." *CIV/n*, No. 6 (Sept. 1954), pp. 23–24. Rpt. in *CIV/n: A Literary Magazine of the 50's.* Ed. Aileen Collins. Montreal: Véhicule, 1983, pp. 187–88.

C677 Cohen, Leonard. "To I.P.L." In his *Let Us Compare Mythologies.* McGill Poetry Series, No. 1. Toronto: Contact, 1956, p. 61.

C678 Dudek, Louis. "For I.P.L." In his *The Transparent Sea.* Toronto: Contact, 1956, pp. 104–05.

C679 Dudek, Louis. "The Want of Criticism." *The Canadian Forum*, May 1956, p. 39.

C680 Ellenbogen, George. "The Archbishop to Irving Layton." In his *Winds of Unreason.* McGill Poetry Series, No. 3. Toronto: Contact, 1957, p. 39.

C681 Ellenbogen, George. "Layton's Reply." In his *Winds of Unreason.* McGill Poetry Series, No. 3. Toronto: Contact, 1957, p. 40.

C682 Hine, Daryl. "Aere Perennius: For Irving Layton." In his *The Carnal and the Crane.* Toronto: Contact, 1957, p. 43. Rpt. in *Jaw Breaker* [Westmount, P.Q.], No. 2 (Oct. 1971), p. 5.

C683 Ross, W.W.E. "Air with Variations: Irving Layton." *The Canadian Forum*, April 1957, p. 22.

C684 Smith, A.J.M. "On Reading Certain Poems and Epistles of Irving Layton and Louis Dudek." *The Canadian Forum*, May 1957, pp. 41–42.

C685 Dobbs, Kildare. "O Montreal!". *The Canadian Forum*, Jan. 1958, p. 228.

C686 Dudek, Louis. "Irving Layton's Poem in Early Spring." In his *Laughing Stalks.* Toronto: Contact, 1958, p. 28. Rpt. in *The Human Voice Quarterly* [Miami], 2, No. 3 (Aug. 1966), 47. Rpt. in *Collected Poetry.* By Louis Dudek. Montreal: Delta, 1971, pp. 173–74.

C687 Dudek, Louis. "Reply to Envious Arthur." In his *Laughing Stalks*. Toronto: Contact, 1958, pp. 43–45.

C688 Dudek, Louis. "Tar and Feathers." In his *Laughing Stalks*. Toronto: Contact, 1958, pp. 40–42. Rpt. in his *Collected Poetry*. Montreal: Delta, 1971, pp. 178–79.

C689 Souster, Raymond. "Irving Layton at Ryerson." In his *Crepehanger's Carnival*. Toronto: Contact, 1958, p. 28. Rpt. ("Irving Layton at Ryerson Polytechnical") in his *Collected Poems of Raymond Souster. Vol. 2, 1955–62*. Ottawa: Oberon, 1981, p. 118.

C690 Francis, Wynne. "For Irving Layton (On Rereading His Poems)." *The Canadian Forum*, June 1959, p. 69.

C691 Grubb, H. Eugene. "Cocktail Party for a Poet." *The Dalhousie Review*, 40 (Summer 1960), 233.

C692 Cohen, Leonard. "Last Dance at the Four Penny." In his *The Spice-Box of Earth*. Toronto: McClelland and Stewart, 1961, pp. 65–66. Rpt. in his *Selected Poems 1956–1968*. Toronto: McClelland and Stewart, 1968, p. 69.

C693 Smith, A.J.M. "To Irving Layton (On His Passion for the First Lady)." *The Canadian Forum*, April 1961, p. 4. Rpt. (revised — "To Irving Layton, on His Love Poem to Mrs. Jacqueline Kennedy, Then First Lady") in *The Classic Shade: Selected Poems*. By A.J.M. Smith. Toronto: McClelland and Stewart, 1978, p. 66.

C694 Swayze, Fred. "Canadians Seen — Irving Layton." *The Fiddlehead*, No. 49 (Summer 1961), p. 3.

C695 Miller, Malcolm. "I Sing of the Fat Old Jewish Woman." *Delta*, No. 15 (Aug. 1961), p. 4.

C696 O'Hearne, Walter. "To a Slopshire Lad." *The Montreal Star*, 21 Oct. 1961, Sec. Entertainments, p. 5. Rpt. in *Engagements: The Prose of Irving Layton*. Ed. Seymour Mayne. Toronto: McClelland and Stewart, 1972, pp. 168–69.

C697 Purdy, Al. "Towns." In his *The Blur in Between: Poems 1960–61*. Toronto: Emblem, 1962, p. 9.

C698 Hertz, K.V. "No Prophet." *Queen's Quarterly*, 69 (Autumn 1962), 376–77. Rpt. in *Poésie / Poetry 64*. Ed. Jacques Godbout and John Robert Colombo. Montréal / Toronto: Jour / Ryerson, 1963, pp. 137–38.

C699 Lone, Kelly. "Alcides (Irving Layton)." *The Fiddlehead*, No. 54 (Fall 1962), pp. 28–29.

C700 Smith, A.J.M. "The Devil Take Her — and Them." *The Tamarack Review*, No. 26 (Winter 1963), p. 95. Rpt. in *Delta*, No. 20 (Feb. 1963), p. 23. Rpt. (revised) in his *Poems: New and Collected*. By A.J.M. Smith. Toronto: Oxford Univ. Press, 1967, p. 99. Rpt. ["The Devil Take Her — and Them (1962)"] in his *On Poetry and Poets: Selected Essays of A.J.M. Smith*. New Canadian Library Original, No. 143. Toronto: McClelland and Stewart, 1977, p. 87. Rpt. ("The Devil Take Her — and Them") in his *The Classic Shade: Selected Poems*. Toronto: McClelland and Stewart, 1978, p. 66.

C701 Spivak, Michael, and V.A. Coleman. "The Soot and Lard Disappear." *The Canadian Forum*, Nov. 1963, p. 191.

C702 Cohen, Leonard. "For My Old Layton." *Catapult*, 1, No. 2 (Summer 1964), 8. Rpt. in *Flowers for Hitler*. By Leonard Cohen. Toronto: McClelland and Stewart, 1964, pp. 36–37. Rpt. in his *Selected Poems 1956–1968*. Toronto: McClelland and Stewart, 1968, p. 102.

C703 [Hibbard, Dale.] "On Irving Layton's Desire to Leave Lusting Impressions." *Encore* [Prevost, P.Q.], No. 5 (Jan.–Feb. 1965), p. 8.

C704 [Macpherson, Jay.] "Sour Grapes for Scurvy Capon." *Yes*, No. 14 (Sept. 1965), n. pag.
  Signed: Donna Jaime.

C705 Gustafson, Ralph. "For Arthur Smith and Irving Layton: As if They Were All Dead." In his *Sift in an Hourglass*. Toronto: McClelland and Stewart, 1966, p. 41.

C706 Gustafson, Ralph. "The Parabola in the Mirror: For Irving Layton." In his *Sift in an Hourglass*. Toronto: McClelland and Stewart, 1966, p. 48.

C707 [Fraser, Raymond?]. "Buck Layton." *Intercourse*, No. 1 (Spring 1966), p. 18.

C708 Marshall, Tom. "Keewaydin." *Yes*, No. 15 (Sept. 1966), n. pag.

C709 Rath, Dorothy H. "The Day Layton Came to London." *Other Voices* [London, Ont.], 2, No. 2 (Fall 1966), n. pag. Rpt. in *Cross-Canada Writer's Quarterly*, 3, No. 1 (Winter 1981), 15.

C710 Smith, A.J.M. "The Country Lovers: A Little Eclogue for Irving Layton and Aviva." In his *Poems New and Collected*. Toronto: Oxford Univ. Press, 1967, p. 90.

C711 Sullivan, D.H. "Proclamation for Yonge Street." *The Canadian Forum*, Aug. 1967, p. 116.

C712 Lane, Red. "Irving Layton (An Epitaph for the Walking Dead)." In his *Collected Poems of Red Lane*. Ed. Patrick Lane and Seymour Mayne. Vancouver: Very Stone House, 1968, p. 84.

C713 Lane, Red. "Irving Layton (Twofold Tribute for the Prodigal Son)." In his *Collected Poems of Red Lane*. Ed. Patrick Lane and Seymour Mayne. Vancouver: Very Stone House, 1968, p. 85.

C714 Acorn, Milton. "The Lost Leader." In his *I've Tasted My Blood: Poems 1956 to 1968*. Ed. and introd. Al Purdy. Toronto: Ryerson, 1969, p. 17.

C715 "To irving sans love." *The Ontarion* [Univ. of Guelph], 23 Jan. 1969.
  See Layton's version of this poem, "To Irving Layton Sans Love" (B414).

C716 Osterlund, Steven. "For Irving Layton." *The Massachussetts Review* [Amherst, Mass.], 11 (Spring 1970), 272.

C717 Blaikie, John. "On hearing Irving Layton read Irving Layton." *The Fiddlehead*, No. 85 (May–June–July 1970), p. 116.

C718 MacCulloch, Clare. "After Meeting with Irving Layton." *Alive* [Guelph, Ont.], Nov. 1970, pp. 12–13. Rpt. in *Manido, the Windmaker*. By Clare MacCulloch. Guelph: Alive, 1971, pp. 20–21.

C719 McCrae, A. "Nobody Loves a Fat Poet." *Poesis* [St. Catharines, Ont.], 1 (1971), 4.

C720 Blayton, Scurving [Geggie, Mary, and Peter Whalley]. "A Poet's Non-Abject Plea to the Canada Council." In *Northern Blights: More Than Anyone Needs to Know about Canadian Poetry and Painting.* By Mary Geggie and Peter Whalley. Morin Heights, P.Q.: Upbank, 1972, p. 31.

Geggie and Whalley also include satirical bio-critical material (C199).

C721 Layton, Max. "Reflection." *Impulse*, 1, No. 3 (Spring 1972), 33.

C722 Lever, Bernice. "Irving, You Have Magic." *Waves*, 1, No. 1 (Spring 1972), 39. Rpt. in *Yet Woman I Am.* By Bernice Lever. Cobalt, Ont.: Highway Book Shop, 1979, p. 59.

C723 Bowering, George. "Irving Layton." In his *Curious.* Toronto: Coach House, 1973, n. pag. Rpt. in his *Selected Poems.* Vancouver: Talonbooks, 1980, p. 108. Rpt. in his *West Window.* Toronto: General, 1982, p. 36.

C724 Brown, Denys. "About Women: A Prophecy." *Excalibur* [York Univ.], 15 March 1973, p. 9.

C725 Ryan, Angeline. "Irvingsdrockh on Gurus." *Excalibur* [York Univ.], 15 March 1973, p. 9.

C726 Hanson, Joan. "Layton." *The Canadian Forum*, March 1974, p. 38.

C727 Milnes, I.D. "Poem." *Emergency Librarian*, 2, No. 2 (Dec. 1974), 18.

C728 Friedman, Irena. "Irving Layton Comes to Visit." *Northern Journey*, Nos. 7-8 (1976), p. 106.

C729 Smith, A.J.M. "On Reading Layton's 'Poetry as the Fine Art of Pugilism.'" *Northern Journey*, No. 6 (1976), p. 97.

C730 Parlow, Lela. "For My Brother Layton." *Books in Canada*, Aug. 1976, p. 26.

C731 Osterlund, Steven. *Paradise in a Warm Climate.* Akron, Ohio: Poetry Postcard, No. 1, 1977. 1 leaf.

C732 McFadden, David. "How I Came to Understand Irving Layton." *The Canadian Forum*, Dec.–Jan. 1977-78, p. 55.

C733 DiCicco, Pier Giorgio. "Casa Loma Birthday." In *Tributaries. An Anthology: Writer to Writer.* Ed. Barry Dempster. Oakville, Ont.: Mosaic / Valley, 1978, p. 53.

C734 Dimitroff, Philip. "A Seasonal Bird." In *Handouts from the Mountain.* Ed. Irving Layton. Toronto: York Poetry Workshop, 1978, p. 25.

C735 Gustafson, Ralph. "Irving Layton." In *Tributaries. An Anthology: Writer to Writer.* Ed. Barry Dempster. Oakville, Ont.: Mosaic / Valley, 1978, p. 53.

C736 Katz, Gertrude. "After the Whole Bloody Bird. For Irving Layton." *Poesie de Montreal Poems*, No. 4 (1978), p. 47.

C737 MacLulich, T.D. "Two Canadian Poets." In *Aurora: New Canadian Writing 1978.* Ed. Morris Wolfe. Toronto: Doubleday, 1978, pp. 51-53.

C738 Solway, David. "In Praise of Prophets." *Matrix*, Nos. 6-7 (1978), p. 99.

C739 Solway, David. "Portrait of a Poet." *Matrix*, Nos. 6–7 (1978), p. 95.

C740 Ahearne, Catharine. "Divine Pigeon: For Irving Layton, In Praise of Older Poets." *Poetry Canada Poésie*, 1, No. 1 (Fall 1979), 4.

C741 Singer, D.K. "For Irving Layton." *Concerning Poetry* [Western Washington Univ.], 12, No. 2 (Fall 1979), 44.

C742 Rath, Dorothy. "Avant-Midi avec un faun." In *An Unlikely Affair: The Irving Layton-Dorothy Rath Correspondence*. By Irving Layton and Dorothy Rath. Oakville, Ont.: Mosaic / Valley, 1980, pp. 3–4.

C743 Rath, Dorothy. "Bargain." In *An Unlikely Affair: The Irving Layton-Dorothy Rath Correspondence*. By Irving Layton and Dorothy Rath. Oakville, Ont.: Mosaic / Valley, 1980, p. 57.

C744 Rath, Dorothy. "Because I measure time . . . ." In *An Unlikely Affair: The Irving Layton-Dorothy Rath Correspondence*. By Irving Layton and Dorothy Rath. Oakville, Ont.: Mosaic / Valley, 1980, p. 124.

C745 Rath, Dorothy. "Collector." In *An Unlikely Affair: The Irving Layton-Dorothy Rath Correspondence*. By Irving Layton and Dorothy Rath. Oakville, Ont.: Mosaic / Valley, 1980, p. 131.

C746 Rath, Dorothy. "Creation." In *An Unlikely Affair: The Irving Layton-Dorothy Rath Correspondence*. By Irving Layton and Dorothy Rath. Oakville, Ont.: Mosaic / Valley, 1980, p. 18.

C747 Rath, Dorothy. "[If I step softly]." In *An Unlikely Affair: The Irving Layton-Dorothy Rath Correspondence*. By Irving Layton and Dorothy Rath. Oakville, Ont.: Mosaic / Valley, 1980, pp. 21–22.

C748 Rath, Dorothy. "Shalom." In *An Unlikely Affair: The Irving Layton-Dorothy Rath Correspondence*. By Irving Layton and Dorothy Rath. Oakville, Ont.: Mosaic / Valley, 1980, p. 71.

C749 Rath, Dorothy. "[To grow to ripeness]." In *An Unlikely Affair: The Irving Layton-Dorothy Rath Correspondence*. By Irving Layton and Dorothy Rath. Oakville, Ont.: Mosaic / Valley, 1980, pp. 119–20.

C750 Rath, Dorothy. "Water Poem." In *An Unlikely Affair: The Irving Layton-Dorothy Rath Correspondence*. By Irving Layton and Dorothy Rath. Oakville, Ont.: Mosaic / Valley, 1980, p. 131.

C751 Rath, Dorothy. "[When I commune]." In *An Unlikely Affair: The Irving Layton-Dorothy Rath Correspondence*. By Irving Layton and Dorothy Rath. Oakville, Ont.: Mosaic / Valley, 1980, p. 9.

C752 Loeb, Kurt. "['I am,' says Irv Layton]." Letter. *The Globe and Mail* [Toronto], 23 April 1980, p. 6.

C753 Mayne, Seymour. "The Interruption: For Irving Layton." In his *The Impossible Promised Land: Poems New and Selected*. Oakville, Ont.: Mosaic / Valley, 1981, p. 119.

C754 Nelson, Sharon H. "Waiting for Layton." *Poesie de Montreal Poems*, No. 5 (1981), p. 59.

C755 Zend, Robert. "Ditto Poem: Irving Layton." In his *Beyond Labels*. Toronto: Hounslow, 1982, p. 99.

C756 Tsimicalis, Stavros. "Waiting for Layton." *Descant*, No. 47 [15, No. 4] (Winter 1984), pp. 80–81.

C757 Brooks, Jack. "Irving Layton Returns to Montreal." *Tidepool: An Anthology of Haiku and Short Poetry* [Hamilton], No. 3 (1986), p. 27.

C758 Crossley, Don. "On Irving Layton's Immortality." *Toronto*, June 1986, p. 8.

C759 Linder, Norma West. "Second Poem for Irving." *Tidepool: An Anthology of Haiku and Short Poetry* [Hamilton], No. 4 (1987), p. 36.

C760 Acorn, Milton. "I Am the Real Irving Layton." In *The Uncollected Acorn*. Ed. and introd. James Deahl. Toronto: Deneau, 1987, p. 58. Rpt. in *Poetry Canada Review*, 8, Nos. 2–3 (Spring 1987), 7.

C761 Layton, Boschka. "Brief to Irving." *Studies in Canadian Literature*, 13, No. 2 (1988), 142.

C761a Scavetta, Tony. "A Tribute to Irving Layton." *The Plowman* [Humber College], No. 3 (Jan. 1989), p. 9.

C762 Johnson, Andrew. "He Spoke of Death and Claimed to Have Shattered Windows." *Surface* [Queen's Univ.], Jan. 1990.

C763 Weber, Faye. "Lazarovitch — Aye!". In her *Wings for My Metronome*. Edmonton: P.S. Presse, 1990, p. 12.

C764 Wilt, Kurt Van. "For I. Layton." *The Georgian* [Sir George Williams Univ.], n.d., p. 15.

Miscellaneous

C765 Cicero, Morgan. "Results of Canwit No. 7." *Books in Canada*, March 1976, p. 34.
Cicero's contribution to "sepulchral wit" includes the following memorial lines: "HERE LIES / IRVING LAYTON / WHO'S GONE TO BE WITH FRIENDS."

C766 Editors. "Canwit No. 18." *Books in Canada*, Dec. 1976, p. 42.

Irving Layton, as "Not any Virgil," is used as an example for a contest to make anagrams out of the names of Canadian authors.

C767 Editors. "Results of Canwit No. 18." *Books in Canada*, Feb. 1977, p. 33.
The editors note that "As expected, there were plenty of duplications in our anagram contest. Poor old IRVING LAYTON, who was NOT ANY VIRGIL in our example, kept popping up as LAY NOT VIRGIN."

C768 Murdoch, Derrick. "Results of Canwit No. 18." *Books in Canada*, Feb. 1977, p. 33.
Murdoch's contribution to the "anagram contest" includes the following: "IRVING LAYTON: ARTY IN LOVING."

C769 "CanWit No. 32." *Books in Canada*, April 1978, p. 33.
The authors of the "CanWit" contest use "Irving 'Lovable' Layton" as an example of the 'nicknames' that will make Canadian writers "truly popular."

C770 Layton, Aviva. *Nobody's Daughter*. Toronto: McClelland and Stewart, 1982.
Aviva Layton's novel includes fictional and biographical elements pertaining to Layton.

Awards and Honours

C771 Canada Foundation Award (1957).

C772 Canada Council Senior Fellowship (1959).

C773 Governor-General's Award for Poetry for *A Red Carpet for the Sun* (1959).

C774 Quebec Literary and Scientific Competition — 1st prize in the English language category (1963).

C775 Veteran A Award from *Catapult* (1963).
       This was a spoof award.

C776 Canada Council Special Arts Award (1967).

C777 Univ. of Western Ontario President's Medal in poem
       category for "Keine Lazarovitch 1870–1959."

C778 D.C.L. Bishop's Univ. (1970).

C779 Honourary D.Litt. Concordia Univ. (1976).

C780 Officer in the Order of Canada (1976).

C781 Award from J.J. Segal Fund for Jewish Culture in the
       category "English Literature on a Jewish Theme"
       (date unknown).

C782 Life Achievement Award, Encyclopaedia Britannica
       (1979).

C783 Honourary D.Litt. York Univ. (1979).

C784 Canada Council Arts Award (1979–81).

C785 Nomination for Nobel Prize in Literature (1982).

C786 Nomination for Nobel Prize in Literature (1983).

D   Selected Book and Record Reviews

Selected Book Reviews

Here and Now

D1   Avison, Margaret. Rev. of *Here and Now*. *The Canadian Forum*, May 1945, pp. 47–48.
        Although "Mother, This Is Spring" has "intelligibility and impact," Layton needs more "technical competence or developing conviction" for the necessary fusion of "intelligibility and impact." (For Layton's reply see B840.)

D2   Klein, A.M. "New Writers Series, No. 1." *The Canadian Jewish Chronicle* [Montreal], 8 May 1945, p. 8. Rpt. (rev. of *Here and Now*) in *Irving Layton: The Poet and His Critics*. Ed. Seymour Mayne. Toronto: McGraw-Hill Ryerson, 1978, pp. 23–26. Rpt. in *A.M. Klein: Literary Essays and Reviews*. Ed. Usher Caplan and M.W. Steinberg. Toronto: Univ. of Toronto Press, 1987, pp. 212–15.
        Layton reveals "a power of expression which is unique and personal, and a social awareness which endows poetic utterance with base and substance."

His "signature locution" and his ability to convey complex concepts in simple words are marks of his talent.

D3   Dupee, F.W. "Verse Chronicle." Rev. of *Flight into Darkness*, by Ralph Gustafson; *Overture*, by F.R. Jones [sic]; *A Tent for April*, by Patrick Anderson; and *Here and Now*, by Irving Layton. *The Nation* [New York], 1 Sept. 1945, p. 210. Rpt. (excerpt) in *Modern Commonwealth Literature: A Library of Literary Criticism*. Ed. John H. Ferres and Martin Tucker. New York: Frederick Ungar, 1977, p. 298.
        Patrick Anderson and Irving Layton are "the most interesting poets of the group." Layton writes "descriptive satires" "out of a stark plebeian experience; . . . for all their snarling bottom-dog attitudes they often succeed in convincing us of their reality."

D4   Ames, Alfred C. "From Left to Right." Rev. of *Ballad of the Bones and Other Poems*, by Byron Herbert Reece; *Here and Now*, by Irving Layton; and *The Task*, by Robert Bhain Campbell. *Poetry* [Chicago], 67 (Feb. 1946), 282, 284, 285.
        Layton's book "is proletarian in form and in content." His politics dominate his poetry; he needs more "disciplined expression" and "elevation of feeling" to write "poetry of a high order."

D5   Brown, E.K. "Letters in Canada: 1945. Poetry." *University of Toronto Quarterly*, 15 (April–July 1946), 274–75. Rpt. ("Poetry") in *Letters in Canada: 1945*. Ed. A.S.P. Woodhouse. Toronto: [*University of Toronto Quarterly*, offprint] Univ. of Toronto Press, 1946, pp. 274–75. Rpt. ("Canadian Poetry: 1945") in *Responses and Evaluations: Essays on Canada*. Ed. David Staines. New Canadian Library, No. 137. Toronto: McClelland and Stewart, 1977, pp. 246–47.

While Layton's poetry has little "passion," he is not "tame." His poems are "saturated . . . with the political and social problems of the immediate present."

The Black Huntsmen

D6   Birney, Earle. Rev. of *The Black Huntsmen*, by Irving Layton; *The Tight-Rope Walker*, by Norman Levine; *Footnote to the Lord's Prayer*, by Kay Smith; and *Counterpoint to Sleep*, by Anne Wilkinson. *Critically Speaking*. CBC Radio, 15 July 1951.

"Schoolboy scribblings," such as "Intransitive Verb," are compensated for by "socially pungent" poems, such as "Newsboy."

D7   Souster, Raymond. Rev. of *The Black Huntsmen*. *Contact*, 1, No. 1 (Jan. 1952), 9. Rpt. in *Irving Layton: The Poet and His Critics*. Ed. Seymour Mayne. Toronto: McGraw-Hill Ryerson, 1978, pp. 31-32.

Because he is hard to categorize, Layton has been ignored by the Canadian critics. But he is a poet "with something to say."

D8   Marriott, Anne. Rev. of *Counterpoint to Sleep*, by Anne Wilkinson; *The Black Huntsmen*, by Irving Layton; *How Smoke Gets into the Air*, by Terence Heywood; and *The Queen of Sheba*, by Michael Hornyansky. *The Canadian Forum*, Feb. 1952, p. 262.

"Disappointingly strained and weak," Layton falls back unsuccessfully on the use of four letter words for effect.

D9   Frye, Northrop. "Letters in Canada: 1951. Poetry." *University of Toronto Quarterly*, 21 (April 1952), 255. Rpt. ("Letters in Canada: 1951") in *The Bush Garden: Essays on the Canadian Imagination*. By Northrop Frye. Toronto: House of Anansi, 1971,

p. 8. Rpt. (excerpt — rev. of *The Black Huntsmen*) in *Irving Layton: The Poet and His Critics*. Ed. Seymour Mayne. Toronto: McGraw-Hill Ryerson, 1978, pp. 32-33.

Layton has real poetic talent, but contrived "violent rhetoric" mars much of the book. "One can get as tired of buttocks in Mr. Layton as of buttercups in the *Canadian Poetry Magazine* . . . ."

D10   M., A.[Creeley, Robert]. Rev. of *Contact*, ed. Raymond Souster; *Cerberus*, by Irving Layton, Louis Dudek, and Raymond Souster; *Twenty-Four Poems*, by Louis Dudek; *The Black Huntsmen* and *Love the Conqueror Worm*, by Irving Layton; and *Canadian Poems 1850-1952*, ed. Irving Layton. *The Black Mountain Review* [Black Mountain, N.C.], 1, No. 1 (Spring 1954), 53. Rpt. ("Canadian Poetry 1954") in *A Quick Graph: The Collected Notes & Essays*. By Robert Creeley. Ed. Donald Allen. San Francisco: Four Seasons Foundation, 1970, pp. 231-32. Rpt. (excerpt — rev. of *Cerberus*, *The Black Huntsmen*, *Love the Conqueror Worm*, and *Canadian Poems 1850-1952*) in *Irving Layton: The Poet and His Critics*. Ed. Seymour Mayne. Toronto: McGraw-Hill Ryerson, 1978, pp. 35-36.

Creeley comments on Layton's work in general, rather than reviewing any of his books in particular. "Layton may well be . . . the first Great Canadian Poet." He has a "sharp ear, and a hard, clear head for rhythms." His idiom has "much of the old and even 'traditional' way of it."

Cerberus, by Irving Layton, Louis Dudek, and Raymond Souster

D11   Williams, William Carlos. Letter to Raymond Souster. 28 June 1952. Printed in *Island* [Toronto], No. 1 (Sept. 1964), p. 47.

Williams responds to a copy of *Cerberus* sent to him by Louis Dudek. "I read Irving Layton but, try as I may, it doesn't come off."

D12 Reaney, James. Rev. of *Cerberus*. *The Canadian Forum*, Dec. 1952, p. 213.
This book has an "amazing unity of tone." Despite "the terrible lapses of taste," the book has a saving humour and energy.

D13 Rev. of *Cerberus*. *Inferno*, No. 9 (1953), p. 32.
These poets have drive and sincerity, but they need more "thoughtful purpose and construction," rather than "clinging to a dated Pound."

D14 Compton, Neil. Rev. of *Cerberus*. CIV/n, No. 2 (April 1953), pp. 21–22. Rpt. in CIV/n: *A Literary Magazine of the 50's*. Ed. Aileen Collins. Montreal: Véhicule, 1983, pp. 59–60.
The poetry here is "the liveliest and the most certain" of any in Canada, but they are "limited by the grey and fuzzy unloveliness of our national tongue."

D15 Frye, Northrop. "Letters in Canada: 1952. Poetry." *University of Toronto Quarterly*, 22 (April 1953), 279–80. Rpt. ("Letters in Canada: 1952") in *The Bush Garden: Essays on the Canadian Imagination*. By Northrop Frye. Toronto: House of Anansi, 1971, pp. 20–21. Rpt. (excerpt — rev. of *Cerberus*) in *Irving Layton: The Poet and His Critics*. Ed. Seymour Mayne. Toronto: McGraw-Hill Ryerson, 1978, p. 34.
Layton inveighs "against the inhibitions of prudery, exploitation, and philistinism." A number of fallacies mar his writing, but "To a Very Old Woman" is a good poem.

D16 E[ckman]., F[rederick]. Rev. of *Cerberus*. *Golden Goose* [Columbus, Ohio], No. 6 (Sept. 1953), pp. 84–85.
This book has more "verve and forthrightness" than "poetic maturity." All three poets have "clarity and concision."

D17 M., A. [Creeley, Robert]. Rev. of *Contact*, ed. Raymond Souster; *Cerberus*, by Irving Layton, Louis Dudek, and Raymond Souster; *Twenty-Four Poems*, by Louis Dudek; *The Black Huntsmen* and *Love the Conqueror Worm*, by Irving Layton; and *Canadian Poems 1850–1952*, ed. Irving Layton. *The Black Mountain Review* [Black Mountain, N.C.], 1, No. 1 (Spring 1954), 51, 53. Rpt. ("Canadian Poetry 1954") in *A Quick Graph: The Collected Notes & Essays*. By Robert Creeley. Ed. Donald Allen. San Francisco: Four Seasons Foundation, 1970, pp. 231–32. Rpt. (excerpt — rev. of *Cerberus*, *The Black Huntsmen*, *Love the Conqueror Worm*, and *Canadian Poems 1850–1952*) in *Irving Layton: The Poet and His Critics*. Ed. Seymour Mayne. Toronto: McGraw-Hill Ryerson, 1978, pp. 35–36.
Creeley comments on Layton's work in general, rather than reviewing any of his books in particular. See D10 for annotation.

D18 Raymund, Bernard. "Contact." *Miscellaneous Man*, No. 7 (June 1956), pp. 24–25.
Complacency is challenged by these three poets, although nothing here by Layton is as good as what he has published in American magazines.

Love the Conqueror Worm

D19 Marriott, Anne. Rev. of *Love the Conqueror Worm*, by Irving Layton; *The House* and *Third Poems*, by Anthony Frisch; and *Black-Panther-Search*, by

Charles H. Howe. *The Canadian Forum*, May 1953, p. 46. Rpt. (excerpt — rev. of *Love the Conqueror Worm*) in *Irving Layton: The Poet and His Critics*. Ed. Seymour Mayne. Toronto: McGraw-Hill Ryerson, 1978, pp. 34–35.

Although Layton's poems generally have something to say, they are "surprisingly thin and forced."

D20 M., A. [Creeley, Robert]. Rev. of *Contact*, ed. Raymond Souster; *Cerberus*, by Irving Layton, Louis Dudek, and Raymond Souster; *Twenty-Four Poems*, by Louis Dudek; *The Black Huntsmen* and *Love the Conqueror Worm*, by Irving Layton; and *Canadian Poems 1850–1952*, ed. Irving Layton. *The Black Mountain Review* [Black Mountain, N.C.], 1, No. 1 (Spring 1954), 51, 53. Rpt. ("Canadian Poetry 1954") in *A Quick Graph: The Collected Notes & Essays*. By Robert Creeley. Ed. Donald Allen. San Francisco: Four Seasons Foundation, 1970, pp. 231–32. Rpt. (excerpt — rev. of *Cerberus*, *The Black Huntsmen*, *Love the Conqueror Worm*, and *Canadian Poems 1850–1952*) in *Irving Layton: The Poet and His Critics*. Ed. Seymour Mayne. Toronto: McGraw-Hill Ryerson, 1978, pp. 35–36.

Creeley comments on Layton's work in general, rather than reviewing any of his books in particular. See D10 for annotation.

D21 Frye, Northrop. "Letters in Canada: 1953. Poetry." *University of Toronto Quarterly*, 23 (April 1954), 260. Rpt. ("Letters in Canada: 1953") in *The Bush Garden: Essays on the Canadian Imagination*. By Northrop Frye. Toronto: House of Anansi, 1971, p. 31.

A few poems of "freshness and originality" are outweighed by much "forced language and flaccid rhythm" in *Love the Conqueror Worm*.

In the Midst of My Fever

D22 Woodcock, George. "Recent Canadian Poetry." *Queen's Quarterly*, 62 (Spring 1955), 111, 112. Rpt. (excerpt — rev. of *The Long Pea-Shooter* and *In the Midst of My Fever*) in *Irving Layton: The Poet and His Critics*. Ed. Seymour Mayne. Toronto: McGraw-Hill Ryerson, 1978, pp. 39–41.

Woodcock discusses the poems in *In the Midst of My Fever* and *The Long Pea-Shooter* together, rather than specifically commenting on one book or the other. Layton's poetry is rhetorical and boring, neglecting sensibility and poetic craft as much as the stagnant neo-Georgians.

D23 Frye, Northrop. "Letters in Canada: 1954. Poetry." *University of Toronto Quarterly*, 24 (April 1955), 253–54. Rpt. ("Letters in Canada: 1954") in *The Bush Garden: Essays on the Canadian Imagination*. By Northrop Frye. Toronto: House of Anansi, 1971, pp. 41–42. Rpt. (excerpt — rev. of *In the Midst of My Fever* and *The Long Pea-Shooter*) in *Irving Layton: The Poet and His Critics*. Ed. Seymour Mayne. Toronto: McGraw-Hill Ryerson, 1978, pp. 38–39.

These poems show "a new excitement and intensity in the process of writing." Layton is an "erudite elegiac poet" of "genuine dignity and power."

D24 Wilson, Milton. "Turning New Leaves." Rev. of *Pressed on Sand*, by Alfred W. Purdy; *The Second Silence*, by Miriam Waddington; *Europe*, by Louis Dudek; and *In the Midst of My Fever* and *The Cold Green Element*, by Irving Layton. *The Canadian Forum*, Oct. 1955, pp. 163–64.

Wilson discusses the poems in *In the Midst of My Fever* and *The Cold Green Element* together, rather than specifically commenting on one book or the other. The best of these poems "are equal to the best written by a Canadian" and an immense advance on his previous work. They reveal a "combination of poise, severity and purity with a devil-may-care casualness."

D25 Denney, Reuel. "Invitations to the Listener: Nine Young Poets and Their Audiences." *Poetry* [Chicago], 89 (Oct. 1956), 46, 51–52.
    Layton captures W.H. Auden's "still-life atmosphere." His best poems, such as "First Snow: Lake Michigan" [sic], combine "freshness and direction of language" with a conviction that "something that needed to be said" has been communicated.

The Long Pea-Shooter

D26 Cogswell, Fred. Rev. of *The Long Pea-Shooter. The Fiddlehead*, Nos. 23–24 (Feb. 1955), p. 22. Rpt. in *Irving Layton: The Poet and His Critics*. Ed. Seymour Mayne. Toronto: McGraw-Hill Ryerson, 1978, p. 37.
    While Layton is technically accomplished, his "emotional and intellectual attitudes" are less appealing. Too many poems employ "inverted didacticism," although others possess "fine workmanship and wit."

D27 Woodcock, George. "Recent Canadian Poetry." *Queen's Quarterly*, 62 (Spring 1955), 111, 112. Rpt. (excerpt — rev. of *The Long Pea-Shooter* and *In the Midst of My Fever*) in *Irving Layton: The Poet and His Critics*. Ed. Seymour Mayne. Toronto: McGraw-Hill Ryerson, 1978, pp. 39–41.
    Woodcock discusses the poems in *In the Midst of My Fever* and *The Long Pea-Shooter* together, rather than specifically commenting on one book or the other. See D22 for annotation.

D28 Levitt, A. "Layton's Peashooter Stings Waste Land Recurrent Theme." *The Georgian* [Sir George Williams Univ.], 22 March 1955, p. 8.
    Layton has achieved a greater simplicity in this book. His best poems, particularly "For an Older Poet in Despair with the Times," transcend social criticism. They are negative, yet vigorous.

D29 Frye, Northrop. "Letters in Canada: 1954. Poetry." *University of Toronto Quarterly*, 24 (April 1955), 253. Rpt. ("Letters in Canada: 1954") in *The Bush Garden: Essays on the Canadian Imagination*. By Northrop Frye. Toronto: House of Anansi, 1971, pp. 40–41. Rpt. (excerpt — rev. of *In the Midst of My Fever* and *The Long Pea-Shooter*) in *Irving Layton: The Poet and His Critics*. Ed. Seymour Mayne. Toronto: McGraw-Hill Ryerson, 1978, p. 38.
    Much of this book "is oppressed by a conscience-driven and resentful mind." Still, the fact that much of Layton's poetry sticks in the mind suggests that he is a "genuine poet."

The Blue Propeller

D30 Pacey, Desmond. Rev. of *The Cold Green Element* and *The Blue Propeller. The Fiddlehead*, No. 26 (Nov. 1955), p. 28.
    Pacey comments generally, rather than noting anything specifically related to *The Blue Propeller* or *The Cold Green Element*. Layton would be a better poet if he were more discriminate in his criticism. Some of his better poems, like "Song for Naomi" and "Metamorphosis" are the quieter ones.

D31 Frye, Northrop. "Letters in Canada: 1955. Poetry." *University of Toronto Quarterly*, 25 (April 1956), 298. Rpt. ("Letters in Canada: 1955") in *The Bush Garden: Essays on the Canadian Imagination*. By

Northrop Frye. Toronto: House of Anansi, 1971, p. 53. Rpt. (excerpt — rev. of *The Cold Green Element* and *The Blue Propeller*) in *Irving Layton: The Poet and His Critics*. Ed. Seymour Mayne. Toronto: McGraw-Hill Ryerson, 1978, p. 42.

Apart from two or three poems, *The Blue Propeller* is "a dark tunnel of noisy dullness."

The Cold Green Element

D32 Wilson, Milton. "Turning New Leaves." Rev. of *Pressed on Sand*, by Alfred W. Purdy; *The Second Silence*, by Miriam Waddington; *Europe*, by Louis Dudek; and *In the Midst of My Fever* and *The Cold Green Element*, by Irving Layton. *The Canadian Forum*, Oct. 1955, pp. 163–64.

Wilson discusses the poems in *In the Midst of My Fever* and *The Cold Green Element* together, rather than specifically commenting on one book or the other. See D24 for annotation.

D33 Pacey, Desmond. Rev. of *The Cold Green Element* and *The Blue Propeller*. *The Fiddlehead*, No. 26 (Nov. 1955), p. 28.

Pacey comments generally, rather than noting anything specifically related to either *The Blue Propeller* or *The Cold Green Element*. See D30 for annotation.

D34 Frye, Northrop. "Letters in Canada: 1955. Poetry." *University of Toronto Quarterly*, 25 (April 1956), 297–98. Rpt. ("Letters in Canada: 1955") in *The Bush Garden: Essays on the Canadian Imagination*. By Northrop Frye. Toronto: House of Anansi, 1971, pp. 52–53. Rpt. (excerpt — rev. of *The Cold Green Element* and *The Blue Propeller*) in *Irving Layton: The Poet and His Critics*. Ed. Seymour Mayne. Toronto: McGraw-Hill Ryerson, 1978, pp. 41–42.

The poems, "polarized between personal associa-

tion and a direct reaction to experience," produce a book that is "remarkable" in its "intricate unity." Layton combines "humour with technical competence."

The Bull Calf and Other Poems

D35 MacLure, Millar. "Poets in Review." Rev. of *The Bull Calf and Other Poems*, by Irving Layton; and *Friday's Child*, by Wilfred Watson. *The Canadian Forum*, May 1956, pp. 35–36.

These poems are the outcome of a love of sensuous experience. He has assimilated the influences of Ezra Pound and others. "No other poet writing now in this country can manage so well the marriage of the big word and the little one in a poem, the genius of English for the mixed metaphor."

D36 Graham, Kathleen. "This Week I Read." *The Leader-Post* [Regina], 5 May 1956, p. 19.

These poems reveal a sense of form, "a keenly intellectual and highly original turn of mind and phrase. . . . They require, and merit, thought and concentration."

D37 Pacey, Desmond. Rev. of *The Bull Calf and Other Poems*. *The Fiddlehead*, No. 29 (Aug. 1956), pp. 30, 32. Rpt. in *Irving Layton: The Poet and His Critics*. Ed. Seymour Mayne. Toronto: McGraw-Hill Ryerson, 1978, pp. 54–55.

"Vitality" and "honesty" inform Layton's poetry. Tenderness is the keynote of this book; he can make "sexual desire seem very real." But, while his honest arrogance is attractive, his vindictive side is less so.

D38 Pacey, Desmond. "A Group of Seven." *Queen's Quarterly*, 63 (Autumn 1956), 441–43.

Layton has a "spiritual affinity" for W.B. Yeats in

his "mellow mixture of illusion and disillusion. . . . He has honesty and energy and an infectious vitality."

D39   Frye, Northrop. "Letters in Canada: 1956. Poetry." *University of Toronto Quarterly*, 26 (April 1957), 310–11. Rpt. (excerpt — rev. of *Music on a Kazoo, The Bull Calf and Other Poems,* and *The Improved Binoculars*) in *Congress Bulletin* [Canadian Jewish Congress], May 1959, p. 3. Rpt. (expanded, original — "Letters in Canada: 1956") in *The Bush Garden: Essays on the Canadian Imagination.* By Northrop Frye. Toronto: House of Anansi, 1971, pp. 68–69. Rpt. (rev. of *Music on a Kazoo, The Bull Calf and Other Poems,* and *The Improved Binoculars*) in *Irving Layton: The Poet and His Critics.* Ed. Seymour Mayne. Toronto: McGraw-Hill Ryerson, 1978, pp. 56–57.

    The best of the poems reveal "growing serenity and precision" and "his power of telling the whole disinterested imaginative truth about his subject."

D40   Lochhead, D.G. Rev. of *The Bull Calf and Other Poems,* by Irving Layton; *Even Your Right Eye,* by Phyllis Webb; and *Let Us Compare Mythologies,* by Leonard Cohen. *The Dalhousie Review,* 36 (Winter 1957), 425.

    Despite "a disturbing hardness of heart" and tedious "swipes at organized religion," Layton communicates "a natural tenderness." He "realizes a searching and arresting directness through the clever and sophisticated manipulation of detail," particularly in poems like "The Bull Calf."

The Improved Binoculars

D41   Rev. of *The Improved Binoculars. The Poet 15: Reviews* [Glasgow], 1957, pp. 4–5.

"A prime exponent of Fart for Fart's sake," Layton is an impressive poet, particularly successful in his tone of "sardonic candour."

D42   Eberhart, Richard. "The Form Is New." *The New York Times Book Review,* 24 Feb. 1957, p. 37.

    Although too diffuse, Layton has a wide emotional range. He has a youthful exuberance and freedom, a blend of "English, European, Greek and American feeling."

D43   Frye, Northrop. "Letters in Canada: 1956. Poetry." *University of Toronto Quarterly,* 26 (April 1957), 310. Rpt. (excerpt — rev. of *Music on a Kazoo, The Bull Calf and Other Poems,* and *The Improved Binoculars*) in *Congress Bulletin* [Canadian Jewish Congress], May 1959, p. 3. Rpt. (expanded, original — "Letters in Canada: 1956") in *The Bush Garden: Essays on the Canadian Imagination.* By Northrop Frye. Toronto: House of Anansi, 1971, p. 68. Rpt. (excerpt — rev. of *Music on a Kazoo, The Bull Calf and Other Poems,* and *The Improved Binoculars*) in *Irving Layton: The Poet and His Critics.* Ed. Seymour Mayne. Toronto: McGraw-Hill Ryerson, 1978, p. 56.

    William Carlos Williams' Introduction to *The Improved Binoculars* displays "commendable enthusiasm" for this "strongly recommended" volume.

D44   "Poets of Prairie and Backwoods." Rev. of *In the Rose of Time,* by Robert Fitzgerald; *The Improved Binoculars,* by Irving Layton; *A Vision of Ceremony,* by James McAuley; and *A Mortal Pitch,* by Vernon Scannell. *The Times Literary Supplement* [London], 19 April 1957, p. 239. Rpt. (excerpt) in *Modern Commonwealth Literature: A Library of Literary Criticism.* Ed. John H. Ferres and Martin Tucker. New York: Frederick Ungar, 1977, pp. 299–300.

While, at his best, Layton has "a sweet and unforced vein of lyricism," "a weakness for philosophical speculation" mars some poems. ". . . there is no mistaking his leaping vitality, or his real and evident delight in words . . . ."

D45 Duncan, Chester. Rev. of *The Improved Binoculars*, by Irving Layton; *Selected Poems 1926–1956*, by Dorothy Livesay; *The Carnal and the Crane*, by Daryl Hine; and *The Boatman*, by Jay Macpherson. *Critically Speaking*. CBC Radio, 14 June 1957.

The accomplishment of these poets may herald a "new era" in Canadian writing. Layton's rebelliousness gets tiresome and detracts from the "tenderness and power" of his best poetry, but there is everything here from "instinctive image-filled flow" to "mature and demon-driven high rhetoric" to "exact description."

D46 Dobbs, Kildare. Rev. of *The Improved Binoculars*. *The Canadian Forum*, Aug. 1957, pp. 115–16. Rpt. in *Irving Layton: The Poet and His Critics*. Ed. Seymour Mayne. Toronto: McGraw-Hill Ryerson, 1978, pp. 58–59.

Layton is at his best when he forgets his role as a poet and simply captures "the fleetingness . . . of all that's warm and alive." His worst poems portray "the poet slobbering over girls," indulging in "lofty pity for his suffering fellow-men," or those in which he " 'swears by the gods,' or roars, or names the authors of Great Books, or more simply says 'Ah!' "

D47 Eckman, Frederick. "Neither Tame nor Fleecy." *Poetry* [Chicago], 90 (Sept. 1957), 386, 388–90.

"Layton has the savage wit, the erotic preoccupations, and the frequent unevenness of an E.E. Cummings." One of his finest poems is "Enemies." He is least successful in his diatribes on "the cultural backwardness of Canadians."

D48 Waddington, Miriam. Rev. of *The Improved Binoculars*. *Congress Bulletin* [Canadian Jewish Congress], 11, Nos. 8–9 (Oct.–Nov. 1957), 4, 5.

Layton's poetry is related to that written by younger American writers, as well as Vladimir Mayakovsky, Walt Whitman, and D.H. Lawrence. While too many of his poems are written out of hatred for humanity, he "redeems himself" as a sensualist. Too many of his poems emphasize the biological imperatives of sex to the neglect of its emotional and spiritual dimensions.

Music on a Kazoo

D49 Frye, Northrop. "Letters in Canada: 1956. Poetry." *University of Toronto Quarterly*, 26 (April 1957), 310. Rpt. (excerpt — rev. of *Music on a Kazoo*, *The Bull Calf and Other Poems*, and *The Improved Binoculars*) in *Congress Bulletin* [Canadian Jewish Congress], May 1959, p. 3. Rpt. (expanded, original — "Letters in Canada: 1956") in *The Bush Garden: Essays on the Canadian Imagination*. By Northrop Frye. Toronto: House of Anansi, 1971, p. 68. Rpt. (excerpt — rev. of *Music on a Kazoo*, *The Bull Calf and Other Poems*, and *The Improved Binoculars*) in *Irving Layton: The Poet and His Critics*. Ed. Seymour Mayne. Toronto: McGraw-Hill Ryerson, 1978, p. 56.

Many of the poems in *Music on a Kazoo* are "expressions of Layton's poetic personality," which tends to be "stereotyped and predictable." "The Dwarf" is the best poem here.

D50 Reaney, James. Rev. of *Music on a Kazoo*. *The Canadian Forum*, Jan. 1958, p. 239. Rpt. in *Irving Layton: The Poet and His Critics*. Ed. Seymour Mayne. Toronto: McGraw-Hill Ryerson, 1978, pp. 57–58.

These poems are "violently satirical, deliberately vulgar and often very funny." Layton makes sex into "something mad and amusing."

A Laughter in the Mind

D51 Ciardi, John. "SRS Quarterly Roundup." *Saturday Review* [New York], 27 Sept. 1958, p. 31.
"Cain" is especially memorable, as are those poems in which ". . . Layton identifies with his subject instead of assaulting it."

D52 Rosenthal, M.L. "The Naked and the Clad." Rev. of *Selected Poems 1928–1958*, by Stanley Kunitz; *A Laughter in the Mind*, by Irving Layton; and *A Coney Island of the Mind*, by Lawrence Ferlinghetti. *The Nation* [New York], 11 Oct. 1958, pp. 214–15. Rpt. (excerpt) in *Modern Commonwealth Literature: A Library of Literary Criticism*. Ed. John H. Ferres and Martin Tucker. New York: Frederick Ungar, 1977, p. 300.
"His [Layton's] struggle to bring a not-quite-related malice out into the open" makes him interesting. He sometimes strikes "pure notes of suffering at the awareness of life gone sour," although sometimes there is an unworthy malice for its own sake.

D53 Wilson, Milton. "Canadian Poetry in 1958." Rev. of *The Deficit Made Flesh*, by John Glassco; *En Mexico*, by Louis Dudek; and *A Laughter in the Mind*, by Irving Layton. *Anthology*. Prod. Robert Weaver. CBC Radio, 13 Jan. 1959. (2 min.)
These poems show Layton developing "by discovering with surprise, delight and horror what his previous poems really meant and then writing new ones to prove it." "Côte des Neiges Cemetery," "Paging Mr. Superman," "Cain," and "The Swimmer" are especially worthy of note. The frog or toad image,

partaking of both land and water, becomes important in this book.

D54 Colombo, John Robert. "Three Poets." Rev. of *The Season's Lovers*, by Miriam Waddington; *The Deficit Made Flesh*, by John Glassco; and *A Laughter in the Mind*, by Irving Layton. *The Tamarack Review*, No. 11 (Spring 1959), pp. 91, 93–95.
Although "Cat Dying in Autumn" and a few others are fine poems, this collection is too uneven to indicate any advance in Layton's talent.

D55 Mandel, E.W. Rev. of *A Laughter in the Mind*. *The Dalhousie Review*, 39 (Spring 1959), 119, 121, 123. Rpt. in *Irving Layton: The Poet and His Critics*. Ed. Seymour Mayne. Toronto: McGraw-Hill Ryerson, 1978, pp. 60–62.
Layton is surprisingly traditional, often recalling Robert Browning. His work is "not a reversion to an outdated metaphysics, nor an anarchistic sensuality, but a serious and determined effort to solve in particularly native imagery and diction a problem that has baffled poets from the Romantics on." He is concerned with "the tension between imagination, fact, and convention, visualized as a conflict between poet, nature, and society."

D56 Byrne, Peter. "La Poésie d'Irving Layton." Trans. Jacques Archambault. *Situations* [Montreal], mai–juin 1959, pp. 38–40.
Layton is wrong in saying that his poetry is freedom. "Pour être libre, le poète doit être capable de prendre conscience de son moi veritable et des conventions littéraires qui lui permettent de s'exprimer; il doit être prêt et capable de créer de lui-même, une image profonde et authentique."

D57 Frye, Northrop. "Letters in Canada: 1958. Poetry." *University of Toronto Quarterly*, 28 (July 1959),

352–53. Rpt. ("Letters in Canada: 1958") in *The Bush Garden: Essays on the Canadian Imagination*. By Northrop Frye. Toronto: House of Anansi, 1971, pp. 95–97. Rpt. (excerpt — rev. of *A Laughter in the Mind*) in *Irving Layton: The Poet and His Critics*. Ed. Seymour Mayne. Toronto: McGraw-Hill Ryerson, 1978, pp. 62–64.

Layton uses more strict metres in *A Laughter in the Mind*. His point of view is Nietzschean; ". . . to Mr. Layton the poetic imagination leads one outside society." Heraclitean images of "fire and dry light" balance images of "mist and damp."

D58 Kenner, Hugh. "Beast-Type Sockdolagers." *Poetry* [Chicago], 94 (Sept. 1959), 413–18. Rpt. (excerpt) in *Modern Commonwealth Literature: A Library of Literary Criticism*. Ed. John H. Ferres and Martin Tucker. New York: Frederick Ungar, 1977, pp. 300–01. Rpt. (expanded, original — rev. of *A Laughter in the Mind*) in *Irving Layton: The Poet and His Critics*. Ed. Seymour Mayne. Toronto: McGraw-Hill Ryerson, 1978, 64–69.

Layton's poetry has a fine "directness" and "violence of imagination." Most poems are flawed, but most remain "indomitably interesting." He "has the exceedingly rare energy that can fill a void with its own strength."

A Red Carpet for the Sun

D59 Fuller, Roy. "Three Canadian Poets: A View from England." Rev. of *A Red Carpet for the Sun*, by Irving Layton; *The Deficit Made Flesh*, by John Glassco; and *The Wandering World*, by Ronald Bates. *Canadian Literature*, No. 1 (Summer 1959), pp. 69–70. Rpt. (excerpt—rev. of *A Red Carpet for the Sun*) in *Irving Layton: The Poet and His Critics*. Ed. Seymour Mayne. Toronto: McGraw-Hill Ryerson, 1978, pp. 78–80.

Layton's "celebration of his virility" and "intellectual protest" are unconvincing; he is not a didactic poet. His best poems are those in which fresh images and penetrating observation prevail. "There are tropes in this book as remarkable as any I remember during many years of reviewing . . . ."

D60 Davies, Robertson. "A Writer's Diary Layton's Poems Not for Puritans." *The Toronto Star*, 12 Sept. 1959, p. 31. Rpt. (excerpt—rev. of *A Red Carpet for the Sun*) in *Irving Layton: The Poet and His Critics*. Ed. Seymour Mayne. Toronto: McGraw-Hill Ryerson, 1978, pp. 80–83. Rpt. in *The Well-Tempered Critic: One Man's View of Theatre and Letters in Canada*. By Robertson Davies. Ed. Judith Skelton-Grant. Toronto: McClelland and Stewart, 1981, pp. 217–19.

Layton writes in a blunt and even coarse manner, but his views are refreshing. "His range is not wide, and he lacks music, but he has passion and poetic sincerity."

D61 Mandel, Eli. "Layton, Cogswell, Bates." Rev. of *A Red Carpet for the Sun*, by Irving Layton; *Descent from Eden*, by Fred Cogswell; and *The Wandering World*, by Ronald Bates. *The Tamarack Review*, No. 13 (Autumn 1959), pp. 124–26. Rpt. (excerpt — rev. of *A Red Carpet for the Sun*) in *Irving Layton: The Poet and His Critics*. Ed. Seymour Mayne. Toronto: McGraw-Hill Ryerson, 1978, pp. 86–88.

In *A Red Carpet for the Sun*, Layton combines a great variety with a unity of vision, which comes from Layton's personality. ". . . it is the intensely personal Layton, throwing haphazard lyrics at us, who achieves coherence, and the mythmakers who crack at the seams."

D62 Marcotte, Gilles. "Le Poète Irving Layton vu d'ici." *Le Devoir* [Montréal], 17 oct. 1959, p. 11. Rpt. (rev.

of *A Red Carpet for the Sun*) in *Irving Layton: The Poet and His Critics*. Ed. Seymour Mayne. Toronto: McGraw-Hill Ryerson, 1978, pp. 83–86.

Layton lives in Quebec, but sees with different eyes from French-Canadians. He is "très consciemment organisé, en possession d'une culture variée, passant avec aisance des formes traditionelles aux contemporaines." "Le drame profond que manifeste cette poésie est celui d'une double obsession: obsession du péché originel — colorée par un judaïsme officiellement rejeté mais intérieurement subi — et obsession sexuelle."

D63 Dudek, Louis. "Layton on the Carpet." *Delta*, No. 9 (Oct.–Dec. 1959), pp. 17–19. Rpt. in *Selected Essays and Criticism*. By Louis Dudek. Ottawa: Tecumseh, 1978, pp. 136–40. Rpt. (rev. of *A Red Carpet for the Sun*) in *Irving Layton: The Poet and His Critics*. Ed. Seymour Mayne. Toronto: McGraw-Hill Ryerson, 1978, pp. 88–92. Rpt. (excerpt) in *Contemporary Literary Criticism: Excerpts from Criticism of Today's Novelists, Poets, Playwrights, and Other Creative Writers*. Ed. Sharon R. Gunton and Laurie Lanzen Harris. Vol. xv. Detroit: Gale, 1980, 320–21.

Dudek indicts Layton for "illiteracy," "barbarism," and lack of craft. While some of his earlier poems have merit, especially those from the decade before 1953 with more of a social-realist orientation, his later poetry suffers from Frygian and other negative influences. Contemporary critics vastly overrate his work.

D64 P[urdy]., A.W. Rev. of *A Red Carpet for the Sun*. *Moment* [New Glasgow, P.E.I.], No. 3 (1960), pp. 7–8.

"Layton is essentially a poet of amazing invective protest." He is a man of vision, trying "to destroy prudery and sexual superstition." In his best poems, he "disappears into the world his poem creates."

D65 Wilson, Milton. "Turning New Leaves (1)." *The Canadian Forum*, Jan. 1960, pp. 231–32. Rpt. (excerpt — rev. of *A Red Carpet for the Sun*) in *Irving Layton: The Poet and His Critics*. Ed. Seymour Mayne. Toronto: McGraw-Hill Ryerson, 1978, pp. 92–95.

Layton's poetry is more complex than his "simple-minded public pronouncements." He is both "a sensitive and alienated soul" and a forceful "antagonistic spirit." His image of the poet is the dancer, existing in a precarious balance.

D66 Nowlan, Alden A. Rev. of *A Red Carpet for the Sun*. *The Fiddlehead*, No. 44 (Spring 1960), pp. 42–44. Rpt. in *Irving Layton: The Poet and His Critics*. Ed. Seymour Mayne. Toronto: McGraw-Hill Ryerson, 1978, pp. 96–99.

While Layton's concept of poetry as "the realization and communication of immediate experience" sometimes leads to banality, poems such as "Divinity" are full of "awesome wonder, honesty, joy, beauty, and brutality." His view "that lust is basically good and clean and wonderful" is salutary for our society.

D67 Hope, A.D. Rev. of *A Red Carpet for the Sun*. *The Dalhousie Review*, 40 (Summer 1960), 271, 273, 275, 277. Rpt. in *Irving Layton: The Poet and His Critics*. Ed. Seymour Mayne. Toronto: McGraw-Hill Ryerson, 1978, pp. 101–04.

". . . if Layton sometimes falls flat on his face he is more often magnificently justified in the risks he takes." The "intrinsic gaiety" of his work is delightful. "In the best of his poems a tremendous exuberance and a huge irony work together to produce a new and arresting vision of things."

D68 Mandel, E.W. "Poetry Chronicle: Giants, Beasts, and Men in Recent Canadian Poetry." *Queen's*

Quarterly, 67 (Summer 1960), 286, 287–88.

Layton's work combines "massive vigour" and "articulate grace." His concern for "the tension between imagination, fact, and convention" is a recurrent one in English poetry. This book is "continuously exciting and disturbing." The "ambiguity of art and life threads through the whole pattern."

D69 Frye, Northrop. "Letters in Canada: 1959. Poetry." *University of Toronto Quarterly*, 29 (July 1960), 447–48. Rpt. ("Letters in Canada: 1959") in *The Bush Garden: Essays on the Canadian Imagination*. By Northrop Frye. Toronto: House of Anansi, 1971, pp. 115–18. Rpt. (excerpt — rev. of *A Red Carpet for the Sun*) in *Irving Layton: The Poet and His Critics*. Ed. Seymour Mayne. Toronto: McGraw-Hill Ryerson, 1978, pp. 99–101.

While the achievement of this book is remarkably varied, Layton "seems tired of his present achievement." Layton has perhaps a "too insistent speaking voice." His "variety of theme" is not matched by a "variety of tone."

D70 Ciardi, John. "The Rhythm and the Beat." Rev. of *A Red Carpet for the Sun*, by Irving Layton; and *Mexico City Blues (242 Choruses)*, by Jack Kerouac. *Saturday Review* [New York], 6 Aug. 1960, pp. 24–25. Rpt. (excerpt — rev. of *A Red Carpet for the Sun*) in *Irving Layton: The Poet and His Critics*. Ed. Seymour Mayne. Toronto: McGraw-Hill Ryerson, 1978, pp. 104–06.

". . . Layton is a true poet, a marriage of heaven and hell." "The bright young men" should "put the book into their pockets and Layton into their minds."

D71 Peter, John. Rev. of *A Red Carpet for the Sun*. *Alphabet*, No. 1 (Sept. 1960), pp. 84–86.

Like D.H. Lawrence, Layton explores neglected areas of experience, although he is too often attracted to the intolerantly assertive side of Lawrence. Too many of the poems "are mere footnotes and impulses," insufficiently detached from his poetic personality.

D72 Creeley, Robert. "Ways of Lou King." *Poetry* [Chicago], 98 (June 1961), 196–97.

Layton is both tender and satiric, holding to a Jewish "tradition of intelligence and compassion." Creeley quotes approvingly "The Madonna of the Magnificat."

Balls for a One-Armed Juggler

D73 O'H[earn]., W[alter]. "Points About a Poet." *The Montreal Star*, 9 Feb. 1963, Sec. Entertainments, p. 6.

Layton is explicit about his hates, but there is no love here. "It's a bore."

D74 O' Broin, Pádraig. "Testy." *The Canadian Forum*, March 1963, pp. 285–86.

The genuine poetry in this book is too often obscured by an obsession with the negative or perverted side of life. Layton has it in his power, if he so wishes, to transcend the hell he has fashioned here.

D75 Lane, Jr., Lauriat. "A Comic Poet." *The Fiddlehead*, No. 56 (Spring 1963), pp. 64–65.

Comic techniques help give this book much of its "special force." Layton has a "sure personal accent," which is "somewhere between [D.H.] Lawrence and [Jonathan] Swift."

D76 Purdy, A.W. "Message from Olympus." *Canadian Literature*, No. 16 (Spring 1963), pp. 81–82. Rpt.

(rev. of *Balls for a One-Armed Juggler*) in *Irving Layton: The Poet and His Critics*. Ed. Seymour Mayne. Toronto: McGraw-Hill Ryerson, 1978, pp. 130–32.

Layton is Canada's best poet. "I don't think I've ever met a human being with such impressive qualities of being right all the time . . . ." His poems are "solidified passion," with savage humour, vital philosophic moments, and flashes of lyricism.

D77 Blostein, David. Rev. of *Balls for a One-Armed Juggler*. *Alphabet*, No. 6 (June 1963), pp. 71–73.

"Layton's true originality . . . rests in his capacity for spontaneous verbal reaction to specific events . . . ." While too many poems are "shapeless effusions," his personal vitality is commendable.

D78 Bowering, George. "Layton Shakes Loose." *Evidence*, No. 7 (Summer 1963), pp. 101–04.

Layton's targets are the same here, but he now attacks them with more brutal directness. He seeks "authenticity in the feelings of a man who is engaged in trying to preserve something trustworthy out of the horror of immoral deterioration." Within the terms he has set for himself, Layton succeeds.

D79 Skelton, Robin. "Canadian Poetry?". *The Tamarack Review*, No. 29 (Autumn 1963), pp. 73–75.

Unlike Layton's previous "lusty, vital poetry," the poems here are "egotistical exhibitionism." Apart from "There Were No Signs," "Silence," and "Butterfly on Rock," the poems are self-indulgent and sloppy.

D80 Farley, Tom. Rev. of *Balls for a One-Armed Juggler*. *The Canadian Author & Bookman*, 39, No. 2 (Winter 1963), 15.

Although more of a continuation than an advance from his previous work, this book "contains spirited and genuine poetry." Unfortunately, the power of many poems is vitiated by the dominating presence of an angry Layton.

D81 Wilson, Milton. "Letters in Canada: 1963. Poetry." *University of Toronto Quarterly*, 33 (July 1964), 376–77. Rpt. (excerpt — rev. of *Balls for a One-Armed Juggler*) in *Irving Layton: The Poet and His Critics*. Ed. Seymour Mayne. Toronto: McGraw-Hill Ryerson, 1978, pp. 132–33.

Ephemera and memorable pieces are here mixed together, with the main points of reference, "acting, creating, killing," much as in Layton's previous books. But the book could go further in fulfilling the vigorous prophecies of the Foreword; the evil the book confronts is too "sporadic and occasional."

The Laughing Rooster

D82 Bukowski, Charles. "The Corybant of Wit." *Evidence* [Toronto], No. 9 [1964], pp. 112–17. Rpt. (rev. of *The Laughing Rooster*) in *Irving Layton: The Poet and His Critics*. Ed. Seymour Mayne. Toronto: McGraw-Hill Ryerson, 1978, pp. 134–40.

Although the Preface does not succeed, and some of the poems are romantically self-indulgent, poems like "Portrait of a Genius" and "I Saw a Faun" are Layton's art at its best. Layton is one of the "few real writers around."

D83 Dudek, Louis. "Peripatetic Poets Show Their Wares." Rev. of *Flowers for Hitler*, by Leonard Cohen; *The Laughing Rooster*, by Irving Layton; *Near False Creek Mouth*, by Earle Birney; and *Within the Zodiac*, by Phyllis Gotlieb. *The Montreal Star*, 31 Oct. 1964, [Entertainments], p. 8.

While this book of Layton's is better than his last, which was "pure rubbish," ". . . there is nothing here you could not as well do without."

D84 Watt, F.W. "Barnstorming Poets Create in Solitude." Rev. of *The Laughing Rooster*, by Irving Layton; *Flowers for Hitler*, by Leonard Cohen; *Near False Creek Mouth*, by Earle Birney; and *Within the Zodiac*, by Phyllis Gotlieb. *The Globe Magazine* [*The Globe and Mail*] [Toronto], 19 Dec. 1964, p. 20.

Layton's masks "range from the pose of global cockiness" to "wry self-awareness." The poet must be "heroic and vital."

D85 Howith, Harry. "The Sadness After." *The Canadian Author & Bookman*, 40, No. 2 (Winter 1964), 14.

This is a more hopeful book than *Balls for a One-Armed Juggler*. Layton is "our genuine major poet," writing in poems like "A Dedication" with great warmth and compassion, although evil is not ignored.

D86 Skelton, Robin. "The Personal Heresy." *Canadian Literature*, No. 23 (Winter 1965), pp. 63–65. Rpt. (excerpt) in *Modern Commonwealth Literature: A Library of Literary Criticism*. Ed. John H. Ferres and Martin Tucker. New York: Frederick Ungar, 1977, p. 301. Rpt. (expanded, original — rev. of *The Laughing Rooster*) in *Irving Layton: The Poet and His Critics*. Ed. Seymour Mayne. Toronto: McGraw-Hill Ryerson, 1978, pp. 140–43.

Layton's poetry is marred by an egocentricity that too often estimates "a poem's worth in terms of the feelings which caused it rather than of the feelings it displays." While he can express "sexual exuberance with delightful directness," concentration on "sensual simplicities" denies "the complexities of human relationship." Layton's deficient craft harms many poems.

D87 Wilson, Milton. "Letters in Canada: 1964. Poetry." *University of Toronto Quarterly*, 35 (July 1965), 355–56.

This "is a characteristic book" with a number of good poems. Layton likes to publish everything "because he's the sort of poet who thinks that his poems ought to stick together."

D88 Lane, Jr., Lauriat. "Parody and Earnest." Rev. of *The Laughing Rooster*, by Irving Layton; and *Laytonic Love*, by Brian Robinson. *The Fiddlehead*, No. 67 (Winter 1966), pp. 73–74.

Most of these poems are "readable but unexciting." They will not "add much to Layton's stature."

D89 Gnarowski, Michael. "Canadian Poetry Today 1964–66." *Culture*, No. 27 (March 1966), pp. 75–76.

The shock value of Layton's approach has become badly dated in these poems. The Introduction is weakened by a peculiar understanding of culture and a lack of "awareness of the community of international literary values."

Collected Poems

D90 Campbell, Gary. "Irving Layton: The Genital Poet." *The McGill Daily*, 22 Oct. 1965, pp. 9–10.

Layton's use of a persona often enables him to keep his ego separate from his art. His message is that "True life is a force which is creative, biological as well as spiritual." The best poems, such as "The Day Aviva Came to Paris," or "Why I Don't Make Love to the First Lady," fuse his roles of "wit, prophet, lyricist, and social critic" into "a kind of whimsical or fanciful poetry."

D91 Dudek, Louis. "Irving Layton — A Vicarious Rebel." *The Gazette* [Montreal], 23 Oct. 1965, p. 7. Rpt. (rev. of *Collected Poems*) in *Irving Layton: The Poet and His Critics*. Ed. Seymour Mayne. Toronto:

McGraw-Hill Ryerson, 1978, pp. 144–46.

Layton's poetry is "spurious," full of "crudity and vulgarity," and consisting "almost entirely of dramatizations of his own ego." Such distorted ego-worship can have no permanent value, but will be "only another sad, Canadian puffed-up reputation."

D92 Colombo, John Robert. "High Praise for *Collected Poems* of Irving Layton." *The Montreal Star*, 13 Nov. 1965, p. 12.

Layton's poetry has become less concerned with political, philosophical, and religious themes than private matters. "Rather than the revolutionary poet, we have a sweet-voiced Theodore Roethke." Layton is among the best poets in the English-speaking world.

D93 Purdy, Al. "On the *Collected Poems* of Irving Layton." *Quarry*, 15, No. 3 (March 1966), 40–44. Rpt. (rev. of *Collected Poems*) in *Irving Layton: The Poet and His Critics*. Ed. Seymour Mayne. Toronto: McGraw-Hill Ryerson, 1978, pp. 146–50.

While Layton was a "great trail-blazer in Canadian poetry," the daringness of his early work has become commonplace. Despite an inability to enter into Layton's poems with complete sympathy, Purdy finds this book "the most substantial body of good work published in the country."

D94 Carruth, Hayden. "That Heaven-Sent Lively Rope-Walker, Irving Layton." *The Tamarack Review*, No. 39 (Spring 1966), pp. 68–73. Rpt. (rev. of *Collected Poems*) in *Irving Layton: The Poet and His Critics*. Ed. Seymour Mayne. Toronto: McGraw-Hill Ryerson, 1978, pp. 151–55.

Layton's book gives the impression "of having been written off the cuff by an intelligent, well-educated, observant, cheerful gas-meter-inspector," but his innate verbal sense keeps him from "bad rhetoric, flabby metric, or stereotyped imagery." Layton's poetry is "very interesting," although he lacks the "Great Style." He has a unique ability "to deflate himself," showing us that he is a man like the rest of us.

D95 MacCallum, Hugh. "Letters in Canada: 1965. Poetry." *University of Toronto Quarterly*, 35 (July 1966), 369–70.

Although Layton states that joy is the chief characteristic of his work, satirical and tragic poems dominate. He "underestimates the passionate wit and indignation of his poetry."

D96 Nesbitt, Bruce. "Five Aspects of the Canadian Vision." Rev. of *Selected Poems 1940–1966*, by Earle Birney; *The Spice-Box of Earth*, by Leonard Cohen; *Within the Zodiac*, by Phyllis Gotlieb; *Collected Poems*, by Irving Layton; and *Smoking the City*, by Bryan McCarthy. *Poetry Australia* [Sydney], No. 14 (Feb. 1967), pp. 40–41.

"Despite obvious rhetorical faults," this is one of the half-dozen of the most important volumes of Canadian poetry since 1950. "His witty, sprawling and uninhibited book is a Dionysiac feast."

D97 Braybrooke, David. Rev. of *Collected Poems*. *Dalhousie Review*, 47 (Spring 1967), 117, 119, 121.

Layton's best work satirizes "vanity and sexual frailty," while also showing "how inextricably both are bound up with human efforts at being good and human successes at being kind to one another." "Surrealistic bombast" detracts from many poems.

D98 Taylor, Michael. "God's and the Poet's Poet." Rev. of *Collected Poems*, by Irving Layton; and *Selected Poems 1940–1966*, by Earle Birney. *Edge* [Edmonton], No. 6 (Spring 1967), pp. 100–04.

Layton's poetry is "less impressive" than Earle Birney's. His frequent failure in epigrams suggests that he is often "the victim of his own image." A handful of poems are memorable, but "self-indulgence" weakens much of his work.

D99 Lane, Jr., Lauriat. Rev. of *Collected Poems*. *The Fiddlehead*, No. 72 (Summer 1967), pp. 88–89.

Layton is "a great poet." The test of this greatness comes both through a personal experience of his work and "organized critical and scholarly scrutiny."

D100 Woodman, Ross. "Six Poets." *Alphabet*, No. 13 (June 1967), pp. 73–75.

Layton "is in some respects our finest poet"; his best lyrics, like "The Swimmer," "are altogether self-contained in their highly wrought imagistic structure." The more personal poems are less successful.

Periods of the Moon

D101 Callaghan, Barry. "Eggs for a One-Armed Juggler." *The Telegram* [Toronto], 28 Jan. 1967, Showcase, p. 20.

Layton is gentle and unashamed, not the "womanizer and loudmouth" of popular legend. He has a unique "willingness to risk absurdity" and a freedom from guilt, which has enabled him to write memorable poems. The confidence of his verse parallels "the triumph of his life."

D102 Waddington, Miriam. "Anthologist, Nerve Poet and Bard of the Buttocks." Rev. of *Periods of the Moon*, by Irving Layton; *Abracadabra*, by John Robert Colombo; and *New Wings for Icarus*, by Henry Beissel. *The Globe Magazine* [*The Globe and Mail*] [Toronto], 18 March 1967, p. 35.

Layton's poetry here is "careless, cliché-ridden and complacent," especially distasteful in its attitude toward women. His only saving grace is that he "hasn't yet been caught by the electronic mood of the time."

D103 Francis, Wynne. "Five Poets." Rev. of *The Glass Trumpet*, by Miriam Waddington; *New Wings for Icarus*, by Henry Beissel; *Selected Poems*, by F.R. Scott; *Periods of the Moon*, by Irving Layton; and *Parasites of Heaven*, by Leonard Cohen. *The Tamarack Review*, No. 43 (Spring 1967), pp. 82–84.

Layton, "a moralist and teacher," is primarily didactic. He is "like a prophet stalking through crowds." He records his "personal joy" and "anguish," as well as the poetic role ". . . he is compelled to play."

D104 Pacey, Desmond. Rev. of *Periods of the Moon*. *The Fiddlehead*, No. 71 (Spring 1967), pp. 69–72. Rpt. in *Irving Layton: The Poet and His Critics*. Ed. Seymour Mayne. Toronto: McGraw-Hill Ryerson, 1978, pp. 174–77.

Layton's prolific publication is a sign of his humility. In these poems "bitterness overshadows gaiety." Those in which these opposites are balanced, as in "An Old Niçoise Whore," are best. Layton "responds passionately to the mingled terror and beauty of the world."

D105 Downes, Gwladys V. "Writing Poems 'In' Like LSD." *Victoria Times*, 3 June 1967, p. 8.

"A little pruning" and the elimination of "sentimentality," an "irritating flipness," and an inappropriate sexual vocabulary may have strengthened this volume, but, in general, Layton's complex sensibility produces excellent poetry.

D106 Davey, Frank. "Layton and Isaiah." *Canadian Literature*, No. 34 (Autumn 1967), pp. 88–90.

Layton's poems are devoid of the "visionary experience" he claims for them. They lack a "fusion of sound and sense" and are too often examples of the "tired anecdote," against which he inveighs in his Introduction. Layton is "more a man of ideas than an artist." He is at best "a charming minor poet."

D107 Helwig, David. "Canadian Poetry: Seven Recent Books." *Queen's Quarterly*, 74 (Winter 1967), 75–76.

These poems are "harsher" and more "vitriolic" than Layton's earlier work. Their imagery brings poems like "Clochards" and "Sun-Bathers" to eloquent life.

D108 MacCallum, Hugh. "Letters in Canada: 1967. Poetry." *University of Toronto Quarterly*, 37 (July 1968), 369–70.

"An undercurrent of melancholy" in the book "points in the direction of pathos rather than defiance." His "personal enthusiasm" imparts freshness to the well-worn topics from his European tour.

The Shattered Plinths

D109 Mandel, Eli. "Dark Visions of Blood and Race." *The Globe Magazine* [*The Globe and Mail*] [Toronto], 24 Feb. 1968, p. 18. Rpt. (rev. of *The Shattered Plinths*) in *Irving Layton: The Poet and His Critics*. Ed. Seymour Mayne. Toronto: McGraw-Hill Ryerson, 1978, pp. 178–79.

This work is only "superficially political"; Layton is more interested in "psychological atmosphere." The chaos of present society is used to suggest that the road to a fuller humanity lies through brutality. His is one of "the most powerful, fantastic and gifted imaginations in this country."

D110 Sommer, Richard. "The Civilized Killer." *Canadian Dimension*, 5, No. 5 (June–July 1968), 33–35. Rpt. (rev. of *The Shattered Plinths*) in *Irving Layton: The Poet and His Critics*. Ed. Seymour Mayne. Toronto: McGraw-Hill Ryerson, 1978, pp. 179–84.

This book is interesting but offensive in Layton's "nostalgia for mass violence." When Layton writes good poems, it is not because of his message, but his joy in life.

D111 Helwig, David. "Poetry East, West and Centre." Rev. of *The Unquiet Bed*, by Dorothy Livesay; *Phrases from Orpheus*, by D.G. Jones, *The Shattered Plinths*, by Irving Layton; and *Bread, Wine and Salt*, by Alden Nowlan. *Queen's Quarterly*, 75 (Autumn 1968), 534–35.

Although "unpleasant," this book "has a remarkable vitality and unity of tone." While the political attitudes are "incoherent or contradictory, . . . they demand attention and argument." "The Graveyard" is one of Layton's finest poems.

D112 M[ills]., J[ohn]. Rev. of *The Shattered Plinths*. *West Coast Review* [Simon Fraser Univ.], 3, No. 2 (Fall 1968), 46–49. Rpt. ("A Plinth for L.B.J.") in *Lizard in the Grass*. By John Mills. Downsview, Ont.: ECW, 1980, pp. 171–75.

While Layton's best poetry "has that indefinable grace of the best poetry anywhere," his poetic targets are out of date. Many poems are limited by Layton's "gloating over violence" and "political naïveté."

D113 Bowering, George. "Eli and Irving." Rev. of *The Shattered Plinths*, by Irving Layton; and *An Idiot Joy*, by Eli Mandel. *Canadian Literature*, No. 39 (Winter 1969), pp. 74–76.

This "could be the worst book published in Canada in 1968." "The Red Moujhik" is "the worst poem ever published in Canada." Layton's celebration of violence is disturbing, particularly in regard to Israeli expansion.

D114 Wiebe, G.M. Rev. of *The Shattered Plinths. Quarry*, 18, No. 2 (Winter 1969), 46–47.

Although Layton rejects the WASP tradition, he falls back on it because he sees no viable alternative. He has an "ability to see and make beauty in a desperate world."

D115 MacCallum, Hugh. "Letters in Canada: 1968. Poetry." *University of Toronto Quarterly*, 38 (July 1969), 346–47.

In many of these poems, Layton effectively criticizes various aspects of "contemporary barbarism," although the high degree of violence is disturbing. "Elegy for Strul" is a fine poem.

D116 Barbour, Douglas. Rev. of *The Shattered Plinths, The Whole Bloody Bird (Obs, Aphs & Pomes)*, and *Selected Poems. Dalhousie Review*, 49 (Autumn 1969), 439, 441.

"The Graveyard" is an excellent poem, but the "mass of messy and jejeune material far outweighs the few good poems."

D117 Scott, Peter Dale. "A Canadian Chronicle." *Poetry* [Chicago], 115 (Feb. 1970), 354–56.

Layton is at his best when he works his vein of "irony and compassion," rather than adopting a false voice that violates his "intelligence and sensitivity."

Selected Poems

D118 Weaver, Robert. "Twenty Years of Irving Layton and 40 of Dorothy Livesay." Rev. of *Selected Poems*, by Irving Layton; and *The Documentaries*, by Dorothy Livesay. *The Toronto Star*, 1 Feb. 1969, Insight: Books, p. 15.

Layton's poetry benefits from Wynne Francis' editing. This book "is a neat and handy introduction" to his work.

D119 Mandel, Eli. "Nothing at All but Poetry." Rev. of *Selected Poems* and *The Whole Bloody Bird (Obs, Aphs & Pomes). The Globe Magazine* [*The Globe and Mail*] [Toronto], 22 March 1969, p. 13. Rpt. [rev. of *Selected Poems* and *The Whole Bloody Bird (Obs, Aphs & Pomes)*) in *Irving Layton: The Poet and His Critics*. Ed. Seymour Mayne. Toronto: McGraw-Hill Ryerson, 1978, pp. 185–86.

Selected Poems misrepresents Layton by making him too clean and respectable.

D120 Barbour, Douglas. Rev. of *The Shattered Plinths, The Whole Bloody Birds (Obs, Aphs & Pomes)*, and *Selected Poems. Dalhousie Review*, 49 (Autumn 1969), 439, 441.

The judicious editing of Wynne Francis makes the *Selected Poems* the best of these three books reviewed.

D121 Marshall, Tom. Rev. of *Selected Poems* and *The Whole Bloody Bird (Obs, Aphs & Pomes). Queen's Quarterly*, 76 (Autumn 1969), 548–49. Rpt. in *Irving Layton: The Poet and His Critics*. Ed. Seymour Mayne. Toronto: McGraw-Hill Ryerson, 1978, pp. 187–88.

Layton is a "visionary" poet, although he often fuses this vision with direct observation. While a "fine craftsman," Layton has shown little evidence of technical development.

D122 Mallinson, Jean. Rev. of *Selected Poems. Monday Morning* [Toronto], Sept. 1969, pp. 34–35.

Wynne Francis' editing has served Layton well. His essential quality is his ability to identify with everything he perceives to be like him. Like all of us, he is "extremist, prince and victim."

D123 Junkins, Donald. Rev. of *Selected Poems. The Far Point*, No. 3 (Fall–Winter 1969), pp. 61–69.

At their best, Layton's poems have "timing, juxtaposition, tone, measure, proportion." But too many are marred by empty bombast, and much of his subject matter is irrelevant. Still, ". . . one feels that Layton is greater than the sum of the weaknesses in many of his poems."

D124 Hornyansky, Michael. "Letters in Canada: 1969. Poetry." *University of Toronto Quarterly*, 39 (July 1970), 328–29.

Wynne Francis' choice in the *Selected Poems* shows Layton's "range and versatility."

The Collected Poems of Irving Layton

D125 Purdy, Al. "Don't Quibble — A Poet as Close to Genius as Any Alive." *The Globe and Mail* [Toronto], 18 Dec. 1971, Entertainment, p. 29. Rpt. (rev. of *The Collected Poems of Irving Layton*) in *Irving Layton: The Poet and His Critics*. Ed. Seymour Mayne. Toronto: McGraw-Hill Ryerson, 1978, pp. 202–05.

Purdy pays a personal tribute to Layton, who with Margaret Atwood and Earle Birney he considers one of the top three poets in Canada, and an important "trail-blazer" in Canadian poetry. Purdy comments on various critical statements that have been made on Layton's work. ". . . I disagree with nearly everything Layton says or does, but I applaud him for being a poet as close to genius as any alive . . . ."

D126 Stewart, Robert. "Letters: Life with Father." *Time*, Can. Ed., 20 Dec. 1971, p. 11.

Layton is a little ahead of his time in both technique and content, which "is where a true poet should always be."

D127 Weaver, Robert. "Sum Total." *Books in Canada*, 1, No. 7 (Jan. 1972), 1–2.

Layton reveals himself here as "more of a humanist than he himself might want to admit." Unfortunately, the quality of the book's production does not match the quality of the poetry.

D128 Callaghan, Barry. "A Poet in His Pride: Layton as Messiah." *Saturday Night*, March 1972, pp. 31–35.

Layton lacks "ethical affirmation." His sexual swagger has "a comic charm," but is not believable. He fears women, equating them with death. A new note of "patience and softness" is now being heard in Layton's poetry; he has found "a wry tolerance of himself in his poet's pride."

D129 D[avey]., F[rank]. Rev. of *The Collected Poems of Irving Layton. Open Letter*, Ser. 2, No. 2 (Summer 1972), pp. 50–52. Rpt. in *Irving Layton: The Poet and His Critics*. Ed. Seymour Mayne. Toronto: McGraw-Hill Ryerson, 1978, pp. 205–07.

Layton helped shatter the post-war "conception of the poem as an aesthetic object" and break "the Puritan embargo on image, magic, and sexuality." His poetry, concerned with "opinions, thoughts, feelings," is different from that of the next generation, which is more concerned with "the tone of the reflections and the nature of the consciousness they project."

D130 Gibbs, Robert. Rev. of *The Collected Poems of Irving Layton. The Fiddlehead*, No. 94 (Summer 1972), pp. 129–31.

In Layton's Preface, he describes his power as a child to still the tumult of his upstairs' neighbours with a broomstick. Similarly, his poems are "ordered intervals in noisy chaos." "A Tall Man Executes a Jig" is an especially "important poem," although all are "essential to Layton's large imagination."

D131 Hornyansky, Michael. "Letters in Canada: 1971. Poetry." *University of Toronto Quarterly*, 41 (Summer 1972), 330–31.

Layton is "good company . . . but with time he has become a fixture." "What needs to be asked . . . is whether the first person is big enough."

D132 Levenson, Christopher. Rev. of *The Collected Poems of Irving Layton*, by Irving Layton; and *Collected Poetry*, by Louis Dudek. *Queen's Quarterly*, 69 (Summer 1972), 272–74.

Stylistically, Layton's poetry shows little significant change; his best poems are those in freer forms. Sometimes his "gay misanthropy" becomes "simplistic rant," and there is some "predictable bourgeois-baiting," but the net result is "largely favourable."

D133 Watt, F.W. Rev. of *The Collected Poems of Irving Layton*. *The Canadian Forum*, Sept. 1972, p. 38. Rpt. in *Irving Layton: The Poet and His Critics*. Ed. Seymour Mayne. Toronto: McGraw-Hill Ryerson, 1978, pp. 208–10.

The Collected Poems of Irving Layton is one of the most important poetic achievements in English-Canadian poetry this century. This book combines Layton's "posturing," "vanity," and "silliness" with his "energy, insight, anguish, passion, eloquence."

D134 Mayne, Seymour. Rev. of *The Collected Poems of Irving Layton*. *West Coast Review* [Simon Fraser Univ.], 7, No. 2 (Oct. 1972) 59–60.

Mayne discusses the book's arrangement, the symbol of the stave of the clown-king-poet, and the ways in which the book suggests possibilities for further growth. "The speaker has actualized himself through many guises, but the creative potential will always remain to be fulfilled."

D135 Kennedy, X.J. Rev. of *The Collected Poems of Irving Layton*. *Counter / Measures* [Bedford, Mass.], No. 3 (1974), pp. 182–85. Rpt. in *Irving Layton: The Poet and His Critics*. Ed. Seymour Mayne. Toronto: McGraw-Hill Ryerson, 1978, pp. 210–13.

Layton is "torn between an abiding disgust for the human race and a deep compassion for that same animal." "Letter to a Librarian" is an excellent poem "of execration." Layton is at his best as an observer, rather than as a "pagan oracle." His work has a good chance of making himself and his subjects immortal.

Nail Polish

D136 Stevens, Peter. "Great Lust and Love in a Milder Image." *The Globe Magazine* [*The Globe and Mail*] [Toronto], 6 Feb. 1971, p. 20.

This book combines "mature strength" with "powerful rhetoric." "The Haunting" and "Dionysus in Hampstead" summarize the tone of his book, one of the "paradoxical process that continues as mankind waits for the violent end of the world."

D137 Richmond, John. "Elegant and Nasty." *The Montreal Star*, 13 March 1971, p. 28.

Layton has always had a "devotion to craft." *Nail Polish* is a fine book, which combines the rough old Layton with a new "inspired sagacity."

D138 Vernon, Lorraine. "Sometimes Silence Is Golden, Layton." Rev. of *Nail Polish*, by Irving Layton; and

Mandalas, by John Douglas. *The Vancouver Sun*, 2 April 1971, p. 34A.

The Layton of this book is "bitter, cynical and self-indulgent." His romanticism is superficial, and he is only "vicariously sensual."

D139 Wainwright, Andy. "Two Hoary Old Poets." Rev. of *Rag & Bone Shop*, by Earle Birney; and *Nail Polish*, by Irving Layton. *Saturday Night*, May 1971, pp. 25, 26–27.

Layton has transcended the ordinary, so that the reader is profoundly moved or altered. Layton, more than Birney, has entered the "alien territory" of high art, making his experience meaningful and universal.

D140 Cogswell, Fred. Rev. of *Acknowledgement to Life: The Collected Poems of Bertram Warr*, by Bertram Warr, ed. Len Gasparini; *Selected Poems 1920–1970*, by R.G. Everson; *Nail Polish*, by Irving Layton; and *Time Touch Me Gently*, by Mel Thistle. *Queen's Quarterly*, 78 (Summer 1971), 326.

"Time and lack of energy" lead Layton here to "inevitable conformity," although "The Haunting" and "Dionysus in Hampstead" are of exceptional quality.

D141 Hunt, Russell A. Rev. of *Nail Polish*. *The Fiddlehead*, No. 91 (Fall 1971), pp. 102–04.

Layton is a Canadian Walt Whitman, although, unlike Whitman, his powers do not appear to be declining with age. His best poems, like "End of the White Mouse," succeed because of his attention "to the real world," while his least successful are those that are "slackly observed."

D142 Waterston, Elizabeth. "New-Found Eyes." *Canadian Literature*, No. 52 (Spring 1972), pp. 102, 104–05. Rpt. (rev. of *Nail Polish*) in *Irving Layton: The Poet and His Critics*. Ed. Seymour Mayne. Toronto: McGraw-Hill Ryerson, 1978, pp. 199–201.

Layton's anger is becoming more muted. His vision is more sardonic, now combined with a greater awareness of his own attitudes. Some poems "have a casual delicacy and shapeliness," but the style is generally much more cool and detached.

D143 Hornyansky, Michael. "Letters in Canada: 1971. Poetry." *University of Toronto Quarterly*, 41 (Summer 1972), 330–31.

At this point, with his ability to shock wearing thin, Layton has two roads open — to be a "Delphic sage with pointed ears," or "a lurching Silenus leering on his ass."

Lovers and Lesser Men

D144 Engel, Marian. "The Greek Light Suits Him." *The Globe and Mail* [Toronto], 10 March 1973, Entertainment, p. 31.

Layton has added to his customary approach "a real engagement with aging and death." The Greek background suits these poems.

D145 Ringrose, Christopher Xerxes. Rev. of *Lovers and Lesser Men*. *Dalhousie Review*, 53 (Spring 1973), 160–63.

This is a "noisy book." Most of the poems are "rhythmically dull." " 'Rage' is rather a dignified term for the flatulent rumblings and self-pity Mr. Layton usually gives us."

D146 Musgrave, Susan. "The Eternal Adolescent." *Victoria Times*, 14 April 1973, p. 36.

Layton combines innocent vitality with brash arrogance. He is an "incurable innocent," which makes it hard to take seriously or to take offence at his many outrageous statements. He is most notable for "his street-fighting energy."

D147 Hosein, Clyde. "Kicking against the Pricks." *Books in Canada*, 2, No. 2 (April–May–June 1973), 4–5.
Layton's "feel for the fire of distant realities" can be felt in only a few of these poems. Petty squabbles spoil many poems; Layton needs to have more concern for "inner excellence."

D148 MacCulloch, Clare. "Irving again Layton." *Alive* [Guelph, Ont.], 11 May 1973, pp. 46–47.
Too many outworn subjects and "trite statements" make this book a disappointment, preventing it from showing us the poetic direction of which Layton is capable.

D149 McSweeney, Kerry. Rev. of *Lovers and Lesser Men* and *Engagements: The Prose of Irving Layton*. *Queen's Quarterly*, 80 (Summer 1973), 325.
Layton's "bellicosity and egocentricity" remain unchanged. "The subjects are predictable," although a few of the pieces are more than "mere jottings."

D150 Dragland, Stan. Rev. of *Lovers and Lesser Men. The Fiddlehead*, No. 99 (Fall 1973), pp. 99–102. Rpt. in *Irving Layton: The Poet and His Critics*. Ed. Seymour Mayne. Toronto: McGraw-Hill Ryerson, 1978, pp. 237–41.
This is a poorly edited "pipsqueak of a book." While some poems like "A Tale of Two Cities" have a new freedom of language, others depend on abstractions, "sneering," or "unleavened vituperation. . . . The book as a whole is flaccid, a hodgepodge of poems that fit together indifferently . . . ."

D151 Stevens, Peter. "The Perils of Majority." *The University of Windsor Review*, 9, No. 2 (Spring 1974), 102.

"A paean of praise for individualism," this book is a not always successful attempt "to embrace a whole world of polarities. . . . What shines through despite the flaws is a shouting rage to live that can also give sweet expression to quiet and simple joys . . . ."

D152 Lacey, Edward. "Canadian Bards and South American Reviewers." *Northern Journey*, No. 4 (June 1974), pp. 83, 84–89, 91, 92, 94, 95, 97, 99, 108, 119. Rpt. (excerpt — rev. of *Lovers and Lesser Men*) in *Irving Layton: The Poet and His Critics*. Ed. Seymour Mayne. Toronto: McGraw-Hill Ryerson, 1978, pp. 241–45.
Lacey discusses a number of Canadian poets from the perspective of one who has been out of the country for most of the 1959–73 period. While Layton is "the greatest poet Canada has yet produced," he is past his peak. Although he is never resolved whether poetry is a lie or the truth, his iambic pentameter is suited more for "a faded romantic sensibility. . . . Layton . . . is the Canadian Hemingway."

D153 Warkentin, Germaine. "Layton's World." Rev. of *Lovers and Lesser Men* and *Engagements: The Prose of Irving Layton. The Lakehead University Review*, 7, No. 1 (Summer 1974), 149–50, 152–53.
Lovers and Lesser Men is comparatively unsuccessful. "Poem after poem is lax, longwinded, out of focus, bored."

Il freddo verde elemento

D154 "Incontro con uomini di cultura italiana per la presentazione di due 'best-sellers' canadesi nella nostra lingua." *Corriere illustrato* [Toronto], [2 Nov. 1974], p. 10.
This review in Italian appears on the occasion of the publication in Italian of Layton's poems and

Farley Mowat's *A Whale for the Killing*. "La sua poesia si muove su due diversi filoni, quello satirico e quello lirico. La sua poesia ha sferzato e ha sorpreso la borghesia canadese con l'uso di immagini esplicitamente sessuali e di vocaboli che altri poeti evitano accuratamente."

The Pole-Vaulter

D155 Pearson, Alan. "Gardener vs. Gartersnapper." Rev. of *The Pole-Vaulter*, by Irving Layton; and *Fire on Stone*, by Ralph Gustafson. *The Globe and Mail* [Toronto], 31 Aug. 1974, p. 29.

Layton's poetry has a greater immediacy than that of Ralph Gustafson. His political views do not generally make good poetry; he is better when he explores his lyrical vein. A photograph of Layton is included.

D156 Scott, Andrew. Rev. of *The Pole-Vaulter*, by Irving Layton; and *Fire on Stone*, by Ralph Gustafson. *The Georgia Straight* [Vancouver], 10 Oct. 1974, pp. 13, 22.

Layton's tirades against Communism are outdated, and his defense of himself against chauvinism will not hold water. Still, some poems like "The Shadow" or "Lines for My Grandchildren," where "his excoriating rage is turned inward," show him to be an expert at the craft.

D157 Fraser, Keath. "Creative Juices Swift and Slow." Rev. of *The Pole-Vaulter*, by Irving Layton; and *Fire on Stone*, by Ralph Gustafson. *Books in Canada*, Nov. 1974, p. 16.

Gustafson is more aware of the artistic aspect of poetry, Layton of its political aspect. The latter is less reflective; his "egoism is in turn redeemed by others who show an equal disdain for breaking down" under the pressures of our world.

D158 Namjoshi, Suniti. "A Would-Be Pole Vaulter." *The Canadian Forum*, Dec. 1974, p. 19.

This is a competent book, full of "an essential honesty." However, it breaks no new ground and suggests no new directions.

D159 Sorestead, Glen. Rev. of *The Pole-Vaulter*. *Skylark* [The Saskatchewan Teachers Association], 11, No. 2 (Winter 1975), 74–75.

Most of what Layton says here he has said as well earlier. Some excellent poems do emerge, especially those in which ". . . he refrains from taking a cudgel to us to tell us about love."

D160 Baglow, John. "The Day Is Too Ordinary." *The Canadian Review*, 2, No. 1 (Jan.–Feb. 1975), 28–30.

Like Norman Mailer, Layton has lost the authenticity he once had. Apart from a few poems, this book is full of "romantic, sexual and political clichés." Layton can no longer find suitable targets for his rage.

D161 Mundwiler, Leslie. "Layton and Wayman: Poets and the History of Joe Blow." Rev. of *The Pole-Vaulter*, by Irving Layton; and *For and against the Moon: Blues, Yells, and Chuckles*, by Tom Wayman. *Canadian Dimension*, 10, No. 7 (March 1975), 60.

Layton's poems are full of clichés, embarrassing nonsense, and "self-indulgent moralizing." He puts "self-expression ahead of self-criticism" to produce a total failure.

D162 Marshall, Tom. "Pole-Vaulting Over the Grave." *CV/II*, 1, No. 1 (Spring 1975), 4.

While Layton is not a "technical innovator," he is a "fine craftsman." The two main themes of his poetry are "liberation into a larger life" and an increasingly "tragic vision."

D163 Musgrave, Susan. Rev. of *The Pole-Vaulter*. *Open Letter*, Ser. 3, No. 2 (Spring 1975), pp. 102–03. Rpt. in *Irving Layton: The Poet and His Critics*. Ed. Seymour Mayne. Toronto: McGraw-Hill Ryerson, 1978, pp. 255–56.
Layton's Preface is marred by "adolescent prejudice, smugness and sheer irrelevance." In his poetry, ". . . his gifts of language, structure and economy seem to be sinking slowly under his posturing . . . ."

D164 Bagchee, Shyamal. "Two Poets and a Half." Rev. of *In Search of Owen Roblin*, by Al Purdy; *The Pole-Vaulter*, by Irving Layton; and *Fire on Stone*, by Ralph Gustafson. *Essays on Canadian Writing*, No. 3 (Fall 1975), pp. 65, 66–69.
While the book suffers from inept editing, and many of the poems remain ideas insufficiently poeticized, the best of Layton's poems pursue interesting new directions in their more "questioning" and "tentative" stance. But Layton remains "unwilling to invest a sufficient amount of his creative energy in this voice that he barely understands and hesitates to embrace."

D165 Gibbs, Robert. "Presiding Voices: Purdy, Layton and Gustafson." Rev. of *In Search of Owen Roblin*, by Al Purdy; *The Pole-Vaulter*, by Irving Layton; and *Fire on Stone*, by Ralph Gustafson. *Dalhousie Review*, 56 (Summer 1976), 356, 359–62, 363, 365.
Al Purdy, Irving Layton, and Ralph Gustafson all use masks, and all follow patterns that "are those of speech rather than those of action." Unlike "ruminative" Purdy, Layton "is almost clear and his persona certain of itself." Unlike Gustafson, whose forms lead him to speak with "wry bemusement," Layton's poems are more angry than bitter.

The Darkening Fire: Selected Poems 1945–1968

D166 MacSkimming, Roy. "Layton Collection Tidies His House." *The Toronto Star*, 18 Oct. 1975, p. F6.
The tone of Layton's writing changes about 1959 as he becomes more aware of himself as a public figure. This change from his earlier "intensely lyrical" voice has led to a new "immediacy," but also a "dilution of language." But his best fifty or sixty poems rank him among the best poets in the world.

D167 Nodelman, Perry. "Much-Selected Poems." *Winnipeg Free Press*, 1 Nov. 1975, p. 17.
While there is little need for yet another selection of almost the same Layton poems, this book does contain some good poetry, especially when Layton "directs his anger and his irony at himself."

D168 Lincoln, Robert. Rev. of *The Darkening Fire: Selected Poems 1945–1968*. *Canadian Book Review Annual: 1975*. Ed. Dean Tudor, Nancy Tudor, and Linda Biesenthal. Toronto: Peter Martin, 1976, p. 143.
This "richly varied selection" shows Layton as "a good interpreter of life, a free spirit and a predator of the language."

D169 Such, Peter. "Three Grand Old Parties: Writers in Canada Must Play Many Roles — and Livesay, Layton, and Woodcock Have Played Them All." Rev. of *Notes on Visitations*, by George Woodcock; *Ice Age*, by Dorothy Livesay; and *The Darkening Fire: Selected Poems 1945–1968*, by Irving Layton. *Books in Canada*, Feb. 1976, pp. 9, 10–11.
Layton's most important legacy to Canadian poetry is his total commitment to his art. His poetry "is magic on the most human and sensitive level."

D170 Morley, Patricia. "Layton: Flawed Prophet, Superb Poet." Rev. of *The Darkening Fire: Selected Poems 1945-1968* and *For My Brother Jesus. The Ottawa Journal*, 8 May 1976, p. 40.

The Darkening Fire: Selected Poems 1945-1968 collects some of Layton's best poetry.

D171 Barbour, Douglas. "Canadian Poetry Chronicle: III." Rev. of *The Darkening Fire: Selected Poems 1945-1968* and *The Unwavering Eye: Selected Poems 1969-1975. Dalhousie Review*, 56 (Autumn 1976-77), 563.

Because ". . . the worst of the dung has already been removed," these two books are the best approach to Layton's poetry. ". . . at his best Layton achieves a diction which articulates the courage of looking death in the face and smiling."

The Unwavering Eye: Selected Poems 1969-1975

D172 MacEwen, Gwendolyn. "Praise Be Guts and Bombast." *The Globe and Mail* [Toronto], 12 April 1975, Entertainment, p. 23. Rpt. (rev. of *The Unwavering Eye: Selected Poems 1969-1975*) in *Irving Layton: The Poet and His Critics*. Ed. Seymour Mayne. Toronto: McGraw-Hill Ryerson, 1978, pp. 257-59.

Layton is good, even in his lesser poems. He is able to "blow the mind with inner associations, internal parallels," writing with "a deceptive starkness, a stunning simplicity."

D173 Evans, J.A.S. "Undertows and Ovid Tones." Rev. of *Double-Header*, by Raymond Souster; and *The Unwavering Eye: Selected Poems 1969-1975*, by Irving Layton. *Books in Canada*, Aug. 1975, p. 19.

Although Layton is becoming more reflective than he once was, he still emanates a tremendous zest for life.

D174 Oliver, Michael Brian. "Dionysos the Jew." *The Antigonish Review*, No. 24 (Winter 1975), pp. 91-93.

Layton's work is not so much Jewish "in a political or philosophical sense" as full of "vituperation and vitriolic wit and rage for life." He is "downright Byronic" in his attitude to Greek life. Most of his best poems "have nothing to do with politics or philosophy."

D175 Adamson, Arthur. "The Poet as Split Infinity." CV/II, 2, No. 1 (Jan. 1976), 47-49.

Layton is both "a descendant of the poets of despair" and an affirmer of life. He can write intense "satirical or dramatic poetry," often combining "simplicity with the strange, allusive quality that makes art at once naive and mysterious." Major themes include "death and aging" and "the nature of the poet's mission and the realm of the imagination." The Jew in his poetry is "the Hamlet of today. . . . He is split: flesh and blood on the one hand, ghost on the other."

D176 Lincoln, Robert. Rev. of *The Unwavering Eye: Selected Poems 1969-1975. Canadian Book Review Annual: 1975*. Ed. Dean Tudor, Nancy Tudor, and Linda Biesenthal. Toronto: Peter Martin, 1976, p. 129.

While the political poems are at times weak, all are "well constructed." "Layton's mood and poetic stance" are foremost in this volume.

D177 Elliot, C.A.S. "Layton: Shocked by Modern Man's Savagery." *The United Church Observer* [Toronto], Feb. 1976, p. 47.

Layton celebrates sex, rages against evil, and believes in the significance of the Jewish experience for Western civilization. While he could communicate more of his love of life, his cynicism is that "of an angry and lonely faith."

D178 Novik, Mary. "The Gospel, According to Irving." Rev. of *The Unwavering Eye: Selected Poems 1969–1975* and *For My Brother Jesus*. *The Vancouver Sun*, 2 April 1976, Leisure & TV Week, p. 34A.

Layton's references to "the fleshy side of human nature" in *The Unwavering Eye: Selected Poems 1969–1975* often suggest a "Swiftian misanthropy." ". . . sex is no longer the panacea it once was . . . ."

For My Brother Jesus

D179 Fulford, Robert. "Irving Layton Blames Christianity for Nazi Horrors That Killed Millions." *The Toronto Star*, 20 March 1976, p. F5.

Layton's "strutting confidence" does not fit with the "ungraspable tragedy" of the holocaust. Mass murder has been practised by many societies other than the European. His diatribes here are often "glib and unearned."

D180 Amiel, Barbara. "Layton, the Lion of Judaism, Feeding Christians to Himself." *Maclean's*, 22 March 1976, pp. 64–65.

Layton avoids being channelled into the stereotypes of right-or-left-wing ideology. His linking of Christianity with anti-Semitism has some foundation, but many of the poems seem written for shock value. He is set apart from other Canadian poets by "passion and the relentless search for truth."

D181 Gibson, Shirley. "He Barges Like a Behemoth and One Could Pick Many a Nit Off His Back." *The Globe and Mail* [Toronto], 27 March 1976, Entertainment, p. 35.

Layton conveys humour and a prodigious ego, is "generous, sly, compassionate, savage, boring, intolerant." The Foreword can well be bypassed, but the poetry is "exciting and provocative."

D182 Novik, Mary. "The Gospel, According to Irving." Rev. of *The Unwavering Eye: Selected Poems 1969–1975* and *For My Brother Jesus*. *The Vancouver Sun*, 2 April 1976, Leisure & TV Week, p. 34A.

In *For My Brother Jesus*, the misanthropic "poems are little more than an excuse for the magnificently polemical preface." In turning from poetry to prophecy, Layton writes little more than "doggerel."

D183 Harrison, Ernest. "The Church Morbid." *Books in Canada*, May 1976, pp. 12–14.

The theme of this book may not be original, but as Layton is the first Jewish poet to state it, the emotional note is new. He celebrates sexuality as opposed to Christian repressiveness. His emphasis on Auschwitz and Gulag as the key experiences of our time produces poetry that is "clear, beautifully balanced, and true." His only deficiency is his lack of understanding of women.

D184 Morley, Patricia. "Layton: Flawed Prophet Superb Poet." Rev. of *The Darkening Fire: Selected Poems 1945–1968* and *For My Brother Jesus*. *The Ottawa Journal*, 8 May 1976, p. 40.

For My Brother Jesus contains mostly "fatuous" poems whose simplistic ideas detract from their poetic qualities.

D185 Jonas, George. "Irving Layton on the Cross." *Saturday Night*, June 1976, pp. 69–70.

This book fulfils even Layton's "own grandiose claims to significance." The Christian sun of transcendence leaves little room for love of others. "There is a painful link between the Council of Nicea and Dachau."

D186 Russell, Kenneth. "Irving Layton's Latest." *The Chelsea Journal*, 2, No. 5 (Sept.–Oct. 1976), 250–51.

The simplistic anti-Christian bias of this book pulls the level far below that of which Layton is capable. His Nietzschean plea for "zestful, earthy living" leads to "rampant egotism," which can result in war.

D187 O'Flaherty, Patrick. "Nothing Stands." *The Canadian Forum*, Oct. 1976, p. 30.

Focusing on "For My Incomparable Gypsy," O'Flaherty laments Layton's decline "into the spleen of senescence."

D188 Rushton, Alfred. "Balancing the Books." GVT, No. 6 (Winter 1977), pp. 10–11.

Christianity was at least in part responsible for the Jewish extermination, but people are also dying today in the Third World because of the economic policies of the Western world. The Jews are not unique in their mistreatment. It is not possible for "one poet to alter the tide of history before it runs its course."

D189 Hatfield, Stephen. "The Sword Sleeps in the Hand: Lazy Aim with the Long Pea-Shooter." Rev. of *For My Brother Jesus* and *The Covenant*. Waves, 6, No. 2 (Winter 1978), 72–76.

Hatfield discusses *For My Brother Jesus* and *The Covenant* together, in general terms. Layton's "indifferent use of language" causes these books to be "watery, pleonastic and unengaging." The feelings behind the poems are vitiated by "sloppiness," "awkward rhythms," and "tedious clichés." Only a few glittering fragments suggest the presence of an artistic mind that once wrote fine poems.

D190 McNamara, Eugene. "In a High Clean Style." Rev. of *For My Brother Jesus*, by Irving Layton; *The Death of Harold Ladoo*, by Dennis Lee; and *Poems for American Daughters*, by C.H. Gervais. *Canadian Literature*, No. 78 (Autumn 1978), pp. 88–89.

While the premise of *For My Brother Jesus*, that Christianity was the prime force in history for anti-Semitism, is not new, a number of the best poems are not related to this idea. Many are "distinguished additions to the Layton canon."

The Covenant

D191 Adachi, Ken. "Layton Can't Be Ignored." *The Toronto Star*, 1 Oct. 1977, p. D7.

These poems have great power, with "the compression and the sour taste of truth." The book does, however, suffer from a sameness, "a poleaxing lack of subtlety," which is fortunately balanced by more lyrical poems.

D192 Geddes, Gary. "Our Most Erotic Puritan." *Books in Canada*, Dec. 1977, pp. 13–14.

Many of these poems fail to fuse thought and feeling; they are more content than form; "care and precision" are often conspicuously absent. "Laurentia" and "Catacombe dei Cappucini," however, have the imaginative poetic sense that is lacking in the overstated poems about the slaughter of the Jews.

D193 Van Wilt, Kurt. "Layton's Covenant with Art." *Essays on Canadian Writing*, No. 9 (Winter 1977–78), pp. 62–65.

Van Wilt praises Layton's intellectual integrity and emotional sensitivity. "No current poet has probed the intricacies of individuality and freedom as finely as Irving Layton." Layton's emphasis on the persecution of the Jews by the Christians is an important reminder of the life-denying nature of Christianity. "No other current poet can say so much, so well, in so few words as Layton."

D194 Charles, J.W. Rev. of *The Covenant*. *Canadian Book Review Annual: 1977*. Ed. Dean Tudor, Nancy Tudor, and Linda Biesenthal. Toronto: Peter Martin, 1978, p. 172.

This is a "dismal" book of "inspired puerility." The subject matter of the holocaust is not suited to the poetic medium.

D195 Hatfield, Stephen. "The Sword Sleeps in the Hand: Lazy Aim with the Long Pea-Shooter." Rev. of *For My Brother Jesus* and *The Covenant*. *Waves*, 6, No. 2 (Winter 1978), 72–76.

Hatfield discusses *For My Brother Jesus* and *The Covenant* together, in general terms. See D189 for annotation.

D196 Lecker, Robert. Rev. of *Out of Place*, by Eli Mandel; *The Covenant*, by Irving Layton; and *Corners in the Glass*, by Ralph Gustafson. *The Fiddlehead*, No. 117 (Spring 1978), pp. 122–24.

Much of Layton's rage and passion appears contrived and insincere. His anti-Christian poems are weak, because here ". . . he is working against his own recognition that complacency and evil are characteristics of men in general, not of a religion." Poems such as "Scylla" and "A Song for Ancients" are successful because they are more honest, with the speaker more directly involved in the poem.

D197 Brown, Russell. "Layton's Quarrel." *Canadian Literature*, No. 80 (Spring 1979), pp. 90–92.

These poems are too close to the language of common speech. While a few succeed, most are neither good poetry nor good rhetoric. There is nothing here of the "magnificent language" that Layton has created in earlier poems.

The Poems of Irving Layton / The Selected Poems of Irving Layton

D198 Smith, A.J.M. "Wandering Gentile, Homebody Jew." Rev. of *Return to Canada: Selected Poems*, by Patrick Anderson; and *The Poems of Irving Layton*, by Irving Layton, ed. Eli Mandel. *Books in Canada*, June–July 1977, p. 19.

Layton's poetry deserves a broader and more complete selection than Mandel's restricted one. Too many of Layton's best poems are absent, although the book still contains many good poems.

D199 Tovey, Roberta. Rev. of *The Selected Poems of Irving Layton*. *The New Republic* [Washington, D.C.], 2 July 1977, p. 39.

Even Layton's failed poems have merit. "When the casual is contained by the barely perceptible rhyme and metric structure his voice joins the oldest poets."

D200 Michaels, Leonard. "Talk and Laments." Rev. of *The Selected Poems of Irving Layton*, by Irving Layton, ed. Eli Mandel; and *Lucky Life*, by Gerald Stern. *The New York Times Book Review*, 9 Oct. 1977, pp. 15, 34.

"Layton manages an extraordinary range of mood and style." "Lillian Roxon," "Song for Naomi," and "Berry Picking" are especially fine.

D201 Nowlan, Michael O. Rev. of *The Poems of Irving Layton*. *Canadian Book Review Annual: 1977*. Ed. Dean Tudor, Nancy Tudor, and Linda Biesenthal. Toronto: Peter Martin, 1978, p. 139.

While the purpose of this volume is hard to ascertain, it provides a good introduction to Layton. Eli Mandel's Introduction is the book's most valuable part.

D202 Barbour, Douglas. "Poetry Chronicle v." *Dalhousie Review*, 58 (Spring 1978), 157–58.

Eli Mandel's Introduction is "witty, intelligent and useful." His selection gives a good impression of Layton's varied poetic personality and "the irrepressible range of Layton's endeavours as a writer."

D203 Smith, Patricia Keeney. "Some Recent Layton Items." Rev. of *The Poems of Irving Layton*, by Irving Layton, ed. Eli Mandel; *The Tightrope Dancer*, by Irving Layton; *Taking Sides: The Collected Social and Political Writings*, ed. Howard Aster; and *There Were No Signs*, by Irving Layton; "The Farting Jesus: Layton and the Heroic Vitalists," by Wynne Francis; "Irving Layton, Pseudo-Prophet — A Reappraisal," by Peter Hunt; *Irving Layton: The Poet and His Critics*, ed. Seymour Mayne; "An Interview with Irving Layton," by Kenneth Sherman; "Nietzsche and Overcoming," by Kurt Van Wilt; and "Jewish Themes in the Works of Irving Layton," by Howard Baker. *Canadian Poetry: Studies, Documents, Reviews*, No. 4 (Spring–Summer 1979), pp. 125–26.

Layton's poetry is "intense, authentic, personal, universal." "The book richly displays Layton's lyric and dramatic gifts, his far-reaching concerns."

The Tamed Puma

D204 Barker, Edna. Rev. of *The Tamed Puma*. *Canadian Book Review Annual: 1979*. Ed. Dean Tudor, Nancy Tudor, and Kathy Vanderlinden. Toronto: Peter Martin, 1980, p. 122.

The beautiful drawings in this book "form a stunning contrast to the poems. . . . Women are, to Layton, a mirror in front of which he basks in his reflected glory."

The Love Poems of Irving Layton

D205 Gervais, Marty. "Layton a Delight for Literary Voyeurs." *The Windsor Star*, 1 March 1980, Book Page, p. 35.

This book is "funny, tragic, and authentic." It is filled with "the jealousy, the anger, the emotional disappointments, the highs, charismatic loyalties, the undulating motions of love and the sexual escapades and erotic voyeurism of the young and old."

D206 Dempster, Barry. Rev. of *The Love Poems of Irving Layton*. *Quill & Quire*, May 1980, pp. 32–33.

These poems display a suitable variety of style. "Annoying, shocking, provocative and amusing," Layton "writes from his soul."

D207 Barbour, Douglas. "Canadian Poetry Chronicle: IX, Part I." *West Coast Review* [Simon Fraser Univ.], 15, No. 1 (June 1980), 74.

There is too much misogyny and not enough joy in these poems. The overall effect of the book is "decidedly anerotic."

D208 Sutherland, Fraser. "The Rooster, the Hen, and the Ego." Rev. of *The Love Poems of Irving Layton*, *For My Neighbours in Hell*, and *An Unlikely Affair*. *Books in Canada*, June–July 1980, p. 8.

"The dialectic between lyricism and irony" contributes to the success of *The Love Poems of Irving Layton*. "I Would for Your Sake Be Gentle" has the quality of "a gifted translation from the classical Greek of a great poet," while a number of other poems also demonstrate Layton's talent.

D209 Smith, Patricia Keeney. "In Love & Hell." Rev. of *The Love Poems of Irving Layton* and *For My Neighbours in Hell*. *Canadian Literature*, No. 88 (Spring 1981), pp. 153–54.

Layton's best love poems "ring out their notes of exultation with the fearless touch of one who has loved both wisely and too well." He is in command of his craft and understands his subject. Some poems convey their message through "metaphysical imagery," while others have the directness of D.H. Lawrence at his best.

D210 Herman, Peter. "Heaven and Hell." Rev. of *The Love Poems of Irving Layton* and *For My Neighbours in Hell*. CV/II, 5, No. 3 (Summer 1981), 43–44, 45.

Layton's love poems achieve a remarkable accuracy and an unusual range of feeling. His "consciousness of himself as a poet" provides a "fascinating element."

D211 Cook, John. Rev. of *The Love Poems of Irving Layton*. *Canadian Book Review Annual: 1980*. Ed. Dean Tudor, Nancy Tudor, and Betsy Struthers. Toronto: Simon & Pierre, 1982, pp. 118–19.

All Layton's poems are love poems, so the collection is at once "fragmentary and central." While many of his best poems are not included, ". . . I can't think of another volume of his poetry which gives a clearer and a more loving glimpse of Layton's essential self."

The Tightrope Dancer

D212 Pyke, Linda. "New Works from Three Seasoned Poets." Rev. of *The Tightrope Dancer*, by Irving Layton; *Fall by Fury & Other Makings*, by Earle Birney; and *Being Alive: Poems 1958–1978*, by Al Purdy. *Quill & Quire*, Sept. 1978, p. 8.

Irving Layton, Earle Birney, and Al Purdy all comprehend "the beauty and horror of existence." For Layton, the poet is on a tightrope, performing defiantly in the face of death.

D213 Gasparini, Len. "Of Imagination All Compact." Rev. of *The Tightrope Dancer*, by Irving Layton; *Fall by Fury & Other Makings*, by Earle Birney; and *Being Alive: Poems 1958–1978*, by Al Purdy. *Books in Canada*, Dec. 1978, p. 36.

Reading Layton "is a sensuous experience that evokes the blood-throb of life." Many poems are "lyrical and inventive."

D214 Kent, David A. Rev. of *The Tightrope Dancer*. *Canadian Book Review Annual: 1978*. Ed. Dean Tudor, Nancy Tudor, and Linda Biesenthal. Toronto: Peter Martin, 1979, p. 105.

Layton unsuccessfully attempts to compensate for his clichés and prosaic efforts with a shocking explicitness. ". . . his megalomania, his pretension and condescension, the borrowed ideas, the name-dropping . . . cannot disguise a shallow intellect . . . ."

D215 Barbour, Douglas. "Canadian Poetry Chronicle: VII." *Dalhousie Review*, 59 (Spring 1979), 158–59.

While the frequent celebration of life helps make this Layton's best collection for some time, his "moods and violent emotions" make his achievement here uneven.

D216 Smith, Patricia Keeney. "Some Recent Layton Items." Rev. of *The Poems of Irving Layton*, by Irving Layton, ed. Eli Mandel; *The Tightrope Dancer*, by Irving Layton; *Taking Sides: The Collected Social and Political Writings*, ed. Howard Aster; *There Were No Signs*, by Irving Layton; "The Farting Jesus: Layton and the Heroic Vitalists," by Wynne Francis; "Irving Layton, Pseudo-Prophet — A Reappraisal," by Peter Hunt; *Irving Layton: The Poet and His Critics*, ed. Seymour Mayne; "An Interview with Irving Layton," by Kenneth Sherman; "Nietzsche and Overcoming," by Kurt Van Wilt; and "Jewish

Themes in the Works of Irving Layton," by Howard Baker. *Canadian Poetry: Studies, Documents, Reviews*, No. 4 (Spring–Summer 1979), p. 126.

"... Layton is a poet of the personality . . . ." His "speaking voice redeems what may otherwise be read as sentimental, anarchic, even fussily fabricated."

D217 Gatenby, Greg. "Poetry Chronicle." *The Tamarack Review*, No. 77–78 (Summer 1979), p. 79.

This book contains some fine lyrics. Layton's attitude to death has changed from fear to a joking acceptance. His life and work are instructive to those who wish "to be fearless and scrupulously honest."

D218 Nicoll, Sharon. Rev. of *The Tightrope Dancer*, by Irving Layton; *Hanging In*, by Raymond Souster; and *Fall by Fury & Other Makings*, by Earle Birney. *The Fiddlehead*, No. 123 (Fall 1979), pp. 103–06.

The few good poems here are outnumbered by those that are vapid, banal, or petty. But some, such as "The Oracle," have a "control of language and sureness of rhythm." "Mishnah and the Eternal Shmuck" acquires power through a restraint which is all too rare in Layton's poetry.

D219 Edwards, Mary Jane. "Falling." Rev. of *Fall by Fury & Other Makings*, by Earle Birney; and *The Tightrope Dancer*, by Irving Layton. *Canadian Literature*, No. 86 (Autumn 1980), pp. 113–14.

These poems are a mixture of successes and failures. Some are closer to " 'rhetoric or journalism,' " but the best achieve " 'concision and intensity.' "

Droppings from Heaven

D220 Geddes, Gary. "Love and Curses." *The Gazette* [Montreal], 1 Sept. 1979, p. 55.

Layton is at his best when, as in most of this volume, he forgets to be controversial and becomes "the gentle author of elegies, love poems and self-mocking meditations." "Canadian Epic" and "Inverness" are two of the book's delightful poems.

D221 Colombo, John Robert. "Polemics and Lyrics." Rev. of *Droppings from Heaven*, by Irving Layton; and *Another Mouth*, by George Bowering. *The Globe and Mail* [Toronto], 15 Sept. 1979, p. 43.

Although Layton indicts Canadians for not addressing the problems of an age marked by Auschwitz and Gulag, many of his poems are "joyful, even in vituperation." "All are sparked by a sense of injustice and the need for compassion."

D222 Gervais, Marty. "Big Themes Tackled with Both Pitchforks Blazing." *The Windsor Star*, 6 Oct. 1979, The Book Page, p. 37.

Layton's importance comes from his "writing about things that matter." This book "is an indictment of all those who turn away from the unpleasant."

D223 Abley, Mark. "Poetry That Fell from the Sky." Rev. of *The Gods*, by Dennis Lee; *Droppings from Heaven*, by Irving Layton; *Another Mouth*, by George Bowering; *A Balancing Act*, by Florence McNeil; and *The Tough Romance*, by Pier Giorgio di Cicco. *Maclean's*, 8 Oct. 1979, pp. 54, 56.

While many of these poems are "irritated scribbles," Layton answers a need through his Dylan Thomas-like unconventionality. Some lyrics combine "fierce energy with a rare and handsome gentleness."

D224 Purdy, Al. "Layton and Lee: A Bulldozer Versus a Subtle Quester." Rev. of *Droppings from Heaven*, by Irving Layton; and *The Gods*, by Dennis Lee. *The Toronto Star*, 27 Oct. 1979, p. F7.

As a poet and mentor, Layton has done great work, but the present book shows no development. Only a few poems, including "A Wild Peculiar Joy" and "Senile, My Sister Sings," are "echoes of a lost authenticity." Layton lacks "Lee's thoughtfulness and calm reason."

D225 Aubert, Rosemary. Rev. of *Droppings from Heaven*. *Quill & Quire*, Nov. 1979, p. 33.
Layton's poetic power remains undiminished; his blasts at Canadian gentility are managed with "technical ease." "Senile, My Sister Sings," with its "tender but nonetheless vigorous emotion," is the best poem here.

D226 Smith, Patricia Keeney. "A Wild Peculiar Joy." *The Canadian Forum*, Dec.–Jan. 1979–80, p. 32.
These poems are not in the tradition of Layton's best works, which fuse "singer and satirist." Still, the passion remains intense, with many of his lyrics "engendered by a deep feeling for individuals." The most surprising "are those in which a new setting has given fresh impetus to the satiric image."

D227 Thompson, Michael. "Mannafest Destiny." *Books in Canada*, Feb. 1980, pp. 17–18.
Layton is guilty of "carelessness of craft sometimes, the wrong kind of vulgarity, posturing, opacity." But he is also intensely alive, much preferable to those characterized, in Layton's words, by "the colonial cringe and ever-prevalent gentility."

D228 Amprimoz, Alexandre L. Rev. of *Droppings from Heaven*. *Quarry*, 29, No. 2 (Spring 1980), 77–78.
Amprimoz sarcastically examines Layton's exaggerated claims and lack of originality. "It is sad to see that academics . . . persist in studying and teaching Layton just to embarrass him with honours, royalties and fame — things that the humble poet really dislikes . . . ."

D229 Linder, Norma West. "Strong Words Indeed." Rev. of *Echoes from Labour's War*, by Dawn Fraser; and *Droppings from Heaven*, by Irving Layton. *The Canadian Author & Bookman*, 55, No. 3 (May 1980), 24.
At times, Layton's poetry is too "strong" or "egocentric," but it also has great "vitality" and "unforgettable imagery."

D230 Barbour, Douglas. "Canadian Poetry Chronicle: IX, Part 1." *West Coast Review* [Simon Fraser Univ.], 15, No. 1 (June 1980), 74.
While this book has a few good poems, Layton's work in general suffers from a "failure in technique." He has talent, but produces at a far lower level than he is capable.

D231 Trethewy, Eric. Rev. of *Droppings from Heaven*. *The Fiddlehead*, No. 126 (Summer 1980), pp. 144–46.
Even the best of the poems in this volume are marred by faulty craft. Layton's poetry is too rhetorical, too seldom introspective. A streak of "gratuitous savagery and malice" sometimes leads him to a "pettiness of . . . response."

D232 Daniel, Lorne. "Gems & Ashes." Rev. of *Hanging In*, by Raymond Souster; and *Droppings from Heaven*, by Irving Layton. *Canadian Literature*, No. 87 (Winter 1980), pp. 128, 129–30.
While Layton writes in much the same manner as his previous work, his use of new angles, locales, and settings keeps the poetry fresh. "Rhetoric and bombast" mar some of his work, but Layton is best enjoyed whole.

There Were No Signs

D233 Littman, Sol. "Now, Layton with Pictures." *The Toronto Star*, 15 April 1979, p. B6.

Aligi Sassu's etchings help universalize Layton's poems, while Francesca Valente's translations show "a remarkable ear for Layton's modern cadences and interrupted rhythms." The result is "magnificent."

D234   Cherry, Zena. "Art Forms Blend in Book." *The Globe and Mail* [Toronto], 19 April 1979, p. 73.
   This collaboration is a "rare bargain," as the etchings alone are worth $1,500 of the $2,000 price.

D235   Smith, Patricia Keeney. "Some Recent Layton Items." Rev. of *The Poems of Irving Layton*, by Irving Layton, ed. Eli Mandel; *The Tightrope Dancer*, by Irving Layton; *Taking Sides: The Collected Social and Political Writings*, ed. Howard Aster; *There Were No Signs*, by Irving Layton; "The Farting Jesus: Layton and the Heroic Vitalists," by Wynne Francis; "Irving Layton, Pseudo-Prophet — A Reappraisal," by Peter Hunt; *Irving Layton: The Poet and His Critics*, ed. Seymour Mayne; "An Interview with Irving Layton," by Kenneth Sherman; "Nietzsche and Overcoming," by Kurt Van Wilt; and "Jewish Themes in the Works of Irving Layton," by Howard Baker. *Canadian Poetry: Studies, Documents, Reviews*, No. 4 (Spring–Summer 1979), pp. 129–30.
   The special issue of *There Were No Signs*, illustrated by Aligi Sassu, is a "marriage of imaginations [that] should engender new insight." ". . . Sassu's sensibility seems darkly romantic by contrast to Layton's more usual irony and exuberance."

For My Neighbours in Hell

D236   Sutherland, Fraser. "The Rooster, the Hen, and the Ego." Rev. of *The Love Poems of Irving Layton*, *For My Neighbours in Hell*, and *An Unlikely Affair*. *Books in Canada*, June–July 1980, p. 8.
   In *For My Neighbours in Hell*, ". . . the poet resembles a rancorous rooster atop the 20th century's dunghill." A few successful poems, like "Apocalypse" and "The Abyss," are mixed in with many unsuccessful poems.

D237   Dempster, Barry. Rev. of *For My Neighbours in Hell*. *Quill & Quire*, Aug. 1980, p. 31–32.
   While some pieces "are more sermon than verse," Layton's poems show "few lapses and a multitude of strange yet believable shapes" in their emotional and poetic reaction.

D238   Smith, Patricia Keeney. "In Love & Hell." Rev. of *The Love Poems of Irving Layton* and *For My Neighbours in Hell*. *Canadian Literature*, No. 88 (Spring 1981), pp. 154–55.
   The poems in *For My Neighbours in Hell* are "hard as onyx, they admit that pity has not the power of plain talk, in perilous times." But hell is not without its "dash of glitter."

D239   Herman, Peter. "Heaven and Hell." Rev. of *The Love Poems of Irving Layton* and *For My Neighbours in Hell*. CV/II, 5, No. 3 (Summer 1981), 43, 44–45.
   For My Neighbours in Hell is full of bad poetry and marred with "abject misanthropy," "racial epithets," and "blanket statements." A few good poems, like "Dracula" and "Florida Nights," are insufficient to "redeem what is basically a hellishly bad book."

Europe and Other Bad News

D240   Morley, Patricia. "Layton: Beyond the Prime." *The Citizen* [Ottawa], 7 March 1981, Book Page, p. 35.
   "We've heard it before, not once but many times." The targets are the same, and the content is tired.

D241   Abley, Mark. "Bitter Wisdom of Moral Concern." Rev. of *True Stories*, by Margaret Atwood; *The Stone*

Bird, by Al Purdy; and *Europe and Other Bad News*, by Irving Layton. *Maclean's*, 30 March 1981, pp. 52, 53.

Margaret Atwood, Al Purdy, and Irving Layton combine "moral concern" with a "lyric voice" in these three books. Layton's poems suffer from predictability and a carelessness with language, which even his righteous indignation about Gulag and the Holocaust cannot rescue.

D242 Stromberg-Stein, Susan. "Hubris and Hype." *The Gazette* [Montreal], 11 April 1981, p. 61.

Too much ego and name-dropping mar the poems. Layton is still a colourful figure, but ". . . can he dance?"

D243 Crosby, Tecca. "Old Enough to Know Better." *Books in Canada*, May 1981, pp. 33–34.

Layton's stance as the wise old man is unconvincing; his personal poems sound more "like the mutterings of the village idiot rather than of the local philosopher." Poems on the larger issues of our time are "stuck in a groove" and fail to progress to "a more profound assessment. . . . He is a man grown old with bitterness, guilt, and lack of forgiveness."

D244 Aubert, Rosemary. Rev. of *Europe and Other Bad News*. *Quill & Quire*, June 1981, p. 35.

A few successful poems do not salvage this book, in which ". . . his signal anger almost seems forced . . . ." But apart from a few flaws, the book is technically accomplished.

D245 Whiteman, Bruce. Rev. of *Europe and Other Bad News*. *Journal of Canadian Studies / Revue d'études canadiennes* [Trent Univ.], 17, No. 2 (Summer 1982), 150, 154.

As are many of Layton's recent books, *Europe and Other Bad News* is filled with "weak and bad poems." While his persistence is admirable, his craft is not; the few good poems are buried in a mass of bad ones.

D246 Mitcham, Peter. "Nutgalls & Sunbursts." Rev. of *Europe and Other Bad News*, by Irving Layton; and *The Stone Bird*, by Al Purdy. *Canadian Literature*, No. 94 (Autumn 1982), pp. 122–24.

Layton has something here for every taste, "the joyless, the joyful, and those in which the two moods sometimes meet." He is a great entertainer and an "absurd and fabulous" legend.

D247 Oliver, Michael Brian. "Layton and Purdy, Again." Rev. of *Europe and Other Bad News*, by Irving Layton; and *The Stone Bird*, by Al Purdy. *The Fiddlehead*, No. 134 (Oct. 1982), pp. 105–06, 110.

"Verbal verve" and "felicity with language" help make Layton a genuine poet. He conveys the "feeling that beauty is the greatest, and rarest, grace available to man and . . . that man is seldom capable of seeing even truth, let alone beauty."

D248 Nowlan, Michael O. Rev. of *Europe and Other Bad News*. *Canadian Book Review Annual: 1981*. Ed. Dean Tudor and Ann Tudor. Toronto: Simon & Pierre, 1983, p. 164.

These poems confirm Layton's status as "our greatest poet." Many reveal his scorn for "man's contradictions and hypocritical nature."

A Wild Peculiar Joy: Selected Poems 1945–1982

D249 Helwig, David. "Irving Layton: Orator Howling in an Empty Stadium." Rev. of *A Wild Peculiar Joy: Selected Poems 1945–1982*, by Irving Layton; and *The Beauty of the Weapons: Selected Poems 1972–*

82, by Robert Bringhurst. *The Toronto Star*, 31 Dec. 1982, Books, p. E10.

Layton writes some fine poems, but a curious coldness pervades much of his work; he seldom seems aware of the reader's presence.

D250 Keith, W.J. Rev. of *A Wild Peculiar Joy: Selected Poems 1945–1982. Canadian Book Review Annual: 1982.* Ed. Dean Tudor and Ann Tudor. Toronto: Simon & Pierre, 1983, pp. 182–83.

The "careful winnowing" that went into the preparation of this volume has resulted in a fine selection. Layton's "extraordinary variety of language" and "control of tone" make him an impressive poet.

D251 Djwa, Sandra, and R.B. Hatch. "Letters in Canada: 1982. Poetry." *University of Toronto Quarterly*, 52 (Summer 1983), 343.

Layton's poetry, like Margaret Avison's, is "replete with myth and allusion" and fuses "a traditional poetic mode with a freer, North American form."

D252 Berry, Reginald. "Natural & Unnatural." Rev. of *The Beauty of the Weapons: Selected Poems 1972–82*, by Robert Bringhurst; *A Throw of Particles: The New and Selected Poetry of D.G. Jones*, by D.G. Jones; *Winter Sun / The Dumbfounding: Poems 1940–66*, by Margaret Avison; *A Wild Peculiar Joy: Selected Poems 1945–82*, by Irving Layton; and *Mostly Coast People: Selected Verse*, by Hubert Evans. *Canadian Literature*, No. 102 (Autumn 1984), p. 137.

With so many other collections of Layton's work available, this volume is not necessary. The absence of information as to what volumes the poems first appeared in, or of a justifying Foreword, limit its usefulness to the reader. The nine poems here published for the first time "reveal a new, touchingly mellow Layton."

The Gucci Bag

D253 Mirolla, Michael. "'Gucci Bag' Ode to the Bard's Passion, Reputation." *The Gazette* [Montreal], 26 Nov. 1983, p. I1.

Though too many second-rate poems prevent this book from being one of Layton's best, he remains our most "expansive," "life-affirming" poet. The book "abounds with metaphors having to do with decay, with rot, with leaves falling, with insects."

D254 Adachi, Ken. "Irving Layton: The 'howling beast' in *The Gucci Bag*." *The Toronto Star*. "Books," 3 Dec. 1983, p. H3.

Layton shows "raw hatred" and "unbridled invective" in this book, although "rapt affirmation" is also present. Poetry, Layton says, has little hope; filmmakers are the ones now making "great statements on the human condition."

D255 Fitzgerald, Judith. "Covering the Poetic Bases." Rev. of *The Gucci Bag*, by Irving Layton; *Predators of the Adoration*, by Christopher Dewdney; and *Settlements*, by David Donnell. *The Globe and Mail* [Toronto]. "Books," 10 Dec. 1983, Entertainment, p. 23.

Beneath Layton's "wrath, indignation and despair," a note of poignancy and longing balances his vision of the world.

D256 Rizzardi, Alfredo. "Una letteratura da scoprire." *L'indice dei Libri del Mese* [Bologna?], No. 3 [c.1984], p. 21.

"Stupisce la inalterata vitalita de questo poeta ormai settantatreenne che unisce alla corposita visionaria una sottile intelligenza satirica e un'abilita straordinaria nell'usare linguaggio e ritmi; stupisce soprattutto l'inesausta creativita."

D257 Girard, Louise H. Rev. of *The Gucci Bag*, by Irving Layton; and *Pearls*, by Fred Cogswell. *Canadian Book Review Annual: 1983*. Ed. Dean Tudor and Ann Tudor. Toronto: Simon and Pierre, 1984, pp. 218–19.

The best of Layton's poems are those in which he reacts simply as a human being; others suffer from being "self-centred" and "self-indulgent."

D258 Hunter, Bruce. "Rage, Lust and City Living." Rev. of *The Gucci Bag*, by Irving Layton; and *Settlements*, by David Donnell. *Cross-Canada Writer's Quarterly*, 6, No. 2 (1984), 20.

Layton has a keen eye for evil and the "irony and whimsy in the order of things." His craft is "clean" and "meticulous," expressing "our hidden selves that only the artist seems able to live."

D259 Kertes, Joseph. "Layton's Inferno." *Books in Canada*, Jan. 1984, pp. 19–20.

"More like a sustained poetic treatise than Layton's previous works," this book shows a more subdued Layton writing poems that combine a remarkable "roundness of vision" with "unprecedented wisdom." Some fine poems on death are included.

D260 Martindale, Sheila. Rev. of *The Gucci Bag*. *The Canadian Author & Bookman*, 59, No. 4 (Summer 1984), 24–25.

Layton is never "pretentious" or "boring," which helps redeem some of the quirky ideas in this book. Layton "has lost none of his brilliance and fire," although more "sadness and loneliness" and "bitterness" pervade this book.

A Spider Danced a Cosy Jig

D261 Robinson, B.A. Rev. of *A Spider Danced a Cosy Jig*. *Canadian Book Review Annual: 1984*. Ed. Dean Tudor and Ann Tudor. Toronto: Simon and Pierre, 1985, pp. 334–35.

Some of these poems "will bring a chuckle to the reader," while others "are realistic but nonetheless upsetting."

D262 Norrie, Helen. Rev. of *Anno's Hat Tricks*, by Akihiro Nozaki and Mitsumasa Anno; *The Moonbear*, by Bettina Ansorge; *The Little Stick Boy*, by Simon Stern; and *A Spider Danced a Cosy Jig*, by Irving Layton. *Winnipeg Free Press*, 12 Oct. 1985, p. 62.

These poems will appeal only to children with a sense of black humour. Miro Malish's illustrations are enjoyable, but the book should be examined "carefully before purchase."

D263 Ferns, John. "Poems for Children?". Rev. of *A Spider Danced a Cosy Jig*, by Irving Layton; and *Flight of the Roller-Coaster: Poems for Younger Readers*, by Raymond Souster. *Canadian Children's Literature / Littérature canadienne pour la jeunesse: A Journal of Criticism & Review / Une revue de critiques et de comptes rendus*, No. 41 (1986), pp. 68–69.

Layton's book is preferable to Raymond Souster's, since he is a better poet, and the illustrations are effective. Compared to Souster, Layton's "rhythms are stronger, his language livelier."

D264 Chanin, Lawrence. Rev. of *A Spider Danced a Cosy Jig*. *The Canadian Author & Bookman*, 61, No. 3 (Spring 1986), 47–48.

These poems convey a dark vision of mankind; "tough-minded readers" may enjoy this book, but "others might find it causes nightmares."

Dance with Desire: Love Poems

D265 Geddes, Gary. "Love Poems Lay Bare Irving Layton." *The Gazette* [Montreal], 17 May 1986, p. B7.

The best poems perceive in their subjects a quality that will endure in Layton's work. Too many give way to vulgarity and abuse; a poet's quarrel must always be with his language rather than his subject.

D266 Fitzgerald, Judith. "2 Great Poets of Our Times." Rev. of *Dance with Desire: Love Poems*, by Irving Layton; and *The Night the Dog Smiled*, by John Newlove. *The Toronto Star*, 6 July 1986, p. A14.

This book has "a sense of tradition." Each poem is "crafted with tiny brilliant allusions and literary echoes." "Layton is one of our greatest poets."

D267 Filip, Ray. "Beasts of the Field." Rev. of *Dance with Desire: Love Poems*, by Irving Layton; *The Beekeeper's Daughter*, by Bruce Hunter; and *Small Horses and Intimate Beasts*, by Michel Garneau. *Books in Canada*, Nov. 1986, p. 20.

Even the best of these love poems are not completely successful. "Layton's language is as fresh as a fossil in stone."

D268 Heller, Liane. "WQ Reviews: Poetry." Rev. of *Dance with Desire: Love Poems*. *Cross-Canada Writers' Quarterly*, 9, No. 1 (1987), 22–23.

Many of these poems have an "uncompromising frankness," which makes their author vulnerable. His exploration of love and hate lead the reader to a recognition of "the complexity of the infinite but earth-bound heart."

D269 Heft, Harold. Rev. of *Dance with Desire: Love Poems*. RUBICON [McGill Univ.], No. 8 (Spring 1987), pp. 184–85.

The poems in this book fall into three categories. In the first, he congratulates himself "for being so irresistible and potent." In the second, he develops "his views on the nature of women and why they

hold him, as a poet, captive." In the third, "a vein of wit" shows itself "in short, snazzy poems or in distinct sections of longer poems."

D270 Noyes, Steve. "Tin Memory." Rev. of *Dance with Desire: Love Poems*, by Irving Layton; and *It Takes All Kinds*, by Raymond Souster. *The Fiddlehead*, No. 155 (Spring 1988), pp. 106–09.

While Layton writes some honest poems, too many are "awkward and deliberate odes to male ego, pretentious reimaginings of myth, [or] thinly disguised misogyny."

Final Reckoning: Poems 1982–1986

D271 Fitzgerald, Judith. "With Best Wishes, to Irving Layton." *The Toronto Star*, 31 May 1987, Books, p. A23.

Layton has made himself "too vulnerable to the public in the name of art." But he is to be applauded for his "unswerving vision, . . . dedication to the best of ideals, . . . [and] terrific insistence upon truly great art."

D272 Ferguson, Trevor. "Spleen May Write the Poem, but Layton's Heart Will Speak Tomorrow." Rev. of *Final Reckoning: Poems 1982–1986*, by Irving Layton; *I Shout Love and Other Poems*, by Milton Acorn; *Corpses, Brats and Cricket Music*, by George Faludy; and *Brick* [Tribute to Frank R. Scott], No. 30. *The Gazette* [Montreal], 26 Sept. 1987, p. J11.

Layton refuses to leave this life calmly. Here we have "the irascible ruffian in all his glory, spittle, and bile."

D273 Owens, Judith. "Love's Trials." Rev. of *K. in Love*, by Don Coles; and *Final Reckoning: Poems 1982–1986*, by Irving Layton. *Canadian Literature*, Nos.

124–25 (Spring–Summer 1990), pp. 371–73.

Layton "makes large claims for art's enduring vitality and efficacy." At other times he regards human endeavour as transitory or takes a messianic stand. Love remains central, "standing like a kind of sanctuary for the poet."

Fortunate Exile

D274 Precosky, Don. Rev. of *Fortunate Exile. Canadian Book Review Annual: 1987*. Ed. Dean Tudor. Toronto: Simon and Pierre, 1988, p. 160.

This book, "the finest distillation of his voluminous output," is moving and often anguished. "Layton's anger and pain are like a fire that purges him of the egotism that marks too much of his poetry."

D275 Shepherd, Victor. Rev. of *Fortunate Exile. The United Church Observer*, Feb. 1988, p. 53.

These poems not only confront the depravity of humanity but affirm the joy of life. Reading these poems will bring Christians a "step closer to the peculiar passion and pathos which is Israel."

D276 Rosenblatt, Joe. "In the Smithy of His Soul." *Books in Canada*, April 1988, pp. 28–29.

Layton's best poems, like "Keine Lazarovitch: 1870–1959" are "deeply moving in intensity and charged with original language." The poems that are more didactic or fixated on Jews are less successful, but this book "is a must if one is to know what makes the artist tick."

D277 Hatch, Ronald B. "Letters in Canada 1987: Poetry." *University of Toronto Quarterly*, 58 (Fall 1988), 48.

While Layton often writes well about public issues, his own personality too often takes over with a voice that is "slightly flat and somewhat naïve."

D278 Messenger, Cynthia. Rev. of *Fortunate Exile. Queen's Quarterly*, 95 (Winter 1988), 942–43.

These poems form a powerful statement on the suffering of Jews and the existence of evil. "Anarch" is the most interesting poem "because it explores the place of the poem in a world that is both supremely beautiful and deeply sorrowful."

D279 Keeney, Patricia. Rev. of *Weathering It: Complete Poems 1948–1987*, by Douglas LePan; *Winter Prophesies*, by Ralph Gustafson; and *Fortunate Exile*, by Irving Layton. *Cross-Canada Writers' Quarterly*, 11, No. 2 (1989), 22–23.

Some of these poems slip into "complaint and harangue," but others like "Parque de Montjuich" and "Cain" combine "moral and pagan points of view" in a "lyric and visionary" manner. "It is the pagan celebratory mode that renders the exile truly fortunate."

D280 Johnson, Rick. "Voices of Experience." Rev. of *Selected Poems*, by Patrick Lane; *Winter Prophecies*, by Ralph Gustafson; and *Fortunate Exile*, by Irving Layton. *The Canadian Forum*, Feb.–March 1989, pp. 28, 29–30.

These poems "celebrate a passion, a cultural integrity, and a gritty defiance." Layton's "control of language and syntax makes even the most grotesque imagery have a rightness that fits the ear and eye."

Now Is the Place

D281 S[utherland]., J[ohn]. "Mr. Layton's Talents." *Northern Review*, 2, No. 2 (July–Aug. 1948), 34–35. Rpt. in *Essays, Controversies and Poems*. By John Sutherland. Ed. Miriam Waddington. New Canadian Library Original, No. 81. Toronto: McClelland and Stewart, 1972, pp. 112–14. Rpt. ["Two Reviews of

Now Is the Place (1948)"] in *Irving Layton: The Poet and His Critics*. Ed. Seymour Mayne. Toronto: McGraw-Hill Ryerson, 1978, pp. 29–30.

Layton's short stories, "the best yet written by a Canadian," show his talents to lie more in fiction than poetry. Only about four of the poems have any value. Layton is too much the rebel, too blunt and direct, to be accepted by the Canadian critical establishment.

D282 Roskolenko, Harry. "Post-War Poetry in Canada." *here and now*, 2, No. 4 (June 1949), 24, 27. Rpt. [excerpt — "Two Reviews of *Now Is the Place* (1948)"] in *Irving Layton: The Poet and His Critics*. Ed. Seymour Mayne. Toronto: McGraw-Hill Ryerson, 1978, pp. 27–29.

Roskolenko finds Layton's exclusion from the first and second editions of A.J.M. Smith's *The Book of Canadian Poetry: A Critical and Historical Anthology* "odd." Layton shares common traits with Roy Daniells, but does not sustain emotion or employ satire as neatly as the latter. He is, however, "the most exciting equator of speech uses, with a harder core of social relationships."

The Swinging Flesh

D283 Woodcock, George. "Top Canadian Poet Short Story Master." *The Sun* [Vancouver], 10 May 1961, First Sec., p. 5.

The "involvement," "compassion," "humour," and "magnificently controlled prose" make this book "one of the best collection of stories yet published in Canada."

D284 Glover, Guy. "Look Ma! No Hands." *The Montreal Star*, 20 May 1961, Entertainment and the Arts, p. 6.

Layton's boyishness gives him a freshness and vig-

our, but also an unnecessary salaciousness. The poetry is uneven in quality, although "Keine Lazarovitch" is magnificent. The stories are conventional, but possess "a subtlety of expression and richness of theme."

D285 Hale, Barrie. "Baggy-Pants Rhetoric." *Canadian Literature*, No. 9 (Summer 1961), pp. 66–67.

While the stories in this collection are "strangely passive" and more statement than story, the poems have "verve" and "rhetoric." While Layton's performances do not always work, he is "fun to watch."

D286 Pacey, Desmond. Rev. of *The Swinging Flesh*. *The Fiddlehead*, No. 49 (Summer 1961), pp. 61–62. Rpt. in *Irving Layton: The Poet and His Critics*. Ed. Seymour Mayne. Toronto: McGraw-Hill Ryerson, 1978, pp. 119–21.

Layton's Foreword to this book makes some good points, but overstates and overgeneralizes. Layton has lost his "sense of direction"; he is unable "to see beyond the present discontents." But his stories are "steadily improving," and the poems are "full of warmth, tenderness, humanity and love."

D287 Webb, Phyllis. Rev. of *The Swinging Flesh*, by Irving Layton; and *The Spice-Box of Earth*, by Leonard Cohen. *Critically Speaking*. CBC Radio, 30 July 1961. Printed in *Irving Layton: The Poet and His Critics*. Ed. Seymour Mayne. Toronto: McGraw-Hill Ryerson, 1978, pp. 117–19. Rpt. ("Curses and Lamentations") in *Talking*. By Phyllis Webb. Montreal: Quadrant, 1982, pp. 75–77.

The surfeit of anger in this book offends the reader. While the stories occasionally achieve a Dostoevskian mood, they are "neither technically nor stylistically interesting." The only interesting poems are those which, like "The Day Aviva Came to Paris," verge on fantasy.

D288 Daniells, Roy. Rev. of *The Swinging Flesh*. *The Canadian Forum*, Oct. 1961, pp. 162–63.

Layton has little sympathy for the characters in his stories. The best of the poems, however, celebrate with "genuine exuberance."

D289 Dudek, Louis. "Three Major Canadian Poets — Three Major Forms of Archaism." Rev. of *The Devil's Picture Book*, by Daryl Hine; *The Spice-Box of Earth*, by Leonard Cohen; and *The Swinging Flesh*, by Irving Layton. *Delta*, No. 16 (Nov. 1961), pp. 22, 24–25. Rpt. (rev. of *The Swinging Flesh*) in *Irving Layton: The Poet and His Critics*. Ed. Seymour Mayne. Toronto: McGraw-Hill Ryerson, 1978, pp. 121–22.

The poems are typical Layton fare. Though often "original and genuine," the book lacks "technical proficiency." A drawing of Layton by Louis Dudek is included.

D290 Rans, Geoffrey. Rev. of *The Swinging Flesh*. *Alphabet*, No. 3 (Dec. 1961), pp. 79–81.

The "occasional banality" in these poems is a small price to pay for the finer achievements. The stories, at their best, "have such finesse, both in detail and over-all, that they disarm criticism."

D291 Ripley, J.D. Rev. of *The Swinging Flesh*. *The Dalhousie Review*, 41 (Winter 1961–62), 567–72.

Neither the prose nor the poetry in *The Swinging Flesh* will advance Layton's reputation. While the poems contain "immense energy," they are often marred by his "sustained cursing; . . . the idea is more important than the vehicle of conveyance." The stories have warmth and power, but are often weakened by "the far-fetched image," or "stereotyped or overlush" language.

D292 Wilson, Milton. "Letters in Canada: 1961. Poetry." *University of Toronto Quarterly*, 31 (July 1962), 452–54.

Although in the stories the "style is sometimes laboured," and the plots threaten to become formulaic, the best, especially "The Philistine" and "A Plausible Story," are memorable achievements. The poems are "a scattered, transitional lot," although there are some excellent additions to the Layton cannon.

D293 Mandel, E.W. "Poetry and Prose." *Queen's Quarterly*, 68 (Winter 1962), 690–91. Rpt. (rev. of *The Swinging Flesh*) in *Irving Layton: The Poet and His Critics*. Ed. Seymour Mayne. Toronto: McGraw-Hill Ryerson, 1978, pp. 122–24.

This volume shows "the powerful unity of Layton's mind"; poems and stories complement each other. A sense of terror is more evident in the stories than in the poems, in which the terror appears "ironically in the laughter of a clown."

The Whole Bloody Bird (Obs, Aphs & Pomes)

D294 Mandel, Eli. "Nothing at All but Poetry." Rev. of *Selected Poems* and *The Whole Bloody Bird (Obs, Aphs & Pomes)*. *The Globe Magazine* [*The Globe and Mail*] [Toronto], 22 March 1969, p. 13. Rpt. [rev. of *Selected Poems* and *The Whole Bloody Bird (Obs, Aphs, & Pomes)*] in *Irving Layton: The Poet and His Critics*. Ed. Seymour Mayne. Toronto: McGraw-Hill Ryerson, 1978, p. 186.

The Whole Bloody Bird (Obs, Aphs & Pomes) is a much better representation of Layton's wide-ranging genius than *Selected Poems*. He has the "ability to repeat himself endlessly in theme and technique without losing the enormous energy that endlessly renews his work."

D295 Callaghan, Barry. "A Letter to Irving Layton." *The Telegram* [Toronto], 5 April 1969, Weekend / Showcase, p. 5.

This book contains much insight, but in general is too easily won. Layton needs to push himself further to show the madness in himself that he speaks of experiencing.

D296 McCuaig, Norman. Rev. of *The Whole Bloody Bird (Obs, Aphs & Pomes)*. *The Canadian Forum*, June 1969, p. 66.

Layton's view of the world is wildly removed from reality, and his poems are far from what poetry should be. "Somebody's gotta be kidding."

D297 Barbour, Douglas. Rev. of *The Shattered Plinths*, *The Whole Bloody Bird (Obs, Aphs & Pomes)*, and *Selected Poems*. *Dalhousie Review*, 49 (Autumn 1969), 441.

Apart from a few poems, this book tempts one "to dismiss Layton as a washed-up poet."

D298 Gustafson, Ralph. "Virtue Is Not Enough." Rev. of *All There Is of Love*, by Sandra Kolber; *Passage of Summer*, by Elizabeth Brewster; *Heaven Take My Hand*, by David Weisstub; *Rocky Mountain Foot*, by George Bowering; and *The Whole Bloody Bird (Obs, Aphs & Pomes)*, by Irving Layton. *Canadian Literature*, No. 42 (Autumn 1969), pp. 72, 76–77.

The prose sections of this book are "arrogant and observant." His aphorisms are "memorably cogent." The poems, while not among his best, confirm his position as "one of the three poets in Canada who command the grand style."

D299 Marshall, Tom. Rev. of *Selected Poems* and *The Whole Bloody Bird (Obs, Aphs & Pomes)*. *Queen's Quarterly*, 76 (Autumn 1969), 548–49. Rpt. in *Irving Layton: The Poet and His Critics*. Ed. Seymour Mayne. Toronto: McGraw-Hill Ryerson, 1978, pp. 187–88.

While the poems are uneven in quality, Layton's "general observations and aphorisms are usually challenging."

D300 Mallinson, Jean. Rev. of *The Whole Bloody Bird (Obs, Aphs & Pomes)*. *Monday Morning* [Toronto], April–May 1970, pp. 23–24.

At times, the "Observations" have a "vigour and flair." The poems are often "linear and flaccid," but the aphorisms provide a discipline for Layton, flourishing "on the soil of bias and strong opinion."

D301 Hornyansky, Michael. "Letters in Canada: 1969. Poetry." *University of Toronto Quarterly*, 39 (July 1970), 329.

The Whole Bloody Bird (Obs, Aphs, & Pomes) shows Layton as good company, although it tells us little that is new about the world.

D302 Dowden, Graham. Rev. of *The Whole Bloody Bird (Obs, Aphs & Pomes)*. *Quarry*, 20, No. 1 (Winter 1971), 45–48.

Layton writes "frequent diatribes against targets either too complex to be touched by them or too vulnerable to need them." The best part of the book is the "Pomes," particularly "Elephant," but, in general, Layton needs a stronger sense of self-criticism.

Engagements: The Prose of Irving Layton

D303 Ages, Arnold. "Layton's Honor Roll of Literary Crucified." *The Globe and Mail* [Toronto], 11 Nov. 1972, p. 32.

This welcome collection shows Layton writing in "hard-hitting cogent prose" with "universal appeal."

D304 Fulford, Robert. "Prose of Irving Layton: It's Both an Appalling and Interesting Volume." *The Toronto Star*, 11 Nov. 1972, p. 57. Rpt. (rev. of *Engagements: The Prose of Irving Layton*) in *Irving Layton: The Poet and His Critics*. Ed. Seymour Mayne. Toronto: McGraw-Hill Ryerson, 1978, pp. 214–16.

This book is appalling "because it brings us the ego of Irving Layton in a pure state, unadulterated by the poetic process." Yet it is interesting because here is "Canadian literary history in raw form." Layton "remains one of the most absorbing figures in Canadian letters."

D305 Friis-Baastad, Erling. "Cheaper by the Dozen." *Books in Canada*, Nov.–Dec. 1972, p. 15.

Layton comes across as a petty, overbearing person in his polemical prose, which makes the short stories a welcome relief. While he has done much to give poets and poetry their due, these articles better served their purpose when they first appeared.

D306 Adams, Richard. "Layton: The Writer as Radical." *Journal of Canadian Fiction*, 2, No. 1 (Winter 1973), 96–97. Rpt. (excerpt) in *Modern Commonwealth Literature: A Library of Literary Criticism*. Ed. John H. Ferres and Martin Tucker. New York: Frederick Ungar, 1977, pp. 303–04. Rpt. (expanded, original — rev. of *Engagements: The Prose of Irving Layton*) in *Irving Layton: The Poet and His Critics*. Ed. Seymour Mayne. Toronto: McGraw-Hill Ryerson, 1978, pp. 216–20.

This book reminds us of many forgotten aspects of Layton. Much of his prose is tied together by "the opposition between the prophetic poet and philistine society. . . . Layton has done a lot of things few Canadian Poets have done, including writing some fine short stories and an interesting body of criticism."

D307 Dawe, Alan. "Frustrated Poets Critically Cranky." Rev. of *Engagements: The Prose of Irving Layton*, by Irving Layton; and *The Cow Jumped Over the Moon: The Writing and Reading of Poetry*, by Earle Birney. *The Vancouver Sun*, 12 Jan. 1973, p. 32A.

Both Earle Birney and Irving Layton "wish to celebrate a sense of joy in life that they seldom find manifest in the world that surrounds them." Layton's prose was worth collecting, but is best taken in small doses.

D308 Kurth, Burton. Rev. of *Engagements: The Prose of Irving Layton*. *The Malahat Review* [Univ. of Victoria], No. 26 (April 1973), pp. 229–31.

Layton's conflicting love and hate is well revealed in his changing attitude to Louis Dudek. "Fascinating but sometimes painful," Layton too often descends to pointless vituperation, which is a waste of his powers.

D309 McSweeney, Kerry. Rev. of *Lovers and Lesser Men* and *Engagements: The Prose of Irving Layton*. *Queen's Quarterly*, 80 (Summer 1973), 325.

Engagements: The Prose of Irving Layton is a useful collection, although more judicious editing would have eliminated some of the more "ephemeral" and "puerile" pieces.

D310 Christy, Jim. "Down for the Count." *Canadian Literature*, No. 60 (Spring 1974), pp. 126–28.

Layton's prose is boring and pedestrian, ranging from the "ridiculous" to "workaday mediocre"; his verbal attacks lack openness. His views on sex and women are out of date, and his political views exalt American multinational corporations at the expense of the suffering of the world.

D311 Warkentin, Germaine. "Layton's World." Rev. of *Lovers and Lesser Men* and *Engagements: The Prose* of *Irving Layton. The Lakehead University Review*, 7, No. 1 (Summer 1974), 149–51.

Layton's prose is unified by an obsessive concern with defending the poet against a philistine society. Unlike his poetry, his prose has a "wearying consistency."

Taking Sides: The Collected Social and Political Writings

D312 Jonas, George. "Enlightening Thunderer." *Books in Canada*, May 1978, p. 15.

Layton's extreme self-confidence is attractive, even if it does lead him into positions that are hard to defend. He is most likeable for being a "militant democrat," least likeable for "his demands for unconditional homage."

D313 Fetherling, Doug. "The Ornery Essays of Citizen Layton." *Saturday Night*, June 1978, pp. 67–68. Rpt. ("Poetry Chronicle: viii") in *The Blue Notebook: Reports on Canadian Culture*. By Doug Fetherling. Oakville, Ont.: Mosaic, 1985, pp. 62–64.

This book is valuable for its biographical perspective on Layton's career, but the entries are generally dated and transient. In contrast with *Engagements: The Prose of Irving Layton*, this collection is "slapdash." The techniques Layton uses to break down the resistance that many have to poetry and what it tells them does not work so well in his political writing, although it does make him a more complete figure.

D314 Solecki, Sam. Rev. of *Taking Sides: The Collected Social and Political Writings. The Canadian Forum*, June–July 1978, pp. 38–39.

Apart from an interview with Eli Mandel and four articles on film, the volume is generally trivia that is not worth repeating. Most of Layton's comments on politics and social issues are neither interesting nor perceptive.

D315 Smith, Patricia Keeney. "Some Recent Layton Items." Rev. of *The Poems of Irving Layton*, by Irving Layton, ed. Eli Mandel; *The Tightrope Dancer*, by Irving Layton; *Taking Sides: The Collected Social and Political Writings*, ed. Howard Aster; *There Were No Signs*, by Irving Layton; "The Farting Jesus: Layton and the Heroic Vitalists," by Wynne Francis; "Irving Layton, Pseudo-Prophet — A Reappraisal," by Peter Hunt; *Irving Layton: The Poet and His Critics*, ed. Seymour Mayne; "An Interview with Irving Layton," by Kenneth Sherman; "Nietzsche and Overcoming," by Kurt Van Wilt; and "Jewish Themes in the Works of Irving Layton," by Howard Baker. *Canadian Poetry: Studies, Documents, Reviews*, No. 4 (Spring–Summer 1979), pp. 126–27.

Taking Sides: The Collected Social and Political Writings is not as impressive as other works by Layton, since it contains much of his ephemeral journalism and is poorly edited. Layton's prose is "contradictory and arbitrary, the style alternately careless and inspired, creating a maddeningly uneven combination."

D316 Djwa, Sandra. "Letters in Canada: 1978. Humanities." *University of Toronto Quarterly*, 18 (Summer 1979), 447–51.

This collection "chronicles Layton's concept of the function of the artist within the context of his changing political and social thought," as well as "his preoccupation with the Holocaust." It also helps explain his assumption of Nietzschean ideas. The editing, however, could be more thorough.

D317 Robinson, John. "A Myth-Making Bug." Rev. of *Taking Sides: The Collected Social and Political*

Writings, ed. Howard Aster; and *The Universe Ends at Sherbourne & Queen*, by Ted Plantos. *Canadian Literature*, No. 84 (Spring 1980), pp. 127–28.

Layton's attempts to mythologize himself through his writings fail because of his self-contradictions. The book is a curious mixture of fine criticism and astute comments with inaccurate statements and impressionistic generalities.

D318 Harding, Anthony John. "In Debate." *Canadian Literature*, No. 98 (Autumn 1983), pp. 102–04.

Much of Layton's political writing is marred by insupportable backing of American and Israeli right-wing militaristic policies. Some of the articles contradict each other, and careless editing leads to frequent errors and inconsistencies; ". . . an accurate bibliography of Layton's writings would have been far more useful."

An Unlikely Affair

D319 Duffy, Dennis. "An Unlikely Affair." *The Globe and Mail* [Toronto], 5 April 1980, Entertainment, p. E13.

These letters were not worth publishing. On Rath's side they are full of "hero-worshipping, loyal, self-effacing, frustrated pleadings and praises." Layton's are full of "complaints at the invincible ignorance, callousness and contrariety of the universe."

D320 Sutherland, Fraser. "The Rooster, the Hen, and the Ego." Rev. of *The Love Poems of Irving Layton, For My Neighbours in Hell*, and *An Unlikely Affair. Books in Canada*, June–July 1980, pp. 8–9.

The lack of an Index and editorial notes limits the usefulness of *An Unlikely Affair*. Both Layton and Rath come across as decent, sincere people. Layton only rarely lapses into bombast or diatribe.

D321 Dempster, Barry. Rev. of *An Unlikely Affair. Quill & Quire*, July 1980, p. 58.

The Irving Layton-Dorothy Rath relationship was more interesting to the participants than to the observers and would have been better served by their writing a poem about each other.

D322 McClung, Ellen. Rev. of *An Unlikely Affair. Canadian Book Review Annual: 1980*. Ed. Dean Tudor, Nancy Tudor, and Betsy Struthers. Toronto: Simon & Pierre, 1982, pp. 156–57.

Dorothy Rath's "menopausal hysteria" and Irving Layton's "flourishing self-interest" prevent the reader from any appreciation of their relationship. Her letters seem to have been written with publication in mind, while Layton wrote because he saw Rath as "a fan and a useful press clipper." Few of the letters have any literary or historical value.

Wild Gooseberries: The Selected Letters of Irving Layton

D323 Sutherland, Fraser. "Ecstasy and Terror." *The Globe and Mail* [Toronto], 14 Oct. 1989, p. C9.

These letters are "a witch's brew of inconsistencies and contradictions." "Dichotomies fuel his [Layton's] poetic motor and, misfire though it often does, what a powerful engine it is."

D324 Taylor, Noel. "Stinging Letters from Mellowing Poet." *The Citizen* [Ottawa], 28 Oct. 1989, p. H3.

These letters "reveal the poet Layton in all his aspects." More recent letters have less passion than the earlier ones.

D325 Yanofsky, Joel. "Irving Layton's Contradictions." *The Gazette* [Montreal], 28 Oct. 1989, p. K12.

These letters, chronicling Layton's continuous battle with the literary establishment, show him "happiest when he is talking about himself." He "has grown old and weary fighting a losing battle" with a world indifferent to poetry.

D326 Wayne, Joyce. "Canlit's Lone Wolf." *Saturday Magazine* [*The Toronto Star*], 18 Nov. 1989, p. M13.

While the book would have benefited from a more objective editorial stance, these letters are important for showing how Layton's battles altered the course of Canadian literature. The split with Louis Dudek is particularly important. But only in the letters to Desmond Pacey is there any introspection or self-doubt.

Irving Layton & Robert Creeley: The Complete Correspondence, 1953–1978

D327 Bowering, George. "Poets' Letters Open Window on Post-War CanLit." *The Globe and Mail* [Toronto], 1 Sept. 1990, p. C8.

At last the attention to more recent Canadian literature is being balanced by more attention to the 1945–60 period. In these letters, Layton comes across as naïve, "eager for publication and somewhat self-absorbed." This book is a "significant contribution to the historical and critical study of Canadian and American poetry."

D328 Beardsley, Doug. Rev. of *Irving Layton & Robert Creeley: The Complete Correspondence, 1953–1978*. *The Victoria Times-Colonist*, 2 Sept. 1990, p. B5.

This book is notable for "Creeley's post modern eye and ear," its reminder of the important role Raymond Souster played in introducing postmodern writing to Canada, and many profiles of people and issues of this time.

Waiting for the Messiah: A Memoir

D329 Skelton, Robin. "Two Looks at Irving Layton: Warts and All, and All but Warts." Rev. of *Waiting for the Messiah: A Memoir*, by Irving Layton; and *Irving Layton: A Portrait*, by Elspeth Cameron. *Quill & Quire*, Oct. 1985, p. 44.

Viewing Elspeth Cameron's biography of Layton (C9) along with Layton's memoir, one gets "a curiously stereoscopic effect, the Layton passion and self-regard bringing solidity to the sharp outlines of Cameron's picture." While Layton's autobiography has a few minor flaws, he "writes with such vitality that his sins may be excused."

D330 Adachi, Ken. "Looking at Layton from Inside and Out." Rev. of *Waiting for the Messiah: A Memoir*, by Irving Layton; and *Irving Layton: A Portrait*, by Elspeth Cameron. *The Toronto Star*, 19 Oct. 1985, p. M4.

Layton "has had the nerve to show himself just as he was in his youth.... The most powerful moments come in Layton's anguished pondering of his relationship with Faye Lynch ...," his first wife.

D331 Yanofsky, Joel. "Irving Layton: Canada's Legendary Poet Shows How Much He Is His Own Invention." Rev. of *Waiting for the Messiah: A Memoir*, by Irving Layton; and *Irving Layton: A Portrait*, by Elspeth Cameron. *The Gazette* [Montreal], 19 Oct. 1985, p. H1.

Layton's "excess and overdramatization" is sometimes provocative, sometimes tiresome. Aggressiveness and disgust pervade the book; his position is so well defended as to make sympathy with his position superfluous.

D332 Mills, Allen. "Two Views of Irving Layton." Rev. of *Irving Layton: A Portrait*, by Elspeth Cameron; and

Waiting for the Messiah: A Memoir, by Irving Layton. *Winnipeg Free Press*, 26 Oct. 1985, p. 74.

While there are "some loving accounts of his [Layton's] early life and some useful descriptions of literary and political friendships," *Waiting for the Messiah: A Memoir* is disappointing, marred by a "cold cynicism" to his friends and himself.

D333 Johnson, Brian D. "A Bull in the Literary China Shop." Rev. of *Irving Layton: A Portrait*, by Elspeth Cameron; and *Waiting for the Messiah: A Memoir*, by Irving Layton. *Maclean's*, 28 Oct. 1985, p. 64.

Layton "now seems obsessed with bronzing his ego for posterity." He "warms himself by the fire of his own flamboyant delusions; . . . his account bristles with passion and conceit."

D334 Powe, B.W. "Waiting for Israel Lazarovitch." Rev. of *Irving Layton: A Portrait*, by Elspeth Cameron; and *Waiting for the Messiah: A Memoir*, by Irving Layton. *Books in Canada*, Nov. 1985, pp. 16–18.

Layton is as guilty here of the racialist stereotyping as is Elspeth Cameron in her book. While *Waiting for the Messiah: A Memoir* has some good passages, helping to illuminate Layton's links with nineteenth century writing, it is not the "unmasking many had hoped for."

D335 Precosky, Don. Rev. of *Waiting for the Messiah: A Memoir. Canadian Book Review Annual: 1985*. Ed. Dean Tudor and Ann Tudor. Toronto: Simon and Pierre, 1986, pp. 65–66.

The contents of this book are surprisingly controlled. "The last 30 pages" are especially effective at conveying "his own sense of youthful excitement and optimism."

D336 Jackson, Marni. "Another Nose-Thumbing Gesture from Irving Layton." *Chatelaine*, Feb. 1986, Showtime, p. 4.

This book is "alarmingly candid, boastful and true to Layton's lifelong vocation as a poet." Readers may not always approve, but they will be "at least enthralled."

D337 Drache, Sharon. Rev. of *Waiting for the Messiah: A Memoir. Poetry Canada Review*, 7, No. 4 (Summer 1986), 40–41.

This "splendidly vital autobiography" "tries to assess with candour and wisdom who he [Layton] is." His is "a life remarkably and daringly lived for the sake of art and for the sake of his unique, yet, Jewish self."

D338 Wiens, Erwin. Rev. of *Irving Layton: A Portrait*, by Elspeth Cameron; and *Waiting for the Messiah: A Memoir*, by Irving Layton. *Journal of Canadian Poetry*, 2 (1987), 148–52, 154.

The centre of this book "is the political street-life of Jewish Montreal in the thirties." Its weakest parts illustrate Layton "consciously allegorizing the people and events of his life." At its best, he is shown "ruminating among the fragments of his memory and making new discoveries about himself," engaging "the conflicts and contradictions" that pervade his life and work.

D339 Forst, Graham. "Zarathustran." Rev. of *Waiting for the Messiah: A Memoir*, by Irving Layton; and *Nietzsche: Life as Literature*, by Alexander Nehamas. *Canadian Literature*, No. 112 (Spring 1987), pp. 109–10.

Both Nietzsche and Layton insist "on the obligation of the artist to 'create himself' out of the fabric of his life and work." Both believe that the artist must continually fashion his life as he fashions his work, "thereby continually creating and recreating the Messiah."

D340 Herman, Peter. Rev. of *Waiting for the Messiah: A Memoir*. RUBICON [McGill Univ.], No. 8 (Spring 1987), pp. 181-83.

Layton's "thoughtful, even elegiac approach" is a welcome change from his usually bitterly polemical prose. It is hard to know how much he has fictionalized, but he avoids "self-panegyric." The book is especially valuable for Layton's tracing of his formative years as a poet.

D341 Smith, Patricia Keeney. "Elspeth Cameron and Irving Layton." Rev. of *Irving Layton: A Portrait*, by Elspeth Cameron; and *Waiting for the Messiah: A Memoir*, by Irving Layton. *University of Toronto Quarterly*, 56 (Spring 1987), 468-70.

Layton's *Waiting for the Messiah: A Memoir* is often "thrilling" in the way Layton traces the origins of his positions that "have remained unchanged throughout . . . [his] creative lifetime," although much of it is spoiled by Layton's doing the reader's thinking. His dedication to poetry is revealed as "the fact that would control his existence."

D342 Kirshner, Sheldon. "Layton's Turbulent Early Years." *The Canadian Jewish News* [Toronto], 26 Nov. 1987, p. 8.

"Writing in a sparkling prose style, Layton paints a vivid picture of a budding poet who must overcome many obstacles before he can fulfill himself artistically." Kirshner summarizes Layton's early life as presented in this book.

Canadian Poems 1850-1952

D343 Crawley, Alan. Rev. of *Canadian Poems 1850-1952*, ed. Irving Layton and Louis Dudek; *Trial of a City*

and Other Verse, by Earle Birney; and *Border River*, by A.G. Bailey. *Critically Speaking*. CBC Radio, 1 Feb. 1952.

Canadian Poems 1850-1952 may prove useful for future generations, although it would have been better if some of the older poems had been omitted and some "promising new species" included. This book demonstrates "close agreement in opinion and taste between the editors."

D344 Sandwell, B.K. "Our Poets: New Anthology." *Saturday Night*, 20 Dec. 1952, p. 7.

Compared to John Garvin's anthology, this book includes more women and more recent poets. It rejects the "genteel tradition," but avoids vulgarity.

D345 May, James Boyer. "Cum Laude." CIV/n, No. 2 (April 1953), pp. 20-21. Rpt. in *CIV/n: A Literary Magazine of the 50's*. Ed. Aileen Collins. Montreal: Véhicule, 1983, pp. 57-59.

Editors Irving Layton and Louis Dudek have done an excellent job in winnowing the best of Canadian poetry. "Practically everything here has elements of validity for today's intelligent study." Phyllis Webb's poetry is especially praiseworthy.

D346 M., A. [Creeley, Robert]. Rev. of *Contact*, ed. Raymond Souster; *Cerberus*, by Irving Layton, Louis Dudek, and Raymond Souster; *Twenty-Four Poems*, by Louis Dudek; *The Black Huntsmen* and *Love the Conqueror Worm*, by Irving Layton; and *Canadian Poems 1850-1952*, ed. Irving Layton. *The Black Mountain Review* [Black Mountain, N.C.], 1, No. 1 (Spring 1954), 51, 53. Rpt. ("Canadian Poetry 1954") in *A Quick Graph: The Collected Notes & Essays*. By Robert Creeley. Ed. Donald Allen. San Francisco: Four Seasons Foundation, 1970, pp. 231-32. Rpt. (excerpt — rev. of *Cerberus, The Black*

Huntsmen, Love the Conqueror Worm, and *Canadian Poems 1850–1952*) in *Irving Layton: The Poet and His Critics.* Ed. Seymour Mayne. Toronto: McGraw-Hill Ryerson, 1978, pp. 35–36.

Creeley comments on Layton's work in general, rather than reviewing any of his books in specific. See D10 for annotation.

D347 Frye, Northrop. "Letters in Canada: 1953. Poetry." *University of Toronto Quarterly,* 23 (April 1954), 261. Rpt. ("Letters in Canada: 1953") in *The Bush Garden: Essays on Canadian Imagination.* By Northrop Frye. Toronto: House of Anansi, 1971, p. 31.

This book presents "fresh insights and discoveries" and is "well worth examining."

Poems for 27 Cents

D348 Bowering George. "A Quarter's Worth of Poetry." *TISH,* Feb. 1962, p. 12. Rpt. in *TISH: No. 1–19.* Ed. Frank Davey. Vancouver: Talonbooks 1975, pp. 127–28.

Layton's Introduction is "extrapoetical ranting." Of the four poets included, "Gertrude Katz works with sound better than anyone in the book . . . ," while Alan Pearson is the most "promising."

D349 Scott, Peter Dale. "Turning New Leaves." *The Canadian Forum,* Feb. 1962, p. 260.

Some of the poems, especially those by Alan Pearson, augur well for the future, but Layton's "intolerant low-brow truculence" would be better out of it.

D350 Cogswell, Fred. "Two Anthologies." Rev. of *Poems for 27 Cents,* ed. Irving Layton; and *Poetry 62,* ed. Eli Mandel. *The Fiddlehead,* No. 52 (Spring 1962), p. 62.

Poems for 27 Cents "contains a sound and lively introduction by Irving Layton, and a group of economically written, neat poems by young Montreal poets."

Love Where the Nights Are Long: An Anthology of Canadian Love Poems

D351 Jones, Paul P.H. "Canadian Love Poems." *The Gazette* [Montreal], 12 Jan. 1963, p. 26.

Layton's Introduction is excessive in its "honest enthusiasm," but the poems are "good and surprisingly catholic." Harold Town's illustrations are "uniformly excellent" in their suggestiveness of the "half-recalled reality of passion."

D352 Rowe, Percy. "50 Below Zero." *The Telegram* [Toronto], 12 Jan. 1963, p. 35.

Layton's Introduction "is the daftest thing I've ever read. . . . his arguments are as misguided as his prose is mellifluous." There is nothing here "that I could remember the next day."

D353 P[ercy]., H.R. Rev. of *Poet's Choice,* ed. Paul Engle and Joseph Langland; and *Love Where the Nights Are Long: An Anthology of Canadian Love Poems,* ed. Irving Layton, illus. Harold Town. *The Canadian Author & Bookman,* 8, No. 3 (Spring 1963), pp. 12–13.

Layton's Introduction takes "a glorious and rebellious stand." "We go into this book apparelled in our own memories, hugging close our own secret splendours, and if our equipment is adequate we meet the poets on their own terms . . . . If it is not adequate, we . . . go our own way . . . never knowing what we have missed."

Selected Record Reviews

Irving Layton (Caedmon)

D354 "The Voice of Canadian Poetry." Rev. of *Irving Layton* (Caedmon), by Irving Layton; *Pictures from a Dying Landscape*, by David Watmough; *Live Songs*, by Leonard Cohen; *Canadada*, by The Four Horsemen; and *Four Kingston Poets in a Reading Prepared for the National Arts Centre*, by Tom Marshall, Stuart MacKinnon, Gail Fox, and David Helwig. *Quill & Quire*, Aug. 1973, p. 10.

Layton presents himself "without bombast and haranguing." "His poetry can sing as well as snarl, and should be heard to be best appreciated."

D355 Rockett, W.R. "CBC Now Offering Poets on Record." Rev. of *Open Secret*, by Gwendolyn MacEwen; *Maritimes*, by Alden Nowlan; *Ontario*, by Al Purdy; and *Irving Layton* (Caedmon), by Irving Layton. *The Toronto Star*, 25 Aug. 1973, p. H6.

While it is good to have this record, Layton is "a terrible reader." His comments "are arrogant, often annoying, sometimes grandiose."

D356 Swan, Susan. "Wholly Moses." Rev. of *Irving Layton* (Caedmon), by Irving Layton; and *Live Songs*, by Leonard Cohen. *Books in Canada*, Oct. 1973, p. 11.

"Both poets are evangelists," although it would be possible to imagine Layton without an audience. The subject matter comprises the standard Layton range from the apocalyptic to the beautiful.

Index to Critics Listed in the Bibliography

Lust, Peter C83, C140
Lyons, Roberta C526

M., A. [Creeley, Robert] [see also Creeley, Robert] D10, D17, D20, D346
Maag, Trudy C54
MacCallum, Hugh D95, D108, D115
MacCulloch, Clare C213, C214, C718, D148
MacEwen, Gwendolyn D172
MacFadden, David C732
MacLulich, T.D. C737
MacLure, Millar D35
Macpherson, Jay C704
MacSkimming, Roy D166
Mader, Phil C510
Maggs, Arnaud C670
Malka, prod. C667
Mallinson, Jean D122, D300
Maltby, G.M. C102
Mandel, Eli C3, C8, C183, C233, C252, C259, C277, C286, C287, C288, C400, C663, C667, D55, D61, D68, D109, D119, D293, D294
Mandel, Eli, ed. C27
Mannis, Harry, host C611
Mansbridge, Francis C504, C515
Mantle, K. C207
Mantz, Douglas C266, C613
Marchand, Blaine C357
Marchand, Philip C658
Marcotte, Gilles D62
Marriott, Anne D8, D19
Marsh, Bruce C595
Marshall, Tom C325, C708, D121, D162, D299
Martin, Donald C648
Martin, Robert C209
Martindale, Sheila D260
Mason, Grace A. C95
Mathews, John Pengwerne C70

Mathews, Robin C297, C298
Matson, Patricia C505
May, James Boyer D345
Mayne, Seymour C221, C243, C267, C299, C300, C425, C532, C667, C753, D134
Mayne, Seymour, ed. C4, C6, C24, C26, C29, C42, C51, C55, C141, C189, C227, C232, C244, C281, C299, C300, C425, C553, C587, C696, C712, C713, D2, D7, D9, D10, D15, D17, D19, D20, D22, D23, D26, D27, D29, D31, D34, D37, D39, D43, D46, D49, D50, D55, D57, D58, D59, D60, D61, D62, D63, D65, D66, D67, D69, D70, D76, D81, D82, D86, D91, D93, D94, D104, D109, D110, D119, D121, D125, D129, D133, D135, D142, D150, D152, D163, D172, D281, D282, D286, D287, D289, D293, D294, D299, D304, D306, D346
McClung, Ellen D322
McCracken, Melinda C142
McCrae, A. C719
McCuaig, Norman D296
McCullagh, Joan C268
McCulloch, Peter B. C360
McDonald, Marci C170
McFadden, David C732
McGoogan, Kenneth C454
McGregor, Gaile C426
McKeown, Bob C605
McLean, Ross, prod. and dir. C556
McLeod, A.L., ed. C62, C327
McNamara, Eugene D190
McPherson, David C599
McPherson, Hugo C133
McQuarrie, Jane C407
McSweeney, Kerry D149, D309
McWhirter, George C457
Mercer, Anne V. C387, C407
Messenger, Cynthia D278

Dennis Lee
An Annotated Bibliography

Mary MacPherson

Acknowledgements

The author gratefully acknowledges Ellen Quigley for the years of detailed work she has contributed, the Social Sciences and Humanities Research Council of Canada for their generosity and acknowledgement of the significance of the work, and Dennis Lee for his friendship and inspiration over the years.

Introduction

Dennis Lee is renowned among children (and their parents) for such works as *Alligator Pie* and *Garbage Delight*. They have found pleasure in Lee's playfulness and his experimentation with words and sounds and might be surprised to learn that this same author writes "serious" works. Lee has written extensively for adults as well as children, and in all cases his fascination with language is apparent. Although his writing is often amusing, he treats the job of writing and editing seriously.

While generally favourable, critical reception of Lee's work has been somewhat mixed. This reaction is not surprising for Lee is somewhat unusual in his desire to write for children as well as adults, experimenting with and employing several different formats, and covering a broad range of topics. Doug Fetherling describes Lee as one of Canada's most respected and influential poets and also one of the most popular, but not for the same books. He is valued by colleagues for his rare abilities as poet, critic, and editor and beloved as the writer of children's verse (C230).

With the publication of his first book of adult poetry, *Kingdom of Absence* (1967), Lee came to the attention of the critics who were quick to point out that he had not yet found an "adequate poetic medium," he lacked consistent "authentic voice" and mastery of form, nor did he know "the difference between rhetoric and poetry" (D6, C233, D5). Despite the inadequacies of form, his powerful imagery evokes a "terrifyingly dark world view" through the themes of alienation and recognition of the void (D2, D6). It is a "single poem depicting one man's . . . search for meaning"

but there is also "some of the funniest poetry" (C4). In later works the criticism of Lee's form is tempered by praise but there are other similarities to *Kingdom* in the types of themes he explores, the evocative nature of his imagery, and the amusing quality of his work.

Lee's pessimistic view of the world and of Canada in particular colours many of his poems. He laments for his country, and sees it as being destroyed by Americans (D12). Through his poetry he links his "spiritual anguish to Canada's political indecisions and to a technology and empire belonging to the United States of America" (C196). R.D. MacDonald compares Lee's *Civil Elegies* to George Grant's *Lament for a Nation* and notes the differences in form of language as well as "attitudes toward and accounts of Canada's history, the failure of a colonial people to achieve an independent nation of their own." He is critical of Lee, claiming that he "does not confront the complexities and consequences of our own industrial society" and that ". . . his poem seems insufficiently thought out" (C146).

Many of Lee's poems suggest that he has "given up on Canada" but the founding of the House of Anansi Press helped increase independent publishing in Canada and is a tangible example of Lee's desire to improve things in his country (D11). It's also an indication of his view of the importance of the writer in society. This idea is explored in several of his poems, and in particular in "The Death of Harold Ladoo." The death of the young writer initiates Lee's search for the importance of the poet in a technological age, a theme that is reiterated in the shorter poems in *The Gods* (D20). It places the poet in the context of contemporary society, going beyond elegy to what it means to be a writer, and grappling with the inadequacies of poetry in the face of death (D29, D27, D19). It is an honest and humane poem, balancing contentment and anger, combining subjective reaction with factual details and biography to produce a work that will probably become a classic (D22). Gail Fox describes "Ladoo" as Lee's finest poem to date, David Cavanagh says that it is his most powerful work, and Ian

Pearson claims that it is the most significant Canadian poem of the decade (D21, D27, D19). Those who knew Harold Ladoo will be "touched deeply by this poem" (D29).

Lee steps out of his role of poet with *Savage Fields: An Essay in Literature and Cosmology*, in which he analyzes Leonard Cohen's *Beautiful Losers* and Michael Ondaatje's *The Collected Works of Billy the Kid*. His theme is too ambitious, however, and his "overview of western civilization suffers from being based on a very limited and highly idiosyncratic sampling of its contemporary products" (D131). Charles Steele agrees that the generalizations are questionable, based on a discussion of only two texts, but his analysis of the two works is "thorough and productive" (D139). J.J. Healy finds the work "enigmatic . . . dense . . . difficult," while to Scott Symons it is a book possessing "breadth, scope, profundity, force, insight" (D136, D132). Lee describes a "perfect system of philosophical analysis which is brilliant and challenging and utterly wrongheaded" based on misuse of Heidegger's cosmology and backed up by distortions of Cohen's and Ondaatje's works (C233). Even Perry Nodelman, one of Lee's most stalwart defenders, finds Lee's arguments unconvincing and accuses him of misrepresenting the authors' intentions. It is really "about Dennis Lee trying to come to terms with his own version of the universe" (D133).

The area in which no one can criticize Lee is in his work as an editor, where he excels. He does much more than most editors would, and often uses unique methods, being "devious, insightful, gaining his means by misdirection and mind-reading brilliance" (C137). He "probably comes closest to Canada's version of the legendary editor . . . coaxing and bullying along the way" in order to "push the writer towards a truth . . . questioning you . . . himself . . . the universe" (C140, C136). Graeme Gibson recalls how lucky he was to be rejected by mainstream publishers only to be accepted by Anansi and helped by Lee to make the most of his book *Five Legs* (C127). Lee's allegiance is to the book, not the author, his goal not necessarily to make the book a success but to produce the best one possible. "Lee-as-editor . . . [is] a National asset" (C138).

Through his work as editor, publisher, poet, and critic, Lee has done a lot to shape the current literary world, but that is recognized only by others in the field, not the general public. To them he is a children's writer, and it is through his children's poetry that he can best accomplish some of his goals. One of them is to try to bridge the gap between poetry's traditional readership and a wider, less sophisticated audience. His sense of exploration and experimentation has free rein here. Sometimes his use of slang combined with poetic expressions works well and sometimes it falls short, but even when unsuccessful, Lee is expanding the frontiers (D29). His first big success with children's poetry was *Alligator Pie*, which has sold over 100,000 copies and is Canada's best-selling children's book since *Anne of Green Gables* (C103). It "may rewardingly be read by people of almost any age" and demonstrates Lee's "fine sense of the strangeness of words" (D53). It was popular with the critics as well, most of whom praised his playfulness, his sense of humour and fun, his originality, and his sense of rhythm. In fact his early works are regarded so highly that there is very little negative criticism. One critic gives *Alligator Pie* a "borderline" recommendation and another claims that "humour is rare in this uneven poetry collection" (D72, D77). This contrasts sharply with such praise as "well constructed verse with powerful word usage and considerable originality . . . marvelously diverting, lyrically beautiful, or funny" (D76). His work shows "honest craft, originality and an understanding of children" (C117). Lee has actually created a "Canadian body of . . . poetry for young children." His verse is very lively, filled with puns, tongue-twisters, and inverted words. His strong repetitious rhythms are similar to Mother Goose, R.L. Stevenson, and A.A. Milne (C185). The poems are filled with "wonder" and "excitement," creating a world full of entrancing jingles, sprightly humour, and flights of fancy (D54, D56). He displays a "fine poetic imagination and sensitivity to language" resulting in "fresh, contemporary and Canadian books" which are "major events in our literary life" (D57).

Later works win equally high praise although there is more of a mixture of criticism as well. *Garbage Delight* won the CLA Book of the Year Award in 1977 and although it is described by some as Lee's best book of children's poetry, it also includes "conventional, old-time juvenile jingles" (D88, D89). It has some "quiet, inward poems" and those in *Nicholas Knock* have a "philosophical and thought-provoking quality" (C57, C185). *Jelly Belly* is a "quaintly gentle, evocative book" described as "brilliant" and containing "exactly the right blend of simplicity, fantasy and outrageousness" (D98, D104, D103). It is also called a "mixed blessing" with poetry "marred by loose diction" (C229). *The Ordinary Bath* does not meet the standards set by earlier works and lacks the light humour expected from Lee, despite its vigorous and colourful imagery (D110, D118). Its exuberant tastelessness may offend some adults but, as always, Perry Nodelman finds Lee's writing "hilarious" (D119).

The rhythmic, almost musical quality of his work is also a major factor in his popularity. Whenever Lee gives a poetry reading, his audience is captivated by the magic and vividness of his imagery, and the "musical rhythm that gets one's foot tapping" (C125). James Reaney says that the "magic effect of Lee's poetry for children is to get them chanting and dancing" and Denise Levertov compares Lee's poems to musical scores (C161, C131). He uses a "structured and consistent rhyme scheme that is pleasing to the ear" and "infectious rhythms" to produce poems that "bounce and jog along in the best child-approved manner" (C125, D94, D78).

Lee's children's poetry contrasts sharply with the themes of his serious adult poetry but his "concept of voice or cadence" provides the link between his writing for adults and children (C208). His theory of cadence has been compared to Heidegger's *Mozart's Briefe*, since both emphasize "hearing and seeing" and to Claude Lévi-Strauss'

Mythologiques, although Lee denies any affinity. Whether or not he has been influenced by others, it is an important component of his poetry and helps to make it more accessible to the general public.

Lee is a complex writer whose works generate discussion and commentary. His love of language and talent for using it, whether writing for adult or child, to amuse or criticize, to deal with serious issues or frivolity, have earned him the description as a "poet of sunlight and shadow, of whimsy and despair" (C194).

[That is not the ground — the objects limping]," "xiii [Trees fall back out of meaning;]," "xiv [I dangling in my mundane fever, hanged]," "xv [My first apocalypse was on a Wednesday.]" (B35), "xvi [If there's one thing that really cleans you out]," "xvii [Can do can]" (B25), "xviii [Now they come silently]," "xix [Larry, you were the wild one.]," "xx [Brave boys, good night. What darkness lights your way?]," "xxi [Strung in toronto again,]," "xxii [When I review my troop of scruffy selves]" (B20), "xxiii [I woke on the floes.]" (B26), "xxiv [Where is she now, my slim and driven comrade?]," "xxv [The heroes rode beside me. One was lame]," "xxvi [I drift between two images. An icy plane]" (B27), "xxvii [Absence, be utter. Vacancy, what journeys?]" (B28), "xxviii [The slack air locks and throbs]" (B29), "xxix [Eliot as he passed me]" (B30), "xxx [I seen a]," "xxxi [How I got up here was I could not stand the body-blows on my sensitive]" (B31), "xxxii [I know a lady sabotaged by love,]," "xxxiii [You can not declare but what I speak I know.]," "xxxiv [My subject is the absence of the real]," "xxxv [Lady, in tuition]" (B33), "xxxvi [How often, in muskoka, bedded down]" (B32), "xxxvii [Yes. Only in this absence. When the spring]," "xxxviii [There is a route of secular purgation,]," "xxxix [Until God riddle our cankered souls with light]" (B13), "xl [When, panic-stricken at the praise men give]," "xli [Not sample handfuls of the world's galore,]," "xlii [One beauty —]," and "xliii [Cities of light, and every time]" (B34).

Part I

Works by Dennis Lee

A   Books (Poetry, Children's Poetry, Children's Tales, Poetry Chapbooks, Poetry Chapbooks for Children, Criticism, Prose Chapbooks, Drama, Miscellaneous, and Books Edited), Librettos, Lyrics, Broadsides, Calendars, Audio-Visual Material, Editorial Work, and Manuscripts

Poetry

A1   *Kingdom of Absence.* Preface and back cover W.D. Godfrey. HAP, No. 1. Toronto: House of Ananse [sic; Anansi], 1967. 60 pp.
——— . Back cover Al Purdy and Milton Wilson. Toronto: House of Anansi, 1967. 60 pp.
Includes "i [Lady, till the curfew rings]" (B22), "ii [Dusk, and the bright air falls]" (B19), "iii [Sudden among the grass the]" (B23), "iv [Shad flies bash full tilt against the screen.]" (B24), "v [Like shunting boxcars on a run-down line]," "vi [The great constructs of the mind recede,]," "vii [Of witty desecrations, and the slow]" (B15), "viii [The trumpets of the randy Renaissance]" (B16), "ix [Looney with sunlight, van Gogh stood and stared]" (B14), "x [No, nothing is preserved, in counterplay]," "xi [We explicate the trees but they go sorrowing]" (B21), "xii

A2   *Civil Elegies.* HAP, No. 4. Toronto: House of Anansi, 1968. [48] pp.
Includes "First Elegy [Often I sit in the sun and brooding over the city, always]" (B39), "Second Elegy [The light rides easy on people dozing at noon in Toronto, or]" (B38), "Third Elegy [It would be

343

better maybe if we could stop loving the children]"
(B36), "Fourth Elegy [Among the flaws that mar my
sleep I harbour more than war for I have friends and
lacerations]," "Fifth Elegy [I am one for whom the
world is constantly proving too much —]" (B37),
"Sixth Elegy [I come to the square each time there is
nothing and once, made calm again]," and "Seventh
Elegy [Withdrawal in the gut, accompanied by a]."

A3   *Civil Elegies and Other Poems.* HAP, No. 23. Tor-
      onto: House of Anansi, 1972. 59 pp.
      ——— . [Paperback.] Toronto: House of Anansi,
      1972. 59 pp.
      Includes "Brunswick Avenue" (B42), "Civil Ele-
gies: 1 [Often I sit in the sun and brooding over the
city, always] [B39], 2 [Master and Lord, where]
[B48], 3 [The light rides easy on people dozing at
noon in Toronto, or] [B38], 4 [Among the things
which], 5 [It would be better maybe if we could stop
loving the children] [B36], 6 [I am one for whom the
world is constantly proving too much —] [B37], 7
[Among the flaws that mar my sleep I harbour more
than wars for I have friends and lacerations] [A2 —
"Fourth Elegy"], 8 [I come to the square each time
there is nothing and once, made calm again] [A2 —
"Sixth Elegy"], 9 [Here, as I sit and watch, the rusty
leaves hang taut with departure.]," "Coming Back"
(B53), "400: Coming Home" (B54), "Glad for the
Wrong Reasons" (B55), "He Asks Her," "Heaven
and Earth" (B40), "High Park, by Grenadier Pond"
(B43), "In a Bad Time" (B45), "More Claiming,"
"The Morning of the Second Day: He Tells Her,"
"Night" (B56), "Recollection" (B44), "Sibelius
Park" (B46), "Thursday," "When It Is Over" (B41),
and "Words for the Given" (B47).
      ——— . *Elégies civiles et autres poèmes.* Trans. Marc
Lebel. "Notes de l'Auteur et du Traducteur" Dennis
Lee and Marc Lebel. "Lee, Poète du Processus"

Dennis Lee. Montréal: L'Hexagone, 1980. 107–08,
109–11, 111 pp.
      Includes the original English- and French-language
translation on facing pages: "Brunswick Avenue"
(B42), "Civil Elegies/Élégies Civiles: 1 [Often I sit in
the sun and brooding over the city, always/Souvent
au soleil assis à ruminer la ville, en déploiements]
[B39], 2 [Master and Lord, where/Maître et Seigneur,
où] [B48], 3 [The light rides easy on people dozing
at noon in Toronto, or/La lumière tangue doucement
sur les gens qui roupillent à midi dans Toronto, ou]
[B38], 4 [Among the things which/Parmi les choses
qui], 5 [It would be better maybe if we could stop
loving the children/Ce serait mieux peut-être si nous
pouvions cesser d'aimer les enfants] [B36], 6 [I am
one for whom the world is constantly proving too
much — /Je suis de ceux que le monde finit toujours
par sursaturer —] [B37], 7 [Among the flaws that
mar my sleep I harbour more than wars for I have
friends and lacerations/Parmi les accrocs qui dé-
figurent mon sommeil je couve plus que des guerres
car j'ai des amis et des lacérations] [A2 — "Fourth
Elegy"], 8 [I come to the square each time there is
nothing and once, made calm again/Je m'amène sur
la place chaque fois que c'est le vide et une fois,
rasséréné] [A2 — "Sixth Elegy"], 9 [Here, as I sit and
watch, the rusty leaves hang taut with departure./
Pendant qu'ici je suis assis à regarder, les feuilles
rouillées pendent tendues de départ.]," "Coming
Back/ M'en revenant" (B53), "400: Coming Home/
Route 400: le retour" (B54), "Glad for the Wrong
Reasons/Heureux pour de fausses raisons" (B55),
"He Asks Her/Il lui demande," "Heaven and Earth/
Ciel et terre" (B40), "High Park, by Grenadier Pond/
Quoi que je dise" (B43), "In a Bad Time/Par temps
difficiles" (B45), "More Claiming/Repossession,"
"The Morning of the Second Day: He Tells Her/Au
matin du second jour: il lui dit," "Night/La nuit"

(B56), "Recollection/Je me rappelle" (B44), "Sibelius Park" (B46), "Thursday/Jeudi," "When It Is Over/ Quand c'est fini" (B41), and "Words for the Given/ Mots pour le donné" (B47).

A4   *The Gods.* Toronto: McClelland and Stewart, 1979. 63 pp.
   Includes "Ache of the Real," "After Dinner Music," *The Death of Harold Ladoo* (B63), "1838" (B49), "The Gods" (B65), "Not Abstract Harmonies But" (B60), "Of Eros, in Shiny Degree" (B51), "On a Kazoo," "Remember, Woman," "Song" (B61), "Song: Lay Down" (B62), "Summer Song" (B108), "When I Went Up to Rosedale" (B57), "Yip Yip," and "You Can Climb Down Now" (B67).

A5   *The Difficulty of Living on Other Planets.* Illus. Alan Daniel. Toronto: Macmillan, 1987. 112 pp.
   Includes "The Abominable Fairy of Bloor Street" (B82), "The Academic Odyssey of Wendell Grebe" (see B471), "The Ant and the Elephant," "Ballad of the Bonny Bind," "The Bard of the Universe" (see B467), "Because in Ecstasy," "The Bubble Ring," "The Cat and the Wizard" (B99), "The Coat" (B83), "The Difficulty of Living on Other Planets" (B79), "The Dive of the Ten-Ton Turd," "The Doughnut Hole," "1838" (B49), "Forty Mermaids" (A7), "The Golden Rule" (see B468), "Greatheart and the Brain Drain" (B80), "High Blue Meadows" (see B469), "The Mouse and the Maid" (see B477), "Mr Green and Ms Levine," "Nicholas Knock" (A8), "Odysseus and Tumbleweed" (see B472), "The Presence of Pioneers" (B52), "The Protocol" (see B473), "The Revenge of Santa Clause" (see B478), "The Soul of My Wombat," "Suzie Saw the Blue Balloon," "Tales from 'Sir Blunderbuss'" (see B475), "There Was a Man" (B109), "The Thing" (A8), "A Trip to the Hardware," "When I Went Up to Ottawa" (see

B470), "When I Went Up to Rosedale" (B57), and "Yer Blues" (see B474).

Children's Poetry

A6   *Wiggle to the Laundromat.* Illus. Charles Pachter. Toronto: new, 1970. [32] pp.
   ——. Deluxe ed. Illus. Charles Pachter. Toronto: new, 1970. [32] pp.
   ——. [Paperback.] Illus. Charles Pachter. Toronto: new, 1975. [32] pp.
   Includes "Alligator Pie" (B96), "The Coat" (B83), "The Difficulty of Living on Other Planets" (B79), "The Fishes of Kempenfeldt Bay" (B151), "Flying Out of Holes" (B95), "Holidays" (A20), "In Kamloops" (B102), "Kahshe or Chicoutimi" (B103), "Ookpik" (B88), "Skyscraper" (B105), "Street Song," "Wiggle to the Laundromat" (B89), "Willoughby Wallaby Woo" (see B288), and "The Windypuff Song" (B86).

A7   *Alligator Pie.* Illus. Frank Newfeld. Boston: Houghton Mifflin, 1974. 64 pp.
   ——. Illus. Frank Newfeld. Toronto: Macmillan, 1974. 64 pp.
   ——. [Paperback.] Illus. Frank Newfeld. Toronto: Macmillan, 1974. 64 pp.
   Includes "Alligator Pie" (B96), "Bed Song," "Billy Batter" (B115), "Bouncing Song" (B97), "Bump on Your Thumb" (B98), "The Fishes of Kempenfelt Bay" (B151), "Flying Out of Holes" (B95), "The Friends" (B100), "Higgledy Piggledy," "The Hockey Game (With thanks to A.A. Milne)," "I Found a Silver Dollar" (B87), "If You Should Meet" (B84), "In Kamloops" (B102), "Kahshe or Chicoutimi" (B103), "Like a Giant in a Towel," "Lying on Things," "Mumbo, Jumbo" (B118), "Nicholas Grouch," "On Tuesdays I Polish My Uncle" (B112),

"Ookpik" (B88), "Peter Rabbit," "Psychapoo" (B90), "Rattlesnake Skipping Song," "Singa Songa," "The Sitter and the Butter and the Better Batter Fritter" (B104), "Skyscraper" (B105), "The Special Person" (B107), "Street Song" (A5), "Thinking in Bed," "Tongue Twister" (B110), "Tony Baloney," "Tricking" (B113), "Wiggle to the Laundromat" (B89), "William Lyon Mackenzie King," "Willoughby Wallaby Woo" (see B288), and "Windshield Wipers."

Includes the following prose: "Hockey Sticks and High-Rise: A Postlude."

A8   *Nicholas Knock and Other People*. Illus. Frank Newfeld. Boston: Houghton Mifflin, 1974. 64 pp.

Includes the same contents as the following two editions, except that "Ookpik" is changed to "Nimpkin" in "Ookpik and the Animals," "Ookpik Dancing," and "A Song for Ookpik."

——. Illus. Frank Newfeld. Toronto: Macmillan, 1974. 64 pp.

——. [Paperback.] Illus. Frank Newfeld. Toronto: Macmillan, 1974. 64 pp.

Includes "The Abominable Fairy of Bloor Street" (B82), "The Cat and the Wizard" (B99), "A Child's Song," "The Coat" (B83), "Curse: On a Driver, Who Splashed His New Pants When He Could Have Just as Easily Driven Around the Puddle," "The Cyclone Visitors" (B94), "The Difficulty of Living on Other Planets" (B79), "1838" (B49), "Forty Mermaids," "Going Up North" (B101), "Homage to Moose Factory, Ont," "I Have My Father's Eyes," "Mister Hoobody," "Nicholas Knock," "Oilcan Harry," "Ookpik and the Animals," "Ookpik Dancing," "The Poodle and the Grundiboob," "The Question" (B119), "The Saint's Lament," "A Song for Ookpik" (B106), "Spadina" (B50), "Summer Song" (B108), "There Was a Man" (B109), "The Thing," "To Rec-

ognize the Lesser Glunk . . . ," "Wellington the Skeleton" (B120), "Winter Song," "With My Foot in My Mouth" (B111), and "You Too Lie Down."

A9   *Garbage Delight*. Illus. Frank Newfeld. Boston: Houghton Mifflin, 1977. 64 pp.

——. Illus. Frank Newfeld. Toronto: Macmillan, 1977. 64 pp.

Includes "The Aminals [sic]" (B121), "Bath Song," "Beat Me and Bite Me," "The Bedtime Concert," "Being Five" (B122), "The Big Blue Frog and the Dirty Flannel Dog" (B123), "The Big Molice Pan and the Bertie Dumb," "Bigfoot," "Bike-Twister," "Bloody Bill," "The Bratty Brother (Sister)," "The Coming of Teddy Bears" (B126), "The Fly-Nest," "Garbage Delight" (B91), "Goofus" (B92), "Goofy Song," "Half Way Dressed" (B116), "I Eat Kids Yum Yum!" (B114), "Inspector Dogbone Gets His Man," "The Last Cry of the Damp Fly," "McGonigle's Tail," "The Moon," "The Muddy Puddle," "Muffin and Puffin and Murphy and Me" (B117), "One Sunny Summer's Day" (B124), "The Operation," "The Pair of Pants," "Periwinkle Pizza," "Peter Was a Pilot," "Quintin and Griffin," "A Sasquatch from Saskatchewan," "The Secret Song," "Skindiver," "Smelly Fred," "The Snuggle Bunny," "The Summerhill Fair," "Suzy Grew a Moustache" (B125), "The Swing," "The Tickle Tiger," "The Tiniest Man in the Washing Machine," "What Will You Be?" (B93), and "Worm" (B127).

A10   *Jelly Belly*. Illus. Juan Wijngaard. London, Eng.: Blackie and Son, 1983. 64 pp.

——. Illus. Juan Wijngaard. Toronto: Macmillan, 1983. 64 pp.

——. London, Eng.: Picturemac, 1983. 64 pp.

Includes "Anna Banana" (B135), "The Army Went A-Marching," "The Bear and the Bees," "Bigamy

Bill," "The Birthday Present," "Boogie Tricks," "Bundle-Buggy Boogie" (B131), "Can You Canoe?", "Carey Cut," "Catching," "Chicoutimi Town," "Christmas Tree" (see B479), "Counting Out," "Dawdle, Dawdle, Dawdle," "Dickery Dean," "The Dinosaur Dinner" (see B481), "Dirty Georgie" (A61), "Doctor, Doctor," "Doodle-y-Doo," "Dopey the Dinosaur," "Double-Barrelled Ding-Dong-Bat" (B136), "The Dreadful Doings of Jelly Belly," "Easy, Peasy," "Eh, Mon," "The Excellent Wedding of the Broom and the Mop," "Five Fat Fleas," "Freddy" (B137), "The Garbage Men" (A62), "The Gentle Giant" (A62), "The Ghost and Jenny Jemima," "Going, Going, Gone," "Good Night, Good Night," "Granny Spider" (B129), "Hugh, Hugh" (B142), "Jenny Shall Ride," "The Kitty Ran Up the Tree," "Kitty-Cat, Kitty-Cat," "Knock! Knock!", "Lazy Liza Briggs" (B143), "Little Miss Dimble" (B144), "Little Mr Mousiekin," "The Little Old Man," "The Maple Tree," "Meet Me," "Mr Lister's Dog" (B145), "Mrs Magee," "Mrs Murphy, and Mrs Murphy's Kids" (B132), "My Doodle-Bug Won't Come Home," "News of the Day," "No," "Over and Over," "Peter Stampeder," "Peterkin Pete" (B146), "Pussy-Willow," "The Puzzle" (B152), "The Queen of Sheba's Daughter," "Robber J Badguy" (A62), "Rock Me Easy," "Sailing to Sea" (B149), "The Seven Kinds of Bees," "Shoo, Doggie, Shoo!", "Silverly" (B141), "Skit, Scat," "The Snowstorm," "Spaghetti-O!" (A62), "There Was an Old Lady" (B139), "Three Tickles" (see B483), "Thumbelina," "The Tiny Perfect Mayor," "Torontosaurus Rex," "Under the Garden Hose" (A62), "Up in North Ontario" (B147), "The Voyage" (B150), "William Lyon Mackenzie" (B148), and "Zinga, Zinga."

A11   *The Dennis Lee Big Book*. Illus. B. Klunder. Toronto: Gage, 1985. 34 pp.

Includes "Alligator Pie" (B96), "Being Five" (B122), "Billy Batter" (B115), "The Coming of Teddy Bears" (B126), "Dickery Dean" (A10), "The Dinosaur Dinner" (see B481), "Dirty Georgie" (A61), "The Gentle Giant" (A62), "Good Night, Good Night" (A10), "I Eat Kids Yum Yum!" (B114), "I Found a Silver Dollar" (B87), "The Kitty Ran Up the Tree" (A10), "Little Miss Dimble" (B144), "The Muddy Puddle" (A9), "My Doodle-Bug Won't Come Home" (A10), "Psychapoo" (B90), "Skyscraper" (B105), "There Was an Old Lady" (B139), and "Tony Baloney" (A7).

A12   *The Ice Cream Store*. Illus. David McPhail. Toronto: Alligator-HarperCollins, 1991. [64] pp.

Includes "Aki," "Antelope, a Cantaloupe," "Bappy Earthday!", "Betty, Betty," "Big Bad Billy," "The Butterfly," "By the Light of the Moon," "Chica," "Chickadee, Fly!", "Chillybones," "Chitter-Chatter-Chipmunk" (B128), "Cool Pillow," "Cops and Robbers," "Cowardy, Cowardy Custard," "The Dangerous Tale of the Dinosaurus Dishes," "Digging a Hole to Australia," "Dimpleton the Simpleton," "Ding, Dong," "Doh-Si-Doh," "Dooby, Dooby," "Down in Patagonia," "The Fib," "Fog Lifting," "Follow That Whale," "Goof on the Roof," "Green for Go," "Gumbo Stew," "Hammy, the Escape Hamster," "Herman the Hoofer," "A Home Like a Hiccup," "I Know It's Time," "The Ice Cream Store," "I'm Not a Naughty Daughter," "I'm Not Coming Out," "Jenny the Juvenile Juggler" (B138), "Jumbo," "The Kitsilano Kid," "Lickety-Split," "The Lottery Dream of Miss Patricia Pig," "Lucy Go Lightly," "Lulu," "Mabel," "Mary Ellen Montague," "Maxie and the Taxi," "The Motorcycle Driver," "The Mouse That Lives on the Moon," "Mrs. Mitchell's Underwear," "My Life in a Shoe," "Night Song," "Nine Black Cats," "The Perfect

Pets," "Peter Ping and Patrick Pong," "The Pig in Pink Pyjamas," "Polliwogs," "Popping Corn," "Queen for a Day," "Rose Petals Pink," "The Secret Place," "Secrets," "Shake-'n'-Bake a Jelly," "Skinny Marinka Dinka," "Skipping (Olga)," "Snick, Snack," "Stinky," "The Visit," "Waiter, Dear Waiter," "The Water-Go-Round," "Wild!", and "A Wonderful Trip in a Rocketship."

Children's Tales

A13   *The Ordinary Bath.* Illus. Jon McKee. [Instigator Lou Fedorkow.] Toronto: Magook/McClelland and Stewart, 1979. [48] pp.
       See A70.

A14   *Lizzy's Lion.* Illus. Marie-Louise Gay. Toronto: Stoddart, 1984. [28] pp.
       See B153.

Poetry Chapbooks

A15   *Not Abstract Harmonies But.* Kanchenjunga Chapbook, No. 1. San Francisco: Kanchenjunga, 1974. [4] pp.
       Includes "Not Abstract Harmonies But" (B60).

A16   *The Death of Harold Ladoo.* New York: *boundary 2: a journal of postmodern literature* [State Univ. of New York at Binghamton] Offprint, 1976. 26 pp.
       ——— . Kanchenjunga Chapbook, No. 6. San Francisco: Kanchenjunga, 1976. 25 pp.
       Includes *The Death of Harold Ladoo* (B63).

A17   *Miscellany.* Toronto: n.p., 1977. [24] pp.
       Includes "Another Love Song," "The Dark," "1838" (B49), "Greatheart and the Brain Drain" (B80), "If I Could Fly," "King of the Broken Castle,"

"Lady Zero" (B64), "Love Song," "Of Eros, in Shiny Degree" (B51), "The Presence of Pioneers" (B52), "The Saint's Lament" (A8), "Song for His Imaginary Lady," "The Stopover," "Summer Song" (B108), "Wendigo," "When I Went Up to Rosedale" (B57), and "Winter Song" (A8).

A18   *The Gods.* Kanchenjunga Chapbook, No. 9. San Francisco: Kanchenjunga, 1978. [8] pp.
       Includes "The Gods" (B65).

A19   *The Difficulty of Living on Other Planets.* Illus. Alan Daniel. Toronto: Canadian Booksellers Association, [1987]. 8 pp.
       Includes "The Bard of the Universe" (see B467), "The Difficulty of Living on Other Planets" (B79), "The Golden Rule" (see B468), and "When I Went Up to Ottawa" (see B470).

Poetry Chapbooks for Children

A20   WIGGLE TO THE LAUNDROMAT: *Rhymes, Chants, Jingles and Poems.* [Toronto: Rochdale College, 1967?]. 17 leaves.
       Includes "The Abominable Wizard of Bloor Street" (B82), "Alligator Pie" (B96), "Bed Song" (A7), "Bouncing Song" (B97), "Candy Two, Candy Four," "The Coat" (B83), "The Cyclone Visitors" (B94), "The Difficulty of Living on Other Planets" (B79), "1838" (B49), "The Fishes of Kemperfeldt Bay" (B151), "Flying Out of Holes" (B95), "Greatheart and the Brain Drain" (B80), "Holidays," "I Found a Silver Dollar" (B87), "I Liked You in the Morning" (B81), "If You Should Meet" (B84), "In Kamloops" (B102), "In Praise of Moose Factory," "Inch and Pinch," "Kahshe or Chicoutimi" (B103), "Nathan Phillips Square [The clamshell towers go up.]," "Nicholas Grouch" (A7), "Ookpik" (B88), "Ookpik

in Heaven," "Paul Bunyan and the CPR," "The Poodle and the Grundiboob" (A8), "The Portable Grouch," "Psychapoo" (B90), "Skyscraper" (B105), "Song for My Lady Away" (A17 — "Song for His Imaginary Lady"), "The Song of Ookpik," "The Stopover," "Street Song" (A6), "Time Song," "Tweedle and Twidle," "The Warning" (B85), "Wendigo," "What Am I?", "Wiggle to the Laundromat" (B89), "Willoughby Wallaby Woo" (see B288), "The Windypuff Song" (B86), and "Winter Song" (A8).

A21 *Nicholas Knock.* Illus. Frank Newfeld. Toronto: Macmillan, [1975]. [12] pp.
Includes "Nicholas Knock" (A8).

Criticism

A22 "Principles of Ekstatic Form." M.A. Thesis Toronto 1965. 126 leaves.

A23 *Savage Fields: An Essay in Literature and Cosmology.* Toronto: House of Anansi, 1977. 125 pp.
——— . [Paperback.] Toronto: House of Anansi, 1977. 125 pp.

Prose Chapbooks

A24 *Notes on Rochdale.* [Toronto]: Privately printed, [1966?]. 20 pp. [Mimeographed.]
Includes "Notes on Rochdale" (B221).

A25 *A Statement on Rochdale College.* Toronto: Privately printed, 1966. 10 pp. [Mimeographed.]

A26 *Innocents and Tories: A Personal Vaudeville in Five Acts.* Toronto: Privately printed, 1967. 26 pp. [Mimeographed.]
Includes "Innocents and Tories: A Personal Vaudeville in Five Acts" (B197).

A27 *Report on the 1967* CUS *Seminar.* Ottawa: Canadian Union of Students/Union canadienne des étudiants, Secretariat, 1967. 10 pp. [Mimeographed.]

A28 *Rochdale College* [goals]. [Toronto: Rochdale College, 1967.] 1 p.

A29 *Rochdale College* [history, direction, philosophy]. [Toronto: Rochdale College, 1967–68.] [8] pp.

A30 *Notes on Rochdale.* Ottawa: Canadian Union of Students/Union canadienne des étudiants, [1968]. 13 pp. [Mimeographed.]

A31 *Reading* Savage Fields. Winnipeg: *Canadian Journal of Political and Social Theory/Revue canadienne de théorie politique et sociale* Offprint, 1979. 22 pp.
Includes "Reading *Savage Fields*" (B206).

A32 ——— , Rick Archbold, Doug Gibson, John Pearce, and Jan Walter. *Author & Editor: A Working Guide.* Toronto: Book and Periodical Development Council, 1983. 36 pp.
Includes Lee's "Writer to Publishing House" and "The Mechanic's Handbook: How the Book Is Costed," which Lee co-wrote with Rick Archbold.

A33 *Adonis.* Toronto: International Festival of Authors, 1987. 21 pp.
Includes "Adonis" (B254).

Drama

A34 *Mushroom Malady.* Music Peter Grant. [*The Bob Revue* (Victoria College, Univ. of Toronto), Fall 1961]. 55 pp. [Mimeographed.]
Includes "Dithyramb in Springtime" (B11), "The Fey's First Theme" (B281), "The Fey's Second

Theme" (B282), "Jed's Finale Speech" (B283), "Song for a Wedding: To John and Judy" (B285), and "Spring Song" (B284).

Miscellaneous

A35 ——, and Roberta A. Charlesworth. *A Teacher's Manual for The Second Century Anthology of Verse.* Toronto: Oxford Univ. Press, 1968. 88 pp.

A36 ——, and Roberta A. Charlesworth. *A Teacher's Manual for The Second Century Anthologies of Verse Book 2.* Toronto: Oxford Univ. Press, 1968. 88 pp.

Books Edited

A37 ——, and Roberta A. Charlesworth, eds. *An Anthology of Verse.* Toronto: Oxford Univ. Press, 1964. 549 pp.

A38 ——, and Roberta A. Charlesworth, eds. *The Second Century Anthologies of Verse: Book 2.* Toronto: Oxford Univ. Press, 1967. 281 pp.
Although Lee is identified as co-editor, he disclaims co-editorship of this publication.

A39 ——, and Howard Adelman, eds. and introd. *The University Game.* Toronto: House of Anansi, 1968, 1–3, 178 pp.

A40 ——, and introd. *T.O. Now: The Young Toronto Poets.* HAP, No. 8. Toronto: House of Anansi, 1968. i–iv, 101 pp.

A41 ——, and Margaret Atwood, eds. *Nobody Owns Th Earth.* By bill bissett. HAP, No. 22. Toronto: House of Anansi, 1971. 91 pp.

Although Lee acted as editor for most Anansi books between 1967 and 1972, the back cover explicitly states, "Pomes herein chosen Togethr by Margaret Atwood & Dennis Lee." Thus, though arbitrary from a literary-historical standpoint, this entry is included.

A42 ——, and Margaret Atwood, eds. *Crusoe: Poems Selected and New.* By Eli Mandel. HAP, No. 25. Toronto: House of Anansi, 1973. 108 pp.
Although Lee acted as editor for most Anansi books between 1967 and 1972, the verso of the title page explicitly states, "The poems in CRUSOE were selected by Margaret Atwood and Dennis Lee." Thus, though arbitrary from a literary-historical standpoint, this entry is included.

A43 ——, and foreword. *Moving to the Clear: Poems from Trent University, Peterborough.* [Peterborough]: n.p., 1976. 3, 44 pp.
——, and foreword. [Toronto]: n.p., 1976. 3, 35 pp.

A44 ——, and introd. *The New Canadian Poets, 1970–1985.* Toronto: McClelland and Stewart, 1985. xvii–liii, 383 pp.

Librettos

A45 *Place of Meeting.* Music John Beckwith. Toronto: Canadian Music Centre/W.R. Draper, 1967. 47 pp.
Commissioned by the Toronto Mendelssohn Choir with the collaboration of the Canadian Music Centre under a grant from the Centennial Commission for premiere performance during Canada's centennial year, 1967.

A46 *Nicholas Knock.* Music Derek Holman. Arranged The Aldeburgh Connection. In *Scenes from Child-*

hood. Music at Sharon. Sharon, Ont. 23 July 1988. [55] pp.

Lee's "Nicholas Knock" (A7) is arranged for treble, soprano, tenor, and piano duet.

Lyrics

A47 *1838*. Music John Beckwith. Sevenoaks, Eng.: Novello, 1971. 7 pp.

Includes the poem "1838" (B49) set to music.

A48 *Musical Notes from Jim Henson's Fraggle Rock*. Music Philip Balsam. Toronto: Muppet Music/Cherry Lane, 1982. (8" disc; 33-1/3 rpm; one side only.)

———. Music Philip Balsam. New York: Home Box Office, 1982.

Includes "Follow Me" (B313), "Fraggle Rock Rock" (B310), "Fraggle Rock Theme" (B290), and "Lost and Found" (B296).

A49 *Fraggle Rock*. Music Philip Balsam. Prod. Philip Balsam and Don Gillis. Exec. prod. Jim Henson. With Philip Balsam, Dave Goelz, Jim Henson, Richard Hunt, Kathryn Mullen, Jerry Nelson, Karen Prell, and Steve Whitmire. New York: Muppet Music/Cherry Lane (ASCAP), Henson & Associates, Columbia Records/CBC Records, 1983. (L.p., 33-1/3 rpm; cassette.)

———. Toronto: Home Box Office, 1982.

———. New York: Muppet Music, Columbia Records/CBC Records, 1983.

Includes "Beetle Song" (B306), "Brave Boy, Jump Up" (B346), "Catch the Tail by the Tiger" (B303), "Convincing John" (B299), "Do It on My Own," "Doozer Knitting Song" (B336), "Easy Is the Only Way to Go," "Follow Me" (B313), "Fraggle Rock Rock" (B310), "Fraggle Rock Theme" (B290),

"Friendship Song" (B329), "Lost and Found" (B296), "Muck and Goo" (B341), "Our Melody" (B335), "Wemblin Fool" (B347), and "Why?".

"Muck and Goo" is co-written with bpNichol.

———. Music Philip Balsam. Prod. Philip Balsam and Don Gillis. Paris: RCA, 1984.

———. *De Freggels*. Music Philip Balsam. Prod. Philip Balsam and Don Gillis. Nederland: RCA, 1984.

A50 *Fraggle Songs V. 1*. Music Philip Balsam. Musical dir. Don Gillis. With the Muppet performers. Toronto: CBC, 1983. (Videotape; VHS cassette; colour; stereo; 51 min.)

Includes "Beetle Song" (B306), "Brave Boy Jump Up" (B346), "Catch a Tail by the Tiger" (B303), "Convincing John" (B299), "Dixie Wailing" (B325), "Doozer Knitting Song" (B336), "Dumb of a Son" (B340), "Easy Is the Only Way" (A49 — "Easy Is the Only Way to Go"), "Fireman Song" (B291), "Follow Me" (B313), "Fraggle Rock, Rock" (B310), "Friendship Song" (B329), "Get Blue" (B327), "Here to There" (B311), "I Can Do It on My Own" (A49 — "Do It on My Own"), "I Seen Trouble" (B316), "I'm Not Scared," "Let Me Be Your Song" (B334), "Lost and Found" (B296), "Music Box Song," "Our Melody" (B335), "Pantry Song" (B297), "Ragtime Queen" (B349), "Rollin Rollin" (B305), "Terrible Tunnel," "Why?" (A49), "Workin Workin" [(B292 — "Work Song")?], and "Yucky" (B317).

A51 *Fraggle Rock Sing-Along Book*. Music Philip Balsam. Vol. 1. New York: Henson & Associates/Cherry Lane Music, 1984. 24 pp. (Cassette included.)

Includes "Beetle Song" (B306), "Catch the Tail by the Tiger" (B303), "Dumb of a Son of a Gun" (B340), "Lost and Found" (B296), "Muck and Goo" (B341), and "Wemblin' Fool" (B347).

A52   *Theme from Fraggle Rock*. Music Philip Balsam. Music direction Philip Balsam and Don Gillis. Prod. Tony Cox. [Toronto]: Muppet Music/Cherry Lane Music, Henson & Associates, RCA, 1984. (6-3/4" disc; 45 rpm.)

   Includes "Fraggle Rock Theme" (B290) and "Workin' " [(B292 — "Work Song")?].

A53   *Fraggle Rock: Perfect Harmony*. Music Philip Balsam. Arranged and prod. Philip Balsam and Don Gillis. With Dave Goelz, Richard Hunt, Kathryn Mullen, Jerry Nelson, Karen Prell, and Steve Whitmire. Exec. prod. Jim Henson. Illus. Larry Di Fiori. New York: Muppet Music (ASCAP), Columbia Records/CBC Records, 1986. (L.p.; 33-1/3 rpm; cassette.)

   Includes "Closing Theme" (B290), "Dreaming of Someone" (B307), "Dum De Dum," "The Fraggle Rock Theme" (B290), "Go With the Flow" (B331), "Helping Hand," "Here to There" (B311), "I Seen Troubles" (B316), "Music Box," "Pantry Chant" (B297), "Perfect Harmony" (B338), "Ragtime Queen" (B349), "Sail Away" (B333), "Time to Live as One" (B318), "Without a Hat" (B298), and "Workin" [(B292 — "Work Song")?].

Broadsides

A54   *Sibelius Park*. [Toronto: Coach House, 1968.] 1 leaf.
   Includes "Sibelius Park" (B46).

A55   *1838*. Illus. Dennis Crossfield. Kingston, Ont.: Quarry, [1971]. 1 leaf.
   Includes "1838" (B49) and a portrait of William Lyon Mackenzie.

A56   ———, trans. *Death of a Chleuch Dancer*. Toronto: Dreadnaught, 1976. 1 leaf.

Includes "Death of a Chleuch Dancer" (B262). Lee adapted the literal translation, by George Faludy, of the original Hungarian poem entitled "Chleuch táncos halála," by George Faludy.

A57   *Dennis Lee*. Writers in Brief, No. 14. London: National Book League, 1980. 1 leaf.
   Includes "After Dinner Music" (A4), "Alligator Pie" (B96), "400: Coming Home" (B54), "The Friends" (B100), "Master and Lord (Second Elegy)" (B48), "Of Eros, In Shiny Degree" (B51), "Suzy Grew a Moustache" (B125), and "There Was a Man" (B109).
   Also includes an author statement and a biographical note.

A58   *As She Grows Older (For a difficult old lady, senile; and for her daughters)*. Albion Broadsheet Nine. Toronto: Barbarian, 1981. 1 leaf.

A59   *The Rhyme of the Three Cuddly Bombs*. Toronto: Coach House, 1983. 1 leaf.
   Includes "The Rhyme of the Three Cuddly Bombs" (B71).

A60   *Owed to Peter Downie*. [Toronto: Peter Sibbald Brown], 1986. 1 leaf.

Calendars

A61   *The Dennis Lee & Frank Newfeld 1979 Alligator Pie Calendar*. Illus. Frank Newfeld. Featuring Uncle Bumper. Toronto: Macmillan, 1978. [32] pp.
   Includes "Alligator Pie" (B96), "Billy Batter" (B115), "The Bully," "The Coming of Teddy Bears" (B126), "The Dinosaurs' Dinner" (see B481), "Dirty Georgie," "Goofy Song" (A9), "Half Way Dressed" (B116), "The Muddy Puddle" (A9), "The Question" (B119), "The Secret," and "Tongue Twister" (B110).

A62 *The Dennis Lee & Frank Newfeld 1980 Alligator Pie Calendar*. Illus. Frank Newfeld. Toronto: Macmillan, 1979. [32] pp.

Includes "Being Five" (B122), "Christmas Tree" (see B479), "The Garbage Men," "The Gentle Giant," "In Kamloops" (B102), "Johnny the Juvenile Juggler," "Robber J. Badguy," "Spaghetti-O!", "Suzy Grew a Moustache" (B125), "Three Tickles" (see B483), "Tricking" (B113), "Under the Garden Hose," and "The Visit."

Audio-Visual Material

A63 *Dennis Lee*. Narr. Dennis Lee. Toronto: High Barnet, 1970. (Cassette; 1 hr.)

Includes "The Abominable Wizard of Bloor Street" (see B82), "A Bed Song" (see A7), "Brunswick Avenue" (see B42), "Civil Elegies (In Seven Parts)" (see A2), "The Coat" (see B83), "The Cyclone Visitors" (see B94), "The Difficulty of Living on Other Planets" (see B79), "Fishes of Kempenfelt Bay" (see B151), "Glad for the Wrong Reasons" (see B55), "Holidays" (see A20), "I Found a Silver Dollar" (see B87), "In Kamloops" (see B102), "Inch and Pinch" (see A20), "Kahshe or Chicoutimi" (see B103), "Late Night Monologue," "The Morning of the Second Day" (see A3 — "The Morning of the Second Day: He Tells Her"), "On Tuesdays I Polish My Uncle" (see B112), "Psychapoo" (see B90), "Recollection" (see B44), "When It Is Over" (see B41), "Wiggle to the Laundromat" (see B89), "Willoughby, Wallaby, Woo" (see B289), and "The Windypuff Song" (see B86).

A64 *Civil Elegies and Other Poems*. Narr. Dennis Lee. Toronto: Toronto Public Libraries, 1972. (Cassette; 1-1/2 hr.)

Includes "Brunswick Avenue" (see B42), "Civil Elegies: 1 [Often I sit in the sun and brooding over the city, always] [see B39], 2 [Master and Lord, where] [see B48], 3 [The light rides easy on people dozing at noon in Toronto, or] [see B38], 4 [Among the things which] [see A3], 5 [It would be better maybe if we could stop loving the children] [see B36], 6 [I am one for whom the world is constantly proving too much —] [see B37], 7 [Among the flaws that mar my sleep I harbour more than wars for I have friends and lacerations] [see A2 — "Fourth Elegy"], 8 [I come to the square each time there is nothing and once, made calm again] [see A2 — "Sixth Elegy"], 9 [Here, as I sit and watch, the rusty leaves hang taut with departure.] [see A3]," "Coming Back" (see B53), "400: Coming Home" (see B54), "Glad for the Wrong Reasons" (see B55), "He Asks Her" (see A3), "Heaven and Earth" (see B40), "High Park, by Grenadier Pond" (see B43), "In a Bad Time" (see B45), "More Claiming" (see A3), "The Morning of the Second Day: He Tells Her" (see A3), "Night" (see B56), "Recollection" (see B44), "Sibelius Park" (see B46), "Thursday" (see A3), "When It Is Over" (see B41), and "Words for the Given" (see B47).

A65 *Alligator Pie*. Narr. Helene Grice. Toronto: CNIB, 1975. (Cassette; 1-1/2 hr.).

Includes "Alligator Pie" (see B96), "Bed Song" (see A7), "Billy Batter" (see B115), "Bouncing Song" (see B97), "Bump on Your Thumb" (see B98), "The Fishes of Kempenfelt Bay" (see B151), "Flying Out of Holes" (see B95), "The Friends" (see B100), "Higgledy Piggledy" (see A7), "The Hockey Game (With thanks to A.A. Milne)" (see A7), "I Found a Silver Dollar" (see B87), "If You Should Meet" (see B84), "In Kamloops" (see B102), "Kahshe or Chicoutimi" (see B103), "Like a Giant in a Towel" (see A7), "Lying on Things" (see A7), "Mumbo, Jumbo" (see B118), "Nicholas Grouch" (see A7), "On Tuesdays I Polish My Uncle" (see B112), "Ookpik" (see

B88), "Peter Rabbit" (see A7), "Psychapoo" (see B90), "Rattlesnake Skipping Song" (see A7), "Singa Songa" (see A7), "The Sitter and the Butter and the Better Batter Fritter" (see B104), "Skyscraper" (B482), "The Special Person" (see B107), "Street Song" (see A6), "Thinking in Bed" (see A7), "Tongue Twister" (see B110), "Tony Baloney" (see A7), "Tricking" (see B113), "Wiggle to the Laundromat" (see B89), "William Lyon Mackenzie King" (see A7), "Willoughby Wallaby Woo" (see B289), and "Windshield Wipers" (see A7).

Includes the following prose: "Hockey Sticks and High-Rise: A Postlude" (see A7).

A66 *Alligator Pie and Other Poems.* Narr. Dennis Lee, with Danny Allan, Danny Aneca, Jeff Arch, Julie Booth, Andrea Botsford, Andre Brewster, Tracey Brock, David Brown, Laura Chapman, Lisa Chapman, Tony DaSilva, Bobby Deans, Denise Desrocher, Michelle Dunn, Haniff Dwyer, Barbara Gavin, Bobby Gavin, Jennifer Gavin, Robbie Grewal, Tammy Grimard, Tanya Kaluta, Jason Kempton, Robert Kouyoumjian, Paulette LeBlanc, Brent Lewis, Steven Mallon, Ryan Marshall, Penny Martin, Randy Martins, Candy Masters, Donovan McDowall, Richard McIntosh, Anju Mistry, Nancy Nadeau, Karen Naisbitt, James Niosi, Leasa Niosi, Christina Palhetas, Dwayne Paul, Steven Pitt, John Pombert, Angele Provencher, Marcel Raab, Jeff Riel, Matthew Rudnicki, Karen Shelestynsky, Chris Shelton, Muriel Squire, Geoffrey Stahl, Jacqueline Stahl, Janine Terry, Mark Topping, Ann Varickanickal, Terry Walker, Michael Watson, Emily Pohl Weary, Carrie Williams, Michael Williams, and Shannon Williams. Music Don Heckman. Front container illus. Frank Newfeld. Back container notes Sheila A. Egoff. New York: Caedmon, TC1530, 1978. (L.p., 33-1/3 rpm; 37 min., 36 sec.)

Includes the following poems narrated by Lee: "Bath Song ('A Biscuit, a Basket')" (see A9), "Being Five" (see B122), "The Big Molice Pan and the Bertie Dumb" (see A9), "Billy Batter" (see B115), "Bloody Bill" (see A9), "Bouncing Song ('Hambone, Jawbone')" (see B97), "Bump on Your Thumb" (see B98), "The Coming of Teddy Bears" (B480), "The Fishes of Kempenfelt Bay" (see B151), "The Friends" (see B100), "Garbage Delight" (see B91), "Half Way Dressed" (see B116), "Higgledy Piggledy" (see A7), "I Eat Kids Yum Yum!" (see B114), "In Kamloops" (see B102), "Inspector Dogbone Gets His Man" (see A9), "The Moon" (see A9), "Mr. Hoobody" (see A8), "The Question" (see B119), "Rattlesnake Skipping Song" (see A7), "The Sitter and the Butter and the Better Batter Fritter" (see B104), "Skyscraper" (B482), "Smelly Fred" (see A9), "The Special Person" (see B107), "Suzy Grew a Moustache" (see B125), "Tricking" (see B113), "Wellington the Skeleton" (see B120), and "Windshield Wipers" (see A7).

Includes the following poems narrated by Lee and the children: "Alligator Pie" (excerpt; first stanza; read twice) (see B96), "The Big Molice Pan and the Bertie Dumb" (see A9), "Mumbo, Jumbo" (see B118), "On Tuesdays I Polish My Uncle" (see B112), "Skyscraper" (see B105), and "Tongue Twister ('Someday I'll Go to Winnipeg')" (see B110).

Includes the following poems read by children: "Alligator Emily" [Emily's version of the first stanza of "Alligator Pie"], "Alligator Pie" (full poem) (see B96), and "Peter Was a Pilot" (see A9).

A67 *Keynote Speaker.* Narr. Dennis Lee. Prod. Audio Archives. Markham, Ont.: Ontario Library Association, Jan.–Feb. 1980. (Cassette; 1-1/2 hrs.)

Adult and children's poetry reading with critical reflections, recorded live.

A68 *A Reading with Dennis Lee and Friends*. Narr. Dennis Lee. Prod. D'Allen Film and Video Productions. Toronto: Macmillan, 1984. (Videotape; 30 min.)

Includes "Alligator Pie" (see B96), "Alligator Pie — Reprisal," "Bath Song" (see A9), "Being Five" (see B122), "Billy Batter" (see B115), "Bump on Your Thumb" (see B98), "Bundle-Buggy Boogie" (see B131), "The Dinosaur Dinner" (B481), "The Gentle Giant" (see A62), "The Ghost and Jenny Jemima" (see A10), "Good Night, Good Night" (see A10), "Halfway Dressed" (see B116), "I Eat Kids Yum Yum" (see B114), "In Kamloops" (see B102), "Jelly Belly" (see A10 — "The Dreadful Doings of Jelly Belly"), "Mrs Murphy, and Mrs Murphy's Kids" (see B132), "Robber J. Badguy" (see A62), "Skyscraper" (B482), "Suzy Grew a Moustache" (see B125), "Three Tickles" (B483), and "Tricking" (see B113).

A69 *The Ordinary Bath*. Illus. Jon McKee. Music Philip Balsam. Narr. Dennis Lee. Prod. and dir. Paul Caulfield. Brampton, Ont.: Mirus Films, 1985. (Videotape; 16 mm.; 11 min.)

———. Illus. Jon McKee. Music Philip Balsam. Narr. Dennis Lee. Prod. and dir. Paul Caulfield. Brampton, Ont.: Mirus Films, 1985. (Videotape; 3/4" u-matic.)

———. Illus. Jon McKee. Music Philip Balsam. Narr. Dennis Lee. Prod. and dir. Paul Caulfield. Brampton, Ont.: Mirus Films, 1985. (Videotape; 1/2" VHS.)

See A13.

A70 ———, and Jim Henson (story). *Labyrinth*. Screenplay Terry Jones. Dir. Jim Henson. Prod. Eric Rattray. Exec. prod. George Lucas. Exec. supervising prod. David Lazer. Henson Associates and Lucasfulm, 1986.

A71 *Willoughby Wallaby*. Music Michael Lobel. Script Jean Richards. Illus. Vickie M. Learner. Bantam Sing-a-Story. With Lance Brodie, Liz Corrigan, and Lenny Roberts. Toronto: Parachute, 1987. [24] pp. (Cassette; 20 min.)

Editorial Work

A72 Co-Founder, director, editor. House of Anansi, 1967–72.

A73 Consulting editor. Macmillan of Canada, 1972–78.

A74 Poetry consultant. McClelland and Stewart, 1981–84.

Manuscripts

A75 The Dennis Lee Papers
Thomas Fisher Rare Book Library
University of Toronto
Toronto, Ontario

In January 1979 (and again in 1984), the Thomas Fisher Rare Book Library in Toronto acquired from the author his correspondence, editing files and notes, literary manuscripts, drafts, and related materials (reviews, clippings, publicity, etc.), lecture notes, tapes, and memorabilia, for the period 1948–84. The collection fills 155 boxes, approximately 75 linear feet. The papers provide for the study of both Lee's writing career and his career generally, which includes his affiliations with Rochdale College, SUPA, House of Anansi Press, The League of Canadian Poets, Stop Spadina, the Ontario Royal Commission on Book Publishing, to name some of the more predominant. In addition, the papers are a source of information for the Canadian literary scene from the mid-1960s to the end of the 1970s, during which time Lee helped to found the House of Anansi and worked there in an editorial capacity. There is a great deal of correspondence and literary manuscripts of many of the young writers published by House of Anansi Press. The collection has been catalogued; a finding aid outlining the organization of the papers and a listing, by container, of the contents of each box has been printed. In addition, the library houses first editions of the published monographs. The large *Fraggle Rock* section of the collection contains scripts by a variety of writers for shows one to fifty-four. Five boxes of children's letters and art work sent to Lee are included.

B Contributions to Periodicals and Books (Poems, Children's Poems, Children's Tale, Short Story, Juvenile Prose, Reprinted Anthology Contributions: A Selection, Essays, Articles, Translations, and Reviews), Lyrics, Published Correspondence, Ghostwriter, Miscellaneous, Press Releases and Flyers, and Audio-Visual Material

Note: When an item is reprinted in one of Lee's books, this fact is noted in the entry through one of the following abbreviations:

Adonis	*Adon.*
Alligator Pie	*AP*
Alligator Pie (cassette)	*AP* (cass.)
Alligator Pie and Other Poems	*APOP*
Civil Elegies	*CE*
Civil Elegies and Other Poems	*CEOP*
Civil Elegies and Other Poems (cassette)	*CEOP* (cas.)
Death of a Chleuch Dancer	*DCD*
The Death of Harold Ladoo	*DHL*
Dennis Lee	*DL*
Dennis Lee (cassette)	*DL* (cas.)
The Dennis Lee & Frank Newfeld 1979 Alligator Pie Calendar	*DLFN79*
The Dennis Lee & Frank Newfeld 1980 Alligator Pie Calendar	*DLFN80*
The Dennis Lee Big Book	*DLBB*
The Difficulty of Living on Other Planets	*DLOP*
The Difficulty of Living on Other Planets (chapbook)	*DLOP* (chap.)
1838 (broadside)	*1838* (broad.)
1838. Music John Beckwith	*1838* (music)
Elégies civiles et autres poèmes	*Ecap*
Fraggle Rock	*FR*
Fraggle Rock: Perfect Harmony	*FR:PH*
Fraggle Rock Sing-Along Book	*FRS-A*
Fraggle Songs V. 1	*FS*
Garbage Delight	*GD*
The Gods	*Gods*
The Gods (chapbook)	*Gods* (chap.)
The Ice Cream Store	*ICS*
Innocents and Tories: A Personal Vaudeville in Five Acts	*IT*
Jelly Belly	*JB*
Kingdom of Absence	*KA*
Lizzy's Lion	*LL*
Miscellany	*Misc.*
Mushroom Malady	*MM*
Musical Notes from Jim Henson's Fraggle Rock	*MNJH*
Nicholas Knock and Other Poems	*NKOP*
Not Abstract Harmonies But	*NAHB*
Notes on Rochdale [1966?]	*NR*
Reading Savage Fields	*RSF*
A Reading with Dennis Lee and Friends	*RDLF*
The Rhyme of the Three Cuddly Bombs	*RTCB*

Poems

B1 ———, and Margaret Atwood. "Spratire." *Acta Victoriana* [Victoria College, Univ. of Toronto], 83, No. 2 (Dec. 1958), 22.
Signed: Shakesbeat Latweed.

B2 "Dirge at a Wake." *Acta Victoriana* [Victoria College, Univ. of Toronto], 85, No. 1 (Nov. 1960), 7.

B3 "Song of Seasons." *Acta Victoriana* [Victoria College, Univ. of Toronto], 85, No. 1 (Nov. 1960), 6.

B4 "Titanic." *Acta Victoriana* [Victoria College, Univ. of Toronto], 85, No. 1 (Nov. 1960), 6.

B5 ———, and Margaret Atwood. "Discursive Verse . . . ." *The Strand* [Victoria College, Univ. of Toronto], 9 Dec. 1960, p. 2.
Signed: Shakesbeat Latweed.

B6 "Three Poems: Anima." *Acta Victoriana* [Victoria College, Univ. of Toronto], 85, No. 3 (Feb. 1961), 5.

B7 "Three Poems: The Fire of Eros." *Acta Victoriana* [Victoria College, Univ. of Toronto], 85, No. 3 (Feb. 1961), 5.

B8 "Three Poems: Tigerlily." *Acta Victoriana* [Victoria College, Univ. of Toronto], 85, No. 3 (Feb. 1961), 4. Rpt. *Jargon* [Univ. of Toronto], 2 (Spring 1961), 12.

B9 "Never, I Say Not Once in Greece Ago." *Jargon* [Univ. of Toronto], 1 (1961–62) [30]. Rpt. ("Three Poems Dennis Lee: Poem") in *Acta Victoriana* [Victoria College, Univ. of Toronto], 86, No. 2 (Spring 1962), 13.

B10 "Winter Has My Heart in Hand." *Jargon* [Univ. of Toronto], 1 (1961–62), 18.

B11 "Three Poems by Dennis Lee: Dithyramb in Springtime (from the Bob) (poem from 'Mushroom Malady')." *Acta Victoriana* [Victoria College, Univ. of Toronto], 86, No. 2 (Spring 1962), 13. *MM* ("Dithyramb in Springtime").

B12 "Three Poems by Dennis Lee: For a Child." *Acta Victoriana* [Victoria College, Univ. of Toronto], 86, No. 2 (Spring 1962), 14.

B13 "Poem [Until God riddle our cankered souls with light]." *Acta Victoriana* [Victoria College, Univ. of Toronto], 88, No. 2 (1963), 18. *KA* ("xxxix [Until God riddle our cankered souls with light]").

B14 "Three Sonnets from a Sequence [Loony with sunlight, van Gogh stood and stared]." *Alphabet* [London, Ont.], No. 7 (Dec. 1963), p. 9. *KA* ("ix [Looney with sunlight, van Gogh stood and stared]").

B15 "Three Sonnets from a Sequence [Now God is dead I gnaw upon my heart]." *Alphabet* [London, Ont.], No. 7 (Dec. 1963), p. 8. *KA* (revised — "vii [Of witty desecrations, and the slow]").

B16 "Three Sonnets from a Sequence [The trumpets of the randy Renaissance]." *Alphabet* [London, Ont.], No. 7 (Dec. 1963), p. 8. *KA* ("viii [The trumpets of the randy Renaissance]").

B17 "At a Writers' Conference." *The Varsity* [Univ. of Toronto] [Literary Issue], 7 Dec. 1963, p. 2.

B18 "The Stopover." *The Varsity* [Univ. of Toronto] [Literary Issue], 7 Dec. 1963, p. 2.

B19 "[Dusk, and the bright air falls]." *The Canadian Forum*, April 1964, p. 4. Rpt. ("Kingdom of Absence: 2") in *The Canadian Forum*, April 1966, p. 292. *KA* ("II [Dusk, and the bright air falls]").

B20 "Sonnet [The view from the parade square]." *The Canadian Forum*, April 1964, p. 4. Rpt. ("Kingdom of Absence: 22") in *The Canadian Forum*, April 1966, p. 292. *KA* (revised — "XXII [When I review my troop of scruffy selves]").

B21 "Sonnet [We explicate the trees but they go sorrowing]." *The Canadian Forum*, April 1965, p. 16. *KA* ("XI [We explicate the trees but they go sorrowing]").

B22 "Kingdom of Absence: 1." *The Canadian Forum*, April 1966, p. 292. *KA* ("I [Lady, till the curfew rings]").

B23 "Kingdom of Absence: 3." *The Canadian Forum*, April 1966, p. 292. *KA* ("III [Sudden among the grass the]").

B24 "Kingdom of Absence: 4." *The Canadian Forum*, April 1966, p. 292. *KA* ("IV [Shad flies bash full tilt against the screen.]").

B25 "Kingdom of Absence: 5." *The Canadian Forum*, April 1966, p. 292. *KA* ("XVII [Can do can]").

B26 "Kingdom of Absence: 8." *The Canadian Forum*, April 1966, p. 293. Rpt. (excerpt — "Sonnet XXIII")

in *Saturday Night*, April 1967, p. 44. Rpt. trans. Virgil Teodorescu and Petronela Negosanu ("Regatul Absentei XXIII") in *Întelegînd Zâpada: Antolgie a poetilor canadieni de limbâ engleza*. Ed. Virgil Teodorescu and Petronela Negosanu. Bucharest: Univers, 1977, p. 198. *KA* ("XXIII [I woke on the floes.]").

B27 "Kingdom of Absence: 9." *The Canadian Forum*, April 1966, p. 293. Rpt. trans. Virgil Teodorescu and Petronela Negosanu ("Regatul Absentei XXVI") in *Întelegînd Zâpada: Antolgie a poetilor canadieni de limbâ engleza*. Ed. Virgil Teodorescu and Petronela Negosanu. Bucharest: Univers, 1977, p. 198. *KA* (revised — "XXVI [I drift between two images. An icy plane]").

B28 "Kingdom of Absence: 10." *The Canadian Forum*, April 1966, p. 293. Rpt. ("Absence, Be utter. Vacancy, what Journeys?") in ANYTHING BUT SON OF ROCHDALE [Toronto], 1, No. 4 (Dec. 1967), [10]. *KA* ("XXVII [Absence, be utter. Vacancy, what journeys?]").

B29 "Kingdom of Absence: 11." *The Canadian Forum*, April 1966, p. 293. Rpt. trans. Virgil Teodorescu and Petronela Negosanu ("Regatul Absentei XXVIII") in *Întelegînd Zâpada: Antolgie a poetilor canadieni de limbâ engleza*. Ed. Virgil Teodorescu and Petronela Negosanu. Bucharest: Univers, 1977, p. 199. *KA* ("XXVIII [The slack air locks and throbs]").

B30 "Kingdom of Absence: 12." *The Canadian Forum*, April 1966, p. 293. *KA* ("XXIX [Eliot as he passed me]").

B31 "Kingdom of Absence: 13." *The Canadian Forum*, April 1966, p. 293. *KA* ("XXXI [How I got up here was I could not stand the body-blows on my sensitive]").

B32 "Kingdom of Absence: 14." *The Canadian Forum*, April 1966, pp. 293–94. *KA* ("xxxvi [How often, in muskoka, bedded down]").

B33 "Kingdom of Absence: 15." *The Canadian Forum*, April 1966, p. 294. *KA* ("xxxv [Lady, in tuition]").

B34 "Kingdom of Absence: 16." *The Canadian Forum*, April 1966, p. 294. *KA* ("xliii [Cities of light, and every time]").

B35 "My First Apocalypse Was on a Wednesday." *Acta Victoriana* [Victoria College, Univ. of Toronto], 90, No. 4 (April 1966), 19. Rpt. ("Kingdom of Absence: 7") in *The Canadian Forum*, April 1966, pp. 292–93. *KA* ("xv [My first apocalypse was on a Wednesday.]").

B36 "Third Elegy (Nathan Phillips Square, Toronto) [It would be better maybe if we could stop loving the children]." *Canadian Dimension*, 4, No. 6 (Oct. 1967), 32–33. *CE* ("Third Elegy [It would be better maybe if we could stop loving the children]"); *CEOP* ("Civil Elegies: 5 [It would be better maybe if we could stop loving the children]"); *Ecap* ("Civil Elegies/Élégies Civiles: 5 [It would be better maybe if we could stop loving the children/Ce serait mieux peut-être si nous pouvions cesser d'aimer les enfants]").

See *CEOP* (cas.) ("Civil Elegies: 5 [It would be better maybe if we could stop loving the children]").

B37 "Sixth Elegy [I am one for whom the world is constantly proving too much –]." *Acta Victoriana* [Victoria College, Univ. of Toronto], 92, No. 3 (Feb. 1968), 18. *CE* ("Fifth Elegy [I am one for whom the world is constantly proving too much –]"); *CEOP*

("Civil Elegies: 6 [I am one for whom the world is constantly proving too much —]"); *Ecap* ("Civil Elegies/Élégies Civiles: 6 [I am one for whom the world is constantly proving too much — /Je suis de ceux que le monde finit toujours par sursaturer –]").

See *CEOP* (cas.) ("Civil Elegies: 6 [I am one for whom the world is constantly proving too much –]").

B38 "Second Elegy [The light rides easy on people dozing at noon in Toronto, or]." *The Canadian Forum*, May 1968, pp. 38–39. Rpt. in *Impulse*, 1, No. 1 (Fall 1971), 7–10. *CE*; *CEOP* ("Civil Elegies: 3 [The light rides easy on people dozing at noon in Toronto, or]"); *Ecap* ("Civil Elegies/Élégies Civiles: 3 [The light rides easy on people dozing at noon in Toronto, or/La lumière tangue doucement sur les gens qui roupillent à midi dans Toronto, ou]").

See *CEOP* (cas.) ("Civil Elegies: 3 [The light rides easy on people dozing at noon in Toronto, or]").

B39 "Of Big Buildings . . . and Little Men." *Toronto Daily Star*, 3 Aug. 1968, Entertainment, p. 34. Rpt. ("Civil Elegies: 1 [Often I sit in the sun and brooding over the city, always]") in *Vanderbilt Poetry Review* [Vanderbilt Univ., Nashville, Tenn.], 1, No. 2 (Fall-Winter 1972), 3–6. Rpt. trans. Virgil Teodorescu and Petronela Negosanu ("Elegii Civile") in *Întelegînd Zâpada: Antologie a poetilor canadieni de limbâ engleza*. Ed. Virgil Teodorescu and Petronela Negosanu. Bucharest: Univers, 1977, pp. 199–204. *CE* ("First Elegy [Often I sit in the sun and brooding over the city, always]"); *CEOP* ("Civil Elegies: 1 [Often I sit in the sun and brooding over the city, always]"); *Ecap* ("Civil Elegies/Élégies Civiles: 1 [Often I sit in the sun and brooding over the city, always/Souvent au soleil assis à ruminer la ville, en déploiements]").

See *CEOP* (cas.) ("Civil Elegies: 1 [Often I sit in the sun and brooding over the city, always]").

B40 "Heaven and Earth." *Black Moss* [Windsor, Ont.], 1, No. 1 (1969), 4. Rpt. trans. Thor Sorheim ("Himmel Og Jord") in *Gylendals Aktuelle Magasin* [Oslo, Norway], No. 2 (1979), p. 76. *CEOP* ("Heaven and Earth"); *Ecap* ("Heaven and Earth/Ciel et terre").
See *CEOP* (cas.) ("Heaven and Earth").

B41 "When It Is Over." *Black Moss* [Windsor, Ont.], 1, No. 1 (1969), 4. Rpt. ("When It's Over") in *Impulse*, 1, No. 1 (Fall 1971), 6. Rpt. in *Vanderbilt Poetry Review* [Vanderbilt Univ., Nashville, Tenn.], 1, No. 2 (Fall–Winter 1972), 10. *CEOP* ("When It Is Over"); *Ecap* ("When It Is Over/Quand c'est fini").
See *DL* (cas.) ("When It Is Over") and *CEOP* (cas.).

B42 "Brunswick Avenue." *Pro-ject* [Toronto/Detroit], 1 (Winter–Spring 1969), 47–48. *CEOP*; *Ecap*.
See *DL* (cas.) and *CEOP* (cas.).

B43 "High Park, by Grenadier Pond." *Pro-ject* [Toronto/Detroit], 1 (Winter–Spring 1969), 49. *CEOP*; *Ecap* ("High Park, by Grenadier Pond/Quoi que je dise").
See *CEOP* (cas.) ("High Park, by Grenadier Pond").

B44 "Recollection." *Pro-ject* [Toronto/Detroit], 1 (Winter–Spring 1969), 48. Rpt. trans. Stein Petter Guvag and Arne Ruste ("Erindring") in *Gylendals Aktuelle Magasin* [Oslo, Norway], No. 2 (1979), p. 76. *CEOP* ("Recollection"); *Ecap* ("Recollection/Je me rappelle").
See *DL* (cas.) ("Recollection") and *CEOP* (cas.).

B45 "In a Bad Time." *The Canadian Forum*, April–May 1970, p. 116. Rpt. trans. ("En Mala Epoca") in *Antología de la poesia actual Canadiense inglesa*. Ed. Manuel Betanzos Santos. Mexico City: Universidad Autonoma de San Luis Potosi, 1978, pp. 81–84. Rpt. trans. Stein Petter Guvag and Arne Ruste ("I En Vond Tid") in *Gylendals Aktuelle Magasin* [Oslo, Norway], No. 2 (1979), p. 76. *CEOP* ("In a Bad Time"); *Ecap* ("In a Bad Time/Par temps difficiles").
See *CEOP* (cas.) ("In a Bad Time").

B46 "Sibelius Park." *The Canadian Forum*, April–May 1970, p. 103. *CEOP*; *Ecap*; *SP*.
See *CEOP* (cas.).

B47 "A Conversation with the Given." *BlewOintment* [blewointmentpress Oil Slick Speshul], [1971], p. 1. *CEOP* ("Words for the Given"); *Ecap* ("Words for the Given/Mots pour le donné").
See *CEOP* (cas.) ("Words for the Given").

B48 "Third Elegy [Master and Lord, where]." Illus. Whyte. *Saturday Night*, June 1971, p. 35. Rpt. ("Civil Elegies: 2 [Master and Lord, where]") in *Vanderbilt Poetry Review* [Vanderbilt Univ., Nashville, Tenn.], 1, No. 2 (Fall–Winter 1972), 7–8. Rpt. ("Master and Lord, Where / Are You?") in *Vic report* [Victoria College, Univ. of Toronto], 4, No. 2 (March 1976), 4. Rpt. ("Master and Lord") in *New Departures* [Piedmont, Eng.] [Special Anthology Issue], No. 12 (Sept. 1980), p. [27]. *CEOP* ("Civil Elegies: 2 [Master and Lord, where]"); *Ecap* (Civil Elegies/Élégies Civiles: 2 [Master and Lord, where/Maître et Seigneur, où]"); *DL* ["Master and Lord (Second Elegy)"].
See *CEOP* (cas.) ("Civil Elegies: 2 [Master and Lord, where]").

B49 "1838." Illus. Gail Ashby. *This Magazine Is about Schools*, 5, No. 4 (Fall–Winter 1971), 124–27. Rpt. (excerpt) in *Proceedings and Book Catalog: Children's Books International 2*. Ed. Jane Manthorne and Irenemarie H. Cullinane. Boston: Boston Public Library, 1977, p. 47. *Gods; DLOP* (revised); *NKOP* (revised); *Misc.* (revised); *WL:RC; 1838* (music); *1838* (broad.).

See B287 ["1838 (Ontario)"].

B50 "Spadina." Illus. C. Oszusko. *Earth and You; Vehicle of Current Ideas for Modern People* [Toronto], 3, Nos. 17–18 (1971 [sic; 1972]), 14. Rpt. (expanded — "2 Notes from Tory Toronto: Spadina") in *White Pelican*, 3, No. 2 (Spring 1973), 52. *NKOP* ("Spadina").

B51 "Of Eros, in Shiney Degree." *blewointmentpress poverty isshew*, March 1972, p. 87. Rpt. in *Toronto Life*, Sept. 1977, p. 179. Rpt. in *Saturday Night*, July–Aug. 1979, p. 60. *Gods; Misc.; DL*.

B52 "The Presence of Pioneers." *Impulse*, 2, No. 1 (Autumn 1972), 45. Rpt. trans. ("La Presencia de los pioneros") in *Antología de la poesia actual Canadiense inglesa*. Ed. Manuel Betanzos Santos. Mexico City: Universidad Autonoma de San Luis Potosi, 1978, pp. 81–84. *DLOP* (revised — "The Presence of Pioneers"); *Misc.* (revised).

B53 "Coming Back." *Vanderbilt Poetry Review* [Vanderbilt Univ., Nashville, Tenn.], 1, No. 2 (Fall–Winter 1972), 9. *CEOP; Ecap* ("Coming Back/M'en revenant").

See *CEOP* (cas.) ("Coming Back").

B54 "400: Coming Home." *ellipse*, No. 12 (1973), pp. 88, 90. Rpt. trans. Louise Pelletier ("400: Retour") in *ellipse*, No. 12 (1973), pp. 89, 91. *CEOP* ("400: Coming Home"); *Ecap* ("400: Coming Home/Route 400: le retour"); *DL*.

See *CEOP* (cas.) ("400: Coming Home").

B55 "Content pour de fausses raisons." Trans. Monique Grandmangin. *ellipse*, No. 12 (1973), p. 93. Rpt. ("Glad for the Wrong Reasons") in *ellipse*, No. 12 (1973), p. 92. *CEOP; Ecap* ("Glad for the Wrong Reason/Heureux pour de fausses raisons").

See *DL* (cas.) ("Glad for the Wrong Reasons") and *CEOP* (cas.).

B56 "Night." *ellipse*, No. 12 (1973), p. 90. Rpt. trans. Chantal Airanda ("La Nuit") in *ellipse*, No. 12 (1973), p. 91. Rpt. trans. Stein Petter Guvag and Arne Ruste ("Natt") in *Gylendals Aktuelle Magasin* [Oslo, Norway], No. 2 (1979), p. 76. *CEOP* ("Night"); *Ecap* ("Night/La nuit").

See *CEOP* (cas.) ("Night").

B57 "2 Notes from Tory Toronto: When I Went Up to Rosedale." *White Pelican*, 3, No. 2 (Spring 1973), 53. Rpt. ("When I Went Up to Rosedale") in *Toronto Life*, July 1977, p. 53. *Gods; DLOP; Misc.*

B58 "Talking Graffiti Magnificat." *BlewOintment* [TH BLEWOINTMENTPRESS WHAT ISINT TANTRIK SPESHUL], Dec. 1973, p. 61.

B59 "Beggars of Yonge." In *A Book of Process*. Ed. and introd. Eldon Garnet. [Toronto]: rumblestill/La Club Foot, [1974?], p. 28.

B60 "Not Abstract Harmonies But." *White Pelican*, 4, No. 4 (Autumn 1974), pp. 7–8. Rpt. in *Scarborough Fair* [Scarborough College, Univ. of Toronto], 1975–76, pp. 68–69. *Gods; NAHB*.

B61 "Song." *White Pelican*, 4, No. 4 (Autumn 1974), p. 6. Rpt. in *Scarborough Fair* [Scarborough College, Univ. of Toronto], 1975–76, p. 71. *Gods*.

B62 "Song: Lay Down." *White Pelican*, 4, No. 4 (Autumn 1974), 5. Rpt. in *Scarborough Fair* [Scarborough College, Univ. of Toronto], 1975–76, p. 70. *Gods*.

B63 *The Death of Harold Ladoo. boundary 2: a journal of postmodern literature* [State Univ. of New York at Binghamton], 5, No. 1 (Fall 1976), 213–28. *Gods*; *DHL*.

B64 "Lady Zero." *Toronto Life*, Oct. 1977, p. 123. *Misc.*

B65 "The Gods." *Acta Victoriana* [Victoria College, Univ. of Toronto] [Centennial 1878–1978], 102, No. 2 (Fall 1978), 22–23. Rpt. in *Poetry Australia* [Sydney], No. 69 (Feb. 1979), pp. 16–19. Rpt. in *Aquarius* [London, Eng.] [Canadian Issue], Nos. 13–14 (1981–82), pp. 57–60. Rpt. trans. Jacques Darras ("Les Dieux") in *in"hui 18* [Amiens, France] [Multiples], 25 oct. 1983, pp. 81–87. *Gods* ("The Gods"); *Gods* (chap.).

B66 "Percy." *Canadian Literature*, No. 78 (Autumn 1978), pp. 8–11.

B67 "You Can Climb Down Now." *Liberté*, 20, No. 6 [No. 120] (déc. 1978), 77. Rpt. in *Poetry Australia* [Sydney], No. 69 (Feb. 1979), p. 20. Rpt. in *Ariel: A Review of International English Literature* [Univ. of Calgary], 10, No. 3 (July 1979), 55. *Gods*.

B68 "Riffs: 1 [When I lurched like a blizzard of wants through the networks of plenty,], 2 [But she is an], 3 [When you're up to yr], 4 [Nudge of her snuggled head], 5 [Those perfect], 6 [Capo and], 7 [. . . I'll tell you what's the matter.], 8 [So I'll cook me some], 9 [Hot po-], 10 [Acey deucey], 11 [Multifarious dodos:], 12 [One thing], 13 [Take me again —], 14 [Pen-], 15 [It is], 16 [Aw, nobody's], 17 [Not marble, nor the], 18 [Ho hum you], 19 [For months before we lay down,], 20 [Will pass your place.], 21 [Heaven was plain &], 22 [We swam into], 23 [Why else do I squat like a rainbow], 24 [Stir me again.], 25 [Smelting head foundries of ozone gravity breakage I], 26 [The angels'], 27 [How far can I], 28 [Aw, shd I], 29 [Music of], 30 [Clear tracings in], 31 [Twirls on the face of], 32 [Am I in], 33 [To guzzle], 34 [Look maw — no mind &], 35 [Inch by], 36 [Suppose a couple of], 37 [Just], 38 [Hey I scraped the], 39 [Awright], 40 [You would not be-], 41 [Put it on Body controls, and fly the limit.], 42 [SKID skid, dopey li'l], 43 [Hey I'm too far headed.], 44 [Goin' t'], 45 [There is a pure], 46 [Crank it or], 47 [All the left-out], 48 [My], 49 [Downward of roses,], 50 [Can't hold them together:], 51 [We two were given to emerge], 52 [From one half-wasted by], 53 [How am I to live?], 54 [Barely, be], 55 [Just now I thought to your], 56 [One month of], 57 [There's a], 58 [If not for you], 59 [Blood on], 60 [The dolphins of need be-], 61 [Deciduate, on grounds.], 62 [Am going soon, and I aspire to hear], 63 [Have walked some], 64 [Radiance came and], 65 [Nobody asked us], 66 [Egg-], 67 [Lady, this is no-]." *Descant* [Dennis Lee Special Issue], No. 39 [14, No. 1] (Winter 1982), pp. 201–26. Rpt. in *Tasks of Passion: Dennis Lee at Mid-Career*. Ed. Karen Mulhallen, Donna Bennett, and Russell Brown. Toronto: Descant, 1982, pp. 201–26. Rpt. (revised, expanded, and excerpted — "*from Riffs*: [When I lurched like a blizzard of wants through the networks of plenty,] [For months before we lay down], [Those perfect], [Hot po-], [There were], [One thing], [Take me again —], [Pen-], [Inch by], [Look maw — no mind &], [We swam into], [Why do I squat like a rainbow], [Smelting head foundries of ozone gravity breakage I], [Goin' t'], [There is a pure], [Just now I thought to your], [Blood on], [Nobody asked us], [Lady, this is no-]") in *Epoch* [Cornell Univ.], 33, No. 3 (Summer–Fall 1984), 310–18.

B69 "Riff [Darling, when we are]." *Canadian Literature*, No. 100 (Spring 1984), p. 199.

B70 "After Sabra, After Shatila." *This Magazine*, 16, No. 4 (Dec.–Jan. 1982–83), 20–21.

B71 "The Rhyme of the Three Cuddly Bombs." *Dismantler* [Ottawa], 3, No. 3 (July 1983), insert. Rpt. in CV/II, 7, No. 4 (Jan. 1984), 18. *RTCB*.

B72 "13 Blues for E." *Island* [Lantzville, B.C.], Nos. 15–16 (1985), pp. 38–43.

B73 "New Lives for Old." *Event: Journal of the Contemporary Arts* [Douglas College, New Westminster, B.C.] [15th Anniversary Issue], 15, No. 1 (1986), 28–29.

B74 "Try Panic." *Event: Journal of the Contemporary Arts* [Douglas College, New Westminster, B.C.] [15th Anniversary Issue], 15, No. 1 (1986), 30.

B75 "Unlucky Once." *Event: Journal of the Contemporary Arts* [Douglas College, New Westminster, B.C.] [15th Anniversary Issue], 15, No. 1 (1986), 31.

Children's Poems

B76 "If." *Wee Wisdom* [Kansas, Mo.], March 1948, Writers' Guild.

B77 "Free Verse." *The Twig* [Univ. of Toronto Schools] (1955), 44.

B78 "The Vision." Illus. J.S. *The Twig* [Univ. of Toronto Schools] (1956), 47.

B79 "The Difficulty of Living on Other Planets." *Campus Co-Op Newsletter* [Rochdale College, Toronto], 3, No. 1 (Summer 1967), 8. Rpt. in *This Magazine Is about Schools*, 2, No. 2 (Spring 1968), 119. *DLOP* (revised); *WL* (revised); *NKOP*; *DLOP* (chap.); *WL:RC*.
    See *DL* (cas.).

B80 "Greatheart and the Brain Drain." *Campus Co-Op Newsletter* [Rochdale College, Toronto], 3, No. 1 (Summer 1967), 8. *DLOP*; *Misc.*; *WL:RC*.

B81 "I Liked You in the Morning." *Campus Co-Op Newsletter* [Rochdale College, Toronto], 3, No. 1 (Summer 1967), 8. *WL:RC*.

B82 "The Abominable Wizard of Bloor Street." *Catalyst* [Univ. of Toronto], No. 1 (Autumn 1967), p. 15. Rpt. (revised — "The Abominable Fairy of Bloor Street") in *Canadian Children's Literature: A Journal of Criticism & Review*, No. 4 (1976), pp. 32–33. *DLOP* (revised); *NKOP* (revised); *WL:RC* (revised — "The Abominable Wizard of Bloor Street").
    See *DL* (cas.).

B83 "The Coat." *Catalyst* [Univ. of Toronto], No. 1 (Autumn 1967), p. 17. *DLOP* (revised); *WL* (revised); *NKOP*; *WL:RC*.
    See *DL* (cas.).

B84 "If You Should Meet." *Catalyst* [Univ. of Toronto], No. 1 (Autumn 1967), p. 16. *AP*; *WL:RC*.
    See *AP* (cas.).

B85 "The Warning." *Catalyst* [Univ. of Toronto], No. 1 (Autumn 1967), p. 15. *WL:RC*.

B86 "The Windypuff Song." *Catalyst* [Univ. of Toronto], No. 1 (Autumn 1967), p. 16. *WL*; *WL:RC*.
    See *DL* (cas.).

B87 "I Found a Silver Dollar." *This Magazine Is about Schools*, 2, No. 1 (Winter 1968), 35. *AP*; *DLBB*; *WL:RC*.
See *DL* (cas.) and *AP* (cas.).

B88 "Ookpik." *This Magazine Is about Schools*, 2, No. 1 (Winter 1968), 35. Rpt. (excerpt) in *Proceedings and Book Catalog: Children's Books International 2*. Ed. Jane Manthorne and Irenemarie H. Cullinane. Boston: Boston Public Library, 1977, p. 47. *WL*; *AP*; *WL:RC*.
See *AP* (cas.) and B286.

B89 "Wiggle to the Laundromat." *This Magazine Is about Schools*, 2, No. 1 (Winter 1968), 35. *WL*; *AP*; *WL:RC*.
See *DL* (cas.) and *AP* (cas.).

B90 "Psychapoo." *This Magazine Is about Schools*, 2, No. 2 (Spring 1968), pp. 118–19. *AP*; *DLBB*; *WL:RC*.
See *DL* (cas.) and *AP* (cas.).

B91 "Garbage Delight." In *Explore, Express*. Edmonton: Alberta School Broadcast Publication, 1973, p. 57. Rpt. illus. Frank Newfeld in *The Canadian* [*The Toronto Star*], 10 Sept. 1977, p. 17. Rpt. illus. Frank Newfeld in *Reader's Digest* [Montreal], March 1978, p. 76. *GD*.
See *APOP*.

B92 "Goofus." In *Explore, Express*. Edmonton: Alberta School Broadcast Publication, 1973, p. 55. *GD*.

B93 "What Will You Be?". In *Explore, Express*. Edmonton: Alberta School Broadcast Publication, 1973, p. 70. Rpt. illus. Frank Newfeld in *Reader's Digest* [Montreal], March 1978, p. 77. *GD*.

B94 "The Cyclone Visitors." *Toronto Life*, Sept. 1973, p. 37. Rpt. in *Canadian Children's Literature: A Journal of Criticism and Review*, No. 4 (1976), p. 51. *NKOP*; *WL:RC*.
See *DL* (cas.).

B95 "Flying Out of Holes." *The Citizen* [Ottawa], 26 Oct. 1974, p. 68. *WL*; *AP*; *WL:RC*.
See *AP* (cas.).

B96 "Once Upon an Alligator Pie . . . : There Was a Beautiful Young Poem That Had Never Been Written . . . : Alligator Pie." Illus. Frank Newfeld. *Weekend Magazine*, 6 Dec. 1975, p. 6. Rpt. ("Alligator Pie") in *Kid's Report*, 11 Jan. 1980. Rpt. in *Math Quest*. By Brendan Kelly. Don Mills, Ont.: Addison-Wesley, 1986, p. 137. Rpt. in *When You've Made It Your Own . . . .* By Gregory A. Denman. Foreword Bill Martin, Jr. Portsmouth, N.H.: Heinemann Education Books, 1988, p. 99. *WL*; *AP*; *DLBB*; *WL:RC*; *DL*; *DLFN79*.
See *AP* (cas.), *APOP*, and *RDLF*. For Gregory A. Denman's comments on "Alligator Pie," see C193.

B97 "Bouncing Song." *Canadian Children's Literature: A Journal of Criticism and Review*, No. 4 (1976), p. 48. *AP*; *WL:RC*.
See *AP* (cas.) and *APOP* ["Bouncing Song ('Hambone, Jawbone')"].

B98 "Bump on Your Thumb." *Canadian Children's Literature: A Journal of Criticism and Review*, No. 4 (1976), pp. 41–42. *AP*.
See *AP* (cas.), *APOP*, and *RDLF*.

B99 "The Cat and the Wizard." *Canadian Children's Literature: A Journal of Criticism and Review*, No. 4 (1976), pp. 53–58. *DLOP* (revised); *NKOP* (revised).
See B476.

B100 "The Friends." *Canadian Children's Literature: A Journal of Criticism and Review*, No. 4 (1976), pp. 33–34. *AP; DL*.
See *AP* (cas.) and *APOP*.

B101 "Going Up North." *Canadian Children's Literature: A Journal of Criticism and Review*, No. 4 (1976), pp. 30–31. Rpt. in *Proceedings and Book Catalog: Children's Books International 2*. Ed. Jane Manthorne and Irenemarie H. Cullinane. Boston: Boston Public Library, 1977, p. 46. *NKOP*.

B102 "In Kamloops." *Canadian Children's Literature: A Journal of Criticism and Review*, No. 4 (1976), p. 41. Rpt. in *Proceedings and Book Catalog: Children's Books International 2*. Ed. Jane Manthorne and Irenemarie H. Cullinane. Boston: Boston Public Library, 1977, p. 45. *WL; AP; WL:RC; DLFN80*.
See *DL* (cas.), *AP* (cas.), *APOP*, and *RDLF*.

B103 "Kahshe or Chicoutimi." *Canadian Children's Literature: A Journal of Criticism and Review*, No. 4 (1976), p. 40. *WL; AP; WL:RC*.
See *DL* (cas.) and *AP* (cas.).

B104 "The Sitter and the Butter and the Better Batter Fritter." *Canadian Children's Literature: A Journal of Criticism and Review*, No. 4 (1976), pp. 46–47. *AP*.
See *AP* (cas.) and *APOP*.

B105 "Skyscraper." *Canadian Children's Literature: A Journal of Criticism and Review*, No. 4 (1976), p. 36. *WL; AP; DLBB; WL:RC*.
See *AP* (cas.), *APOP*, *RDLF*, and B482.

B106 "A Song for Ookpik." *Canadian Children's Literature: A Journal of Criticism and Review*, No. 4 (1976), p. 52. Rpt. trans. ("La Cancion de Ookpik") in *Antología de la poesia actual Canadiense inglesa*. Ed. Manuel Betanzos Santos. Mexico City: Universidad Autonoma de San Luis Potosi, 1978, pp. 81–84. *NKOP*.

B107 "The Special Person" (excerpt). *Canadian Children's Literature: A Journal of Criticism and Review*, No. 4 (1976), p. 43. Rpt. (expanded) in *Proceedings and Book Catalog: Children's Books International 2*. Ed. Jane Manthorne and Irenemarie H. Cullinane. Boston: Boston Public Library, 1977, p. 46. *AP*.
See *AP* (cas.) and *APOP*.

B108 "Summer Song." *Canadian Children's Literature: A Journal of Criticism and Review*, No. 4 (1976), pp. 36–37. *Gods; NKOP; Misc*.

B109 "There Was a Man." *Canadian Children's Literature: A Journal of Criticism and Review*, No. 4 (1976), p. 48. *DLOP* (revised); *NKOP* (revised); *DL*.

B110 "Tongue Twister." *Canadian Children's Literature: A Journal of Criticism and Review*, No. 4 (1976), p. 41. *AP; DLFN79*.
See *AP* (cas.) and *APOP* ["Tongue Twister ('Someday I'll Go to Winnipeg')"].

B111 "With My Foot in My Mouth." *Canadian Children's Literature: A Journal of Criticism and Review*, No. 4 (1976), pp. 44–45. *NKOP*.

B112 "The Second Great Alligator Pie Contest: On Tuesdays I Polish My Uncle." Illus. Frank Newfeld. *Weekend Magazine*, 11 Dec. 1976, p. 15. *AP* ("On Tuesdays I Polish My Uncle").
See *DL* (cas.), *AP* (cas.), and *APOP*.

B113 "The Second Great Alligator Pie Contest: Tricking." *Weekend Magazine*, 11 Dec. 1976, p. 15. *AP* ("Tricking"); *DLFN80*.
See *AP* (cas.), *APOP*, and *RDLF*.

B114 "I Eat Kids Yum Yum!". Illus. Frank Newfeld. *Magook* [Toronto], No. 1 (1977), pp. 40–41. *GD*; *DLBB*.
See *APOP* and *RDLF*.

B115 "Billy Batter." Illus. Marylin Hafner. *Cricket* [La Salle, Ill.], Aug. 1977, p. 16. *AP*; *DLBB*; *DLFN79*.
See *AP* (cas.), *APOP*, and *RDLF*.

B116 "Half Way Dressed." Illus. Marylin Hafner. *Cricket* [La Salle, Ill.], Aug. 1977, p. 13. *GD*; *DLFN79*.
See *APOP* and *RDLF*.

B117 "Muffin and Puffin and Murphy and Me." Illus. Marylin Hafner. *Cricket* [La Salle, Ill.], Aug. 1977, p. 17. *GD*.

B118 "Mumbo Jumbo." Illus. Marylin Hafner. *Cricket* [La Salle, Ill.], Aug. 1977, p. 17. *AP* ("Mumbo, Jumbo").
See *AP* (cas.) and *APOP*.

B119 "The Question." Illus. Marylin Hafner. *Cricket* [La Salle, Ill.], Aug. 1977, p. 18. *NKOP*; *DLFN79*.
See *APOP*.

B120 "Wellington the Skeleton." Illus. Marylin Hafner. *Cricket* [La Salle, Ill.], Aug. 1977, pp. 14–15. *NKOP*.
See *APOP*.

B121 "The Aminals [sic]." Illus. Frank Newfeld. *The Canadian* [*The Toronto Star*], 10 Sept. 1977, p. 18. *GD*.

B122 "Being Five." Illus. Frank Newfeld. *The Canadian* [*The Toronto Star*], 10 Sept. 1977, p. 17. Rpt. illus.

Frank Newfeld in *Reader's Digest* [Montreal], March 1978, pp. 76–77. *GD*; *DLBB*; *DLFN80*.
See *APOP* and *RDLF*.

B123 "The Big Blue Frog and the Dirty Flannel Dog." Illus. Frank Newfeld. *The Canadian* [*The Toronto Star*], 10 Sept. 1977, p. 16. *GD*.

B124 "One Sunny Summer's Day." Illus. Frank Newfeld. *The Canadian* [*The Toronto Star*], 10 Sept. 1977, p. 18. *GD*.

B125 "Suzy Grew a Moustache." Illus. Frank Newfeld. *The Canadian* [*The Toronto Star*], 10 Sept. 1977, p. 17. *GD*; *DL*; *DLFN80*.
See *APOP* and *RDLF*.

B126 "The Coming of Teddy Bears." *Cricket* [La Salle, Ill.], Dec. 1977, p. 88. *GD*; *DLBB*; *DLFN79*.
See *APOP* and *B480*.

B127 "Worm." Illus. Frank Newfeld. *Reader's Digest* [Montreal], March 1978, p. 77. *GD*.

B128 "Chitter-Chatter-Chipmunk." Illus. Frank Newfeld. *Chickadee*, 1, No. 2 (Feb. 1979), 8. *ICS*.

B129 "Granny Spider." Illus. Frank Newfeld. *Chickadee*, 1, No. 2 (Feb. 1979), 8. *JB*.

B130 "The Three Little Nippers." Illus. Frank Newfeld. *Chickadee*, 1, No. 2 (Feb. 1979), 8–9.

B131 "A Love Affair with Dennis Lee: Bundle-Buggy Boogie." *The Medium* [Estevan, Sask.], 21, No. 2 (Fall 1980), p. 32. *JB* ("Bundle-Buggy Boogie").
See *RDLF*. *The Medium* also includes letters from Lee (B446, B447, and B448) and notes by Shirley Andrist (C109).

B132 "A Love Affair with Dennis Lee: Mrs. Murphy and Mrs. Murphy's Kids." *The Medium* [Estevan, Sask.], 21, No. 2 (Fall 1980), pp. 30–31. Rpt. (*"Three Poems*: Mrs. Murphy and Mrs. Murphy's Kids") in PRISM *international*, 20, No. 4 (Summer 1982), 83–84. Rpt. illus. Juan Wijngaard ("Mrs. Murphy, and Mrs. Murphy's Kids") in *Chickadee*, Feb. 1984, pp. 22–23. *JB* ("Mrs Murphy, and Mrs Murphy's Kids").
　　See *RDLF. The Medium* also includes letters by Lee (B446, B447, and B448) and notes by Shirley Andrist (C109).

B133 "A Love Affair with Dennis Lee: My Pet." *The Medium* [Estevan, Sask.], 21, No. 2 (Fall 1980), p. 29.
　　Also includes letters by Lee (B446, B447, and B448) and notes by Shirley Andrist (C109).

B134 "A Love Affair with Dennis Lee: The Tree." *The Medium* [Estevan, Sask.], 21, No. 2 (Fall 1980), 28.
　　Also includes letters by Lee (B446, B447, and B448) and notes by Shirley Andrist (C109).

B135 "Anna Banana." In *Poem Stew*. Ed. William Cole. Illus. Karen Ann Weinhaus. New York: Lippincott, 1981, p. 64. Rpt. in *The Globe and Mail* [Toronto]. "The Features Page," 24 Dec. 1983, p. 10. *JB*.

B136 "Double-Barrelled Ding-Dong-Bat." In *A Day in Verse: Breakfast, Books, and Dreams*. Ed. Michael Patrick Hearn. New York: Frederick Warne, 1981, n. pag. *JB*.

B137 "Freddy." In *A Day in Verse: Breakfast, Books, and Dreams*. Ed. Michael Patrick Hearn. New York: Frederick Warne, 1981, n. pag. *JB*.

B138 "Jenny the Juvenile Juggler." In *A Day in Verse: Breakfast, Books, and Dreams*. Ed. Michael Patrick Hearn. New York: Frederick Warne, 1981, n. pag.

Rpt. illus. Jillian Hulme-Gilliland in *Quarry*, 34, No. 1 (Winter 1985), 7. ICS.

B139 "There Was an Old Lady." In *Poem Stew*. Ed. William Cole. Illus. Karen Ann Weinhaus. New York: Lippincott, 1981, pp. 28–29. *JB*; *DLBB*.

B140 "*Three Poems*: The Doughnut Hole." PRISM *international*, 20, No. 4 (Summer 1982), 85.

B141 "*Three Poems*: Silverly." PRISM *international*, 20, No. 4 (Summer 1982), 86. *JB* ("Silverly").

B142 "Hugh, Hugh." *The Globe and Mail* [Toronto]. "The Features Page," 24 Dec. 1983, p. 10. *JB*.

B143 "Lazy Liza Briggs." *The Globe and Mail* [Toronto]. "The Features Page," 24 Dec. 1983, p. 10. *JB*.

B144 "Little Miss Dimble." *The Globe and Mail* [Toronto]. "The Features Page," 24 Dec. 1983, p. 10. *JB*; *DLBB*.

B145 "Mr. Lister's Dog." *The Globe and Mail* [Toronto]. "The Features Page," 24 Dec. 1983, p. 10. *JB* ("Mr Lister's Dog").

B146 "Peterkin Pete." *The Globe and Mail* [Toronto]. "The Features Page," 24 Dec. 1983, p. 10. *JB*.

B147 "Up in Northern Ontario." *The Globe and Mail* [Toronto]. "The Features Page," 24 Dec. 1983, p. 10. *JB* ("Up in North Ontario").

B148 "William Lyon Mackenzie." *The Globe and Mail* [Toronto]. "The Features Page," 24 Dec. 1983, p. 10. *JB*.

B149 "Sailing to Sea." Illus. Juan Wijngaard. *Chickadee*, Feb. 1984, p. 24. *JB*.

B150 "The Voyage." Illus. Juan Wijngaard. *Chickadee*, Feb. 1984, p. 25. *JB*.

B151 "The Fishes of Kempenfelt Bay." In *Math Quest*. By Brendan Kelly. Don Mills, Ont.: Addison-Wesley, 1986, p. 221. *WL* ("The Fishes of Kempenfeldt Bay"); *AP* ("The Fishes of Kempenfeldt Bay"); *WL:RC* ("The Fishes of Kempenfeldt Bay").
   See *DL* (cas.) ("Fishes of Kempenfeldt Bay"), *AP* (cas.) ("The Fishes of Kempenfeldt Bay"), and *APOP*.

B152 "The Puzzle." In *Math Quest*. By Brendan Kelly. Don Mills, Ont.: Addison-Wesley, 1986, p. 77. *JB*.

Children's Tale

B153 "Lizzy's Lion." Illus. Terry Oakes. In *Gangsters, Ghosts and Dragonflies: A Book of Story Poems*. Ed. Brian Patten. London: George Allen & Unwin, 1981, pp. 100–02. *LL*.
   For reprinted contributions to this anthology, see B178.

Short Story

B154 "The Present." *Acta Victoriana* [Victoria College, Univ. of Toronto], 83, No. 3 (Jan. 1959), 5–6.

Juvenile Prose

B155 "Hmmmm." *The Twig* [Univ. of Toronto Schools] (1953), 39.

B156 "Small Person." *The Twig* [Univ. of Toronto Schools] (1954), 52.

B157 "Valedictory, 1957." *The Twig* [Univ. of Toronto Schools] (1957), 99–100.

Reprinted Anthology Contributions: A Selection

B158 "Free Verse." In *First Flowering: A Selection of Prose and Poetry by the Youth of Canada*. Ed. and preface Anthony Frisch. Toronto: Kingswood House, 1956, pp. 26–27.

B159 "The Children in Nathan Phillips Square" [i.e., "Third Elegy," 1968]. In *The New Romans: Candid Canadian Opinions of the U.S.* Ed. and introd. A.W. Purdy. Edmonton: Hurtig, 1968, pp. 144–47.

B160 "Getting to Rochdale" (essay — "Innocents and Tories: A Personal Vaudeville in Five Acts"). In *The University Game*. Ed. and introd. Howard Adelman and Dennis Lee. Toronto: House of Anansi, 1968, pp. 69–94.

B161 "400: Coming Home" and "He Asks Her." In *Fifteen Winds: A Selection of Modern Canadian Poems*. Ed. and introd. A.W. Purdy. Toronto: Ryerson, 1969, pp. 55–57.

B162 "400: Coming Home," "Glad for the Wrong Reasons," and "When It Is Over." In *Made in Canada: New Poems of the Seventies*. Ed. and introd. Douglas Lochhead and Raymond Souster. [Ottawa]: Oberon, 1970, pp. 119–21.

B163 "Glad for the Wrong Reasons." In *How Do I Love Thee: Sixty Poets of Canada (and Quebec) Select and Introduce Their Favourite Poems from Their Own Work*. Ed. and preface John Robert Colombo. Edmonton: Hurtig, 1970, p. 139.

B164 "Brunswick Avenue," "400: Coming Home," "He Asks Her," and "High Park, by Grenadier Pond." In *The Book Cellar Anthology*. Ed. Randall Ware. Introd. Doug Fetherling. Toronto: Peter Martin, 1971, pp. 43–47.

B165 "1883" [sic; "1838"], "More Claiming," "Third Elegy," and "Thursday." In *Storm Warning: The New Canadian Poets*. Ed. and introd. Al Purdy. Toronto: McClelland and Stewart, 1971, pp. 90–95.

B166 "From *First Elegy*" [i.e., "Civil Elegies: 1," 1972] (excerpt) and "Spadina." In *The City: Attacking Modern Myths*. Ed. and introd. Alan Powell. Toronto: McClelland and Stewart, 1972, pp. 93, 114.

B167 "Here, as I Sit" [i.e., "Civil Elegies: 9," 1972] and "Master and Lord" [i.e., "Civil Elegies: 2," 1972]. In *The Oxford Anthology of Canadian Literature*. Ed. and preface Robert Weaver and William Toye. Toronto: Oxford Univ. Press, 1973, pp. 280–83.

B168 "When It Is Over." In *Mirrors: Recent Canadian Verse*. Ed. and introd. Jon Pearce. Toronto: Gage, 1975, p. 129.

B169 "1838" (excerpt). In *1837: William Lyon Mackenzie and the Canadian Revolution*. Ed. Rick Salutin. Toronto: James Lorimer, 1976, p. 180.

B170 "W.L.M./1838" [i.e., "1838"] and "When I Went Up to Rosedale." In *The Toronto Book: An Anthology of Writings Past and Present*. Ed. and introd. William Kilbourn. Toronto: Macmillan, 1976, pp. 31–32, 119–20.

B171 "Civil Elegy 5" [1972 ed.], "1838," "400: Coming Home," and "Thursday." In *Canadian Poetry: The Modern Era*. Ed. and preface John Newlove. Toronto: McClelland and Stewart, 1977, pp. 132–37.

B172 "Tricking." In *What's to Eat?*. Ed. and introd. Edith Down and Sharon Pisesky. Family Study Series/Introductory. Toronto: Copp Clark, 1977, p. 134.

B173 "When I Went Up to Rosedale." In *Toronto in Words and Pictures*. Ed. William Kilbourn and Rudi Christl. Toronto: McClelland and Stewart, 1977, pp. 88–89.

B174 "The Coming of Teddy Bears." In *The Poets of Canada*. Ed. and preface John Robert Colombo. Edmonton: Hurtig, 1978, pp. 234–35.

B175 "Roots and Play: Writing as a 35-Year-Old Children [sic]" (essay; excerpt). In *Children's Literature Review: Excerpts from Reviews, Criticism, and Commentary on Books for Children and Young People*. Ed. Gerard J. Senick. Vol. III. Detroit: Gale, 1978, 113–15.

B176 "Alligator Pie." In *Farewell to the 70s*. Ed. and note Anna Porter and Marjorie Harris. A Discovery Book. Toronto: Thomas Nelson & Sons, 1979, p. 63.

B177 "Being Five," "Billy Batter," "Forty Mermaids," "Mumbo, Jumbo," "Street Song," and "Tricking." In *Storytellers' Rendezvous: Canadian Stories to Tell Children*. Ed. and preface Lorrie Anderson, Irene Aubrey, and Louise McDiarmid. Foreword Paul Kitchen. Ottawa: Canadian Library Association, 1979, pp. 97, 99, 101.

B178 "Mrs. Murphy and Mrs. Murphy's Kids," "Oilcan Harry," and "On Tuesdays: I Polish My Uncle." In *Gangsters, Ghosts and Dragonflies: A Book of Story*

Poems. Ed. Brian Patten. London: George Allen & Unwin, 1981, pp. 11, 24–25, 48–49.

See B153 for an original publication in this anthology.

B179 "The Sitter and the Butter and the Better Batter Fritter" and "William Lyon Mackenzie King." In *The Maple Laugh Forever: An Anthology of Comic Canadian Poetry.* Ed. and "Prologue" Douglas Barbour and Stephen Scobie. Edmonton: Hurtig, 1981, pp. 23, 88–89.

B180 "After Sabra, After Shatila." In *And Not Surrender: American Poets on Lebanon.* Ed. Kamal Boullata. Washington, D.C.: Arab American Cultural Foundation, 1982, pp. 58–60.

B181 "As She Grows Older" and "Downward of Roses." In *New Directions 44: An International Anthology of Poetry and Prose.* Ed. J. Laughlin, Peter Glassgold, and Frederick R. Martin. New York: New Directions, 1982, pp. 180–81.

B182 "Coming Home" [i.e., "400: Coming Home"] and "Summer Song." In *The Heath Introduction to Literature.* Canadian ed. Ed. Alice S. Landy and Dave Martin. Lexington, Mass.: D.C. Heath, 1982, pp. 889–91.

B183 "400: Coming Home, "FROM Civil Elegies: 2, 9" [i.e., "Civil Elegies: 2, 9" 1972], "The Gods," "1838," "Thursday," "Remember, Woman," and "Summer Song." In *Canadian Poetry.* Ed. Jack David and Robert Lecker. Introd. George Woodcock. New Press Canadian Classics. Toronto/Downsview, Ont.: General/ECW, 1982. Vol. II, 218–31.

B184 "From 'Civil Elegies' " [i.e., "Civil Elegies: 1" 1972],

and "The Gods." In *The New Oxford Book of Canadian Verse: In English.* Ed. and introd. Margaret Atwood. Toronto: Oxford Univ. Press, 1982, pp. 367–74.

B185 "Alligator Pie," "Double-Barrelled Ding-Dong-Bat," "Freddy," "The Muddy Puddle," and "Tony Balony." In *The Random House Book of Poetry for Children.* Ed. and introd. Jack Prelutsky. New York: Random House, 1983, pp. 28, 104, 109–10, 180.

B186 *The Death of Harold Ladoo,* "From 'Cadence, Country, Silence: Writing in Colonial Space' " (excerpt; essay), and "When I Went Up to Rosedale." In *An Anthology of Canadian Literature in English.* Ed. and introd. Donna Bennett and Russell Brown. Vol. II. Toronto: Oxford Univ. Press, 1983, 505–32.

B187 "The Gods." In *Modernity and Responsibility: Essays for George Grant.* Ed. Eugene Combs. Toronto: Univ. of Toronto Press, 1983, pp. 3–6.

B188 "From Civil Elegies" [i.e., "Civil Elegies: 2" 1972 and "Civil Elegies: 6" 1972] and "You Can Climb Down Now." In *The Penguin Book of Canadian Verse.* 4th rev. ed. Ed. and introd. Ralph Gustafson. Markham, Ont.: Penguin, 1984, pp. 312–14.

B189 "W.L.M./1838" and "When I Went Up to Rosedale." In *Toronto Remembered: A Celebration of the City.* Ed. and introd. William Kilbourn. Toronto: Stoddart, 1984, pp. 36, 96–97.

B190 "Cadence, Country, Silence: Writing in Colonial Space" (essay). In *1940–1983.* Vol. II of *Towards a Canadian Literature: Essays, Editorials and Manifestos.* Ed. Douglas M. Daymond and Leslie G. Monkman. Ottawa: Tecumseh, 1985, pp. 497–520.

B191 "Alligator Pie," "I Eat Kids Yum Yum!", and "The Sitter and the Butter and the Better Batter Fritter." In *The CanLit Foodbook: From Pen to Palate — A Collection of Tasty Literary Fare.* Ed., introd., and illus. Margaret Atwood. Toronto: Totem, 1987, pp. 128, 144, 160.

B192 "1838." In *The Northern Red Oak: Poems for and about Milton Acorn.* Ed. and introd. James Deahl. Toronto: Unfinished Monument, 1987, p. 42.

B193 "Jenny the Juvenile Juggler." In *Rhythm Road: Poems to Move To.* Ed. Lillian Morrison. New York: Lothrop, Lee & Shepard, 1988, p. 81.

B194 "Little Miss Dimble" and "Sailing to Sea." In *Singing in the Sun.* Ed. Jill Bennett. Illus. Vanessa Julian-Ottie. Markham, Ont.: Penguin, 1988, pp. 67, 76.

Essays

B195 "U of T: Full of Competent Mediocrity." Photograph Mike Lloyd. *Toronto Life,* Feb. 1967, pp. 40–41, 52–53. Rpt. (excerpt) in *The Strand* [Victoria College, Univ. of Toronto], 16 Feb. 1967, pp. 2, 4–5.
Continued in "The Unreformed University" (B196).

B196 "The Unreformed University: Part II." *Toronto Life,* March 1967, pp. 28–29, 41, 52, 57.
Continued from "U of T: Full of Competent Mediocrity" (B195).

B197 "Innocents and Tories: A Personal Vaudeville in Five Acts." U.L.S.R. Conference, Rochdale College, Toronto. 6 Oct. 1967. Printed ("Getting to Rochdale"). Photographs Pamela Harris. *This Magazine Is about Schools,* 2, No. 1 (Winter 1968), 72–96.

Rpt. in *This Book Is about Schools.* Ed. Satu Repo. New York: Pantheon, 1970, pp. 354–80. *IT.*

B198 "Notes on a WASP Canadian Nationalist." In *Notes for a Native Land: A New Encounter with Canada.* Ed. Andy Wainwright. Ottawa: Oberon, 1969, pp. 19–25.

B199 "Dennis Lee: Glad for the Wrong Reasons." In *How Do I Love Thee: Sixty Poets of Canada (and Quebec) Select and Introduce Their Favourite Poems from Their Own Work.* Ed. John Robert Colombo. Edmonton: Hurtig, 1970, pp. 139–40.

B200 "Modern Poetry." In *Read Canadian: A Book about Canadian Books.* Ed. Robert Fulford, David Godfrey, and Abraham Rotstein. Toronto: James Lewis and Samuel, 1972, pp. 228–36.

B201 "Cadence, Country, Silence." Rencontre québécoise internationale des Ecrivains, Montréal. 28 May–4 June 1972. Printed (expanded) in *Liberté,* 14, No. 6, [No. 84] (1972), 65–68. Rpt. ("Cadence, Country, Silence: Writing in a Colonial Space") in *Open Letter,* Ser. 2, No. 6 (Fall 1973), pp. 34–53. Rpt. ("Cadence, Country, Silence: Writing in Colonial Space") in *boundary 2: a journal of postmodern literature* [State Univ. of New York at Binghamton], 3, No. 1 (Fall 1974), 151–68. Rpt. (excerpt) in *Cencrastus: Scottish & International Literature Arts & Affairs* [Edinburgh], No. 4 (Winter 1980–81), pp. 1–6.

B202 "Running and Dwelling: Homage to Al Purdy." Illus. Pilsworth. *Saturday Night,* July 1972, pp. 14–16.

B203 "Rejoinder." Letter. *Saturday Night,* Sept. 1972, pp. 32–33.

A response to Robin Mathews' letter (C11), which criticizes Lee's "Running and Dwelling: Homage to Al Purdy."

B204 "Loughborough 1975: A Coming of Age in Canadian Children's Literature?". *The Canadian Author & Bookman*, 51, No. 2 (Winter 1975), 9–10.

Includes an excerpt from Lee's presentation at Loughborough 1975, the 8th International Summer Seminar on Children's Literature.

B205 "Roots and Play: Writing as a 35-Year-Old Children [sic]." *Canadian Children's Literature: A Journal of Criticism and Review*, No. 4 (1976), pp. 28–58.

B206 "Reading *Savage Fields*." *Canadian Journal of Political and Social Theory/Revue canadienne de théorie politique et sociale* [Winnipeg], 3, No. 2 (Spring–Summer 1979), 161–82. Rpt. (revised) in *Brick* [Ilderton, Ont.], No. 13 (Fall 1981), pp. 32–39. *RSF* (revised).

Lee also responds to criticism by Leah Bradshaw (C98) and David Godfrey (C99).

B207 "Polyphony, Enacting a Meditation." *Descant* [Dennis Lee Special Issue], No. 39 [14, No. 1] (Winter 1982), pp. 82–99. Rpt. in *Tasks of Passion: Dennis Lee at Mid-Career*. Ed. Karen Mulhallen, Donna Bennett, and Russell Brown. Toronto: Descant, 1982, pp. 82–99.

A reconsideration of "An Interview with Dennis Lee" (C221).

B208 "Writer to Publishing House." In *Author & Editor: A Working Guide*. By Rick Archbold, Doug Gibson, Dennis Lee, John Pearce, and Jan Walter. Toronto: Book and Periodical Development Council, 1983, pp. 27–32.

See also B251.

B209 Contributor. "Making Strange Poetics: Discussion." Long-liners Conference on the Canadian Long Poem, Calumet College, York Univ., Toronto. 29 May–1 June 1984. Printed in *Open Letter* [Long-liners Conference Issue], Ser. 6, Nos. 2–3 (Summer–Fall 1985), pp. 222, 223, 229.

B210 "For and Against Pound: Polyphony and Ekstatic Form." Long-liners Conference on the Canadian Long Poem, Calumet College, York Univ., Toronto. 29 May–1 June 1984. Printed (revised) in *Open Letter* [Long-liners Conference Issue], Ser. 6, Nos. 2–3 (Summer–Fall 1985), pp. 191–202, 204–12.

Following this essay in *Open Letter*, the editors note that this "essay is an extensive revision of the partially extemporaneous paper which Lee presented to the Conference." (See C174.)

B211 Introduction. In *The New Canadian Poets, 1970–1985*. Ed. Dennis Lee. Toronto: McClelland and Stewart, 1985, pp. xvii–liii.

B212 "The Poery of Al Purdy: An Afterword." In *The Collected Poems of Al Purdy*. Ed. Russell Brown. Toronto: McClelland and Stewart, 1986, pp. 371–91. Rpt. ("Singing in the Dark: 'Poetry' by Al Purdy 'Essay' by Dennis Lee") in *The Canadian Forum*, Aug.–Sept. 1986, pp. 16–18.

B213 "Labyrinth" (essay). *Crackers* [Richmond, Ont.], No. 2 (Fall 1986), pp. 8–9.

See also *Labyrinth* (video) (A70).

Articles

B214 "The Poetry of the People." *Acta Victoriana* [Victoria College, Univ. of Toronto], 84, No. 1 (Dec. 1959), 9–11.

Signed: Shakesbeat Latweed. Satirical prose.

B215 "Call to Blood, Sweat and Learning." *The Varsity* [Univ. of Toronto], 2 Feb. 1961.

B216 "Dry Ground Defended." Letter. *Varsity Weekend Review* [Univ. of Toronto], 9 Dec. 1961, pp. 4–5.

B217 "The Academics." *The Telegram* [Toronto], 11 Dec. 1965, p. 9.

B218 "Rochdale College." *Rochdale College Bulletin* [Toronto], 10 Dec. 1966, pp. 6–7.

B219 "A Start." *Rochdale College Bulletin* [Rochdale College, Toronto], 10 Dec. 1966, pp. 3–6.

B220 "Statement of Aims." *Rochdale College Bulletin* [Rochdale College, Toronto], 10 Dec. 1966, pp. 8–11.

B221 "Notes on Rochdale." *Rochdale College Bulletin* [Rochdale College, Toronto], 30 Jan. 1967, pp. [17–31]. *NR.*

B222 "Rochdale Education." *Campus Co-Op News Letter* [Rochdale College, Toronto], 3, No. 1 (Summer 1967), 7–8.

B223 "Bookstores." ANYTHING BUT SON OF ROCHDALE [Rochdale College, Toronto], 1, No. 1 (Sept. 1967), 1.

B224 "Rochdale Is Free. Wow!!". ANYTHING BUT SON OF ROCHDALE [Rochdale College, Toronto], 1, No. 1 (Sept. 1967), 10–12.

B225 "What You Need Is a Glossary." ANYTHING BUT SON OF ROCHDALE [Rochdale College, Toronto], 1, No. 1 (Sept. 1967), 21–25.

B226 "Phone This Number." ANYTHING BUT SON OF ROCHDALE [Rochdale College, Toronto], 1, No. 2 (Oct. 1967), 7–8.

B227 ——, and Howard Adelman. Introduction. In *The University Game*. Ed. Howard Adelman and Dennis Lee. Toronto: House of Anansi, 1968, pp. 1–3.

B228 Contributor. *Rochdale College Catalogue*. [Toronto: Rochdale College], 1968, pp. 3–4.
Lee discusses his year, 1967, as resource person at Rochdale College.

B229 "A Warning Against This Kind of Anthology Being an Introduction Which Discusses the Reader." In *T.O. Now: The Young Toronto Poets*. Ed. Dennis Lee. HAP, No. 8. Toronto: House of Anansi, 1968, pp. i–iv.

B230 "The Joys of Junk." Photographs William E. Smith. *Toronto Life*, Feb. 1969, pp. 56–57.

B231 "Education Next Year." *Rochdale Daily* [Rochdale College, Toronto], 10 Feb. 1969, pp. 2–3. Rpt. (condensed — *Education Next Year: A Proposal*) n.p.: n.p., [Dec. 1968]. 1 leaf. [Mimeographed.]

B232 "When Will We Have a Second Year?". *Rochdale Daily* [Rochdale College, Toronto], 14 Feb. 1969, p. [1].

B233 "Non-Confidence in Council." *Maysay* [Rochdale College, Toronto], No. 5, 11 May 1969, pp. 1–3.

B234 "Question of the Week: Dennis Lee, Resource Person, Rochdale College: Will President Nixon's Peace Proposals Speed Up the Paris Talks?". *Toronto Daily Star*, 17 May 1969, Insight, p. 6.

B235 "Spadina Expressway/Are the Experts Misleading Us?". Illus. *Toronto Daily Star*, 29 Sept. 1969, Sec. One, p. 6.

B236 " 'Thank You Mr. Blumenfeld for Arguing against Spadina.' " *Toronto Daily Star*, 1969.

B237 " 'Stop Work on the Spadina Expressway Until We've Reconsidered the Alternatives.' " Illus. *Toronto Daily Star*, 19 Feb. 1970, Sec. One, Voice of the People, p. 7.

B238 "Draft Notes on English Trade Publishing." An unpublished brief submitted to the Royal Commission on Book Publishing, Toronto, 1971. [Mimeographed, 11 pp.]
  See also B239.

B239 "A Regulatory Body for Canadian Publishing: A Brief to the Ontario Commission on Book Publishing." Written and submitted to the Royal Commission on Book Publishing on behalf of the House of Anansi Press, Toronto, 1971. [Mimeographed, 6 pp.] Printed (excerpts — "A Brief to the Royal Commission on Book Publishing") in *BlewOintment* [Blewointmentpress Poverty Isshew], March 1971, pp. 79–85.
  See also B238.

B240 "Brunswick Elects Heap . . . Oh Well!". *The Sunday Brunswick* [Toronto], 24 Oct. 1971, p. [3].

B241 "Election Irregularities." *The Sunday Brunswick* [Toronto], 24 Oct. 1971, p. [3].

B242 "Once Upon an Alligator Pie . . . : There Was a Beautiful Young Poem That Had Never Been Written . . . ." Illus. Frank Newfeld. *Weekend Magazine*, 6 Dec. 1975, pp. 3, 6, 9.

B243 Foreword. In *Moving to the Clear: Poems from Trent University, Peterborough*. Ed. Dennis Lee. [Peterborough]: n.p., 1976, p. 3. Rpt. [Toronto]: n.p., 1976, p. [3].

B244 "The Second Annual Great Alligator Pie Contest." Illus. Frank Newfeld. *Weekend Magazine*, 11 Dec. 1976, pp. 14–16.

B245 "Reaping Their Promise: Dennis Lee." *Books in Canada*, April 1977, p. 4.

B246 "Meet Your Poet: Dennis Lee." Illus. *Cricket* [La Salle, Ill.], Aug. 1977, p. 19.

B247 "Author's Choice." *The Toronto Star*. "Books in the Star," 10 Dec. 1977, p. D8.

B248 Foreword. In *It Scares Me but I Like It: Creating Poetry with Children*. By Russell Hazzard. All about Us/Nous autres. Don Mills, Ont.: Fitzhenry & Whiteside, 1979, pp. 4–5.

B249 "Apprenticed to Truth and Uncertainty." *University of Toronto Graduate*, 6, No. 3 (Spring 1979), 6. Rpt. in *Bulletin* [Univ. of Toronto], 2 April 1979, p. 6.

B250 "TWUC and the Crisis in Trade-Book Publishing." In *Book Committee Report*. Toronto: Writers' Union of Canada, 1980, pp. 1–8.

B251 ———, and Rick Archbold. "How a Book Is Costed." In *Author & Editor: A Working Guide*. By Rick Archbold, Doug Gibson, Dennis Lee, John Pearce, and Jan Walter. Toronto: Book and Periodical Development Council, 1983, pp. 10–13.
  See also B208.

B252 Introduction. In *The New Canadian Poets, 1970–1985*. Toronto: McClelland and Stewart, 1985, pp. xvii–liii.

B253 Preface. In *Book Show: A Celebration of Reading*. Ed. John O'Leary and Katharine Reynolds. Toronto: Frontier College, [1986], p. 3.

B254 "Reading Adonis." *Poetry Canada Review*, 9, No. 2 (Winter–Spring 1988), 8–10. *Adon*. ("Adonis").

Translations

B255 "First Elegy." *Quarry*, 19, No. 1 (Fall 1969), 6–9.
Translated from the original German poem, "Die Erste Elegie," by Rainer Maria Rilke.

B256 "Second Elegy." *Contemporary Literature in Translation*, 6 (Winter 1969), 9–11.
Translated from the original German poem, "Die Zweite Elegie," by Rainer Maria Rilke.

B257 "White Mice." In *Moving to the Clear: Poems from Trent University, Peterborough*. Ed. and foreword Dennis Lee. [Peterborough]: n.p., 1976, pp. 16–17. Rpt. [Toronto]: n.p., 1976, pp. 16–17. Rpt. in *The Canadian Forum*, Feb. 1978, p. 22. Rpt. in *Learn This Poem of Mine by Heart*. By George Faludy. Ed. John Robert Colombo. Toronto: Hounslow, 1983, pp. 55–57. Rpt. in *George Faludy Selected Poems 1933–1980*. Ed. Robin Skelton. Toronto: McClelland and Stewart, 1985, p. 48.
Adapted from the literal translation, by George Faludy and Eric Johnson, of the original Hungarian poem entitled "Fehér egerek" by George Faludy.

B258 ———, and A. Bantas. "Remnants." In *Modern Romanian Poetry*. Ed. Nicholas Catanoy. Oakville, Ont.: Mosaic, 1977, p. 21.

Adapted from the literal translation, by A. Bantas, of the original Romanian poem by Adrian Pavnescu.

B259 ———, and M. Damboiu. "This World." In *Modern Romanian Poetry*. Ed. Nicholas Catanoy. Oakville, Ont.: Mosaic, 1977, pp. 72–73.
Adapted from the literal translation, by M. Damboiu, of the original Romanian poem by Virgil Gheorghiu.

B260 "Apocalyptica." In *East and West: Selected Poems of George Faludy*. Ed. John Robert Colombo. Toronto: Hounslow, 1978, p. 128. Rpt. in *The Canadian Forum*, Feb. 1978, p. 22.
Adapted from the literal translation, by George Faludy, of the original Hungarian poem by George Faludy.

B261 "Chief Censor and Secretary of State for Culture Han Ju Visits Li Ho to Commission a Poem." In *East and West: Selected Poems of George Faludy*. Ed. John Robert Colombo. Toronto: Hounslow, 1978, pp. 138–39.
Adapted from the literal translation, by George Faludy, of the original Hungarian poem by George Faludy.

B262 "Death of a Chleuch Dancer." In *East and West: Selected Poems of George Faludy*. Ed. John Robert Colombo. Toronto: Hounslow, 1978, p. 48. Rpt. in *The Canadian Forum*, Feb. 1978, p. 21. Rpt. in *George Faludy Selected Poems 1933–1980*. Ed. Robin Skelton. Toronto: McClelland and Stewart, 1985, p. 49. *DCD*.
Adapted from the literal translation, by George Faludy, of the original Hungarian poem entitled "Chleuch táncos halála" by George Faludy.

B263 "Love Poems to Her, Dying: 3–4." In *East and West: Selected Poems of George Faludy*. Ed. John Robert Colombo. Toronto: Hounslow, 1978, pp. 97–98. Rpt. (excerpt — "Love Poem to Her Dying: Three") in *George Faludy Selected Poems 1933–1980*. Ed. Robin Skelton. Toronto: McClelland and Stewart, 1985, p. 127.

Adapted from the literal translation, by George Faludy, of the original Hungarian poem by George Faludy.

B264 "Morocco." In *East and West: Selected Poems of George Faludy*. Ed. John Robert Colombo. Toronto: Hounslow, 1978, p. 45. Rpt. in *The Canadian Forum*, Feb. 1978, p. 21. Rpt. in *George Faludy Selected Poems 1933–1980*. Ed. Robin Skelton. Toronto: McClelland and Stewart, 1985, p. 48.

Adapted from the literal translation, by George Faludy, of the original Hungarian poem by George Faludy.

B265 "On the Tower of the Casbah, Above the River Draa." In *East and West: Selected Poems of George Faludy*. Ed. John Robert Colombo. Toronto: Hounslow, 1978, p. 49. *The Canadian Forum*, Feb. 1978, p. 22. Rpt. in *George Faludy Selected Poems 1933–1980*. Ed. Robin Skelton. Toronto: McClelland and Stewart, 1985, p. 57.

Adapted from the literal translation, by George Faludy, of the original Hungarian poem by George Faludy.

B266 "Sonnets: 3." In *East and West: Selected Poems of George Faludy*. Ed. John Robert Colombo. Toronto: Hounslow, 1978, p. 105.

Adapted from the literal translation, by George Faludy, of the original Hungarian poem by George Faludy.

B267 ———, George Faludy, and Eric Johnson. "Pitiless and Alone." *The Canadian Forum*, Feb. 1978, p. 23. Rpt. in *George Faludy Selected Poems 1933–1980*. Ed. Robin Skelton. Toronto: McClelland and Stewart, 1985, pp. 72–75.

Adapted from the literal translation, by George Faludy and Eric Johnson, of the original Hungarian poem by George Faludy.

B268 "Alba Three." In *George Faludy Selected Poems 1933–1980*. Ed. Robin Skelton. Toronto: McClelland and Stewart, 1985, pp. 69–70.

Adapted from the literal translation, by George Faludy and Eric Johnson, of the original Hungarian poem by George Faludy.

B269 "Hungary, 1950." In *George Faludy Selected Poems 1933–1980*. Ed. Robin Skelton. Toronto: McClelland and Stewart, 1985, p. 87.

Adapted from the literal translation, by George Faludy and Eric Johnson, of the original Hungarian poem by George Faludy.

B270 "Lorenzo De Medici." In *George Faludy Selected Poems 1933–1980*. Ed. Robin Skelton. Toronto: McClelland and Stewart, 1985, pp. 129–30.

Adapted from the literal translation, by George Faludy and Eric Johnson, of the original Hungarian poem by George Faludy.

Reviews

B271 "Insects Gain Upper Hand." Rev. of *The Life of the Insects* (play), by Josef Kapek and Karl Kapek. *Charles St. Cheshire Cat* [*The Strand*] [Victoria College, Univ. of Toronto], Dec. 1963, pp. 1–2.

B272 "Lacey Talented." Rev. of *The Forms of Loss*, by

Edward Lacey. *The Varsity* [Univ. of Toronto], 19 March 1965, p. 14.

B273 "U of T Poet's First Book." Rev. of *Man in a Window*, by Wayne Clifford. *The Varsity* [Univ. of Toronto], 19 March 1965, p. 15.

B274 "Multiversity: Efficient, but the Education Is Lousy." Rev. of *The Multiversity*, by Nicholas von Hoffman. Illus. Ken Gray. *Toronto Daily Star*, 27 Aug. 1966, Toronto Daily Star Book Page, p. 27.

B275 "Figures." Rev. of *Figures in a Landscape*, by David Helwig. *The Tamarack Review*, No. 48 (Summer 1968), pp. 79–82.

B276 Rev. of *Black Night Window*, by John Newlove. *Bust* [Toronto], Nos. 2–3 (Summer 1968), pp. 26–29.

B277 "Poet or Man?". Rev. of *The Silences of Fire*, by Tom Marshall. *The Tamarack Review*, No. 54 (Spring 1970), pp. 81–84.

B278 "Poetic Gravity." Rev. of *Collected Poetry*, by Louis Dudek. *Books in Canada*, 1, No. 3 (Oct. 1971), 14, 19–20.

B279 "The New Poets: Fresh Voices in the Land." Rev. of *Clearing*, by Dale Zieroth; *Headwaters*, by Sid Marty; *Wood Mountain Poems*, by Andy Suknaski; *Waiting for Wayman*, by Tom Wayman; *Three*, by Charles Noble, J.O. Thompson, and Jon Whyte; *Waterloo Express*, by Paulette Jiles; *Blue Sky Notebook*, by Richard Sommer; *In Guildenstern Country*, by Peter Van Toorn; and *At the Edge of the Chopping There Are No Secrets*, by John Thompson. Illus. Jon Whyte. *Saturday Night*, Dec. 1973, pp. 33–35. Rpt. (excerpt — Rev. of *Sex and Death*, by Al Purdy) in *Contemporary Literary Criticism: Excerpts from Criticism of the Works of Today's Novelists, Poets,*

Playwrights, and Other Creative Writers. Ed. Carolyn Riley and Phyllis Carmel Mendelson. Vol. VI. Detroit: Gale, 1976, 428. Rpt. (excerpt — Rev. of *Waterloo Express*, by Paulette Jiles) in *Contemporary Literary Criticism: Excerpts from Criticism of the Works of Today's Novelists, Poets, Playwrights, and Other Creative Writers*. Ed. Dedria Bryfonski. Vol. XIII. Detroit: Gale, 1980, 304.

B280 "Touching the Marvellous." Rev. of *Sometimes All Over*, by Don Coles. *Brick* [Ilderton, Ont.], No. 14 (Winter 1982), pp. 32–37.
Signed: Ann Gunnarsson.

Lyrics

Note: The date of broadcasts for the *Fraggle Rock* series cannot be located. However, since I did obtain some of the recording dates, I have included these and generally entered the lyrics under those dates. But for finer tuning, I have followed the program order rather than the recording order, listing episode 1 before episode 2, and so on, even though this does not necessarily follow for the recording dates.

B281 "Lyrics from The Bob: The Fey's First Theme." *Acta Victoriana* [Victoria College, Univ. of Toronto], 86, No. 1 (Autumn 1961), p. 17. *MM* ("The Fey's First Theme").

B282 "Lyrics from The Bob: The Fey's Second Theme (Epithalamion)." *Acta Victoriana* [Victoria College, Univ. of Toronto], 86, No. 1 (Autumn 1961), pp. 17–18. *MM* ("The Fey's Second Theme").

B283 "Lyrics from The Bob: Jed's Finale Speech." *Acta Victoriana* [Victoria College, Univ. of Toronto], 86, No. 1 (Autumn 1961), p. 18. *MM* ("Jed's Finale Speech").

B284 "Spring Song." *Acta Victoriana* [Victoria College, Univ. of Toronto], 86, No. 1 (Autumn 1961), p. 39. *MM*.

B285 "Song for a Wedding: To John and Judy." Music Peter Grant. *Acta Victoriana* [Victoria College, Univ. of Toronto], 88, No. 1 (1963), 13–15. *MM*.

B286 "Ookpik." Music Harry Freedman. Canadian Children's Opera Chorus. 1969. [Ms. Canadian Music Centre.] *WL* (poem); *AP*; *WL:RC*.
See also B88.

B287 "1838 (Ontario)." Music Harry Freedman. [From *Nicholas Knock and Other People*, 1974.] In *Green . . . Blue . . . White . . . Songs of the Eastern Provinces*. Toronto: Canadian Music Centre, 1978, pp. 43–52. Rpt. Music Harry Freedman. Toronto: Anerca Music, 1982.
Commissioned by the Canadian Music Centre with the assistance of the Ontario Arts Council. See B49 ("1838"). Since *1838* (music) includes Lee's poem and music by John Beckwith, not Harry Freedman, I have considered these quite different publications. All reprints of "1838" are listed in B49.

B288 "Willoughby Wallaby Woo." In *Singable Songs for the Very Young*. Sung Raffi and Ken Whiteley. Music Larry Miyata. Toronto: Troubadour Records, 1976. (L.p.; 33-1/3] rpm.)
Music is added to Lee's poem of the same title. See B289.

B289 "Willoughby, Wallaby, Woo." Music Larry Miyata. In *The Raffi Singable Songbook: A Collection of 51 Songs from Raffi's First Three Records for Young Children*. Illus. Joyce Yamamoto. Toronto: Chappell, 1979, p. 92. *WL* (poem); *AP*; *WL:RC*.
See *DL* (cas.), *AP* (cas.), and B288.

B290 "Fraggle Rock Theme." Music Philip Balsam. *Fraggle Rock*. [Taped 4, 8 March 1982.] Rerecorded (revised — "Opening Theme"). *Fraggle Rock*. [Taped 11 May 1982.] *MNJH* ("Fraggle Rock Theme"); *FR*; *TFR*; *FR:PH* ("Closing Theme" and "Fraggle Rock Theme").

B291 "Fireman's Song." Music Philip Balsam. In "Wembley Finds a Job." *Fraggle Rock*, 1. [Taped 4, 8 March 1982.] *FS* ("Fireman Song").

B292 "Work Song." Music Philip Balsam. In "Wembley Finds a Job." *Fraggle Rock*, 1. [Taped 4, 8 March 1982.] [*FS* ("Workin Workin"); *TFR* ("Workin' "); *FR:PH* ("Workin")?].

B293 "Feel So Bad." Music Philip Balsam. In "One of Our Fraggles Is Missing." *Fraggle Rock*, 2. [Taped 13 April 1982.]

B294 "Feel So Glad." Music Philip Balsam. In "One of Our Fraggles Is Missing." *Fraggle Rock*, 2. [Taped 13 April 1982.]

B295 "Kick a Stone." Music Philip Balsam. In "One of Our Fraggles Is Missing." *Fraggle Rock*, 2. [Taped 13 April 1982.] Rerecorded in "All Work and All Play." *Fraggle Rock*, 32. [Taped 1983.]

B296 "Lost and Found." Music Philip Balsam. In "If You Want to Get Ahead, Get a Hat." *Fraggle Rock*, 3. [Taped 20 April 1982.] *MNJH*; *FR*; *FS*; *FRS-A*.

B297 "Pantry Chart [sic; Chant]." Music Philip Balsam. In "If You Want to Get Ahead, Get a Hat." *Fraggle Rock*, 3. [Taped 20 April 1982.] *FS* ("Pantry Song"); *FR:PH* ("Pantry Chant").

B298 "Without a Hat." Music Philip Balsam. In "If You Want to Get Ahead, Get a Hat." *Fraggle Rock*, 3. [Taped 20 April 1982.] *FR:PH*.

B299 "Convincing John." Music Philip Balsam. In "Save the Doozer Building." *Fraggle Rock*, 4. [Taped 27 April 1982.] *FR*; *FS*.

B300 "Mokey's Song." Music Philip Balsam. In "Save the Doozer Building." *Fraggle Rock*, 4. [Taped 27 April 1982.] Printed in *Annual Report 1984–1985: Cultural Property Export and Import Act*. Ottawa: Dept. of Communications, 1985, p. 42.
A photograph of Lee's manuscript copy of the poem from the Thomas Fisher Rare Book Library superimposed over a photograph of Lee.

B301 "Please Water Run." Music Philip Balsam. In "Quest for Water." *Fraggle Rock*, 5. [Taped 4 May 1982.]

B302 "Red Superstar." Music Philip Balsam. In "Quest for Water." *Fraggle Rock*, 5. [Taped 4 May 1982.]

B303 "Catch a Tail by the Tiger." Music Philip Balsam. In "Only the Brave." *Fraggle Rock*, 6. [Taped 11 May 1982.] *FR*; *FS*; *FRS-A*.

B304 "Gobo's Goodbye." Music Philip Balsam. In "Only the Brave." *Fraggle Rock*, 6. [Taped 11 May 1982.]

B305 "Rollin' On." Music Philip Balsam. In "Only the Brave." *Fraggle Rock*, 6. [Taped 11 May 1982.] *FS* ("Rollin' Rollin' ").

B306 "Beetle Song." Music Philip Balsam. In "Better Red Than a Talking Bush or Something." *Fraggle Rock*, 7. [Taped 26 June 1982.] *FR*; *FS*; *FRS-A*.

B307 "Dreamin'." Music Philip Balsam. In "Better Red Than a Talking Bush or Something." *Fraggle Rock*, 7. [Taped 26 June 1982.] *FR:PH* ("Dreaming of Someone").

B308 "Junior Gorg's Gong." Music Philip Balsam. In "Better Red Than a Talking Bush or Something." *Fraggle Rock*, 7. [Taped 26 June 1982.]

B309 "La La Song." Music Philip Balsam. In "Better Red Than a Talking Bush or Something." *Fraggle Rock*, 7. [Taped 26 June 1982.]

B310 "Fraggle Rock Rock." Music Philip Balsam. In "The Gorgification of Wembley." *Fraggle Rock*, 8. [Taped 6 July 1982.] *MNJH*; *FR*; *FS* ("Fraggle Rock, Rock").

B311 "Here to There." Music Philip Balsam. In "The Gorgification of Wembley." *Fraggle Rock*, 8. [Taped 6 July 1982.] *FS*; *FR:PH*.

B312 "Recruiting Song." Music Philip Balsam. In "The Gorgification of Wembley." *Fraggle Rock*, 8. [Taped 6 July 1982.]

B313 "Follow Me." Music Philip Balsam. In "Beginnings." *Fraggle Rock*, 10. [Taped 20 July 1982.] Rerecorded. Music Philip Balsam. In "Uncle Matt Comes Home." *Fraggle Rock*, 30. [Taped 20 July 1983.] *MNJH*; *FR*; *FS*.

B314 "Hip Hip I." Music Philip Balsam. In "Beginnings." *Fraggle Rock*, 10. [Taped 20 July 1982.]

B315 "Hip Hip II." Music Philip Balsam. In "Beginnings." *Fraggle Rock*, 10. [Taped 20 July 1982.]

B316 "I Seen Troubles." Music Philip Balsam. In "Beginnings." *Fraggle Rock*, 10. [Taped 20 July 1982.] *FS* ("I Seen Trouble"); *FR:PH* ("I Seen Troubles").

B317 "Feelin' Yucky." Music Philip Balsam. In "The Finger of Light." *Fraggle Rock*, 12. [Taped 3 Aug. 1982.] *FS* ("Yucky").

B318 "Time to Live as One." Music Philip Balsam. In "The Finger of Light." *Fraggle Rock*, 12. [Taped 3 Aug. 1982.] *FR:PH*.

B319 "Take 'Em Away." In *John Denver & The Muppets Rocky Music Holiday*. RCA, AFLI-4721, 1983. (L.p.; 33-1/3 rpm.)
Includes printed lyrics.

B320 "Help Me for a Change." Music Philip Balsam. In "We Love You Wembley." *Fraggle Rock*, 13. [Taped 2 Feb. 1983.]

B321 "Lover, Lover #9." Music Philip Balsam. In "We Love You Wembley." *Fraggle Rock*, 13. [Taped 2 Feb. 1983.]

B322 "Wembley #9." Music Philip Balsam. In "We Love You Wembley." *Fraggle Rock*, 13. [Taped 2 Feb. 1983.]

B323 "The Wimp Duet." Music Philip Balsam. In "We Love You Wembley." *Fraggle Rock*, 13. [Taped 2 Feb. 1983.]

B324 "The Wimp Song." Music Philip Balsam. In "We Love You Wembley." *Fraggle Rock*, 13. [Taped 2 Feb. 1983.]

B325 "Dixie Wailing." Music Philip Balsam. In "The Challenge." *Fraggle Rock*, 14. [Taped 1 Feb. 1983.] *FS*.

B326 "Dum De Dum #2." Music Philip Balsam. In "The Challenge." *Fraggle Rock*, 14. [Taped 1 Feb. 1983.]

B327 "Get Blue." Music Philip Balsam. In "I Don't Care." *Fraggle Rock*, 15. [Taped 22 Feb. 1983.] *FS*.

B328 "Swear to Be Fair." Music Philip Balsam. In "I Don't Care." *Fraggle Rock*, 15. [Taped 22 Feb. 1983.]

B329 "The Friendship Song." Music Philip Balsam. In "Marooned." *Fraggle Rock*, 16. [Taped 1 March 1983.] *FR* ("Friendship Song"); *FS*.

B330 "Friendship Song — Reprise." Music Philip Balsam. In "Marooned." *Fraggle Rock*, 16. [Taped 1 March 1983.]

B331 "Go With the Flow." Music Philip Balsam. In "Marooned." *Fraggle Rock*, 16. [Taped 1 March 1983.] *FR:PH*.

B332 "Moon Come Soon." Music Philip Balsam. In "Capture the Moon." *Fraggle Rock*, 17. [Taped 8 March 1983.]

B333 "Sail Away With Me." Music Philip Balsam. In "Capture the Moon." *Fraggle Rock*, 17. [Taped 8 March 1983.] *FR:PH* ("Sail Away").

B334 "Let Me Be Your Song." Music Philip Balsam. In "The Minstrels." *Fraggle Rock*, 18. [Taped 1 March 1983.] Rebroadcast. In "The Honk of Honks." *Fraggle Rock*, 94. [Taped 30 April 1986.] *FS*.

B335 "Our Melody." Music Philip Balsam. In "The Minstrels." *Fraggle Rock*, 18. [Taped 1 March 1983.] *FR; FS*.

B336 "Doozer Knitting Song." Music Philip Balsam. In "The Great Radish Famine." *Fraggle Rock*, 19. [Taped 22 March 1983.] *FR*; *FS*.

B337 "Doozer Marching Song." Music Philip Balsam. In "The Great Radish Famine." *Fraggle Rock*, 19. [Taped 22 March 1983.]

B338 "Perfect Harmony." Music Philip Balsam. In "The Great Radish Famine." *Fraggle Rock*, 19. [Taped 22 March 1983.] *FR:PH*.

B339 "Afraid to Be Afraid." Music Philip Balsam. In "The Garden Plot." *Fraggle Rock*, 20. [Taped 5 April 1983.]

B340 "Dumb of a Son of a Gun." Music Philip Balsam. In "The Garden Plot." *Fraggle Rock*, 20. [Taped 5 April 1983.] *FS* ("Dumb of a Son"); *FRS-A* ("Dumb of a Son of a Gun").

B341 ———, and bpNichol. "One, Two, Muck and Goo." Music Philip Balsam. In "The Garden Plot." *Fraggle Rock*, 20. [Taped 5 April 1983.] *FR* ("Muck and Goo"); *FRS-A*.

B342 "Once Upon a Time I Knew My Name." Music Philip Balsam. In "Gobo's Discovery." *Fraggle Rock*, 21. [Taped 12 April 1983.]

B343 "The Me I Wanna Be." Music Philip Balsam. In "Gobo's Discovery." *Fraggle Rock*, 21. [Taped 12 April 1983.]

B344 "What If?". Music Philip Balsam. In "Gobo's Discovery." *Fraggle Rock*, 21. [Taped 12 April 1983.]

B345 "Brave Alone." Music Philip Balsam. In "The Beast of Bluestock." *Fraggle Rock*, 22. [Taped 19 April 1983.]

B346 "Brave Boy Jump Up." Music Philip Balsam. In "The Beast of Bluestock." *Fraggle Rock*, 22. [Taped 19 April 1983.] *FR* ("Brave Boy, Jump Up"); *FS* ("Brave Boy Jump Up").

B347 "Wemblin' Fool." Music Philip Balsam. In "The Beast of Bluestock." *Fraggle Rock*, 22. [Taped 19 April 1983.] *FR* ("Wemblin Fool"); *FRS-A* ("Wemblin' Fool").

B348 "The Joke Isn't Funny Anymore." Music Philip Balsam. In "Mokey's Funeral." *Fraggle Rock*, 23. [Taped 26 April 1983.]

B349 "Ragtime Queen." Music Philip Balsam. In "Mokey's Funeral." *Fraggle Rock*, 23. [Taped 26 April 1983.] *FS*; *FR:PH*.

B350 "Fly to the Sky." Music Philip Balsam. In "Wembley's Egg." *Fraggle Rock*, 25. [Taped 20 Sept. 1983.]

B351 "Light of the Moon." Music Philip Balsam. In "Wembley's Egg." *Fraggle Rock*, 25. [Taped 20 Sept. 1983.]

B352 "I'm Never Alone." Music Philip Balsam. In "Booberock." *Fraggle Rock*, 26. [Taped 27 Sept. 1983.]

B353 "Remembering Song." Music Philip Balsam. In "Booberock." *Fraggle Rock*, 26. [Taped 27 Sept. 1983.]

B354 "Garbage of Time." Music Philip Balsam. In "The Trash Heap Doesn't Live Here Any More." *Fraggle Rock*, 27. [Taped 4 Oct. 1983.]

B355 "Perfect Day." Music Philip Balsam. In "The Trash Heap Doesn't Live Here Any More." *Fraggle Rock*, 27. [Taped 4 Oct. 1983.]

B356 "Trash Is Back in Town." Music Philip Balsam. In "The Trash Heap Doesn't Live Here Any More." *Fraggle Rock*, 27. [Taped 4 Oct. 1983.]

B357 "Bring Back the Wonder." Music Philip Balsam. In "Red's Sea Monster." *Fraggle Rock*, 28. [Taped 11 Oct. 1983.]

B358 "Sing It and Say." Music Philip Balsam. In "Red's Sea Monster." *Fraggle Rock*, 28. [Taped 11 Oct. 1983.]

B359 "Sorrow and Shame." Music Philip Balsam. In "Red's Sea Monster." *Fraggle Rock*, 28. [Taped 11 Oct. 1983.]

B360 "Dream a Dream." Music Philip Balsam. In "Boober's Dream." *Fraggle Rock*, 29. [Taped 1983.]

B361 "Everybody's Doin' It." Music Philip Balsam. In "Boober's Dream." *Fraggle Rock*, 29. [Taped 1983.]

B362 "Party Hard in My Own Backyard." Music Philip Balsam. In "Boober's Dream." *Fraggle Rock*, 29. [Taped 1983.]

B363 "Welcome Home Ding-a-Ling." Music Philip Balsam. In "Uncle Matt Comes Home." *Fraggle Rock*, 30. [Taped 1983.]

B364 "Lose Your Heart." Music Philip Balsam. In "Mokey and the Minstrels." *Fraggle Rock*, 31. [Taped 1983.]

B365 "Music Makes Us Real." Music Philip Balsam. In "Mokey and the Minstrels." *Fraggle Rock*, 31. [Taped 1983.]

B366 "Rumble Bug Hum." Music Philip Balsam. In "All Work and All Play." *Fraggle Rock*, 32. [Taped 1983.]

B367 "Yes We Do." Music Philip Balsam. In "All Work and All Play." *Fraggle Rock*, 32. [Taped 1983.]

B368 "Doom-De-Doom." Music Philip Balsam. In "Sir Hubris and the Gorgs." *Fraggle Rock*, 33. [Taped 1983.]

B369 "Only Way Home." Music Philip Balsam. In "Sir Hubris and the Gorgs." *Fraggle Rock*, 33. [Taped 1983.]

B370 "Is It True." Music Philip Balsam. In "The Wizard of Fraggle Rock." *Fraggle Rock*, 34. [Taped 1983.]

B371 "Doozer Building Song." Music Philip Balsam. In "The Doozer Contest." *Fraggle Rock*, 35. [Taped 1983.]

B372 "Count on Me." Music Philip Balsam. In "A Friend in Need." *Fraggle Rock*, 36. [Taped 1984.]

B373 "Knew I Was Good." Music Philip Balsam. In "A Friend in Need." *Fraggle Rock*, 36. [Taped 1984.]

B374 "Wise to Myself." Music Philip Balsam. In "A Friend in Need." *Fraggle Rock*, 36. [Taped 1984.]

B375 "One and One." Music Philip Balsam. In "Red's Club." *Fraggle Rock*, 37. [Taped 25 Jan. 1984.]

B376 "Rules Song." Music Philip Balsam. In "Red's Club." *Fraggle Rock*, 37. [Taped 25 Jan. 1984.]

B377 "Choose Right Blues." Music Philip Balsam. In "The Secret of Convincing John." *Fraggle Rock*, 38. [Taped 31 Jan. 1984.]

B378 "Convincing John." Music Philip Balsam. In "The Secret of Convincing John." *Fraggle Rock*, 38. [Taped 31 Jan. 1984.]

B379 "Follow the Road." Music Philip Balsam. In "Manny's Land of Carpets." *Fraggle Rock*, 39. [Taped 8 Feb. 1984.]

B380 "Goodbye." Music Philip Balsam. In "Manny's Land of Carpets." *Fraggle Rock*, 39. [Taped 8 Feb. 1984.]

B381 "Dream-Girl Lover." Music Philip Balsam. In "Junior Sells the Farm." *Fraggle Rock*, 40. [Taped 15 Feb. 1984.]

B382 "The Gorg's Lament." Music Philip Balsam. In "Junior Sells the Farm." *Fraggle Rock*, 40. [Taped 15 Feb. 1984.]

B383 "Shine on Me." Music Philip Balsam. In "The Day the Music Died." *Fraggle Rock*, 41. [Taped 21 Feb. 1984.]

B384 "Stuff Samba." Music Philip Balsam. In "The Day the Music Died." *Fraggle Rock*, 41. [Taped 21 Feb. 1984.]

B385 "Ho Ho Ho." Music Philip Balsam. In "Fraggle Wars." *Fraggle Rock*, 42. [Taped 29 Feb. 1984.]

B386 "Sunlight and Shadow." Music Philip Balsam. In "Fraggle Wars." *Fraggle Rock*, 42. [Taped 29 Feb. 1984.]

B387 "Warped Theme." Music Philip Balsam. In "Fraggle Wars." *Fraggle Rock*, 42. [Taped 29 Feb. 1984.]

B388 "Home." Music Philip Balsam. In "Home Is Where the Trash Is." *Fraggle Rock*, 50. [Taped 15 May 1984.]

B389 "Manic McMooch." Music Philip Balsam. In "Home Is Where the Trash Is." *Fraggle Rock*, 50. [Taped 15 May 1984.]

B390 "Now You See Me." Music Philip Balsam. In "Believe It or Not." *Fraggle Rock*, 51. [Taped 22 May 1984.]

B391 "Talkin' Bout Germs." Music Philip Balsam. In "Pebble Pox Blues." *Fraggle Rock*, 52. [Taped 30 May 1984.]

B392 "There's a Promise." Music Philip Balsam. In "The Bells of Fraggle Rock." *Fraggle Rock*, 53. [Taped 28 May 1984.]

B393 "Blanket of Woe." Music Philip Balsam. In "Blanket of Snow, Blanket of Woe." *Fraggle Rock*, 54. [Taped 4 June 1984.]

B394 "Goombah Soup." Music Philip Balsam. In "Blanket of Snow, Blanket of Woe." *Fraggle Rock*, 54. [Taped 4 June 1984.]

B395 "Bunny Go High and Go Low" (lyrics only). In *The Bunny Picnic: A Picturebook Special*. By Jocelyn Stevenson. N.p.: Henson Associates, 1985, p. 69. Recorded. Music Philip Balsam. In *The Tale of Bunny Picnic*. New York: Muppet Music, ASCAP, 1986. Telecast. Prod. Henson Associates. BBC-HBO [Home Box Office], 26, 29 March 1986. Air dates 30 March, 1, 3, 7 April 1986. (1 min., 18 sec.)

B396 "Bunny Stew" (lyrics only). In *The Bunny Picnic: A Picturebook Special*. By Jocelyn Stevenson. N.p.: Henson Associates, 1985, p. 44. Recorded. Music Philip Balsam. In *The Tale of Bunny Picnic*. New York: Muppet Music, ASCAP, 1986. Telecast. Prod. Henson Associates. BBC-HBO [Home Box Office], 26, 29 March 1986. Air dates 30 March, 1, 3, 7 April 1986. (1 min., 46 sec.)

B397 "Drum of Time" (lyrics only). In *The Bunny Picnic: A Picturebook Special*. By Jocelyn Stevenson. N.p.: Henson Associates, 1985, p. 119. Recorded. Music Philip Balsam. In *The Tale of Bunny Picnic*. New York: Muppet Music, ASCAP, 1986. Telecast. Prod. Henson Associates. BBC-HBO [Home Box Office], 26, 29 March 1986. Air dates 30 March, 1, 3, 7 April 1986. (1 min., 38 sec.)

B398 "Hello Springtime" [opening signature tune] (lyrics only). In *The Bunny Picnic: A Picturebook Special*. By Jocelyn Stevenson. N.p.: Henson Associates, 1985, p. 1. Recorded. Music Philip Balsam. In *The Tale of Bunny Picnic*. New York: Muppet Music, ASCAP, 1986. Telecast. Prod. Henson Associates. BBC-HBO [Home Box Office], 26, 29 March 1986. Air dates 30 March, 1, 3, 7 April 1986. (2 min., 5 sec.)

B399 "Hello Springtime" [closing signature tune] (lyrics only). In *The Bunny Picnic: A Picturebook Special*. By Jocelyn Stevenson. N.p.: Henson Associates, 1985, p. 129. Recorded. Music Philip Balsam. In *The Tale of Bunny Picnic*. New York: Muppet Music, ASCAP, 1986. Telecast. Prod. Henson Associates. BBC-HBO [Home Box Office], 26, 29 March 1986. Air dates 30 March, 1, 3, 7 April 1986. (1 min., 48 sec.)

B400 "I Had a Dream" (lyrics only). In *The Bunny Picnic: A Picturebook Special*. By Jocelyn Stevenson. N.p.: Henson Associates, 1985, p. 12. Recorded. Music Philip Balsam. In *The Tale of Bunny Picnic*. New York: Muppet Music, ASCAP, 1986. Telecast. Prod. Henson Associates. BBC-HBO [Home Box Office], 26, 29 March 1986. Air dates 30 March, 1, 3, 7 April 1986. (1 min., 1 sec.)

B401 "The Story Show" (lyrics only). In *The Bunny Picnic: A Picturebook Special*. By Jocelyn Stevenson. N.p.: Henson Associates, 1985, p. 53. Recorded. Music Philip Balsam. In *The Tale of Bunny Picnic*. New York: Muppet Music, ASCAP, 1986. Telecast. Prod. Henson Associates. BBC-HBO [Home Box Office], 26, 29 March 1986. Air dates 30 March, 1, 3, 7 April 1986. (1 min., 34 sec.)

B402 "This Way." Music Philip Balsam. In "Sprocket's Big Adventure." *Fraggle Rock*, 73. [Taped 15 Oct. 1985.]

B403 "A Time to Build." Music Philip Balsam. In "Sprocket's Big Adventure." *Fraggle Rock*, 73. [Taped 15 Oct. 1985.]

B404 "I Don't Understand Him." Music Philip Balsam. In "Uncle Matt's Discovery." *Fraggle Rock*, 74. [Taped 22 Oct. 1985.]

B405 "Ball of Fire." Music Philip Balsam. In "Junior Faces the Music." *Fraggle Rock*, 75. [Taped 24 Oct. 1985.]

B406 "Pass It On." Music Philip Balsam. In "The Perfect Blue Rollie." *Fraggle Rock*, 76. [Taped 5 Nov. 1985.]

B407 "Take Away the Sunlight." Music Philip Balsam. In "The Perfect Blue Rollie." *Fraggle Rock*, 76. [Taped 5 Nov. 1985.]

B408 "Children of Tomorrow." Music Philip Balsam. In "A Tune for Two." *Fraggle Rock*, 77. [Taped 12 Nov. 1985.] Printed in *Poets for Africa: An International Anthology for Hunger Relief*. Ed. Susann Flammang. Las Vegas: Family of God, 1986.

B409 "Song for Two." Music Philip Balsam. In "A Tune for Two." *Fraggle Rock*, 77. [Taped 12 Nov. 1985.]

B410 "Show Me." Music Philip Balsam. In "A Brush with Jealousy." *Fraggle Rock*, 78. [Taped 26 Nov. 1985.]

B411 "Sure Ain't Junk." Music Philip Balsam. In "A Brush with Jealousy." *Fraggle Rock*, 78. [Taped 26 Nov. 1985.]

B412 "Free and High." Music Philip Balsam. In "Wembley's Flight." *Fraggle Rock*, 79. [Taped 3 Dec. 1985.]

B413 "Heart in a Hanky." Music Philip Balsam. In "Wembley's Flight." *Fraggle Rock*, 79. [Taped 3 Dec. 1985.]

B414 "Do the Sashay." Music Philip Balsam. In "Wonder Mountain." *Fraggle Rock*, 80. [Taped 10 Dec. 1985.]

B415 "Don't Know What Time It Is." Music Philip Balsam. In "Wonder Mountain." *Fraggle Rock*, 80. [Taped 10 Dec. 1985.]

B416 "People Don't Know." Music Philip Balsam. In "Red in the Land of the Blue Dragons." *Fraggle Rock*, 81. [Taped 17 Dec. 1985.]

B417 "Insect Rock." Music Philip Balsam. In "Space Frog Follies." *Fraggle Rock*, 82. [Taped 1 Jan. 1986.]

B418 "Gors in Glory." Music Philip Balsam. In "Boober Gorg." *Fraggle Rock*, 83. [Taped 14 Jan. 1986.]

B419 "I'm a Little Stew Pot." Music Philip Balsam. In "Boober Gorg." *Fraggle Rock*, 83. [Taped 14 Jan. 1986.]

B420 "Happy Birthday to Me." Music Philip Balsam. In "Mirror Mirror." *Fraggle Rock*, 84. [Taped 21 Jan. 1986.]

B421 "Make a Friend." Music Philip Balsam. In "Mirror Mirror." *Fraggle Rock*, 84. [Taped 21 Jan. 1986.]

B422 "The Secret Rhyme." Music Philip Balsam. In "The Riddle of Rhyming Rock." *Fraggle Rock*, 85. [Taped 28 Jan. 1986.]

B423 "Travellin' Free." Music Philip Balsam. In "The Voice Inside." *Fraggle Rock*, 86. [Taped 4 Feb. 1986.]

B424 "You're on Your Own." Music Philip Balsam. In "The Voice Inside." *Fraggle Rock*, 86. [Taped 4 Feb. 1986.]

B425 "Sing That Law Again." Music Philip Balsam. In "The Trial of Cotterpin Doozer." *Fraggle Rock*, 87. [Taped 26 Feb. 1986.]

B426 "River Roll On." Music Philip Balsam. In "The River of Life." *Fraggle Rock*, 88. [Taped 3 March 1986.]

B427 "Sister and Brother." Music Philip Balsam. In "The River of Life." *Fraggle Rock*, 88. [Taped 3 March 1986.]

B428 "Tree of Life." Music Philip Balsam. In "Beyond the Pond." *Fraggle Rock*, 89. [Taped 10 March 1986.]

B429 "Just a Dream Away." Music Philip Balsam. In "Gone, but Not Forgotten." *Fraggle Rock*, 90. [Taped April 1986.]

B430 "Still So Far." Music Philip Balsam. In "Mokey Then and Now." *Fraggle Rock*, 91. [Taped 7 April 1986.]

B431 "Voodoo." Music Philip Balsam. In "Mokey Then and Now." *Fraggle Rock*, 91. [Taped 7 April 1986.]

B432 "I Give to Thee." Music Philip Balsam. In "Ring Around the Rock." *Fraggle Rock*, 92. [Taped April 1986.]

B433 "There's a Lot I Want to Know." Music Philip Balsam. In "Inspector Red." *Fraggle Rock*, 93. [Taped 22 April 1986.]

B434 "The Rock Goes On." Music Philip Balsam. In "The Honk of Honks." *Fraggle Rock*, 94. [Taped 30 April 1986.]

B435 "Boss of Just Yourself." Music Philip Balsam. In "The Gors Who Would Be King." *Fraggle Rock*, 95. [Taped 6 May 1986.]

B436 "How Wide, How Far, How Long." Music Philip Balsam. In "The Gors Who Would Be King." *Fraggle Rock*, 95. [Taped 6 May 1986.]

B437 "Magic Be With You." Music Philip Balsam. In "Change of Address." *Fraggle Rock*, 96. [Taped 6 May 1986.]

B438 "Petals of the Rose." Music Philip Balsam. In "Change of Address." *Fraggle Rock*, 96. [Taped 6 May 1986.]

B439 "Child Power." In *Jacob Two-Two Meets the Hooded Fang*. By Mordecai Richler. Music Philip Balsam. Arranged and prod. Andy Krehm and Stephen Woodjetts. With William Colgate, Jeff Jones, and Vivienne Williams. Illus. San Murata. Toronto: Young People's Theatre/Silverbirch Productions, 1987. (45 rpm.)

B440 "Things Go Bump." In *Jacob Two-Two Meets the Hooded Fang*. By Mordecai Richler. Music Philip Balsam. Arranged and prod. Andy Krehm and Stephen Woodjetts. With William Colgate, Jeff Jones, and Vivienne Williams. Illus. San Murata. Toronto: Young People's Theatre/Silverbirch Productions, 1987. (45 rpm.)

Published Correspondence

B441 "Book Publishing." Letter. *The Globe and Mail* [Toronto], 14 Sept. 1971, p. 6.

B442 "Letter to David Helwig." *Quarry*, 21, No. 3 (Summer 1972), 67–70.
A response to David Helwig's letter regarding *Civil Elegies and Other Poems* (C10).

B443 "Reclaim Canadian Independence without a Purge." Letter. *Excalibur* [York Univ.], 16 Nov. 1972, p. 7.
Regarding a speech made at York University.

B444 "Dennis Lee Wrote in July . . . ." Letter. *Alive Magazine* [Guelph, Ont.], 23 Oct. 1976, p. 1.
Lee explains why he no longer subscribes to *Alive Magazine*.

B445 "Dennis Lee's Thanks." Letter. *The Globe and Mail* [Toronto], 28 Nov. 1977, p. 6.
Lee clarifies several statements by Adele Freedman in "Separating Dennis Lee's Psyches" (C214).

B446 Letter to Grade 4 students at Estevan Hillside School. 10 May 1978. Printed ("A Love Affair with Dennis Lee: 10 May 1978") in *The Medium* [Estevan, Sask.], 21, No. 2 (Fall 1980), 28.
Includes "My Pet" (B133) and "The Tree" (B134). Also includes notes by Shirley Andrist (C109).

B447 Letter to Grade 5 students at Estevan Hillside School. 1 May 1979. Printed ("A Love Affair with Dennis Lee: 1 May 1979") in *The Medium* [Estevan, Sask.], 21, No. 2 (Fall 1980), 29–30.

Includes "Mrs. Murphy and Mrs. Murphy's Kids" (B132). Also includes notes by Shirley Andrist (C109).

B448 Letter to Grade 6 students at Estevan Hillside School. 31 March 1980. Printed ("A Love Affair with Dennis Lee: 31 March 1980") in *The Medium* [Estevan, Sask.], 21, No. 2 (Fall 1980), 31–32.
Includes "Bundle-Buggy Boogie" (B131). Also includes notes by Shirley Andrist (C109).

B449 ———, and George Bowering. "Towards Polyphony: Extracts from a Conversation between Dennis Lee and George Bowering." *Descant* [Dennis Lee Special Issue], No. 39 [14, No. 1] (Winter 1982), pp. 191–98. Rpt. in *Tasks of Passion: Dennis Lee at Mid-Career*. Ed. Karen Mulhallen, Donna Bennett, and Russell Brown. Toronto: Descant, 1982, pp. 191–98.
Selections from letters written June 1979–March 1981.

B450 Letter. *The Globe and Mail* [Toronto], 1 June 1983, p. 6.
Concerning the receivership position of Clarke, Irwin.

B451 "Important Point." Letter. *The Globe and Mail* [Toronto], 15 Dec. 1983, p. 6.
Lee corrects Judith Fitzgerald's review of poetry by David Donnell.

B452 "The Wrong Tunesmith." Letter. *The Globe and Mail* [Toronto], 30 Dec. 1983, p. 7.
Lee corrects Judy Steed's "Jelly Belly's Jolly Gems. An Intellectual Strikes Pay Dirt: Wacky Rhymes Are Now a Hit on Kid's TV" (C227).

B453 "Reading Beyond Belief." Letter. *The Globe and Mail* [Toronto], 23 Feb. 1985, p. 7.
Lee criticizes Don Downey's obituary of Marian Engel.

B454 Letter. In *Mr. Jourdenais*. Ottawa: n.p., 1987, p. 14.
The letter to Fernand Jourdenais, M.P. for La Prairie, about his stand on Bill C-84 was published in Jourdenais' handbook to his constituents.

B455 "Dear John . . . ." Letter to John Newlove. In *Words for John Newlove: On the Occasion of His Fiftieth Birthday*. N.p.: Privately printed, 1988, n. pag.

Ghostwriter

B456 Reid, Tim, MPP (Liberal, Scarborough East). "The Spadina Expressway System Is Going to Cost the Provincial Government Half a Billion Dollars More Than Is Necessary." Throne Debate, Ontario Legislature. 10 March 1970. [Press release; ts. 6 pp.; mimeographed.] Rpt. ("Speech from the Throne") in *Legislature of Ontario Debates*. Official Report. Daily Ed. Third Session of the Twenty-Eighth Legislature. Afternoon Session. No. 11. Toronto: Queen's Printer, 10 March 1970, pp. 426–29. Rpt. Evening Session. No. 12. Toronto: Queen's Printer, 10 March 1970, pp. 433–37.

Miscellaneous

B457 ———, ed. "A Perception of Poets." *University of Toronto Graduate*, 6, No. 3 (Spring 1979), 6–8. Rpt. in *Bulletin* [Univ. of Toronto], 2 April 1979, pp. 6–8.
Includes poems by Roo Borson, Susan Glickman, Kim Maltman, Theresa Moritz, Suzanne Nussey, Polly Thompson, Bruce Whiteman, and Jan Zwicky. Lee's introduction, "Apprenticed to Truth and Uncertainty" (B249) is also included.

Press Releases and Flyers

B458 "Acquisition of Macmillan by Gage." [Toronto: Writers' Union of Canada], 18 April 1980. 3 pp. [Brief and press release.]

B459 "Macmillan Purchase: National Cultural Asset in Jeopardy?". Toronto: Writers' Union of Canada, 22 April 1980. 4 pp. [Press release.]

B460 ———, and Timothy Findley. "A Statement on Macmillan/Gage." Toronto: Writers' Union of Canada, 8 May 1980. 3 pp. [Statement to union members and press release.]

B461 Rev. of *Incognito*, by David Young. Press release for *Incognito*. Toronto: Coach House, 10 Aug. 1982. 2 pp.

B462 ———, and Walter Walker. "About Authors and Books." Toronto: McClelland and Stewart, Nov. 1982. 3 leaves. [Press release.]

B463 "The Summerhill Fair" (poem). In *Summerhill Fair* [Toronto], June 1984. 1 leaf. [Flyer.]

Audio-Visual Material

Note: Several audio-visual publications are included in the Lyrics category of Section B.

B464 "Civil Elegies: 1–9." Narr. Gordon Pinsent. *Anthology*. CBC Radio, 29 Dec. 1973.

B465 From *Civil Elegies and Other Poems*. Narr. Dennis Lee. In *Speaking of Books: Dennis Lee*. Toronto: OECA, 1975. (Videotape.)
Also includes an interview by Robert Fulford (C209).

B466 Dialogue (parts). *The Dark Crystal*. Narr. Dennis Lee. Dir. Jim Henson. Universal Pictures, 1982.

B467 "Universe." Narr. Dennis Lee. *Morningside*. Host Peter Gzowski. CBC Radio, 21 Oct. 1987.
The broadcast includes an interview by Peter Gzowski (C236). See also *DLOP* and *DLOP* (chap.).

B468 "The Golden Rule." Narr. Dennis Lee. *Morningside*. Host Peter Gzowski. CBC Radio, 21 Oct. 1987.
The broadcast includes an interview by Peter Gzowski (C236). See also *DLOP* and *DLOP* (chap.).

B469 "High Blue Meadows." Narr. Dennis Lee. *Morningside*. Host Peter Gzowski. CBC Radio, 21 Oct. 1987.
The broadcast includes an interview by Peter Gzowski (C236). See also *DLOP* and *DLOP* (chap.).

B470 "When I Went Up to Ottawa." Narr. Peter Gzowski. *Morningside*. Host Peter Gzowski. CBC Radio, 21 Oct. 1987.
The broadcast includes an interview by Peter Gzowski (C236). See also *DLOP* and *DLOP* (chap.).

B471 "The Academic Odyssey of Wendell Grebe." Narr. Stephen Scobie. *Fine Lines*. CFUV Radio [Univ. of Victoria], 28 Oct. 1987.
The broadcast includes an interview by Stephen Scobie (C237). See also *DLOP*.

B472 "Odysseus and Tumbleweed." Narr. Dennis Lee. *Fine Lines*. CFUV Radio [Univ. of Victoria], 28 Oct. 1987.
The broadcast includes an interview by Stephen Scobie (C237). See also *DLOP*.

B473 "The Protocol." Narr. Dennis Lee. *Fine Lines*. CFUV Radio [Univ. of Victoria], 28 Oct. 1987.

The broadcast includes an interview by Stephen Scobie (C237). See also *DLOP*.

B474 "Yer Blues." Narr. Dennis Lee. *Fine Lines*. CFUV Radio [Univ. of Victoria], 28 Oct. 1987.
The broadcast includes an interview by Stephen Scobie (C237). See also *DLOP*.

B475 "Tales from 'Sir Blunderbluss.' " Narr. Dennis Lee. *Morningside*. Host Peter Gzowski. CBC Radio, 11 Nov. 1987.
See *DLOP*.

B476 "The Cat and the Wizard." Narr. Dennis Lee. *Morningside*. Host Peter Gzowski. CBC Radio, 19 Nov. 1987.
See *DLOP* and B99.

B477 "The Mouse and the Maid: Epithalamium for Susan." Narr. Dennis Lee. *Morningside*. Host Peter Gzowski. CBC Radio, 30 Nov. 1987.
See *DLOP* ("The Mouse and the Maid").

B478 "The Revenge of Santa Claus." Narr. Dennis. Lee. *Morningside*. CBC Radio, 22 Dec. 1987.
See *DLOP*.

B479 "Christmas Tree." In *First Impressions Listening Program*. Narr. Jack Booth, Willa Pauli, Jo Phenix, and Larry Swartz. Toronto: Holt, Rinehart and Winston, 1988. Tape 3, Side A. (57 sec.)
See *JB* and *DLFN80*.

B480 "The Coming of Teddy Bears." In *First Impressions Listening Program*. Narr. Jack Booth, Willa Pauli, Jo Phenix, and Larry Swartz. Toronto: Holt, Rinehart and Winston, 1988. Tape 3, Side B. (1 min., 40 sec.) (*APOP*.
See B126, *GD*, and *DLFN79*.

B481 "The Dinosaur Dinner." In *First Impressions Listening Program*. Narr. Jack Booth, Willa Pauli, Jo Phenix, and Larry Swartz. Toronto: Holt, Rinehart and Winston, 1988. Tape 5, Side A. (1 min., 35 sec.) *RDLF*.
See *JB*, *DLBB*, and *DFLN79* ("The Dinosaurs' Dinner").

B482 "Skyscraper." In *First Impressions Listening Program*. Narr. Jack Booth, Willa Pauli, Jo Phenix, and Larry Swartz. Toronto: Holt, Rinehart and Winston, 1988. Tape 3, Side A. (1 min., 11 sec.) *AP* (cas.); *APOP*; *RDLF*.
See also B105, *WL*, *AP*, *DLBB*, and *WL:RC*.

B483 "Three Tickles." In *First Impressions Listening Program*. Narr. Jack Booth, Willa Pauli, Jo Phenix, and Larry Swartz. Toronto: Holt, Rinehart and Winston, 1988. Tape 5, Side B. (31 sec.) *RDLF*.
See *JB* and *DLFN80*.

Part II

Works on Dennis Lee

C   Books, Articles and Sections of Books, Theses and Dissertations, Interviews and Profiles, Adaptations, Miscellaneous, Poems and Illustrations Based on Lee's Work, and Awards and Honours

Books

C1   *Descant* [Dennis Lee Special Issue], No. 39 [14, No. 1] (Winter 1982). 247 pp. Rpt. *Tasks of Passion: Dennis Lee at Mid-Career*. Ed. Karen Mulhallen, Donna Bennett, and Russell Brown. Toronto: Descant, 1982. 247 pp.
    Since this book includes material by and about Lee, each piece is listed separately in the appropriate section of the bibliography.
    Includes Alison *Acker*'s "Dennis Lee's Children's Poetry" (C117), Margaret *Atwood*'s "Dennis Revisited" (C118), Ted *Blodgett*'s "Authenticity and Absence: Reflections on the Prose of Dennis Lee" (C119), George *Bowering*'s "Detachment from Self" (C302), Robert *Bringhurst*'s "At Home in the Difficult World" (C120), Matt *Cohen*'s "Dennis Lee and Andy Warhol" (C121), Don *Coles*'s "The Sheer Extent of It" (C122), Stan *Dragland*'s "On *Civil Elegies*" (C123), Sheila *Egoff*'s "Dennis Lee's Poetry

for Children" (C125), Marian *Engel*'s "Working with Dennis Lee" (C126), Graeme *Gibson*'s "Kind of Squash" (C127), George *Grant*'s "Dennis Lee, Poetry and Philosophy" (C128), Sean *Kane*'s "The Poet as Shepherd of Being" (C129), Irving *Layton*'s "A Chess Master in Control" (C130), Denise *Levertov*'s "The Poem as Score" (C131), Mary *MacPherson*'s "Chronology and Bibliography" (C132), Ann *Munton*'s "Simultaneity in the Writings of Dennis Lee" (C135), Michael *Ondaatje*'s "Cut Down the Middle" (C136), Al *Purdy*'s "Dennis the Ed" (C137), and Scott *Symons*'s "Generalissimo Lee" (C138).
    Also includes Dennis *Lee*'s and George *Bowering*'s "Towards Polyphony: Extracts from a Conversation between Dennis Lee and George Bowering" (B449) and Dennis *Lee*'s "Polyphony, Enacting a Meditation" (B207) and "Riffs" (B68).

C2   Middlebro', T.G. *Dennis Lee and His Works.* [Toronto: ECW, 1985. 39 pp.]
    An offprint of C169.

Articles and Sections of Books

C3   Walker, Alan. "Rochdale — The College the Students Already Run." Photographs Kryn Taconis. *The Star Weekly Magazine* [Toronto Daily Star], Jan. 1968, pp. [8]–13
    Walker discusses the founding and the philosophy of Rochdale College. Two photographs of Lee are included.

C4   Baxter, Marilyn. "I Patched My Coat with Darkness." *Acta Victoriana* [Victoria College, Univ. of Toronto], 92, No. 4 (April 1968), 18–24.
    Kingdom of Absence is a "single poem depicting one man's honest and penetrating search for meaning." Lee "moves through doubt, fear, bitterness,

irony, apathy and humility to an absolute honesty that both debilitates and enriches." He explores the "inauthenticity" of city and country life, "time the destroyer," the human intellect, despair "that forces the poet to acknowledge his own culpability," and the void. There is an image of hanging or being pulled in two different directions, but also "some of the funniest poetry."

C5   Cameron, Donald. "Quick, Name 55 New Canadian Writers . . . Dennis Can." *Maclean's*, July 1971, p. 72.

In this article, which is based on an interview, Cameron summarizes Lee's comment that ". . . English Canada has produced no fewer than 55 serious novelists since the advent of Margaret Laurence and Mordecai Richler." The new writers vary greatly in form, locale, and content. According to Lee, ". . . the cognoscenti may view Canada — like Nigeria and the West Indies in the recent past — as the place where the exciting new fiction is coming from."

C6   Hughes, Campbell B. "Book Publishing." Letter. *The Globe and Mail* [Toronto], 18 Sept. 1971, p. 6.

Hughes accuses Lee of distorting his statements in his letter to the editor (B441) to support his own view of the current state of book publishing. Lee should not "attempt to polarize book publishers into groupings of 'good guy' Canadian publishers and 'bad guy' subsidiary publishers . . . ."

C7   Owen, I.M. "Book Publishing." Letter. *The Globe and Mail* [Toronto], 18 Sept. 1971, p. 6.

Owen agrees with Lee "in supporting the Third Interim Report of the Rohmer Commission" but not with Lee's letter to the editor (B441) attacking Cambell Hughes, whose information was at the time incomplete.

C8   Atwood, Margaret. *Survival: A Thematic Guide to Canadian Literature*. Toronto: House of Anansi, 1972, pp. 61, 123, 173–74, 242–44.

Civil Elegies connects various oppressions with various liberations. The poetry contains two poles, "Hell," or "servitude," and "Paradise," a "form of freedom." Lee presents and "investigates" the images as well as "the process of transition." Lee places himself " 'inside' " the society and "embodies its plight."

C9   Beau[lieu?], Ivanhoé. "Dennis Lee, poète et éditeur torontois: A la recherche de l'enracinement." *Le Soleil* [Québec], 10 juin 1972, p. 64.

". . . pour moi, la poésie de Dennis Lee compte parmi les plus belles choses que j'ai lues en anglais." The author discusses meeting with Lee, House of Anansi Press, and the surge of Canadian writers (including Lee) for whom writing (not teaching) is their life and work.

C10   Helwig, David. Letter. *Quarry*, 21, No. 3 (Summer 1972), 66–67.

Helwig is unable to review *Civil Elegies and Other Poems* because he prefers the version published in 1968. "The new elegies are longer, more discursive, more resolved, somehow less personal or with less sense of a crucial moment." Helwig does not listen to the "voice" the same way he did in the original elegies. The "marriage poems" are too personal. Lee replies to Helwig's letter (B442).

C11   Mathews, Robin. "Rejoinder." Letter. *Saturday Night*, Sept. 1972, pp. 31–32.

Mathews criticizes Lee for discussing Al Purdy in terms of the George Grant/Northrop Frye sense of alienation in Canadian literature (B202).

C12 Jones, D.G. "Myth, Frye and Canadian Writers." *Canadian Literature*, No. 55 (Winter 1973), p. 20.
Jones refers to Lee's "Glad for the Wrong Reasons" in a passing reference.

C13 Geddes, Gary. "Lee, Dennis (1939–   )." In *Supplement to The Oxford Companion to Canadian History and Literature*. Ed. William Toye. Toronto: Oxford Univ. Press, 1973, pp. 186–87.
Geddes notes Lee's educational background, his involvement with Rochdale College and House of Anansi Press. Some of his works are mentioned, but *Kingdom of Absence* and *Civil Elegies* are discussed in more detail.

C14 Grantham, Ron. " 'Elegies' Prove Topical." *The Citizen* [Ottawa], 12 July 1973, p. 69.
Lee's reading from *Civil Elegies* was "unexpectedly topical" "in reference to the Pentagon Papers version of Canada's role as messenger for the United States early in the Vietnam War." Grantham briefly outlines Lee's co-founding with Dave Godfrey of House of Anansi Press. Despite the growing market for Canadian literature, Lee believes "federal and provincial help is essential . . . ."

C15 Colombo, John Robert. "Lee, Dennis." In his *Colombo's Canadian Quotations*. Edmonton: Hurtig, 1974, p. 343.
Colombo cites several of Lee's works.

C16 Davey, Frank. "Dennis Lee (1939–)." In his *From There to Here: A Guide to English-Canadian Literature since 1960*. Vol. II of *Our Nature — Our Voices*. Erin, Ont.: Porcepic, 1974, pp. 165–67.
Lee has a Canadian nationalist "unity of political and artistic action." The " 'void' " is "one of the dominant ideas of his work." Apart from the promi-sing new lyrics in *Civil Elegies and Other Poems*, Lee's style is "awkwardly conservative," abstract, and generalizing, rather than vividly particular. In *Civil Elegies*, ". . . the peaceful march of his long line tends to give the lie to [his] . . . claims of anguish and despair." Lee uses "empty and pretentious phrases." The 1972 revisions "do not grapple with the graver weaknesses of the work." Bibliographical data are included.

C17 Allen, Bob. "Peter Rabbit Strikes Again." *The Vancouver Province*, 28 Jan. 1974.
Lee's reading at the University of British Columbia "was a solid performance." *Civil Elegies* "is sombre stuff — full of musings about the poet's inner struggles to come to terms with himself." Lee's style is "direct" and "mercifully free of sentimental or sloppy excesses." His delivery was "casual but forceful." His children's poetry shows his "ability to play with language."

C18 Poupard, Denise. "I Could Have Danced? Chanced? Pranced? All Night." *Charlatan* [Univ. of Ottawa], 27 Sept. 1974, p. 37.
In this report of a reading that Lee gave in Ottawa, Poupard notes that "A delightful, rollicking set was provided by Dennis Lee." Lee's " 'children's' poems . . . were magical and vivid" and captured the audience. All his works were strikingly illustrated by his lively voice and smooth-flowing rhythms, even his "more serious" poetry.

C19 Smith, Erith. "No More Jolly Millers or Tuffets: He Gives Children's Rhymes a Modern Meaning." *Colonist Times* [Victoria], 9 Oct. 1974, p. 23.
Smith comments on Lee's reading for children in Victoria, British Columbia. Photographs are included.

C20 Stusiak, Marilyn. "Time to Return to the Joy of Books." *The Vancouver Sun*, 10 Oct. 1974, Children's World, p. 46.

Lee "brought squeals of joy and laughter from young audiences" in Vancouver this week. He "has the ability to play with the language creating pieces of whimsy, rhymes and poems that are relevant for urban youngsters living in the nuclear age."

C21 McAlpine, Mary. "Just a Kid of 35." *The Vancouver Sun*. "Living Today," 11 Oct. 1974, p. 38.

McAlpine mentions some of Lee's readings. Some of his children's poems "smack of [Hillaire] Belloc, [W.B.] Yeats, [Thomas] Hardy — only [Edward] Lear is absent." If Lee tries consciously to write a children's poem he is "condescending." Instead, he becomes "a 35-year-old" child and follows his "nose." Lee believes Margaret Laurence is Canada's best novelist and admires the work of Alice Munro. For poetry, he chooses Al Purdy. A photograph is included.

C22 "Poet at Play." *The Calgary Herald*, 15 Oct. 1974, p. 39.

For this reading in Calgary, "The children were eager to learn new rhymes that include many Canadian place names and situations and objects with which all children are familiar." A photograph of Lee with some children is accompanied by a caption.

C23 McDonald, Marguerite. "Poetry Is about Us." *Calgary Albertan*, 16 Oct. 1974, p. 10.

Lee gave a reading in Calgary.

C24 Wardle, Rob. "Dennis . . . Lee." *Arthur* [Trent Univ.], 16 Oct. 1974, p. 10.

Reading from *Alligator Pie* and *Nicholas Knock and Other People* at Otonabee College, Trent Uni-

versity, Lee entertained the audience of "twenty year old" kids with what he calls his " 'writing playfully.' " At intermission, Lee spoke to individuals "of his two diverse styles . . . ." Later, he showed his more formal side, reading three unpublished works and from *Civil Elegies*. A photograph of Lee is included.

C25 Vickers, Reg. "Books and Bookmen." *Herald Magazine* [*The Calgary Herald*], 18 Oct. 1974, p. 11.

Lee visited Calgary as part of an eight-week Canada-wide reading tour. *Alligator Pie* and *Nicholas Knock and Other People* have become so popular that the publisher is having difficulty securing enough paper for a second printing for Christmas. A photograph of Lee is also included.

C26 Fowlie, Vern. "His Verse Tells of Here, Today." *Winnipeg Free Press*, 22 Oct. 1974, p. 19.

Fowlie comments on Lee's reading in Winnipeg. A photograph is included.

C27 Carson, Catherine. "Once Upon Time, Daddy Wrote Poems for Bedtime Tales . . . and Now They're in Books." *Edmonton Journal*, 26 Oct. 1974, p. 26.

Lee read for children in Edmonton. A photograph of Lee with some children is included.

C28 "Alligator Pie and Other Poems." *Our Schools: The Winnipeg School Division No. 1*, 3, No. 3 (Nov. 1974), p. 19.

Lee read for children in Winnipeg. A photograph of Lee with some children is included.

C29 "Gift of Poetry." *Mail-Star* [Halifax], 16 Nov. 1974, p. 3.

Lee's "young audience is the result of his switch recently to devoting his attention to Children's verse, which he feels should become more indicative of modern day realities." A photograph of Lee with some children is accompanied by a caption.

C30 "Canadian Poet Visiting Area Schools." *Western Star* [Corner Brook, Nfld.], 19 Nov. 1974, p. 9.
Lee visited several schools in Corner Brook and St. Albans as part of Young Canada's Book Week. Lee keeps "in close contact with children in order to write good poetry. 'If I try to calculate what they want, the results are boring.' " A photograph of Lee with some children is included.

C31 Doyle, Pat. "Poet Says Children Need Verse More Suitable to Daily Lives." *The Evening Telegram* [St. John's, Nfld.], 19 Nov. 1974, p. 16.
While reading to his two-year-old daughter, Lee realized "that children needed some updated verse." In a cross-Canada tour, he spent two days in Newfoundland. In Lee's collections, ". . . children will discover 'boys and girls who are joyful; adventurous, funny, and brave poems that will scare them; poems that will lull them to sleep.' " Lee has been well-received by children and adults. A photograph of Lee with some children is included.

C32 McCormick, Christy. "Zesty Kids Give Poetry Reading Lots of Bounce." *The Gazette* [Montreal], 27 Nov. 1974, p. 19.
Lee reads in Montreal. A photograph of Lee with some children is included.

C33 Lowe, Patricia. "Why Dennis Lee Went from Elegies to Alligator Pie: Sugar and Spice of the Children's Life." *The Montreal Star*, 28 Nov. 1974, p. C9.
Lee reads for children in Montreal. A photograph of Lee with a child is included.

C34 Whittaker, Herbert. "Joyful Jingles Come Alive." *The Globe and Mail* [Toronto], 23 Dec. 1974, p. 10.
"Many of Lee's best jingles are short, not meant to test the shortest of attention spans." In *Alligator Pie in Your Eye* (C238) we see "some dramatic continuity . . . . What emerges from all this is a contemporary, contrary child's-eye view of the world we live in, and at the first performance yesterday it obviously passed muster . . . ."

C35 Kareda, Urjo. "Alligator Pie a Plus for Children's Theatre." *The Toronto Star*, 30 Dec. 1974, p. D6.
Alligator Pie in Your Eye (C238), "a Theatre Passe Muraille 'seed' show, is a beguiling dramatic adaptation of some of Dennis Lee's exceptional poems for children. . . . The poems themselves, from Alligator Pie and Wiggle to the Laundromat, are delightful, and the show makes them positively shine."

C36 Egoff, Sheila. *The Republic of Childhood: A Critical Guide to Canadian Children's Literature in English.* 2nd ed. Toronto: Oxford Univ. Press, 1975, pp. 243–45, 253, 268, 269.
Egoff refers to *Alligator Pie* and *Nicholas Knock and Other People.*

C37 Cherry, Zena. "Poet Dennis Lee Wins $500 IODE Award." *The Globe and Mail* [Toronto], 4 March 1975, p. 12.
Lee won the National Chapter of Canada IODE [Imperial Order of the Daughters of the Empire] Book Award for *Alligator Pie.*

C38 Watt, Keith. "Dennis Lee: The Wizard Is Me." *Arthur* [Trent Univ.], 24 Nov. 1975, p. 2.
Lee gave a reading for adults in Peterborough, Ontario.

C39 "Once Upon a Winner." Illus. Frank Newfeld. *Weekend Magazine*, 20 March 1976, p. 10.

The first Annual Alligator Pie Contest, which includes poems by others based on Lee's *Alligator Pie* (C269–C291), is introduced. See also B96 and B242.

C40 Jones, D.G. "A Post Card from Chicoutimi." *Studies in Canadian Literature* [Univ. of New Brunswick], 1 (Summer 1976), 177, 179–81.

"As a Canadian and as a writer, Lee identifies with Gaston Miron: his problem in relation to American culture is much the same as Miron's in relation to anglophone America." Passages from *Civil Elegies* "echo an older Québec literature." Like Paul-Marie Lapointe, Lee "would place a new emphasis on the particular body in space and the particular moment in time."

C41 Adilman, Sid. "Alligator Pie Sales a Plum for the Poet." *The Toronto Star*, 22 Dec. 1976, p. F7.

Adilman discusses the success of *Alligator Pie* and *Nicholas Knock and Other People*. A photograph of Lee is included.

C42 Jones, D.G. "Grounds for Translation." *ellipse*, No. 21 (1977), p. 82. Rpt. trans. ("Raisons d'être de la traduction") in *ellipse*, No. 21 (1977), p. 83.

In "Cadence, Country, Silence: Writing in Colonial Space," Lee "discovered that his identification was less with Americans than with Quebeckers. . . . he shared the acute problems of how to live and write when you do not appear to exist, or when your existence, first in the eyes of others, finally in your own, is an illusion." This is the central theme of *Civil Elegies*. "Garneau lives on in Lee."

C43 Mandel, Eli. *Another Time*. Three Solitudes: Contemporary Literary Criticism in Canada, No. III. Erin, Ont.: Porcepic, 1977, pp. 121–22, 156.

Toronto "shows itself as the void" in Lee's poetry. Lee's *Civil Elegies* (1968) "is a book of seven brooding meditations on civility, civitas, the possibility of life in the modern city. ". . . Lee turns the nationalist argument into a question of literary language . . . . His theory of decolonization turns out to be as much a literary as a political solution. Form itself is here a political matter . . . ."

C44 Sullivan, Rosemary. "Breaking the Circle." *The Malahat Review* [Univ. of Victoria, B.C.], No. 41 (Jan. 1977), p. 30.

Lee is the most "radical" of the "young generation of poets in Canada who insist that a poet must be grounded in his or her own culture." Lee insists "that poets write out of a civic space."

C45 "Children Enjoy Poem Session." *The Chronicle-Herald* [Halifax], 22 Jan. 1977, p. 17.

Lee reads for children in Truro, Nova Scotia. A photograph is included.

C46 "Canada's Best English-Canadian Books for Children." *The World of Children's Books: A Review of Children's Literature in English* [Univ. of Alberta], 2, No. 1 (Spring 1977), 2.

In a survey of 170 Canadian children's librarians, *Alligator Pie* came in first place; *Nicholas Knock* was voted sixteenth.

C47 "Uncle Polishers Sweep Alligator Contest!". *Weekend Magazine*, 26 March 1977, p. 14.

The second Annual Great Alligator Pie Contest, which includes poems by others based on Lee's *Alligator Pie*, is introduced. See B244 and C292–C301.

C48 Ruston, Ruth Ellen. "Not Your Average Tortured Writer: When Things Are Not Nice Oonah McFee

Takes the Sting Out by Making Them Beautiful."
The Canadian [Toronto], 2 July 1977, pp. 12–13.
Ruston quotes Lee and discusses his early encouragement of Oonah McFee.

C49 French, William. "Alligator Pie Is the Librarians' Choice but Children May Not Agree." *The Globe and Mail* [Toronto], 5 July 1977, p. 14.
In a survey of librarians, *Alligator Pie* was voted the best Canadian children's book. A photograph of Lee with children is included.

C50 Worthington, Helen. "Experts List Their Favorites." *The Toronto Star*, 26 July 1977, p. F1.
Alligator Pie and *Garbage Delight* are named in a list of the best Canadian children's books.

C51 "Scarboro Public Library Week Is Set for Sept. 19 to 25." *The Mirror* [Scarborough, Ont.]. "At the Library," 14 Sept. 1977, pp. 30–31.
Lee holds a pre-publication reading of *Garbage Delight* in Scarborough, Ontario.

C52 Montgomery, John. "Dennis Lee Signs Books." *Stouffville Tribune*, 29 Sept. 1977.
"Mr. Lee's verses, irreverent and funny, are refreshing in that they avoid the type of treacly pap often foisted off as children's literature." Two photographs of Lee with children are included.

C53 Stevens, Victoria. "Children's Author and Authors-to-Be Meet at Harborfront." *The Toronto Star*. "Starship: A Special Space for Children," 29 Sept. 1977, p. D1.
Lee reads for children in Toronto. A photograph of Lee with children is included.

C54 "Dennis Lee Poetry Contest." *Apple* [Hamilton Public School System], Oct. 1977, p. 13.

Lee presents Hamilton public school classes prizes for The Bookcellar's poetry contest. A photograph is included.

C55 Hunt, Jacquie. "Dennis Lee Delights Children Again." *The Citizen* [Ottawa], 4 Oct. 1977, p. 47.
"The same rollicking rhythms and audacious view of the real concerns of childhood, the same brilliant color and sly visual humor that characterized the earlier two volumes are again apparent in the latest edition of nursery rhymes for modern Canadians, *Garbage Delight*." "Lee, like A.A. Milne, has exactly captured the child's tendency to imbue his favorite toys with a life of their own . . . ." The true appeal of the work is "their uninhibited gusto and uncensored honesty."

C56 Earl, Marjorie. "Author of Alligator Pie Serves Up More Fantasy." *Tribune* [Winnipeg], 11 Oct. 1977, p. 37.
Garbage Delight will succeed on its own merit, although success is inevitable because of Lee's previous work. An "underlying note of seriousness" and political undertones are found in Lee's poems. Lee has not studied children's poetry as a craft. He says, " '. . . I learned from reading to my kids.' "

C57 Matchan, Linda. " 'Alligator Pie' Delights Kids." *Tribune* [Winnipeg], 22 Oct. 1977, p. 33.
Lee says that *Garbage Delight* "breaks away from the 'wild and woolly' style of *Alligator Pie* . . . . The book contains 'more quiet, inward poems' than the other books . . . ." When Lee reads his poems to a young audience, he has " 'a sense of their being in league with the poem.' " Although the poems have a "simple, lyric style," Lee often writes between fifteen and twenty drafts. One photograph of Lee and four photographs of children are included.

C58   Finlayson, Judith. "Canadian Juvenile Publishing Comes of Age." *Quill & Quire*, Nov. 1977, pp. 6, 8.
Alligator Pie and *Nicholas Knock and Other People* have had successful sales. A photograph is included.

C59   Fulford, Robert. "The Politics of Publishing: Why Do They All Hate Lorimer?". *Saturday Night*, Nov. 1977, p. 21.
Fulford refers to Lee and publishing with House of Anansi Press.

C60   Hohenadel, Peter. "Creative Writing a Spark in Need of Focus." *The Varsity* [Univ. of Toronto], 14 Nov. 1977, p. 3.
Hohenadel mentions the avant garde phase of *Acta Victoriana* in the early 1960s, when Lee and Margaret Atwood were its editors.

C61   Lownsbrough, John. "Kids' Books." *The Financial Post Magazine* [*The Financial Post*] [Toronto], 19 Nov. 1977, p. 17.
Lownsbrough quotes Lee on children's books and refers to his recent cross-Canada reading tour.

C62   Pullan, Diane. "Record Sales for Caedmon Canada." *Quill & Quire*, Dec. 1977, p. 18.
Pullan discusses the April release of Lee's children's poetry on the Caedmon label (A66). A photograph is included.

C63   Stewart, Walter. "Author! Author!". *Maclean's*, 12 Dec. 1977, p. 56.
Stewart refers to Lee signing autographs at a bookstore in the Maritimes.

C64   Maxwell, Ward, and Riley Tench. "Lee et Fricassee." Illus. Frank Newfeld. *Arthur* [Trent Univ.]. "CS Review," 16 Dec. 1977, p. 16.

At Trent University, Lee read some children's poems and gave a seminar on *Savage Fields: An Essay in Literature and Cosmology*. He used the image of iron filings in a magnetic field to illustrate the tension between "earth" and "world." He believes his views cannot "be understood in terms of Western Logic." His "new spirit of thought . . . must, by its existence and relative importance, develop its own logic." While reading his poetry, he "works well with children" in the audience. When the children and their parents left, the "Santa figure . . . was replaced by a young-old man reading strong, almost solemn poetry in quiet, serious tones."

C65   N[ew]., W.H. "The Loss of Zed." Editorial. *Canadian Literature*, No. 75 (Winter 1977), pp. 3, 4.
New refers to Lee's *Alligator Pie* and *Garbage Delight*.

C66   Bilan, R.P. "Canadian Poet-Critics." *Dalhousie Review*, 57 (Winter 1977–78), 765, 770–74.
This is a review-article of Eli Mandel's *Another Time* and Lee's *Savage Fields: An Essay in Literature and Cosmology*, an "ambitious" and "unusual" book. Lee "lacks the theoretical, certainly philosophical, capability necessary for what he undertakes." His speculation is "highly questionable" and his literary criticism, "while often perceptive and fascinating, suffer[s] from the abstract nature of his approach." The terms "world" and "earth" "never become sufficiently precise." Bilan questions Lee's omission of "imagination, creativity, art, intellectual vision, compassion and love" from Lee's category of "world." Lee's literary proof is "extremely limited" and shows "extraordinary provinciality." His "account of savage fields seems . . . imposed" and often "misleading." "It is Lee [not Michael Ondaatje] who denies that any positive features belong

to the world." "Lee's deep conservativism causes him to limit too drastically man's capacity to *create* meaning." "The problem with Lee's position is that he seems essentially to want to return to the world displaced by the liberal cosmology," the "sacramental universe," though ". . . he does remark that it would be 'almost impossible' . . . . By the end of his book Lee appears to have thought himself into a corner. . . . Nonetheless, Lee has extended the boundaries of Canadian criticism" beyond "Canadian themes, images, and patterns, towards the mainstream of criticism and towards an engagement with the major questions of our time."

C67   Egoff, Sheila A. Back container notes. In *Alligator Pie and Other Poems*. Narr. Dennis Lee. Music Don Heckman. Front container illus. Frank Newfeld. New York: Caedmon, TC 1530, 1978. (L.p.; 33-1/3.)
Egoff examines Lee's children's poetry in its contemporary context and in the tradition of oral folklore.

C68   Steele, James. "The Literary Criticism of Margaret Atwood." In *In Our Own House: Social Perspectives on Canadian Literature*. Ed. Paul Cappon. Toronto: McClelland and Stewart, 1978, p. 79.
Steele includes Lee in a list of "idealist critics and poets of the archetypal school."

C69   McCarthy, Arlene H. "The Literary Revolution — Its Causes and Effects." *Canadian Author & Bookman*, 53, No. 2 (Jan. 1978), 14.
Experimental writing, like that of Dennis Lee and Dave Godfrey "was too unconventional and risky for the established publishing houses to accept . . . ." They founded the House of Anansi Press to publish their own work and that of others who had been rejected, including Harold Ladoo, Graeme Gibson, Margaret Atwood, and Marian Engel.

C70   Nodelman, Perry. "The Silver Honkabeest: Children and the Meaning of Childhood." *Canadian Children's Literature/Littérature canadienne pour la jeunesse*, No. 12 (1978), pp. 26–34.
Nodelman examines some of the poems in *Nicholas Knock and Other People* in view of Lee's own theory of writing children's poems, which he expresses in his "Roots and Play: Writing as a 35-Year-Old Children [sic]" (B205).

C71   Yaffe, Phyllis. "More on the Kids' Book Fest." *Book and Periodical Development Council Newsletter* [Toronto], No. 3 (Jan. 1978), p. 7.
Yaffe refers to Lee's cross-country reading tour during the Children's Book Festival.

C72   Fetherling, Doug. "The Savage Cosmos of Dennis Lee." Illus. William Kettlewell. *Saturday Night*, Jan.–Feb. 1978, pp. 74–75. Rpt. (expanded — "Notes on Dennis Lee") in *The Blue Notebook: Reports on Canadian Culture*. By Doug Fetherling. Oakville, Ont.: Mosaic, 1985, pp. 72–75.
Lee has done much to shape the present literary world. Yet, because his adult works are complex, he is known best to the general public as a children's poet. Some biographical material is outlined. *Kingdom of Absence* explores "the sense of being lost in the crack between his background and his environment" in England at the time of writing. Back in Canada, Lee still rejected "this artificial and alien tradition. . . . He came to see himself eventually as more or less a red tory . . . ." In *Civil Elegies*, Lee says "no to liberalism." In *The Death of Harold Ladoo*, ". . . he spoke from the same private source on more public matters that plagued him." In *Savage Fields: An Essay in Literature and Cosmology*, Lee points to the no-man's land between "world" and "earth." Philosophers, especially George Grant and Martin

Heidegger, have influenced Lee. Lee's struggles for voice and clarity have had "varying results." This critical book is most rewarding for "the incredible range of isolated ideas . . . ." A caricature of Lee by William Kettlewell is included in *Saturday Night*.

C73   F[reedman]., A[dele]. "Close Encounters of Various Kinds." *Quill & Quire*, Feb. 1978, p. 8.
      In this article, which is based on interviews with several editors (including Lee) about the editor-author relationship, Freedman notes that Lee is generally regarded as the best editor in Canada." He waits for the book to tell him " 'about itself.' " His work as an editor is " 'too intimate to be divulged.' " Many writers, including Marian Engel, have become dependent on Lee during the course of the editorial process. A photograph of Lee is included.

C74   Jones, D.G. Session Three: Panelist. The Calgary Conference on the Canadian Novel, Univ. of Calgary, Calgary. 17 Feb. 1978. Printed in *Taking Stock: The Calgary Conference on the Canadian Novel*. Ed. Charles R. Steele. Downsview, Ont.: ECW, 1982, p. 95.
      ". . . English-Canadian poets — Al Purdy, Margaret Atwood, Dennis Lee — have increasingly focussed on the past . . . . In Lee's 'Civil Elegies' the ancestral shades swarm like the eumenides, furies, into the square in front of Toronto's City Hall."

C75   Mandel, Eli. "The Regional Novel: Borderline Art." The Calgary Conference on the Canadian Novel, Univ. of Calgary, Calgary. 17 Feb. 1978. Printed in *Taking Stock: The Calgary Conference on the Canadian Novel*. Ed. Charles R. Steele. Downsview, Ont.: ECW, 1982, p. 109.
      In a discussion of nationalism, separatism, and "the *language* of regionalism," Mandel notes that

". . . presumably if one were to follow an argument like Dennis Lee's in 'Cadence, Country, Silence,' the distinction between nationalism and separatism loses some of its force."

C76   Jones, D.G. "In Search of Canada: Dennis Lee's Ironic Vision." ARC [Carleton Univ.], 1 (Spring 1978), 23–28.
      Civil Elegies and Other Poems and "Cadence, Country, Silence: Writing in Colonial Space" "are two of the most significant publications" of the decade. They draw into question previous works by Jones himself, Eli Mandel, and Warren Tallman, which "emphasize . . . myth as opposed to history." Jones discusses Lee's ability to maintain "an ironic middle ground" between a Humanist and a Modernist stance, which is the basis of Lee's centrally Canadian vision.

C77   "Canada Day: A CanLit Event. Dennis Lee." *Early Canadian Life* [Milton, Ont.], April 1978, Canadian Bookworm, pp. 3, 17.
      A brief biographical sketch of Lee is accompanied by a photograph.

C78   Ryval, Michael. "Cornering a Clamour of Critics." *Quill & Quire*, May 1978, pp. 4, 12.
      Ryval refers to Lee and *Savage Fields: An Essay in Literature and Cosmology*.

C79   "Awards." *Quill & Quire*, June 1978, p. 24.
      Lee has won the Canadian Library Association Book of the Year Award for *Garbage Delight*.

C80   "Awards Honour Children's Authors, Illustrators." *Feliciter* [Ottawa], 24, No. 6 (June 1978), 1.
      Lee has won the Canadian Library Association Book of the Year Award for *Garbage Delight*. A photograph of Lee with some children is included.

C81 Kilpatrick, Ken. "Author's Move for Freedom Was Worth It." *The Spectator* [Hamilton, Ont.], 10 June 1978, p. 18.

Kilpatrick's article includes an announcement that Lee has won the Ruth Schwartz Children's Book Award, sponsored by the Canadian Booksellers Association in co-operation with the Ontario Arts Council.

C82 Kilpatrick, Ken. "Macmillan Had Four Top Books." *The Spectator* [Hamilton], 17 June 1978, p. 16.

Lee has won the Canadian Library Association Book of the Year Award for *Garbage Delight*.

C83 Brown, Russell M. "Critic, Culture, Text: Beyond Thematics." *Essays on Canadian Writing*, No. 11 (Summer 1978), pp. 174–79, 180, 183.

With *Savage Fields: An Essay in Literature and Cosmology*, "Lee is the first important Canadian critic to publish a work which shows clear influence of structuralist methodology." However, his thesis "becomes less an act of speculative theory and more a controversial evaluation of man's condition" when he describes the regrettable " 'savage strife' " in this " 'terrible era of modernity.' " "Values are introduced under the guise of . . . terminology": the dualism of "*earth*" and "*world*," traditionally "nature/civilization," becomes lost in "*planet*." Lee "exempts several Canadian authors from having relevance to his discussion . . . ." His application of "the *world/earth* overlap" to the "content *and* structure" of Michael Ondaatje's book works well, but the theory is imposed on Leonard Cohen's book. "He is less interested in offering insight into this work than he is in showing how . . . Cohen fails to find the visionary resolution Lee seeks." This leads Lee to "dismissive evaluation" and Brown to sense that Lee is bent on editing Cohen's book post-publication. Nonethe-

less, Lee's "discovery of a grammar of violence in *Billy the Kid* . . . shows us the way to a thematic analysis which does not lose sight of the specifics of a given work."

C84 "CACL Awards." *Quill & Quire*, July 1978, p. 34.

Lee has won the Canadian Library Association Book of the Year Award for *Garbage Delight*. A photograph of Lee with some children is included.

C85 Simpson, Sheila. "Have Another Piece of Alligator Pie." Illus. Frank Newfeld. *Our Books Atlantic* [Halifax]. "Books Now," 31 July 1978. Rpt. *Casket* [Halifax]. "Books Now," 22 Nov. 1979, p. B4.

Lee arrives by garbage truck to the Halifax Regional Library amid cheers of several hundred school children. They chant the words to "Alligator Pie" and several other poems by heart. Lee is here to read from *Garbage Delight*, which has just won the Canadian Library Association Book of the Year Award and the Canadian Booksellers Award.

C86 McDonough, Irma. "CACL Children's Book Awards, 1947–1978." *Canadian Library Journal*, 35, No. 4 (Aug. 1978), 262, 266.

Lee won the Canadian Library Association Book of the Year Awards in 1975 for *Alligator Pie* and in 1978 for *Garbage Delight*. A photograph of Lee is included.

C87 "Writers in Residence." *Q & Q update*, 8 Sept. 1978, p. 3.

Lee is the writer-in-residence at the University of Toronto for the academic year 1978–79.

C88 Scobie, Stephen. "A Scheme Is Not a Vision." *Canadian Literature*, No. 78 (Autumn 1978), pp. 53–58.

Lee's *Savage Fields: An Essay in Literature and*

Cosmology presents "a System, which is . . . over-generalized and oversimplified . . . ." Lee's "initial and fatal preconception" is the " 'savage' " field, "the fundamental misconception of the whole book." Viewing strife as the "*only* reality . . . is . . . extreme pessimism . . . . In Lee, we see the Puritan guilty conscience of a disillusioned liberal run wild . . . ." As a philosophical theory, the book is "simplistic, contradictory, and inadequate." It also fails in its literary criticism. His "view of Billy as the chief exponent and illustration of the destructive nature of 'world' leads him into an almost ludicrous distortion of the character [Michael] Ondaatje presents." Lee does not allow Billy to emerge as an artist — the individual who "brings 'world' and 'earth' into harmony" — because Lee "cannot admit this possibility." He "gets off to a bad start with his assertion that [Leonard Cohen's] *Beautiful Losers* presents a myth of Canadian history in which Catherine Tekakwitha marks the Fall. Lee reads "*Beautiful Losers* as a fractured failure, in which Book Three makes no sense . . ." rather than "a successful unity, crowned by Book Three."

C89 Woodman, Dianne. "Canadian Children's Books: A Bookseller's Point of View." *Canadian Literature*, No. 78 (Autumn 1978), pp. 16, 17, 19.

The runaway success of *Alligator Pie, Nicholas Knock and Other People*, and *Garbage Delight* demonstrates that people are "willing to support Canadian children's books . . . of quality . . . ."

C90 Nathan, Paul S. "Alligator Uproar." *Publishers Weekly* [New York]. "Rights & Permissions," 2 Oct. 1978, p. 96.

Nathan discusses the popularity of Lee's collections of children's poems.

C91 "Alligator Pie Day a 'Snappy' Success!". *Maclean-Hunter Newsweekly* [Toronto], 3 Nov. 1978, p. 2.

Alligator Pie Day, a celebration of the 1979 *Alligator Pie Calendar* on 28 October 1978, was a success.

C92 Twigg, Alan. "Interview with Leonard Cohen." *Georgia Straight* [Vancouver], 10–17 Nov. 1978, p. 6. Rpt. in *For Openers: Conversations with 24 Canadian Writers*. By Alan Twigg. Madeira Park, B.C.: Harbour, 1981, p. 58.

Leonard Cohen refers to Lee's analysis of *Beautiful Losers* in *Savage Fields: An Essay in Literature and Cosmology*.

C93 O'Malley, Martin. "On Writing for Kids: Saying 'Bum' for Easy Laughs, and Other Literary Gaffes." Illus. Joe Salina. *The City* [*The Sunday Star*] [Toronto], 19 Nov. 1978, pp. 4–6.

O'Malley is promoting the Children's Book Festival, whose director, Phyllis Yaffe, declared Lee "a legend." One of Lee's favourite children's books is Pierre Burton's *The Secret World of Og*, and Lee was also influenced by the work of E.B. White.

C94 Mandel, Eli. "Academic and Popular: Public Demand and Classroom Realities." *Indirections* [OCTE, Toronto], 3, No. 2 (Winter 1978), 19–22.

In *Savage Fields: An Essay in Literature and Cosmology*, Lee gives a "lucid and bitter account of modernism" and "a new way of looking at the world or assuming its character." When "neither technology nor ecology offer solutions," as Lee says, " 'to go thinking within the models that rule in our civilization' " is not good. "When . . . popular and academic change roles, what remains?" Lee says, " '. . . thought is running up against one of its limits the instant it begins to think.' " Lee's view is not "as inevitable, as deterministic, as conclusive as its experiments make out."

C95 Marshall, Tom. *Harsh and Lovely Land: The Major Canadian Poets and the Making of a Canadian Tradition.* Vancouver: Univ. of British Columbia Press, 1979, pp. xiv, 90–91, 138, 147, 163, 171–72.

Marshall agrees with Lee's assessment of Al Purdy. He does not agree that Lee's perspective in *Savage Fields: An Essay in Literature and Cosmology* is "the whole truth about the world or about human life . . . but it is . . . a tremendous vision . . . ." Marshall alludes to Lee's use of the terms "absence" or "cadence" for "the ultimately mysterious larger rhythm of things." Lee is among the "more ambitious" poets "thinking in terms of larger structures" with *Civil Elegies* and *The Death of Harold Ladoo. Civil Elegies* "is one of the most timely and interesting . . . longer poems." His idiom is "persuasive and flowing."

C96 Pearce, Jon. "Enacting a Meditation: Dennis Lee." *Journal of Canadian Poetry,* 2, No. 1 (Winter 1979), 5.

Pearce introduces and explains Lee's self-interview, "An Interview with Dennis Lee" (C221).

C97 Hearn, John. "Classic Children's Books." *The Globe and Mail* [Toronto]. "The Collector's Column," 9 Feb. 1979, Better Living, p. BL6. Rpt. ("Identifying First Editions") in *The Globe and Mail* [Toronto]. "The Collector's Column," 16 March 1979, Better Living, p. BL12. Rpt. ("Children's Book Editions a Problem") in *The London Free Press.* "Collectables," 24 March 1979, p. E10.

Hearn comments on correspondence from Mary MacPherson that identifies the first and subsequent printings of *Alligator Pie* and prints most of the letter.

C98 Bradshaw, Leah. "A Second Look at *Savage Fields.*" *Canadian Journal of Political and Social Theory/Revue canadienne de théorie politique et sociale,* 3, No. 2 (Spring–Summer 1979), 139–51.

". . . while Lee has accurately identified the *malaise* of contemporary thought, his model does not go far enough towards an inquiry into the process of human understanding. Consequently, he places too much hope in the possibility of a recovery of 'meaningful' existence." In the first section, Bradshaw provides "a brief synopsis of Lee's theoretical viewpoint . . . ." She wonders why Lee has "chosen to describe his world as hell . . . . Lee obviously finds no solace in the argument that history has worked out its course in such a way that the result is the savage field. . . . What he is suggesting is that we reach out beyond ourselves as world-creatures and embrace the pre-conceptual source of our being: earth." In the second section, Bradshaw poses a dualistic model in which world confronts world in the form of competing ideologies. In the third section, she demonstrates that Michael Ondaatje's *The Collected Works of Billy the Kid: Left Handed Poems* and Leonard Cohen's *Beautiful Losers* are patterned after this theory.

C99 Godfrey, David. "On *Savage Fields* and the Act of Criticism." *Canadian Journal of Political and Social Theory/Revue canadienne de théorie politique et sociale,* 3, No. 2 (Spring–Summer 1979), 152–59.

Godfrey outlines shortcomings in Lee's analysis of both Leonard Cohen's and Michael Ondaatje's books. Lee's criticism is unscientific. "It could say that 57% of Caucasians trained at the University of Toronto lost interest in *Beautiful Losers* halfway through part II." However, Lee "presents no other proof than his own interpretation of the book, and his own emotional response rooted in that interpretation, for the 'failure' of the book. . . . If one lets *Savage Fields* be seen as a narrative, or narrative autobiography . . ." then Godfrey "enjoyed the story." Theoretically, process can be described as "strife whether or not mind is involved. . . . Consciousness is itself a process, but it does not necessarily affect the world of matter in process." Conscious and unselfconscious material energy are difficult to firmly distinguish from each other. "From the human point of view . . . no action is value-free and Lee has always followed Grant firmly and properly in attacking that fallacy of the social sciences."

C100 Cornell, Pamela. "The Art of Telling Tales." Illus. Frank Newfeld. *Graduate* [Univ. of Toronto]. "Books," 6, No. 4 (May–June 1979), 12–13.
Cornell refers to Lee's four children's books.

C101 Adachi, Ken. "Small Booksellers Band Together." *The Toronto Star*, 23 July 1979, p. C4.
Adachi notes that Lee will throw the ceremonial first pitch, for the Blue Jays's and Detroit Tigers' game, 28 July 1979, announcing "Book Night" at the CNE stadium.

C102 Parr, Susan. "Youngster Meets Favorite Poet." *Star-Phoenix* [Saskatoon], 24 Oct. 1979, p. D1.
Parr comments on Lee's book-signing session in Saskatoon. A photograph of Lee with some children is included.

C103 Adilman, Sid. "Kid's Book Chalks Up 100,000 Sales." *The Toronto Star*, 3 Dec. 1979, p. C1.
Alligator Pie, with 100,000 copies sold to date, is Canada's best-selling children's book since *Anne of Green Gables*.

C104 "Children Choose Their Own Literature." *The Vancouver Sun*. "Books," 7 Dec. 1979, p. 43L.
Lee's *Alligator Pie* is listed among books for young readers that "more than 80 percent of the children found outstanding."

C105 Suknaski, Andrew. "Pedestalled Woman." *Edmonton Journal*. "Readers' Journal," 15 Dec. 1979, p. A5.
Suknaski responds to Heather Pringle's review of *The Gods* in the *Edmonton Journal* (D26). Lee's "You Can Climb Down Now" "finally redeems the poet who gives back woman her rightful dignity and place in the ordinary reality of earth."

C106 Freeman, Alan. "Lee-Miron: apprendre de l'autre." *Le Devoir* [Montreal], 5 avril 1980, p. 22.
Lee gave a reading with Gaston Miron in Quebec City.

C107 Lesynski, Loris. "Warm about 'Bath.'" Letter. *Books in Canada*, May 1980, p. 32.
Lesynski criticizes Mary Ainslie Smith's review of *The Ordinary Bath* (D117). The book is "written as a touching, probing story with a dance of a rhythm." It will "probably turn into a classic."

C108 Arnason, David, Dennis Cooley, and Robert Enright. "Interview with Eli Mandel, March 16/78." *Essays on Canadian Writing*, Nos. 18–19 (Summer–Fall 1980), pp. 76, 78. Rpt. in *RePlacing*. Ed. Dennis Cooley. Downsview, Ont.: ECW, 1980, pp. 76, 78.
Eli Mandel notes that Lee "tackles" the question of "What can the writer write?" wrongly in *Savage Fields: An Essay in Literature and Cosmology*. Lee has said that Mandel's "Writing West" "was *the* essay for him."

C109 Andrist, Shirley. "A Love Affair with Dennis Lee." *The Medium* [Estevan, Sask.], 21, No. 2 (Fall 1980).
Andrist comments on Lee's poems for children. Includes letters by Lee (B446, B447, B448), which also include poems (B131–B134).

C110 Johnston, R.F. Ontario Legislative Assembly. *Debates: Official Report (Hansard)*. 31st Parliament, 4th sess. 6 Nov. 1980. Toronto: Queen's Printer, pp. 4158–59.

Civil Elegies prophesies "the end of Canada if we do not take action." Johnston reads eleven lines from "Civil Elegies 1" to the legislature. Living in the "foothills of the shield," as Johnston did, "gives one . . . a sense of the spiritual that Dennis Lee speaks about . . . ." Lee writes about how Canada has "sold out our nationhood, our resources and our guts to achieve a standard of living, and in so doing somehow missed nationhood and somehow maintained ourselves as colonials."

C111 Kroetsch, Robert. "Canadian Literature: What Happened in the Seventies?". MLA Conference, Houston, Tex. 29 Dec. 1980. Printed ("For Play Entrance: The Contemporary Canadian Long Poem") in *Dandelion*, 8, No. 1 (1981), 78.

Kroetsch refers to *The Death of Harold Ladoo* and describes Lee as "the aging white male dark and dangerous and wild and *poetic*."

C112 Egoff, Sheila A. In *Thursday's Child: Trends and Patterns in Contemporary Children's Literature*. Ed. Sheila A. Egoff. Chicago: American Library Association, 1981, p. 27.

Lee writes in the C.S. Lewis "tradition."

C113 Saltman, Judith. "Poetry." In *Thursday's Child: Trends and Patterns in Contemporary Children's Literature*. Ed. Sheila A. Egoff. Chicago: American Library Association, 1981, pp. 228, 230, 231.

Dennis Lee, John Ciardi, and Shel Silverstein have rehoned light verse. Like the traditionalists, ". . . their work is both a release of pure pleasure and a tool of acerbic social observation." However, their writing is more sophisticated. Lee's work reflects the physical and emotional terrain of Canada. His first three collections for children "create a poetry of pure play, jumping with puns and molding the oral language and codes of childhood into original verse."

C114 Woodcock, George. "To Dennis Lee." Letter. In his *Taking It to the Letter*. Montreal: Quadrant, 1981, p. 55.

Woodcock agrees with Lee that more criticism is needed on the new writing of the last decade. However, "graduate student critics" are not taking up this task. Woodcock's files are "clogged" with criticism of Leonard Cohen, F.P. Grove, E.J. Pratt, and Malcolm Lowry. In the final analysis, Woodcock distrusts "all literature that needs explication."

C115 Wayne, Joyce. "The Atwood Generation: Notes on Surfacing from the Underground." *Quill & Quire*, Feb. 1981, pp. 4, 6, 8.

Wayne discusses the current state of literature in Canada and the emergence of writers in the 1960s. Lee was among the new wave of literary writers. "As Dennis Lee demonstrates in *Civil Elegies*, the intense attraction to the new literature reflected both a fascination with stylistic experimentation and a social commitment to a radically different idea of Canada." Initially, many of the writers founded publishing houses in order to publish their books. Reporting to The Writers Union conference, Lee advised writers to take initiative in problem solving.

C116 French, William. "Committed McClelland Is a Sign of Good Times." *The Globe and Mail* [Toronto], 27 Oct. 1981, p. 16.

French notes Lee's appointment as senior literary consultant at McClelland and Stewart.

C117 Acker, Alison. "Dennis Lee's Children's Poetry." *Descant* [Dennis Lee Special Issue], No. 39 [14, No. 1] (Winter 1982), pp. 48–51. Rpt. in *Tasks of Passion: Dennis Lee at Mid-Career*. Ed. Karen Mulhallen, Donna Bennett, and Russell Brown. Toronto: Descant, 1982, pp. 48–51.

"Study of Dennis Lee's work . . . shows not only honest craft, originality and an understanding of children, but a delicate balance between anarchy and compliance with contemporary mores." "Lee's poems dive deepest into . . . childhood fears and desires . . . ," but never get "out of hand. . . . After all, Lee's world is still a very nice WASP world . . . . It is a far cry from the world of many Canadian children, especially the immigrant kids . . . ." Lee has great "rhythms," "skill with words," and "diction." His "rhyming is solid." "All these poems encourage language learning . . . the joy of words . . . ."

C118 Atwood, Margaret. "Dennis Revisited." *Descant* [Dennis Lee Special Issue], No. 39 [14, No. 1] (Winter 1982), pp. 13–15. Rpt. in *Tasks of Passion: Dennis Lee at Mid-Career*. Ed. Karen Mulhallen, Donna Bennett, and Russell Brown. Toronto: Descant, 1982, pp. 13–15.

Atwood discusses meeting Lee, their collaborations under the pseudonym Shakesbeat Latweed, and the development of House of Anansi Press. As an editor, Lee "can give another writer not only generous moral support but also an insightful, clear view of where a given book is trying to go," with "pages and pages of single-spaced, detailed and amended notes." Too much of "his own time and the attention and acclaim of others has often gone to the editing when it could or should have gone to the writing."

C119 Blodgett, Ted. "Authenticity and Absence: Reflections on the Prose of Dennis Lee." *Descant* [Dennis Lee Special Issue], No. 39 [14, No. 1] (Winter 1982), pp. 103–17. Rpt. in *Tasks of Passion: Dennis Lee at Mid-Career*. Ed. Karen Mulhallen, Donna Bennett, and Russell Brown. Toronto: Descant, 1982, pp. 103–17.

"Lee's fundamental concern is not the literary text but the problem of discourse itself." His approach is not "anti-modern," but "pre-modern" — "theological . . . and medieval." Discussing Lee's theoretical and practical uses of Heideggerian theory, Blodgett says that Lee is impatient with language's connection to the "real" and "language as a creative instrument." Drawing on George Grant, the theories that language is "in need of repair," that consciousness interprets the "real" "according to the kind of model employed," Blodgett discusses Lee's theory of "Cadence . . . , [which] takes its departure from Being," authenticity, and " 'presence.' Cadence becomes obstructed when the space of the writer becomes colonized," resulting in empty "signs" and silence "if one chooses to remain authentic." Lee wrote many drafts to move beyond the structuralist model he began with. He refuses "play and possibility" and embraces "closure" and silence. The binary model of " 'earth' " and " 'world' " are "mediated by 'planet,' a proposal that, so far from being radical, appears merely to tinker with the system." ". . . it is a kind of mystification to assert that 'savage fields figure planet as "dual," but not as "dichotomous" ' . . . . Lee's notion of cadence is surprisingly close to Derrida's notion of the trace . . . ," although it becomes subject to ontology and once again draws back before freedom. With consciousness situated as " 'world,' " "What must be preserved is the model within which Being may hide. . . . neurobiology has eliminated the subject . . . ." "The obverse of colonial, however, is imperial (American), and [for Lee] to abandon white mythology would be to give up the assurance that Nonbeing always implies its opposite. . . . Lee's model, as closed as any other cosmos, is totalitarian . . . . Only those texts that contain a certain duplicity are admissible as characteristic of our era. . . . The last, perhaps the ultimate, problem with Lee's model is that while it purports to speak for 'our' era, its synchronic character forbids its validity." Blodgett concludes, questioning human interpretation of the world, "For that is one of the fundamental failures of Western (white) thought, its human closure."

C120 Bringhurst, Robert. "At Home in the Difficult World." *Descant* [Dennis Lee Special Issue], No. 39 [14, No. 1] (Winter 1982), pp. 57–81. Rpt. in *Tasks of Passion: Dennis Lee at Mid-Career.* Ed. Karen Mulhallen, Donna Bennett, and Russell Brown. Toronto: Descant, 1982, pp. 57–81.

Bringhurst outlines personal and cultural differences between Lee and himself and the respect he holds for Lee as a writer. Lee has "welcomed without reserve [many varied] immigrant writers" and is modest. In the face of "rootlessness" and "western civilization," Lee has maintained "perpetual, attentive wonder." As a writer and an editor, Lee's "method of working" is extensive rewriting. Although Lee denies any affinity, Bringhurst compares Claude Lévi-Strauss's *Mythologiques* to Lee's theory of cadence. Lee "is an urban poet," yet "the presence of the earth" is "deep and central" to his writing. In his poetry, "earth *and* the human world; void *and* being; gods *and* godlessness" shine "into and out of the face of the other." Lee's larger poems are "meditations." Bringhurst outlines how the poems correspond with various Buddhist, or Mahayana, meditations. "Meditation . . . has something to do not with melting dualities down, but with kindling them into illuminations . . . . It is also the

process of casting off selves [and voices] until none remain . . . ," which Lee calls "polyphonies." Lee has a "sometimes meditative, sometimes tantric, sometimes frayed multiplicity of selves . . . ." "*Savage Fields*, [however] . . . is a work of . . . monophonic prose . . . . Moreover, it masquerades . . . [as] literary criticism . . . ." The dual but coextensive system of "world" and "earth" does not follow the rule: "everything that is, is both . . ." and at war. "*Savage Fields* is a work in progress," but ". . . it names no escape . . . . It is written in the world's language, thinking the thoughts of the world." In the epilogue, ". . . the expository form of the book breaks down, another voice at last begins to sound." But only in the poems is Lee ultimately able to balance "world" and "earth."

C121 Cohen, Matt. "Dennis Lee and Andy Warhol." *Descant* [Dennis Lee Special Issue], No. 39 [14, No. 1] (Winter 1982), pp. 32–36. Rpt. in *Tasks of Passion: Dennis Lee at Mid-Career.* Ed. Karen Mulhallen, Donna Bennett, and Russell Brown. Toronto: Descant, 1982, pp. 32–36.

Cohen discusses phoning Ann Gunnarson [a pseudonym Lee has used], who used to babysit Lee. "*The Death of Harold Ladoo* is Dennis Lee's finest poem . . . because it is his most personal poem." It is "the ultimate Toronto poem" in technique, themes, and rhythm. "*The Death of Harold Ladoo* is an act of biography that mines the particular instead of trying to deny and transcend it." As an editor, Lee's participation is often "far beyond the role normally assigned to an editor," often fundamentally affecting the book. "Lee also edited numerous books with which his involvement was more peripheral." Cohen describes the drastic alteration of a book of his through the editing by Margaret Atwood and Lee and questions whether it was "a triumph or a tragedy."

C122 Coles, Don. "The Sheer Extent of It." *Descant* [Dennis Lee Special Issue], No. 39 [14, No. 1] (Winter 1982), pp. 37–38. Rpt. in *Tasks of Passion: Dennis Lee at Mid-Career*. Ed. Karen Mulhallen, Donna Bennett, and Russell Brown. Toronto: Descant, 1982, pp. 37–38.

Commenting on Lee's editing, Coles is amazed by "the sheer extent of it, the patience and the spend-thrift offering and re-offering of all that taste and tact and banked-up expertise." Coles gives examples of Lee's commentary.

C123 Dragland, Stan. "On *Civil Elegies*." *Descant* [Dennis Lee Special Issue], No. 39 [14, No. 1] (Winter 1982), pp. 170–88. Rpt. in *Tasks of Passion: Dennis Lee at Mid-Career*. Ed. Karen Mulhallen, Donna Bennett, and Russell Brown. Toronto: Descant, 1982, pp. 170–88.

Two centres, the narrator and Nathan Phillips Square, focus the diverse history, rural and urban geography, and politics that can be called Canada without succumbing to homogeneity. The void is "a continuous thread through the poem" that is "pro-tean" — regenerative and abominable. It supplies an absolute "alternative" to godlessness and focuses being. Lee's eccentric style is flexible and "purpose-fully manipulated." His language is "instantly responsive" and "always *engaged*, totally . . . with its environment." Dragland discusses Lee's length of line, punctuation, grammatical construction, and repetition. Lee "has found his own shaky ground to stand firmly on," though ". . . he is light years away" from a nation built on these premises. Lee "is nowhere imprisoned by the impotence that is part of its [the poem's] subject . . . not only because it moves through and beyond that, but also because it is always throwing up those curls of wave which con-tradict placelessness."

C124 Duffy, Dennis. *Gardens, Covenants, Exiles: Loyal-ism in the Literature of Upper Canada/Ontario*. Toronto: Univ. of Toronto Press, 1982, pp. 119–24.

"Lee's '1838' and 'When I Went Up to Rosedale' . . . present a diptych of failed Canadas." Lee's strength as a poet lies in his "simplicity, clarity, and cadence." In "Cadence, Country, Silence," a gloss of *Civil Elegies*, Lee acknowledges his "debt" to George Grant and explains the difficulty of the artist " 'not to fake a space of our own and write it up, but rather to find words for our space-lessness' . . . ." Duffy discusses Lee's development of the image of "the void." Lee examines the "role our culture has played in its own destruction." In *The Death of Harold Ladoo*, the ". . . world has banished the gods only to have them return as demons." The cycle of Lee's poems "can be seen as a dialogue between political and religious concepts of void." In *Savage Fields: An Essay in Literature and Cosmology*, man lives in "a world of his own making . . . and an earth marked by non-man . . . ." The despair of living in both, simultaneously, is the kind of feeling associated with religious experience.

C125 Egoff, Sheila. "Dennis Lee's Poetry for Children." *Descant* [Dennis Lee Special Issue], No. 39 [14, No. 1] (Winter 1982), pp. 41–47. Rpt. in *Tasks of Pas-sion: Dennis Lee at Mid-Career*. Ed. Karen Mul-hallen, Donna Bennett, and Russell Brown. Toronto: Descant, 1982, pp. 41–47.

Egoff elaborates on the technical skill required in nonsense and light verse. Lee's "physical and emo-tional geography" are Canadian, but ". . . such places as Winnipeg and Nipigon take on an aura of make-believe." In his poetry for young children, Lee "is a traditionalist." He "has retained all the qualities that make Lear and Carroll and Milne and Stevenson still appealing to to-day's child — a structured and consistent rhyme scheme that is pleasing to the ear; a musical rhythm that gets one's foot tapping . . . ; a good deal of humour and fun often combined with recognizable, gentle child situations." Lee "is more concerned with the inner world of childhood than were his predecessors." He "goes beyond the chiefly idyllic aspects of childhood."

C126 Engel, Marian. "Working with Dennis Lee." *Descant* [Dennis Lee Special Issue], No. 39 [14, No. 1] (Winter 1982), pp. 29–30. Rpt. in *Tasks of Passion: Dennis Lee at Mid-Career*. Ed. Karen Mulhallen, Donna Bennett, and Russell Brown. Toronto: Descant, 1982, pp. 29–30.

Engel alludes to a family relationship with Lee and recalls his extensive editing of *The Honeyman Festival*. When they worked on *Monodromos*, "We got into wrangles, not big ones," but they had to separate because Engel would have grown "dependent. I have to have my own way with my work or I lose my sense of direction."

C127 Gibson, Graeme. "Kind of Squash." *Descant* [Dennis Lee Special Issue], No. 39 [14, No. 1] (Winter 1982), pp. 16–19. Rpt. in *Tasks of Passion: Dennis Lee at Mid-Career*. Ed. Karen Mulhallen, Donna Bennett, and Russell Brown. Toronto: Descant, 1982, pp. 16–19.

Gibson recalls Lee's editing of *Five Legs*. ". . . I came to see I was lucky to have ben turned down by those mainstream Canadian, English and American publishers — none of them, at that time, could have helped me make the most of the book in the way Dennis did." Lee is a "complex and driven man." Recalling the "enthusiasm" as well as the "tortuous and imperfect energy" at House of Anansi, Gibson notes, ". . . more often than not we find Dennis near the centre — as he was indeed with so many of the triumphs."

C128 Grant, George. "Dennis Lee, Poetry and Philosophy." *Descant* [Dennis Lee Special Issue], No. 39 [14, No. 1] (Winter 1982), pp. 229–35. Rpt. in *Tasks of Passion: Dennis Lee at Mid-Career*. Ed. Karen Mulhallen, Donna Bennett, and Russell Brown. Toronto: Descant, 1982, pp. 229–35.

Poetry and philosophy require openness, receptivity, and imitation, not "creation." During the Vietnam war, Lee was the only one who perceived that "The rampaging decadence of imperial war" could not be explained within liberalism or Marxism, but that "In the very roots of western civilization lay a particular apprehension of 'being.' " This "affirmation of 'being' " influenced the universities and language itself. In his description of language, Lee as a North American is "slightly" less "cosy" than Martin Heidegger. Grant compares Lee's theory of cadence with *Mozart's Briefe*, since both emphasize "hearing and seeing." Lee's openness is also evident "in his work as an editor." ". . . *Civil Elegies* is written out of the struggle which makes human beings existentialists . . . ." *The Gods* and *The Death of Harold Ladoo* partake of traditional philosophy, which "believed that the truth present in existentialism was only a preparation for its transcending." "*The Death of Harold Ladoo* moves back and forth with the fluidity of music" from the particular to the universal. In *Savage Fields: An Essay in Literature and Cosmology*, ". . . the joy of eternity must be more substantially present, if the ravages of fate are to be looked on, and one is not to be turned to stone."

C129 Kane, Sean. "The Poet as Shepherd of Being." *Descant* [Dennis Lee Special Issue], No. 39 [14, No. 1] (Winter 1982), pp. 121–42. Rpt. in *Tasks of Passion: Dennis Lee at Mid-Career*. Ed. Karen Mulhallen, Donna Bennett, and Russell Brown. Toronto: Descant, 1982, pp. 121–42.

Kane outlines the modernist "retreat from Voice" that began with Vico and the "break-up of a uniform Christian-Classical world-view with its belief in a reality alive with God-given value." Kane discusses modernism and experimental writing as reactions to the separation of words and being. Lee's "declaration of the essential living otherness of a poem" is anti-modern. Theoretically and technically, Friedrich Hölderlin "is Lee's spiritual ancestor. The role of the poet as Orpheus envoicing creation becomes in modern Canada the task of enacting the cadence of civil and spiritual belonging in a colonized space that recognizes neither citizenship nor the sacred." Kane draws some allusions to Samuel Beckett. The "poly-determinacy" of "Enactment" or Cadence "is what disintegrates the act of conscious purpose that would give it [ego-defined] meaning . . ." and subject language to human control. The modern role of "poet as primordial namer" is "tenuous," and in *Kingdom of Absence* Lee is restricted by the "iron hand of symmetrization." "The result was an utter silencing of his writing. . . . Lee often relies on pairs of opposing terms in his thinking . . . ." The simplification of a complex problem into an artificial "either/or," self and other dilemma leads to a paralysis of thought and action. "The letting-go could be honest only if Lee let the experience of complete deprival direct both sides of the crisis of naming — what is God-given, what is man-made?" In the last elegy, the speakers are "undivided from each other" and the either/or stances break down in polyphony, revealing "the fragile words and gestures of being human in a space without authentic beings or belonging."

C130 Layton, Irving. "A Chess Master in Control." *Descant* [Dennis Lee Special Issue], No. 39 [14, No. 1] (Winter 1982), p. 31. Rpt. in *Tasks of Passion: Dennis Lee at Mid-Career.* Ed. Karen Mulhallen, Donna Bennett, and Russell Brown. Toronto: Descant, 1982, p. 31.

In editing Layton's *A Wild Peculiar Joy: The Selected Poems 1945–82*, "There was wariness at the beginning, on his part, on mine. After all, we come from opposite ends of the literary and cultural spectrum: WASP and Jew. . . . Lee's devotion to literature . . . was perfect. Also he had an excellent ear and superb taste. . . . the disagreements were clearly stated and understood and ranged widely over theme, craft and everything else that delights literary chess masters."

C131 Levertov, Denise. "The Poem as Score." *Descant* [Dennis Lee Special Issue], No. 39 [14, No. 1] (Winter 1982), pp. 55–56. Rpt. in *Tasks of Passion: Dennis Lee at Mid-Career.* Ed. Karen Mulhallen, Donna Bennett, and Russell Brown. Toronto: Descant, 1982, pp. 55–56.

Lee's poems "manifest a full awareness of the poem as a form of musical score, in which melody — the pitch patterns of the voice — is indicated . . . by means of the deployment of the words on the page. . . . His diction, too, is very characteristic in its bold incorporation of unexpected words, often ugly in themselves, but accurate . . . ." Lee's syntax also "reflects the movement of *inner speech*, that is, neither the broken and casual habits of our common utterance nor the articulation of preformed ideas that characterize prose but the fluent processes of a mature mind talking its way along interior paths."

C132 MacPherson, Mary. "Chronology and Bibliography." *Descant* [Dennis Lee Special Issue], No. 39 [14, No. 1] (Winter 1982), pp. 239–47. Rpt. in *Tasks of Passion: Dennis Lee at Mid-Career.* Ed. Karen Mulhallen, Donna Bennett, and Russell Brown. Toronto: Descant, 1982, pp. 239–47.

Bio-bibliographical data. The bibliography was originally presented as a thesis (C199).

C133 Metcalf, John. *Kicking against the Pricks.* Downsview, Ont.: ECW, 1982, p. 78.

Metcalf briefly remembers Ray Smith saying "that his editor, Dennis Lee, had somehow managed to read the story ["Symbols in Agony," a "dour farce,"] without quite grasping that its intention was comic."

C134 Middlebro', Tom. "Dennis Lee 1939– ." In *Canadian Poetry*. Ed. Jack David and Robert Lecker. Vol. II. New Press Canadian Classics. Toronto/ Downsview, Ont.: General/ECW, 1982, 312–13.

After a brief biographical sketch, Middlebro' notes the "anguish" in Lee's poetic subject and comments on the influence of Martin Heidegger and George Grant in Lee's work. Bibliographical data is included.

C135 Munton, Ann. "Simultaneity in the Writings of Dennis Lee." *Descant* [Dennis Lee Special Issue], No. 39 [14, No. 1] (Winter 1982), pp. 143–69. Rpt. in *Tasks of Passion: Dennis Lee at Mid-Career*. Ed. Karen Mulhallen, Donna Bennett, and Russell Brown. Toronto: Descant, 1982, pp. 143–69.

"Throughout Lee's writing there are numerous seeming opposites . . . . Whether it be in subject matter, cosmological views, conditions of creativity, political or social programmes of action, or the actual form of his poetic meditations and 'enactments,' Lee proposes a way out of paradoxes through a vision of simultaneity," which "goes beyond contemporary patterns of logic." Munton explores these aspects in Lee's poetic works from *Kingdom of Absence* to *The Gods* as well as in *Savage Fields: An Essay in Literature and Cosmology.*

C136 Ondaatje, Michael. "Cut Down the Middle." *Descant* [Dennis Lee Special Issue], No. 39 [14, No. 1] (Winter 1982), pp. 20–21. Rpt. in *Tasks of Passion: Dennis Lee at Mid-Career*. Ed. Karen Mulhallen, Donna Bennett, and Russell Brown. Toronto: Descant, 1982, pp. 20–21.

Lee is "Intensely private" and desires "to change the world." His "grandest moment" as a critic was when ". . . he approached . . . [Leonard Cohen's *Beautiful Losers*] as if it was still in manuscript, saying what *he* would do in editing the work." Lee is a Platonist and "takes what is *being said*" very seriously. "He won't necessarily make the book a success but he will push the writer towards a truth . . . . If something is bothering him about a section he will write you a four page (single spaced) letter questioning you, questioning himself, questioning the universe, questioning the liberal party, God, early jazz violinists, plant life in Argentina, the immorality of Basho, the failure of the villanelle in the 20th century. This can be exhausting" and infuriating.

C137 Purdy, Al. "Dennis the Ed." *Descant* [Dennis Lee Special Issue], No. 39 [14, No. 1] (Winter 1982), pp. 22–24. Rpt. in *Tasks of Passion: Dennis Lee at Mid-Career*. Ed. Karen Mulhallen, Donna Bennett, and Russell Brown. Toronto: Descant, 1982, pp. 22–24.

"Our editorial meetings [about Purdy's *Being Alive* and *Selected Poems*] would be like a coming together of two mild zephyrs that wouldn't stir the curtains of an outhouse. Dennis and I are simply too much alike . . . ." Although, at times, Lee would bring "a different and fresh viewpoint" to the poems. "And sometimes because of what he didn't say, I had a pretty good idea of what he was thinking." *Being Alive* is a "much better book than it would have been without Dennis . . . . He didn't re-write them [the poems] . . . . He was tactfully dissatisfied. He was simply Dennis, devious, insightful, gaining his ends by misdirection and mind-reading brilliance."

C138 Symons, Scott. "Generalissimo Lee." *Descant* [Dennis Lee Special Issue], No. 39 [14, No. 1] (Winter 1982), pp. 25–28. Rpt. in *Tasks of Passion: Dennis Lee at Mid-Career.* Ed. Karen Mulhallen, Donna Bennett, and Russell Brown. Toronto: Descant, 1982, pp. 25–28.

Working with Lee as an editor is like "fighting a jungle-battle. . . . With yourself, the author, as guerilla warrior. And your subject matter, the jungle, full of hidden devils. And Lee . . . the hidden Generalissimo . . . ." Lee is "totally committed to the book — not to the author . . . ." He "cajoles, bludgeons and drags the protesting, awed, frightened, irritated author after him. Thank God! . . . At his worst, dealing with Lee is a bit like being lectured by a Moderator of the United Church." Lee "is probably the finest extant exemplar of . . . the Grit tradition . . . ." Lee's missives "present themselves as simple, ho-hum, innocent commentary. But they're not." His " 'small point' " usually requires two to three months of work and ". . . your entire book has been put into question. . . . Lee-as-editor . . . [is] a National Asset . . . ."

C139 French, William. "A Timely Reminder of the Censorship Battle." *The Globe and Mail* [Toronto], 9 Nov. 1982, p. 25.

French notes that "a special program will be staged to honor poet, critic and editor Dennis Lee. An all-star cast of readers will do their stuff for the occasion . . ." that "marks the launching" of *Tasks of Passion: Dennis Lee at Mid-Career* (C1).

C140 Adachi, Ken. "Authors Paying Tribute to Their Editor/Hero." Rev. of *Tasks of Passion: Dennis Lee at Mid-Career*, ed. Karen Mulhallen, Donna Bennett, and Russell Brown. *The Toronto Star*, 16 Nov. 1982, p. F3.

In this review, Adachi also comments that Lee "probably comes closest to Canada's version of the legendary editor, the *rara avis* who has that talent for unswerving attention to the work of others . . . coaxing and bullying along the way . . . . And when the book is ready for distribution, he's also known to persuade reviewers to pay special attention."

C141 Adilman, Sid. "Children's Author, Fraggle Rocker. More Alligator Pie and The Muppets: Dennis Lee Is at It Again." *The Toronto Star*, 18 Dec. 1982, p. F3.

Adilman mentions Lee's involvement with *Fraggle Rock* and notes Lee's revisions and voice-over in *The Dark Crystal*. Lee had many offers to produce *Alligator Pie* on stage, but " 'turned them all down' " until Janet Amos and Theatre Passe Muraille (see C238). A photograph of Lee with some children is included.

C142 Lane, M. Travis. "Contemporary Canadian Verse: The View from Here." *University of Toronto Quarterly*, 52 (Winter 1982–83), 180, 184, 185, 189.

Lane comments on Lee's use of form, rather than "dull, disorderly, meaningless art." Lee's meditative poems, "although eloquent and deeply moving, are . . . weakened by what may be a reluctance to appear old-fashionedly rational." Lee's "ability to . . . qualify his spontaneous expressions . . . is a strength too rarely found in our poetry."

C143 Bennett, Donna, and Russell Brown. "Dennis Lee, b. 1939." In *An Anthology of Canadian Literature in English*. Ed. Donna Bennett and Russell Brown. Vol. II. Toronto: Oxford Univ. Press, 1983, 504–05.

Bennett and Brown discuss Lee's educational background, his early days at Rochdale College and House of Anansi Press, and his work as an editor and as writer-in-residence. They comment on Lee's adult poetry in terms of nationalism, modernism, German philosophy, and his interest in meditation and music. Lee is a popular children's poet, and the authors note his television work for *Fraggle Rock*.

C144 Adachi, Ken. "National Book Festival Keeps Sights High." *The Toronto Star.* "Books," 19 April 1983, p. F7.

Adachi notes that Lee and other poets "take to the stage to read poems on the ethics of nuclear energy and disarmament."

C145 Thomas, Clara. "Festschrifts for Frye and Lee: Instruction and Delight." Rev. of *Centre and Labyrinth: Essays in Honour of Northrop Frye*, ed. Eleanor Cook, Chaviva Hošek, Jay Macpherson, Patricia Parker, and Julian Patrick; and *Tasks of Passion: Dennis Lee at Mid-Career*, ed. Karen Mulhallen, Donna Bennett, and Russell Brown. *Quill & Quire*, July 1983, p. 59.

"A new long poem, Riffs, is here, as is his Polyphony, a luminous series of meditations moving towards and centring on Cadence, a manifestation of cosmic energy . . . . The range of Lee's talents is" evident. Lee's own inclusions in the book are worth lingering over.

C146 MacDonald, R.D. "Lee's 'Civil Elegies' in Relation to Grant's 'Lament for a Nation.'" *Canadian Literature*, No. 98 (Autumn 1983), pp. 10–30.

In *Civil Elegies*, Lee and George Grant "express very different meanings and faiths. . . . Not only is the form of their language different . . . not only are their Gods different . . . but their attitudes toward and accounts of Canada's history, the failure of a colonial people to achieve an independent nation of their own, are also quite different: Grant emphasizes our failure to perpetuate what was good in our heritage while Lee, the modern liberal, makes much of becoming 'our own,' achieving independence from an out-moded past." Lee's poems "show a dialectical scepticism with little sign of 'awe' " and "little historical sense." "One is left asking: if the quiet [compliant or quiescent] Canadian is the source of our failure to be, is Lee's own quietness any more legitimate?" Is it merely dictated by the style of a distorting literary convention? Lee "does not adequately face what it has meant to live the Shield, . . . the historical necessity, the economic and human necessities . . . ." The third elegy "is little more than a recycling of the polemical slogans of Canadian nationalists . . ." and "does not confront the complexities and consequences of our own industrial society . . . ." After considering "various aspects of the void," Lee commits himself to "the diverse stir of the mundane world," but "He does not show in the texture of his poetry a close or loving concern for the actual and nearest . . . ." Lee is "unaware of . . . [the catastrophic] implications" of being "less cautious, less worried about consequences . . . ." Thus, ". . . his poem seems insufficiently thought out . . . ."

C147 N[ew]., W[illiam]. "The Flowers That Bloom in L.A." Editorial. *Canadian Literature*, No. 98 (Autumn 1983), pp. 3–4.

New values "the joyful inventiveness of Lee's lyrics" in *Fraggle Rock*. The "programme offers us a satiric glimpse of others and a creative distance from ourselves."

C148 Zieroth, Dale. "Reclaiming the Body/Reclaiming the Nation: A Process of Surviving Colonization in Dennis Lee's 'Civil Elegies and Other Poems.'" *Canadian Literature*, No. 98 (Autumn 1983), pp. 35–43.

In *Civil Elegies and Other Poems*, the separation of mind and body mirrors the "problem with the nation." In the "liberal cosmology . . . the body becomes value-free . . ." along with other objects for technological manipulation. "While Lee is aware that he is part of this cosmology, he does not share its values . . ." and the world and body become meaningless. In *Civil Elegies*, Lee engages "in the process of examining and articulating some of its [the mind-body problem] aspects in the particular context of a colonized Canada . . . . the body becomes a metaphor for society," the "civic body." In the resolution, the "act of resolving to honour the body and the world more fully reclaims them from meaninglessness . . . . In the final elegy, it becomes clear that reclaiming the body is necessarily a reclamation of speech itself."

C149 Fitzgerald, Judith. "Outside the Mainstream but Going Places." *The Globe and Mail* [Toronto], 12 Nov. 1983, Sec. Entertainment, p. 7.

In this profile of Christopher Dewdney, Fitzgerald reports Lee's reaction to Dewdney and Lee's mandate, at McClelland and Stewart, to publish "poets between the ages of 30 and 40 who would otherwise be lost in the national visibility shuffle." Lee's risk-taking has proved rewarding.

C150 Giguère, Richard. *Exil, révolte et dissidence: étude comparée des poésies québécoise et canadienne (1925–1955)*. Vie des Lettre québécoises, No. 23. Québec: Les Presses de l'Univ. Laval, 1984, pp. 124, 222.

Lee is cited among the emerging writers of the 1960s and 1970s who are concerned with nationalism.

C151 Jones, D.G. "The Mythology of Identity: A Canadian Case." In *Driving Home: A Dialogue Between Writers and Readers*. Ed. Barbara Belyea and Estelle Dansereau. Waterloo: Wilfrid Laurier Univ. Press, 1984, pp. 39–41, 42, 44, 45, 47–48.

Lee's "400: Coming Home" and *Civil Elegies* are part of an English-Canadian tradition: "occasional, descriptive, discursive." The tone is "elegiac and ironic." As Lee says, "space is primal": ". . . English-Canadians live in a divided home" — empire builders and "perverse" pastoral dwellers. For the latter, ". . . home is dominated by an alien authority . . . ."

C152 Nodelman, Perry. "Cadence and Nonsense: Dennis Lee's Poems for Children and for Adults." *Canadian Children's Literature/Littérature canadienne pour la jeunesse*, No. 33 (1984), pp. 22–31.

Nodelman discusses the imagery of "selves" in Lee's poetry and his multiplicity of roles as "poet, theorist, and an editor." In response to past criticism, Nodelman wonders "if Lee's children's poetry is so separate from the rest of his work that the two can't be discussed together. . . . few of Lee's children's poems are nonsensical. Most of them are, rather, absurdist fantasies . . . ." The fact that "1838" appears in both *The Gods* and *Nicholas Knock and Other People* shows that "Lee himself does not mark the boundary between his adult . . . and children's poems . . . ." The concept of "cadence," which Lee describes in his essays, can be applied to some of his verse for children. Other pieces "are clearly intended to be dramatic monologues . . . ." As a whole, Lee's poems for children "describe cadence," while his adult poems "seek cadence." A photograph of Lee is included.

C153 Powe, B.W. *A Climate Charged*. Oakville, Ont.: Mosaic, 1984, pp. 77–79.

Savage Fields: An Essay in Literature and Cosmology "is a dense literary-philosophical inquiry where, in veiled terms, Heidegger and Nietzsche collide on the pages like metaphysical mastodons." The title is a metaphor for "order and disorder on our planet." Lee is trying to give Canadian literature "an identity." The " 'nature-civilization' conflict" seems conventional. "Lee's thick manner . . . appears to be a deliberate rhetorical device . . . ." His definition of liberalism is confusing. "The problem is that *Savage Fields* is a work for initiates familiar with the assumptions." Lee is at his best in the areas of "practical criticism." His examination of Leonard Cohen's *Beautiful Losers* is "specific . . . clear, even useful . . . ." Lee deserts "what he should be excelling at: language and perception."

C154 Wesley, David. "Jelly Belly's the Best Yet." *The Hamilton Spectator*, 7 Jan. 1984, p. 3.

Jelly Belly, with "a depth of folklore . . . missing in Lee's earlier work," seems to be Lee's best work yet. The book reads like a familiar classic, but has a contemporary basis. Canadian references are "obvious, yet non-self-conscious . . . ." The poems cover "the panorama of childhood experience . . . ." Juan Wijngaard's pictures "enhance the spell cast by Lee's verses." Lee says play is as " 'crucial to human life as sleeping, congregating and appropriating.' " A photograph of Lee is included.

C155 Wade, Barbara. "Mokey, Boober, and bp: What Does Writing a Sonnet Have in Common with Writing Lyrics for Television's *Fraggle Rock*? Perhaps More Than One Might Guess." *Books in Canada*, April 1984, pp. 11–13.

Wade discusses how Lee came to write lyrics for the songs on *Fraggle Rock*. She discusses the "collaborative" nature of the program, and Lee comments on the differences and difficulties of writing for television. A photograph of Dennis Lee, David Young, and bpNichol is included.

C156 Adachi, Ken. "New Technology Hooks Up Writers." *The Toronto Star*. "Books," 9 April 1984, p. D3.

Adachi notes that Lee is expected to be among the contributors to *Swift Current*, the computerized literary magazine co-ordinated by Frank Davey.

C157 Brown, Russell. Contributor. "Locality as Writing: A Preface to the 'Preface' of *Out of Place*. Discussion." Long-liners Conference on the Canadian Long Poem, Calumet College, York Univ., Toronto. 29 May–1 June 1984. Printed in *Open Letter* [Long-liners Conference Issue], Ser. 6, Nos. 2–3 (Summer–Fall 1985), pp. 293–94.

Brown notes that in conversations outside of the conference, Lee has said that "the short poem is an exhausted form."

C158 Dudek, Louis. Contributor. "Making Strange Poetics: Discussion." Long-liners Conference on the Canadian Long Poem, Calumet College, York Univ., Toronto. 29 May–1 June 1984. Printed in *Open Letter* [Long-liners Conference Issue], Ser. 6, Nos. 2–3 (Summer–Fall 1985), p. 230.

Dudek notes that ". . . Lee's discussion of Pound [see B227] left out the thought that Pound always pushed forward that the poem was written for those who like to *think*," so that the reader makes the connections between the various elements.

C159 Lane, M. Travis. "Alternatives to Narrative: The Structuring Concept." Long-liners Conference on the Canadian Long Poem, Calumet College, York Univ., Toronto. 29 May–1 June 1984. Printed in *Open Letter* [Long-liners Conference Issue], Ser. 6, Nos. 2–3 (Summer–Fall 1985), pp. 146–47.

"The end of 'The Death of Harold Ladoo' achieves the sense of exhaustion and release psychiatrists seem to desire when they encourage their patients to 'talk it out.' " Like Phyllis Webb's "Failed Poems" and "A

Question of Questions," Lee's poem has "the nagging, obsessional quality we recognize from serious thought."

C160 Miki, Roy. "The Lang Poem: The Cosmology of the Long Poem in Contemporary Canadian Poetry." Long-liners Conference on the Canadian Long Poem, Calumet College, York Univ., Toronto. 29 May–1 June 1984. Printed in *Open Letter* [Long-liners Conference Issue], Ser. 6, Nos. 2–3 (Summer–Fall 1985), pp. 73–74, 84.

In a discussion of "a desacrilization of the material world," Miki notes that Lee, in *Savage Fields: An Essay in Literature and Cosmology*, follows George Grant's "lead" in attributing the "triumph of technological form, in which things are nothing more than 'objects' to be conquered" to "the vast 'liberalization' process made possible through the rise of technological modes of thought."

C161 Reaney, James. "Long Poems." Long-liners Conference on the Canadian Long Poem, Calumet College, York Univ., Toronto. 29 May–1 June 1984. Printed in *Open Letter* [Long-liners Conference Issue], Ser. 6, Nos. 2–3 (Summer–Fall 1985), pp. 117, 119.

"The most important victory in this poet-into-the popular wilds is that won by Dennis Lee's *Alligator Pie*. Uninfluenced by Heidegger, perhaps because of this, *Alligator Pie* is Lee's most effective poem . . . . For the magic effect of his poetry for children is to get them chanting and dancing, and to have their own verse-reading and composing festivals! . . . *Alligator Pie* is our local important long poem since it revives that epos rhythm on a primitive, engaging level."

C162 Zekas, Rita. "Man Who Gave Us Alligator Pie Makes Howling Success of Jacob." *The Toronto Star*, 5 June 1984, p. B3.

Zekas notes that Lee wrote the lyrics for the play *Jacob Two-Two Meets the Hooded Fang*; Philip Balsam wrote the music. Lee and Balsam have worked together for "five or six years." Lee has a new Muppet movie "in the works." A photograph of Lee, Balsam, and actors from the production is included.

C163 Adachi, Ken. "Lee 'Tickled Pink' with New Literary Prize." *The Toronto Star*. "Books," 22 Oct. 1984, p. D2.

Adachi notes that Lee won the Philips Information Systems Literary Prize, the "first . . . in English-speaking Canada to be awarded specifically for general contribution to Canadian letters as opposed to awards for individual works."

C164 French, William. "Lee Receives $5,000 Literary Prize." *The Globe and Mail* [Toronto], 22 Oct. 1984, p. M11.

French notes that Lee won the Philips Information Systems Literary Prize. For an award "based on general contribution to Canadian letters," Lee "is eminently qualified" as a "serious poet," a critic, a "creator of children's verses," a co-founder of House of Anansi Press, "one of the most astute editors in the country," a lyricist, and "director of the poetry program at McClelland and Stewart."

C165 V[anderhoof]., A[nn]. "Lee Awarded Philips Prize." *Quill & Quire*, Dec. 1984, p. 20.

Lee has been awarded the first Philips Information Systems Literary Prize of $5,000, a word processor, and a stone sculpture. The word processor will make revisions easier, since, Lee says, " 'I revise endlessly — anywhere from 20 to 50 revisions.' " A photograph of Lee is included on the cover.

C166 Goldie, Terry. "Riffs of Criticism." Rev. of *Invocations: The Poetry and Prose of Gwendolyn*

MacEwen, by Jan Bartley; *On F.R. Scott: Essays on His Contributions to Law, Literature, and Politics,* ed. Sandra Djwa and R. St. J. MacDonald; and *Tasks of Passion: Dennis Lee at Mid-Career,* ed. Karen Mulhallen, Donna Bennett, and Russell Brown. *Canadian Literature,* No. 103 (Winter 1984), pp. 146–47, 148–49.

In the review of *Tasks of Passion: Dennis Lee at Mid-Career,* Goldie also comments on Lee's contribution, " 'Riffs.' " The "jazzy tone . . . seems forced . . . . Towards the end, however, either he comes closer to me or I to him . . . ." Goldie also mentions that he grew up in Lee's shadow.

C167 Middlebro', Tom. "Knowledge in the Making." Rev. of *Tasks of Passion: Dennis Lee at Mid-Career,* ed. Karen Mulhallen, Donna Bennett, and Russell Brown. *Essays on Canadian Writing* [10th Anniversary Issue], No. 30 (Winter 1984–85), pp. 140–41, 142–45.

Although the volume of Lee's work is not large, it is significant. Lee's meaning of cadence, "a dynamic version of Spinoza's one intellectual substance, that is, God, whose knowable attributes are thought and extension," is central to many of his poems. Lee has fused the problems concerning English writers "from the Renaissance on . . . . For Dennis Lee the failure to establish authentic human relationships as lovers, workers, or citizens is a consequence of a failure to be at home in the world. Lee's work deals with "central traditional themes."

C168 Ferguson, Ted. "Once Upon a Time in Canada." *The Review* [Imperial Oil Limited], 69, No. 4 (1985), 26, 27–28.

Ferguson discusses the surge in Canadian children's literature since the publication of *Alligator Pie* in 1974 and notes Lee's international recognition. Profiles of Lee and Robert Munsch are given, and a brief history of children's writing in Canada is outlined. Lee explains that, in order to write children's poetry, he must get in touch with the child in himself while, at the same time, applying his adult writing skills. An illustration, by Frank Newfeld, from *Alligator Pie* is included.

C169 Middlebro', T.G. "Dennis Lee (1939–)." Illus. Isaac Bickerstaff. In *Canadian Writers and Their Works.* Ed. Robert Lecker, Jack David, and Ellen Quigley. Poetry Series. Vol. IX. Toronto: ECW, 1985, 188–228.

In the first three sections of this four-part essay, Middlebro' includes biographical material, outlines the tradition and milieu in which Lee's writing has developed, and the evolution of a critical consensus about Lee's work. In the section on Lee's work, Middlebro' discusses in detail the influence on Lee's works of Martin Heidegger's theology and George Grant's politics, as well as the influence of Rainer Maria Rilke's *Duino Elegies* on Lee's elegiac form. Middlebro' follows Lee's concept of the "artist as diagnostician" and discusses "Lee's thesis [in *The Death of Harold Ladoo*] . . . that the only transcendent forces now at work in the world are malignant . . . ." Lee's love poetry and odes are "introspective lyrics." "Riffs" "reads like a rough first draft." "The Gods" is "Lee's closest approach to the classical ode in form" and "Lee's most interesting ode . . . ." Middlebro' discusses it in detail. Generally, Lee's work "reveals a strong mind under painful self-scrutiny, and there is a laboured precision of expression, with an obvious attention to the weight of each word." A caricature-sketch by Isaac Bickerstaff precedes the article. Reprinted as a self-contained offprint (C2).

C170 Stott, Jon C. "The Marriage of Pictures and Text in Alligator Pie and Nicholas Knock." Illus. Frank Newfeld. *Canadian Children's Literature/Littérature canadienne pour la jeunesse*, Nos. 39–40 (1985), pp. 72–79.

In illustrating *Alligator Pie* and *Nicholas Knock and Other People*, Frank Newfeld tried to "present a reaction" to the poems. In *Alligator Pie*, Lee explores the linguistical "elements of play . . . of young children." In *Nicholas Knock and Other People*, for older children, Lee involves "the conflicts between the inner liberating impulses and the social constraints . . . ." In *Alligator Pie*, Lee began with "a plea and then went on to celebrate life and play . . . . *Nicholas Knock* concludes with one [a plea], an indication of lack of fulfilment." The two books also contrast visually. Lee met Newfeld only after the books had been illustrated.

C171 Woodcock, George. Introduction. In *Canadian Writers and Their Works*. Ed. Robert Lecker, Jack David, and Ellen Quigley. Poetry Series. Vol. IX. Toronto: ECW, 1985, 1, 2, 8, 9–10, 12.

Lee is one of a handful of Canadian poets belonging to "the second generation of the modern movement in Canadian writing." A contemporary of Margaret Atwood, the two collaborated to write for *Acta Victoriana* while at Victoria College, University of Toronto. Both are "politically concerned" writers. Lee "has laboured perhaps more than any other Canadian poet in our time to achieve 'the correctness of our sentiments.' " His form is didactic. *Civil Elegies* will remain a "literary monument to the nationalist generation to which he belongs." Lee's "other self," best known for children's poetry, is interesting.

C172 Posesorski, Sherie. "Neighbourhood Gossip: Once a Garrison for the Rich, Toronto's Multicultural Annex District Now Provides a Wealth of Material for the City's Writers." *Books in Canada*, May 1985, pp. 11, 12.

Lee's "Sibelius Park" is mentioned among works that describe Toronto's Annex district.

C173 Deshaw, Rose. "Samaritan of Rhyme." Letter. *The Globe and Mail* [Toronto], 24 July 1985, p. 7.

Deshaw disagrees with Fraser Sutherland's description of Lee as a "power broker of extreme arrogance" (D148) and praises Lee's "insightful critiques" and "helping hand."

C174 Davey, Frank, and Ann Munton. Introduction. *Open Letter* [Long-liners Conference Issue], Ser. 6, Nos. 2–3 (Summer–Fall 1985), pp. 6–7, 212.

Davey and Munton note that Lee, "at his request, substitutes a later-written text for the largely extemporaneous address he gave to the conference" (see B210). In an editorial note following Lee's paper, the editors note that "In the original, he suggested that many poems by Al Purdy contain subtle and graduated shifts of voice that are very similar to the kind of polyphony Lee would himself like to achieve."

C175 Adachi, Ken. "Book Festival Celebrates Illustrators' Powerful Art." *The Toronto Star*. "Books," 16 Nov. 1985, Kids' Culture, p. F2.

Lee will be present at the Children's Book Festival. A movie based on his *The Ordinary Bath* will be shown at the festival (A69). A photograph of Lee is included.

C176 Posesorski, Sherie. "Listening to Lee." *Books in Canada*, Dec. 1985, pp. 5–6.

Lee reads from *Lizzy's Lion* in Toronto. "The audience is like a roomful of Mexican jumping beans . . . ." Lee says, "I feel like the medium for their collective energy, . . . and I'm riding the wave of their energy."

C177 Sutherland, Fraser. "Frisking Laura Secord." In *The Bumper Book*. Ed. John Metcalf. Toronto: ECW, 1986, pp. 16, 18, 22–23.

Sutherland notes Lee among the "spear-carriers of the 1960s" who "are now encamped." He comments on Lee's "arrogance" in his introduction to *The New Canadian Poets: 1970–1985.*

C178 "Dennis Lee Wins Metcalf Award." *The Toronto Star*, 30 May 1986, p. D21.

Lee has won the "Vicky Metcalf Award for a body of work deemed inspirational to Canadian youth." The prize is worth $2,000.00. Lee "was praised for having encouraged other writers and publishers to produce Canadian books for children."

C179 "Dennis Lee Leads Spring Awards List." *Children's Book News* [Toronto], 9, No. 1 (June 1986), 1.

A photograph of Lee and a Muppet character is included. Lee wins the Vicky Metcalf Award for the children's author with a noteworthy body of work over a period of several years.

C180 *What's News* [Annapolis Royal, N.S.], Sept. 1986, p. 1.

"Dennis Lee Week" was one of the highlights of the month at the Arts Festival in Annapolis Royal, Nova Scotia. Three photographs of Lee and children are included.

C181 Ferres, John H. "Debating Destinations." Rev. of *Driving Home: A Dialogue between Writers and Readers*, ed. Barbara Belyea and Estelle Dansereau. *Essays on Canadian Writing*, No. 33 (Fall 1986), p. 188.

In this review of an anthology, Ferres notes that Lee's poem, "400: Coming Home," is related to William Carlos Williams' "Spring and All."

C182 *Al-Iraq*, 27 Nov. 1986. [Translation.]

Lee has never seen a poetry gathering in such a volume in his life as that in Mirbad. He was not expecting to receive an invitation to take part in a festival of this type. He did not believe the invitation came down upon him from the sky. It was a good coincidence that he found a book containing poems of Arab poets and was able to get acquainted with ancient Arabic poems. A photograph of Lee is included.

C183 *Al-Gadissia* [Baghdad], 30 Nov. 1986.

Canadian poet Dennis Lee, author of fifteen books of adult and children's poetry and winner of many Canadian awards, presented his poem. It was a piece from a long work, written in the days of the Viet Nam War. A photograph of Lee is included.

C184 Helwig, David. "The Genesis of Poet Purdy." Rev. of *Collected Poems of Al Purdy*, ed. Russell Brown. *The Whig-Standard* [Kingston], 20 Dec. 1986, Magazine, p. 21.

In this review of *Collected Poems of Al Purdy*, Helwig notes that Lee's Afterword is "an excellent essay."

C185 Saltman, Judith. *Modern Canadian Children's Books*. Toronto: Oxford Univ. Press, 1987, pp. 7, 12, 117–19, 122.

The success of *Alligator Pie* stimulated the "burgeoning interest in children's books" in Canada. *Alligator Pie* was "unique" in creating a "Canadian body of . . . poetry for young children." Lee's poetic roots "are the oral traditions of early childhood." His strong, repetitive rhythms are similar to the rhymes of Mother Goose, Robert Louis Stevenson, and A.A. Milne. ". . . Lee observes closely the self-absorbed, inner life of the very young." Friendship, play, imagination, and emotion are key elements. His domestic poems have "warmth," and his nonsense verse is spirited, breaking "taboos." While the verse is simple, Lee's language is an "indefatigable jumbling of puns, tongue-twisters, and inverted words." Saltman briefly discusses the illustrators and notes that Marie-Louise Gay's "zany" pictures in *Lizzy's Lion* "distance the reader from the literary violence." Many poems in *Nicholas Knock and Other People*, an unequalled collection, "have a philosophical and thought-provoking quality."

C186 Sutherland, Fraser. "The Cosmic Ruminant's Vision." Rev. of *Collected Poems of Al Purdy*, ed. Russell Brown. *The Globe and Mail* [Toronto], 3 Jan. 1987, p. E16.

In a review of *Collected Poems of Al Purdy*, Sutherland notes that Lee's Afterword is "long, mildly helpful."

C187 Galt, George. "Giant Steps." Rev. of *Collected Poems of Al Purdy*, ed. Russell Brown. *Books in Canada*, Jan.–Feb. 1987, pp. 16–17.

In this review of *Collected Poems of Al Purdy*, Galt notes that Lee's Afterword is an essay that is "as brilliant an exposition of Purdy's work as we may ever have. Lee's interpretation locates Purdy's uniqueness in his sense of process and his ability to mimic the nuances of life-as-process in a poem."

C188 Smith, Dan. "Depressing Revelations: Finding Cheer Between the Lines." *The Toronto Star*, 21 March 1987, Books in Store for Spring, p. M5.

Smith asked several authors what they read when depressed. Lee phoned "back and let us know that he never reads anything else when he is deep into a new book — as he was then."

C189 Meyer, Bruce, and Brian O'Riordan. "Two Windows: An Interview with D.G. Jones." *Poetry Canada Review*, 8, Nos. 2–3 (Spring 1987), 3, 5.

In this interview, Jones uses Lee's *Civil Elegies* as an example of English-Canadian "poets and . . . people . . . always trying to organize space into something, or along some civil lines," unlike the French-Canadian feeling that ". . . space is almost meaningless . . . ." Meyer and O'Riordan mention Lee's discovery of Saint-Denys Garneau as an example of "the kind of discoveries" that no longer happen.

C190 Adilman, Sid. "Henson's Gift a Sneak Peek at the Fraggles." *The Toronto Star*. "Eye on Entertainment," 28 March 1987, Entertainment, p. J1.

Fraggle Rock will continue "as a weekly animated series for NBC Saturday mornings starting this fall. . . . 'The only thing from this series we're going to keep is the music (written by Toronto's Dennis Lee and Phil Balsam). I love the music.' "

C191 Skelton, Robin. "Poetry: Packing All the Power into Two of Seven Titles." *Quill & Quire*. "Feature Review," May 1987, p. 24.

In this review of, among other books, *The Collected Poems of Al Purdy*, edited by Russell Brown, Skelton notes that Lee's Afterword is unnecessary and "profoundly irritating" and "gives the impression that the speaker is superior to the poet . . . ."

C192 Pitman, Teresa. " 'I Am Not a Dennis Lee Factory!'". *The Oakville Beaver*, 23 Oct. 1987, Weekend, p. 9.

Lee had "instant rapport" with the kids at a poetry reading, many of whom recite his poems by heart. *The Difficulty of Living on Other Planets* "is something in between his children's poetry and his more serious work." Lee refers to it as " 'folk poetry.' " Two photographs of Lee and children and one of a child are included.

C193 Denman, Gregory A. *When You've Made It Your Own* . . . . Foreword Bill Martin, Jr. Portsmouth, N.H.: Heinemann Educational Books, 1988, pp. 24–25, 99.

Denman explains rhyme in poetry as the "golden thread" and uses "Alligator Pie" as an example. He also shows how the poem is used by children as a "model" for writing poems. (See B96 for the poem included.)

C194 Scrivener, Leslie. "Dennis Lee: Man and Boy." *The Toronto Star*, 3 Jan. 1988, People, pp. H1, H2.

Lee "is a poet of sunlight and shadow, of whimsy and despair." Scrivener profiles these two sides of Lee with references to his popular poetry for children, his affiliation with Rochdale College, his work as an editor, *The Death of Harold Ladoo*, and *The Difficulty of Living on Other Planets*. A photograph of Lee is included.

C195 Grant, Janet. "Dennis Lee: From Alligators to Fraggles." In her *Kids' Writers*. Canadian Lives. Markham, Ont.: Fitzhenry & Whiteside, 1989, pp. 3–17.

Grant divides this biographical chapter into five brief sections: 1) how Lee came to write children's poems and invigorate the Canadian children's literature industry; 2) Lee's childhood years; 3) Lee's high school and university years; 4) Lee's development as publisher, editor, and poet; and 5) Lee's song lyrics and writing for film and television.

Theses and Dissertations

C196 Grant, Robert Stuart. "Negative Nationalism and the Poetry of Dennis Lee." M.A. Thesis Windsor 1971.

Lee's poetry fits Louis Dudek's description of " 'nationalism-in-reverse.' " Grant outlines "the parallel histories of political and literary nationalism in English Canada" in order to "provide a prospective from which to view this negative nationalism to which Dudek alludes." He then shows "that as Lee's poetry developed (both in terms of craft and sensitivity) he tended more and more to link his spiritual anguish to Canada's political indecisiveness and to a technology and empire belonging to the United States of America. This sentiment found its culmination in Lee's *Civil Elegies* in which he laments the death of Canada as a nation. Lee does not, however, approach the ideological vehemence of contemporary prose statements of this sentiment, but rather views the fate of Canadians and Canada with an understanding that is derived from sharing that same fate."

C197 Burman, Patrick. "The Dialectics of English-Canadian Nationalism." Diss. Notre Dame 1979.

Burman includes an analysis of *Civil Elegies and Other Poems*, chapter viii.

C198 Lebel, Marc. "Elégies civiles et autres poèmes." M.A. Thesis Sherbrooke 1979.

Lebel's translation of *Civil Elegies and Other Poems* was later published (A3).

C199 MacPherson, Mary. "An Annotated Bibliography of Dennis Lee." M.A. Thesis Toronto 1981.

Bibliographical data from March 1948 to September 1981. Published in revised form in C132.

C200 Munton, Ann. "The Paradox of Silence in Modern Canadian Poetry: Creativity or Sterility?". Diss. Dalhousie 1981.

In a chapter entitled "Silence and Simultaneity in the Writings of Dennis Lee," Munton notes that "Silence as associated with social and political situations — the suppression of classes, nations, or races — is a concern of all four poets [Dorothy Livesay, Eli

Mandel, A.M. Klein, and Dennis Lee]. Dennis Lee, for instance, correlates his own actual silence with his perception of Canada's mute colonial status and with the inner silence of creativity."

C201 Crandall, Kathy. "Writing in a Colonized Country: A Comparative Study of the Work and Writing of the Poets Dennis Lee and Gaston Miron." M.A. Thesis Sherbrooke 1982.

"The thesis is a comparative study of the lives and writing of the poets Dennis Lee and Gaston Miron as they struggle with the realities of writing in colonized space."

Interviews and Profiles

C202 Anderson, Allan. "Poets of Canada: 1920 to the Present." Interview with George Bowering, Leonard Cohen, John Robert Colombo, Louis Dudek, Joan Finnigan, Northrop Frye, Michael Gnarowski, Phyllis Gotlieb, Ralph Gustafson, David Helwig, D.G. Jones, Dennis Lee, Tom Marshall, John Newlove, Milton Wilson. *Anthology.* Supervising prod. Alex Smith. Ed. Robert Weaver. CBC Radio, 22 May 1971.

Part II of a seven-part series. Anderson discusses with a number of poets and critics what makes poets and their poetry Canadian.

C203 Anderson, Allan. "Poets of Canada: 1920 to the Present." Interview with Milton Acorn, George Bowering, Leonard Cohen, Victor Coleman, Doug Fetherling, Northrop Frye, Len Gasparini, Irving Layton, Dennis Lee, Gwendolyn MacEwen, David McFadden, bpNichol, and Michael Ondaatje. *Anthology.* Supervising prod. Alex Smith. Ed. Robert Weaver. CBC Radio, 12 June 1971.

Part V of a seven-part series. Anderson discusses concrete and experimental poetry with a number of poets.

C204 Anderson, Allan. "Poets of Canada: 1920 to the Present." Interview with Margaret Atwood, Margaret Avison, Nelson Ball, Victor Coleman, Northrop Frye, John Glassco, Irving Layton, Dennis Lee, Dorothy Livesay, Gwendolyn MacEwen, Eli Mandel, Anne Marriott, John Newlove, Glen Siebrasse, Francis Sparshott, Peter Stevens, Miriam Waddington, Milton Wilson, and George Woodcock. *Anthology.* Supervising prod. Alex Smith. Ed. Robert Weaver. CBC Radio, 19 June 1971.

Part VI of a seven-part series. Anderson discusses small presses and literary criticism with a number of poets and critics.

C205 Stedingh, R.W. "An Interview with Dennis Lee." *The Canadian Fiction Magazine*, No. 7 (Summer 1972), pp. 42–54.

Recording and tape transcription by Gyorgy Porkolab.

C206 Anderson, Allan. "Aspects of the Canadian Novel." Interview with Matt Cohen, Lawrence Garber, Hugh Garner, Graeme Gibson, Dave Godfrey, Dennis Lee, George Payerle, Ray Smith, David Lewis Stein, and Sheila Watson. *Anthology.* Prod. Doug MacDonald. CBC Radio, 25 Nov. 1972. (8 min.)

In section A of part IV of a seven-part series, Anderson interviews the above authors. Lee, as a writer and a publisher with the House of Anansi Press, gives an account of the experimental novel to date. In another segment of this interview, he discusses the group of novelists who are concerned with the form of writings, mentioning Lawrence Garber and Ray Smith as the best examples of this group. Later, he talks about Margaret Laurence's *The Stone Angel*, the best novel that English Canada has ever produced.

C207 Woodcock, George. "New Wave in Publishing." Interview with Dennis Lee, Shirley Gibson, Michael Macklem, David Robinson, James Lorimer, Victor Coleman, and Mel Hurtig. *Canadian Literature*, No. 57 (Summer 1973), pp. 50, 52–53, 54–55, 57, 59–60, 61.

Lee notes that most of the small presses in Canada have been started by writers who could not get published by the established houses. Many of these small presses will "close down or go much more commercial" as the "writer/founders . . . withdraw to their own work," as Lee did. Although the volume of publications is increasing, the proportion of high-quality work remains the same. Lee founded House of Anansi Press with a nationalist idealism. Established and new publishing is predominantly centralized in Ontario because people here feel it is important and are willing to make the sacrifice to do it. House of Anansi Press has been a success because it has published good writers.

C208 Taylor, Charles. "A Heavyweight Poet Becomes Children's Troubadour." *The Globe and Mail* [Toronto], 28 Sept. 1974, Entertainment, p. 27.

Lee's role as children's troubadour is a great contrast to the serious nationalist poet he is. While his "political and philosophical concerns are implicit in his children's poetry . . . ," adults can discover the "profound and mythic qualities" of the children's verse. One link between the writing for adults and children is Lee's "concept of voice or cadence." He was able to free himself from "colonizing" influences after reading George Grant's works. He then revised *Civil Elegies* and inserted nationalistic references into his work for children. A photograph of Lee and children is included.

C209 Fulford, Robert. *Speaking of Books: Dennis Lee.* Toronto: OECA, 1975. (Videotape; 30 min.)

Robert Fulford interviews Lee about the renaissance in Canadian writing and publishing. Lee reads poems from *Civil Elegies and Other Poems* (B465).

C210 Watt, Keith. "An Interview with Dennis Lee." *Arthur* [Trent Univ.], 22 Sept. 1975, p. 5.

Lee reflects on a range of subjects including the role of a writer-in-residence, his own method of working, and his approach to children's poetry. "These poems were not written for children in the sense that I see children out there, and I see my job as a poet to make up poems for them . . . . I see them as written by a 35-year-old child." Lee views *Civil Elegies* as a "hard act to follow." He examines Rochdale in retrospect and speaks of current projects, the paradox of trying to publish in Canada, and the House of Anansi Press. The interview captures the mood of Lee as a full-time writer freed of teaching responsibilities and looking forward to sharing time with people who write and want to learn more.

C211 McDonough, Irma. "Profile: Dennis Lee." Illus. Frank Newfeld. *In Review: Canadian Books for Children*, 9, No. 1 (Winter 1975), 12–14. Rpt. in *Profiles*. Rev. ed. Ed. Irma McDonough. Ottawa: Canadian Library Association, 1975, pp. 96–98.

McDonough discusses *Alligator Pie*, *Nicholas Knock*, Lee's readings, and children's delighted response. Biographical material is included. A photograph of Lee is also included.

C212 Plaskett, John. "Interview with Dennis Lee." *Vic report* [Victoria College, Univ. of Toronto], 4, No. 2 (March 1976), [1], 4–7.

Lee talks about growing up in Toronto, how the city influenced him, and his experiences studying and teaching at Victoria College, University of Toronto. He discusses the failure of Rochdale College, the relationship between his university experience and his writing, and the circumstances surrounding the founding of the House of Anansi Press in 1967. He speaks about the state of Canadian publishing and the population's lack of self-respect — a theme expressed in *Civil Elegies and Other Poems*. He discusses what prompted him to write children's poetry and elaborates on the poem "Nicholas Knock." A cover sketch, two photographs of Lee, and the poem "[Master and Lord, where]" (B48) are included.

C213   Atwood, Margaret. "Uncle Dennis' Hat Trick; Dennis Lee — the Pied Piper of *Alligator Pie* and *Nicholas Knock* — Returns with More Magic Rhymes." Illus. Frank Newfeld. *The Canadian* [*The Toronto Star*], 10 Sept. 1977, pp. 16, 18–19.

Atwood first met Lee at a "freshman mixer" in 1957 at the University of Toronto. She recounts with personal anecdotes her friendship with Lee during their college days, Lee's involvement with Rochdale College and "Stop Spadina," his editorial work with House of Anansi Press and Macmillan, and his current status as the "Pied Piper" of Canadian children's poetry. In *Garbage Delight*, "The permission to play has been given by the poems to their audience, but it has also been given by Dennis to himself." Six poems by Lee are also included (B91, B121–B125).

C214   Freedman, Adele. "Separating Dennis Lee's Psyches." *Fanfare* [*The Globe and Mail*] [Toronto], 23 Nov. 1977, p. 11.

Lee has a "brooding, Kierkegaardian side" and a "jolly side that loves a good romp." In this article, which is based on an interview with Lee, Freedman recounts Lee's early days at Victoria and Rochdale colleges. Lee's involvement with nationalism and House of Anansi Press caused his own writing to halt

and then prompted the revisions to *Civil Elegies*. Lee's children's poems "present a comic version of a world which rejects nothing, including violence and hate. Lee is present in them as in everything he writes . . . ." Even if one is "skeptical about Lee's theory" in *Savage Fields: An Essay in Literature and Cosmology* of the "constant state of strife" in the world, his "searching accent" is troublesome. The book is altogether "idiosyncratic." Generally, Lee works "out of an 'impulse to wholeness . . . .' " This bio-bibliographical portrait includes photographs of Lee. Lee responds to this article in a letter to the editor (B445).

C215   Witten, Mark. "The Case of the Midwife Lode." *Books in Canada*, Dec. 1977, pp. 6–8.

Witten discusses the significance of Lee's editorial work "with a score of poets and novelists, established and unknown . . . ." Witten speaks with Michael Ondaatje, Oonah McFee, Graeme Gibson, Margaret Atwood, Matt Cohen, Eli Mandel, and Pier Giorgio Di Cicco regarding their experiences with Lee. A photograph of Lee is included.

C216   "Meet the Author." *The Children's Book News*, 1, No. 2 (June 1978), [2].

Lee discusses how he got started writing children's poetry, getting in touch with "the child" in himself, and his method of writing, which includes endless re-writing. A photograph of Lee is included.

C217   "Looking for People with 'The Passion.' " *Bulletin* [Univ. of Toronto], 23 Oct. 1978, p. 3.

Lee is the University of Toronto's writer-in-residence for 1978–79. He prefers to see people on an individual basis as opposed to writing workshops. Good editing is an intuitive thing with Lee. While a student himself at Victoria College, University of Toronto, Lee showed his work to Jay Macpherson. A photograph of Lee with a student is included.

C218 "Dennis Lee." *Author Kit No. 1*. Toronto: Children's Book Centre, 1979. 1 leaf.

Includes a poster portrait of Lee and bio-bibliographical data.

C219 Pearce, Jon. "An Interview with Dennis Lee." *Journal of Canadian Poetry*, 2, No. 1 (Winter 1979), 6–22. Rpt. in *Twelve Voices: Interviews with Canadian Poets*. Ed. Jon Pearce. Ottawa: Borealis, 1981, pp. 45–59.

An essay by Lee cast in the form of an interview between Lee and Jon Pearce. See C96, an introduction by Jon Pearce. See also B207 for Lee's reconsideration of this piece.

C220 Morley, Rose, and Bruce Meyer. "Interview with Dennis Lee." *University of Toronto Review*, No. 3 (Spring 1979), pp. 29–31.

Lee describes his function as writer-in-residence at the University of Toronto as "Very much reactive." Oonah McFee, one of his students, astonished Lee with her "incredible hard work and perseverance." He does not "think U. of T. is full of gigantic explosions of talent but it's certainly not barren land . . . ." Lee comments on his use, in his children's poems, of Canadian place names, which are "fun in their own rank." He talks about his involvement with House of Anansi Press between 1967 and 1972, which led to his "four year dry spell" and his approach to editing — to see "good stuff" published — which remained unchanged at Macmillan. A photograph is included.

C221 Anderson, Jon. "Dennis Lee: The Muppets' Minstrel." Illus. Muriel Wood. *Reader's Digest* [Montreal], Aug. 1980, pp. 82–86.

Lee gave a poetry reading in Toronto. Lee, the most popular writer for children since Lucy Maud Montgomery, gets " 'in touch with' " the kid in himself and follows his instinct. He captures a child's world, including the pressures they face and their "violent emotions and fears." Publicity tours, readings, and interviews are discussed. Lee works slowly with many rewrites of individual poems.

C222 Kent, John. "John Kent Interviews Dennis Lee." CV/II 5, No. 1 (Autumn 1980), 14–17.

With specific reference to *The Death of Harold Ladoo*, Lee discusses the process of endlessly revising his poetry. He analyses *Kingdom of Absence* and *Civil Elegies and Other Poems* in terms of elegiac poetry and voice. He comments on *Savage Fields: An Essay in Literature and Cosmology* and addresses the criticism that a poet's attempt at literary criticism is "only comments on their own writing." He talks about where he stands in terms of Northrop Frye, who epitomizes "the liberal thinker and the escape from value judgement . . . ." He touches briefly on the impetus behind the ideas expressed in "Cadence, Country, Silence: Writing in Colonial Space" and highlights his involvement in Rochdale College and House of Anansi Press.

C223 "The Visiting Poet Wants a Link-Up with Scots." *Glasgow Evening Times*, City Ed., 2 Oct. 1980, p. 19.

Lee hopes to devise a scheme by which the work of Scottish poets and novelists can circulate among Canadian critics and writers and vice-versa.

C224 Twigg, Alan. "When to Write." In his *For Openers: Conversations with 24 Canadian Writers*. Madeira Park, B.C.: Harbour, 1981, pp. 241–52.

Lee waits for a poem to present itself, rather than setting out to be "socially useful" or "cathartic." Craft becomes necessary with the "scores of drafts" generated "from the multiplicity of what-is." The sacredness of the "what-is" was lost with "the advent of the [value-free] 'objective world' of Descartes . . . ." Art, not life, becomes the pattern for artistic creation. The substitution of "sensation for meaning" is "decadence." Lee is "anti-romantic." His "vista" for his writing is "the last few centuries." "The suburban United Church" shaped his sense "of lacking a concrete sense of the sacramental." Now he is attracted to "the older Methodist/Presbyterian tradition," although he has "backed away from churches completely." In his teens and early twenties, he read the Christian mystics. Lee's children's poetry began as a release for repressed feelings. In terms of time, psychic space, and authority, Lee is "pretty dissatisfied with my way of being a parent." Lee "would like to pedal back in time or psychic space, and disconnect from all that shallow, secular, trendy downtown Toronto civilization." A photograph of Lee is included.

C225 Swail, David. "Dennis Lee: A Poet's Progress at Mid-Career." *Vic report* [Victoria College, Univ. of Toronto], 12, No. 1 (Fall 1983), 6–10.

    Jelly Belly will appear in the fall. Lee's work with Jim Henson in *The Dark Crystal* and *Fraggle Rock* is discussed. Lee is running the poetry program for McClelland and Stewart, and he discusses their fall releases. His adult poetry, *Kingdom of Absence* and *Civil Elegies*, were influenced by his years at Victoria College and House of Anansi Press, nationalism, and George Grant. Rochdale College was founded as an alternative to "museum culture." Lee mentions his earlier plans for United Church ministry and the profound influence of Northrop Frye's *Anatomy of Criticism: Four Essays. Tasks of Passion: Dennis Lee at Mid-Career* is also discussed.

C226 Grady, Wayne. "A Man's Garden of Verse." *Saturday Night.* "Books," Nov. 1983, pp. 73, 74.

    This profile of Lee is based on an interview and occasioned by the release of *Jelly Belly.* Lee speaks of the success of "his earlier 'light-weight, kibitzing poems.'" Not since Mother Goose has there been "a collection of free, unassociated, almost anonymous nursery rhymes." Grady gives a biographical profile of Lee, including his early years at Victoria and Rochdale Colleges and at House of Anansi Press. In relation to Lee's adult poetry and criticism, Grady highlights Lee's "dislocation from the present," the "battle between nature and civilization," and Lee's explanation of his adult poetry as " 'meditative.' " Lee is " 'compelled by nursery rhymes — which are among the purest challenges a poet can pursue.' " A photograph of Lee is included.

C227 Steed, Judy. "Jelly Belly's Jolly Jems. An Intellectual Strikes Paydirt: Wacky Rhymes by Dennis Lee Are Now a Hit on Kids' TV." Illus. Juan Wijngaard. *The Globe and Mail* [Toronto]. "The Features Page," 24 Dec. 1983, p. 10.

    Lee "is a serious, intense . . . intellectual who speaks haltingly about the struggle to find his own voice . . . ." Writing songs for Fraggle Rock may prove economically successful. The children's work "dominates his life." Lee is surprised that *Jelly Belly* appeals so much to adults. In this profile, which is based on an interview, Lee says he " 'went back to the beginning, when sound and rhythm start to have meaning,' " when he wrote this book. Considering the pitfalls of success, Lee says " 'The thing is to be of world stature without denying your own roots.' " Eight of Lee's poems are printed next to this article (B135, B142–B148). Lee also responds in a letter (B452).

C228 Davies, Cory Bieman, and Catherine Ross. "Re-realizing Mother Goose: An Interview with Dennis Lee on *Jelly Belly*." *Canadian Children's Literature/ Littérature canadienne pour la jeunesse*, No. 33 (1984), pp. 6–14.

Lee discusses *Jelly Belly* in terms of its sales. He talks about some of the influences on his writing, including A.A. Milne, Mother Goose, and *The Oxford Dictionary of Nursery Rhymes*, and gives details about his general process of revision. The contributions of illustrators Juan Wijngaard, Charles Pachter, and Frank Newfeld are discussed. Lee concludes by outlining the difference in form between the poetry he writes for children and that for adults.

C229 Thompson, M.A. "Jelly Belly in the Perilous Forest." *Canadian Children's Literature/Littérature canadienne pour la jeunesse*, No. 33 (1984), pp. 15–21.

Most people agree that Lee's poetry is fun, though that "may mean honest foolery" or "a brash imitation of it." Lee's popular appeal is "based on a few of his best-known poems." *Jelly Belly* "is a mixed blessing." Juan Wijngaard's drawings "lift the poems into fantasy." The poetry is "marred by loose diction." Some verses "barely exist." In "re-doing" Mother Goose, there should be something "new, or better, or at least different." *Alligator Pie* "was a mixture of fun and serious, simple and complex." *Nicholas Knock and Other People*, "the least popular of Mr. Lee's children's books," has a religious theme. *Garbage Delight* is more like *Alligator Pie*. Lee "is in danger of becoming another Santa Claus — restricted to the very young . . . inoffensive to adults, cross-cultural, fun, marketable."

C230 Fetherling, Doug. "Dennis Lee: A Confessional and Religious Poet Who Also Wows the Kids." *The Graduate* [Univ. of Toronto], May–June 1984, pp. 20–22.

Rpt. (expanded — "Notes on Dennis Lee") in *The Blue Notebook: Reports on Canadian Culture*. By Doug Fetherling. Oakville, Ont.: Mosaic, 1985, pp. 75–76.

In addition to being one of Canada's most respected and influential poets, Lee is also one of the most popular, although not for the same books. His contemporaries "practically worship him" for his rare qualities of being a confessional and religious poet and for his key role as editor and critic. Beloved on another plane is the writer of children's verse. ". . . Lee has always appeared torn between his meditative side and his liturgical side." There are "elements of both" in both spheres of his writing.

C231 Gzowski, Peter. Interview with Dennis Lee and Philip Balsam. *Morningside*. Host Peter Gzowski. CBC Radio, 29 Aug. 1984.

Gzowski talks to Dennis Lee (the lyricist) and Philip Balsam (the music writer) about *Jacob Two-Two Meets the Hooded Fang*.

C232 Flohil, Richard. "Philip Balsam and Dennis Lee: Writing Songs for Fraggles." *The Canadian Composer/Le Compositeur Canadien* [Toronto], Oct. 1984, pp. 16, 18, 20. Rpt. trans. ("Des chansons connues dans 87 pays à travers le monde") in *The Canadian Composer/Le Compositeur Canadien*, Oct. 1984, pp. 17, 19, 21.

Dennis Lee and Philip Balsam are an unlikely pair to have written about 150 songs for a children's television program. Lee discusses the more "serious" side of the process of his writing and his ability to write " 'in the popular mode.' " Balsam describes his collaboration with Lee and the Balsamettes — an informal gathering of friends who played music together. Lee initially declined Jim Henson's request to write a script for the Muppets but suggested that

Henson might consider their musical talent for future productions. Once Balsam has a melody, he gets together with Lee, who writes the lyrics. Two photographs of Dennis Lee and Philip Balsam and one photograph of Fraggle Rock characters are included.

C233 Barbour, Douglas. "Dennis Lee." *Dictionary of Literary Biography*. Vol. 53. Canadian Writers since 1960, First Series. 1986.

Barbour describes Lee as ". . . an almost archetypal Toronto poet of the Canadian nationalist type." Lee's educational background is outlined and his affiliations with Rochdale, the House of Anansi Press, Macmillan of Canada, and McClelland and Stewart. *Kingdom of Absence*, although "an ambitious book . . . is a failure" lacking consistent "authentic voice" and mastery of form. *Civil Elegies* (1968) is "a bold step forward." Although Lee's ideas are somewhat "imposed," his "new free-form line is . . . a much more flexible instrument for his voice . . . ." Lee's reading of George Grant during a four-year dry spell influenced a revised and extended version of *Civil Elegies* (1972) with "stronger explorations of the meaning of both Canadian and human citizenship . . . ." The personal poems in *Civil Elegies and Other Poems* provide "a context out of which the philosophical meditator . . . can speak with greater human authority." Despite human failure, there is "hope amid despair." In the children's books of poetry, ". . . Lee displays a knack for the absurd similar to Edward Lear's . . . ." *Savage Fields: An Essay in Literature and Cosmology* shows Lee "still trapped in a heady, perfect system of philosophical analysis which is brilliant and challenging and utterly wrongheaded . . . ." Lee misuses the cosmology derived from Martin Heidegger and distorts the literary works by Leonard Cohen and Michael Ondaatje, used as exemplars of Lee's arguments. "The Gods" raises "interesting questions about the formal and psychological freedoms poetry allows," while the love poems in *The Gods* demonstrate "human possibility" despite the state of the political world. *The Death of Harold Ladoo* "resolutely affirms life in all its complexity." "Riffs," "a meditation emerging from a love affair," is written with an exhilarating range of voices.

C234 Jaber, In'am N. "No Competition Between Fiction and Poetry, Says Poet." *Baghdad Observer*, 27 Nov. 1986, p. 8.

Jaber interviews Lee who is attending the seventh al-Mirbad Poetry Festival in Baghdad, 23 November to 2 December 1986. Jaber comments on Lee's popularity as a poet for children and adults. "The inseparability between Lee and his poetry seems to be the product of his full faith in poetry." Lee has read translated Arabic poetry by Adonis, Nizar Qabbani, and Mahmoud Darweesh. A photograph of Lee is included.

C235 Buchanan, Alison, Harriet Law, Garfield Reeves-Stevens, and Alastair Sweeny. "Dennis Lee: Keeping the Child in Me." In their *Canadians All 7: Portraits of Our People*. Toronto: Methuen, 1987, pp. 70–76.

Lee's personal background is highlighted, from his childhood days, through university, to his editorial consulting at Macmillan and McClelland and Stewart.

C236 Gzowski, Peter. Interview with Dennis Lee. *Morningside*. Host Peter Gzowski. CBC Radio, 21 Oct. 1987.

The first of a five-part reading series. Gzowski discusses *The Difficulty of Living on Other Planets* with Lee. Four of Lee's poems are also read (B467–B470).

C237 Scobie, Stephen. Interview with Dennis Lee. *Fine Line*. CFUV Radio [Univ. of Victoria], 28 Oct. 1987.

In a discussion that revolves primarily around the poems in *The Difficulty of Living on Other Planets*, Lee says that he is not satirizing post-structural thought in his writing. He talks about the capacity for "play" in rhyme and free verse, as well as poetry as public address versus personal. He discusses some of his poetry for children in terms of tapping currents of greater inwardness to get at the quietness in the child. Lee and Scobie also read four poems (B471–B474).

Adaptations

C238 Theatre Passe Muraille, adapted. *Alligator Pie in Your Eye*. Dir. Janet Amos. Prod. Theatre Passe Muraille. Toronto, 21 Dec. 1974–5 Jan. 1975. Reproduced (revised). *Alligator Pie*. Dir. Miles Potter. Prod. Theatre Passe Muraille. Toronto, 26 Dec. 1982–2 Jan. 1983, 17–31 Dec. 1983, 7, 14 Jan. 1984. Reproduced. Dir. Miles Potter. Prod. National Arts Centre. Toronto, 19–31 Dec. 1983. Reproduced. Dir. Michel Lefebvre. Prod. Theatre Passe Muraille. Blyth, Ont., 28 Sept. 1984; Owen Sound, Ont., 29 Sept. 1984; Markdale, Ont., 30 Sept. 1984; Barrie, Ont. (area), 1–3 Oct. 1984; Parry Sound, Ont. (area), 4–5 Oct. 1984; North Bay, Ont., 6 Oct. 1984; Elliot Lake, Ont., 7 Oct. 1984; Sault Ste. Marie, Ont., 9 Oct. 1984; Blind River/Elliot Lake, Ont., 10 Oct. 1984; Elliot Lake/Espanola, Ont., 11 Oct. 1984; Nairn Centre, Ont., 12 Oct. 1984; Creighton/Copper Cliff, Ont., 13 Oct. 1984; Sudbury, Ont., 14 Oct. 1984; Matawa, Ont., 15 Oct. 1984; Quebec City, 18–21 Oct. 1984; Lennoxville, P.Q., 22–23 Oct. 1984; Oswego, N.Y., 25 Oct. 1984; Syracuse, N.Y., 26–27 Oct. 1984; Utica, N.Y., 28 Oct. 1984; Swift Current, Sask., 31 Oct. 1984; Lethbridge, Alta., 2–3 Nov. 1984; Brooks, Alta., 4 Nov. 1984; Medicine Hat, Alta., 5 Nov. 1984; Calgary, 7–11 Nov. 1984; Red Deer, Alta., 12 Nov. 1984; St. Albert, Alta., 14–15 Nov. 1984; Edmonton, 16–20 Nov. 1984; Spruce Grove, Alta., 23 Nov. 1984; North Battleford, Sask., 24 Nov. 1984; Prince Albert, Sask., 25 Nov. 1984; Broadway Theatre, Saskatoon, 26–27 Nov. 1984; Regina, 28–29 Nov. 1984; Morden, Man. (area), 1–3 Dec. 1984; Winnipeg, 6–9 Dec. 1984; Brandon, 11–12 Dec. 1984; Cowichan, B.C., 14 Dec. 1984; Victoria, 15–16 Dec. 1984; Vancouver, 18–23 Dec. 1984; Orillia Opera House, Orillia, Ont., 10 Feb. 1985; Hamilton Place, Hamilton, Ont., 11–15, 25–28 Feb. 1985; Peterborough, Ont., 18 Feb. 1985; Port Dover, Ont., 19–20 Feb. 1985; Waterloo, Ont., 21 Feb. 1985; Univ. of Waterloo, Waterloo, Ont., 22–23 Feb. 1985; Oakville, Ont., 24 Feb. 1985; Rochester, N.Y., 2 March 1985. Reproduced. Dir. Micheline Chevrier. Muskoka Festival July–Oct. 1986.

The cast includes Clare Coulter, Geza Kovacs, Eric Peterson, and Miles Potter, musician John Roby, in the Janet Amos production. The cast includes Geoff Bowes, Seana McKenna, and Dixie Seattle in the first Miles Potter production. The cast includes Norma Dell'agnese, Jan Kudelka, and Michel Lefebvre in the second Miles Potter production. The cast includes Peggy Coffey, Doug Hughes, and Howard Aaron Shrier, musician Matt Horner, in the Michel Lefebvre production. The cast includes Silver Brobst, Glen Peloso, and Fred Pitt in the Micheline Chevrier production. A play based on Lee's *Alligator Pie*.

C239 Adapted to stage. *Garbage Delight*. Muskoka Festival. Bala, Gravenhurst, and Port Carling. Summer 1987.

Lee's *Garbage Delight* is adapted to stage.

C240 Warren, Myles. *Paper, Planets . . . and Things!*. Muskoka Festival. Prod. Young Company. Gravenhurst, Port Carling, and Huntsville. 5 July–1 Sept. 1988.

The following poems by Lee are adapted into Myles Warren's play: "The Coat," "The Garbage Men," "Goofus" (excerpt), "Jelly Belly," "The Maple Tree," "Mrs. Maggee," "The Muddy Puddle," "News of the Day," "On Tuesdays I Polish My Uncle," "The Secret Song," "The Secret Song" (excerpt), "The Seven Kinds of Bees," "Skyscraper," "Summer Song," "There Was a Man," "The Thing," "Thinking in Bed," and "What Will You Be?".

Miscellaneous

C241 "For the Kids." *The Leader-Post* [Regina], 19 Oct. 1974, p. 3.

Lee reads for children at the Central Library. A photograph with a caption is included.

C242 "Students Present Mayor with Book." *Western Star* [Corner Brook, Nfld.], 16 Nov. 1974, p. 9.

A photograph of Mayor Patrick Griffin and children is accompanied by a caption that announces Lee's visit as part of Young Canada Book Week celebrations in Newfoundland.

C243 "Poet's Visit Helps Observe Young Canada's Book Week." *Western Star* [Corner Brook, Nfld.], 18 Nov. 1974, p. 2.

Lee holds an autographing party at Glynmill Inn in Corner Brook, Newfoundland. A photograph of Lee with three adults and a caption is included.

C244 "Poetry Reading." *Telegraph-Journal* [St. John and Lancaster, N.B.], 21 Nov. 1974.

Lee reads for children in Fredericton, Sackville, and Moncton. A photograph of Lee with a child and a caption are included.

C245 "Reading to Kids." *Westmount Examiner* [Montreal], 28 Nov. 1974, p. 3.

Lee reads for children at Westmount Public Library and the Double Hook Bookstore in Montreal. A photograph of Lee with some children and a caption are included.

C246 Franklin. Caricature. *The Globe and Mail Entertainment Guide* [*The Globe and Mail*] [Toronto], 11–17 April 1975, p. 1.

A caricature of Lee and children to announce the *Dennis Lee* videotape in Robert Fulford's *Speaking of Books* series (C206).

C247 Photograph. *Canadian Library Journal*, 33, No. 2 (April 1976), 179.

This photograph of Lee reading to children is accompanied by a caption announcing that Lee was awarded the Canadian Library Association Book of the Year Award for the best Canadian children's book written in English, for *Alligator Pie*.

C248 Photograph. *Quill & Quire*, May 1977, p. 29.

A photograph of Dennis Lee, Frank Newfeld, and George Gilmour is accompanied by an announcement that Lee and Newfeld are signing their contracts with Macmillan for *Garbage Delight*.

C249 "Bringing the Book Business to a Young Market." *The Citizen* [Ottawa], 4 Oct. 1977, p. 4.

Lee visits an Ottawa bookstore. A photograph of Lee with some children are included.

C250 Photograph. *Quill & Quire*, Nov. 1977, p. 27.

A photograph of Dennis Lee and Frank Newfeld arriving at Boys' and Girls' House in Toronto in a garbage truck, to promote *Garbage Delight*, is accompanied by a caption.

C251 "Canada Book Week." *Bay News* [Pickering, Ont.], 16 Nov. 1977, p. 1.
A photograph of Lee.

C252 "Oh Me, Oh My." *The Toronto Sun*, 7 May 1978, p. 6.
A photograph of Lee and a child at the Toronto's Children's bookstore is accompanied by a caption.

C253 Amos, Robert. Caricature. CV/II, 4, No. 1 (Winter 1979), 9.
A caricature of Lee.

C254 Sandford, Robert. "Pie Poetry by Dennis Lee." *St. Louis Post-Dispatch*. "Everyday/Weeders and Seeders," 17 May 1979, p. 5.
A photograph of Lee and one of the children at his reading in St. Louis are included.

C255 "Some Pitch!". *The City* [*The Toronto Star*], 22 July 1979, p. 9.
Lee will throw the first pitch of the Blue Jays's and Detroit Tigers' game at "Book Night at the Ball Park" on 28 July 1979. A photograph of Lee and a caption are included.

C256 Cartoon. *Bracebridge Herald-Gazette*, 8 Aug. 1979, p. 23.
This cartoon announces a children's poetry reading on Saturday 11 August at the Gravenhurst Opera House in Gravenhurst, Ontario.

C257 "Kids of All Ages." *Westmount Examiner* [Montreal], 8 Nov. 1979, p. 12.
A photograph from Lee's reading at the Westmount Children's Library in Montreal and a caption are included.

C258 Rae, Carole. "Reading to Children a Most Important Task." *Saskatchewan Bulletin*, 16 Nov. 1979, p. 5.
A photograph of Lee at the Early Childhood Education Council in Saskatoon is included.

C259 "Rapt Expressions." *Richmond Review* [Richmond, B.C.], 28 Nov. 1979, p. 12.
A photograph from Lee's reading during the Children's Book Festival in Richmond, British Columbia, and a caption are included.

C260 "Nanaimo Goes Garbage Delight!". *Christmas Newsletter* [Vancouver Island Regional Library], Dec. 1979, pp. [1, 9].
Two photographs from Lee's reading at the Nanaimo Public Library are included.

C261 "Childcult: New Energy in Entertainment for the Young." *Saturday Night*. "The Inside Track," July–Aug. 1980, p. [3].
The author notes the publication of Lee's children's books and calendars.

C262 Boos, Josephine "Jodine" Beynon. *The Descendants of John Beynon*. Barrie, Ont.: Privately printed, 1984, n. pag..
Boos outlines Lee's maternal family tree.

C263 Photograph. *Canadian Bookseller*, Feb. 1985, Booking Space, p. 16.
A photograph and caption announces that Lee's reading opened the Children's Book Festival at Roy Thomson Hall in Toronto.

C264 Photograph. *Quill & Quire*, Jan. 1987, p. 9.
Lee is pictured with Amiri Baraka and David Young. A caption announces that they are attending The International Festival of Authors.

C265 Photograph. *Gravenhurst News*, 19 Aug. 1987, p. A3.

This photograph of Lee and his daughter, Hilary, is accompanied by a note that, while vacationing in Muskoka, Lee attended the performance adapting his *Garbage Delight* at the Opera House (C239).

C266 "Poet Pleased with 'Garbage Delight.'" *The Gravenhurst Banner*, 19 Aug. 1987, p. 3.

This photograph of Lee and the performers from *Garbage Delight* is accompanied by a note that Lee joined an enthusiastic crowd of five year olds for the one-hour production of *Garbage Delight*, a Muskoka Festival production (C239).

C267 Hesse, Cheryl. "About Dinosaur Knees and Cans of Peas." Illus. Juan Wijngaard. *The St. Albert Gazette*, 28 Oct. 1987, Scene, p. B.

Lee entertained children at the St. Albert public Library, reading poems from his children's books while on tour to promote *The Difficulty of Living on Other Planets*. A photograph of Lee and children is included.

C268 Photograph. *The Toronto Star*, 3 Jan. 1988, p. 1.

Poems and Illustrations Based on Lee's Work

C269 Andru, Gordon. "[Alligator pizza, alligator pizza if I don't]." *Weekend Magazine*, 20 March 1976, p. 11.

C270 Bernie, Cindy. "[Alligator Cherry,]." *Weekend Magazine*, 20 March 1976, p. 13.

C271 Connolly, Tara. "[Miss X was a fat, old thing,]." Illus. Tara Connolly. *Weekend Magazine*, 20 March 1976, p. 12.

C272 Crossley, Paul. "[Alligator ice, alligator ice,]." *Weekend Magazine*, 20 March 1976, p. 13.

C273 Edwards, Tim. "[Alligator mush, alligator mush]." *Weekend Magazine*, 20 March 1976, p. 13.

C274 Fever, Andrew. "[Alligator bun, alligator bun,]." Illus. Andrew Fever. *Weekend Magazine*, 20 March 1976, p. 13.

C275 Fleischer, Sara. "[Alligator knishes, alligator knishes,]." *Weekend Magazine*, 20 March 1976, p. 13.

C276 Grinnell, Michael. "[Alligator meat, alligator meat]." *Weekend Magazine*, 20 March 1976, p. 13.

C277 Helwig, Maggie. "[Miss X flies through the air]." *Weekend Magazine*, 20 March 1976, p. 10.

C278 Klippenstein, Noreen. "[I'm thinking of you,]." *Weekend Magazine*, 20 March 1976, p. 11.

C279 Macdonald, Marcus. *Alligator Float* [illus.]. *Weekend Magazine*, 20 March 1976, p. 10.

C280 Mao, John. Illus. *Weekend Magazine*, 20 March 1976, p. 10.

C281 Monteith, Maureen. Illus. *Weekend Magazine*, 20 March 1976, p. 12.

C282 Morrison, Andy. "[Alligator Crumble, alligator Crumble,]." *Weekend Magazine*, 20 March 1976, p. 13.

C283 Morton, Alistair. Illus. *Weekend Magazine*, 20 March 1976, p. 13.

C284 Mullin, Richard. "[Alligator spaghetti, alligator spaghetti,]." *Weekend Magazine*, 20 March 1976, p. 13.

C285 Newell, Michelle. "[Miss X flies through the air]." *Weekend Magazine*, 20 March 1976, p. 10.

C286 Parsons, Peter. "[Miss X flies through the air,]." *Weekend Magazine*, 20 March 1976, p. 12.

C287 Pollard, Rachael. Illus. *Weekend Magazine*, 20 March 1976, p. 12.

C288 Shiner, Judy. "[Alligator sauce, alligator sauce,]." *Weekend Magazine*, 20 March 1976, p. 13.

C289 Thomas, Justine. "[Alligator honey,]." *Weekend Magazine*, 20 March 1976, p. 11.

C290 Towler, David. "[Miss X flies through the air]." *Weekend Magazine*, 20 March 1976, p. 12.

C291 Watson, Andrew. *Alligator Pancakes* [illus.]. *Weekend Magazine*, 20 March 1976, p. 11.

C292 Clifford, Anne. "[Grown-ups speak funny]." *Weekend Magazine*, 26 March 1977, p. 19.

C293 Findlay, David. "Lunch." *Weekend Magazine*, 26 March 1977, p. 17.

C294 Kennedy, Bill. "The Mickey Rooney Songbook." *Weekend Magazine*, 26 March 1977, p. 18.

C295 Konrad, Denise. "[I went to play on the moon]." *Weekend Magazine*, 26 March 1977, p. 19.

C296 Smyth, Sheila. "The Bonfire." *Weekend Magazine*, 26 March 1977, p. 14.

C297 Spira, David. "On Tuesdays I Polish My Uncle". *Weekend Magazine*, 26 March 1977, p. 14.

C298 Squire, Denise. "Nonsense." *Weekend Magazine*, 26 March 1977, p. 17.

C299 Steinberg, Michael. "On Tuesdays I Polish My Uncle." *Weekend Magazine*, 26 March 1977, p. 18.

C300 Van Horne, Ann. "[All day long I]." *Weekend Magazine*, 26 March 1977, p. 18.

C301 Wells, Marian. "The Sad Tale of the Lonely Rhubarb Plant." *Weekend Magazine*, 26 March 1977, p. 18.

C302 Bowering, George. "Detachment from Self." *Descant* [Dennis Lee Special Issue], No. 39 [14, No. 1] (Winter 1982), p. 9. Rpt. in *Tasks of Passion: Dennis Lee at Mid-Career*. Ed. Karen Mulhallen, Donna Bennett, and Russell Brown. Toronto: Descant, 1982, p. 9.

Awards and Honours

C303 Governor-General's Award for Poetry for *Civil Elegies and Other Poems* (1972).

C304 Canadian Library Association Book of the Year Award for the best Canadian children's book written in English for *Alligator Pie* (1974).

C305 National Chapter of Canada IODE [Imperial Order of the Daughters of the Empire] Book Award for children's books for *Alligator Pie* (1974).

C306 Hans Christian Andersen Honour List for *Alligator Pie* (1975).

C307 Canadian Library Association Book of the Year Award for the best Canadian children's book written in English for *Garbage Delight* (1977).

C308 The Ruth Schwartz Foundation Award for *Garbage Delight* (1977).

C309 Canadian Booksellers Award for *Garbage Delight* (1978).

C310 Scottish-Canadian exchange fellowship in Edinburgh, Scotland (1980–81).

C311 Philips Information Systems Literary Prize, for outstanding contribution to Canadian letters by a Canadian author under the age of 50 (1984).

C312 Vicky Metcalf Award, Canadian Authors Association, for a body of work deemed inspirational to Canadian youth (1986).

What characterizes Mr. Lee's poetry, however, is the tone of almost unrelieved resignation." The imagery is concentrated and powerful. The most recurrent image is the "Void." Some poems give a microscopic view of the world, while others give a kaleidoscope. "Negatives" in the form of words like "unselve, dissemble, dismantled, undone, unclaimed, disinherited" are characteristic of the poetry and its message. The journey into Lee's web of pessimism is often an intellectual exercise.

D Selected Book Reviews, Selected Calendar Reviews, Selected Lyrics Reviews, and Selected Audio-Visual Reviews

Selected Book Reviews

Kingdom of Absence

D1 Jackson, Marni. "The Dark Is Light Enough." *Acta Victoriana* [Victoria College, Univ. of Toronto], 92, No. 1 (Nov. 1967), 10–12.
All but perhaps three of the poems are variations on the sonnet form. Lee expresses his artistic frustration as a writer and examines isolation and otherness. Lee is often "darkly amusing" sounding like Bob Dylan. "There are also echoes of [Leonard] Cohen, [Al] Purdy, [Robert] Creeley and others . . . ." Jackson watches "the poet's focus on the void sharpen and close in."

D2 Harland, Cathy. Rev. of *Kingdom of Absence*. *Quarry*, 17, No. 2 (Winter 1968), 42–43.
We see "the patterned hell a mind can weave in conjunction with a tormented spirit." In places, *Kingdom of Absence* is good poetry, even beautiful; in others, it is a "terrifyingly dark world view. . . .

D3 Kearns, Lionel. "If There's Anything I Hate It's Poetry." Rev. of *bp/Journeyings and the Return*, by bpNichol; *Poems: New and Collected*, by A.J.M. Smith; *Kingdom of Absence*, by Dennis Lee; and *A Silent Green Sky*, by Florence McNeil. *Canadian Literature*, No. 36 (Spring 1968), p. 68.
Dennis Lee and A.J.M. Smith have the same concept of poetic form. "Lee's problem, however, lies in the fact that he has considerably less skill, subtlety, and literary background than Smith, and consequently the effect of his effort is often ludicrous . . . ."

D4 Purdy, Alfred W. "Aiming Low." *The Tamarack Review*, No. 47 (Spring 1968), pp. 84–85.
Lee is a "black" poet with "very wry humour, . . . and while often very good [he] has still a distance to go before reaching full development."

D5 Thompson, Eric. Rev. of *The Circle Game*, by Margaret Atwood; and *Kingdom of Absence*, by Dennis Lee. *The Fiddlehead*, No. 75 (Spring 1968), p. 78.
Lee asks to be read not only in a "literal sense" but in an "intuitive sense." He is "self-ruminating" with a "fondness for literary name-dropping" and a "penchant for the world 'abyss.' " Lee is "haunted by spectres of the City." In trying to "clarify man's essential problems in poetic terms," Lee "doesn't

appear to know the difference between rhetoric and poetry."

D6 MacCallum, Hugh. "Letters in Canada: 1967. Poetry." *University of Toronto Quarterly*, 37 (July 1968), 374.
   Kingdom of Absence is a collection of sonnet-length poems. Alienation, recognition of the void or abyss, and the quality of absence are central to the poetry. "No solution is reached, but the signs point in the direction of love and a kind of secular mysticism." W.B. Yeats, T.S. Eliot, and Dylan Thomas are in evidence in the poetry. The poet is, in his own words, "hung between styles" and does not always succeed in finding an "adequate poetic medium."

Civil Elegies

D7 Montagnes, Ann. "Seven Canadian Poets of Varying Style and Talent Offer a Non-Transistorised Service to Piece Together Our Fragmented Times." *Saturday Night.* "Books in Review," July 1968, pp. 27, 28.
   "Of the younger poets only Dennis Lee is old enough to have outgrown social jaundice. Only thus can he put his dry, cynical, bitter record of his recovering in a package so appealing to touch and sight."

D8 Marshall, Tom. Rev. of *The Animals in That Country*, by Margaret Atwood; *The Dumbfounding*, by Margaret Avison; *Winter of the Luna Moth*, by Joe Rosenblatt; and *Civil Elegies*, by Dennis Lee. *Quarry*, 18, No. 3 (Spring 1969), 54.
   Although "intelligent and aware," Lee "has not quite achieved himself." *Civil Elegies* is sometimes "boring," yet "other times very exciting . . . . [T.S.] Eliot, [Theodore] Rilke, [E.J.] Pratt, Frank Scott" are evident in the work. "Lee's effort to be a public poet

is commendable . . . ." Sometimes Lee seems uncertain of "form," with "long, sprawling, uninteresting lines."

D9 Lacey, Edward A. "Poetry Chronicle IV." *Edge* [Edmonton], No. 9 (Summer 1969), 135–38.
   Civil Elegies is a meditation "on Canada and the quality of Canadian life." Lacey is "surprised by the grave and sombre tone [of] this work." Lee's theme is "the sense of void, of non-significance, of life in 'that great lacuna, Canada' . . . ." *Civil Elegies* is "an important and thoughtful poem." However, ". . . what is the motive for the sudden introduction of the figure of Sir John A. Macdonald?" The "long line" of the poetry serves Lee's "purposes here well." He "is to be congratulated for having caught this tone of nervous, frustrated impotence, which may well be the characteristic tone of the civilised human being of our times."

D10 MacCallum, Hugh. "Letters in Canada: 1968. Poetry." *University of Toronto Quarterly*, 38 (July 1969), 347.
   The speaker in *Civil Elegies* locates himself in the external world of Nathan Phillips Square, yet ". . . the heart of each meditation is intensely inward, a probing of the interior life." The force of the poems is "sombre," arising from the poetry as a "kind of therapy, a cathartic activity."

Civil Elegies and Other Poems

D11 Fulford, Robert. "A Poet's View of Canada: A Nation of Losers and Quislings." *The Toronto Star*, 15 April 1972, p. 77.
   In *Civil Elegies and Other Poems*, Lee like other nationalists says that Canadians have sold out to America, ". . . yet they refuse to surrender."

Although Lee's poems suggest that he has "given up on Canada," his work with House of Anansi Press has helped create a resurgence of independent publishing in Canada. George Grant's theme of liberalism is influential in Lee's poetry. The new poems focus on "imperfect love and imperfect marriage." A "hard-won affirmation" brings the elegies and the love poems together.

D12 Dickson, Robert. "À travers ses 'Élégies.'" *Le Soleil* [Québec], 10 juin 1972, p. 64.
Civil Elegies and Other Poems is one of the most significant books of poetry in contemporary Canadian letters. Using the traditional elegiac form, Lee laments, on behalf of the entire nation, for his country. Ordinary experiences are intensified by the use of irony and "l'humour noir." The poet is in exile in his own country, witnessing its destruction by Americans. Lee says he would cherish " 'a civil habitation that is human and our own.' " Lee "admire le courage d'un homme qui est allé au bout de lui-même," like Saint-Denys Garneau. But we live in a divided world with a " 'singleness of eye,' " which Lee would give anything to make whole.

D13 Fetherling, Doug. "A Poet-Publisher with a Voice Like No One Else's." *Saturday Night*, June 1972, p. 37. Rpt. (revised, expanded — "Notes on Dennis Lee") in *The Blue Notebook: Reports on Canadian Culture*. By Doug Fetherling. Oakville, Ont.: Mosaic, 1985, pp. 71, 72.
The achievement of poet-publisher Dennis Lee lies somewhere between his two professions. His reputation as a poet has suffered at the hand of his editors because he has been seldom published. *Civil Elegies and Other Poems* perhaps evens the score. The semantics of the elegiac poems, written in "loping, sweeping lines," are significant. For example, the word "civil" depicts the "impetus" behind the poems in terms of the city and the narrator, a "civilian." The "other" poems of the title "are mainly love-desperation poems in which Lee's technical mastery is at its best and most obvious." Lee's language is "both colloquial and intellectual," but it is his voice that "is like no one else's."

D14 Newman, Christina. "Feeling for the Nation That Made Him." *Maclean's*, June 1972, p. 88.
Lee "is a fine poet writing well and truthfully out of a sensibility that is contemporary . . . [and] painful . . . ." He is one of the new nationalist poets. As an urban being, he points out "what's wrong with his times, his place and himself." Lee combines the view of the "public poet" in the elegies with those of the "private poet" in the other poems, bringing "new meaning out of the Joycean notion of the artist as a forger of the conscience of his race." A photograph is included.

D15 Nodelman, Perry. "Toughminded." *Winnipeg Free Press*. "The World of Books," 12 Aug. 1972, pp. 20–21.
Lee's *Civil Elegies and Other Poems* are "unwieldy, toughminded, shot through with passages of a knotty and uncompromising beauty." A reader must work at the poems, but is rewarded. The poems are personal, referring to House of Anansi Press, Lee's family's Muskoka cottage, and Rochdale. Lee is a "thoughtful" human being trying to cope in a distressing environment, trying to resolve his dislike of cities and his lack of a sense of wholeness. The first section of the book emphasizes the poet's own attitudes; the second places them in a wider context. He ends up trying to accept things as they are. Lee is "a poet superior to most of those he edits for Anansi . . . ."

D16 Schroeder, Andreas. "Difficult Sanities." *Canadian Literature*, No. 55 (Winter 1973), pp. 102–05.

Lee's *Civil Elegies and Other Poems* is an exceptional book. Foremost, it is honest because Lee "admits that lies exist in his own perception . . . ." A paradox exists because Lee is both observer and participant of the human condition. The poems are Lee's own exploration and search for direction and sanity. The private poems of the first section of the book dove-tail nicely with the elegies because they depict sell-out on a personal level. The transformation of the elegies in this edition is extensive. The voice is better modulated and more assured. In short, Lee has outdone himself.

The Gods

D17 Abley, Mark. "Poetry That Fell from the Sky." Rev. of *The Gods*, by Dennis Lee; *Droppings from Heaven*, by Irving Layton; *Another Mouth*, by George Bowering; *A Balancing Act*, by Florence McNeil; and *A Tough Romance*, by Pier Giorgio Di Cicco. *Maclean's*. "Books," 8 Oct. 1979, p. 54.

This "is a book of remarkable honesty, force and wit." Lee covers many topics in varied styles. He is also "self-critical" and can be "earthy and funny as well as contemplative." The elegy for Harold Ladoo "allows Lee to examine his own ambitions and illusions." A photograph of Lee is included.

D18 Helwig, David. "From Ondaatje to Lee: Words That Live as Poetry." *Saturday Night*, Nov. 1979, p. 61.

The Death of Harold Ladoo is "an honorable poem in which Lee mixes colloquial speech with high rhetoric," attempting to combine "personal and public experience." The writing is ambitious, but does not deliver. The "complex history" of the poem demands prose. "In '1838' and 'When I Went Up to Rosedale,' Lee adapts the wit and rhyme of his children's poems to the purpose of serious social comment . . . ."

D19 Pearson, Ian. Rev. of *The Gods*. *Quill & Quire*, Nov. 1979, pp. 33–34.

Lee is not trapped by the mundane. "But his vision is too far-reaching and intense . . . ." The long elegy on Harold Ladoo is the most significant Canadian poem of the decade. It is a crucial re-evaluation of nationalism that, at the same time, grapples with the inadequacies of poetry in the face of real death.

D20 MacGregor, Tom. "A Moving Elegy." *Sunday Sun* [Edmonton]. "Books," 4 Nov. 1979, p. S6.

The Death of Harold Ladoo says more "about the mourner than the mourned." It "has all the rambling and indulgence one expects from the graveside and, at the same time, is chockful of moving and taut passages." Ladoo's death initiates Lee's search for the importance of the poet in a technological age. This theme is reiterated in the shorter poems.

D21 Fox, Gail. "Lee's Best in 'Wangy, Wonderful' Collection." *Toronto Clarion*, 31 Oct.–13 Nov. 1979, p. 7.

". . . *The Gods* . . . is wangy, tough, and wonderful." The poems explore a myriad of themes. Some of the love poems are "rhythmically inventive"; others "stagger under unnecessarily long prosy meters . . . ." *The Death of Harold Ladoo* is Lee's finest poem to date. It changes moods frequently, yet does not lose the "manic, gentle and anguished order" of Lee's 1960s and early 1970s. A photograph of Lee is included.

D22 Gervais, Marty. "Dennis Lee Strikes Balance with Latest Book of Poems." *The Windsor Star*. "The Book Page," 10 Nov. 1979, p. 28.

In *The Gods*, Lee continually balances contentment and anger. In exploring this philosophical dilemma, Lee takes on the world as it is, ultimately, demanding an answer to death. Lee is not negative or fatalistic. There is contentment and a sense of the absurd. In the long meditative piece, "The Gods," Lee "tackles the notion of Gods on earth, their behaviour, misgivings and humanness." In the longer Ladoo poem, Lee's anger shows with the injustice of death. Lee combines subjective reaction and factual details with biography. The poem will probably go down as a classic. A photograph of Lee is included.

D23 Dudek, Louis. Rev. of *The Gods*. *The Globe and Mail* [Toronto]. "Entertainment, Books," 24 Nov. 1979, p. 14.

The Gods is "arresting." It undertakes some serious thinking about our times — the "devaluation and trivialization of life brought about by the disappearance of the numinous . . . ." This theme relates to work by Theodore Rilke and T.S. Eliot. Lee tends to write it as an essay, but he is highly emotive. His reasoning is very similar to C.G. Jung: if the "primitive unconscious" is suppressed, ". . . it manifests itself in the perversions of violent politics and subcultural actuality." This argument may be suspect. The unsatisfied need for " 'the gods' " is only one theory. The poetry is an elegy on the absence of gods; ". . . it is not yet a struggle toward a statement of how the gods can be reborn." Lee's development will be fascinating to follow. A photograph of Lee is included.

D24 Ruebssat, Norbert. "Dennis Lee: The Poet in Public." *The Vancouver Sun*. "Books," 30 Nov. 1979, p. 43L.

Lee is a "public poet." He uses words "to create community understanding." The content and style of *The Gods* is "more varied" than *Civil Elegies*. Part

of Lee's success is that he works at the "craft" of writing. In *The Gods*, "Lee is concerned about the lack of spiritual coherence in the world . . . ." His images are religious, yet his message is social and political. He is critical "about how art and poetry" stand "in relation to life." This is most evident in *The Death of Harold Ladoo*, "a blending of personal history and cultural awareness that goes quite deep . . . ." Three photographs of children and one of Lee with a child are included.

D25 Prosser, David. "Gods of the Bathtub." Rev. of *The Ordinary Bath* and *The Gods*. *The Whig-Standard* [Kingston]. "Book Section," 1 Dec. 1979, p. 24.

Lee expresses "complex artistic and philosophical positions." The creatures that invade the bath, in *The Ordinary Bath*, are versions of the beings in *The Gods*. The language of religion is incompatible with the modern world and must be made more compatible. Technology, though good, reduces human stature, leaving a sense of deprivation. Lee says his work is also about idolatry. We make a false god of intensity of experience and, for example, sex. A photograph of Lee is included.

D26 Pringle, Heather. "Intensity of Vision Not Sustained by Lee." *The Edmonton Journal*. "Books Journal," 8 Dec. 1979, p. C4.

In *The Gods*, Lee attempts to trace the divine world in modern life. Lee's lines of poetry are often too stiff, awkward, and fuzzy, lacking the graceful phrases of *Civil Elegies and Other Poems*. The book begins on a weak note with flat ballads, love poems, and songs, which are uninspired, sometimes embarrassing. In the meditative poems, Lee is convincing in his depiction of the vision of divinity, which is refined in the elegiac *The Death of Harold Ladoo*. The intensity of the apocalyptic fervour of the images of Lee's gods is not sustained. Andrew Suknaski responds to this review (C105).

D27 Cavanagh, David. "Confronting the Famine." *The Whig-Standard Magazine* [*The Whig-Standard*] [Kingston], 29 Dec. 1979, p. 25.

Lee's gods are "mutants," deformed leftovers in an age that has slaughtered two ingredients of faith: awe and passion. One of the madnesses, the death of Trinidadian writer Harold Ladoo, forms Lee's most powerful work to date. The poem moves beyond elegy to an examination of what it means to be a writer. The poem is honest and humane, with many double-edges. The creative double-bind torments Lee and kills Ladoo. Lee faces the feeling that he (Lee) and his world are playing out a suicidal drama as a result of lost faith. But he rejects fatalism and confronts the dilemma squarely; there is no victory, just humanity. The first part of the book is a mixture of shorter philosophical, political, and love poems. "Sometimes they work. Sometimes they don't." In *The Gods*, ". . . Lee consciously acknowledges the danger of abstract absolutes."

D28 Graham, Barbara. Rev. of *The Gods*. *Canadian Materials* [Ottawa], 8, No. 1 (Winter 1980), 32.

"Lee is searching for new gods who will add meaning and richness . . ." to life. Lee rejects "youth" and "the here and now." Eros at least provides the universe with continuity. Lee "regrets the passage of the ancient gods." The Ladoo poem continues the search for the gods in a personal way and comes "to terms with the significance of the life and death of the young writer tragically murdered while visiting Trinidad." The poetry is "significant" reading for "senior secondary students and staff."

D29 Moritz, Albert. "Visions of a High Clean Style." *Books in Canada*, Jan. 1980, pp. 16–17.

In writing about personal experience and social commentary and in attempting to understand creativity, Lee places the poet in the context of contemporary society. His vision for the poet is to comprehend the past and the undigested present. Lee's flaw is in trying to bridge the gap between poetry's traditional readership and a wider, less sophisticated audience. Sometimes the "confrontation" of slang with "traditional," "idiomatic," and " 'poetic' " expressions "explodes into new meaning, but sometimes it just flattens into prosaic narrative, or wanders off in a confusion of directions . . . ." When Lee catches the appropriate rhythm of speech, it is satisfying. Even when he does not, he expands the frontiers. *The Gods* is an important Canadian document.

D30 Watling, Doug. Rev. of *The Gods*, by Dennis Lee; and *Droppings from Heaven*, by Irving Layton. *Tribune* [Campbellton, N.B.]. "Books Now," 2 Jan. 1980, p. 4.

In *The Death of Harold Ladoo*, Lee creates "levels of insight" and "awareness." He wrestles with emotions and denies metaphysical double-talk to establish a more personal vision. The title poem uses "the gods" "as a collective metaphor for the unknowable in life." In other poems, he works out philosophies or states of being. These light poems seem trite when compared to the elegy on Ladoo. However, Lee's honesty and ease with a variety of poetic forms is absorbing and a little unsettling.

D31 Cooley, Dennis. "Loss and Confusion." *The Canadian Forum*, March 1980, pp. 34–36.

The Gods lacks editorial judgement. "Though Lee takes chances in writing poems that run between proclamation and confession, for the most part his attempts fall into dullness or bombast." Sometimes he is more flaccid than flamboyant. In *The Death of*

Harold Ladoo, the writing can be woeful. However, Lee's vulnerability, the shifts in emotion, and the occasional eloquence are impressive. His personal and domestic voice gives the poem power and credibility. Lee gets in trouble with the loose lines and diffuse structure he adopts. His rhetoric is vague and over-wrought. Lee's recurring weakness is his addiction to abstraction, exaggeration, and rhetoric. He has a greater talent for more traditional forms, especially satire and parody. The plain language and facetious tone of the short poems in the first half of the book are good. "On a Kazoo," which works on jazz rhythms and has a whimsical sense of sexual play, may be the best in the collection. Lee has the itch to overreach his material. Hopefully, he will continue to write with the clear, fresh grace of his best poetry.

D32 Banting, Pamela. "Poet's Message about 'The Gods.' " *Calgary Albertan Magazine* [*Calgary Albertan*]. "Books," 13 April 1980, p. 15.

The central question of *The Gods* is "how to be in this world" of "technology." ". . . we now think in abstract terms that deaden our perception . . ." and destroy any link to " 'the gods,' . . . whom we now know only by their absence." The poet, as medium, is especially vulnerable to their wrath. Lee's language is direct and accessible. It works best in the longer "elegy" poem. The songs at the beginning of the book are easy with their relaxed rhythms and conversational tones, but sometimes fall flat. The poems are held together by metaphors of currents of power and energy fields.

D33 Dragišic, Peggy. "Between the Intolerable and the Inscrutable." Rev. of *Savage Fields: An Essay in Literature and Cosmology* and *The Gods*. *Brick* [Ilderton, Ont.], No. 11 (Winter 1981), pp. 8, 11–12.

Rpt. in *Brick* [Ilderton, Ont.], [A Brick Sampler, with Index], No. 12 (Spring 1981), pp. 57, 60–61.

Lee adds "a wry humour, a quizzical distance" to the themes previously developed in *Civil Elegies and Other Poems*. He "acts out a poetics that goes beyond . . . *Savage Fields* . . . ." Lee "finds a unity of mind and body, a peace that is more than just a moment of respite from strife; mind is full of 'a hungry kind of thanks' that evokes a source of being greater than the machinery of strife, but not cancelling strife; just containing it . . . ." Other poems "suffer all the inconsistencies of feeling, all the tortures of difficult thought that vex Lee as an essayist," though ". . . they achieve more clarity . . . ."

The Difficulty of Living on Other Planets

D34 DiManno, Rosie. "Lee's Whimsy Cuts into Heavy Issues." *The Toronto Star*, 1 Nov. 1987, p. C2.

Lee "starts out by tweaking you with whimsy, but ends up wielding an ideological cleaver" that is often "sombre" and "pessimistic." DiManno notes the revisions of earlier publications and the approximate date of composition for original publications. The rhymes are "almost the exclusive domain of children's verse." A photograph of Lee is included.

D35 Kelly, Deirdre. "Playful Poetry for Adults, 'What a Subversive Idea.' " *The Globe and Mail* [Toronto], 3 Nov. 1987, Entertainment, p. D8.

Lee reaches for "the child" in most adults. The book grew out of Lee's desire to revise nine poems from *Nicholas Knock and Other People*. He experiments with form, "Thus quatrains . . . share metric space with sonnets. Octets and couplets abound." Lee hopes the first reading will be for fun before themes like good and evil surface with subsequent readings. A photograph of Lee is included.

D36 McGoogan, Kenneth. "Lee Cooks Up Alligator Pie for Adults." *Sunday Herald* [*The Calgary Herald*], 8 Nov. 1987, Books, p. E6.

In *The Difficulty of Living on Other Planets*, Lee is "a thinking-man's Ogden Nash." The "rhyme and regular rhythms" make the poems "accessible." On another level, the book is "organized in Blakean terms, and traces a movement from innocence to experience."

D37 Bemrose, John. "A Garden of Adult Verse." *Maclean's*, 16 Nov. 1987, p. 64b.

". . . *The Difficulty of Living on Other Planets* is a far cry from Lee in full flight." It is "padded" with work from earlier books. Some of the new verses are "fine . . . . But Lee's most fetching quality is metaphysical playfulness, the ability to juggle with the illogical." Some rhyming is "tiresome," and several poems are surprisingly sentimental.

D38 Trowell, Ian. "A Case of How to Fall between Stools." *The London Free Press.* "Perspective on Books," 21 Nov. 1987, p. B7.

This is "Gilbert-and-Sullivan-like rhythm for all ages," with shades of British poet John Betjeman. ". . . Lee's originality lies entirely in his localizing — using domestic scenes and places — the expressions of greater talents." A photograph of Lee is included.

D39 Smart, Carolyn. "This Bard Is a Card!". *The Whig-Standard* [Kingston], 28 Nov. 1987, p. 26.

The Difficulty of Living on Other Planets made Smart laugh and moved her to "ponder many things in a different light." Lee "has the most incredible ear for rhythms and for language, both formal and colloquial." Illustrator Alan Daniel's work is "gently whimsical."

D40 Blizzard, Christine. "The Alligators Are Back for the Crunch!". *The Sunday Star* [*The Toronto Star*], 29 Nov. 1987, p. C10.

Themes in *The Difficulty of Living on Other Planets* are the "mellowed" concerns of Lee in the 1960s. This time he uses "wit" and "a keen eye for the absurd." His style of poetry will allow people to get over the " 'cultural hurdle of reading poetry,' " making " 'them feel at home.' " A photograph of Lee is included.

D41 Yanofsky, Joel. "Poetic Successes." Rev. of *The Difficulty of Living on Other Planets*, by Dennis Lee; and *Fortunate Exile*, by Irving Layton. *The Gazette* [Montreal], 19 Dec. 1987, Books, p. J-11.

In *The Difficulty of Living on Other Planets*, ". . . Lee is a court jester poking fun at the quirkiness of daily life . . . with fanciful tales of growing old." Lee can be philosophical or whimsical. ". . . what Lee's poems occasionally lack in wit, they make up for in warmth and wisdom."

D42 Fitzgerald, Judith. "No Poetic Problems with Love . . . But Some Difficulties with 'The Difficulty of Living.' " Rev. of *Lovhers*, by Nicole Brossard, trans. Barbara Godard; *The Eyes of Love*, by Raymond Souster; and *The Difficulty of Living on Other Planets*, by Dennis Lee. *The Toronto Star*, 3 Jan. 1988, Books, p. A16.

". . . although charming, the intended marriage of form and content does not always yield to good light verse." The rhyming structure distracts the reader. A few poems are eloquent. A photograph of Lee is included.

D43 Burrows, Malcolm. "Lee's Poetry and Post-Modernism Point Out Extraterrestrial Landscape Within." Illus. Alan Daniel. *The Varsity.* "The Review," 6 Jan. 1988, p. 13.

Lee uses "a comfortable incessant rhythm and an unfailing use of rhyme," injecting "witty barbs at the woes of our society . . . ." There is an Edward Lear "feel for things nonsensical." Lee offers "solace and community," touching "on all the BIG themes."

D44 Eriksen, Shelley. "Lee's Witty New Rhymes Delightful Bedtime Reading." *The Vancouver Sun*. "Books," 9 Jan. 1988, p. C5.
The poems "are pure delightful storytelling not limited to the enjoyment of specific age groups." The rhythms are "infectious," and many poems are "distinctively Canadian." A photograph of Lee is included.

Wiggle to the Laundromat

D45 Swann, Susan. "Lee Writes Poetry for Canadian Kids." *Toronto Citizen*. "Books," 8 Oct. 1970, p. 9.
Wiggle to the Laundromat "is a kid's book and probably one of the first with Canadian content, not to mention its references to such unromantic things as skyscrapers and laundromats." Lee began writing for his two children and friends began to ask for mimeographed copies. *Wiggle to the Laundromat* is a small selection of these poems. Lee discovers the "beauty in Canadian place names." A photograph of Lee and his children, Kevin and Hilary, is included.

D46 "New Nursery Rhymes Charm." *The Citizen* [Ottawa], 31 Oct. 1970, p. 40.
Wiggle to the Laundromat is a book that can amuse most adults as well as youngsters. "The whimsical charming verses have the rhythms and the rhyming of the traditional nursery chants."

D47 Rev. of *Wiggle to the Laundromat*. *The Montreal Star*, 14 Nov. 1970, p. 26.

Wiggle to the Laundromat "is as urban and vital as downtown on a Saturday night."

D48 Lunn, Janet. "Some Good. Some Loved. Some So-So." *The Globe Magazine* [*The Globe and Mail*] [Toronto]. "Children's Books," 21 Nov. 1970, p. 23.
"The verses are silly, and use a lot of funny Canadian place names, but they're like the ones we make up around the dinner table with our children. They don't quite scan and aren't funny enough not to."

D49 Montgomery, Margot. Rev. of *Wiggle to the Laundromat*. *In Review: Canadian Books for Children*, 5, No. 2 (Spring 1971), 25–26.
Wiggle to the Laundromat suggests a Canadian Mother Goose. "The tone and rhythm of the poems vary from rollicking nonsense verse and street rhyme to whimsical song." The quality of the poetry also varies. Most succeed, but one or two seem contrived. Some are rather sophisticated for the young child.

Alligator Pie

D50 Coles, Don. "A Child's Garden of Modern Verse without the Elves." Rev. of *Alligator Pie* and *Nicholas Knock and Other People*. Illus. Frank Newfeld. *The Toronto Star*. "Books in the Star," 28 Sept. 1974, p. G7.
Coles comments generally on Lee's books, rather than specifically on a particular book. Several of the poems with a political overtone in *Alligator Pie* and *Nicholas Knock and Other People* should be omitted in subsequent printings.

D51 Lampard, E.H. "These Enchanting Tales Are Sure to Delight Children of All Ages." Rev. of *Alligator Pie* and *Nicholas Knock and Other People*. Illus. Frank Newfeld. *The St. Catharines Standard*, 28 Sept. 1974, p. 34.

Lampard comments generally on Lee's books, rather than specifically on a particular book. The collaboration of Dennis Lee and Frank Newfeld in *Alligator Pie* and *Nicholas Knock and Other People* "can best be described as enchanting." Lee's poems move "in the direction of A.A. Milne, Lewis Carroll, Edward Lear and indeed . . . all the Mother Goose rhymes beloved of children for generations." The poems have "swing," a "strong lilt," and extensive "use of alliteration and repetition of words, the sort of thing that children love." Caricatures of Lee and Newfeld are drawn by Newfeld.

D52 N., J.R. "Nicholas Knock: Poetic Stroll Through Universe." Rev. of *Alligator Pie* and *Nicholas Knock and Other People*. *Star-Phoenix* [Saskatoon], 4 Oct. 1974.

The author comments generally on Lee's books, rather than specifically on a particular book. Reading both *Nicholas Knock and Other People* and *Alligator Pie* is "A simple and entertaining experience . . . ." Some poems have a "Canadian flavor," with places and names that are Canadian.

D53 Laurence, Margaret. "You Can Almost Hear the Skipping Rope Slapping." Rev. of *Alligator Pie* and *Nicholas Knock and Other People*. Illus. Frank Newfeld. *The Globe and Mail* [Toronto]. "Books," 5 Oct. 1974, p. 35.

For the most part, Laurence comments generally on the books, rather than specifically on a particular book. There is no such thing as "children's literature." *Alligator Pie* and *Nicholas Knock and Other People* are "written with no down-putting condescension [and] . . . may rewardingly be read by people of almost any age . . . ." *Alligator Pie*, with its "chants" and "skipping songs," should be read aloud. *Nicholas Knock and Other People* "is filled with fabulous characters" and "zany" humour. Lee "has a fine sense of the strangeness of words, the ways in which the social meanings assigned to certain words contrast kookily with the meaning-in-itself of the same words." Frank Newfeld's "bizarre" pictures are a perfect compliment to Lee's poems.

D54 Kiely, John. "Nursery Rhymes Contain a Canadian Flavor." Rev. of *Alligator Pie* and *Nicholas Knock and Other People*. Illus. Frank Newfeld. *Kitchener-Waterloo Record*, 12 Oct. 1974, p. 48.

Kiely comments generally on Lee's books, rather than specifically on a particular book. *Alligator Pie* and *Nicholas Knock and Other People* are full of "wonder" and "excitement," "tongue twisters and rhymes . . . . There are poems to skip rope to and poems to say goodnight to . . . ." Frank Newfeld's drawings "are consistently good and occasionally exceptional . . . ." The poems "touch a child's fears and joys . . . ."

D55 Reid, Rob. "Grundibooks, Honkabusts and Wombats." Rev. of *Alligator Pie* and *Nicholas Knock and Other People*. *Arthur* [Trent Univ.], 16 Oct. 1974, p. 14.

Reid comments generally on Lee's books, rather than specifically on a particular book. Lee writes with "a child's perception of the universe." He balances the "extravagant and the ordinary." There are "exotic animals" and "weird places." Reality and fantasy are interwoven. Themes are subtle. They are "suggestive rather than didactic," thus stimulating our own speculation.

D56 Herron, Marjorie. "Hey Diddle Diddle." Rev. of *Alligator Pie* and *Nicholas Knock and Other People*. *Winnipeg Free Press*. "Books," 19 Oct. 1974, p. 21.

Herron comments generally on Lee's books, rather

than specifically on a particular book. *Alligator Pie* and *Nicholas Knock and Other People* are Lee's celebration of "objects, places and events belonging peculiarly to Canada's children." The poems create a "world full of entrancing jingles, sprightly humor and flights of fancy."

D57 Barbour, Douglas. "In Love with His Audience." Rev. of *Alligator Pie* and *Nicholas Knock and Other People*. *The Edmonton Journal*, 26 Oct. 1974, p. 26.

Barbour comments generally on Lee's books, rather than specifically on a particular book. Lee's "fine poetic imagination and sensitivity to language" results in "fresh, contemporary and Canadian" books. The illustrations are "vibrant and colourful." His books "are not meant to replace Mother Goose or A.A. Milne, but to stand with them." The poetry encompasses a child's environment and uses Canadian place names, past times, and people. This is good literature that appeals to children of all ages and adults. Lee's voice is "individualistic." These works are "major events in our literary life."

D58 Hunt, Jacquie. "Fun Verse for Young Canadians." Rev. of *Alligator Pie* and *Nicholas Knock and Other People*. Illus. Frank Newfeld. *The Citizen* [Ottawa], 26 Oct. 1974, p. 68.

"In *Alligator Pie* . . . Lee exhibits the exuberant rhyming facility of a Dr. Seuss, the madcap imagination of a Maurice Sendak, the inventiveness of a Tove Janssen . . . ." Some poems are reminiscent of street songs, some of familiar nursery rhymes, others tell a story. Frank Newfeld draws a caricature of himself and Lee. "Flying Out of Holes" (B95) is also included.

D59 Innes, Lorna. "The Colourful World of Nicholas Knock." Rev. of *Alligator Pie* and *Nicholas Knock and Other People*. Illus. Frank Newfeld. *Chronicle-Herald* [Halifax], 9 Nov. 1974, p. 10.

Innes comments generally on Lee's books, rather than specifically on a particular book. "Violence, which has been a staple of children's verse and writing and which has been served up by such experts as Lewis Carroll, Hilaire Belloc and W.S. Gilbert . . . is found in Lee's poems." Much of the "Canadian flavor" of the writing is Toronto-based. *Alligator Pie* and *Nicholas Knock and Other People* may become classics.

D60 Johnston, Margaret E. Rev. of *Alligator Pie*. *In Review: Canadian Books for Children*, 9, No. 1 (Winter 1975), 35.

Lee's invitation to children "to add their own words and verses" is generous. Lee's writing is "light but not empty, nonsensical but not farcical, bubbling but of lasting pleasure." The illustrations are "well-designed" and "perceptive."

D61 Rev. of *Alligator Pie*. *Kirkus Reviews* [New York], 15 Aug. 1975, p. 912.

Lee's Canadian place names "will be just as exotic" in the United States as the archaic nursery rhymes he wants to supplement. ". . . but as the rhymes are almost all sound and no sense that won't matter . . . ." The influence of A.A. Milne and Laura E. Richards is obvious. Frank Newfeld's "harsh, designer-like cartoons . . . are a real handicap . . . ."

D62 Hearne, Betsy. Rev. of *Alligator Pie*. *Sun-Times* [Chicago], 31 Aug. 1975.

Lee's *Alligator Pie* manages "to be original and bounce along nonsense verses that do and don't make sense. Most attempts to update nursery rhymes are unsuccessfully self-conscious, but these are loose and chantable with a tricky twist."

D63 Rumley, Larry. Rev. of *Alligator Pie. Seattle Times*, 16 Nov. 1975, p. 15.

Lee has created poems "designed to suit a child's fancy regardless of 'meaningfulness.' " The poems with place names add extra "fun" for local residents. Lee says the poems are " 'meant to be used.' " When children pass poems around creating their own versions, " '. . . the changes always make sense — to the tongue and ear if not necessarily to the mind.' " Frank Newfeld's drawings are "most appropriate."

D64 Heins, Ethel L. Rev. of *Alligator Pie. Horn Book Magazine* [Boston], 51 (Dec. 1975), 608.

Alligator Pie "introduces American children to a fresh, new voice from Canada. Percussive rhythms, an acrobatic use of language, and a fine variety of form, meter, and subject matter distinguish the verses." The poems in the first half of the book will appeal to younger children, the second half to older ones. Many of these latter poems "are as dexterously nonsensical as those of Laura E. Richards." The "humor" in the pictures is not as "spontaneous" as the poems.

D65 Thiele, Barbara. Rev. of *Alligator Pie. School Library Journal* [New York], 22, No. 4 (Dec. 1975), 47.

The thirty-six nursery rhymes in *Alligator Pie* "play on the things children live with every day. The most successful verses here combine catchy rhythm with nonsensical subject . . . ." Some illustrations are "inappropriate." However, the poems "will be thoroughly enjoyed by young listeners."

D66 Rev. of *Alligator Pie. Curriculum Advisory* [New York], Feb. 1977.

Lee says, "There is a class of poem whose only virtue is that it Contains a Worthy Sentiment, or Deals With the Child's Real World. Adults sometimes tolerate these wretched exercises, thinking they must be Literature." Children do not. Lee's poetry is anything but a "wretched exercise." The "real world" is there in the writing.

D67 Lorenzi, Wendy. "Alligator Pie — Bouncing Rhymes." *Early Canadian Life* [Milton, Ont.], July 1977, p. 22.

"The bouncing rhymes and cadences of the poems collected in *Alligator Pie* account for . . . its rapid ascent to classic status . . . ." The poems "catch the exuberance and energy of the small child." They should be "read aloud, chanted, skipped to and giggled over." The "nonsense" "appeals to the child's sense of the ridiculous." Lee also acknowledges "the anxieties inherent in a small person's world." Frank Newfeld's illustrations "capture the mood of the poems" and the child's "imagination."

Nicholas Knock and Other People

Note: A number of reviewers comment generally on *Alligator Pie* and *Nicholas Knock and Other People*, rather than specifically on each book. Rather than fill this section with meaningless entries, refer to Don *Coles* (D50), E.H. *Lampard* (D51), J.R.N. (D52), Margaret *Laurence* (D53), John *Kiely* (D54), Rob *Reid* (D55), Marjorie *Herron* (D56), Douglas *Barbour* (D57), and Lorna *Innes* (D59).

D68 Hunt, Jacquie. "Fun Verse for Young Canadians." Rev. of *Alligator Pie* and *Nicholas Knock and Other People.* Illus. Frank Newfeld. *The Citizen* [Ottawa], 26 Oct. 1974, p. 68.

Nicholas Knock and Other People, written for older children, has "nonsense rhymes, but . . . often an undercurrent of serious intent . . . ." Its "greatest appeal" lies in Lee's "instinctive and sensitive celebration of the child's view." A Frank Newfeld draws a caricature of himself and Lee. "Flying Out of Holes" (B95) is also included.

D69 Wernick, Kathleen. "These Children's Poems Truly Canadian." Rev. of *Alligator Pie* and *Nicholas Knock and Other People*. *The Spectator* [Hamilton], 2 Nov. 1974, p. 4.

Nicholas Knock and Other People, for older children, has "zest" and "fantasy," with "more substantial" subject matter than *Alligator Pie*. Lee appreciates "a child's sense of fair play and freedom." Frank Newfeld's illustrations also demonstrate his understanding of a child's perspective.

D70 Montagnes, Ann. "Behold the Ultimate Virtue." Rev. of *Alligator Pie* and *Nicholas Knock and Other People*. Illus. Frank Newfeld. *The Globe and Mail* [Toronto], 7 Dec. 1974, p. 35.

Among children's books that will stand the test of time are Lee's *Alligator Pie* and *Nicholas Knock and Other People*. "In *Nicholas Knock and Other People*, for older children and adults, you no longer want to meddle with the author's . . . unusual rhymes, timing and vocabulary . . . ." Frank Newfeld's drawings are as "assertive and gripping" as Lee's poetry.

D71 English, Betsy. Rev. of *Nicholas Knock and Other People*. *In Review: Canadian Books for Children*, 9, No. 1 (Winter 1975), 35–36.

The poetry in *Nicholas Knock and Other People* is "not simple at all." It is "delightful," "funny," "joyous." Throughout, there is a "sense of gaiety . . . something for everyone." The illustrations are "gorgeous."

D72 Rev. of *Nicholas Knock and Other People*. *Kirkus Reviews* [New York], 1 Aug. 1977, p. 786.

Nicholas Knock and Other People "bounces along less evenly than . . . *Alligator Pie*." However, its "Milne-ish rhythms," "outlandishness," and "pure silliness" are similar. The book is given a "Borderline" recommendation, with a note that ". . . the harsh illustrations don't place it anywhere."

D73 Rev. of *Nicholas Knock and Other People*. *Booklist* [Chicago], 1 Nov. 1977, p. 478.

While Canadian place names are not a problem for American children, political and historical references may be. The "poster-type graphics" give the book "dramatic unity."

D74 Willard, Nancy. Rev. of *Nicholas Knock and Other People*. *The New York Times Book Review*. "Poet's Corner," 13 Nov. 1977, p. 47.

Lee's poetry contains "the sensical as well as the nonsensical . . . ." The ". . . references to Canadian places and politics may escape Lee's American readers . . . ."

D75 H[eins]., P[aul]. Rev. of *Nicholas Knock and Other People*. *Horn Book Magazine* [Boston], 53 (Dec. 1977), 675.

Drawing on traditional poetics, ". . . the Canadian poet . . . uses the simplest means to attain amusingly outrageous effects." Lee "invents words . . . and constantly indulges in the verbally unexpected . . . ." Some verses are "purely lyrical." The illustrations "suggest comics" from an "art deco world . . . deliberately garish."

D76 Cater, June B. Rev. of *Nicholas Knock and Other People*. *School Library Journal* [New York], 24, No. 6 (Feb. 1978), 59.

"Well constructed verse with powerful word usage and considerable originality, this collection contains a number of selections which are marvelously diverting, lyrically beautiful, or funny." Canadian historical references and "local culture or events . . . may be unintelligible to American children." The "collection may prove controversial . . . never dull or trite."

D77 Rev. of *Nicholas Knock and Other People. Children's Book Review Service* [Brooklyn], March 1978, p. 78.

"Grotesque imagery abounds but humor is rare in this uneven poetry collection." Some poems are amusing, "but most . . . are too sophisticated in their references . . . cynical and anti-establishment in tone . . . ."

Garbage Delight

D78 Landsberg, Michele. "Boisterous Burps and Bums. Slap-Bang Hectic Merriment. Maybe Lee's Ready for Riskier Territory." Illus. Frank Newfeld. *The Globe and Mail* [Toronto], 17 Sept. 1977, p. 38.

Unlike other poetry, Lee's writing has been "taken over by the kids themselves. . . . the poems bounce and jog along in the best child-approved manner . . . ." Several poems demonstrate "Lee's willingness and capacity to venture into . . . riskier, more challenging territory."

D79 Davis, Lesia. "Poems and Pictures for Little Ones 'In the Middle.' " Illus. Frank Newfeld. *Calgary Albertan*, 8 Oct. 1977, p. 31.

The appeal of *Garbage Delight* is the "catchy rhyme. Commonplace and not so commonplace things are imprinted on our minds . . . ." Lee also deals with "real concerns of a five year old . . . ." The poem "Suzy Grew a Moustache" ends unnecessarily in violence. The illustrations are humorous, stylish, and imaginative.

D80 Bennett, Michael. "Some Kids Refuse to Grow Up." *The Vancouver Province.* "Entertainment," 21 Oct. 1977, p. 28.

Dennis Lee and Frank Newfeld both remember what it is like to be a kid — "to wiggle and squiggle" and say words that rhyme and words that grownups do not like. A photograph of Lee and a child is also included.

D81 Heward, Burt. "Dennis Lee: Serious in Two Worlds." Rev. of *Garbage Delight* and *Savage Fields: An Essay in Literature and Cosmology.* Illus. Frank Newfeld. *The Citizen* [Ottawa], 22 Oct. 1977, p. 37.

This review is based on an interview. Lee says, " '. . . rhythms and traditional rhymes and stanzas are part of the hugging, physical feeling . . . of the bedtime-story experience.' " The full range of being human is covered in the poetry. In *Savage Fields: An Essay in Literature and Cosmology* Lee says, " '. . . the strife of the world and earth may define the fundamental being in our era.' " The things that once were a sign of progress are a mark of decay. Lee says, " 'You just *need* bare bums and bratty brothers to subsume such serious stuff in children's poetry. It's all part of life as "garbage delight." ' "

D82 Newson, Bryan. "Let's Ear It for Aural Lee." *Books in Canada*, Nov. 1977, p. 11.

Garbage Delight is another "winner." The poetry captures "Sound and rhythm, the elements of language children learn first . . . ." Lee writes "without condescension or embarrassment of the child's world from the child's point of view." Newfeld's drawings "counterpoint" and "extend" the poems.

D83 Ashby, Adele. Rev. of *Garbage Delight. Canadian Materials*, 6, No. 2 (Spring 1978), 87–88.

Garbage Delight is a "gorgeous, forbidden fantasy . . . ." The place is "very real and it alternates between fear and aggression . . . . The language has that 'quality of memorableness' which places Lee firmly in the nonsense tradition of Mother Goose, Edward Lear, Hillaire Belloc, Lewis Carroll and Ogden Nash." Lee's words are "lovely" and "unexpected," the poetry "loaded with Canadian references." Lee explores "violence" in a "light-hearted" way. This is also apparent in Frank Newfeld's illustrations.

D84 A[nderson]., A[nne]. M[arie]. Rev. of *Garbage Delight. Reviewing Librarian*, 4, No. 1 (Jan. 1978), 15–16.
   Garbage Delight is a "collection of infectious, fantastic children's poems . . . . The poet's moods shift and reshape themselves many times." The reader will both empathize and identify with the characters. "Outrageous behaviour, as usual, abounds . . . ." The rhythm is great for "oral reading." Frank Newfeld's illustrations create "moods and visual drama . . . ."

D85 Kelly, Elinor. Rev. of *Garbage Delight. In Review: Canadian Books for Children*, 12, No. 1 (Winter 1978), 55.
   "*Alligator Pie* is a milestone in Canadian publishing for children." Now *Garbage Delight* is on the best-seller list. The sound of the words are delightful. Frank Newfeld's drawings are fun. Note the portrait of Lee with the poem "Goofus" and the book design itself.

D86 Reaney, James S. "How Much Garbage Delight?". *Canadian Children's Literature/Littérature canadienne pour la jeunesse*, No. 12 (1978), pp. 72–74.
   Since the publication of *Alligator Pie* in 1974, Lee's work has been commercially and artistically successful. *Garbage Delight* "seems a refinement of what he has accomplished previously." The poetry is dra-

matic, and children are able to act it out. Adults will find echoes of Rudyard Kipling and Robert Service in the poetry's "superheroics." One common denominator in the poems is the metaphor of food as "immediate gratification" or the subject of rebellion. The ominous undercurrents of the poetry are introduced with subtle irony. Lee has acquired his audience of adults and children honestly.

D87 Rev. of *Garbage Delight*, by Dennis Lee, illus. Frank Newfeld; *My Feet Roll*, illus. Winnie Mertens; and *Children of the Yukon*, by Ted Harrison, illus. Ted Harrison. *Children's Book News* [London, Eng.]. "The Children's Book News Choice," No. 1 (1978), 1.
   "The light-hearted spirit of these poems" will appeal to the young, while ". . . the devilish sense of humour will make them enjoyable for an older reader."

D88 Stott, Jon. Rev. of *Garbage Delight. World of Children's Books* [Edmonton], 3, No. 1 (Spring 1978), 52–53.
   Garbage Delight explores new poetic experiences. It may be Lee's best book of children's poetry. Many of the poems are "silly and rousing." The most original poems are the lyrics that explore the "quiet inner life" of the child. Lee calls this the "homing instinct" in children. The rest of the volume is potpourri.

D89 Rev. of *Garbage Delight. Kirkus Reviews* [New York], 1 Dec. 1978, p. 1309.
   Many of Lee's "latest inventions . . . are more in the nature of outlandish burlesques than inspired nonsense, while some are conventional, old-time juvenile jingles . . . ." The illustrations "are overstyled and excruciatingly colored."

D90 Geringer, Laura. Rev. of *Garbage Delight*. *School Library Journal* [New York], 25, No. 5 (Jan. 1979), 55.

Garbage Delight has "a few pleasing sound capers and tongue twisters. . . . The collection, however, is more than half waste, with several flat take-offs on traditional verse . . . ." Some poems are "self-consciously cute" and "coy." Frank Newfeld's drawings are "unattractively colored" and "strain for absurdity and humor."

D91 Rev. of *Garbage Delight*. *Center for Children's Books: Bulletin* [Chicago], 32 (April 1979), 140, 141.

Garbage Delight "is a collection of nonsense poems that only rarely go beyond humor to achieve mood or imagery." They are appealing in terms of "rhyme, a pronounced rhythm, and exaggeration."

D92 Rev. of *Garbage Delight*. *Language Arts* [Urbana, Ill.], 56 (Sept. 1979), 685.

Garbage Delight is "a daffy book of sense, nonsense, and poems somewhere in between. Spoonerisms, internal rhymes, tongue twisters, and unusual meter (not to speak of topics) turn the language topsy-turvy."

D93 Cutcliffe, Susan. Rev. of *Garbage Delight*. *Book Times* [Toronto], 4, No. 1 (Summer 1981), 1.

Ten-year-old Susan Cutcliffe says *Garbage Delight* is about "things that happen in real life." Lee's style is "refreshing" and "fun" to read.

Jelly Belly

D94 Granfield, Linda. "Fanciful, Factual, or Fruitless? Let the Buyer Discriminate." Illus. Juan Wijngaard. *Quill & Quire*, Nov. 1983, p. 25.

Jelly Belly surmounts "all categories." In this "engaging collection," the poetry recalls "Mother Goose classics." The rhythms are "infectious." "There are action rhymes to play with toddlers, tongue-twisting poems full of Canadian geographical references, and sweet lullabies." Juan Wijngaard's illustrations "match the spirit of the poetry . . . ."

D95 Martin, Sandra. "Explosions from Munsch." Rev. of *Favorite Stories* (cassette), by Robert Munsch; *David's Father*, by Robert Munsch, illus. Michael Martchenko; and *Jelly Belly*, by Dennis Lee, illus. Juan Wijngaard. *The Globe and Mail* [Toronto]. "Children's Books," 5 Nov. 1983, Entertainment, p. 15.

Jelly Belly is " 'a new sort of Mother Goose.' " It "encompasses the mythic and the contemporary, the cosmopolitan and the homegrown, the serious and the silly, the chant and the lullaby, the poem and the rhyme." The poems do not always work. Juan Wijngaard's illustrations enhance the "mythic poems," but look "English," where they should look "Canadian."

D96 Innes, Lorna. "Children's Book Festival — Lot of Reasons to Celebrate." *The Chronicle Herald* [Halifax], 12 Nov. 1983, p. 32.

Jelly Belly is a "fine" book and is "strikingly illustrated." One poem is a "variation on the Old Mother Hubbard theme . . . ." There are "clapping" and "marching" rhymes.

D97 Cohen, Elaine. "What's Good for the Goose Is Good for the Gander." *The Suburban* [Montreal]. "Arts & Entertainment," 23 Nov. 1983, p. A-29.

Jelly Belly is "fascinating." Juan Wijngaard captures "the message in each poem." Lee's poetry has a "folksy quality." His "action rhymes, prehistoric creatures, ceremonial occasions, animal tales, nonsense jingles, lullabies and of course Mr. *Jelly Belly* 'with a big fat frown' " interest children. Unlike traditional poetry, Lee makes reference to "modern technology." He does not use his poetry to moralize, although, he says, " '. . . there are values of tolerance, compassion and courage implied in' " his poetry.

D98 Wayne, Joyce. "Father Goose." *Books in Canada*, Dec. 1983, p. 15.
  Jelly Belly contains traditional nursery rhymes. The simplest rhymes are often the most difficult to write. For Lee, it is "a challenge, not an escape from the concerns of his adult verse." As in *The Death of Harold Ladoo*, there is a "tug-of-war between creativity and devastation." Lee does not write " '*for* children, but as one of them.' " In his best poems, ". . . nothing artificial, nothing consciously adult and intellectual, intervenes between the words and the child. . . . For all its rowdiness, *Jelly Belly* is a quaintly gentle, evocative book." A photograph of Lee is included.

D99 Rosen, Michael. "Rhymeo Nasties." *New Statesman* [London, Eng.]. "Verse for Children," 2 Dec. 1983, p. 27.
  "I've just had a row with my three-year-old because I won't read *Jelly Belly* . . . for the 200th time." There are countless characters in "a torrent of new rhymes, jingles and finger rhymes." If you're tired of *Humpty Dumpty*, this book is for you.

D100 Scobie, Stephen. "Poems for the Very Young." *Monday Magazine* [Victoria], 9 Dec. 1983, p. C-13.
  Jelly Belly was even more demanding and difficult for Lee than his earlier books. "Many of the poems are little more than basic rhythm and sound . . . . Lee doesn't sanitize his world: the kids in these poems get

dirty, smell bad, wear Walkmen, and even occasionally die." The "absurd grace when his imagination runs to the fantastic . . ." distinguishes Lee's work.

D101 "Nonsense, Irreverence Captured for the Young." Rev. of *Jelly Belly*, by Dennis Lee, illus. Juan Wijngaard; and *The Witches*, by Roald Dahl. *Times-Colonist* [Victoria]. "Books for Children," 10 Dec. 1983, p. C-13.
  Dennis Lee, like Roald Dahl, "relies heavily for his comedy on shock effects . . . . Both Dahl and Lee operate at the high-wire level of fantasy, nonsense . . ." not unlike Lewis Carroll's. In *Jelly Belly*, Lee's writing is "relaxed, spontaneous and lyrical. . . . There is variety of metre, lightness of touch and rhythm, plenty of humor but also more melancholy and gentleness."

D102 Galloway, Priscilla. Rev. of *Jelly Belly*. *Canadian Book Review Annual: 1983*. Ed. Dean Tudor and Ann Tudor. Toronto: Simon & Pierre, 1984, p. 291.
  "*Jelly Belly* is vintage Dennis Lee. . . . the zany jingles, the chants, the wonderful place name poems . . ." all have the "irreverence and the lyricism" of Lee's earlier books. The illustrations "are good fun or pleasant, though occasionally [Juan] Wijngaard seems to be straining for effect . . . ." Lee is in touch with the child in himself while, at the same time, he "brings to his craft the skills of his experience."

D103 Millar, Mary. Rev. of *Jelly Belly*. Illus. Juan Wijngaard. *The Whig-Standard Magazine* [*The Whig-Standard*] [Kingston], 7 Jan. 1984, p. 22.
  Jelly Belly "is just as funny, vigorous and appealing as" Lee's other children's books. Lee has "hit exactly the right blend of simplicity, fantasy and outrageousness . . . . The rhythms are strong, the rhyme-schemes catchy, the terms of reference part of chil-

dren's everyday experience . . . ." Canadianisms are both "implicit and explicit . . . ."

D104 Nodelman, Perry. "For & about Children." Rev. of *A Child's Anne*, by Deirdre Kessler, illus. Floyd Trainor; *Jelly Belly*, by Dennis Lee, illus. Juan Wijngaard; and *The Genesis of Grove's The Adventure of Leonard Broadus: A Text and Commentary*, ed. Mary Rubio. *Canadian Literature*, No. 103 (Winter 1984), pp. 150–51.

Jelly Belly is an international publishing project. Juan Wijngaard's illustrations give the book a British flavour, while Lee's lyrics provide "Canadian slang." The poetry is "brilliant." With Lee's "pleasing and insidiously unforgettable rhythms" and rhymes, Lee has come close to the oral tradition of original nursery rhymes. Like Mother Goose, the poetry has a national identity yet remains "anonymous." Lee pleases children and elicits "childlike moods."

D105 C., B. Rev. of *Jelly Belly*. *Junior Bookshelf* [Huddersfield, Eng.], 48, No. 1 (Feb. 1984), 26, 27.

"These modern nonsense rhymes" contain "a wide variety of what the poet calls his " 'rumbunctious' work." They could easily "be mistaken for traditional nursery lore." The "Canadian place-names" will be more significant for Canadian children. Juan Wijngaard's illustrations "match the text very well." The cover, however, is a little grotesque.

D106 Klause, Annette Curtis. Rev. of *Jelly Belly*. *School Library Journal*, 32, No. 4 (Dec. 1985), 77.

The cover of *Jelly Belly* "is an immediate turn-off . . . . The pictures are more original than the poems . . . ," some of which resemble Mother Goose rhymes. Other poems are "original and clever," some "silly," others "pointless." This book will never compete with those by Shel Silverstein or Jack Prelutsky.

D107 R., H. Rev. of *Jelly Belly*. *Booklist* [Chicago], 15 May 1985, pp. 1334, 1335.

Lee's "contemporary nursery rhymes . . . have the solemn nonsense, vigor, and chanting rhythms of Mother Goose along with some echoes of Edward Lear and Lewis Carroll." There are "lullabies . . . counting, bouncing, and tickling rhymes." The settings are "home, farm, and playground." The poetry is "close to the child's experience." Juan Wijngaard's illustrations are lively, capturing "the immediate and the surreal."

The Dennis Lee Big Book

D108 Gould, Allan. "Bonanza for Young Readers." *Barrie Examiner*, 27 Nov. 1985.

Lee is "the best Canadian poet for children." *The Dennis Lee Big Book* is a "collection of some of Lee's best from most of his earlier collections."

D109 Wynne-Jones, Tim. "From Scrooge to Fantasies: A Child's Treasures of Reading." *The Globe and Mail* [Toronto]. "Children's Books," 14 Dec. 1985, Literary Supp., p. E8.

Wynne-Jones briefly notes that ". . . there is nothing new in the 19 entries, [but] none of the whacky poems has grown stale."

The Ordinary Bath

D110 Ackerman, Marianne. "An Ordinary Book: An Amusing Price." Illus. Jon McKee. *Sunday Post of Canada* [Ottawa], 18 Nov. 1979.

The Ordinary Bath does not meet the standards set by Lee's previous work and is over-priced. In this review, which is based on an interview, Lee explained, " 'It is about what one does with aggression, with free-floating Dionysian forces.' " The child learns the " 'compromise between freedom and authority.' " The idea for the book originated with unpublished author and artist Lou Fedorkow. Lee contemplated it for about a year.

D111 Peterson, Leslie. Rev. of *The Ordinary Bath*. Illus. Jon McKee. *The Vancouver Sun*. "Books," 30 Nov. 1979, p. 43L.
 Though ordinary on the surface, "Beneath the murky waters of this innocent little tale . . . lies a splashingly exotic world." Jon McKee's illustrations interact with Lee's words, "shifting their perspective." In this review, which is based on an interview, Lee says, " 'I don't think I'll be cranking out children's poetry indefinitely.' "

D112 Hunt, Jacquie. "Younger Children." *The Globe and Mail* [Toronto]. "Children's Books," 1 Dec. 1979, Entertainment, p. 11.
 Lee explores a fascination with being bad. Adult analysis of this children's story reveals the themes of the sorcerer's apprentice and "archetypal coming of age." Jon McKee's illustrations are "explosive." For the child, the experience is a familiar one.

D113 Robb, Edith. "Rub a Dub Dub Monsters in a Tub?". *Moncton Transcript*, 1 Dec. 1979.
 "The Ordinary Bath leaves a critic in a tie . . . . there is adventure and fun for some, but certainly no reassurance or understanding for the already timid."

D114 Uteck, Barbara. "For Christmas: Kids' Taste Is Quite Old-Fashioned." Illus. Jon McKee. *The Gazette* [Montreal], 8 Dec. 1979, Montreal Gazette Books, p. 52.
 In *The Ordinary Bath*, crude and violent poems take over completely. ". . . parents might well wonder about a book that seems more *Mad* magazine or

Sesame Street than poetry." Still, Uteck's five year old delighted in the book.

D115 Johnston, Ann. "Bring Up Baby on Homegrown Heroes." *Maclean's*, 17 Dec. 1979, p. 49.
 The story is a version of the sorcerer's apprentice. It reaches and maintains a great crescendo. The pace is frantic and the illustrations are "poster-bright." For very young children, it could be as frightening as *Jaws*. This is not Lee at his best.

D116 Roberts, Ken. "The 'Stuff' of Life." Rev. of *Canadian Children's Annual 1980*, ed. Robert Nielson; *Six Darn Cows*, by Margaret Laurence, illus. Ann Blades; *The Ordinary Bath*, by Dennis Lee, illus. Jon McKee; *The Olden Days Coat*, by Margaret Laurence, illus. Muriel Wood; and *The River Runners*, by James Houston. *Lethbridge Herald*. "Books in Review," 19 Jan. 1980, p. 50.
 The text of *The Ordinary Bath* is enjoyable, but the illustrations are disappointing. The book does work, but it could have been much better.

D117 Smith, Mary Ainslie. Rev. of *The Ordinary Bath*, by Dennis Lee, illus. Jon McKee; *There's a Rainbow in My Closet*, by Patti Stern; and *The Fire Stealer*, by William Toye, illus. Elizabeth Cleaver. *Books in Canada*, Feb. 1980, p. 21.
 Lee's new book is a disappointment. The text is short, only 650 words. The language, though "rhythmic, full of alliteration and rhyming words," is not written in the regular verse that made his earlier books so much fun. Jon McKee's drawings are "effective." Loris Lesynski responds to this review (C107).

D118 Osler, Ruth. Rev. of *The Ordinary Bath*. *In Review: Canadian Books for Children*, 14, No. 2 (April 1980), Reviews: Picture Books, 48–49.

The short text of *The Ordinary Bath* plays with word, rhythm, and rhyme. Illustrator Jon McKee catches the mood with his action-filled drawings. Reminiscent of Dr. Seuss, the book is vigorous and colourful. It lacks the light humour one normally expects from Lee.

D119 Nodelman, Perry. "Shakespeare Takes a Bath." Rev. of *Shakespeare and the Flying Bed*, by Mark Coté, illus. Mark Coté; and *The Ordinary Bath*, by Dennis Lee, illus. Jon McKee. *Canadian Children's Literature/Littérature canadienne pour la jeunesse*, Nos. 15–16 (1980), pp. 91–93.

Lee's writing has the demonic energy of four year olds and is also rather vulgar. His exuberant tastelessness may offend adults, but Nodelman finds Lee's writing "hilarious." Jon McKee's illustrations in *The Ordinary Bath* are as unrestrained and tasteless as Lee's writing, making a more satisfactory combination than Lee and Frank Newfeld. *The Ordinary Bath* is about the boundaries between freedom and anarchy. The bathtub creature that emerges represents the boy's ability to imagine and his desire for unrepressed freedom. Lee occasionally uses poetic rhythms. This orderliness balances the anarchy of the story.

Lizzy's Lion

D120 Wynne-Jones, Tim. Rev. of *Lizzy's Lion*. *Quill & Quire*, Nov. 1984, p. 11.

Lee's " 'first story book in verse' " has some of the "punchy, springy rhythm" of *Jelly Belly*. Typical of Lee's work, the book is easy to learn and remember. The words are meaningful despite the fact that they rhyme. Marie-Louise Gay's drawings are equal in verve.

D121 Adilman, Sid. "Lee Goes Romping On with a Wonderful Lion." Rev. of *Lizzy's Lion*, by Dennis Lee, illus. Marie-Louise Gay; and *The Violin-Maker's Gift* and *Uncle Jacob's Ghost Story*, by Donn Kushner. Illus. Marie-Louise Gay. *The Toronto Star*. "Children's Books," 30 Sept. 1984, p. G11.

As usual, Lee "knows the private imaginings of little children. His scale of operation is smaller this time, his story quite slight, but his whimsy, clever rhyming scheme and artistic collaborator are all a delight."

D122 Martin, Sandra. "The Ticklish Art of Children's Poetry." Rev. of *The New Wind Has Wings*, ed. Mary Alice Downie, illus. Elizabeth Cleaver; *Lizzy's Lion*, by Dennis Lee, illus. Marie-Louise Gay; *A Spider Danced a Cosy Jig*, by Irving Layton, illus. Miro Malish; and *Blink (a strange book for children)*, by sean o huigin, illus. Barbara de Lella. *The Globe and Mail* [Toronto]. "Children's Books," 27 Oct. 1984, Entertainment, p. 20.

"Nobody reads his own work as well as Dennis Lee, but he's in danger of becoming a performer more than a poet and of having his children's books descend to the level of commodities." *Lizzy's Lion* "is so contrived that I doubt it could hold children's attention for more than a couple of readings without the boost of Marie-Louise Gay's wonderfully scratchy and wonky drawings."

D123 Fasick, Adele M. Rev. of *Lizzy's Lion*. *Canadian Materials* [Ottawa], 2 Feb. 1985, p. 86.

". . . Lee can do no wrong when it comes to writing rhymes for small children." Adults should not worry "about the morality of chewing up a robber . . . ."

D124 Foster, Roy. "Apocalyptic Escapades." Illus. Patrick Benson. *The Times Literary Supplement* [London, Eng.], 13 Dec. 1985, p. 1435.

Lizzy "resembles those grim schoolgirls drawn by Ronald Searle, who used to keep vigil by the chimney on Christmas Eve armed with clubs and man-traps." The story "is firmly in the tradition of [Hillaire] Belloc's *Cautionary Tales*, which inexhaustibly go on brightening the lives of children bored by the clichés of everyday existence."

D125 Noonan, Gerald. "Literary, and Enforcer, Lions Have a Place in the Bedroom." Illus. Marie-Louise Gay. *Canadian Children's Literature/Littérature canadienne pour la jeunesse*, No. 41 (1986), 74–76.

Lizzy's Lion is Lee's " 'first storybook in verse.' " The book itself is lavish. With only fourteen four-line verses, there is not much reading. However, the illustrations are "generous." The reaction to the story, by real children, is very positive.

The Death of Harold Ladoo

D126 Fulford, Robert. "Memorial Poem Becomes a Bitter Confessional." *The Toronto Star*, 7 Aug. 1976, p. F5. Rpt. (revised — "Gangs of Honking Egos") in *The Montreal Star*, 14 Aug. 1976, p. D3.

The Death of Harold Ladoo is a "memorial poem" that turns "into a work of bitter confessional autobiography, a disillusioned view of the artist's place in the world, and a criticism of Lee's own generation of Canadian literary nationalists . . . ." It is one of the "most interesting" and "most eloquent" Canadian poems. Lee remembers first meeting Ladoo. They were immediate "friends and allies." Ladoo used people, and Lee used Ladoo. Yet "Lee affectionately mourns Ladoo's death . . . ." The theme of the poem is similar to that in *Civil Elegies*, but is expressed in more personal terms. Photographs of Lee and Ladoo are included in *The Toronto Star*.

D127 MacEwen, Gwendolyn. Rev. of *The Death of Harold Ladoo*. *Q & Q update* [*Quill & Quire*], 9 Sept. 1976, p. 13.

". . . Dennis Lee's work on the whole has been ignored because it has not been *understood*." Lee is "ahead of his/our times" and is "prophetic." There are strains of W.B. Yeats and Hart Crane in *The Death of Harold Ladoo*. This is a significant work. Lee is "an exponent of the *real*. . . . Here, the truth is spoken and the speaker is a very skilled craftsman, as well as a complex and major poet of our times."

D128 McNamara, Eugene. "In a High Clean Style." Rev. of *For My Brother Jesus*, by Irving Layton; *The Death of Harold Ladoo*, by Dennis Lee; and *Poems for American Daughters*, by C.H. Gervais. *Canadian Literature*, No. 78 (Autumn 1978), pp. 89, 90.

The Death of Harold Ladoo is "an elegy, a eulogy, a diary, a love letter, a cry of pain, an attempt at exorcism." The honesty is painful. Although Lee is writing fact, he maintains the persona of a "white liberal academic." Lee's diction is "spare, dry and minimal, befitting the pervasive tone of loss and grief." Although the style and subject of the poem is different from *Civil Elegies and Other Poems*, there are similarities like "the use of the self-mocking mask," and the "life-denying urban" contemporary society.

D129 Such, Peter. "Requiem for the Way It Was." *Books in Canada*, Nov. 1976, pp. 34, 36.

Lee "captures with eerie truth the contradictions in novelist Ladoo himself and the 'tough caring' that grew between him and those who encouraged him in his hectic, self-destructive literary career." Those who knew Ladoo will be "touched deeply by this poem." It could easily be a "postscript" to *Civil Elegies*. "Here are the same discursive philosophical lines, the same jazz-like alternations of different voices, the colloquial changes and rhythmic surprises . . . ." The "riskiness and honesty" is revelatory.

Savage Fields: An Essay in Literature and Cosmology

D130 Stuewe, Paul. Rev. of *Savage Fields: An Essay in Literature and Cosmology. Q & Q update* [*Quill & Quire*], 13 Oct. 1977, pp. 5–6.

Lee's criticism of Michael Ondaatje's *The Collected Works of Billy the Kid: Left Handed Poems*, "in terms of the 'world/earth' dichotomy," is commendable. But then Lee becomes "speculative," the results, less satisfactory. Lee is specific again in his appreciation of Leonard Cohen's *Beautiful Losers*. However, the structure of Lee's book does not reflect his "thought processes." Also, "relevant intellectual history" is missing in the book. Lee should have included others like Sigmund Freud and Georg Simmel "who anticipated most of the contents of its speculative sections." Nonetheless, this is the best criticism of Cohen and Ondaatje to date.

D131 Solecki, Sam. "In a Bad Time." *The Canadian Forum*, Oct. 1977, pp. 28–29.

Lee's book "moves beyond research and explication towards a statement about culture and society." He finds the "ontological and epistemological assumptions" of dominant liberalism to be "logically and psychologically untenable." In the footsteps of George Grant and Martin Heidegger, Lee argues that "civilization and instinct . . . remain in perpetual strife even within man himself." Lee's theme is too ambitious for the small amount of space in which he examines it. His "overview of western civilization suffers from being based on a very limited and highly idiosyncratic sampling of its contemporary prod-

ucts." Despite the book's shortcomings, Lee's "readings of *Billy the Kid* and *Beautiful Losers* are consistently intelligent and satisfying." Charles Steele responds to this review (D139).

D132 Symons, Scott. Rev. of *Savage Fields: An Essay in Literature and Cosmology. The Globe and Mail*, 12 Nov. 1977, Books, p. 43.

Lee's book possesses "Breadth, scope, profundity, force, insight . . . ." His analysis of Michael Ondaatje's *The Collected Works of Billy the Kid: Left Handed Poems* is "pungent." ". . . Lee provides us with a detected, analyzed, and confirmed new cosmology (and ontology) . . . for which Auschwitz seems a paradigm! . . . Lee is not as relentlessly honest as he needs to be" in recognizing "Occidental gliberalism" as the source of the savage fields. "At best . . . Lee half-admits this liberal parentage and in a footnote only." *Savage Fields: An Essay in Literature and Cosmology* "marks the coming-of-age of literary criticism in Canada. CanLitCrit can no longer be merely GritLitCrit; can no longer be merely the self-apotheosis of Methodist bush-gardeners."

D133 Nodelman, Perry. "Thinking against Thought: An Astonishing Book of Criticism." *Winnipeg Free Press*, 19 Nov. 1977, Leisure/Books, p. 6.

"*Savage Fields* is a book of paradoxes." It is a "thoughtful" book that "comes out against thought itself." This is "an agonizing" confession. "Lee's arguments . . . are not convincing." For example, he suggests "that the private hell Billy creates for himself to live in is the one we all inhabit." This is a misrepresentation of what Michael Ondaatje intended. The book is really "about Dennis Lee trying to come to terms with his own vision of the universe . . . ."

D134 Skelton, Robin. "The Element of Fire Is Not Quite Put Out." *Books in Canada*, Nov. 1977, p. 35.

"In this lucidly written and courageously speculative essay, Dennis Lee suggests that the 'liberal' cosmology . . . is no longer credible." Skelton examines Lee's use of Martin Heidegger's terms "world" and "earth" for the two forces we inhabit. Lee's analysis of Michael Ondaatje's *The Collected Works of Billy the Kid: Left Handed Poems* and Leonard Cohen's *Beautiful Losers* is "fascinating and perceptive." The problem Lee sets forth "may only be solvable" if man has a " 'soul' . . . distinct from . . . brain . . . ."

D135 Czarnecki, Mark. "Literature, Cosmology Fail to Unite." *The Toronto Star*, 3 Dec. 1977, p. D8.

Czarnecki notes, ". . . literature and cosmology have not been successfully united in Savage Fields." Lee provides "an enlightening framework" for Michael Ondaatje's *The Collected Works of Billy the Kid: Left Handed Poems*. However, ". . . his analysis diffuses and confuses itself by creating too many categories with not enough in them." Lee is convincing when he explains how, in *Beautiful Losers*, Leonard "Cohen wrote himself into a corner by writing his hero into an insane asylum." The book reflects a "poetic vision in the most encompassing senses of the term."

D136 Healy, J.J. "Literature and Cosmology: Lee's Provocative Prose Poem." *The Citizen* [Ottawa], 31 Dec. 1977, p. 41.

"*Savage Fields* is . . . enigmatic," "dense at times; difficult always. It teeters constantly on the thin edge of pretension." Lee's "genuine insight nibbles and wrestles with such persistent integrity that the hint of jargon recedes and we are left with a provocative prose-poem." Lee points to "conceptual problems beyond the domain of literary criticism," perhaps "beyond the range of any science of man so far developed."

D137 Jones, D.G. "Lee's Cosmology." *The Montreal Star*, 11 March 1978, p. D3.

In *Savage Fields: An Essay in Literature and Cosmology* ". . . our whole planetary reality is simultaneously a human construct and a natural phenomenon, 'world' and 'earth.' 'To be is to be in strife.' " Lee's reading of Michael Ondaatje's *The Collected Works of Billy the Kid: Left Handed Poems* and Leonard Cohen's *Beautiful Losers* is "highly illuminating," though controversial (see Stephen Scobie [C88]). This is an important book "giving to a familiar argument a radical new definition."

D138 Kertzer, J.M. "Letters in Canada: 1977. Humanities." *University of Toronto Quarterly*, 47 (Summer 1978), 454-55.

Savage Fields: An Essay in Literature and Cosmology "is interesting often simply because of its daring. . . . its strength is literary not philosophical." Lee quotes Martin Heidegger and Friedrich Nietzsche, but "D.H. Lawrence is a continual, unacknowledged, and perhaps unrecognized presence in the book, and Lee aims at a salvation for modern man no less radical or elusive than Lawrence's 'spontaneous-creative fullness of being.' " Margaret Atwood and Northrop Frye are two influences that "may explain why Lee refers only to Canadian authors though he takes as his province all modern literature, and why he finds Canadians in the vanguard of the avant-garde of modern thought." After a "competent" analysis of Michael Ondaatje's *The Collected Works of Billy the Kid: Left Handed Poems* and a "fine analysis of [Leonard] Cohen's *Beautiful Losers*, the essay falls off, and ends with a combination of confession, sermon, and pep talk."

D139 Steele, Charles. "A Map of Metaphor: The Poetic Vision of Canadian Criticism." Rev. of *Savage Fields*:

An Essay in Literature and Cosmology, by Dennis Lee; *Survival: A Thematic Guide to Canadian Literature*, by Margaret Atwood; *Butterfly on Rock: A Study of Themes and Images in Canadian Literature*, by D.G. Jones; *Sex and Violence in the Canadian Novel: The Ancestral Present*, by John Moss; and *The Haunted Wilderness: The Gothic and the Grotesque in Canadian Fiction*, by Margot Northey. *Book Forum* [Rhinecliff, N.Y.], 4, No. 1 (1978), 144–50.

Lee "unabashedly undertakes to oversee . . . modernism itself." Discussing only two texts, his generalizations are questionable. However, his analysis of Michael Ondaatje's *The Collected Works of Billy the Kid: Left Handed Poems* and Leonard Cohen's *Beautiful Losers* is "thorough and productive." Lee "confronts and explains" the "structural difficulties" of Cohen's novel. "Lee's cosmology . . . is structurally coherent." His vision is "bleak" but convincing. Steele responds to Sam Solecki's review (D131).

D140 Ross, Catherine. "5 Looks at Canadian Literature." Rev. of *Canadian Literature: Surrender or Revolution*, by Robin Mathews, ed. Gail Dexter; *The New Hero: Essays in Comparative Quebec/Canadian Literature*, by Ronald Sutherland; *Another Time*, by Eli Mandel; *Savage Fields: An Essay in Literature and Cosmology*, by Dennis Lee; and *Sex and Violence in the Canadian Novel: The Ancestral Present*, by John Moss. *Brick* [Ilderton, Ont.], No. 7 (Fall 1979), pp. 40, 41, 42–43.

Savage Fields: An Essay in Literature and Cosmology "is a work in which criticism can be a form of fiction with the critic as his own central protagonist." It is "a novel about the agonizing quest of a central consciousness to escape the implications of consciousness itself."

D141 Barbour, Douglas. " 'Fields' with Hope." *Brick* [Ilderton, Ont.], No. 11 (Winter 1981), pp. 6–7.

Savage Fields: An Essay in Literature and Cosmology is "both philosophically provocative and critically frustrating. . . . Lee's application of the term 'field' . . . is a brilliant stroke." Barbour does not agree that Lee's "interpenetrating fields" must be defined by a " 'savage play' . . . in irreconcilable conflict." Lee "singlemindedly" uses the concept of savage fields as a "method" of interpreting Michael Ondaatje's *The Collected Works of Billy the Kid: Left Handed Poems* and Leonard Cohen's *Beautiful Losers*. These "books are more multiplex" than Lee's system allows, although his commentaries are "interesting and provocative."

D142 Dragišic, Peggy. "Between the Intolerable and the Inscrutable." Rev. of *Savage Fields: An Essay in Literature and Cosmology* and *The Gods*. *Brick* [Ilderton, Ont.], No. 11 (Winter 1981), pp. 8–11, 12. Rpt. in *Brick* [Ilderton, Ont.], [A Brick Sampler, with Index], No. 12 (Spring 1981), pp. 57–61.

Lee has neither "Grant's faith" nor "a philosopher's learning and toughmindedness . . . ." Lee's system "is absolutist, undifferentiated, admitting of no exceptions, too breathtakingly simple to allow for judicious and critical discrimination, or to accommodate even *his own* 'philosophically inconsistent' objections and qualifications." Lee's analysis of Michael Ondaatje's *The Collected Works of Billy the Kid: Left Handed Poems* adds some clarity to the poem, "But, ultimately, the core meaning . . . its emotional and philosophical range is definitely truncated by a number of Lee's conclusions" and misread passages. In some instances, "a genius for killing can be seen to be kind." Lee omits many images "of human making that [are] not exploitive of earth, but cherishing . . . ." Lee "fails to distinguish among kinds of consciousness . . ." and is "paradoxically silent about poetic processes" and the imagination. He also neglects "choice," the creative act of " 'will.' " "Again, the wit of F's failure-that-is-nevertheless-a-success eludes Lee" in his analysis of Leonard Cohen's *Beautiful Losers*. And, "Because he feels he can't rest upon Cohen's Isis Continuum as a viable and true pattern for human being, he quite despairs, loses all critical flexibility, misreads the third section, . . . and bad-temperedly suggests much of the book should have been blotted." Nonetheless, ". . . *Savage Fields* invites critical thought . . . ."

Author & Editor: A Working Guide

D143 Wolfe, Morris. "Dramatic Readings: From Radio's Role in Canadian Theatre to the NFB's Annoying Habit of Dubbing French-Language Films." *Books in Canada*. "The Browser," May 1983, p. 29.
"No one who writes or edits books will want to be without *Author & Editor: A Working Guide* . . . ."

T.O. Now: The Young Toronto Poets

D144 Colombo, John Robert. "T.O. Now?". *The Tamarack Review*, No. 48 (Summer 1968), pp. 71–73.
Lee "conceived of *T.O. Now* as an extension of three earlier anthologies of contemporary poetry, Ryerson's *Poetry 62* and *Poetry 64* and Contact's *New Wave Canada*, and included the work of thirteen various young poets." Some of the poetry is good, but, as a whole, the book is "not a good guide to what is being written by the younger poets in Toronto these days." Lee has failed to include writing from the New Writers' Workshop at Three Schools, from Coach House Press (bpNichol and David Aylward in particular), and work of "unaffiliated poets" like Doug Enid and Lee himself.

D145 Barbour, Douglas. "Young Toronto Poets." *Canadian Literature*, No. 42 (Autumn 1969), pp. 87–88.
Not all the poets in *T.O. Now: The Young Toronto Poets* "are good poets, or even show signs of becoming so." Eight are enjoyable, and, of those eight, four are worth "re-reading."

D146 Purdy, A.W. Rev. of *T.O. Now: The Young Toronto Poets*. *The Canadian Forum*, Nov. 1968, pp. 181–82.
The age range, sixteen to twenty-five, of the thirteen poets in this anthology is "remarkable." Most of their styles are "modern," and most are "free from sentimentality." The world of these poets "is a black and dismal" one. They are, for the most part, superior writers to those in Raymond Souster's *New Wave Canada: The New Explosion in Canadian Poetry*.

The New Canadian Poets: 1970–1985

D147 Adachi, Ken. "Putting Honor Before Profit." *The Toronto Star*. "Books," 29 June 1985, p. M7.
Lee has included those with a first book published after 1970. This is an anthology "of riches prodigally offered." The poets "exhibit no common social or political schools of thought, no similar patterns of structure or semantics," which is exciting. A photograph of Lee is included.

D148 Sutherland, Fraser. "Poetry from the Flabby Generation." *The Globe and Mail* [Toronto], 13 July 1985, Entertainment, p. 13.
Sutherland decries the lack of "artistic principle" and innovation in today's poets. The anthology promotes poets akin to Lee's own circle. His introduction is "long" and "disjointed." He has chosen poets less for " 'quality' " than for "historical" and "esthetic concerns." A few poems "are spectacularly good." A photograph of Lee is included.

D149 Skelton, Robin. "Eclectic Poetic Energy Fires Lee's Anthology." *Quill & Quire*, Aug. 1985, p. 44.

The poets in this collection "reveal 'the confident and exuberant variety' of the period, and the poems chosen show the poets at their very best." However, a number of writers who "display approaches not represented elsewhere in the collection" are not included. The "schools of content" that Lee suggests — "Prairie Documentary, Feminist, Immigrant, and Daily Work" — are not likely used deliberately by the poets. "Lee is on more solid ground" in his discussion of the dominant use of vernacular. Skelton agrees with Lee that "This is an eclectic generation."

D150 King-Edwards, Lucille. "Class Distractions." *Books in Canada*, Oct. 1985, pp. 30, 32.

King-Edwards is suspicious of a book that "establishes a two-class ranking within itself." The first section consists of "20 poets at length. Part two contains the usual anthology coup de grâce of two to three poems each." It is a "safe" anthology, "not too many important toes have been stepped on here yet . . . readers and writers from each pocket of poetry across Canada will find at least one very fine poet neglected while someone with a bigger name in Toronto has taken their place."

D151 Keith, W.J. Rev. of *The New Canadian Poets, 1970–1985. Canadian Book Review Annual: 1985.* Ed. Ann Tudor and Dean Tudor. Toronto: Simon & Pierre, 1986, pp. 189–90.

Lee's book updates and supplements Eli Mandel's *Poets of Contemporary Canada: 1960–1970.* ". . . the book is most valuable for Lee's long, remarkable introduction, which is full of fresh observation and useful facts." This anthology demonstrates that ". . . there are numerous young and talented poets jockeying for attention, though it fails to identify any that can be described as pre-eminent."

D152 Smith, Patricia Keeney. "Poet Pie." *The Canadian Forum*, Feb. 1986, pp. 38, 39.

Lee gives us a "representative range" and a "discernible rhythm" in *The New Canadian Poets, 1970–1985.* The book has "shape and form. . . . contrast and connection, . . . enlightenment and surprise. . . . The book's major strengths are its belief in the art of poetry and its female voices." In Part II, ". . . some fine poets are either badly or far too briefly represented." Lee's introduction is mainly "helpful but highly provocative."

Selected Calendar Reviews

The Dennis Lee & Frank Newfeld 1979 Alligator Pie Calendar

D153 L., E.H. "This Calendar Is a Real Gem." *The St. Catharines Standard*, 18 Nov. 1978, p. 42.

This calendar, in addition to being a date-keeping device, is a gem of comic inspiration that will appeal to children of all ages as well as to adults.

D154 Amey, J. Larry. Rev. of *The Dennis Lee & Frank Newfeld 1979 Alligator Pie Calendar. In Review: Canadian Books for Children*, 13, No. 2 (Spring 1979), 42.

This is more than just a calendar. Uncle Bumper launches the year "by declaring that Dennis Lee and Frank Newfeld do not exist." The pictures are stilted but colourful, and the poems are terrific. Most of them are from *Alligator Pie* and *Garbage Delight*, although there are some new ones. The calendar is "A funny, clever, energetic and satisfying production."

D155 McGrath, Joan. Rev. of *The Dennis Lee & Frank Newfeld 1979 Alligator Pie Calendar. Canadian Materials*, 7, No. 1 (Winter 1979), 44.

Dennis Lee and Frank Newfeld have departed from their previous book format with this calendar. It is a good-humoured collection of new and old poems by Lee, vividly coloured drawings by Newfeld, and listings of historic events with a strong Canadian emphasis. The dates of important festivals of many nations are included. It will support the "classroom emphasis on multiculturalism in the cheeriest possible way . . . ."

The Dennis Lee & Frank Newfeld 1980 Alligator Pie Calendar

D156 Rev. of *The Gnomes Calendar 1980*, by R. Poortvliet and W. Huygen; and *The Dennis Lee & Frank Newfeld 1980 Alligator Pie Calendar*, by Dennis Lee, illus. Frank Newfeld. *St. John's Daily News*, 12 Oct. 1979.

Regardless of age, you will enjoy this calendar. It features the delightfully dizzy lines of Lee's poetry and the special events of each month. There are "great lines to learn and history to remember."

D157 "This Will Last All Year Long." *The St. Catharines Standard*, 27 Oct. 1979, p. 46.

The Dennis Lee & Frank Newfeld 1980 Alligator Pie Calendar is a real treasure for youngsters. The poems and drawings are delightful for young and old. The calendar is packaged for mailing. There is a folded sheet of Uncle Bumper's hand-puppets and puzzles. It is a great gift that will last all year long.

D158 Maynard, Fredelle. "Bright 1980 Beginning." *Chatelaine*. "Your Kids and Mine," Jan. 1980, p. 26.

Frank Newfeld's illustrations are bold and fanciful. The calendar includes the usual holidays, plus celebrations from around the world. There is an assortment of useful and utterly useless facts. It is "A crazy, captivating, authentically Canadian production."

D159 Heaney, Ellen. "Calendars." *In Review: Canadian Books for Canadian Children*, 14, No. 1 (Feb. 1980), 38.

Newfeld's brightly coloured illustrations and more of Lee's verses are included in this 1980 edition. Each month includes important dates along with fictitious information. Although it is not a library purchase, it is great for all fans.

Selected Lyrics Reviews

Fraggle Rock (L.p.; 1983)

D160 Hume, Christopher. Rev. of *Fraggle Rock*. *The Toronto Star*, 15 Sept. 1984, Audio/Video, p. F12.

Lee's lyrics "positively sparkle . . . . whatever Lee does he does well." These songs confirm Lee's reputation as one of the finest children's writers.

D161 Perry, Richard. "Choosing Concertos . . . Tunes for Tots . . . Adventures on Tape." *Quill & Quire*. "Juvenile," Nov. 1984, p. 29.

The *Fraggle Rock* songs show "a kind of musical Muppet anarchy clearly beloved by regimented school kids and office workers with Miss Piggy pinned to their corkboards." The lyrics are "clever enough," and the tunes ensure "the widest possible appeal." A photograph of five Fraggles is included.

Selected Audio-Visual Reviews

Alligator Pie and Other Poems

D162 Ryval, Michael. "Strictly Speaking." *Maclean's*, 6 Feb. 1978, p. 48b.

Even if distribution is not widespread, Caedmon believes the record is a "labour of love," which "should be available." A photograph is included.

D163 Goddard, Peter. "Alligator Pie and More Nutty Stories Are on Record." *The Toronto Star*. "Starship," 22 May 1978, p. D6.

This album is "full of crazy rhymes, nutty stories and all sorts of wonderful, weird things. . . . there's all kinds of word games, tongue twisters and brain busters that can drive you crazy." A photograph of Lee is included.

D164 Goddard, Peter. "Platters for Kids." Rev. of *Alligator Pie and Other Poems* (Caedmon), by Dennis Lee, music Don Heckman; *Sesame Street Fever* (Sesame Street), by Bee Gees et al.; and *Sgt. Pepper* (Capitol), by The Beatles. *Chatelaine*. "What's New," Dec. 1978, p. 12.

This album is "full of the kind of craziness that only a closet-kid like Lee would conjure up." Don Heckman contributed "interlude" music, ". . . but the real music comes from the ebb and flow of Lee's verse and the kids' reactions to it."

The Ordinary Bath

D165 Crew, Robert. "Alligator Pie a Holiday Feast." *The Toronto Star*, 16 Dec. 1983, p. D9.

". . . the show is liberally-flavored with wit and spiced with broad, childish humor. It's firmly rooted in the age-old tradition of nursery rhymes and Mother Goose, with unmistakable echoes of such people as Hilaire Belloc, Edward Lear and W.S. Gilbert."

D166 Thompson, Pat. Rev. of *The Ordinary Bath*. *Cinema Canada* [Toronto]. "Mini-Reviews," Jan. 1986, p. 37.

The film is a "cunning little kid-gem from Mirus Films." Although the film appears to be animated, ". . . in reality, Jon McKee's drawings for the book are manipulated to give them life." Lee's language is "gorgeous."

Index to Critics Listed in the Bibliography

Duncan Campbell Scott
An Annotated Bibliography

Laura Groening

Part II

Works on Duncan Campbell Scott

Acknowledgements

I would like to thank the many people whose work helped make this bibliography possible. Robert McDougall first introduced me to D.C. Scott and to the complexities of bibliographic studies in Canada, and the Department of English at Carleton University under Ian Cameron's chairmanship funded the initial research for the project. A Killam Postdoctoral Fellowship and an S.S.H.R.C. Canada Research Fellowship at Dalhousie University facilitated subsequent work. Leon Slonim located the place of first publication for most of Scott's poems in his remarkable Ph.D. dissertation, and Carole Gerson's ongoing commitment to Scott's fiction uncovered several previously undiscovered short stories in *The Christmas Globe* [Toronto]. The inter-library-loans staff at Carleton University and librarians throughout Canada (and one from the Maine State Public Library) have been unflaggingly helpful: I particularly appreciated being able to work with the National Library of Canada's collection of glorious nineteenth- and early twentieth-century periodicals. Stanley Dragland and Catherine E. Kelly, S.C.I.C., provided the first bibliographies that paved the way for so much Scott scholarship. Finally, thanks to Jennifer Boire and Rebecca Ansley for their aid with the final stages of the manuscript and to Ellen Quigley and the staff at ECW for their assistance.

Introduction

In his 1952 reminiscence "Travelling with a Poet" (C68), Pelham Edgar describes his 1906 journey into the wilderness with the poet D.C. Scott to sign Treaty No. 9 with the Ojibway and the Cree. Scott, a poet, and Edgar, with the soul of a poet, enjoyed the blissful, lazy canoe trip, their spirits becalmed by the extraordinary scenery: "We gloat over things — cloud effects, peeps of vistas through the islands as they shift past us, and lights and shadows on the water." They passed their time reading the *Oxford Book of Poetry*. Edgar had brought along *Shirley*, Charlotte Brontë's class-conscious novel, but it lay unread at the bottom of the canoe. The signing of an Indian Treaty was for these two men an experience of nature as the sublime. Social worries did not seem appropriate, for, as Edgar put it some forty-six years later,

> Ontario treats its Indian population with a fairness that amounts to generosity. Quebec refuses to recognize the Indian title to the waste lands of the Province, pays no annuities, and withholds reserves. Ontario, on the other hand, has purchased almost all its lands with a price and has conceded the Indians all the hunting and trading privileges which they have ever possessed.

According to Edgar, among the truly significant results of the Treaty expedition was the creation of a number of major poems by the hand of a man whose "authoritative experience" meant he had "no need to fabricate a spurious image of the 'noble savage.' "

Fifty years later, Brian Titley, in an article entitled "Duncan Campbell Scott and the Administration of Indian Affairs" (C236), describes his experience of reading through documents of treaty trips like the one Edgar recalls. Scott is presented by Titley as a man who misrepresents his attitudes and his power as a civil servant. He was — Titley uses the word three times in the one article — "draconian" in his implementation of the assimilationist aims and policies of the government that Edgar praised for moving with "slow dignity." Titley dismisses Scott's poetry and those who read his poetry. Most of the criticism, he says, "is of little value." Analysis of poetry is "an esoteric exercise at best." He would have us search for Scott's attitudes to the Native people "in readily comprehensible prose."

The story of Scott's reputation as a writer that lies between the extreme, opposite reactions of Pelham Edgar's aestheticism and Brian Titley's pragmatism suggests an interesting snapshot of the shifting intellectual response towards the indigenous peoples of Canada. Scott's career as a poet and civil servant spanned the first half of the twentieth century, a period relatively complacent about the lives of Native people even while it was somewhat anguished about non-Native cultural identity. Scott's long and varied career sheds light on both attitudes. (The best biography of Scott remains E.K. Brown's "Memoir" in his *Selected Poems of Duncan Campbell Scott*.) Born in Ottawa in 1862, he wrote poems, short stories, biography, criticism, and even an unpublished novel (now published and edited with an afterword by John Flood). He was a diligent editor who published four volumes of Archibald Lampman's poetry and co-edited the *Makers of Canada* series with Pelham Edgar. And he worked for the Department of Indian Affairs for over fifty years.

In 1879, Scott's father, a Methodist missionary to the Natives along the eastern shore of Lake Huron, on Manitoulin Island, and at Amherstburg, wrote to Prime Minister John A. Macdonald to request employment for a son he could not afford to educate further. Scott, at the age of seventeen, was installed at his civil service desk, where, as an employee of the government, he met the man who would shape his destiny: Archibald Lampman. It was Lampman who fired Scott's initial interest in poetry and it was Lampman's early death in 1899 that turned Scott into one of Canada's most dependable editors as he worked throughout his life to keep his friend's literary reputation alive. Together Scott and Lampman canoed into the wilderness that would engage so much of their best poetry. After Lampman's death, Scott continued to voyage out into reserve communities where he met many of the Native peoples who would inspire much of his creative writing.

Scott's writing, however, was slow to capture the critical acclaim awarded much more readily to Lampman, or even to other contemporaries such as Charles G.D. Roberts and Bliss Carman. Although the few early critics who chose to write about Scott often did so in superlatives, when Edgar first began to celebrate the work of a man who was also a friend and colleague (1919: C17), his was an almost solitary voice on behalf of an unusual poet, a poet whose work, A.J.M. Smith surmises (C40), was "quieter than that of any other poet of the group." How much easier it was to understand the idealist nature portraits of Archibald Lampman or the pure descriptive sonnets of Charles G.D. Roberts than it was to comprehend the difficult mysticism of "The Piper of Arll" (not addressed as such until 1960) (C84), the complexity of "The Height of Land" (C87), the apocalyptic nature of "Powassan's Drum" (C155), or the Darwinian regret of "The Onondaga Madonna" (C163). When Archibald MacMechan published *Headwaters of Canadian Literature* in 1924 (by which time Scott had published seven books of poetry), he devoted eight pages of discussion to Lampman, nine to Roberts, and seven to Carman. Scott appears only in passing as the biographer of Governor Simcoe: he is not mentioned as a poet.

The difficulty critics had with Scott's poetry can perhaps be illustrated by Bernard Muddiman's 1914 well-intentioned but contradictory article on four of Scott's poetry books and his first book of stories (C16). Noting the imita-

tive quality of *The Magic House*, Muddiman terms Scott's first book of poems "a volume of delightful minor verse." But he also qualifies his sense of influence by insisting that "it must not be thought that Duncan Scott is merely an imitator. These echoes are really not worth a second consideration. He is, when at his best, purely himself." It is with some surprise, therefore, that one encounters Muddiman praising Scott's second volume of verse precisely because of the presence of Browning, Meredith, Keats, and even Swift and Pope. To add to the confusion, while Muddiman says at the beginning of his review that Scott's work on French Canadians and Indians became the "body of his best work," when he turns to *New World Lyrics and Ballads*, he is tempted to call the volume as a whole a "temporary relapse" because of what he sees as the weaknesses in such Native poems as "The Mission of the Trees" and "The Forsaken."

In 1943, however, when E.K. Brown set out to recuperate and legitimize the Confederation poets in *On Canadian Poetry* (C41), he was captivated by the "restrained intensity" of the man who was also at this point the head of the Indian Affairs Department. Interestingly, Brown's interpretation of Scott's poetry is filled with echoes of earlier critics (Muddiman's "austerity," O.J. Stevenson's "restraint combined with intensity," the often noted uniqueness of the poems about Native peoples), but Brown's work on Scott is the first to gather together these fugitive words of praise and apply them in a systematic, critical fashion to Scott's body of work. "Of all Canadian poets," Brown writes, "indeed of all Canadian imaginative writers, he has best succeeded in making great literature out of such distinctively Canadian material as our aborigines supply." With Brown, attention focused on the "Indian" poems. A.J.M. Smith, who had called "At Gull Lake" a masterpiece in *The Book of Canadian Poetry* (1943), Desmond Pacey (C62), and Roy Daniells (C97) joined Brown in an enthusiastic response to what they identified as sympathetic images of a threatened people. Even Northrop Frye (C70), sceptical of Scott's work as a whole ("Whatever one thinks of the total merit of Scott's very uneven output . . ."), called the existence of a body of poetry that encompassed both "The Forsaken" and "Ode on a Seventeenth Century Theme" an "imaginative balance that is characteristic of so much of the best in Canadian culture down to the present generation."

From 1961 on, there has been the kind of steady, critical investigation of Scott's writing that suggests an established, canonical writer. Although Scott is most valued as a poet, his reputation as a short story writer is quietly consistent, with commentary extending from Raymond Knister's early enthusiasm in 1927 (C27) to William New's sophisticated handling of the genre in 1987 (C244). Stan Dragland reissued several of Scott's short stories as *In the Village of Viger and Other Stories* (A16), and he edited *Duncan Campbell Scott: A Book of Criticism* (C2). The University of Ottawa devoted its 1979 annual symposium to Scott (C3). In addition to publishing the conference proceedings, the University has published a second selection of Scott's stories (A15). Carole Gerson has done serious work uncovering many of the uncollected short stories. Nevertheless, Dragland's comment in the introduction to *A Book of Criticism* (1974) is still relevant today. There is "too little" criticism of Scott's fiction, he said, "to balance the larger body of poetry critiques."

The body of poetry critiques, on the other hand, is indeed quite healthy, with articles devoted to all aspects of Scott's poetry, from his thematics to his prosody (C195, C215, C259). If any one poem has been singled out for significant attention, it would have to be "The Piper of Arll." This poem aside, the most sustained study has been devoted to Scott's writing about Native peoples. Much of the criticism devoted to this now-controversial work has shown an awareness of the complexities of the highly charged social questions implicitly raised by Scott's writing. Gerald Lynch, for example, seeks to answer the questions

> do the Indian poems reveal a *fixed* attitude on Scott's part? Is it the literary critic's province to reconcile or

to emphasize discrepancies between Scott the Deputy Superintendent General of Indian Affairs, Scott the wilderness traveller negotiating treaties, and Scott the poet? And finally, what does an examination of the Indian poems tell us about their success or failure on their own terms? (C209).

Glenys Stowe takes a more psychological approach to Scott's writing, arguing that the Native poems reveal "psychic conflict" between reason and emotion. "In the deaths of Akoose and Keejigo, as in that of the woman in "The Forsaken," Scott seems to reach a reconciliation of his warring elements, and an acceptance of both his instinctive and his cerebral drives" (C142). Lee Meckler believes that "The Forsaken" consciously demonstrates "the encroachment and effect of European values on those of the Indians" (C164). Leon Slonim, among others investigating the historical basis of many of the poems (and stories), explains the dynamic relationship between Scott's retelling and the original versions of the tales (C170, C171, C174, C189).

Running alongside this solid appreciation of Scott's literary representations of Native peoples, however, has been a small, discontented voice in response to the depictions of indigenous Canadians. Some critics, literary and social, have begun to study Scott less as a writer than as a civil servant, even to the point of marvelling, as S.D. Grant (C223) and Brian Titley do, that Scott the poet is better known than Scott the civil servant. E. Palmer Patterson suggests John Collier's respect for the Pueblo culture of the United States as an alternative to Scott's views on Canadian Indians (C112), and Keiichi Hirano defines Scott as having a "humane society" attitude (C91). John Flood has written a volume of poems (C149) inspired by what he calls elsewhere Scott's "duplicity" (C158). Perhaps it is symptomatic of this frustration that *Copperfield* has published under the title "Extracts from D.C. Scott's Own Journal of 1905 & 1906" passages recorded during the 1906 James Bay Treaty Expedition that were in fact Pelham Edgar's, not Scott's (B264).

It is an oddity of Scott criticism that Brian Titley's carefully researched *A Narrow Vision* is at this point the only full-length, single author study of Duncan Campbell Scott and the book is devoted to his career as a civil servant.

The story of Scott's relationship to the Native peoples is every bit as complicated as the many critical responses outlined here might suggest. Scott was indeed a white assimilationist who, as Ojibway poet Armand Garnet Ruffo writes, "Asks much about yesterday, little about today / and acts as if he knows tomorrow."[1] But he was also a man who urged inter-racial marriage and voting rights at a period in history when the most obvious social alternative was provided by his American neighbours who relegated their African-American population to a system of racial segregation. He was a civil servant who implemented the residential school system and cut the health budget for Native Canadians, but he was also enraged by the injustice manifested by the fact that for the non-Native trader, the Native was "but a slave, used . . . as a tool to provide wealth, and therefore to be kept in good condition as cheaply as possible." Perhaps most important, for purposes of this literary bibliography, Scott was a poet who argued that "Working without conscious plan and merely repeating to themselves, as it were, what they have learned of life from experience, or conveying the hints that intuition has whispered to them, [poets] awaken in countless souls sympathetic vibrations of beauty and ideality." As such a poet, he tried, among other things, to capture the moment of transition that he saw as definitive in the life of Native peoples: he saw not just government "charges" but a New World illustration of what Matthew Arnold, *his* favourite poet, described as "Wandering between two worlds, one dead, / The other powerless to be born."

NOTE

[1] "Poems for Duncan Campbell Scott," *Gatherings: The En'owkin Journal of First North American Peoples* 2 (1991), 173.

Part 1

Works by Duncan Campbell Scott

A   Books (Poetry, Short Stories, Novel, Miscellaneous Non-Fiction, Mixed Genre Collection, Criticism, Published Letters, and Books Edited), Pamphlets, Poems Privately or Separately Printed (Including Christmas-Card Poems), Lyrics, Adaptation, Editorial Work, and Manuscripts

Poetry

A1   *The Magic House and Other Poems*. London: Methuen, 1893. 95 pp.
_____ . Ottawa: J. Durie, 1893. 95 pp.
_____ . Boston: Copeland and Day, 1895. 95 pp.
    Includes "Above St. Irénée" (A34), "At Les Eboulements [The bay is set with ashy sails,]" (B6), "At Scarboro' Beach" (B32), "At the Cedars," "At the Lattice," "La Belle Feronière," "By the Willow Spring," "The End of the Day" (B21), "The Fifteenth of April," "The First Snow," "A Flock of Sheep" (B34), "For Remembrance" (B15), "From the Farm on the Hill" (B9), "The Hill Path" (B1), "The Ideal," "An Impromptu [The stars are in the ebon sky,]," "In an Old Quarry," "In November" (B17), "In the Country Churchyard," "In the House of Dreams," "Life and Death," "A Little Song," "The Magic

House" (B8), "Memory," "A Memory of the 'Inferno,'" "The Message," "Night and the Pines," "A Night in June" (B25), "A Night in March," "A November Day" (B12), "Off Rivière du Loup" (B58), "Off the Isle Aux Coudres" (B30), "Ottawa [City about whose brow the north winds blow]," "A Portrait," "The Reed-Player" (B13), "The River Town" (B16), "September" (B29), "The Silence of Love," "The Sleeper" (B33), "Song [Here's the last rose,]" (B18), "Song [I have done,]" (B4), "A Summer Storm," "To Winter [Come, O thou conqueror of the flying year;]," "To Winter [Come, O thou season of intense repose;]," "The Voice and the Dusk" (B19), "Written in a Copy of Archibald Lampman's Poems" (B5), and "Youth and Time" (B3).

A2   *Labor and the Angel*. Boston: Copeland and Day, 1898. 59 pp.
    Includes the following poems: "Adagio," "Afterwards," "Angelus," "At Les Éboulements [A glamour on the phantom shore]" (A34), "Avis," "The Cup" (A37), "The Dame Regnant," "Dirge for a Violet," "Equation," "From Shadow," "A Group of Songs: The Canadian's Home-Song [A39 — "The Canadian's Home Song from Abroad"], Madrigal [B49], A Song [In the ruddy heart of the sunset,], Song [Sorrow is come like a swallow to nest,], A Song ['Tis autumn and down in the fields] [B47], A Song. To B.W.B. [The world is spinning for change,], Song [When the ash-tree buds and the maples,] [B45], Song [The wind is wild to-night,], Spring Song [Sing me a song of the early spring,] [B37], Summer Song [B42], Autumn Song [B11], Winter Song [B36], Words after Music," "The Happy Fatalist," "The Harvest" (B35), "In May" (B40), "Labor and the Angel," "The Lesson [When the great day is done,], [Dear God! to whom the bravest of us is a child],"

"March" (B44), "On the Mountain" (B41), "The Onondaga Madonna" (B39), "The Piper of Arll" (B43), "Rain and the Robin" (B38), "Stone Breaking" (B51), "The Violet Pressed in a Copy of Shakespeare," "Watkwenies," "When Spring Goes By," and "The Wolf."

A3   *New World Lyrics and Ballads.* Notes Duncan Campbell Scott. Toronto: Morang, 1905. 65–66, 66 pp.

Includes "At the End," "The Builder," "Catnip Jack," "Dominique de Gourgues," "Dulce [sic] Gathering," "The Forgers," "The Forsaken" (B63), "The House of the Broken-Hearted," "Indian Place-Names," "Life and a Soul," "The Mission of the Trees," "A Nest of Hepaticas," "Night Hymns on Lake Nepigon [sic]" (B52), "On the Way to the Mission," "Peace," "Rapids at Night" (B61), "Roses on the Portage" (B65), "The Sea by the Wood" (B56), "Twin-Flowers on the Portage" (B53), "The Wood by the Sea" (B57), and "The Wood Peewee."

A4   *Via Borealis.* Decorations A.H. Howard. Toronto: Wm. Tyrrell, 1906. 21 pp.

Includes "Dream Voyageurs," "Ecstasy" (B68), "The Half-Breed Girl" (B70), "An Impromptu [Here in the pungent gloom]," "Night Burial in the Forest," "Song [Creep into my heart, creep in, creep in,]," and "Spring on Mattagami."

A5   *Lundy's Lane and Other Poems.* New York: George H. Doran, 1916. 194 pp.

————. Toronto: McClelland, Goodchild and Stewart, 1916. 194 pp.

Includes "Angel," "The Apparition" (B92), "At Sea," "At the Gill-Nets," "At William MacLennan's Grave" (B69), "The Battle of Lundy's Lane," "The Beggar and the Angel," "By a Child's Bed," "Christ-mas Folk-Song," "The Closed Door," "Elizabeth Speaks," "Fantasia," "Feuilles d'Automne," "Fragment of an Ode to Canada" (B80), "From Beyond," "Frost Magic: I–II," "The Ghost's Story" (B59), "The Height of Land," "Improvisation on an Old Song," "In Snow-Time" (B72), "The Leaf," "A Legend of Christ's Nativity" (B50), "Lines in Memory of Edmund Morris" (A42), "A Love Song [I gave her a rose in early June]" (B60), "The Lover to His Lass" (B76), "Madonna with Two Angels," "Meditation at Perugia" (B71), "Mid-August," "Mist and Frost," "A Mystery Play," "New Year's Night, 1916," "Night" (B67), "The November Pansy," "O Turn Once More," "Retrospect," "The Sailor's Sweetheart," "Three Songs: I [Where love is life], II [Nothing came here but sunlight], III [I have songs of dancing pleasure]," "To a Canadian Lad Killed in the War" (B78), "To the Heroic Soul [I. Nurture thyself, O Soul! II. Be strong, O Warring Soul!]" (B66), *Via Borealis*: Dream Voyageurs [A4], Ecstasy [B68], The Half-Breed Girl [B70], An Impromptu [Here in the pungent gloom] [A4], Night Burial in the Forest [A4], Song: Creep into My Heart [A4], Spring on Mattagami [A4]," "Willow Pipes" (B75), and "The Wood-Spring to the Poet."

A6   *To the Canadian Mothers and Three Other Poems.* Toronto: Mortimer, 1917. 18 pp.

Sold for the Benefit of the Prisoners of War Fund.

Includes "Somewhere in France," "To a Canadian Aviator Who Died for His Country in France" (B79), "To a Canadian Lad Killed in the War" (B78), and "To the Canadian Mothers."

A7   *Beauty and Life.* Toronto: McClelland and Stewart, 1921. 96 pp.

Includes "After a Night of Storm" (B84), "After Battle," "Afterwards" (A2), "The Anatomy of Melancholy" (B85), "Bells," "By the Shore," "The Eagle Speaks" (B83), "The Enigma," "The Fallen" (B111), "The Flight," "The Fragment of a Letter," "Idle to Grieve," "Impromptu [Bring your cherished beauty]," "In Grenada," "In the Selkirks," "In Winter," "Last Year," "Leaves" (B86), "Lilacs and Humming Birds," "Lines on a Monument," "The Lovers" (B94), "A Masque," "Ode for the Keats Centenary," "On the Death of Claude Debussy," "Portrait of Mrs. Clarence Gagnon," "Question and Answer," "Reverie" (B87), "A Road Song" (B82), "Senza Fine," "Somewhere in France," "Song [Lay thy cheek to mine, love,]," "Spirit and Flesh," "Threnody [Now the only debt that can be paid to her]," "To a Canadian Aviator who Died for his Country in France" (B79), "To the Canadian Mothers" (A6), "The Tree, the Birds, and the Child," "Variations on a Seventeenth Century Theme," "A Vision," and "The Water Lily."

A8   *The Poems of Duncan Campbell Scott*. Toronto: McClelland and Stewart, 1926. 341 pp.

_____ . Foreword John Masefield. London: J.M. Dent, 1927. [1–4], 341 pp.

Includes "Above St. Irénée" (A34), "Adagio" (A2), "After a Night of Storm" (B84), "After Battle" (A7), "Afterwards" (A2), "The Anatomy of Melancholy" (B85), "Angel" (A5), "Angelus" (A2), "The Apparition" (B92), "At Dawning," "At Les Eboulements [The bay is set with ashy sails,]" (B6), "At Sea," "At the Cedars" (A1), "At the End" (A3), "At the Gill-Nets" (A5), "At the Piano," "At William Maclennan's Grave" (B69), "An August Mood" (A43), "Avis" (A2), "The Battle of Lundy's Lane" (A5), "Bells" (A7), "The Builder" (A3), "By a Child's Bed" (A5), "By the Shore" (A7), "By the Willow Spring" (A1), "The Canadian's Home-Song" (A39 — "The Canadian's Home Song from Abroad"), "Catnip

Jack" (A3), "Christmas Folk-Song" (A5), "The Closed Door" (A5), "The Cup" (A37), "The Dame Regnant" (A2), "Dedication of 'In the Village of Viger,' 1896," "Dedication of Labour and the Angel, 1898, to my Wife," "Dirge for a Violet" (A2), "Dominique de Gourgues" (A3), "Dream Voyageurs" (A4), "Dreams and Memories," "Dulse Gathering" (A3), "The Eagle Speaks" (B83), "Early Morning," "Ecstasy" (B68), "Elizabeth Speaks" (A5), "The End of the Day" (B21), "The Enigma" (A7), "Equation" (A2), "The Fallen" (B111), "Fantasia" (A5), "The Fifteenth of April" (A1), "The First Snow" (A1), "A Flock of Sheep" (B34), "The Flight" (A7), "For Remembrance" (B15), "The Forgers" (A3), "The Forsaken" (B63), "The Fragment of a Letter" (A7), "Fragment of an Ode to Canada" (B80), "Frost Magic: I–II" (A5), "The Ghost's Story" (B59), "The Half-Breed Girl" (B70), "The Happy Fatalist" (A2), "The Harvest" (B35), "The Height of Land" (A5), "The Hill Path" (B1), "The House of the Broken-Hearted" (A3), "I Do Not Ask," "The Ideal" (A1), "Idle to Grieve" (A7), "An Impromptu [Here in the pungent gloom]" (A4), "An Impromptu [The stars are in the ebon sky,]" (A1), "Improvisation on an Old Song," "In Grenada" (A7), "In May" (B40), "In November" (B17), "In Snow-Time" (B72), "In the Country Churchyard" (A1), "In the House of Dreams" (A1), "In the Selkirks" (A7), "In Winter" (A7), "Indian Place-Names" (A3), "The Journey" (B99), "June Lyrics," "Labour and the Angel" (A2), "Last Year" (A7), "The Leaf" (A5), "Leaves" (B86), "A Legend of Christ's Nativity" (B50), "The Lesson [When the great day is done,], [Dear God! to whom the bravest of us is a child]" (A2), "Life and a Soul" (A3), "Life and Death" (A1), "Lilacs and Humming Birds" (A7), "Lines in Memory of Edmund Morris" (A42), "Lines on a Monument" (A7), "A Little While," "The Lovers" (B94), "The Lower St. Lawrence," "The Mad Girl's Song," "Madonna with Two Angels" (A5), "Madrigal" (B49), "The Magic House" (B8), "March" (B44), "A Masque" (A7), "Meditation at Perugia" (B71), "Memory" (A1), "Mid-August" (A5), "The Mission of the Trees" (A3), "Mist and Frost" (A5), "A Mood," "The Mower," "Morning at Paramé" (B97), "A Mystery Play" (A5), "A Nest of Hepaticas" (A3), "The New Moon with the Old Moon," "New Year's Night, 1916" (A5), "Night" (B67), "Night and the Pines" (A1), "Night Burial in the Forest" (A4), "Night Hymns on Lake Nipigon" (B52), "A Night in June" (B25), "A Night in March" (A1), "The November Pansy" (A5), "O Turn Once More" (A5), "Ode for the Keats Centenary" (A7), "Off Rivière du Loup" (B58), "Off the Isle Aux Coudres" (B30), "An Old Tune" (B95), "On the Death of Claude Debussy" (A7), "On the Mountain" (B41), "On the Way to the Mission" (A3), "The Onondaga Madonna" (B39), "Ottawa [City about whose brow the north winds blow]" (A1), "Permanence" (B90), "The Piper of Arll" (B43), "Portrait of Mrs. Clarence Gagnon" (A7), "Powassan's Drum," "Prairie Wind," "Prayer and Answer," "Prologue," "Question and Answer" (A7), "Rain and the Robin" (B38), "Rapids at Night" (B61), "The Reed-Player" (B13), "Retrospect" (A5), "Reverie" (B87), "A Road Song" (B82), "Roses on the Portage" (B65), "The Sailor's Sweetheart" (A5), "The Sea by the Wood" (B56), "Senza Fine" (A7), "September" (B29), "Somewhere in France" (A7), "Song [Creep into my heart, creep in, creep in,]" (A4), "Songs of Four Seasons: Spring [B37], Summer [B42], Autumn [B11], Winter [B36]," "Spirit and Flesh" (A7), "Spring Night" (B96), "Spring on Mattagami" (A4), "A Summer Storm" (A1), "Thirteen Songs: I, II, III, IV, V, VI [B45], VII, VIII, IX, X [B18], XI [B4], XII, XIII [A7 — "Song (Lay thy cheek to mine, love,)"]," "Thoughts," "To a Canadian Aviator Who Died for His Country in France" (B79), "To a Canadian Lad Killed in the War" (B78), "To the Canadian Mothers, 1914–1918" (A6), "To the Heroic Soul [I. Nurture thyself, O Soul! II. Be strong, O Warring Soul!]" (B66), "The Tree, the Birds, and the Child" (A7), "Twin-Flowers on the Portage" (B53), "Two Lyrics: I [Echo on the moonlit hill] [B88], II [If my heart were never moved to sadness] [B89]," "Variations on a Seventeenth Century Theme" (A7), "The Violet pressed in a Copy of Shakespeare" (A2), "A Vision" (A7), "The Voice and the Dusk" (B19), "The Water Lily" (A7), "Watkwenies" (A2), "When Spring Goes By" (A2), "Willow-Pipes" (B75), "The Wolf" (A2), "The Wood by the Sea" (B57), "The Wood Peewee" (A3), "The Wood-Spring to the Poet" (A5), "Words after Music," and "Youth and Time" (B3).

A9   *The Green Cloister: Later Poems*. Toronto: McClelland and Stewart, 1935. 96 pp.

Includes "At East Gloucester," "At Gull Lake: August 1810," "At Lodore," "At Palma," "At Sunset," "Autumn Evening," "The Bells: Sleep and Sleeplessness," "A Blackbird Rhapsody," "By the Sea" (B98), "By the Sea Shore," "Chiostro Verde," "Como," "Compline," "The Dreaming Eagle," "Earliest Morning," "En Route" (A47), "Enigma," "Evening at Ravello," "The Faithful," "A Fancy" (B102), "The Fields of Earth," "From the Headland," "A Group of Lyrics: I [O Wave that breaks far out at sea!], II [Where there was sea the mountains stand], III [Twilight had formed a lovely rose,], IV [The rose shall fade]," "Imogen's Wish," "In Algonquin Park," "In the Rocky Mountains," "January Evening," "Kensington Gardens," "The Nightwatchman," "On a Drawing of a Hand," "On Ragleth Hill," "Past and Present" (B120), "A Prairie Water Colour," "Reality" (B103), "A Scene at Lake

Manitou," "A Secret," "A Song [Moments fall from the hour]," "The Spider and the Rose," "Spring in the Valley," "Time, the Victor," "The Touch of Winter," "Twilight," "Under Stars," and "The Wise Men from the East" (B101).

A10   *Selected Poems of Duncan Campbell Scott.* Ed. and memoir E.K. Brown. Toronto: Ryerson, 1951. xi–xlii, 176 pp.

    Includes "Above St. Irénée" (A34), "Adagio" (A2), "After Battle" (A7), "Amanda" (B112), "At Gull Lake: August, 1810" (A9), "At Sunset" (A9), "At the Gill-Nets" (A5), "At the Piano" (A8), "At William Maclennan's Grave" (B69), "An August Mood" (A43), "Avis" (A2), "Before the Silence" (B119), "Bells" (A7), "A Blackbird Rhapsody" (A9), "By a Child's Bed" (A5), "By the Shore" (A7), "The Canadian's Home-Song" (A39 — "The Canadian's Home Song from Abroad"), "The Closed Door" (A5), "Como" (A9), "Compline" (A9), "Early Morning" (A8), "The End of the Day" (B21), "The Fallen" (B111), "Fantasia" (A5), "The Fields of Earth" (A9), "The Fifteenth of April" (A1), "For Remembrance" (B15), "The Forsaken" (B63), "Frost Magic: I–II" (A5), "The Half-Breed Girl" (B70), "The Harvest" (B35), "The Height of Land" (A5), "The Ideal" (A1), "An Impromptu [Here in the pungent gloom]" (A4), "In May" (B40), "In Snow-Time" (B72), "In the Country Churchyard" (A1), "In the Selkirks" (A7), "Indian Place-Names" (A3), "June Lyrics" (A8), "Last Year" (A7), "Leaves" (B86), "The Lesson [When the great day is done,], [Dear God! to whom the bravest of us is a child]" (A2), "Life and a Soul" (A3), "Lines in Memory of Edmund Morris" (A42), "The Lovers" (B94), "The Mad Girl's Song" (A8), "The Magic House" (B8), "March" (B44), "Meditation at Perugia" (B71), "Memory" (A1), "Mid-August" (A5), "Morning at Paramé" (B97), "A Nest of Hepaticas" (A3), "New Year's Night, 1916" (A5), "Night" (B67), "Night and the Pines" (A1), "Night Burial in the Forest" (A4), "Night Hymns on Lake Nipigon" (B52), "A Night in March" (A1), "The November Pansy" (A5), "O Turn Once More" (A5), "Ode for the Keats Centenary" (A7), "Off the Isle Aux Coudres" (B30), "Old Olives at Bordighera" (B106), "On the Death of Claude Debussy" (A7), "On the Way to the Mission" (A3), "The Onondaga Madonna" (B39), "Permanence" (B90), "The Piper of Arll" (B43), "Powassan's Drum" (A8), "Prairie Wind" (A8), "Rapids at Night" (B61), "Reality" (B103), "The Reed-Player" (B13), "Retrospect" (A5), "The Sailor's Sweetheart" (A5), "The Sea by the Wood" (B56), "A Song [In the air there are no coral-]" (B105), "Songs of Four Seasons: Spring [B37], Summer [B42], Autumn [B11], Winter [B36]," "The Spider and the Rose" (A9), "Spring Night" (B96), "Spring on Mattagami" (A4), "Thirteen Songs: III [A8], VI [B45], VIII [A8], XI [B4], XIII [A7 — "Song (Lay thy cheek to mine, love,)"]," "Thoughts" (A8), "To a Canadian Aviator Who Died for His Country in France" (B79), "To a Canadian Lad Killed in the War" (B78), "To the Canadian Mothers, 1914–1918" (A6), "To the Heroic Soul [I. Nurture thyself, O Soul! II. Be strong, O Warring Soul!]" (B66), "Twelfth Anniversary" (A20), "Veronique Fraser" (B107), "The Voice and the Dusk" (B19), "The Water Lily" (A7), "Watkwenies" (A2), "The Wood by the Sea" (B57), "The Wood Peewee" (A3), "The Wood-Spring to the Poet" (A5), and "Youth and Time" (B3).

A11   *Duncan Campbell Scott: Selected Poetry.* Ed. and biog. note Glenn Clever. Ottawa: Tecumseh, 1974. v–viii, 121 pp.

    Includes "After Battle" (A7), "Amanda" (B112), "At Delos" (B108), "At Gull Lake, 1810" (A9),

"Autumn Evening" (A9), "By a Child's Bed" (A5), "By the Sea Shore" (A9), "The Canadian's Home-Song" (A39 — "The Canadian's Home Song from Abroad"), "Chiostro Verde" (A9), "The Closed Door" (A5), "Como" (A9), "Compline" (A9), "Evening at Ravello" (A9), "The Forsaken" (B63), "The Half-Breed Girl" (B70), "The Harvest" (B35), "The Height of Land" (A5), "The Ideal" (A1), "In May" (B40), "In the Country Churchyard" (A1), "In the Selkirks" (A7), "Indian Place-Names" (A3), "Kensington Gardens" (A9), "The Lesson [When the great day is done,], [Dear God! to whom the bravest of us is a child]" (A2), "Life and Soul" (A3), "Lines in Memory of Edmund Morris" (A42), "Man to Nature" (A20), "Meditation at Perugia" (B71), "Nature to Man" (A20), "Night and the Pines" (A1), "Night Burial in the Forest" (A4), "Night Hymns on Lake Nipigon" (B52), "O Turn Once More" (A5), "Ode for the Keats Centenary" (A7), "Old Olives at Bordighera" (B106), "On a Drawing of a Hand" (A9), "On the Way to the Mission" (A3), "The Onondaga Madonna" (B39), "The Piper of Arll" (B43), "Powassan's Drum" (A8), "Rapids at Night" (B61), "Reality" (B103), "Retrospect" (A5), "The Sailor's Sweetheart" (A5), "A Scene at Lake Manitou" (A9), "The Sea by the Wood" (B56), "The Sea-Witch" (A20), "A Song [In the air there are no coral-]" (B105), "Song [When the ash-tree buds and the maples,]" (B45), "Songs of Four Seasons: Spring [B37], Summer [B42], Autumn [B11], Winter [B36]," "Spring on Mattagami" (A4), "Thirteen Songs: XIII [A7 — "Song (Lay thy cheek to mine, love,)"], "To the Heroic Soul [I. Nurture thyself, O Soul! II. Be strong, O Warring Soul!]" (B66), "Veronique Fraser" (B107), "Watkwenies" (A2), "The Wise Men from the East" (B101), "The Wood by the Sea" (B57), and "Youth and Time" (B3).

A12   *Powassan's Drum: Poems of Duncan Campbell Scott.* Ed. Raymond Souster and Douglas Lochhead. Foreword Raymond Souster. Preface Douglas Lochhead. Ottawa: Tecumseh, 1985. ix–x, xi–xii, 200 pp.

Includes "Afterwards" (A2), "Amanda" (B112), "Angelus" (A2), "At Gull Lake: August, 1810" (A9), "At the Cedars" (A1), "At the End" (A3), "At William Maclennan's Grave" (B69), "The Battle of Lundy's Lane" (A5), "By a Child's Bed" (A5), "By the Willow Spring" (A1), "The Canadian's Home-Song" (A39 — "The Canadian's Home Song from Abroad"), "Catnip Jack" (A3), "The Closed Door" (A5), "The Cup" (A37), "Dedication of 'In the Village of Viger,' 1896" (A13 — "To My Daughter Elizabeth Duncan Scott"), "Dirge for a Violet" (A2), "Dulce [sic] Gathering" (A3), "The Eagle Speaks" (B83), "Ecstasy" (B68), "The Fifteenth of April" (A1), "The First Snow" (A1), "A Flock of Sheep" (B34), "For Remembrance" (B15), "The Forsaken" (B63), "The Fragment of a Letter" (A7), "From the Farm on the Hill" (B9), "The Ghost's Story" (B59), "The Half-Breed Girl" (B70), "The Harvest" (B35), "The Height of Land" (A5), "An Impromptu [Here in the pungent gloom]" (A4), "In May" (B40), "In Snow-Time" (B72), "In the Country Churchyard" (A1), "In Winter" (A7), "Indian Place-Names" (A3), "June Lyrics" (A8), "Labour and the Angel" (A2), "Last Year" (A7), "Leaves" (B86), "The Lesson [Dear God! to whom the bravest of us is a child]" (A2), "The Lesson [When the great day is done,]" (A2), "Life and a Soul" (A3), "Life and Death" (A1), "Lines in Memory of Edmund Morris" (A42), "March" (B44), "Meditation at Perugia" (B71), "Mid-August" (A5), "A Nest of Hepaticas" (A3), "New Year's Night, 1916" (A5), "Night and the Pines" (A1), "Night Burial in the Forest" (A4), "Night Hymns on Lake Nipigon" (B52), "A Night in June" (B25), "A November Day" (B12), "The

November Pansy" (A5), "O Turn Once More" (A5), "Off Rivière du Loup" (B58), "Off the Isle Aux Coudres" (B30), "Old Olives at Bordighera" (B106), "On the Death of Claude Debussy" (A7), "On the Way to the Mission" (A3), "The Onondaga Madonna" (B39), "The Orchard in Moonlight" (A20), "Ottawa [City about whose brow the north winds blow]" (A1), "The Piper of Arll" (B43), "A Portrait" (A1), "Portrait of Mrs. Clarence Gagnon" (A7), "Powassan's Drum" (A8), "Rapids at Night" (B61), "Reality" (B103), "The Reed-Player" (B13), "Retrospect" (A5), "Reverie" (B87), "Roses on the Portage" (B65), "The Sailor's Sweetheart" (A5), "The Sea by the Wood" (B56), "Senza Fine" (A7), "September" (B29), "A Song [In the air there are no coral-]" (B105), "Song [Sorrow is come like a swallow to nest]" (A2 — "A Group of Songs: Song [Sorrow is come like a swallow to nest,]"), "Spring on Mattagami" (A4), "A Summer Storm" (A1), "To the Heroic Soul [I. Nurture thyself, O Soul! II. Be strong, O Warring Soul!]" (B66), "The Tree, the Birds, and the Child" (A7), "Twelfth Anniversary" (A20), "Twin Flowers on the Portage" (B53), "Veronique Fraser" (B107), "The Violet Pressed in a Copy of Shakespeare" (A2), "The Water Lily" (A7), "Watkwenies" (A2), "Willow-Pipes" (B75), "The Wood Peewee" (A3), "The Wood-Spring to the Poet" (A5), and "Written in a Copy of Archibald Lampman's Poems" (B5).

Short Stories

A13 *In the Village of Viger*. Boston: Copeland and Day, 1896. 135 pp.
_____ . Illus. Thoreau MacDonald. Toronto: Ryerson, 1945. 114 pp.
Includes "The Bobolink" (B133), "The Desjardins" (B123), "Josephine Labrosse" (B124),

"The Little Milliner" (B125), "No. 68 Rue Alfred de Musset," "Paul Farlotte," "The Pedler [sic]" (B134), "Sedan" (B135), "The Tragedy of the Seigniory" (B128), and "The Wooing of Monsieur Cuerrier" (B127).
Also includes poem-dedication "To My Daughter Elizabeth Duncan Scott."

A14 *The Witching of Elspie: A Book of Stories*. New York: George H. Doran, 1923. 248 pp.
_____ . Toronto: McClelland and Stewart, 1923. 248 pp.
_____ . New York: Books for Libraries, 1972. 248 pp.
Includes "An Adventure of Mrs. Mackenzie's" (B149), "At Plangeant's Locks," "The Escapade of the Rev. Joshua Geer," "Expiation" (B154), "In the Year 1806," "Labrie's Wife" (B161), "A Legend of Welly Legrave" (B143), "Spirit River," "The Vain Shadow" (B147), "Vengeance Is Mine" (B153), "The Winning of Marie-Louise" (B145), and "The Witching of Elspie" (B146).

A15 *Selected Stories of Duncan Campbell Scott*. Ed., introd., and bibliography Glenn Clever. Ottawa: Univ. of Ottawa Press, 1972. ix–xv, 131–35, 135 pp.
Includes "The Bobolink" (B133), "Charcoal" (B152), "The Circle of Affection" (B160), "Clute Boulay" (B157), "Expiation" (B154), "Labrie's Wife" (B161), "No. 68 Rue Alfred de Musset" (A13), "Paul Farlotte" (A13), "Spirit River" (A14), "The Winning of Marie-Louise" (B145), and "The Wooing of Monsieur Cuerrier" (B127).

A16 *In the Village of Viger and Other Stories*. Introd. S.L. Dragland. New Canadian Library, No. 92. Toronto: McClelland and Stewart, 1973. 9–16, 137 pp.
Includes "The Bobolink" (B133), "Charcoal"

(B152), "Clute Boulay" (B157), "The Desjardins" (B123), "In the Year 1806," "Josephine Labrosse" (B124), "Labrie's Wife" (B161), "The Little Milliner" (B125), "No. 68 Rue Alfred de Musset" (A13), "Paul Farlotte" (A13), "The Pedler [sic]" (B134), "Sedan" (B135), "Tête-Jaune" (B159), "The Tragedy of the Seigniory" (B129), "Vengeance Is Mine" (B153), "The Winning of Marie-Louise" (B145), and "The Wooing of Monsieur Cuerrier" (B127).

Novel

A17 *Untitled Novel, ca. 1905*. Ed. and afterword John Flood. Moonbeam, Ont.: Penumbra, 1979. 317–27, 327 pp.

Miscellaneous Non-Fiction

A18 *John Graves Simcoe*. The Makers of Canada Series. Vol. 7. Toronto: Morang, 1905. 241 pp.

———. Parkman ed. Toronto: Morang, 1910. 241 pp.

　　With this is bound: Edgar, Matilda. *General Brock*. Toronto: Morang, 1910. 322 pp.

———. The Makers of Canada Series. Vol. 4. Toronto: Morang, 1912. 241 pp.

———. Illus. A.G. Doughty. Toronto: Oxford Univ. Press, 1926. 247 pp.

　　With this is bound: Edgar, Matilda. *General Brock*. Toronto: Oxford Univ. Press, 1926. 324 pp.

A19 *Walter J. Phillips*. The Canadian Art Series. Toronto: Ryerson, 1947. 59 pp.

Mixed Genre Collection

A20 *The Circle of Affection and Other Pieces in Prose and Verse*. Illus. Thoreau MacDonald. Toronto:

McClelland and Stewart, 1947. 237 pp.

　　Includes the following poems: "Amanda" (B112), "At Delos" (B108), "At Derwentwater," "At Murray Bay" (B22), "The Cascades of the Gatineau" (A50), "The Days of a Rose," "Early Summer Song," "Farewell to Their Majesties" (B109), "A Fragment," "Frost," "Hymn for Those in the Air" (B118), "Intermezzo" (B115), "A Love Song [It is not I alone]" (B54), "Man to Nature," "Nature to Man," "Ode on the Centenary of Florence Nightingale," "Old Olives at Bordighera" (B106), "On Hearing Bach's 'Sheep May Safely Graze'" (A54), "The Orchard in Moonlight," "Power" (B110), "Remembrance," "Rondeau," "The Sea-Witch," "Slumber Song," "A Song [In the air there are no coral-]" (B105), "Song [Keep me safe within your heart]," "Song [To go with March amarching]," "Spring Midnight: Deepwood," "These Are in the Beginning" (B113), "Time," "To Deaver Brown," "To Jane Edgar: For Her Album," "To My Friend — Leonard W. Brockington," "Twelfth Anniversary," and "Veronique Fraser" (B107).

　　Includes the following short stories: "Charcoal" (B152), "The Circle of Affection" (B160), "Clute Boulay" (B157), "Coquelicot," "The Flashlight" (B158), "The *Lark*," "A Night in Cordoba" (B156), "The Return," "The Rose of Hope," and "Tête-Jaune" (B159).

　　Includes the following articles: "Clarence A. Gagnon: Recollection and Record" (B257), "The Last of the Indian Treaties" (B234), "Poetry and Progress" (B242), "The Tercentenary of Quebec," and "Wayfarers."

Criticism

A21 ———, A. Lampman, and W.W. Campbell. *At the Mermaid Inn, Conducted by A. Lampman, W.W.*

Campbell, *Duncan C. Scott: Being Essays on Life and Literature which appeared in the Toronto* Globe *1892–1893.* Ed. and introd. Arthur S. Bourinot. Ottawa: Bourinot, 1958. 1–5, 96 pp.

Includes reprints and excerpts of several pieces from Scott's "At the Mermaid Inn" (B162, B166, B168–B169, B172, B176, B179, B181, B184, B189, B191, B197–B198, B204–B206, B211–B214, B220, and B228).

Includes the following poems by Scott: "Death and the Young Girl" (B24) and "From Amiel's Journal — (Six O'clock)" (B27).

A22 _____ , Wilfred Campbell, and Archibald Lampman. *At the Mermaid Inn: Wilfred Campbell, Archibald Lampman, Duncan Campbell Scott in* The Globe *1892–93.* Ed. and introd. Barrie Davies. Literature of Canada: Poetry and Prose in Reprint, No. 21. Toronto: Univ. of Toronto Press, 1979. vii–xxi, 353 pp.

Includes all of Scott's columns from "At the Mermaid Inn," 6 Feb. 1892–1 July 1893 (B162–B228).

Includes the following poems by Scott: "Death and the Young Girl" (B24) and "From Amiel's Journal — (Six O'clock)" (B27).

Includes the following short story by Scott: "Sister Ste Colombe" (B131–B132).

Published Letters
NOTE: See also "Letters" section, B327–B333.

A23 _____ , Archibald Lampman, J.G. Bourinot, E.W. Thomson, and E.K. Brown. *Some Letters of Duncan Campbell Scott, Archibald Lampman, and Others.* Ed. Arthur S. Bourinot. Ottawa: Bourinot, 1959. 63 pp.

Includes letters by Scott and others, as well as Scott's poem "Spring / Midnight: Deepwood. Written for My Friend Arthur S. Bourinot August 1944" (first version) and "Spring Midnight: Deepwood. F[irst] Written for My Friend Arthur S. Bourinot" (second version) (A20).

A24 *More Letters of Duncan Campbell Scott.* Ed. and introd. Arthur S. Bourinot. Ottawa: Bourinot, 1960. 1–7, 106 pp.

Includes letters by Scott as well as his "Appendix: Some Excerpts from a Decade of Canadian Poetry, by Duncan Campbell Scott, *The Canadian Magazine,* 1901" (B231) and Arthur S. Bourinot's "Some Personal Recollections of Duncan Campbell Scott" (C64).

Also includes Arthur S. Bourinot's "A Note on Yeats at Hart House" and "Some Recollections of Sir Gilbert Parker, Bart., the Canadian Novelist," neither of which relate to Scott.

A25 _____ , and E.K. Brown. *The Poet and the Critic: A Literary Correspondence between D.C. Scott and E.K. Brown.* Ed., introd., and notes Robert L. McDougall. Ottawa: Carleton Univ. Press, 1983. 1–15, 206–77, 308 pp.

Books Edited

A26 _____ , and memoir. *The Poems of Archibald Lampman.* By Archibald Lampman. Toronto: Morang, 1900. xi–xxv, 473 pp.
_____ , and memoir. 2nd ed. Toronto: Morang, 1900. xi–xxv, 473 pp.
_____ . Holiday ed. Toronto: Morang, 1901. 2 vols.
_____ , and memoir. 3rd ed. Toronto: Morang, 1905. xi–xxv, 473 pp.
_____ , and memoir. 4th ed. Toronto: Morang, 1915. xi–xxv, 473 pp.

_____, and memoir. *The Poems of Archibald Lampman (Including At the Long Sault)*. Introd. Margaret Coulby Whitridge. Toronto: Univ. of Toronto Press, 1974. xi–xxv, vii–xxix, 473 pp.

A27   _____, and introd. *The People of the Plains*. By Amelia M. Paget. Toronto: William Briggs, 1909. 5–15, 199 pp.

A28   _____, and introd. *Lyrics of Earth: Sonnets and Ballads*. By Archibald Lampman. Toronto: Musson, 1925. 3–47, 276 pp.

A29   _____, and E.K. Brown, eds. Foreword D.C. Scott. *At the Long Sault and Other New Poems*. By Archibald Lampman. Introd. E.K. Brown. Toronto: Ryerson, 1943. vii–x, xi–xxix, 45 pp.

A30   _____, foreword, and memoir. *Selected Poems of Archibald Lampman*. Toronto: Ryerson, 1947. v, xiii–xxvii, 176 pp.

Pamphlets

A31   *Poetry and Progress: Presidential Address*. Ottawa: Royal Society of Canada, [1922]. 18 pp.
    Includes "Poetry and Progress: Presidential Address" (B242).

A32   *The Administration of Indian Affairs in Canada*. Toronto: Canadian Institute of International Affairs, 1931. 27 pp.
    "Prepared for the fourth bi-annual conference of the Institute of Pacific Relations to be held at Hangchow from October 18th–November 3rd, 1931."

A33   _____, et al. *James Bay Treaty: Treaty No. 9 (Made in 1905 and 1906) and Adhesions Made in 1929 and 1930*. Ottawa: Queen's Printer and Controller of Stationery, 1931. 35 pp.

Poems Privately or Separately Printed (Including Christmas-Card Poems)

A34   "Above St. Irénée," "From Les Eboulements [A glamour on the phantom shore]," and "To Helen Douglas Macoun." Printed with Archibald Lampman's "The Meadow" and "Sunset at Les Eboulements." 1890.

A35   "At Scarboro' Beach" (B32). Printed with Archibald Lampman's "A Thunderstorm." 1892.

A36   "A Song ['Tis Autumn and down in the fields]" (B47). Printed with Archibald Lampman's "Earth: The Stoic." 1892.

A37   "The Cup." Printed with Archibald Lampman's "The Hermit Thrush." 1894.

A38   "Two Poems." By D.C. Scott and A. Lampman. 1896. Includes "[We plough the field]" by Scott and "[The bees are busy]" by Lampman.

A39   "These Poems." By D.C. Scott and A. Lampman. 1897. Includes "The Canadian's Home Song from Abroad" by Scott and "Temagami" and "In the Wilds" by Lampman.

A40   "A Love Song [I gave her a rose in early June]" (B60). Printed with Archibald Lampman's "Yarrow." 1898.

A41   "Canada to the Duke and Duchess of Cornwall and York Representing King Edward VII on Their Visit to the Canadian People." Sept. 1901. [Thomas Fisher Rare Book Library, Toronto; National Library, Ottawa.]

Also includes Edward VII's "To My People Beyond the Seas." Windsor Castle, 4 Feb. 1901, presented to the readers of *The Montreal Star*.

A42 "Lines in Memory of Edmund Morris." 1915. [20] pp.

A43 "An August Mood." 1924.

A44 "Byron on Wordsworth, Being Discovered Stanzas of Don Juan: To My Friend Colonel Henry C. Osborne for the Byron Centenary 1824 April Nineteenth 1924" (B121). 1924. 4 pp.

A45 "Prologue." Spoken by Dorothy White at the opening of the Ottawa Little Theatre. 4 January 1928. 5 pp.

A46 "[When twilight walks in the west]." 1929–30.

A47 "En Route." 1930–31.

A48 "[Lifted up from the heart of Earth]." [Mount Temple, Aug.] 1931.

A49 "[All day long the valiant mountains]." [1932?].

A50 "The Cascades of the Gatineau." 1935–36.

A51 "[O Time that like a flower unfolds]." 1936–37.

A52 "A Song [In the air there are no coral-]" (B105). 1938–39.

A53 "A Farewell to Their Majesties" (B109). CBC, 1939. The poem is printed with the following annotation: "This poem was written for the CBC by Dr. Duncan Campbell Scott, Canadian author and poet, on the occasion of the departure of Their Majesties the King and Queen from Canada on June 15, 1939."

A54 "On Hearing Bach's 'Sheep May Safely Graze': To E.B. & R.R." 1940–41.

A55 "Intermezzo" (B115). 1941.

A56 "The Wren." 1946–47.

A57 "Impromptu." 1947–48.

A58 "The Anatomy of Melancholy" (B85) and "Lilacs and Humming Birds" (A7). N.d.

A59 "[Be strong O warring soul!]." N.d.

A60 "A Carol (To Bethlehem beneath the star)." N.d.

A61 "Christmas Folk-Song." N.d.

A62 "[Lifted up from the heart of the earth]." N.d.

A63 "Reality" (B103). N.d.

A64 "Spring Night" (B96). N.d.

Lyrics

A65 "Three Songs of the West Coast: Na Du — Na Du Du (Lullaby); Outsiders, Behold Geedaranits (A Spirit Song); Stop All This Idle Chatter! Aguhlen Hagweeyaha." Recorded from Singers of Nass River Tribes Canada by Marius Barbeau. English versions Duncan Campbell Scott. Transcribed and arranged Ernest MacMillan. London, Eng.: Frederick Harris, 1928. 14 pp.

A66   "Last Year." Music W.H. Anderson. Vancouver: Western Music Company, 1940. 4 pp.

A67   "Ecstasy." Words for *Spring Rhapsody: A Song Cycle for Contralto and Piano*. Music Jean Coulthard. First Festival of the Arts, Vancouver, 1958. Don Mills, Ont.: BMI Canada, 1969. 7 pp.

A68   "The Sailor's Sweetheart" (A5). Music Nancy Telfer. Oakville, Ont.: Frederick Harris Music, 1985. 14 pp.

A69   "The Wind and the Flower." Music Nancy Telfer. Oakville, Ont.: Frederick Harris Music, 1985. 12 pp.
       The words are taken from "At Gull Lake: August 1810" (A9).

Adaptation

A70   *Good-Night Marie.* Music Elinore Cooper Bartlett and Kate Vannah. Boston: O. Ditson, c.1896. 5 pp.
       Adapted from Hungarian.

Editorial Work

A71   General editor (with Pelham Edgar). The Makers of Canada. First series. Toronto: Morang, 1903–11.

Manuscripts

A72   Duncan Campbell Scott Papers
       National Archives of Canada
       Ottawa, Ontario

       In the Duncan Campbell Scott Papers, there are 87 letters from E.K. Brown, most of which concern Brown's *On Canadian Poetry* and the edition of Archibald Lampman's poetry that Scott and Brown worked on together (*At the Long Sault and Other New Poems*). There is also correspondence with Earle Birney, Arthur Bourinot, Sir John George Bourinot, Rupert Brooke, Audrey Alexandra Brown, the Canadian Broadcasting Corporation, about *The Circle of Affection and Other Pieces in Prose and Verse*, with William Arthur Deacon, Ira Dilworth, W.H. Drummond, Pelham Edgar, Scott's daughter Elizabeth, Clarence Gagnon, J.M. Gibbon, about *The Green Cloister: Later Poems*, with Ralph Gustafson, Lawren Harris, Lampman's mother, William Dawson Le Sueur, about *Lundy's Lane and Other Poems*, with Andrew MacPhail, John Masefield, Vincent Massey, the editors of *Massey's Magazine*, and assorted individual letters about literary matters. The collection also contains copies of Scott's contributions to "A Book Lover's Corner," notes on Emily Brontë and a clipping of a review of Elizabeth Gaskell's biography of Charlotte Brontë, a carbon copy of the CBC "Message to students from Duncan Campbell Scott," a copy of a Scott manuscript entitled "Readers take over," 2 clippings from William Wilfred Campbell, clipping of a Wilson MacDonald article "Is Carman Supreme?", clipping of B.K. Sandwell's "The Professional Conspiracy to Destroy Canadian Literature," a small booklet of poetry inscribed "With Compliments of Pelham Edgar," a price list of sketches in oil by Clarence Gagnon, reviews and clippings about *The Green Cloister: Later Poems*, a copy of the manuscript of "Joy, Joy, Joy," handwritten address by Scott concerning the Lampman poems donated to Trinity College, reviews and clippings concerning Lampman, a manuscript on Walter Savage Landor, a booklet by Le Sueur entitled "Culture and Character," limericks and doggerel written by Scott, 2 copies of the prologue Scott wrote for the opening of the Ottawa Little Theatre, reviews and clippings concerning John Masefield, clippings from *The Times*

Literary Supplement [London], clippings from Scott's contributions to "At the Mermaid Inn," miscellaneous literary clippings, clipped poems, clippings concerning modern poetry, and clipped articles about Scott (some of which are newspaper articles not included in this bibliography).

A73 E.K. Brown Papers
National Archives of Canada
Ottawa, Ontario

In the E.K. Brown Papers, there are 95 letters from Scott to Brown, the other half of the Scott-Brown correspondence (see A72).

A74 Photograph Archives
National Archives of Canada
Ottawa, Ontario

In the Department of Indian Affairs file, there are over 200 photographs of Scott's trip to settle the James Bay Indian Treaty in 1906. The collection consists of both prints and lantern slides.

A75 Records of the Department of Indian Affairs
National Archives of Canada
Ottawa, Ontario

The National Archives hold papers from the Department of Indian Affairs (RG 10), which include Scott correspondence, documents signed by Scott, and photographs taken by Scott. There are 37 pages of pictures of Scott's Western tour (1910) and 38 pictures of Scott's Maritime tour (1911). There is a leather-bound journal in which Scott kept a record of his 1905 trip to sign the James Bay Treaty (Treaty 9). The second part of the journal contains a record, probably written by Pelham Edgar, of Scott's 1906 trip to conclude the signing of Treaty 9.

A76 Arthur Bourinot Papers
National Library of Canada
Ottawa, Ontario

In the Arthur Bourinot papers, there are 8 boxes of Scott papers.

Box 1:
Correspondence, poems for Elise Scott, poems torn out of *The Magic House and Other Poems*, and photocopies of introductory pages of various editions of *The Magic House and Other Poems*.

Box 2:
Reprints of articles by and about Scott, a reprint of "Spring Midnight: Deepwood," clippings about Scott's marriage to Elise and his Doctor of Laws degree from Queen's, general correspondence between Scott and Thoreau MacDonald and McClelland and Stewart, 2 letters from Scott to Sir John G. Bourinot, and correspondence with Macmillan.

Box 3:
Photos of trips to Indian reserves.

Box 4:
Articles and clippings about Scott.

Boxes 5 and 6:
Materials used in the preparation of "The Letters of Duncan Campbell Scott," which remains unpublished, and *More Letters of Duncan Campbell Scott*.

Box 7:
Material used in the preparation of "At the Mermaid Inn."

Box 8:
Assorted biographical material.

The Bourinot Papers also contain Belle Scott's social scrapbooks and a scrapbook in which Scott kept copies of reviews of his books, reviews of books by other Canadian poets, and newspaper articles about Canadian poetry.

A77   G.H. Clarke Papers
Queen's University Archives
Douglas Library
Queen's University
Kingston, Ontario

The G.H. Clarke Papers include 43 letters from Scott, written between 1938 and 1946.

A78   Lorne Pierce Papers
Queen's University Archives
Douglas Library
Queen's University
Kingston, Ontario

The Lorne Pierce Papers include letters to or from Scott, written between 1922–1936 and 1938–1940.

A79   Duncan Campbell Scott Papers
Queen's University Archives
Douglas Library
Queen's University
Kingston, Ontario

The Duncan Campbell Scott Papers include 7 assorted letters from Scott, printed copies of poems, biographical and critical articles written about Scott (all of which have been published), a photograph of Scott as a young man, and pen and ink sketches by A.H. Howard for *Via Borealis*.

A80   W.D. Lighthall Papers
Rare Book Room
McLennan-Redpath Library
McGill University
Montreal, Quebec

The Lighthall Papers include 60 letters and notes from Scott to Lighthall and carbon copies of 6 letters from Lighthall to Scott. Most of the correspondence concerns the Royal Society of Canada and the Canadian Authors' Association. There are also 4 Christmas-card poems from Scott to Lighthall and a carbon copy of a letter from Scott to Laurence J. Burpee (attached to a letter from Burpee to Lighthall).

A81   Duncan Campbell Scott Papers
McLennan-Redpath Library
McGill University
Montreal, Quebec

The Duncan Campbell Scott papers include a typescript of "The Battle of Lundy's Lane" and a holograph of "At the Cedars."

A82   Duncan Campbell Scott Papers
Thomas Fisher Rare Book Library
University of Toronto
Toronto, Ontario

The Duncan Campbell Scott Papers include letters from Scott to Archibald Lampman, John Masefield, Arthur Bourinot and notebooks containing drafts of poems written between 1899 and 1943. There are some typed poems, a holograph copy of "Spring Midnight: Deepwood," and a typewritten copy of the unpublished novel.

A83   Pelham Edgar Collection
E.J. Pratt Library
Victoria College
University of Toronto
Toronto, Ontario

The Duncan Campbell Scott papers in the Pelham Edgar Collection include:

Folder 19:
Holograph of "The Poetry of Duncan Campbell Scott," by Pelham Edgar.

Folder 20:
Holograph of "Duncan Campbell Scott," by Pelham Edgar (unpublished).

Folder 21:
Typescript of "Duncan Campbell Scott," by Pelham Edgar (unpublished).

Folders 36–46:
Correspondence from Scott, written between 1890 and 1946.

Folder 47:
Poems in holograph, typescript, or Xerox copy (31 leaves).

Folders 48–49:
"Duncan Campbell Scott" (autobiographical notes).

Folder 50:
An appreciation of Scott, supposedly written by Percy H. Wright.

Folder 51:
Framed photo of Scott and Rupert Brooke.

A84 A.J.M. Smith Papers
Thomas Fisher Rare Book Library
University of Toronto
Toronto, Ontario

   The A.J.M. Smith Papers include 9 letters from Scott.

A85 J.E. Wetherell Papers
Thomas Fisher Rare Book Library
University of Toronto
Toronto, Ontario

The J.E. Wetherell Papers include 9 letters from Scott.

A86 Mazo de la Roche Papers
Thomas Fisher Rare Book Library
University of Toronto
Toronto, Ontario

   The Mazo de la Roche Papers include 3 letters from Scott.

A87 Alan Crawley Papers
Queen's University Archives
Douglas Library
Queen's University
Kingston, Ontario

   The Alan Crawley Papers include letters from Scott.

A88 Raymond Knister Papers
Queen's University Archives
Douglas Library
Queen's University
Kingston, Ontario

   The Raymond Knister Papers include letters from Scott.

A89 Earle Birney Papers
Thomas Fisher Rare Book Library
University of Toronto
Toronto, Ontario

   The Earle Birney Papers include 2 letters from Scott.

A90 Archibald Lampman Papers
Queen's University Archives
Douglas Library

Queen's University
Kingston, Ontario

The Archibald Lampman Papers include the type-script of *At the Long Sault and Other New Poems*, including Scott's Foreword.

A91 Duncan Campbell Scott Papers
Special Collections and Archives
Carleton University
Ottawa, Ontario

The Scott papers in the rare book room include "On a Portrait of Judge Haliburton," signed and dated 4 March 1899 and handwritten on the flyleaf of *Haliburton: A Centenary Chaplet*. The collection also contains 5 Christmas card poems: "Above Saint Irénée," "From Les Eboulements," and "To Helen Douglas Macoun" with Archibald Lampman's "The Meadow" and "Sunset at Les Eboulements," dated 1890; "At Scarboro' Beach" with Lampman's "A Thunderstorm," dated 1892; "Two Poems [We plough the field]" with Lampman's ["The bees are busy]," dated 1896; "These Poems: The Canadian's Home Song from Abroad" with Lampman's "Temagami" and "In the Wilds," dated 1897; and "Two Poems: A Love Song" with Lampman's "Yarrow," dated 1898; and a signed copy of "A Song ['Tis Autumn and down in the fields]," printed with Lampman's "Earth: The Stoic." The papers also include abstracts collected by Scott from *The Fortnightly Review* and a collection of articles from various magazines, both of which were bound by Scott with typed tables of contents. They are not annotated. The volume of magazine articles contains 4 selections by Scott: "George Meredith, Dean of English Novelists," "Lord Strathcona," "The Last of the Indian Treaties," and "A Walk to Swanston."

A92 Ottawa Little Theatre Papers
National Archives of Canada
Ottawa, Ontario

The Ottawa Little Theatre Papers contain correspondence to and from Scott about the administration of the theatre and the incorporation of the Ottawa Drama League (incorporated 23 June 1927). There are documents surrounding the acquisition of the theatre's new home and the annual selection of plays that indicate Scott's extensive involvement in all aspects of the Little Theatre: he raised the $75,000 necessary for the purchase and renovation of the church that became the new theatre, oversaw all details of the building from the architect's plans to the awarding of the contract for wiring, and was instrumental in the production of each season. Under Scott, membership rose from 49 (during World War I) to 1800 in 1928 when the new theatre opened. There are brief histories of the Ottawa Little Theatre, which include Scott's role in its development, newspaper clippings about the theatre, and a poem of love and admiration addressed to Scott and signed from "The Little Theatre, Ottawa."

A93 M.O. Hammond Papers
Queen's University Archives
Douglas Library
Queen's University
Kingston, Ontario

The M.O. Hammond Papers include letters from Scott.

A94 William Arthur Deacon Papers
Thomas Fisher Rare Book Library
University of Toronto
Toronto, Ontario

The William Arthur Deacon Papers include 31 letters from Scott, as well as 3 Christmas card poems. The material dates 1924–46.

A95 Robert Borden Papers
National Archives of Canada
Ottawa, Ontario

There are letters between Scott and Borden (dated 1913–21 and 1927–36) concerning the Department of Indian Affairs, the Ottawa Little Theatre, and general matters of culture.

A96 John A. Macdonald Papers
National Archives of Canada
Ottawa, Ontario

There are letters from Scott to members of John A. Macdonald's staff about matters concerning the Department of Indian Affairs.

A97 Arthur Meighen Papers
National Archives of Canada
Ottawa, Ontario

There are letters from Scott (dated 1918–32) to Arthur Meighen and members of Meighen's staff about matters concerning the Department of Indian Affairs.

A98 Canadian Authors' Association Papers
National Archives of Canada
Ottawa, Ontario

The Canadian Authors' Association Papers contain an autographed copy of Scott's poem "After Battle."

A99 Elise Aylen Scott Papers
National Archives of Canada
Ottawa, Ontario

The collection contains letters written by Scott to Elise Aylen between 1927 and 1930, the years just prior to their marriage in 1931. There are also letters from publishers to Elise Aylen Scott, requesting permission to republish Scott's poems, and there are three Christmas-card poems ("When twilight walks in the west," "The Meadow," and "Les Eboulements") and "Above St. Irénée," "From les Eboulements," and "To Helen Douglas Macoun."

B   Contributions to Periodicals and Books (Poems, Short Stories, Articles and Reviews, Governmental Reports, Reprinted Anthology Contributions: A Selection, Drama, and Letters) and Audio-Visual Material

Note: When an item is reprinted in one of Scott's books, this fact is noted in the entry through one of the following abbreviations:

"The Anatomy of Melancholy" and "Lilacs and Hummingbirds" .... "AM"
"At Scarboro' Beach" .... "ASB"
At the Mermaid Inn: Wilfred Campbell, Archibald Lampman, Duncan Campbell Scott in The Globe *1892–93* .... AMI
At the Mermaid Inn, Conducted by A. Lampman, W.W. Campbell, Duncan C. Scott: Being Essays on Life and Literature which appeared in the Toronto Globe *1892–1893* .... AMIC
Beauty and Life .... BL
"Byron on Wordsworth, Being Discovered Stanzas of Don Juan: To My Friend Colonel Henry C. Osborne for the Byron Centenary 1824 April Nineteenth 1924" .... "BW"

The Circle of Affection and Other Pieces in Prose and Verse .... CAOP
Duncan Campbell Scott: Selected Poetry . DCS
"A Farewell to Their Majesties" .... "FTM"
The Green Cloister: Later Poems .... GC
In the Village of Viger VV
In the Village of Viger and Other Stories VVOS
"Intermezzo" .... "Inter."
Labor and the Angel .... LA
"A Love Song [I gave her a rose in early June]" .... "LS"
Lundy's Lane and Other Poems .... LLOP
The Magic House and Other Poems ... MHOP
More Letters of Duncan Campbell Scott MLDC
New World Lyrics and Ballads .... NWLB
The Poems of Duncan Campbell Scott .. PDCS
Poetry and Progress: Presidential Address .. PP
Powassan's Drum: Poems of Duncan Campbell Scott .... PD
"Reality" .... "Reality"
Selected Poems of Duncan Campbell Scott . SPDC
Selected Stories of Duncan Campbell Scott . SSDC
Some Letters of Duncan Campbell Scott, Archibald Lampman, and Others .... SLDC
"A Song [In the air there are no coral-]" . "Song"
"A Song ['Tis Autumn and down in the fields]" .... "Song"
"Spring Night" .... "SN"
To the Canadian Mothers and Three Other Poems .... TCMT
Via Borealis .... VB
The Witching of Elspie: A Book of Stories .. WE

Poems

B1   "The Hill Path." *Scribner's Magazine,* May 1888, p. 532. *MHOP; PDCS.*

B2 "Ballade. To Sandra, in Absence." *Scribner's Magazine*, July 1889, p. 63.

B3 "Youth and Time." *Scribner's Magazine*, Sept. 1889, p. 298. *MHOP; PDCS; SPDC; DCS.*

B4 "Song [I have done]." *Scribner's Magazine*, Oct. 1889, p. 435. *MHOP; PDCS* ("Thirteen Songs: xi"); *SPDC.*

B5 "Written in a Copy of Archibald Lampman's Poems." *The Week: A Canadian Journal of Politics, Literature, Science and Arts* [Toronto], 4 Oct. 1889, p. 698. *MHOP; PD.*

B6 "At Les Éboulements [The bay is set with ashy sails,]." *Scribner's Magazine*, Dec. 1889, p. 759. *MHOP; PDCS* ("At Les Eboulements").

B7 "Ottawa: *Before Dawn* [The stars are stars of morn; a keen wind wakes]." In *Songs of the Great Dominion: Voices from the Forest and Waters, the Settlements and Cities of Canada.* Ed. William Douw Lighthall. London: Walter Scott, 1889, p. 314. See B286 for reprinted material in this book.

B8 "The Magic House." *Scribner's Magazine*, June 1890, pp. 713–14. *MHOP; PDCS; SPDC.*

B9 "From the Farm on the Hill." *The Independent* [New York], 3 July 1890, p. 901. *MHOP; PD.*

B10 "In August." *The Independent* [New York], 28 Aug. 1890, p. 1181.

B11 "Autumn Song." *Scribner's Magazine*, Oct. 1890, p. 436. *LA* ("A Group of Songs: Autumn Song"); *PDCS* ("Songs of Four Seasons: Autumn"); *SPDC; DCS.*

B12 "A November Day." *The Week: A Canadian Journal of Politics, Literature, Science and Arts* [Toronto], 14 Nov. 1890, p. 794. *MHOP; PD.*

B13 "The Reed Player." *Scribner's Magazine*, Dec. 1890, p. 720. Rpt. in *The Week: A Canadian Journal of Politics, Literature, Science and Arts* [Toronto], 26 Dec. 1890, p. 66. Rpt. ("The Reed-Player: *to B.C.*") in *Poets of the Younger Generation.* By William Archer. London: John Lane, 1902, p. 395. *MHOP* ("The Reed-Player"); *PDCS; SPDC; PD.*

B14 "From the Hungarian." *Scribner's Magazine*, May 1891, p. 562. *MHOP* ("At the Lattice").

B15 "For Remembrance." *Scribner's Magazine*, Sept. 1891, p. 336. Rpt. in *The Week: A Canadian Journal of Politics, Literature, Science and Arts* [Toronto], 16 Oct. 1891, p. 741. *MHOP; PDCS; SPDC; PD.*

B16 "The River Town." *The Week: A Canadian Journal of Politics, Literature, Science and Arts* [Toronto], 18 Sept. 1891, p. 670. *MHOP.*

B17 "In November." *Scribner's Magazine*, Nov. 1891, p. 562. Rpt. in *The Week: A Canadian Journal of Politics, Literature, Science and Arts* [Toronto], 13 Nov. 1891, p. 805. *MHOP; PDCS.*

B18 "Song [Here's the last rose,]." *Scribner's Magazine*, Jan. 1892, p. 25. *MHOP; PDCS* ("Thirteen Songs: x").

B19 "The Voice and the Dusk." *The Independent* [New York], 7 Jan. 1892, p. 1. *MHOP; PDCS; SPDC.*

B20 "April." *Youth's Companion* [Boston], 7 April 1892, p. 172.

B21 "The End of the Day." *Youth's Companion* [Boston], 14 April 1892, p. 190. *MHOP; PDCS; SPDC.*

B22 "At Murray Bay." *The Week: A Canadian Journal of Politics, Literature, Science and Arts* [Toronto], 22 April 1892, p. 328. *CAOP.*

B23 "Domenico Scarlatti." *Arcadia: A Journal Devoted to Art, Music and Literature* [Montreal], 15 June 1892, p. 75.

B24 "Death and the Young Girl." *The Globe* [Toronto]. "At the Mermaid Inn," 18 June 1892, p. 9. *AMIC; AMI.*
   Originally signed: S.

B25 "A Night in June." *The Cosmopolitan* [New York], July 1892, p. 313. Rpt. in *Current Literature: A Magazine of Record and Review* [New York], 10 (Aug. 1892), 606–07. *MHOP; PDCS; PD.*

B26 "To the Hills." *The Independent* [New York], 21 July 1892, p. 1.

B27 "From Amiel's Journal — (Six O'Clock)." *The Globe* [Toronto]. "At the Mermaid Inn," 30 July 1892, p. 8. *AMIC* ("From Amiel's Journal — Six O'clock"); *AMI.*
   Originally signed: S.

B28 "The Dream [I had a dream last night,]." *The Week: A Canadian Journal of Politics, Literature, Science and Arts* [Toronto], 19 Aug. 1892, p. 603.

B29 "September." *The Cosmopolitan* [New York], 13 (Sept. 1892), 526. Rpt. in *Current Literature: A Magazine of Record and Review* [New York], 11 (Oct. 1892), 206. *MHOP; PDCS; PD.*

B30 "Off the Isle Aux Coudres." *The Independent* [New York], 22 Sept. 1892, p. 1. *MHOP; PDCS; SPDC; PD.*

B31 "An East Wind." *Youth's Companion* [Boston], 29 Dec. 1892, p. 692.

B32 "At Scarboro' Beach." *The Canadian Magazine of Politics, Science, Art and Literature* [Toronto], June 1893, p. 272. *MHOP;* "ASB."

B33 "The Sleeper." *The Independent* [New York], 15 June 1893, p. 835. *MHOP.*

B34 "A Flock of Sheep." *Youth's Companion* [Boston], 6 July 1893, p. 246. *MHOP; PDCS; PD.*

B35 "The Harvest." *The Globe* [Toronto], 2 Sept. 1893, p. 9. Rpt. in *Scribner's Magazine*, Sept. 1893, pp. 370–73. *LA; PDCS; SPDC; DCS; PD.*

B36 "Winter Song." *Scribner's Magazine*, Dec. 1893, p. 748. Rpt. in *The Week: A Canadian Journal of Politics, Literature, Science and Arts* [Toronto], 22 Dec. 1893, p. 91. *LA* ("A Group of Songs: Winter Song"); *PDCS* ("Songs of Four Seasons: Winter"); *SPDC; DCS.*

B37 "Spring Song [Sing me a song of the early spring,]." *Scribner's Magazine*, April 1894, p. 476. Rpt. in *The Week: A Canadian Journal of Politics, Literature, Science and Arts* [Toronto], 13 April 1894, p. 475. *LA* ("A Group of Songs: Spring Song [Sing me a song of the early spring,]"); *PDCS* ("Songs of Four Seasons: Spring"); *SPDC; DCS.*

B38 "Rain and the Robin." *St. Nicholas Magazine* [New York], June 1894, p. 747. *LA; PDCS.*

B39 "An Onondaga Mother and Child." *The Atlantic Monthly* [Boston], Sept. 1894, p. 325. *LA* (revised — "The Onondaga Madonna"); *PDCS*; *SPDC*; *DCS*; *PD*.

B40 "In May." *The Week: A Canadian Journal of Politics, Literature, Science and Art* [Toronto], 31 May 1895, p. 640. *LA*; *PDCS*; *SPDC*; *DCS*; *PD*.

B41 "On the Mountain." *Youth's Companion* [Boston], 13 June 1895, p. 290. *LA*; *PDCS*.

B42 "Summer Song." *Scribner's Magazine*, Aug. 1895, p. 194. Rpt. in *The Week: A Canadian Journal of Politics, Literature, Science and Art* [Toronto], 9 Aug. 1895, p. 878. *LA* ("A Group of Songs: Summer Song"); *PDCS* ("Songs of Four Seasons: Summer"); *SPDC*; *DCS*.

B43 "The Piper of Arll." *Truth* [New York], 14 Dec. 1895, pp. 8–9. *LA*; *PDCS*; *SPDC*; *DCS*; *PD*.

B44 "March." *Massey's Magazine* [Toronto], March 1896, p. 151. Rpt. in *Acta Victoriana* [Victoria College, Univ. of Toronto], 25, No. 6 (March 1902), 316. *LA*; *PDCS*; *SPDC*; *PD*.

B45 "Spring Song [When the ash tree buds, and the maples,]." *Truth* [New York], 4 April 1896, p. 6. *LA* ("A Group of Songs: Song [When the ash-tree buds and the maples,]"); *PDCS* ("Thirteen Songs: VI"); *SPDC*; *DCS* ("Song [When the ash-tree buds and the maples,]").

B46 "When the Cows Come Home." *St. Nicholas Magazine* [New York], June 1896, p. 648.

B47 "A Song ['Tis Autumn and down in the fields,]." *The Week: A Canadian Journal of Politics, Literature, Science and Art* [Toronto], 6 Nov. 1896, p. 1188. *LA* ("A Group of Songs: A Song ['Tis autumn and down in the fields]"); "Song" ("A Song ['Tis Autumn and down in the fields]").

B48 "A Song for Winter." *Truth* [New York], 26 Dec. 1896, p. 9. Rpt. (expanded) in *Acta Victoriana* [Victoria College, Univ. of Toronto], 23, No. 3 (Dec. 1899), 154–55.

B49 "Madrigal." *Truth* [New York], 22 April 1897, p. 7. *LA* ("A Group of Songs: Madrigal"); *PDCS* ("Madrigal").

B50 "A Legend of Christ's Nativity." *The Independent* [New York], 23 Dec. 1897, p. 1677. *LLOP*; *PDCS*.

B51 "Stone Breaking." *Acta Victoriana* [Victoria College, Univ. of Toronto], 22, No. 3 (Dec. 1898), 126. *LA*.

B52 "Night Hymns on Lake Nepigon [sic]." *The Atlantic Monthly* [Boston], Aug. 1900, pp. 179–80. *NWLB*; *PDCS* ("Night Hymns on Lake Nipigon"); *SPDC*; *DCS*; *PD*.
See B335.

B53 "Twin Flowers on the Portage." *The Atlantic Monthly* [Boston], July 1901, pp. 137–38. *NWLB* ("Twin-Flowers on the Portage"); *PDCS* ("Twin-Flowers on the Portage"); *PD* ("Twin Flowers on the Portage").

B54 "A Love Song (Seventeenth Century) [It is not I alone]." *The Independent* [New York], 21 Nov. 1901, p. 2775. Rpt. in *The Independent* [New York], 11 Feb. 1904, p. 309. *CAOP* ("A Love Song [It is not I alone]").

B55 "The Coming of Winter." *Munsey's Magazine* [New York], Dec. 1901, p. 362.

B56 "The Sea by the Wood." *The Canadian Magazine of Politics, Science, Art and Literature* [Toronto], Dec. 1901, pp. 142–43. *NWLB; PDCS; SPDC; DCS; PD.*

B57 "The Wood by the Sea." *The Canadian Magazine of Politics, Science, Art and Literature* [Toronto], Dec. 1901, p. 143. *NWLB; PDCS; SPDC; DCS.*

B58 "Off Rivière du Loup." In *Poets of the Younger Generation.* By William Archer. London: John Lane, 1902, p. 394. Rpt. in *Saturday Magazine [The Globe]* [Toronto], 4 March 1905, p. 8. *MHOP; PDCS; PD.*

B59 "The Ghost's Story." *Acta Victoriana* [Victoria College, Univ. of Toronto], 25, No. 8 (June 1902), 420. *LLOP; PDCS; PD.*

B60 "A Love Song [I gave her a rose in early June]." *The Delineator* [New York], July 1902, p. 75. *LLOP;* "LS."

B61 "Rapids at Night." *The Atlantic Monthly* [Boston], Aug. 1902, pp. 259–60. *NWLB; PDCS; SPDC; DCS; PD.*

B62 "Heine." *Reader: An Illustrated Monthly Magazine* [New York], Dec. 1902, p. 166.

B63 "The Forsaken." *The Outlook* [New York], 25 April 1903, pp. 960–61. *NWLB; PDCS; SPDC; DCS; PD.*

B64 "The Home Comers." *The Daily Mail and Empire* [Toronto], 28 May 1903, p. 7.

B65 "Roses on the Portage." *Acta Victoriana* [Victoria College, Univ. of Toronto], 27, No. 3 (Dec. 1903), 223. *NWLB; PDCS; PD.*

B66 "To the Heroic Soul [Be strong, O Warring Soul!]." [Pt. II.] *The Atlantic Monthly* [Boston], Sept. 1904, p. 413. Rpt. (expanded — "To the Heroic Son [sic] [I. Nurture thyself, O Soul! II. Be strong, O Warring Soul!]") in *Current Literature* [New York], 38 (Feb. 1905), 140. Rpt. ("To the Heroic Soul [I. Nurture thyself, O Soul! II. Be strong, O Warring Soul!]") in *The Literary Digest* [New York], 25 Jan. 1919, p. 36. *LLOP; PDCS; SPDC; DCS; PD.*

B67 "Night." *The Smart Set: A Magazine of Cleverness* [New York], 17, No. 3 (Nov. 1905), 128. *LLOP; PDCS; SPDC.*

B68 "Ecstasy." *The Smart Set: A Magazine of Cleverness* [New York], 20, No. 3 (Nov. 1906), 160. *VB; LLOP* ("*Via Borealis*: Ecstasy"); *PDCS* ("Ecstasy"); *PD.*

B69 "At William Maclennan's Grave." *The Canadian Magazine of Politics, Science, Art and Literature* [Toronto], Dec. 1906, pp. 151–52. *LLOP* ("At William MacLennan's Grave"); *PDCS* ("At William Maclennan's Grave"); *SPDC; PD.*

B70 "The Half-Breed Girl." *The Smart Set: A Magazine of Cleverness* [New York], 20, No. 4 (Dec. 1906), 84–85. *VB; LLOP* ("*Via Borealis*: The Half-Breed Girl"); *PDCS* ("The Half-Breed Girl"); *SPDC; DCS; PD.*

B71 "At Perugia." *The University Magazine* [McGill Univ., Univ. of Toronto, Dalhousie College], 6 (April 1907), 152–53. *LLOP* ("Meditation at Perugia"); *PDCS; SPDC; DCS; PD.*

B72 "In Snow-Time." *Scribner's Magazine*, April 1907, p. 496. *LLOP; PDCS; SPDC; PD.*

B73 "On a Portrait of Judge Haliburton." *The Canadian Magazine of Politics, Science, Art and Literature* [Toronto], Dec. 1909, p. 187.

B74 "Ode of Welcome to the Duke and Duchess of Connaught." *Canada: An Illustrated Weekly Journal for All Interested in the Dominion* [London, Eng.], 28 Oct. 1911, p. 113.

B75 "Willow Pipes." *The Canadian Magazine of Politics, Science, Art and Literature* [Toronto], May 1913, p. 72. *LLOP; PDCS* ("Willow-Pipes"); *PD.*

B76 "The Lover to His Lass." *The Canadian Magazine of Politics, Science, Art and Literature* [Toronto], July 1913, p. 292. *LLOP.*

B77 "Threnody [Sing we a dirge for our heros]." In *The Band of Purple: A Collection of Canadian Poems.* Ed. Lillie A. Brooks. Toronto: Oxford Univ. Press, 1915, n. pag.

B78 "To a Canadian Lad Killed in the War." *The University Magazine* [McGill Univ., Univ. of Toronto, Dalhousie College], 14 (Oct. 1915), 346. *LLOP; TCMT; PDCS; SPDC.*

B79 "To a Canadian Aviator Who Died for His Country in France." *Scribner's Magazine*, Aug. 1917, p. 246. *TCMT; BL* ("To a Canadian Aviator who Died for his Country in France"); *PDCS* ("To a Canadian Aviator Who Died for His Country in France"); *SPDC.*

B80 "Fragment of an Ode to Canada." *Manitoba Free Press* [Winnipeg], 9 Aug. 1918, p. 13. Rpt. (revised) in *Manitoba Free Press* [Winnipeg], 1 July 1922, p. 9. *LLOP; PDCS.*

B81 "Ode on the Hundredth Anniversary of the Birth of James Russell Lowell." *Boston Evening Transcript*, 19 Feb. 1919, Sec. 2, p. 5.

B82 "A Road Song." *The Sewanee Review* [Univ. of the South, Sewanee, Tenn.], 29 (Jan. 1921), 1. Rpt. in *Saturday Night*, 1 Aug. 1942, p. 25. *BL; PDCS.*

B83 "The Eagle Speaks." *The London Mercury*, June 1921, pp. 127–28. *BL; PDCS; PD.*

B84 "After a Night of Storm." *The Dalhousie Review*, 1 (July 1921), 122. *BL; PDCS.*

B85 "The Anatomy of Melancholy." *The Canadian Forum*, Nov. 1921, p. 430. *BL; PDCS;* "AM."

B86 "Leaves." *The Canadian Magazine of Politics, Science, Art and Literature* [Toronto], Nov. 1921, pp. 28–29. *BL; PDCS; SPDC; PD.*

B87 "Poem [Then something moves]." *Queen's Quarterly*, 29 (Oct.–Nov.–Dec. 1921), 181. *BL* ("Reverie"); *PDCS; PD.*

B88 "Two Lyrics: I [Echo on the moonlit hill]." *Acta Victoriana* [Victoria College, Univ. of Toronto], 46, No. 5 (Feb. 1922), 214. *PDCS.*

B89 "Two Lyrics: II [If my heart were never moved to sadness]." *Acta Victoriana* [Victoria College, Univ. of Toronto], 46, No. 5 (Feb. 1922), 214. *PDCS.*

B90 "Permanence." *The London Mercury*, March 1922, pp. 458–59. Rpt. in *The Dalhousie Review*, 2 (Jan. 1923), 443. *PDCS; SPDC.*

B91 "Song [Nothing came here but sunlight]." *Manitoba Free Press* [Winnipeg], 18 July 1922, p. 13.

B92 "An Apparition." *Manitoba Free Press* [Winnipeg], 19 July 1922, p. 13. *LLOP* ("The Apparition"); *PDCS*.

B93 "Lines on the Peace Arch." *The Vancouver Sun*, 4 Aug. 1922, p. 4.

B94 "The Lovers." *Scribner's Magazine*, May 1923, p. 528. *BL*; *PDCS*; *SPDC*.

B95 "An Old Tune: To Percy Grainger." *The Canadian Forum*, July 1925, p. 309. *PDCS* ("An Old Tune").

B96 "Spring Night: To Leo Smith." *The Canadian Forum*, July 1925, p. 309. *PDCS* ("Spring Night"); *SPDC*; "SN."

B97 "Morning at Parame." *Acta Victoriana* [Victoria College, Univ. of Toronto], 50, No. 3 (Dec. 1925), 28. *PDCS* ("Morning at Paramé"); *SPDC*.

B98 "By the Sea." *The Dalhousie Review*, 7 (April 1927), 96. *GC*.

B99 "The Journey." *The London Mercury*, Dec. 1927, pp. 130–31. Rpt. in *The Literary Digest* [New York], 7 Jan. 1928, p. 32. *PDCS*.

B100 "Song [To go with March amarching]." *Saturday Night*, 17 March 1928, p. 1.

B101 "The Wise Men from the East." *The Globe* [Toronto], 25 Dec. 1929, p. 12. *GC*; *DCS*.
This poem was commissioned by the R. Simpson Co.

B102 "A Fancy." *Queen's Quarterly*, 38 (Summer 1931), 505–06. *GC*.

B103 "Reality." *Queen's Quarterly*, 38 (Summer 1931), 507–08. *GC*; *SPDC*; *DCS*; *PD*; "Reality."

B104 "First Class Car." *Saturday Night*, 8 May 1937, p. 2. Signed: Oliver Gascoigne.

B105 "A Song [In the air there are no coral-]." *Canadian Poetry Magazine*, 2, No. 2 (Oct. 1937), 11. *SPDC*; *DCS*; *PD*; *CAOP*; "Song" ("A Song [In the air there are no coral-]").

B106 "Old Olives at Bordighera." *Queen's Quarterly*, 45 (Winter 1938), 460–61. *SPDC*; *DCS*; *PD*; *CAOP*.

B107 "Veronique Fraser." *Saturday Night*, 4 Feb. 1939, p. 2. *SPDC*; *DCS*; *PD*; *CAOP*.

B108 "At Delos." *Queen's Quarterly*, 46 (Spring 1939), 65. *DCS*; *CAOP*.

B109 "A Farewell to Their Majesties." *Saturday Night*, 17 June 1939, p. 2. *CAOP*; "FTM."
This poem was introduced with the following comment: "Thanks to the Canadian Broadcasting Corporation, Canada now has the equivalent of a Poet Laureate. The CBC with excellent judgement selected Dr. Duncan Campbell Scott to furnish the following dignified verses to be read at the Royal departure from Canada."

B110 "Power." *Poetry* [Chicago], 58 (April 1941), 5. *CAOP*.

B111 "The Fallen." *Saturday Night*, 1 Aug. 1942, p. 25. *BL*; *PDCS*; *SPDC*.

B112 "A Dream [Lovely Amanda running through the cool]." *Voices* [New York], No. 113 (Spring 1943), pp. 6–8. *SPDC* ("Amanda"); *DCS*; *PD*; *CAOP*.

B113 "These Are in the Beginning." *Queen's Quarterly*, 50 (Spring 1943), 63. *CAOP*.

B114 "To Helen." *The Canadian Forum*, April 1943, p. 10.

B115 "Intermezzo." *Queen's Quarterly*, 50 (Summer 1943), 200. *CAOP*; "Inter."

B116 "Lines to Be a Last Song." *The Canadian Forum*, March 1944, p. 274.

B117 "The Rite." *Canadian Poetry Magazine*, 10, No. 3 (March 1947), 30.

B118 "Hymn for Those in the Air." *Saturday Night*, 25 Dec. 1943, p. 15. Rpt. in *The Ottawa Journal*, 17 March 1945, p. 6. *CAOP*.

B119 "Before the Silence." *Queen's Quarterly*, 55 (Autumn 1948), 290–91. *SPDC*.

B120 "Past and Present." *The Canadian Author & Bookman*, 38, No. 1 (Summer 1962), [front cover]. *GC*.

B121 "Byron on Wordsworth, Being Discovered Stanzas of Don Juan: To My Friend Colonel Henry C. Osborne for the Byron Centenary 1824 April Nineteenth 1924." *Canadian Poetry: Studies, Documents, Reviews*, No. 22 (Spring–Summer 1988), pp. 59–62. "BW."
This poem is reprinted in full in Stan Dragland's analysis (C248).

Short Stories

B122 "The Ducharmes of the Baskatonge." *Scribner's Magazine*, Feb. 1887, pp. 236–43.

B123 "In the Village of Viger: The Desjardins." *Scribner's Magazine*, Oct. 1887, pp. 498–501. *VV* ("The Desjardins"); *VVOS*.

B124 "In the Village of Viger: Josephine Labrosse." *Scribner's Magazine*, Oct. 1887, pp. 501–04. *VV* ("Josephine Labrosse"); *VVOS*.

B125 "In the Village of Viger: The Little Milliner." *Scribner's Magazine*, Oct. 1887, pp. 493–98. *VV* ("The Little Milliner"); *VVOS*.

B126 "Coiniac Street." *The Globe* [Toronto], 23 Nov. 1889, p. 11.

B127 "The Wooing of Monsieur Cuerrier: A Sketch in Viger." *Scribner's Magazine*, March 1891, pp. 373–76. *VV* ("The Wooing of Monsieur Cuerrier"); *SSDC*; *VVOS*.

B128 "John Scantleberry, Working Merchant Tailor, Great Specialty of Pantaloons." *The Dominion Illustrated Monthly* [Montreal/Toronto], Feb. 1892, pp. 37–45.

B129 "The Tragedy of the Seigniory." *Two Tales* [Boston], April 1892, pp. 105–12. *VV*; *VVOS*.

B130 "The Triumph of Marie Laviolette." *Scribner's Magazine*, Aug. 1892, pp. 232–41.

B131 "Sister Ste Colombe." *The Globe* [Toronto]. "At the Mermaid Inn," 6 May 1893, p. 7. "AM"; *AMI*.
Originally unsigned. Continued in 13 May edition. Also includes an article (B222).

B132 "Sister Ste Colombe." *The Globe* [Toronto]. "At the Mermaid Inn," 13 May 1893, p. 11. *AMI*.
Originally signed: S. Continued from 6 May edition.

B133 "In Viger Again: The Bobolink." *Scribner's Magazine*, Oct. 1893, pp. 462–64. *VV* ("The Bobolink"); *SSDC*; *VVOS*.

B134 "In Viger Again: The Pedler [sic]." *Scribner's Magazine*, Oct. 1893, pp. 461–62. *VV* ("The Pedler [sic]"); *VVOS*.

B135 "In Viger Again: Sedan." *Scribner's Magazine*, Oct. 1893, pp. 457–61. *VV* ("Sedan"); *VVOS*.

B136 "The Mystery of the Red Deeps." *Massey's Magazine* [Toronto], April 1896, pp. 232–40.
Continued in the May 1896 issue (B137).

B137 "The Mystery of the Red Deeps." *Massey's Magazine* [Toronto], May 1896, pp. 309–15.
Continued from the April 1896 issue (B136).

B138 "John Greenlaw's Story." *Massey's Magazine* [Toronto], July 1896, pp. 30–34.

B139 "The Nest of Imposture." *Massey's Magazine* [Toronto], Aug. 1896, pp. 102–06.
Continued in the September 1896 issue (B140).

B140 "The Nest of Imposture." *Massey's Magazine* [Toronto], Sept. 1896, pp. 203–08.
Continued from the August 1896 issue (B139).

B141 "Ends Rough Hewn." *Massey's Magazine* [Toronto], Oct. 1896, pp. 276–82.

B142 "The Return." *Massey's Magazine* [Toronto], Nov. 1896, pp. 352–57.
This story was later dramatized as *Pierre: A Play in One Act* (B326).

B143 "A Legend of Welly Legrave." *Scribner's Magazine*, April 1898, pp. 470–79. *WE*.

B144 "Their Wedding Eve: A Story of the War of 1812." *The Globe Christmas Number* [Toronto], [24?] Dec. 1898, pp. 14–16.

B145 "The Winning of Marie-Louise." *The Outlook* [New York], 1 July 1899, pp. 523–27. Rpt. in *The Canadian Magazine of Politics, Science, Art and Literature* [Toronto], Sept. 1903, pp. 417–21. *WE*; *SSDC*; *VVOS*.

B146 "The Witching of Elspie." *The Christmas Globe* [Toronto], [25 Dec.?] 1899, pp. 31–32. *WE*.

B147 "The Vain Shadow: [Being an Excerpt from the Manuscript Journal of Archibald Muir, Clerk of the Honourable the [sic] Hudson's Bay Company at Nepigon [sic] House in the year of our Lord 1815]." *Scribner's Magazine*, July 1900, pp. 72–82. Rpt. in *The Canadian Magazine* [Toronto], Jan. 1928, pp. 10–11, 44–45, 48. *WE* ("Vain Shadow").

B148 "Coquelicot." *The Christmas Globe* [Toronto], [25 Dec.?] 1901, pp. 21–24.

B149 "An Adventure of Mrs. Mackenzie's: Being a Variation on a Theme of Thackeray's." *The Canadian Magazine of Politics, Science, Art and Literature* [Toronto], July 1903, pp. 260–69. *WE* ("An Adventure of Mrs. Mackenzie's").

B150 "The Stratagem of Terrance O'Halloran." *The Canadian Magazine of Politics, Science, Art and Literature* [Toronto], Jan. 1904, pp. 283–86.

B151 "A Sacred Trust: A Story of the Upper Ottawa." *The Christmas Globe* [Toronto], [25 Dec.?] 1906, pp. 40–41, 43.

B152 "Star-Blanket." *The Canadian Magazine of Politics, Science, Art and Literature* [Toronto], July 1904, pp. 251–56. *SSDC* ("Charcoal"); *VVOS*; *CAOP*.

B153 "Vengeance Is Mine." *Munsey's Magazine* [New York], 36 (March 1907), 777–84. *WE*; *VVOS*.

B154 "Recompense." *Munsey's Magazine* [New York], Oct. 1907, pp. 25–28. *WE* ("Expiation"); *SSDC*.

B155 "How Uncle David Rouse Made His Will." *The Christmas Globe* [Toronto], [25 Dec.?] 1907, pp. 32–33.

B156 "A Night in Cordoba." *Civil Service Review*, 1, No. 4 (March 1929), 277–78. *CAOP*.

B157 "Clute Boulay." *Queen's Quarterly*, 41 (Summer 1934), 206–17. Rpt. in *Boréal: Journal of Northern Ontario Studies/Revue du nord de l'Ontario* [Univ. College of Hearst], No. 9 (1978), pp. 23–30. *SSDC*; *VVOS*; *CAOP*.

B158 "The Flashlight." *Queen's Quarterly*, 41 (Winter 1934), 487–92. *CAOP*.

B159 "Tête-Jaune." *Queen's Quarterly*, 46 (Autumn 1939), 267–79. *VVOS*; *CAOP*.

B160 "The Circle of Affection." *Queen's Quarterly*, 52 (Summer 1945), 141–57. *SSDC*; *CAOP*.

B161 "Labries Frau." Trans. Armin Arnold. In *Kanadische Erzähler der Gegenwart*. Ed. Armin Arnold and Walter Riedel. Zürich: Manesse, 1986, pp. 247–71. *WE* ("Labrie's Wife"); *SSDC*; *VVOS*.

Articles and Reviews

Note: Most of Scott's book reviews were published in the "At the Mermaid Inn" column, where they often provided him with an occasion to muse on some aspect of culture that interested him. Consequently, to avoid weakening the continuity and the topicality of the column, book reviews and articles are combined in this bibliography.

B162 "At the Mermaid Inn." *The Globe* [Toronto], 6 Feb. 1892, p. 9. *AMIC* (excerpt); *AMI*.
Originally signed: S. A discussion of Algernon Swinburne's appreciation (in *The Fortnightly Review*, February 1892) of Victor Hugo's poem "Dieu"; Scott muses on the use of "local colour" in Canadian and Australian verse; a discussion of Richard Watson Gilder's *Poems of Two Worlds* and Hamlin Garland's *Main-Travelled Road*.

B163 "At the Mermaid Inn." *The Globe* [Toronto], 13 Feb. 1892, pp. 8–9. *AMI*.
Originally signed: S. Scott and a companion muse on " 'a verse from the great bible of human life' "; a general discussion of playwriting, with a specific reference to *Athelwold: A Drama in Five Acts and in Verse*, by Amelie Rives, and to *Hedda Gabler*, by Henrik Ibsen.

B164 "At the Mermaid Inn." *The Globe* [Toronto], 20 Feb. 1892, pp. 8–9. *AMI*.
Originally signed: S. Scott quotes from *The Prelude, or Growth of a Poet's Mind*, by William Words-

worth; an anecdote on Methodism and Protestantism; the Shelley Society plans a performance of *The Cenci* on the centenary of the birth of Percy Bysshe Shelley; a discussion of Helmuth von Moltke's *Letters of Field-Marshall Count Helmuth von Moltke to His Mother and His Brothers*.

B165 "At the Mermaid Inn." *The Globe* [Toronto], 27 Feb. 1892, p. 8. *AMI.*

Originally signed: S. A letter to "Francesca" on Edmond Scherer's *Essays on English Literature*, with specific reference to Scherer's evaluations of George Eliot and Matthew Arnold; two anecdotes on Byron taken from Sir Walter Scott's journal.

B166 "At the Mermaid Inn." *The Globe* [Toronto], 5 March 1892, p. 9. *AMIC* (excerpt); *AMI.*

Originally signed: S. A story illustrating that a "duke exists by reason of his documents," not by virtue of his innate superiority; a discussion of Henry B. Fuller's *The Chevalier of Pensieri-Vani* and the February 1892 issue of *The Fortnightly Review*, with specific reference to James Thomson's "The City of Dreadful Night" and Francis Adams' "Some Australian Men of Mark."

B167 "At the Mermaid Inn." *The Globe* [Toronto], 12 March 1892, p. 9. *AMI.*

Originally signed: S. A discussion of the novels of George Meredith, with specific reference to *Harry Richmond*.

B168 "At the Mermaid Inn." *The Globe* [Toronto], 19 March 1892, pp. 8-9. *AMIC; AMI.*

Originally signed: S. A "sermon" on Victor Hugo's statement that "One service more is one more beauty"; a whimsical discussion on the dangers of book borrowers.

B169 "At the Mermaid Inn." *The Globe* [Toronto], 26 March 1892, p. 8. *AMIC; AMI.*

Originally signed: S. A parody of post-Romantic blank verse and theories of poetic inspiration.

B170 "At the Mermaid Inn." *The Globe* [Toronto], 2 April 1892, p. 8. *AMI.*

Originally signed: S. Commentary on the Percy Bysshe Shelley centenary; notes on forthcoming publications by Algernon Swinburne, John Florio, W.E. Henley, and Robert Louis Stevenson; a discussion of Thomas Hardy's *Tess of the d'Urbervilles*.

B171 "At the Mermaid Inn." *The Globe* [Toronto], 9 April 1892, p. 8. *AMI.*

Originally signed: S. A refutation of views of history that debunk the heroic; a refutation of prosaic literal interpretations of poetic diction.

B172 "At the Mermaid Inn." *The Globe* [Toronto], 16 April 1892, pp. 8-9. *AMIC; AMI.*

Originally signed: L. & S. A discussion of a recent art exhibition at the Royal Canadian Academy, Ottawa.

B173 "At the Mermaid Inn." *The Globe* [Toronto], 23 April 1892, p. 8. *AMI.*

Originally signed. S. A discussion of *The Collected Poems of Philip Bourke Marston*, ed. Louise Chandler Moulton.

B174 "At the Mermaid Inn." *The Globe* [Toronto], 30 April 1892, p. 8. *AMI.*

Originally signed: S. Calls attention to Louis Moreau Gottschalk's derogatory remarks in *Notes of a Pianist* on French Canadians; in a search for true poetry, he attacks books, such as Edward Robert Bulwer Lytton's *Glenaveril*, which are "immensely dull and have no touch of poetry from cover to cover."

B175 "At the Mermaid Inn." *The Globe* [Toronto], 7 May 1892, p. 8. *AMI.*

Originally signed: S. Comments on the relationship between people's social class and their ability to respond to a work of art.

B176 "At the Mermaid Inn." *The Globe* [Toronto], 14 May 1892, p. 8. *AMIC* (excerpt); *AMI.*

Originally signed: S. Book tariffs as a further impediment to acquiring a library in Canada where books are expensive; a humorous letter to Alexis on the advisability of publishing under one's own name, no matter how ill-liked it may be.

B177 "At the Mermaid Inn." *The Globe* [Toronto], 21 May 1892, p. 8. *AMI.*

Originally signed: S. Uses Robert Louis Stevenson's "Letter to a Young Gentleman Who Proposed to Embrace the Career of Art" to muse on the nature of the creative spirit.

B178 "At the Mermaid Inn." *The Globe* [Toronto], 28 May 1892, pp. 8–9. *AMI.*

Originally signed: S. A defence of George Meredith's poem *Modern Love.*

B179 "At the Mermaid Inn." *The Globe* [Toronto], 4 June 1892, pp. 8–9. *AMIC* (excerpt); *AMI.*

Originally signed: S. Cites Arthur Hugh Clough's poem "In a London Square" to make the point that the "final test of the highest poetry" is "its power of comforting and sustaining the spirit"; a note on Robert Louis Stevenson's forthcoming work.

B180 "At the Mermaid Inn." *The Globe* [Toronto], 11 June 1892, p. 8. *AMI.*

Originally signed: S. Uses the fate of a "crippled Scotch tutor" who sought solace from life in the writing of unsuccessful poetry to chastise those of smaller spirit.

B181 "At the Mermaid Inn." *The Globe* [Toronto], 25 June 1892, pp. 8–9. *AMIC; AMI.*

Originally signed: S. A volume of selected Canadian literature should be published for the exhibition at Chicago in 1893; the qualities of a good critic.

B182 "At the Mermaid Inn." *The Globe* [Toronto], 2 July 1892, p. 9. *AMI.*

Originally signed: S. Accuses Rudyard Kipling, especially in *Barrack-Room Ballads*, of intolerable coarseness.

B183 "At the Mermaid Inn." *The Globe* [Toronto], 9 July 1892, p. 12. *AMI.*

Originally signed: S. Discussion of *The Life of Thomas Cooper, Written by Himself.*

B184 "At the Mermaid Inn." *The Globe* [Toronto], 16 July 1892, p. 8. *AMIC; AMI.*

Originally signed: S. Letter to "Francesca" on the satisfaction of keeping a journal.

B185 "At the Mermaid Inn." *The Globe* [Toronto], 23 July 1892, p. 8. *AMI.*

Originally signed: S. Narrates the Scandinavian myth of how the art of poetry arose.

B186 "At the Mermaid Inn." *The Globe* [Toronto], 6 Aug. 1892, p. 8. *AMI.*

Originally signed: S. A pirated edition of *Diana of the Crossways* provides Scott with another occasion to endorse George Meredith's writing.

B187 "At the Mermaid Inn." *The Globe* [Toronto], 13 Aug. 1892, p. 6. *AMI*.

Originally signed: S. Reprints Algernon Charles Swinburne's sonnet "The Centenary of Shelley."

B188 "At the Mermaid Inn." *The Globe* [Toronto], 20 Aug. 1892, p. 8. *AMI*.

Originally signed: S. A discussion of *The Siege of Lucknow: A Diary*, by Julia Selina, Lady Inglis (Thesiger).

B189 "At the Mermaid Inn." *The Globe* [Toronto], 27 Aug. 1892, p. 8. *AMIC*; *AMI*.

Originally signed: S. A humorous aside on the possible consequences of newspapers adopting the magazine practice of dating their issues well in advance of the date at which they actually appear.

B190 "At the Mermaid Inn." *The Globe* [Toronto], 3 Sept. 1892, p. 8. *AMI*.

Originally signed: S. A semi-serious look at the possible abuses of hypnotism.

B191 "At the Mermaid Inn." *The Globe* [Toronto], 10 Sept. 1892, p. 8. *AMIC*; *AMI*.

Originally signed: S. Poetry and the poetic temperament, with reference to Arthur Symons' article "Mr. Henley's Poetry"; a discussion of *The Life and Times of Sir George Grey, K.C.B.*, by William Lee Rees and Lily Rees.

B192 "At the Mermaid Inn." *The Globe* [Toronto], 17 Sept. 1892, pp. 8-9. *AMI*.

Originally signed: S. A discussion of *Poems of Wordsworth (From Arnold's Selections)*, edited by J.E. Wetherell.

B193 "At the Mermaid Inn." *The Globe* [Toronto], 24 Sept. 1892, p. 8. *AMI*.

Originally signed: S. An annoyed response to prosaic critics whose criticism of literature helps ensure that writers will be unable to earn their living by writing in Canada.

B194 "At the Mermaid Inn." *The Globe* [Toronto], 1 Oct. 1892, p. 8. *AMI*.

Originally signed: S. Appreciation of the late George William Curtis.

B195 "At the Mermaid Inn." *The Globe* [Toronto], 8 Oct. 1892, pp. 8-9. *AMI*.

Originally signed: S. A discussion of *Poems by the Way*, by William Morris.

B196 "At the Mermaid Inn." *The Globe* [Toronto], 15 Oct. 1892, p. 8. *AMI*.

Originally signed: S. Letter to "Francesca" on the death of Alfred Lord Tennyson.

B197 "At the Mermaid Inn." *The Globe* [Toronto], 22 Oct. 1892, pp. 8-9. *AMIC*; *AMI*.

Originally signed: S. Appreciation of the late Canadian artist Paul Peel; a discussion of *The Naulahka: A Story of West and East*, by Rudyard Kipling and Wolcott Balestier.

B198 "At the Mermaid Inn." *The Globe* [Toronto], 29 Oct. 1892, p. 8. *AMIC* (excerpt); *AMI*.

Originally signed: S. A discussion of W.E. Henley's *The Song of the Sword and Other Verses*.

B199 "At the Mermaid Inn." *The Globe* [Toronto], 12 Nov. 1892, pp. 8-9. *AMI*.

Originally signed: S. A discussion of Henrik Ibsen's *The Lady from the Sea*.

B200 "At the Mermaid Inn." *The Globe* [Toronto], 19 Nov. 1892, p. 9. *AMI*.

Originally signed: S. On ideality.

B201 "At the Mermaid Inn." *The Globe* [Toronto], 3 Dec. 1892, p. 9. *AMI*.

Originally signed: S. A skating expedition provides Scott with an excuse to write a vivid description of a Canadian winter night.

B202 "At the Mermaid Inn." *The Globe* [Toronto], 10 Dec. 1892, p. 9. *AMI*.

Originally signed: S. The passion for reading and writing plays.

B203 "At the Mermaid Inn." *The Globe* [Toronto], 17 Dec. 1892, pp. 8–9. *AMI*.

Originally signed: S. A note on R.K. Kernighan's poem "A Convert to Theosophy"; evaluation of Harriet Monroe's poem "Columbian Ode."

B204 "At the Mermaid Inn." *The Globe* [Toronto], 31 Dec. 1892, p. 8. *AMIC; AMI*.

Originally signed: S. On the growth of a "vigorous national life" in Canada.

B205 "At the Mermaid Inn." *The Globe* [Toronto], 7 Jan. 1893, p. 6. *AMIC; AMI*.

Originally signed: S. An examination of the career of Gilbert Parker.

B206 "At the Mermaid Inn." *The Globe* [Toronto], 14 Jan. 1893, p. 6. *AMIC; AMI*.

Originally signed: S. Using Michel Eyquem de Montaigne's *Essays* as an example, Scott condemns those who read "the old authors out of pruriency" and are thus misled as to the purpose of the work.

B207 "At the Mermaid Inn." *The Globe* [Toronto], 21 Jan. 1893, p. 6. *AMI*.

Originally signed: S. The forthcoming works by George Meredith and R.D. Blackmore; on the unusual and alarming picture of the past provided by constables' accounts, such as *The Constable's Accounts of the Manor of Manchester*, edited by J.P. Earwaker.

B208 "At the Mermaid Inn." *The Globe* [Toronto], 28 Jan. 1893, p. 6. *AMI*.

Originally signed: S. On our schools' need of a Canadian history textbook that is "based in sympathy" and that teaches both "the great deeds" and "the heroic sufferings" of Canadians.

B209 "At the Mermaid Inn." *The Globe* [Toronto], 4 Feb. 1893, p. 6. *AMI*.

Originally signed: S. On Gustave Flaubert's impassioned search for "the absolute fusion of form and content."

B210 "At the Mermaid Inn." *The Globe* [Toronto], 11 Feb. 1893, p. 6. *AMI*.

Originally signed: S. Letter to "Francesca" on the pointlessness of coveting literary fame.

B211 "At the Mermaid Inn." *The Globe* [Toronto], 18 Feb. 1893, p. 6. *AMIC; AMI*.

Originally signed: S. On the "spirit of ideal liberty," which characterizes Harriet Monroe's *Valeria and Other Poems*.

B212 "At the Mermaid Inn." *The Globe* [Toronto], 25 Feb. 1893, p. 7. *AMIC; AMI*.

Originally signed: S. The role of unconventional religious opinions in poetry.

B213 "At the Mermaid Inn." *The Globe* [Toronto], 4 March 1893, p. 6. *AMIC; AMI*.

Originally signed: S. The writing of poetry and the meaning of "success."

B214 "At the Mermaid Inn." *The Globe* [Toronto], 11 March 1893, p. 6. *AMIC; AMI.*

Originally signed: S. On achieving a distinctive literary style by combining one's "native gift" with a study of prose masters such as Shakespeare, Walter Savage Landor, and Matthew Arnold.

B215 "At the Mermaid Inn." *The Globe* [Toronto], 18 March 1893, p. 6. *AMI.*

Originally signed: S. The decline of humour in literature.

B216 "At the Mermaid Inn." *The Globe* [Toronto], 25 March 1893, p. 6. *AMI.*

Originally signed: S. A letter in *The Athenaeum* reveals that a series of portraits painted by Peter Lely in 1672 had become scattered and misnamed in their different locations.

B217 "At the Mermaid Inn." *The Globe* [Toronto], 1 April 1893, p. 9. *AMI.*

Originally signed: S. The art of book-making in Canada; note regarding Gilbert Parker's *The Chief Factor* and *Mrs. Falchion.*

B218 "At the Mermaid Inn." *The Globe* [Toronto], 8 April 1893, p. 6. *AMI.*

Originally signed: S. The recent failing of the magazine *Arcadia.*

B219 "At the Mermaid Inn." *The Globe* [Toronto], 15 April 1893, p. 6. *AMI.*

Originally signed: S. The American characteristic of impatience and its impact on art and literature; a discussion of Anthonie Cornelis Oudemans' *The Great Sea-Serpent: An Historical and Critical Treatise.*

B220 "At the Mermaid Inn." *The Globe* [Toronto], 22 April 1893, p. 6. *AMIC; AMI.*

Originally signed: S. Poetic feeling in the paintings of childhood by Paul Peel.

B221 "At the Mermaid Inn." *The Globe* [Toronto], 29 April 1893, p. 6. *AMI.*

Originally signed: S. On Archibald Geikie's article "Scenery and the Imagination."

B222 "At the Mermaid Inn." *The Globe* [Toronto], 6 May 1893, p. 7. *AMI.*

Originally signed: S. A discussion of idealism and ethics. Also includes "Sister Ste Colombe" [Pt. 1] (B131).

B223 "At the Mermaid Inn." *The Globe* [Toronto], 20 May 1893, p. 6. *AMI.*

Originally signed: S. Excerpts from "How I Write My Books: Related in a Letter to a Friend" (*The Globe* [Toronto], 26 Nov. 1887), by Wilkie Collins, in which Collins describes his method of writing and constructing novels.

B224 "At the Mermaid Inn." *The Globe* [Toronto], 3 June 1893, p. 6. *AMI.*

Originally signed: S. Books as walking companions; a comparison of Henry Francis Cary's and Dante Gabriel Rossetti's translations of Dante's *Divina Commedia.*

B225 "At the Mermaid Inn." *The Globe* [Toronto], 10 June 1893, p. 6. *AMI.*

Originally signed: S. The "problems or conditions of human life [that] are fit and proper subjects for the novelist's art"; note that Thomas McIlwraith is contemplating a new and enlarged edition of *The Birds of Ontario.*

B226 "At the Mermaid Inn." *The Globe* [Toronto], 17 June 1893, p. 5. *AMI*.
Originally signed: S. Typical June weather.

B227 "At the Mermaid Inn." *The Globe* [Toronto], 24 June 1893, p. 7. *AMI*.
Originally signed: S. The music criticism of Henri Frédéric Amiel in his *Journal Intime*; human perception and appreciation of natural scenery, as demonstrated in William Wordsworth's *The Prelude, or Growth of a Poet's Mind*.

B228 "At the Mermaid Inn." *The Globe* [Toronto], 1 July 1893, p. 6. *AMIC; AMI*.
Originally signed: S. A discussion of Frank Yeigh's *Ontario's Parliament Buildings; or, A Century of Legislation, 1792–1892. A Historical Sketch*.

B229 "Canadian Feeling toward the United States." *The Bookman: A Literary Journal* [New York], 3, No. 4 (June 1896), 333–36.

B230 Memoir. In *The Poems of Archibald Lampman*. By Archibald Lampman. Ed. Duncan Campbell Scott. Toronto: Morang, 1900, pp. xi–xxv. Rpt. in *The Poems of Archibald Lampman (Including At the Long Sault)*. By Archibald Lampman. Ed. Duncan Campbell Scott. Introd. and Bibliographical Note Margaret Coulby Whitridge. Toronto: Univ. of Toronto Press, 1974, pp. xi–xxv.

B231 "A Decade of Canadian Poetry." *The Canadian Magazine of Politics, Science, Art and Literature* [Toronto], June 1901, pp. 153–58. *MLDC* (excerpts — "Appendix: Some Excerpts from a Decade of Canadian Poetry, by Duncan Campbell Scott, *The Canadian Magazine*, 1901").

B232 "Lord Strathcona." *Ainslee's Magazine* [New York], 8 (1901–02), 552–60.

B233 "A Walk to Swanston." *The Reader: An Illustrated Monthly Magazine* [New York], 1 (Nov. 1902–May 1903), 502–06.

B234 "The Last of the Indian Treaties." Photograph Duncan Campbell Scott. *Scribner's Magazine*, Nov. 1906, pp. 573–83. *CAOP*.

B235 "George Meredith, Dean of English Novelists." *Munsey's Magazine* [New York], Feb. 1908, pp. 798–802.

B236 Introduction. In *The People of the Plains*. By Amelia M. Paget. Ed. Duncan Campbell Scott. Toronto: William Briggs, 1909, pp. 5–15.

B237 Introduction. In "Traditional History of the Confederacy of the Six Nations." By Committee of the Chiefs. *The Royal Society of Canada Proceedings and Transactions*, Ser. 3, 5, Sec. II (May 1911), 195–97. Rpt. in *Traditional History of the Confederacy of the Six Nations*. By Committee of the Chiefs. Ottawa: Royal Society of Canada, 1912, pp. 195–97.

B238 "Indian Affairs, 1763–1841." In *Canada and Its Provinces*. Gen. ed. Adam Shortt and Arthur G. Doughty. Toronto: Glasgow, Brook, 1913. Vol. IV, 695–725.

B239 "Indian Affairs, 1840–1867." In *Canada and Its Provinces*. Gen. ed. Adam Shortt and Arthur G. Doughty. Toronto: Glasgow, Brook, 1913. Vol. V, 331–62.

B240 "Indian Affairs, 1867–1912." In *Canada and Its Provinces*. Gen. ed. Adam Shortt and Arthur G.

Doughty. Toronto: Glasgow, Brook, 1913. Vol. VII, 593–626.

B241 "Notes on the Meeting Place of the First Parliament of Upper Canada and the Early Buildings at Niagara." *The Royal Society of Canada Proceedings and Transactions*, Ser. 3, 7, Sec. II (May 1913), 175–91.

B242 "Poetry and Progress." [Presidential Address.] Royal Society of Canada, Ottawa. 17 May 1922. Printed in *The Royal Society of Canada Proceedings and Transactions*, Ser. 3, 16 (May 1922), xlix–lxvii. Rpt. in *The Canadian Magazine of Politics, Science, Art and Literature* [Toronto], Jan. 1923, pp. 187–95. Rpt. ("Poetry and Progress: *Presidential Address delivered before the Royal Society of Canada, May 17, 1922*") in *Duncan Campbell Scott: A Book of Criticism*. Ed. S.L. Dragland. Ottawa: Tecumseh, 1974, pp. 7–27. *CAOP* ("Poetry and Progress"); *PP* ("Poetry and Progress: Presidential Address").

B243 Rev. of *The Ninth Vibration*, by L. Adams Beck. *The Canadian Bookman: A Monthly Devoted to Literature, the Library and the Printed Book*, Dec. 1922, p. 323.

B244 "The Aboriginal Races." *Annals of the American Academy of Political and Social Science* [Philadelphia], 107 (May 1923), 63–66.

B245 Introduction. In *Lyrics of the Earth: Sonnets and Ballads*. By Archibald Lampman. Ed. Duncan Campbell Scott. Toronto: Musson, 1925, pp. 3–47.

B246 "Who's Who in Canadian Literature: Archibald Lampman." *The Canadian Bookman: A Journal Devoted to Literature and the Creative Arts*, April 1926, pp. 107–09.

B247 Introduction. In *Ten Canadian Colour Prints*. By Walter J. Phillips. Toronto: Thomas Nelson, 1927, pp. 3–5.

B248 Rev. of *Anatole France, the Parisian*, by Herbert L. Stewart. *The Dalhousie Review*, 7 (Jan. 1928), 545–47.

B249 "My Best Piece of Work: Canadian Authors Tell Why. Duncan C. Scott." *Toronto Star Weekly* [*Toronto Daily Star*], 2 Nov. 1929, General Section Number One, p. 9.

B250 "Archibald Lampman." In *Addresses Delivered at the Dedication of the Archibald Lampman Memorial Cairn at Morpeth, Ontario*. By William Sherwood Fox, E.A. Cruikshank, J.H. Cameron, Arthur Stringer, Nathaniel A. Benson, and Duncan Campbell Scott. London, Ont.: Western Ontario Branch of the Canadian Authors' Association, 1930, pp. 12–16. Rpt. in the *Civil Service Review* [Ottawa], 3, No. 2 (Sept. 1930), 172–76.

B251 Foreword. In *Roses of Shadow*. By Elise Aylen. Toronto: Macmillan, 1930, pp. iii–vi.

B252 Foreword. In *Catalogue of the Manoir Richelieu Collection of North American Indians (1830–1840)*. By Percy F. Godenrath. Montreal: Canada Steamship Lines, 1932, pp. 1–3.

B253 "Booklover's Corner." *The Ottawa Journal*, 10 July 1937, p. 19.
A commentary on "A Leechbook of the Fifteenth Century."

B254 "Booklover's Corner." *The Ottawa Journal*, 17 July 1937, p. 19.

A commentary on Alfred Einstein's *A Short History of Music* and Edgar Lee Masters' *Life of Walt Whitman*.

B255 "Booklover's Corner." *The Ottawa Journal*, 31 July 1937, p. 17.
A commentary on George Borrow and Sir Thomas Browne of Norfolk.

B256 "Booklover's Corner." *The Ottawa Journal*, 7 Aug. 1937, p. 19.
This column was devoted to a commentary on Edward Gibbon.

B257 "Clarence A. Gagnon: Recollection and Record." *Maritime Art: A Canadian Art Magazine*, 3, No. 1 (Oct.–Nov. 1942), 5–8. CAOP.

B258 Foreword. In *At the Long Sault and Other New Poems*. By Archibald Lampman. Ed. E.K. Brown and D.C. Scott. Toronto: Ryerson, 1943, pp. vii–x.

B259 "Archibald Lampman." *Educational Record* [Quebec], 59, No. 4 (Oct.–Dec. 1943), 221–25. Rpt. in *Leading Canadian Poets*. Ed. W.P. Percival. Toronto: Ryerson, 1948, pp. 98–106.

B260 "Memoir of Sir Charles G.D. Roberts." *Full Tide* [Vancouver], 5 Feb. 1944, p. 11.

B261 Foreword. In *Selected Poems of Archibald Lampman*. By Archibald Lampman. Ed. Duncan Campbell Scott. Toronto: Ryerson, 1947, p. v.

B262 Memoir. In *Selected Poems of Archibald Lampman*. By Archibald Lampman. Ed. Duncan Campbell Scott. Toronto: Ryerson, 1947, pp. xiii–xxvii.

B263 "Copy of a Letter by Duncan Campbell Scott to Ralph Gustafson." *The Fiddlehead*, No. 41 (Summer 1959), pp. 12–14. Rpt. in *Archibald Lampman*. Ed. Michael Gnarowski. Critical Views on Canadian Writers. Toronto: Ryerson, 1970, pp. 154–58.

B264 "Extracts from D.C. Scott's Own Journal of 1905 & 1906." *Copperfield* [Temagami, Ont.], 5 (1974), 37–45.
In fact, these extracts are not all from "Scott's Own Journal." The 1906 journal was not kept by Scott. Kathy Mezei believes Pelham Edgar wrote it (see C262), an opinion with which I concur. Edgar was the secretary for the 1906 trip. In the journal he actually describes things that Scott did. For example, he refers to Scott's taking photographs. Furthermore, the handwriting is quite different from Scott's.

Governmental Reports

B265 "Report of the Superintendent of Indian Education." *Sessional Papers*. Vol. XIX. Government of Canada. Session 1911, 269–341.

B266 "Report of the Superintendent of Indian Education." *Sessional Papers*. Vol. XX. Government of Canada. Session 1911–12, 289–393.

B267 "Report of the Superintendent of Indian Education." *Sessional Papers*. Vol. XXI. Government of Canada. Session 1912–13, 299–401.

B268 "Report of the Superintendent of Indian Education." *Sessional Papers*. Vol. XXIII. Government of Canada. Session 1914, 305–413.

B269 "Report of the Deputy Superintendent General of Indian Affairs." *Sessional Papers*. Vol. XXIII. Government of Canada. Session 1915, xvii–xxxii.

B270 "Report of the Deputy Superintendent General of Indian Affairs." *Sessional Papers*. Vol. XXIII. Government of Canada. Session 1916, xix–xxxv.

B271 "Report of the Deputy Superintendent General of Indian Affairs." *Sessional Papers*. Vol. XVIII. Government of Canada. Session 1917, xxix–xli.

B272 "Report of the Deputy Superintendent General of Indian Affairs." *Sessional Papers*. Vol. XII. Government of Canada. Session 1918, 9–32.

B273 "Report of the Deputy Superintendent General of Indian Affairs." *Sessional Papers*. Vol. IX. Government of Canada. Session 1919, 9–40.

B274 "Report of the Deputy Superintendent General of Indian Affairs." *Sessional Papers*. Vol. VIII. Government of Canada. Session 1920, 7–54.

B275 "Report of the Deputy Superintendent General of Indian Affairs." *Sessional Papers*. Vol. VIII. Government of Canada. Session 1921, 7–30.

B276 "Report of the Deputy Superintendent General of Indian Affairs." *Sessional Papers*. Vol. VIII. Government of Canada. Session 1922, 7–36.
Unsigned.

B277 "Report of the Deputy Superintendent General of Indian Affairs." *Sessional Papers*. Vol. IV. Government of Canada. Session 1923, 7–32.

B278 "Report of the Deputy Superintendent General of Indian Affairs." *Sessional Papers*. Vol. IV. Government of Canada. Session 1924, 7–22.

B279 "Report of the Deputy Superintendent General of Indian Affairs." *Sessional Papers*. Vol. II. Government of Canada. Session 1925, 7–26.

B280 "Report of the Deputy Superintendent General of Indian Affairs." *Annual Departmental Reports*. Vol. III. 1924–25, 7–25.

B281 "Report of the Deputy Superintendent General of Indian Affairs." *Annual Departmental Reports*. Vol. II. 1925–26, 7–30.

B282 "Report of the Deputy Superintendent General of Indian Affairs." *Annual Departmental Reports*. Vol. II. 1926–27, 7–26.

B283 "Report of the Deputy Superintendent General of Indian Affairs." *Annual Departmental Reports*. Vol. II. 1927–28, 7–25.

B284 "Report of the Deputy Superintendent General of Indian Affairs." *Annual Departmental Reports*. Vol. II. 1928–29, 7–41.

B285 "Report of the Deputy Superintendent General of Indian Affairs." *Annual Departmental Reports*. Vol. II. 1929–30, 7–52.

Reprinted Anthology Contributions: A Selection

B286 "At the Cedars." In *Songs of the Great Dominion: Voices from the Forests and Waters, the Settlements and Cities of Canada*. Ed. and introd. William Douw Lighthall. London: Walter Scott, 1889, pp. 91–93.
See B7 for an original publication in this collection.

B287 "Above St. Irénée," "At Les Éboulements," "Autumn Song," "The End of the Day," "The Fifteenth of April," "For Remembrance," "Life and

Death," "Off Rivière du Loup," "Ottawa," "The Reed-Player," "September," and "Song [Here's the last rose]." In *Later Canadian Poems*. Ed. J.E. Wetherell. Toronto: Copp Clark, 1893, pp. 121–26.

B288 "Above St. Irénée," "The End of the Day," "The Fifteenth of April," "A Flock of Sheep," "Home Song" [A2 — "The Canadian's Home-Song"], "Life and Death," "Memory," "Off Rivière du Loup," and "Ottawa." In *A Treasury of Canadian Verse; With Brief Biographical Notes*. Ed. and preface Theodore H. Rand. Toronto: William Briggs, 1900, pp. 322–30.

B289 "Off Rivière du Loup," "A Portrait," and "A Summer Storm." In *Selections from the Canadian Poets*. Ed. and introd. E.A. Hardy. Morang's Literature Series, No. 9. Toronto: Morang, 1906, pp. 72–76.

B290 "Autumn Song," "The End of the Day," "The Fifteenth of April," "For Remembrance," "The Forsaken," "The Half-Breed Girl," "The House of the Broken-Hearted," "A Little Song," "The Reed-Player," and "A Summer Storm." In *The Oxford Book of Canadian Verse*. Ed. and preface Wilfred Campbell. Toronto: Oxford Univ. Press, 1912, pp. 220–24.

B291 "At the Cedars," "The Builder," "The Forgers," "The Half-Breed Girl," "Lines in Memory of Edmund Morris" (excerpts), "The Sea by the Wood," "The Voice and the Dusk," and "The Wood by the Sea." In *Canadian Poets*. Ed. and foreword John W. Garvin. Toronto: McClelland, Goodchild, and Stewart, 1916, pp. 135–44.

B292 "Bells," "Ecstasy," "In the Selkirks," "Rapids at Night," and "The Voice and the Dusk." In *Our Canadian Literature: Representative Prose and Verse*. Ed. and introd. Albert Durrant Watson and Lorne Pierce. Toronto: Ryerson, 1922, pp. 21, 31, 74–75, 91–92, 105.

B293 "The Fifteenth of April," "The Half-Breed Girl," "Off Rivière du Loup," and "To the Heroic Soul." In *The Golden Treasury of Canadian Verse*. Ed. and introd. A.M. Stephen. Toronto: J.M. Dent, 1928, pp. 51–57.

B294 "Labrie's Wife" (story). In *Canadian Short Stories*. Ed. and introd. Raymond Knister. Toronto: Macmillan, 1928, pp. 255–75.
    Knister's book is dedicated to Scott.

B295 "At the Cedars," "Bells," "Ecstasy," "The Forsaken," "The Half-Breed Girl," "In the Selkirks," "On the Way to the Mission," "The Piper of Arll," "Rapids at Night," "The Reed-Player," and "The Voice and the Dusk." In *Our Canadian Literature: Representative Verse English and French*. Ed. and foreword Bliss Carman and Lorne Pierce. Toronto: Ryerson, 1935, pp. 124–40.
    Carman and Pierce's book is dedicated to Sir Charles G.D. Roberts and Scott.

B296 "Powassan's Drum." In *New Harvesting: Contemporary Canadian Poetry, 1918–1938*. Ed. and preface Ethel Hume Bennett. Toronto: Macmillan, 1938, pp. 162–67.

B297 "After Battle," "At Delos," "The Half-Breed Girl," "The Sailor's Sweetheart," and "Watkwenies." In *Anthology of Canadian Poetry (English)*. Ed. and preface Ralph Gustafson. Harmondsworth, Eng.: Penguin, 1942, pp. 37–40.

B298 "At Delos," "At Gull Lake: August, 1810," "At the Cedars," "Night Burial in the Forest," and "The Piper of Arll." In *The Book of Canadian Poetry: A Critical and Historical Anthology*. Ed., preface, and introd. A.J.M. Smith. Toronto: Gage, 1943, pp. 214–25.

B299 "The Forsaken," "Night Hymns on Lake Nipigon," and "The Onondaga Madonna." In *A Pocketful of Canada*. Ed. and preface John D. Robins. Introd. H.M. Tory. Toronto: Collins, 1946, pp. 172–73, 181, 229–31.

B300 "Paul Farlotte" (story). In *A Book of Canadian Stories*. Ed., introd., and preface Desmond Pacey. Toronto: Ryerson, 1947, pp. 79–90.

B301 "The Forsaken" and "Power." In *Twentieth Century Canadian Poetry: An Anthology*. Ed. and introd. Earle Birney. Toronto: Ryerson, 1953, pp. 81–83, 100.

B302 "Indian Place-Names," "The Journey," "The Mad Girl's Song," and "The Sailor's Sweetheart." In *Canadian Poems 1850–1952*. 2nd rev. ed. Ed. and introd. Louis Dudek and Irving Layton. Toronto: Contact, 1953, pp. 48–51.

B303 "At the Cedars," "Bells," "Ecstasy," "The Forsaken," "The Half-Breed Girl," "In the Selkirks," "On the Way to the Mission," and "Rapids at Night." In *Canadian Poetry in English*. Ed. Bliss Carman, Lorne Pierce, and V.B. Rhodenizer. Introd. V.B. Rhodenizer. Foreword Lorne Pierce. Toronto: Ryerson, 1954, pp. 120–29.

B304 "At Delos," "At Gull Lake: August, 1810," "At the Cedars," "By a Child's Bed," "The Cup," "The Forsaken," "The Half-Breed Girl," "The Height of Land," "Lilacs and Humming-Birds," "Night Burial in the Forest," "On the Way to the Mission," "The Onondaga Madonna," "Ottawa," "The Piper of Arll," "Powassan's Drum," "The Sea by the Wood," "Senza Fine," "Spring on Mattagami," "A Vision," and "The Wood by the Sea." In *Poets of the Confederation: Carman/Lampman/Roberts/Scott*. Ed. and introd. Malcolm Ross. New Canadian Library Original, No. O1. Toronto: McClelland and Stewart, 1960, pp. 88–122.

B305 "At Gull Lake: August, 1810," "En Route," "Night and the Pines," "Night Hymns on Lake Nipigon," "A Night in June," "Off Rivière du Loup," and "A Prairie Water Colour." In *The Oxford Book of Canadian Verse: In English and French*. Ed. and introd. A.J.M. Smith. Toronto: Oxford Univ. Press, 1960, pp. 93–104.

B306 "Paul Farlotte" (story). In *Canadian Short Stories*. Ed. and introd. Robert Weaver. London: Oxford Univ. Press, 1960, pp. 15–27.

B307 "The Desjardins" (story) and "En Route." In *A Book of Canada*. Ed. and introd. William Toye. Toronto: Collins, 1962, pp. 172–77, 284–85.

B308 "Labrie's Wife" (story). In *Modern Canadian Stories*. Ed. Giose Rimanelli and Roberto Ruberto. Foreword Earle Birney. Toronto: Ryerson, 1966, pp. 1–15.

B309 "At Delos," "The Onondaga Madonna," "The Piper of Arll," "The Sailor's Sweetheart," "A Song [In the air there are no coral-]," "Thoughts," and "Watkwenies." In *The Penguin Book of Canadian Verse*. Ed. and introd. Ralph Gustafson. Rev. ed. Harmondsworth, Eng.: Penguin, 1967, pp. 98–106.

B310 "The Mad Girl's Song." In *A Century of Canadian Literature/Un Siècle de Littérature Canadienne.* Ed. H. Gordon Green and Guy Sylvestre. Foreword and introd. H. Gordon Green. Préface and introd. Guy Sylvestre. Toronto: Ryerson, 1967, pp. 75–76.

B311 "The Forsaken" (excerpt). In *The Wind Has Wings: Poems from Canada.* Ed. Mary Alice Downie and Barbara Robertson. Illus. Elizabeth Cleaver. Toronto: Oxford Univ. Press, 1968, pp. 62–63.

B312 "Labrie's Wife" (story). In *Great Canadian Short Stories: An Anthology.* Ed. and introd. Alec Lucas. New York: Dell, 1971, pp. 36–50.

B313 "The Desjardins" (story), "The Forsaken," and "A Night in June." In *The Oxford Anthology of Canadian Literature.* Ed. and preface Robert Weaver and William Toye. Toronto: Oxford Univ. Press, 1973, pp. 471–78.

B314 "The Last of the Indian Treaties" (article). In *The Canadian Century: English-Canadian Writing since Confederation.* [Vol. II of *The Book of Canadian Prose.*] Ed. and introd. A.J.M. Smith. Toronto: Gage, 1973, pp. 135–46.

B315 "At Gull Lake: August, 1810," "At the Cedars," "The Closed Door," "The Forsaken," "The Height of Land" (excerpt), "Night Burial in the Forest," "Night Hymns on Lake Nipigon," "The Onondaga Madonna," "The Pedlar" (story), "The Piper of Arll," "The Sea by the Wood," and "The Wood by the Sea." In *Canadian Anthology.* Ed. and preface Carl F. Klinck and Reginald E. Watters. 3rd rev. ed. Toronto: Gage, 1974, pp. 148–61.

B316 "At the Cedars," "At Delos," "At Les Eboulements," "At Murray Bay," "The Closed Door," "The Desjardins" (story), "Ecstasy," "The Forsaken,"

"The Half-Breed Girl," "The Leaf," "Memory," "On the Way to the Mission," "The Onondaga Madonna," "The Piper of Arll," and "Thirteen Songs: I–XIII." In *Canadian Literature: The Beginnings to the 20th Century.* Ed., preface, and introd. Catherine M. McLay. Toronto: McClelland and Stewart, 1974, pp. 313–36.

B317 "Expiation" (story). In *Stories from Ontario.* Ed. and introd. Germaine Warkentin. Toronto: Macmillan, 1974, pp. 78–85.

B318 "A Decade of Canadian Poetry" (article). In *The Search for English-Canadian Literature: An Anthology of Critical Articles from the Nineteenth and Early Twentieth Centuries.* Literature of Canada: Poetry and Prose in Reprint, No. 16. Ed. and introd. Carl Ballstadt. Toronto: Univ. of Toronto Press, 1975, pp. 187–90.

B319 "A Decade of Canadian Poetry" (article). In *Twentieth Century Essays on Confederation Literature.* Ed. and introd. Lorraine McMullen. Ottawa: Tecumseh, 1976, pp. 111–19.

B320 "Labrie's Wife" (story). In *Nineteenth Century Canadian Stories.* Ed. and introd. David Arnason. Toronto: Macmillan, 1976, pp. 188–203.

B321 "At Delos," "At Gull Lake: August, 1810," "The Forsaken," "The Height of Land," "Night and the Pines," "On the Way to the Mission," "The Piper of Arll," "The Sea by the Wood," "Watkwenies," and "The Wood by the Sea." In *Literature in Canada.* Ed. and preface Douglas Daymond and Leslie Monkman. Toronto: Gage, 1978. Vol. I, 378–99.

B322 "Paul Farlotte" (story). In *The Penguin Book of Canadian Short Stories.* Ed. and preface Wayne Grady. Harmondsworth, Eng.: Penguin, 1980, pp. 62–71.

B323 "At The Cedars," "At Gull Lake: August, 1810," "En Route," "The Forsaken," and "On the Way to the Mission." In *The New Oxford Book of Canadian Verse: In English*. Ed. and introd. Margaret Atwood. Toronto: Oxford Univ. Press, 1982, pp. 47–57.

B324 "At the Cedars," "At Gull Lake: August, 1810," "The Forsaken," "On the Way to the Mission," "The Onondaga Madonna," and "The Piper of Arll." In *Canadian Poetry*. Ed. Jack David and Robert Lecker. Introd. George Woodcock. New Press Canadian Classics. Toronto/Downsview, Ont.: General/ECW, 1982, pp. 99–116.

B325 "At the Cedars," "En Route," "The Forsaken," "The Height of Land," "Labrie's Wife" (story), "Night and the Pines," "Night Hymns on Lake Nipigon," "The Onondaga Madonna," "The Piper of Arll," and "Rapids at Night." In *An Anthology of Canadian Literature in English*. Ed. and introd. Russell Brown and Donna Bennett. Vol. 1. Toronto: Oxford Univ. Press, 1982, 195–220.

Drama

B326 *Pierre: A Play in One Act*. In *Canadian Plays from Hart House Theatre*. Ed. Vincent Massey. Toronto: Macmillan, 1926. Vol. 1, 51–76.

This is a dramatized version of the story "The Return" (B142).

Letters

Note: See also "Published Letters" section, A23–A25.

B327 "Reading for the Indians." Letter. *The Week: A Canadian Journal of Politics, Literature, Science and Arts* [Toronto], 12 Jan. 1894, p. 157.

The letter is dated 2 Jan. 1894.

B328 "Scott to Thoreau MacDonald." *Boréal: Journal of Northern Ontario Studies/Revue du nord de l'Ontario* [Univ. College of Hearst], No. 9 (1978), pp. 19–21, 23.

B329 *Dear Bill: The Correspondence of William Arthur Deacon*. Ed. John Lennox and Michele Lacombe. Toronto: Univ. of Toronto Press, 1988, pp. 72, 73–74, 76–77, 129, 130.

The book publishes three letters from Scott to Deacon and two from Deacon to Scott.

B330 "Views of Canadian Literature." *The Week: A Canadian Journal of Politics, Literature, Science and Arts* [Toronto], 16 March 1894, p. 369.

B331 "Letter of Presentation." *The Trinity University Review*, 58, No. 3 (Christmas 1945), 18.

Printed with *Two Autograph Poems*, by Archibald Lampman.

B332 Letters. *Canadian Poetry*, 29 (Feb. 1966), 16–18. SLDC.

B333 Letters. *Canadian Poetry*, 30 (May 1967), 61–64. SLDC.

Audio-Visual Material

B334 *Night Hymn on Lake Nipigon*. Illus. Norval Morriseau. Prod. Trevor Davies and George Macey. Canadian Filmmakers Distribution Centre. 1971. (Colour; 7 min.)

Scott's poem "Night Hymn on Lake Nipigon" (B52) is accompanied by the paintings of Norval Morriseau.

Part II

Works on Duncan Campbell Scott

C   Books, Articles and Sections of Books, Theses
     and Dissertations, Miscellaneous, and Awards
     and Honours

Books

C1   Watson, Dorothy. *Duncan Campbell Scott: A Bibli-
     ography*. Toronto: St. John's Press, 1945. 8 pp.
       Bibliographical data.

C2   Dragland, S.L., ed. *Duncan Campbell Scott: A Book
     of Criticism*. Ottawa: Tecumseh, 1974. 199 pp.
       Each entry is listed separately in the appropriate
     section of the bibliography. See E.K. *Brown*'s "Dun-
     can Campbell Scott" (C41), Melvin H. *Dagg*'s "Scott
     and the Indians" (C127), Stan *Dragland*'s Introduc-
     tion (C141) and Bibliography (C139), Gary *Geddes*'
     "Piper of Many Tunes: Duncan Campbell Scott"
     (C113), Raymond *Knister*'s "Duncan Campbell Scott"
     (C23), J.D. *Logan*'s and Donald G. *French*'s "Dun-
     can Campbell Scott" (C21), Bernard *Muddiman*'s
     "Duncan Campbell Scott" (C16), Desmond *Pacey*'s
     "The Poetry of Duncan Campbell Scott" (C62), G.
     Ross *Roy*'s "Duncan Campbell Scott" (C85), A.J.M.
     Smith's "Duncan Campbell Scott" (C83) and "The

Poetry of Duncan Campbell Scott" (C61), and Milton *Wilson*'s "Scott's Drowned Poet" (C84).
  Also includes Duncan Campbell *Scott*'s "Poetry
and Progress: *Presidential Address delivered before
the Royal Society of Canada, May 17, 1922*" (B242).

C3   Stich, K.P., ed. *The Duncan Campbell Scott Sympo-
     sium*. Re-Appraisals: Canadian Writers, No. 6.
     Ottawa: Univ. of Ottawa Press, 1980. 157 pp.
       Each entry is listed separately in the appropriate
     section of the bibliography. See C.M. *Armitage*'s
     "The Letters of Duncan Campbell Scott to Lionel
     Stevenson" (C191), Sandra *Campbell*'s "A Fortunate
     Friendship: Duncan Campbell Scott and Pelham
     Edgar" (C194), Glenn *Clever*'s "Duncan Campbell
     Scott's Fiction: Moral Realism and Canadian Iden-
     tity" (C183), Fred *Cogswell*'s "Symbol and Decora-
     tion: 'The Piper of Arll'" (C177), James *Doyle*'s
     "Duncan Campbell Scott and American Literature"
     (C178), Stan *Dragland*'s "'Spring on Mattagami': A
     Reconsideration. Duncan Campbell Scott's 'Spring
     on Mattagami' and Some Contexts" (C184) and
     "'Spring on Mattagami': A Reconsideration. 'Spring
     on Mattagami': Second Thoughts" (C185), John
     Flood's "Native People in Scott's Short Fiction"
     (C186), Gordon *Johnston*'s "Epilogue: 'Piano, to
     D.C.S.'" (C273) and "The Significance of Scott's
     Minor Poems" (C179), Catherine E. *Kelly*'s "Mean-
     ings Held in a Mist: The Major Poems" (C180) and
     "Selected Bibliography" (C197), John P. *Matthews*'
     "Duncan Campbell Scott and 'the Moment of
     Becoming'" (C181), Robert L. *McDougall*'s "D.C.
     Scott: A Trace of Documents and a Touch of Life"
     (C182), Kathy *Mezei*'s "From Lifeless Pools to the
     Circle of Affection: The Significance of Space in the
     Poetry of D.C. Scott" (C198), K.P. *Stich*'s Introduc-
     tion (C199), and Martin *Ware*'s "'Spring on Matta-
     gami': A Reconsideration. 'Spring on Mattagami' in

a Dramatic Context" (C187) and " 'Spring on Mattagami': A Reconsideration. 'Spring on Mattagami': A Further Comment" (C188).

C4 Johnston, Gordon. *Duncan Campbell Scott and His Works*. [Downsview, Ont.: ECW, 1983.] 54 pp.

This is an offprint of Johnston's essay in *Canadian Writers and Their Works* (C215).

C5 Titley, E. Brian. *A Narrow Vision: Duncan Campbell Scott and the Administration of Indian Affairs in Canada*. Vancouver: Univ. of British Columbia Press, 1986. 245 pp.

"This book is essentially a study of the personnel and policies of the Department of Indian Affairs in a particularly turbulent and eventful era. As the leading official of the department and the principal arbiter of policy during that time, Scott provides a convenient focus." In a thematic, rather than a chronological, study Titley argues that "Canadian Indian policy found its principal inspiration in the assumptions of nineteenth-century evangelical religion, cultural imperialism, and laissez-faire economics." Scott's implementation of the policies was not marked by the ". . . corrupt practices that had abruptly terminated the careers of some of his predecessors. Nonetheless, he lacked the vision to transcend the account books and the narrow strictures of the Indian policy that he inherited."

Articles and Sections of Books

Note: I have not searched for all articles that refer to Scott as a civil servant.

C6 Stafford, Ezra Hurlburt. "The Poet of Summer." *The Week: A Canadian Journal of Politics, Literature, Science and Arts* [Toronto], 20 July 1894, pp. 801–02.

"A nation's literature is not the collection of literary works produced by writers born in that country, but the books which that nation reads." "There is perhaps no writer in the English language who brings to one's mind more vividly, and with more sweetness, the rich scents and colours of the summertime than Mr. Duncan Campbell Scott." Stafford concludes "For years I have been reading his poems and naïve prose papers in the American magazines, without imagining for a moment that the author was a resident of Canada . . . ."

C7 Brodie, Allan Douglas. "Canadian Short-Story Writers." *The Canadian Magazine of Politics, Science, Art and Literature* [Toronto], Feb. 1895, pp. 334–44.

Scott is a short story teller "thrice welcome." He has contributed work to such major American periodicals as *Scribner's Magazine* and the *Youth's Companion*.

C8 Horning, Lewis Emerson, and Lawrence J. Burpee. *A Bibliography of Canadian Fiction (English)*. Toronto: William Briggs, 1899, p. 56.

Bibliographical data.

C9 James, C.C. *A Bibliography of Canadian Poetry (English)*. Toronto: William Briggs, 1899, p. 52.

Bibliographical data.

C10 Archer, William. "Duncan Campbell Scott." In his *Poets of the Younger Generation*. London: John Lane, 1902, pp. 385–93.

Scott, while writing much good philosophic and romantic poetry, is primarily a descriptive poet. Inspired by the "cyclic drama of life and death" so evident in the extreme Canadian climate, Scott creates nature poetry with "a rare intensity of imaginative vision."

C11 "The Home-Comer." *Toronto Daily Star*, 28 May 1903, p. 6.

"Two hundred persons competed for the prizes offered by the Toronto Home-Comers Festival Committee, and the first prize has been won by Duncan Campbell Scott of Ottawa, one of the recognized Canadian poets." There is a $100.00 prize.

C12 "Life, Literature, and Education: Duncan Campbell Scott." *The Farmer's Advocate and Home Magazine* [Winnipeg and London], 16 Aug. 1905, p. 1247.

Scott's poetry is "unique" in "conception," "expression," and "arrangement." "Like Walt Whitman, he has taken language and the conventional standards of rhyme and rhythm into his own hands, hacked them, pared them to his liking, manufacturing short lines or long regular rhythms, or irregular, as suited his mood and added to the strength of his presentation."

C13 MacMurchy, Archibald. *Handbook of Canadian Literature (English)*. Toronto: William Briggs, 1906, pp. 210–13.

"Very few Canadians know that we have such a writer as Mr. Scott, and fewer still know that we have a writer of such high talent. His volumes come upon us unannounced, unheralded like the quiet dew at eventide. He is a poet of acute observation and of imagination of no common quality and capacity."

C14 "Literary Landmarks of Canada." *The Globe* [Toronto], 11 Jan. 1908, p. 5.

A picture of Scott's birthplace at the corner of Queen and Metcalfe, Ottawa.

C15 "Scott, Duncan Campbell." *Canadian Who's Who*. Toronto: Musson, 1910, p. 204.

Bio-bibliographic data.

C16 Muddiman, Bernard. "Duncan Campbell Scott." *The Canadian Magazine of Politics, Science, Art and Literature* [Toronto], May 1914, pp. 63–72. Rpt. in *Duncan Campbell Scott: A Book of Criticism*. Ed. S.L. Dragland. Ottawa: Tecumseh, 1974, pp. 31–40.

Muddiman looks at the influences that echo throughout Scott's poetry: Alfred Tennyson in *The Magic House and Other Poems* and Robert Browning in *Labor and the Angel*. He praises Scott's keeping of "the vow of passionate refrainment" that is characteristic of such great writers as Thomas Browne and Walter Pater. It is by his prose that Scott will be remembered. There is "no page in Canadian prose so perfect as the conclusion" of "Sedan."

C17 Edgar, Pelham. "Canadian Poetry." *Canadian Bookman*, 49, No. 5 (July 1919), 623–28. Rpt. in *Twentieth Century Essays on Confederation Literature*. Ed. Lorraine McMullen. Ottawa: Tecumseh, 1976, pp. 121, 122, 124–25.

"The most significant of our Canadian poets is Duncan Campbell Scott, and no contemporary work in Canada or elsewhere interests me more. He has a securer sense of form and more musical variety than is possessed by any of those I have named [Charles G.D. Roberts, Bliss Carman, Archibald Lampman, William Wilfred Campbell, Isabella Valency Crawford], as rich a fund of emotional energy, and more of the 'fundamental brainwork' upon which Rossetti asserted that great poetry must necessarily rest."

C18 Edgar, Pelham. "Recent Canadian Poets." *Ontario Library Review*, 5 (Aug. 1920), 5.

Scott is "the greatest of our Canadian poets" because there is "more actual development" in his work than in the work of his contemporaries. He also "seems to have more contact with life."

C19 Langford, Howard D. "A Defence of Canadian Poetry as Represented in the Works of Duncan Campbell Scott." *Ontario Library Review and Book-Selection Guide*, 5 (May 1921), 96–101.

Langford studies Scott's poetry in order to demonstrate that "The ability to produce good art and the ability to appreciate it develop simultaneously in a nation, and the measure of their development is one of the surest indications of national progress."

C20 French, Donald G. *The Appeal of Poetry*. Toronto: McClelland and Stewart, 1923, pp. 54, 120, 135.

". . . instead of using Nature to surround the experience or mood with a harmonious atmosphere, the poet may make it serve as a foil, and heighten the effect of the mood by using contrast instead of harmony." French illustrates his point by quoting from Scott's "By the Shore."

C21 Logan, J.D., and Donald G. French. "Duncan Campbell Scott." In *Highways of Canadian Literature: A Synoptic Introduction to the Literary History of Canada (English) from 1760 to 1924*. Ed. J.D. Logan and Donald G. French. Toronto: McClelland and Stewart, 1924, pp. 159–83. Rpt. in *Duncan Campbell Scott: A Book of Criticism*. Ed. S.L. Dragland. Ottawa: Tecumseh, 1974, pp. 43–64.

Scott's abilities as a poet are unsurpassed. Logan and French emphasize that Scott's *differentia* — the quality or power which distinguishes his poetic genius and craftsmanship from the mind and art of all other Canadian poets — is *Style*." They are particularly concerned to demonstrate Scott's musical ear, and, to that end, they trace the ten "movements" of "Variations on a Seventeenth Century Theme" ("the most ingeniously conceived poem, if not in English poetry, at least in continental American

poetry"). Scott's gifts as a poet of nature are also affirmed, and his intellectualism is second only to that of Matthew Arnold.

C22 Stevenson, Lionel. *Appraisals of Canadian Literature*. Toronto: Macmillan, 1926, pp. vii, 9, 12, 13, 35, 45, 48, 50, 66, 85, 96, 115, 117, 176, 178, 181, 192.

In a discussion of the way in which nature is treated by the poets of the Confederation, Stevenson points out that Scott "lays most emphasis on the evidences of order in nature."

C23 Knister, Raymond. "Duncan Campbell Scott." *Willison's Monthly* [Toronto], Jan. 1927, pp. 295–96. Rpt. in *Duncan Campbell Scott: A Book of Criticism*. Ed. S.L. Dragland. Ottawa: Tecumseh, 1974, pp. 66–71. Rpt. in *The First Day of Spring: Stories and Other Prose*. By Raymond Knister. Ed. Peter Stevens. Literature of Canada: Poetry and Prose in Reprint, No. 17. Toronto: Univ. of Toronto Press, 1976, pp. 398–404.

Knister, who has always appreciated Scott's fiction (he dedicated his 1928 *Canadian Short Stories* to Scott), finds that *The Poems of Duncan Campbell Scott* "gains by the careful arrangement . . . which gives the effect of a unity through variety unusual in such collections." Knister acknowledges the presence of musical influence in "Variations on a Seventeenth Century Theme," but it is not "especially fruitfully [sic]." "Ode for the Keats Centenary" is "a contribution hardly to be surpassed in English literature." The volume as a whole is "interesting to all lovers of poetry" and "important and permanent" for Canadian literature.

C24 Masefield, John. Foreword. In *The Poems of Duncan Campbell Scott*. By Duncan Campbell Scott. London: Dent, 1927, n. pag.

"... Mr. Scott uses the verse-forms of Europe; but in all his most distinctive work his subjects are Canadian." "The Piper of Arll," Masefield's favourite, "has perhaps given me pleasure more frequently than any poem."

C25 Pierce, Lorne. *An Outline of Canadian Literature (French and English)*. Toronto: Ryerson, 1927, pp. 7, 80, 82, 84–86, 116–17, 120, 171, 194, 198, 236.

In a largely biographical sketch based on the premise that Scott (in 1927) is not accorded the recognition he deserves, Pierce argues that the many ideas in Scott's poems "deal with Canadian landscape and historical tradition, music and mystery, Indian life and lore, with death, but more with humanity and multiform life, idylls of Quebec, adventure in the unexplored places, vagabondia songs and more."

C26 Stevenson, O.J. *A People's Best*. Illus. Robert Ross. Toronto: Musson, 1927, pp. 109–18. Rpt. ("Music's Magic Spell") in *Ontario Library Review*, 13 (Aug. 1928), 10–13.

In his treatment of Scott, Stevenson blends biographical details with a critical appreciation of the poems which reveal Scott the musician and the painter. "In all of Scott's poems there is restraint combined with intensity." A portrait by Robert Ross is included.

C27 Edgar, Pelham. "Duncan Campbell Scott." *The Dalhousie Review*, 7 (April 1927), 38–46.

In a largely biographical essay written on the occasion of Scott's winning the Lorne Pierce medal, Edgar praises the poet for his technique and his meditative power. Scott's poem on the centenary of the death of Keats is "a revelation at once of Keats and of himself." It is the best poem he ever wrote.

C28 Burrell, Martin. "A Canadian Poet." In his *Betwixt Heaven and Charing Cross*. Toronto: Macmillan, 1928, pp. 253–61.

Writing in response to the publication of *The Poems of Duncan Campbell Scott*, Burrell stresses the importance of the "man within" the poet. He points out the numerous musical influences on Scott and traces poetic influences to John Milton, Alfred Tennyson, Robert Browning, and John Keats — all poets noted for the musical quality of their verse. He praises the "fine imaginative quality of this Canadian poet" and cites the story of John Masefield's being turned to poetry as a result of his reading "The Piper of Arll."

C29 Connor, Carl Y. *Archibald Lampman: Canadian Poet of Nature*. New York: Louis Carrier, 1929, pp. 82, 84, 91, 93, 95, 99, 103, 112, 114, 120, 168, 190, 197. Rpt. Ottawa: Borealis, 1977, pp. 82, 84, 91, 93, 95, 99, 103, 112, 114, 120, 168, 190, 197.

In this biography of Archibald Lampman, Connor studies the intellectual and social milieu that Scott and Lampman shared and offers insights into their friendship.

C30 Stevenson, Lionel. "Who's Who in Canadian Literature: Duncan Campbell Scott." *The Canadian Bookman: A Monthly Devoted to Literature and the Creative Arts*, March 1929, pp. 59–62.

Stevenson praises Scott's success in marrying the tradition of English poetry to the Canadian reality. Scott depicts "many aspects of Canadian life — dramatic, habitant and Indian studies, lovely landscapes colored with all the variations of seasons, interpretations of the very spirit of forest and river and prairie.... Though the subjects are often of the new world, the technique has been acquired and perfected by the only method — long and sensitive study of the masterpieces of the past." Stevenson is particularly interested in the influence of George Meredith that he detects in Scott's metres.

C31   Rhodenizer, V.B. *A Handbook of Canadian Literature*. Ottawa: Graphic, 1930, pp. 146, 148, 158, 186, 201, 216–23, 243, 259, 261, 264.

Scott's work contains that which Canadian literature "stands in the greatest need, namely artistic conscience." Scott's poetry reveals that he "has studied with critical care the best literature of the world" and that he "has acquired in addition a discriminating appreciation of painting and music."

C32   Collin, W.E. *The White Savannahs*. Toronto: Macmillan, 1936, pp. 20, 34, 36.

Collin looks at Scott's "A Psalm of Life" as a contrast to the "depersonalized landscape and impersonal pentameter line" of Archibald Lampman. "Scott's art is not purely naturalistic, he is separated from nature by an intermediary." "When poets feel landscape through their emotions . . . we no longer have naturalistic art."

C33   Wright, Percy H. "Who Is Our Poet Laureate?". *Saturday Night*, 4 Dec. 1937, p. 20.

Scott is becoming recognized as "Canada's foremost poet." That there has been a tendency to underestimate his work can be attributed to the fact that the country "is very poor in larger works of criticism" (larger than periodical articles). In order to demonstrate the quiet power of Scott's poetry, Wright quotes in full "Variations on a Seventeenth Century Theme."

C34   Sykes, W.J. "The Poetry of Duncan Campbell Scott." *Queen's Quarterly*, 46 (Spring 1939), 51–64.

In a "brief survey, which aims only to call attention to some of the characteristics" of Scott's poetry, Sykes speculates "whether in the years to come Duncan Campbell Scott will be regarded as the foremost Canadian poet of his time." The poems which express the poet's "insight into the customs and instincts" of Canadian Indians are particularly satisfying, while those which he classes as dream poems "seem too tenuous, too unsubstantial."

C35   Masefield, John. *In the Mill*. London: Heinemann, 1941, pp. 59–60, 79, 97.

Citing as his first adult, literary influences George DuMaurier's *Trilby* and *Peter Ibbetson*, Thomas De Quincey's *The Confessions of an Opium Eater*, and D.C. Scott's *The Piper of Arll*, Masefield describes his encounter with Scott's poem in the pages of *Truth*.

C36   Brown, E.K. "Duncan Campbell Scott: An Individual Poet." *The Manitoba Arts Review*, 2, No. 3 (Spring 1941), 51–54.

Brown proposes four ways in which Scott's poetry differs from that of Charles G.D. Roberts, Bliss Carman, and Archibald Lampman. First his "profound imaginative sympathy" endows his Indian poems with unusual power. Second, "The nature passages that one remembers in his poetry . . . are wild and furious," rather than tamed, as they are in the poetry of the other three poets of the Confederation. Third, his poetry is filled with an original use of music. Finally, his "method of thought" suggests an "intellectual maturity, and a spiritual development far beyond the scope of Lampman and Carman."

C37   Edgar, Pelham. "The Poetry of Duncan Campbell Scott." *The Educational Record of the Province of Quebec*, 58 (1942), 8–11.

In an article written for "younger readers," Edgar reviews the position he has taken on Scott in his other published articles. He also includes a list of the specific dates on which Scott wrote the poems that comprise *Via Borealis*.

C38 Klinck, Carl F. *Wilfred Campbell: A Study in Late Provincial Victorianism*. Toronto: Ryerson, 1942, pp. 4, 19, 54, 61, 74, 75, 80, 81, 83, 86, 90, 92, 93, 94, 96, 103, 168, 215, 217–18, 224, 228–34. Rpt. Ottawa: Tecumseh, 1977, pp. 4, 19, 54, 61, 74, 75, 80, 81, 83, 86, 90, 92, 93, 94, 96, 103, 168, 215, 217–18, 224, 228–34.

Klinck examines the intellectual ideas current in turn-of-the-century Canada. He compares the treatment of nature in the poetry of Archibald Lampman, W.W. Campbell, and D.C. Scott: all three begin with the central idea of the Earth as Mother, with all her children kin. Unlike Campbell, however, Scott "subordinates teaching to esthetic re-creation, a subtle transmutation of Nature's colours, lines and music into colourful, delineative, musical words which take a different route to the consciousness but achieve the same essential effect."

C39 Brockington, Leonard W. "Duncan Campbell Scott's Eightieth Birthday." *Saturday Night*, 1 Aug. 1942, p. 25.

On the occasion of Scott's eightieth birthday, Brockington creates the portrait of a man at ease in a world of culture. He cites Scott's collections of books and Canadian paintings and refers to his love of music, calling him "a humble artist and not a little of a saint." The poet (whom he classes with Charles Lamb, Walter Bagehot, Austin Dobson, Walter de la Mare, and Archibald Lampman) was also an administrator who "brought human and humane understanding to the problems of the Indian wards of the federal government."

C40 Smith, A.J.M. " 'Our Poets': A Sketch of Canadian Poetry in the Nineteenth Century." *University of Toronto Quarterly*, 12 (Oct. 1942), 88–89, 92–93. Rpt. (revised — Introduction) in *The Book of Canadian Poetry: A Critical and Historical Introduction*. Ed. A.J.M. Smith. Chicago: Univ. of Chicago Press, 1943, pp. 18–24.

Scott, unlike Bliss Carman and Charles G.D. Roberts, "has not won as wide acclaim as he deserves" because he "is a scholarly poet, a conscientious and unassuming artist." "His talent is quieter than that of any other poet of the group, but he is the one who shows the liveliest interest in human beings and dramatic action." As a group, the poets of the Confederation were limited in that they ignored "the coarse bustle of humanity." On the other hand, their theme ("the impingement of nature in Canada upon the human spirit") if "narrow" was also "important."

C41 Brown, E.K. "Duncan Campbell Scott." In his *On Canadian Poetry*. Toronto: Ryerson, 1943, pp. 108–32. Rev. ed., 1944, pp. 118–43. Rpt. in *Duncan Campbell Scott: A Book of Criticism*. Ed. S.L. Dragland. Ottawa: Tecumseh, 1974, pp. 74–93.

Scott is a poet whose combined "restraint and intensity" rendered his verse too original to be readily appreciated by critics enraptured with the other poets of the Confederation. Because Scott's work was truly rooted in the untamed Canadian landscape, the poet was in search of a "form suitable and adequate for his novel matter," a search which kept some of his early work from being truly successful. Brown then traces the "emotional centre of Scott's work" through a number of what he considers important poems and concludes the chapter with the now famous anecdote of Scott's " 'perfectly tolerable, perfectly beautiful old age.' "

C42   Smith, A.J.M. Introduction. In *The Book of Canadian Poetry: A Critical and Historical Anthology.* Toronto: Gage, 1943, pp. 15, 18, 19, 20, 213. Rev. and enl. ed., 1948, pp. 18, 21, 22, 208. Rev. and enl. ed., 1957, pp. 16, 19, 20, 207.

"Unlike Roberts and Carman, Duncan Campbell Scott has not received the full measure of admiration he deserves." "His talent is quieter than that of Carman or Roberts, yet he shows a deeper interest in human beings and in dramatic action, and he is more fastidious and accurate in feeling."

C43   Frye, Northrop. "Canada and Its Poetry." *The Canadian Forum*, Dec. 1943, pp. 207–10. Rpt. in *The Bush Garden: Essays on the Canadian Imagination.* By Northrop Frye. Toronto: House of Anansi, 1971, p. 139.

Discussing the theme of death in Canadian poetry, Frye writes, "D.C. Scott's 'Piper of Arll' is located in an elusive fairyland, but the riddle of inexplicable death is still at the heart of the poem."

C44   S., E. "Popular Canadian Poet Celebrates 83rd Birthday." *The Ottawa Journal*, 4 Aug. 1945, p. 5.

Excerpts from an interview Scott granted *The Ottawa Journal* make up a large portion of this article.

C45   Thomas, Clara. *Canadian Novelists, 1920–1945.* Toronto: Longmans, Green, 1946, pp. 112–13.

Bio-bibliographical data.

C46   Brown, E.K. "L'âge d'or de notre poésie." Trans. Guy Sylvestre. *Gants du Ciel*, 11 (printemps 1946), 7–17. Rpt. trans. in *Responses and Evaluations: Essays on Canada.* Ed. David Staines. New Canadian Library, No. 137. Toronto: McClelland and Stewart, 1977, pp. 87–96.

Asserting that ". . . the most admirable body of poetry which has yet been written in English-speaking Canada within a short period belongs not to 1935–1945, but to 1885–1900," Brown then looks at the poetry of Archibald Lampman, Bliss Carman, and D.C. Scott. He singles out "The Height of Land," "Variations on a Seventeenth Century Theme," and "The Forsaken" to support his contention that Scott wrote his best poetry after 1900. Brown, who earlier in the article commends Lampman's "social idealism," praises Scott's Indian poems because "The Indian for him is not a noble savage, nor yet the sordid victim of the potlatch: the Indian is simply a human being belonging to a class which has had difficulty in adjusting to a complicated social structure for which its background has not been a preparation." Brown suggests that the poets of Scott's generation have suffered from a critical reaction against romanticism.

C47   Frye, Northrop. "La tradition narrative dans la poésie canadienne-anglais." Trans. Guy Sylvestre. *Gants du Ciel*, No. 11 (printemps 1946), pp. 19–30. Rpt. (trans. — "The Narrative Tradition in English-Canadian Poetry") in *The Bush Garden: Essays on the Canadian Imagination.* By Northrop Frye. Toronto: House of Anansi, 1971, pp. 149, 152, 154.

Comparing Canadian poetry to Old English poetry, Frye writes, "Consider too the subjects of many of D.C. Scott's finest poems, the lovers destroyed in a log jam, the lonely Indian murdered in the forest for his furs, the squaw who baits a fish hook with her own flesh to feed her children. These are ballad themes; and his longest poem *Dominique de Gourges*, a narrative filled with the sombre exaltation of revenge, is curiously archaic in spirit for the author of a poem on Debussy."

C48 Edgar, Pelham. "A Criticism and an Appreciation of Duncan Campbell Scott's Poetry." *The Ottawa Journal*, 30 March 1946, p. 15.

Edgar cites "A Scene on Lake Manitou" to emphasize Scott's mastery of "primitivism." "The Closed Door" is "a tribute so poignantly tender that comment on its matchless art would be a sacrilege." He also praises the "musical variations" in Scott's poetry.

C49 Sutherland, John. Introduction. In *Other Canadians: An Anthology of the New Poetry in Canada 1940–1946*. Ed. John Sutherland. Montreal: First Statement, 1947, pp. 9, 12. Rpt. ("Mr. Smith and the 'Tradition' ") in *John Sutherland: Essays, Controversies and Poems*. Ed. Miriam Waddington. New Canadian Library, No. 81. Toronto: McClelland and Stewart, 1972, pp. 59, 60.

"He [A.J.M. Smith] has divided the sober, restrained and classical poetry of D.C. Scott and Archibald Lampman from the suspiciously heady lyricism of Carman and the barnyard regionalism of Sir Charles Roberts . . . ."

C50 Pomeroy, Elsie M. "Duncan Campbell Scott." The Annual Roberts Night, Canadian Authors' Association, Toronto Branch, Toronto. 10 Jan. 1947. Printed in *The Maritime Advocate and Busy East*, Aug. 1947, pp. 5–7, 29.

Pomeroy quotes from several British, American, and Canadian reviews of Scott's work in support of her belief in the poet's genius. She notes how favourably Scott's first book was received outside Canada.

C51 Edgar, Pelham. "Duncan Campbell Scott: An Appreciation." *The Ottawa Journal*, 27 Dec. 1947, p. 14.

In a brief attempt to sum up the significance of Scott's work, Edgar concludes that "Fine in substance and in artistry as his prose undoubtedly is, his poetry remains his surest passage to immortality." Although Scott did not enjoy popular success during his lifetime, his future reputation will rest secure because of his native poems ("Never has aboriginal character been more faithfully portrayed.") and "the impeccable sense of cadence that pervades his poetry throughout."

C52 "Duncan Campbell Scott's 85th Birthday." *The Canadian Author & Bookman*, 23, No. 3 (Dec. 1947), 35.

In this biographical tribute, the author notes that Scott "would resent being tagged 'the dean of Canadian writers.' "

C53 Brown, E.K. "In Memoriam: Duncan Campbell Scott." *Winnipeg Free Press*, 29 Dec. 1947, p. 11.

Brown, who writes that the death of Scott "breaks the last personal link with the greatest movement in our literature," notes that Scott was "evolving an art more masculine, more original, and perhaps more remarkable" than any of the other poets of the Confederation. He briefly documents Scott's life as a writer and civil servant, concluding with a reference to his own friendship with the poet.

C54 Clarke, George Herbert. "Duncan Campbell Scott (1862–1947)." *Proceedings and Transactions of the Royal Society of Canada*, Ser. 3, 42 (1948), 115–19.

Clarke writes a chiefly biographical article on the occasion of the death of Scott, a poet who "honoured truth in life and art." A portrait of Scott is included.

C55 Edgar, Pelham. "Duncan Campbell Scott." In *Leading Canadian Poets*. Ed. W.P. Percival. Toronto: Ryerson, 1948, pp. 213–19.

Edgar provides some notes on Scott's poems, particularly those poems that grew out of the 1906 trip to James Bay that he made with the poet. The essay is aimed at younger readers.

C56 Percival, W.P. "What Is the Character of Canadian Poetry." In *Leading Canadian Poets*. Ed. W.P. Percival. Toronto: Ryerson, 1948, p. 4.

In an essay that attempts to define the essence of individual Canadian poets in a line or two each, Percival singles out Scott for his use of metaphor.

C57 "Obituary Notes: Duncan C. Scott." *Publishers Weekly*, 10 Jan. 1948, p. 170.

The writer refers to Scott's work as a civil servant, poet, short story writer, and editor of The Makers of Canada series.

C58 "Great Poet, Great Man." *Saturday Night*, 24 Jan. 1948, p. 5.

Given the fact that Scott's poetry "attracted comparatively little attention" when the poets of the Confederation were in "their great vogue," the writer is glad to see that Scott lived long enough to realize that his literary reputation was secure. Scott was a gifted amateur in the field of music and theatre, and "In personal relations he was the warm friend of every sincere literary craftsman who came his way . . . ."

C59 "Duncan Campbell Scott." *The Canadian Forum*, Feb. 1948, p. 244.

The author of this obituary notes that Scott was "near the Canadian top." However, "His taste is far from faultless, and some of his best known poems, notably 'At the Cedars,' would hardly look out of place in *Sarah Binks*."

C60 "Memorial to a Great Soul." *The Canadian Author & Bookman*, 24, No. 2 (March 1948), 17.

A commemorative gathering was held at Carleton College by the Ottawa branch of the Canadian Authors' Association. (A full account of this evening is given by Wilfrid Eggleston [C195].)

C61 Smith, A.J.M. "The Poetry of Duncan Campbell Scott." *The Dalhousie Review*, 28 (April 1948), 12–21. Rpt. in *Duncan Campbell Scott: A Book of Criticism*. Ed. S.L. Dragland. Ottawa: Tecumseh, 1974, pp. 104–14. Rpt. ["The Poetry of Duncan Campbell Scott (1948)"] in *On Poetry and Poets: Selected Essays of A.J.M. Smith*. By A.J.M. Smith. New Canadian Library, No. 143. Toronto: McClelland and Stewart, 1977, pp. 48–58.

National sentiment after 1890 was responsible for the poets of the Confederation "being overpraised or at least being praised in terms that transcended and hence failed to perceive correctly their special and limited goodness." Smith turns his attention to Scott, whose work was spared "excessive adulation," because of the "absence of an obvious and easily demonstrated Canadianism." Scott's poetry reveals "the classical virtues of restraint and precision," and, while his work often reflects the influence of Matthew Arnold, the Pre-Raphaelites, or William Wordsworth, it always bears the "indications of an individual sensibility . . . which is so hard to describe." Smith singles out the Indian poems which are rendered "most original" by the union of "emotional intensity and perfection of form."

C62 Pacey, Desmond. "The Poetry of Duncan Campbell Scott." *The Canadian Forum*, Aug. 1948, pp. 107–09. Rpt. in *Essays in Canadian Criticism 1938–1968*. By Desmond Pacey. Toronto: Ryerson, 1969, pp. 39–44. Rpt. in *Duncan Campbell Scott: A Book of Criticism*. Ed. S.L. Dragland. Ottawa: Tecumseh, 1974, pp. 97–102.

Pacey points out that Scott's "conception of Nature as wild and threatening sets . . . [him] apart from the other members of the Group of the Sixties." Although he finds Scott "less capable" of achieving musical effects than Charles G.D. Roberts or Bliss Carman, he states that his poetry presents "an authentic glimpse of the Canadian spirit at its finest."

C63   Macbeth, Madge. "A Word of Remembrance about Duncan Campbell Scott." *The Canadian Author & Bookman*, 24, No. 4 (Fall Supplement 1948), 13.
    Scott "was not a man one could criticize, rationalize, analyze. He was a man to stir the finest impulses of the heart." Macbeth comments on Scott's sense of humour, revealing that he was a "convincing, if kindly, mimic."

C64   Bourinot, Arthur S. "The Ever-Eager Heart." *The Canadian Author & Bookman*, 25, No. 3 (Autumn 1949), 8–9. Rpt. [expanded — "The Ever-Eager Heart (Some Personal Recollections of Duncan Campbell Scott)"] in *Five Canadian Poets: Duncan Campbell Scott, Archibald Lampman, William E. Marshall, Charles Sangster, George Frederick Cameron*. By Arthur S. Bourinot. Ottawa: Bourinot, 1954, pp. 1–3. Rpt. (revised — "Some Personal Recollections of Duncan Campbell Scott") in *More Letters of Duncan Campbell Scott*. Ed. Arthur S. Bourinot, 1960, pp. 1–7.
    Bourinot writes a reminiscence of "growing up on Scott" and gives a sense of the place and time in which Scott began to write. He talks of Scott's love and knowledge of music and painting and discusses the kind of literature which most interested the poet.

C65   Brown, E.K. "Duncan Campbell Scott." *Chambers Encyclopaedia*, 12 (1950).
    Brown identifies Scott as a "Canadian poet and civil servant" whose "association with Archibald Lampman brought him awareness of his poetic powers." Brown notes that "Both in the prose and in the greater poetry there is an architecture which expresses a strong intelligence and conscious aesthetic."

C66   Brown, E.K. "The Causerie." *Winnipeg Free Press*, 24 June 1950, p. 21.
    Brown provides some of the historical detail surrounding the famous canoe trip made by Scott to settle "the last of the Indian treaties" in the James Bay area. The poems of *Via Borealis* were composed at this time, and, in fact, the journey continued to provide inspiration for some of Scott's later poetry: "It was in November 1915 that he [Scott] wrote 'The Height of Land' in which he has worked out with every resource of his art the illumination that comes to a person of imaginative insight in the heart of the north."

C67   Brown, E.K. "Memoir of Duncan Campbell Scott." In *Selected Poems of Duncan Campbell Scott*. By Duncan Campbell Scott. Ed. E.K. Brown. Toronto: Ryerson, 1951, pp. xi–xlii. Rpt. ("Duncan Campbell Scott: A Memoir") in *Responses and Evaluations: Essays on Canada*. By E.K. Brown. Ed. David Staines. New Canadian Library, No. 137. Toronto: McClelland and Stewart, 1977, pp. 112–44.
    In a biographical sketch, Brown relates Scott's poetry to his life, including both the traditional look at the influence of British poets and the less-acknowledged influence of Canadian poets on Scott's work. Thomas Carlyle, Alfred Tennyson, and Matthew Arnold are much loved by Scott, George Meredith less so. Scott took his "stimulus" to write from Archibald Lampman with whom he shared an "interest in nature, in music, and in books," and, although the poetry never reflects the art of W.W. Campbell,

"... no one could associate with Campbell without being provoked to harder thinking and sharper statement." Scott's theory of poetry evolved into a belief that "The poet has value in so far as he expresses illuminations . . . ," and "In sharing or offering to share his illuminations he has his part, and it is a high one, in the progress that is coupled with poetry in the title of the ['Poetry and Progress'] address." The memoir makes clear the vast range of Scott's talents: poet, fiction writer, editor, playwright, and "reluctant biographer."

C68 Edgar, Pelham. "Travelling with a Poet." In his *Across My Path*. Ed. Northrop Frye. Toronto: Ryerson, 1952, pp. 58–74.

In a two-part chapter, Edgar first describes the canoe trip he and Scott made in 1906 to settle the James Bay Treaty with the Cree. From this trip came the poems that comprise *Via Borealis* and the inspiration for "The Height of Land" and "Lines in Memory of Edmund Morris." In the second part of the chapter, Edgar turns to the poetry itself, arguing that "... no one in the range of our literature or any literature has approached Scott in his mastery of primitive themes." Edgar also praises Scott's poems of "Coleridgean weirdness" for their musical quality.

C69 Pacey, Desmond. *Creative Writing in Canada: A Short History of English-Canadian Literature*. Toronto: Ryerson, 1952, pp. 2, 34, 37, 53, 56–62, 65, 68, 80, 84, 112, 115, 200. Rev. and enl. ed., 1961, pp. 2, 38, 41, 57, 61–68, 70, 73, 87, 91, 121, 124, 125, 278.

"The poetry of Duncan Campbell Scott is a poetry of conflict. His pictures of nature are predominantly those of nature in storm, with man withstanding its pressure by virtue either of an inner moral strength or a supreme outer assurance." "The vision of a world in violent conflict also finds expression in Scott's love poems." Scott was never as famous as the other poets of the Confederation, perhaps because "He was altogether a quieter, less spectacular artist. In spite of the violent content of so many of his poems, the dominant tone is quiet. There is usually a turbulent climax, but there is always a peaceful close."

C70 Frye, Northrop. "Letters in Canada: 1951." *University of Toronto Quarterly*, 21 (April 1952), 257. Rpt. in *The Bush Garden: Essays on the Canadian Imagination*. By Northrop Frye. Toronto: House of Anansi, 1971, p. 9. Rpt. ("Letters in Canada: 1952") in *Masks of Poetry: Canadian Critics on Canadian Verse*. Ed. A.J.M. Smith. New Canadian Library Original, No. O3. Toronto: McClelland and Stewart, 1962, pp. 96–97.

"Whatever one thinks of the total merit of Scott's very uneven output, he achieved the type of imaginative balance that is characteristic of so much of the best in Canadian culture down to the present generation, when altered social conditions are beginning to upset it. On one side he had the world of urbane and civilized values; on the other, the Quebec forest with its Indians and lonely trappers."

C71 Klinck, Carl F., and Reginald E. Watters. "Duncan Campbell Scott 1862–1947." In *Canadian Anthology*. Toronto: Gage, 1955, pp. 142–43. Rpt. ["Duncan Campbell Scott (1862–1947)"] in rev. ed., 1966, pp. 149–50. 3rd ed., 1974, p. 147.

Brief bio-bibliographical data.

C72 Watters, R.E. "Duncan Campbell Scott 1862–1947." In *Canadian Anthology*. Ed. Carl F. Klinck and Reginald E. Watters. Toronto: Gage, 1955, pp. 548–49. Rpt. ["Duncan Campbell Scott (1862–1947)"] in rev.

ed., 1966, pp. 609–11. 3rd ed., 1974, pp. 712–14. Bibliographical data.

C73 Daniells, Roy. "Literature: Poetry and the Novel." In *The Culture of Contemporary Canada*. Ed. Julian Park. Toronto: Ryerson/Ithaca, N.Y.: Cornell Univ. Press, 1957, pp. 51–52.

"If we look very briefly at the history of Canadian poetry — that is, of Canadian poetry in English — seeking first for an early corpus of reputable verse having some coherence within itself and some relation to the Canadian scene, we might well commence with three Victorians who were close contemporaries: Sir Charles G.D. Roberts (1860–1943), Archibald Lampman (1861–1899), and Duncan Campbell Scott (1862–1947)." Scott "worked in the department of Indian Affairs and many of his poems deal with wild people and wild places."

C74 Eggleston, Wilfrid. *The Frontier & Canadian Letters*. Toronto: Ryerson, 1957, pp. 127, 129, 130–31, 133, 135. Rpt. Carleton Library Series. Toronto: McClelland and Stewart, 1977, pp. 127, 129, 130–31, 133, 135.

In his discussion of "The sons and daughters of manse, parsonage and rectory in Canadian letters . . . ," Eggleston briefly describes the cultural influence of Scott's home. "Prepared, spiritually conditioned, no doubt, by the home influence, Scott recalled that the 'first perception or what might be called pang of poetry came to him in the classroom at Smith's Falls, when the master wrote on the blackboard a splash of verbal colour from Tennyson's "Dream of Fair Women." ' "

C75 Frye, Northrop. "Preface to an Uncollected Anthology." In *Studia Varia: Royal Society of Canadian Literary and Scientific Papers*. Ed. E.G.D. Murray. Toronto: Royal Society of Canada-Univ. of Toronto Press, 1957, pp. 30, 35. Rpt. in *The Bush Garden: Essays on the Canadian Imagination*. By Northrop Frye. Toronto: House of Anansi, 1971, pp. 174, 179.

"We are concerned here, however, not so much with mythopoeic poetry as with myth as a shaping principle of poetry. Every good lyrical poet has a certain structure of imagery as typical of him as his handwriting, held together by certain recurring metaphors, and sooner or later he will produce one or more poems that seem to be at the centre of that structure. . . . My anthology is largely held together by such poems: they start approximately with D.C. Scott's 'Piper of Arll' . . . ."

C76 Pacey, Desmond. "The Canadian Writer and His Public." In *Studia Varia: Royal Society of Canadian Literary and Scientific Papers*. Ed. E.G.D. Murray. Toronto: Royal Society of Canada-Univ. of Toronto Press, 1957, pp. 11, 12.

"Of the 'big five' of Canadian poetry [Archibald Lampman, Charles G.D. Roberts, Bliss Carman, Duncan Campbell Scott, and William Wilfred Campbell], only D.C. Scott and W.W. Campbell were still writing verse in Canada [in 1903], and they had not shown any significant improvement since 1893."

C77 Bourinot, Arthur S. Introduction. In *At the Mermaid Inn, Conducted by A. Lampman, W.W. Campbell, Duncan C. Scott: Being Essays on Life and Literature which appeared in the Toronto* Globe *1892–1893*. Ed. Arthur S. Bourinot. Ottawa: Bourinot, 1958, pp. 1–5.

Bourinot quotes briefly from critical responses to "At the Mermaid Inn" to show that "Of the merits and demerits of the column there are thus some conflicting opinions." "Scott's essays, as one would expect, were on a more intellectual level [than William Wilfred Campbell's], but were sometimes lacking in warmth and human interest, the homey 'down to earth tone' of some of Lampman's."

C78 Frye, Northrop. "Poetry." In *The Arts in Canada: A Stock-Taking at Mid-Century*. Ed. Malcolm Ross. Toronto: Macmillan, 1958, 84, 85, 86.

Frye cites Scott's *The Magic House* as one of four volumes signalling the arrival of the "new literary age."

C79 Pacey, Desmond. "Duncan Campbell Scott." In his *Ten Canadian Poets: A Group of Biographical and Critical Essays*. Toronto: Ryerson, 1958, pp. 141–64.

The chapter on Scott, following the general format of the book, is divided into two sections: biography and criticism. In an attempt to illustrate how life informs art, Pacey roots the criticism of the poetry in the biography of the poet. He is particularly interested in "the central tension in Scott's poetry, that between passionate intensity and austere restraint," a tension that was originated by "the conflict in his parentage between the enthusiasm and emotionalism of Methodism on the one hand and the dourness of the Scot and [sic; on] the other." He traces this tension through a number of Scott's poems, concluding that "The essence of Scott's view of the world seems to be a vision of a battleground where nature is in conflict with itself, man in conflict with nature, and man in conflict with man." But "Out of the conflict emerges . . . peace and beauty" because of his faith "in a presiding spirit which in the long run has a beneficent purpose, and in man's capacity to endure."

C80 Rashley, R.E. *Poetry in Canada: The First Three Steps*. Toronto: Ryerson, 1958, pp. 49, 64, 81–88, 91, 94, 97, 98, 102, 112, 157, 158.

Rashley writes that the "sixties group" could not write "without reference to nature." For Scott, nature was the "spring of happiness and spiritual well-being," and, consequently, "the world of man" was unattractive. Scott differed from his contemporaries, however, because of his contact with the Indians. In spite of this contact, "There is no evidence in the poems that Scott examined the nature of these cultures; the service they performed was to enable him to objectify his ideas of life in a way which seems to have been denied to the period in the study of its own life." Rashley demonstrates the ways in which Canadian poetry is and always has been "a proper and adequate voice of its times."

C81 "Along Poet's Row: Duncan Campbell Scott." *The Canadian Author & Bookman*, 34, No. 1 (Spring 1958), 11.

The author of this biographical note refers to Scott's presidency of the Royal Society of Canada, the Doctor of Letters he received from the University of Toronto in 1922, and *The Circle of Affection*.

C82 Magee, William H. "Local Colour in Canadian Fiction." *University of Toronto Quarterly*, 28 (Jan. 1959), 181, 182, 185. Rpt. in *Twentieth Century Essays on Confederation Literature*. Ed. Lorraine McMullen. Ottawa: Tecumseh, 1976, pp. 82–83, 91.

"The basic challenge to . . . [local colour] storytellers, the difficulty of finding a fictional frame of plot and characterization appropriate to lauding local colour atmosphere, baffled Scott more than it did many a mediocre writer." Scott relies too heavily "on a purely fictional tradition of life." Rather than depending on "general trends in the parent literatures," he might have profited from the Canadian example of Susanna Moodie's *Roughing It in the Bush; or, Life in Canada*.

C83 Smith, A.J.M. "Duncan Campbell Scott." In *Our Living Tradition: Second and Third Series*. Ed. Robert L. McDougall. Toronto/Ottawa: Carleton Univ./Univ. of Toronto, 1959, pp. 73–94. Rpt. (excerpt — "Duncan Campbell Scott: A Reconsideration") in *Canadian Literature*, No. 1 (Summer 1959), pp. 13–25. Rpt. ("The Poetry of Duncan Campbell Scott") in *Towards a View of Canadian Letters: Selected Critical Essays 1928–1971*. By A.J.M. Smith. Vancouver: Univ. of British Columbia Press, 1973, pp. 79–96. Rpt. ("Duncan Campbell Scott") in *Duncan Campbell Scott: A Book of Criticism*. Ed. S.L. Dragland. Ottawa: Tecumseh, 1974, pp. 115–34.

Smith takes an historical look at Scott's work in order to demonstrate that he wrote poetry "that one might well call modern, if it were not timeless." Smith's Modernist perspective leads him to examine Scott's less well-known poems, while enabling him to capitalize on Brown's theme of "intensity." Smith argues that it is the intensity arising from a clarity of vision that makes Scott a truly original writer.

C84 Wilson, Milton. "Klein's Drowned Poet: Canadian Variations on an Old Theme." *Canadian Literature*, No. 6 (Autumn 1960), pp. 5–17. Rpt. (excerpt — "Scott's Drowned Poet") in *Duncan Campbell Scott: A Book of Criticism*. Ed. S.L. Dragland. Ottawa: Tecumseh, 1974, pp. 136–38.

Wilson looks at "The Piper of Arll" in the context of the drowned poet in Canadian literature. The poem is "a sort of pre-Raphaelite lyrical ballad, whose piper (poet, singer, artist, what you will, Scott was never one to separate the arts) sinks with his complete retinue: audience, palace of art, and all. The tone may be elegiac, but the poem's cycle is closed; in the end there is nothing to be mourned and no one left to mourn."

C85 Roy, G. Ross. "Duncan Campbell Scott." In his *Le Sentiment de la Nature dans la Poésie Canadienne Anglaise, 1867–1918*. Paris: A.G. Nizet, 1961, pp. 73–98. Rpt. trans. Peggy Dragísíc in *Duncan Campbell Scott: A Book of Criticism*. Ed. S.L. Dragland. Ottawa: Tecumseh, 1974, pp. 140–61.

Roy begins his analysis of the poetry of Duncan Campbell Scott by asserting that "The measure of his poetic genius is to have known how, while using his immediate experience of things Canadian, to create a poetry that is as valuable for the English or American reader as it is for the Canadian. That is to say, he produced works whose interest is universal but whose elements are Canadian."

C86 Watt, F.W. "The Literature of Canada." In *The Commonwealth Pen: An Introduction to the Literature of the British Commonwealth*. Ed. A.L. McLeod. Ithaca, N.Y.: Cornell Univ. Press, 1961, pp. 21, 22, 24.

"Not one of . . . [the Group of the Sixties] was a serious innovator. . . . but each could, when he wished, evoke with clarity and simplicity impressions of a natural world which was familiar, accepted and understood." "In poems like 'At Gull Lake' and 'The Forsaken' Scott largely escaped a dangerous tendency to moralize in Victorian fashion and achieved a sternly impersonal vision of the beauty and terror of primitive life."

C87 Matthews, John Pengwerne. *Tradition in Exile: A Comparative Study of Social Influences on the Development of Australian and Canadian Poetry in the Nineteenth Century*. Toronto: Univ. of Toronto Press, 1962, pp. 101, 106, 112, 117, 129–31.

Matthews is particularly interested in Scott's "The Height of Land," which he compares with the Australian poet Bernard O'Dowd's "The Bush." In "The Height of Land," "one obtains a greater sense of the force of Canada's sheer size applying a type of moral pressure against the insignificance of the small area man has yet managed to make his own." Both Scott and O'Dowd "are the interpreters of the mystical significance to their societies of the gigantic empty spaces which surround them."

C88 Bourinot, Arthur S. "The Poet's Scrapbooks." *The Canadian Author & Bookman*, 38, No. 1 (Summer 1962), 6.
Bourinot, seeking "something new" to say about Scott, comments on parts of the poet's scrapbooks. The scrapbooks contain "relatively unimportant" book reviews, a newspaper picture of Scott's birthplace at the corners of Queen and Metcalfe Streets in Ottawa (*The Globe* [Toronto], 11 Jan. 1908), the letter from Sir John A. MacDonald to Scott's father confirming the son's appointment to the public service, and letters and clippings that tell the story of John Masefield's deep respect for Scott and his love for Scott's poem "The Piper of Arll."

C89 Macbeth, Madge. "Duncan Campbell Scott: A Few of My Memories." *The Canadian Author & Bookman*, 38, No. 1 (Summer 1962), 2.
Macbeth recalls Scott as a "gentle man, a sensitive man, a man with deep fondness for his friends." She discusses his sense of humour and gift of mimicry. He was "a magician with words and a connoisseur of all things beautiful."

C90 Wilton, Margaret Harvey. "Duncan Campbell Scott: Man and Artist." *The Canadian Author & Bookman*, 38, No. 1 (Summer 1962), 3-5, 20.
Quoting liberally from such critics as Pelham Edgar (C68), E.K. Brown (C67), and A.J.M. Smith (C61) on Scott's affinity for nature, Wilton suggests that perhaps Scott's "most outstanding quality is primi-

tiveness," not the primitiveness of the eighteenth century, but of enlightened first-hand observation.

C91 Hirano, Keiichi. "The Aborigene [sic] in Canadian Literature: Notes by a Japanese." *Canadian Literature*, No. 14 (Autumn 1962), pp. 44-47.
In a literary canon where Indians "belong to the peripheral or the merely ornamental," Scott's Indian poems remain unsurpassed in power, marred only occasionally by his "Christian moralizing." Nevertheless, ". . . on the whole his attitude does not seem to have gone much beyond that of a well-meaning and conscientious governmental official. (Or should I say white man official?)."

C92 Wallace, W.S. *The Macmillan Dictionary of Canadian Biography*. 3rd ed. London: Macmillan, 1963, p. 674. Rev. and enl. ed., updated W.A. McKay, 1978, p. 752.
Bio-bibliographical data.

C93 Sylvestre, Guy, Brandon Conron, and Carl F. Klinck, eds. *Canadian Writers/Écrivains Canadiens: A Biographical Dictionary/Un dictionnaire biographique*. Toronto: Ryerson, 1964, p. 125. Rev. and enl. ed., 1966, pp. 139-40.
Biographical data.

C94 Bailey, Alfred G. "Overture to Nationhood." In *Literary History of Canada: Canadian Literature in English*. Gen. ed. Carl F. Klinck. Toronto: Univ. of Toronto Press, 1965, p. 67. 2nd ed., 1976. I, 81.
". . . with the advent of the school of Roberts, Lampman, Carman, Campbell, and Scott, the formative period of Canadian literary history may be regarded as having passed into one of a national achievement from which the country has never seriously receded, and from which it has advanced to the ampler perspectives of our own day."

C95 Beattie, Munro. "Poetry 1920–1935." In *Literary History of Canada: Canadian Literature in English*. Gen. ed. Carl F. Klinck. Toronto: Univ. of Toronto Press, 1965, p. 727. 2nd ed., 1976. II, 238.

In a discussion of the rise of free verse and the general departure "from conventional metrics and stanza forms," Beattie makes the point that "Some of Duncan Campbell Scott's finest poems . . . were composed in lines that eschewed traditional prosody, though not in a way that would astonish readers of Matthew Arnold."

C96 Beattie, Munro. "Poetry 1950–1960." In *Literary History of Canada: Canadian Literature in English*. Gen. ed. Carl F. Klinck. Toronto: Univ. of Toronto Press, 1965, p. 801. 2nd ed., 1976. II, 313.

In a discussion of Fred Cogswell, Beattie claims that ". . . his ballads recall some of the narrative lyrics of Duncan Campbell Scott . . . ."

C97 Daniells, Roy. "Confederation to the First World War." In *Literary History of Canada: Canadian Literature in English*. Gen. ed. Carl F. Klinck. Toronto: Univ. of Toronto Press, 1965, pp. 198, 207. 2nd ed., 1976. I, 212, 221.

W.D. Lighthall's anthology *Songs of the Great Dominion* (1889) contains much mediocre verse, but "A few pieces by [Isabella Valancy] Crawford, [Archibald] Lampman, [Bliss] Carman, and D.C. Scott, filled with an appreciation of nature, stand above the general undistinguished level."

C98 Daniells, Roy. "Crawford, Carman, and D.C. Scott." In *Literary History of Canada: Canadian Literature in English*. Gen. ed. and introd. Carl F. Klinck. Toronto: Univ. of Toronto Press, 1965, pp. 416–21; 2nd ed., 1976. I, 432–37.

Scott's "central perception [is] that nature is on the whole good, if not always beneficent, and he holds to the hope that man's future is one of ceaseless evolution towards better things, however repellent some stages of the journey may prove to be." "All the poems for which he is likely to be remembered are concerned with the northern wilderness, Canada's Indian territory." The "technique of his verse, more astringent and more uncertain than that of his contemporaries, delayed recognition of his achievement."

C99 Frye, Northrop. "Conclusion." In *Literary History of Canada: Canadian Literature in English*. Gen. ed. Carl F. Klinck. Toronto: Univ. of Toronto Press, 1965, pp. 825, 843, 844, 845. 2nd ed., 1976. II, 337, 355, 356, 357. Rpt. *The Bush Garden: Essays on the Canadian Imagination*. Toronto: House of Anansi, 1971, pp. 219, 242, 243, 245.

In his discussion of "the impact of the sophisticated on the primitive," Frye cites Scott's poetry. "He [Scott] writes of a starving squaw baiting a fish-hook with her own flesh, and he writes of the music of Debussy and the poetry of Henry Vaughan. In English literature we have to go back to Anglo-Saxon times to encounter so incongruous a collision of cultures." Scott is also given as an example of "The nineteenth-century Canadian poet [who] can hardly help being preoccupied with physical nature; the nature confronting him presents him with the riddle of unconsciousness, and the riddle of unconsciousness in nature is the riddle of death in man."

C100 Gundy, H. Pearson. "Literary Publishing." In *Literary History of Canada: Canadian Literature in English*. Gen. ed. Carl F. Klinck. Toronto: Univ. of Toronto Press, 1965, p. 186. 2nd ed., 1976. I, 200.

The Week, which began publication in 1883, published some of Scott's earliest verse.

C101 Pacey, Desmond. "Fiction 1920–1940." In *Literary History of Canada: Canadian Literature in English.* Gen. ed. Carl F. Klinck. Toronto: Univ. of Toronto Press, 1965, p. 661. 2nd ed., 1976. II, 171.

Pacey cites Scott's enthusiastic review of L. Adams Beck's novel *The Ninth Vibration* "as an example of how readily the Canadian literary public of the twenties could mistake grandiosity for greatness." Scott's *The Witching of Elspie: A Book of Stories* is one of several books that prove that "Books of short stories were rare in the period and, with a few conspicuous exceptions, of low quality. Their generally escapist quality is suggested by the popularity of stories about the old days in rural Quebec . . . ."

C102 Pacey, Desmond. "The Writer and His Public 1920–1960." In *Literary History of Canada: Canadian Literature in English.* Gen. ed. Carl F. Klinck. Toronto: Univ. of Toronto Press, 1965, pp. 479, 491. 2nd ed., 1976. II, 5, 17.

As an example of "the extremes to which [the *Canadian Bookman*] carried literary nationalism," Pacey cites Scott's review of L. Adams Beck's *The Ninth Vibration*, in which Scott approves the fact that Beck has " 'added to his signature . . . the word Canada . . . .' "

C103 Rhodenizer, Vernon Blair. *Canadian Literature in English.* Montreal: n.p., 1965, p. 894.
Bibliographical data.

C104 Roper, Gordon, Rupert Schieder, and S. Ross Beharriell. "The Kinds of Fiction (1880–1920)." In *Literary History of Canada: Canadian Literature in English.* Gen. ed. Carl F. Klinck. Toronto: Univ. of Toronto Press, 1965, p. 289. 2nd ed., 1976. I, 303.

"The fictional form that rivalled historical romance in popularity in these years was the local colour story or sketch." "Duncan Campbell Scott published one of the most skilful collections in his *In the Village of Viger* (1896), and his later collection, *The Witching of Elspie* (1923)."

C105 Tait, Michael. "Drama and Theatre." In *Literary History of Canada: Canadian Literature in English.* Gen. ed. Carl F. Klinck. Toronto: Univ. of Toronto Press, 1965, pp. 636–37. 2nd ed., 1976. II, 146.

Discussing the rise of the little theatre in the 1920s, Tait dismisses the value of the plays that grew out of the movement, preferring to cite "a few collections and single plays," one of which was Scott's *Pierre.* "*Pierre* is a domestic tragedy set in rural Quebec. Its plot is over-familiar, the return after many years of the ne'er-do-well son, and the dialogue is written in the specious idiom English Canadians always seem to attribute to the French. The play, however, has dignity and there is genuine pathos in the last scene as Madame Durocher, the universal mother, speaks of the happy future in store for her son, unaware that Pierre has departed again having stolen the meagre savings of the family."

C106 Watt, F.W. "Literature of Protest." In *Literary History of Canada: Canadian Literature in English.* Gen. ed. Carl F. Klinck. Toronto: Univ. of Toronto Press, 1965, pp. 462, 466. 2nd ed., 1976. I, 478, 482.

"Among those late Victorian poets whose work retains most literary value, Archibald Lampman and D.C. Scott were almost alone in demonstrating social and ideological concerns of an unorthodox nature. Both reputedly took part in Fabian discussion groups in Ottawa; both wrote poems of revolutionary or utopian inspiration. The title of Scott's second book of verse, *Labor and the Angel* (1896), is a sign of his temper and interest at this period: his sympathy with the underprivileged and dismay and indignation at social squalor and injustice were evidently strong;

but after 1900 Scott turned away almost entirely in his verse from social preoccupations."

C107 Jones, D.G. "The Sleeping Giant or the Uncreated Conscience of the Race." Association of Canadian University Teachers of English, Univ. of British Columbia, Vancouver. June 1965. Printed in *Canadian Literature*, No. 26 (Autumn 1965), pp. 9–10. Rpt. in *A Choice of Critics: Selections from* Canadian Literature. Ed. George Woodcock. Toronto: Oxford Univ. Press, 1966, pp. 11–12. Rpt. in *Butterfly on Rock: A Study of Themes and Images in Canadian Literature*. By D.G. Jones. Toronto: Univ. of Toronto Press, 1970, pp. 19–20.

Tracing a movement whereby "Eden becomes Ark" and "Adam in the snow becomes the poet in the sea," Jones argues, "A vivid transition is provided by Duncan Campbell Scott's 'The Piper of Arll.' " "The piper in the little cove of Arll is a lonely shepherd. With the arrival of a mysterious ship, he hears the music of a larger life . . . . He strives to learn the music, but when the ship sails away without him he is heartbroken and accordingly breaks his pipe. Yet he mends it again, and as the mysterious ship returns he sings his soul out and expires. The crew takes his body to the ship, whereupon piper, crew, and all sink beneath the sea." "The ship is another ark, and the sunken ark and the piper are one."

C108 Watters, Reginald Eyre, and Inglis Freeman Bell. *On Canadian Literature 1806–1960: A Check List of Articles, Books and Theses on English-Canadian Literature, Its Authors, and Language*. Toronto: Univ. of Toronto Press, 1966, pp. 43, 150–51.

Bibliographical data.

C109 Gustafson, Ralph. Introduction. In *The Penguin Book of Canadian Verse*. Rev. ed. Harmondsworth, Eng.: Penguin, 1967, pp. 24, 25.

"The poetry of Duncan Campbell Scott is of a man who loved life wholly, affectionately, and at all times; where the word in Lampman is dream, the word in Scott is memory; he is a technician of refinement."

C110 Kirkconnell, Watson. *A Slice of Canada: Memoirs*. Toronto: Acadia Univ.-Univ. of Toronto Press, 1967, pp. 50, 235, 291, 306.

Scott was among those who nominated Kirkconnell for the Royal Society of Canada in 1936. Scott was national president of the Canadian Authors' Association in 1933–35.

C111 Story, Norah. "Scott, Duncan Campbell." In her *The Oxford Companion to Canadian History and Literature*. Toronto: Oxford Univ. Press, 1967, pp. 749–50.

In a brief outline of Scott's life and work, Story points out that "Scott's interest in music and art is revealed in his poetry in the verbal colour of his sensitive descriptions of nature and in the strong lyrical quality that he sustained in a variety of rhythms and in free verse."

C112 Patterson II, E. Palmer. "Poet and the Indian: Indian Themes in the Poetry of Duncan Campbell Scott and John Collier." *Ontario History*, 59 (June 1967), 69–78.

Patterson's article is based on the "hypothesis" that the "unofficial writings" of D.C. Scott and John Collier (an American Indian Affairs administrator and poet) "will give clues to the attitudes towards Indians which influenced them as they carried out their duties." Both Scott and Collier maintained consistent attitudes throughout their writing careers. Scott's attitudes were rooted in nineteenth-century "notions of Social Darwinism and the survival of the fittest, and the highest confidence in Western Civilization's achievement and its future," while Collier insisted "that Indians have retained the power to live, and this power consists of the 'ancient, lost reverence and passion for the earth and its web of life.' "

C113 Geddes, Gary. "Piper of Many Tunes: Duncan Campbell Scott." *Canadian Literature*, No. 37 (Summer 1968), pp. 15–27. Rpt. in *Duncan Campbell Scott: A Book of Criticism*. Ed. S.L. Dragland. Ottawa: Tecumseh, 1974, pp. 165–77. Rpt. in *Colony and Confederation: Early Canadian Poets and Their Background*. Ed. George Woodcock. Vancouver: Univ. of British Columbia Press, 1974, pp. 148–60.

Geddes, rejecting a critical tendency to "modernize" Scott, insists on the importance of reading him as a nineteenth-century poet if his "larger significance" is not to be overlooked. For Scott, "...nature is not a repository of 'truth,' but rather the means by which man's own important sensations are elicited and activated." Much of the article is devoted to an explication of that much misunderstood poem, "The Piper of Arll," wherein Geddes finds that "The nature of the poetic experience . . . is essentially religious . . . ."

C114 Smith, A.J.M. "The Canadian Poet: Part 1. To Confederation." *Canadian Literature*, No. 37 (Summer 1968), p. 8. Rpt. (revised — "The Canadian Poet: To Confederation") in *Towards a View of Canadian Letters: Selected Critical Essays 1928–1971*. By A.J.M. Smith. Vancouver: Univ. of British Columbia Press, 1973, pp. 56–57.

"The Forsaken" and "At Gull Lake: August, 1810" are examples of "genuine poetry out of the native mythology of Canada" that is concerned "dramatically and sympathetically with the Indian."

C115 Livesay, Dorothy. "The Documentary Poem: A Canadian Genre." Association of Canadian University Teachers of English, Learned Societies, York Univ., Downsview, Ont. 12 June 1969. Printed in *Contexts of Canadian Criticism: A Collection of Critical Essays*. Ed. Eli Mandel. Patterns of Literary Criticism, No. 9. Chicago: Univ. of Chicago Press, 1971, pp. 275–77. Rev. ed. Toronto: Univ. of Toronto Press, 1977, pp. 275–77.

In a brief outline of the Canadian documentary poem, Livesay comments that Scott made "use of his files in the Department of Indian Affairs to create the dramatic narratives such as 'The Forsaken.' " In the Indian poems, Scott's characters are either "objectified" or, "as in the powerful 'Powassan's Drum,' " turned into myth.

C116 Jones, D.G. *Butterfly on Rock: A Study of Themes and Images in Canadian Literature*. Toronto: Univ. of Toronto Press, 1970, pp. 6, 19–20, 47–49, 50, 69, 70, 90, 94, 102–10, 112, 117, 165, 166.

Scott is "preoccupied with the problem of Job, with the destructive violence of such a world, particularly as it is exacerbated by the activity of man." Looking at the paralysis which is embodied in the Indian poems, Jones points out that "The condition of the Indians is but a specific and notable instance of a condition which preoccupies Scott in a number of poems. 'The Piper of Arll' has no connection with Indians nor, in its pastoral form, with any particular group in actual society; yet it dramatizes much the same theme: the suppression of passion leading to a consequent stagnation or paralysis of life." (Part of this was originally published in 1965. See C107.)

C117 Jones, Joseph, and Johanna Jones. *Authors and Areas of Canada*. People and Places in World-English Literature, No. 1. Austin, Tex.: Steck-Vaughan, 1970, pp. 64–65.

"An 'advanced' poet for his day, experimenting

with numerous rhythms and with free verse, Scott ... turned to the primitive for his themes." "Drawn thus towards the wilderness, Scott nevertheless was socially active and played a leading part in professional organizations such as the Royal Society of Canada."

C118 Woodcock, George. *Canada and the Canadians*. Toronto: Macmillan, 1970, pp. 246–47. Rev. ed. 1973, pp. 246–47.

"In literature the consciousness of setting first began to appear with the group of writers generally known as the Confederation Poets, ... all of them occasionally rose above mere derivativeness, and Duncan Campbell Scott did so frequently."

C119 Thomson, Peter. "Scott, Duncan Campbell." *Britain and the Commonwealth*. Vol. 1 of *The Penguin Companion to Literature*. Ed. David Daiches. London, Eng.: Allen Lane Penguin, 1971, p. 463.

Bio-bibliographical data.

C120 Livesay, Dorothy. "The Native People in Our Canadian Literature." *English Quarterly*, 4, No. 1 (Spring 1971), 28–29.

Tracing the image of the Native in Canadian literature from the work of Frances Brooke to that of George Bowering, Livesay writes that Scott "was not merely a civil servant concerned with bringing the Indians' status more and more into line with that of the white population. He deeply questioned the 'civilizing' of an ancient pattern of life. We know this from his Indian poems, which reveal an appreciation of the dichotomy between darkness and light, summer and winter, peace and storm. Poems like 'The Forsaken,' 'Night Burial in the Forest,' and 'On the Way to the Mission' are objective narratives, with no moral or judgmental overtones."

C121 Atwood, Margaret. *Survival: A Thematic Guide to Canadian Literature*. Toronto: House of Anansi, 1972, pp. 55, 62, 119.

Scott's "At the Cedars" is an example of death by nature, and "The Piper of Arll" is an example of the "doomed exploration poem." Poets like Scott and Archibald Lampman were the first to find "a language appropriate to its objects" of description.

C122 Clever, Glenn. Introduction. In *Selected Stories of Duncan Campbell Scott*. By Duncan Campbell Scott. Ed. Glenn Clever. Ottawa: Univ. of Ottawa Press, 1972, pp. ix–xv.

"Duncan Campbell Scott's poetry receives more comment than does his fiction, yet his thirty-two stories ..., distinctively Canadian and distinguished by quiet power, deserve attention." A variety of themes recur in the stories, "such as the growth of self-knowledge, the effects of emotion and time, the devotion and tensions of family life, the commitment to one's fellows." Scott produced fiction "tended and nurtured by ... understanding and tolerance."

C123 [Clever, Glenn.] "Selected Bibliography." In *Selected Stories of Duncan Campbell Scott*. By Duncan Campbell Scott. Ed. Glenn Clever. Ottawa: Univ. of Ottawa Press, 1972, pp. 131–35.

Bibliographical data.

C124 Reference Division, McPherson Library, University of Victoria, B.C., comp. *Creative Canada: A Biographical Dictionary of Twentieth-Century Creative and Performing Artists*. Vol. II. Toronto: Univ. of Toronto Press, 1972, 246–47.

Bio-bibliographical data.

C125 Thomas, Clara. *Our Nature — Our Voices: A Guidebook to English-Canadian Literature*. Vol. 1 of *Our*

Nature — Our Voices. Toronto: new, 1972, pp. 61–64.

"... Scott had first-hand experience of the Indians, the French Canadians and the half-breeds who were the north's half-forgotten citizens. He was the first of our writers to see them and to put them down, in poem and story, as real men and women with a grim doom and a tragic dignity in living and in dying."

C126 Watters, Reginald Eyre. *A Checklist of Canadian Literature and Background Materials, 1628–1960*. 2nd ed. Toronto: Univ. of Toronto Press, 1972, pp. 176, 229, 387, 447, 574, 639, 732.

Bibliographical data.

C127 Dagg, Melvin H. "Scott and the Indians." *The Humanities Association Bulletin*, 23 (Fall 1972), 3–11. Rpt. in *Duncan Campbell Scott: A Book of Criticism*. Ed. S.L. Dragland. Ottawa: Tecumseh, 1974, pp. 181–92.

Addressing Chipman Hall's (C255) and Keiichi Hirano's (C91) belief that Scott's attitude to the Indians was condescending, perhaps racist, Dagg looks at some lesser known poems on the Indians in order to demonstrate the difference in Scott the Indian Affairs administrator and Scott the poet. Admitting that the "nobility, the pride, power, above all, the innate wisdom of the Indian, is not to be found in his popular 'doomed figures,'" Dagg turns our attention to the passages in "Lines in Memory of Edmund Morris" concerned with the deaths of Crowfoot and Akoose and to "Watkwenies" in an attempt to disprove Hirano's assertion that "'... there is no evidence that privately as a poet, he took a completely different view from Scott the government official.'"

C128 Dragland, S.L. Introduction. In *In the Village of Viger and Other Stories*. By Duncan Campbell Scott.

Gen. ed. Malcolm Ross. New Canadian Library, No. 92. Toronto: McClelland and Stewart, 1973, pp. 9–16.

After reviewing Scott's reputation as a short-story writer, Dragland discusses how the integrated nature of the stories of *In the Village of Viger and Other Stories* proves Scott's commitment to the idea of the book as a whole. The "detailed realization of its [the book's] human and physical geography," the "careful delineation of the season, with its natural phenomena, in which each story takes place," the reappearance of the "motif of the city," and the "image of a bird, caged or free" appear throughout the book. The later stories "take a further step in the direction of realism, whether it is the psychological realism of 'In the Year 1806' or the documentary realism of 'Charcoal.'" Scott is often at his best when writing of the wilderness: "Life in the North is as elemental as the North itself, and Scott knew what it could do to a man ...." Scott, "By writing honestly about people and places he knew from experience, ... helped engineer the revolution to realism in Canadian fiction for which Sara Jeannette Duncan, Frederick Philip Grove, Sinclair Ross, and Ringuet are better known."

C129 Gnarowski, Michael. *A Concise Bibliography of English-Canadian Literature*. Toronto: McClelland and Stewart, 1973, pp. 107–09. Rev. ed., 1978, pp. 125–27.

Bibliographical data.

C130 MacCulloch, Clare. *The Neglected Genre: The Short Story in Canada*. Guelph, Ont.: Alive, 1973, pp. 37–39.

"'Paul Farlotte' is the objective correlative for D.C. Scott to show the dual cultural concept in French Canada immediately following Confederation."

When Paul's mother dies and Paul survives without her, we witness "the final break with the motherland which our pioneers had to make."

C131 Peel, Bruce Braden. *A Bibliography of the Prairie Provinces to 1953.* 2nd ed. Toronto: Univ. of Toronto Press, 1973, p. 442.
Bibliographical data.

C132 Strickland, David. *"Quotations" from English Canadian Literature.* Modern Canadian Library. Toronto: Pagurian, 1976, pp. 17, 25, 32, 36, 47, 50, 72, 169.
Quotations from Scott's works are placed under various thematic headings.

C133 Walsh, William. Introduction. In *Commonwealth Literature.* Ed. William Walsh. London: St. James, 1973, p. 3.
"In Canada, a more positive effort than in New Zealand, a less truculent one than in Australia, to arrive at the same kind of thing, the development of a separate Canadian tradition, was one of the consequences of the work of the post-Confederation poets, Lampman, Roberts, Crawford, Carman, and Scott."

C134 Waterston, Elizabeth. *Survey: A Short History of Canadian Literature.* Methuen Canadian Literature Series. Toronto: Methuen, 1973, pp. 26–27, 40, 80, 83, 85, 86, 153, 163.
Scott as one of the Confederation poets "revealed not only the conflict between conservation and change, wilderness and technology, but also the tension between poetic integrity and the patriotic impulse." In a discussion of the problems that arise in the use of Indian materials by poets, Waterston describes Scott as "by temperament mystic, aesthetic." "Perhaps as an escape from the routine of his

Ottawa life as a civil servant, Scott created poetry which has the hypnotic beat and the powerful story line of Indian legends." Like W.H. Drummond, he "also exploited the comic value of the superstitious [Quebec] villagers in *In the Village of Viger,* 1896, and other stories."

C135 Woodcock, George. "Scott, Duncan Campbell." In *Commonwealth Literature.* Ed. William Walsh. London: St. James, 1973, pp. 223–25.
Bio-bibliographical data.

C136 Waterston, Elizabeth. "Canadian Cabbage, Canadian Rose." *Journal of Canadian Fiction,* 2, No. 3 (Summer 1973), 129, 130, 131. Rpt. in *Twentieth Century Essays on Confederation Literature.* Ed. Lorraine McMullen. Ottawa: Tecumseh, 1976, pp. 93, 95–96, 98.
Waterston describes the choice faced by early Canadian fiction writers: ". . . should the artist fix his eye on the kail, the rank, unpoetic reality of subsistence living? Or should he focus on the rosebush, the touch of sentiment, of romance, of perhaps hopeless aspiration?" Scott, "in his stories of Archie Muir and of Trader Nairn" and of *In the Village of Viger,* chose the first option.

C137 Beckmann, Susan. "A Note on Duncan Campbell Scott's 'The Forsaken.'" *The Humanities Association Review,* 25, No. 1 (Winter 1974), 32–37.
"The Forsaken" owes as much to William Wordsworth's "The Complaint (of a Forsaken Indian Woman)" as it does to Scott's personal experiences with the Indians. However, ". . . the Scott poem is not in the least derivative in any pejorative sense of the term," because Scott, unlike Wordsworth, made no attempt to undermine the dignity of the "lives of the Indian people."

C138 Clever, Glenn. Preface. In *Duncan Campbell Scott: Selected Poetry*. Ed. Glenn Clever. Ottawa: Tecumseh, 1974, pp. v–viii.

Clever introduces the selection of poems with a brief but useful chronology of Scott's life.

C139 [Dragland, S.L.] Bibliography. In *Duncan Campbell Scott: A Book of Criticism*. Ed. S.L. Dragland. Ottawa: Tecumseh, 1974, pp. 193–99.

Bibliographical data.

C140 Colombo, John Robert. *Colombo's Canadian Quotations*. Edmonton: Hurtig, 1974, p. 527.

Colombo includes five quotations from Scott's poetry and prose.

C141 Dragland, S.L. Introduction. In *Duncan Campbell Scott: A Book of Criticism*. Ed. S.L. Dragland. Ottawa: Tecumseh, 1974, pp. 1–3.

Dragland helps provide an historical context for the criticism by writing a general introduction to the book and a brief commentary before each of the selections. Of the book as a whole, Dragland says that biography "is not part of the present concern, or the primary inclusion would be E.K. Brown's Memoir in the *Selected Poems*. Nor does the scope of this book extend to criticism of Scott's fiction, of which there has been too little to balance the larger body of poetry critiques."

C142 Stow, Glenys. "The Wound Under the Feathers: Scott's Discontinuities." In *Colony and Confederation: Early Canadian Poets and Their Background*. Ed. George Woodcock. Canadian Literature Series. Vancouver: Univ. of British Columbia Press, 1974, pp. 161–77.

Stow explores the cultural and personal tensions present (in both resolved and unresolved forms) in Scott's poetry. "Keejigo, star of the morning, victim of the battle between the instinctive and the cerebral worlds, is perhaps the most striking emblem of the tension which gives dark power to the best of Duncan Campbell Scott's work." After examining a number of the better known poems, Stow suggests that, in the "image of a sun-ripened fruit" at the conclusion of "Lines in Memory of Edmund Morris," Scott achieves a symbol of "his own desire for completion. The world, and man within it, ripening, will set free a platonic essence where opposites blend and reconcile . . . ."

C143 Ballstadt, Carl. Introduction. In *The Search for English-Canadian Literature: Anthology of Critical Articles from the Nineteenth and Early Twentieth Centuries*. Ed. Carl Ballstadt. Literature of Canada: Poetry and Prose in Reprint, No. 16. Toronto: Univ. of Toronto Press, 1975, p. 187, xl.

"Unlike many of the critics represented in this volume, Duncan Campbell Scott (1862–1947) needs no introduction. He is well known as a poet, short story writer, and essayist." Scott's essay, "A Decade of Canadian Poetry," "suggests that the mental affinities of Canadians and Americans has resulted in a serious consideration of Canadian poetry by Americans."

C144 New, William H. *Critical Writings on Commonwealth Literatures: A Selective Bibliography to 1970, with a List of Theses and Dissertations*. University Park: Pennsylvania State Univ. Press, 1975, pp. 138, 161, 184.

Bibliographical data.

C145 Harrison, Dick. " 'So Deathly Silent': The Resolution of Pain and Fear in the Poetry of Lampman and D.C. Scott." The Lampman Symposium, Univ. of Ottawa,

Ottawa. 3 May 1975. Printed in *The Lampman Symposium*. Ed. Lorraine McMullen. Re-Appraisals: Canadian Writers [No. 3]. Ottawa: Univ. of Ottawa Press, 1976, pp. 63–74.

Harrison compares the "resolution of pain and fear" in Archibald Lampman's and D.C. Scott's works. "In Scott's poetry, pain and fear are less likely to be the subject of a lyric outcry [as they are in Lampman's] than the source of tension in a dramatic narrative." "Where pain and fear in Scott have an active and violent resolution, in Lampman they are resolved passively, through escape of [sic] through a slow, organic process."

C146 Colombo, John Robert. *Colombo's Canadian References*. Toronto: Oxford Univ. Press, 1976, pp. 474–75.

"He [Scott] was a fine poet whose lyrics catch the essentially hostile quality of the northern landscapes and whose narrative poems depict the Indians as the most enduring of people . . . ."

C147 Farley, T.E. *Exiles & Pioneers: Two Visions of Canada's Future 1825–1975*. Ottawa: Borealis, 1976, pp. 74–78.

Farley classes Scott as a poet of exile because of the "condition of stasis" which is manifested in his poetry: he "could not denounce society categorically, as Lampman did in 'The City of the End of Things.' As a result, his poetry moves toward, and often achieves, a condition of stasis, checkmated between a stormy society to which he is bound, and the idealized stars he yearns for but cannot reach . . . ."

C148 Fee, Marjorie, and Ruth Cawker. *Canadian Fiction: An Annotated Bibliography*. Toronto: Peter Martin, 1976, pp. 100–01, 122, 125, 126, 128, 130, 134, 141, 142, 147, 149, 151, 152, 154, 162, 165, 166, 167.

Bibliographical data pertaining to Scott's short stories. "These nineteenth-century stories [of *In the Village of Viger*] are still lively and suspenseful, and sustain a mood of high adventure and mystery." "The lives of trappers and marginally genteel villagers [in *The Witching of Elspie*] provide the centres for mysterious or passionate legends."

C149 Flood, John. *The Land They Occupied*. Erin, Ont.: The Porcupine's Quill, 1976, pp. 26–46.

In this book of poetry inspired by what he believes is the treachery embodied in the signing of Treaty No. 9 that he describes in his preface, Flood devotes thirteen poems to Scott and the Indians. The book includes photographs taken during the trip to sign the treaty.

C150 Gerson, Carole. "The Piper's Forgotten Tune: Notes on the Stories of D.C. Scott and a Bibliography." *Journal of Canadian Fiction*, No. 16 (1976), pp. 138–43.

Gerson hails the publication of two new collections of Scott's stories as proof that the value of his fiction is finally being recognized. As a short story writer, ". . . Scott's consistent rejection of both sentimentality and sensationalism and his maintenance of a detached narrative style impart an essentially modern tone to his central theme of psychic and physical survival." Gerson concludes with a bibliography of Scott's stories, including those at present uncollected.

C151 McMullen, Lorraine. Introduction. *Twentieth Century Essays on Confederation Literature*. Ed. Lorraine McMullen. Ottawa: Tecumseh, 1976, pp. 2, 3, 5, 7, 8.

Rehearsing the approaches taken by the articles she has included in her book and outlining some important moments in the making of a Canadian literature,

McMullen notes Scott's address to the Royal Society of Canada ("Poetry and Progress" 1922), his poetic contributions to newspapers and periodicals in the later nineteenth century, his inclusion with six other poets in J.R. Wetherell's anthology *Later Canadian Poets* (1893), his participation in the development of a tradition of local colour stories, his adoption of the "Kailyard School," and his co-writing of the column "At the Mermaid Inn" in *The Globe* [Toronto]. In her selections, she includes Scott's "A Decade of Canadian Poetry," in which Scott "looks back at the most important decade for poetry in the confederation period, the nineties, from the point of view of one directly involved . . . ."

C152 Moyles, R.G. *English-Canadian Literature to 1900: A Guide to Information Sources*. Detroit: Gale, 1976, pp. 93–97.
Bibliographical data.

C153 Pacey, Desmond. "The Course of Canadian Criticism." In *Literary History of Canada: Canadian Literature in English*. Gen. ed. Carl F. Klinck. Toronto: Univ. of Toronto Press, 1976. III, 21.
A.J.M. Smith's essay on Scott (published in *Our Living Tradition*) is proof that "Smith has most distinguished himself as a practical critic."

C154 Thomas, Clara. "Biography II." In *Literary History of Canada: Canadian Literature in English*. Gen. ed. Carl F. Klinck. Toronto: Univ. of Toronto Press, 1976. III, 187, 188, 189.
"The first concerted effort towards providing biographies of Canadians and the most successful Canadian publishing venture to that time was George Morang's Makers of Canada series. Between 1903 and 1908 twenty volumes of biography were published under the editorship of two of Canada's lead-ing literary men, Duncan Campbell Scott and Pelham Edgar."

C155 Cogswell, Fred. "No Heavenly Harmony: A Reading of Powassan's Drum." *Studies in Canadian Literature* [Univ. of New Brunswick], 1 (Summer 1976), 233–37.
Attempting to account for Scott's representation of the creator in the figure of an Indian medicine man, Cogswell explains that Scott must have realized "that the harmony created by the musician, the poet, and the artist was of an order different from the details of daily life. By comparison, the latter were a flawed creation. When, therefore, he attempted an apocalyptic poem, dealing with his vision of these things, he found it necessary to posit a flawed creator." Cogswell takes us through part of the imagery of "Powassan's Drum" — Powassan's "physical shape (his body) is severed from his culture (his head), and he is unable to navigate his canoe (his power over his environment) through the 'dead' water, and he therefore must perish in the first inevitable great storm." Cogswell concludes that Scott's poem embodies his belief that artistic vision, "severed from the rest of mankind and distorted by external passion, is both inaccurate and powerless to avert the violence which is the only answer that nature can give to the malevolent power expressed when hatred is unleashed."

C156 Dragland, S.L. "Duncan Campbell Scott as Literary Executor for Archibald Lampman: 'A Labour of Love.'" *Studies in Canadian Literature* [Univ. of New Brunswick], 1 (Summer 1976), 143–57.
Scott's devotion to Archibald Lampman's work was an unselfish and life-long activity. Lampman "*inspired* the friendship in Scott that was to last so long after his death." Dragland includes a number of little-known anecdotes: Scott, in spite of thinking

well of Lorne Pierce, "wrote to at least two people telling them, in capital letters, to be sure to keep copies of all correspondence with Pierce."

C157 Waterston, Elizabeth. "The Missing Face: Five Short Stories by Duncan Campbell Scott." *Studies in Canadian Literature* [Univ. of New Brunswick], 1 (Summer 1976), 223–29.

Waterston looks at five short stories from *The Witching of Elspie: A Book of Stories* in which Scott "brought out . . . the most subtle and self-torturing situations in which a northern form of Puritanism might embroil itself." The tone and structure of the stories differ from those of the poetry because Scott "was following his times in separating poetry from prose, leaving to poetry the romantic effects of lyrics about landscape, while using prose to probe into social science or psychology."

C158 Flood, John. "The Duplicity of D.C. Scott and the James Bay Treaty." *Black Moss* [Coatsworth, Ont.], Ser. 2, No. 2 (Fall 1976), pp. 50–63.

Flood compares the humanitarian views of Scott the poet with the pragmatic actions of Scott the civil servant, noting that ". . . what should have most concerned Scott as an agent negotiating with Native people is a humane approach to the issue of survival through the preservation of their integrity rather than through a perpetuation of a climate of endurance and tolerance." Flood looks at a number of documents prepared by Scott during his tenure with the Department of Indian Affairs and argues that "The duplicity from which Scott suffers as a poet whose humanitarian support his critics say is in favor of the Indians and as a civil servant whose allegiance is to the white, christian government is that, while occupying the middle ground, he plays both ends against the middle . . . ."

C159 Adaskin, Harry. *A Fiddler's World: Memoirs to 1938.* Vancouver: November House, 1977, pp. 168–69.

Adaskin provides a few memories of Scott and his wife Belle Botsford, of the death of the Scotts' daughter, and of Scott's marriage to his second wife Elise Aylen.

C160 Davies, Barrie. "Lampman Could Tell His Frog from His Toad: A Note on Art Versus Nature." *Studies in Canadian Literature* [Univ. of New Brunswick], 2 (Winter 1977), 129–30.

Scott's comment that Archibald Lampman's frogs were really toads prompted Davies' brief note on Lampman's general interest in metamorphosis as a poetic convention. ". . . Lampman's intentions were lost on D.C. Scott . . . ."

C161 Frye, Northrop. "Haunted by Lack of Ghosts: Some Patterns in the Imagery in Canadian Poetry." In *The Canadian Imagination.* Ed. David Staines. Cambridge, Mass.: Harvard Univ. Press, 1977, pp. 33–34.

Frye cites "The Forsaken" as proof that "The nostalgic and elegiac are the inevitable emotional responses of an egocentric consciousness locked into a demythologized environment." "In such a setting the Indian appears as a noble savage in the sense that his life is so largely one of stoically enduring both the sufferings imposed by nature and those he inflicts on himself and others."

C162 Marshall, Tom. "The Major Canadian Poets: Between Two Worlds, Duncan Campbell Scott." *The Canadian Forum*, June–July 1977, pp. 20–24. Rpt. (revised — "Half-Breeds: Duncan Campbell Scott") in *Harsh and Lovely Land: The Major Canadian Poets and the Making of a Canadian Tradition.* By Tom Marshall. Vancouver: Univ. of British Columbia Press, 1979, pp. 23–33.

Marshall argues that, "least appreciated of the

Confederation poets in his lifetime, Scott is, nonetheless, the best and most important of them, since he goes further technically, emotionally, and intellectually towards an idiom that can embody the Canadian situation." To demonstrate his point, Marshall looks at "The Piper of Arll," Scott's "symbolic fable of the artist in exile," and at the Indian poems, which avoid "a mellifluous pseudo-Wordsworthian sentimentalizing." Scott's attitude to the Indians is rooted in his religion, which "inclines him to refer (or defer) the more creative and potentially progressive possibilities of the Canadian situation to another world, or at least to a distant future."

C163 Bentley, D.M.R. " 'The Onondaga Madonna': A Sonnet of Rare Beauty." CV/II, 3, No. 2 (Summer 1977), 28–29.

Bentley examines the way ironic intention in the poem was strengthened when Scott changed its title from "An Onondaga Mother and Child" to "The Onondaga Madonna." "Scott's choice of the Petrarchan sonnet form, coupled with his masterful handling of imagery, rhythm, and rhyme, reinforces the theme of his poem [of the tension between Indian and European] in such a manner that, in the full sense of the terms, form reflects content and art conceals artifice. What we are left with is a feeling that the poem is a marvellously ironic fusion of vision and technique, of subject and treatment."

C164 Meckler, Lee B. "Rabbit-Skin Robes and Mink-Traps: Indian and European in 'The Forsaken.' " *Canadian Poetry: Studies, Documents, Reviews*, No. 1 (Fall–Winter 1977), pp. 60–65.

"The Forsaken" is a "carefully wrought artefact with a strategy that is more consciously thought out than might first be supposed." The word "slunk" in Part 11 of the poem is indicative of what Meckler

believes to be Scott's overall theme: the encroachment and effect of European values on those of the Indians.

C165 Endres, Robin. "Marxist Literary Criticism and English Canadian Literature." In *In Our Own House: Social Perspectives on Canadian Literature*. Ed. Paul Cappon. Toronto: McClelland and Stewart, 1978, pp. 95–96, 98.

Applying the Christopher Caudwell theory of "the bourgeois illusion of freedom" to Canadian poetry, Endres argues that, while the first generation of Canadian poets is "celebrating and heralding the establishment of Canadian industrial society," the "second generation of Canadian poets," including Scott, sees "man as instinctively free, but bound by the oppressive conditions of industrial society."

C166 Mathews, Robin. *Canadian Literature: Surrender or Revolution*. Toronto: Steel Rail, 1978, pp. 56, 123, 124, 125, 161, 196.

Mathews argues that George Grant's position "that white men in Canada must be alienated from the land" is countered by "Scott's statement that when he left the religion of his fathers he went into the wilderness and found he could manage." Furthermore, Scott's "The Height of Land," "one of the great poems of the last hundred years, . . . speaks itself with a perfect sense of being, as Leacock says ' "home" now.' " Mathews cites Scott as an example of a poet whose "handling of the native people" has been ignored by poets working since 1945. He also points out that Scott "calls the men in commerce who practised the liberal ideology of individualist exploitation the white men-servants of greed."

C167 Naaman, Antoine. *Répertoire des thèses littéraires canadiennes de 1921 à 1976*. Sherbrooke: Naaman, 1978, p. 257.

Bibliographical data.

C168 Stevens, Peter. *Modern English-Canadian Poetry: A Guide to Information Sources*. Vol. xv of *American Literature, English Literature, and World Literatures in English Information Guide Series*. Detroit: Gale, 1978, pp. 58, 60, 61.

Bibliographical data.

C169 McDougall, Robert L. "D.C. Scott: The Dating of the Poems." *Canadian Poetry: Studies, Documents, Reviews*, No. 2 (Spring–Summer 1978), pp. 13–27.

In spite of Scott's decision in *The Poems of Duncan Campbell Scott* to "present his work outside the framework of chronology," McDougall affirms the "general utility for precise dates for the composition of poems," and publishes a chart which documents when many of the poems in *The Green Cloister: Later Poems* and *The Poems of Duncan Campbell Scott* were composed.

C170 Slonim, Leon. "Notes on Duncan Campbell Scott's 'Lines in Memory of Edmund Morris.'" *Canadian Poetry: Studies, Documents, Reviews*, No. 2 (Spring–Summer 1978), pp. 38–42.

Slonim's purpose is "to shed more light on the historical and biographical context of 'Lines,' first with reference to the poem as a whole and then with reference to specific allusions within the poem."

C171 Slonim, Leon. "A Source for Duncan Campbell Scott's 'On the Way to the Mission.'" *Canadian Poetry: Studies, Documents, Reviews*, No. 3 (Fall–Winter 1978), pp. 62–64.

Exploring the possibility of Major Robert Rogers' *Ponteach: or the Savages of America* (cited in Francis Parkman's writing) as a source for "On the Way to the Mission," Slonim argues that the changes Scott made to the original "increase the reader's sympathy for the victimized characters."

C172 Davies, Barrie. Introduction. In *At the Mermaid Inn: Wilfred Campbell, Archibald Lampman, Duncan Campbell Scott in The Globe 1892–93*. Ed. Barrie Davies. Literature of Canada: Poetry and Prose in Reprint, No. 21. Toronto: Univ. of Toronto Press, 1979, pp. vii–xxi.

At the Mermaid Inn: Wilfred Campbell, Archibald Lampman, Duncan Campbell Scott is important "because it reflects many of the issues, conflicts, and general temper of the age." Davies' introduction is designed to emphasize "the centrality of much of the material to the time and place in which it was written; to trace through themes which seem especially pertinent now." In characterizing the contributions of the three poets, Davies points out that "Campbell and Lampman provided the more outspoken and controversial pieces. Scott tended to hold aloof from contemporary issues and his voice is more arcane and monotone."

C173 Kelly, Catherine. "In the Listening World: The Poetry of Duncan Campbell Scott." *Studies in Canadian Literature* [Univ. of New Brunswick], 4 (Winter 1979), 71–94.

"Consciousness of large, essential life at the core of being seems basic to Duncan Campbell Scott's poetry." Kelly seeks to establish "some sense of the transcendent base in Scott's work," looks at "some of the formal aspects of the poetry by which it is communicated" (she is particularly interested in Scott's use of the word "cold" as image and idea), and demonstrates the effect of the "fundamental experience" "in personal life." Kelly surveys a number of poems and concentrates on "The Height of Land."

C174 Slonim, Leon. "The Source of Duncan Campbell Scott's 'Charcoal.'" *Studies in Canadian Literature*

[Univ. of New Brunswick], 4 (Winter 1979), 162–66.

Although "Charcoal" is based on a factual event, the fact that Scott changed certain details suggests that his story is "less an example of documentary realism than a blend of realism and romance, a blend which is characteristic of Scott's narratives."

C175 Woodcock, George. *The Canadians.* Don Mills, Ont.: Fitzhenry and Whiteside, 1979, pp. 160, 260.

"When a clear Ontarian poetic tradition did begin to develop . . . , it was represented by poets like . . . Duncan Campbell Scott whose work was so largely dominated by his experiences among Indians far out from the settled centres in the north country."

C176 Woodcock, George. "Duncan Campbell Scott." In *Great Writers of the English Language: Poets.* Ed. James Vinson. London: Macmillan, 1979, pp. 859–61.

Bio-bibliographical data.

C177 Cogswell, Fred. "Symbol and Decoration: 'The Piper of Arll.'" The Duncan Campbell Scott Symposium, Univ. of Ottawa, Ottawa. 28 April 1979. Printed in *The Duncan Campbell Scott Symposium.* Ed. K.P. Stich. Re-Appraisals: Canadian Writers, No. 6. Ottawa: Univ. of Ottawa Press, 1980, pp. 47–54.

In a reading of "The Piper of Arll," Cogswell explains "(1) the relation of beach, cove and bay to the ocean; (2) the relation of the poet to the ocean throughout the poem; (3) the relation of the poet to the ship during and immediately after its first appearance; and (4) the final appearance and sinking of the ship."

C178 Doyle, James. "Duncan Campbell Scott and American Literature." The Duncan Campbell Scott Symposium, Univ. of Ottawa, Ottawa. 28 April 1979.

Printed in *The Duncan Campbell Scott Symposium.* Ed. K.P. Stich. Re-Appraisals: Canadian Writers, No. 6. Ottawa: Univ. of Ottawa Press, 1980, pp. 101–09.

Doyle concentrates on Scott's short stories to demonstrate in what ways the "English Victorian" Scott was influenced by American literature.

C179 Johnston, Gordon. "The Significance of Scott's Minor Poems." The Duncan Campbell Scott Symposium, Univ. of Ottawa, Ottawa. 28 April 1979. Printed in *The Duncan Campbell Scott Symposium.* Ed. K.P. Stich. Re-Appraisals: Canadian Writers, No. 6. Ottawa: Univ. of Ottawa Press, 1980, pp. 11–21.

Johnston attributes some of the problems in Scott's poetry to what he calls "the doubleness of rational thought" that led Scott "to want to resolve ambiguities."

C180 Kelly, Catherine E. "Meanings Held in a Mist: The Major Poems." The Duncan Campbell Scott Symposium, Univ. of Ottawa, Ottawa. 28 April 1979. Printed in *The Duncan Campbell Scott Symposium.* Ed. K.P. Stich. Re-Appraisals: Canadian Writers, No. 6. Ottawa: Univ. of Ottawa Press, 1980, pp. 37–46.

Kelly discusses the "mystery, transcendence, supernatural reality," which is the "unifying element" throughout the poetry. She then applies her theory to "Lines in Memory of Edmund Morris."

C181 Matthews, John P. "Duncan Campbell Scott and 'the Moment of Becoming.'" The Duncan Campbell Scott Symposium, Univ. of Ottawa, Ottawa. 28 April 1979. Printed in *The Duncan Campbell Scott Symposium.* Ed. K.P. Stich. Re-Appraisals: Canadian Writers, No. 6. Ottawa: Univ. of Ottawa Press, 1980, pp. 1–10.

In an article indebted to A.J.M. Smith and A.M. Klein, Matthews traces the "moment of becoming" through a number of Scott's poems. He defines his term as "the point of synthesis which does not consist of a small range in the middle of the spectrum of apparently opposed opposites, but which contains the entire range, equally, and at the same time." If the moment of becoming is a universal condition, ". . . its perception is a peculiarly Canadian talent, and its continuance a vital Canadian necessity."

C182 McDougall, Robert L. "D.C. Scott: A Trace of Documents and a Touch of Life." The Duncan Campbell Scott Symposium, Univ. of Ottawa, Ottawa. 28 April 1979. Printed in *The Duncan Campbell Scott Symposium*. Ed. K.P. Stich. Re-Appraisals: Canadian Writers, No. 6. Ottawa: Univ. of Ottawa Press, 1980, pp. 127–41.

McDougall outlines the details of his discovery of Scott's correspondence with E.K. Brown. He has since published the letters as *The Poet and the Critic: A Literary Correspondence between D.C. Scott and E.K. Brown 1940–47*. McDougall also looks at some incidents in Scott's life.

C183 Clever, Glenn. "Duncan Campbell Scott's Fiction: Moral Realism and Canadian Identity." The Duncan Campbell Scott Symposium, Univ. of Ottawa, Ottawa. 29 April 1979. Printed in *The Duncan Campbell Scott Symposium*. Ed. K.P. Stich. Re-Appraisals: Canadian Writers, No. 6. Ottawa: Univ. of Ottawa Press, 1980, pp. 85–100.

Clever surveys the moral realism of Scott's fiction in order to "place Scott as a primary figure in the shift in Canadian fiction away from the tradition he inherited and to show his part in the development of a Canadian sensibility."

C184 Dragland, Stan. " 'Spring on Mattagami': A Reconsideration. Duncan Campbell Scott's 'Spring on Mattagami' and Some Contexts." The Duncan Campbell Scott Symposium, Univ. of Ottawa, Ottawa. 29 April 1979. Printed in *The Duncan Campbell Scott Symposium*. Ed. K.P. Stich. Re-Appraisals: Canadian Writers, No. 6. Ottawa: Univ. of Ottawa Press, 1980, pp. 55–61.

"Spring on Mattagami," far from being a derivative poem with annoying echoes of George Meredith's "Love in the Valley," is "one of Scott's major poems" because ". . . it represents a thorough absorption and an individualized recreation of an inherited form." Dragland compares the poem's vision of the North with the demonic one in "Powassan's Drum" to make the point that Scott's presentation of his protagonist is ironic and psychologically more complex than earlier critics believed.

C185 Dragland, Stan. " 'Spring on Mattagami': A Reconsideration. 'Spring on Mattagami': Second Thoughts." The Duncan Campbell Scott Symposium, Univ. of Ottawa, Ottawa. 29 April 1979. Printed in *The Duncan Campbell Scott Symposium*. Ed. K.P. Stich. Re-Appraisals: Canadian Writers, No. 6. Ottawa: Univ. of Ottawa Press, 1980, pp. 66–70.

Dragland explores the relationship between the protagonist and the lady in "Spring on Mattagami" "to demonstrate further aspects of the richness" of the poem. The protagonist's "wishful vision [of the lady] involves a sort of negative capability, a decision not to bother solving the problem of who she is and what motivates her . . . ."

C186 Flood, John. "Native People in Scott's Short Fiction." The Duncan Campbell Scott Symposium, Univ. of Ottawa, Ottawa. 29 April 1979. Printed in *The Duncan Campbell Scott Symposium*. Ed. K.P. Stich. Re-Appraisals: Canadian Writers, No. 6. Ottawa: Univ. of Ottawa Press, 1980, pp. 73–83.

Flood looks at the role of the Indian in the short stories. He argues the presence of the "Representative Indian," who is used at best to "offer some insight into the motives or thoughts of other characters," and the "Individual Indian," whom Scott attempts and fails to portray realistically.

C187 Ware, Martin. " 'Spring on Mattagami': A Reconsideration. 'Spring on Mattagami' in a Dramatic Context." The Duncan Campbell Scott Symposium, Univ. of Ottawa, Ottawa. 29 April 1979. Printed in *The Duncan Campbell Scott Symposium*. Ed. K.P. Stich. Re-Appraisals: Canadian Writers, No. 6. Ottawa: Univ. of Ottawa Press, 1980, pp. 62–66.

"Spring on Mattagami" is one of a group of "essentially dramatic poems which deal with the adventures of the troubled white soul: adventures which are in significant ways the obverse of those presented in Scott's well-known and much studied Indian poems." Ware agrees that "Spring on Mattagami" is "surely to be read in an ironic light."

C188 Ware, Martin. " 'Spring on Mattagami': A Reconsideration. 'Spring on Mattagami': A Further Comment." The Duncan Campbell Scott Symposium, Univ. of Ottawa, Ottawa. 29 April 1979. Printed in *The Duncan Campbell Scott Symposium*. Ed. K.P. Stich. Re-Appraisals: Canadian Writers, No. 6. Ottawa: Univ. of Ottawa Press, 1980, pp. 70–72.

Ware disagrees with Dragland's interpretation that the "speaker's wishful vision of his beloved's surrender involves 'a form of negative capability' " (C185). He further disagrees with Dragland's contrast of "Spring on Mattagami" with "Powassan's Drum" (C184) because both poems are "demonic": "We leave them not filled but purged of nightmare, and with a grateful sense of the boundless energy of Scott's Northern world . . . ."

C189 Slonim, Leon. "D.C. Scott's 'At Gull Lake: August, 1810.' " *Canadian Literature*, No. 81 (Summer 1979), pp. 142–43.

Scott's poem is based on Alexander Henry's *New Light on the Early History of the Greater Northwest*. Slonim quotes in full the relevant passage so that a comparison can be made of the two narratives in order to reveal how Scott "confronted and transformed his material."

C190 Doyle, James. "Canadian Poetry and American Magazines, 1885–1905." *Canadian Poetry: Studies, Documents, Reviews*, No. 5 (Fall–Winter 1979), pp. 73–82.

Doyle outlines the pervasive influence of American magazines on the Canadian literary scene from 1885 to 1905, noting that the young Canadian poets were particularly drawn to such periodicals as *Scribner's Magazine* and *The Atlantic Monthly* because they both paid for contributions (which Canadian magazines were seldom able to do) and welcomed unknown writers (which British magazines preferred not to do). However, Canadian poets achieved success over the border only by "the whole-hearted acceptance of the standards of American poets and editors." Fortunately, by 1905, Scott was "spending more of his time preparing editions of his poems and offering his work to Canadian periodicals," so he was able to break away from the strict demands of the American market. The situation symbolizes "the perennial cultural dilemma of English-Canadians, who must pursue an elusive compromise between the recognition of their affinities with the United States, and their urge to create an autonomous society and culture."

C191 Armitage, C.M. "The Letters of Duncan Campbell Scott to Lionel Stevenson." In *The Duncan Campbell*

Scott Symposium. Ed. K.P. Stich. Re-Appraisals: Canadian Writers, No. 6. Ottawa: Univ. of Ottawa Press, 1980, pp. 111–12.

Armitage briefly describes the letters that Scott wrote to Lionel Stevenson between 1923 and 1940.

C192 Bentley, D.M.R. "Duncan Campbell Scott." In *Profiles in Canadian Literature.* Ed. Jeffrey M. Heath. Vol. 1. Toronto: Dundurn, 1980, 25–33.

Scott occupies "a broadly humanist and idealist position . . . ." His poetry "organizes itself into opposing yet related pairs such as Indian and European, primitive and sophisticated, intensity and restraint." "When we also consider" such examples as the paired poems of "The Sea by the Wood" and "The Wood by the Sea," ". . . it becomes abundantly clear that Scott's habitual way of thinking was dialectical, that he thought in terms of pairs, opposites, mirror images, and juxtapositions." Furthermore, "For Scott, it would seem, the movement of individual life, as well as of art and mankind too, was ideally towards a state of reconciliation, peace and beauty."

C193 Birney, Earle. *Spreading Time: Remarks on Canadian Writing and Writers, Book I: 1904–1949.* Montreal: Véhicule, 1980, pp. 10, 16, 84, 97, 102–03, 129. Rpt. (revised, excerpt — "Struggle against the Old Guard: Editing the *Canadian Poetry Magazine*") in *Essays on Canadian Writing,* No. 21 (Spring 1981), pp. 15, 19, 21, 23.

Scott's poetry is "precise and delicate in form and feeling" and is "worth any Canadian reader's attention."

C194 Campbell, Sandra. "A Fortunate Friendship: Duncan Campbell Scott and Pelham Edgar." In *The Duncan Campbell Scott Symposium.* Ed. K.P. Stich. Re-Appraisals: Canadian Writers, No. 6. Ottawa: Univ. of Ottawa Press, 1980, pp. 113–26.

Campbell provides details about Scott's friendship with Pelham Edgar. She also comments on their joint editorship of the Makers of Canada series.

C195 Eggleston, Wilfrid. *Literary Friends.* Ottawa: Borealis, 1980, pp. 106–24.

In a chapter on D.C. Scott and Pelham Edgar, Eggleston recalls his earliest encounters with the poet. He includes anecdotes about the Scott Commemoration Nights at the Public Archives ("Scott had of course been invited but he was too shy to attend") and Carleton College. Some of his wife's memories about her first meeting with Scott and Elise Aylen Scott are quoted.

C196 Grady, Wayne. Preface. In *The Penguin Book of Canadian Short Stories.* Ed. Wayne Grady. Harmondsworth, Eng.: Penguin, 1980, p. vi.

"The direct, pared style of the stories in *In the Village of Viger,* and their naturalistic examination of real people in real situations, provided the first breath of the modern spirit in the Canadian short story."

C197 Kelly, Catherine E. "Selected Bibliography." In *The Duncan Campbell Scott Symposium.* Ed. K.P. Stich. Re-Appraisals: Canadian Writers, No. 6. Ottawa: Univ. of Ottawa Press, 1980, pp. 147–55.

Bibliographical data.

C198 Mezei, Kathy. "From Lifeless Pools to the Circle of Affection: The Significance of Space in the Poetry of D.C. Scott." In *The Duncan Campbell Scott Symposium.* Ed. K.P. Stich. Re-Appraisals: Canadian Writers, No. 6. Ottawa: Univ. of Ottawa Press, 1980, pp. 23–35.

Mezei begins with the idea that "in Scott's poems . . . the recreation of the natural landscape into the form of a poem provided a structure for exploring and viewing his own subjective states and the primal forces moving man and the universe." She then examines "the symbolic significance of [Scott's recurring] spatial images," most of which are "drawn from the landscape, especially the northern Canadian wilderness." She divides the spatial images into two primary categories, those of the (female) circles, which represent the paradoxical "nature of existence," and those of the (masculine) heights, which represent the "ascent to the ideal."

C199 Stich, K.P. Introduction. In *The Duncan Campbell Scott Symposium.* Ed. K.P. Stich. Re-Appraisals: Canadian Writers, No. 6. Ottawa: Univ. of Ottawa Press, 1980, pp. xi–xiv.

"Coincidentally," Stich points out, "the Symposium took place within only a short walk from where Scott lived and worked in Ottawa." "With Scott such reappraisals [as the Symposium provides] were particularly timely because our faith in late nineteenth-century Canadian poets needs the support of microscopes . . . ."

C200 Adamson, Arthur. "Notes from a Dark Cellar: Ruminations on the Nature of Regionalism and Metaphor in Mid-Western Canadian Poetry." *Essays on Canadian Writing,* Nos. 18–19 (Summer–Fall 1980), pp. 223, 224.

Adamson briefly describes Keejigo as "a metaphor for Tabashaw's vision" in "At Gull Lake, 1810."

C201 Jones, Joseph, and Johanna Jones. *Canadian Fiction.* Twayne's World Authors Series, No. 630. Boston: Twayne, 1981, pp. 47, 92, 105.

"The work of Duncan Campbell Scott, who became closely acquainted with Indian life through his post as a public servant, brings us nearer a time when Canadian aboriginals . . . came to be viewed less distantly."

C202 Monkman, Leslie. *A Native Heritage: Images of the Indian in English-Canadian Literature.* Toronto: Univ. of Toronto Press, 1981, pp. 33–34, 51, 67, 70–74, 88, 98.

Monkman identifies Scott as "the white writer of the late nineteenth and early twentieth centuries who is most closely identified with the culture of the Indian." Monkman examines Scott's work from the perspective of a critic who recognizes that Scott "accepted the eventual disappearance of the red man as inevitable" and "the distinction between Indian cultures of the past and the present."

C203 Roberts, Carolyn. "Words after Music: A Musical Reading of Scott's 'Night Hymns on Lake Nipigon.' " *Canadian Poetry: Studies, Documents, Reviews,* No. 8 (Spring–Summer 1981), pp. 56–63.

"Clearly, Scott's poetry demands a close analysis of his explicitly musical poems," a critical task which Roberts states has not yet been done. Consequently, she traces the musical techniques and structures of "Night Hymns on Lake Nipigon," where Scott's "brilliance lies in the fact that he has united this tradition of using the Sapphic stanza to write odes, hymns and other musical verse forms with the familiar Latin hymn 'Adeste Fidelis,' itself quoted at the central point of the poem, the last line of the fifth stanza."

C204 Bentley, D.M.R. "A Stretching Landscape: Notes on Some Formalistic Continuities in the Poetry of the Hinterland." *CV/II,* 5, No. 3 (Summer 1981), 6, 7, 8–9, 11.

In an article exploring the relationship between poetic form and the hinterland in a range of Canadian poets, Bentley looks at Scott's Indian poems to demonstrate how the poet alternated between "closed and traditional forms, beliefs, and landscapes" and "the freer and more open techniques, thoughts, and terrains which he had encountered in his travels through the wilderness and through the works of, amongst others, [Walt] Whitman, [Ralph Waldo] Emerson, [Matthew] Arnold, [Coventry] Patmore, and the European *symbolistes*."

C205 Atwood, Margaret. Introduction. In *The New Oxford Book of Canadian Verse: In English*. Ed. Margaret Atwood. Toronto: Oxford Univ. Press, 1982, pp. xxxii–xxxiii.

"Though these [Confederation] poets . . . are usually lumped together, within their convention they are quite different in tone. . . . This editor has a sneaking preference for Duncan Campbell Scott. Although I recognize that the other poets are lusher and more graceful, Scott's condensed tragedies have a starkness and a moral jaggedness that evoke darkness rather than the light and half-lights of Lampman."

C206 Brown, Russell, and Donna Bennett. "Duncan Campbell Scott, 1862–1947." In *An Anthology of Canadian Literature in English*. Ed. Russell Brown and Donna Bennett. Vol. 1. Toronto: Oxford Univ. Press, 1982, 194–95.

Brown and Bennett provide a brief overview of Scott's life.

C207 Cockburn, R.H. "A Note on the Probable Source of Duncan Campbell Scott's 'The Forsaken.'" *Studies in Canadian Literature* [Univ. of New Brunswick], 7 (1982), 139–40.

Cockburn cites Thomas Anderson's story of the abandoned old Algonquin woman as a possible source for "The Forsaken" because ". . . stories of the sort travelled rapidly and widely in the North" during the period when both Anderson and Scott worked there.

C208 Frye, Northrop. "National Consciousness." In *Divisions on a Ground: Essays on Canadian Culture*. Ed. James Polk. Toronto: House of Anansi, 1982, p. 53.

"In Canadian poetry there is a special pathos in dying animals and falling trees, and in many tragic narratives, such as Duncan Campbell Scott's 'At the Cedars' . . . there is a lurking sense not only of the indifference of nature to man, but almost of its exasperation with this parasite of humanity that has settled on it."

C209 Lynch, Gerald. "An Endless Flow: D.C. Scott's Indian Poems." *Studies in Canadian Literature* [Univ. of New Brunswick], 7 (1982), 27–54.

In a chronological study of the Indian poems concerned with " 'the impact of the primitive on the sophisticated,' " Lynch argues that ". . . Scott's understanding of and compassion for the Indians, and of what was being done to them in the process of assimilation, grew from poem to poem . . . ." Pointing out that, as an administrator, Scott was "a white man writing for other white men," especially those who constitute the "official, white, government bureaucracy," Lynch is interested in audience as a crucial aspect of context and as a way to account for apparent inconsistencies in Scott's writings.

C210 Mezei, Kathy. "D.C. Scott: 1862–1947." In *Canadian Poetry*. Ed. Jack David and Robert Lecker. New Press Canadian Classics. Toronto/Downsview, Ont.: General/ECW, 1982. 1, 288–90.

"Scott's long life spanned several artistic movements from *fin de siècle* to Modernism and while he was unreceptive to the rebellious 'New Movement in Poetry,' he experimented with many forms — sonnets, quatrains, rhyming couplets, dramatic verse, narrative, musical structures, blank verse, odes, elegies."

C211 Woodcock, George. Introduction. In *Canadian Poetry*. Ed. Jack David and Robert Lecker. New Press Canadian Classics. Toronto/Downsview, Ont.: General/ECW, 1982. 1, 20, 21, 22, 23.

"... in Charles G.D. Roberts and Archibald Lampman, in Duncan Campbell Scott and at times in Bliss Carman, we see not only a strange luminous factualism in evoking the landscape, but also a new use of imagery, of language, of poetic forms."

C212 Woodcock, George. *Northern Spring: The Flowering of Canadian Literature* [pamphlet]. Introd. Victor Howard. Images of/du Canada, No. 1. Washington, D.C.: Canadian Embassy, 1982, p. 3.

Scott and the other poets of the Confederation "wrote the first poetry that took the Canadian landscape and the life people lived in it as the source of their imagery . . . ," realizing that "... their new content demanded a new idiom." "The first experimental Canadian poetry in a modernist sense was written by [Charles G.D.] Roberts and Scott in their later years ...."

C213 Bentley, D.M.R. "Drawers of Water; Notes on the Significance and Scenery of Fresh Water in Canadian Poetry." Pt. I. *CV/II*, 6, No. 4 (Aug. 1982), 17, 21–22, 23, 24, 27, 28.

Beginning with the idea that "Frye's myth of the St. Lawrence as an immigrant-devouring whale" is only one of many possible myths, Bentley looks at patterns of river imagery to show how "... rivers have entered imaginatively and mimetically into Canadian poetry." Quoting "The Lower St. Lawrence," Bentley argues that for Scott, "... the voyage up and down the St. Lawrence is evocative of the emotionally charged departures and returns that accompany travel between old and new worlds."

C214 Bentley, D.M.R. "Drawers of Water; The Significance and Scenery of Fresh Water in Canadian Poetry." Pts. II–III. *CV/II*, 7, No. 1 (Nov. 1982), 26, 32–33, 35, 39, 40, 42, 44, 46.

In the two-part conclusion to an article tracing the use of water imagery in Canadian poetry, Bentley looks at waterfalls and lakes. Bentley studies "Rapids at Night" and "At the Cedars" to demonstrate Scott's use of form and metre to mimic the nature of the rapids. He also shows Scott's placing "fresh water scenery at the service of spiritual or dramatic themes." Scott's equation of fixed forms with European culture is examined, as is the fact that "... the obscuring and tantalizing mists of lake scenery were suggestive of the imaginative and spiritual mysteries" with which Scott was "deeply concerned."

C215 Johnston, Gordon. "Duncan Campbell Scott (1862–1947)." In *Canadian Writers and Their Works*. Ed. Robert Lecker, Jack David, and Ellen Quigley. Poetry Series. Vol. II. Downsview, Ont.: ECW, 1983, 235–89.

After a brief look at Scott's life, the tradition and milieu in which he wrote, and the critical reception of his work, Johnston provides a detailed study of the poet's prosody. "The practical question" for Scott was "how to find a form adequate to express his reality and his relation to it." "It is in the creation of rhythmic patterns that Scott is boldest and most significant." Johnston isolates two rhythmic structures (the stanza and the "cadential line") and traces their presence in the major poems. Johnston concludes by examining Scott's fiction, both the short stories, which, "like much of his poetry, are poised between the nineteenth and twentieth centuries," and the unpublished novel, which, in addition to being a novel of manners, "also attempts to portray large forces in Canadian society: culture, religion, politics, and business." Also published as an offprint (C4).

C216 Kelly, Catherine. "In the Vague Spaces of Duncan Campbell Scott's Poetry." *Studies in Canadian Literature* [Univ. of New Brunswick], 8 (1983), 61–92.

Citing the idealistic diction in "Poetry and Progress," Kelly argues the existence of "three major kinds of experience of transcendent presence" in Scott's poetry. First, there is the "compelling and ineffable encounter recreated in 'The Height of Land.'" Second, there is the "delightful visitation of intimate love imparted in 'The Water Lily.'" Third, there is reality "presented as mystery encountered on its own ground unsupported by the external sense." In this article, Kelly explores the third.

C217 Kelly, Catherine. "Tremoured with Fire: Duncan Campbell Scott's Love Poetry." *Studies in Canadian Literature* [Univ. of New Brunswick], 8 (1983), 194–220.

In this, the third article in a trilogy exploring the "principle of transcendence" in Scott's poetry, Kelly shows how "Scott's love poetry is also a transcendental recreation of human experience." Beginning with a study of the diction, structure, and imagery of "The Water Lily," she ranges freely throughout the love poetry to conclude that ". . . it is notable that Scott deals in depth with this loving relationship present in transcendental experience."

C218 McDougall, Robert L. Introduction. In *The Poet and the Critic: A Literary Correspondence between D.C.*

Scott and E.K. Brown. Ed. Robert L. McDougall. Ottawa: Carleton Univ. Press, 1983, pp. 1–15.

McDougall provides us with "capsule portraits" of E.K. Brown and D.C. Scott and outlines his discovery of the Scott-Brown correspondence. He also describes the friendship between "a young critic of immense energy and talent and an old poet, rich in honours, whose roots went back to the Confederation period."

C219 McDougall, Robert L. Notes. In *The Poet and the Critic: A Literary Correspondence between D.C. Scott and E.K. Brown.* Ed. Robert L. McDougall. Ottawa: Carleton Univ. Press, 1983, pp. 206–77.

McDougall annotates the letters.

C220 Wicken, George. "Scott, Duncan Campbell." In *The Oxford Companion to Canadian Literature.* Ed. William Toye. Toronto: Oxford Univ. Press, 1983, pp. 740–42.

"Scott confronted an issue that, to a greater or lesser extent, troubled all the Confederation Poets: how does a writer reconcile the literary and philosophical traditions of Western civilization with the Canadian landscape and its inhabitants?" Scott's "reputation rests largely on his Indian poems."

C221 Stich, K.P. "North of Blue Ontario's Shore: Spells of Emerson and Whitman in D.C. Scott's Poetry." *Canadian Poetry: Studies, Documents, Reviews*, No. 12 (Spring–Summer 1983), pp. 1–12.

Stich traces Scott's interest in Walt Whitman and Ralph Waldo Emerson and then goes on to "show how comparisons as well as contrasts to Emerson and Whitman are particularly helpful for a reading of Scott's poems about poets or poetry like 'The Height of Land,' 'The Woodspring to the Poet,' 'In the Rocky Mountains,' and 'The Dreaming Eagle.'"

C222 Deahl, James, and Terry Barker. "New Canada or True North." *CV/II*, 7, No. 3 (Sept. 1983), 34.

Deahl and Barker briefly survey the use of nature in a number of poets, arguing that "in the northern part of the continent New Canada and Mere Canada overshadowed the True North, and in the south, Manifest Destiny and the Pursuit of Happiness obscured the Redeemer Nation." Scott and Hector de Saint-Denys Garneau "wished to retain the unity of form represented by the tradition that flowed from the True North." However, "These poets, and many others of their generation, retreat into a sentimental-ized and *artificial* nature markedly different from the hard, but good, *real* nature of [Isabella Valency] Crawford."

C223 Grant, S.D. "Indian Affairs Under Duncan Campbell Scott: The Plains Cree of Saskatchewan 1913–1931." *Journal of Canadian Studies*, 18, No. 3 (Fall 1983), 21–39.

Making clear what a confusion of "protection and discrimination" Indian policy was during the period when Scott served as deputy superintendent general, Grant provides a context for the poet's beliefs and actions as an administrator. Ironically, ". . . neither absorption nor integration of the native into Cana-dian society were advanced appreciably during the lifetime of Duncan Campbell Scott," despite Scott's avowed faith in assimilation.

C224 Daymond, Douglas M., and Leslie G. Monkman. "At the Mermaid Inn 1892–1893." In *Towards a Canadian Literature: Essays, Editorials & Manifes-tos*. Ed. Douglas M. Daymond and Leslie G. Monk-man. Vol. 1. Ottawa: Tecumseh, 1984, 138.

The editors note that "Although the columns ["At the Mermaid Inn"] appeared for only eighteen months, they reveal the intellectual and cultural milieu of three of the most important Canadian writers of the late nineteenth century."

C225 McGill, Jean S. *Edmund Morris: Frontier Artist*. Toronto: Dundurn, 1984, pp. 61–67, 112, 129, 159, 165–68, 183.

Scott invited Morris to participate in the 1906 trip to sign Treaty No. 9 (the James Bay Treaty), and it was during this trip that Morris painted so many of his Indian portraits. Morris kept a diary of the expe-dition. Scott was also responsible for arranging to have Rupert Brooke meet Morris. It was Brooke who, having seen a notice of Morris' death in *The Globe* [Toronto], accidentally broke the news of the painter's drowning to Scott. McGill reprints excerpts from "Lines in Memory of Edmund Morris."

C226 Titley, E. Brian. "Duncan Campbell Scott and Indian Education Policy." In *An Imperfect Past: Education and Society in Canadian History*. Ed. J. Donald Wilson. Vancouver: Centre for the Study of Curric-ulum and Instruction, Univ. of British Columbia, 1984, pp. 141–53.

Scott's ideas "were rooted in the notions of cultural and racial superiority that permeated late Victorian society and which precluded tolerance for that which was foreign or different." Briefly describing the three types of schools provided by the government (day, boarding, and industrial schools), Titley argues that the Native peoples were initially hostile to the edu-cational experiment, the "*raison d'être*" of which was "cultural transformation." Scott's educational policy as it developed did eventually result in the increased enrolment of Indian children in school. However, ". . . numbers in school did not automat-ically translate into numbers being assimilated." "The vast majority [of young Indians] remained distinctly Indian and only marginally in the work-force, if indeed at all."

C227 Livesay, Dorothy. "The Canadian Documentary: An Overview." The Long-liners Conference on the Canadian Long Poem, Calumet College, York Univ., Downsview, Ont. 29 May–1 June 1984. Printed in *Open Letter* [Long-liners Conference Issue], Ser. 6, Nos. 2–3 (Summer–Fall 1985), 128.

"It was left to Duncan Campbell Scott to make use of his files in the Department of Indian Affairs to create the dramatic narratives such as 'The Forsaken.' However, in these realistic accounts his characters are objictified, seen at a distance. Or else, as in the powerful 'Powassan's Drum,' Scott becomes a myth-maker."

C228 Kilpatrick, R.S. "Scott's 'Night Hymns on Lake Nipigon': 'Matins' in the Northern Midnight." *Canadian Poetry: Studies, Documents, Reviews*, No. 14 (Spring–Summer 1984), pp. 64–68.

Building on Carolyn Roberts' "Words After Music: A Musical Reading of Scott's 'Night Hymns on Lake Nipigon'" (C203), Kilpatrick demonstrates that ". . . there could be an even deeper relationship between 'Night Hymns' and Gregory's [Gregory the Great] Sapphic hymn . . . for [Percy] Dearmer's adaptation obscures the possibility that Scott might have been familiar with the original Latin. An examination of links between the two suggests shades of meaning and allusions, otherwise hidden, which underscore the importance of Robert's [sic] musical analysis."

C229 McLeod, Les. "Canadian Post-Romanticism: The Context of Late Nineteenth-Century Canadian Poetry." *Canadian Poetry: Studies, Documents, Reviews*, No. 14 (Spring–Summer 1984), pp. 1–37.

Positing "a massive critical failure to understand Canada's nineteenth-century poets because, for a long time, we could not develop a language of criti-

cism appropriate to them," McLeod argues for the adoption of the term "post-romantic" to discuss late nineteenth-century Canadian poetry. He applies the term to Scott's "Adagio" and "The November Pansy."

C230 Bentley, D.M.R. "Alchemical Transmutation in Duncan Campbell Scott's 'At Gull Lake: August, 1810,' and Some Contingent Speculations." *Studies in Canadian Literature* [Univ. of New Brunswick], [Tenth Anniversary Issue], 10 (1985), 1–23.

Searching Scott's poetry for "various images and ideas which are evocative of hermeticism," Bentley proves the validity of arguing that Scott "may have been acquainted with certain hermetical writings, particularly those of Thomas Vaughan, and that he may have found attractive certain hermetical ideas, including that of the presence in nature and in man of a divine spirit."

C231 Keith, W.J. *Canadian Literature in English*. Longman Literature in English. London: Longman, 1985, pp. 32, 39–40, 46, 53, 54, 58, 60, 108, 271.

Keith looks briefly at Scott's Indian poems (in which "It seems as if Scott deflected . . . the emotional sympathies he was unable to display as an official") and "The Piper of Arll" ("a lyrical, richly mysterious narrative poem"). He points out the Arnoldian quality of Scott's sensibility.

C232 Lochhead, Douglas. Preface. In *Powassan's Drum: Poems of Duncan Campbell Scott*. Ed. Raymond Souster and Douglas Lochhead. Ottawa: Tecumseh, 1985, pp. xi–xii.

"In retrospect [the period of the 1920s and 1930s] was a heady time to have lived in Ottawa." What struck Lochhead "was the strength, the understanding and the nobility of [Scott's] poems about nature." Furthermore, Scott "speaks in his best poems in a language we use and understand and, indeed, expect from our contemporary poets." For Lochhead, ". . . these poems represent the way we look at our Canadian environment now, and Duncan Campbell Scott saw it first."

C233 McDougall, R.L. "Scott, Duncan Campbell." *The Canadian Encyclopedia* (1985).
 In a largely biographical sketch, McDougall writes, "Precise in imagination, intense yet disciplined, flexible in metre and form, Scott's poems weathered well the transition from traditional to modern poetry in Canada."

C234 McGregor, Gaile. *The Wacousta Syndrome: Explorations in the Canadian Langscape.* Toronto: Univ. of Toronto Press, 1985, pp. 34, 35, 37, 291.
 "In Canada . . . the use of conventions to structure experience would seem to be . . . justified by the extent to which so much of the land was in *fact*, not just in imagination, an amorphous mass inherently resistant to both humanization and aesthetic ordering. The protagonist in Duncan Campbell Scott's story 'Vengeance Is Mine,' for instance, characterizes his northern environment as almost mythically formless . . . ." Scott's attempts as a poet "to transcend the Darwinian world by means of a more positive romantic world vision" largely failed because he "perceived something in Canadian nature that gave an uncomfortable immediacy to the most disturbing aspects of the amoral universe implied by Darwin."

C235 Souster, Raymond. Foreword. In *Powassan's Drum: Poems of Duncan Campbell Scott.* Ed. Raymond Souster and Douglas Lochhead. Ottawa: Tecumseh, 1985, pp. ix–x.
 "Nature was [for Scott] not merely as it was for Lampman — a friendly refuge from the meanness of

man and the growing encroachments of a vulgar new mechanization of life, but a stage on which human dramas were enacted in all their nobleness and ignominious failure." He is the "most interesting, most challenging and technically the most venturesome of the Confederation poets, . . . the true bridge between the Victorian and the modern tradition in Canada."

C236 Titley, E. Brian. "Duncan Campbell Scott and the Administration of Indian Affairs." British Association for Canadian Studies Conference. Edinburgh, 9–12 April 1985. Printed in *Canadian Story and History 1885–1985.* Ed. Colin Nicholson and Peter Easingwood. Edinburgh: Edinburgh Univ. Centre of Canadian Studies, n.d., 47–60.
 Titley examines Scott's career as the "principal arbiter of Indian policy for almost twenty years." Rehearsing various critical responses to Scott's poems about Natives, Titley concludes that ". . . to rely on Scott's poetry as the key to his true feelings regarding the native population is a rather dubious proposition. Nor is it really necessary. Scott's pronouncements on Indians in readily comprehensible prose, in both an official and unofficial capacity, are legion." Looking at some of these pronouncements, he claims that Scott was guilty of "historical misrepresentation" and "ethnocentricism" and that his writing echoed the "rhetoric of nineteenth century imperialism." "Like his fellow poet, Kipling, Scott attempted to rationalize the subjugation of colonized peoples by cloaking it in the aura of 'responsibility' and 'duty.' "

C237 Doyle, James. "The Confederation Poets and American Publishers." *Canadian Poetry: Studies, Documents, Reviews*, No. 17 (Fall–Winter 1985), 59–67.
 Citing as one of his examples Copeland and Day's publication of Scott's *In the Village of Viger*, Doyle

outlines the attractions and perils of "persistently" seeking "American book publication." "Canadian [Confederation] poets benefitted for a time from a mild American curiosity about the northern country, and from the enthusiasm for local colour writing, but in the long run their hard-won successes with American publishers usually led to the same obscurity that engulfed most of the poetry produced in the United States at the time."

C238 Matthews, John. "'Redeem the Time': Imaginative Synthesis in the Poetry of Duncan Campbell Scott and Christopher Brennan." *Australian/Canadian Literatures in English: Comparative Perspectives.* Ed. Russell McDougall and Gillian Whitlock. Sydney: Methuen, 1987, pp. 187–204.

Exploring the "sea change" that British culture underwent in its migration to the colonies, Matthews argues that "The images of Scott and Brennan . . . remain basic for any who would seek to understand the adaptation of the imaginative vision in Canada and Australia." Significantly, "In both countries the Romantic tradition of an animate, benign nature was abandoned." Scott's poem "Thoughts," for example, provides a landscape first of ". . . death reflecting death, where no sea change seems possible . . . ," and then of ". . . a sea change in which the dead trees and their equally dead mirror-image become cancerous to the imagination."

C239 Simpson, Janice C. "Healing the Wound: Cultural Compromise in D.C. Scott's 'A Scene at Lake Manitou.'" *Canadian Poetry: Studies, Documents, Reviews*, No. 18 (Spring–Summer 1986), pp. 66–76.

Taking as her starting point Gerald Lynch's belief that Scott showed a "complex and changing attitude" towards the Native peoples (C209), Simpson reads "A Scene at Lake Manitou" as evidence of "a great development in Scott's attitude towards Indians from such early poems as 'Watkwenies' and 'The Onondaga Madonna.'"

C239a Gerson, Carole. "The *Christmas Globe*: Lampman, Scott, Wood, et al." *Canadian Notes and Queries*, No. 36 (Autumn 1986), pp. 10–12.

Gerson identifies previously unknown printings of Scott's stories in the *Globe Christmas Number* (Toronto): "Their Wedding Eve: A Story of the War of 1812" (B144); "The Witching of Elspie" (B146); "Coquelicot" (B148); "A Sacred Trust: A Story of the Upper Ottawa" (B151); "How Uncle David Rouse Made His Will" (B155).

C240 Groening, Laura. "Critic and Publisher: Another Chapter in E.K. Brown's Correspondence." *Canadian Literature*, No. 110 (Fall 1986), pp. 46, 48, 49, 50, 53, 54, 55–56, 56–57, 58.

In an analysis of the E.K. Brown-Lorne Pierce Correspondence, Groening uses Brown's letters to Scott as a counterpoint to those he exchanged with Pierce. Brown believed Scott and Archibald Lampman to be better poets than Pierce's favourites, Charles G.D. Roberts and Bliss Carman. Groening includes an account of the publication of the *Selected Poems of Duncan Campbell Scott*, which Brown edited and introduced.

C241 Ware, Tracy. "D.C. Scott's 'The Height of Land' & the Greater Romantic Lyric." *Canadian Literature*, No. 111 (Winter 1986), pp. 10–25.

Ware uses "[M.H.] Abrams' conception of the greater Romantic lyric" as an "important point of departure" in his close reading of "The Height of Land." ". . . 'The Height of Land' ends inconclusively, with a long series of five questions expressing Scott's reservations about the concept of progress. An awareness of the differences between Abrams' account of the greater Romantic lyric and Scott's poem makes it difficult to agree with Pelham Edgar and others that the conclusion of Scott's poem is triumphant." Rather, the poem "ends by calling attention to the gap between the 'imaginative idea' and the disappointing natural 'fact,' and by tentatively equating a consciousness of that gap with 'the zenith of our wisdom' . . . ."

C242 Weis, L.P. "D.C. Scott's View of History & the Indians." *Canadian Literature*, No. 111 (Winter 1986), pp. 27–40.

Arguing that ". . . critics of Duncan Campbell Scott's literary portrayals of the Indian usually agree on a basic point: Scott held one set of ideals as a bureaucrat and another as an artist," Weis attempts to demonstrate that in fact there is no disjunction between the attitudes of the civil servant and those of the poet. "Like a significant number of his contemporaries in Canada, Scott accepted current Victorian concepts of history and change. . . . A lifelong admirer of Matthew Arnold, Scott undoubtedly saw in the Indians a clear illustration that, caught in the shifts of historical change, many people would become pathetic creatures 'Wandering between two worlds, one dead, / The other powerless to be born.'" Consequently, even though progress destroyed individual Indians, Scott still "believed that historical process necessitated the death of old orders, and that Indian culture was one of these archaic forms."

C243 Moritz, Albert, and Theresa Moritz. *The Oxford Illustrated Literary Guide to Canada*. Toronto: Oxford Univ. Press, 1987, pp. 95, 105, 132, 136–40, 154.

Biographical data with photographs of Scott at the Archibald Lampman Memorial in Morpeth, Ontario, and with Rupert Brooke.

C244 New, W.H. *Dreams of Speech and Violence: The Art of the Short Story in Canada and New Zealand*. Toronto: Univ. of Toronto Press, 1987, pp. 4, 20, 29–30, 42–51, 55, 57, 58, 66, 72, 95, 98, 100, 110, 177–86, 243.

Arguing on behalf of Scott's originality and attempting to account for the lack of influence his fiction has had on the short-story tradition in Canada, New asserts that Scott's Viger stories are more than the local colour sketches that critics describe. ". . . in Scott's hands the sketch came to *embody* story, to find irony in real life, and through it convey an implied narrative of attitudinal and social changes which carried more than regional reverberations." New goes on to explore the cohesiveness of the individual stories.

C245 Weis, Lyle P. "Bipolar Paths of Desire: D.C. Scott's Poetic and Narrative Structures." *Studies in Canadian Literature* [Univ. of New Brunswick], 12 (1987), 35–52.

Weis emphasizes the "importance of ambivalence as a formal strategy in the writer's work" to argue the presence in Scott's writing of a "recurring pattern," "a bipolar path of desire," which "captures symbolically a dynamic moral ambivalence" in several poems. He demonstrates that several works of fiction are marked by characters "torn between the private self and the outer world." Scott's "idealistic vision of a better life drew him, finally, to accept self-sacrifice and compromise as a price for a fuller existence."

C246 Woodcock, George. *Northern Spring: The Flowering of Canadian Literature*. Vancouver: Douglas & McIntyre, 1987, pp. 10–11, 36–37, 94, 132, 186–87, 198, 224.

Citing Margaret Atwood in *The New Oxford*

Book of Canadian Verse (C205), Woodcock writes, "But I find Scott interesting also because, like Roberts to a certain extent but unlike the metrically conservative Lampman, he felt uneasily that a new approach to the Canadian land needed a new formal expression, and in the end went very near to free verse."

C247 Stouck, David. *Major Canadian Authors: A Critical Introduction to English Literature in Canada.* Rev. enl. ed. Lincoln, Neb.: Univ. of Nebraska Press, 1988, pp. 29, 31, 33, 38, 313–14.

"With Ottawa's Department of Indian Affairs for more than fifty years, Scott was a Victorian poet whose best verse was inspired by his work with the Indians and his direct experience with the northern wilderness."

C248 Dragland, Stan. "Byron on Wordsworth: Light and Occasional Verse in the Scott/Aylen Papers." *Canadian Poetry: Studies, Documents, Reviews*, No. 22 (Spring–Summer 1988), pp. 49–67.

In a full description of the light and occasional verse in the Scott/Aylen Papers at the National Archives of Canada, Dragland focuses on Scott's "Byron on Wordsworth, Being Stanzas of Don Juan: To My Friend Colonel Henry C. Osborne for the Byron Centenary 1824 April Nineteenth 1924." The article also reprints the poem (B121).

C249 Morrison, James. "The Poet and the Indians." *The Beaver* [Winnipeg], Aug.–Sept. 1988, pp. 4–16.

Morrison provides a summary of Scott's 1905 and 1906 trips to sign the James Bay Treaty No. 9 with the Cree. The article includes nine photographs, a map, and a reproduction of the cover of *Via Borealis*.

Theses and Dissertations

C250 MacRae, C.F. "The Victorian Age in Canadian Poetry." M.A. Thesis Toronto 1953.

Canadian poetry lacks ideas. The "narrative is the fundamental form [of poetry]. If it proves weak, the entire tradition is weak . . . . In Canadian poetry the narrative element is unusually weak." Scott, however, "succeeded better than any of his fellows in integrating the descriptive with the narrative."

C251 Wilcox, John William. "The Poetry of Duncan Campbell Scott." M.A. Thesis Toronto 1958.

Wilcox divides Scott's poetry into the categories of "Dream Poetry" and "Nature Poetry."

C252 Crozier, Daniel F. "The Imagery and Symbolism in the Poems of Duncan Campbell Scott." M.A. Thesis New Brunswick 1963.

Crozier demonstrates that "Scott in his selection of symbols was a conventional product of late Victorianism, but that in a few poems, notably 'The Piper of Arll,' he showed considerable originality and skill in his manipulation of conventional images."

C253 Denham, William Paul. "Music and Painting in the Poetry of Duncan Campbell Scott." M.A. Thesis Western Ontario 1964.

Denham studies the influence of music on Scott's poetry in order to demonstrate that one of Scott's main concerns lay with "imposing a musical pattern on a structure of meaning."

C254 Rogers, Robert Amos. "American Recognition of Canadian Authors Writing in English 1890–1960." Diss. Michigan 1964.

Bibliographical data.

C255 Djwa, Sandra Ann. "Metaphor, World View and the Continuity of Canadian Poetry: A Study of the Major English Canadian Poets with a Computer Concordance to Metaphor." Diss. British Columbia 1968.

In a thesis which posits the continuity of Canadian poetry, Djwa devotes Chapter II to describing "the movement away from the dream as a metaphor of romantic transcendentalism in the works of Sir Charles G.D. Roberts, Archibald Lampman and Duncan Campbell Scott. The 'dream' in Roberts' canon emerges as a vehicle for transcendence which fuses Christian romanticism and Darwinian progress; in the later works of Duncan Campbell Scott this transcendence is denied and evil is admitted, and the dream emerges in relationship to the temporal world." The selected computer concordance to metaphor includes Scott's poems.

C256 Hall, Chipman. "A Survey of the Indian's Role in English Canadian Literature to 1900." M.A. Thesis Dalhousie 1969.

The "white English-speaking authors' attitudes toward the Indian and the Eskimo were influenced by the nature of the contact that they made with these native people." However, "All the poets and novelists, regardless of the roles they accord the Indians, leave them at the end of the work, either dead or facing the impending demise of their race."

C257 Miller, Judith. "Towards a Canadian Aesthetic: Descriptive Colour in the Landscape Poetry of Duncan Campbell Scott, Archibald Lampman, and William Wilfred Campbell." M.A. Thesis Waterloo 1970.

Looking at words of colour in the poetry of D.C. Scott, Archibald Lampman, and W.W. Campbell, Miller has tabulated and determined "patterns of organization" in nine colour groupings "in an effort to discover some of the dynamics of the development of a Canadian aesthetic, as these Canadian artists emerged from the influence of the old world, moving toward a more native expression of their experience."

C258 Dragland, S.L. "Forms of Imaginative Perception in the Poetry of Duncan Campbell Scott" ("Poetics and Related Themes in the Poetry of Duncan Campbell Scott"). Diss. Queen's 1971.

Dragland "concentrates on the theme of imaginative perception or the creative act in the various explicit and implicit guises in which it appears in Scott's poetry." After an initial chapter exploring the poetic theory of the poets of the 1860s, he analyzes Scott's poetry under the themes of "Poems on Poetry," "Resolution," "Aspiration," "Limitation," "The Old and New Lands," "The Primitive and the Civilized" (which focuses on the Indian poems), and "Innocence and Experience."

C259 Monk, Patricia. "The Role of Prosodic and Structural Elements in the Poetry of Duncan Campbell Scott." M.A. Thesis Carleton 1971.

Monk surveys nineteenth-century British theories of prosody and then provides a detailed prosodic study of Scott's poems, arguing on behalf of his "thorough understanding of the appropriate nature of verse forms." She uses her study to show that "prosodic analysis can identify Scott's individual poetic fingering" and "that it can characterize his use of versification as meaning." By looking at "five patterns of technical development," she discovers "insights into Scott's poetic personality and the shape of his writing career." Finally, she uses prosodic analysis "to place Scott in perspective with respect to three groups of poets: those of the nineteenth-century English tradition, the Canadian poets of his immediate circle, and the modernists who emerged during the early years of the twentieth century."

C260 Godo, Margaret Anne. "The Indian in Poetry and His Relationship to Canadian Nationalism: A Study of the Late Nineteenth Century and the Mid Twentieth Century." M.A. Thesis McMaster 1973.

Opening with a quotation from Margaret Atwood's *Survival: A Thematic Guide to Canadian Literature*, Godo posits that "The varying roles of the Indian symbolically represent both the innocent promise and the terror offered by the Canadian landscape to its new inhabitants." Godo looks at "The Half-Breed Girl," "At Gull Lake," and "The Forsaken."

C261 Kelly, Catherine E. "The Short Stories of Duncan Campbell Scott." M.A. Thesis New Brunswick 1973.

Kelly studies the short stories in order to demonstrate Scott's "primary concern with the essentials of human happiness and suffering," in which she detects a "sense of difficulty in reconciling life's contradictions in the effort to achieve peace." The "net result is a body of work finally unresolved in the tensions created by the ambivalence of the author's vision."

C262 Mezei, Kathy. "A Magic Space Wherein the Mind Can Dwell: Place and Space in the Poetry of Archibald Lampman, Emile Nelligan, and Duncan Campbell Scott." Diss. Queen's 1977.

"All three poets seem to be searching for a magic space wherein they can dwell and create. But the journey towards the magic space as well as the dimensions of the space itself are developed out of details of place." Mezei ". . . centre[s] on the poets' use of different details of place to create the dimensions of a mental, ideal (magic), and poetic space."

The title of the dissertation is taken from Scott's "The Fragment of a Letter," in *Beauty and Life*.

C263 Kelly, Catherine E. "The Foreappointed Quest: A Study of Transcendence in the Poetry of Duncan Campbell Scott." Diss. New Brunswick 1978.

Scott's poetry "records a religious journey which is still in progress after the final poem is read." If studied chronologically, the poems reveal a "maturing of spiritual life." If studied according to the arrangement of *The Poems of Duncan Campbell Scott*, the poems "shape the body of Scott's creative effort into a circle by which early work is affirmed and made one with the later work." "The Height of Land" is examined as an embodiment of the "central experience" of transcendence.

C264 Slonim, Leon. "A Critical Edition of the Poems of D.C. Scott." Diss. Toronto 1978.

In addition to preparing a critical edition of Scott's poems, Slonim has compiled a bibliography which includes a listing of the first place of publication for the individual poems.

C265 Kostjuk, Dwight Thomas. "Poetic Meter and Form in the Poetry of Duncan Campbell Scott." M.A. Thesis New Brunswick 1980.

Kostjuk studies selected poems "in terms of prosodic and structural components" under the categories of the short lyric, the short fixed lyric, the extended lyric, the narrative, and the dramatic. He concludes that Scott controls "an extensive range of poetic devices" and is a master of syntax and diction.

C266 Welage, Patricia A. "The Divided Worlds of Duncan Campbell Scott." M.A. Thesis Concordia 1981.

Welage finds that "empirical analysis of the chronology of [Scott's] creative output reveals that his work falls into five periods of productivity" (1887–93, 1894–1907, 1907–27, 1927–35, and 1935–47). This "impressive time span of sixty years" shows "a gradual maturing of the writer as his vision becomes clearer to him."

C267 Weis, Lyle Percy. "D.C. Scott and the Desire for a Sense of Order." Diss. Alberta 1983.

Weis establishes an historical and intellectual framework for studying Scott in an attempt to refute "current critical opinion [which] often describes Scott as . . . one who achieved a claim to greatness because he rejected the assumptions of a stifling tradition." Each chapter is designed to clarify the fact that Scott valued a rational, historical, and moral interpretation of life.

C268 Ware, Tracy. "A Generic Approach to Confederation Romanticism." Diss. Western Ontario 1984.

Ware provides "A study of the often-noted but never thoroughly examined influence of the English Romantics" on Bliss Carman, Archibald Lampman, Charles G.D. Roberts, and Duncan Campbell Scott. The dissertation "is organized in terms of the genres that best reflect both the Romantic influence and the achievements of the four poets: the commemorative poem, the return poem, and the greater Romantic lyric." The poems "show that the Confederation poets were conscious of their positions in both space and time, and that the critical notion of the inapplicability of Romanticism to the Canadian landscape should be reconsidered."

Miscellaneous

C269 Thomson, Theresa E. "Duncan Campbell Scott." *Canadian Poetry Magazine*, 12, No. 2 (Dec. 1948), 8.

A poem in honour of Scott.

C270 Bourinot, Arthur S. "Duncan Campbell Scott — Archibald Lampman." In his *This Green Earth*. Gananoque, Ont.: Carillon Poetry Chap-Books, 1953, p. 16. Rpt. in *The Canadian Author & Bookman*, 38, No. 1 (Summer 1962), 6.

A poem dedicated to Archibald Lampman and D.C. Scott.

C271 Karsh, Yousuf. Portrait. *The Canadian Author & Bookman*, 38, No. 1 (Summer 1962), [front cover].

A photograph of Scott.

C272 Flood, John. "Scott Talks to his Wards, Warns Them." In his *The Land They Occupied*. Erin, Ont.: The Porcupine's Quill, 1976, p. 37.

A poem about Scott's Indian poetry.

C273 Johnston, Gordon. "Epilogue: 'Piano, to D.C.S.'" In *The Duncan Campbell Scott Symposium*. Ed. K.P. Stich. Re-Appraisals: Canadian Writers, No. 6. Ottawa: Univ. of Ottawa Press, 1980, p. 145.

A poem dedicated to Scott.

C274 Dragland, Stan. *Journeys through Bookland and Other Passages*. Toronto: Coach House, 1984, pp. 112–13.

Dragland's narrator recounts his personal experience of a rainbow such as Scott describes at the end of "At Gull Lake, August 1810."

Awards and Honours

C275 Fellow of the Royal Society of Canada [FRSC] (1899).

C276 President Section II Royal Society of Canada (1902–03).

C277 Honourary Secretary, Royal Society of Canada (1911–21).

C278 President, Royal Society of Canada (1921–22).

C279 Honourary Litt.D. Univ. of Toronto (1922).

C280 Fellow of the Royal Society of Literature (Great Britain) (1927).

C281 Lorne Pierce Medal (1927).

C282 C.M.G. (King's Birthday Honour List) (1934).

C283 Honourary LL.D. Queen's Univ. (1939).

C284 Commemorative Evening [for Scott] Public Archives of Canada (1943).

C285 Commemorative Evening [for Scott] Carleton College (1948).

D Selected Book Reviews

The Magic House and Other Poems

D1 Edgar, Pelham. "Duncan Campbell Scott." *The Week: A Canadian Journal of Politics, Literature, Science and Art* [Toronto], 15 March 1895, pp. 370–71.

Edgar's evaluation of Scott's poetry is rooted in the premise that "It is a misplaced sentiment which demands that the work of our poets should be distinctively Canadian, for a narrow provincialism would be the inevitable result." Scott is "excellently equipped" for poetry, and Edgar looks forward to more poems "of a lyrical nature."

Labor and the Angel

D2 Payne, William Morton. Rev. of *Labor and the Angel. The Dial: A Semi-Monthly Journal of Literary Criticism, Discussion, and Information* [Chicago], 16 Jan. 1899, pp. 54–55.

Payne quotes "Winter Song" and writes that "Few poets get so near as Mr. Duncan Campbell Scott to the very heart of nature."

D3 Edgar, Pelham. "Some Canadian Poets: Duncan Campbell Scott." *Saturday Magazine* [*The Globe*] [Toronto], 4 March 1905, p. 3.

Somewhat disappointed with the poems of *The Magic House and Other Poems* where ". . . brain and heart do not always work together," Edgar says that *Labor and the Angel* "marks an advance in strength." Scott's best work lies in the meditative poems, and "It is refreshing to point to one at least among our Canadian writers whose fame may be enhanced, but need not be limited, by his descriptive talent."

New World Lyrics and Ballads

D4 Edgar, Pelham. "A New Volume of Canadian Verse by Duncan Campbell Scott." *Saturday Magazine* [*The Globe*] [Toronto], 25 Nov. 1905, p. 4.

"Mr. Scott's intimate knowledge of the life and traditions of our native Indian tribes has furnished him with material that he has used to good purpose in several of the shorter narrative poems . . . ." "The most ambitious poem in the collection [as a whole] is 'Dominique de Gourgues,' and Mr. Scott's treatment of this inspiring theme displays a masterly skill in the conduct of a complicated narrative and a dramatic vigor which we already knew him to possess, but which had not hither to revealed itself so convincingly." The poem owes its subject matter to Francis Parkman's "Pioneers of France in the New World." From Tennyson's "The Revenge" it perhaps derives "the secret of swift dramatic movement relieved by interludes of lyrical repose . . . ."

D5 Payne, William Morton. Rev. of *New World Lyrics and Ballads. The Dial: A Semi-Monthly Journal of Literary Criticism, Discussion, and Information* [Chicago], 16 Feb. 1906, pp. 127–28.

"... Canadian poets certainly hold their own with our minstrels on this side of the border." Payne singles out "The House of the Broken-Hearted" as evidence that *New World Lyrics and Ballads* contains "a few poems as good as any that the author has previously published."

D6 Rev. of *New World Lyrics and Ballads*. *The New York Times Saturday Review of Books*, 7 July 1906, p. 434.

Scott's poems "belong to the newer world which is too busy doing to tolerate idle doubts."

Lundy's Lane and Other Poems

D7 Rev. of *Lundy's Lane and Other Poems*. *The Canadian Magazine of Politics, Science, Art and Literature* [Toronto], Dec. 1916, pp. 192–93.

The reviewer begins by asserting that "If for nothing else than the beautiful love poem, 'Spring on Mattagami,' this volume could be regarded as one of the important poetry publications of the year." Several stanzas from the poem are quoted.

Beauty and Life

D8 Bourinot, Arthur S. "New Poems by Dr. Scott." *The Canadian Bookman: A Monthly Devoted to Literature, the Library and the Printed Book*, Jan. 1922, pp. 55–56.

"*Beauty and Life* shews Dr. Scott's power of word music, his philosophical trend and his scholarly attainments." The book is "deeply tinctured with an indulging streak of profound and penetrating philosophy of life" and reveals that Scott "has confidence in the power of Beauty and her immortality."

D9 Rev. of *Beauty and Life*. *The Canadian Magazine of Politics, Science, Art and Literature* [Toronto],

March 1922, pp. 459–61.

Scott's overall "small output is due to constant distraction from literary effort and also to what must be the artist's sense shivering at the very possibility of submitting anything unworthy .... One scarcely could say too much of this poet's superb fancy [in "Ode for the Keats Centenary"] wrought for our dull understanding by sheer craftsmanship under infinite pain."

The Poems of Duncan Campbell Scott

D10 Garvin, John W. "The Poems of Duncan Campbell Scott." *The Canadian Bookman: A Monthly Devoted to Literature and the Creative Arts*, Dec. 1926, pp. 364–65.

In a favourable review which begins by quoting liberally from William Archer's *Poets of the Younger Generation*, which includes poems by Scott, Garvin warns that "With the everyday reader, poetry of such perfection and distinction [as Scott's] is not always popular." He emphasizes the fact that Scott is an "outstanding master" at *vers libre* and cites an extract from "Powassan's Drum" to illustrate the point.

D11 Deacon, William Arthur. "The Bookshelf." *Saturday Night*, 2 July 1927, p. 9.

Scott is "the representative Canadian poet of his generation." His poetry "has won favor because of its artistry, its intellectual and emotional depth, and the natural, yet austere, simplicity of his nobler passages." A photograph of Scott is included.

D12 Rev. of *The Poems of Duncan Campbell Scott*. *The Times Literary Supplement* [London], 20 Oct. 1927, p. 737.

Scott finds "in the adventures of Indians and of

Canadians and in the wild scenery of his country a subject for ballads and poems, which are romantic because they are not self centred, but subsist and live upon the new and strange." However, Scott's diction "is too full of words that we commonly meet with in poetry and which naturally elevate a poet's ideas to fit the elevation of his language, whereas of course the elevation of the ideas should come first and at rare moments, and be attended by a suitable elevation of diction."

The Green Cloister: Later Poems

D13   Clarke, George Herbert. Rev. of *The Green Cloister: Later Poems. Queen's Quarterly*, 42 (Winter 1935), 556–57.

Clarke, praising *The Green Cloister: Later Poems* as "vertebrate," with "structure and . . . thighs and thews to sustain and carry it," asserts that Scott "has long known — and felt — what it means to be a poet, and the fineness of his fibre is reflected in the austere charm (austere in the Arnoldian sense) and the generally firm character of his work."

D14   Edgar, Pelham. "Recent Verse." Rev. of *Lilies and Leopards*, by Annie Charlotte Dalton; and *The Green Cloister: Later Poems*, by Duncan Campbell Scott. *Saturday Night*, 21 Dec. 1935, p. 8.

Scott "hovers momentarily over some fair plot of this charted earth, and the lyrical ecstasy of that moment is touched with the wistfulness of one who is taking his last look on beauty. Here is no fierceness of regret, no angry protest, no recrimination. We pass, and the world endures."

D15   Martin, Burns. Rev. of *The Green Cloister: Later Poems. The Dalhousie Review*, 16 (April 1936), 125–26.

Scott "is as felicitous as of yore in making a scene live before our eyes, and at the same time adding a deeper meaning to it."

Selected Poems of Duncan Campbell Scott

D16   Bourinot, Arthur S. Rev. of *Selected Poems of Duncan Campbell Scott. Canadian Poetry Magazine*, 14, No. 4 (Summer 1951), 30–31.

Looking more at the makeup of the book than at the poems within it, Bourinot notes that *Selected Poems of Duncan Campbell Scott* is "so close to perfection" that "It is a privilege to review it." He praises Scott for fulfilling his own belief that one must toil "for the last perfection," and he praises E.K. Brown for the memoir, M.O. Hammond for the frontispiece, Elise Aylen Scott for the selections in the book, and Ryerson for the format. "It is a book that every lover of poetry should possess, for in it is the quintessence of the spirit of a great man and a great soul."

D17   McLaren, Floris. Rev. of *The Selected Poems of Duncan Campbell Scott. Contemporary Verse*, No. 35 (Summer 1951), p. 23.

McLaren notes that "The sudden death of E.K. Brown, just before the books [sic] publication makes the volume a double memorial, to a poet of scholarship and achievement and a fine contemporary critic."

D18   Daniells, Roy. Rev. of *Selected Poems of Duncan Campbell Scott. The Canadian Forum*, Sept. 1951, p. 140.

After comparing Brown's loving labours over Scott's poetry to Arnold's over Wordsworth's, Daniells points out that "The selection of poems in this volume is made to reveal — his great unevenness admitted — how genuine a poet Scott was at his best;

to relate, through a memoir, to Scott's life and to the period; to persuade us to apply the standards of his own age to his diction and rhythm, and to enjoy him as we enjoy the Victorians; to help us feel our way into that combination of simple realism and of elemental, terrifying dream that distinguishes his best Indian pieces. Finally, certain poems emerge, fit to stand on their own feet in the great company of beautiful and permanent things . . . ."

D19 Clarke, George Herbert. Rev. of *The Selected Poems of Duncan Campbell Scott*. *Queen's Quarterly*, 58 (Autumn 1951), 455–58.

"This is an appropriate and welcome collection of poems chosen from the works of one of Canada's most cherished and influential poets . . . ." Clarke emphasizes Scott's "joy in light and colour" and cites his able interpretations of "the Indian soul," the "lives of Nature's teeming tribes," and "seasonal aspects." Scott's poems, like all true art, contain "that unknown *x* that suggests character, quality, the man-in-himself, the way in which his mind and spirit regard the world."

Powassan's Drum: Poems of Duncan Campbell Scott

D20 McDougall, R.L. Rev. of *Powassan's Drum: Poems of Duncan Campbell Scott*. *Journal of Canadian Poetry*, 2 (1987), 90–93.

McDougall speculates on "What happened in the relatively short space of ten years or so to make a second collection of the poetry of D.C. Scott (who died in 1947) necessary, or even desirable . . . ?" Perhaps it is simply, as Douglas Lochhead and Raymond Souster suggest (C232, C235), Scott's fairly recent ranking as a "classic." The title of the volume is a "kind of come-on" because the poem for which

it is named is not typical of Scott's work as a whole. The book is presumably aimed at the "general reader."

D21 Hatch, Ronald. Rev. of *Powassan's Drum: Poems of Duncan Campbell Scott*, ed. Raymond Souster and Douglas Lochhead; *Windflower: Poems of Bliss Carman*, ed. Raymond Souster and Douglas Lochhead; and *Bliss Carman: Quest & Revolt*, by Muriel Miller. *Canadian Literature*, No. 115 (Winter 1987), pp. 223–24.

The selection from Scott's work is more interesting than that from Bliss Carman's because "The editors chose to begin with seven Indian and Metis poems which capture the plight of these peoples poised between different cultures and time periods. These poems are undoubtedly among Scott's most original." "*Powassan's Drum* leaves the impression that Scott overworks the moonlight-and-roses motif, that he too often indulges in derivative language. Still, in his Indian poems, and especially with the hesitations in which he couches his later work, one feels that here was a genuine poet in the making."

In the Village of Viger

D22 Martin, Burns. Rev. of *In the Village of Viger*. *The Dalhousie Review*, 25 (July 1945), 262.

Martin, reviewing the Ryerson reprint of *In the Village of Viger*, states that "There is faultless choice of language, the quiet use of suspense in telling a story, and above all the insight into, and sympathy with, the common French-Canadian . . . ." The Ryerson edition is particularly satisfying because of the presence of Thoreau MacDonald's illustrations.

D23 Edgar, Pelham. "Short-Story Object Lesson." *The Canadian Author & Bookman*, 21, No. 4 (Dec. 1945), 18.

"These sketches are minor masterpieces of delicate evocation, creating atmosphere by touches so elusive as to discourage the young writer who might wish to make them models for his art." Edgar goes on to illustrate his point with a detailed description of the story "Paul Farlotte."

D24 Galvin, J.F. Rev. of *In the Village of Viger. Culture: Revue Trimestrielle; Sciences Religieuses et Sciences Profanes au Canada*, 6 (Dec. 1945), 508.

Galvin briefly, but favourably, compares Scott's stories to the work of William Henry Drummond and Charles Dickens and to *Maria Chapdelaine*.

The Witching of Elspie: A Book of Stories

D25 Rev. of *The Witching of Elspie: A Book of Stories. The New York Times Book Review*, 18 Nov. 1923, pp. 19, 22.

The reviewer refers to a "certain vividness of characterization," to a "powerful analysis of situation and character," and to "an undercurrent of fatalism akin to Scandinavian fiction, or the Russian."

Selected Stories of Duncan Campbell Scott

D26 Waterston, Elizabeth. "A Small Mercy." *Canadian Literature*, No. 61 (Summer 1974), pp. 111–13.

The "*Viger* volume is generally veiled in prettiness." "The *Witching of Elspie* volume, 1923, shows a major change in tone. It is tempting to explain the shift from village idylls to wilderness scenes of primitive suffering and endurance as the result of changes in the author's life. The deaths of Lampman and of Scott's daughter and the accretion of heavy official duties in the Department of Indian affairs did darken the imaginative screen." Overall, we would be better served by a collection, rather than a selection, of Scott stories.

In the Village of Viger and Other Stories

D27 Stow, Glenys. "Of North and South: D.C. Scott." *Journal of Canadian Fiction*, 2, No. 3 (Summer 1973), 123–24.

Stan Dragland's edition of Scott's short stories is "a rescue mission," given the fact that ". . . many readers are probably less aware of Scott's pastoral side than of his obsession with storms, passion and death." "The calm surface" of Viger is, however, "deceptive," for beneath this surface we find that the villagers "suffer from physical and mental ailments, frustrations and sorrows which are rarely resolved except by resignation or death. . . . Reason and classical restraint, craftsmanship and pattern were civilized qualities which Scott laboured to attain, and which the editor admires in him; yet the poems and short stories in which he is most effective combine these skills with some element of the supernatural or the wilderness world which lingers in the memory after the rational pattern has faded."

Untitled Novel, ca. 1905

D28 Stevens, Peter. Rev. of *Untitled Novel, ca. 1905. Windsor Star*. "The Book Page," 21 June 1980, p. E7.

The novel "is a melodrama of revenge, thwarted passion, infidelity, murder, illegitimacy, betrayal, braggadocio without any real foundation. Characters appear and disappear at an alarming and illogical rate, and often there is little credible motivation assigned to characters. . . . Some scenes work well enough. . . . the brief incursion into politics is handled in a gently ironic fashion. . . . It is a plodding and earnest novel that is generally too dull to sustain interest . . . ."

John Graves Simcoe

D29 Rev. of *John Graves Simcoe*. *Review of Historical Publications Relating to Canada*, 11 (1907), 72–74.
". . . Mr. Scott has presented in simple and rather pleasing literary form the chief incidents of Governor Simcoe's career. He has not, however, made any serious effort to interpret Simcoe's place in history, as one of the 'Makers of Canada.'"

The Circle of Affection and Other Pieces in Prose and Verse

D30 Compton, Neil M. "Sensitive Poetry." *The Gazette* [Montreal], 28 June 1947, p. 23.
Scott is a "sensitive poet . . . , an excellent essayist and an indifferent writer of short stories." Although the stories "suffer from over-elaboration," the verse "represents some of the best qualities of the older school of Canadian poetry," and the essays possess ideas "still . . . relevant."

D31 Birney, Earle. Rev. of *The Circle of Affection and Other Pieces in Prose and Verse*. *Canadian Poetry Magazine*, 11, No. 1 (Sept. 1947), 39–40.
Scott "is one of those rare writers who, always careful and distinguished in utterance, has grown in power with his years." He defines Scott's growth in terms of "depth of feeling and economy." The ten stories are "surely as polished and indigenous a group as any Canadian writer can offer in that form."

D32 Clarke, George Herbert. "Lampman and Scott." Rev. of *Archibald Lampman: Selected Poems*, ed. D.C. Scott; and *The Circle of Affection and Other Pieces in Prose and Verse*, by D.C. Scott. *Queen's Quarterly*, 54 (Autumn 1947), 392–94.
Archibald Lampman: Selected Poems and *The Circle of Affection and Other Pieces in Prose and Verse* are "closely related, since the editor of the one is the author of the other . . . ." Clarke lauds the efforts of both Scott the editor and Scott the artist. "It was a happy thought . . . to vary the contents [in *The Circle of Affection and Other Pieces in Prose and Verse*], to make more directly accessible some contributions previously printed in periodicals, and to give his readers a sufficiently balanced selection from his work in prose and verse to enable them to trace in some degree the development of a Canadian literary artist distinguished in both poetry and fiction."

At the Mermaid Inn, Conducted by A. Lampman, W.W. Campbell, Duncan C. Scott: Being Essays on Life and Literature which appeared in the Toronto Globe 1892–1893

D33 Mullins, S.G. "Les Livres Canadiens: Littérature." *Culture: Revue Trimestrielle; Sciences Religieuses et Sciences Profanes au Canada*, 19 (Dec. 1958), 451–52.
Arthur S. Bourinot's edition of *At the Mermaid Inn* "sheds further light on the Confederation Period of Canadian literature." Scott's voice "sounds the most intellectual note. Lacking the warmth and human touch of [Archibald] Lampman, Scott makes up for this deficiency by weightier subject matter." The editor's preference for Lampman is understandable: ". . . one will forgive him his prejudice" in selecting so many more pieces by Lampman than by Scott or William Wilfred Campbell.

D34 McDougall, Robert L. Rev. of *At the Mermaid Inn, Conducted by A. Lampman, W.W. Campbell, Duncan C. Scott: Being Essays on Life and Literature which appeared in the Toronto Globe 1892–1893*.

The Dalhousie Review, 39 (Summer 1959), 283, 285.

McDougall, although stressing the crucial nature of the material, laments the "variety of irregularities in method." He is particularly concerned by Arthur S. Bourinot's favouring of Archibald Lampman over Scott and William Wilfred Campbell, an unjustified editorial bias.

D35 Roper, Gordon. "Turning New Leaves (1)." *The Canadian Forum*, Sept. 1959, pp. 134–36.

"Judging from these selections, one is struck by how much [Archibald] Lampman, [William Wilfred] Campbell and Scott had in common in age, interest, background, education, occupation, residence, and literary activity." "They are young literary men well read in and respectful of the British, American, and classical past. But they also have a strong sense of the uniqueness of their own place and time, and they are responding to the new literary winds blowing up from South of the Border . . . ." "Had Mr. Bourinot reprinted all the *Globe* columns decided differences of temperament and opinion probably would have been more evident."

D36 Swayze, Fred. Rev. of *At the Mermaid Inn, Conducted by A. Lampman, W. W. Campbell, Duncan C. Scott: Being Essays on Life and Literature which appeared in the Toronto* Globe *1892–1893*. *Queen's Quarterly*, 65 (Winter 1959), 715–16.

"Here are fascinating glimpses of an Ottawa that is still just recognizable and unexpected sidelights on almost forgotten painters, poets, musicians and magazines. . . . It is period Canadian." Scott's "appreciation of art and music adds grace notes to these pages. . . . We leave him unread to our own cost." The editorial bias in favour of Archibald Lampman is "an editor's privilege."

At the Mermaid Inn: Wilfred Campbell, Archibald Lampman, Duncan Campbell Scott in The Globe 1892–93

D37 Abley, Mark. "Distant Shades of Things to Come." *Maclean's*, 28 May 1979, pp. 48, 50.

W.W. Campbell, Archibald Lampman, and D.C. Scott "had eloquence, courage and wit." Abley welcomes Barry Davies' edition for collecting the series of articles which continue to "read with remarkable freshness."

D38 Wicken, George. "Rediscovering the Fourth Estate." *Essays on Canadian Writing*, No. 16 (Fall–Winter 1979–80), pp. 70–77.

Wicken heralds the publication as "one of the most welcome reprints of nineteenth-century Canadian literature" and reviews the book's importance with an eye to elaborating the historical context in which the column was originally written. ". . . Lampman, Campbell, and Scott were careful to point out the advantages of developing a national literature and art without alienating the large audience which the circulation of *The Globe* guaranteed them." He concludes, "To a great extent, the press mirrors the spirit of an age. Let us have more reprints drawn from nineteenth-century Canadian newspapers so that we may better understand the literature which that age produced."

D39 Keith, W.J. "Letters in Canada: 1979. Humanities." *University of Toronto Quarterly*, 49 (Summer 1980), 447–49.

Keith writes that ". . . while the appearance of this edition is to be welcomed, both contents and editing fall short of Scott's much-touted 'ideal.'" Archibald Lampman, W.W. Campbell, and D.C. Scott generally fail to embody in their own writing the high critical standards for which they called in their columns. The three tend to write with "all the earnestness of Matthew Arnold and distressingly little of his wit and profundity."

More Letters of Duncan Campbell Scott

D40 Mullins, S.G. "Les Livres Canadiens: Littérature." *Culture: Revue Trimestrielle; Sciences Religieuses et Sciences Profanes au Canada*, 21 (Dec. 1960), 443–44.

"That D.C. Scott was not only a fine nature poet but also a well-read scholar, a sympathetic friend, and a keen critic of poetry emerges from these pages."

D41 Wilson, Milton. "Letters in Canada: 1960. Humanities/Literary Studies." *University of Toronto Quarterly*, 30 (July 1960–61), 422–23.

"Arthur S. Bourinot's practice as an editor may be eccentric and inconsistent, but he assembles documents that no one else seems able or willing to print, and students of Canada's literary history are bound to be grateful as well as exasperated." This volume provides "plenty of evidence of Scott's mental and physical curiosity, industry as an editor, and capacity for friendship. The evidence of Scott's poetic taste is less detailed . . . ."

D42 Roper, Gordon. Rev. of *More Letters of Duncan Campbell Scott*, ed. Arthur S. Bourinot; and *Mark Twain — Howells Letters*, ed. Henry Nash Smith and William S. Gibson. *The Canadian Forum*, April 1961, p. 22.

"The [Pelham] Edgar and [E.K.] Brown letters afford many glimpses of Scott's literary taste." Arthur S. Bourinot "published these letters because no publisher would risk producing them in one single, large volume." "Unfortunately, he has selected,

edited, and printed the texts of these letters in an early 20th Century fashion. The reader must accept what is on the page before him on faith, without means of knowing how accurately the actual text of the letters has been reproduced."

The Poet and the Critic: A Literary Correspondence between D.C. Scott and E.K. Brown

D43 Garebian, Keith. Rev. of *The Poet and the Critic: A Literary Correspondence Between D.C. Scott and E.K. Brown*. *Quill & Quire*, July 1984, pp. 74–75.

"One of the drawbacks of the correspondence" is that ". . . there is such shared taste that the benignity is totally undramatic. Instead of the drama of personality, we have sensible, literary pioneering."

D44 Jeays, Linda. Rev. of *The Poet and the Critic: A Literary Correspondence between D.C. Scott and E.K. Brown*. *The Canadian Author & Bookman*, 60, No. 3 (Spring 1985), 22–23.

"Scott is the perfect role-model: he was persistent in the preparation of manuscripts, determined in the pursuit of publication, and meticulous in attention to word-choice. . . . A common love of Archibald Lampman's poetry and a strong desire to develop the national characteristics of Canadian literature led . . . [E.K. Brown and D.C. Scott] into a mutually stimulating correspondence . . . ."

D45 Monkman, Leslie. "Understanding." *Canadian Literature*, No. 104 (Spring 1985), pp. 162–63.

Monkman stresses the book's value, both for the completeness of the correspondence, which "reveals new facets of two of the finest writers in our literature," and for the extensive textual apparatus, which "makes the collection more useful and reliable for students of both men."

D46 Keith, W.J. "Letters in Canada: 1984. Humanities." Rev. of *Isabella Valancy Crawford: The Life and the Legends,* by Dorothy Farmiloe; *Dry Water: A Novel of Western Canada,* by Robert Stead, ed. Prem Varma; and *The Poet and the Critic: A Literary Correspondence between D.C. Scott and E.K. Brown,* ed. Robert L. McDougall. *University of Toronto Quarterly,* 54 (Summer 1985), 437–38.

The book is "exemplary, an admirable example of sound scholarship, good writing, and careful editing." Both D.C. Scott and E.K. Brown were "good letter-writers, and both emerge, in different ways, as congenially humane people." There are "numerous gobbets of information and gossip about the literary establishment of the time. But the relationship between old and isolated poet on the one hand and energetic but careful academic on the other carries its own interest."

D47 Dragland, Stan. "The Scott/Brown Letters." *Canadian Poetry: Studies, Documents, Reviews,* No. 17 (Fall–Winter 1985), pp. 99–104.

Dragland notes that, while the letters themselves do not discuss "great issues," and neither man (Brown nor Scott) "sustains a style that rises very much above the ordinary," the volume with its complete two-sided conversation is "a significant document in Canadian literary history . . . ."

D48 Ford, George. Rev. of *The Poet and the Critic: A Literary Correspondence between D.C. Scott and E.K. Brown. Journal of Canadian Poetry,* 1 (1986), 129–32.

"These letters will be especially interesting to students of Canadian poetry and its history, for much of the correspondence includes not only the poetry of Scott but also that of his friend [Archibald] Lampman." "The appeal of this collection of letters is not limited, however, to issues of the Canadian poetry scene; it has universal dimensions in its touchingly tender exhibition of a warm friendship between persons of different generations."

Index to Critics Listed in the Bibliography

Farley, T.E. C147
Fee, Marjorie C148
Flood, John C149, C158, C186, C272
Ford, George D48
French, Donald G. C20, C21
Frye, Northrop C43, C47, C70, C75, C78, C99, C161, C208
Frye, Northrop, ed. C68

Galvin, J.F. D24
Garebian, Keith D43
Garvin, John W. D10
Geddes, Gary C113
Gerson, Carole C150, C239a
Gnarowski, Michael C129
Godo, Margaret Anne C260
Grady, Wayne C196
Grant, S.D. C223
Groening, Laura C240
Gundy, H. Pearson C100
Gustafson, Ralph C109

Hall, Chipman C256
Harrison, Dick C145
Hatch, Ronald D21
Heath, Jeffrey M., ed. C192
Hirano, Keiichi C91
Horning, Lewis Emerson C8
Howard, Victor C212

James, C.C. C9
Jeays, Linda D44
Johnston, Gordon C4, C179, C215, C273
Jones, D.G. C107, C116
Jones, Johanna C117, C201
Jones, Joseph C117, C201

Karsh, Yousuf C271

Keith, W.J. C231, D39, D46
Kelly, Catherine E. C173, C180, C197, C216, C217, C261, C263
Kilpatrick, R.S. C228
Kirkconnell, Watson C110
Klinck, Carl F. C38, C71
Klinck, Carl F., ed. C72, C93, C94, C95, C96, C97, C98, C99, C100, C101, C102, C104, C105, C106, C153, C154
Knister, Raymond C23
Kostjuk, Dwight Thomas C265

Langford, Howard D. C19
Lecker, Robert, ed. C210, C211, C215
Livesay, Dorothy C115, C227
Lochhead, Douglas C232
Lochhead, Douglas, ed. C235
Logan, J.D. C21
Lynch, Gerald C209

Macbeth, Madge C63, C89
MacCulloch, Clare C130
MacMurchy, Archibald C13
MacRae, C.F. C250
Magee, William H. C82
Mandel, Eli, ed. C115
Marshall, Tom C162
Martin, Burns D15, D22
Masefield, John C24, C35
Mathews, Robin C166
Matthews, John Pengwerne C87, C181, C238
McDougall, Robert L. C169, C182, C218, C219, C233, D20, D34
McDougall, Robert L., ed. C83, D46
McDougall, Russell, ed. C238
McGill, Jean S. C225
McGregor, Gaile C234
McLaren, Floris D17

Toye, William, ed.   C133, C220

Vinson, James, ed.   C176

Waddington, Miriam, ed.   C49
Wallace, W.S.   C92
Walsh, William   C133
Walsh, William, ed.   C135
Ware, Martin   C187, C188
Ware, Tracy   C241, C268
Waterston, Elizabeth   C134, C136, C157, D26
Watson, Dorothy   C1
Watt, F.W.   C86, C106
Watters, Reginald Eyre   C71, C72, C108, C126
Watters, Reginald Eyre, ed.   C73
Weis, Lyle Percy   C242, C245, C267
Welage, Patricia A.   C266
Whitlock, Gillian, ed.   C238
Wicken, George   C220, D38
Wilcox, John William   C251
Wilson, J. Donald, ed.   C226
Wilson, Milton   C84, D41
Wilton, Margaret Harvey   C90
Woodcock, George   C118, C135, C175, C176, C211,
   C212, C246
Woodcock, George, ed.   C107, C113, C142
Wright, Percy H.   C33